Practical Skills in
Forensic Science

ALAN M. LANGFORD
JOHN R. DEAN
ROB REED
DAVID HOLMES
JONATHAN WEYERS
ALLAN JONES

Third Edition

Harlow, England • London • New York • Boston • San Francisco • Toronto • Sydney
Dubai • Singapore • Hong Kong • Tokyo • Seoul • Taipei • New Delhi
Cape Town • São Paulo • Mexico City • Madrid • Amsterdam • Munich • Paris • Milan

Pearson

Other books in the series published by Pearson Education

Practical Skills in Biology
(Fourth edition)
Jones, Reed, Weyers

Practical Skills in Biomolecular Sciences
(Third edition)
Reed, Holmes, Weyers and Jones

Practical Skills in Chemistry
Dean, Jones, Holmes, Reed, Weyers and Jones

Practical Skills in Environmental Sciences
Duck, Jones, Reed and Weyers

Pearson Education Limited
KAO Two
KAO Park
Harlow CM17 9NA
United Kingdom
Tel: +44 (0)1279 623623
Web: www.pearson.com/uk

First published 2005 (print)
Second edition published 2010 (print)
Third edition published 2019 (print and electronic)

ISBN: 978-1-292-13946-3 (print)
       978-1-292-14049-0 (PDF)
       978-1-292-14050-6 (ePub)

British Library Cataloguing-in-Publication Data
A catalogue record for the print edition is available from the British Library

Library of Congress Cataloging-in-Publication Data

Names: Langford, Alan, 1969- author.
Title: Practical skills in forensic science / Alan Langford [and five others].
Description: Third edition. | Harlow, United Kingdom : Pearson Education, [2019]
Identifiers: LCCN 2017050771| ISBN 9781292139463 (Print) | ISBN 9781292140490 (PDF) | ISBN 9781292140506 (ePub)
Subjects: LCSH: Forensic sciences.
Classification: LCC HV8073 .P685 2018 | DDC 363.25--dc23
LC record available at https://lccn.loc.gov/2017050771

10 9 8 7 6 5 4 3 2 1
23 22 21 20 19
Cover image © TEK IMAGE/Getty Images

Print edition typeset in 10/12pt Times LT Pro by Spi Global

Printed in Slovakia by Neografia

NOTE THAT ANY PAGE CROSS REFERENCES REFER TO THE PRINT EDITION

Contents

Contents

List of boxes

List of boxes

Preface

'Forensic Science is defined as the application of science to serve the purposes of the law. The sciences used in the analysis of physical evidence include many aspects of chemistry, biology, physics, mathematics and statistics. This multidisciplinary nature is a core feature of forensic science.'

QAA for HE Subject Benchmark Statement for Forensic Science (2012).

Practical skills form the cornerstone of forensic science. However, the diversity of skills required in the laboratory means that a student's experience may be limited. While some techniques do require specific skills, many of them are transferable generic skills that are required throughout the subject area.

Limited time constraints of the modern curriculum often preclude or minimise laboratory time. It is the aim of this book to provide a general guidance for use in and out of practical sessions and also to cover a range of techniques from the basic to the more advanced.

In creating the third edition of *Practical Skills in Forensic Science*, we have maintained the approach of the previous editions, with the aim of providing support to students taking forensic science based courses in a concise and user-friendly manner. Key points, definitions, illustrations, 'how to' boxes, checklists, worked examples, tips and hints are included where appropriate. However, we have also used this opportunity of the new edition to restructure the layout, to literally start at the beginning of the laboratory process and progress to the end, with the dissemination of results.

In updating and thoroughly revising the book to include a 'taste' of the latest developments in methodology, we have considered carefully the Quality Assurance Agency UK Subject Benchmarking statements for Forensic Science, reviewed and updated in 2012, and have attempted to cover all the generic skills, along with the practical aspects of the subject specific topics in forensic science. With that in mind we have carefully arranged sections to cover the following themes: crime scene investigation; forensic biology; and, forensic chemistry. We have also been mindful to support one of the QAA's aims for forensic science degrees (under- and post-graduate) programmes in the context of practical skills. Specifically, "to develop a sound knowledge of science and of laboratory and other transferable skills which are of value in areas of employment other than forensic science, such as schools, hospitals, analytical science-based companies, the pharmaceutical industry, the Home Office and other government agencies".

To students who buy this book, we hope you will find it useful in the laboratory during your practical classes and in your project work – this is not a book to be left on the bookshelf.

We would like to take this opportunity to thank our wives (Jules, Lynne, Polly, Gill, Mary and Angela) and families for their continued support, and to recognise the following colleagues and friends who have provided assistance, comment and food for thought at various points during the production of all editions: James Abbott, Gary Askwith, Chris Baldwin, Dave Bannister, Jon Bookham, Samantha Bowerbank, Susan Carlile, Michelle Carlin, Jim Creighton, Sarah Cresswell, Martin Davies, Mike Deary, Sylvain Denieul, Les Dix, Marcus Durrant, Jackie Eager, Gordon Forrest, Laura Heath, Kris Heath, Derek Holmes, Helen Hooper, Alan Jones, Ed Ludkin, Ton Nelson, Tom Marshall, Dave Osborne, Justin Perry, Lee Rounds, Jane Shaw, Tony Simpson, Dave Wealleans and Ian Winship. We would also like to thank the staff of Pearson Education for the friendly support over the years, and would wish to acknowledge Richelle Zakrewski, Rufus Cornow, Pat Bond, Owen Knight, Simon Lake, Alex Seabrook and Pauline Gillett.

As with previous editions, we would be grateful to hear of any errors you might notice, so that these can be put right at the earliest opportunity.

Alan Langford (alan.langford@northumbria.ac.uk)
John R. Dean (john.dean@northumbria.ac.uk)
Rob Reed (r.reed@cqu.edu.au)
David Holmes (david.holmes@northumbria.ac.uk)
Allan M Jones (a.m.jones@dundee.ac.uk)
Jonathon Weyers (j.d.b.weyers@dundee.ac.uk)

Guided tour

Definitions of key terms and concepts are highlighted in the text margin.

Key points highlight critical features of methodology.

Tips and hints provide useful hints and practical advice, and are highlighted in the text margin.

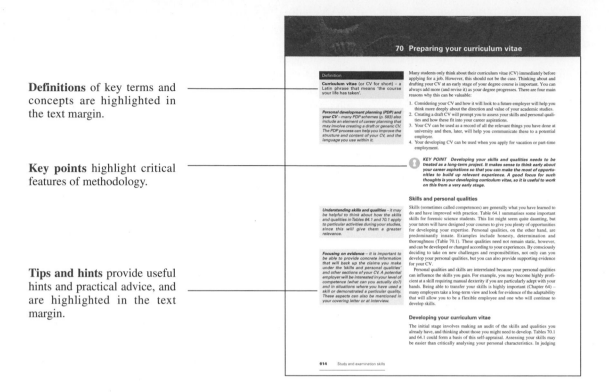

Examples are included in the margin to illustrate important points without interrupting the flow of the main text.

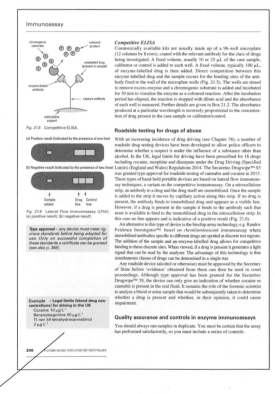

Worked examples and **'How to' boxes** set out the essential procedures in a step-by-step manner.

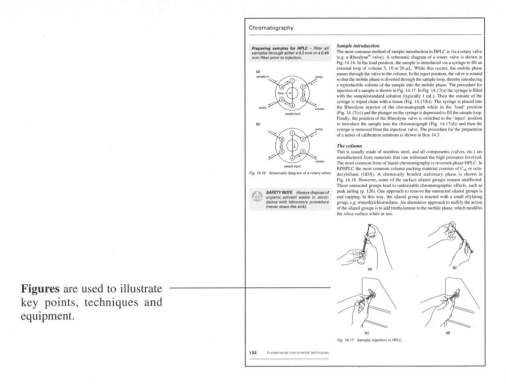

Figures are used to illustrate key points, techniques and equipment.

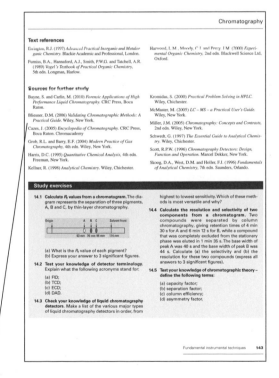

Sources for further study – every chapter is supported by a section giving printed and electronic sources for further study.

Study exercises are included in every chapter to reinforce learning with problems and practical exercises.

For the student

This book aims to provide guidance and support over the broad range of your undergraduate course, including laboratory classes, project work, lectures, tutorials, seminars and examinations, as outlined below:

Chapters 1–44 cover a wide range of specific practical skills required in forensic science

These are based on the authors' experience of the questions students often ask in practical classes, and the support that is needed in order to get the most out of particular exercises. The text includes tips, hints, definitions, worked examples and 'how to' boxes that set out the key procedures in a step-by-step manner, with appropriate comments on safe working practice. The material ranges from basic laboratory procedures, such as experimental design (Chapter 5) and preparing solutions (Chapters 6–8), through the fundamentals of crime scene investigation and scientific support (Chapters 23–29) to the more advanced practical procedures that you might use during a final-year project, for example analytical methods such as chromatography (Chapter 14) and spectroscopy (Chapters 16–20).

Chapters 30–44 cover the major sub-disciplines within forensic chemistry and forensic biology

As with the chapters on specific skills and techniques, these chapters are designed to provide practical guidance and advice on the various aspects of forensic analysis from a student's perspective. Many of the chapters contain 'how to' boxes and worked examples along with specific case examples, to illustrate how the individual disciplines operate in relation to particular criminal cases.

Chapters 45–49 deal with IT and library resources

These chapters will help you get the most out of the resources and information available in your library, and online resources and the Internet, as well as providing helpful guidance on the use of software packages for data analysis.

Chapters 50–57 explain data analysis and presentation

This will be an important component of your course and you will find that these chapters guide you through the skills and techniques required, ranging from the presentation of results as graphs or tables through to the application of statistical tests. Worked examples are used to reinforce the numerical aspects wherever possible.

Chapters 58–63 deal with evaluating and communicating data

These chapters will help you with preparing assignments, essays and laboratory reports, alongside support in relation to oral, visual and written forms of communication. The ability to evaluate information is an increasingly important skill in contemporary society, and practical guidance is provided here, as well as more specific advice, for example on preparing and presenting a forensic report.

Chapters 64–70 cover general skills

These include a number of transferable skills that you will develop during your course, for example self-evaluation, time management, teamwork, preparing for examinations and creating a CV.

We hope that you will find this book a helpful guide throughout your course, and beyond.

Acknowledgements

Figures

Figure 2.3 from http://www.sigmaaldrich.com/safety-center/understanding-the-label.html#67-548-ec-pictograms, Sigma-Aldrich. Used with permission of Merck KGaA, Darmstadt Germany and/or its affiliates; Figure 22.10 from http://www.sciex.com/Documents/brochures/MDQPlus_brochure.pdf page 5, Image provided by SCIEX © 2017; Figure 23.3 adapted from *Digital Imaging Procedure. V2.1. Publication number: 58/07* Home Office Scientific Development Branch (Cohen, N. and Maclennan-Brown, K. 2007) p.36, https://www.gov.uk/government/uploads/system/uploads/attachment_data/file/378451/DIP_2.1_16-Apr-08_v2.3—Web_2835.pdf, © Crown copyright. Contains public sector information licensed under the Open Government Licence (OGL) v3.0. http://www.nationalarchives.gov.uk/doc/open-government-licence/version/3/; Figure 23.4 from Image Authentication for Digital Image Evidence, 5, pp. 1–11 (2006), Figure 8, *Forensic Science Journal*, 5, pp1–11 (Wen, C. and Yang, K. 2006), Central Police University Taiwan, ROC Taiwan Academy of Forensic Sciences, Taiwan, R.O.C; Figure 30.1 from Laura Barnes, With permission of L. Barnes; Figure 36.3 after *Phytoplankton* 2ed., Edward Arnold (Boney, D.A 1989) Reprinted by permission of Cambridge University Press.

Screenshots

Screenshot 48.1 from https://support.office.com/, Used with permission from Microsoft, Microsoft product screenshot(s) reprinted with permission from Microsoft Corporation; Screenshot 49.2 from https://www.microsoft.com/en-gb/, Microsoft, Microsoft product screenshot(s) reprinted with permission from Microsoft Corporation

Tables

Table 38.3 from Therapeutic and toxic blood concentrations of nearly 1000 drugs and other xenobiotics, *Critical care* 16(4), R136 (Schulz, M., Iwersen-Bergmann, S., Andresen, H and Schmoldt, A. 2012), https://doi.org/10.1186/cc11441 © Schulz et al.; licensee BioMed Central Ltd. 2012 https://creativecommons.org/licenses/by/2.0/legalcode; Table on page 383 from https://www.gov.uk/government/statistics/seizures-of-drugs-in-england-and-wales-financial-year-ending-2015, © Crown copyright. Contains public sector information licensed under the Open Government Licence (OGL) v3.0. http://www.nationalarchives.gov.uk/doc/open-government-licence/version/3/; Table 44.1 from www.gov.uk/government/collections/fire-statistics, © Crown copyright. Contains public sector information licensed under the Open Government Licence (OGL) v3.0. http://www.nationalarchives.gov.uk/doc/open-government-licence/version/3/; Table 66.1 from http://www.belbin.com/belbin-for-teams/, © Belbin® 2012

Text

General Displayed Text on page 37 from Pastettes®, Copyright © Alpha Laboratories; General Displayed Text on page 38 from Pi-pump®, © Pi-Pump.co.uk; General Displayed Text on page 38 from Gilson Pipetman®, Copyright © Gilson, Inc; General Displayed Text on page 40 from Parafilm®, Copyright® Bemis Company, Inc.; General Displayed Text on page 41 from Pyrex®, © Corning Incorporate; General Displayed Text on page 41 from AnalaR®, © VWR International, LLC; General Displayed Text on page 41 from Chloros®, Copyright by Chloros Environmental; General Displayed Text on page 41 from Virkon®, © LANXESS; General Displayed Text on page 52 from Millipore®, Copyright © Merck KGaA; General Displayed Text on page 79 from Celite™, © Imerys; General Displayed Text on page 79 from ASE™, Thermo Fisher Scientific; General Displayed Text on page 88 from Teflon®, © The Chemours Company; General Displayed Text on page 97 from driBlok™, © Techne; General Displayed Text on page 97 from ReactiVial®, Thermo Fisher Scientific; Extract on page 109 from SYBR® Safe, Thermo Fisher Scientific; General Displayed Text on page 118 from AmpFLSTR®SGM Plus™, Thermo Fisher Scientific Applied Biosystems; General Displayed Text on page 125 from Sephadex®, © GE Healthcare; General Displayed Text on page 125 from Sepharose®, © GE Healthcare; General Displayed Text on page 125 from Bio-gel®, Copyright © Bio-Rad Laboratories, Inc; General Displayed Text on page 132 from Rheodyne® Rheodyne LLC; General Displayed Text on page 177 from Mylar™ film, Dupont Teijin Films U.S. Limited Partnership; General Displayed Text on page 177 from DuPont™ Kapton®, Copyright © DuPont; General Displayed Text on page 179 from SpectroBlend®, © Chemplex Industries, Inc; General Displayed Text on page 179 from Securetec Drugwipe™ S5, Securetec AG; General Displayed Text on page 214 from Gel Doc™, Copyright © Bio-Rad Laboratories, Inc; General Displayed Text on page 216 from Bio-Rad® Bio-Safe Coomassie Stain, Copyright © Bio-Rad Laboratories, Inc; General Displayed Text on page 243 from J-LAR®, ©NITTO DENKO CORPORATION; General Displayed Text on page 248 from Sellotape™, Copyright Sellotape; General Displayed Text on page 254 from Encase® Forensic, © OpenText Corp; General Displayed Text on page 257 from SupraNano™, © ArroGen Forensics Ltd.; General Displayed Text on page 258 from Zephyr® brush, Zephyr Mfg Co; General Displayed Text on page 258 from Maglite®, © Mag Instrument Inc; General Displayed Text on page 258 from Lightning Powder, Armor Holding Forensics LLC; General Displayed Text on page 259 from magna brush®, Michael McCarthy; General Displayed Text on page 260 from MVC®Lite, BVDA International BV; General Displayed Text on page 260 from Super Glue®, Copyright © Super Glue Corp; General Displayed Text on page 268 from Crime-lite®, Foster + Freeman Ltd; General Displayed Text on page 271 from Snow Print Wax™, © Safariland, LLC; General Displayed Text on page 274 from SICAR6®, Foster & Freeman Ltd; General Displayed Text on page 277 from Silmark™, Siltech Ltd; General Displayed Text on page 295 from Haemastix®, © Ascensia Diabetes Care Holdings AG; General Displayed Text on page 297 from Chelex 100®,Bio-Rad Laboratories Inc.; General Displayed Text on page 300 from Phadebas®, Magle Life Sciences ©; General Displayed Text on page 285 from AmpFLSTR®NGM SElect™, Thermo Fisher Scientific; General Displayed Text on page 303 from NDNAD®, Crown Copyright, © Crown copyright. Contains public sector information licensed under the Open Government Licence (OGL) v3.0. http://www.nationalarchives.gov.uk/doc/open-government-licence/version/3/; General Displayed Text on

Acknowledgements

page 305 from AmpliTaqGold®, Roche Molecular Diagnostics; General Displayed Text on page 305 from SGM Plus®, Thermo Fisher Scientific Applied Biosystems; General Displayed Text on page 306 from Powerplex®, © Promega UK, an affiliate of Promega Corporation; General Displayed Text on page 306 from Minicon®, Copyright © Merck KGaA.; General Displayed Text on page 306 from Amplitype®, Thermo Fisher Scientific Applied Biosystems; General Displayed Text on page 310 from Fluoroscan®, Hologic; General Displayed Text on page 310 from StepOne™, Thermo Fisher Scientific Applied Biosystems; General Displayed Text on page 331 from Isomet™, Copyright © Isomet Corporation; General Displayed Text on page 358 from Lion Alcolmeter®, Lion Laboratories Limited; General Displayed Text on page 358 from Lion Intoximeter®, Lion Laboratories Ltd; General Displayed Text on page 384 from Tylenol®, Johnson & Johnson Inc; General Displayed Text on page 388 from Spherisorb™, © Waters.; General Displayed Text on page 391 from Inertsil ODS2™, Copyright GL Sciences, Inc., USA; General Displayed Text on page 396 from GEM®, © Edgewell Personal Care; General Displayed Text on page 398 from Meltmount®, © Copyright By Cargille-Sacher Laboratories Inc; General Displayed Text on page 403 from Benchkote®, © GE Healthcare; General Displayed Text on page 405 from adidas™, © adidas AG; General Displayed Text on page 430 from Dionex®, Thermo Fisher Scientific; General Displayed Text on page 430 from Carbotrap 300®, Copyright © Sigma-Aldrich Co.; General Displayed Text on page 436 from Science Direct®, © Elsevier; General Displayed Text on page 439 from Google Scholar™ scholarly texts search, © 2015 Google Inc. All rights reserved. Google Scholar™ is a trademark of Google Inc., © 2015 Google Inc. All rights reserved. Google and the Google Logo are registered trademarks of Google Inc.; General Displayed Text on page 449 from Amazon®, © Amazon.com, Inc.; General Displayed Text on page 458 from Mac® is a registered trademark of Apple Inc. registered in the U.S. and other countries; General Displayed Text on page 458 from Microsoft Word® and WordPerfect® https://www.microsoft.com/en-us/legal/intellectualproperty/trademarks/usage/general.aspx, Used with permission from Microsoft; General Displayed Text on page 459 from Microsoft® Office, used with permission from Microsoft; General Displayed Text on page 462 from EndNote™, Clarivate Analytics; General Displayed Text on page 463 from Statgraphics®, Statpoint Technologies, Inc; General Displayed Text on page 463 from Minitab®, Copyright 2017 Minitab Inc All rights reserved, Portions of the input and output contained in this publication/book are printed with permission of Minitab Inc. All material remains the exclusive property and copyright of Minitab Inc., All rights reserved.; General Displayed Text on page 463 from Freelance Graphics®, IBM Corporation; General Displayed Text on page 463 from Harvard Graphics®, Copyright © The President and Fellows of Harvard College; General Displayed Text on page 463 from Microsoft Powerpoint®, used with permission from Microsoft; General Displayed Text on page 463 from Sigmaplot®, © SPSS Inc and IBM Corporation, screenshots reprinted courtesy of International Business Machines Corporation, © International Business Machines Corporation. SPSS was acquired by IBM in October, 2009. IBM, the IBM logo, ibm.com, and SPSS are trademarks of International Business Machines Corp., registered in many jurisdictions worldwide. Other product and service names might be trademarks of IBM or other companies. A current list of IBM trademarks is available on the Web at "IBM Copyright and trademark information" at www.ibm.com/legal/copytrade.shtml.; General Displayed Text on page 464 from Dreamweaver® software application, web development tool, Adobe Systems, Inc., Adobe product screenshot(s) reprinted with permission from Adobe Systems Incorporated.; General Displayed Text on page 464 from Mind Genius®, Copyright MindGenius Ltd; General Displayed Text on page 464 from Adobe Photoshop® image-editing software, Adobe Systems, Inc, Adobe product screenshot(s) reprinted with permission from Adobe Systems Incorporated.; General Displayed Text on page 464 from PaintShop Pro®, Copyright Corel Corporation; General Displayed Text on page 465 from Microsoft Excel®, used with permission from Microsoft; General Displayed Text on page 546 from GraphPad Prism®, ©GraphPad Software, Inc; General Displayed Text on page 586 from Filofax®, © Copyright Filofax; General Displayed Text on page 586 from TMI®, Time Manager; General Displayed Text on page 586 from Day-timer®, Day Timer; General Displayed Text on page 592 from Belbin®, © BELBIN Associates.

Abbreviations

AAS	atomic absorption spectrometer
AES	atomic emission spectrometer
AC	affinity chromatography
ACS	American Chemical Society
AMPFLP	amplified fragment-length polymorphisms
ANOVA	analysis of variance
AP	acid phosphatase
APCI	atmospheric pressure chemical ionisation
A_r	relative atomic mass
ASO	allele specific oligonucleotide
ATP	adenosine triphosphate
BMI	body mass index
b.pt.	boiling point
Cb	measured blood or breath alcohol concentration
CDT	carbohydrate-deficient transferrin
CE	capillary electrophoresis
CEC	capillary electrochromatography
CGE	capillary gel electrophoresis
CO	carbon monoxide
CoA	calculated alcohol concentration in blood or breath
CODIS	combined DNA index system
COSHH	control of substances hazardous to health
CoV	coefficient of variation
CRM	certified reference material
CSM	crime scene manager
CZE	capillary zone electrophoresis
DAD	diode array detection
DCM	dichloromethane
DFSA	drug-facilitated sexual assault
DMAC	p dimethylaminocinnamaldehyde
DNA	deoxyribonucleic acid
DTT	dithiothreitol
ECD	electron capture detector
EDTA	ethylenediaminetetraacetic acid
EI	electron impact (ionisation)
ELISA	enzyme-linked immunosorbent assay
EMR	electromagnetic radiation
en	ethylenediamine
EOF	electro-osmotic flow
ESDA	electrostatic detection apparatus
ESI	electrospray ionisation
FAAS	flame atomic absorption spectrometer
FID	flame ionisation detector
FOA	first officer attending
FSS	Forensic Science Service
FT	Fourier transform
FT–IR	Fourier transform – infrared spectroscopy
GC	gas chromatography
GC–MS	gas chromatography–mass spectrometry
GFC	gel filtration chromatography
GGT	γ glutamyl transferase
GHB	γ hydroxy butyrate
GPC	gel permeation chromatography
GRIM	glass refractive index measurement
GSR	gunshot residue

Abbreviations

HASAW	hazards at work
H&E	haemotoxylin and eosin
HCB	hexachloro-1,3-butadiene
HCL	hollow cathode lamp
HFBA	heptafluorobutyric anhydride
HIC	hydrophobic interaction chromatography
HPLC	high-performance liquid chromatography
HV	hypervariable region
ICP	inductively coupled plasma
ICP-MS	inductively coupled plasma–mass spectrometry
IEC	ion exchange chromatography
IEF	isoelectric focusing
IR	infrared (radiation)
ISE	ion selective electrode
IUPAC	International Union of Pure and Applied Chemistry
kg	kilogram
KM	Kastle Meyer
LC–MS	liquid chromatography–mass spectrometry
LCN	low copy number
LGC	Laboratory of the Government Chemist
LMG	leuco malachite green
LSD	lysergic acid
m	mass
MDL	minimum detectable level
MDMA	3,4-methylenedioxymethylamphetamine (ecstasy)
MEKC	micellar electrokinetic chromatography
MEL	maximum exposure limit
m.pt.	melting point
M_r	relative molecular mass
MS	mass spectrometry
MSTFA	N-methyl-N-trimethylsilyltrifluoroacetamide
mtDNA	mitochondrial DNA
NCA	National Crime Agency
NDNAD	National DNA Database
NH	null hypothesis
NIST	National Institute of Standards and Technology
NMR	nuclear magnetic resonance
NP-HPLC	normal phase high-performance liquid chromatography
ODS	octadecylsilane
OEL	occupational exposure standard
PAGE	polyacrylamide gel electrophoresis
PCIA	phenol/chloroform/isoamyl alcohol
PCR	polymerase chain reaction
PDT	pyridyldiphenyl triazine
PFA	perfluoroalkoxyvinylether
PTFE	polytetrafluoroethylene
PLOT	porous layer open tubular (column)
PMT	photomultiplier tube
PPE	personal protection equipment
r	Widmark factor
R_f	relative frontal mobility
RNA	ribonucleic acid
RP-HPLC	reversed phase high-performance liquid chromatography
rpm	revolutions per minute
SAX	strong anion exchange
SCOT	support coated open tubular (column)
SCX	strong cation exchange
SDS	sodium dodecyl sulphate

SE	standard error (of the sample mean)
SEM	scanning electron microscopy
SGM	second generation multiplex
SI	Système International d'Unités
SIO	senior investigating officer
SLR	single lens reflex
SNP	single nucleotide polymorphism
SOCO	scene of crime officer
SOP	standard operating procedure
STR	short tandem repeat
TCA	trichloroacetic acid
TCD	thermal conductivity detector
TE	Tris/EDTA
TEA	thermal energy analyser
TG	thermogravimetry
TLC	thin-layer chromatography
TMS	tetramethylsilane
TRIS	tris(hydroxymethyl)aminomethane or 2-amino-2-hydroxymethyl-1,3-propane-diol
UK	United Kingdom
UKAS	United Kingdom Accreditation Services
URL	uniform resource locator
USEPA	United States Environmental Protection Agency
UV	ultraviolet (radiation)
Vd	volume of distribution
VNTR	variable number of tandem repeats
WCOT	wall-coated open tubular (column)

Fundamental approaches to science

Developing practical skills – these will include:

- *designing experiments;*
- *observing and measuring;*
- *recording data;*
- *analysing and interpreting data;*
- *reporting/presenting.*

All knowledge and theory in science has originated from practical observation and experimentation – this is equally true for disciplines as diverse as chromatography and molecular genetics. Practical work is an important part of most courses and often accounts for a significant proportion of the assessment marks. The abilities developed in practical classes will continue to be useful throughout your course and beyond, some within science and others in any career you choose.

Being prepared

 KEY POINT *You will get the most out of practicals if you prepare well in advance. Do not go into a practical session assuming that everything will be provided, without any input or involvement on your part.*

The main points to remember are:

- **Read any handouts in advance** – make sure you understand the purpose of the practical and the particular skills involved. Does the practical relate to, or expand on, a current topic in your lectures? Is there any additional preparatory reading that will help?
- **Take along appropriate textbooks,** to explain aspects of the practical.
- **Consider what safety hazards might be involved,** and any precautions you might need to take before you begin (p. 6).
- **Listen carefully to any introductory guidance and note any important points** – adjust your schedule/handout as necessary.
- **During the practical session, organise your bench space** – make sure your lab book is adjacent to, but not within, your working area. You will often find it easier to keep clean items of glassware, etc. on one side of your working space, with used equipment on the other side.
- **Write up your work as soon as possible** and submit it on time, or you may lose marks.
- **Catch up on any work you have missed as soon as possible** – preferably, before the next practical session.

Using textbooks in the lab – *take this book (or photocopies of relevant pages) along to the relevant classes, so that you can make full use of the information during your practical sessions.*

 SAFETY NOTE Using mobile phones – *these should never be used in a lab class, as there is a risk of contamination from hazardous substances. Always switch off your mobile phone before entering a laboratory.*

Ethical and legal aspects of laboratory work

You will need to consider the ethical and legal implications of forensic science work throughout your degree studies:

- **Safe working in the laboratory** means following a code of safe practice, supported by legislation, alongside a moral obligation to avoid harm to yourself and others, as discussed in Chapter 2.
- **Any laboratory work that involves working with animal or human tissues** must be considered carefully and must be performed in accordance with the relevant rules/legislation, including appropriate disposal after use.

In addition to the above, forensic science throws up some moral and legal dilemmas, and students are increasingly likely to be asked to reflect on ethical topics, for example in group discussions on current issues or recent cases in the media. For many topics, you will find that there are not always 'right' or 'wrong' answers, and it is important to be able to consider these issues in a rational and logical manner, and to provide reasoned argument in support of a particular viewpoint.

Basic requirements for laboratory work

Recording practical results

An A4 loose-leaf ring binder offers flexibility, since you can insert laboratory handouts or lined and graph paper at appropriate points. The danger of losing one or more pages from a loose-leaf system is the main drawback. Bound books avoid this problem, although those containing alternating lined/graph or lined/blank pages tend to be wasteful – it is often better to paste sheets of graph paper into a bound book as required.

All of your forensic examination notes should be written in ink. Any mistakes should simply be scored out and initialled. Buy a black, spirit-based (permanent) marker for labelling lab glassware, etc. Fibre-tipped fine line drawing/lettering pens are useful for preparing final versions of graphs and diagrams for assessment purposes. Use a see-through ruler (with an undamaged edge) for graph drawing, so that you can see data points and information below the ruler as you draw.

Presenting results – *although you don't need to be a graphic designer to produce work of a satisfactory standard, presentation and layout are important and you will lose marks for poorly presented work.*

Using inexpensive calculators – *many unsophisticated calculators have a restricted display for exponential numbers and do not show the 'power of 10', e.g. displaying 2.4×10^{-5} as 2.4^{-05}, or $2.4E{-}05$, or $2.4{-}05$.*

Using calculators for numerical problems – *Chapter 54 gives further advice.*

Calculators

These range from basic machines with no pre-programmed functions and only one memory, to sophisticated programmable minicomputers with many memories. The following may be helpful when using a calculator:

- **Power sources** – choose a battery-powered machine, rather than a mains-operated or solar-powered type. You will need one with basic mathematical/scientific operations, including powers, logarithms (p. 503), roots and parentheses (brackets), together with statistical functions such as sample means and standard deviations (Chapter 55).
- **Mode of operation** – the older operating system used by, for example, Hewlett-Packard calculators, is known as the reverse Polish notation. To calculate the sum of two numbers, the sequence is 2 [enter] 4 + and the answer 6 is displayed. The more usual method of calculating this equation is as 2 + 4 =, which is the system used by the majority of modern calculators. Most newcomers find the latter approach to be more straightforward. Spend some time finding out how a calculator operates, for example does it have true algebraic logic ($\sqrt{}$ then number, rather than number then $\sqrt{}$)? How does it deal with scientific notation (p. 502)?
- **Display** – some calculators will display an entire mathematical operation (e.g. '2 + 4 = 6'), while others simply display the last number/operation. The former type may offer advantages in tracing errors.
- **Complexity** – in the early stages, it is usually better to avoid the more complex machines, full of impressive-looking but often unused pre-programmed functions. Go for more memory, parentheses or statistical functions rather than engineering or mathematical constants. Programmable calculators may be worth considering for more advanced studies. However, it is important to note that such calculators are often unacceptable for exams.

Presenting more advanced practical work

In some practical reports and in project work, you may need to use more sophisticated presentation equipment. Computer-based graphics packages can be useful – choose easily-read fonts such as Arial or Helvetica for posters and

Presenting graphs and diagrams – *ensure these are large enough to be easily read – a common error is to present graphs or diagrams that are too small, with poorly chosen scales.*

Printing on acetates – *standard overhead transparencies are not suitable for use in laser printers or photocopiers – you need to make sure that you use the correct type.*

consider the layout and content carefully (p. 573). Alternatively, you could use fine-line drawing pens and dry-transfer lettering/symbols, such as those made by Letraset, although this approach can be more time-consuming than computer-based systems.

To prepare overhead transparencies for spoken presentations, you can use spirit-based markers and acetate sheets. An alternative approach is to print directly from a computer-based package, using a laser printer and special acetates, or use a digital projector with, for example, PowerPoint (p. 547). You can also photocopy on to special acetates. Advice on content and presentation is given in Chapter 59.

Sources for further study

Barnard, C.J., Gilbert, F.S. and MacGregor, P.K. (2007) *Asking Questions in Biology: Key Skills for Practical Assessments and Project Work,* 3rd edn. Prentice Hall, Harlow.

Bonner, P. and Hargreaves, A. (2011) *Basic Bioscience Laboratory Techniques: A Pocket Guide.* Wiley, New York.

Mappes, T. and Degrazia, D. (2005) *Biomedical Ethics,* 6th edn. W.C. Brown/McGraw-Hill, New York.

Meah, M. and Kebede-Weshead, E. (2012) *Essential Laboratory Skills for Biosciences.* Wiley, Chichester.

Mier-Jedrzejowicz, W.A.C. (2007) *A Guide to HP Handheld Calculators and Computers,* 5th edn. Wilson-Barnett, Tustin. [Provides further guidance on the use of Hewlett-Packard calculators (reverse Polish notation).]

Overton, J., Johnson, S. and Scott, J. (2015) *Study and Communication Skills for the Chemical Sciences,* 2nd edn. Open University Press, Oxford.

Study exercises

1.1 **Consider the value of practical work.** Spend a few minutes thinking about the purpose of practical work within a specific part of your course (e.g. a particular first-year module) and then write a list of the six most important points.

1.2 **Make a list of items required for a particular practical exercise.** This exercise is likely to be most useful if you can relate it to an appropriate practical session on your course, e.g. bulk drug examination.

1.3 **Check your calculator skills.** Carry out the following mathematical operations, using either a hand-held calculator or a PC with appropriate 'calculator' software.

(a) $5 \times (2 + 6)$

(b) $(8.3 \div [6.4 - 1.9]) \times 24$ (to four significant figures)

(c) $(1 \div 32) \times (5 \div 8)$ (to three significant figures)

(d) $1.2 \times 10^5 + 4.0 \times 10^4$ in scientific notation (see p. 44)

(e) $3.4 \times 10^{-2} - 2.7 \times 10^{-3}$ in 'normal' notation (i.e. conventional notation, not scientific format) and to three decimal places.

(See also the numerical exercises in Chapter 54.)

2 Health and safety

Health and Safety legislation – In the UK, the **Health and Safety at Work etc. Act 1974** provides the main legal framework for health and safety. **The Control of Substances Hazardous to Health (COSHH) Regulations 2002** impose specific legal requirements for risk assessment wherever hazardous chemicals or biological agents are used, with approved codes of practice for the control of hazardous substances, carcinogens and biological agents, including pathogenic microbes.

Health and safety legislation requires institutions to provide a working environment that is safe and without risk to health. Where appropriate, training and information on safe working practices must be provided. Students and staff must take reasonable care to ensure the health and safety of themselves and of others, and must not misuse any safety equipment.

 KEY POINT *All practical work must be carried out with safety in mind, to minimise the risk of harm to yourself and to others – safety is everyone's responsibility.*

Risk assessment

A risk assessment is a systematic approach to hazard identification and control. It is essential to consider what aspects of a laboratory or crime scene investigation activity can cause injury (to people) and then to control measures that will reduce the risk of injury to an acceptable level. Important aspects to consider are:

- substance hazards;
- how the substance is to be used;
- how it can be controlled;
- who is exposed;
- how much exposure;
- how long the exposure duration is.

 KEY POINT *It is important to distinguish between the HAZARD of a substance and the RISK resulting from exposure.*

The risk assessment process

The five-step process requires you to:

1. **Identify the hazards and risk**: One way to do this is by using 'PEME', i.e. People, Equipment, Materials and Environment:
   (a) **'People' hazards** can cover a range of issues including the individual themselves and the systems that people have to use. In this 'people' context, consider the following terms: training, capabilities/restrictions, supervision, communication, adequate numbers and human error.
   (b) **'Equipment' hazards** relate to the equipment to be used, e.g. injection port of a gas chromatograph (GC) is typically 270°C (Chapter 14); it will also consider related aspects of the equipment including repair, maintenance, handling, storage, cleaning and operation of the equipment.
   (c) **'Materials' hazards** cover any liquid, solid or gas associated with the task, e.g. using controlled drugs to determine their concentration in blood (Chapter 38). This aspect also covers any by-products or waste generated by the activity.
   (d) **'Environment' hazards** relate to the surrounds you are working in, e.g. in crime scene investigation you may encounter poor lighting, heating and ventilation, poor access and egress, tripping/slipping hazards, restricted space/visibility and other activities taking place nearby.

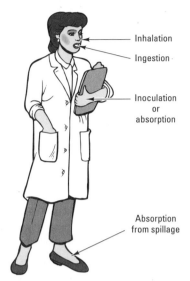

Fig. 2.1 Major routes of entry of harmful substances into the body.

Definitions

Hazard – the potential of a substance or biological agent to cause harm.

Likelihood – the assessment of the likelihood of harm prior to any control measures being in place, given the amount/nature of substance used and the environment/manner it's used in.

Risk – a measure of the likelihood and severity prior to any control measures being in place, calculated by likelihood × severity.

Severity – this is a substance-specific rather than activity-specific measurement that can be indicated on the MSDS. In each instance, the highest numerical assessment should be used to calculate the risk.

---

2. **Identify who can be harmed and how:**
   (a) **Who** – Although a task may seem to be well managed, if control measures fail then a whole range of people could be injured, e.g. co-workers in the area or people visiting the area. Your risk assessment should consider all those people who could potentially be harmed if the control measures fail.
   (b) **How** – the major routes of chemical exposure (Fig. 2.1) are:
      i **inhalation** – breathing in small particles or chemical vapours is the most common pathway;
      ii **dermal** – some chemicals can be absorbed into the body;
      iii **eye contact** – rubbing your eyes after chemical exposure with your hands (with or without gloves);
      iv **ingestion** – inadvertent hand to mouth transmission;
      v **subcutaneous penetration** – improper use of glass pipettes/syringes and their disposal can lead to injury and exposure of the underlying skin tissue.

3. **Identify the current controls and decide if more is required:**
   (a) **Identify the control measures currently in place** for each hazard you have identified: physical controls (i.e. local exhaust ventilation); procedural controls (i.e. a safe working procedure for the task); and behavioural controls (i.e. adequate supervision and monitoring of behaviour).
   (b) **Identify the risks and decide on precautions** – a risk matrix analysis. A risk analysis is a qualitative estimate of risk associated with each applicable task; it assumes that the planned or existing controls are in place. Box 2.1 shows you how to undertake a risk matrix analysis. The risk matrix evaluates the risk by allocating a numeric risk level and the tolerability of the hazard.

4. **Record your findings** – you will need to record your assessments. You will need to:
   (a) State clearly what task/activity the risk assessment covers.
   (b) Ensure that the hazards and controls are clearly listed.
   (c) Consider all those people who could potentially be harmed.
   (d) Ensure that the appropriate member of staff signs off the assessment.
   (e) Make sure the completed risk assessments are readily available to those who might need them.

5. **Review as necessary**. Risk assessments should be reviewed on a regular basis. The period of review should reflect the hazards: the greater the hazards the more frequent the review.

Box 2.1   How to perform a risk matrix analysis

A risk matrix analysis allows you to prioritise the likelihood and severity of risk to an individual from the hazard identified.

1 **Using the form** in Fig. 2.2 (illustration is for superglue fuming of fingerprints using cyanoacrylate) conduct a COSHH assessment of the chemical to be used in a practical laboratory class.

2 **First consult the Material Safety Data Sheet** (MSDS) supplied; all manufacturers of hazardous chemicals are required to provide one of these sheets for all products that they sell.

3 **Consult the hazard pictograms** (Fig. 2.3) for visible relevant information. In addition, H (hazard) statements and P (precautionary) statements are

Box 2.1 (Continued)

available on the MSDS sheets and/or at http://www
.sigmaaldrich.com/help-welcome/hazard-and-
precautionary-statements.html (click on the Hazard
statement overview or Precautionary statement
overview tabs).

4 **Assess the 'likelihood' of harm** prior to any control
measures being in place, given the amount/nature
of substance used and the environment/manner it
is used in (Table 2.1)

5 **Assess the severity** using the MSDS sheets for guidance (Table 2.1).

6 **Calculate the risk using the risk matrix** (Table 2.1)
This calculation should quote the highest risk
associated with the substance. You should consider
additional control measures to further reduce the
final risk's numerical value.

Experiment Record - short COSHH record form

COSHH Assessments for   **Experiment Title:**   Chemical Enhancement of latent fingerprints

Name of Assessor__ Alan Langford____   Signed __*A Langford*__ Date__01/10/15 _____

Substance	H Statement[1]	Hazard[2] Key hazard(s) associated with the substance	Signal Word?[3]	Likelihood[4]	Severity[5]	Risk[6] (before additional control measures)	Specific Risk Control Measures[7]	Controlled Risk[8]
Basic yellow 40	H315, 319, 335	Causes skin, respiratory and serious eye irritation	WARNING	3	4	12	GLP, PPE, gloves safety glasses	4
Ethyl-2-cyanoacrylate	H315, 319, 335	Causes skin, respiratory and serious eye irritation	WARNING	3	4	12	GLP, PPE, gloves safety glasses, used in dedicated fingerprint fuming cabinet	4
Basic yellow working solution Ethanol (100ml+0.2g dye)	H225	Highly flammable liquid and vapour	WARNING (for neat ethanol)	2	3	6	GLP, PPE, use in fume hood	3

Substance	P Statement[9]	Storage[10]	Emergency Procedures (in event of spillage, fire etc.)[11] Detail	Disposal[12]
Basic yellow 40	P261, 305, 351, 338	Cool, sealed container, dry well ventilated	Fire: wear S/C breathing apparatus if necessary; extinguish; water or CO_2 Spillage: water; do not let enter drain First aid: wash with water for 15 mins	In solvent; to flammable waste for incineration;
Basic yellow working solution	P210, 261, 305, 351, 338	Store in cool place. Keep container tighty closed in a dry and well-ventilated place. Containers which are opened must be carefully resealed and kept upright to prevent leakage.	Fire: water, CO_2, powder, foam Spillage: wear gloves, Absorb material, wash area with water First aid: IF IN EYES: Rinse cautiously with water for several minutes. Remove contact lenses, if present and easy to do. Continue rinsing.	Flammable waste for incineration

Fig. 2.2 Risk matrix analysis for chemical enhancement of fingerprints using cyanoacrylate fuming and Basic Yellow 40.

Box 2.1   (Continued)

Description	Pictogram	Hazard class and hazard category:
Exploding Bomb		Unstable explosives Explosives of Divisions 1.1, 1.2, 1.3, 1.4 Self reactive substances and mixtures, Types A,B Organic peroxides, Types A,B
Flame		Flammable gases, category 1 Flammable aerosols, categories 1,2 Flammable liquids, categories 1,2,3 Flammable solids, categories 1,2 Self-reactive substances and mixtures, Types B,C,D,E,F Pyrophoric liquids, category 1 Pyrophoric solids, category 1 Self-heating substances and mixtures, categories 1,2 Substances and mixtures, which in contact with water, emit flammable gases, categories 1,2,3 Organic peroxides, Types B,C,D,E,F Pyrophoric gas (US only)
Flame Over Circle		Oxidizing gases, category 1 Oxidizing liquids, categories 1,2,3
Gas Cylinder		Gases under pressure: - Compressed gases - Liquefied gases - Refrigerated liquefied gases - Dissolved gases
Corrosion		Corrosive to metals, category 1 Skin corrosion, categories 1A,1B,1C Serious eye damage, category 1
Skull and Crossbones		Acute toxicity (oral, dermal, inhalation), categories 1,2,3
Exclamation Mark		Acute toxicity (oral, dermal, inhalation), category 4 Skin irritation, category 2 Eye irritation, category 2 Skin sensitisation, category 1 Specific Target Organ Toxicity – Single exposure, category 3
Health Hazard		Respiratory sensitization, category 1 Germ cell mutagenicity, categories 1A,1B,2 Carcinogenicity, categories 1A,1B,2 Reproductive toxicity, categories 1A,1B,2 Specific Target Organ Toxicity – Single exposure, categories 1,2 Specific Target Organ Toxicity – Repeated exposure, categories 1,2 Aspiration Hazard, category 1
Environment		Hazardous to the aquatic environment - Acute hazard, category1 - Chronic hazard, categories 1,2

Fig. 2.3   Hazard warning pictograms. Sigma Aldrich. Available at: http://www.sigmaaldrich.com/safety-center/understanding-the-label.html#67-548-ec-pictograms.

Box 2.1   (Continued)

Table 2.1   An example of a risk matrix analysis – assessing the likelihood and severity of the hazard to determine the overall risk

Likelihood of harm		Severity of harm		Risk: the risk in using the substance = Likelihood × Severity		
Remote	1	Negligible (no injury)	1	**Low**	**1 to 10**	**Good lab practice required**
Unlikely	2	Minor injury	2	**High**	**12 to 18**	**Specific identified control measures must be used**
May occur	3	Lost time injury	3	**Very High**	**20 +**	**Trained personnel only**
Likely	4	Major injury	4			
Very likely	5	Single fatality	5			
Certain	6	Multiple fatalities	6			

 SAFETY NOTE   *Protective clothing* is worn as a first barrier to spillages of chemicals onto your clothing.

Lab coats are for protection of you and your clothing.

Eye protection – special spectacles with side pieces to protect your eyes. If you are a spectacle wearer, eye protection with prescription lenses are available from your optician.

Contact lenses should not be worn in the laboratory. Chemicals can get under the lens and damage the eye before the lens can be removed.

Shoes should cover the feet; no open-toed sandals should be worn.

Long hair should be tied back and hats should not be worn.

Basic rules for laboratory work

- **Wear appropriate protective clothing at all times** – a clean lab coat (buttoned up), eye protection, appropriate footwear – and ensure your hair does not constitute a hazard
- **Never smoke, eat or drink** in any laboratory because of the risks of contamination by inhalation or ingestion (Fig. 2.1).
- **Never work alone** in a laboratory.
- **Make sure you know what to do in case of fire**, including where to find the exit routes, how to raise the alarm and where to gather on leaving the building. Remember that the most important consideration at all times is human safety – do not attempt to fight a fire unless it is safe to do so.
- **All laboratories display notices** telling you where to find the first aid kit and who to contact in case of accident/emergency. Report all accidents, even those appearing insignificant – your department will have a formal recording procedure to comply with safety legislation.
- **Know the hazard warning pictograms** for specific hazards (see Fig. 2.3).
- **Never touch chemicals** unless they are known to have minimal hazard: use a spatula to transfer and manipulate solids, and pipettes for liquids (see p. 38).
- **Never mouth pipette any liquid** – use a pipette filler or, if appropriate, a pipettor (pp. 38–39).
- **Take care when handling glassware** – see p. 41 for details.
- **Use a fume cupboard for hazardous chemicals**. Make sure that it is working and then open the front only as far as is necessary – many fume cupboards are marked with a maximum opening.
- **Always use the minimum quantity** of any hazardous materials.
- **Work in a logical, tidy manner** and minimise risks by thinking ahead.
- **Always clear up at the end of each session**. This is an important aspect of safety, encouraging a responsible attitude towards laboratory work.
- **Dispose of waste in appropriate containers**. Most labs will have bins for sharps, glassware, hazardous solutions and radioactive waste.

Material Safety Data Sheets (MSDS) should contain the following information:

Identification of the substance and the company/supplier

Hazards associated with the product

First aid measures

Firefighting measures

Accidental release procedures

Handling and storage

Exposure controls and personal protection

Physical and chemical properties

Stability and reactivity

Toxicological and ecological information

Disposal practices

Other miscellaneous information

Basic rules for crime scene investigation

A full risk assessment of the scene must be carried out to ensure the health and wellbeing of the crime scene examiners is not compromised. Consider the types of hazards that may be present – these may include:

- **Physical hazards** – consider whether the scene is safe before you enter. For example, fire damage to a building may make the structure unsafe, or the presence of drug paraphernalia including used syringes poses a risk of needle stick injury.
- **Chemical hazards** – consider large-scale cannabis cultivation and the risk of exposure of the drug by inhalation or fingerprint visualisation using powdering techniques (see p. 257).
- **Biological hazards** – consider the presence of any biological fluid (see p. 291) and the risk of exposure to an unknown pathogenic risk.

Your work must be designed carefully to allow for the experience of the participants and the locations visited. Don't overestimate what can be achieved – crime scene work is often more demanding than laboratory work, especially if the location is remote/exposed. Any physical disabilities must be brought to the attention of the organiser, so that appropriate precautions can be taken. A comprehensive first aid kit should be available and your clothing and equipment must be suitable for all of the weather conditions likely to be encountered during the work.

 KEY POINT *As you are likely to encounter biological evidence you should treat any biological hazard as a potential high risk of infection; therefore you must wear full personal protective equipment (PPE) as appropriate to the scene (see Chapter 23).*

The assessment of risk should also extend to how any evidence is to be recovered and packaged (Chapter 24) to ensure the safety of the exhibit in transport but also the safety of anyone who will handle the exhibit from its recovery from the crime scene to its potential presentation in a courtroom.

Sources for further study

Anon (2016) *Biological Hazards at Work.* Available at: http://www.hse.gov.uk/biosafety/information.htm. Last accessed 12/08/2017.

Anon (2016) *Control of Substances Hazardous to Health (COSHH)* Health and Safety Executive. Available at: http://www.hse.gov.uk/coshh/. Last accessed 12/08/2017.

Anon (2016) *Health and Safety Essentials. Learn Chemistry, Enhancing Learning and Teaching. Control of Hazardous Chemicals in the Laboratory: COSHH.* Available at: http://www.rsc.org/learn-chemistry/resource/res00001116/coshh-resource?cmpid=CMP00002777. Last accessed 12/08/2017.

Day, R., Reader, J.A. and Rowland, E. (2003) *Health, Safety and Environmental Legislation.* Royal Society of Chemistry, Cambridge.

Picot, A. and Grenouillet, P. (1995) *Safety in the Chemistry and Biochemistry Laboratory.* Wiley, New York.

Sutton, P. and Trueman K. (eds) (2009) *Crime Scene Management; Scene Specific Methods.* Wiley, West Sussex.

Study exercises

2.1 Test your knowledge of safe working procedures. After reading the appropriate sections of this book, can you remember the following?

(a) The five main steps involved in the process of risk assessment.
(b) The major routes of entry of harmful substances into the body.
(c) The warning labels for the major chemical hazard symbols (either describe them or draw them from memory).
(d) The international symbol for a biohazard.

2.2 Locate relevant health and safety features in a laboratory. Find each of the following in one of the laboratories used as part of your course (draw a simple location map if this seems appropriate):

(a) fire exit(s);
(b) fire-fighting equipment;
(c) first aid kit;
(d) 'sharps' container;
(e) container for disposal of broken glassware;
(f) eye wash station (where appropriate).

2.3 Investigate the health and safety procedures in operation at your university. Can you find out the following:

(a) your university's procedure in case of fire;
(b) the colour coding for fire extinguishers available in your department and their recommendations for use;
(c) the accident reporting procedure used in your department;
(d) your department's Code of Safe Practice relating to a specific aspect of biology or chemistry.

2.4 Carry out risk assessments for specific chemical hazards. Look up the hazards associated with the use of the following chemicals and list the appropriate protective measures required to minimise risk during use in a laboratory class:

(a) Cocaine dissolved in methanol, used as standard for a calibration (Chapters 39, 51).
(b) Phenolphthalein, e.g. for use as a presumptive test for blood (Chapter 30).
(c) Sulphuric acid, used in the preparation of an HPLC mobile phase (Chapter 14).

Definitions

Statistic – an estimate of a parameter, obtained from a sample (e.g. the height of 18-year-old females based on those in your class).

Variable – any characteristic or property which can take one of a range of values. (Contrast this definition with that for a **parameter,** which is a numerical constant in any particular instance.)

*Working with discontinuous variables –
note that while the original data values must
be integers, derived data and statistical values do not have to be whole numbers. Thus,
it is perfectly acceptable to express the
mean number of children per family as 2.4.*

There are a variety of skills required for accurate recording in forensic science. This chapter describes the general principles applying to several of these skills. The term 'data' (singular = datum, or data value) refers to items of information, and you will use different types of data from a wide range of sources during your practical work. Consequently, it is important to appreciate the underlying features of data collection and measurement.

Variables

Scientific variables (Fig. 3.1) can be classified as follows (see also p. 31).

Quantitative variables

These are characteristics whose differing states can be described by means of a number. They are of two basic types:

- **Continuous variables,** such as length – these are usually measured against a numerical scale. Theoretically, they can take any value on the measurement scale. In practice, the number of significant figures of a measurement is directly related to the precision of your measuring system – for example, dimensions measured with Vernier calipers will provide readings of greater precision than a millimetre ruler. Many of the variables measured in forensic science are continuous and quantitative, for example mass, temperature, time, amount of product formed by an enzyme.
- **Discontinuous (discrete) variables** – these are always obtained by counting and therefore the data values must be whole numbers (integers), with no intermediate values.

Ranked variables

These provide data that can be listed in order of magnitude (i.e. ranked), often expressed as a numbered series, for example from 1 to 5. When such data are given numerical ranks, rather than descriptive terms, they are sometimes called 'semi-quantitative data'. Note that the difference in magnitude between ranks need not be consistent. For example, regardless of whether there was a one-year or a five-year gap between offspring in a family, their ranks in order of birth would be the same (Fig. 3.1).

Qualitative variables (attributes)

These are non-numerical and descriptive – they have no order of preference and, therefore, are not measured on a numerical scale nor ranked in order of magnitude, but are described in terms of categories. Examples include viability (i.e. dead or alive), shape (e.g. round, flat, elongated), presence/absence of a particular molecule in a sample.

Variables may be independent or dependent. Usually, the variable under the control of the experimenter (e.g. time) is the independent variable, while the variable being measured is the dependent variable. Sometimes it is inappropriate to describe variables in this way and they are then referred to as interdependent variables (e.g. the length and breadth of an organism).

The majority of data values are recorded as direct measurements, readings or counts, but there is an important group, called derived (or computed), that

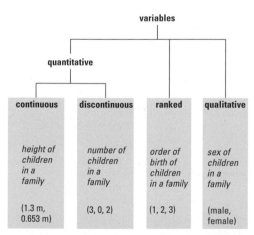

Fig. 3.1 Example to illustrate the different types of variables as used to describe some characteristics of families.

Examples A **nominal scale** for temperature is not feasible, since the relevant descriptive terms can be ranked in order of magnitude.

An **ordinal scale** for temperature measurement might use descriptive terms, ranked in ascending order, e.g. cold = 1, cool = 2, warm = 3, hot = 4.

The **Celsius scale** is an interval scale for temperature measurement, since the arbitrary zero corresponds to the freezing point of water (0°C).

The **Kelvin scale** is a ratio scale for temperature measurement since 0K represents a temperature of absolute zero (for information, the freezing point of water is 273.15K on this scale).

result from calculations based on two or more data values – for example ratios, percentages, indices and rates.

Measurement scales

Variables may be measured on different types of scale:

- **Nominal scale** – this classifies objects into categories based on a descriptive characteristic. It is the only scale suitable for qualitative data.
- **Ordinal scale** – this classifies by rank. There is a logical order in any number scale used.
- **Interval scale** – this is used for quantitative variables. Numbers on an equal unit scale are related to an arbitrary zero point.
- **Ratio scale** – this is similar to the interval scale, except that the zero point now represents an absence of that character (i.e. it is an absolute zero).

The measurement scale is important in determining the mathematical and statistical methods used to analyse your data. Table 3.1 presents a summary of the important properties of these scales. Note that you may be able to measure a characteristic in more than one way, or you may be able to convert data collected in one form to a different form, as in the example given in the margin (temperature), or you could find out the dates of birth of individuals (interval scale) but then use this information to rank them in order of birth (ordinal scale). Where there are no other constraints, you should use a ratio scale to measure a quantitative variable, since this will allow you to use the broadest range of mathematical and statistical procedures (Table 3.1).

Table 3.1 Some important features of scales of measurement

	Measurement scale			
	Nominal	Ordinal	Interval	Ratio
Type of variable	Qualitative (Ranked)* (Quantitative)*	Ranked (Quantitative)*	Quantitative	Quantitative
Examples	Species Sex Colour	Abundance scales Reproductive condition Optical assessment of colour development	Fahrenheit temperature scale Date (BC/AD)	Kelvin temperature scale Weight Length Response time Most physical measurements
Mathematical properties	Identity	Identity Magnitude	Identity Magnitude Equal intervals	Identity Magnitude Equal intervals True zero point
Mathematical operations possible on data	None	Rank	Rank Addition Subtraction	Rank Addition Subtraction Multiplication Division
Typical statistics used	Only those based on frequency of counts made: contingency tables, frequency distributions, etc. Chi-square test	Non-parametric methods, sign tests. Mann–Whitney U-test (check distribution before using, Chapter 56)	Almost all types of test, t-test, analysis of variance (ANOVA), etc. (check distribution	Almost all types of test, t-test, ANOVA, etc. (check distribution before using, Chapter 56)

*In some instances (see text for examples).

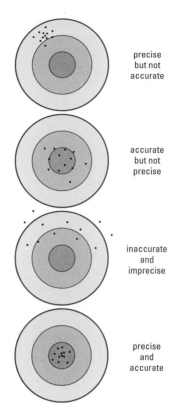

precise
but not
accurate

accurate
but not
precise

inaccurate
and
imprecise

precise
and
accurate

Fig. 3.2 'Target' diagrams illustrating precision and accuracy.

Accuracy and precision

Accuracy is the closeness of a measured or derived data value to its true value, while precision is the closeness of repeated measurements to each other (Fig. 3.2). A balance with a fault in it (i.e. a bias, see below) could give precise (i.e. very repeatable) but inaccurate (i.e. untrue) results. Unless there is bias in a measuring system, precision will lead to accuracy and it is precision that is generally the most important practical consideration, if there is no reason to suspect bias. You can investigate the precision of any measuring system by repeated measurements of individual samples.

Absolute accuracy and precision are impossible to achieve, due to both the limitations of measuring systems for continuous quantitative data and the fact that you are usually working with incomplete data sets (samples). It is particularly important to avoid spurious accuracy in the presentation of results – include only those digits that the accuracy of the measuring system implies. This type of error is common when changing units (e.g. inches to metres) and in derived data, especially when calculators give results to a large number of decimal places. Further advice is given on p. 501 and for validation on pp. 473–474.

Bias (systematic error) and consistency

Bias is a systematic or non-random distortion and is one of the most troublesome difficulties in using numerical data. Biases may be associated with incorrectly calibrated instruments, for example a faulty pipettor, or with experimental manipulations, for example shrinkage during the preservation of a specimen. Bias in measurement can also be subjective, or personal – for example, an experimenter's preconceived ideas about an 'expected' result.

Bias can be minimised by using a carefully standardised procedure, with fully calibrated instruments. You can investigate bias in 'trial runs' by measuring a single variable in several different ways, to see whether the same result is obtained.

To avoid personal bias, 'blind' measurements should be made where the identity of individual samples is not known to the operator – for example, using a coding system.

Measurement error

All measurements are subject to error, but the dangers of misinterpretation are reduced by recognising and understanding the likely sources of error and by adopting appropriate protocols and calculation procedures.

A common source of measurement error is carelessness – for example, reading a scale in the wrong direction or parallax errors. This can be reduced greatly by careful recording and may be detected by repeating the measurement. Other errors arise from faulty or inaccurate equipment, but even a perfectly functioning machine has distinct limits to the accuracy and precision of its measurements. These limits are often quoted in manufacturers' specifications and are applicable when an instrument is new; however, you should allow for some deterioration with age. Further errors are introduced when the subject being studied is open to influences outside your control. Resolving such problems requires appropriate experimental design and representative sampling.

One major influence virtually impossible to eliminate is the effect of the investigation itself – even putting a thermometer in a liquid may change the temperature of the liquid. The very act of measurement may give rise to a

Minimising errors *– determine early in your study what the dominant errors are likely to be and concentrate your time and effort on reducing these.*

Working with derived data *– special effort should be made to reduce measurement errors because their effects can be magnified when differences, ratios, indices or rates are calculated.*

confounding variable, as discussed in Chapter 55. You should include descriptions of possible sources of errors and estimates of their likely importance in any report. However, do not use 'natural variability' as a catch-all excuse for poor technique or inadequacies in your experimental design or analytical procedures.

Collecting and recording primary data

When carrying out advanced lab work or research projects, you will need to master the important skill of managing data and observations and learn how to keep a record of your studies in a lab book. This is important for the following reasons:

Understanding what is expected of you in note-taking – especially when taking notes for a lab-based practical. Pay special attention to the aims and learning objectives of the session, as these will indicate the sorts of notes you should be taking, including content and diagrams, and the ways in which you should present these for assessment.

- **An accurate and neat record** helps when using information later, perhaps for exam purposes or when writing a report.
- **It allows you to practise important skills** such as scientific writing, drawing diagrams, preparing graphs and tables and interpreting results.
- **Analysing and writing up your data** as you go along prevents a backlog at the end of your study time.
- **You can show your work to a future employer** to prove you have developed the skills necessary for writing up properly. In industry, this is vital so that others in your team can interpret and develop your work.

Recording primary data – never be tempted to jot down data on scraps of paper – you are likely to lose them, or to forget what individual values mean.

 KEY POINT *A good set of lab notes should:*
- *outline the purpose of your experiment or observation;*
- *set down all the information required to describe your materials and methods;*
- *record all relevant information about your results or observations and provide a visual representation of the data;*
- *note your immediate conclusions and suggestions for further experiments.*

Recording numerical data – write down only those figures that can be justified by the measurement technique (significant figures).

Individual observations (e.g. laboratory temperature) can be recorded in the text of your notes, but tables are often the most convenient way to collect large amounts of information. When preparing a table for data collection, you should:

1. **Use a concise title** or a numbered code for cross referencing.
2. **Decide on the number of variables** to be measured and their relationship with each other, and lay out the table appropriately:
   (a) The first column of your table should show values of the independent (controlled) variable, with subsequent columns for the individual (measured) values for each replicate or sample.
   (b) If several variables are measured for the same organism or sample, each should be given a row.
   (c) In time-course studies, put the replicates as columns grouped according to treatment, with the rows relating to different times.
3. **Make sure the arrangement reflects the order** in which the values will be collected. Your table should be designed to make the recording process as straightforward as possible in order to minimise the possibility of mistakes. For final presentation, a different arrangement may be best (Chapter 53).
4. **Consider whether additional columns** are required for subsequent calculations. Create a separate column for each mathematical manipulation, so the step-by-step calculations are clearly visible. Use a computer spreadsheet (pp. 495–6) if you are manipulating lots of data.

Designing a table for data collection – use a spreadsheet or the table-creating facility in a word processor to create your table. This will allow you to reorganise it easily if required. Make sure there is sufficient space in each column for the values – if in doubt, err on the generous side.

Identifying your notes – always put a date and time on each of your primary record sheets. You may also wish to add your name and details of the type of observation or experiment.

Recording observations – write down the actual observation, not your interpretation of it. For example, the colour of a presumptive test, rather than whether the test was positive or negative.

Choosing a notebook for primary recording – a spiral-bound notebook is good for making a primary record – it lies conveniently open on the bench and provides a simple method of dealing with major mistakes!

Choosing a book for secondary recording – a hard-backed A4 size lined book is good because you will not lose pages. Graphs, printouts, etc. can be stuck in, as required.

Formal aspects of keeping a record – the diary aspect of the record can be used to establish precedence (e.g. for patentable research where it can be important to 'minute' where and when an idea arose and whose it was); for error tracing (e.g. you might be able to find patterns in the work affecting the results); or even for justifying your activities to a supervisor.

5. **Take sufficient time to record quantitative data unambiguously** – write large clear numbers, making sure that individual numerals cannot be confused.

6. **Record numerical data to an appropriate number of significant figures,** reflecting the accuracy and precision of your measurement. Do not round off data values, as this might affect the subsequent analysis of your data.

7. **Record discrete or grouped data as a tally chart,** each row showing the possible values or classes of the variable. Provided that tally marks are of consistent size and spacing, this method has the advantage of providing an 'instant' frequency distribution chart.

8. **Prepare duplicated recording tables** if your experiments or observations will be repeated.

9. **Explain any unusual data values or observations** in a footnote. Don't rely on your memory.

Recording details of project and research work

One approach to recording your project work (see Chapter 61) at university is to make dual records.

Primary record

The primary record is made at the lab bench. In this, you must concentrate on the detail of materials, methods and results. Include information that would not be used elsewhere, but which would prove useful in error tracing – for example, if you note how a solution was made up (exact volumes and weights used rather than concentration alone), this could reveal whether a miscalculation had been the cause of a rogue result. Note the origin, type and state of the chemicals and organism(s) used. Make rough diagrams to show the arrangement of replicates, equipment, etc. If you are forced to use loose paper to record data, make sure each sheet is dated and taped to your lab book, collected in a ring binder or attached with a treasury tag. The same applies to traces, printouts and graphs.

The basic order of the primary record for a lab project should mirror that of a research report (see p. 560), including the title and date, brief introduction, comprehensive materials and methods, the data and short conclusions.

Secondary record

You should make a secondary record concurrently or later in a bound book and it ought to be neater, in both organisation and presentation. This book will be used when discussing results with your project supervisor, and when writing up a report or thesis, and may be part of your course assessment. While these notes should retain the essential features of the primary record, they should be more concise and the emphasis should move towards interpretation and analysis of the experiment. Outline the aims more carefully at the start and link the experiment to others in a series (e.g. 'Following the results of Expt.D24, it was decided to test whether...'). You should present data in an easily digestible form, for example as tables of means or as summary graphs. Use appropriate statistical tests (Chapter 56) to support your analysis of the results. The choice of a bound book ensures that data are not easily lost.

Note that the dual method of recording deals with the inevitable untidiness of notes taken at the bench or in the field – these often have to be made rapidly, in awkward positions and in a generally complex environment. Writing a second, neater version forces you to consider again details that might have been overlooked in the primary record, and provides a duplicate in case of loss or damage.

Analyse your data as soon as possible – always analyse and think about data immediately after collection as this may influence your subsequent activities.

- A graphical indication of what has happened can be particularly valuable.
- Carry out statistical analyses before moving on to the next experiment because apparent differences among treatments may not turn out to be statistically significant when tested.
- Write down any conclusions you make while analysing your data – sometimes those which seem obvious at the time of doing the work are forgotten when the time comes to write up a report or thesis.
- Note ideas for further studies as they occur to you – these may prove valuable later. Even if your experiment appears to be a failure, suggestions as to the likely causes might prove useful.

 SAFETY NOTE *Maintaining and consulting communal lab records – these activities may form a part of the safety requirements for working in a laboratory.*

If you find it difficult to decide on the amount of detail required in Materials and Methods, the basic ground rule is to record enough information to allow a reasonably competent scientist to repeat your work exactly. You must tread a line between the extremes of pedantic, irrelevant detail and the omission of information essential for a proper interpretation of the data – better perhaps to err on the side of extra detail to begin with. An experienced worker can help you decide which subtle shifts in technique are important (e.g. batch numbers for an important chemical, or when a new stock solution is made up and used). Many important scientific advances have been made because of careful observation and record taking, or because coincident data were recorded that did not seem of immediate value.

When creating a primary record, take care not to lose any of the information content of the data. For instance, if you only write down means and not individual values, this may affect your ability to carry out subsequent statistical analyses.

There are numerous ways to reduce the labour of keeping a record. Don't repeat Materials and Methods for a series of similar experiments; use devices such as 'method as for Expt. B4'. A photocopy might suffice if the method is derived from a text or article (check with your supervisor). To save time, make up and copy a checklist in which details such as chemical batch numbers can be entered.

Using communal records

If working with a research team or in a shared laboratory, you may need to use communal databases. These avoid duplication of effort and ensure uniformity in techniques. They may also form part of the legal safety requirements for your lab work. You will be expected to use the databases carefully and to contribute to them properly. They might include:

- **a shared notebook of common techniques** – e.g. how to make up media or solutions;
- **a set of simplified step-by-step instructions** for use of equipment – manuals are often complex and poorly written and it may help to redraft them, incorporating any differences in procedure adopted by the group;
- **an alphabetical list of suppliers** of equipment and consumables – perhaps held on a card index system;
- **a list of chemicals** required by the group and where they are stored;
- **the risk assessment sheets** for dangerous procedures (Chapter 2);
- **the record book** detailing the use of radioisotopes and their disposal;
- **Standard Operating Procedure (SOP)** – necessary to ensure the quality and operational procedures used in the laboratory.

Making observations

Observations provide the basic information leading to the formulation of hypotheses, an essential step in the scientific method (see Fig. 5.1). Observations are obtained either directly by our senses or indirectly through the use of instruments that extend our senses and may be either:

- **qualitative** – described by words or terms rather than by numbers and including subjective descriptions in terms of variables such as colour, shape and smell; often recorded using photographs and drawings;
- **quantitative** – numerical values derived from counts or measurements of a variable (see Chapter 54), frequently requiring use of some kind of instrument.

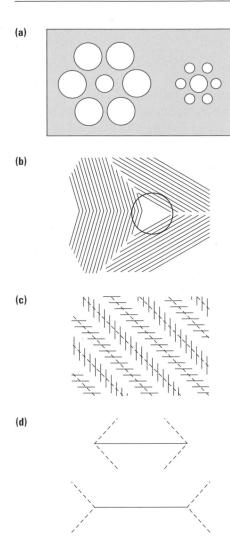

Fig. 3.3 Examples of 'optical illusions' caused by problems of perception. Image (a) shows how the sizes of adjacent objects can distort a simple comparison of size – the central circles in either hexagonal pattern are the same size. Image (b) reveals how shapes can be distorted by adjacent linear objects – the inner shape is a perfect circle. Image (c) illustrates how directional cues can lead to confusion – the dashed lines are parallel. Image (d) shows how adjacent shapes can make comparison of simple linear dimensions difficult – the two solid lines are the same length. In all cases, the correct perception can only be confirmed with a measurement aid such as a ruler or compass.

> **Preparation** – *thorough theoretical groundwork before a practical class or examination is vitally important for improving the quality of your observations (see Fig. 3.3).*

> **KEY POINT** *Although qualitative and quantitative observations are useful in science, you should try to make numerical counts or measurements wherever possible – this allows you to define your observations more rigorously and make objective comparisons using statistical tools.*

Factors influencing the quality of observations

Perception   Observation is highly dependent on the perception of the observer (Fig. 3.3). Perception involves both visual and intuitive processes, so your interpretation of what you see is very dependent on what you already know or have seen before. Thus, two persons observing the same event or object may 'see' it differently, a good example of bias. This is frequently true in microscopy where experience is an important factor in interpretation.

When you start forensic science, your knowledge base will be limited and your experience restricted. Practical training in observation provides the opportunity to develop both aspects of your skills in a process that is effectively a positive feedback loop – the more you know/see as a result of practice, the better your observations become.

Precision and error   Obviously very important for interpretive accuracy, with both human and non-human components (see Fig. 3.2).

Artefacts   These are artificial features introduced usually during some treatment process such as chemical fixation prior to microscopic examination. They may be included in the interpretive process if their presence is not recognised – again, prior experience and knowledge are important factors in spotting artefacts (see Chapter 10 in relation to microscopy).

Developing observational skills

In forensic science, you cannot rely solely on photography or video recordings, therefore you must be able to observe and to accurately draw what you see. You must develop your knowledge and observational skills to benefit properly from your practical work. The only way to acquire these skills is through extensive practice.

Make sure your observations are:

- **relevant** – directed towards a clearly defined objective;
- **accurate** – related to a scale whenever possible;
- **repeatable** – as error free (precise) as possible.

Much forensic science work attempts to relate action to deed, often through careful analysis of the crime scene. One of the best ways to develop observational skills is by making accurate drawings or diagrams, forcing you to look more carefully than is usual. An important observational skill to develop is the interpretation of two-dimensional images, such as footprint or fingerprint impressions and photographs, in terms of the three-dimensional forms from which they are derived. This requires a clear understanding of the nature of the image in terms of both scale and orientation.

Counting

Counting is an observational skill that requires practice to become both accurate and efficient. It is easy to make errors or to lose count when working with large numbers of objects. Use a counting aid whenever human error might be significant. There are many such aids – tally counters, tally charts and specialised counting devices such aas colony counters or drug tablet counters (see Fig. 3.4). It is important to avoid counting items twice, for example when counting hairs or fibres recovered from a jumper.

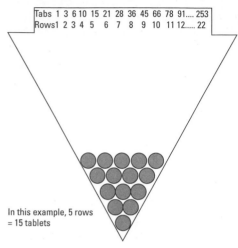

| Tabs | 1 | 3 | 6 | 10 | 15 | 21 | 28 | 36 | 45 | 66 | 78 | 91..... | 253 |
| Rows | 1 | 2 | 3 | 4 | 5 | 6 | 7 | 8 | 9 | 10 | 11 | 12..... | 22 |

In this example, 5 rows = 15 tablets

Fig. 3.4 A drug counter allows you to quickly and accurately count large numbers of tablets (Chapter 39).

Another valuable technique is to use a grid system to organise the counting procedure, for example when counting sperm heads under a microscope. Remember that you must decide on a protocol for sampling, particularly with regard to the direction of counting within the grid and for dealing with boundary overlaps to prevent double counting at the edges of the grid squares.

Observation during examinations

Making appropriate observations during practical examinations often causes difficulty, particularly when qualitative observations are needed. Answering such questions clearly requires specific knowledge, but also requires a strategy to provide the relevant observations. You should set out your observations in a logical sequence so that you show the examiner how you arrived at your conclusion.

Drawing diagrams

Drawing has an important place in forensic science because of its role in developing observation skills. You need to look at an object or crime scene very carefully to be able to draw it accurately, while labelling a diagram forces you to think about components and their positions. If your observation of an object or scene is poor, so too will be your diagram (see Chapter 23).

 KEY POINT *You may not feel confident about being able to produce quality art work in laboratory practicals, especially when the time allowed is limited. However, the requirements of drawing in forensic science are not as demanding as you might think and the skills required can be learned. By following the guidelines and techniques described below, most students should be able to produce good diagrams.*

Apparatus diagrams (laboratory work)

Here, your aim is to portray the components of some experimental set-up as a diagram (Fig. 12.20). Note that these figures are normally drawn as a section or in simplified schematic format (e.g. Fig. 12.2) rather than as a perspective drawing. Also, you may be more concerned with the relationship between parts than with showing them to a uniform scale.

Graphs and histograms

These are used to display numerical information (data) in a form that is easily assimilated. Chapter 52 covers the main types of graph and how they should be constructed.

Steps towards drawing a good diagram

To produce good figures, both planning and careful execution are needed (Box 3.1 gives useful practical advice).

Drawing materials While some diagrams for basic lab practical reports might be drawn in pencil, to allow corrections to be made, your crime scene sketches and examination notes must be made in ink, to prevent them from being altered or tampered with. Always use plain paper for drawing and, if you are asked to supply your own, make sure it is of good quality.

Use pen and ink to create line drawings for illustration purposes in posters, project reports, etc. Computer drawing programs can also provide good quality output suitable for these tasks, often giving a more professional end result.

Box 3.1 Checklist for making a good diagram

1. **Decide exactly what you are going to draw and why.**

2. **Decide how large the diagram should be and where you are going to place it on the page.**

3. **Start drawing:**
    (a) Draw exactly what you see, not what you expect to see.
    (b) Avoid shading and excessive detail.

(c) Use conventions and symbols where appropriate.

4. **Label the drawing/diagram carefully and comprehensively** including the date, where appropriate.

5. **Give the diagram a title and legend** to include any explanation of symbols/abbreviations, and a scale, if necessary.

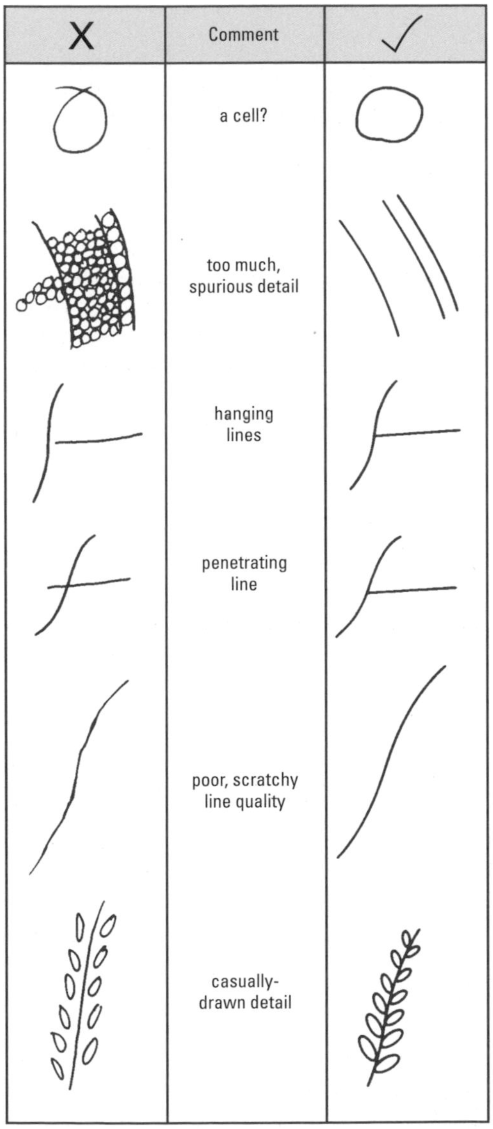

X	Comment	✓
◯	a cell?	◯
	too much, spurious detail	
	hanging lines	
	penetrating line	
	poor, scratchy line quality	
	casually-drawn detail	

Fig. 3.5 Examples of common errors in drawings of biological material, e.g. plant components (Chapter 36). Most of these mistakes are due to lack of care or attention to detail – easily solved!

Drawing from the microscope   Begin by positioning the paper beside your drawing hand and use the 'opposite' eye for examining the specimen – for a right-handed person, the paper is placed on the right of the microscope and you use your left eye. With a binocular microscope, use only one of the eyepieces – if you keep both eyes open, it is possible, with practice, to learn to draw and see the page with one eye while observing the specimen with the other. For specimens that need to be drawn very accurately a projection device may be required.

An alternative to drawing from the microscope is to capture the image using a specialist camera mounted onto the microscope. The general principles of photography are further described in Chapter 23.

Photomicrography   This requires the use of special equipment mounted on a microscope. Consult the manual(s) for the particular system you are using since most of the operations will be semi-automatic. The important operations for successful photomicrography are outlined below:

1. **Carefully prepare the object** – ensure thorough cleanliness of any slides or coverslips used.
2. **Choose the correct film type** and any filters required for alteration of colour balance, depending on the type of light source available (see pp. 233–4).
3. **Decide on the magnification to be used** – make sure that you know how this relates to the magnification of the negative/transparency.
4. **Carefully focus the object on to the film plane** – there will be a system-specific method for doing this but it may require practice to get it right.
5. **Make extra exposures above and below** the one indicated (called 'bracketing'), even when using an automatic exposure system – exposures of at least +1 and −1 stop are recommended, especially for colour photography.
6. **Include a photograph of a stage micrometer** (p. 74) so that the final magnification can be calculated and shown on the photograph.

Avoiding mistakes   There are three main categories of error in student diagrams:

1. **Incorrect positioning and proportions** – take care when representing individual components in a diagram.
2. **Forgetting to add a title, scale or a full set of labels** – use a checklist like that provided in Box 3.1 to ensure your diagram is complete.
3. **Untidiness in presentation** – avoid this type of error by using the correct materials as discussed above and by taking care – untidiness is frequently due to lack of attention to detail, as illustrated in Fig. 3.5.

Finally, it is important to realise that you cannot expect your drawing skills to develop overnight. This skill, like any other, requires much practice. Try to learn from any feedback your tutor may provide, and if your marks are consistently low without explanation, seek advice.

Sources for further study

Edwards, B. (2000) *The New Drawing on the Right Side of your Brain.* Souvenir Press, London.

Graziano, A.M. and Raulin, M.L. (2013) *Research Methods: A Process of Inquiry,* 8th edn. Available at: http://www.graziano-raulin.com/. Last accessed 13/08/2017.

Kanare, H.M. (1988) *Writing the Laboratory Notebook.* American Chemical Society, Washington.

Nussbeck, S.Y., Weil, P.W., Menzel, J., Marzec, B., Lorberg, K. and Schwappach, B. (2014) *The Laboratory Notebook in the 21st Century* EMBO Reports **15**(6): 631–634.

Oldfield, R., Dickes, F.W. and Rost, F.W.D. (2000) *Photography with a Microscope.* Cambridge University Press, Cambridge.

Stanford University. *Suggestions for Keeping Laboratory Notebooks* (2016) Available at: http://otl.stanford.edu/inventors/resources/inventors_labnotebooks.html. Last accessed 13/08/2017. [A Stanford University website which looks at the laboratory notebook from the patenting perspective.]

Zweifel, F.W. (1988) *A Handbook of Biological Illustration,* 2nd edn. University of Chicago Press, Chicago.

Study exercises

3.1 Classify variables. Decide on the type of variables used for the following measures, indicating whether they are quantitative or qualitative, continuous or discontinuous, and the type of scale that would be used.

(a) number of different organisms in a sample;
(b) height of individuals in a sample;
(c) eye colour of individuals in a sample;
(d) species present in a sample;
(e) date of a sample.

3.2 Investigate types of error. Before weighing out a controlled drug, the electronic balances need to be checked and calibrated. A set of certified standard masses were weighed on two electronic balances and gave the readings shown in the table. Explain these results in terms of the type of error involved in each case.

Comparison of weights of masses on two balances

	\multicolumn{5}{c}{Standard mass (mg)}				
	10	25	50	100	250
Reading (balance A)	10.050	25.049	50.051	100.048	250.052
Reading (balance B)	10.004	25.011	50.021	100.039	250.102

3.3 Design a table to record results from an experiment aimed at determining the concentration of a drug in a blood sample and the precision of an analytical instrument, e.g. HPLC. Six standards were used for the calibration curve and 10 replicates each for a low, mid and high concentration for precision data. Assume that you need to calculate means, relative standard deviation, r^2 etc.

4 SI units and their use

Dimensionless measurements – some quantities can be expressed as dimensionless ratios or logarithms (e.g. pH), and in these cases you do not need to use a qualifying unit.

Table 4.1 The base units and supplementary SI units

Measured quantity	Name of SI unit	Symbol
Base units		
Length	metre	m
Mass	kilogram	kg
Amount of substance	mole	mol
Time	second	s
Electric current	ampere	A
Temperature	kelvin	K
Luminous intensity	candela	cd
Supplementary units		
Plane angle	radian	rad
Solid angle	steradian	sr

When describing a measurement, you normally state both a number and a unit (e.g. 'the length is 1.85 metres'). The number expresses the ratio of the measured quantity to a fixed standard, while the unit identifies that standard measure or dimension. Clearly, a single unified system of units is essential for efficient communication of such data within the scientific community. The Système International d'Unités (SI) is the internationally ratified form of the metre–kilogram–second system of measurement and represents the accepted scientific convention for measurements of physical quantities.

Another important reason for adopting consistent units is to simplify complex calculations where you may be dealing with several measured quantities. Although the rules of the SI are complex and the scale of the base units is sometimes inconvenient, to gain the full benefits of the system you should observe its conventions strictly.

The description of measurements in SI involves:

- **seven base units and two supplementary units,** each having a specified abbreviation or symbol (Table 4.1);
- **derived units,** obtained from combinations of base and supplementary units, which may also be given special symbols (Table 4.2);
- **a set of prefixes** to denote multiplication factors of 10^3, used for convenience to express multiples or fractions of units (Table 4.3).

Table 4.2 Some important derived SI units

Measured quantity	Name of unit	Symbol	Definition in base units	Alternative in derived units
Energy	joule	J	m^2kgs^{-2}	Nm
Force	newton	N	$mkgs^{-2}$	Jm^{-1}
Pressure	pascal	Pa	$kgm^{-1}s^{-2}$	Nm^{-2}
Power	watt	W	m^2kgs^{-3}	Js^{-1}
Electric charge	coulomb	C	As	JV^{-1}
Electric potential difference	volt	V	$m^2kgA^{-1}s^{-3}$	JC^{-1}
Electric resistance	ohm	Ω	$m^2kgA^{-2}s^{-3}$	VA^{-1}
Electric conductance	siemens	S	$s^3A^2kg^{-1}m^{-2}$	AV^{-1} or Ω^{-1}
Electric capacitance	farad	F	$s^4A^2kg^{-1}m^{-2}$	CV^{-1}
Luminous flux	lumen	lm	cdsr	
Illumination	lux	lx	$cdsrm^{-2}$	lmm^{-2}
Frequency	hertz	Hz	s^{-1}	
Radioactivity	becquerel	Bq	s^{-1}	
Enzyme activity	katal	kat	mol substrate s^{-1}	

Table 4.3 Prefixes used in the SI

Multiple	Prefix	Symbol	Multiple	Prefix	Symbol
10^{-3}	milli	m	10^3	kilo	k
10^{-6}	micro	μ	10^6	mega	M
10^{-9}	nano	n	10^9	giga	G
10^{-12}	pico	p	10^{12}	tera	T
10^{-15}	femto	f	10^{15}	peta	P
10^{-18}	atto	a	10^{18}	exa	E
10^{-21}	zepto	z	10^{21}	zetta	Z
10^{-24}	yocto	y	10^{24}	yotta	Y

Recommendations for describing measurements in SI units

Basic format

> **Example**   10 mg is correct, while 10mg, 10 mg. and 10m g are incorrect. 2.6 mol is right, but 2.6 mols is wrong.

- **Express each measurement as a number** separated from its units by a space. If a prefix is required, no space is left between the prefix and the unit it refers to. Symbols for units are only written in their singular form and do not require full stops to show that they are abbreviated or that they are being multiplied together.

> **Example**   n stands for nano and N for newtons.

- **Give symbols and prefixes appropriate upper or lower case initial letters** as this may define their meaning. Upper case symbols are named after persons, but when written out in full they are not given initial capital letters.

> **Example**   1 982 963.192 309 kg (perhaps better expressed as 1.983 Gg).

- **Show the decimal sign** as a full point on the line. Some metric countries continue to use the comma for this purpose and you may come across this in the literature – therefore commas should not be used to separate groups of thousands. In numbers that contain many significant figures, you should separate multiples of 10^3 by spaces rather than commas.

Compound expressions for derived units

- **Take care to separate symbols** in compound expressions by a space to avoid the potential for confusion with prefixes. Note, for example, that 200 m s (metre-seconds) is different from 200 ms (milliseconds).
- **Express compound units** using negative powers rather than a solidus (/): for example, write molm^{-3} rather than mol/m^3. The solidus is reserved for separating a descriptive label from its units (see p. 380).
- **Use parentheses** to enclose expressions being raised to a power if this avoids confusion.
- **Where there is a choice, select relevant (natural) combinations of derived and base units** – for example you might choose units of Pam^{-1} to describe a hydrostatic pressure gradient rather than kgm^{-2}s^{-2}, even though these units are equivalent and the measurements are numerically the same.

Use of prefixes

- **Use prefixes** to denote multiples of 10^3 (Table 4.3) so that numbers are kept between 0.1 and 1,000.
- **Treat a combination of a prefix and a symbol as a single symbol.** Thus, when a modified unit is raised to a power, this refers to the whole unit including the prefix.

- **Avoid the prefixes** deci (d) for 10^{-1}, centi (c) for 10^{-2}, deca (da) for 10 and hecto (h) for 100 as they are not strictly SI.
- **Express very large or small numbers** as a number between 1 and 10 multiplied by a power of 10 if they are outside the range of prefixes shown in Table 4.3.
- **Do not use prefixes in the middle of derived units** – they should be attached only to a unit in the numerator (the exception is in the unit for mass, kg).

 KEY POINT *For the foreseeable future, you will need to make conversions from other units to SI units as much of the literature quotes data using imperial, c.g.s. or other systems. You will need to recognise these units and find the conversion factors required. Examples relevant to forensic science are given in Box 4.1. Table 4.4 provides values of some important physical constants in SI units.*

Some implications of SI in forensic science

Volume

The SI unit of volume is the cubic metre, m^3, which is rather large for practical purposes. The litre (L) and the millilitre (mL) are technically obsolete, but are widely used and glassware is still calibrated using them. Note also that the US spelling is liter. Use of the symbol L for litre, rather than l, avoids confusion with 1 and I.

Mass

The SI unit for mass is the kilogram (kg) rather than the gram (g) – this is unusual because the base unit has a prefix applied.

Amount of substance

You should use the mole (mol, i.e. Avogadro's constant; see Table 4.4) to express very large numbers. The mole gives the number of atoms in the atomic mass, a convenient constant.

Concentration

The SI unit of concentration, molm^{-3}, is quite convenient for biological systems. It is equivalent to the non-SI term 'millimolar' (mM ≡ Kmmol L^{-1})

Table 4.4 Some physical constants in SI terms

Physical constant	Symbol	Value and units
Avogadro's constant	N_A	6.022 174 × 10^{23} mol^{-1}
Boltzmann's constant	k	1.380 626 × 10^{-23}
Charge on electron	e	1.602 192 × 10^{-19} C
Gas constant	R	8.314 43 J K^{-1} mol^{-1}
Faraday's constant	F	9.648675 × 10^4 C mol^{-1}
Molar volume of ideal gas at STP	V_0	0.022 414 m^3 mol^{-1}
Speed of light *in vacuo*	c	2.997 924 × 10^8 ms^{-1}
Planck's constant	h	6.626 205 × 10^{-34} Js

Box 4.1 Conversion factors between some redundant units and the SI

Quantity	SI unit/symbol	Old unit/symbol	Multiply number in old unit by this factor for equivalent in SI old unit*	Multiply number in SI unit by this factor for equivalent in old unit*
Area	square metre/m^2	acre	4.04686×10^3	0.247105×10^{-3}
		hectare/ha	10×10^3	0.1×10^{-3}
		square foot/ft^2	$0.092\,903$	10.7639
		square inch/in^2	645.16×10^{-9}	$1.550\,00 \times 10^6$
		square yard/yd^2	$0.836\,127$	$1.195\,99$
Angle	radian/rad	degree/°	17.4532×10^{-3}	$57.295\,8$
Energy	joule/J	erg	0.1×10^{-6}	10×10^6
		kilowatt hour/kWh	3.6×10^6	0.277778×10^{-6}
		calorie/cal	4.1868	0.2388
Length	metre/m	Ångstrom/Å	0.1×10^{-9}	10×10^9
		foot/ft	$0.304\,8$	$3.280\,84$
		inch/in	$25.4-10^{-3}$	$39.370\,1$
		mile	1.60934×10^3	0.621373×10^{-3}
		yard/yd	$0.914\,4$	$1.093\,61$
Mass	kilogram/kg	ounce/oz	28.3495×10^{-3}	$35.274\,0$
		pound/lb	$0.453\,592$	$2.204\,62$
		stone	6.35029	$0.157\,473$
		hundredweight/cwt	$50.802\,4$	19.6841×10^{-3}
		ton (UK)	1.01605×10^3	0.984203×10^{-3}
Pressure	pascal/Pa	atmosphere/atm	$101\,325$	9.86923×10^{-6}
		bar/b	$100\,000$	10×10^{-6}
		millimetre of mercury/ mmHg	133.322	7.50064×10^{-3}
			133.322	7.50064×10^{-3}
		torr/Torr		
Radioactivity	becquerel/Bq	curie/Ci	$37-10^9$	27.0270×10^{-12}
Temperature	kelvin/K	centigrade (Celsius)	°C−273.15	K−273.15
		degree/°C	(°F−459.67) × 5/9	(K × 9/5)−459.67
		Fahrenheit degree/°F		
Volume	cubic metre/m^3	cubic foot/ft^3	$0.028\,316\,8$	$35.314\,7$
		cubic inch/in^3	16.3871×10^{-6}	61.0236×10^3
		cubic yard/yd^3	$0.764\,555$	$1.307\,95$
		UK pint/pt	$0.568\,261 \times 10^{-3}$	$1\,759.75$
		US pint/liq pt	$0.473\,176 \times 10^{-3}$	$2\,113.38$
		UK gallon/gal	$4.546\,09 \times 10^{-3}$	219.969
		US gallon/gal	$3.785\,41 \times 10^{-3}$	264.172

* In the case of temperature measurements, use formulae shown.

***Converting between concentration units** – being able to express concentrations in different units is important as this skill is frequently used when following instructions and interpreting data.*

while 'molar' (MK $\equiv$ mol L^{-1}) becomes kmolm^{-3}. Note that the symbol M in the SI is reserved for mega and hence should not be used for concentrations. If the solvent is not specified, then it is assumed to be water (see Chapter 9). Typically a concentration of a drug found in a biological sample (blood, urine or vitreous humour) will be expressed in mg L^{-1} ($\equiv$ ppm $\equiv$ μg ml^{-1}), in hair as

---

Converting mol L^{-1} to g L^{-1} by using the equation

$$mole = \frac{mass}{relative\ molecular\ mass\ (RMM)}$$

Definition

STP – Standard temperature and pressure = 293.15 K and 0.101 325 MPa.

---

ng g^{-1} and in tissues as mg kg^{-1} (see Chapter 38). If alcohol has been found in a blood sample, it is reported as mg 100 ml^{-1} (see Chapter 37).

Time

In general, use the second (s) when reporting physical quantities having a time element (e.g. rates of respiration in mol O_2 m^{-2} s^{-1}). Hours (h), days (d) and years should be used if seconds are clearly absurd (e.g. samples were taken over a 5-year period). Note, however, that you may have to convert these units to seconds when doing calculations.

Temperature

The SI unit is the kelvin, K. The degree Celsius scale has units of the same magnitude, °C, but its zero is at 273.15K, the melting point of ice at STP. Temperature is similar to time in that the Celsius scale is in widespread use, but note that conversions to K may be required for calculations. Note also that you must not use the degree sign (°) with K and that this symbol must be in upper case to avoid confusion with k for kilo; however, you *should* retain the degree sign with °C to avoid confusion with the coulomb, C.

Light

While the first six base units in Table 4.1 have standards of high precision, the SI base unit for luminous intensity, the candela (cd) and the derived units lm and lx (Table 4.2), are defined in 'human' terms. They are, in fact, based on the spectral responses of the eyes of 52 American soldiers measured in 1923! Clearly, few organisms 'see' light in the same way as this sample of humans. Also, light sources differ in their spectral quality. For these reasons, it is better to use expressions based on energy or photon content (e.g. W m^{-2} or mol photons m^{-2} s^{-1}) in studies other than those on human vision, specifying the wavelength spectrum involved.

Sources for further study

Anon (2000) *The NIST Reference on Constants, Units and Uncertainty; International System of Units (SI).* Available at: http://www.physics.nist.gov/cuu/Units/index.html. Last accessed 13/08/2017.

Anon (2014) *Measurement Units: The SI.* Available at: http://www.bipm.org/en/measurement-units/. Last accessed 13/08/2017.

Blackman, A. and Gahan, L (2014) *Aylward and Findlay's SI Chemical Data,* 7th edn. Wiley, Chichester.

Rowlett, R. (2004) *How Many? A Dictionary of Units of Measurement.* Available at: http://www.unc.edu/~rowlett/units/. Last accessed 13/08/2017.

SI units and their use

Study exercises

4.1 Practise converting between units. Using Box 4.1 and p. 26 as a source, convert the following amounts into the units shown. Give your answers to three significant figures.

(a) 6 foot 3 inches into centimetres
(b) One UK pint into millilitres
(c) 37 °C into kelvin
(d) 11 stone 6 pounds into kilograms.

4.2 Practise using prefixes appropriately. Simplify the following number/unit combinations using an appropriate prefix so that the number component lies between 0.1 and 1,000.

(a) 10,000 mm
(b) 0.015 mL

(c) 5×10^9 J
(d) 65,000 ms^{-1}
(e) 0.000 000 000 1 g

4.3 Practise calculating mass or moles.

(a) Calculate the mass of sucrose in g L^{-1} (RMM = 342.29). For the purpose of this calculation assume a concentration of 6×10^{-3} mol L^{-1}.
(b) Calculate the moles of caffeine (RMM = 194.19). For the purpose of this calculation assume a mass of caffeine of 4.3 g.
(c) Calculate the mass of nicotine in mg 100 mL^{-1} (RMM = 185.67). For the purpose of this calculation, assume a concentration of $1.43 - 10^{-3}$ mol L^{-1}.

5 Scientific method and design of experiments

Definitions

There are many interpretations of the following terms. For the purposes of this chapter, the following will be used.

Hypothesis – an explanation tested in a specific experiment or by a set of observations. Tends to involve a 'small-scale' idea.

Paradigm – theoretical framework so successful and well-confirmed that most research is carried out within its context and doesn't challenge it – even significant difficulties can be 'shelved' in favour of its retention.

(Scientific) Law – this concept can be summarised as an equation (law) that provides a succinct encapsulation of a system, often in the form of a mathematical relationship. The term is often used in the physical sciences (e.g. 'Beer's Law', p. 154).

Theory – a collection of hypotheses that covers a range of natural phenomena – a 'larger-scale' idea than a hypothesis. Note that a theory may be 'hypothetical', in the sense that it is a tentative explanation.

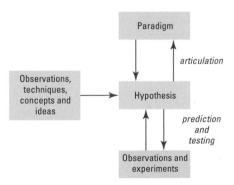

Fig. 5.1 A model of scientific method as used when testing hypotheses on a small scale. Hypotheses can arise as a result of various thought-processes on the part of the scientist, and are consistent with the overlying paradigm. Each hypothesis is testable by experiment or observation, leading to its confirmation or rejection. Confirmed hypotheses act to strengthen the status of the paradigm, but rejected ones do not immediately result in the paradigm's replacement.

Science is a body of knowledge based on observation and experiment. Scientists attempt to explain their observations in terms of theories and hypotheses. They make predictions from these hypotheses and test them by experiment or further observations. The philosophy and sociology that underlie this process are complex topics (see, e.g., Chalmers, 2013). Any brief description must involve simplifications.

Figure 5.1 models the scientific process you are most likely to be involved in – testing 'small-scale' hypotheses. These represent the sorts of explanation that can give rise to predictions that can be tested by an experiment or a series of observations. For example, you might put forward the hypothesis that the rate of loss of a substance from a biological tissue is dependent on the concentration of calcium ions. This might then lead to a prediction that the application of a substance known to decrease the concentration of calcium ions in the tissue would reduce K^+ efflux. An experiment could be set up to test this hypothesis, and the results would either confirm or refute the hypothesis.

If confirmed, a hypothesis is retained with greater confidence. If refuted, it is either rejected outright as false, or modified and retested. Alternatively, it might be decided that the experiment was not a valid test of the hypothesis – perhaps because it was later found that the applied substance could not penetrate the tissue to a presumed site of action.

Nearly all scientific research deals with the testing of small-scale hypotheses. These hypotheses operate within a theoretical framework that has proven to be successful – i.e. is confirmed by many experiments and is consistently predictive. This operating model or 'paradigm' is not changed readily, and, even if a result appears that seems to challenge the conventional view, would not be overturned immediately. The conflicting result would be 'shelved' until an explanation was found after further investigation. In the example used above, a relevant paradigm could be the notion that life processes are ultimately chemical in nature.

Although changes in paradigms are rare, they are important, and the scientists who recognise them become famous. For example, a 'paradigm shift' can be said to have occurred when Mendel's ideas about genetics replaced earlier explanations. Generally, however, results from hypothesis-testing tend to support and develop ('articulate') this paradigm, enhancing its relevance and strengthening its status. Thus, research in the area of molecular genetics has developed and refined Mendel's ideas.

Where do ideas for small-scale hypotheses come from? They arise from one or more thought processes on the part of a scientist:

- analogy with other systems;
- recognition of a pattern;
- recognition of departure from a pattern;
- invention of new analytical methods;
- development of a mathematical model;
- intuition;
- imagination.

Recently, it has been recognised that the process of science is not an entirely objective one. For instance, the choice of analogy that led to a new hypothesis might well be subjective, depending on past knowledge or understanding. Also, science is a social activity, where researchers put forward and defend viewpoints

Deciding whether to accept or reject a hypothesis – this is sometimes clear-cut, as in some areas of genetics where experiments can be set up to result in a binary outcome. In many other cases, the existence of 'biological variation' means that statistical techniques need to be employed (Chapters 55 and 56; Box 13.2).

against those who hold an opposing view; where groups may work together towards a common goal; and where effort may depend on externally dictated financial opportunities and constraints. As with any other human activity, science is bound to involve an element of subjectivity.

How are decisions made about whether to accept or reject a hypothesis? This is sometimes clear-cut, as in some areas of genetics where experiments can be set up to result in a binary outcome. In many other cases, the existence of 'natural variation' means that statistical techniques need to be employed (Chapters 55–57).

No hypothesis can ever be rejected with certainty. Statistics might allow us to quantify as vanishingly small the probability of an erroneous conclusion, but we are nevertheless left in the position of never being 100% certain that we have rejected all relevant alternative hypotheses, nor 100% certain that our decision to reject some alternative hypotheses was correct! However, despite these problems, experimental science has yielded and continues to yield many important findings.

 KEY POINT *The fallibility of scientific 'facts' is essential to grasp. No explanation can ever be 100% certain as it is always possible for a new alternative hypothesis to be generated. Our understanding of science changes all the time as new observations and methods force old hypotheses to be retested.*

Quantitative hypotheses, those involving a mathematical description of the system, have become very important, because they can be formulated concisely by mathematical models. Formulating models is often useful because it forces deeper thought about mechanisms and encourages simplification of the system. A mathematical model:

- is inherently testable through experiment;
- identifies areas where information is lacking or uncertain;
- encapsulates many observations;
- allows you to predict the behaviour of a system.

Remember, however, that assumptions and simplifications required to create a model may result in it being unrealistic. Further, the results obtained from any model are only as good as the information put into it.

Definition

Mathematical model – an algebraic summary of the relationship between the variables in a system.

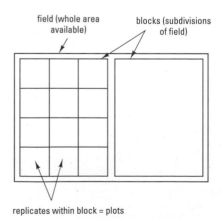

Fig. 5.2 Terminology and physical arrangement of elements in an experiment. Each block should contain the complete range of treatments (treatments may be replicated more than once in each block).

The terminology of experimentation

In many experiments, the aim is to provide evidence for causality. If x causes y, we expect, repeatedly, to find that a change in x results in a change in y. Hence, the ideal experiment of this kind involves measurement of y, the dependent (measured) variable, at one or more values of x, the independent variable, and subsequent demonstration of some relationship between them. Experiments therefore involve comparisons of the results of treatments – changes in the independent variable as applied to an experimental subject. The change is engineered by the experimenter under controlled conditions.

Subjects given the same treatment are known as replicates. A 'block' is a grouping of replicates. The blocks are contained in a 'field', i.e. the whole area (or time) available for the experiment (Fig. 5.2). These terms originated from the statistical analysis of agricultural experiments, but they are now used for many other areas of science.

Why you need to control variables in experiments

Interpretation of experiments is seldom clear-cut because uncontrolled variables always change when treatments are given.

Confounding variables

These variables increase or decrease systematically as the independent variable increases or decreases. Their effects are known as systematic variation. This form of variation can be disentangled from that caused directly by treatments by incorporating appropriate controls in the experiment. A control is really just another treatment where a potentially confounding variable is adjusted so that its effects, if any, can be taken into account. The results from a control may therefore allow an alternative hypothesis to be rejected. There are often many potential controls for any experiment.

The consequence of systematic variation is that you can never be certain that the treatment, and the treatment alone, has caused an observed result, especially when using biological material. By careful design you can, however, 'minimise the uncertainty' involved in your conclusion. Methods available include:

Reducing edge effects – one way to do this is to incorporate a 'buffer zone' of untreated subjects around the experiment proper.

- **ensuring, through experimental design,** that the independent variable is the only major factor that changes in any treatment;
- **incorporating appropriate controls** to show that potential confounding variables have little or no effect;
- **selecting experimental subjects randomly** to cancel out systematic variation arising from biased selection;
- **matching or pairing individuals among treatments** so that differences in response due to their initial status are eliminated;
- **arranging subjects and treatments randomly** so that responses to systematic differences in conditions do not influence the results;
- **ensuring that experimental conditions are uniform** so that responses to systematic differences in conditions are minimised; when attempting this, beware of 'edge effects' where subjects on the periphery of the layout experience substantially different conditions from those in the centre.

Nuisance variables

These are uncontrolled variables that cause differences in the value of y independently of the value of x, resulting in random variation. Experimental science is characterised by the high number of nuisance variables that are found and their relatively great influence on results – biological data tend to have large errors! To reduce and assess the consequences of nuisance variables:

- **incorporate replicates** to allow random variation to be quantified;
- **choose subjects** that are as similar as possible;
- **control random fluctuations** in environmental conditions.

Constraints on experimental design

Evaluating design constraints – a good way to do this is by processing an individual subject through the experimental procedures – a 'preliminary run' can help to identify potential difficulties.

Box 5.1 outlines the important stages in designing an experiment. At an early stage, you should find out how resources may constrain the design. For example, limits may be set by availability of subject materials, cost of treatment, availability of a chemical or bench space. Logistics may be a factor (e.g. time taken to record or analyse data).

Box 5.1   Checklist for designing and performing an experiment

1. Preliminaries

(a) **Read background material** and decide on a subject area to investigate.

(b) **Formulate a simple hypothesis to test** – it is preferable to have a clear answer to one question than to be uncertain about several questions.

(c) **Decide which dependent variable you are going to measure and how** – is it relevant to the problem? Can you measure it accurately, precisely and without bias?

(d) **Think about and plan the statistical analysis of your results** – will this affect your design?

2. Designing

(a) **Find out the limitations on your resources.**

(b) **Choose treatments and conditions that alter the minimum of confounding variables.**

(c) **Incorporate as many effective controls as possible.**

(d) **Keep the number of replicates as high as is feasible.**

(e) **Ensure that the same number of replicates is present in each treatment.**

(f) **Use effective randomisation and blocking arrangements.**

3. Planning

(a) **List all the materials you will need** – order any chemicals and make up solutions; obtain the experimental material you require; check equipment is available.

(b) **Organise space and/or time** in which to do the experiment.

(c) **Account for the time taken to apply treatments and record results** – make out a timesheet if things will be hectic.

4. Carrying out the experiment

(a) **Record the results and make careful notes of everything you do** (see p. 16) – make additional observations to those planned if interesting things happen.

(b) **Repeat the experiment** if time and resources allow.

5. Analysing

(a) **Graph data as soon as possible** (during the experiment if you can) – this will allow you to visualise what has happened and make adjustments to the design if this seems appropriate (e.g. timing of measurements).

(b) **Carry out the planned statistical analysis.**

(c) **Jot down conclusions and new hypotheses** arising from the experiment.

Your equipment or facilities may affect design because you cannot regulate conditions as well as you might desire. For example, you may be unable to ensure that the temperature is constant over an experiment laid out in an open laboratory.

Use of replicates

Deciding the number of replicates in each treatment – try to:

- *maximise the number of replicates in each treatment;*
- *make the number of replicates even.*

Replicate results show how variable the response is within treatments. They allow you to compare the differences among treatments in the context of the variability within treatments – you can do this *via* statistical tests such as analysis of variance (Chapter 56). Larger sample sizes tend to increase the precision of estimates of parameters and increase the chances of showing a significant difference between treatments, if one exists. For statistical reasons (weighting, ease of calculation, fitting data to certain tests), it is often best to keep the number of replicates even. Remember that the degree of independence of replicates is important – sub-samples cannot act as replicate samples, they tell you about variability in the measurement method but not in the quantity being measured.

If the total number of replicates available for an experiment is limited by resources, you may need to compromise between the number of treatments and the number of replicates per treatment. Statistics can help here, for it is possible to work out the minimum number of replicates you would need to show a certain difference between pairs of means (say 10%) at a specified level of significance (say $P = 0.05$). For this, you need to obtain a prior estimate of variability within treatments, perhaps from an initial trial run (e.g. Sokal and Rohlf, 2012).

Multi-factorial experiments

The simplest experiments are those in which one treatment (factor) is applied at a time to the subjects. This approach is likely to give clear-cut answers, but it could be criticised for lacking realism. In particular, it cannot take account of interactions among two or more conditions that are likely to occur in real life. A multi-factorial experiment (Fig. 5.3) is an attempt to do this – the interactions among treatments can be analysed by specialised statistics.

Multi-factorial experiments are economical on resources because of 'hidden replication'. This arises when two or more treatments are given to a subject because the result acts statistically as a replicate for each treatment. Choice of relevant treatments to combine is important in multi-factorial experiments – for instance, an interaction may be present at certain concentrations of a chemical but not at others (perhaps because the response is saturated). It is also important that the measurement scale for the response is consistent, otherwise spurious interactions may occur. Beware when planning a multi-factorial experiment that the number of replicates do not get out of hand – you may have to restrict the treatments to 'plus' or 'minus' the factor of interest (as in Fig. 5.3).

Repetition of experiments

Even if your experiment is well designed and analysed, you should understand that only limited conclusions can be made. Firstly, what you can say is valid for a particular place and time, with a particular investigator, experimental subject and method of applying treatments. Secondly, if your results were significant at the 5% level of probability (p. 518), there is still an approximately one-in-twenty chance that the results did arise by chance. To guard against these possibilities, it is important that experiments are repeated. Ideally, this would be done by an independent scientist with independent materials. However, it makes sense to repeat work yourself so that you can have full confidence in your conclusions. Many scientists recommend that experiments are done three times in total, but this may not be possible in undergraduate work.

Definition

Interaction – where the effect of treatments given together is greater or less than the sum of their individual effects.

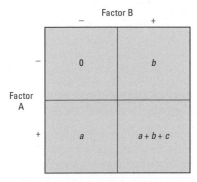

Fig. 5.3 Design of a simple multifactorial experiment. Factors A and B have effects *a* and *b* when applied alone. When both are applied together, the effect is denoted by *a* + *b* + *c*.

- If *c* = 0, there is no interaction (e.g. 2 + 2 + *c* = 4).
- If *c* is positive, there is a positive interaction (synergism) between A and B (e.g. 2 + 2 + *c* = 5).
- If *c* is negative, there is a negative interaction (antagonism) between A and B (e.g. 2 + 2 + *c* = 3).

Reporting correctly – it is good practice to report how many times your experiments were repeated (in Materials and Methods). In the Results section, you should add a statement saying that the illustrated experiment is representative.

Text references

Chalmers, A.F. (2013) *What is this Thing called Science?* 4th edn. Open University Press, Buckingham.

Sokal, R.R. and Rohlf, F.J. (2012) *Biometry,* 4th edn. W.H. Freeman and Co., San Francisco.

Sources for further study

Bird, C.L., Willoughby, C. and Frey, J.G. (2013) Laboratory notebooks in the digital era: the role of ELNs in record keeping for chemistry and other sciences. *Chemical Society Review* **42**: 8157–8175.

Heath, D. (1995) *An Introduction to Experimental Design and Statistics for Biology.* UCL Press Ltd, London.

Mansfield, N. (2007) *Key Skills for Scientists: Getting the Message Across. Section 2 Keeping a Laboratory Notebook* Available at: http://www.rsc.org/learn-chemistry/resource/res00001029/key-transferable-skills-for-science-students?cmpid=CMP00001721. Last accessed 13/08/2017.

Quinn, G.P. and Keough, M.J. (2002) *Experimental Design and Data Analysis for Biologists.* Cambridge University Press, Cambridge.

Ruxton, G. and Colegrave, N. (2009) *Experimental Design for the Life Sciences.* Oxford University Press, New York.

Study exercises

5.1 Generate random numbers. Produce a list of 20 random whole numbers between 1 and 5 using a spreadsheet. If using Excel, investigate the RAND( ) and INT functions. The RAND( ) function produces a random number between 0 and 1, so you will need to multiply by a constant factor to scale your final output appropriately. Copy your test formula(e) to several cells to test empirically whether it works.

5.2 Design and plan an experiment 1. Using one of your practicals, determine the purpose of the experiment and what it aims to achieve. List anything else could you do to make the results more robust.

5.3 Design and plan an experiment 2. Design an experiment to determine the growth rates of *Calliphora vicina* when feeding on cadaveric material. List all the confounding variables that you could encounter.

Fundamental laboratory techniques

Measuring and dispensing liquids

The equipment you should choose to measure out liquids depends on the volumes being dispensed, the accuracy required and the number of times the job must be done (Table 6.1).

Certain liquids may cause problems:

- **High-viscosity liquids are difficult to dispense** – allow time for all the liquid to transfer.
- **Organic solvents may evaporate rapidly,** making measurements inaccurate – work quickly; seal containers without delay.
- **Solutions prone to frothing** (e.g. protein and detergent solutions) are difficult to measure and dispense – avoid forming bubbles due to overagitation; do not transfer quickly.
- **Suspensions (e.g. cell cultures) may sediment** – thoroughly mix them before dispensing.

Pasteur pipettes

Hold correctly during use (Fig. 6.1) – keep the pipette vertical, with the middle fingers gripping the barrel while the thumb and index finger provide controlled pressure on the bulb. Squeeze gently to dispense individual drops.

Pasteur pipettes should be used with care for hazardous solutions. Remove the tip from the solution before fully releasing pressure on the bulb – the air taken up helps prevent spillage. To avoid the risk of cross-contamination, take care not to draw up solution into the bulb or to lie the pipette on its side. Plastic disposable 'Pastettes®' are safer and avoid cross-contamination.

Reading any volumetric scale – make sure your eye is level with the bottom of the liquid's meniscus and take the reading from this point.

Measuring cylinders and volumetric flasks

These must be used on a level surface so that the scale is horizontal. You should first fill with solution until just below the desired mark; then fill slowly

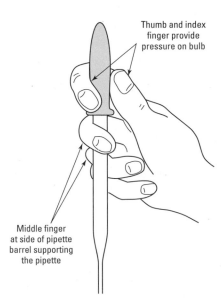

Thumb and index finger provide pressure on bulb

Middle finger at side of pipette barrel supporting the pipette

Fig. 6.1 How to hold a Pasteur pipette.

Table 6.1 Criteria for choosing a method for measuring out a liquid

Method	Best volume range	Accuracy	Usefulness for repetitive measurement
Pasteur pipette	1–5 m	Low	Convenient
Conical flask/beaker	25–5,000 m	Very low	Convenient
Measuring cylinder	5–2,000 m	Medium	Convenient
Volumetric flask	5–2,000 m	High	Convenient
Burette	1–100m	High	Convenient
Glass pipette	1–100 m	High	Convenient
Mechanical pipettor	5–1,000 m	High*	Convenient
Syringe	0.5–20 m	Medium**	Convenient
Microsyringe	0.5–50 m	High	Convenient
Weighing	Any (depends on accuracy of balance)	Very high	Inconvenient

*If correctly calibrated and used properly (see p. 39).
**Accuracy depends on width of barrel: large volumes are less accurate.

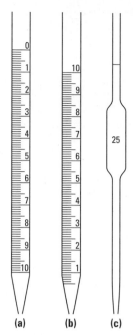

Fig. 6.2 Glass pipettes – (a) graduated pipette, reading from zero to maximum; (b) graduated pipette, reading from maximum to tip, by gravity; (c) bulb (volumetric) pipette, showing volume (calibration mark to tip, by gravity) on bulb.

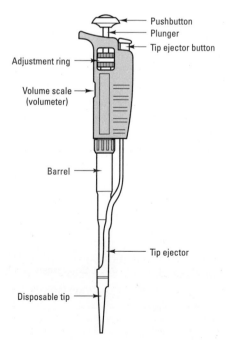

Fig. 6.3 A pipettor – the Gilson Pipetman.

(e.g. using a Pasteur pipette) until the meniscus is level with the mark. Allow time for the solution to run down the walls of the vessel.

Burettes

These should be mounted vertically on clamp stands – don't overtighten the clamp. First ensure the tap is closed and fill the body with solution using a funnel. Open the tap and allow some liquid to fill the tubing below the tap before first use. Take a meniscus reading, noting the value in your notebook. Dispense the solution via the tap and measure the new meniscus reading. The volume dispensed is the difference between the two readings. Titrations using a burette are usually performed using a magnetic stirrer to ensure thorough mixing.

Pipettes

These come in various designs, including graduated and bulb (volumetric) pipettes (Fig. 6.2). Take care to look at the volume scale before use – some pipettes empty from full volume to zero, others from zero to full volume; some scales refer to the shoulder of the tip, others to the tip by gravity or to the tip after blowing out.

 KEY POINT *For safety reasons, never mouth pipette – various aids are available, such as the Pi-pump®.*

Pipettors (autopipettors)

These come in two basic types:

- **Air displacement pipettors** – for routine work with dilute aqueous solutions. One of the most widely used examples is the Gilson Pipetman® (Fig. 6.3). Box 6.1 gives details on its use.
- **Positive displacement pipettors** – for non-standard applications, including dispensing viscous, dense or volatile liquids, or certain procedures in molecular genetics, for example the PCR (p. 114), where an air displacement pipettor might create aerosols, leading to errors.

Air displacement and positive displacement pipettors may be:

- **Fixed volume** – capable of delivering a single factory-set volume.
- **Adjustable** – where the volume is determined by the operator across a particular range of values. Make sure you are familiar with the working range of the pipettes so you can choose the appropriate pipette for your application.

 KEY POINT *Only use the adjustment ring (see Fig. 6.3) to change the volume. Do not use the push button.*

- **Pre-set** – movable between a limited number of values.
- **Multi-channel** – able to deliver several replicate volumes at the same time.

Whichever type you use, you must ensure that you understand the operating principles of the volume scale and the method for changing the volume delivered – some pipettors are easily misread.

A pipettor must be fitted with the correct disposable tip before use – each manufacturer produces different tips to fit particular models. Specialised tips are available for particular applications.

Box 6.1 Using a pipettor to deliver accurate, reproducible volumes of liquid

A pipettor can be used to dispense volumes with accuracy and precision, by following this step-wise procedure:

1. **Select a pipettor that operates over the appropriate range.** Most adjustable pipettors are accurate only over a particular working range and should not be used to deliver volumes below the manufacturer's specifications (minimum volume is usually 10–20% of maximum value). Do not attempt to set the volume above the maximum limit, or the pipettor may be damaged.

2. **Set the volume to be delivered.** In some pipettors, you 'dial up' the required volume. Types like the Gilson Pipetman have a system where the scale (or 'volumeter') consists of three numbers, read from top to bottom of the barrel, and adjusted using the black knurled adjustment ring (Fig. 6.3). This number gives the first three digits of the volume scale and thus can only be understood by establishing the maximum volume of the Pipetman, as shown on the push-button on the end of the plunger (Fig. 6.3). The following examples illustrate the principle for two common sizes of Pipetman®:

P1000 Pipetman
(maximum volume 1000 µL)
if you dial up

the volume is set at 1000 µL

P20 Pipetman
(maximum volume 20 µL)
if you dial up

the volume is set at 10.0 µL

3. **Fit a new disposable tip to the end of the barrel.** Make sure that it is the appropriate type for your pipettor and that it is correctly fitted. Press the tip on firmly using a slight twisting motion – if not, you will take up less than the set volume and liquid will drip from the tip during use. Tips are often supplied in boxes, for ease of use – if sterility is important, make sure you use appropriate sterile technique at all times (p. 41). *Never, ever, try to use a pipettor without its disposable tip.*

4. **Check your delivery.** Confirm that the pipettor delivers the correct volume by dispensing volumes of distilled water and weighing on a balance, assuming 1 mg = µL = mm³. The value should be within 1% of the selected volume. For small volumes, measure several 'squirts' together (e.g. 20 'squirts' of 5 µL = 100 mg). If the pipettor is inaccurate (p. 15, 474) giving a biased result (e.g. delivering significantly more or less than the volume set), you can make a temporary correction by adjusting the volumeter scale down or up accordingly (the volume *delivered* is more important than the value *displayed* on the volumeter), or have the pipettor recalibrated. If the pipettor is imprecise (p. 15, 38), delivering a variable amount of liquid each time, it may need to be serviced. After calibration, fit a clean (sterile) tip if necessary.

5. **Draw up the appropriate volume.** Holding the pipettor *vertically,* press down on the plunger/push-button until a resistance (spring-loaded stop) is met. Then place the end of the tip in the liquid. Keeping your thumb on the plunger/push-button, release the pressure slowly and evenly – watch the liquid being drawn up into the tip, to confirm that no air bubbles are present. Wait a second or so, to confirm that the liquid has been taken up, then withdraw the end of the tip from the liquid. Inexperienced users often have problems caused by drawing up the liquid too quickly/carelessly. If you accidentally draw liquid into the barrel, seek assistance from your demonstrator or supervisor as the barrel will need to be cleaned before further use.

6. **Make a quick visual check on the liquid in the tip.** Does the volume seem reasonable (e.g. a 100 mL volume should occupy approximately half the volume of a P200 tip)? The liquid will remain in the tip, without dripping, as long as the tip is fitted correctly and the pipettor is not tilted too far from a vertical position.

7. **Deliver the liquid.** Place the end of the tip against the wall of the vessel at a slight angle (10–15° from vertical) and press the plunger/push-button slowly and smoothly to the first (spring-loaded) stop. Wait a second or two, to allow any residual liquid to run down the inside of the tip, then press again to the final stop, dispensing any remaining liquid. Remove from the vessel with the plunger/push-button still depressed.

8. **Eject the tip.** Press the tip ejector button if present (Fig. 6.3). If the tip is contaminated, eject directly into an appropriate container, for example a beaker of disinfectant for microbiological work, or a labelled container for hazardous solutions (p. 9). For repeat delivery, fit a new tip if necessary and begin again at step 5 above. Always make sure that the tip is ejected before putting a pipettor on the bench.

Syringes

Syringes should be used by placing the tip of the needle in the solution, and drawing the plunger up slowly to the required point on the scale. Check the barrel to make sure no air bubbles have been drawn up. Expel slowly and touch the syringe on the edge of the vessel to remove any liquid adhering to the end of the needle. Microsyringes should always be cleaned before and after use by repeatedly drawing up and expelling pure solvent. The dead space in the syringe needle can occupy up to 4% of the nominal syringe volume. A way of avoiding such problems is to fill the dead space with an inert substance (e.g. silicone oil) after sampling. An alternative is to use a syringe where the plunger occupies the needle space (available for small volumes only).

Balances

These can be used to weigh accurately how much liquid you have dispensed. Convert mass to volume using the equation:

Example Using eqn [6.1], weighing 9 g of liquid with a density of 1.2 g mL^{-1} will give a volume of $9 \div 1.2 = 7.5$ mL.

$$\frac{\text{mass}}{\text{density}} = \text{volume} \qquad [6.1]$$

Densities of common solvents can be found in Haynes (2015). You will also need to know the liquid's temperature, as density is temperature dependent.

Holding and storing liquids

Test tubes

These are used for colour tests, small-scale reactions, blood for drug analyses, etc. The tube can be sterilised by heating and maintained in this state with a cap or cotton wool plug.

Beakers

Beakers are used for general purposes – for example, heating a solvent while the solute dissolves, carrying out a titration, etc.

Conical (Erlenmeyer) flasks

Working with beakers and flasks – *remember that volume graduations, where present, are often inaccurate and should be used only where approximations will suffice.*

These are used for storage of solutions. Their wide base makes them stable, while their small mouth reduces evaporation and makes them easier to seal. Volume gradations, where present, are often inaccurate.

Bottles and vials

These are used when the solution needs to be sealed for safety, for sterility or to prevent evaporation or oxidation. They usually have a screw top or ground glass stopper to prevent evaporation and contamination. Many types are available, including 'bijou', 'McCartney', 'universal' and 'Winkler'.

Storing light-sensitive chemicals – *use a coloured vessel or wrap aluminium foil around a clear vessel.*

You should clearly label all stored solutions, including relevant hazard information, preferably marking with hazard warning tape. Seal vessels in an appropriate way, for example using a stopper or a sealing film such as Parafilm® or Nescofilm to prevent evaporation. To avoid degradation, store your solution in a fridge, but allow it to reach room temperature before use. Unless a solution containing organic constituents has been sterilised or is toxic, microbes will start growing, so older solutions may not give reliable results.

Table 6.2 Spectral cut-off values for glass and plastics (λ_{50} = wavelength at which transmission of EMR is reduced to 50%)

Material	λ_{50} (nm)
Routine glassware	340
Pyrex® glass	292
Polycarbonate	396
Acrylic	342
Polyester	318
Quartz	220

Special cleaning of glass – for an acid wash use dilute acid, e.g. 100 mmol L^{-1} (100 mol m^{-3}) HCl. Rinse thoroughly at least three times with distilled or deionised water. Glassware that must be exceptionally clean (e.g. for a micro-nutrient study) should be washed in a chromic acid bath, but this involves toxic and corrosive chemicals and should only be used under supervision.

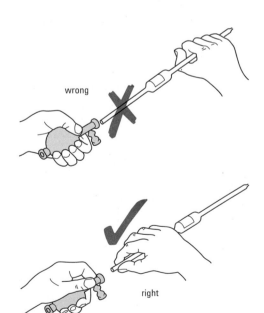
wrong

right

Fig. 6.4 Handling glass pipettes and tubing.

Creating specialised apparatus

Glassware systems incorporating ground glass connections such as Quickfit are useful for setting up combinations of standard glass components – for example, for chemical reactions. In project work, you may need to adapt standard forms of glassware for a special need. A glassblowing service (often available in chemistry departments) can make special items to order.

Choosing between glass and plastic

Bear in mind the following points:

- **Reactivity** – plastic vessels often distort at relatively low temperatures; they may be inflammable, may dissolve in certain organic solvents and may be affected by prolonged exposure to ultraviolet (UV) light. Some plasticisers may leach from vessels and have been shown to have biological activity. Glass may adsorb ions and other molecules and then leach them into solutions, especially in alkaline conditions. Pyrex® glass is stronger than ordinary soda glass and can withstand temperatures up to 500°C.
- **Rigidity and resilience** – plastic vessels are not recommended where volume is critical as they may distort through time. Use class A volumetric glassware for accurate work, for example preparing solutions (Chapter 7). Glass vessels are more easily broken than plastic, which is particularly important for centrifugation (see p. 82).
- **Opacity** – both glass and plastic absorb light in the UV range of the EMR spectrum (Table 6.2) Quartz should be used where this is important, for example in cuvettes for UV spectrophotometry (see p. 156).
- **Disposability** – plastic items may be cheap enough to make them disposable, an advantage where there is a risk of chemical or microbial contamination.

Cleaning glass and plastic

Take care to avoid the possibility of contamination arising from prior use of chemicals or inadequate rinsing following washing. A thorough rinse with distilled or deionised water immediately before use will remove dust and other deposits and is good practice in quantitative work, but ensure that the rinsing solution is not left in the vessel. 'Strong' basic detergents (e.g. Pyroneg) are good for solubilising acidic deposits. If there is a risk of basic deposits remaining, use an acid wash. If there is a risk of contamination from organic deposits, a rinse with AnalaR® grade ethanol is recommended. Glassware can be disinfected by washing with a sodium hypochlorite bleach such as Chloros®, with sodium metabisulphite or a blended commercial product such as Virkon® – dilute as recommended before use and rinse thoroughly with sterile water after use. Alternatively, to sterilise, heat glassware to at least 121°C for 15 min in an autoclave or 160°C for 3 h in an oven.

Safety with glass

Many minor accidents in the laboratory are due to lack of care with glassware. You should follow these general precautions:

- **Wear safety glasses when there is *any* risk of glass breakage** – for example when using low pressures or heating solutions.
- **If heating glassware, use a 'soft' Bunsen flame** – this avoids creating a hot spot where cracks may start. Always use tongs or special heat-resistant gloves when handling hot glassware.

- **Don't use chipped or cracked glassware** – it may break under very slight strains and should be disposed of in the broken glassware bin.
- **Never carry large bottles by their necks** – support them with a hand underneath or, better still, carry them in a basket.
- **Take care when attaching tubing to glass tubes and when putting glass tubes into bungs** – always hold the tube and 'hole' close together (Fig. 6.4) and wear thick gloves when appropriate.
- **Don't force bungs too firmly into bottles** – they can be very difficult to remove. If you need a tight seal, use a screw-top bottle with a rubber or plastic seal.
- **Dispose of broken glass thoroughly and with great care** – use disposable paper towels and wear thick gloves. Always put pieces of broken glass into the correct bin.

Text reference

Haynes, W.M. (2015) *CRC Handbook of Chemistry and Physics,* 96th edn. CRC Press, Boca Raton.

Sources for further study

Anon (2016) *Gilson Guide to Pipetting,* 3rd edn. Available at: http://www.gilson.com/en/Pipette/Categories/86/Default. aspx#.WEGD39KLRpg. Last accessed 14/08/2017.

Boyer, R.F. (2011) *Biochemistry Laboratory: Modern Theory and Techniques,* 2nd edn. Prentice Hall, New Jersey.

CHEMnet BASE. Available at: http://www.chemnetbase.com. Last accessed 14/08/2017. [Online access to the *Handbook of Chemistry and Physics*]

Henrickson, C., Byrd, L.C. and Hunter, N.W. (2005) *A Laboratory Manual for General, Organic and Biochemistry,* 5th edn. McGraw-Hill, New York.

Seidman, L.A. and Moore, C.J. (2008) *Basic Laboratory Methods for Biotechnology: Textbook and Laboratory Reference,* 2nd edn. Benjamin Cummings, San Francisco.

Study exercises

6.1 Decide on the appropriate methods and equipment for the following procedures.

(a) Preparing one litre of ethanol at approximately 70% v/v in water for use as a general-purpose reagent.

(b) Adding 200 μL of a sample to the well of an ELISA plate (Chapter 21).

(c) Preparing a calibration standard from a 1 mg mL^{-1} stock solution of methadone, to contain 2.0 mg L^{-1}.

6.2 Write a protocol for calibrating and using a pipettor. After reading this chapter, prepare a detailed stepwise protocol explaining how to use a pipettor to deliver a specific volume, say of 500 μL (e.g. using a Gilson Pipetman, or an alternative if your department does not use this type). Ask another student to evaluate your protocol and provide you with written feedback – either simply by reading through your protocol, or by trying it out with a pipettor as part of a class exercise (check with a member of staff before you attempt this in a laboratory).

6.3 Determine the accuracy and precision of a pipette. Using the following data for three different models of pipettor, determine which pipettor is most accurate and which is most precise (see p. 15 if you are unsure of the definitions of these two terms). All three pipettors were set to deliver 1,000 μL (1.000 mL) and 10 repetitive measurements of the weight of the volume of water in grams delivered were made using a three-place balance:

Model A pipettor: 0.986; 0.971; 0.993; 0.964; 0.983; 0.996; 0.977; 0.969; 0.982; 0.974

Model B pipettor: 1.013; 1.011; 1.010; 1.009; 1.011; 1.010; 1.011; 1.009; 1.011; 1.012

Model C pipettor: 0.985; 1.022; 1.051; 1.067; 0.973; 0.982; 0.894; 1.045; 1.062; 0.928

In your answer, you should support your conclusions with appropriate numerical (statistical) evidence (see Chapter 56 for appropriate measures of location and dispersion).

Using chemicals

Safety aspects

In practical classes, the person in charge has a responsibility to inform you of any hazards associated with the use of chemicals. In project work, your first duty when using an unfamiliar chemical is to find out about its properties, especially those relating to safety. For routine practical procedures, a risk assessment (p. 6) will have been carried out by a member of staff and relevant safety information will be included in the practical schedule – an example is shown in Table 7.1 for the chemical enhancement of fingerprints.

Table 7.1 Representative risk assessment information for a practical exercise in chemical enhancement of fingerprints using superglue and BY40

Experimental record – short COSHH record form

COSHH Assessments for: Chemical Enhancement of latent finger prints

Name of assessor ___ Alan Langford_____   Signed A Langford Date 01/10/17

Substance	H statement	Hazard Key hazard(s) associated with the substance	Signal word?	Likelihood	Severity	Risk (before additional control measures)	Specific risk control measures	Controlled risk
Basic yellow 40	H315, 319, 335	Causes skin, respiratory and **serious** eye irritation	**WARNING**	3	4	12	GLP, PPE, gloves safety glasses	4
Ethyl-2-cyanoacrylate	H315, 319, 335	Causes skin, respiratory and **serious** eye irritation	**WARNING**	3	4	12	GLP, PPE, gloves, safety glasses, used in dedicated fingerprint fuming cabinet	4
Basic yellow working solution Ethanol (100 mL + 0.2 g dye)	H225	Highly flammable liquid and vapour	**WARNING (for neat ethanol)**	2	3	6	GLP, PPE, use in fume hood	3

Substance	P Statement	Storage	Emergency procedures (in event of spillage, fire etc.) Detail	Disposal
Basic yellow 40	P261, 305, 351,338	Cool, sealed container, dry, well ventilated	Fire; wear s/c breathing apparatus if necessary; extinguish: water or CO_2 Spillage: water; do not let enter drain First aid: wash with water for 15 mins	In solvent; to flammable waste for incineration
Basic yellow working solution	P210, 261, 305, 351,338	Store in cool place. Keep container tightly closed in a dry and well-ventilated place. Containers that are opened must be carefully resealed and kept upright to prevent leakage.	Fire: water, CO_2, powder, foam Spillage: wear gloves, Absorb material, wash area with water First aid: IF IN EYES: Rinse cautiously with water for several minutes. Remove contact lenses, if present and easy to do. Continue rinsing.	Flammable waste for incineration

Finding out about chemicals – *The Merck Index (O'Neil et al., 2013) and the CRC Handbook of Chemistry and Physics (Haynes, 2015) are useful sources of information on the physical and biological properties of chemicals, including melting and boiling points, solubility, toxicity, etc. (see Fig. 7.1).*

Fig. 7.1 The Merck Index on-line can be used to search for information on specific chemicals e.g. sodium chloride.

KEY POINT *Before you use any chemical you must find out whether safety precautions need to be taken and complete the appropriate forms confirming that you appreciate the risks involved.*

Your department or school must provide the relevant information to allow you to do this. If your supervisor has filled out the form, read it carefully before signing.

Key safety points when handling chemicals are:

- **Treat all chemicals as potentially dangerous** – for lab classes, you should carefully read all hazard and risk information provided before you start work. In project work, you may need to be involved in the risk assessment process with your supervisor.
- **Wear a laboratory coat, with buttons fastened, at all times** – it should be cleaned appropriately should any chemical compound be spilled on it. Closed-toe footwear will protect your feet should any spillages occur.
- **Make sure you know where safety devices such as eye bath, fire extinguisher, first aid kit, are kept** before you begin work in the lab.
- **Wear gloves and safety glasses** for toxic, irritant or corrosive chemicals and carry out procedures with them in a fume cupboard – make sure you understand the hazard warning signs (p. 9), along with any specific hazard coding system used in your department. Carry out procedures with solid material in a fume cupboard.
- **Use aids such as pipette fillers** to minimise risk of contact.
- **Extinguish all naked flames** when working with flammable substances.
- **Never smoke, eat, drink or chew gum** in a lab where chemicals are handled.
- **Label solutions appropriately.**
- **Report all spillages and clean them up properly.**
- **Dispose of chemicals and biological samples in the correct manner** – if unsure, ask a member of staff (do not assume that it is safe to use the lab waste bin or the sink for disposal).
- **Always wash your hands** after any direct contact with chemicals or biological material at the end of a lab session.

Selection

Chemicals are supplied in various degrees of purity and this is always stated on the manufacturer's containers. Suppliers differ in the names given to the grades and there is no conformity in purity standards. Very pure chemicals cost more, sometimes a lot more, and should only be used if the situation demands. If you need to order a chemical, your department will have a defined procedure for doing this.

Preparing solutions

Using chemicals – *be considerate to others. Always return store room chemicals promptly to the correct place. Report when supplies are getting low to the person responsible for looking after the store. If you empty an aspirator or wash bottle, fill it up from the appropriate source!*

Solutions are usually prepared with respect to their molar concentrations (e.g. mmol L^{-1}, or mol m^{-3}), or mass concentrations (e.g. gL^{-1}, or kgm^{-3}). Both can be regarded as an amount of *substance* per unit volume of *solution*, in accordance with the relationship:

$$\text{concentration} = \frac{\text{amount}}{\text{volume}} \qquad [7.1]$$

The most important aspect of eqn [7.1] is to recognise clearly the units involved, and to prepare the solution accordingly. For molar concentrations, you will need the relative molecular mass of the compound, so that you can determine the mass of substance required. Further advice on concentrations and interconversion of units is given on p. 26.

Box 7.1 shows the steps involved in making up a solution. The concentration you require is likely to be defined by a protocol you are following and the grade of chemical and supplier may also be specified. Success may depend on using the same source and quality, for example with enzyme work. To avoid waste, think carefully about the volume of solution you require, though it is always a good idea to err on the high side because you may spill some or make a mistake when dispensing it. Try to choose one of the standard volumes for vessels, as this will make measuring-out easier.

Box 7.1 How to make up an aqueous solution of known concentration from solid material

1. **Find out or decide the concentration of chemical required** and the degree of purity necessary.

2. **Decide on the volume of solution required.**

3. **Find out the relative molecular mass of the chemical (M_r).** This is the sum of the atomic (elemental) masses of the component elements and can be found on the container. If the chemical is hydrated, i.e. has water molecules associated with it, these must be included when calculating the mass required.

4. **Work out the mass of chemical that will give the concentration desired in the volume required.**

    Suppose your procedure requires you to prepare 250 mL of 0.1 mol L^{-1} NaCl.
    (a) Begin by expressing all volumes in the same units, either millilitres or litres (e.g. 250 mL as 0.25 litres).
    (b) Calculate the number of moles required from eqn [7.1]: 0.1 = amount (mol) ÷ 0.25. By rearrangement, the required number of moles is thus 0.1 × 0.25 = 0.025 mol.
    (c) Convert from mol to g by multiplying by the relative molecular mass (M_r for NaCl = 58.44).
    (d) Therefore, you need to make up 0.025 × 58.44 = 1.461 g to 250 mL of solution, using distilled water.

In some instances, it may be easier to work in SI units, though you must be careful when using exponential numbers.

    Suppose your protocol states that you need 100 mL of 10 mmol L^{-1} KCl.
    (e) Start by converting this to 100 × 10^{-6}m^3 of 10 molm^{-3} KCl.
    (f) The required number of mol is thus (100 × 10^{-6}) × (10) = 10^3.
    (g) Each mol of KCl weighs 72.56g (M_r, the relative molecular mass).

(h) Therefore you need to make up 72.56 × 10^{-3}g = 72.56 mg KCl to 100 × 10^{-6}m^3 (100 mL) with distilled water.

See Box 8.1 for additional information.

5. **Weigh out the required mass of chemical to an appropriate accuracy.** If the mass is too small to weigh to the desired degree of accuracy, consider the following options:
    (a) Make up a greater volume of solution.
    (b) Make up a stock solution that can be diluted at a later stage (p. 46).
    (c) Weigh the mass first, then calculate what volume to make the solution up to using eqn [7.1].

6. **Add the chemical to a beaker or conical flask then add a little less water than the final amount required.** If some of the chemical sticks to the paper, foil or weighing boat, use some of the water to wash it off.

7. **Stir and, if necessary, heat the solution to ensure all the chemical dissolves.** You can determine when this has happened visually by observing the disappearance of the crystals or powder.

8. **If required, check and adjust the pH of the solution when cool** (see p. 58).

9. **Make up the solution to the desired volume.** If the concentration needs to be accurate, use a class A volumetric flask; if a high degree of accuracy is not required, use a measuring cylinder (class B).
    (a) Pour the solution from the beaker into the measuring vessel using a funnel to avoid spillage.
    (b) Make up the volume so that the meniscus comes up to the appropriate measurement line. For accurate work, rinse out the original vessel and use this liquid to make up the volume.

10. **Transfer the solution to a reagent bottle or a conical flask and label the vessel clearly.**

Use distilled or deionised water to make up aqueous solutions and stir to make sure all the chemical is dissolved. Magnetic stirrers are the most convenient means of doing this – carefully drop a clean magnetic stirrer bar ('flea') in the beaker, avoiding splashing; place the beaker centrally on the stirrer plate, switch on the stirrer and gradually increase the speed of stirring. When the crystals or powder have completely dissolved, switch off and retrieve the flea with a magnet or another flea. Take care not to contaminate your solution when you do this and rinse the flea with distilled water.

'Obstinate' solutions may require heating but do this only if you know that the chemical will not be damaged at the temperature used. Use a stirrer-heater to keep the solution mixed as you heat it. Allow the solution to cool down before you measure its volume or pH as these are affected by temperature.

Stock solutions

Stock solutions are valuable when making up a range of solutions containing different concentrations of a reagent, or if the solutions have some common ingredients. They also save work if the same solution is used over a prolonged period (e.g. a nutrient solution). The stock solution is more concentrated than the final requirement and is diluted as appropriate when the final solutions are made up. The principle is best illustrated with an example (Table 7.2).

Preparing dilutions

Making a single dilution

In analytical work, you may need to dilute a stock solution to give a particular mass concentration, or molar concentration. Use the following procedure to prepare a solution in a volumetric flask:

1. **Transfer an accurate volume of stock solution** to a volumetric flask, using appropriate equipment (Table 6.1).
2. **Make up to the calibration mark with solvent** – add the last few drops from a pipette or solvent bottle, until the meniscus is level with the calibration mark.
3. **Mix thoroughly,** either by repeated inversion (holding the stopper firmly) or by prolonged stirring, using a magnetic stirrer. Make sure you add the magnetic flea *after* the volume adjustment step.

For routine work using dilute aqueous solutions where the highest degree of accuracy is not required, it may be acceptable to substitute test tubes or conical

---

Solving solubility problems – if your chemical does not dissolve after a reasonable time:

- check the limits of solubility for your compound (see Merck Index, O'Neil et al., 2013);
- check the pH of the solution – solubility often changes with pH, e.g. you may be able to dissolve the compound in an acidic or a basic solution.

Making a dilution – use the relationship $[C_1]V_1 = [C_2]V_2$ to determine volume or concentration (see p. 54).

Table 7.2 Use of stock solutions. Suppose you need a set of solutions 10 mL in volume containing differing concentrations of KCl, with and without reagent Q. You decide to make up a stock of KCl at twice the maximum required concentration (50 mmol L^{-1} = 50 mol m^{-3}) and a stock of reagent Q at twice its required concentration. The table shows how you might use these stocks to make up the media you require. Note that the total volumes of stock you require can be calculated from the table (end column).

Stock solutions	Volume of stock required to make required solutions (mL)						Total volume of stock required (mL)
	No KCl plus Q	No KCl minus Q	15 mmol L^{-1} KCl plus Q	15 mmol L^{-1} KCl minus Q	25 mmol L^{-1} KCl plus Q	25 mmol L^{-1} KCl minus Q	
50 mmol L^{-1} KCl	0	0	3	3	5	5	16
[reagent Q] $\times$ 2	5	0	5	0	5	0	15
Water	5	10	2	7	0	5	29
Total	10	10	10	10	10	10	60

Removing a magnetic flea from a volumetric flask – *use a strong magnet to bring the flea to the top of the flask, to avoid contamination during removal.*

Using the correct volumes – *it is important to distinguish between the volumes of the various liquids. A one-in-ten dilution is obtained using 1 volume of stock solution plus 9 volumes of diluent (1 + 9 = 10). Note that when this is shown as a ratio, it may represent the initial and final volumes (e.g. 1:10) or, sometimes, the volumes of stock solution and diluent (e.g. 1:9).*

Using diluents – *various liquids are used, including distilled or deionised water, salt solutions, buffers, Ringer's solution, etc., according to the specific requirements of the procedure.*

flasks for volumetric flasks. In such cases, you would calculate the volumes of stock solution and diluent required, with the assumption that the final volume is determined by the sum of the individual volumes of stock and diluent used (e.g. Table 7.2). Thus, a two-fold dilution would be prepared using 1 volume of stock solution and 1 volume of diluent. The dilution factor is obtained from the ratio of the initial concentration of the stock solution and the final concentration of the diluted solution. The dilution factor can be used to determine the volumes of stock and diluent required in a particular instance. For example, suppose you wanted to prepare 100 mL of a solution of NaCl at 0.2 mol L^{-1}. Using a stock solution containing 4.0 mol L^{-1} NaCl, the dilution factor is $0.2 \div 4.0 = 0.05 = 1/20$ (a twenty-fold dilution). Therefore, the amount of stock solution required is 1/20th of 100 mL = 5 mL and the amount of diluent needed is 19/20th of 100 mL = 95 mL.

Preparing a dilution series

Dilution series are used in a wide range of procedures, including the preparation of standard curves for calibration of analytical instruments (p. 478), and immunoassay, where a range of dilutions of a particular sample is often required. A variety of different approaches can be used.

Linear dilution series

Here, the concentrations are separated by an equal amount – for example, a series containing protein at 0, 0.2, 0.4, 0.6, 0.8, 1.0 μg mL^{-1}. Such a dilution series might be used to prepare a calibration curve for spectrophotometric assay of protein concentration, or an enzyme assay. Use $[C_1]V_1 = [C_2]V_2$ (p. 54) to determine the amount of stock solution required for each member of the series, with the volume of diluent being determined by subtraction.

Logarithmic dilution series

Here, the concentrations are separated by a constant proportion, often referred to as the step interval. This type of serial dilution is useful when a broad range of concentrations is required, for example for titration of biologically active substances, or when a process is logarithmically related to concentration.

The most common examples are:

- **Doubling dilutions** – where each concentration is half that of the previous one (two-fold step interval, $\log_2$ dilution series). First, make up the most concentrated solution at twice the volume required. Measure out half of this volume into a vessel containing the same volume of diluent, mix thoroughly and repeat, for as many doubling dilutions as are required. The concentrations obtained will be 1/2, 1/4, 1/8, 1/16, etc., times the original (i.e. the dilutions will be two, four, eight and sixteen-fold, etc.).
- **Decimal dilutions** – where each concentration is one-tenth that of the previous one (ten-fold step interval, $\log^{10}$ dilution series). First, make up the most concentrated solution required, with at least a 10% excess. Measure out one-tenth of the volume required into a vessel containing nine times as much diluent, mix thoroughly and repeat. The concentrations obtained will be 1/10, 1/100, 1/1,000, etc., times the original (i.e. dilutions of 10^{-1}, 10^{-2}, 10^{-3}, etc.). To calculate the actual concentration of solute, multiply by the appropriate dilution factor.

When preparing serial doubling or decimal dilutions, it is often easiest to add the appropriate amount of diluent to several vessels beforehand, as shown in

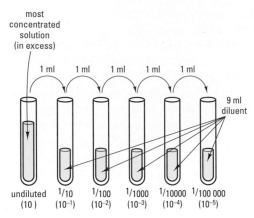

most concentrated solution (in excess)

1 ml 1 ml 1 ml 1 ml 1 ml

9 ml diluent

undiluted (10⁰)   1/10 (10⁻¹)   1/100 (10⁻²)   1/1000 (10⁻³)   1/10000 (10⁻⁴)   1/100 000 (10⁻⁵)

Fig. 7.2 Preparation of a dilution series. The example shown is a decimal dilution series, down to 1/100,000 (10^{-5}) of the solution in the first (left-hand) tube. Note that all solutions must be mixed thoroughly before transferring the volume to the next in the series. In microbiology and cell culture, sterile solutions and appropriate aseptic technique will be required.

Preparing a dilution series using pipettes or pipettors – use a fresh pipette or disposable tip for each dilution, to prevent carry-over of solutions.

 SAFETY NOTE
Using a vortex mixer with open and capped test tubes – do not vortex too vigorously or liquid will spill from the top of the tube, creating a contamination risk.

 SAFETY NOTE
Cleaning up chemical spillages – you must always clean up any spillages of chemicals because you are the only person who knows the risks from the spilled material.

the worked example in Fig. 7.2. When preparing a dilution series, it is essential that all volumes are dispensed accurately, for example using calibrated pipettors (p. 39), otherwise any inaccuracies will be compounded, leading to gross errors in the most dilute solutions.

Harmonic dilution series

Here, the concentrations in the series take the values of the reciprocals of successive whole numbers, for example 1, 1/2, 1/3, 1/4, 1/5, etc. The individual dilutions are achieved by a stepwise increase in the volume of diluent in successive vessels, for example by adding 0, 1, 2, 3, 4 and 5 times the volume of diluent to a set of test tubes, then adding a constant unit volume of stock solution to each vessel. Although there is no dilution transfer error between individual dilutions, the main disadvantage is that the series is non-linear, with a step interval that becomes progressively smaller as the series is extended.

Solutions must be thoroughly mixed before measuring out volumes for the next dilution. Use a fresh measuring vessel for each dilution to avoid contamination, or wash your vessel thoroughly between dilutions. Clearly label the vessel containing each dilution when it is made – it is easy to get confused! When deciding on the volumes required, allow for the aliquot removed when making up the next member in the series. Remember to discard any excess from the last in the series if volumes are critical.

Mixing solutions and suspensions

Various devices may be used, including:

- **Magnetic stirrers and fleas** – magnetic fleas come in a range of shapes and sizes, and some stirrers have integral heaters. During use, stirrer speed may increase as the instrument warms up.
- **Vortex mixers** – for vigorous mixing of small volumes of solution, for example when preparing a dilution series in test tubes. Take care when adjusting the mixing speed – if the setting is too low, the test tube will vibrate rather than create a vortex, giving inadequate mixing. If the setting is too high, the test tube may slip from your hand.
- **Orbital shakers and shaking water baths** – these are used to provide controlled mixing at a particular temperature, for example for long-term incubation and cell-growth studies.
- **Bottle rollers** – for cell-culture work, ensuring gentle, continuous mixing.

Storing chemicals and solutions

Labile chemicals may be stored in a fridge or freezer. Take special care when using chemicals that have been stored at low temperature – the container and its contents must be warmed up to room temperature before use, otherwise water vapour will condense on the chemical. This may render any weighing you do meaningless and it could ruin the chemical. Other chemicals may need to be kept in a desiccator, especially if they are deliquescent.

 KEY POINT Label all stored chemicals clearly with the following information: the chemical name (if a solution, state solute(s), concentration(s) and pH if measured), plus any relevant hazard warning information, the date made up, and your name.

Weighing – never weigh anything directly on to a balance's pan: you may contaminate it for other users. Use a weighing boat or a slip of aluminium foil. Otherwise, choose a suitable vessel like a beaker, conical flask or aluminium tray.

Deciding on which balance to use – select a balance that weighs to an appropriate number of decimal places, e.g. you should use a top-loading balance weighing to one decimal place for less accurate work. Note that a weight of 6.4 g on such a balance may represent a true value of between 6.350 g and 6.449 g (to three decimal places).

Using a balance – it is poor technique to use a large container to weigh out a small amount of a chemical. You are attempting to make accurate measurements of a small difference between two large numbers. Instead, use a small weighing container.

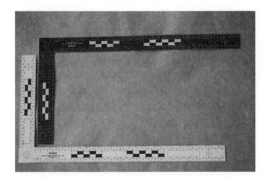

Fig. 7.3 Example of a black and white reversible L-shaped photographic scale for use on light and dark backgrounds.

Using balances

Electronic balances with digital readouts are now favoured over mechanical types – they are easy to read and their self-taring feature means the mass of the weighing boat or container can be subtracted automatically before weighing an object. The most common type offers accuracy down to 1 mg over the range 1 mg to 160 g, which is suitable for most scientific applications.

To operate a standard self-taring balance:

1. **Check that the balance is level,** using the adjustable feet to centre the bubble in the spirit level (usually at the back of the machine). For accurate work, make sure a draught shield is on the balance.
2. **Place an empty vessel in the middle of the balance pan** and allow the reading to stabilise. *If the object is larger than the pan, take care that no part rests on the body of the balance or the draught shield as this will invalidate the reading.* Press the tare bar to bring the reading to zero.
3. **Place the chemical or object carefully in the vessel** (powdered chemicals should be dispensed with a suitably sized clean spatula). Take care to avoid spillages.
4. **Allow the reading to stabilise** and make a note of the value.
5. **If you add excess chemical,** take great care when removing it. Switch off if you need to clean any deposit accidentally left on or around the balance.

Larger masses should be weighed on a top-loading balance to an appropriate degree of accuracy. Take care to note the limits for the balance – while most have devices to protect against overloading, you may damage the mechanism. In the field, spring or battery-operated balances may be preferred. Try to find a place out of the wind to use them. For extremely small masses, there are electrical balances that can weigh down to 1 mg, but these are very delicate and must be used under supervision.

Measuring length and area

When measuring linear dimensions, the device you need depends on the size of object you are measuring and the precision demanded (Table 7.3). Typically, in forensic science an accurate black and white reversible L shaped photographic scale is used (Fig. 7.3).

For many regularly shaped objects, area can be estimated from linear dimensions. The areas of irregular shapes can be measured with an optical measuring device or a planimeter. These have the benefits of speed and ease of use – instructions are machine specific. A simple 'low-tech' method is to trace objects on to good-quality paper or to photocopy them. If the outline is then cut round, the area can be estimated by weighing the cutout and comparing to the mass of a piece of the same paper of known area. Avoid getting any moisture from the specimen on to the paper as this will affect the reading.

Table 7.3 Suitability of devices for measuring linear dimensions

Measurement device	Suitable lengths	Degree of precision
Eyepiece graticule (light microscopy)	1 μm to 10 mm	0.5 μm
Vernier calipers	1–100 mm	0.1 mm
Ruler	10 mm to 1 m	1.0 mm
Tape measure	10 mm to 30 m	1.0 mm
Optical surveying devices	1 m to 100 m	0.1 m

See Box 7.2 for method of using Vernier calipers

Box 7.2 How to use Vernier calipers

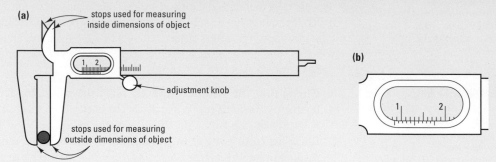

Fig. 7.4 (a) Vernier caliper; (b) Vernier measurement scale.

Note that numbers on the scale refer to centimetres. Vernier scales consist of two numerical scales running side by side, the moving one being shorter with ten divisions compressed into the length for nine on the longer, static one. Use Vernier calipers to measure objects to the nearest 0.1 mm.

1. **Clamp the stops lightly over the object** as in Fig. 7.4(a), taking care not to deform it.

2. **Read off the number of whole millimetres** by taking the value on the fixed scale lying to the left of the first line on the moving (short) scale, i.e. 8 mm in Fig. 7.4(b).

3. **Read off 0.1 mm value** by finding which line in the moving scale corresponds most closely with a line on the fixed scale, i.e. 0.5 mm in Fig. 7.4(b). If the zero of the short scale corresponded to a whole number on the static scale, then record 0.0 mm as this shows fully the accuracy of the measurement.

4. **Add these numbers to give the final reading,** i.e. 8.5 mm in Fig. 7.4(b).

Measuring and controlling temperature

Heating specimens

Care is required when heating specimens. Safety glasses should always be worn. Use a thermostatically controlled electric stirrer-heater if possible. If using a Bunsen burner, keep the flame well away from yourself and your clothing (tie back long hair). Use a non-flammable mat beneath a Bunsen to protect the bench. Switch off when no longer required. To light a Bunsen, close the air hole first, then apply a lit match or lighter. Open the air hole if you need a hotter, more concentrated flame – the hottest part of the flame is just above the apex of the blue cone in its centre.

Ovens and drying cabinets may be used to dry specimens or glassware. They are normally thermostatically controlled. If drying organic material for dry weight measurement, do so at about 80°C to avoid caramelising the specimen. Always state the actual temperature used as this affects results. Check that all water has been driven off by weighing until a constant mass is reached.

Cooling specimens

Fridges and freezers are used for storing stock solutions and chemicals that would either break down or become contaminated at room temperature. Normal fridge and freezer temperatures are about 4°C and −15°C respectively. Ice baths can be used when reactants must be kept close to 0°C. Most science departments will have a machine that provides flaked ice for use in these baths. If common salt is mixed with ice, temperatures below 0°C can be achieved. A mixture of ethanol and solid carbon dioxide will provide a temperature of −72°C if required. To freeze a specimen quickly, immerse in liquid nitrogen (−196°C)

SAFETY NOTE
There is a danger of fire whenever organic material is heated and a danger of scalding from heated liquids.

Heating/cooling glass vessels – *take care if heating or cooling glass vessels rapidly as they may break when heat stressed. Freezing aqueous solutions in thin-walled glass vessels is risky because ice expansion may break the glass.*

using tongs and wearing an apron and thick gloves, as splashes will damage your skin. Always work in a well-ventilated room.

Maintaining cultures or specimens at constant temperature

Thermostatically controlled temperature rooms and incubators can be used to maintain temperature at a desired level. Always check with a thermometer or thermograph that the thermostat is accurate enough for your study. To achieve a controlled temperature on a smaller scale, use a water bath. These usually incorporate heating elements, a circulating mechanism and a thermostat. Baths for sub-ambient temperatures have a cooling element.

Controlling atmospheric conditions

Gas composition

The atmosphere may be 'scrubbed' of certain gases by passing through a U-tube or Dreschel bottle containing an appropriate chemical or solution.

For accurate control of gas concentrations, use cylinders of pure gas – the contents can be mixed to give specified concentrations by controlling individual flow rates. The cylinder head regulator (Fig. 7.5) allows you to control the pressure (and hence flow rate) of gas – adjust using the controls on the regulator or with spanners of appropriate size. Before use, ensure the regulator outlet tap is off (turn anticlockwise), then switch on at the cylinder (turn clockwise) – the cylinder dial will give you the pressure reading for the cylinder contents. Now switch on at the regulator outlet (turn clockwise) and adjust to desired pressure/flow setting. To switch off, carry out the above directions in reverse order.

Pressure

Many forms of pump are used to pressurise or provide partial vacuum, usually to force gas or liquid movement. Each has specific instructions for use. Many laboratories are supplied with 'vacuum' (suction) and pressurised air lines that are useful for procedures such as vacuum-assisted filtration. Make sure you switch off the taps after use. Take special care with glass items kept at very low or high pressures. These should be contained within a metal cage to minimise the risk of injury.

Measuring time

Many experiments and observations need to be carefully timed. Large-faced stopclocks allow you to set and follow 'experimental time' and remove the potential difficulties in calculating this from 'real time' on a watch or clock. Some timers incorporate an alarm that you can set to warn when readings or operations must be carried out; 24-h timers are available for controlling light and temperature regimes.

Miscellaneous methods for treating samples

Homogenising

This involves breaking up and mixing specimens, e.g. liver samples taken from a *post mortem,* to give a uniform preparation. Blenders are used to homogenise animal and plant material and they work best when an adequate volume of liquid is present – buffer solution may be added to specimens for this purpose. Use in short bursts to avoid overheating the motor and the sample. A pestle and mortar is used for grinding up specimens. Acid-washed sand grains can be

Using thermometers – some are calibrated for use in air, others require partial immersion in liquid and others total immersion – check before use. If a mercury thermometer is broken, report the spillage because mercury is a poison.

Example Water vapour can be removed by passing a gas over dehydrated $CaCO_3$ and CO_2 may be removed by bubbling it through KOH solution.

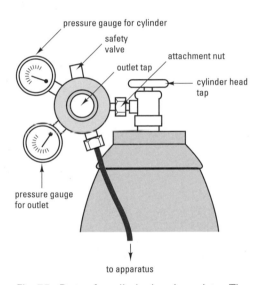

pressure gauge for cylinder

safety valve

outlet tap

attachment nut

cylinder head tap

pressure gauge for outlet

to apparatus

Fig. 7.5 Parts of a cylinder head regulator. The regulator is normally attached by tightening the attachment nut clockwise. The exception is with cylinders of hydrogen, where the special regulator is tightened anticlockwise to avoid the chance of this potentially explosive gas being incorrectly used.

Using a timer – always set the alarm before the critical time, so that you have adequate time to react.

added to help break up the tissues. For quantitative work with brittle samples, care must be taken not to lose material when the sample breaks into fragments.

Separation of components of mixtures and solutions

Particulate solids (e.g. soils) can be separated on the basis of size using sieves. These are available in stacking forms that fit on automatic shakers. Sieves with the largest pores are placed at the top and the assembly is shaken for a fixed time until the sample separates. Suspensions of solids in liquids may be separated out by centrifugation (see p. 82) or filtration. Various forms of filter paper are available, having different porosities and purities. Vacuum-assisted filtration speeds up the process and is best carried out with a filter funnel attached to a filter flask. Filtration through pre-sterilised membranes with very small pores (e.g. the Millipore® type) is an excellent method of sterilising small volumes of solution. Solvents can be removed from solutes by heating, by using rotary film evaporation under low pressure and, for water, by freeze drying. The last two are especially useful for heat-labile solutes – refer to the manufacturers' specific instructions for use.

Text references

Haynes, W.M. (ed.) (2015) *CRC Handbook of Chemistry and Physics,* 96th edn. CRC Press, Boca Raton.

O'Neil, M.J., Smith, A. and Heckelman, P.E. (2013) *The Merck Index: An Encyclopedia of Chemicals, Drugs and Biologicals,* 15th edn. Merck & Co. Inc., Whitehouse Station.

Sources for further study

CHEMnet BASE. Available at: http://www.chemnetbase.com. Last accessed 14/08/2017. [Online access to the *Handbook of Chemistry and Physics*]

Meah, M. and Kebede-Weshead, E. (2012) *Essential Laboratory Skills for Biosciences.* John Wiley & Sons, Chichester.

Seidman, L.A. and Moore, C.J. (2000) *Basic Laboratory Methods for Biotechnology: Textbook and Laboratory Reference.* Prentice-Hall, New Jersey.

Study exercises

7.1 Practise the calculations involved in preparing dilutions (answer in each case to three significant figures – you may wish to refer to p. 501 as well).

(a) If you added 1.0 mL of an aqueous solution of NaCl at 0.4 mol L^{-1} to 9.0 mL of water, what would be the final concentration of NaCl in mmol L^{-1}?

(b) If you added 25 mL of an aqueous solution of DNA at 10 mg mL^{-1} to a 500 mL volumetric flask and made it up to the specified volume with water, what would be the final concentration of DNA, in ng mL^{-1}?

(c) If you added 10 mL of an aqueous solution of caffeine at 10 mg L^{-1} to a 250 mL volumetric flask and made it up to the specified volume with water, what would be the final concentration of caffeine?

(d) How would you prepare 10 mL of the tricyclic antidepressant amitriptyline at a final concentration of 0.2 mg L^{-1} from a solution containing amitriptyline at 200 mg L^{-1}?

Preparing solutions – practical advice is given on p. 44.

SAFETY NOTE *Safety with solutions* – *many solutes and solvents used in science are potentially toxic, corrosive, oxidising or flammable, and they may also be carcinogenic (see p. 9). Further, there is a risk of accident involving the vessels used when preparing, storing and dispensing solutions (see pp. 44–5).*

Definitions

Electrolyte – a substance that dissociates, either fully or partially, in water to give two or more ions.

Mole (of a substance) – the equivalent in mass to relative molecular mass in grams.

Relative atomic mass (A_r) – the mass of an atom relative to $^{12}C = 12$.

Relative molecular mass (M_r) – the mass of a compound's formula unit relative to $^{12}C = 12$.

Expressing solute concentrations – *you should use SI units wherever possible. However, you are likely to meet non-SI concentrations and you must be able to deal with these too.*

A solution is a homogeneous liquid, formed by the addition of solutes to a solvent (usually water in biological systems). The behaviour of solutions is determined by the type of solutes involved and by their proportions, relative to the solvent. Many laboratory exercises involve calculation of concentrations – for example, when preparing an experimental solution at a particular concentration, or when expressing data in terms of solute concentration. Make sure that you understand the basic principles set out in this chapter before you tackle such exercises.

The effect of solutes on solutions

Solutes can affect the properties of solutions in several ways, including:

Electrolytic dissociation

This occurs where individual molecules of an electrolyte dissociate to give charged particles (ions). For a strong electrolyte (e.g. NaCl), dissociation is essentially complete. In contrast, a weak electrolyte (e.g. acetic acid), will be only partly dissociated, depending on the pH and temperature of the solution (p. 57).

Osmotic effects

These are the result of solute particles lowering the effective concentration of the solvent (water). These effects are particularly relevant to biological systems since membranes are far more permeable to water than to most solutes. Water moves across biological membranes from the solution with the higher effective water concentration to that with the lower effective water concentration (osmosis).

Ideal/non-ideal behaviour

This occurs because solutions of real substances do not necessarily conform to the theoretical relationships predicted for dilute solutions of so-called ideal solutes. It is often necessary to take account of the non-ideal behaviour of real solutions, especially at high solute concentrations (see Haynes (2015) and Robinson and Stokes (2002) for appropriate data).

Concentration

In SI units (p. 25), the concentration of a solute in a solution is expressed in $mol\ m^{-3}$, which is convenient for most biological purposes. The concentration of a solute is usually symbolised by square brackets, for example [NaCl]. Details of how to prepare a solution using SI and non-SI units are given on p. 45.

A number of alternative ways of expressing the relative amounts of solute and solvent are in general use, and you may come across these terms in your practical work or in the literature.

Molarity

This is the term used to denote molar concentration, [C], expressed as moles of solute per litre volume of solution ($mol\ L^{-1}$). This non-SI term continues to find widespread usage, in part because of the familiarity of working scientists with the term, but also because laboratory glassware is calibrated in millilitres and

Example A 1.0 molar solution of NaCl would contain 58.44 g NaCl (the relative molecular mass) per litre of solution.

litres, making the preparation of molar and millimolar solutions relatively straightforward. However, the symbols in common use for molar (M) and millimolar (mM) solutions are at odds with the SI system and many people now prefer to use mol L^{-1} and mmol L^{-1}, respectively, to avoid confusion. Box 8.1 gives details of some useful approaches to calculations involving molarities.

Molality

Example A 0.5 molal solution of NaCl would contain $58.44 \times 5 = 29.22$ g NaCl per kg of water.

This is used to express the concentration of solute relative to the *mass* of solvent, i.e. mol kg^{-1}. Molality is a temperature-independent means of expressing solute concentration, rarely used except when the osmotic properties of a solution are of interest.

Per cent composition (% w/w)

Example A 5% w/w sucrose solution contains 5 g sucrose and 95 g water (= 95 mL water, assuming a density of 1 g mL^{-1}) to give 100 g of solution.

This is the solute mass (in g) per 100g solution. The advantage of this expression is the ease with which a solution can be prepared, since it simply requires each component to be pre-weighed (for water, a volumetric measurement may be used, e.g. using a measuring cylinder) and then mixed together. Similar terms are parts per thousand (‰), i.e. mgg^{-1}, and parts per million (ppm), i.e. $\mu g\ g^{-1}$.

Box 8.1   Useful procedures for calculations involving molar concentrations

1. **Preparing a solution of defined molarity.** For a solute of known relative molecular mass, M_r, the following relationship can be applied:

$$[C] = \frac{\text{mass of solute/relative molecular mass}}{\text{volume of solution}} \quad [8.1]$$

So, if you wanted to make up 200 mL (0.2 L) of an aqueous solution of NaCl (M_r 58.44) at a concentration of 500 m mol L^{-1} (0.5 mol L^{-1}), you could calculate the amount of NaCl required by inserting these values into eqn [8.1]:

$$0.5 = \frac{\text{mass of solute/58.44}}{0.2}$$

which can be rearranged to

$$\text{mass of solute} = 0.5 \times 0.2 \times 58.44 = 5.844 \text{ g}$$

The same relationship can be used to calculate the concentration of a solution containing a known amount of a solute. For example, if 21.1 g of NaCl were made up to a volume of 10 0mL (0.1 L), this would give

$$[\text{NaCl}] = \frac{21.1/58.44}{0.1} = 3.61 \text{ mol } L^{-1}$$

2. **Dilutions and concentrations.** The following relationship is very useful if you are diluting (or concentrating) a solution:

$$[C_1]V_1 = [C_2]V_2 \quad [8.2]$$

where $[C_1]$ and $[C_2]$ are the initial and final concentrations, whereas V_1 and V_2 are their respective volumes – each pair must be expressed in the same units. Thus, if you wanted to dilute 200 mL of 0.5 mol L^{-1} NaCl to give a final molarity of 0.1 mol L^{-1}, then, by substitution into eqn [8.2]:

$$0.5 \times 200 = 0.1 \times V_2$$

Thus $V_2 = 1,000$ mL (in other words, you would have to add water to 200 mL of 0.5 mol L^{-1} NaCl to give a final volume of 1,000 mL to obtain a 0.1 mol L^{-1} solution).

3. **Interconversion.** A simple way of interconverting amounts and volumes of any particular solution is to divide the amount and volume by a factor of 10^3. Thus, a molar solution of a substance contains 1 mol L^{-1}, which is equivalent to 1 mmol mL^{-1}, or 1 μmol μL^{-1}, or 1 nmol nL^{-1}, etc. You may find this technique useful when calculating the amount of substance present in a small volume of solution of known concentration. For example, to calculate the amount of NaCl present in 50 μL of a solution with a concentration (molarity) of 0.5 μmol L^{-1} NaCl:

(a) this is equivalent to 0.5 μmol μL^{-1};
(b) therefore 50 μL will contain 50×0.5 μmol $= 25$ μmol.

Alternatively, you may prefer to convert to primary SI units, for ease of calculation (see Box 7.1).
The 'unitary method' (p. 504) is an alternative approach to these calculations.

> **Example** A 5% w/v sucrose solution contains 5 g sucrose in 100 mL of solution. A 5% v/v glycerol solution would contain 5 mL glycerol in 100 mL of solution.
>
> Note that when water is the solvent this is often not specified in the expression, e.g. a 20% v/v ethanol solution contains 20 mL of ethanol made up to 100 mL of solution using water.

Per cent concentration (% w/v and % v/v)

For solutes added in solid form, this is the number of grams of solute per 100 mL solution. This is more commonly used than per cent composition, since solutions can be accurately prepared by weighing out the required amount of solute and then making this up to a known volume using a volumetric flask. The equivalent expression for liquid solutes is % v/v.

The principal use of mass/mass or mass/volume terms (including $g L^{-1}$) is for solutes whose relative molecular mass is unknown (e.g. cellular proteins), or for mixtures of certain classes of substance (e.g. total salt in sea water). You should *never* use the per cent term without specifying how the solution was prepared, i.e. by using the qualifier w/w, w/v or v/v. For mass concentrations, it is simpler to use mass per unit volume, for example $mg L^{-1}$, $\mu g\, \mu L^{-1}$, etc.

Parts per million concentration (ppm)

This is a non-SI weight per volume (w/v) concentration term commonly used in quantitative analysis such as flame photometry, atomic absorption spectroscopy and gas chromatography, where low concentrations of solutes are analysed. The term ppm is equivalent to the expression of concentration as $mg\, mL^{-1}$ ($10^{-6} g\, mL^{-1}$) and a 1.0 ppm solution of a substance will have a concentration of $1.0 mg\, mL^{-1}$ ($1.0 \times 10^{-6} g\, mL^{-1}$).

Parts per billion (ppb) is an extension of this concentration term as $\mu g\, mL^{-1}$ ($10^{-9} g\, mL^{-1}$) and is commonly used to express concentrations of very dilute solutions. For example, the allowable concentration of arsenic in water is 0.05 ppm, but it is more conveniently expressed as 50 ppb.

Activity (a)

This is a term used to describe the *effective* concentration of a solute. In dilute solutions, solutes can be considered to behave according to ideal (thermodynamic) principles – i.e. they will have an effective concentration equivalent to the actual concentration. However, in concentrated solutions (≥ 500 mol m^{-3}), the behaviour of solutes is often non-ideal, and their effective concentration (activity) will be less than the actual concentration [C]. The ratio between the effective concentration and the actual concentration is called the activity coefficient (γ), where

> **Example** A solution of NaCl with a molality of 0.5 mol kg^{-1} has an activity coefficient of 0.681 at 25°C and a molal activity of 0.5 × 0.681 = 0.340 mol kg^{-1}.

$$\gamma = \frac{a}{[C]} \qquad [8.3]$$

Equation [8.3] can be used for SI units (mol m^{-3}), molarity (mol L^{-1}) or molality (mol kg^{-1}). In all cases, γ is a dimensionless term, since a and [C] are expressed in the same units. The activity coefficient of a solute is effectively unity in dilute solution, decreasing as the solute concentration increases (Table 8.1). At high concentrations of certain ionic solutes, γ may increase to become greater than unity.

Table 8.1 Activity coefficient of NaCl solutions as a function of molality. Data from Robinson and Stokes (2002)

Molality	Activity coefficient at 25°C
0.1	0.778
0.5	0.681
1.0	0.657
2.0	0.668
4.0	0.783
6.0	0.986

 KEY POINT *Activity is often the correct expression for theoretical relationships involving solute concentration (e.g. where a property of the solution is dependent on concentration). However, for most practical purposes, it is possible to use the actual concentration of a solute rather than the activity, since the difference between the two terms can be ignored for dilute solutions.*

> **Examples** For carbonate ions (CO_3^{2-}), with a relative molecular mass of 60.00 and a valency of 2, the equivalent mass is 60.00/2 = 30.00 g eq^{-1}.
>
> For sulphuric acid (H_2SO_4, relative molecular mass 98.08), where 2 hydrogen ions are available, the equivalent mass is 98.08y2 = 49.04 g eq^{-1}.

> **Example** A 0.5 N solution of sulphuric acid would contain 0.5 × 49.04 = 24.52 g L^{-1}.

Equivalent mass (equivalent weight)

Equivalence and normality are outdated terms, although you may come across them in older texts. They apply to certain solutes whose reactions involve the transfer of charged ions – for example, acids and alkalis (which may be involved in H^+ or OH^- transfer), and electrolytes (which form cations and anions that may take part in further reactions). These two terms take into account the valency of the charged solutes. Thus, the equivalent mass of an ion is its relative molecular mass divided by its valency (ignoring the sign), expressed in grams per equivalent (eq) according to the relationship:

$$\text{equivalent mass} = \frac{\text{relative molecular mass}}{\text{valency}} \qquad [8.4]$$

For acids and alkalis, the equivalent mass is the mass of substance that will provide 1 mol of either H^+ or OH^- ions in a reaction, obtained by dividing the molecular mass by the number of available ions (n), using n instead of valency as the denominator in eqn [8.4].

Normality

A 1 normal solution (1N) is one that contains one equivalent mass of a substance per litre of solution. The general formula is:

$$\text{normality} = \frac{\text{mass of substance per litre}}{\text{equivalent mass}} \qquad [8.5]$$

Text references

Haynes W.M. (ed.) (2015) *Handbook of Chemistry and Physics,* 96th edn. CRC Press, Boca Raton.

Robinson, R.A. and Stokes, R.H. (2002) *Electrolyte Solutions.* Dover Publications, New York.

Sources for further study

Burtis, C.A. and Ashwood, E.R. (2001) *Fundamentals of Clinical Chemistry,* 5th edn. Saunders, Philadelphia.

Chapman, C. (1998) *Basic Chemistry for Biology.* McGraw-Hill, New York.

O'Neil, M.J., Smith, A. and Heckelman, P.E. (2006) *The Merck Index: An Encyclopedia of Chemicals,* *Drugs and Biologicals,* 14th edn. Merck & Co. Inc., Whitehouse Station.

Seidman, L.A. and Moore, C.J. (2000) *Basic Laboratory Methods for Biotechnology: Textbook and Laboratory Reference.* Prentice Hall, New Jersey.

9 pH and buffer solutions

SAFETY NOTE
Working with strong acids or alkalis – these can be highly corrosive; rinse with plenty of water, if spilled.

SAFETY NOTE
Preparing a dilute acid solution using concentrated acid – always add the concentrated acid to water slowly, not the reverse, since the strongly exothermic process can trigger a violent reaction with water.

SAFETY NOTE
Preparing an alkali solution – typically, the alkali will be in solid form (e.g. NaOH) and addition to water will rapidly raise the temperature of the solution. Use only heat-resistant glassware, cooled with water, if necessary.

Example Human plasma has a typical H^+ concentration of approximately 0.4×10^{-7} mol L^{-1} ($=10^{-7.4}$ mol L^{-1}), giving a pH of 7.4.

pH is a measure of the amount of hydrogen ions (H^+) in a solution. This affects the solubility of many substances and the activity of most biological systems, from individual molecules to whole organisms. It is usual to think of aqueous solutions as containing H^+ ions (protons), though protons actually exist in their hydrated form as hydronium ions (H_3O^+). The proton concentration of an aqueous solution $[H^+]$ is affected by several factors:

- **Ionisation (dissociation) of water,** which liberates protons and hydroxyl ions in equal quantities, according to the reversible relationship:

$$H_2O \rightleftharpoons H^+ + OH^- \tag{9.1}$$

- **Dissociation of acids** according to the equation:

$$H{-}A \rightleftharpoons H^+ + A^- \tag{9.2}$$

where H–A represents the acid and A^- is the corresponding conjugate base. The dissociation of an acid in water will increase the amount of protons, reducing the amount of hydroxyl ions as water molecules are formed (eqn [9.1]). The addition of a base (usually, as it's salt) to water will decrease the amount of H^+, due to the formation of the conjugate acid (eqn [9.2]).

- Dissociation of alkalis according to the relationship:

$$X{-}OH \rightleftharpoons X^+ + OH^- \tag{9.3}$$

where X–OH represents the undissociated alkali. Since the dissociation of water is reversible (eqn [9.1]), in an aqueous solution the production of hydroxyl ions will effectively act to 'mop up' protons, lowering the proton concentration.

Many compounds act as acids, bases or alkalis. Those that are almost completely ionised in solution are usually called strong acids or bases, while weak acids or bases are only slightly ionised in solution.

In an aqueous solution, most of the water molecules are not ionised. In fact, the extent of ionisation of pure water is constant at any given temperature and is usually expressed in terms of the ion product (or ionisation constant) of water, K_w:

$$K_w = [H^+][OH^-] \tag{9.4}$$

where $[H^+]$ and $[OH^-]$ represent the molar concentration (strictly, the activity) of protons and hydroxyl ions in solution, expressed in mol L^{-1}. At 25 °C, the ion product of pure water is 10^{-14} mol^2 L^{-2} (i.e. 10^{-8} mol^2 m^{-6}). This means that the concentration of protons in solution will be 10^{-7} mol L^{-1} (10^{-4} mol m^{-3}), with an equivalent concentration of hydroxyl ions (eqn [9.1]). Since these values are very low and involve negative powers of 10, it is customary to use the pH scale, where:

$$pH = -\log_{10}[H^+] \tag{9.5}$$

and $[H^+]$ is the proton activity in mol L^{-1} (see p. 55).

***KEY POINT** While pH is strictly the negative logarithm (to the base 10) of H^+ activity, in practice H^+ concentration in mol L^{-1} (equivalent to kmol m^{-3} in SI terminology) is most often used in place of activity, since the two are virtually the same given the limited dissociation of H_2O. The pH scale is not SI – nevertheless, it continues to be used widely in biological science.*

Table 9.1 Effects of temperature on the ion product of water (K_w), H^+ ion concentration and pH at neutrality. Values calculated from Haynes (2015)

Temp. (°C)	K_w (mol^2 L^{-2})	[H$^+$] at neutrality (nmol L^{-1})	pH at neutrality
0	0.11×10^{-14}	33.9	7.47
4	0.17×10^{-14}	40.7	7.39
10	0.29×10^{-14}	53.7	7.27
20	0.68×10^{-14}	83.2	7.08
25	1.01×10^{-14}	100.4	7.00
30	1.47×10^{-14}	120.2	6.92
37	2.39×10^{-14}	154.9	6.81
45	4.02×10^{-14}	199.5	6.70

Table 9.2 Properties of some pH indicator dyes

Dye	Acid–base colour change	Useful pH range
Thymol blue (acid)	red–yellow	1.2–6.8
Bromophenol blue	yellow–blue	1.2–6.8
Congo red	blue–red	3.0–5.2
Bromocreso green	yellow–blue	3.8–5.4
Resazurin	orange–violet	3.8–6.5
Methyl red	red–yellow	4.3–6.1
Litmus	red–blue	4.5–8.3
Bromocreso purple	yellow–purple	5.8–6.8
Bromothymo blue	yellow–blue	6.0–7.6
Neutral red	red–yellow	6.8–8.0
Phenol red	yellow–red	6.8–8.2
Thymol blue (alkaline)	yellow–blue	8.0–9.6
Phenol-phthalein	none–red	8.3–10.0

Definition

Buffer solution – one that resists a change in H^+ concentration (pH) on addition of acid or alkali.

The value where an equal amount of H^+ and OH^- ions are present is termed neutrality – at 25 °C the pH of pure water at neutrality is 7.0. At this temperature, pH values below 7.0 are acidic while values above 7.0 are alkaline. However, the pH of a neutral solution changes with temperature (Table 9.1), due to the enhanced dissociation of water with increasing temperature. This must be taken into account when measuring the pH of any solution and when interpreting your results.

Always remember that the pH scale is a *logarithmic* one, not a *linear* one – a solution with a pH of 3.0 is not twice as acidic as a solution of pH 6.0, but 1,000 times as acidic (i.e. contains 1,000 times the amount of H^+ ions). Therefore, you may need to convert pH values into proton concentrations before you carry out mathematical manipulations. For similar reasons, it is important that pH change is expressed in terms of the original and final pH values, rather than simply quoting the difference between the values – a pH change of 0.1 has little meaning unless the initial or final pH is known.

Measuring pH

pH electrodes

Accurate pH measurements can be made using a pH electrode, coupled to a pH meter. The pH electrode is usually a combination electrode, comprising two separate systems – an H^+-sensitive glass electrode and a reference electrode, which is unaffected by H^+ ion concentration (Fig. 9.1). When this is immersed in a solution, a pH-dependent voltage between the two electrodes can be measured using a potentiometer. In most cases, the pH electrode assembly (containing the glass and reference electrodes) is connected to a separate pH meter by a cable, although some hand-held instruments (pH probes) have the electrodes and meter within the same assembly, often using an H^+-sensitive field effect transistor in place of a glass electrode, to improve durability and portability.

Box 9.1 gives details of the steps involved in making a pH measurement with a glass pH electrode and meter.

pH indicator dyes

These compounds (usually weak acids) change colour in a pH-dependent manner. They may be added in small amounts to a solution, or they can be used in paper strip form. Each indicator dye usually changes colour over a restricted pH range, typically 1–2 pH units (Table 9.2). Universal indicator dyes/papers make use of a combination of individual dyes to measure a wider pH range. Dyes are not suitable for accurate pH measurement as they are affected by other components of the solution including oxidising and reducing agents and salts. However, they are useful for:

- **estimating the approximate pH** of a solution;
- **determining a change in pH** – for example at the end-point of a titration or the production of acids during bacterial metabolism;
- **establishing the approximate pH** of intracellular compartments – for example, the use of neutral red as a 'vital' stain.

Buffers

Rather than simply measuring the pH of a solution, you may wish to *control* the pH – for example, in metabolic experiments, or in a growth medium for cell culture. In fact, you should consider whether you need to control pH in any

Box 9.1   Using a glass pH electrode and meter to measure the pH of a solution

The following procedure should be used whenever you make a pH measurement – consult the manufacturer's handbook for specific information, where necessary. Do not be tempted to miss out any of the steps detailed below, particularly those relating to the effects of temperature, or your measurements are likely to be inaccurate.

1. **Stir the test solution thoroughly before you make any measurement.** It is often best to use a magnetic stirrer. Leave the solution for sufficient time to allow equilibration at lab temperature.

2. **Record the temperature of every solution you use,** including all calibration standards and samples, since this will affect K_w, neutrality and pH.

3. **Set the temperature compensator on the meter to the appropriate value.** This control makes an allowance for the effect of temperature on the electrical potential difference recorded by the meter – it does *not* allow for the other temperature-dependent effects mentioned elsewhere. Basic instruments have no temperature compensator, and should only be used at a specified temperature, either 20 °C or 25 °C, otherwise they will not give an accurate measurement.

More sophisticated systems have automatic temperature compensation.

4. **Rinse the electrode assembly with distilled water.** Gently dab off the excess water on to a clean tissue – check for visible damage or contamination of the glass electrode (consult a member of staff if the glass is broken or dirty). Also check that the solution within the glass assembly is covering the metal electrode.

5. **Calibrate the instrument.** Set the meter to 'pH' mode, if appropriate, and then place the electrode assembly in a standard solution of known pH, usually pH 7.00. This solution may be supplied as a liquid, or may be prepared by dissolving a measured amount of a calibration standard in water – calibration standards are often provided in tablet form, to be dissolved in water to give a particular volume of solution. Adjust the calibration control to give the correct reading. Remember that your calibration standards will only give the specified pH at a particular temperature, usually either 20 °C or 25 °C. If you are working at a different temperature, you must establish the actual

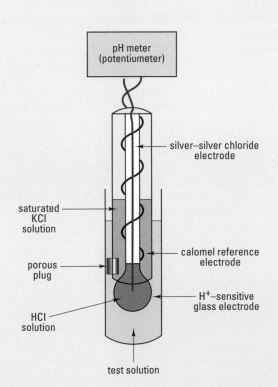

Fig. 9.1 Measurement of pH using a combination pH electrode and meter. The electrical potential difference recorded by the potentiometer is directly proportional to the pH of the test solution.

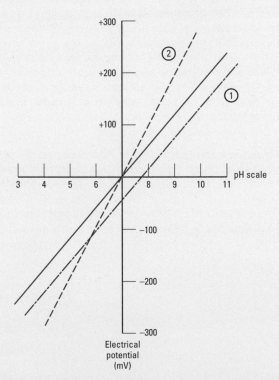

Fig. 9.2 The relationship between electrical potential and pH. The solid line shows the response of a calibrated electrode, while the other plots are for instruments requiring calibration: 1 has the correct slope but incorrect isopotential point (calibration control adjustment is needed); 2 has the correct isopotential point but incorrect slope (slope control adjustment is needed).

Box 9.1 (Continued)

pH of your calibration standards, either from the supplier or from literature information.

6. **Remove the electrode assembly from the calibration solution and rinse again with distilled water.** Dab off the excess water. Basic instruments have no further calibration steps (single-point calibration), while the more refined pH meters have additional calibration procedures.

If you are using a basic instrument, you should check that your apparatus is accurate over the appropriate pH range by measuring the pH of another standard whose pH is close to that expected for the test solution. If the standard does not give the expected reading, the instrument is not functioning correctly – consult a member of staff.

If you are using an instrument with a slope control function, this will allow you to correct for any deviation in electrical potential from that predicted by the theoretical relationship (at 25°C, a change in pH of 1.00 unit should result in a change in electrical potential of 59.16 mV) by performing a two-point calibration. Having calibrated the instrument at pH 7.00, immerse in a second standard at the same temperature as that of the first standard, usually buffered to either pH 4.00 or pH 9.00, depending on the expected pH of your samples. Adjust the slope control until the exact value of the second standard is achieved (Fig. 9.2). A pH electrode and meter calibrated using the two-point method will give accurate readings over the pH range from 3 to 11. Laboratory pH electrodes are not accurate outside this range, since the theoretical relationship between electrical potential and pH is invalid.

7. **Once the instrument is calibrated, measure the pH of your solution(s).** Make sure that the electrode assembly is rinsed thoroughly between measurements. You should be particularly aware of this requirement if your solutions contain organic biological material (e.g. soil, tissue fluids, protein solutions) since these may adhere to the glass electrode and affect the calibration of your instrument. If your electrode becomes contaminated during use, check with a member of staff before cleaning – avoid touching the surface of the glass electrode with abrasive material. Allow sufficient time for the pH reading to stabilise in each solution before taking a measurement – for unbuffered solutions, this may take several minutes, so do not take inaccurate pH readings due to impatience!

8. **After use, the electrode assembly must not be allowed to dry out.** Most pH electrodes should be stored in a neutral solution of KCl, either by suspending the assembly in a small beaker, or by using an electrode cap filled with the appropriate solution (typically 1.0 mol L^{-1} KCl buffered at pH 7.0). However, many labs simply use distilled water as a storage solution, leading to loss of ions from the interior of the electrode assembly. In practice, this means that pH electrodes stored in distilled water will take far longer to give a stable reading than those stored in KCl.

9. **Switch the meter to zero (where appropriate), but do not turn off the power.** pH meters give more stable readings if they are left on during normal working hours. Problems (and solutions) include: inaccurate and/or unstable pH readings caused by cross-contamination (rinse electrode assembly with distilled water and blot dry between measurements); development of a protein film on the surface of the electrode (soak in 1% w/v pepsin in 0.1 mol L^{-1} HCl for at least an hour); deposition of organic or inorganic contaminants on the glass bulb (use an organic solvent, such as acetone, or a solution of 0.1 mol L^{-1} disodium ethylenediaminetetraacetic acid, respectively); drying out of the internal reference solutions (drain, flush and refill with fresh solution, then allow to equilibrate in 0.1 mol L^{-1} HCl for at least an hour); cracks or chips to the surface of the glass bulb (use a replacement electrode).

experiment involving a biological system, be they whole organisms, isolated cells, subcellular components or biomolecules. One of the most effective ways to control pH is to use a buffer solution.

A buffer solution is usually a mixture of a weak acid and its conjugate base. Added protons will be neutralised by the anionic base while a reduction in protons, for example due to the addition of hydroxyl ions, will be counterbalanced by dissociation of the acid (eqn [9.2]) – thus the conjugate pair acts as a 'buffer' to pH change. The innate resistance of most biological fluids to pH change is due to the presence of cellular constituents that act as buffers, for example proteins, which have a large number of weakly acidic and basic groups in their amino acid side chains.

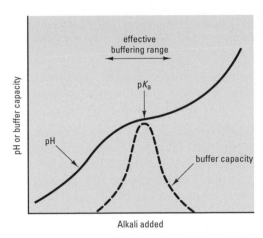

Fig. 9.3 Theoretical pH titration curve for a buffer solution. pH change is lowest and buffer capacity is greatest at the pK_a of the buffer solution.

An ideal buffer – *for biological purposes would possess the following characteristics:*

- *impermeability to biological membranes;*
- *biological stability and lack of interference with metabolic and biological processes;*
- *lack of significant absorption of ultra violet or visible light;*
- *lack of formation of insoluble complexes with cations;*
- *minimal effect of ionic composition or salt concentration;*
- *limited pH change in response to temperature.*

Table 9.3 pK_a values at 25 °C of some acids and bases (upper section) and some large organic zwitterions (lower section) commonly used in buffer solutions. For polyprotic acids, where more than one proton may dissociate, the pK_a values are given for each ionisation step. Only the trivial acronyms of the larger molecules are provided – their full names can be obtained from the catalogues of most chemical suppliers

Acid or base	pK_a value(s)
Acetic acid	4.8
Carbonic acid	6.1, 10.2
Citric acid	3.1, 4.8, 5.4
Glycylglycine	3.1, 8.2
Phthalic acid	2.9, 5.5
Phosphoric acid	2.1, 7.1, 12.3

Buffer capacity and the effects of pH

The extent of resistance to pH change is called the buffer capacity of a solution. The buffer capacity is measured experimentally at a particular pH by titration against a strong acid or alkali – the resultant curve will be strongly sigmoidal, with a plateau where the buffer capacity is greatest (Fig. 9.3). The mid-point of the plateau represents the pH where equal quantities of acid and conjugate base are present, and is given the symbol pK_a, which refers to the negative logarithm (to the base 10) of the acid dissociation constant, K_a, where

$$K_a = \frac{[H^+][A^-]}{[HA]} \qquad [9.6]$$

By rearranging eqn [9.6] and taking negative logarithms, we obtain:

$$pH = pK_a + \log_{10}\frac{[A^-]}{[HA]} \qquad [9.7]$$

This relationship is known as the Henderson–Hasselbalch equation and it shows that the pH will be equal to the pK_a when the ratio of conjugate base to acid is unity, since the final term in eqn [9.7] will be zero. Consequently, the pK_a of a buffer solution is an important factor in determining the buffer capacity at a particular pH. In practical terms, this means that a buffer solution will work most effectively at pH values about one unit either side of the pK_a.

Selecting an appropriate buffer

When selecting a buffer, you should be aware of certain limitations to their use. Citric acid and phosphate buffers readily form insoluble complexes with divalent cations, whereas phosphate can also act as a substrate, activator or inhibitor of certain enzymes. Both of these buffers contain biologically significant quantities of cations, for example Na^+ or K^+. TRIS (Table 9.3) is often toxic to biological systems – due to its high lipid solubility it can penetrate membranes, uncoupling electron transport reactions in whole cells and isolated organelles. In addition, it is markedly affected by temperature, with a tenfold increase in H^+ concentration from 4 °C to 37 °C. A number of zwitterionic molecules (possessing both positive and negative groups) have been introduced to overcome some of the disadvantages of the more traditional buffers. These newer compounds are often referred to as 'Good buffers', to acknowledge the early work of Dr N.E. Good and co-workers: HEPES is one of the most useful zwitterionic buffers, with a pK_a of 7.5 at 25 °C.

These zwitterionic substances are usually added to water as the free acid – the solution must then be adjusted to the correct pH with a strong alkali, usually NaOH or KOH. Alternatively, they may be used as their sodium or potassium salts, adjusted to the correct pH with a strong acid (e.g. HCl). Consequently, you may need to consider what effects such changes in ion concentration may have in a solution where zwitterions are used as buffers. In addition, zwitter ionic buffers can interfere with protein determinations (e.g. Lowry method).

Figure 9.4 shows a number of traditional and zwitterionic buffers and their effective pH ranges. When selecting one of these buffers, aim for a pK_a which is in the direction of the expected pH change (Table 9.3). For example, HEPES buffer would be a better choice of buffer than PIPES for use at pH 7.2 for experimental systems where a pH increase is anticipated, whereas PIPES would be a better choice where acidification is expected.

Table 9.3 Continued

Acid or base	pK_a value(s)
Succinic acid	4.2, 5.6
TRIS*	8.3
Boric acid	9.2
MES	6.1
PIPES	6.8
MOPS	7.2
HEPES	7.5
TRICINE	8.1
TAPS	8.4
CHES	9.3
CAPS	10.4

*Note that this compound is hygroscopic and should be stored in a desiccator; also see text regarding its biological toxicity.

Table 9.4 Preparation of sodium phosphate buffer solutions for use at 25 °C. Prepare separate stock solutions of (a) disodium hydrogen phosphate and (b) sodium dihydrogen phosphate, both at 200 mol m^{-3}. Buffer solutions (at 100 mol m^{-3}) are then prepared at the required pH by mixing together the volume of each stock solution shown in the table, then diluting to a final volume of 100 mL using distilled or deionised water

Required pH (at 25 °C)	Volume of stock (a) Na$_2$HPO$_4$ (mL)	Volume of stock (b) NaH$_2$PO$_4$ (mL)
6.0	6.2	43.8
6.2	9.3	40.7
6.4	13.3	36.7
6.6	18.8	31.2
6.8	24.5	25.5
7.0	30.5	19.5
7.2	36.0	14.0
7.4	40.5	9.5
7.6	43.5	6.5
7.8	45.8	4.2
8.0	47.4	2.6

Preparation of buffer solutions

Having selected an appropriate buffer, you will need to make up your solution to give the desired pH. You will need to consider two factors:

- **the ratio of acid and conjugate base** required to give the correct pH;
- **the amount of buffering required** – buffer capacity depends on the absolute quantities of acid and base, as well as their relative proportions.

In most instances, buffer solutions are prepared to contain between 10 mmol L^{-1} and 200 mmol L^{-1} of the conjugate pair. Although it is possible to calculate the quantities required from first principles using the Henderson–Hasselbalch equation, there are several sources which tabulate the amount of substance required to give a particular volume of solution with a specific pH value for a wide range of traditional buffers (e.g. Perrin and Dempsey, 2012). For traditional buffers, it is customary to mix stock solutions of acidic and basic components in the correct proportions to give the required pH (Table 9.4). For zwitterionic acids, the usual procedure is to add the compound to water, then bring the solution to the required pH by adding a specific amount of strong alkali or acid (obtained from tables). Alternatively, the required pH can be obtained by dropwise addition of alkali or acid, using a meter to check the pH, until the correct value is reached. When preparing solutions of zwitterionic buffers, the acid may be relatively insoluble. Do not wait for it to dissolve fully before adding alkali to change the pH – the addition of alkali will help bring the acid into solution (but make sure it has all dissolved before the desired pH is reached).

Remember that buffer solutions will only work effectively if they have sufficient buffering capacity to resist the change in pH expected during the course of the experiment. Thus a weak solution of HEPES (e.g. 10 mmol L^{-1}, adjusted to pH 7.0 with NaOH) will not be able to buffer the growth medium of a dense suspension of cells for more than a few minutes.

Finally, when preparing a buffer solution based on tabulated information, always confirm the pH with a pH meter before use.

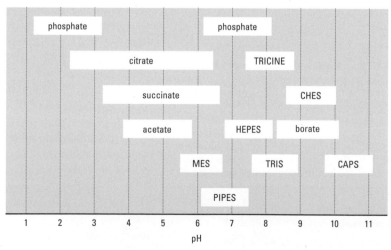

Fig. 9.4 Useful pH ranges of some commonly used buffers.

Text references

Haynes, W.M. (ed.) (2015) *CRC Handbook of Chemistry and Physics,* 96th edn. CRC Press, Boca Raton.

Perrin, D.D. and Dempsey, B. (2012) *Buffers for pH and Metal Ion Control.* Springer Science and Business Media, London.

Sources for further study

Clark, J. (2000) *Calculations in AS/A Level Chemistry.* Longman, Harlow, Essex.

Galster, H. (1991) *pH Measurement: Fundamentals, Methods, Applications, Instrumentation.* Wiley, New York.

Rilbe, H. (1996) *pH and Buffer Theory: A New Approach.* Wiley, New York.

Study exercises

9.1 Practise interconverting pH values and proton concentrations. Express all answers to three significant figures.

(a) What is pH 7.4 expressed as $[H^+]$ in mol L^{-1}?

(b) What is pH 4.1 expressed as $[H^+]$ in mol m^{-3}?

(c) What is the pH of a solution containing H^+ at 2×10^{-5} mol L^{-1}?

(d) What is the pH of a solution containing H^+ at $10^{-12.5}$ mol L^{-1}?

Many types of evidence in forensic science are too small to be seen by the naked eye and can only be observed with a microscope. All microscopes consist of a co-ordinated system of lenses arranged so that a magnified image of a specimen is seen by the viewer (Fig. 10.1 and Photo 10.1). The main differences are the wavelengths of electromagnetic radiation used to produce the image, the nature and arrangement of the lens systems and the methods used to view the image.

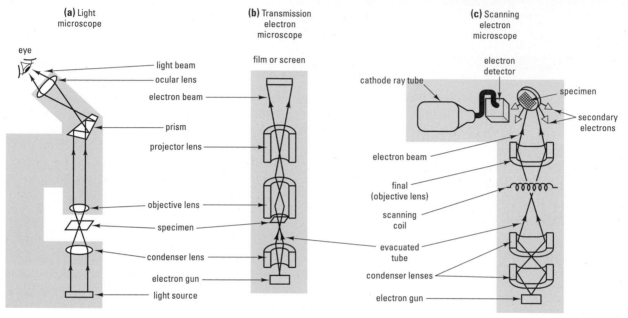

(a) Light microscope   **(b)** Transmission electron microscope   **(c)** Scanning electron microscope

Fig. 10.1 Simplified diagrams of light and electron microscopes. Note that the electron microscopes are drawn upside-down to aid comparison with the light microscope.

Table 10.1 Comparison of microscope types. Resolution is that obtained by a skilled user. LM, light microscope; SEM, scanning electron microscope; TEM, transmission electron microscope

Property	Type of microscope		
	LM	SEM	TEM
Resolution	200 nm	10 nm	1 nm
Depth of focus	Low	High	Medium
Field of view	Good	Good	Limited
Specimen preparation (ease)	Easy	Easy	Skilled
Specimen preparation (speed)	Rapid	Quite rapid	Slow
Relative cost of instrument	Low	High	High

Microscopes allow objects to be viewed with increased resolution and contrast. Resolution is the ability to distinguish between two points on the specimen – the better the resolution, the 'sharper' the image. This is affected by lens design and inversely related to the wavelength of radiation used. Contrast is the difference in intensity perceived between different parts of an image. This can be enhanced (a) by the use of stains, and (b) by adjusting microscope settings, usually at the expense of resolution.

The three main forms of microscopy are light microscopy, transmission electron microscopy (TEM) and scanning electron microscopy (SEM). Their main properties are compared in Table 10.1.

Light microscopy

Two forms of the standard light microscope, the binocular (compound) microscope and the dissecting or stereoscopic microscope, are described in detail in Chapter 11. These are the instruments most likely to be used in routine practical work. Photo 10.1(b) shows a typical image from a light microscope. In more advanced project work, you may use one or more of the

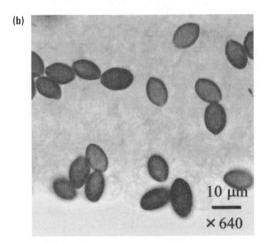

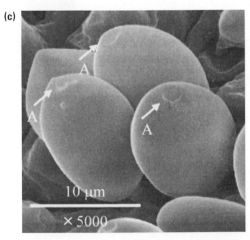

Photo 10.1 Examples of images of a specimen (spores of *Psilocybe cubensis,* also known as the hallucinogenic or 'magic' mushroom) obtained using different techniques: (a) macroscopic surface view of the fruiting body (unmagnified); (b) light microscopy; and (c) scanning electron microscopy (images from Tsujikawa *et al.,* 2003, Copyright © 2003, with permission from Elsevier).

following more sophisticated variants of light microscopy to improve image quality:

- **Dark field illumination** involves a special condenser that causes reflected and diffracted light from the specimen to be seen against a dark background. The method is particularly useful for near-transparent specimens. Care must be taken with the thickness of slides used – air bubbles and dust must be avoided and immersion oil must be used between the dark field condenser and the underside of the slide.
- **Ultraviolet microscopy** uses short-wavelength UV light to increase resolution. Fluorescence microscopy uses radiation at UV wavelengths to make certain fluorescent substances (e.g. fluorescent dyes that bind to specific cell components) emit light of visible wavelengths. Special light sources, lenses and mountants are required for UV and fluorescence microscopy and filters must be used to prevent damage to users' eyes.
- **Phase contrast microscopy** is useful for increasing contrast when viewing transparent specimens. It is superior to dark field microscopy because a better image of the interior of specimens is obtained. Phase contrast operates by causing constructive and destructive interference effects in the image, visible as increased contrast. Adjustments must be made, using a phase telescope in place of the eyepiece, for each objective lens and a matching phase condenser, and the microscope must be set up carefully to give optimal results.
- **Nomarski or Differential Interference Contrast (DIC) microscopy** gives an image with a three-dimensional quality. However, the relief seen is optical rather than morphological, and care should be taken in interpreting the result. One of the advantages of the technique is the extremely limited depth of focus that results – this allows 'optical sectioning' of a specimen.
- **Polarised light microscopy** can be used to reveal the presence and orientation of optically active components within specimens (e.g. paint pigments, fibres), showing them brightly against a dark background.
- **Confocal microscopy** allows three-dimensional views of cells or thick sections. A finely focused laser is used to create electronic images of layered horizontal 'slices', usually after fluorescent staining. Images can be viewed individually or reconstructed to provide a 3D computer-generated image of the whole specimen.
- **Comparison microscopy** involves two microscopes side by side (Photo 10.2). These two instruments are connected by an optical bridge to allow both samples to be viewed at the same time by means of projection on to a video screen. By manipulating the position of each image the two samples can be compared. This technique is commonly utilised for hair and fibre examinations (Chapters 32 and 42), tool mark comparisons (Chapter 28) and ballistics evidence (Chapter 43).

Applications of light microscopy in forensic science

A stereoscopic microscope, also known as a dissecting microscope (p. 73), is used predominantly to search and recover trace evidence, such as hair, fibre and other surface debris from items of clothing. A standard binocular microscope (p. 69) is then used to examine the recovered items in greater detail.

Light microscopy is used for the examination of cellular material, most commonly for the identification of plant material, for example cannabis (see p. 391) or toxic mushrooms, for example *Psilocybe* sp. (Photo 10.1), in forensic chemistry cases, as well as identification of biological cellular material (for example blood,

Introduction to microscopy

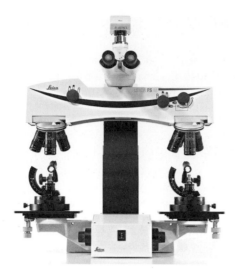

Photo 10.2 Photograph of Leica FS M comparison microscope. (Image courtesy of Leica Microsystems).

Identification of blood – this can be performed with light microscopy, using Takayama's reagent:

1. From the blood-stained exhibit, scrape a small quantity of the stain on to a microscope slide.
2. Add one drop of Takayama's reagent and add a coverslip.
3. Gently warm the slide by carefully passing through a Bunsen flame.
4. When cool, observe under low-power magnification (×10 objective).

The appearance of pink needle-like crystals indicates a positive result for blood.

---

sperm, epithelial cells) during the investigation of sexual assaults in forensic biology cases. When an exhibit is tested for semen using acid phosphatase (see Chapter 30) and gives a positive result, the presence of spermatozoa can be confirmed by light microscopy (p. 297). The sample can be stained (e.g. with haematoxylin and eosin stain), and sperm heads can be looked for under medium-power magnification (340 objective). Occasionally, a sample may give a positive acid phosphatase test, but no sperm heads are subsequently observed using light microscopy. In such cases, a choline test (p. 298) is used to confirm or refute a positive result. Evidence of fungal infection can be determined in intimate biological samples by staining the cells with acridine orange. The light microscope should be fitted with a blue fluoroscope (p. 296) prior to observation. Yeast, under these conditions, will appear red, whereas spermatozoa will appear yellow or green.

Electron microscopes

Electron microscopes offer an image resolution up to 200 times better than light microscopes (Table 10.1) because they utilise radiation of shorter wavelength in the form of an electron beam. The electrons are produced by a tungsten filament operating in a vacuum and are focused by electromagnets. TEM and SEM differ in the way in which the electron beam interacts with the specimen – in TEM the beam passes through the specimen (Fig. 10.1(b)), while in SEM the beam is scanned across the specimen and is reflected from the surface (Fig. 10.1(c)). In both cases, the beam must fall on a fluorescent screen before the image can be seen. Permanent images ('electron micrographs') are produced after focusing the beam on photographic film (Photo 10.1(c)). Electron microscopy can be coupled with energy dispersive X-ray detection (SEM-EDXRF, see Chapter 18) to characterise glass and paint fragments, and gunshot residue, and to discriminate between different soil samples and other complex materials.

The electron microscope may be demonstrated as part of undergraduate practical work but it is unlikely that you will be allowed to operate such a complex and expensive instrument.

Text reference

Tsujikawa, K., Kanamori, T., Iwata, Y., Ohmae, Y., Sugita, R., Inoue, H. and Kishi, T. (2003) Morphological and chemical analysis of magic mushrooms in Japan. *Forensic Science International* **138**, 85–90.

Sources for further study

Bradbury, S. (1989) *An Introduction to the Optical Microscope,* 2nd edn. Bios, Abingdon.

Murphy, D.B. (2012) *Fundamentals of Light Microscopy and Electronic Imaging,* 2nd edn. Wiley-Liss, New York.

Wheeler, B. and Wilson, L.J. (2008) *Practical Forensic Microscopy: A Laboratory Manual.* Wiley, New York.

Study exercises

10.1 Test your microscopy knowledge. Indicate whether the following statements about light microscopy, scanning electron microscopy (SEM) or transmission electron microscopy (TEM) are true or false.

(a) TEM allows you to see at finer resolution than light microscopy.

(b) TEM allows you to see surface features of specimens.

(c) SEM always requires staining of specimens.

(d) The resolution of TEM is about 200 times better than that of light microscopy.

(e) The resolution of a microscope is linked to the wavelength of electromagnetic radiation employed.

(f) The specimen in both TEM and SEM is viewed under near-vacuum conditions.

(g) Specimens for light microscopy can be living or dead.

(h) SEM provides better resolution than TEM.

(i) The depth of focus in light microscopy is greater than that in SEM.

(j) Light microscopy, SEM and TEM all involve the use of a condenser lens within the microscope.

10.2 Fill in the blanks in the following paragraph.

Dark field microscopy involves shining reflected and _____ light on the specimen against a dark background. It is particularly useful for _____ specimens. Ultraviolet microscopy uses short wavelength UV light in order to increase image _____. Phase contrast microscopy utilises constructive and destructive _____ effects to increase image _____. Nomarski microscopy provides a pseudo ____ image, with a very small depth of _____, allowing _____ _____ to be carried out. _____ light microscopy allows visualisation of optically active components in the specimen. Confocal microscopy involves the use of a _____ light source and can yield computer-generated 3D images.

Preparative techniques are crucial to successful microscopical investigation because the chemical and physical processes involved have the potential for making the material difficult to work with and for producing artefacts. It is usually best to follow a recipe that has worked in the past for your material (see Grimstone and Skaer, 1972; Kiernan, 2001).

Staining

The purpose of staining in microscopy is to:

- **add contrast to the image**;
- **identify chemical components of interest**;
- **locate particular tissues, cells or organelles**.

This is achieved in different ways for different types of microscopy. In standard light microscopy, contrast is achieved by staining the structure of interest with a coloured dye (e.g. Photo 11.1); in ultraviolet microscopy, contrast is obtained using fluorescent stains. Physico-chemical properties of the stain cause it to attach to certain structures preferentially or be taken up across cell membranes.

Stains for light microscopy are categorised according to the charge on the dye molecule. Stains like haematoxylin, whose coloured part is a cation (i.e. basic dye), stain acidic, anionic substances like nucleic acids – such structures are termed basophilic. Stains like eosin, whose coloured part is an anion (i.e. acid dye), stain basic, cationic substances – such structures are termed acid ophilic. Acid dyes tend to stain all tissue components, especially at low pH, and are much used as counterstains. Staining is progressive if it results in some structures taking up the dye preferentially. Staining is regressive if it involves initial overstaining followed by decolorisation (differentiation) of those structures that do not bind the dye tightly.

Stains and staining procedures

There is a huge range of stains for light microscopy. Consult appropriate texts for full details of (a) how to make up stains and (b) the protocol to use. Results depend on technique – follow the recommended procedures carefully. There

---

Definitions

Counterstains – stains that apply a background colour to contrast with stained structures.

Metachromic stains – have the capacity to stain different structures different colours.

Mordants – chemicals (salts and hydroxides of divalent and trivalent metals) that increase the efficiency of stains usually by forming complexes with the stain.

Negative staining – where the background is stained rather than the structure of interest.

Orthochromic stains – never change colour whatever they stain.

(a)

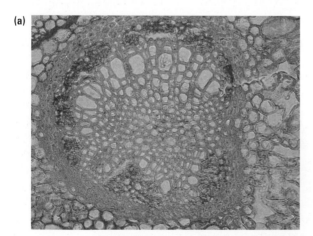

(b)

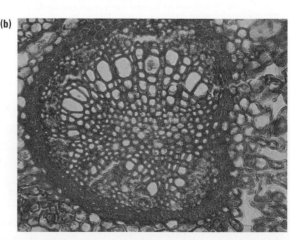

Photo 11.1 Simulation of the introduction of contrast into a biological specimen by staining. Leaf midrib transverse section showing in greyscale the effects 'before' (a) and 'after' (b) staining xylem tissue red with phloroglucinol. In colour, the effects of staining are even more distinct.

Using coverslips – all wet specimens for microscopic examination must be covered with a coverslip to protect the objective lens from water, oil, stains and dirt.

Haemotoxylin and Eosin – the principal stain used for histological staining of biological samples for medical diagnosis. The nucleus stains blue/purple, cytoplasm stains pink.

Using mountants – most mountants require that all water is removed from the section by transfer through increasing concentrations of ethanol until 100% ethanol is reached.

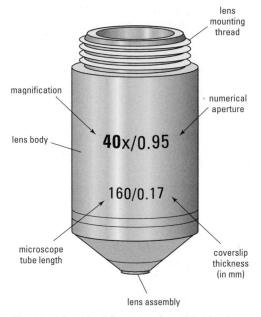

Fig. 11.1 Standard features of an objective lens. Most lenses are inscribed to show the details labelled above. The numerical aperture is a measure of the light-gathering power of the lens.

are many stains used in histochemistry for identifying various classes of macromolecules such as DNA. Consult specialist texts for methods (e.g. Grimstone and Skaer, 1972; Lillie, 1977; Horobin and Kiernan, 2002).

 KEY POINT   Consideration must be given as to whether the stain would affect DNA recovery (see Simons and Vintiner, 2011).

Mounting sections

These protect sections during examination and allow storage without deterioration. A permanent mount involves sealing your section under a coverslip in a mountant. The mountants used are clear resins dissolved in a slowly evaporating solvent that will remain clear through time, is chemically inert and will harden quickly, for example Meltmount™ p. 396. The newer synthetic resins and plastics such as DPX mountant dry quickly, are available in a range of refractive indices and do not yellow with age. This type of mountant can be used for the preparation of a cannabis microscope slide (p. 391).

Setting up and using a light microscope

The light microscope is one of the many important instruments used and its correct use is one of the basic and essential skills of forensic science. A standard undergraduate binocular microscope consists of three main types of optical unit – eyepiece, objective (Fig. 11.1) and condenser. These are attached to a stand that holds the specimen on a stage (Photo 11.2). A monocular microscope is constructed similarly but has one eyepiece lens rather than two.

Setting up a binocular light microscope
Before using any microscope, familiarise yourself with its component parts.

 KEY POINT   Never assume that the previous person to use your microscope has left it set up correctly. Apart from differences in users' eyes, the microscope needs to be properly set up for each lens combination used.

The procedures outlined below are simplified to allow you to set up microscopes like those of the Olympus CX series (Photo 11.2). For monocular microscopes, disregard instructions for adjusting eyepiece lenses in step 5.

1. **Place the microscope at a convenient position on the bench.** Adjust your seating so that you are comfortable operating the focus and stage controls. Unwind the power cable, plug in and check that the lamp setting is at a minimum before you switch on. Then adjust the lamp setting to about two-thirds of the maximum.
2. **Select a low-power (e.g. ×10) objective.** Make sure that the lens clicks home.
3. **Set the eyepiece (ocular) lenses to your interpupillary distance** – this can usually be read off a scale on the turret. You should now see a single circular field of vision. If you do not, try adjusting in either direction.
4. **Put a prepared slide on the stage.** Examine it first against a light source and note the position, colour and rough size of the specimen. Place the slide on the stage (coverslip up!) and, viewing from the side, position it with the stage adjustment controls so that the specimen is illuminated.

Photo 11.2 Diagram of the Olympus binocular microscope model CX41.

- The lamp in the base of the stand (**1**) supplies light; its brightness is controlled by an on–off switch and voltage control (**2**). Never use maximum voltage or the life of the bulb will be reduced – a setting two-thirds to three-quarters of maximum should be adequate for most specimens. A field–iris diaphragm may be fitted close to the lamp to control the area of illumination (**3**).
- The condenser control focuses light from the condenser lens system (**4**) on to the specimen and projects the specimen's image on to the front lens of the objective. Correctly used, it ensures optimal resolution.
- The condenser–iris diaphragm (**5**) controls the amount of light entering and leaving the condenser; its aperture can be adjusted using the condenser–iris diaphragm lever (**6**). Use this to reduce glare and enhance image contrast by cutting down the amount of stray light reaching the objective lens.
- The specimen (normally mounted on a slide) is fitted to a mechanical stage or slide holder (**7**) using a spring mechanism. Two controls allow you to move the slide in the x and y planes. Vernier scales (see p. 74) on the slide holder can be used to return to the same place on a slide. The fine and coarse focus controls (**8**) adjust the height of the stage relative to the lens systems. Take care when adjusting the focus controls to avoid hitting the lenses with the stage or slide.
- The objective lens (**9**) supplies the initial magnified image; it is the most important component of any microscope because its qualities determine resolution, depth of field and optical aberrations. The objective lenses are attached to a revolving nosepiece (**10**). Take care not to jam the longer lenses on to the stage or slide as you rotate the nosepiece. You should feel a distinct click as each lens is moved into position. The magnification of each objective is written on its side; a normal complement would be ×4, ×10, ×40 and ×100 (oil immersion).
- The eyepiece lens (**11**) is used to further magnify the image from the objective and to put it in a form and position suitable for viewing. Its magnification is written on the holder (normally ×10). By twisting the holder for one or both of the eyepiece lenses you can adjust their relative heights to take account of optical differences between your eyes. The interpupillary distance scale (**12**) and adjustment knob allow compensation to be made for differences in the distance between users' pupils.

(Photograph courtesy of Olympus UK Ltd.)

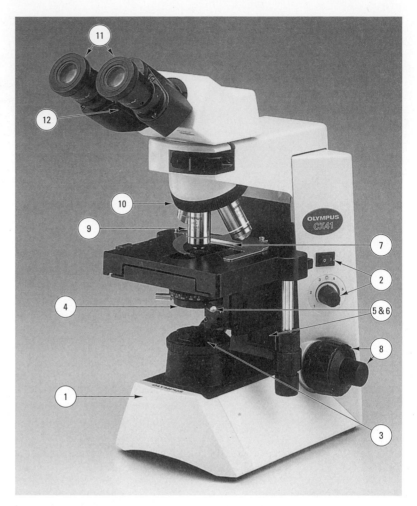

5. **Focus the image of the specimen** using first the coarse and then the fine focusing controls (Photo 11.3). The image will be reversed and upside-down compared to that seen by viewing the slide directly.
   (a) If both eyepiece lenses are adjustable, set your interpupillary distance on the scale on each lens. Close your left eye, look through the right eyepiece with your right eye and focus the image with the normal controls. Now close your right eye, look through the left eyepiece with your left eye and focus the image by rotating the eyepiece holder. Take a note of the setting for future use.
   (b) If only the left eyepiece is adjustable, close your left eye, look with the right eye through the static right eyepiece and focus the image with the normal controls. Now close your right eye, look through the left eyepiece with your left eye and focus the image by rotating the eyepiece holder. Take a note of the setting for future use.
6. **Close the condenser–iris diaphragm** (aperture–iris diaphragm), then open it to a position such that further opening has no effect on the brightness of the image (the 'threshold of darkening'). The edge of the diaphragm should not be in view. Turn down the lamp if it is too bright.
7. **Focus the condenser**. Place an opaque pointed object (the tip of a mounted needle or a sharp pencil point) on the centre of the light source. Adjust the condenser setting until both the specimen and needle tip/pencil point are in focus together. Check that the condenser–iris diaphragm is just outside the field of view.

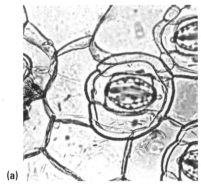 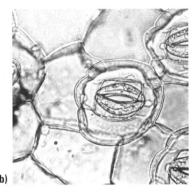

(a)   (b)

Photo 11.3 Importance of correct focus in light microscopy. Stomatal complex of *Commelina communis* L., a specimen that is a monolayer of cells approximately 30–50 mm thick. (a) Focal plane is on 'internal' walls of the cells; (b) focal plane is on the 'external' walls and stomatal pore. The two images are different and while it would not be possible to measure the stomatal pore in (a), it would not be possible to see the vacuolar crystals in (b). When looking at specimens, always use the fine focus control to view different focal planes. (From a photograph of Olympus Model CX41 binocular microscope, supplied by Olympus microscopes, Olympus Optical Company (UK) Limited, published courtesy of Olympus UK Ltd.)

Using binocular eyepieces – *if you do not know your interpupillary distance, ask someone to measure it with a ruler. You should stare at a fixed point in the distance while the measurement is taken in millimetres. Take a note of the value for future use.*

Issues for spectacle and contact lens wearers – *those who wear glasses can remove them for viewing, as microscope adjustments will accommodate most deficiencies in eyesight (except astigmatism). This is more comfortable and stops the spectacle lenses being scratched by the eyepiece holders. However, it creates difficulties in focusing when drawing diagrams.*

Adjusting a microscope with a field–iris diaphragm – *adjust this before the condenser–iris diaphragm. Close it until its image appears in view as a circle of light, if necessary focusing on the edge of the circle with the condenser controls and centring it with the centring screws. Now open it so the whole field is just illuminated.*

High-power objectives – *never remove a slide while a high-power objective lens (i.e. ×40 or ×100) is in position. Always turn back to the ×10 first. Having done this, lower the stage and remove the slide.*

8. **For higher magnifications**, swing in the relevant objective (e.g. ×40), carefully checking that there is space for it. Adjust the focus using the fine control only. If the object you wish to view is in the centre of the field with the ×10 objective, it should remain in view (magnified, of course) with the ×40. Adjust the condenser–iris diaphragm and condenser as before – the correct setting for each lens will be different.

9. **When you have finished using the microscope**, remove the last slide and clean the stage if necessary. Turn down the lamp setting to its minimum, then switch off. Clean the eyepiece lenses with lens tissue. Check that the objectives are clean. Unplug the microscope from the mains and wind the cable round the stand and under the stage. Replace the dust cover.

If you have problems in obtaining a satisfactory image, refer to Box 11.1 – if this doesn't help, refer the problem to the class supervisor.

Procedure for observing transparent specimens

Some stained preparations and all colourless objects are difficult to see when the microscope is adjusted as above (Photo 11.4). Contrast can be improved by closing down the condenser–iris diaphragm. Note that when you do this, diffraction haloes appear round the edges of objects. These obscure the image of the true structure of the specimen and may result in loss of resolution. Nevertheless, an image with increased contrast may be easier to interpret.

Procedure for oil immersion objectives

These provide the highest resolution of which the light microscope is capable. They must be used with immersion oil filling the space between the objective lens and the top of the slide. The oil has the same refractive index as the glass lenses, so loss of light by reflection and refraction at the glass–air interface is reduced. This increases the resolution, brightness and clarity of the image and reduces aberration. Use oil immersion objective(s) as follows:

1. **Check that the object of interest is in the field of view** using, for example the ×10 or ×40 objective.

2. **Apply a single small droplet of immersion oil** to the illuminated spot on the top of the slide, having first swung the ×40 objective away. Never use too much oil – it can run off the slide and mess up the microscope.

3. **Move the high power (×100) oil immersion objective into position carefully,** checking first that there is space for it. Focus on the specimen using the fine control only. You may need a higher brightness setting.

4. **Perform condenser–iris diaphragm and condenser focusing adjustments** as for the other lenses.

5. **When finished, clean the oil immersion lens** by gently wiping it with clean lens tissue. If the slide is a prepared one, wipe the oil off with lens tissue.

Box 11.1   Problems in light microscopy and possible solutions

No image; very dark image; image dark and illuminated irregularly:

- Microscope not switched on (check plug and base).
- Illumination control at low setting or off.
- Objective nosepiece not clicked into place over a lens.
- Diaphragm closed down too much or off-centre.
- Lamp failure.

Image visible and focused but pale and indistinct:

- Diaphragm needs to be closed down further (see Photo 11.4).
- Condenser requires adjustment.

Image blurred and cannot be focused:

- Dirty objective.
- Dirty slide.

- Slide upside-down.
- Slide not completely flat on stage.
- Eyepiece lenses not set up properly for user's eyes.
- Fine focus at end of travel.
- Oil immersion objective in use, without oil.

Dust and dirt in field of view:

- Eyepiece lenses dirty.
- Objective lens dirty.
- Slide dirty.
- Dirt on lamp glass or upper condenser lens.

(a) 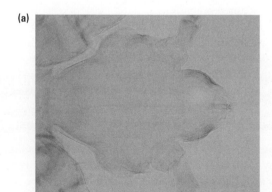   (b)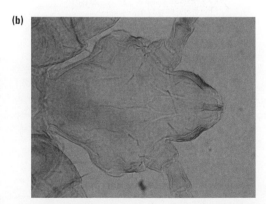

Photo 11.4   Effect of closing the condenser–iris diaphragm on contrast. Head of human head louse, *Pediculus humanus capitus* DeGeer; (a) with condenser–iris diaphragm open; (b) with condenser–iris diaphragm closed (all other settings the same). Note the difference in detail that can be seen in (b), but also that image (b) is darker – when using the condenser–iris diaphragm in this way you may need to compensate by increasing the light setting.

You should take great care when working with oil immersion lenses as they are the most expensive to replace. Because the working distance between the lens and coverslip is so short (less than 2 mm), it is easy to damage the lens surface by inadvertently hitting the slide or coverslip surface. You must also remember that they need oil to work properly. If working with an unfamiliar microscope, you can easily recognise oil immersion lenses. They will either carry a black ring on the lens barrel near to the lens, or will state 'oil' clearly on the barrel.

Care and maintenance of your microscope

Microscopes are delicate precision instruments. Handle them with care and never force any of the controls. Never touch any of the glass surfaces with anything other than clean, dry lens tissue. Bear in mind that a replacement would be very expensive.

When moving a microscope, hold the stand above the stage with one hand and rest the base of the stand on your other hand. Always keep the microscope vertical (or the eyepieces may fall out). Put the microscope down gently.

Clean the lenses by gently wiping with clean, dry lens tissue. Use each piece of tissue once only. Try not to touch lenses with your fingers as oily fingerprints are difficult to clean off. Do not allow any solvent (including water) to come into contact with a lens – sea water is particularly damaging.

The dissecting (stereoscopic) microscope

The dissecting microscope (Photo 11.5) is a form of stereoscopic microscope used for observations at low total magnification (34 to 350) where a large working distance between objectives and stage is required, perhaps because the specimen is not flat or dissecting instruments are to be used. A stereoscopic microscope essentially consists of two separate lens systems, one for each eye. Some instruments incorporate zoom objectives. The eyepiece–objective combinations are inclined at about 15° to each other and the brain resolves the compound image in three dimensions as it does for normal vision. The image is right-side up and not reversed, which is ideal for dissections. Specimens are often viewed in a fresh state and need not be placed on a slide – they might be in a Petri dish or on a white tile. Illumination can be from above or below the specimen, as desired.

Most of the instructions for the binocular microscope given above apply equally well to dissecting microscopes, although the latter do not normally have adjustable condensers or diaphragms. With stereoscopic microscopes, make especially sure to adjust the eyepiece lenses to suit your eyes so that you can take full advantage of the stereoscopic effect.

Interpreting microscope images

Microscope images, whether viewed directly or as photomicrographs, need to be interpreted with extreme care. This is not only because of the potentially damaging procedures involved in specimen preparation, but also because scale, section orientation and staining combine to create images that can be misinterpreted by the human mind.

Eliminating artefacts

There are several types of artefacts (e.g. those shown in Photo 11.6). It is only through experience that you can learn to recognise these. Sometimes they are mistaken for specimens, because the specimen itself is hard to see. A useful tip is to look at your slide carefully before placing it on the stage – if you do this against a light background, you may be able to see the specimen and judge its

SAFETY NOTE *Take care when moving microscopes, not only because of the replacement cost if damaged, but also because they weigh several kilograms and could cause injury if dropped. Always carry a microscope using two hands.*

Measuring specimens using a dissecting microscope – because of the low magnification, sizes can generally be estimated by comparison with a ruler placed alongside the specimen. If accurate measurements are required, eyepiece graticules can be used.

Calculating the magnification of a microscopic image – multiply the objective magnification by the eyepiece magnification

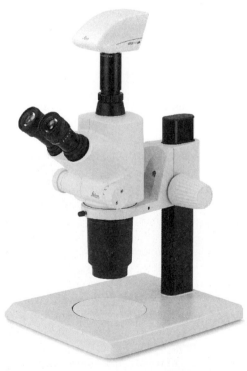

Photo 11.5 Photograph of Leica S8 APO Stereomicroscope. (Image courtesy of Leica Microsystems.)

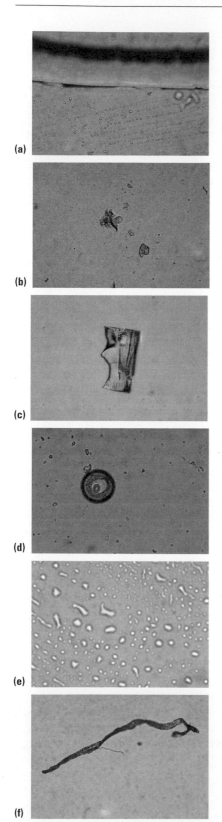

(a)

(b)

(c)

(d)

(e)

(f)

Photo 11.6 Artefacts in microscopy. Do not mistake any of the following for biological specimens: (a) edge of coverslip; (b) dust on slide; (c) shard of glass; (d) air bubble; (e) grease spots; (f) cellulose fibre.

location as you move the slide under the objective. For slides where specimens are tiny and spread out, such as blood or semen, it can be useful to focus on the edge of the coverslip (as in Photo 11.6(a)) to determine the correct focal plane before searching. Correctly setting up the microscope is crucial in such cases.

Establishing scale and measuring objects

Working out the length of objects on photomicrographs On a micrograph, the scale will usually be provided as a magnification factor (e.g. ×500) or in the form of a bar of defined length (e.g. 100 nm). If you need to estimate the dimensions of an object in the micrograph, follow the steps below:

1. **Measure the object as it appears on the micrograph** with a ruler or set of Vernier calipers (see p. 50). It may be difficult to decide exactly where the boundary of a structure lies – rather than a discrete boundary, you may be dealing with shades of grey. It is essential to be consistent!
2. **If the scale is given as a bar, measure the bar too** and find the object's size by proportion. For example, if the object measures 32 mm and a bar representing 100 nm is 20 mm long, then the size of the object is 32/20 × 100 nm = 160 nm.
3. **If the scale is given as a magnification factor,** divide your measurement by this number to obtain the object's size, taking care to enter the correct units in your calculator. For example, if the object measures 32 mm and the print magnification is stated as ×200,000, then its size is 32×10^{23} m/200,000 = 1.6×10^{27} m = 160 nm.

Avoid putting too many significant figures in any estimates of dimensions – there may be quite large errors in estimating print magnifications, which could make the implied accuracy meaningless.

Adding linear scales to drawings

The magnification of a light microscope image is calculated by multiplying the objective magnification by the eyepiece magnification. However, the magnification of the image bears no certain relation to the magnification of any drawing of the image – you may equally well choose to draw the same image 10 mm or 10 cm long. For this reason, *it is essential to add a scale to all your diagrams.* You can provide either a bar giving the estimated size of an object of interest, or a bar of defined length (e.g. 100 μm).

The simplest method of estimating linear dimensions is to compare the size of the image to the diameter of the field of view. You can make a rough estimate of the field diameter by focusing on the millimetre scale of a transparent ruler using the lowest power objective. Estimate the diameter of this field directly, then use the information to work out the field diameters at the higher powers *pro rata.* For example, if the field at an overall magnification of 340 is 4mm, at an overall magnification of ×100 it will be: 40/100 × 4 mm = 1.6 mm (1600 μm).

Greater accuracy can be obtained if an eyepiece micrometer (graticule) is used. This carries a fine scale and fits inside an eyepiece lens. The eyepiece micrometer is calibrated using a stage micrometer, basically a slide with a fine scale on it. Figure 11.2 shows how to calibrate an eyepiece micrometer, along with a worked example. Once you have calibrated your eyepiece micrometer for each objective lens used, you can use it to measure objects. In the example shown in Fig. 11.2, the scale reading is multiplied by 2.65 μm to give the value in micrometres. So, if you measured the width of a human hair at 34 eyepiece micrometer units, then this will be equal to 34 × 2.65 = 90.1 mm. An alternative approach is to put a scale bar on a diagram, for example a 100 mm scale bar would be equivalent to the length of almost 38 eyepiece micrometer divisions.

Using an eyepiece graticule – *choose the eyepiece lens corresponding to your stronger eye (usually the same side as the hand you write with) and check that you have made the correct adjustments to the eyepiece lenses as detailed on p. 71.*

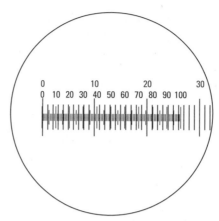

Fig. 11.2 Calibrating an eyepiece micrometer (graticule). Align the two scales and read the number of stage micrometer divisions (shown in colour) for a particular number of eyepiece micrometer divisions (shown in black). In this case 26.5 scale divisions of 0.01 mm (= 2.65 mm) are equivalent to 100 eyepiece divisions, so each eyepiece division 0.265 ÷ 100 = 0.00265 mm = 2.65 μm. This is a typical value for a total magnification of ×400 (e.g. ×40 objective and ×10 eyepiece).

Text references

Grimstone, A.V. and Skaer, R.J. (1972) *A Guidebook to Microscopical Methods.* Cambridge University Press, Cambridge.

Horobin, R.W. and Kiernan, J.A. (eds) (2002) *Conn's Biological Stains: A Handbook of Dyes, Stains and Fluorochromes for use in Biology and Medicine,* 10th edn. BIOS Scientific Publishers Ltd, Oxford.

Kiernan, J.A. (2001) *Histological and Histochemical Methods: Theory and Practice,* 3rd edn. Pergamon Press, Oxford.

Lillie, R.D. (ed.) (1977) *H.J. Conn's Biological Stains,* 9th edn. Williams and Wilkins, Baltimore.

Simons, J.L. and Vintiner, S.K. (2011) Effects of histological staining on the analysis of human DNA from archived slides. *Journal of Forensic Sciences* **56**(1) Suppl. 1: S223–228.

Sources for further study

Bradbury, S. and Bracegirdle, B. (1998) *Introduction to Light Microscopy.* Bios Scientific Publishers, Oxford.

Crang, R.F.E. and Klomparens, K.L. (1988) *Artefacts in Biological Electron Microscopy.* Plenum Press, New York.

Nikon MicroscopyU – The Source for Microscopy Education (2016) *Microscopy Basics, Techniques and Applications.* Available at: https://www.microscopyu.com/. Last accessed 15/08/2017.

Wheeler, B. and Wilson, L.J. (2008) *Practical Forensic Microscopy: A Laboratory Manual.* Wiley, New York.

Study exercises

11.1 Test your knowledge of the parts of a binocular light microscope. Cover up the legend on the left of Photo 11.2 with a piece of paper or card. Now identify the parts of the light microscope numbered on the diagram. Check your answers against the legend.

11.2 Identify roles of parts of a binocular light microscope. State briefly the primary role of each component of a standard binocular light microscope:

(a) condenser;
(b) objective lens;
(c) condenser–iris diaphragm;
(d) interpupillary distance scale;
(e) Vernier scales on the mechanical stage.

11.3 Identify the correct sequence of adjustments when setting up a light microscope.

(a) *Focus specimen:* set interpupillary distance – adjust condenser–iris diaphragm – make individual eyepiece adjustment – focus condenser – focus specimen.

(b) *Make individual eyepiece adjustment:* set interpupillary distance – focus condenser – focus specimen – adjust condenser–iris diaphragm – focus specimen.

(c) *Set interpupillary distance:* focus specimen – make individual eyepiece adjustment – adjust condenser–iris diaphragm – focus condenser – focus specimen.

(d) *Make individual eyepiece adjustment:* set interpupillary distance – focus specimen – adjust condenser–iris diaphragm – focus condenser – focus specimen.

(e) *Focus specimen:* make individual eyepiece adjustment – set interpupillary distance – focus condenser – adjust condenser–iris diaphragm.

12 Sample preparation

The preparation of a sample for subsequent analysis is critical to the forensic scientist. Often the key steps in the sample preparation are to ensure that the sample acquired is:

- **not mislaid or lost**;
- **converted to a form that is suitable for subsequent analysis**;
- **not contaminated.**

 KEY POINT *Sample preparation is also used for removal of target analyte(s) from a sample matrix, and for their pre-concentration prior to analysis.*

Solvent extraction (p. 87) and solid phase extraction (p. 89) are the most commonly encountered in forensic science; however, there is a range of analytical procedures that can be used depending on whether the sample can be classified as either solid (or semi-solid), a gas (air) sample or an aqueous solution. In any situation, a range of sample preparation techniques can be used.

 KEY POINT *Note that the techniques described prepare the sample for the subsequent measurement stage – they do not record any signal response.*

Preparation of solid (or semi-solid) samples

Soxhlet extraction

In this process, the components of a solid mixture are extracted into a solvent. The 'batch process', analogous to liquid–liquid extraction, involves grinding the solid to a fine powder, mixing it with the appropriate solvent and filtering off the solid by gravity or under vacuum and then evaporating the solvent (p. 94) from the extract solution. However, a more elegant 'continuous extraction process', called Soxhlet extraction, is available when the most appropriate solvent is known.

The apparatus for Soxhlet extraction is shown in Fig. 12.1 and comprises a flask containing the solvent, a Soxhlet extractor and a reflux condenser. The solid to be extracted is placed in a porous thimble, made from hardened filter paper, and the solvent is heated so that its vapour flows past the thimble, condenses and fills the extractor with hot solvent to extract the solid. When the extractor is full, the solvent (together with the extracted material) siphons back into the solvent flask and the process is repeated automatically. The advantage of this procedure is that fresh solvent continually extracts the solid, which is concentrated in the flask. The disadvantage is that the compound extracted is kept at the boiling point of the solvent for a prolonged period. Soxhlet extractors come in sizes of 10 mL to 5,000 mL, based on the volume of solvent contained in the extractor. The procedure for using a Soxhlet extraction system is described in Box 12.1.

A more modern version of Soxhlet extraction is Soxtec extraction. As with Soxhlet, the sample is weighed (approximately 5 g) along with anhydrous sodium sulphate and placed into a cellulose extraction thimble. The thimble is immersed into boiling solvent (for example, 60 mL acetone:dichloromethane, 1:1 v/v) for 60 mins. The thimble is raised above the solvent for a further 60 mins, before the final stage of solvent evaporation.

Samples encountered in forensic science include, for example:

Biological	Chemical
Blood	Paint
Urine	Glass
Semen	Fibres
Saliva	Drugs
Plant material	Accelerants

Sample preparation *techniques for solid samples –*

- *soxhlet extraction;*
- *supercritical fluid extraction;*
- *microwave-assisted extraction;*
- *pressurised fluid extraction.*

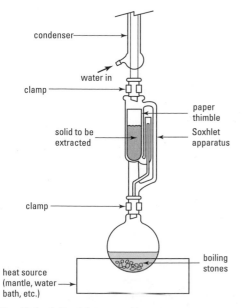

Fig. 12.1 A Soxhlet extraction system.

Box 12.1 How to set up a Soxhlet extraction system

1. **Select apparatus of the appropriate size for the amount of solid to be extracted.** Specifically, the Soxhlet thimble should fit below the siphon outlet and the volume of the solvent reservoir should be such that it is never more than half-full when all the solvent has siphoned from the extractor.

2. **Assemble the apparatus as shown in Fig. 12.1.** Clamp at the joints of the flask and the *top* of the Soxhlet extractor. The best heat source to use for continuous operation over a long period is a mantle.

3. **Disassemble the apparatus.** Leave the clamps in position.

4. **Fill the flask to about one-third of its volume with solvent.** Add some anti-bumping granules (or a magnetic 'flea', if a stirrer-mantle is being used) and clamp it into position in the mantle.

5. *Lightly* **grease the 'male' joint of the Soxhlet extractor.** Attach it to the reservoir flask. Clamp the top of the extractor.

6. **Add solvent to the extractor until it siphons.** This ensures that the reservoir will never be dry. Check that the reservoir is now no more than half-full – if it is, replace with a larger flask.

7. **Half-fill the extraction thimble with the solid to be extracted.** Plug the top of the thimble with white cotton wool to prevent any solid being carried over into the solvent.

8. **Place the thimble in the extractor.**

9. **Attach a water supply to the reflux condenser.** Lightly grease the male joint and attach the condenser to the top of the extractor. Turn on the water, ensuring a steady flow.

10. **Switch on the heater and turn up the power so that the solvent refluxes** – and drips into the extractor.

11. **Confirm that everything is running smoothly. Watch at least two siphoning cycles** of the extraction and check the apparatus frequently.

12. **When the extraction is complete, allow the apparatus to cool and dismantle it.** Place the extraction thimble in the fume cupboard to allow the solvent to evaporate and then dispose of it appropriately. Gravity filter or decant the solvent in the reservoir flask to remove the anti-bumping granules of magnetic 'flea' and remove the solvent by distillation or rotary evaporation (p. 95).

Example: Soxhlet extraction has been used as the preparative method for the identification of fatty acids from adipocere in soil samples (Algarra et al., 2010)

Example: SFE using CO_2 has been shown to be successful in the extraction of pharmaceutical drugs (Dean, 1993).

This has the advantages of:

- rapid extraction (approximately 2 h per sample);
- less organic solvent usage (up to 80% less than Soxhlet);
- sample extract can be concentrated *in situ*.

Other techniques

Several modern techniques can be used, including supercritical fluid extraction, microwave-assisted extraction and pressurised fluid extraction (also known by its trade name of accelerated solvent extraction). These instrumental techniques rely on the use of heat, pressure and solvents to extract organic compounds from solid or semi-solid samples. Supercritical fluid extraction (SFE) exploits the gas-like and liquid-like properties of a supercritical fluid, typically CO_2, to extract organic compounds at temperatures above 31.1 °C at a pressure of 74.8 atm (1070.4 psi). By using combinations of CO_2 mixed with an organic modifier (e.g. methanol), it is possible to extract a range of organic molecules of different polarity. Instrumentally, the system consists of a source of CO_2, which is pumped (after cooling of the pump head) to the extraction cell. A second pump can be added for the organic modifier. The extraction cell is located in an oven while pressure is generated in the system via a back-pressure regulator (Fig. 12.2). Typically, samples are extracted for 10–60 min, depending on the organic compounds present and the temperature and pressure conditions selected, and collected ready for analysis. A procedure for the SFE of organic compounds is described in Box 12.2.

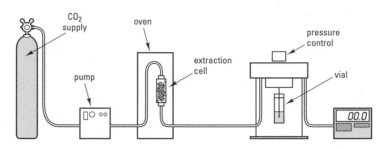

Fig. 12.2 Schematic diagram of a supercritical fluid extraction system.

Box 12.2 How to operate a typical supercritical fluid extraction system

1. **Turn on the electrical supply** of the SFE system including recirculating water bath. Allow 30 mins for cooling of the CO_2 pump head.

2. **Take an extraction cell and tighten an end cap on one end only** using a wrench, and then weigh the cell. Ensure the extraction cell is suitable for its purpose, i.e. able to withstand high pressure and does not leak.

3. **Fill the extraction cell with the sample** mixed 50:50 with an inert matrix (e.g. Celite™), and weigh the cell again.

4. **Tighten the other end cap on to the cell** with the wrench and insert into the oven of the SFE system. This requires the use of a wrench to ensure a suitable connection.

5. **Connect a glass collection vial containing 2 mL of methanol to the outlet** of the back-pressure regulator fitted with a C18 SPE cartridge (p. 89).

6. **Set the SFE operating parameters** – flow rate of liquid CO_2, 2 mL min^{-1} and methanol, 0.2 mL min^{-1}; oven temperature, 60 °C; and, pressure, 2,000 psi. Before the extraction commences, pre-heat the extraction cell containing the sample to the pre-set temperature for 10 min, then undergo a static extraction (no flow of CO_2) at the operating conditions for 5 min, and finally a dynamic extraction (flow of CO_2 and methanol) for one hour.

7. **Remove the collection vial from the system after the allotted extraction time.** Back-flush the C18 SPE cartridge with fresh methanol (2 mL).

8. **Carefully transfer extract to a volumetric flask.** Ensure all the extract is transferred by washing the collection vial with small quantities of solvent.

9. **Analyse the extract using an appropriate technique -** for example, for example gas chromatography.

Example: It has been shown that MAE can be used for the extraction of benzodiazepines (Fernandez et al., 2013) although solvent extraction or SPE (solid phase extraction) remains the preparation method of choice for forensic toxicological analysis (Chapter 38).

In pressurised microwave-assisted extraction (MAE), an organic solvent and the sample are subjected to radiation from the microwave source (i.e. the magnetron) in a sealed vessel (Fig. 12.3). The sample and solvent are placed in an inert vessel liner (100 mL) made from a fluoropolymer and subject to heating for a period of time (thereby resulting in the build-up of pressure). In the event of an extraction cell reaching critical conditions, an automatic system allows venting of excess pressure. If any solvent leaks from an extraction vessel, a solvent-monitoring system will automatically shut off the magnetron but leave the exhaust fan to continue working. Most systems allow up to 14 samples to be extracted simultaneously. A procedure for the extraction of organic compounds by MAE is described in Box 12.3.

Pressurised fluid extraction, available commercially as accelerated solvent extraction, ASE™, is an automated system capable of processing up to 24 samples sequentially (Fig. 12.4). Each sample is placed in an extraction cell and loaded on a carousel. After setting the extraction conditions, typically a temperature of 100 °C and a pressure of 2,000 psi for an extraction time of 10 min, organic solvent is introduced into the extraction cell. Upon completion, the extract is collected in a vial (a flow of nitrogen gas is used to remove trace

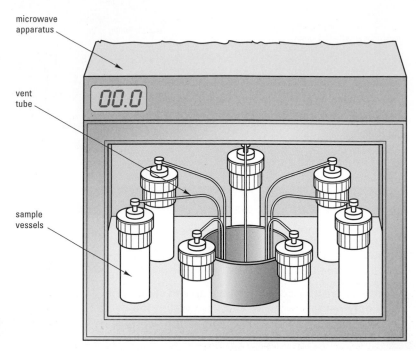

Fig. 12.3 Schematic diagram of a pressurised microwave-assisted extraction system.

Box 12.3　How to operate a typical pressurised microwave-assisted extraction (MAE) system

1. **Take an extraction cell** and then weigh the cell.

2. **Fill each extraction cell with sample,** approximately 2 g, and weigh the cell again.

3. **Add 20–50 mL of organic solvent to each sample.** Typical solvents include dichloromethane, acetone and methanol. Non-polar solvents (e.g. hexane) can be used by mixing them with polar solvents.

4. **Tighten the end cap on to the cell and insert into the microwave oven of the MAE system.** All extraction cells are mounted in a carousel.

5. **Set the MAE operating parameters**: temperature, 200 °C; pressure, 250 psi; extraction time, 10 min. Typically, pressure is continuously measured during

the extraction, while temperature is monitored for all cells every 7 s.

6. **After the allotted extraction time,** remove all the extraction cells on the carousel and allow to cool for approximately 30 min before attempting to open them.

7. **Filter each extract** to remove the sample matrix from the organic solvent containing solvent.

8. **Carefully transfer extract to a volumetric flask.** Ensure that all extract is transferred by washing the collection vial with small quantities of solvent.

9. **Analyse the extract** using an appropriate technique, for example gas chromatography.

---

amounts of solvent) and analysed. A procedure for the extraction of organic compounds by ASE is described in Box 12.4.

Preparation of a headspace sample

Headspace extraction is a term applied to a range of techniques that sample the volume of air above a liquid sample. The nature of the compounds must, by definition, be volatile and be analysed by gas chromatography (Chapter 14). This is the primary preparative technique that is used for forensic alcohol analysis (Chapter 37). Theoretically, the concentration of compound(s) in the headspace is determined by the partition coefficient (K) (p. 81)

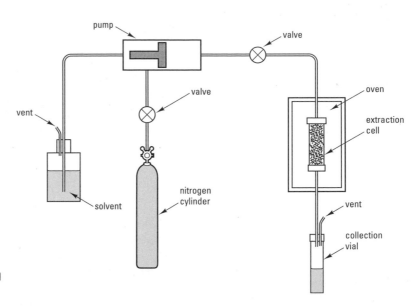

Fig. 12.4 Schematic diagram of an accelerated solvent extraction system.

Box 12.4 How to operate a typical pressurised fluid extraction (PFE) system

1. **Ensure the system is connected to the electrical supply** and is ready for operation with a nitrogen supply and organic solvent. Ensure collection vials are in place.

2. **Take an extraction cell** and finger-tighten an end cap on one end only, and then weigh the cell.

3. **Fill the extraction cell with the sample,** 2–10 g, mixed 50:50 with an inert matrix (e.g. Celite) and weigh the cell again.

4. **Finger-tighten the other end cap on to the cell and place in carousel** and start the extraction programme.

5. **Typical PFE operating parameters** are temperature, 100 °C; pressure, 2,000 psi; extraction time, 10 min.

6. **After the allotted extraction time,** remove the extract-containing collection vial.

7. **Carefully transfer extract to a volumetric flask.** Ensure that all the extract is transferred by washing the collection vial with small quantities of solvent.

8. **Analyse the extract** using an appropriate technique – for example, gas chromatography.

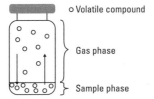

Fig. 12.5 Volatile compound distribution in a sealed container.

Table 12.1 Typical K values for some common solvents at 40 °C

Solvent	K value
Cyclohexane	0.077
Toluene	2.82
Ethanol	1355
Ethyl acetate	62.4

$$K = C_s/C_g \qquad [12.1]$$

where C_s is the concentration of the compound in the sample phase (solid or liquid) and C_g is the concentration of the compound in the gaseous phase (Fig. 12.5). Typical K values for some common solvents are shown in Table 12.1.

The value of K is, however, greatly influenced by both temperature and the addition of a salt (so-called 'salting out'). An increase in temperature, for example raising the temperature of a liquid from 40 °C to 60 °C, will lower the value of K and hence increase the GC signal response. With ethanol this would change the partition coefficient from 1355 at 40 °C to 511 at 60 °C. For forensic alcohol analysis, typically samples are collected into vials containing sodium fluoride and potassium oxalate as a preservative and anticoagulant (Chapter 37). There is therefore the possibility, especially with the collection of a low volume of blood, that the phenomenon of salting out may occur in the presence of sodium fluoride, lowering the value of K and hence increasing the GC signal response to ethanol, thus essentially increasing the reported concentration (Jones and Fransson, 2003).

- *Headspace analysis* – *can also be done above a solid sample.*

A volatile compound will be in the head-space above the sample.

Compounds with a low K value will partition more readily into the gaseous phase.

The 'salting out' effect is most significant with compounds that have high K values.

Working in SI units – *to convert RCF to acceleration in SI units, multiply by 9.80 ms^{-2}.*

Example Suppose you wanted to calculate the RCF of a bench centrifuge with a rotor of r_{av} = 95 mm running at a speed of 3,000 r.p.m. Using eqn [12.3] the RCF would be 1.118 × 95 × (3)^2 = 956 *g*.

You might wish to calculate the speed (r.p.m.) required to produce a relative centrifugal field of 2,000*g* using a rotor of r_{av} = 85 mm. Using eqn [12.4] the speed would be 945.7$\sqrt{(2,000 ÷ 85)}$ = 4,587 r.p.m

KEY POINT *The addition of salt to the aqueous solution decreases the solubility of the compounds; as a result, the concentration of organic compounds in the headspace increases.*

As well as *K* values, the volume of the sample and gaseous phases is also important. These are determined using the phase ratio (β).

$$\beta = V_g/V_s \qquad [12.2]$$

where V_g is the volume of the gaseous phase and V_s is the volume of the sample phase. As a result, a large sample volume will result in a low β value producing a higher GC signal response (and vice versa). Ultimately, seeking to minimise both *K* and *β* values will lead to the highest GC signal response.

Preparation of aqueous samples

Centrifugation

One of the simplest forms of sample preparation for aqueous samples containing particulates is centrifugation. Particles suspended in a liquid will move at a rate that depends on:

- **the applied force** – particles in a liquid within a gravitational field (e.g. a stationary test tube) will move in response to the earth's gravity;
- **the density difference between the particles and the liquid** – particles less dense than the liquid will float upwards, while particles denser than the liquid will sink;
- **the size and shape** of the particles;
- **the viscosity** of the medium.

For most particles (cells, organelles, soil or molecules) the rate of flotation or sedimentation in response to the earth's gravity is too slow to be of practical use in separation.

KEY POINT *A centrifuge is an instrument designed to produce a centrifugal force far greater than the earth's gravity, by spinning the sample about a central axis (Fig. 12.6). Particles of different size, shape or density will thereby sediment at different rates, depending on the speed of rotation and their distance from the central axis.*

How to calculate centrifugal acceleration

The acceleration of a centrifuge is usually expressed as a multiple of the acceleration due to gravity (g = 9.80 ms^{-2}), termed the relative centrifugal field (RCF, or '*g* value'). The RCF depends on the speed of the rotor (*n*, in revolutions per minute, r.p.m.) and the radius of rotation (*r*, in mm) where:

$$RCF = 1.118r\left(\frac{n}{1,000}\right)^2 \qquad [12.3]$$

This relationship can be rearranged, to calculate the speed (r.p.m.) for specific values of *r* and RCF:

$$n = 945.7\sqrt{\left(\frac{RCF}{r}\right)} \qquad [12.4]$$

However, you should note that RCF is not uniform within a centrifuge tube – it is highest near the outside of the rotor (r_{max}) and lowest near the central axis

Table 12.2 Relationship between speed (r.p.m.) and acceleration (relative centrifugal field, RCF) for a typical bench centrifuge with an average radius of rotation, $r_{av} = 115\ mm$

Speed r.p.m.	RCF*
500	1,130
1,000	1,130
1,500	1,290
2,000	1,510
2,500	1,800
3,000	1,160
3,500	1,570
4,000	2,060
4,500	2,600
5,000	3,210
5,500	3,890
6,000	4,630

*RCF values rounded to nearest 10.

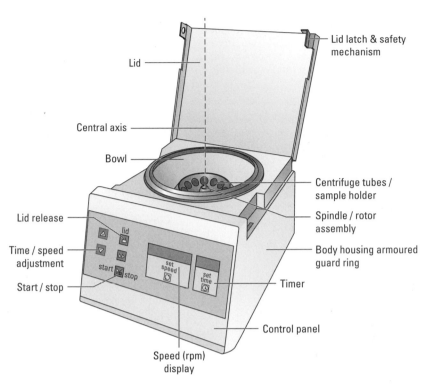

Fig. 12.6 Principal components of a low-speed bench centrifuge.

(r_{min}). In practice, it is customary to report the RCF calculated from the average radius of rotation (r_{av}), as shown in Eqn. 12.3. It is also worth noting that RCF varies as a *squared* function of the speed – thus the RCF will be doubled by an increase in speed of approximately 41% (Table 12.2).

Centrifugal separation methods

Differential sedimentation (pelleting)   By centrifuging a mixed suspension of particles at a specific RCF for a particular time, the mixture will be separated into a pellet and a supernatant (Fig. 12.7). The successive pelleting of a suspension by spinning for a fixed time at increasing RCF is widely used to separate organelles from cell homogenates. The same principle applies when cells are harvested from a liquid medium.

Density gradient centrifugation   The following techniques use a density gradient – a solution that increases in density from the top to the bottom of a centrifuge tube (Fig. 12.8):

- **Rate-zonal centrifugation** – by layering a sample on to a shallow pre-formed density gradient, followed by centrifugation, the larger particles will move faster through the gradient than the smaller ones, forming several distinct zones (bands). This method is time-dependent, and centrifugation must be stopped before any band reaches the bottom of the tube (Fig. 12.9).
- **Isopycnic centrifugation** – this technique separates particles on the basis of their buoyant density. Several substances form density gradients during centrifugation (e.g. sucrose, CsCl, Ficoll®, Percoll®, Nycodenz®). The sample is mixed with the appropriate substance and then centrifuged – particles form bands where their density corresponds to that of the medium (Fig. 12.9). This method requires a steep gradient and sufficient time tow allow gradient formation and particle redistribution, but is unaffected by further centrifugation.

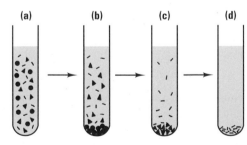

(a)   (b)   (c)   (d)

Fig. 12.7 Differential sedimentation: (a) before centrifugation, the tube contains a mixed suspension of large, medium and small particles of similar density; (b) after low-speed centrifugation, the pellet is predominantly composed of the largest particles; (c) further high-speed centrifugation of the supernatant will give a second pellet, predominantly composed of medium-sized particles; (d) a final ultracentrifugation stop pellets the remaining small particles. Note that all of the pellets apart from the final one will have some degree of cross-contamination.

Sample preparation

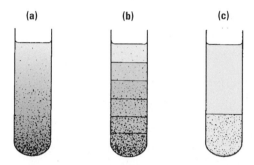

Fig. 12.8 Density gradients: (a) a continuous (linear) density gradient; (b) a discontinuous (stepwise) density gradient, formed by layering solutions of decreasing density on top of each other; (c) a single-step density barrier, designed to allow selective sedimentation of one type of particle.

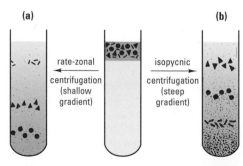

Fig. 12.9 Density gradient centrifugation. The central tube shows the position of the sample prior to centrifugation, as a layer on top of the density gradient medium. Note that particles sediment on the basis of size during rate-zonal centrifugation (a), but form bands in order of their densities during isopycnic centrifugation (b). •, large particles, intermediate density; ◢, medium-sized particles, low density; ▲ small particles, high density.

Bands within a density gradient can be sampled using a fine Pasteur pipette, or a syringe with a long, fine needle. Alternatively, the tube may be punctured and the contents (fractions) collected dropwise in several tubes. For accurate work, an upward displacement technique can be used (see Ford and Graham, 1991).

Density barrier centrifugation A single step density barrier (Fig. 12.8(c)) can be used to separate cells from their surrounding fluid, e.g. using a layer of silicone oil adjusted to the correct density using dinonyl phthalate. Blood cell types can be separated using a density barrier of, for example, Ficoll.

Types of centrifuge and their uses

Low-speed centrifuges These are bench-top instruments for routine use, with a maximum speed of 3,000–6,000 r.p.m. and RCF up to 6,000g (Fig. 12.6). They are used to harvest cells, larger organelles (e.g. nuclei, chloroplasts) and coarse precipitates (e.g. antibody–antigen complexes, p. 204). Most modern machines also have a sensor that detects any imbalance when the rotor is spinning and cuts off the power supply (Fig. 12.6). However, some of the older models do not, and must be switched off as soon as any vibration is noticed to prevent damage to the rotor or harm to the operator.

Microcentrifuges (microfuges) These are bench-top machines, capable of rapid acceleration up to 12,000 r.p.m. and 10,000 g. They are used to sediment small sample volumes (up to 1.5 mL) of larger particles (e.g. cells, precipitates) over short time-scales (typically, 0.5–15 min). They are particularly useful for the rapid separation of cells from a liquid medium (e.g. silicone oil microcentrifugation). Box 12.5 gives details of operation for a low-speed centrifuge.

Continuous flow centrifuges Useful for harvesting large volumes of cells from their growth medium. During centrifugation, the particles are sedimented as the liquid flows through the rotor.

High-speed centrifuges These are usually larger, free-standing instruments with a maximum speed of up to 25,000 r.p.m. and RCF up to 60,000 g. They are used for microbial cells, many organelles (e.g. mitochondria, lysosomes) and protein precipitates. They often have a refrigeration system to keep the rotor cool at high speed. You would normally use such instruments only under direct supervision.

Ultracentrifuges These are the most powerful machines, having maximum speeds in excess of 30,000 r.p.m. and RCF up to 600,000g, with sophisticated refrigeration and vacuum systems. They are used for smaller organelles (e.g. ribosomes, membrane vesicles) and biological macromolecules. You would not normally use an ultracentrifuge, though your samples may be run by a member of staff.

Box 12.5 How to use a low-speed bench centrifuge

1. **Choose the appropriate tube size and material for your application** – with caps where necessary. Most low-speed machines have four-place or six-place rotors – use the correct number of samples to *fill* the rotor assembly whenever possible.

2. **Fill the containers to the appropriate level** – do not overfill, or the sample may spill during centrifugation.

3. **It is vital that the rotor is balanced during use** – therefore, *identical* tubes must be prepared, to be placed opposite each other in the rotor assembly. This is particularly important for density gradient samples, or for samples containing materials of widely differing densities (e.g. soil samples), since the density profile of the tube will change during a run. However, for low-speed work using small amounts of particulate matter in aqueous solution, it is sufficient to counterbalance a sample with a second tube filled with water, or a saline solution of similar density to the sample.

4. **Balance each pair of sample tubes** – (plus the corresponding caps, where necessary) to within 0.1 g using a top-pan balance; add liquid dropwise to the lighter tube, until the desired weight is reached. Alternatively, use a set of scales. For small sample volumes (up to 10 mL) added to disposable, lightweight plastic tubes, accurate pipetting of your solution may be sufficient for low-speed use.

5. **For centrifuges with swing-out rotors** – check that each holder/bucket is correctly positioned in its locating slots on the rotor and that it is able to swing freely. All buckets must be in position on a swing-out rotor, even if they do not contain sample tubes – buckets are an integral part of the rotor assembly.

6. **Load the sample tubes into the centrifuge** – make sure that the outside of the centrifuge tubes, the sample holders and sample chambers are dry. Any liquid present will cause an imbalance during centrifugation, in addition to the corrosive damage it may cause to the rotor. For sample holders where rubber cushions are provided, make sure that these are correctly located. Balanced tubes must be placed opposite each other – use a simple code if necessary, to prevent mix-ups.

7. **Bring the centrifuge up to operating speed** – by gentle acceleration. Do not exceed the maximum speed for the rotor and tubes used.

8. **If the centrifuge vibrates at any time during use, switch off** – find the source of the problem.

9. **Once the rotor has stopped spinning, release the lid and remove all tubes** – if any sample has spilled, make sure you clean it up thoroughly using a non-corrosive disinfectant (e.g. Virkon) so that it is ready for the next user.

10. **Close the lid (to prevent the entry of dust) and return all controls to zero**.

Rotors

Centrifuges can be used with sample tubes of different size and capacity by changing the rotor.

- **Swing-out rotors** – sample tubes are placed in buckets that pivot as the rotor accelerates (Fig. 12.10(a)). Swing-out rotors are used on many low-speed centrifuges. Their major drawback is their extended path length and the resuspension of pellets due to currents created during deceleration.
- **Fixed-angle rotors** – used in many high-speed centrifuges and microcentrifuges (Fig. 12.10(b)). With their shorter path length, fixed rotors are more effective at pelleting particles than swing-out rotors.
- **Vertical tube rotors** – used for isopycnic density gradient centrifugation in high-speed centrifuges and ultracentrifuges (Fig. 12.10(c)). They cannot be used to harvest particles in suspension as a pellet is not formed.

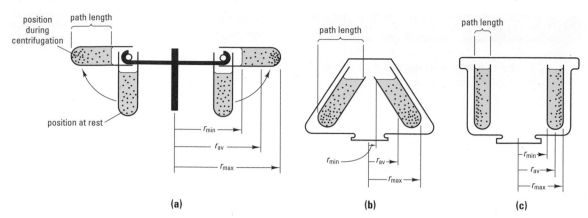

Fig. 12.10 Rotors: (a) swing-out rotor; (b) fixed-angle rotor; (c) vertical tube rotor.

Changing a rotor – *if you ever have to change a rotor, make sure that you carry it properly (don't knock/drop it), that you fit it correctly (don't cross-thread it, and tighten to the correct setting using a torque wrench) and that you store it correctly (clean it after use and don't leave it lying around).*

Safe working practice with centrifuge tubes – *never be tempted to use a tube or bottle that was not designed to fit the machine you are using (e.g. a general-purpose glass test-tube, or a screw-capped bottle), or you may damage the centrifuge and cause an accident.*

Balancing the rotor – *for the safe use of centrifuges, the rotor must be balanced during use, or the spindle and rotor assembly may be damaged permanently. In severe cases, the rotor may fail and cause a serious accident.*

Safe practice – *given their speed of rotation and the extremely high forces generated, centrifuges have the potential to be extremely dangerous if used incorrectly. For safety reasons, all centrifuges are manufactured with an armoured casing that should contain any fragments in cases of rotor failure. Machines usually have a safety lock to prevent the motor from being switched on unless the lid is closed, and to stop the lid from being opened while the rotor is moving.*

Centrifuge tubes

These are manufactured in a range of sizes (from 1.5 mL up to 1,000 mL) and materials. The following aspects may influence your choice:

- **Capacity** – this is obviously governed by the volume of your sample. Note that centrifuge tubes must be completely full for certain applications (e.g. for high-speed work).
- **Shape** – conical-bottomed centrifuge tubes retain pellets more effectively than round-bottomed tubes, while the latter may be more useful for density gradient work.
- **Maximum centrifugal force** – detailed information is supplied by the manufacturers. Standard Pyrex glass tubes can only be used at low centrifugal force (up to 2,000 g).
- **Solvent resistance** – glass tubes are inert, polycarbonate tubes are particularly sensitive to organic solvents (e.g. ethanol, acetone), while polypropylene tubes are more resistant. See manufacturer's guidelines for detailed information.
- **Sterilisation** – disposable plastic centrifuge tubes are often supplied in sterile form. Glass and polypropylene tubes can be repeatedly sterilised. Cellulose ester tubes should not be autoclaved. Repeated autoclaving of polycarbonate tubes may lead to cracking/stress damage.
- **Opacity** – glass and polycarbonate tubes are clear, while polypropylene tubes are more opaque.
- **Ability to be pierced** – if you intend to harvest your sample by puncturing the tube wall, cellulose acetate and polypropylene tubes are readily punctured using a syringe needle.
- **Caps** – most fixed-angle and vertical tube rotors require tubes to be capped, to prevent leakage during use and to provide support to the tube during centrifugation. For low-speed centrifugation, caps must be used for any hazardous samples. Make sure you use the correct caps for your tubes.

 KEY POINT It is vital that you balance your loaded centrifuge tubes before use. As a general rule, balance all sample tubes to within 1% or better, using a top-pan balance or scales. Place balanced tubes opposite each other.

Using microcentrifuge tubes – the integral push-on caps of microcentrifuge tubes must be correctly pushed home before use or they may come off during centrifugation.

Balancing tubes – never balance centrifuge tubes 'by eye' – use a balance. Note that a 35 mL tube full of liquid at an RCF of 3,000 g has an effective weight greater than a large adult man.

Extraction – making a cup of coffee involves the extraction of the flavour chemicals and caffeine from the insoluble vegetable matter using hot water and is an example of liquid–solid extraction.

Sample volume – typically in forensic science you will be working with low weight/volumes. Choose the most appropriate glassware for your application.

To extract drugs from blood or urine – liquid–liquid extraction is typically used. The process involves changing the pH of the sample to facilitate the movement of either acidic (sample pH > 7) or basic (sample pH > 7) components from the aqueous sample into the solvent.

Solvent extraction

This technique separates the components of chemical mixtures by using the dissimilar solubility properties of the components of the mixture in different solvents. Extraction is used mainly to purify a reaction product partially before final purification by recrystallisation or distillation. The two common types of extraction process used in the laboratory are:

1. **Liquid–liquid extraction** – this uses two immiscible solvents; the desired compound in solution or suspension in one solvent is extracted into the other solvent. For example, covalent organic compounds are extracted from aqueous solution into dichloromethane, leaving the ionic by-products or reagents in the aqueous phase.
2. **Solid–liquid extraction** – this involves the use of a solvent to remove solvent-soluble components of a solid mixture.

Liquid–liquid extraction

Several experimental processes in practical chemistry are based on liquid–liquid extraction:

- **Extraction** – where a solid or liquid suspended or dissolved in one solvent is extracted into another. This technique can be used to separate covalent molecules from ionic compounds in an aqueous solution or suspension.
- **Washing** – where ionic species are removed from a non-polar solvent by extraction into water.
- **Acid–base extraction** – where covalent molecules are converted into their salts and thus removed from a non-polar solvent into water, while neutral covalent species will remain in the non-polar solvent, as shown in Table 12.3.

All of these processes involve mixing the two immiscible solvents, one of which contains the mixture, in a separatory funnel (p. 88), or if using test tubes by the use of a low-speed rotating mixer, and shaking the funnel to promote the extraction process. The immiscible layers are allowed to reform and are then separated.

For liquid–liquid extraction, water is usually the polar solvent. Since most extractions involve getting the required compound into the organic solvent (or removing unwanted ionic chemicals from it), it should have good solvent power for the desired compound and a low boiling point for ease of removal and recovery of the compound. The common organic solvents used in liquid–liquid extraction are diethyl ether (ethoxyethane) b.pt.34 °C, dichloromethane (DCM)

Table 12.3 Examples of acid–base extraction chemistry

ArCOOHFF	+	RH	$\xrightarrow[CH_2Cl_2]{NaON}$	ArCOO$^-$Na$^+$	+	RH
Acid insoluble in H_2O soluble in CH_2Cl_2		Neutral insoluble in H_2O soluble in CH_2Cl_2		Salt soluble in H_2O	Neutral insoluble in H_2O soluble CH_2Cl_2
ArNH$_2$	+	RH	$\xrightarrow[CH_2Cl_2]{HCl}$	ArNHCl$^-$	+	RH
Amine insoluble in H_2O soluble in CH_2Cl_2		Neutral insoluble in H_2O soluble in CH_2Cl_2		Salt soluble in H_2O	Neutral insoluble in H_2O soluble in CH_2Cl_2
ArCOOH	+	ArOH	$\xrightarrow[CH_2Cl_2]{NaOH_2CO_3}$	ArCOO$^-$Na$^+$	+	ArOH
Acid insoluble in H_2O soluble in CH_2Cl_2		Weak acid insoluble in H_2O soluble in CH_2Cl_2		Salt soluble in H_2O	Weak acid insoluble in H_2O soluble CH_2Cl_2

Extraction calculations – *it is necessary to calculate volumes of solvents and number of extractions when attempting to maximise the economics of an industrial-scale extraction process.*

Separatory funnels – *the cone-shaped funnels are specifically designed for extractions. Only use parallel-sided funnels when no alternative is available.*

b.pt. 41 °C and ethyl acetate (ethyl ethanoate) b.pt. 77 °C. Dichloromethane is denser than water and forms the lower layer, whereas diethyl ether and ethyl acetate float on water and are the upper layer.

Partition coefficients The theory of liquid–liquid extraction is based on the equilibrium between the concentrations of dissolved component in the two immiscible liquids, when they are in contact. The equilibrium constant for this process is called the partition coefficient (see also p. 81) or distribution coefficient and is given by:

$$K = \frac{\text{concentration of solute in liquid 1}}{\text{concentration of solute in liquid 2}} \qquad [12.5]$$

You only need to calculate such quantities if:

- **you are carrying out specific experiments** to determine partition coefficients, when you will be given specific instructions or references to the appropriate literature;
- **the solute has appreciable solubility** in both solvents.

The reason calculation is not necessary is that, in the overwhelming majority of extractions you will carry out, the conditions used are designed to ensure that the components will be almost totally soluble in one of the liquids and almost insoluble in the other, since complete separation is required. The number of extractions needed to extract a water-soluble solute into an immiscible organic phase can be calculated from the following relationship:

$$w_n = w_0 \left(\frac{Kv}{Kv + s} \right)^n \qquad [12.6]$$

where K = partition coefficient of the solute, v = volume (mL) of aqueous solution of the solute, s = volume (mL) of immiscible organic solvent, w_0 = weight of solute initially in the aqueous layer, w_n = weight of solute remaining in the aqueous layer after n extractions, and n = number of extractions. Evaluation of this expression shows that, for a fixed volume of solvent, it is more efficient to carry out many small extractions than one big one.

Separatory funnels

These come in a range of sizes from 5 mL to 5,000 mL and there are two general types – parallel sided and cone shaped (Fig. 12.11). Cone-shaped separatory funnels are made of thin glass and should be supported in a ring (p. 90). Small-volume cone-shaped funnels (<100 mL capacity) and parallel-sided separatory funnels should be clamped at the ground-glass joint at the neck.

Separatory funnels will have glass or Teflon® taps with a rubber ring and clip or screw cap on the end to prevent the tap slipping from the barrel, or a Rotaflo tap. You must ensure that the tap assembly is in good condition by making the following checks before starting work:

- **For glass taps** – disassemble the tap by first removing the clip and ring or cap from the tap (note the order of the component parts for reassembling). Dry the tap and barrel with tissue, add a light smear of grease to the tap (making sure you do not clog the hole in the tap) and reassemble the tap and fittings, turning the tap to ensure free movement. Support the separatory funnel in position and add some of the organic solvent to be used (2–3 mL) to the funnel, with the tap closed, to check that the tap does not leak. If the tap leaks, disassemble and regrease.

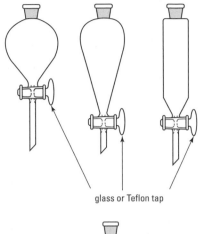

glass or Teflon tap

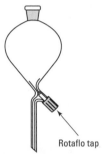

Rotaflo tap

Fig. 12.11 Separatory funnels.

Drying separatory funnels in an oven – *always disassemble the tap and do not place the tap and its plastic components in the oven. Dry them with tissue.*

Batch liquid–liquid extraction – *the process described is inefficient if the material being extracted has appreciable solubility in both of the solvents used. In these situations, a continuous extraction system is necessary and you should consult the specialist textbooks, e.g. Furniss et al. (1989, p. 160).*

SPE cartridges – *these contain a range of sorbents, classified as normal phase, reversed phase or ion exchange.*

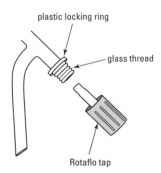

plastic locking ring

glass thread

Rotaflo tap

Fig. 12.12 A Rotaflo tap.

- **For Teflon taps** – disassemble the tap, wipe the tap and barrel with clean tissue, reassemble without grease, check for free movement of the tap and for leakage as described above. When you have finished using the funnel, loosen the clip/cap on the tap since Teflon will flow under pressure and the tap may 'seize' in the barrel.
- **For a Rotaflo tap** – unscrew the tap from the funnel and ensure that the plastic locking thread is in place (Fig. 12.12). If it is not present, consult your instructor and obtain a replacement. Dry the barrel of the tap and the tap with a tissue and reassemble. Do not grease the Rotaflo tap.

The general procedure for using a separatory funnel for extraction is described in Box 12.6 (p. 90) and there are five additional practical tips to aid your success:

1. **Label *all* flasks** to avoid confusion.
2. *Never* **throw away any of the separated liquids** *until you are absolutely sure of their identity.*
3. *Always* **transfer solvents into the separatory funnel using a stemmed filter funnel** so that solids and liquids will not stick to the inside of the joint and prevent a good seal when you insert the stopper and then invert the funnel.
4. *Always* **place a *safety beaker* under the separatory funnel** to collect liquid just in case the tap leaks (Fig. 12.13(a)).
5. *Always* **take the stopper from the separatory funnel** before you attempt to allow liquid to run from the funnel. If you do not remove the stopper from the top of the funnel, a partial vacuum is formed in the funnel after a little of the liquid has run out. Air will be sucked into the funnel through the outlet stem causing bubbles, which will remix your separated layers. If your funnel is equipped with a Quickfit stopper, it is good practice to take the stopper out of the top and put it back upside down (Fig. 12.13(b)). This ensures that no vacuum is formed and that organic vapours do not escape easily from the flask.

Solid phase extraction

Solid phase extraction (SPE) is a technique that can be used for clean-up and pre-concentration of aqueous samples. The aqueous sample is passed through a sorbent (typically the same material as the stationary phase in HPLC, see Chapter 14) via gravity or, more likely, with the aid of a vacuum. The sorbent is usually packed in to small tubes or cartridges (Fig. 12.14). The primary function of the sorbent is to retain the analyte(s) in the aqueous sample, but not to retain any extraneous material present. After this pre-concentration and/or clean-up step the analyte(s) are eluted from the sorbent and collected for subsequent analysis.

SPE cartridge The most common arrangement for SPE is the syringe barrel or cartridge. The cartridge itself is usually made of polypropylene with a wide entrance, through which the sample is introduced, and a narrow exit (male luer tip). The sorbent material, ranging in mass from 50 mg to 10 g, is positioned between two frits, at the base (exit) of the cartridge and on top of the sorbent, which act to both retain the sorbent material and to filter out any particulate matter (Fig. 12.14).

Solvent flow through a single cartridge is typically done using a side-arm flask apparatus (Fig. 12.16, p. 91), whereas multiple cartridges can be simultaneously processed (from 8 to 30 cartridges) using a vacuum manifold (Fig. 12.17, p. 91). Recent advances in automation have allowed modified autosamplers (devices for sample manipulation) to be used to provide unattended operation of an SPE

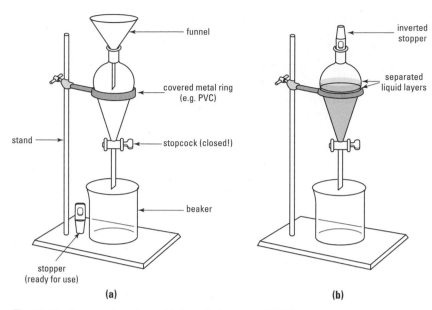

Fig. 12.13   A separatory funnel (a) ready to use and (b) in use.

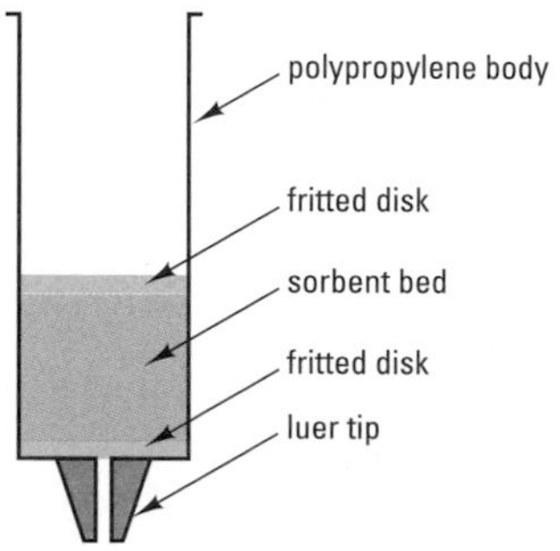

Fig. 12.14   Solid phase extraction cartridge.

Box 12.6   How to separate a carboxylic acid and a hydrocarbon using solvent extraction

This is an example of an acid–base extraction. The solid mixture (e.g. 4.0 g for the solvent volumes used below) of benzoic acid and naphthalene is soluble in dichloromethane, but benzoic acid will dissolve in dilute aqueous sodium hydroxide (2M) by forming the sodium salt (sodium benzoate). Naphthalene is insoluble in water.

1. **Dissolve the mixture in a clean, dry beaker in dichloromethane (50 mL).**

2. **Clean and dry the tap** of a separatory funnel (250 mL) and set up as shown in Fig. 12.13(a).

3. **Make sure that the tap is** *closed* and then add the solution containing the mixture, using a stemmed funnel to prevent contamination of the joint, and rinse out the beaker with dichloromethane (~5 mL).

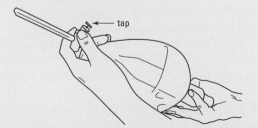

Fig. 12.15   Holding a separatory funnel.

4. **Add sodium hydroxide solution (10 mL) to the separatory funnel,** place the stopper in the separatory funnel and gently invert it and hold it as shown in Fig. 12.15. *Do not shake the separatory funnel* since you do not know how much heat will be produced in the reaction, which will pressurise the separatory funnel.

5. **Open the tap,** to release any pressure caused by the heat of reaction.

6. **Close the tap, shake the mixture once** and open the tap to release any pressure.

7. **Close the tap, shake the mixture twice** and open the tap to release any pressure.

8. **Repeat** until no more vapour is expelled via the tap.

9. **Close the tap** and replace the separatory funnel in the ring or clamp.

10. **Take out the stopper,** place it upside down in the top of the separatory funnel and allow the solvent layers to separate. The upper layer is the aqueous layer (10 mL compared with 50 mL of dichloromethane). Sometimes a few globules of dichloromethane will 'cling' to the surface of the water layer – these can be released by gently swirling the contents of the separatory funnel.

Box 12.6 Continued

11. **When the liquids have stopped swirling, open the tap gently** and *slowly* run the dichloromethane lower layer into a clean conical flask and label it 'dichloromethane layer'. Avoid fast emptying of the funnel because a vortex may be formed which will cause the upper layer to run out with the lower layer.

12. **Run the remaining aqueous layer** into a clean, dry conical flask and label it 'sodium hydroxide layer'.

13. **Return the dichloromethane layer** to the separatory funnel and extract it with another portion (10 mL) of sodium hydroxide. Repeat the extraction process for a total of 40 mL (i.e. 4 × 10 mL) of the alkali, collecting all the sodium hydroxide extracts in the same flask.

14. **Finally, extract the dichloromethane with water (20 mL)** to remove any traces of sodium hydroxide and add these 'washings' to the sodium hydroxide layer' flask.

15. **You now have** a solution of naphthalene in dichloromethane and a solution of sodium benzoate in sodium hydroxide ready for further processing.

16. **If an emulsion forms,** the layers do not have a well-defined boundary – add a few drops of methanol to the upper layer down the inside wall of the funnel. This often 'breaks' the emulsion.

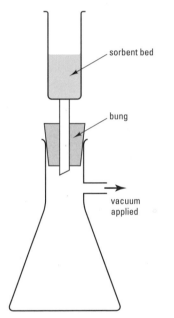

Fig. 12.16 Manifold for a single solid phase extraction cartridge.

Reversed phase sorbents – *these use non-polar sorbents and polar solvents while 'normal' phase sorbents use polar sorbents and non-polar solvents.*

system with the potential to link the system to the analysis stage. The use of automated SPE allows more samples to be extracted (higher sample throughput) with better precision. In addition, it also allows the scientist to perform other tasks or prepare more samples for analysis.

Types of SPE media Sorbents for SPE can be classified as normal phase, reversed phase or ion exchange. The most common sorbents are based on silica particles (see Chapter 14) to which functional groups are bonded to surface silanol groups to alter their retentive properties. In addition to silica, some other common sorbents are based on florisil, alumina and macroreticular polymers.

Normal phase sorbents have polar functional groups (e.g. cyano, amino and diol groups) and hence can retain polar analytes (e.g. drugs, phenols). In contrast, reversed phase sorbents have non-polar functional groups (e.g. octadecyl, octyl and methyl groups) and hence can retain non-polar compounds (e.g. polycyclic aromatic hydrocarbons). Ion-exchange sorbents have either cationic or anionic functional groups that attract compounds of the opposite charge in the ionised

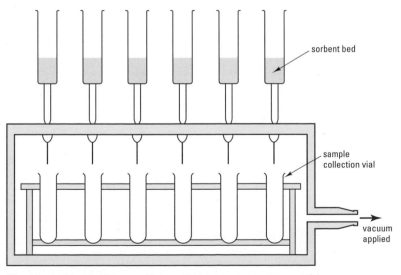

Fig. 12.17 Manifold for multiple solid phase extraction cartridges.

Careful optimisation of the SPE method is required if the approach is to be successful.

Solvent evaporation may be required post-extraction to achieve the greatest sensitivity.

Example   SPE cartridge choices include:

Mixed mode – acidic, neutral and basic compounds, pH stability across a wide range (1–14).

Cation exchanger – enhanced selectivity for aromatic bases (e.g. methadone).

Anion exchanger – enhanced selectivity for acidic analytes.

C18 – low to moderate polarity (e.g. pesticides).

form. For example, a cation-exchange phase, such as benzenesulphonic acid, will extract an analyte with a net positive charge (e.g. a phenoxyacid herbicide).

Method of SPE operation   The mode of operation of SPE can be divided in to five steps (Box 12.7). Each step is characterised by the nature and type of solvent used which in turn is dependent upon the characteristics of the sorbent and the sample. The five steps are:

1. **wetting** the sorbent;
2. **conditioning** the sorbent;
3. **loading** the sample;
4. **rinsing or washing** the sorbent to elute extraneous material;
5. **eluting** and collecting the analyte of interest.

The choice of solvents for SPE is obviously important in the overall success of this method. Further guidance on solvent selection is found on p. 87. In practice, at the wetting stage a solvent is required that will 'activate' the sorbent, whereas the conditioning sorbent is required to prepare the sorbent for the aqueous sample. Perhaps the most difficult solvent to select is the rinsing or washing solvent. In this step, the function of the solvent is to remove any extraneous material but not the analyte(s) of interest. Finally, the choice of elution solvent is one that can both effectively remove the analyte(s) from the sorbent and can also be compatible with the method of analysis to be used. If the eluting solvent proves to be incompatible with the analytical technique of choice, it is possible to carry out a solvent exchange. This can be done by evaporating the analyte(s) containing solvent to dryness, using a solvent evaporation technique (pp. 94–95), and then to reconstitute the analyte(s) in a different solvent. This process can be problematical in that volatile analyte(s) can be lost due to evaporation – it is wise to evaluate the approach on a test sample first.

Solid phase microextraction (SPME)

Solid phase microextraction is a technique for the preparation of samples for chromatography. It uses a coated fused-silica fibre to retain organic compounds – i.e. to pre-concentrate them from the sample matrix, for example air, aqueous or solid.

Box 12.7   How to pre-concentrate a sample using a reversed-phase C18 solid phase extraction (SPE) cartridge

1. **Place the SPE cartridge into a vacuum manifold.** Apply the vacuum at a flow rate of 5 mL min⁻¹.

2. **Wet the sorbent** by passing 1.0 mL of methanol or acetonitrile through the cartridge. This solvent will remove impurities from the C18 sorbent and wet its surface.

3. **Condition the sorbent** by passing 1 mL of water or buffer through the sorbent. Do not allow the sorbent to dry out before applying the sample.

4. **Add the sample to the sorbent** in a high-polarity solvent or buffer.

5. **Remove unwanted, extraneous material** by washing the sample-containing sorbent with a high-polarity solvent or buffer. This process may be repeated.

6. **Elute analytes from the cartridge** with a less polar solvent, for example methanol or the HPLC mobile phase (if this is the method of subsequent analysis).

7. **Carefully transfer extract to a volumetric flask.** Ensure that all the extract is transferred by washing the collection vial with small quantities of solvent.

8. **Analyse the extract** using an appropriate technique – for example, gas chromatography.

9. **Discard the SPE cartridge.**

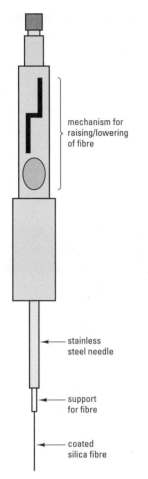

Fig. 12.18 Solid phase microextraction system.

Desorption of organic compounds normally occurs in the hot injection port of a gas chromatograph (GC), although it is possible to use the mobile phase of a high-performance liquid chromatography (HPLC) system to desorb the organic compounds.

The SPME device consists of a fused silica fibre, coated with a stationary phase and mounted in a syringe-type holder (Fig. 12.18). The holder has two functions:

1. **to provide protection** for the fibre;
2. **to allow insertion into the hot environment** of the GC injection port (or injection valve of an HPLC) using a needle.

As samples and standards are normally introduced into chromatographic systems using a syringe (p. 132, 135) the use of an SPME device is straightforward.

When not in use, the fused-silica coated fibre is retracted within the protective needle of the holder. In operation, the fibre (~1 cm long) is exposed to organic compounds within their matrix (air, aqueous, solid) for a specified time. SPME can be used in two ways (Fig. 12.19):

1. **direct**;
2. **headspace SPME** (see also headspace, p. 80).

In direct SPME the coated silica fibre is exposed to the sample matrix directly (e.g. blood plasma). A procedure for the analysis of an organic compound in aqueous solution by SPME is shown in Box 12.8. Improved response time and signal can be achieved by agitation of the sample vial, agitation of the fibre, and/or stirring or sonication of the sample solution. For gaseous samples, the natural convection of air is usually sufficient to aid diffusion of analyte(s)on to the SPME fibre. In headspace SPME, the process relies on the release of volatile compounds from the sample matrix (see also headspace analysis, p. 80). This may be achieved by heat, chemical modification or the inherent volatility of the organic compounds. A procedure for the analysis of an organic compound in the headspace above a sample or air by SPME is shown in Box 12.9. After sampling, the fibre is retracted within its holder for protection until inserted in the hot injector of the GC (or mobile phase of the HPLC) – desorption of analytes occurs due to the influence of temperature in the case of GC or organic solvent in the case of HPLC.

> **KEY POINT** Prior to sampling, the silica-coated SPME fibre should be cleaned. This is done, for example, by exposing the fibre to the hot injection port of the GC. This is particularly important as the fibre can equally adsorb analytes from the atmosphere as well as the sample and in some cases the atmosphere may be the sample.

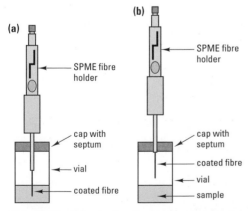

Fig. 12.19 Schematic diagrams representing the two approaches in which SPME can be used: (a) direct SPME involving insertion of the fibre directly into the aqueous sample; and (b) headspace SPME where the fibre is suspended above the sample.

Purge and trap

A specialist form of sample preparation is used for volatile compounds in aqueous samples. The technique, called purge and trap, is widely used for the extraction of volatile compounds, followed by gas chromatography. The method involves the introduction of an aqueous sample into a glass sparging vessel (Fig. 12.20). The sample is then purged with (high-purity) nitrogen at a specified flow rate and time. The extracted volatile is then transferred to a trap (e.g. Tenax) at ambient temperature. This is followed by the desorption step. In this step, the trap is rapidly heated to desorb the trapped volatile in a narrow band. The desorbed volatile is then transferred via a heated transfer line to the injector of a gas chromatograph for separation and detection.

Box 12.8 How to concentrate a sample using direct solid phase microextraction (SPME) of an organic compound in an aqueous sample

1. **Place the sample in a vial.**

2. **Clean the SPME fibre** by inserting it into the hot injection port (220 °C) of the GC.

3. **Expose the SPME fibre** to the aqueous sample. Agitate the sample solution by sonication for 10 min.

4. **Retract the fibre into the SPME holder.**

5. **Pierce the GC septum with the SPME needle** and then expose the silica-coated fibre to the hot temperature (220 °C) of the injection port for 5 min.

6. **Start the GC** isothermal or temperature programme for separation and analysis of the organic compounds.

Box 12.9 How to concentrate a sample using headspace solid phase microextraction (SPME) of an organic compound in an aqueous sample

1. **Place the sample in a septum-sealed vial.**

2. **Clean the SPME fibre** by inserting it into the hot injection port (220 °C) of the GC.

3. **Pierce the septum-sealed vial** with the needle of the SPME.

4. **Expose the fibre to the headspace above the aqueous sample** for 2min. Gentle heating of the sample solution (40 °C) may be beneficial.

5. **Retract the fibre into the SPME holder.**

6. **Pierce the GC septum with the SPME needle** and then expose the fibre to the hot temperature (220 °C) of the injection port for 5min.

7. **Start the GC** isothermal or temperature programme for separation and analysis of the organic compounds.

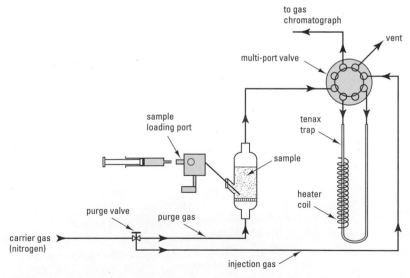

Fig. 12.20 Purge and trap system for the extraction of volatile compounds from aqueous samples.

Example *Tenax is typically used for accelerant analysis in cases involving suspected arson (Chapter 44).*

Solvent evaporation

Often, when the sample preparation step is complete, additional steps are required prior to analysis. The most common approach at this stage is to remove the organic solvent. In all cases, the evaporation method is slow, with a high risk of contamination from the solvent, glassware and any gas used.

There are two commonly used techniques for solvent evaporation:

1. **rotary film evaporation;**
2. **gas 'blow-down'.**

Both techniques have advantages and disadvantages. Where your experimental protocol may simply state 'the solvent is evaporated off', you should select the most appropriate procedure based on:

- **the volume of solvent** to be removed;
- **the amount of solute** in solution;
- **the relative boiling points** of the solvent and solute;
- **the next step** in the experimental procedure.

Rotary film evaporation   This method, which is also known as rotary evaporation, 'rotavap' or 'rovap', is the technique of choice for the removal of large volumes of volatile solvents from solutions, for example from extractions and chromatography (Chapter 14, p.123). Rotary evaporators are common pieces of equipment in the laboratory and the operating principle is that of a reduced-pressure distillation except that the evaporation flask can be rotated. This rotation reduces the risk of 'bumping', inherent in all reduced-pressure distillations, and spreads the solution in a thin film on the walls of the flask. This effectively increases the surface area of the solution and increases the rate of evaporation, which is further enhanced by the use of a vacuum.

 KEY POINT *When using a 'rovap' you must check that the reduced-pressure boiling point of the solute you are trying to isolate is below the temperature of the water bath.*

There are many variations in the details of the form of rotary film evaporators and a typical assembly is illustrated in Fig. 12.21. A general guide to the use of a rotary evaporator is given in Box 12.10.

When using rotary film evaporators, you should take note of the following safety advice:

- **Never use flat-bottom flasks or conical flasks** under reduced pressure.
- **Always check your flask** for 'star' cracks.
- **Always make sure that your solution has cooled** to room temperature before you begin, otherwise it may boil vigorously and 'bump' when you apply the vacuum, before it is lowered into the water bath.
- **Do not rush to lower the flask into the water bath** – wait to see what happens to the extent of evaporation at room temperature.
- **Always have the water bath just warm, not hot, at the start of the procedure** – if the water bath is too hot, allow it to cool or add cold water or ice.
- **Check that all joints are 'sealed' and that the water pump is producing a vacuum** – it will change 'note' as the vacuum is produced, when it is working properly. If there is no vacuum, the solution may not boil and you will overheat it in trying to promote evaporation. The joints may suddenly seal and the solution will then boil vigorously under the reduced pressure and will 'bump' into the condenser and receiving flask.

If it is necessary to evaporate volumes of solvent greater than the capacity of the rotating flask, you can carry out the process batch-wise involving several separate evaporations or the rotary evaporator can be modified for continuous evaporation (Fig. 12.22). A thin Teflon tube is attached to the vacuum inlet

Using 'rovaps' – these are communal so make sure that the 'rovap' is clean before you use it and clean it up after use. Empty the solvent collection flask into the appropriate waste solvent bottles.

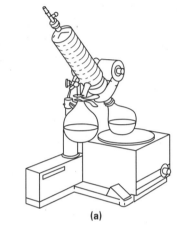

(a)

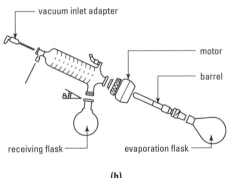

(b)

Fig. 12.21 (a) Typical examples of a rotary evaporator; (b) exploded view of glassware.

Transferring viscous liquids – it is often difficult to transfer small amounts of viscous liquids from a 'rovap' flask to a small sample tube. Dissolve the liquid in a small amount of dry solvent, transfer a little of this solution (1 or 2 mL) to a suitable small tube and 'blow off' the solvent with nitrogen.

Box 12.10   How to use a rotary film evaporator

1. **Check that the apparatus is ready for use by ensuring that:**
   (a) The receiving flask is clipped in place and is empty.
   (b) You have available the correct-size ground-glass joint adapters to connect your flask to the rotating 'barrel' protruding from the motor of the evaporator. Many rotary film evaporators have an 'odd' joint size, usually 29/32, which is not common to the routine ground-glass flasks used in the laboratory. Alternatively, special bulb-shaped flasks with 29/32 joints may be available.
   (c) The rotating barrel is 'clipped' in place in the motor, by pulling it gently. Someone may have had to clean out and reassemble the 'rovap', and if the barrel is not 'clipped' in place it will slide out when you attach your flask. If the barrel slides out of the motor when you pull it, consult your instructor.
   (d) The rotating barrel is clean and dry.
   (e) Water is flowing steadily through the condenser. If it is not, adjust the water tap.
   (f) The temperature of the water in the water bath is about 20 °C below the boiling point of the solvent to be removed.

2. **Open the vacuum inlet adapter** at the top of the condenser, and turn the water pump to maximum.

3. **Fill the rotating flask half-full or less,** using a stemmed filter funnel. You must not contaminate the joint of the rotating flask with solute, which will be deposited there during evaporation, since you may not be able to remove the flask after evaporation. If the flask is too full it may 'bump', sending solution up into the condenser and receiver. You will then have to dismantle and clean out the equipment with an appropriate solvent to recover your compound.

4. **Raise the apparatus using the lifting mechanism** so that when the flask is attached it is not touching the water in the bath. On modern equipment, the lifting system is an electric motor controlled by an 'up-down' pressure switch, but on older apparatus the lifting device is either (i) a manual handle with a trigger, which is pulled to lift and released to lock it in place, or (ii) a lever with a twist-grip on the end. To operate the latter mechanism, twist the grip anticlockwise to release the 'lock', pull the lever down to raise the apparatus and twist the grip clockwise to lock it in place.

5. **Attach the flask to the barrel** and put plastic joint clips on all the joints, while supporting the flask with your hand. If the weight of the flask and contents 'springs' any of the joints, it is too heavy – replace it with a smaller flask or remove some of the solution. *You must not rely on the power of the vacuum to hold your flask in place.*

6. **Turn on the motor,** slowly increasing the speed to the maximum.

7. **Close the vacuum inlet adapter slowly** until it is fully shut and observe the flask for a few seconds. If boiling occurs (liquid is condensed to the receiver flask) continue until boiling stops and then lower the flask so that it just touches the surface of the water, lock it in place and boiling should recommence. As the volume of solution decreases, you may need to lower the flask further into the water bath until all the solvent has been evaporated. If a white coating of frost forms on the flask evaporation may stop, because the flask is too cold – lower the flask into the water bath to warm it and evaporation should begin again.

8. **When evaporation is complete,** raise the flask from the bath, switch the motor off, open the vacuum inlet tap to allow air into the system and allow the flask to cool. Support the flask with your hand, take off the plastic joint clips, put the flask on one side and *only then* turn off the water pump. Turn off the water supply to the condenser.

9. **Unclip the receiving flask,** dispose of the solvent into a waste solvent bottle and reattach the receiving flask to the apparatus.

adapter so that it feeds down the condenser into the 'barrel' and another glass tube, dipping into the solution to be evaporated, is connected to the air inlet on the vacuum adapter. Once the rotary evaporator is operating, the tap on the vacuum adapter is opened a little. Solution is drawn up by the vacuum, runs into the rotating flask and is evaporated. Careful control of the tap allows a constant volume of solution to be sucked into the rotating flask and evaporated without overfilling it.

Gas 'blow-down'   This procedure is useful for removing very small volumes of solvents (about 2–5 mL) from solutes by blowing a stream of nitrogen over the surface of the solution, while warming the solution gently. This is routinely undertaken by placing the sample tube in a temperature-controlled sample concentrator (e.g. Dri-Block™) (Fig. 12.23(b)). The main application of the gas blow-down is in the isolation of small amounts of solute from rotary evaporation or small-scale liquid–liquid extraction, for further analysis by instrumental techniques, where the sample size may be 20 mg or less – for example, infra-red spectroscopy (p. 180), NMR (nuclear magnetic resonance) spectroscopy (p. 194), gas chromatography (p. 135) or liquid chromatography (p. 131).

The simplest system for evaporation by gas blow-down is shown in Fig. 12.23(a). A Pasteur pipette is connected by a flexible tube to a cylinder of nitrogen, which has a gas blow-off safety system. The sample is placed in a special tube with a conical base, such as a ReactiVial®. Hold the Pasteur pipette and direct a gentle stream of nitrogen towards the side of the tube so that it flows over the surface of the liquid. As the solvent evaporates, the liquid and tube will cool and may condense atmospheric water into the tube. To prevent condensation, clamp the tube in a warm sand bath or above a closed steam bath or in the hole of a purpose-designed aluminium heating block. The following points should be noted when using a gas blow-down system:

- **Always carry out the operation** in a fume cupboard.
- **The solute should have negligible vapour pressure at room temperature,** otherwise it may co-evaporate with the solvent.
- **Do not heat the solution to boiling** – only apply enough heat to prevent condensation of atmospheric water vapour.

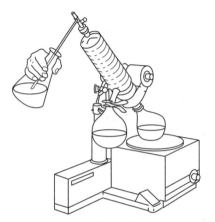

Fig. 12.22 The procedure for continuous solvent removal using a rotary evaporator.

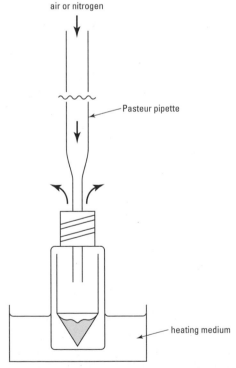

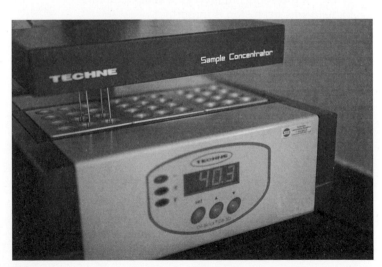

Fig. 12.23 (a) Gas 'blow-down' evaporation; (b) Dri-Block

Text references

Algarra, M., Rodrigues-Borges, J.E. and Esteves da Silva, J.C. (2010) LC-MS identification of derivatised free fatty acids from adipocere in soil samples. *Journal of Separation Science* **3B3**(2): 143–154.

Dean, J.R. (ed) (1993) *Applications of Supercritical Fluids in Industrial Analysis.* Springer Science+Business Media, Dordrecht.

Fernandez, P., M. Lago, I. Alvarez, A. M. Carro and R. A. Lorenzo (2013) Chromatographic determination of benzodiazepines in vitreous humor after microwave-assisted extraction. *Analytical Methods* **5**(19): 4999–5004.

Ford, T.C. and Graham, J.M. (1991) *An Introduction to Centrifugation.* Bios, Oxford.

Jones, A.W. and Fransson, M. (2003) Blood analysis by headspace gas chromatography: Does a deficient sample volume distort ethanol concentration? *Medicine, Science and the Law* **43**(3): 241–247.

Sources for further study

Bayne, S. and Carlin, M.G. (2011) *Forensic Applications of High Performance Liquid Chromatography.* CRC Press, Boca Raton, Florida.

Carlin, M.G. and Dean, J.R. (2013) *Forensic Applications of Gas Chromatography.* CRC Press, Boca Raton, Florida.

Dean, J.R. (2014) *Environmental Trace Analysis: Techniques and Applications.* Wiley, Chichester.

Furniss, B.A., Hannaford, A.J., Smith, P.W.G. and Tatchell, A.R. (1989) *Vogel's Textbook of Practical Organic Chemistry,* 5th edn. Longman, Harlow.

Mitra, S. (ed.) (2001) *Sample Preparation Techniques in Analytical Chemistry.* Wiley-Interscience, New York.

Skoog, D.A., West, D.M., Holler, F.J. and Crouch, S.R. (2014) *Fundamentals of Analytical Chemistry,* 9th edn. Brookes Cole, Belmont, CA

Study exercises

12.1 Identify possible technique(s) that you could use to prepare the following samples for analysis:

(a) cannabis in blood;
(b) pesticides in soil;
(c) accelerants in fire debris;
(d) illicit heroin.

12.2 What are the steps required for a successful SPE? Explain why each step is important.

12.3 Find a peer-reviewed article in a forensic science journal your university subscribes to that details how buprenorphine is extracted from blood. Read the Materials and Methods section and write down a protocol that you would follow in order to replicate the experiment in your laboratory. Ask another student to evaluate your protocol and provide you with written feedback.

Essential vocabulary for Mendelian genetics – make sure you know what the following terms and symbols mean:

- *chromosome, sex chromosome, autosome;*
- *gene, allele;*
- *dominant, recessive, lethal;*
- *haploid, diploid, gamete, zygote;*
- *heterozygous, homozygous;*
- *P, F1, F2. ☿, ♂.*

Genomes and chromosome numbers – remember that mitochondria and chloroplasts contain DNA molecules, but these are not included when calculating the chromosome number.

This chapter gives a general overview of the techniques involved in DNA analysis, but it should be noted that the principle application adopted in forensic science for routine casework is the polymerase chain reaction (PCR) (p. 114).

Mendelian genetics

Gregor Mendel, an Austrian monk, made pioneering studies of the genetics of eukaryotic organisms in the middle of the nineteenth century. He made crosses between different forms of flowering plants. Through careful examination and numerical analysis of the observable characteristics, or phenotype, of the parents and their progeny, Mendel was able to deduce much about their genetic characteristics, or genotype. The principles derived from these experiments explain the basis of heredity, and hence underpin our understanding of sexual reproduction, biodiversity and evolution. Mendelian genetics is concerned primarily with the transmission of genetic information, as opposed to molecular genetics, which deals with the molecular details of the genome and techniques for altering genes.

 KEY POINT *A common initial stumbling block in genetics is terminology. In many cases the definitions are interdependent, so your success in this subject depends on your grasp of all of the definitions and underlying ideas explained below.*

Important terms and concepts

Each character in the phenotype is controlled by the organism's genes, the basic units of inheritance. Each gene includes the 'genetic blueprint' (DNA), which usually defines the amino acid sequence for a specific polypeptide or protein – often an enzyme or a structural protein. The protein gives rise to the phenotype through its activity in metabolism or its contribution to the organism's structure. The full complement of genes in an individual is known as its genome. Individual genes can exist in different forms, each of which generally leads to a different form of the protein it codes for. These different gene forms are known as alleles.

In eukaryotes, the genes are located in a particular sequence on chromosomes within the nucleus. The number of chromosomes per cell is characteristic for each organism (its chromosome number, n). For example, the chromosome number for man is 23. In cells of most 'higher' organisms, there are two of each of the chromosomes ($2n$). This is known as the diploid state. As a result of the process of meiosis, which precedes reproduction, special haploid cells are formed (gametes) which contain only one of each chromosome ($1n$). In sexual reproduction, haploid gametes from two individuals fuse to form a zygote, a diploid cell with a new genome, which gives rise to a new individual through the process of mitosis. Cell numbers are increased by this process, producing genetically identical cells.

Organisms vary in the span of the diploid and haploid phases. In some 'lower' organisms, the haploid phase is the longer lasting form; in most 'higher' organisms, the diploid phase is dominant. Since each diploid individual carries two of each chromosome, it has two copies of each gene in every cell. The number of alleles of each character present depends on whether the relevant genes are the same – the homozygous state – or whether they are different – the heterozygous state. Hence, while there may be many alleles for any given gene, an individual could have two at most, and might only have one if it were homozygous. This will depend on the alleles present in the parental gametes that fused when the zygote was formed. Offspring that inherit a different combination of alleles at the two loci compared with their parents are known as recombinants.

The basis of Mendel's experiments and of many exercises in genetics are *crosses,* where individuals showing particular phenotypes are mated and the phenotypes of the offspring, or F_1 generation, are studied (see Box 13.1). If homozygous individuals carrying alternative alleles for a character are crossed, one of the alleles may be *dominant*, and all the F_1 generation will show that character in their phenotype. The character not evident is said to be *recessive*.

In describing crosses, geneticists denote each character with a letter of the alphabet, a capital letter being used for the dominant allele and lower case for the recessive. Taking, for example, a gene with dominant and recessive forms A and a respectively, there are three possibilities for each individual – it can be (a) homozygous recessive aa; (b) homozygous dominant AA; or (c) heterozygous Aa.

The reasons for dominance might relate to the activity of an enzyme coded by the relevant gene – for example, Mendel's yellow pea allele is dominant because the gene involved codes for the breakdown of chlorophyll. In the homozygous recessive case, none of the functional enzyme will be present, chlorophyll breakdown cannot occur and the seeds remain green. Not all alleles exhibit dominance in this form. In some cases, the heterozygous state results in a third phenotype (incomplete or partial dominance); in others, the heterozygous individual expresses both genotypes (codominance). Another possible situation is epistasis, in which one gene affects the expression of another gene that is independently inherited. Note also that many genes, such as those coding for human blood groups, have multiple alleles.

 KEY POINT *Genetics problems may well involve one of the 'standard' crosses shown in Box 13.1. Before tackling the problem, try to analyse the information provided to see if it fits one of these types of cross. Figure 13.1 is a flowchart detailing the steps you should take in answering genetics problems.*

Unless otherwise stated or it is obvious from the evidence, you should assume that the genes being considered in any given case are on separate chromosomes. This is important because it means that they will assort independently during meiosis. Thus, the fact that an allele of gene A is present in any individual will not influence the possibility of an allele of gene B being present. This allows you to apply simple probability in predicting the genetic make-up of the offspring of any cross (see p. 101).

Where genes are present on the same chromosome, they are said to be linked genes, and thus it would appear that they would not be able to assort independently during metaphase 1 of meiosis, when homologous chromosomes are independently orientated. However, although physically attached to each other, they may become separated when crossing-over occurs between the homologous chromosomes at an early stage of meiosis. Exchange of genetic information between homologous chromosomes is called recombination. Linkage can be detected from a cross between individuals heterozygous and homozygous recessive for the relevant genes (e.g. AaBb × aabb). If the genes A and B are on different chromosomes, we expect the ratio of AaBb, aabb, Aabb and aaBb to be 1:1:1:1 in the F_1. However, if the dominant alleles of both genes occur on the same chromosome, the last two combinations will occur, but rarely. Just how rarely depends on how far apart they lie on the relevant chromosome – the further apart, the more likely it is that crossing over will occur. This is the basis of chromosome mapping (see Box 13.1).

Example In the garden pea, *Pisum sativum,* studied by Mendel, the yellow seed allele Y was found to be dominant over the green seed allele y. A cross of YY × yy genotypes would give rise to Yy in all of the F_1 generation, all of which would thus have the yellow seed phenotype. If the F_1 generation were interbred, this Yy × Yy cross would lead to progeny in the next, F_2, generation with the genotypes YY:Yy:yy in the expected ratio 1:2:1. The expected phenotype ratio would be 3:1 for yellow: green seed.

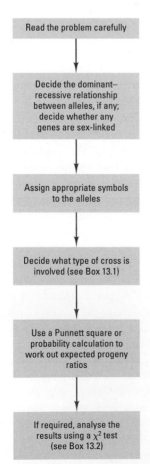

Fig. 13.1 Flowchart for tackling problems in Mendelian genetics.

Pedigree notation:

○   normal female

□   normal male

● ■   female or male with an inherited condition

○—□   mating

     offspring

Example of simple family pedigree:

This diagram shows the offspring of a normal male and female. The two daughters are normal, but the son has the inherited condition.

Fig. 13.2 Pedigree notation and family trees.

Denoting linked genes – *these are often shown diagrammatically, with a double line indicating the chromosome pair. For example, the two possible linkages for the genotype AaBb would be shown as:*

$$\frac{A}{a} \quad \frac{b}{B} \quad or \quad \frac{A}{a} \quad \frac{B}{b}$$

Using probability calculations – *this can be simpler and faster than Punnett squares when two or more genes are considered.*

Hardy–Weinberg principle – *for a population in genetic equilibrium, the genotype frequencies at an autosomal locus will remain at particular equilibrium values, which can be expressed in terms of the allele frequencies at that locus.*

Another complication you will come across is sex-linked genes. These occur on one of the X or Y chromosomes that control sex. Because one or other of the sexes – depending on the organism – is determined as XX and the other as XY (see Box 13.1), this means that rare recessive genes carried on the X chromosome may be expressed in XY individuals. Sex-linked genes are sometimes obvious from differences in the frequencies of phenotypes in male and female offspring. Pedigree charts (Fig. 13.2) are codified family trees that are often used to show the inheritance and expression of sex-linked characteristics through various generations.

Analysis of crosses

There are two basic ways of working out the results of crosses from known or assumed genotypes:

- **The Punnett square method** provides a good visual indication of potential combinations of gametes for a given cross. Lay out your Punnett squares consistently, as shown in Fig. 13.3. Then group together the like genotypes to work out the genotype ratio and proceed to work out the corresponding phenotype ratio if required.
- **Probability calculations** are based on the fact that the chance of a number of independent events occurring is equal to the probabilities of each event occurring, multiplied together. Thus, if the probability P of a child being a boy is 0.5 and the probability of the child of particular parents being blue-eyed is 0.5, then the probability of that couple having a blue-eyed son is $0.5 \times 0.5 = 0.25$, and that of having two blue-eyed boys is:

$$P = (0.5 \times 0.5) \times (0.5 \times 0.5) = 0.0625$$

How do you decide whether the results of an experimental cross fit your expectation from theory as calculated above? This isn't easy, because of the element of chance in gene crossing-over during meiosis. Thus, while you might expect to see a 3:1 phenotype ratio of progeny for a given cross, in 500 offspring you might actually observe a ratio of 379:121, which is a ratio of just over 3.13:1. Can you conclude that this is significantly different from 3:1 in the context of random error? The answer to this problem comes from statistics. However, the answer isn't certain, and your conclusion will be based on a balance of probabilities (see Box 13.2 and Table 13.1)..

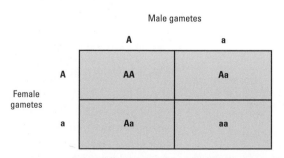

Fig. 13.3 Layout for a simple Punnett square for the cross Aa × Aa. The genotypic ratios for this cross are 1:2:1 for AA:Aa:aa, and the phenotypic ratio would be 3:1 for characteristic A to characteristic a. In this simple Punnett square, the allele frequencies are treated as equal ($f = 0.5$); if different from this, the probability of genotypes in each combination will be the relevant frequencies multiplied together.

DNA analysis – fundamental principles

Box 13.1 Types of cross and what you can (and cannot) learn from them

Monohybrid cross – the simplest form of cross, considering two alleles of a single gene.

Example: AA × aa

If only the parental *phenotypes* are known, you can't always deduce the parental genotypes from the phenotype ratio in the F_1. An individual of dominant phenotype in the F_1 could arise from a homozygous dominant or heterozygous genotype. However, crossing the F_1 generation with themselves to give an F_2 generation may provide useful information from the phenotype ratios that are found.

Dihybrid cross – a cross involving two genes, each with two alleles.

Example: AaBB × AaBb

As with a monohybrid cross, you can't always deduce the parental genotype from the phenotype ratio in the F_1 generation alone.

Test cross – a cross of an unknown genotype with a homozygous recessive.

Example: AABb × aabb

A test cross is one between an individual dominant for A and B with one recessive for both genes. The progeny will all be dominant for A, revealing the homozygous nature of the parent for this gene, but the progeny phenotypes will be split approximately 1:1 dominant to recessive for gene B, revealing the heterozygous nature of the parent for this gene. This type of cross reveals the unknown parental genotype in the proportions of phenotypes in the F_1.

Sex-linked cross – a cross involving a gene carried on the X chromosome; this can be designated as dominant or recessive using appropriate superscripts (e.g. X^A and X^a).

Example: X^AX^a × X^AY

In sex-linked crosses you need to know the basis of sex determination in the species concerned – which of XX or XY is male (e.g. the former in birds, butterflies and moths, the latter in mammals and *Drosophila*). The expected ratios of phenotypes in the offspring will depend on this. Note that the recessive genotype a will be expressed in the X^aY case.

Crosses with linked genes – genes are linked if they are on the same chromosome. This is revealed from a cross between individuals heterozygous and homozygous recessive for the relevant genes.

Example1 (genes on separate chromosomes): expected offspring frequency from the cross AaBb × aabb is AaBb, aabb, Aabb and aaBb in the ratio 1:1:1:1.

Example2 (linked genes): the frequencies of the last two combinations in example1 might be skewed according to the direction of parental linkage.

Chromosome mapping uses the frequency of crossing-over of linked genes to estimate their distance apart on the chromosome on the basis that crossing-over is more likely when the genes are further apart. So-called 'map units' are calculated on the following basis:

$$\frac{\text{no. of recombinant progeny}}{\text{total no. of progeny}} \times 100 = \%\text{ crossing over}$$

[13.1]

By convention, 1% crossing over = 1 map unit (centimorgan, cM). The order of a number of genes can be worked out from their relative distances from each other. Thus, if genes A and B are 12 map units apart, while A and B are respectively 5 and 7 map units from C, the assumed order on the chromosome is ACB (Fig. 13.4).

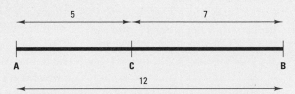

Fig. 13.4 Genetic map showing relative positions of genes A, B and C.

Limitation of the chi² test – the formula cited in Box 13.2 is valid only if expected numbers are greater than 5.

Limitation of the chi² test – the formula cited in Box 13.2 is valid only if expected numbers are greater than 5.

Population genetics

Population genetics is largely concerned with the frequencies of alleles in a population and how these may change in time. The Hardy–Weinberg principle states that the frequency of alleles *f* remains the same between generations, unless influenced by some outside factor(s).

To understand why this is the case, consider alleles H and h for a particular gene, which exists in the breeding population at frequencies *p* and *q* respectively. If the individuals carrying these alleles interbreed randomly, then the

Box 13.2   Example of a chi² (χ^2) test

This test allows you to assess the difference between observed (O) and expected (E) values and is extremely useful in genetics. It is particularly valuable in determining whether progeny phenotype ratios fit your assumptions about their genotypes. The operation of the test is best illustrated by the use of an example. Assume that your null hypothesis (see p. 517) is that the phenotypic ratio is 3:1 and you observe that in 500 offspring the phenotype ratio is 379:121, whereas the expected ratio is 375:125.

Start the test by calculating the test statistic χ^2. The general formula for calculating χ^2 is:

$$\chi^2 = \sum \frac{(O - E)}{E} \qquad [13.2]$$

In this example, this works out as:

$$\chi^2 = \frac{(379 - 375)^2}{375} + \frac{(121 - 125)^2}{125} = \frac{16}{375} + \frac{16}{125} = 0.171$$

The probability associated with this value can be obtained from χ^2 tables for ($n - 1$) degrees of freedom (d.f.), where n = the number of categories = number of phenotypes considered. Here the d.f. value is $2 - 1 = 1$. Since the χ^2 value of 0.171 is lower than the tabulated value for 1 d.f. (3.84, Table 13.1), we therefore accept the null hypothesis and conclude that the difference between observed and expected results is not significant (since $P > 0.05$). Had χ^2 been > 3.84, then $P < 0.05$ and we would have rejected the null hypothesis and concluded that the difference was significant, i.e. that the progeny phenotype did not fit the expected ratio.

Table 13.1   Values of chi2 (χ^2) for which $P = 0.05$. The value for ($n - 1$) degrees of freedom (d.f.) should be used, where $n =$ *the number of categories (= phenotypes)* considered (normally fewer than 4 in genetics problems). If χ^2 is less than this value, accept the null hypothesis that the observed values arose by chance; if χ^2 is greater than this value, reject the null hypothesis and conclude that the difference between the observed and expected values is statistically significant

Degrees of freedom	χ^2 value for which $P = 0.05$
1	3.84
2	5.99
3	7.82
4	9.49

Example   Cystic fibrosis occurs in 0.04% of Caucasian babies. If this condition results from a double recessive allele *aa*, then following the Hardy–Weinberg principle, $q^2 = 0.0004$ (0.04% expressed as a fraction of 1) and so $q = \sqrt{0.0004} = 0.02$, or 2%. Since $p = (1 - q)$, $p = 0.98$, or 98%. The frequency of carriers of cystic fibrosis in the Caucasian population (people having the alleles Aa) is given by $2pq$. From the above, $2pq = 2(0.02 \times 0.98) = 0.0392$. Hence 3.92% of the Caucasian population are carriers (roughly one in 25).

expected phenotype and allele ratios in the F_1 generation can be calculated simply as:

$$f(HH) = p^2$$

$$f(Hh) = 2pq$$

$$f(hh) = q^2$$

If you wish to confirm this, lay out a Punnett square with appropriate frequencies for each allele. Now, by summation, the frequency of H in the $F_1 = p^2 + pq$ (a similar calculation can be made for allele h); and since in this example there are only two alleles, $p + q = 1$ and so $q = (1 - p)$. Substituting $(1 - p)$ for q, the frequency of H in the F_1 is thus:

$$p^2 + p(1 - p) = p^2 + p - p^2 = p$$

i.e. the frequency of the allele is unchanged between generations. A similar relationship exists for the other alleles.

The Hardy–Weinberg principle was named after its first, independent, protagonists. It holds so long as the following criteria are satisfied:

1. **random mating** – so that no factors influence each individual's choice of a mate;
2. **large population size** – so that the laws of probability will apply;
3. **no mutation** – so that no new alleles are formed;
4. **no emigration, immigration or isolation** – so that there is no interchange of genes with other populations nor isolation of genes within the population;
5. **no natural selection** – so that no alleles have a reproductive advantage over others.

Population geneticists use the Hardy–Weinberg principle (p. 101) to gain an idea of the rate of evolution and the influences on evolution. By ensuring that criteria 1–4 hold, if there are any changes in allele frequency between generations, then the rate of change of allele frequencies indicates the rate of evolutionary change (natural selection).

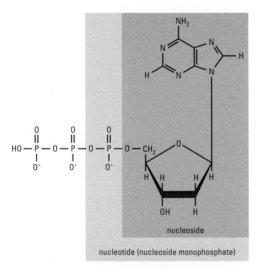

Fig. 13.5 Nitrogenous bases in nucleic acids.

Fig. 13.6 A nucleoside triphosphate – deoxy-adenosine 5′ triphosphate (dATP).

Nucleic acids – general principles

Nucleic acids are nitrogen-containing compounds of high M_r, often found within nucleic acid–protein (nucleoprotein) complexes in cells. The two main groups of nucleic acids are:

1. **Deoxyribonucleic acid (DNA)** – found in chromosomes and the principal molecule responsible for the storage and transfer of genetic information.
2. **Ribonucleic acid (RNA)** – involved with the DNA-directed synthesis of proteins in cells. Three principal types of RNA exist – messenger RNA (mRNA), ribosomal RNA (rRNA) and transfer RNA (tRNA). In some viruses, RNA acts as the genetic material. In eukaryotes, mRNA molecules initially synthesised in the nucleus from genomic DNA (nascent mRNA) will contain several sequences – called introns – that are not transcribed into protein. These are successively excised in the nucleus, leaving only coding sequences (exons) in the mRNA that migrates to the cytoplasm, to be translated at the ribosome.

 KEY POINT *Nucleic acids are important in the transmission of information within cells, and one of the most important aspects of nucleic acid analysis is to 'decipher' the coded information within these molecules.*

The structure of nucleic acids

Nucleic acids are polymers of nucleotides (polynucleotides), where each nucleotide consists of:

- **a nitrogenous base,** of which there are five main types – two have a purine ring structure, i.e. adenine (A) and guanine (G), and three have a pyrimidine ring, i.e. thymine (T), uracil (U) and cytosine (C), as shown in Fig. 13.5. Their carbon atoms are numbered C-1, C-2, etc.;
- **a pentose sugar,** which is ribose in RNA and deoxyribose in DNA – the carbon atoms are denoted as C-1′, C-2′, etc. and deoxyribose has no hydroxyl group on C-2′. The C-1′ of the sugar is linked either to the N-9 of a purine or the N-1 of a pyrimidine;
- **a phosphate group** – which links with the sugars to form the sugar–phosphatebackbone of the polynucleotide chain.

A compound with sugar and base only is called a nucleoside (Fig. 13.6) and the specific names given to the various nucleosides and nucleotides are listed in Table 13.2. The individual nucleotides within nucleic acids are linked by phosphodiester bonds between the 3′ and 5′ positions of the sugars (Fig. 13.7).

 KEY POINT *RNA and DNA differ both in the nature of the pentose sugar residue, and in their base composition – both types contain adenine, guanine and cytosine, but RNA contains uracil while DNA contains thymine.*

Differences also exist in the conformation of the two types of nucleic acid. DNA typically exists as two interwoven helical polynucleotide chains, with their structure stabilised by hydrogen bonds between matching base pairs on the adjacent strands – A always pairs with T (two hydrogen bonds), and G with C (three hydrogen bonds). This complementarity is important since it stabilises the DNA duplex (double helix) and provides the basis for replication and transcription. While most double-stranded (ds) DNA molecules are in this form,

Table 13.2 Nomenclature of nucleosides and nucleotides

Base	Nucleoside	Nucleotide
Adenine	Adenosine	Adenylic acid
Guanine	Guanosine	Guanylic acid
Uracil[1]	Uridine	Uridylic acid
Cytosine	Cytidine	Cytidylic acid
Thymine[2]	Thymidine	Thymidylic acid

[1] In DNA.
[2] In RNA.

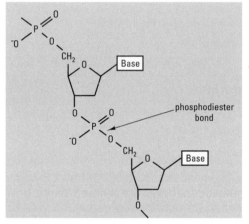

Fig. 13.7 Linkage of nucleotides in nucleic acids.

i.e. as a double helix, some viral DNA is single stranded (ss). Intact DNA molecules are very large indeed, with high M_r values (e.g. 10^9). In the main, RNA is single stranded and in the form of a gentle right-handed helix stabilised by base-stacking interactions, although some sections of RNA (tRNA) have regions of self-complementarity, leading to base pairing. Typical values for M_r of RNA range from 10^4 for tRNA to 10^6 for other types.

Extraction and purification of DNA

Irrespective of the source of DNA, extraction and purification involve the following stages, in sequence:

- disruption of cells to release their contents;
- removal of non-nucleic acid components (e.g. protein), leaving DNA and/or RNA;
- concentration of the remaining nucleic acids.

The following general steps are required to isolate DNA:

1. **Homogenisation** – tissues can be disrupted, for example by lysis in a buffered solution containing the detergent sodium dodecyl sulphate (SDS) or Triton X-100.
2. **Enzymic removal of protein and RNA** – using proteinase (e.g. proteinase K at 0.1 mg mL^{-1}) and ribonuclease (typically at 0.1 mg mL^{-1}) for 1–2 h.
3. **Phenol–chloroform extraction** – to remove any remaining traces of contaminating protein.
4. **Precipitation of nucleic acids** – usually by adding twice the volume of ethanol.
5. **Solubilisation in an appropriate volume of buffer (pH 7.5)** – ribonuclease is often added to remove any traces of contaminating RNA.

Separating nucleic acids   Electrophoresis is the principal method used for separating nucleic acids. At alkaline pH values, linear DNA and RNA molecules have a uniform net negative charge per unit length due to the charge on the phosphoryl group of the backbone. Electrophoresis using a supporting medium that acts as a molecular sieve (e.g. agarose or polyacrylamide, p. 213) enables DNA fragments to be separated on the basis of their relative sizes (see Chapter 22 for further details).

Quantitative analysis of nucleic acids

Measuring nucleic acid content   The concentration of reasonably pure samples of DNA or RNA can be measured by spectrophotometry (p. 154). In contrast, measurement of the nucleic acid content of whole cell or tissue homogenates requires chemical methods, since the homogenates will contain many substances that would interfere with the spectroscopic methods. The principles involved in each technique are as follows:

- **Spectrophotometry** – DNA and RNA both show absorption maxima at ≈ 260 nm, due to the conjugated double bonds present in their constituent bases. At 260 nm, an A_{260} value of 1.0 is given by a 50 μg mL^{-1} solution of dsDNA, or a 40 μg mL^{-1} solution of ssRNA. If the absorbance at 260 nm is also measured, protein contamination can be quantified. Pure nucleic acids give A_{260}/A_{280} ratios of 1.8–2.0, and a value below 1.6 indicates significant protein contamination. Further purification steps are required for contaminated samples (e.g. by repeating the phenol–chloroform extraction step). RNA contamination of a DNA preparation is indicated if A_{260} decreases when the sample is treated with 2.5 μL of RNase at 20 μg mL^{-1}. DNA contamination of an RNA preparation might be suspected if the sample is very viscous, and this can be confirmed by electrophoresis.

- **Spectrofluorimetry** – this is the best approach for samples where the DNA concentration is too low to allow direct assay by the spectrophotometric method described above. The method uses the fluorescent dye ethidium bromide, which binds to dsDNA by insertion between stacked base pairs, a phenomenon termed 'intercalation'. The fluorescence of ethidium bromide is enhanced 25-fold when it interacts with dsDNA. Since ssDNA gives no significant enhancement of fluorescence, dsDNA can be quantified in the presence of denatured DNA. The concentration of dsDNA in solution $[dsDNA]_x$ can be calculated by comparing its fluorescence (excitation wavelength, 525 nm; emission wavelength, 590 nm) with that of a standard dsDNA solution of known concentration $[dsDNA]_{std}$ using the following relationship:

$$[dsDNA]_x = \frac{[dsDNA]_{std} \times \text{fluorescence of unknown}}{\text{fluorescence of standard}}$$
[13.3]

Principles of molecular genetics

In contrast to Mendelian genetics, molecular genetics involves the study of the genetic material itself, i.e. deoxyribonucleic acid (DNA).

 ***KEY POINT** The sequence of the bases A, G, T and C carries the genetic information of the organism. A section of DNA that encodes the information for a single polypeptide or protein is referred to as a gene, while the entire genetic information of an organism is called the genome.*

Organisation and function of DNA

The amount of DNA in the genome is usually expressed in terms of base pairs (bp), rather than M_r, and its size depends on the complexity of the organism – for example, the human papilloma virus has a genome of 8×10^3 base pairs (8 kbp), that of *Escherichia coli* is 4×10^6 base pairs (4 Mbp), while the human haploid genome is very large comprising 3×10^9 base pairs (3,000 Mbp). The human genome contains about 23,000 genes (distributed on 23 pairs of chromosomes), which represent only about 1% of the total amount of genomic DNA (i.e. 99% of human DNA is non-coding). Organisms with smaller genomes have smaller amounts of non-coding DNA – some viral genomes have 'overlapping' genes, where the same base sequences carry information for more than one protein.

The size of each individual gene varies considerably – the largest ones may exceed 10Mbp. Chromosomes represent the largest organisational units of DNA – in eukaryotes, they are usually linear molecules, complexed with protein and RNA, ranging in length from tens to hundreds of Mbp. The unit used to denote physical distance between genes (base pairs) differs from that used to describe genetic distance (centimorgan, cM), which is based on recombination frequency (p. 102). In humans, 1cM $\approx$ 1Mbp, though this relationship varies widely, depending on recombination frequency within particular regions of a chromosome.

Each DNA template for the synthesis of RNA (transcription) begins at a promoter site upstream of the coding sequence and terminates at a specific site at the end of the gene. The base sequence of this RNA is complementary

Measuring nucleic acids by spectrophotometry – ideally, the nucleic acid extracts should be prepared to give A_{260} values of between 0.10 and 0.50, for maximum accuracy and precision.

Safe working with ethidium bromide – this compound is highly toxic and mutagenic. Avoid skin contact (wear gloves) and avoid ingestion. Use a safe method of disposal (e.g. adsorb from solution using an appropriate adsorbant).

Definition

Units of nucleic acid size (length) – kilobase pair (kbp) = 10^3 base pairs megabase pair (Mbp) = 10^6 base pairs.

to the 'template strand' and equivalent to the 'coding strand' of the DNA. In eukaryotic cells, transcription occurs in the nucleus, where the newly synthesised RNA, or primary transcript, is also subject to processing, or 'splicing', in which non-coding regions within the gene (introns) are excised, joining the coding regions (exons) together into a continuous sequence. Further processing results in the addition of a polyadenyl 'tail' at the 3′ end and a 7-methylguanosine 'cap' at the 5′ end of what is now mature eukaryotic messenger RNA (mRNA). The mRNA then migrates from the nucleus to the cytoplasm, where it acts as a template for protein synthesis (translation) at the ribosome – the translated portion of mRNA is read in coding units, termed codons, consisting of three bases.

Each codon corresponds to a specific amino acid, including a codon for the initiation of protein synthesis (Table 13.3). Individual amino acids are brought to the ribosome by specific transfer RNA (tRNA) molecules that recognise particular codons. The amino acids are incorporated into the growing polypeptide chain in the order dictated by the sequence of codons on mRNA until a termination codon is recognised, after which the protein (polypeptide) is released from the ribosome.

The basic techniques described in this chapter are used widely in many aspects of molecular biology, including the identification and characterisation of genes, gene cloning and genetic engineering, medical genetics and genetic fingerprinting.

KEY POINT *An important characteristic of nucleic acids is their ability to hybridise – two single strands with complementary base pairs will hydrogen bond (anneal) to produce a duplex, as in conventional double-stranded (ds) DNA. This duplex can be converted to single-stranded (ss) DNA (i.e. 'melted') by conditions that disrupt hydrogen bonding (e.g. raising the temperature or adding salt) and then reannealed by lowering the temperature or by removal of the salt.*

DNA can be purified and assayed (p. 105), and it is relatively stable in its pure form. Most of the problems of working with such a large biomolecule have been overcome by the following steps:

- **Restriction enzymes** (see below) can be used to cut DNA precisely and reproducibly – mammalian DNA may yield millions of fragments, with sizes ranging from a few hundred base pairs to tens of kbp, whereas small viral genomes may give only a few fragments;
- **Electrophoretic methods** for the separation of DNA fragments on the basis of their sizes (p. 108);
- **Segments of DNA** can be detected by 'probes' that specifically hybridise with the DNA of interest (p. 109);
- **Once separated, specific segments of DNA** can be obtained in almost unlimited quantities by insertion into vectors and multiplication within suitable host cells in a process termed DNA cloning;
- **Methods are now available for rapidly determining the base sequence of DNA segments** (p. 112), together with strategies for combining information from several adjacent segments to give contiguous sequences representing entire genomes in well-studied organisms;
- **Specific target sequences of DNA** within a genome can be amplified by more than a billion-fold by the polymerase chain reaction (PCR, p. 114).

Good practice in molecular genetics – this includes:

- accurate pipetting down to 1 μL, or less;
- steadiness of hand in sample loading;
- keeping enzyme solutions cold during use and frozen during storage;
- using sterile plasticware;
- using double-distilled water;
- wearing disposable gloves to avoid contamination.

Example Multiple sequence alignment – software tools can be downloaded from the European Bioinformatics Institute website at: http://www.ebi.ac.uk/Tools/msa/

Table 13.3 The genetic code – combinations of nucleotide bases coding for individual amino acids

1st base	2nd base				3rd base
	U	C	A	G	
U	F	S	Y	C	U
	F	S	Y	C	C
	L	S	*	*	A
	L	S	*	W	G
C	L	P	H	R	U
	L	P	H	R	C
	L	P	Q	R	A
	L	P	Q	R	G
A	I	T	N	S	U
	I	T	N	S	C
	I	T	K	R	A
	M	T	K	R	G
G	V	A	D	G	U
	V	A	D	G	C
	V	A	E	G	A
	V	A	E	G	G

* = termination codons.
Note that AUG (= M) is the initiation codon. The above codons are given for mRNA – the coding strand of DNA would have T in place of U, while the template strand would have complementary bases to those given above.

DNA analysis – fundamental principles

Producing DNA fragments

Fragments of DNA can be produced by mechanical shearing or ultrasonication (p. 215), producing a random array of fragment sizes. Reproducible cleavage can be achieved using type II restriction endonucleases (commonly called restriction enzymes), which recognise and cleave at a specific palindromic sequence of double-stranded DNA (usually four or six base pairs), known as the restriction site. Each enzyme is given a code name derived from the name of the organism from which it is isolated, for example *Hin* dIII was the third restriction enzyme obtained from *Haemophilus influenzae* strain Rd (Fig. 13.8). Most restriction enzymes will cut each DNA strand at a slightly different position within the restriction site to produce short, single-stranded regions known as cohesive ends, or 'sticky ends', as shown in Fig. 13.8. A few restriction enzymes cleave DNA to give blunt-ended fragments (e.g. *Hin* dII and *Sma* I).

Separation of nucleic acids using gel electrophoresis

Separation of DNA by agarose and polyacrylamide gel electrophoresis Electrophoresis is the term used to describe the movement of ions in an applied electrical field. DNA molecules are negatively charged (p. 105) and migrate through an agarose gel towards the anode at a rate that is dependent on molecular size – smaller, compact DNA molecules can pass through the sieve-like agarose matrix more easily than large, extended fragments (molecular sieving). Electrophoresis of plasmid DNA is usually carried out using a submerged agarose gel (Fig. 13.9). The amount of agarose is adjusted, depending on the size of the DNA molecules to be separated, for example 0.3% w/v agarose is used for large fragments (>20,000 bp), whereas 0.8 % is used for smaller fragments. Very small fragments are best separated using a polyacrylamide gel (Table 13.4).

Note the following practical aspects:

- **Individual samples are added to pre-formed wells using a pipettor.** The volume of sample added to each well is usually less than 25 mL so a steady hand and careful dispensing are needed to pipette each sample.
- **The density of the samples is usually increased** by adding a small amount of glycerol or sucrose, so that each sample is retained within the appropriate well.
- **The use of TAE buffer at pH 8.0** (p. 219) ensures that fragments are negatively charged.
- **A water-soluble anionic tracking dye** (e.g. bromophenol blue) is also added to each sample, so that migration towards the anode can be followed visually.
- **DNA fragment size markers** (molecular weight standards) are added to one or more wells. After electrophoresis, the relative positions of bands of known molecular weight can be used to prepare a calibration curve (usually by

Table 13.4 Gel concentrations for the separation of DNA of various sizes

Type of gel	% (w/v)	Range of resolution of DNA (bp)
Polyacrylamide	20.0	5–100
	15.0	20–150
	5.0	75–500
	3.5	100–1,000
Agarose	2.0	100–5,000
	1.2	200–8,000
	0.8	400–20,000
	0.3	1000–70,000

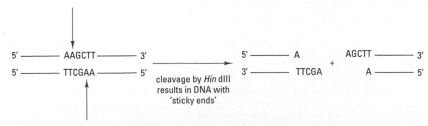

Fig. 13.8 Recognition base sequence and cleavage site for the restriction enzyme *Hin* dIII. This is the conventional representation of double-stranded DNA, showing the individual bases, where A is adenine, C cytosine, G guanine and T thymine. The cleavage site on each strand is shown by an arrow.

Using molecular weight standards – *for accurate molecular weight determination your standards must have the same conformation as the DNA in your sample, i.e. linear DNA standards for linear (restriction) fragments and closed circular standards for plasmid DNA.*

Chromosome walking – *a method for analysing areas of interest in DNA, in which the end of a segment of DNA is used as a probe to locate other segments that overlap the first segment; long stretches of DNA can be analysed by subsequent use of probes made from the ends of successive overlapping segments.*

Assaying nucleic acids in solution – *double-stranded DNA at 50 mgmL^{-1} has an A$_{260}$ of 1, and the same absorbance is obtained for single-stranded DNA at 33 mgmL^{-1} and (single-stranded) RNA at 40 mgmL^{-1}. These values can be used to convert the absorbance of a test solution to a concentration of nucleic acid.*

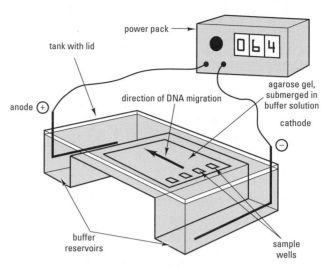

Fig. 13.9 Agarose gel electrophoresis of DNA.

plotting $\log_{10}$ of the molecular weight of each band against the distance travelled).

- The gel should be run until the tracking dye has migrated across 80% of the gel (see manufacturer's instructions for appropriate voltages/times).
- **After electrophoresis, the bands of DNA can be visualised** by soaking the gel for around 5 min in a suitable fluorescent stain e.g. SYBR® Safe or SafeView.
- **Under UV light, bands of DNA are visible** due to the intense fluorescence of the visualising stain, e.g. SYBR® Safe or SafeView fluoresce green in UV and blue light. The limit of detection using this method is around 10 ng DNA per band. Suitable plastic safety glasses or goggles will protect your eyes from the UV light. The migration of each band from the well can be measured using a ruler. Alternatively, a photograph can be taken, using a digital camera and adaptor, or a dedicated system (e.g. GelDoc from Bio-Rad).
- **If a particular band is required for further study** (e.g. a plasmid), the piece of gel containing that band is cut from the gel using a clean scalpel. The DNA can be separated from the agarose by solubilising the gel slice and then binding it to an anion exchange resin, followed by elution in water or buffer (e.g. TE buffer, containing 10 mmol L^{-1} tris/HCl at pH 8.0 plus 1 mmol L^{-1} EDTA). Various commercial kits based on this approach are also available, e.g. from Qiagen.

Pulsed field gel electrophoresis (PFGE) If structural information is to be gained about large stretches of genomic DNA, then the order of the relatively short DNA segments (generated by the restriction enzymes described above) needs to be established. This is technically possible by techniques such as 'chromosome walking', but is time-consuming and potentially difficult, especially when dealing with large chromosomes such as those from yeast (a few Mbp) and humans (50–100 Mb), in contrast to the smaller genomes of bacteria and viruses.

The technique of PFGE allows separation of DNA fragments of up to L12Mb. Very large DNA fragments (> 100kbp) can be generated from chromosomal DNA by the use of certain restriction enzymes that recognise base sequences that are present at relatively low frequency, for example the enzyme *Not* I, which recognises a sequence of 8bp rather than 4–6bp. These enzymes are sometimes called 'rare cutters'. Genomic DNA prepared in the normal way is

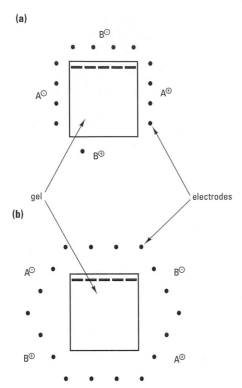

Fig. 13.10 The configuration of electrodes for conventional PFGE (a) and CHEF/PACE (b).

not suitable for digestion by these enzymes, as shearing during extraction fragments the DNA. Therefore, genomic DNA for analysis by PFGE is prepared as follows:

- **cells are embedded** in an agarose block;
- **the block is incubated in solutions** containing detergent, RNase and proteinase K, lysing the cells and hydrolysing RNA and proteins – the products of RNase and proteinase digestion diffuse away, leaving behind genomic DNA molecules exceeding several thousand kbp;
- **the block is incubated** *in situ* in a buffered solution containing an appropriate 'rare cutter': restriction fragments are produced, of up to L800kbp.

PFGE differs from conventional electrophoresis in that it uses two or more alternating electric fields. An explanation for the effectiveness of the technique is that large DNA fragments will be distorted by the voltage gradient, tending to elongate in the direction of the electric field and 'snaking' through pores in the gel. If the original electric field (Fig. 13.10(a)), is removed, and a second is applied at an angle to the first (Fig. 13.10(b)), the DNA must reorientate before it can migrate in the new direction. Larger (longer) DNA molecules will take more time to reorientate than smaller molecules, resulting in size-dependent separations.

The original configuration of electrodes used in PFGE is shown in Fig. 13.10(a) – this tends to produce 'bent' lanes that make lane-to-lane comparisons difficult. This can be overcome by using one of the many variants of the technique, one of which employs contour clamped homogeneous electric fields (CHEF). Here, multiple electrodes are arranged in a hexagonal array around the gel (Fig. 13.10(b)) and these are used to generate homogeneous electric fields with reorientation angles of up to 120°. A further development of CHEF involves programmable, autonomously controlled electrodes (PACE), which allows virtually unlimited variation of field and pulsing configurations, and can fractionate DNA molecules from 100 bp to 6 Mbp.

Identification of specific nucleic acid molecules using blotting and hybridisation techniques

Southern blotting After separation by conventional agarose gel electrophoresis (p. 108), the fragments of DNA can be denatured and immobilised on a filter membrane using a technique named after its inventor, Dr E.M. Southern. The main features of the conventional apparatus for Southern blotting are shown in Fig. 13.11. The principal stages in the procedure are:

1. **To ensure efficient transfer**, the gel is first soaked in HCl, leading to random cleavage of the DNA into smaller fragments.
2. **The gel is subsequently soaked in alkali** to denature the dsDNA to ssDNA, then neutralised – this is necessary to allow hybridisation with probe DNA after blotting.
3. **A nitrocellulose or nylon membrane is then placed directly on the gel**, followed by several layers of absorbent paper. The DNA is 'blotted' on to the filter as the buffer solution soaks into the paper by capillary action.
4. **The filter is baked in a vacuum oven** at 80 °C for 3–5 *h* or exposed to UV light, in order to 'fix' the DNA.
5. **Specific DNA fragments are identified by incubation** (6–24 h) with complementary labelled probes of ssDNA, which will hybridise with a particular sequence, followed by visualisation, often using an enzyme-based system. If radiolabelled probes are used (see below), the desired fragments are located by autoradiography.

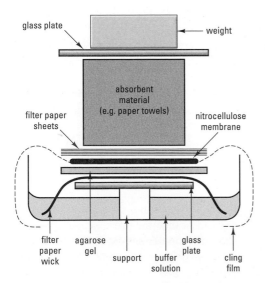

Fig. 13.11 Components of Southern blotting apparatus.

Modifications of the method use either a vacuum apparatus, an electric field ('electroblotting') or positive pressure to transfer the DNA fragments from the gel to the membrane. These modifications reduce the time for transfer by around 10-fold.

Northern blotting This process is similar in principle to Southern blotting, but RNA is the molecule that is separated and probed.

Dot blotting or slot blotting Here, samples containing denatured DNA or RNA samples are applied directly to the nitrocellulose membrane (via small individual round or slot-like templated holes) without prior digestion with restriction enzymes or electrophoretic separation. The 'blot' is then probed in a similar manner to that described for Southern blotting. This allows detection of a particular nucleic acid sequence in a sample – clinical applications include the detection of specific pathogenic microbes and the detection of particular genes.

Types of probe

The probes used in blotting and DNA hybridisation can be obtained from a variety of sources including:

- **cDNA (complementary or copy DNA)**, which is produced from isolated mRNA using reverse transcriptase. This retroviral enzyme catalyses RNA-directed DNA synthesis (rather than the normal transcription of DNA to RNA). After the mRNA has been reverse transcribed, it is degraded by the addition of alkali or ribonuclease, leaving the ssDNA copy. This is then used as a template for a DNA polymerase, which directs the synthesis of the second complementary DNA strand to form dsDNA. This is denatured to ssDNA before use.
- **Oligonucleotide probes (15–30 nucleotides)** can be produced if the amino acid sequence of the gene product is known. Since the genetic code is degenerate, i.e. some amino acids are coded for by more than one codon (see Table 13.3), it may be necessary to synthesise a mixture of oligonucleotides to detect a particular DNA sequence – this mixture of oligonucleotides is termed a 'degenerate probe'.
- **Specific genomic DNA sequences**, where the gene has been characterised.
- **PCR-generated fragments** (p. 114).
- **Heterologous probes**, i.e. sequences for the same gene, or its equivalent, in another organism.

Labelling of probes Detection of very low concentrations of target DNA sequences requires probes that can be detected with high sensitivity. This is achieved by radiolabelling (e.g. using ^{33}P) or by using enzyme-linked methods, which are often available in kit form:

- **Enzyme-linked methods** involve incorporating a modified nucleotide precursor, such as biotinylated dTTP, into the DNA by nick-translation or random priming. When the probe hybridises with the target sequence, it can be detected by addition of an enzyme (e.g. horse radish peroxidase) coupled to streptavidin. The streptavidin binds specifically to the biotin attached to the probe and the addition of a suitable fluorogenic or chromogenic substrate for the enzyme allows the probe to be located. An analogous chemiluminescent system is also available, based on dioxygenin-labelled nucleotides.
- **Radiolabelled probes** can be made by several methods, including the nick-translation technique. This uses DNA polymerase I from *E. coli*, which has an exonuclease activity that 'nicks' dsDNA and removes a nucleotide, and a

---

Definition

Probe – a labelled DNA or RNA sequence used to detect the presence of a complementary sequence (by molecular hybridisation) in a mixture of DNA or RNA fragments.

Example For a simple tripeptide containing methionine, aspartate and phenylalanine, the synthetic oligonucleotide probes would include combinations of the following codons:

1st codon (met): ATG
2nd codon (asp): GAT, GAC
3rd codon (phe): TTT, TTC

Using commercial kits *– do not blindly follow the protocol given by a manufacturer without making sure you understand the principles of the method and the reasons for the procedure. This will help you to recognise when things go wrong and what you might be able to do about it.*

Using labelled probes – an alternative approach is the chemiluminescent system based on dioxygenin-labelled nucleotides.

Example Low-stringency hybridisation can be useful when using a heterologous probe, i.e. from another species.

Example High-stringency conditions could be used for detecting a single base change in a mutant gene using a dot-blot hybridisation procedure with a specific oligonucleotide probe.

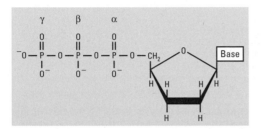

Fig. 13.12 A 2′,3′-dideoxynucleoside triphosphate.

polymerase activity that can replace this with a labelled deoxyribonucleotide. After several cycles of nick-translation, the labelled DNA is denatured to ssDNA for use as probes. Newer approaches include random priming of single-stranded template DNA, followed by the synthesis of radiolabelled DNA fragments complementary to the template using a DNA polymerase and a radiolabelled deoxynucleoside triphosphate (dNTP). Probe hybridisation to a target sequence is detected by autoradiography. Oligonucleotide probes cannot be labelled using the above methods and require 'end labelling', where a kinase is used to replace the 5′ terminal phosphate group with a radiolabelled group.

Hybridisation of probes The stability of the duplex formed between the probe and its target is directly proportional to the number and type of complementary base pairs that can be formed between them – stability increases with the amount of G + C, since these bases form three hydrogen bonds per base pair, rather than two. Duplex stability is also influenced by temperature, ionic strength and pH of the hybridisation buffer, and these can be varied to suit the stringency of hybridisation required:

- In 'low-stringency' hybridisation, duplex formation with less than perfect complementarity is promoted, either by lowering the temperature or increasing ionic strength.
- 'Stringent' hybridisation conditions usually involve high temperatures, or decreased ionic strength, and will sustain only perfectly matched duplexes.

DNA sequencing

By fragmenting target DNA with several restriction enzymes and then sequencing the overlapping fragments, it is possible to determine the nucleotide sequences of very large stretches of DNA, including entire genomes. Sequencing methods rely on polyacrylamide gel electrophoresis (p. 214). The Sanger, or chain termination, method is the most widely used in conventional DNA sequencing. This makes use of dideoxynucleotides (Fig. 13.12), which have no −OH group at either the C-2 or C-3 of ribose. A dideoxynucleoside triphosphate (ddNTP) can be added to a growing DNA chain, but since it lacks an −OH group at the C-3 position it cannot form a phosphodiester bond with the incoming dNTP of the growing chain. Therefore, a dideoxynucleotide acts as a terminator at the site it occupies. Details of the Sanger sequencing method are given in Box 13.3 and Fig. 13.13.

Box 13.3 DNA sequencing using the chain termination (Sanger) method

The DNA to be sequenced must first be obtained as single-stranded fragments, typically around 200 bp, for example using a denatured plasmid. Sequencing is often performed using a commercial kit and the principal stages are as follows:

1. **Set up the strand synthesis reaction** – four separate tubes are required, each containing a small amount of one of the dideoxynucleoside triphosphates. Each tube contains all of the other components required

for DNA synthesis, i.e. (i) the DNA selected for analysis (template DNA, e.g. denatured plasmid), (ii) a DNA polymerase (e.g. thermostable *Taq* polymerase), (iii) an [35S] oligonucleotide primer of known sequence, to allow synthesis of the complementary DNA strand, (iv) dGTP, dATP, dCTP, dTTP (in excess) together with (v) one type of ddNTP (i.e. ddGTP, ddATP, ddCTP or ddTTP) in limited concentration. New DNA strands are synthesised by

Box 13.3 (Continued)

addition of dNTPs to the primer, guided by the template DNA until a ddNTP is added. As an example of the principle of the method, consider the ddTTP tube. When T is required to pair with A on the template DNA strand, the dTTP will be competing with the ddTTP, but because the dTTP is in excess this will normally be added to the chain at the appropriate position. However, on occasions a ddTTP will be inserted at a given site and this will terminate DNA synthesis on the template strand. Thus, synthesis will be halted at all possible sites where ddT has substituted for dT and several strands of different length will be formed in the reaction mixture, each ending with ddT.

2. **Terminate the strand synthesis reaction** – after 5–10 min at 37 °C add a 'stop' solution containing formamide to disrupt hydrogen bonding between complementary bases and incubate at 80 °C for 15 min, to produce ssDNA.

3. **Separate the fragments using polyacrylamide gel electrophoresis** – 4–6% (w/v) denaturing acrylamide gels are used, containing urea (46%w/v) as the denaturing agent. Thin gels (0.35 mm thickness) are used, typically 20 cm wide by 50 cm long. The products in each of the four tubes are placed in four lanes side by side on the same gel and are separated by electrophoresis at 35–40 W (up to 32 mA, 1.5 kV) for 2.5 h. The high voltage raises the gel temperature to L50 °C, helping denaturation. A single gel can separate DNA fragments that differ in length by a single nucleotide.

4. **Locate the positions of individual bands by auto radiography** – the gel is fixed for 15 min with 10% (v/v) acetic acid, covered with Whatman 3MM paper and Saran wrap, then vacuum dried, to avoid quenching the radioisotope signal and to prevent it from sticking to the X-ray film. The gel is unwrapped and placed next to an X-ray film for 24 h.

5. **Read the gel** – the nucleotide sequence can be read directly from the band positions that represent the

newly made DNA segments of varying lengths (Fig. 13.13). The smallest segment is represented by the band at the bottom, since it travels furthest in the gel. The nucleotide sequence of the template strand can be deduced directly from that of the new strand, since the base on the template strand will be represented by an incomplete chain that terminates with the complementary dd nucleotide – i.e. template A with ddT, G with ddC, T with ddA, and C with ddG (Fig. 13.13).

Troubleshooting and other points to note – streaking can be due to damage to wells, air bubbles in wells/gel, or contamination by dirt/dust; faint and fuzzy gels may be due to insufficient template DNA, primer and/or dNTPs, due to poor annealing of primer and template, or to errors in preparing or running the gel; bands in more than one lane can indicate contamination of the template DNA, more than one primer site on the template, or secondary structure of DNA, giving 'ghost' banding.

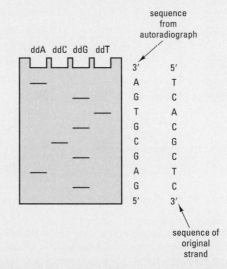

Fig. 13.13 Sanger sequencing gel, showing how the banding pattern is converted into a sequence of nucleotide bases.

The alternative approach to sequencing is based on chemical degradation (the Maxam and Gilbert method), using different reagents to break the target DNA sequence into fragments which are then separated by polyacrylamide gel electrophoresis. The Maxam and Gilbert method is more involved than the Sanger technique, and is reserved for specialised applications – for example, for studying the interaction between DNA and proteins.

DNA analysis – fundamental principles

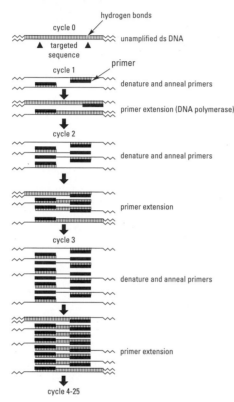

Fig. 13.14 The polymerase chain reaction (PCR).

Automated DNA sequencing The development of automated DNA sequencing machines (so-called 'DNA sequencers') has enabled sequencing to be performed several orders of magnitude faster than with manual methods. Base-specificity is achieved by using primers labelled with fluorophores with different fluorescence characteristics in each of the four reaction tubes (Box 13.3). After the reactions are separately completed, the four sets of products can be pooled and fractionated by electrophoresis in a single lane. The fluorophore-labelled fragments are detected as they pass a scanning laser detector and the DNA sequence is determined by using both the specific wavelength emitted by the fragment (indicating the base) and by the migration time (indicating the fragment size, which corresponds to the base location in the DNA sequence). Such automated DNA sequencing tends to be performed by capillary electrophoresis (p. 220) rather than polyacrylamide gel electrophoresis.

The polymerase chain reaction

The polymerase chain reaction (PCR) is a rapid, inexpensive and simple means of producing mg amounts of DNA from minute quantities of template.

> **KEY POINT** *PCR offers an alternative approach to gene cloning for the production of many copies of an identical sequence of DNA. The starting material may be genomic DNA (e.g. from a single cell), RNA, DNA from archival specimens, cloned DNA or forensic samples.*

The technique uses *in vitro* enzyme-catalysed DNA synthesis to create millions of identical copies of DNA. If the base sequence of the adjacent regions of the DNA to be amplified is known, this enables synthetic oligonucleotide primers to be constructed that are complementary to these so-called 'flanking regions'. Initiation of the PCR occurs when these primers are allowed to hybridise (anneal) to the component single strands of the target DNA, followed by enzymatic extension of the primers (from their 3' ends) using a thermostable DNA polymerase. A single PCR cycle consists of three distinct steps, carried out at different temperatures (Fig. 13.14), as follows:

1. **Denaturation of dsDNA** by heating to 94–98 °C separating the individual strands of the target DNA.
2. **Annealing of the primers,** which occurs when the temperature is reduced to 37–65 °C.
3. **Extension of the primers** by a thermostable DNA polymerase (e.g. *Taq* polymerase, isolated from *Thermus aquaticus*) at 72 °C; this step should last long enough to generate the PCR product – approximately 1 min of reaction time is required per kbp of sequence.

In the first cycle, the product from one primer is extended beyond the region of complementarity of the other primer, so each newly synthesised strand can be used as a template for the primers in the second cycle (Fig. 13.14). Successive cycles will thus generate an exponentially increasing number of DNA fragments, the termini of which are bounded by the 5' ends of the primers (length of each fragment = length of primers + length of target sequence). Since the amount of DNA produced doubles in each cycle, the amount of DNA produced = 2^n, where n is the number of cycles. Up to 1 mg of amplified target DNA can be produced in 25–30 cycles from a single-copy sequence within 50 ng of genomic DNA, assuming close to 100% efficiency during the cycling process. After electrophoresis, the PCR product is normally present in sufficient quantity to be visualised directly with SYBR®Safe (p. 109).

The temperature changes in PCR are normally achieved using a thermal cycler, which is simply a purpose-built incubator block that can be programmed to vary temperatures, incubation times and cycle numbers.

 KEY POINT *PCR is so sensitive that one of the main problems associated with the technique is contamination and amplification of 'foreign' DNA. Great care is required to avoid sample contamination during in vitro amplification (Box 13.4).*

PCR components and conditions

These are readily available in kit form from commercial suppliers – they include a thermostable DNA polymerase, such as *Taq* polymerase, dNTPs, buffer, a detergent (e.g. Triton), KCl, $MgCl_2$ or $MgSO_4$, and primers. Protocols for PCR vary considerably for particular applications – a typical procedure is given in Box 13.4. However, if you are trying to develop your own PCR procedure, the following information may be useful:

- **Primers need to be at least 18 nucleotides long** (primers longer than 18 nucleotides should be unique, even in a large eukaryotic genome) – both primers should have similar annealing temperatures, T_m, with a minimal degree of self-complementarity (to avoid formation of secondary structures), and no complementarity to each other (so that primer dimers are not formed).

 SAFETY NOTE *you must not expose your skin or eyes to any UVC source due to its' mutagenic/carcinogenic properties.*

- **For most applications, the final concentration of each primer should be 0.1–0.5 mmol L^{-1}**, which gives an excess of primers of about 10^7 with respect to the template, for example target genomic DNA at a concentration of 50 ng per 10 mL reaction mixture.

Box 13.4 How to carry out the polymerase chain reaction (PCR)

The protocol given below is typical for a standard PCR. Note that temperatures, incubation times and the number of cycles will vary with the particular application, as discussed in the text.

1. **Make sure you have the required apparatus and reagents to hand** – including: (i)a thermal cycler; (ii) template thermostable DNA ($\geq$ 550 ng/mL); (iii)stock solution of all dNTPs (5 mmol L^{-1} for each dNTP); (iv)a DNA polymerase (at 5 U/mL); (v)primers at, for example, 30 mmol L^{-1}; (vi)stock buffer solution, for example containing 100 mmolL^{-1} tris (pH8.4), 500 mmol L^{-1} KCl, 15 mmol L^{-1} $MgCl_2$, 1% (w/v) gelatin, 1% (v/v) Triton X-100 (this stock is often termed '10x PCR buffer stock').

2. **Prepare a reaction mixture** – for example, a mixture containing: 1.0 mL genomic DNA; 2.5 mL stock buffer solution; 1.0 mL primer 1; 1.0 mL primer 2; 1.0 mL of each of the stock solutions of dNTPs, 0.1 mL *Taq* polymerase; 15.4 mL distilled deionised water, to give a total volume of 25.0 mL.

3. **Use appropriate positive and negative controls** – a positive control is a PCR template that is known to work under the conditions used in the laboratory, for example a plasmid, with appropriate primers, known to amplify at the annealing temperature to be used. A commonly used negative control is the PCR mixture minus the template DNA, though negative controls can be set up lacking any one of the reaction components.

4. **Cycle in the thermal cycler** – for example, an initial period of 5 min at 94 °C, followed by 30 cycles of 94 °C for 1 min (denaturation), then 60 °C for 1 min (primer annealing), then 72 °C for 1 min (chain extension).

5. **Assess the effectiveness of the PCR** – for example, by gel electrophoresis and SYBR®Safe staining.

Troubleshooting

- If no PCR product is detected, repeat the procedure, checking carefully that all components are added to the reaction mixture. If there is still no product, check that the annealing temperature is not too high, or the denaturing temperature is not too low.

- If too many bands are present, this may indicate that (i) the primers may not be specific, (ii) the annealing temperature is too low, (iii) too many cycles have been used, or (iv) there is an excess of Mg^{2+}, dNTPs, primers or enzyme.

Box 13.4 (Continued)

- Bands corresponding to primer-dimers indicate that (i) the 3′ ends of the primers show partial complementarity, (ii) the annealing temperature is not high enough, or (iii) the concentration of primers is too high.

Avoiding contamination in diagnostic PCR

The sensitivity of PCR is also the major drawback in forensic analysis, since the technique is susceptible to contamination, particularly through DNA from the skin and hair of the operator, previous PCR products, airborne microbes and through positive controls. While the same general principles involved in the sterile culture of microbes can be applied a number of specific precautions can also be taken to avoid such contamination:

- **use a laminar-flow cabinet** dedicated to PCR use located in a separate lab from that used to store PCR products;

- **strictly segregate areas** involved in sample preparation, reaction assembly, amplification, electrophoresis and interpretation;

- **keep separate supplies of pipettors, tips, microfuge tubes and reagents** – these should be exclusive to the PCR, with separate sets for sample preparation, reagents and product analysis;

- **use positive-displacement pipettors or aerosol-preventive pipette tips;**

- **autoclave all buffers, use distilled deionised water, pipette tips and tubes prior to use;**

- **wear disposable gloves at all times and change them frequently** – protective coverings for the face and hair are also advisable;

- **avoid contamination due to carry-over** by including dUTP in the PCR mixture instead of dTTP. Thus copies will contain U rather than T. Before the template denaturing step, treat the mixture with uracil-N-glycosylase (UNG, available commercially as AmpEase®) – this will destroy any strands containing U, i.e. any strands carried over from a previous reaction, or any contaminating material from another PCR. The target DNA will contain T, rather than U and will not be degraded by UNG. At the first heating step, the UNG will be denatured, so any newly synthesised U-containing copies will remain intact.

- **for very sensitive work, use a strong UVC light** inside the PCR workstation for 20–30 min before starting your work, to degrade any contaminating DNA.

Storing primers for PCR – primers are best stored in ammonia solution, which remains liquid at −20°C, avoiding the need for repeated freezing and thawing when dispensed. Before use, aliquots of stock solution should be heated in a fume cupboard, to drive off the ammonia.

Using dNTP solutions – make up stock solutions, pool in small volumes (50–100 mL of each dNTP) and store separately at −20°C.

Establishing the optimum concentration of Mg^{2+} – this can be determined by trial and error, and can be a useful starting point for any new PCR; try a range of different Mg^{2+} concentrations and select the one giving the strongest intensity of the target band following gel electrophoresis.

- **Annealing temperatures are based around T_m**, the temperature at which 50% of the primers are annealed to their target sequence. For primers of <20 bases, T_m can be roughly calculated in °C from the equation:

$$T_m = 4(G + C) + 2(A + T)$$ [13.4]

where G, C, A and T are the number of bases in the primer. Using this as a starting point, the optimum annealing temperature can be determined by trial and error. The T_m values of the two primers should be within 5 °C of each other (and, therefore, be ideally identical in G > + > C content). The annealing temperature is then set 5 °C below the lowest T_m of the primer pair.

- **The last two bases at the 3′ end** (where elongation is initiated) should be either G or C (3 hydrogen bonds, giving strong annealing), rather than either A or T (only 2 hydrogen bonds).

- **dNTPs should be used at equal concentrations of 200 mmol L^{-1},** which should provide the initial excess required for incorporation into DNA.

- **One of the key variables in PCR is the Mg^{2+} concentration**; Mg^{2+} is required as a cofactor for the thermostable DNA polymerase (Promega, 2016). Excess Mg^{2+} stabilises dsDNA and may prevent complete denaturation of product at each cycle – it also promotes spurious annealing of primers, leading to the formation of undesired products. However, very low Mg^{2+} concentration impairs polymerisation. The Mg^{2+} concentration that gives optimal yield and

Understanding codes for primers and probes – *oligomeric nucleotides are often referred to by the number of bases; e.g. a 20-mer primer will contain 20 nucleotide bases.*

specificity can be determined by trial and error. The purpose of gelatin and Triton X-100 is to stabilise the DNA polymerase during thermal cycling.

- **The most frequently used thermostable DNA polymerase is *Taq* polymerase**, which extends primers at a rate of 2–4 kbp per min at 72 °C. It should be used at a concentration of ≥ 1 nmol L^{-1} (≥ 0.1 U per 5 mL reaction mixture). A disadvantage of *Taq* polymerase is that it has a relatively high rate of misincorporation of bases (one aberrant nucleotide per 100,000 nucleotides per cycle). Other polymerases are available (e.g. *Pfu* polymerase from *Pyrococcus* sp., VENT polymerase from *T. litoralis* or genetically modified forms of *Taq* polymerase) which have lower misincorporation rates.

PCR variations

Nested PCR This can be used when the target sequence is known, but the number of DNA copies is very small (e.g. a single DNA molecule from a microbial genome), or if the sample is degraded (e.g. some forensic samples). The process involves two consecutive 'rounds' of PCR. The first PCR uses so-called 'external' primers, and the second PCR uses two 'internal' (or 'nested') primers that anneal to sequences within the product of the first PCR. This increases the likelihood of amplification of the target sequences by selecting for it using different primers during each round. Thus, nested PCR also increases the specificity of the reaction, since a single set of primers used in isolation may give a reasonable yield but several bands, while the use of a second set of primers ensures that a unique sequence is amplified, for example in microbial diagnostics.

Inverse PCR This is a useful technique for amplifying a DNA sequence flanking a region of known base sequence (Fig. 13.15) – for example to provide material for characterising an unknown region of DNA. The DNA is cut with a restriction enzyme so that both the region of known sequence and the flanking regions are included. This restriction fragment is then circularised and cut with a second restriction enzyme with specificity for a region in the known sequence. The now linear DNA will have part of the known sequence at each terminus and, by using primers that anneal to these parts of the known sequence, the unknown region can be amplified by conventional PCR. The product can then be sequenced and characterised (p. 112).

Reverse transcriptase-PCR (RT-PCR) This technique is useful for detecting cell-specific gene expression (as evident by the presence of specific mRNA) when the amount of biological material is limited. Using either an oligo-dT primer to anneal to the 3′ polyadenyl 'tail' of the mRNA, or random hexamer primers together with reverse transcriptase, cDNA is produced which is then amplified by PCR. RT-PCR is often a useful method of generating a probe, the identity of which can be confirmed by sequencing (p. 112).

Amplification fragment length polymorphism (AFLP) This term refers to several closely related techniques in which a single oligonucleotide primer of arbitrary sequence is used in a PCR reaction under conditions of low stringency, so that the primer is able to anneal to a large number of different sites within the target DNA. Some of the multiple amplification products will be polymorphic (e.g. the presence or absence of a particular annealing site will result in presence or absence of a particular band on the gel, after PCR and electrophoresis). Such polymorphisms can be used to detect differences between dissimilar DNA sequences.

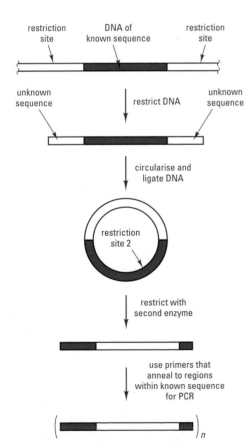

Fig. 13.15 Inverse PCR – basic principles.

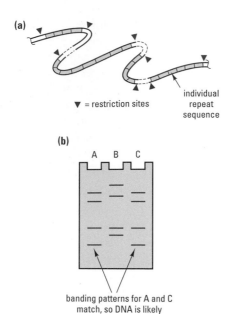

▼ = restriction sites

individual repeat sequence

banding patterns for A and C match, so DNA is likely to be from the same individual

Fig. 13.16 Simplified representation of DNA fingerprinting: (a) tandem repeat sequences within DNA are cut using a restriction enzyme to yield fragments of different size; (b) these fragments are then separated by agarose gel electrophoresis on the basis of their size (M_r), giving a banding pattern that is a characteristic of the DNA used.

PCR and DNA profiling techniques

Genetic mapping and sequencing studies have led to the discovery of highly variable regions in the non-coding regions of DNA between different individuals. These hypervariable regions, often termed 'minisatellite DNA', are found at many sites throughout the genome. Each minisatellite contains a defined sequence of nucleotides which is repeated a number of times in a tandem fashion (Fig. 13.16(a)) – the greater the number of repeats, the longer the mini satellite. The number of tandem repeats in any particular minisatellite varies from one person to another (i.e. they have a variable number of tandem repeats or VNTRs). This is exploited in identifying individuals on the basis of their DNA profile (p. 303) by carrying out the following general steps:

1. **extraction of DNA** from cells of the individual (e.g. white blood cells, buccal cells, spermatozoa);
2. **digestion of the DNA** with a restriction enzyme that cuts at sites other than those within the minisatellite, to produce a series of fragments of different M_r;
3. **electrophoresis and Southern blotting** of the restriction fragments using probes that are specific to the particular minisatellite.

The size of the fragments identified will depend on the number of minisatellites that each fragment contains, and the pattern obtained in the Southern blot is characteristic of the individual being profiled (Fig. 13.16(b)).

PCR is widely used in DNA profiling (Chapter 31) in circumstances where there is a limited amount of starting material. By selecting suitable primers, highly variable regions can be amplified from very small amounts of DNA, and the information from several such regions is used to decide, with a very low chance of error, whether any two samples of DNA are likely to be from the same individual or not (p. 313). PCR products also can be analysed by capillary gel electrophoresis (p. 220).

KEY POINT *You should note that the PCR technique is continually being updated, with subtle new variations being produced on a regular basis – novel approaches and novel acronyms are likely to be reported within the lifetime of this book.*

More recent developments include the use of short tandem repeat (STR) loci. The STR profiling kit routinely used in the UK is the AmpFLSTR®SGM Plus™ PCR amplification kit that uses a gender marker and 12 STR markers. In 2014, the use of DNA17 multiplex kits e.g. NGM SElect™ that uses a gender marker and 16 STR markers have been accredited and validated for use with the National DNA Database (Chapter 31). This new generation DNA technology is the most substantial change in DNA profiling techniques since the introduction of the SGM Plus™ kits and should provide improved sensitivity, discriminatory power and cross border comparability with other European Union databases.

Text references

European Bioinformatics Institute (2016). Available at: http://www.ebi.ac.uk/Tools/msa/. Last accessed 15/08/2017.

Promega (2016) *PCR Optimization.* Available at: https://www.promega.co.uk/resources/product-guides-and-selectors/protocols-and-applications-guide/pcr-amplification/. Last accessed 15/08/2017.

Sources for further study

Forward and reverse e-PCR Available at: https://blast.ncbi.nlm.nih.gov/Blast.cgi. Last accessed 07/09/2017.

Forward and reverse e-PCR instructions: Available at: https://ftp.ncbi.nih.gov/pub/factsheets/HowTo_PrimerBLAST.pdf. Last accessed 07/09/2017.

Online Mendelian Inheritance in Man. Available at: http://www.ncbi.nlm.nih.gov/omim/. Last accessed 15/08/2017.

Blumberg, R.B. (2016) *MendelWeb.* Available at: http://www.mendelweb.org/. Last accessed 15/08/2017.

Brooker, R. (2014) *Genetics: Analysis and Principles,* 5th edn. McGraw-Hill, Burr Hill

Brown, T.A. (2000) *Essential Molecular Biology: A Practical Approach,* Vols 1 and 2, 2nd edn. IRL Press, Oxford.

Burden, D.W. and Whitney, D. (1995) *Biotechnology: Proteins to PCR: A Course in Strategies and Lab Techniques.* Springer-Verlag, Berlin.

Dieffenback, C.W. and Dveksler, G.S. (2003) *PCR Primer: A Laboratory Manual,* 2nd edn. Cold Spring Harbor Laboratory, Cold Spring Harbor.

Dorak, M.T. (2006) *Real-Time PCR.* Taylor and Francis, Abingdon.

Falconer, D.S. and MacKay, T.F.C. (1996) *Introduction to Quantitative Genetics,* 4th edn. Addison-Wesley, New York.

Fletcher, H. and Hickey, I. (2012) *BIOS Instant Notes in Genetics,* 4th edn. Bios, Oxford.

Hames, B.D. and Higgins, S.J. (1995) *Gene Probes: A Practical Approach.* IRL Press, Oxford.

Juo, P.S. (2002) *Concise Dictionary of Biomedicine and Molecular Biology,* 2nd edn. CRC Press, Boca Raton.

Kirby, L.T. (2002) *DNA Fingerprinting: An Introduction. Breakthroughs in Molecular Biology.* Oxford University Press, Oxford.

Klug, W.S. and Cummings, M.R. (2012) *Essentials of Genetics,* 8th edn. Prentice Hall, Upper Saddle River.

McPherson, M.J., Moller, S.G., Benyon, R. and Howe, C. (2000) *PCR Basics: From Background to Bench.* Springer-Verlag, Berlin.

McPherson, M.J. and Moller, S.G. (2006) *PCR Basics.* Taylor and Francis, Abingdon.

Monaco, A.P. (1995) *Pulsed Field Gel Electrophoresis: A Practical Approach.* IRL Press, Oxford.

Sambrook, J. and Russell, D.W. (2001) *Molecular Cloning: A Laboratory Manual,* 3rd edn. Cold Spring Harbor Lab, Cold Spring Harbor.

Schwarzacher, T. and Heslop-Harrison, P. (1999) *Practical in situ Hybridization.* Springer-Verlag, Berlin.

Study exercises

13.1 Carry out a chi^2 test. A geneticist expects the results of a test cross to be in the phenotype ratio 1:2:1. He observes 548 progeny from his cross in the ratio 125:303:120. What should he conclude?

13.2 Investigate the binding properties of ethidium bromide. Find out (a) why ethidium bromide fluorescence is enhanced by DNA, and (b) under what circumstances ethidium bromide can also bind to RNA.

13.3 Select an electrophoretic technique for separating DNA fragments of different sizes. Which technique would you use to separate DNA fragments in the following ranges: (a) 1–70 kbp; (b) 75–500 bp; (c) 100–6 Mbp?

13.4 Investigate the role of magnesium ions in PCR. Find out why optimising the Mg^{2+} concentration is important for successful amplification of target DNA in PCR.

Fundamental instrumental techniques

14 Chromatography

 SAFETY NOTE *The solvents used as the mobile phases of chromatographic systems are often toxic and may produce noxious fumes – where necessary, handle in a fume hood.*

Selecting a separation method – it is often best to select a technique that involves direct interaction between the substance(s) and the stationary phase (e.g. ion-exchange or affinity chromatography), owing to their increased capacity and resolution compared with other methods (e.g. partition or gel permeation chromatography) where the analytes are not bound to the stationary phase.

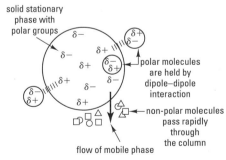

Fig. 14.1 Adsorption chromatography (polar stationary phase).

Chromatography is used to separate the individual components of a mixture on the basis of differences in their physical characteristics – for example, molecular size, shape, charge, volatility, solubility and/or adsorption properties. The essential components of a chromatographic system are:

- **a stationary phase** – where a solid, a gel or an immobilised liquid is held by a support matrix;
- **a chromatographic bed** – the stationary phase may be packed into a glass or metal column, spread as a thin layer on a sheet of glass or plastic, or adsorbed on cellulose fibres (paper);
- **a mobile phase** – either a liquid or a gas which acts as a solvent carrying the sample through the stationary phase and eluting from the chromatographic bed;
- **a delivery system** – to pass the mobile phase through the chromatographic bed;
- **a detection system** – to visualise the test substances.

The individual substances in the mixture interact with the stationary phase to different extents, as they are carried through the system, enabling separation to be achieved.

 KEY POINT *In a chromatographic system, those substances that interact strongly with the stationary phase will be retarded to the greatest extent, while those that show little interaction will pass through with minimal delay, leading to differences in distances travelled or elution times.*

Separation methods

Chromatography is subdivided according to the mechanism of interaction of the solute with the stationary phase.

Adsorption chromatography

This is a form of solid–liquid chromatography. The stationary phase is a porous, finely divided solid that adsorbs molecules of the mixture on its surface by dipole–dipole interactions, hydrogen bonding and/or van der Waals interactions (Fig. 14.1). The range of adsorbents is limited to polystyrene-based resins for non-polar molecules and silica, aluminium oxide and calcium phosphate for polar molecules. Most adsorbents must be activated by heating to 110–120°C before use, since their adsorptive capacity is significantly decreased if water is adsorbed on the surface. Adsorption chromatography can be carried out in column (p. 129) or thin-layer (p. 128) form, using a wide range of organic solvents.

Partition chromatography

This is based on the partitioning of a substance between two liquid phases, in this instance the stationary and mobile phases. Substances that are more soluble in the mobile phase will pass rapidly through the system, while those that favour the stationary phase will be retarded (Fig. 14.2). In normal phase partition chromatography, the stationary phase is a polar solvent, usually water, supported by a solid matrix (e.g. cellulose fibres in paper chromatography) and the mobile phase is an immiscible, non-polar organic solvent. For reversed-phase partition chromatography, the stationary phase is a non-polar solvent (e.g. a C_{18} hydrocarbon such as octadecylsilane), which is chemically bonded to a porous support matrix

Chromatography

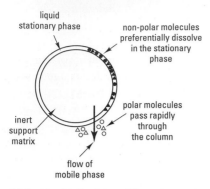

Fig. 14.2 Liquid–liquid partition chromatography, e.g. reversed-phase HPLC.

Maximising resolution in IEC – keep your columns as short as possible. Once the sample components have been separated, they should be eluted as quickly as possible from the column in order to avoid band broadening resulting from diffusion of sample ions in the mobile phase.

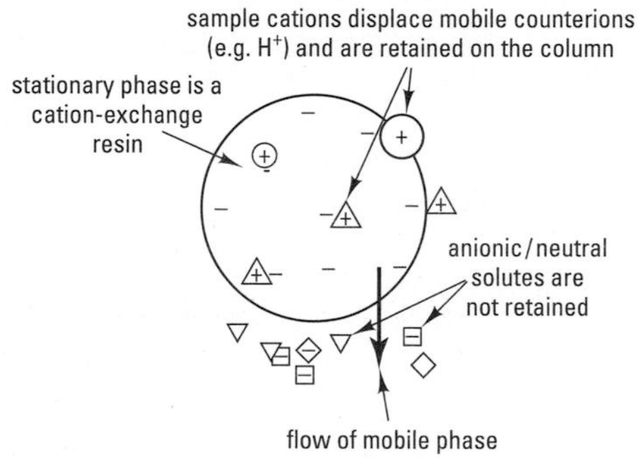

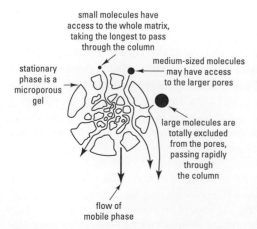

Fig. 14.3 Ion-exchange chromatography (cation exchanger).

small molecules have access to the whole matrix, taking the longest to pass through the column

stationary phase is a microporous gel

medium-sized molecules may have access to the larger pores

large molecules are totally excluded from the pores, passing rapidly through the column

flow of mobile phase

Fig. 14.4 Gel permeation chromatography.

(e.g. silica), while the mobile phase can be chosen from a wide range of polar solvents, usually water or an aqueous buffered solution containing one or more organic solvents, (e.g. acetonitrile). Solutes interact with the stationary phase through non-polar interactions and so the least polar solutes elute last from the column. Solute retention and separation are controlled by changing the composition of the mobile phase (e.g. % acetonitrile). Reverse-phase high-performance liquid chromatography (RPHPLC, p. 131) is used to separate a broad range of non-polar, polar and ionic molecules, including environmental compounds (e.g. phenols) and pharmaceutical compounds (e.g. steroids) and is one of the most commonly encountered separation techniques in forensic analytical science.

Ion-exchange chromatography (IEC)

Here, separations are carried out using a column packed with a porous matrix that has a large number of ionised groups on its surfaces, i.e. the stationary phase is an ion-exchange resin. The groups may be cation or anion exchangers, depending upon their affinity for positive or negative ions. The net charge on a particular resin depends on the pK_a of the ionisable groups and the pH of the solution, in accordance with the Henderson–Hasselbalch equation (p. 61).

For most practical applications, you should select the ion-exchange resin and buffer pH so that the test substances are strongly bound by electrostatic attraction to the ion-exchange resin on passage through the system, while the other components of the sample are rapidly eluted (Fig. 14.3). You can then elute the bound components by raising the salt concentration of the mobile phase, either stepwise or as a continuous gradient, so that exchange of ions of the same charge occurs at oppositely charged sites on the stationary phase. Weakly bound sample molecules will elute first, while more strongly bound molecules will elute at a higher concentration.

Computer-controlled gradient formers are available – if two or more components cannot be resolved using a linear salt gradient, an adapted gradient can be used in which the rate of change in salt concentration is decreased over the range where these components are expected to elute. IEC can be used to separate mixtures of a wide range of anionic and cationic compounds. Electrophoresis (Chapter 22) is an alternative means of separating charged molecules.

Gel permeation chromatography (GPC) or gel filtration

Here, the stationary phase is in the form of beads of a cross-linked gel containing pores of a discrete size (Fig. 14.4). The size of the pores is controlled so that, at the molecular level, the pores act as 'gates' that will exclude large molecules and admit smaller ones (Table 14.1). However, this gating effect is not an all-or-nothing phenomenon – molecules of intermediate size partly enter the pores. A column packed with such beads will have within it two effective volumes that are potentially available to sample molecules in the mobile phase – V_i, the volume surrounding the beads and V_{ii}, the volume within the pores. If a sample is placed at the top of such a column, the mobile phase will carry the sample components down the column, but at different rates according to their molecular size. A very large molecule will have access to all of V_i but to none of V_{ii}, and will therefore elute in the minimum possible volume (the 'void volume', or V_0, equivalent to V_i). A very small molecule will have access to all of V_i and all of V_{ii}, and therefore it has to pass through the total liquid volume of the column (V_t, equivalent to $V_i + V_{ii}$) before it emerges. Molecules of intermediate size have access to all of V_i but only part of V_{ii}, and will elute at a volume between V_0 and V_t, in order of decreasing size depending on their access to V_{ii}.

Table 14.1 Fractionation ranges of selected GPC media

M_r	Medium
50–1,000	Sephadex G15, Biogel P-2
1,000–5,000	Sephadex G-25
1,500–30,000	Sephadex G-50, Biogel P-10
4,000–150,000	Sephadex G-100
5,000–250,000	Sephadex G-200
20,000–1,500,000	Sephacryl S 300
60,000–20,000,000	Sepharose 4B

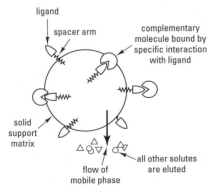

Fig. 14.5 Affinity chromatography.

Cross-linked dextrans (e.g. Sephadex®), agarose (e.g. Sepharose®) and polyacrylamide (e.g. Bio-gel®) can be used to separate mixtures of macro-molecules, particularly enzymes, antibodies and other globular proteins. Selectivity in GPC is solely dependent on the stationary phase, with the mobile phase being used solely to transport the sample components through the column. Thus, it is possible to estimate the molecular mass of a sample component by calibrating a given column using molecules of known molecular mass and similar shape. A plot of elution volume (V_e) against $\log_{10} M_r$ is approximately linear. A further application of GPC is the general separation of components of low molecular mass and high molecular mass, for example 'desalting' a protein extract by passage through a Sephadex G-25 column is faster and more efficient than dialysis.

Affinity chromatography

Affinity chromatography allows biomolecules to be purified on the basis of their biological specificity rather than by differences in physico-chemical properties, and a high degree of purification (more than 1,000-fold) can be expected. It is especially useful for isolating small quantities of material from large amounts of contaminating substances. The technique involves the immobilisation of a complementary binding substance (the ligand) on to a solid matrix in such a way that the specific binding affinity of the ligand is preserved. When a biological sample is applied to a column packed with this affinity support matrix, the molecule of interest will bind specifically to the ligand, while contaminating substances will be washed through with the buffer (Fig. 14.5). Elution of the desired molecule can be achieved by changing the pH or ionic strength of the buffer, to weaken the non-covalent interactions between the molecule and the ligand, or by addition of other substances that have greater affinity for the ligand.

Factors that influence the separation of analytes

A plot of the detector response present at the column outlet as a function of time is called a chromatogram (Fig. 14.6). The time from injection of the sample until the peak elutes from the column is called the retention time, t_r. The amount of compound present for a given peak can be quantified by measuring the peak height or area (most useful) and comparing it with the response for a known amount of the same compound.

The aim of any chromatographic system is to resolve a number of components in a sample mixture – i.e. to ensure that individual peaks do not overlap or coincide. To achieve this, you need to consider several important factors: capacity factor, separation factor or selectivity, column efficiency and asymmetry factor.

Capacity factor, k' – this is a more useful measure of peak retention than retention time, as it is independent of column length and flow rate. To calculate k' you need to measure column dead time, t_o. This is the time it takes an unretained component to pass through the column without any interaction with the stationary phase. It is the time taken from the point of sample injection until the first disturbance in the base line caused by the unretained component. The capacity factor for other components can then be calculated according to the following equation:

$$k' = \frac{t_r - t_o}{t_o} \quad\quad\quad [14.1]$$

Separation factor, α – the separation factor, or selectivity, identifies when the peaks elute relative to each other. It is defined for two peaks as the ratio of the capacity factors ($k'_2 > k'_1$):

Chromatography

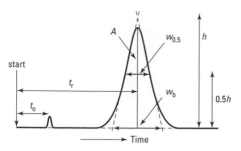

Fig. 14.6 Peak characteristics in a chromatographic separation, i.e. a chromatogram. For symbols, see eqns [14.1] and [14.3].

> **Column efficiency** – *several equations can be used to calculate the column efficiency. Select the correct equation based on the information available.*

> **Learning from experience** – *if you are unable to separate your molecule using a particular method, do not regard this as a failure, but instead think about what this tells you about either the substance(s) or the sample.*

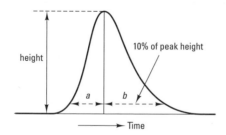

Fig. 14.7 Peak asymmetry.

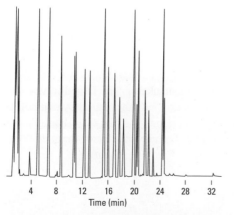

Fig. 14.8 A multicomponent chromatogram. Separation of many compounds, some well resolved, e.g. peaks at 12–13 mins, and others that are not, e.g. peaks at 24–25 mins.

$$\alpha = \frac{k'_2}{k'_1} = \frac{t_{r,2} - t_o}{t_{r,1} - t_o} \qquad [14.2]$$

where $t_{r,1}$ and $t_{r,2}$ are the retention times of peak 1 and peak 2, respectively. If two peaks are present, the separation factor must be greater than 1 to achieve an effective separation.

Column efficiency (plate number), N – an additional parameter used to characterise a separation system. It represents, in general terms, the narrowness of the peak and is often calculated using one of the following equations:

$$N = 5.54 \left(\frac{t_r}{w_{0.5}} \right)^2 \qquad [14.3a]$$

$$N = 16 \left(\frac{tR}{Wb} \right)^2 \qquad [14.3b]$$

$$N = 2\pi \left(\frac{tR.h}{A} \right)^2 \qquad [14.3c]$$

where tR is the retention time of the peak, $w_{0.5}$ Wb are the peak widths at half height and base respectively and h and A are the peak height and peak area respectively. (Fig. 14.6).

For a compound emerging from a column of length L, the number of theoretical plates, N, can be expressed as:

$$N = \frac{L}{H} \qquad [14.4]$$

where H is the plate height (or height equivalent to a theoretical plate). In general, chromatographic columns with larger values of N give the narrowest peaks and generally better separation.

Asymmetry factor, A_s – the plate number, N, assumes that the peak shape is Gaussian, but in practice this is rare. It is more likely that the peak is asymmetrical, i.e. it 'tails'. This is quantified using the asymmetry factor, A_s, calculated as shown in Fig. 14.7.

A vertical line is drawn between the peak maximum and the base line. At 10% of the peak height, the width of the peak to the leading edge and the trailing edge is measured (a and b in Fig. 14.7). The asymmetry factor is then calculated as follows:

$$A_s = \frac{b}{a} \qquad [14.5]$$

In general, A_s values between 0.9 and 1.2 are acceptable. If $A_s < 1$ then peak tailing is in evidence; if $A_s < 1$ then peak fronting is evident. The practical impact of peak tailing or fronting is that adjacent peaks are not as well separated as they would be if they were symmetrical, leading to difficulties in peak quantification.

Resolution

It is often important to be able to separate a large number of compounds. A visual inspection of the chromatogram (Fig. 14.8) will usually indicate whether the separation is appropriate. It is desirable that the valley between adjoining peaks returns to the base line and resolution is a quantitative measure of the separation. The influence of k', a and N on resolution, R, is shown in the following expression:

$$R = \frac{\sqrt{N}}{4} \times \frac{k'}{k' + 1} \times \frac{\alpha - 1}{\alpha} \qquad [14.6]$$

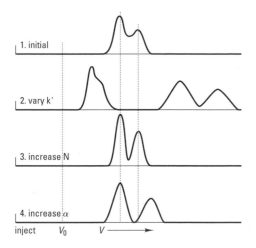

Fig. 14.9 Influence of k', α and N on resolution.

Three conditions must be satisfied in order to achieve some degree of resolution:

1. Peaks have to be retained on the column ($k' < 0$).
2. Peaks have to be separated from each other ($\alpha > 1$).
3. The column must develop some minimum value of N.

These different factors and their influence on resolution are shown in Fig. 14.9, using high-performance liquid chromatography (HPLC) (p. 131) as an example. They are discussed below.

1. **Initial conditions** result in inadequate separation of the two components.
2. **Effect of varying the capacity factor,** k' – from an initial mobile phase of 50% methanol:50% water (v/v) two scenarios are possible. Firstly, on the left-hand side, the influence of increasing the percentage of organic solvent (70% methanol:30% water) allows a faster throughput, but the peaks are unresolved. Secondly, on the right-hand side, the percentage of organic solvent is reduced (30% methanol:70% water) allowing the components to remain in the system for a longer time, giving some separation, but causing peak broadening. This is the easiest change to make and will affect resolution. As a guide, a two- to three-fold change in k' will result for each 10% change in mobile phase composition.
3. **Effect of increasing the plate number,** N – reducing the particle size of the HPLC packing from 5 mm to 3 mm allows a more efficient separation. It should be noted that the retention times of the peaks are not altered (from the initial chromatogram) provided the stationary phase is not altered. Alternatively, N can be increased by placing columns in series with one another. However, you should note from eqn [14.6] that R has a square-root dependence on N, so a four-fold increase in N is required to double R.
4. **Increase separation factor,** α – resolved peaks can be obtained by changing the mobile phase (e.g. methanol to acetonitrile) or the column stationary phase (e.g. C_{18} to C_8). Unfortunately, this is the least predictable approach.

Resolution can be calculated as follows:

$$R = \frac{t_{R_2} - t_{R_2}}{0.5(w_1 + w_2)} \qquad [14.7]$$

where t_R is the retention time and w is the peak width. Baseline separation of symmetrical peaks occur when resolution (R) is greater than 1.5.

Detectors

After separating the components of the mixture, it is necessary to detect them. As chromatography is often used as a quantitative technique it is essential to be familiar with the following terms:

- **Universal detector** – this responds to all compounds eluting from the column, irrespective of their composition.
- **Selective/specific detector** – this responds to certain elements or functional groups. This is a useful approach if the components of the mixture are known.
- **Sensitivity** – the ratio of detector signal to sample size (or detector response per amount of sample).
- **Minimum detectable level (MDL)** – the amount of sample in which the peak height is at least twice the noise height.
- **Linear dynamic range** – the concentration range of the sample that is detectable and where the detector response is linear (between the MDL and detector saturation).

Minimal noise – also known as background noise, arises from column bleed, septa and liners. You can optimise the response of the detector to maximise the analyte response and minimise the noise.

Drift – also known as baseline drift where an alteration in baseline response is seen, especially at high temperatures, usually as a response to column bleed, and is characterised by a rising baseline.

Detectors – a range of detectors are available for chromatography. A mass spectrometer is the only detector that is compatible with GC or LC.

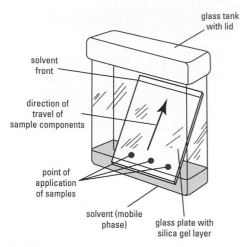

Fig. 14.10 Components of a TLC system.

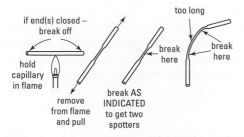

Fig. 14.11 How to make micropipettes.

Types of chromatographic system

Chromatographic systems can be categorised according to the form of the chromatographic bed, the nature of the mobile and stationary phases and the method of separation. The main types of chromatography encountered in forensic science are liquid chromatography (thin layer and column) and gas chromatography.

Liquid chromatography

The basic chromatographic system comprises a stationary phase (adsorbant), usually alumina, silica gel or cellulose, through which a mobile phase travels (elutes). Separation of a mixture of compounds is achieved by a combination of the differing 'adsorption' and solubility characteristics of the components on the stationary phase and in the mobile phase respectively.

Liquid chromatography is used both as an analytical method to determine the complexity of mixtures and the purity of compounds, and as a preparative system for the separation of mixtures. Liquid chromatography is divided into two general types:

1. **Thin-layer chromatography (TLC)** – in which a glass or plastic plate is coated with a thin layer of the stationary phase and the mobile phase *ascends* the plate by capillary action. TLC is essentially an analytical tool and preparative TLC has been largely superseded by flash chromatography. This technique is typically used for preliminary illicit drug testing (p. 384).
2. **Column chromatography** – in which the stationary phase is packed into a glass column and the mobile phase is passed *down* the column, either by gravity (gravity chromatography) or under low pressure from a pump or nitrogen cylinder (flash chromatography). These are the preparative systems.

Thin-layer chromatography

Here, you apply the sample as a single spot near one end of the sheet, by micropipette or microcapillary. This sheet is allowed to dry fully, then it is transferred to a glass tank containing a shallow layer of solvent. The sheet is removed when the solvent front has travelled across 80–90% of its length.

The essential components of a TLC system are:

- **The stationary phase** comprising the layer of adsorbant on a solid backing – the chromatoplate. Aluminium or plastic-backed chromatoplates are now the norm having replaced glass plates, which needed to be prepared 'in-house'. The chromatoplates (20 cm × 20 cm) can be cut down to a more useful size (2 cm × 5 cm) for analytical work, using a guillotine. The adsorbant often contains a fluorescent compound (ZnS) to enable visualisation of the compounds after elution.
- **The development tank** – for plates measuring 2 cm × 5 cm a clean, dry beaker (100 mL) covered with a watch-glass is ideal. The eluting solvent should be about 3 mm deep in the tank to saturate the tank atmosphere with solvent vapour (Fig. 14.10).
- **The application system** – a micropipette or a microsyringe to place the solution of the mixture on the chromatoplate. Micropipettes (Fig. 14.11) are the more common and Box 14.1 gives the instructions for their preparation.
- **The eluent** – finding the eluent that will give the best separation of the components of the mixture is done by experiment. You may need to try several solvents of differing polarity (Table 14.2) or mixtures of solvents to find the best eluent.

Box 14.1 How to make micropipettes for TLC

1. **Heat the middle of an open-ended melting point tube at the tip of the hot flame of a microburner until it begins to sag.** If the melting point tube is sealed at one or both ends, carefully break off the sealed end(s) wearing gloves for protection.

2. **Quickly remove the tube from the flame and pull gently, forming a short capillary.** Do not pull the tube while it is in the flame.

3. **Allow the tube to cool and then break in the centre of the capillary.** You now have two micropipettes. If the capillary is too long, break it near to each end and *immediately* dispose of the fine waste glass into the broken-glass bin. *Do not leave* the waste glass on the laboratory bench.

4. **Make at least 10 micropipettes** – store them in a plastic-capped sample tube for future use.

Solutions of the mixture – the mixture must be applied to the chromatoplate as a solution. If the solvent for the solution is not the same as the eluent to be used, you must evaporate the solvent from the plate, before placing it in the eluent.

Finding an eluent – a medium-polarity solvent such as dichloromethane (DCM) is generally a good starting point.

 SAFETY NOTE *Great care must be taken when using UV light. Do not look directly at the UV source and wear gloves if you put your hands into the UV cabinet.*

- **A visualisation system** – to be able to see colourless separated components on the chromatogram. If the plate contains a fluorescer, it can be viewed under UV light ($\lambda = 254$ nm) in a special box or cabinet. The ZnS in the stationary phase fluoresces green, whereas the 'spots' of separated compounds appear dark. Alternatively, the chromatoplate can be placed in a sealed jar containing a few iodine crystals. The iodine vapour stains the plate light brown and the 'spots' dark brown. In forensic drug analysis, the plates are more commonly sprayed with acidified iodoplatinate spray and the 'spots' of separated compounds appear dark, or using alternative specific visualisation methods for specific drug compounds (Box 39.2), e.g. fast blue BB for cannabis or p-DMAB for LSD.

You can express the movement of an individual compound up the TLC plate in terms of its R_f (relative frontal mobility) value, where:

$$R_f = \frac{\text{distance moved by compound}}{\text{distance moved by solvent}} \qquad [14.8]$$

The R_f value is a constant for a particular substance and eluent system on a specific stationary phase, but variations in chromatographic conditions of adsorbant, eluent (in particular solvent mixtures), temperature and atmosphere make the application of R_f values to absolute identification rather problematical. Usually an authentic sample is run alongside the unknowns in the mixture (Fig. 14.12) or on top of the mixture – 'double spotting' – as shown in Fig. 14.13 (p. 130), to enable identification. The general procedure for running a TLC plate is described in Box 14.2 and for bulk drug analysis in Box 39.2.

Column chromatography

This is used for the preparative scale separation of mixtures of compounds. There are many variations in detail of equipment and technique – such as column type, column packing, sample application and fraction collection – many of which are a matter of personal choice and apparatus available. Typical arrangements are shown in Fig. 14.14 (p. 131) and for a detailed description of all these variations you should consult specialist texts such as Errington (1997, p. 163), Harwood *et al.* (2000, p. 175) and Furniss *et al.* (1989, p. 209).

Gravity chromatography is used to separate the components of a mixture that have a difference in R_f value of at least 0.3. Flash chromatography, because of the smaller size of the adsorbant particles, is more effective at separating mixtures of components of $\Delta R_f = 0.15$, and is also faster.

Table 14.2 The elutropic series of solvents for chromatography

Non-polar	Light petroleum (b.pt. 40–60 °C)
	Cyclohexane
	Toluene
	Dichloromethane
	Diethylether (ether)
	Ethyl ethanoate (ethyl acetate)
	Propanone (acetone)
	Ethanoic acid (acetic acid)
Polar	Methanol

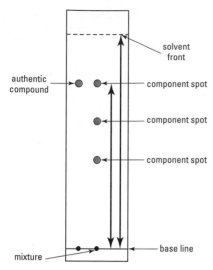

Fig. 14.12 A thin-layer chromatogram.

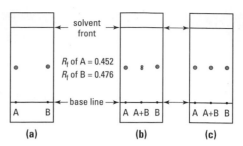

Fig. 14.13 Double-spotting technique: (a) compounds A and B with close R_f values; (b) figure '8' of double spot shows that A and B are different; (c) single spot for double spot shows that A and B could be the same.

KEY POINT *Before attempting a preparative mixture separation by column chromatography, you must always analyse the mixture by TLC to establish the stationary phase and solvent parameters for effective separation and to determine the R_f values of the components.*

Box 14.2 How to run a thin-layer chromatogram

1. **Prepare the TLC development tank using a clean, dry beaker, as shown in Fig. 14.10** – allow it to equilibrate for 10 min.

2. **Prepare the plastic-backed TLC plate** by drawing a fine line (the base line) in *pencil* about 1 cm above the bottom. Take care not to scrape off any of the stationary phase. Put three pencil dots on the base line – one in the centre and the others equidistant on either side, but no closer than 3 mm to the edges of the plate.

3. **Dissolve the mixture (1–3 mg) in two or three drops of a suitable volatile solvent** – dichloromethane or ether are the most common, in a small sample tube.

4. **Dip the tip of a micropipette into the solution** – capillary action will draw the solution into the pipette.

5. **Touch the tip of the micropipette on to one of the pencil spots on the base line** – capillary action will draw the solution from the micropipette on to the plate as a spot. Do not allow the spot to be more than 2 mm in diameter. Put the micropipette back into the sample tube containing the mixture.

6. **Spot other samples** (e.g. reference compounds) on to the plate as appropriate, *using a new micropipette in each case.*

7. **Evaporate the solvent from the plate** – wave it in the air, holding the plate by the edges.

8. **Lower the plate into the developing tank** – hold it by the edges and make sure that *the eluent does not cover the base line.* If it does, discard the plate, prepare another and empty some eluent from the tank.

9. **Put the lid on the tank and allow the eluent to rise up the plate** – to about 1cm from the top of the plate.

10. **Remove the chromatoplate from the tank** – quickly mark the height reached by the eluent, using a pencil.

11. **Wave the chromatoplate in the air** – to evaporate the eluent from the plate.

12. **Visualise the chromatogram** – by either placing the dry chromatoplate in a UV cabinet and using a pencil to draw round the spots (*remember to wear gloves when your hands are in the UV cabinet*) or spray with acidified iodoplatinate in a fume hood until the dark spots develop.

Problems with thin-layer chromatography

Overloading the chromatoplate with sample – TLC is an extremely sensitive technique and it is easy to put too much sample on the plate. The sample solution must not be too concentrated and you must not repeat applications of solutions on the same spot. The result is non-separation of the mixture and a 'smear' up the plate. Dilute the solution or don't put so much on the plate.

Putting the spots of sample too close together – the separated spots 'bleed' into each other and you can't tell from which sample they originate.

Putting the spots too close to the edge of the plate – this results in inaccurate R_f values (spots travel faster up the edge of the plate) and 'bleeding'.

Contamination, which produces unexpected spots – make sure all apparatus is clean, solvents are clean and use a fresh micropipette for each application.

UV visualisation – if you use an eluent such as toluene, which absorbs in the UV region, you must allow all the eluent to evaporate or you will see only a dark plate.

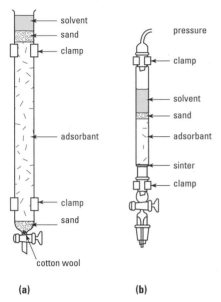

Fig. 14.14 Column chromatography: (a) gravity chromatography; (b) flash chromatography.

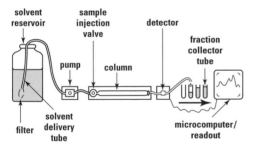

Fig. 14.15 Components of an HPLC system.

HPLC is a versatile form of chromatography, used with a wide variety of stationary and mobile phases, to separate individual compounds of a particular class of molecules on the basis of size, polarity, solubility or adsorption characteristics.

Always use the highest-purity solvents.

High-performance liquid chromatography

High-performance liquid chromatography (HPLC) uses high pressure to force the mobile phase through a closed column packed with micrometre-sized particles. This allows rapid separation of complex mixtures. Several operating modes of HPLC are possible (see also p. 123). These are:

- **Normal phase (NPHPLC)** – the sample should be soluble in a hydrophobic solvent (e.g. hexane) and should be non-ionic. The mobile phase is non-polar while the stationary phase is polar (e.g. silica, cyano, amino).
- **Reversed phase (RPHPLC)** – the most commonly used method in forensic applications, where the sample should be soluble in water or a polar organic solvent (e.g. methanol) and should be non-ionic. The mobile phase is polar while the stationary phase is non-polar (e.g. C18 (ODS), C_8 (octyl), phenyl).
- **Size-exclusion chromatography (SEC)** – this is used when the major difference between compounds in a mixture is their molecular weight. It is normally used for compounds with molecular weights greater than 2,000. The mobile phase should be a strong solvent for the sample. Aqueous SEC is called gel filtration chromatography (GFC) and is used for separation of proteins and other biomolecules, while organic SEC is called gel permeation chromatography (GPC) and is used for the separation of polymers.
- **Ion-exchange chromatography (IEC)** – is used when compounds are ionic, or potentially ionic (e.g. anions, cations, organic acids and bases, amino acids, catecholamines, peptides). The mobile phase is typically a buffer and the choice of pH is critical. Two types can be differentiated – SAX (Strong-Anion eXchange) and SCX (Strong-Cation eXchange).

The essential components of an HPLC system are a solvent delivery system, a method of sample introduction, a column, a detector and an associated readout device (Fig. 14.15).

Solvent delivery system

This should fulfil certain requirements:

- it should be chemically inert;
- it should be capable of delivering a wide flow-rate range;
- it should be able to withstand high pressures;
- it should be able to deliver high flow-rate precision;
- it should have a low internal volume;
- it should provide minimum flow pulsation.

Although several systems are available that meet these requirements, the most common is the reciprocating or piston pump. The choice of solvent delivery system depends on the type of separation to be performed:

- **isocratic separation** – a single solvent (or solvent mixture) is used throughout the analysis;
- **gradient elution separation** – the composition of the mobile phase is altered using a microprocessor-controlled gradient programmer, which mixes appropriate amounts of two different solvents to produce the required gradient.

The main advantage of gradient HPLC is that you can control mobile-phase composition. This allows you to resolve closely related compounds and provides faster elution of strongly retained compounds, thereby producing reduced analysis times and faster method development time. However, this advantage has to be set against some disadvantages, such as the initial higher cost of the equipment compared with an isocratic system. Also, after each gradient run, a re-equilibration of the system is required to return to the initial mobile-phase conditions.

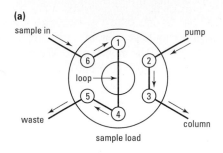

(a)

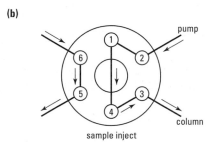

(b)

Fig. 14.16 Schematic diagram of a rotary valve.

Sample introduction

The most common method of sample introduction in HPLC is via a rotary valve (e.g. a Rheodyne® valve). A schematic diagram of a rotary valve is shown in Fig. 14.16. In the load position, the sample is introduced via a syringe to fill an external loop of volume 5, 10 or 20 μL. While this occurs, the mobile phase passes through the valve to the column. In the inject position, the valve is rotated so that the mobile phase is diverted through the sample loop, thereby introducing a reproducible volume of the sample into the mobile phase. The procedure for injection of a sample is shown in Fig. 14.17. In Fig. 14.17(a) the syringe is filled with the sample/standard solution (typically 1 mL). Then the outside of the syringe is wiped clean with a tissue (Fig. 14.17(b)). The syringe is placed into the Rheodyne injector of the chromatograph while in the 'load' position (Fig. 14.17(c)) and the plunger on the syringe is depressed to fill the sample loop. Finally, the position of the Rheodyne valve is switched to the 'inject' position to introduce the sample into the chromatograph (Fig. 14.17(d)) and then the syringe is removed from the injection valve. The procedure for the preparation of a series of calibration solutions is shown in Box 14.3.

The column

This is usually made of stainless steel, and all components (valves, etc.) are manufactured from materials that can withstand the high pressures involved. The most common form of liquid chromatography is reversed-phase HPLC. In RPHPLC the most common column packing material consists of C_{18} or octadecylsilane (ODS). A chemically bonded stationary phase is shown in Fig. 14.18. However, some of the surface silanol groups remain unaffected. These unreacted groups lead to undesirable chromatographic effects, such as peak tailing (p. 126). One approach to remove the unreacted silanol groups is end capping. In this way, the silanol group is reacted with a small silylating group, e.g. trimethylchlorosilane. An alternative approach to nullify the action of the silanol groups is to add triethylamine to the mobile phase, which modifies the silica surface while in use.

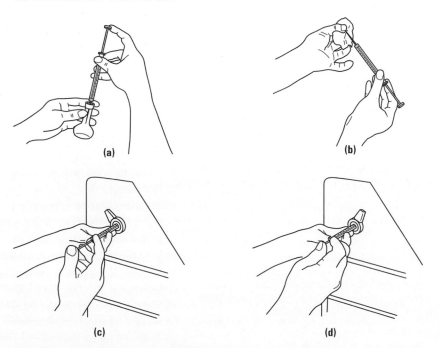

Fig. 14.17 Sample injection in HPLC.

Box 14.3 How to prepare a set of five calibration solutions in the concentration range 0–10 μg mL^{-1} (mg L^{-1})

Assuming that we are starting with a 1,000 μg mL^{-1} stock solution of a particular organic compound (e.g. 2-chlorophenol) you will need 6 × 10.00 mL grade A volumetric flasks and a syringe (0–100.00 μL).

1. Ensure that all the glassware is clean (see p. 41).

2. **Add ≈9 mL of organic solvent** (e.g. dichloromethane) to a 10.00 mL volumetric flask.

3. **Quantitatively transfer 20.00 μL of the stock solution** into the 10.00 mL volumetric flask. Inject the solution from the syringe below the surface of the dichloromethane. Then, dilute to 10.00 mL with dichloromethane.

4. **What is the concentration of this new solution?** Remember that we started with an initial 1,000 μg mL^{-1} 2-chlorophenol stock solution.

$$\frac{1,000\ \mu g}{mL} \times 20 \times 10^{-3}\,mL = \mu g\,2\,chlorophenol \qquad [14.9]$$

So 20 μg 2-chlorophenol was placed in the 10.00 mL volumetric flask. So, the concentration of 2-chloro-phenol is

$$\frac{20\ \mu g}{10\ ml} = 2\ \mu g\ ml^{-1} \qquad [14.10]$$

You now have a 2 μg mL^{-1} calibration solution of 2-chlorophenol.

5. **Similarly transfer 0, 40.00, 60.00, 80.00 and 100.00 μL volumes into separate volumetric flasks** and dilute to 10.00 mL with dichloromethane and label as 0, 4, 6, 8 and 10 μg mL^{-1} 2-chlorophenol calibration solutions.

6. **Take the 0, 2, 4, 6, 8 and 10 μg mL^{-1} 2-chlorophenol calibration solutions** to the chromatograph for analysis.

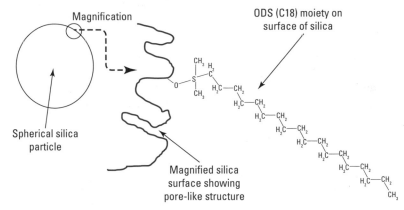

Fig. 14.18 A C$_{18}$ stationary phase.

HPLC detectors

Most HPLC systems are linked to a continuous monitoring detector of high sensitivity – for example, phenols may be detected spectrophotometrically by monitoring the absorbance of the eluent at 280 nm as it passes through a flow cell. Other detectors can be used to measure changes in fluorescence, current or potential, as described below. Most detection systems are non-destructive, which means that you can collect eluent with an automatic fraction collector for further study.

UV/visible detectors are widely used and have the advantages of versatility, sensitivity and stability. Such detectors are of two types – fixed wavelength and variable wavelength. Fixed-wavelength detectors are simple to use, with low operating costs. They usually contain a mercury lamp as a light source, emitting at several wavelengths between 254 nm and 578 nm; a particular wavelength is selected using suitable cutoff filters. The most frequently used wavelengths for analysis of organic molecules are 254 nm and 280 nm. Variable wavelength

Using silica-based HPLC columns – these are limited to a pH range of 2–8 (preferably 3–7). At low pH the bonded phase may be removed; at high pH the silica particles may be dissolved.

UV cutoff for organic solvents:

- *hexane*   *195 nm;*
- *acetonitrile*   *190 nm;*
- *methano*   *205 nm;*
- *water*   *190 nm.*

Chromatography

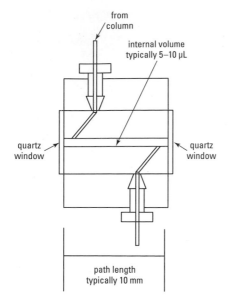

Fig. 14.19 UV detector cell for HPLC.

from column

internal volume typically 5–10 μL

quartz window

quartz window

path length typically 10 mm

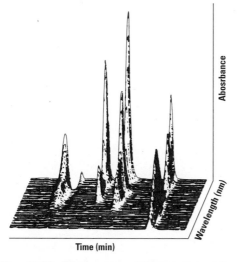

Absorbance

Wavelength (nm)

Time (min)

Fig. 14.20 Diode array detector absorption spectra of the eluent from an HPLC separation of a mixture of four steroids, taken every 15 s.

> **Overcoming interference with fluorescence detectors** – use a dual flow cell to offset background fluorescence due to components of the mobile phase.

> **Maximising sensitivity with fluorescence detectors** – the concentration of other sample components, e.g. pigments, must not be so high that they cause quenching of fluorescence.

> **Optimising electrochemical detection** – the mobile phase must be free of any compounds that might give a response; all constituents must be of the highest purity.

detectors use a deuterium lamp and a continuously adjustable monochromator for wavelengths of 190–600 nm. For both types of detector, sensitivity is in the absorbance range 0.001–1.0 (down to 1ng), with noise levels as low as 4×10^{-5}. Note that sensitivity is partly influenced by the path length of the flow cell, typically 10 mm (see Fig. 14.19). Monitoring at short-wavelength UV (e.g. below 240 nm) may give increased sensitivity but decreased specificity, since many organic molecules absorb in this range. Additional problems with short-wavelength UV detection include instrument instability, giving a variable base line, and absorption by components of the mobile phase (e.g. organic solvents, which often absorb at 210 nm).

An important development in chromatographic monitoring is **diode array detection** (DAD). The incident light comprises the whole spectrum of light from the source, which is passed through a diffraction grating and the diffracted light detected by an array of photodiodes. Typical DAD can measure the absorbance of each sample component at 1–10 nm intervals over the range 190–600 nm. This gives an absorbance spectrum for each eluting substance which may be used to identify the compound and give some indication as to its purity. An example of a three-dimensional diode array spectrum is shown in Fig. 14.20.

Many aromatic organic molecules, including some polycyclic aromatic hydrocarbons, show natural fluorescence, or can be made to fluoresce by pre-column or post-column derivatisation with a fluorophore. **Fluorescence detection** is more sensitive than UV/visible detection, and may allow analysis in the picogram (10^{-12}g) range. A fluorescence detector consists of a light source (e.g. a xenon lamp), a diffraction grating to supply light at the excitation wavelength, and a photomultiplier to monitor the emitted light (usually arranged to be at right angles to the excitation beam). The use of instruments with a laser light source can give an extremely narrow excitation waveband, and increased sensitivity and specificity.

Electrochemical detectors offer very high sensitivity and specificity, with the possibility of detection of femtogram amounts of electroactive compounds such as catecholamines, vitamins, thiols, purines, ascorbate and uric acid. The two main types of detector, amperometric and coulometric, operate on similar principles, i.e. by measuring the change in current or potential as sample components pass between two electrodes within the flow cell. One of these electrodes acts as a reference (or counter) electrode (e.g. calomel electrode), while the other – the working electrode – is held at a voltage that is high enough to cause either oxidation or reduction of sample molecules. In the oxidative mode, the working electrode is usually glassy carbon, while in reductive mode a mercury electrode is used. In both cases, a current flow between the electrodes is induced and detected.

Mass spectrometry (Chapter 15) used in conjunction with chromatographic methods can provide a powerful tool for identifying the components of complex mixtures (e.g. pharmaceuticals). One drawback is the limited capacity of the mass spectrometer – due to its vacuum requirements – compared with the volume of material leaving the chromatography column. Similarly, in HPLC, devices have been developed for solving the problem of large solvent volumes, for example by splitting the eluent from the column so only a small fraction reaches the mass spectrometer.

The computer-generated outputs from the mass spectrometer are similar to chromatograms obtained from other methods, and show peaks corresponding to the elution of particular components. However, it is then possible to select an individual peak and obtain a mass spectrum for the component in that peak to aid in its identification (p. 144). This has helped to identify hundreds of components present in a single sample, including flavour molecules in food, drug metabolites and water pollutants.

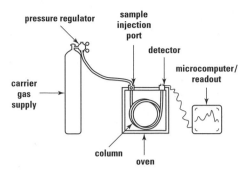

Fig. 14.21 Components of a GC system.

Types of capillary column

- **Wall-coated open tubular (WCOT) column** – liquid stationary phase on inside wall of column.
- **Support-coated open tubular (SCOT) column** – liquid stationary phase coated on solid support attached to inside wall of column.
- **Porous layer open tubular (PLOT) column** – solid stationary phase on inside wall of column.

Applications of gas–liquid chromatography – GLC is used to separate volatile, non-polar compounds. Substances with polar groups must be converted to less polar derivatives prior to analysis, in order to prevent adsorption on the column, resulting in pool resolution and peak tailing.

The main issues to address in the use of Static Headspace (SHS) are:

- Procedure is best done using the autosampler of the GC system, fitted with an incubator.
- Optimising the b value (i.e. sample to headspace vial volumes).
- Whether salting out is required (to improve GC sensitivity).
- Incubation temperature.
- Volume of the gas-tight syringe.
- Potential risk of sample carry-over if a heated gas-tight syringe is not used.
- Gas-tight syringe is heated to the same temperature as the incubation temperature (for the sample vial); prevents sample condensation.
- Influence of sample injection volume on resultant chromatography.
- Check the GC injection port septum regularly; the gas-tight syringe has a wider needle than a typical syringe (for GC injection). The potential for a gas leak to occur is enhanced if the septum is not replaced more regularly.

Gas chromatography

In gas chromatography (GC), a gaseous solute (or the vapour from a volatile liquid) is carried by the gaseous mobile phase. In gas–liquid partition chromatography, the stationary phase is a non-volatile liquid coated on the inside of the column or on a fine support. In gas–solid adsorption chromatography, solid particles that adsorb the solute act as the stationary phase.

The typical components of a gas chromatograph are shown in Fig. 14.21. A volatile liquid is injected through a septum into a heated port, which volatilises the sample. Alternatively, the headspace (p. 80) can also be injected via either static or dynamic headspace systems. A gaseous mobile phase carries the sample through the heated column, and the separated components are detected and recorded. Two types of column are available – packed and capillary. Open tubular capillary columns offer higher resolution, shorter analysis time and greater sensitivity than packed columns, but have lower capacity for the sample.

Sample injection

Samples are injected on to the 'top' of the column, through a sample injection port containing a gas-tight septum. The two common sample injection methods for capillary GC are:

1. **Split/splitless injector** – in the split mode only a portion of the injected sample (typically, 1 part in 50) reaches the column. The rest is vented to waste. A split injector is used for concentrated samples (>0.1 mg mL^{-1} for FID; see p. 137). In the splitless mode all the sample volume injected passes through to the column. It is used in this mode for trace samples (<0.1 mg mL^{-1} for FID).
2. **Cold on-column injector** – all the sample is injected on to the column. It is used for thermally unstable compounds and high-boiling solvents.

In both cases a syringe (1 μL) is used to inject the sample. Examples of each type of injection system are shown in Fig. 14.22. The procedure for injection of a sample is shown in Fig. 14.23. In Fig. 14.23(a) the syringe is filled with the sample/standard solution (typically 0.5 μL). Then the outside of the syringe is wiped clean with a tissue (Fig. 14.23(b)). The syringe is placed into the injector of the gas chromatograph (Fig. 14.23(c)) and, finally, the plunger on the syringe is depressed to inject the sample (Fig. 14.23(d)). The procedure for the preparation of a series of calibration solutions is shown in Box 14.3.

Headspace sampling using static or dynamic headspace analysis.

Headspace analysis (p. 80) can be done in a variety of ways, including via a gas tight syringe (also referred to as static headspace) or dynamic headspace. Static headspace analysis operates by placing the sample vial in a thermostated oven for a period of time (e.g. an incubation temperature of 60 °C for 5 min). This technique is typically used for forensic alcohol analysis (Chapter 37). Static headspace analysis can also be done using solid phase microextraction (p. 93). Both methods allow the opportunity for equilibrium to be achieved in the shortest possible time between the liquid and gaseous phases. A known volume of the gaseous headspace is removed using a gas tight syringe and injected into the injection port of the GC (p. 80, 136).

Dynamic headspace analysis operates by placing the sample vial in a thermostated oven for a period of time (e.g. an incubation period of 80 °C) and passing an inert (purge) gas over the surface; the headspace volatile compounds are removed, at a typical purge flow rate of 15 mL/min and passed through a

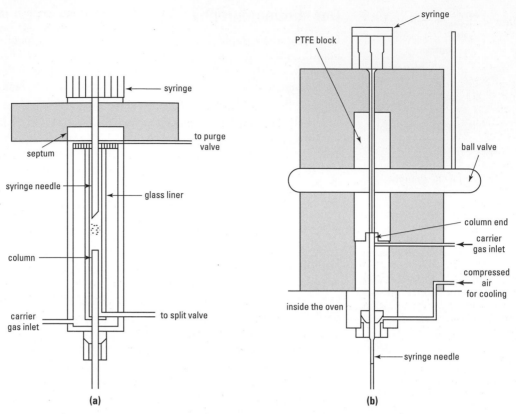

Fig. 14.22   Sample introduction in GC: (a) split/splitless injector; (b) on-column injector.

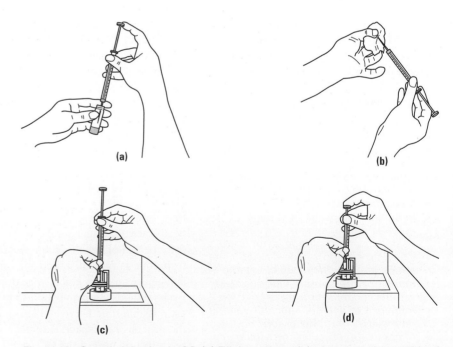

Fig. 14.23   Sample injection in GC. (a) Fill the syringe, (b) wipe clean the outside of the syringe needle, (c) place the syringe needle into the injector and (d) depress the plunger on the syringe to inject the sample.

trap (e.g. Tenax TA, held at e.g. 25 °C) The compounds are then rapidly desorbed from the trap (by heating e.g. 25 °C to 280 °C in 1 min, followed by a hold of 5 min) directly into the injection port of the GC. This technique is typically used for accelerant analysis in fire investigation (Chapter 44).

The column

Modern GC uses capillary columns (internal diameter 0.1–0.5 mm) up to 60 m in length. The stationary phase is generally a cross-linked silicone polymer, coated as a thin film on the inner wall of the fused silica (SiO_2) capillary – at normal operating temperatures, this behaves in a similar manner to a liquid film but is far more robust. Common stationary phases for GC are shown in Fig. 14.24. The mobile phase ('carrier gas') is usually nitrogen or helium. Selective separation is achieved as a result of the differential partitioning of individual compounds between the carrier gas and silicone polymer phases. The separation of most organic molecules is influenced by the temperature of the column, which may be constant during the analysis ('isothermal' – usually 50–250 °C) or, more commonly, may increase in a pre-programmed manner (e.g. from 50 °C to 250 °C at 10 °C per min).

Selecting an appropriate column for capillary GC is a difficult task and one that is usually left to the technician. However, it is important to be aware of some general issues and what influence they can have on the separation. The column internal diameter can affect both resolution and speed of analysis. Smaller internal diameters columns (0.25 mm i.d.) can provide good resolution of early eluting peaks (Fig. 14.25(a)). However, the problem is that the analysis times of the eluting components may be longer, and that the linear dynamic range may be restricted. In contrast, larger internal diameter columns (0.53mm i.d.) provide less resolution for early eluting compounds (Fig. 14.25(b)), but this is reflected in shorter analysis times and a greater linear dynamic range. This type of column may provide sufficient resolution for the analysis of complex mixtures. Figure 14.25 illustrates the effects of column internal diameter.

Another important column effect is the length of the column and the influence this can have on the resolution of eluting components. It was previously shown (p. 126) that resolution was influenced by k', α and N. Substituting eqn [14.4] into eqn [39.6] produces the following equation:

$$R = \frac{1}{4}\sqrt{\frac{L}{H}} \times \frac{k'}{k' + 1} \times \frac{\alpha - 1}{\alpha} \qquad 14.4$$

The importance of this equation can be shown by considering the influence on resolution, R, of column length, L. Under isothermal analysis conditions, i.e. the same column temperature, the retention of eluting compounds is more dependent on column length. For example, doubling the column length doubles the analysis times and increases the resolution by 41%. This is shown in Fig. 14.26 for the analysis of phenols. In contrast, under temperature-programmed analysis (e.g. 130 °C to 250 °C at 4°C min^{-1}) the retention time of eluting components is more dependent on temperature. For example, doubling the column length has minimal effect on analysis times. This is shown in Fig. 14.27 for the analysis of bacterial acid methyl esters.

GC detectors

The output from the GC column is monitored by a detector. The most commonly used detectors for GC analysis of organic molecules are as follows.

The **flame ionisation detector** (FID) is particularly useful for the analysis of a broad range of organic molecules. It involves passing the exit gas stream

The main issues to address in the use of dynamic headspace (DHS) analysis:

- *Procedure is best done using a dedicated DHS system.*
- *Optimising the b value (i.e. sample to headspace to vial volumes).*
- *Whether slating out is required (to improve GC sensitivity)*
- *Incubation temperature.*
- *Selectivity of the trap (for retaining the compounds).*
- *Heated transfer line required; potential for condensation of compounds if not heated sufficiently).*
- *Influence of sample injection volume on resultant chromatography.*

Analysing compounds by GC in the split mode *– make sure that no hazardous materials enter the laboratory atmosphere through the split vent. A charcoal split-vent trap may be required to eliminate potential hazards.*

100% dimethylsiloxane:
the least polar bonded phase. Used for boiling point separations (solvents, petroleum products, etc.).
Typical names: DB–1, HP–1, Rtx–1

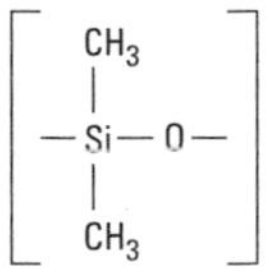

95% dimethylsiloxane–5% diphenylypolysiloxane:
a non-polar phase. Used for separation of environmental samples, e.g. polycyclic aromatic hydrocarbons.
Typical names: DB–5, HP–5, Rtx–5

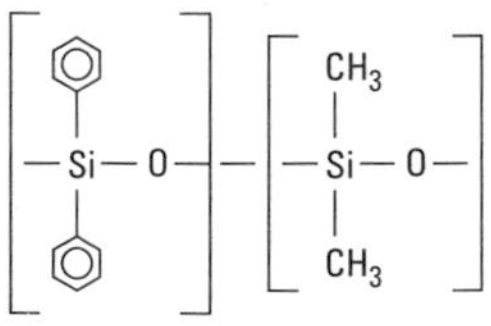

5% 95%

Fig. 14.24 Common stationary phases for capillary GC.

Solvent selection in GC *– choose a solvent with a boiling point at least 20 °C below that of the first eluting compound. Thicker stationary-phase films provide longer retention and higher peak capacity.*

Detectors *– the most appropriate detector depends on the type of chromatography and the application. Ideally, the detector should show high sensitivity, a low detection limit and minimal noise or drift.*

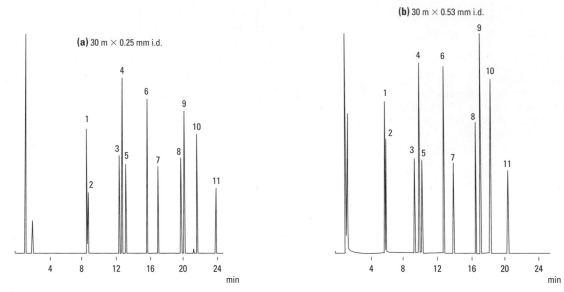

Fig. 14.25 Influence of GC column internal diameter on separation: 1. phenol; 2. 2-chlorophenol; 3. 2-nitrophenol; 4. 2,4-dimethylphenol; 5. 2,4-dichlorophenol; 6. 4-chloro-3-methylphenol; 7. 2,4,6-trichlorophenol; 8. 2,4-dinitrophenol; 9. 4-nitrophenol; 10. 2-methyl-4, 6-dinitrophenol; 11. pentachlorophenol.

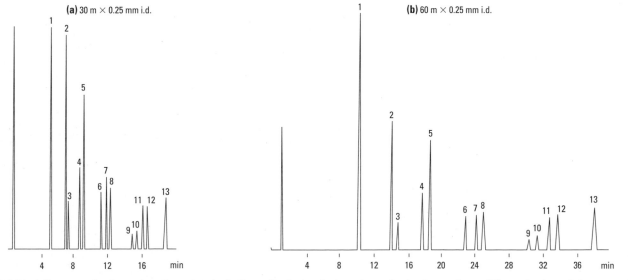

Fig. 14.26 Influence of column length on analysis time. Analysis of phenols under isothermal conditions: 1. phenol; 2. o-cresol; 3. 2,6-xylenol; 4. p-cresol; 5. n-cresol; 6. o-ethylphenol; 7. 2,4-xylenol; 8. 2,5-xylenol; 9. 2,3-xylenol; 10. p-ethylphenol; 11. m-ethylphenol; 12. 3,5-xylenol; 13. 3,4-xylenol.

from the column through a hydrogen flame that has a potential of more than 100V applied across it (Fig. 14.28). Most organic compounds, on passage through this flame, produce ions and electrons that create a small current across the electrodes, and this is amplified for measurement purposes. The FID is very sensitive (typically down to 0.1pg), with a linear response over a wide concentration range. One drawback is that the sample is destroyed during analysis.

The **thermal conductivity detector** (TCD) is based on changes in the thermal conductivity of the gas stream brought about by the presence of separated sample molecules. The detector elements are two electrically heated platinum wires, one

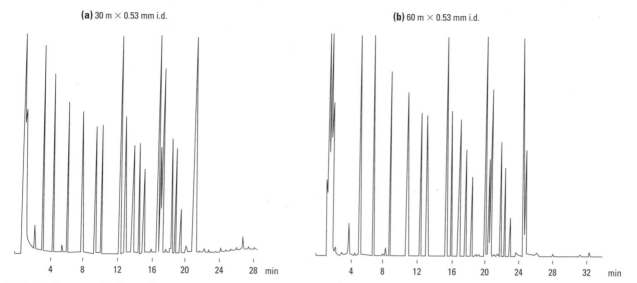

(a) 30 m × 0.53 mm i.d.　　　　　　　　　　　　**(b)** 60 m × 0.53 mm i.d.

Fig. 14.27 Influence of column length on analysis time. Analysis of bacterial acid methyl esters under temperature-programmed conditions.

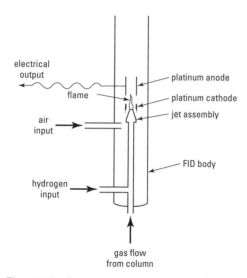

Fig. 14.28 Components of a flame ionisation detector (FID).

in a chamber through which only the carrier gas flows (the reference detector cell), and the other in a chamber that takes the gas flow from the column (the sample detector cell). In the presence of a constant gas flow, the temperature of the wires (and therefore their electrical resistance) is dependent on the thermal conductivity of the gas. Analytes in the gas stream are detected by temperature-dependent changes in resistance based on the thermal conductivity of each separated molecule – the size of the signal is directly related to concentration of the analyte.

The advantages of the TCD include its applicability to a wide range of organic and inorganic molecules and its non-destructive nature, since the sample can be collected for further study. Its major limitation is its low sensitivity (down to ≈ 10 ng) compared with other systems.

The **electron capture detector** (ECD) is highly sensitive (Fig. 14.29) and is useful for the detection of certain compounds with electronegative functional groups (e.g. halogens, peroxides and quinones). The gas stream from the column passes over a β-emitter such as ^{63}Ni, which provides electrons that cause ionisation of the carrier gas (e.g. nitrogen). When carrier gas alone is passing the β-emitter, its ionisation results in a constant current flowing between two electrodes placed in the gas flow. However, when electron-capturing sample molecules are present in the gas flow, a decrease in current is detected. An example of the application of the ECD is in detecting and quantifying chlorinated pesticides.

Mass spectrometry (Chapter 15) used in conjunction with GC provides a powerful tool for identifying the components of complex mixtures, for example environmental pollutants, synthetic products (Fig. 14.30). The procedure requires computer control of the instrument and data storage/analysis. Compounds eluting from the column are bombarded by electrons (electron impact, EI, mode) causing fragmentation and production of charged species. These charged species are separated by the mass spectrometer on the basis of their mass-to-charge ratio. Ions passing through the mass spectrometer are detected by an electron multiplier tube. The mass spectrometer can be used in two modes – total ion and selected ion monitoring. In the former mode, the complete mass spectrum of each of the components of the mixture eluting from the column is recorded. In the latter

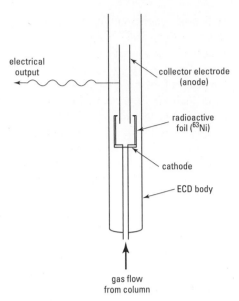

Fig. 14.29 Components of an electron capture detector (ECD).

Problems with peaks – *non-symmetrical peaks may result from column overloading, co-elution of solutes, poor packing of the stationary phase, or interactions between the substance and the support material.*

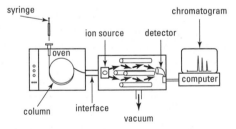

Fig. 14.30 Schematic diagram of a GC–MS instrument.

Interpreting chromatograms – *never assume that a single peak is a guarantee of purity; there may be more than one compound with the same chromatographic characteristics.*

Avoiding problems with air bubbles in liquid chromatography – *always ensure that buffers are effectively degassed by vacuum treatment before use, and regularly clean the flow cell of the detector.*

---

mode, only ions of specified mass-to-charge ratios are detected. Selected ion monitoring offers increased sensitivity and selectivity.

Recording and interpreting chromatograms

For analytical purposes, the detector output is usually connected to a computer-based data acquisition and analysis system. This consists of a personal computer (PC) with data acquisition hardware to convert an analogue detector signal to digital format, plus software to control the data acquisition process, store the signal information and display the resulting chromatogram. The software will also detect peaks and calculate their retention times and sizes (areas) for quantitative analysis. The software often incorporates functions to control the chromatographic equipment, enabling automatic operation. In sophisticated systems, the detector output may be compared with that from a 'library' of chromatograms for known compounds, to suggest possible identities of unknown sample peaks.

In simpler chromatographic systems, you may need to use a chart recorder for detector output. Two important settings must be considered before using a chart recorder:

1. **The base-line reading** – this should be set only after a suitable quantity of mobile phase has passed through the column (prior to injection of the sample) and stability has been established. The chart recorder is usually set a little above the edge of the chart paper grid, to allow for base-line drift.
2. **The detector range** – this must be set to ensure that the largest peaks do not go off the top of the chart. Adjustment may be based on the expected quantity of analyte, or by a trial-and-error process. Use the maximum sensitivity that gives intact peaks. If peaks are still too large on the minimum sensitivity, you may need to reduce the amount of sample used, or prepare and analyse a diluted sample.

Interpreting chromatograms

Make sure you know the direction of the horizontal axis of the chromatogram (usually, either volume or time) – it may run from right to left or vice versa – and make a note of the detector sensitivity on the vertical axis. Ideally, the base line should be 'flat' between peaks, but it may drift up or down because of a number of factors including:

- **changes in the composition of the mobile phase** (e.g. in gradient elution);
- **tailing of material from previous peaks**;
- **carry-over of material from previous samples** – this can be avoided by efficient cleaning of columns between runs. Allow sufficient time for the previous sample to pass through the column before you introduce the next sample;
- **loss of the stationary phase from the column** (column 'bleed'), caused by extreme elution conditions;
- **air bubbles (in liquid chromatography)** – if the buffers used in the mobile phase are not effectively degassed, air bubbles may build up in the flow cell of the detector, leading to a gradual upward drift of the base line, followed by a sharp fall when the accumulated air is released. Small air bubbles that do not become trapped may give spurious small peaks as they pass through the detector.

A peak close to the origin may be due to non-retained sample molecules, flowing at the same rate as the mobile phase, or to artefacts, for example air (GC) or solvent (HPLC) in the sample. Whatever its origin, this peak can be used to measure the void volume and dead time of the column (p. 125). No peaks from genuine sample components should appear before this type of peak.

Peaks can be denoted on the basis of their elution volume (used mainly in liquid chromatography) or their retention times (mainly in GC). If the peaks are not narrow and symmetrical, they may contain more than one component. Where peaks are more curved on the trailing side compared with the leading side (peak tailing, p. 126), this may indicate too great an association between the component and the stationary phase, or overloading of the column.

Optimising chromatographic separations

In an ideal chromatographic analysis, the sample molecules will be completely separated, and detection of components will result in a series of discrete individual peaks corresponding to each type of molecule. However, to minimise the possibility of overlapping peaks, or of peaks composed of more than one substance, it is important to maximise the separation efficiency of the technique, which depends on:

- **The selectivity** – as measured by the relative retention times of the two components (p. 125), or by the volume of the mobile phase between the peak maxima of the two components after they have passed through the column. This depends on the ability of the chromatographic method to separate two components with similar properties.
- **The band-broadening properties** of the chromatographic system – which influence the width of the peaks. These are mainly due to the effects of diffusion.

The resolution of two adjacent components can be defined in terms of k, α and N, using eqn [14.6]. In practical terms, good resolution is achieved when there is a large 'distance' (either time or volume) between peak maxima, and the peaks are as narrow as possible. The resolution of components is also affected by the relative amount of each substance – for systems showing low resolution it can be difficult to resolve small amounts of a particular component in the presence of larger amounts of a second component. If you cannot obtain the desired results from a poorly resolved chromatogram, other chromatographic conditions, or even different methods, should be tried in an attempt to improve resolution. For liquid chromatography, changes in the following factors may improve resolution:

- **Stationary-phase particle size** – the smaller the particle, the greater the area available for partitioning between the mobile phase and the stationary phase. This partly accounts for the high resolution observed with HPLC compared with low-pressure methods.
- **The slope of the salt gradient in eluting IEC columns** – e.g. using computer-controlled adapted gradients.
- **In low-pressure liquid chromatography,** the flow rate of the mobile phase must be optimised because this influences two band-broadening effects which are dependent on diffusion of sample molecules: (i) the flow rate must be slow enough to allow effective partitioning between the mobile

Degassing your mobile phase solvent – this is an important step and the best approach is to prepare the solvent composition (e.g. 50:50 v/v methanol:water, for isocratic RPHPLC) and then filter through a 0.22 mm porosity filter using a Büchner flask arrangement.

Quantifying molecules – note that quantitative analysis often requires assumptions about the identity of separated components and that further techniques may be required to provide information about the nature of the molecules present, e.g. mass spectrometry (see Chapter 15).

phase and the stationary phase: and (ii) it must be fast enough to ensure that there is minimal diffusion along the column once the molecules have been separated. To allow for these opposing influences, a compromise flow rate must be used.

- **If you prepare your own columns,** they must be packed correctly, with no channels present that might result in uneven flow and eddy diffusion.

Quantitative analysis

Most detectors and chemical assay systems give a linear response with increasing amounts of the test substance over a given 'working range' (Chapter 51). Alternative ways of converting the measured response to an amount of substance are:

- **External standardisation** – this is applicable where the sample volume is sufficiently precise to give reproducible results (e.g. HPLC). You measure the peak areas (or heights) of known amounts of the substance to give a calibration factor or calibration curve (Chapter 51) which can be used to calculate the amount of test substance in the sample.
- **Internal standardisation** – where you add a known amount of a reference substance (not originally present) to the sample, to give an additional peak in the elution profile. You determine the response of the detector to the test and reference substances by analysing a standard containing known amounts of both substances, to provide a response factor (r), where:

$$r = \frac{\text{peak area (or height) of test substance}}{\text{peak area (or height) of reference substance}} \qquad [14.12]$$

When using external standardisation – samples and standards should be analysed more than once, to confirm the reproducibility of the technique.

Use this response factor to quantify the amount of test substance (Q_t) in a sample containing a known amount of the reference substance (Q_r), from the relationship:

$$Q_t = \frac{[\text{peak area (or height) of test substance}]}{[\text{peak area (or height) of reference substance}]} \times \frac{Q_r}{r} \qquad [14.13]$$

When using an internal standard – add an internal standard to the sample at the first stage in the extraction procedure, so that any loss or degradation of test substance during purification is accompanied by an equivalent change in the internal standard, as long as the extraction characteristics of the internal standard and the test substance are very similar.

Internal standardisation should be the method of choice wherever possible, since it is unaffected by small variations in sample volume (e.g. for GC microsyringe injection). The internal standard should be chemically similar to the test substance(s) and must give a peak that is distinct from all other substances in the sample. An additional advantage of an internal standard that is chemically related to the test substance is that it may show up problems due to changes in detector response, incomplete derivatisation, etc. A disadvantage is that it may be difficult to fit an internal standard peak into a complex chromatogram.

Text references

Errington, R.J. (1997) *Advanced Practical Inorganic and Metalorganic Chemistry.* Blackie Academic and Professional, London.

Furniss, B.A., Hannaford, A.J., Smith, P.W.G. and Tatchell, A.R. (1989) *Vogel's Textbook of Practical Organic Chemistry,* 5th edn. Longman, Harlow.

Harwood, L.M., Moody, C.J. and Percy, J.M. (2000) *Experimental Organic Chemistry,* 2nd edn. Blackwell Science Ltd, Oxford.

Sources for further study

Bayne, S. and Carlin, M. (2010) *Forensic Applications of High Performance Liquid Chromatography.* CRC Press, Boca Raton.

Bliesner, D.M. (2006) *Validating Chromatographic Methods: A Practical Guide.* Wiley, New York.

Cazes, J. (2005) *Encyclopedia of Chromatography.* CRC Press, Boca Raton. Chromacademy

Grob, R.L. and Barry, E.F. (2004) *Modern Practice of Gas Chromatography,* 4th edn. Wiley, New York.

Harris, D.C. (1995) *Quantitative Chemical Analysis,* 4th edn. Freeman, New York.

Kellner, R. (1998) *Analytical Chemistry.* Wiley, Chichester.

Kromidas, S. (2000) *Practical Problem Solving in HPLC.* Wiley, Chichester.

McMaster, M. (2005) *LC – MS – a Practical User's Guide.* Wiley, New York.

Miller, J.M. (2005) *Chromatography: Concepts and Contrasts,* 2nd edn. Wiley, New York.

Schwedt, G. (1997) *The Essential Guide to Analytical Chemistry.* Wiley, Chichester.

Scott, R.P.W. (1996) *Chromatography Detectors: Design, Function and Operation.* Marcel Dekker, New York.

Skoog, D.A., West, D.M. and Holler, F.J. (1996) *Fundamentals of Analytical Chemistry,* 7th edn. Saunders, Orlando.

Study exercises

14.1 Calculate R_f values from a chromatogram. The diagram represents the separation of three pigments, A, B and C, by thin-layer chromatography.

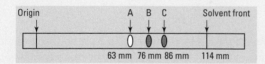

(a) What is the R_f value of each pigment?
(b) Express your answer to 3 significant figures.

14.2 Test your knowledge of detector terminology. Explain what the following acronyms stand for:

(a) FID;
(b) TCD;
(c) ECD;
(d) DAD.

14.3 Check your knowledge of liquid chromatography detectors. Make a list of the various major types of liquid chromatography detectors in order, from highest to lowest sensitivity. Which of these methods is most versatile and why?

14.4 Calculate the resolution and selectivity of two components from a chromatogram. Two compounds were separated by column chromatography, giving retention times of 4 min 30 s for A and 6 min 12 s for B, while a compound that was completely excluded from the stationary phase was eluted in 1 min 35 s. The base width of peak A was 40 s and the base width of peak B was 44 s. Calculate (a) the selectivity and (b) the resolution for these two compounds (express all answers to 3 significant figures).

14.5 Test your knowledge of chromatographic theory – define the following terms:

(a) capacity factor;
(b) separation factor;
(c) column efficiency;
(d) asymmetry factor.

15 Mass spectrometry

Understanding mass spectrometry *– since this technique does not involve the production and measurement of electromagnetic spectra and is not based on quantum principles, it should not really be referred to as a spectroscopic technique.*

Mass-to-charge ratios *– in the overwhelming majority of simple cases, the ion detected is a monopositive cation; thus $z = 1$ and the peaks seen on a low-resolution spectrometer equate to the mass of the ion.*

Determination of exact molecular mass *– high-resolution instruments enable the molecular formula of a compound to be determined by summation of the masses of the individual isotopes of atoms – e.g. both ethane and methanal have integral mass values of 30, but the accurate values are 30.046950 and 30.010565, respectively.*

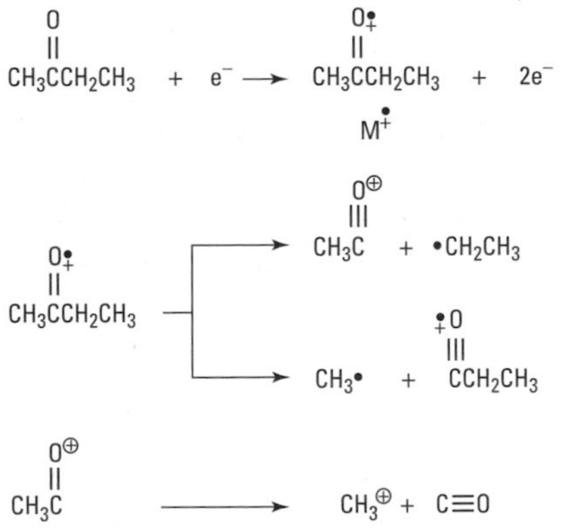

Fig. 15.1 Formation and fragmentation of a molecular ion (M^+).

Mass spectrometry (MS) involves the bombardment of molecules, in the gas phase, with electrons. An electron is lost from a molecule to give a cation, the molecular ion (M^+), which then breaks down in characteristic ways to give smaller fragments, which are cations, neutral molecules and uncharged radicals (Fig. 15.1).

The mixture of molecular ion and fragments is accelerated to specific velocities using an electric field and then separated on the basis of their different masses by deflection in a magnetic or electrostatic field. Only the cations are detected and a mass spectrum is a plot of mass-to-charge ratio (m/z) on the x-axis against the number of ions (relative abundance, RA, %) on the y-axis. A schematic of the components of a mass spectrometer is shown in Fig. 15.2 and an example of a line-graph-type mass spectrum in Fig. 15.3.

There are many types of mass spectrometer, from high-resolution double-focusing instruments, which can distinguish molecular and fragment masses to six decimal places, to 'bench-top' machines with a quadrupole mass detector, which can resolve masses up to about $m/z = 500$, but only in whole-number differences. Routinely you are most likely to encounter data from 'bench-top' instruments and, therefore, only this type of spectrum will be considered.

Basic principles

Sample handling

For low-resolution spectra obtainable from a 'bench-top' MS, samples should be presented in the same form and quantity as demanded for gas chromatographic analysis (p. 135). For high-resolution spectra, contamination of any sort must be avoided and samples (typically less than 500 mg) should be submitted in glass sample tubes with screwcaps containing an aluminium-foil insert. MS is so sensitive that the plasticisers from plastic tubes or plastic push-on caps will be detected, as will contaminating grease from ground-glass joints and taps.

Mass spectra

The standard low-resolution mass spectrum (Fig. 15.3) is computer generated, which allows easy comparison with known spectra in a computer database for identification. The peak at the highest mass number is the molecular ion (M^+), the mass of the molecule minus an electron. The peak at $RA = 100\%$, the base peak, is the most abundant fragment in the spectrum and the computer automatically scales the spectrum to give the most abundant ion as 100%. The mass spectrum of a compound gives the following information about its chemical structure:

- **molecular ion mass** – which includes information on the number of nitrogen atoms and the presence of chlorine and bromine atoms (see below), which is not easily obtained from IR and NMR spectra;
- **the most stable major fragment (base peak)** – which can be correlated to the structure of the molecule;
- **other important fragment ions** – which may give information on the structure;
- **the detailed fragmentation pattern** – which can be used to confirm a structure by reference to a library database, cf. the 'fingerprint' region in IR spectrometry (p. 187).

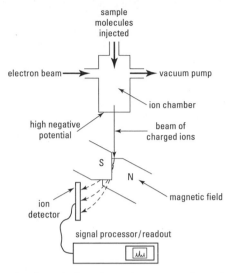

Fig. 15.2 Components of an electron-impact mass spectrometer.

Example In C_2H_5Cl, two isotopes of Cl exist – ^{35}Cl and ^{37}Cl.

For the contribution of ^{35}Cl, m/z 64 (M) = 100%, m/z 65 ($M + 1$) = 2.2%

For the contribution of ^{37}Cl, m/z 66 (M) = 33%, m/z 67 ($M + 1$) = 0.7%

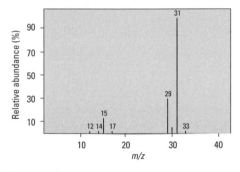

Fig. 15.3 Mass spectrum for methanol; m/z = mass-to-charge ratio.

The nitrogen rule:

- *if no N is present then the molecular ion will have an even m/z value;*
- *if an even number of N are present, then the molecular ion will have an even m/z value;*
- *if an odd number of N are present, then the molecular ion will have an odd m/z value.*

Identification of isotope peaks – the natural abundance of ^{13}C is 1.1%. For a molecule containing n carbon atoms, the probability is that 1.1 × n% of these atoms will be ^{13}C. Thus the mass spectrum of hexane (six carbons) gives a molecular ion (M^+) at $m/z = 86$ and a peak of $m/z = 87$ ($M + 1$) which is 6.6% the intensity of the M^+ peak.

Molecular ions

The m/z value of the molecular ion is the summation of all the atomic masses in the molecule, *including the naturally occurring isotopes*. For organic molecules, you will find a small peak ($M + 1$) above the apparent molecular ion mass (M^+) value due to the presence of ^{13}C. The importance of isotope peaks is the detection of chlorine and bromine in molecules since these two elements have large natural abundances of isotopes (e.g. $^{35}Cl{:}^{37}Cl = 3{:}1$ and $^{79}Br{:}^{81}Br = 1{:}1$). The mass spectra produced by molecules containing these atoms are very distinctive with peaks at $M + 2$ and even $M + 4$ and $M + 6$ depending on how many chlorine or bromine atoms are present. The identification of the number and type of halogen atoms is illustrated in Box 15.1.

Since the low-resolution mass spectrum produces integer values for m/z, the mass of M^+ indicates the number of nitrogen atoms in a nitrogen-containing molecule. If m/z for M^+ is an *odd integer*, there is an *odd number* of N atoms in the molecule and, if the value is an *even number*, then there is an *even number* of N atoms.

Base peak

The molecular ion M^+ fragments into cations, radicals, radical cations and neutral molecules of which only the positively charged species are detected. There are several possible fragmentations for each M^+ but the base peak represents the most *energetically favoured* process with the m/z value of the base peak representing the mass of the most *abundant* (and therefore most stable) positively charged species. The fragmentation of M^+ into the base peak follows the simplified rules outlined in Box 15.2, and for a more detailed interpretation you should consult the correlation tables to be found in the specialist texts referred to at the end of the section.

Fragmentation patterns

The mass spectrum of a molecule is unique and can be stored in a computer. A match of the spectrum with those in the computer library is made in terms of molecular weight and the 10 most abundant peaks and a selection of possibilities will be presented. At this point you need to correlate all the information obtained from the spectroscopic techniques described in Chapters 16, 19 and 20

Box 15.1   How to identify the number of bromine or chlorine atoms in a molecule from the molecular ion

1. Since Cl and Br have isotopes two mass numbers apart, their presence in a molecule will produce peaks at m/z values above M^+, which are two mass numbers apart, i.e. $M + 2$, $M + 4$, etc.

2. The expression for the number and intensities of these peaks is given by the expansion of the formula:

$$(a + b)^n$$

where a and b are the ratio numbers of the two atom isotopes, and n is the number of atoms.

Example 1: If the molecule contains one chlorine atom then:

$$(a + b)^n = (3 + 1)^1 = 3 + 1$$

Thus the mass spectrum of CH_3Cl would show M^+ at $m/z = 50$ ($CH_3{}^{35}Cl$) and $M + 2$ at $m/z = 52$ ($CH_3{}^{37}Cl$) and the heights of these two peaks will be in the approximate ratio 3:1 (Fig. 15.4(a)).

Example 2: If the molecule contains two chlorine atoms then:

$$(a + b)^n = a^2 + 2ab + b^2 = (3 + 1)^2 = 9 + 6 + 1$$

Thus the mass spectrum of CH_2Cl_2 would show M^+ at $m/z = 84$ ($CH_2{}^{35}Cl_2$), $M + 2$ at $m/z = 86$ ($CH_2{}^{35}Cl{}^{37}Cl$) and $M + 4$ at $m/z = 88$ ($CH_2{}^{37}Cl_2$) and the heights of these peaks will be in the approximate ratio 9:6:1 (Fig. 15.4(b)).

Example 3: If the molecule contains one bromine atom then:

$$(a + b)^n = (1 + 1)^1 = 1 + 1$$

Thus the mass spectrum of CH_3CH_2Br would show M^+ at $m/z = 108$ ($CH_3CH_2{}^{79}Br$) and $M + 2$ at $m/z = 110$ ($CH_3CH_2{}^{81}Br$) and the heights of these peaks will be in the approximate ratio 1:1 (Fig. 15.4(c)).

Example 4: If the molecule contains three bromine atoms then:

$$(a + b)^3 = a^3 + 3a^2b + 3ab^2 + b^3$$
$$= (1 + 1)^3 = 1 + 3 + 3 + 1$$

Thus the mass spectrum of $CHBr_3$ would show M^+ at $m/z = 250$ ($CH^{79}Br_3$), $M + 2$ at $m/z = 252$ ($CH^{79}Br_2{}^{81}Br$), $M + 4$ at $m/z = 254$ ($CH^{79}Br^{81}Br_2$) and $M + 6$ at $m/z = 256$ ($CH^{81}Br_3$) and the heights of the peaks will be in the approximate ratio 1:3:3:1 (Fig. 15.4(d)).

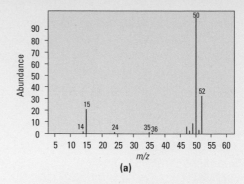

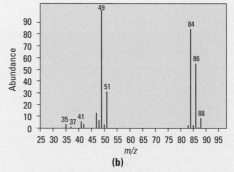

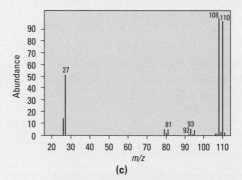

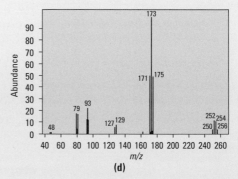

Fig. 15.4 Mass spectra of: (a) CH_3Cl; (b) CH_2Cl_2; (c) CH_3CH_2Br; (d) $CHBr_3$.

Box 15.2 Idealised fragmentation processes for the molecular ion (M^{+})

1. **α-Cleavage** – this involves breaking the 'next but one bond' to a hetero-atom (N, O, Hal, etc.) in the functional group of a molecule. The following examples illustrate the general principles:

2. **σ-Bonds in alkanes** – C—C bonds break in preference to C—H bonds and the most stable carbocation will be formed as the base peak. For example, 2,2-dimethylpentane will give the stable $(CH_3)_3C^+$ cation as the base peak instead of the less stable propyl cation CH_3CH_2.

3. **Aromatic compounds** – simple aromatics cleave to give a phenyl cation, $m/z = 77$, as the base peak, which then loses ethyne to give $m/z = 51$. Aromatics with CH_2 next to the ring give the stable tropylium cation $m/z = 91$, and then lose ethyne to $m/z = 65$.

4. **β-Cleavage or McLafferty rearrangement** – this is applied to molecules with a carbonyl group. If there is a hydrogen atom on the carbon atom four away from the carbonyl oxygen (g carbon atom), a rearrangement of the molecular ion occurs and a neutral alkene is lost from M^{+} This process occurs concurrently with the α-cleavage:

together with the chemistry of the molecule to attempt to identify the structure of the molecule.

When you attempt to interpret the mass spectrum remember that:

- **only the base peak** is almost certain to be derived from the molecular ion;
- **some lesser peaks** may result from alternative fragmentation pathways, but these may be useful in assigning structural features;
- **MS is often used to confirm information** from IR and NMR spectra – interpretation of the mass spectrum alone is very difficult, except for the simplest molecules.

Interfacing chromatography and mass spectrometry

The use and application of low-cost 'bench-top' mass spectrometers has expanded in recent years. The proliferation of this type of instrument, i.e. a chromatograph coupled to a mass spectrometer, is partly due to the lower capital cost of such instrumentation, but also to the value of the additional analytical information that is possible. This section will consider the coupling of gas chromatography to a mass spectrometer (GC–MS) and liquid chromatography to a mass spectrometer (LC–MS). The key differences between the approaches are also discussed.

Gas chromatography–mass spectrometry (GC–MS)

For specific details on capillary gas chromatography see Chapter 14. The coupling of capillary GC to MS is achieved by a heated transfer line, which allows the vapour phase compounds that have been separated by the GC to remain in the gas phase and be transported in the carrier gas, for example helium, directly to the ion source of the MS.

The heated transfer line – *must be at the same temperature as the highest temperature of the oven, otherwise the analyte will not transfer into the ionisation source.*

Ionisation sources for GC–MS

The two most common approaches for ionisation of compounds in GC–MS are those based on either chemical ionisation or electron impact. The latter is the most common. In electron impact (EI) mode, electrons produced from a heated tungsten or rhenium filament (cathode) are accelerated towards an anode, colliding with the vaporised sample (X) and producing (positively) charged ions (Fig. 15.5), which can be separated by MS. This can be expressed in the form of the following equation:

GCMS (EI) *is the most commonly used instrument for the forensic identification of drugs (see Chapters 38 and 39).*

$$X_{(g)} + e^- \rightarrow X_{(g)} + 2e^- \qquad [15.1]$$

Alternatively, in chemical ionisation (CI) mode a reagent gas (e.g. methane), is ionised by electron bombardment to produce a molecular ion (CH_4^+). This molecular ion then reacts with neutral methane to produce a reactant ion (CH_5^+). It is this reactant ion that interacts with the compound molecule to produce a (positively) charged ion which can be separated by MS. The difference, in this mode of ionisation, is that the resultant (positively) charged ion has the molecular weight of the compound plus one (i.e. XH^+). The chemical ionisation mode can be expressed in the form of the following equations:

$$CH_4 + e^- \rightarrow CH_4^+ + 2e^- \qquad [15.2]$$

$$CH_4^+ + CH_4 \rightarrow CH_5^+ + CH_3^* \qquad [15.3]$$

$$X_{(g)} + CH_5^+ \rightarrow XH_{(g)}^+ + CH_4 \qquad [15.4]$$

It is clear from the above that the CI mode is an indirect method of ionisation.

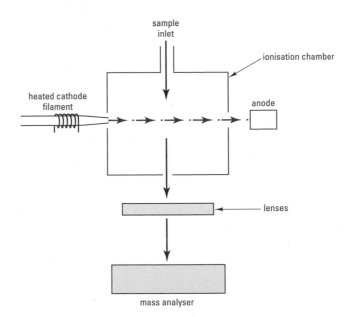

Fig. 15.5 Electron impact ionisation.

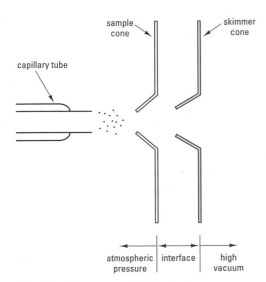

Fig. 15.6 Electrospray ionisation.

Applicability of LC–MS – *APCI is more focused on the analysis of low to moderate molecular weight compounds with low to moderate polarity, whereas ES is focused on large molecular weight compounds of high polarity.*

Liquid chromatography–mass spectrometry (LC–MS)

While developments in interface technology have improved considerably in recent years, it is true to say that it went through many developments including moving belt transport interfaces and thermospray. Modern instruments have relied on the use of two approaches both of which allow ionisation of compounds at atmospheric pressure and outside of the MS. The two approaches are electrospray (ES) ionisation and atmospheric pressure chemical ionisation (APCI).

Electrospray (ES) ionisation

A schematic diagram of the electrospray interface is shown in Fig. 15.6. In operation, solvent from the high-performance liquid chromatography system is pumped through a stainless steel capillary tube, which is held at a high potential (3–5 kV). The presence of this electric field causes the solvent to be sprayed from the end of the capillary tube, hence the name. This action causes highly charged solvent and solute ion droplets to be formed. Solvent from these droplets evaporates, assisted by a flow of warm carrier gas (nitrogen). The generated ions (solvent and solute) are transported into the high-vacuum system of the mass spectrometer via a noz-zle-skimmer arrangement. The electrospray and nozzle-skimmer arrangement are often positioned at right-angles to one another. By allowing a potential gradient to exist between the electrospray and nozzle-skimmer arrangement, the generated ions are 'pulled' into the mass spectrometer, while at the same time allowing some discrimination between the desirable solute ions and unwanted extraneous material, for example salts present in the buffer of the HPLC mobile phase.

Atmospheric pressure chemical ionisation (APCI)

A schematic diagram of the atmospheric pressure chemical ionisation interface is shown in Fig. 15.7. Its operation is similar to that of the ES ionisation approach, except that in APCI the voltage is not applied to the stainless steel capillary tubing but to a corona pin. Solvent from the HPLC system is pumped through a heated stainless steel capillary tube, which is surrounded by a coaxial flow of nitrogen gas. The combination of liquid solvent exiting the capillary

Mass spectrometry

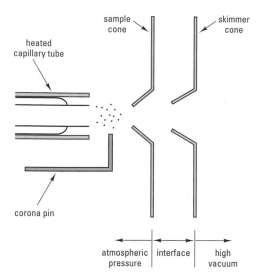

Fig. 15.7 Atmospheric pressure chemical ionisation.

***Understanding units** – 'amu' or atomic mass units are used to represent M_r on mass spectra. An alternative, often used in the biological field, is 'da' or Daltons.*

Definition

Plasma – a hot, ionised gas.

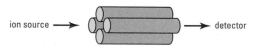

Fig. 15.8 Quadrupole mass spectrometer.

tube and the flow of nitrogen gas produces an aerosol. Desolvation takes place easily due to the heat applied to the solvent via the heated capillary tubing. Located immediately in front of the capillary tube is the probe or corona pin to which is applied a high voltage (2.5–3 kV). In the region around the corona discharge, a plasma is formed due to collisions and charge transfer processes. Therefore, this plasma will be made up of solute and solvent ions. In the same manner as in ES ionisation (p. 149), the generated ions (solvent and solute) are transported into the high-vacuum system of the MS.

In ES ionisation and APCI, molecules can form singly charged ions by loss or gain of a proton (hydrogen atom) – i.e. they can form ions represented as $[M + 1]^+$ or $[M-1]^-$, where M_r = the relative molecular mass of the compound. Therefore, it is possible to operate the mass spectrometer in positive ion mode and determine peaks at m/z ratios of $M + 1$ (e.g. basic compounds typified by amines), or in negative ion mode and determine peaks at m/z ratios of $M - 1$ (e.g. acidic compounds typified by carboxylic acids). Both ES and APCI are regarded as 'soft' ionisation techniques, and as such produce little or no fragmentation patterns. Care is also needed in the interpretation of mass spectra, particularly in the presence of additives (buffer solution) or contaminants. This is because adduct formation is possible. This manifests itself in the form of m/z ratios of $M + 18$ for ammonium adducts or $M + 23$ for sodium adducts.

Types of mass spectrometer

A variety of mass spectrometers are available for the mass/charge separation of charged particles. The most popular are the quadrupole mass spectrometer, ion trap mass spectrometer and the time-of-flight mass spectrometer. While each operates in a different manner, all are capable of separating charged particles on the basis of their m/z ratios.

Quadrupole mass spectrometer

Essentially a quadrupole mass spectrometer consists of four parallel rods (Fig. 15.8). To these rods voltages (both DC and RF) are applied – different voltages are applied to adjacent rods while opposite rods are electrically connected, i.e. have the same voltages applied. By altering the applied voltages, ions of a particular m/z ratio can pass the mass spectrometer to the detector. At the same time, other ions become unstable and are lost. By changing the applied voltages, particles of different m/z ratios can pass through the mass spectrometer.

Ion trap mass spectrometer

The ion trap mass spectrometer consists of three cylindrically symmetrical electrodes to which voltages are applied. By altering the applied voltages, ions of increasing m/z ratios leave the ion trap and travel on to the detector (Fig. 15.9).

Time-of-flight mass spectrometer

In a time-of-flight mass spectrometer, charged particles are separated according to their velocity. Essentially, a charged particle accelerated by application of a voltage has a resulting velocity that is characteristic of its m/z ratio. The ability to separate different charged particles can be improved by increasing the flight time of ions. This is achieved via a reflectron. It is not uncommon to find that

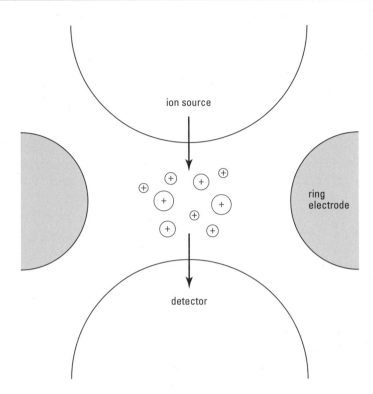

Fig. 15.9 Ion trap mass spectrometer.

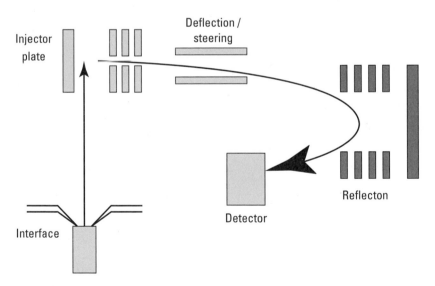

Fig. 15.10 Time-of-flight mass spectrometer.

pre-separation of ions is achieved in a time-of-flight mass spectrometer via an initial quadrupole mass spectrometer (Fig. 15.10).

Detectors for MS

The most common detector of positive ions in chromatography–mass spectrometry is the electron multiplier tube (EMT). The EMT (Fig. 15.11) consists of an open aperture to which is applied a high voltage (3kV). The positive ions are attracted to the high negative potential of the EMT. For each positive ion that strikes the internal surface of the EMT, the semiconductor coating produces

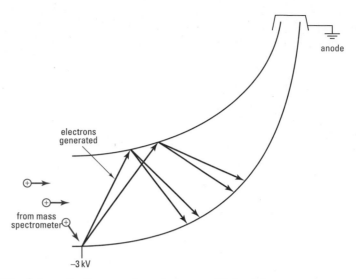

Fig. 15.11 Schematic diagram of an electron multiplier tube.

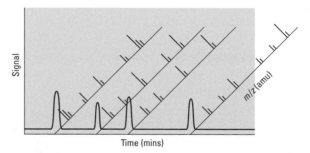

Fig. 15.12 Schematic representation of a typical output from a chromatography–mass spectrometer system.

one electron. The generated electrons (negatively charged) are attracted to an area that is less negative than the open aperture. This is achieved by having the narrow end of the device earthed (zero potential). By this process the generated electrons are drawn deeper into the EMT. On their way, they strike the internal surfaces of the device producing more secondary electrons. All the generated secondary electrons produced from the initial positive ion are collected and measured as an electric current.

Data acquisition

The main reason that mass spectrometry is linked to chromatographic separation is because of the ability of the mass spectrometer to perform quantitative analysis, and allow mass spectral data to be produced. So, while quantitative analysis is possible for a multitude of other detectors (pp. 137–139) it is an additional benefit for the identification of compounds in forensic science. A mass spectrometer produces data that has time, signal intensity and spectral dimensions (Fig. 15.12). Two possible data acquisition modes are possible in mass spectrometry: full scan mode and selected ion monitoring mode.

Full scan mode

In full scan mode, ions produced by the ion source are separated with respect to their *m/z* ratio by the mass spectrometer scanning the entire mass range, typically 0–400 amu, and a mass spectrum is recorded at the detector. In this manner, all ions separated by the mass spectrometer are detected. As the mass spectrometer is coupled up to a chromatographic separation system, all compounds separated with respect to time are monitored in terms of a chromatogram – a plot of signal intensity versus time (p. 126) – and mass spectral information. Depending on the method of ionisation used, it should be possible to identify unknown compounds by their fragmentation patterns or by their molecular weight (see p. 145). The operator is assisted, most notably in GC–MS, by the presence of computer databases that allow searching for particular compounds and comparison of mass spectral information.

Selected ion monitoring (SIM) mode   In contrast to the full scan mode, the SIM mode allows only specified ions to be monitored. This leads to enhanced sensitivity, as the mass spectrometer is not monitoring m/z ratios where no ions are present. The disadvantages of this approach are that only known compounds are monitored in the chromatogram, and no mass spectral information is available. This approach is particularly useful once unknown compounds have been identified via the full scan mode, leading to enhanced sensitivity and selectivity.

> **To identify** any unknown compound in your sample it must be identified in full scan mode.

> **The sensitivity** of the instrument can be improved by converting the analysis to SIM mode, typically with the base peak and two daughter ions BUT only after the identification of the compound in full scan mode.

> **Identification and quantitation in SIM**: the base peak (100%) and two fragment ions (at their respective percentages) based on a full scan mass spectrum would be needed to identify the compound. Quantitation should be performed using the base peak. This allows for sensitive and consistent detection, e.g. PAH's in soil or a drug in a blood sample.

Sources for further study

Dass, C. (2007) *Fundamentals of Contemporary Mass Spectrometry*. Wiley, Chichester.

de Hoffmann, E. and Stroobant, V. (2007) *Mass Spectrometry: Principles and Applications,* 3rd edn. Wiley, Chichester.

McLafferty, F.W. (1993) *Interpretation of Mass Spectra,* 4th edn. University Science Books, Mill Valley.

McMaster, M. (2008) *GC/MS: A Practical User's Guide,* 2nd edn. Wiley, Chichester.

Watson, J.T. and Sparkman, O.D. (2007) *Introduction to Mass Spectrometry: Instrumentation, Applications and Strategies for Data Interpretation,* 4th edn. Wiley, Chichester.

Study exercises

15.1 Calculate the molecular mass and elucidate formula. Using the following information, calculate the molecular mass and predict the formula of compound A.

Compound A

	Abundance		Abundance
m/z 25	13.7%	m/z 60	4.6%
m/z 26	34%	m/z 61	6.8%
m/z 27	100%	m/z 62	76.6%
m/z 35	8.7%	m/z 63	3.8%
m/z 37	2.8%	m/z 64	24.2%

15.2 Test your knowledge of MS terminology. Explain what the following acronyms stand for:

(a) EI^+;
(b) CI^-;
(c) APCI;
(d) ESI.

15.3 Predicting a mass spectrum from a chemical structure. Predict the mass spectrum likely to be observed for MDMA.

3,4-methylene dioxymethyl amphetamine (MDMA)

16 Basic spectroscopy

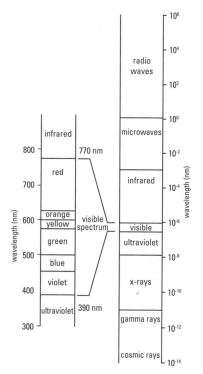

Fig. 16.1 **The electromagnetic spectrum.**

Definition

Absorbance (*A*) – this is given by:

$$A = \log_{10}\left(\frac{I_0}{I}\right).$$

Usually shown as A_x where '*x*' is the wavelength, in nanometres.

As an example, for incident light (I_0) = 1.00 and emergent light (I) = 0.16 (expressed in relative terms), A 5 $\log_{10}(1.00 \div 0.16)$ = $\log_{10} 6.25$ = 0.796 (to three significant figures).

The absorption and emission of electromagnetic radiation (Fig. 16.1) of specific energy (wavelength) are characteristic features of many molecules, involving the movement of electrons between different energy states, in accordance with the laws of quantum mechanics. Electrons in atoms and molecules are distributed at various energy levels, but are mainly at the lowest energy level, usually termed the ground state. When exposed to energy (e.g. from electromagnetic radiation), electrons may be excited to higher energy levels (excited states), with the associated absorption of energy at specific wavelengths giving rise to an absorption spectrum. One quantum of energy is absorbed for a single electron transition from the ground state to an excited state. On the other hand, when an electron returns to its ground state, one quantum of energy is released. This may be dissipated to the surrounding molecules (as heat) or may give rise to an emission spectrum. The energy change (ΔE) for an electron moving between two energy states, E_1 and E_2, is given by the equation:

$$\Delta E = E_1 - E_2 = h\nu \qquad [16.1]$$

where h is the Planck constant (p. 25) and is the frequency of the electromagnetic radiation expressed in Hz or s^{-1}. Frequency is related to wavelength (l, usually expressed in nm) and the speed of electromagnetic radiation, c (p. 25) by the expression:

$$\nu = \frac{c}{\lambda} \qquad [16.2]$$

UV/visible spectrophotometry

This is a widely used technique for measuring the absorption of radiation in the visible and ultraviolet regions of the spectrum. A spectrophotometer is an instrument designed to allow precise measurement at a particular wavelength, while a colorimeter is a simpler instrument that uses filters to measure broader wavebands (e.g. light in the green, red or blue regions of the visible spectrum).

Principles of light absorption

Two fundamental principles govern the absorption of light passing through a solution:

- The absorption of light is exponentially related to the number of molecules of the absorbing solute that are encountered, i.e. the solute concentration [C].
- The absorption of light is exponentially related to the length of the light path through the absorbing solution, *l*.

 KEY POINT *The Beer–Lambert relationship, expressed in mathematical form in eqn [16.3], states that there is a direct linear relationship between the concentration of a substance in a solution, [C], and the absorbance of that solution, A.*

These two principles are combined in the Beer–Lambert relationship (sometimes referred to simply as 'Beer's Law'), which is usually expressed in terms of absorbance (*A*) to:

$$A = \varepsilon l[C] \qquad [16.3]$$

Definition

Transmittance (T) – this is usually expressed as a percentage, where

$$T = \left(\frac{I}{I_0}\right) \times 100(\%)$$

As an example, for incident light (I_0) = 1.00 and emergent light (I) = 0.275 (expressed in relative terms) then transmittance, $T = (0.275 \div 1.00) \times 100 = 27.5\%$.

Examples The molar absorptivity of NADH is 6.22×10^3 L mol^{-1}cm^{-1} at 340 nm. For a test solution giving an absorbance of 0.21 in a cuvette with a light path of 5 mm, using eqn [16.3] this is equal to a concentration of:

$$0.21 = 6.22 \times 10^3 \times 0.5 \times [C]$$

$$[C] = 0.0000675 \text{ mol L}^{-1}$$

(or 67.5 μmol L^{-1}).

The specific absorptivity (10 gL^{-1}) of double-stranded DNA is 200 at 260 nm, therefore a solution containing 1 gL^{-1} will have an absorbance of 200/10=20. For a DNA solution, giving an absorbance of 0.35 in a cuvette with a light path of 1.0 cm, using eqn [16.3] this is equal to a concentration of:

$$0.35 = 20 \times 1.0 \times [C]$$

$$[C] = 0.0175 \text{ gL}^{-1}$$

(equivalent to 17.5 μg mL^{-1}).

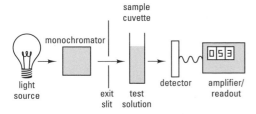

Fig. 16.2 Components of a UV/visible spectrophotometer.

where ε is a constant for the absorbing substance and the wavelength, termed the absorption coefficient or absorptivity, l is the length of the light path through the solution and $[C]$ is the solute concentration. This relationship is extremely useful, since most spectrophotometers are constructed to give a direct measurement of absorbance (A), sometimes also termed extinction (E), of a solution (older texts may use the outdated term optical density, OD). Note that for substances obeying the Beer–Lambert relationship, A is linearly related to $[C]$. Absorbance at a particular wavelength is often shown as a subscript (e.g. A_{550} represents the absorbance at 550 nm). The proportion of light passing through the solution is known as the transmittance (T), and is calculated as the ratio of the emergent and incident light intensities.

Some instruments have two scales:

- **an exponential scale** from zero to infinity, measuring absorbance;
- **a linear scale** from 0 to 100, measuring (per cent) transmittance.

For most practical purposes, the Beer–Lambert relationship applies and you should use the absorbance scale.

UV/visible spectrophotometer

The principal components of a UV/visible spectrophotometer are shown in Fig. 16.2. High-intensity tungsten bulbs are used as the light source in basic instruments, capable of operating in the visible region (i.e. 400–700 nm). Deuterium lamps are used for UV spectrophotometry (200–400 nm); these lamps are fitted with quartz envelopes, since glass does not transmit UV radiation.

A major improvement over the simple colorimeter is the use of a diffraction grating to produce a parallel beam of monochromatic light from the (polychromatic) light source. In practice, the light emerging from such a monochromator is not of a single wavelength, but is a narrow band of wavelengths. This bandwidth is an important characteristic, since it determines the wavelengths used in absorption measurements – the bandwidth of basic spectrophotometers is around 5–10 nm, whereas research instruments have bandwidths of less than 1 nm.

Bandwidth is affected by the width of the exit slit (the slit width), since the bandwidth will be reduced by decreasing the slit width. To obtain accurate data at a particular wavelength setting, the narrowest possible slit width should be used. However, decreasing the slit width also reduces the amount of light reaching the detector, decreasing the signal-to-noise ratio. The extent to which the slit width can be reduced depends on the sensitivity and stability of the detection/amplification system and the presence of stray light.

Most UV/visible spectrophotometers are designed to take cuvettes with an optical path length of 10 mm. Disposable plastic cuvettes are suitable for routine work in the visible range using aqueous and alcohol-based solvents, while glass cuvettes are useful for other organic solvents. Glass cuvettes are manufactured to more exacting standards, so use optically matched glass cuvettes for accurate work, especially at low absorbances (< 0.1), where any differences in the optical properties of cuvettes for reference and test samples will be pronounced. Glass and plastic absorb UV light and quartz cuvettes must be used at wavelengths below 300 nm.

 KEY POINT *Before taking a measurement, make sure that cuvettes are clean, unscratched, dry on the outside, filled to the correct level and located in the correct position in their sample holders.*

Basic spectroscopy

Choosing the appropriate cuvettes – silica and quartz cuvettes can be used for applications across the UV region (200–370 nm) and the visible region (370–850 nm); glass and plastic cuvettes can be used for applications across the visible region (370–850 nm).

Proteins and nucleic acids in biological samples can accumulate on the inside faces of glass/quartz cuvettes, so remove any deposits using acetone on a cotton bud, or soak overnight in 1 mol L^{-1} nitric acid. Corrosive and hazardous solutions must be used in cuvettes with tightly fitting lids, to prevent damage to the instrument and to reduce the risk of accidental spillage.

Basic instruments use photocells similar to those used in simple colorimeters or photodiode detectors. In many cases, a different photocell must be used at wavelengths above and below 550–600 nm, due to differences in the sensitivity of such detectors over the visible waveband. The detectors used in more sophisticated instruments give increased sensitivity and stability when compared to photocells.

Digital displays are increasingly used in preference to needle-type meters, as they are not prone to parallax errors and misreading of the absorbance scale. Some digital instruments can be calibrated to give a direct readout of the concentration of the test substance.

> **KEY POINT Basic spectrophotometers are most accurate within the absorbance range from 0.00 to 1.00 and your calibration standards and test solutions should be prepared to give readings within this range.**

Types of UV/visible spectrophotometer

Basic instruments are single-beam spectrophotometers, in which there is only one light path. The instrument is set to zero absorbance using a blank solution, which is then replaced by the test solution, to obtain an absorbance reading. An alternative approach is used in double-beam spectrophotometers, where the light beam from the monochromator is split into two separate beams, one beam passing through the test solution and the other through a reference blank. Absorbance is then measured by an electronic circuit, which compares the output from the reference (blank) and sample cuvettes. Double-beam spectrophotometry reduces measurement errors caused by fluctuations in output from the light source or changes in the sensitivity of the detection system, since reference and test solutions are measured at the same time (Box 16.1). Recording spectrophotometers are double-beam instruments, designed for use with a chart recorder, either by recording the difference in absorbance between reference and test solutions across a predetermined waveband to give an absorption spectrum (Fig. 16.3), or by recording the change in absorbance at a particular wavelength as a function of time (e.g. in an enzyme assay).

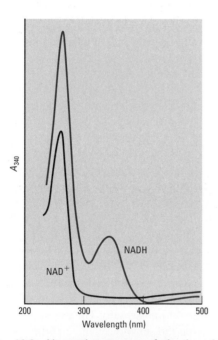

Fig. 16.3 Absorption spectra of nicotinamide adenine dinucleotide in oxidised (NAD+) and reduced (NADH) form. Note the 340nm absorption peak (A 340), used for quantitative work.

Measuring absorbances in colorimetric analysis – if any final solution has an absorbance that is too high to be read with accuracy on your spectrophotometer (e.g. A. > 2), it is bad practice to dilute the solution so that it can be measured. This dilutes both the sample molecules and the colour reagents to an equal extent. Instead, you should dilute the original sample and reassay.

Quantitative spectrophotometric analysis

A single (purified) substance in solution can be quantified using the Beer–Lambert relationship (eqn [16.3]), provided its absorptivity is known at a particular wavelength (usually at the absorption maximum for the substance, since this will give the greatest sensitivity). The molar absorptivity is the absorbance given by a solution with a concentration of 1 mol L^{-1} (= 1 kmol m^{-3}) of the compound in a light path of 1cm. The appropriate value may be available from tabulated spectral data, or it can be determined experimentally by measuring the absorbance of known concentrations of the substance (Box 16.1) and plotting a standard curve (see Chapter 51). This should confirm that the relationship is linear over the desired concentration range and the slope of the line will give the molar absorptivity.

The specific absorptivity is the absorbance given by a solution containing 10 g L^{-1} (i.e. 1% w/v) of the compound in a light path of 1 cm. This is useful

Box 16.1 How to use a spectrophotometer

1. **Switch on and select the correct lamp** for your measurements (e.g. deuterium for UV, tungsten for visible light).

2. **Allow up to 15 min for the lamp to warm up** and for the instrument to stabilise before use.

3. **Select the appropriate wavelength** – on older instruments a dial is used to adjust the mono chromator, whereas newer machines have microprocessor-controlled wavelength selection.

4. **Select the appropriate detector** – some instruments choose the correct detector automatically (on the basis of the specified wavelength), while others have manual selection.

5. **Choose the correct slit width** (if available) – this may be specified in the protocol you are following, or may be chosen on the manufacturer's recommendations.

6. **Insert appropriate reference blank(s)** – single-beam instruments use a single cuvette, while double-beam instruments use two cuvettes (a matched pair for accurate work). The reference blanks should match the test solution in all respects apart from the substance under test, i.e. they should contain all reagents apart from this substance. *Make sure that the cuvettes are positioned correctly, with their polished (transparent) faces in the light path, and that they are accurately located in the cuvette holder(s).*

7. **Check/adjust the 0% transmittance** – most instruments have a control that allows you to zero the detector output in the absence of any light (termed 'dark current' correction). Some microprocessor-controlled instruments carry out this step automatically.

8. **Set the absorbance reading to zero** – usually via a dial, or digital readout.

9. **Analyse your samples** – replace the appropriate reference blank with a test sample, allow the absorbance reading to stabilise (5–10 s) and read the absorbance value from the meter/readout device. For absorbance readings greater than 1 (i.e. > 10% transmission), the signal-to-noise ratio is too low for accurate results. Your analysis may require a calibration curve or you may be able to use the Beer–Lambert relationship (eqn [16.3]) to determine the concentration of test substance in your samples.

10. **Check the scale zero at regular intervals** – using a reference blank (e.g. after every 10 samples).

11. **Check the reproducibility of the instrument** – measure the absorbance of a single solution several times during your analysis. It should give the same value.

Problems (and solutions): inaccurate/unstable readings are most often due to incorrect use of cuvettes – for example dirt, fingerprints or test solution on outside of cuvette (wipe the clear faces using a soft tissue before insertion into the cuvette holder and handle only by the opaque faces); condensation (if cold solutions aren't allowed to reach room temperature before use); air bubbles (which scatter light and increase the absorbance – tap gently to remove); insufficient solution (causing refraction of light at the meniscus); particulate material in the solution (check for 'cloudiness' in the solution and centrifuge before use, where necessary); incorrect positioning in light path (locate in correct position).

for substances of unknown molecular weight (e.g. proteins or nucleic acids), where the amount of substance in solution is expressed in terms of its mass, rather than as a molar concentration. For use in eqn [16.3], the specific absorptivity should be divided by 10 to give the solute concentration in $g\ L^{-1}$.

This simple approach cannot be used for mixed samples where several substances have a significant absorption at a particular wavelength. In such cases, it may be possible to estimate the amount of each substance by measuring the absorbance at several wavelengths, for example protein estimation in the presence of nucleic acids.

Fluorescence

With most molecules, after electrons are raised to a higher energy level by absorption of electromagnetic radiation, they soon fall back to the ground state

Basic spectroscopy

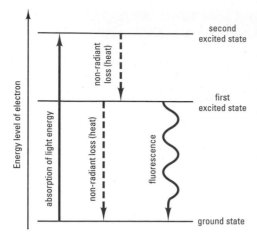

Fig. 16.4 Energy levels and energy transitions in fluorescence.

Table 16.1 Examples of compounds with intrinsic fluorescence

Drugs
Aspirin, morphine, barbiturates, propanalol, ampicillin, tetracyclines

Vitamins
Riboflavin, vitamins A, B6 and E, nicotinamide

Pollutants
Naphthalene, anthracene, benzopyrene

Fig. 16.5 Fluorescein – a widely used fluorescent label, showing (i) a planar conjugated system of fused rings; (ii) heteroatoms within the conjugated structures; (iii) an electron-donating group; and (iv) an electron-attracting group. In fluoregenic enzyme substrates, linkage is usually via one of the two hydroxyl groups, while in fluorescein-labelled proteins, linkage is via an isothiocyanate group (NCS) on the lowermost ring (*).

by radiationless transfer of energy (heat) to the solvent. However, with some molecules, the events shown in Fig. 16.4 may occur – electrons may lose only part of their energy by non-radiant routes and the rest may be emitted as electromagnetic radiation, a phenomenon known as fluorescence. Since not all of the energy that was absorbed is emitted (due to non-radiant loss), the wavelength of the fluorescent light is longer than the absorbed light (longer wavelength = lower energy). Thus, a fluorescent molecule has both an absorption spectrum and an emission spectrum. The difference between the excitation wavelength (λ_{ex}) and the emission wavelength (λ_{em}), measured in nm, is known as the Stokes shift, and is fundamental to the sensitivity of fluorescence techniques. The existence of a Stokes shift means that emitted light can be detected against a low background, independently of the excitation wavelength.

Most fluorescent molecules have the following features:

- **a highly conjugated system** (alternating double and single bonds), involving aromatic or heterocyclic rings, usually containing O or N (as heteroatoms);
- **a condensed system** of fused rings, with one or more heteroatoms;
- **electron-donating groups** such as $-OH$, $-OCH_3$, $-NH_2$ and $-NR_2$, together with electron-attracting groups elsewhere in the molecule, in conjugation with the electron-donating groups;
- **a rigid, planar structure.**

Figure 16.5 illustrates many of these features for fluorescein, used in a range of forensic science applications including visualisation of nucleic acids, fluorescent antibody tests, etc.

Fluorescence spectrophotometry

The principal components of a fluorescence spectrophotometer (fluorimeter) are shown in Fig. 16.6. The instrument contains two monochromators, one to select the excitation wavelength and the other to monitor the light emitted, usually at 90° to the incident beam (though light is actually emitted in all directions). As an example, the wavelengths used to measure the highly fluorescent compound aminomethylcoumarin are 388 nm (excitation) and 440 nm (emission). Some examples of molecules with intrinsic fluorescence are given in Table 16.1.

Compared with UV/visible spectrophotometry, fluorescence spectroscopy has certain advantages, including:

- **enhanced sensitivity (up to 1,000-fold)** – the emitted light is detected against a background of zero, in contrast to spectrophotometry where small changes in signal are measured against a large 'background' (see eqn [16.3]);
- **increased specificity** – not one, but two specific wavelengths are required for a particular compound.

However, there are also certain drawbacks:

- **Not all compounds show intrinsic fluorescence** – limiting its application. However, some non-fluorescent compounds may be coupled to fluorescent dyes, or fluorophores (e.g. proteins may be coupled to fluorescamine).
- **The light emitted can be less than expected due to quenching** – when substances in the sample (e.g. oxygen) either interfere with energy transfer, or absorb the emitted light (in some instances, the sample molecules may self-quench if they are present at high concentration).

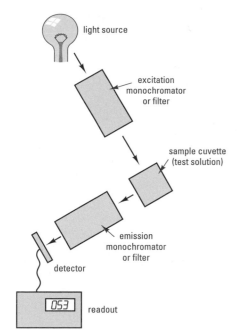

Fig. 16.6 Components of a fluorimeter (fluorescence spectrophotometer). Note that sample cuvettes for fluorimetry must have clear sides all round.

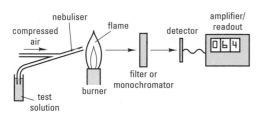

Fig. 16.7 Components of a flame photometer.

Safe working in atomic spectroscopy – *the use of high-pressure gas cylinders can be particularly hazardous. Always consult a member of staff before using such apparatus.*

SAFETY NOTE **Carrying out acid digestion** – *always work within a fume hood and wear gloves and safety glasses throughout the procedure. Rinse any spillages with a large volume of water.*

Plotting calibration curves in quantitative analysis – *do not force your calibration line to pass through zero if it clearly does not. There is no reason to assume that the zero value is any more accurate than any other reading you have made.*

The sensitivity of fluorescence has made it invaluable in techniques in which specific antibodies are linked to a fluorescent dye, including:

- **fluorescence immunoassay (FIA);**
- **immunohistochemistry,** which requires the use of a fluorescence microscope – for example, using fluorescent antibodies, or fluorescent *in situ* hybridisation (FISH) for nucleic acid detection.

Phosphorescence and luminescence

A phenomenon related to fluorescence is phosphorescence, which is the emission of light following inter-system crossing between electron orbitals (e.g. between excited singlet and triplet states). Light emission in phosphorescence usually continues after the exciting energy is no longer applied and, since more energy is lost in inter-system crossing, the emission wavelengths are generally longer than with fluorescence. Phosphorescence has limited applications in forensic science.

Luminescence (or chemiluminescence) is another phenomenon in which light is emitted, but here the energy for the initial excitation of electrons is provided by a chemical reaction rather than by electromagnetic radiation. An example is the action of the enzyme luciferase, extracted from fireflies, which catalyses the following reaction:

$$\text{luciferin} + \text{ATP} + O_2 \Rightarrow \text{oxyluciferin} + \text{AMP}$$
$$+ PP_1 + CO_2 + \text{light} \qquad\qquad [16.4]$$

The light produced is either yellow-green (560 nm) or red (620 nm). This system can be used in biomolecular analysis of ATP (e.g. to determine ATP concentration in a biological sample). Measurement can be performed using the photomultiplier tubes of a scintillation counter to detect the emitted light, with calibration of the output using a series of standards of known ATP content.

Atomic spectroscopy

Atoms of certain metals will absorb and emit radiation of specific wavelengths when heated in a flame, in direct proportion to the number of atoms present. Atomic spectrophotometric techniques measure the absorption or emission of particular wavelengths of UV and visible light to identify and quantify such metals.

Flame atomic emission spectrophotometry (or flame photometry)

The principal components of a flame photometer are shown in Fig. 16.7. A liquid sample is converted into an aerosol in a nebuliser (atomiser) before being introduced into the flame, where a small proportion (typically less than 1 in 10,000) of the atoms will be raised to a higher energy level, releasing this energy as light of a specific wavelength, which is passed through a filter to a photocell detector. Flame photometry can be used to measure the alkali metal ions K^+, Na^+, and Ca^{++} in biological fluids (Box 16.2).

Atomic absorption spectrophotometry (or flame absorption spectrophotometry)

This technique is applicable to a broad range of metal ions, including those of Pb, Cu and Zn. It relies on the absorption of light of a specific wavelength by atoms dispersed in a flame. The appropriate wavelength is provided by a cathode lamp, coated with the element to be analysed, focused through the flame and on

Basic spectroscopy

Practical advantages over flame photometry include:

- *improved sensitivity;*
- *increased precision;*
- *decreased interference.*

to the detector. When the sample is introduced into the flame, it will decrease the light detected in direct proportion to the amount of metal present.

Newer variants of this method include flameless atomic absorption spectrophotometry and atomic fluorescence spectrophotometry, both of which are more sensitive than the flame absorption technique. Chapter 17 gives further details on the practical applications of atomic spectroscopy.

Sources for further study

Christian, G.D., Dasgupta, P.K. and Schug, K.A. (2014) *Analytical Chemistry,* 7th edn. Wiley, Chichester.

Gore, M.G. (ed.) (2000) *Spectrophotometry and Spectrofluorimetry: A Practical Approach,* 2nd edn. Oxford University Press, Oxford.

Harris, D.A. (1996) *Light Spectroscopy.* Bios, Oxford

Harris, D.C. (2010) *Quantitative Chemical Analysis,* 8th edn. Freeman, New York.

Skoog, D.A., West, D.M. and Holler, F.J. (1996) *Fundamentals of Analytical Chemistry,* 7th edn. Brooks Cole, Belmont, CA.

Wilson, K. and Walker, J. (eds.) (2005) *Principles and Techniques of Practical Biochemistry and Molecular Biology,* 6th edn. Cambridge University Press, Cambridge.

Study exercises

16.1 Write a protocol for using a spectrophotometer. After reading this chapter, prepare a detailed stepwise protocol explaining how to use one of the spectrophotometers in your department. Ask another student or a tutor to evaluate your protocol and provide you with feedback.

16.2 Use the Beer–Lambert relationship in quantitative spectrophotometric analysis. Calculate the following (express your answer to three significant figures):

(a) The mass concentration ($\mu g\ mL^{-1}$) of double-stranded DNA in a test solution giving an absorbance at 260 nm (A_{260}) of 0.57 in a cuvette of

path length 5 mm, based on an absorptivity of $20\ g^{-1}\ cm^{-1}$.

(b) The amount (ng) of double-stranded DNA in a 50 μl sub-sample from a test solution where $A_{260} = 0.31$ in a cuvette of path length 1 cm, based on an absorptivity of $20\ g^{-1}\ cm^{-1}$.

16.3 Determine the molar absorptivity of a substance in aqueous solution. A solution of p-nitrophenol containing $8.8\ \mu g\ mL^{-1}$ gave an absorbance of 0.535 at 404 nm in a cuvette of path length 1 cm. What is the molar absorptivity of *p*-nitrophenol at 404 nm, expressed to 3 significant figures? (Note: M_r of *p*-nitrophenol is 291.27.)

17 Atomic spectroscopy

 SAFETY NOTE *In atomic spectroscopy, the use of high-pressure gas sources, e.g. cylinders, can be particularly hazardous. Always consult a demonstrator or technician before use.*

Atomic spectroscopy is a quantitative technique used for the determination of metals in samples. Atomic spectroscopy is characterised by two main techniques – atomic absorption spectroscopy and atomic emission spectroscopy. Atomic absorption spectroscopy (AAS) is normally carried out with a flame (FAAS), although other devices can be used. Atomic emission spectroscopy (AES) is typified by the use of a flame photometer (p. 159) or an inductively coupled plasma. The flame photometer is normally used for elements in groups I and II of the Periodic Table only, i.e. alkali and alkali earth metals.

In both AAS and AES the substance to be analysed must be in solution. In order to do quantitative analysis – i.e. determine how much of the metal is present – the preparation of analytical standard solutions is necessary. Although the concentration range over which the technique can be used may be different, for various instruments, the principles associated with the preparation of analytical standard solutions are the same (Boxes 17.1–5).

AAS

The components of an atomic absorption spectrometer are a radiation source, an atomisation cell, a sample introduction system, a method of wavelength selection and a detector (Fig. 17.1).

Radiation source

The main radiation source for AAS is the hollow-cathode lamp (HCL). The HCL (Fig. 17.3) emits radiation characteristic of a particular element. The choice of HCL for AAS is simple. For example, if you are analysing for lead, you will need a lead-coated HCL. It is normal to pre-warm the HCL for about 10 min prior to use. This can be done either by using a separate pre-heater unit, capable of warming up several HCLs simultaneously, or by inserting the HCL

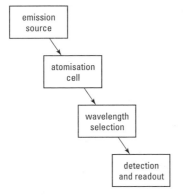

Fig. 17.1 Components of an atomic absorption spectrometer.

Box 17.1 How to prepare a 1,000 μg mL^{-1} stock solution of a metal ion from a metal salt

Stock solutions can be prepared directly from reagent-grade chemicals. It is important to use only reagent-grade chemicals of the highest purity (e.g. AnalaR). This includes the water to be used – distilled and deionised – MilliQ water. (Note: many reagents (solids and liquids) contain metallic impurities in trace amounts. Although you can minimise this risk of contamination by using the highest-purity reagents, it is essential to run 'reagent blanks', especially for elemental determinations trace levels.)

1. **Determine the M_r of the metal salt.** For example, the M_r of Pb(NO$_3$)$_2$ = 331.20 g mol^{-1}.

2. **Determine the A_r of the metal.** The Ar for Pb is 207.19 gmol^{-1}.

3. **Establish the ratio of M_r to A_r.**

$$\frac{331.20}{207.19} = 1.5985 \text{ g of Pb(NO}_3)_2 \text{ in 1 litre}$$

4. **Accurately weigh out the metal salt.** In this case, weigh 1.5985g of Pb(NO$_3$)$_2$.

5. **Quantitatively transfer the metal salt to a pre-cleaned 100 mL beaker** and dissolve in 1% v/v HNO$_3$ (AnalaR or equivalent).

6. **Quantitatively transfer the dissolved metal salt to a 1 L volumetric flask** and make up to the graduation mark with 1% v/v HNO$_3$ (AnalaR or equivalent).

Often, a certified stock standard with a single or multielement composition can be purchased, usually at a concentration (per element) of 1000 mg L^{-1} (1000 μg mL^{-1}).

Box 17.2 How to prepare a set of five calibration solutions in the concentration range 0–10 μg mL^{-1} (mg L^{-1})

Assuming that we are starting with a 1000 μg mL^{-1} stock solution of a particular metal (e.g. lead), then you will need the following: six 100.00 mL grade A volumetric flasks; two 100 mL beakers; and a graduated pipette (0–10.00 mL).

1. **Ensure that all the glassware is clean** (see p. 41).

2. **Transfer ≈ 15 mL of the stock solution into one of the pre-cleaned beakers.**

3. **Quantitatively transfer 10.00 mL of the stock solution** into a 100.00 mL volumetric flask. Then, dilute to 100.00 mL with 1% v/v HNO$_3$ (high purity).

4. **Determine the concentration of this new solution.** Remember that we started with an initial 1000 μg mL^{-1} Pb stock solution.

$$\frac{1000 \ \mu g}{mL} \times mL \equiv 10 \ 000 \ \mu g \ Pb$$

10,000 μg Pb was placed in a 100.00 mL volumetric flask, so:

$$\frac{10 \ 000 \ \mu g}{100 \ mL} \equiv 100 \ \mu g \ mL^{-1} \ Pb$$

You now have a 100 μg mL^{-1} 'working' stock solution of Pb.

5. **Transfer ≈ 15 mL of the working stock solution into the other pre-cleaned beaker.**

6. **Quantitatively transfer 2.00 mL of the solution into a 100.00 mL volumetric flask** and dilute to 100.00 mL with 1% v/v HNO$_3$ (high purity). Label the flask as the 2 μg mL^{-1} Pb calibration solution.

7. **Similarly transfer 0, 4.00, 6.00, 8.00 and 10.00 mL volumes into separate volumetric flasks** and dilute to 100.00 mL with the nitric acid and label as 0, 4, 6, 8 and 10 μg mL^{-1} Pb calibration solutions.

8. **Take the 0, 2, 4, 6, 8 and 10 μg mL^{-1} Pb calibration solutions** for FAAS analysis.

 SAFETY NOTE *Caution is needed when using strong (concentrated) acids. When using concentrated acids always work in a fume cupboard. Wear gloves to protect your hands from 'acid burns'. Always rinse affected areas with copious amounts of water.*

Sample/standard dilutions – all dilutions should be done using appropriate glassware or plastic ware. Typically, this involves the use of grade A pipettes for the transfer of known volumes of liquids and grade A volumetric flasks for subsequent dilutions.

in the AAS instrument and switching on the current. The lamp is typically operated at an electric current between 2 and 30 mA.

Atomisation cell

Several types of atomisation cell are available – flame, graphite furnace, hydride generation and cold vapour. Flame is the most common. In the pre-mixed laminar flame, the fuel and oxidant gases are mixed before they enter the burner (the ignition site) in an expansion chamber. The more commonly used flame in FAAS is the air–acetylene flame (temperature, 2,500 K), while the nitrous oxide–acetylene flame (temperature, 3,150 K) is used for refractory elements (e.g. Al). Both are formed in a slot burner positioned in the light path of the HCL (Fig. 17.4).

In the graphite furnace atomiser, a small volume of sample (5–100 mL) is introduced on to the inner surface of a graphite tube (or on to a platform placed within the tube) through a small opening (Fig. 17.5). The graphite tube is arranged so that light from the HCL passes directly through the centre. Passing an electric current through the tube allows the operator to programme a heating cycle, with several stages (Fig. 17.6) including the elimination of water from the sample (drying), removal of the sample matrix (ashing), atomisation of the analyte (analysis) and removal of extraneous material (cleaning). An internal gas flow of inert gas (N$_2$ or Ar) during the drying and ashing stages removes any extraneous material.

Hydride generation is a sample introduction technique exclusively for elements that form volatile hydrides (e.g. As, Se, Sn). An acidified sample solution is reacted with sodium borohydride solution, liberating the gaseous hydride in a gas–liquid separator. The generated hydride is then transported to an atomisation cell using a carrier gas. The atomisation cell is normally an

Box 17.3   How to analyse a sample using the method of standard additions in FAAS

The method of standard additions is used when the sample matrix may cause difficulties (for example chemical interferences) in sample concentration determination. Standard additions allow any adverse effects to be overcome by incorporating a known amount of the sample in the calibration solutions.

1. **Prepare a 1000 μg mL⁻¹ stock solution** (see Box 17.1).

2. **Then, prepare a 100 μg mL⁻¹ working stock solution** (see Box 17.2).

3. **You will also need to have prepared the sample** – if the sample is a solid you will need to digest the sample (see Box 17.7).

4. **An estimate of the metal concentration in the sample is required prior to carrying out standard additions** so that the linear relationship between signal (absorbance) and concentration is maintained.

5. **You can then prepare the standard addition solutions.** This is most easily done as in Table 17.1.

6. **Analyse the samples using FAAS.**

7. **Plot the graph.** The graphical output should appear as shown in Fig. 17.2.

8. **The graph should contain several features** – it must have a linear response (signal against concentration); it does not pass through the origin; and extrapolation of the graph is required until it intersects the *x*-axis (e.g. 3.2 μg mL⁻¹).

9. **Determine the concentration of the metal in the original sample** – this can be done by taking into account the dilutions involved in the standard additions method and any dilutions used to prepare the sample (see dilution factor, Box 17.5).

Table 17.1   Standard additions solutions

Volumetric flask (100.00 mL capacity)	Volume of 100 μg mL⁻¹ working stock solution (mL)	Volume of aqueous sample solution (mL)
1	0	10
2	1	10
3	3	10
4	5	10
5	7	10

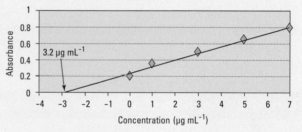

Fig. 17.2   Standard additions graph.

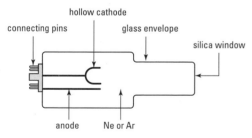

Fig. 17.3   Components of a hollow-cathode lamp (HCL).

electrically heated or flame-heated quartz tube. Using arsenic as an example, it is possible to write the following equation for the generation of arsine (AsH₃):

$$3BH_4^- + 3H^+ + 4H_3AsO_3 \rightarrow 3H_3BO_3 + 4AsH_3 + 3H_2O \qquad 17.1$$

Cold-vapour generation is the term exclusively reserved for mercury. Mercury in a sample is reduced to elemental mercury by tin(II) chloride:

$$Sn^{2+} + Hg^{2+} \rightarrow Sn^{4+} + Hg^0 \qquad 17.2$$

and the mercury vapour produced is transported to an atomisation cell by a carrier gas. The atomisation cell consists of a long-path glass absorption cell located in the path of the HCL. Mercury is monitored at a wavelength of 253.7 nm.

Sample introduction into the flame

Samples are almost exclusively introduced into flames as liquids. Solid samples need to be converted to aqueous solutions using methods such as decomposition (see p. 170). Once in the aqueous form, the sample is introduced into the flame using a nebuliser–expansion chamber.

The pneumatic concentric nebuliser (see also p. 168) consists of a stainless steel tube through which a Pt/Ir capillary tube is located. The aqueous sample

Box 17.4 Sample size and certified reference materials

If a linear calibration graph (plot of concentration against absorbance) has been prepared for lead in FAAS with the concentrations 0, 2, 4, 6, 8 and 10 $\mu g\ mL^{-1}$, the absorbance for the digested sample needs to fall within the linear portion of the graph. This is controlled by two (non-instrumental) factors – the weight of the sample digested and the final volume that the digested sample is made up to. As the volume of the digested sample is limited by the availability of volumetric flasks (10.00, 25.00, 50.00, 100.00 or 250.00 mL are most commonly used, with the 50.00 and 100.00 mL volumetric flasks the most common) it is often easier to alter the sample size. In order to have a representative sample, a minimum sample size is often recommended. For example, if using a certified reference material (CRM) the supplier will recommend a minimum sample size to ensure homogeneity (e.g. not $<$ 0.5 g for a powdered solid steel or alloy sample, or not $<$ 1.0 g for a powdered biological sample such as citrus leaves). Often the maximum sample size is limited by the cost of the CRM. If using a 'real' sample then it is best to take a larger sample size, since a CRM has usually been tested and prepared to a high specification with respect to drying, milling and shelf-life time. A typical minimum sample size for a soil might be 5.00 g. It is important if using 'real' samples to consider the following additional factors:

- **Sampling** – how it is to be done? How will a representative sample be arrived at?

- **Storage of sample** – what containers will be used? Be aware of contamination for the storage container and from the implements used to sample and transfer the sample.

- **Lifetime of stored sample** – how long will the sample remain stable? Is preservation of the sample necessary?

Note: CRMs can be obtained from appropriate suppliers, for example the Laboratory of the Government Chemist in the UK or the National Institute for Science and Technology in the USA. In addition to the CRM, a certificate is provided that contains information on the concentration of various metals within the sample as well as their variation, normally quoted as one standard deviation either side of the mean value (e.g. 2.560 $\pm$ $\mu g\ g^{-1}$ Pb). CRMs are used to test the accuracy of a new method or to enable a quality control scheme to be operated by a commercial laboratory (see also Chapter 50). In practical work they are useful for assessing student performance in preparing and analysing a sample.

Box 17.5 Analysis of a sample: dilution factor

A sample was weighed (0.4998 g) and digested in concentrated nitric acid (20 mL). After cooling, the digested sample was quantitatively transferred into a 100.00 mL volumetric flask and made up with ultrapure water and then analysed for lead by FAAS. Let us suppose that the absorbance obtained corresponds to a concentration of 3.4 $\mu g\ mL^{-1}$. What is the concentration of lead in the original sample?

The method of calculation is most appropriately done as follows:

- **Calculate the dilution factor** – this can be done if the final volume of the sample and its original weight are known. In this case 100 mL and 0.4998 g.

- **You then multiply the concentration** from the graph with the dilution factor:

$$\frac{3.4\ \mu g}{mL} \times \frac{100\ mL}{0.4998\ g} = 680\ \mu g\ g^{-1}$$

Note:

- **The volume of acid used is irrelevant in the calculation** – only the final volume in the volumetric flask matters.

- **The units cancel** (mL on top line cancels with mL on the bottom line) leaving you with units of $\mu g\ g^{-1}$ ($\mu g/g$).

- **Alternatively, the units can be expressed in mg kg^{-1}** (mg/kg), i.e. 680 mg kg^{-1} or % w/w, i.e. 0.068% w/w (see p. 118). (10,000 $\mu g\ g^{-1}$ $\equiv$ 1% w/w or for aqueous samples 10,000 $\mu g\ mL^{-1}$ $\equiv$ 1% w/v.)

is drawn up through the capillary tube by the action of the oxidant gas (air) escaping through the exit orifice that exists between the outside of the capillary tube and the inside of the stainless steel tube. The action of the escaping air and aqueous sample is sufficient to form a coarse aerosol in a process termed the Venturi effect. The typical uptake rate of the nebuliser is between 3 and 6 mL min^{-1}.

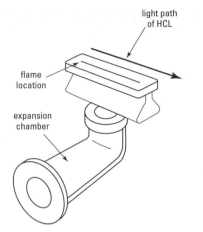

Fig. 17.4 Components of a slot burner for FAAP.

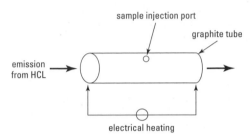

Fig. 17.5 Schematic diagram of a graphite furnace atomiser.

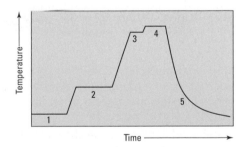

Fig. 17.6 Heating cycle for a graphite furnace atomiser. 1. drying; 2. ashing; 3. analysis; 4. cleaning; 5. cooling

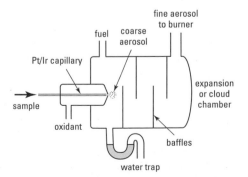

Fig. 17.7 Schematic diagram of a nebuliser–expansion chamber for FAAS.

The expansion chamber (Fig. 17.7) has two functions. The first is concerned with aerosol generation, the objectives of which are:

- to convert the aqueous sample solution into a coarse aerosol using the oxidant gas;
- to disperse the coarse aerosol further into a fine aerosol, by interaction with baffles located within the chamber;
- to condense any residual aerosol particles, which then go to waste.

The second function involves the safe pre-mixing of the oxidant and fuel gases before they are introduced into the laminar flow burner.

Wavelength selection and detection

As AAS is used to monitor one metal at a time, the spectrometer used is termed a monochromator. Two optical arrangements are possible – single and double beam. The latter is preferred as it corrects for fluctuations in the HCL caused by warm up, drift and source noise, thus leading to improved precision in the absorbance measurement. A schematic diagram of the optical arrangement is shown in Fig. 17.8. The attenuation of the HCL radiation by the atomic vapour is detected by a photo multiplier tube (PMT), a device for proportionally converting photons of light to electric current.

Background correction methods

One of the main practical problems with the use of AAS is the occurrence of molecular species that coincide with the atomic signal. One approach to remove this molecular absorbance is by the use of background correction methods. Several approaches are possible, but the most common is based on the use of a continuum source, D_2. In the atomisation cell (e.g. flame), absorption is possible from both atomic species and from molecular species (unwanted interference). By measuring the absorption that occurs from the radiation source (HCL) and comparing it with the absorbance that occurs from the continuum source (D_2) a corrected absorption signal can be obtained. This is because the atomic species of interest absorb the specific radiation associated with the HCL source, whereas the absorption of radiation by the continuum source for the same atomic species will be negligible.

Interferences in the flame

Interferences in the flame can be classified into four categories – chemical, ionisation, physical and spectral.

Chemical interferences occur when the analyte forms a thermally stable compound with a molecular or ionic species present in the sample solution. Examples include the suppression of alkaline earth metals due to the presence of phosphate, silicate or aluminate in the sample solution in the air–acetylene flame. The most well-known example of this is the absorption signal suppression that occurs for Ca at 422.7 nm owing to increasing amounts of phosphate. This signal suppression is due to the formation of calcium pyrophosphate, a thermally stable compound in the flame.

Ionisation interferences occur most commonly for alkali and alkaline earth metals. The low ionisation potential of these metals can lead to their ionisation in the relatively hot environment of the flame. If this occurs, no absorption signal is detected, since FAAS is a technique for measuring atoms not ions. This process can be prevented by the addition of an ionisation suppressor or 'buffer' (e.g. an alkali metal such as caesium). Addition of excess Cs leads to its

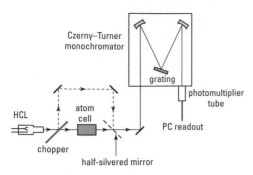

Fig. 17.8 Schematic diagram of the optical arrangement for AAS.

ionisation in the flame in preference to the metal of interest (e.g. Na). This process is termed the 'mass action' effect.

Physical interferences are due to the effects of the sample solution on aerosol formation within the spray chamber. The formation of an aerosol is dependent on the surface tension, density and viscosity of the sample solution. This type of interference can be controlled by the matrix matching of sample and standard solutions – i.e. add the same sample components to the standard solution, but without the metal of interest. If this is not possible, it is then necessary to use the method of standard additions (Box 17.3).

Spectral interferences are uncommon in AAS owing to the selectivity of the technique. However, some interferences may occur, for example the resonance line of Cu occurs at 324.754 nm and has a line coincidence from Eu at 324.753 nm. Unless the Eu is 1,000 times in excess, however, it is unlikely to cause any problems for Cu determination. In addition to atomic spectral overlap, molecular band absorption can cause problems, for example calcium hydroxide has an absorption band on the Ba wavelength of 553.55 nm while Pb at 217.0 nm has molecular absorption from NaCl. Molecular band absorption can be corrected for using background correction techniques (see p. 165). The operation of a flame atomic absorption spectrometer is described in Box 17.6.

Box 17.6   How to operate a flame atomic absorption spectrometer

You should only operate an FAAS system under direct supervision. The instrument should be located under a fume extraction hood. The spectrometer requires approximately 20 min to warm up before switching the gases on and using the instrument.

1. **Adjust the operating wavelength and slit width of the monochromator.** This is done by consulting standard operating conditions, for example for lead see Table 17.2.

2. **Decide what wavelength is to be used for the analysis.** For lead, the maximum sensitivity is achieved by selecting 217.0 nm.

3. **Adjust the wavelength selector to the appropriate wavelength.**

4. **Adjust the gain control** until the energy meter reading reaches a maximum.

5. **Adjust the wavelength selector** for maximum signal reading. You are now ready to ignite the air–acetylene flame.

6. **Turn on the fume extraction hood.** This allows toxic gases to be safely removed from the laboratory environment.

7. **Turn on the air supply** such that the oxidant flow meter is at the desired setting.

8. **Turn on the acetylene supply** such that the fuel flow meter is at the desired setting.

9. **Press the ignite button (or flame button).** The flame should light instantaneously with a 'pop'.

10. **After establishing the flame,** insert the aspirator tube into distilled water. Allow the flame to stabilise for up to 1 min by aspirating distilled water, prior to analysis.

11. **After completing your analysis,** shut off the acetylene first (by closing the cylinder valve) and vent the acetylene gas line while the air is still on. Then, shut off the air compressor and allow the air line to vent.

12. **Finally, switch off the fume extraction hood.**

Table 17.2   Standard operating conditions for lead

Wavelength (nm)	Slit (nm)	Characteristic concentration (mg L^{-1})
283.3	0.7	0.45
217.0	0.7	0.19
205.3	0.7	5.4
202.2	0.7	7.1
261.4	0.7	11.0
368.3	0.7	27.0
364.0	0.7	67.0

Note: Recommended flame is air–acetylene, oxidising (lean, blue).

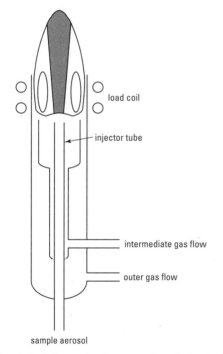

Fig. 17.9 Schematic diagram of an inductively coupled plasma.

Atomic Emission Spectroscopy

The main components of an atomic emission spectrometer are an atomisation and ionisation cell, a method of sample introduction, the spectrometer and detector. In contrast to AAS, no radiation source is required.

Flame photometry (see also p. 159) is almost exclusively used for the determination of alkali metals because of their low excitation potential (e.g. sodium 5.14 eV and potassium 4.34 eV). This simplifies the instrumentation required and allows a cooler flame (air–propane, air–butane or air–natural gas) to be used in conjunction with a simpler spectrometer (interference filter). The use of an interference filter allows a large excess of light to be viewed by the detector. Thus, the expensive photo multiplier tube is not required and a cheaper detector can be used, for example a photodiode or photoemissive detector. The sample is introduced using a pneumatic nebuliser as described for FAAS (p. 162). Flame photometry is therefore a simple, robust and inexpensive technique for the determination of potassium (766.5 nm) or sodium (589.0 nm) in clinical or environmental samples. The technique suffers from the same type of interferences as in FAAS. The operation of a flame photometer is described in Box 16.2.

Inductively coupled plasma

A radio frequency inductively coupled plasma (ICP) is formed within the confines of three concentric glass tubes or plasma torch (Fig. 17.9). Each concentric glass tube has a tangentially arranged entry point through which argon gas enters the intermediate (plasma) and external (coolant) tubes. The inner tube consists of a capillary tube through which the aerosol is introduced from the sample introduction system. Located around the plasma torch is a coil of water-cooled copper tubing. Power input to the ICP is achieved through this copper, load or induction coil, typically in the range 0.5–1.5kW at a frequency of 27 or 40 MHz.

Initiation of the plasma is achieved as follows. The carrier gas flow is first switched off and a spark added momentarily from a Tesla coil (attached to the outer edge of the plasma torch). The spark, a source of 'seed' electrons, causes ionisation of the argon gas. The co-existence of argon, argon ions and electrons constitutes a plasma located within the confines of the plasma torch but protruding from the top in the shape of a bright white luminous bullet. In order to introduce the sample aerosol into the ICP (7000–10,000K) the carrier gas is switched on and punches a hole into the centre of the plasma creating the characteristic doughnut or toroidal shape. The emitted radiation is viewed laterally (side-on) through the luminous plasma.

Sample introduction

The most common method of liquid sample introduction in ICP–AES is the nebuliser (Fig. 17.10). The nebuliser operates in the same manner as that used for FAAS but there are differences in its construction material and manufactured tolerance (the nebuliser for ICP–AES generates a finer aerosol, but is more inefficient). The pneumatic nebuliser consists of a concentric glass tube through which a capillary tube passes (Fig. 17.10(a)). The sample is drawn up through the capillary by the action of the argon carrier gas escaping through the exit orifice that exists between the outside of the capillary tube and the inside of the glass concentric tube. The typical uptake rate of the nebuliser is between 0.5 and 4 mL min^{-1}. In common with FAAS, a means to reduce the coarse aerosol generated to a fine aerosol is required. In ICP–AES terminology this device is called a spray chamber (Fig. 17.11).

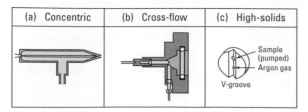

Fig. 17.10 Types of nebuliser: (a) concentric; (b) cross-flow; (c) high-solids.

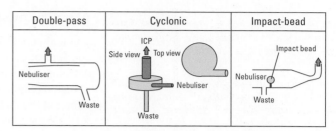

Fig. 17.11 A range of nebuliser spray chamber combinations: (a) double-pass; (b) cyclonic; (c) impact-bead.

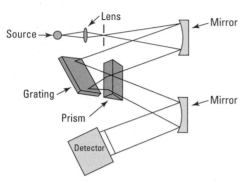

Fig. 17.12 Schematic diagram of the optical layout of an Echelle spectrometer.

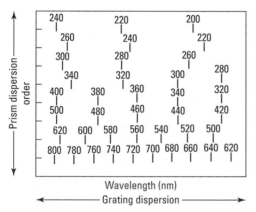

Fig. 17.13 Spectral map generated by the Echelle spectrometer.

Spectrometers

The nature of the ICP is such that all elemental information from the sample is contained within it. The only limitation is whether it is possible to observe all the elemental information at the same time or one element at once. This limitation is associated not with the ICP but with the type of spectrometer used to view the emitted radiation. A monochromator allows measurement of one wavelength, corresponding to one element at a time, while a polychromator allows multiwavelength or multi-element detection. The former can perform sequential multi-element analysis, while the latter carries out simultaneous multielement analysis. The typical wavelength coverage required for a spectrometer is between 167 nm (Al) and 852 nm (Cs). A schematic diagram of a modern Echelle spectrometer is shown in Fig. 17.12.

Detectors

The most common detector for AES is the photo multiplier tube (see p. 167). An alternative approach for the detection of multi-element (multiwavelength) information is the charged-coupled device (CCD). A CCD is essentially an array of closely spaced metal–insulator–semiconductor diodes formed on a wafer of semiconductor material. Incident light striking the CCD is converted into an electrical signal. A typical spectral map output is shown in Fig. 17.13.

Interferences in ICP–AES

Interferences for AES can be classified into two main categories – spectral and matrix interferences. Spectral interference can occur as a result of an interfering emission line from either another element or the argon source gas, or from impurities within or entrained into the source, for example molecular species such as N_2. Such interferences can be eliminated or reduced either by increasing the resolution of the spectrometer or by selecting an alternative spectral emission line.

Matrix interferences are often associated with the sample introduction process. For example, pneumatic nebulisation can be affected by the dissolved-solids content of the aqueous sample, which affects the uptake rate of the nebuliser and hence the sensitivity of the assay. matrix effects in the plasma source typically involve the presence of easily ionisable elements (EIEs, e.g. alkali metals) within the plasma source.

Inductively coupled plasma mass spectrometry

The inductively coupled plasma has been developed as an ion source for mass spectrometry (see also Chapter 15). The plasma is operated in horizontal mode and is positioned at the interface of a mass spectrometer. most common mass spectrometers for ICP–MS are based on a quadrupole instrument. Key to the success of ICP–MS was the development of an interface (Fig. 17.14) that allows

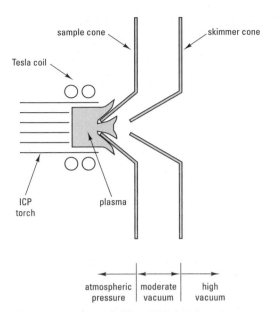

Fig. 17.14 Schematic diagram of an inductively coupled plasma mass spectrometer interface.

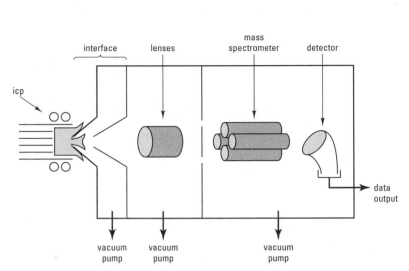

Fig. 17.15 Schematic diagram of an inductively coupled plasma mass spectrometry system.

Table 17.3 Examples of isobaric interferences

Element	Atomic mass unit (amu)												
	108	109	110	111	112	113	114	115	116	117	118	119	120
Pd	26.5		11.7										
Ag		48.2											
Cd	0.9		12.5	12.8	24.1	12.2	28.7		7.5				
In						4.3		95.7					
Sn					1.0		0.6	0.4	14.5	7.7	24.2	8.6	32.6
Te													0.09

an ICP operating at atmospheric pressure to be linked to a mass spectrometer operating under high vacuum (Fig. 17.15).

The ICP operates in much the same way as in AES, and with the same approach to sample introduction. However, the inherent sensitivity of ICP–MS has made it a very useful addition to the methods available for trace metal analysis. Typical sensitivities for metals by ICP–MS are in the trace (ng mL^{-1}) to ultratrace (pg mL^{-1}) range. This ability to measure metals at low concentrations can cause problems, particularly with the grade of reagents used to prepare the standards and the water supply to prepare samples and standards.

Quantitative analysis in ICP–MS is achieved by measurement of element isotopes. Approximately 70% of the elements in the Periodic Table have more than one stable isotope. For example, lead (Pb) has four isotopes with mass:charge ratios of 204, 206, 207 and 208 which have % abundances of 1.4, 24.1, 22.1 and 52.4, respectively. It should therefore be obvious that in order to achieve the largest response for Pb you should choose the isotope with the largest abundance, i.e. 208. However, a mass spectrometer offers additional advantages, including the ability to measure all isotopes very quickly. An ICP–MS can therefore measure almost all the elements in the Periodic Table very quickly. ICP–MS can also use the isotopic information present for an element to provide quantitative information. The typical approach to quantification involves preparing a calibration graph (see Chapter 51); however, ICP–MS can also quantify samples using isotope dilution analysis (IDA). Isotope dilution analysis requires an enriched artificial isotopic standard of the element to be quantified, i.e. a different isotopic abundance to that normally found in nature.

Two classes of interferences occur in ICP–MS:

1. **isobaric interferences;**
2. **molecular interferences** (polyatomic and doubly charged species).

Isobaric interferences occur as a result of direct overlap of isotopes from one element with another. These interferences (Table 17.3) are well known and can be compensated for either by selecting an alternative isotope or by applying a correction based on the isotopic abundance. Molecular interferences, and in particular polyatomic interferences, can be troublesome and result from interactions between the element of interest and other species present (for example argon plasma gas), or the type of acid used to prepare the sample digest. It is therefore possible to produce species, such as $ArCl^+$ or, more correctly in this example, $^{40}Ar^{35}Cl^+$. This may have resulted from the presence of chlorine in the sample matrix or the acid used to digest the sample (e.g. HCl).

The other molecular interference, doubly charged species, can also cause problems. For example, barium has isotopes at mass:charge ratios that include 130, 132, 134, 136 and 138 amu that can form doubly charged species at mass:charge ratios of 65, 66, 67, 68 and 69 amu respectively.

Decomposition techniques for solid inorganic samples

Conversion of a solid matrix into a liquid matrix involves the decomposition of the sample. One of the major problems in preparing solid samples for trace element analysis is the potential risk of contamination. Contamination can arise from several sources – the grade of reagents used, the vessels used for digestion and the subsequent dilution of the sample, and human involvement.

In order to minimise the risk of contamination you should take the following measures:

- **use the highest purity** of reagents and acids, including the water used for sample dilution;
- **use sample blanks** in the analytical procedure, to identify the base level of impurity in the reagents;
- **soak sample vessels in an acid leaching bath** (e.g. 10% v/v nitric acid) for at least 24 h, followed by rinsing in copious amounts of ultrapure water;
- **store cleaned volumetric flasks with their stoppers inserted,** cover beakers with Clingfilm or store upside down to protect from dust;
- **in addition to the wearing of a laboratory coat and safety glasses,** it may be necessary to wear 'contaminant'-free gloves and a close-fitting hat.

Decomposition involves the liberation of the analyte (metal) of interest from an interfering matrix using a reagent (mineral/oxidising acids or fusion flux) and/or heat. An important aspect in the decomposition of an unknown sample is the sample size (Box 17.4). You need to consider two aspects. Firstly, the dilution factor required to convert the solid sample to an aqueous solution (Box 17.5), and secondly, the sensitivity of the analytical instrument (e.g. FAAS or ICP–MS).

Acid digestion

This involves the use of mineral or oxidising acids and an external heat source to decompose the sample matrix. The choice of an individual acid or

---

Reaction types involved in a collision-reaction cell include:

- **Charge exchange** – *this allows the removal of, for example, the argon plasma gas ion interference and the resultant formation of uncharged argon plasma gas, which is then not detected.*

$$Ar^+ + NH_3 \rightarrow NH_3^+ + Ar \qquad 17.3$$

- **Atom transfer: proton transfer** – *this can remove the interference from, for example, ArH^+. This results in the formation of neutral (uncharged) argon plasma gas, which is then not detected.*

$$ArH^+ + H_2 \rightarrow H_3^+ + Ar \qquad 17.4$$

- **Atom transfer: hydrogen-atom transfer** – *this has the ability to alleviate an interference by increasing the mass/charge ratio by one.*

$$Ar^+ + H_2 \rightarrow ArH^+ + H \qquad 17.5$$

- **Adduct formation** – *this allows, for example with ammonia, NH_3, for the mass/charge ratio to increase by 17 amu (atomic weight of N = 14 and atomic weight of H = 1).*

$$Ni^+ + NH_3 \rightarrow Ni^+ + NH_3 \qquad 17.6$$

- **Condensation reaction** – *this also has the ability to increase the mass/charge ratio, for example, creation of the oxide of the element will increase the mass/charge ratio by 16 amu (atomic weight of O = 16).*

$$Ce^+ + N_2O \rightarrow CeO^+ + N_2 \qquad 17.7$$

Table 17.4 Common acids* used for digestion

Acid(s)	Boiling point (°C)	Comments
Hydrochloric acid (HCl)	110	Useful for salts of carbonates, some oxides and some sulphides. A weak reducing agent; not generally used to dissolve organic matter
Hydrofluoric acid (HF)	112	For digestion of silica-based materials only. Cannot be used with glass containers (use plasticware). In addition to laboratory coat and safety glasses, extra safety precautions are needed, e.g. gloves. In case of spill-ages, calcium gluconate gel is required for treatment of skin contact sites and should be available during use; evacuate to hospital immediately if skin is exposed to liquid HF
Nitric acid (HNO_3)	122	Useful for the digestion of metals, alloys and biological samples. Oxidising attack on many samples not dissolved by HCl; liberates trace metals as the soluble nitrate salt
Sulphuric acid (H_2SO_4)	338	Useful for releasing a volatile product; good oxidising properties for ores, metals, alloys, oxides and hydroxides. Often used in combination with HNO_3. Note: sulphuric acid must never be used in PTFE vessels (melting point 327 °C)
Hydrochloric/nitric acids (HCl/HNO_3)	–	A 3:1 v/v mixture of HCl and HNO_3 is called aqua regia. It forms a reactive intermediate, NOCl. Useful for digesting metals, alloys, sulphides and other ores

*All concentrated acids should be used only in a fume cupboard.

Box 17.7 How to acid-digest a sample using a hotplate

1. **Accurately weigh your sample into a beaker (100 mL).** For digestion of a powdered metal sample 0.5000 g is appropriate (for details on how to weigh accurately see p. 49).

2. **Add 20 mL of concentrated acid(s)** (see Table 17.4).

3. **Cover the beaker with a watch glass.** This is done to prevent the loss of sample and to minimise the risk of contamination.

4. **Place the beaker on a pre-heated hotplate.**

5. **Reflux the sample for approx. 30 min to 1 h** – depending on the nature of the sample a coloured, clear solution should result.

6. **Remove the beaker from the heat and allow to cool.** This may take several minutes. Retain the watch-glass cover during this stage to reduce airborne contamination.

7. **Wash the watch-glass cover** into the beaker to 'capture' any splashes of solution.

8. **Dilute the digested sample** with deionised or distilled water.

9. **Quantitatively transfer the diluted, digested sample** to a 100.00 mL volumetric flask (see p. 37). Make up to the graduation mark with de-ionised or distilled water.

10. **Prepare a sample blank using the same procedure** – i.e. perform all of the above tasks but without adding the actual sample.

11. **Prepare samples in at least duplicate.** For statistical work on the results, at least seven sample digests and two sample blanks are recommended.

---

combination of acids depends on the nature of the matrix to be decomposed. For example, the digestion of a matrix containing silica, SiO_2 (e.g. a geological sample), requires the use of hydrofluoric acid (HF). A summary of the most common acids used for digestion and their application is shown in Table 17.4.

Once you have chosen an appropriate acid, place your sample into an appropriate vessel for the decomposition stage. Typical vessels include an open glass beaker or boiling tube for conventional heating (Fig. 17.16) or for microwave

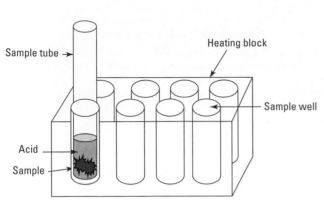

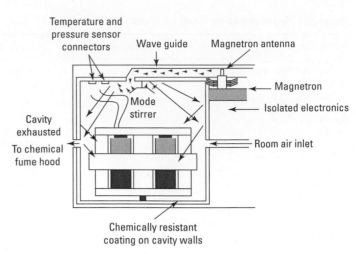

Fig. 17.16 Schematic diagram of a commercial acid-digestion system.

Fig. 17.17 Schematic diagram of a commercial microwave digestion system.

Fig. 17.18 A muffle furnace.

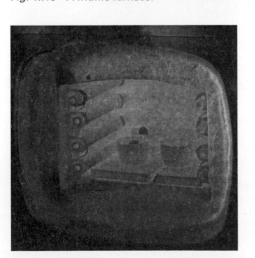

Fig. 17.19 Fusion.

heating (Fig. 17.17), a PTFE or Teflon® PFA (perfluoroalkoxyvinylether) vessel. A typical microwave system operates at 2.45 GHz with up to 14 sample vessels arranged on a rotating carousel. Commercial systems have additional features such as a PTFE-lined cavity; a safety vent (if the pressure inside a vessel is excessive the vent will open, allowing the contents to go to waste); and an ability to measure both the temperature and pressure inside the digestion vessels. The procedure for acid digestion of a sample is shown in Box 17.7.

Other methods of sample decomposition

The use of acid(s) and heat is probably the most common approach to the decomposition of samples. However, several alternatives exist including dry ashing and fusion.

Dry ashing involves heating the sample in air in a muffle furnace (Fig 17.18) at 400–800 °C to destroy the sample matrix (e.g. soil). After decomposition, the sample residue is dissolved in acid and quantitatively transferred to a volumetric flask prior to analysis. The method may lead to the loss of volatile elements (e.g. Hg, As).

Some substances, such as silicates and oxides, are not always destroyed by the direct action of acid and heat. In these situations, an alternative approach is required. Fusion involves the addition of a 10-fold excess of a suitable reagent (e.g. lithium metaborate or tetraborate) to a finely ground sample. The mixture is placed in a metal crucible (e.g. Pt), and then heated in a muffle furnace at 900–1200 °C (Fig. 17.19). After heating (from several minutes to several hours) a clear 'melt' should result, indicating completeness of the decomposition. After cooling, the melt is dissolved in HF (Table 17.4). This process can lead to a higher risk of contamination.

Sources for further study

Dean, J.R. (1997) *Atomic Absorption and Plasma Spectroscopy,* 2nd edn. ACOL series, Wiley, Chichester.

Dean, J.R. (2005) *Practical Inductively Coupled Plasma Spectroscopy.* Wiley, Chichester.

Ebdon, L., Evans, H., Fisher, A. and Hill, S. (1998) *An Introduction to Atomic Absorption Spectrometry.* Wiley, Chichester.

Hill, S.J. (ed.) (2007) *Inductively Coupled Plasma Spectroscopy and its Applications,* 2nd edn. Wiley, Chichester.

Schmidt, W. (2005) *Optical Spectroscopy in Chemistry and Life Sciences: An Introduction.* Wiley, Chichester.

Taylor, H. (2000) *Inductively Coupled Plasma–Mass Spectrometry: Practices and Techniques.* Acade μic Press, London.

Vandecasteele, C. and Block, C.B. (1997) *Modern Methods of Trace Element Determination.* Wiley, Chichester.

Study exercises

17.1 Determine the concentration of metal ions based on atomic spectroscopy of test and standard solutions. The following data represent a set of calibration standards for K^+ in aqueous solution, measured by flame photometry.

Absorbance of standard solutions containing K^+ at up to 0.5 mmol L^{-1}

K^+ concentration (mmol L^{-1})	Absorbance
0	0.000
0.1	0.155
0.2	0.279
0.3	0.391
0.4	0.537
0.5	0.683

Draw a calibration curve using the above data and use this to estimate the amount of K^+ in a test sample prepared by digestion of 0.482 g of tissue in a final volume of 25 mL of solution, giving an absorbance of 0.429 when measured at the same time as the standards shown above. Express your answer in mmol mmol K^+ (g tissue)$^{-1}$, to three significant figures.

17.2 Determine unknowns from a calibration curve. The following data are for a set of calibration standards for Zn, measured by atomic absorption spectrophotometry.

Absorbance measurements for a series of standard solutions containing different amounts of zinc.

Zinc concentration (μg mL^{-1})	Absorbance
0	0.000
1	0.082
2	0.174
3	0.257
4	0.340
5	0.408
6	0.463
7	0.511
8	0.543
9	0.561
10	0.575

Draw a calibration curve by hand using graph paper and estimate the concentration of zinc in the following water samples:

(a) an undiluted sample, giving an absorbance of 0.157;
(b) a 20-fold dilution, giving an absorbance of 0.304;
(c) a 5-fold dilution, giving an absorbance of 0.550.

Give your answer to three significant figures in each case.

Terminology in XRF – *it is common practice to refer to an atom with shells (Fig. 18.1) of electrons, i.e. K, L, M, N, etc., instead of the modern approach using s, p, d and f as descriptors.*

Understanding the relationship between energy and wavelength – *the following equation applies:*

$$E = h \times c/\lambda$$

where E is the energy, h is Planck's constant, c is the velocity of light and λ is the wavelength.

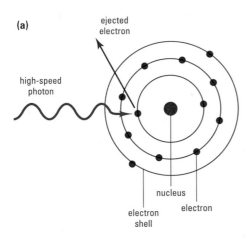

(a)

ejected electron

high-speed photon

nucleus

electron shell

electron

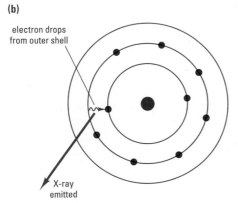

(b)

electron drops from outer shell

X-ray emitted

Fig. 18.1 Operating principle of X-ray fluorescence spectroscopy. Simplified diagrams showing (a) ejection of an electron and (b) the X-ray emitted.

X-ray fluorescence spectrometry (XRF) can be applied to determine the elemental composition of a wide range of objects of importance in forensic science. Its value lies in its non-destructive nature and potential for rapid identification of the elements present in samples. The multi-element nature of XRF allows 'elemental fingerprints' to be generated from samples of known or unknown authenticity. Typical applications areas include paint, glass, pottery and ceramics, metals and alloys, soil, plastics and fabrics. XRF can also be used to identify elements present in drug samples that may give clues as to the manufacturing processes involved and thereby help to further characterise the samples.

X-rays are part of the electromagnetic spectrum (p. 180), with wavelengths between 0.001 and 10 nm. They are produced when high-energy electrons decelerate or when electron transitions occur in the inner shells of atoms. The irradiation of matter with high-energy photons can lead to the ejection of an electron from an inner shell (e.g. the K shell) of an atom (Fig. 18.1(a)) and formation of an ion. This vacancy in the inner shell is filled almost immediately by an electron from a higher energy level (Fig. 18.1(b)). The difference in energy between the two energy levels is released in the form of an X-ray. The energy difference between the two specific orbitals always has the same characteristic value. Therefore, by determining the energy (or wavelength) of the X-ray emitted by a particular element, it is possible to determine the identity of that element. In terms of identification, if the transition is to a K shell, the X-ray produced is described as a K X-ray, if to an L shell, an L X-ray results, and so on. Each X-ray can be further classified as, for example, K_α, K_β, indicating that the energy transition has taken place from the L and M shell, respectively (Fig. 18.2). The intensity of X-rays per unit time at a particular energy (or wavelength) can be counted to allow either qualitative or quantitative analysis to be undertaken.

KEY POINT *The energy of an emitted X-ray is specific to a particular element and allows unequivocal identification, while the strength of the signal allows quantification.*

Instrumentation

An XRF spectrometer requires a source of X-rays (to excite the atoms in the sample), a sample holder and a spectrometer to measure the energy (or wavelength) and intensity of the radiation emitted by the sample. Two types of XRF can be identified – energy-dispersive and wavelength-dispersive XRF. Energy-dispersive X-ray fluorescence (EDXRF) relies on the detector and associated electronics to resolve spectral peaks due to differences in the energy of the generated X-rays. A schematic diagram of an EDXRF is shown in Fig. 18.3. In wavelength-dispersive XRF (WDXRF) a diffractive device such as a crystal is used to investigate the element of interest. A schematic diagram of a WDXRF is shown in Fig. 18.4. This chapter will focus on EDXRF, since this is the most widely used method in analytical science. The analytical performance of EDXRF can be improved by the introduction of additional components, including source filters or secondary targets. In the case of a secondary target, the X-ray tube excites the secondary target. The secondary target fluoresces and excites the

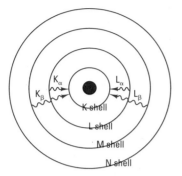

Fig. 18.2 Identification of K and L spectral lines.

Desirable properties of an X-ray source:

- *long-term power stability;*
- *low power-output requirements;*
- *purity of spectral output;*
- *long life;*
- *small size.*

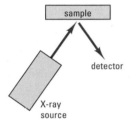

Fig. 18.3 Schematic diagram of an EDXRF system.

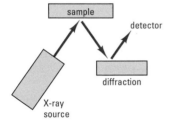

Fig. 18.4 Schematic diagram of an WDXRF system.

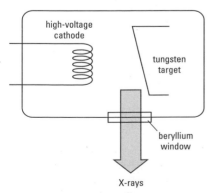

Fig. 18.5 X-ray tube (side window).

sample, and finally the detector measures X-rays from the sample. In addition, detector filters are sometimes positioned between the sample and the detector to remove unwanted X-rays.

Sample chambers in XRF can be operated in air. However, as air absorbs low-energy X-rays from elements below atomic number 20 (calcium), purges are often used. The two most common purge methods are the vacuum system and helium purge. Vacuum systems are preferred for analysis of solids or pressed pellets, whereas helium is preferred for analysis of liquids or powdered materials.

X-ray source

To generate X-rays you need:

- source of electrons;
- means of accelerating the electrons;
- target, to stop the electrons.

X-ray sources are available in a variety of forms, for example side-window X-ray tubes (Fig. 18.5), end-window X-ray tubes and radioisotopes. In the case of X-ray tubes – the most common source of X-rays for laboratory-based instruments – the applied voltage determines which elements can be excited. Also, the more power is applied, then the lower the detection limits achievable.

Detectors

Several types of detectors are available for XRF, including:

- Si(Li) detectors;
- PIN (positive–intrinsic–negative) diodes;
- silicon drift detectors;
- proportional counters;
- scintillation detectors.

For EDXRF, the most common detector has been the Si(Li) detector (Fig. 18.6). The principle of operation of a detector for XRF is as follows:

1. A detector is composed of a non-conducting or semiconducting material between two charged electrodes.
2. X-ray radiation ionises the detector material causing it to become conductive, momentarily.
3. The newly freed electrons are accelerated towards the detector anode to produce an output pulse.
4. The ionised semiconductor produces electron–hole pairs, the number of pairs produced being proportional to the X-ray photon energy.

Evaluating spectra

EDXRF can be used to analyse, for example, the chemical composition of glass (see Chapter 41), either quantitatively or qualitatively. It is important to be able to differentiate between peaks caused by the elements of interest and other spectral anomalies including interferences. The types of anomalies found in XRF are complex and varied, but need to be recognised in order to distinguish them from elemental peaks.

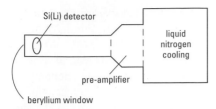

Fig. 18.6 Schematic diagram of a Si(Li) detector.

Escape peaks – *In normal operation, X-rays strike the sample and promote elemental fluorescence. However, escape peaks result from the fact that some silicon (Si) fluorescence at the surface of the detector escapes and is not collected by the detector. The result is a peak that appears in the spectra at an energy that corresponds to silicon, i.e. 1.74 keV.*

Sum peaks – *These occur when two photons strike the detector at exactly the same time. In this situation, fluorescence is captured by the detector and is recognised as a single photon but at twice its normal energy. Sum peaks can be observed in spectra at twice the energy for the element under investigation, i.e. 2 × element keV.*

Bremsstrahlung – *The process of electrons colliding with atoms in the object under investigation results in deceleration of electrons and production of an X-ray photon. The resultant continuum of energy, often called Bremsstrahlung radiation, appears as a broad band across many energies.*

Elemental K and L spectral peaks

These are the most common elemental peaks observed in EDXRF spectra. For example, the L shell electron transition to fill a vacancy in the K shell results in the production of K_α radiation. This is the most frequent transition, and hence produces the most intense peak. However, when an M shell electron transition occurs to fill a vacancy in the K shell it results in the production of K_β radiation, and so on (Fig. 18.2). The ratio of signal intensities between K_α and K_β is normally 20:1.

Similarly, if an M shell electron transition occurs to fill a vacancy in the L shell, it results in the production of L_α radiation. Whereas, an N shell electron transition to fill a vacancy in the L shell produces L_β radiation, and so on (Fig. 18.2). In addition to the elemental peaks, other peaks can also appear in spectra.

Scatter

When some of the source X-rays strike the sample they are scattered back at the detector (often referred to as 'backscatter'). Two types of scatter can be identified:

- **Rayleigh scatter** – X-rays from the X-ray tube or target strike the atom without promoting fluorescence. In this scenario, energy is not lost in the collision process. As a result, this type of scatter appears as a source peak in the line spectrum. It is sometimes referred to as 'elastic' scatter.
- **Compton scatter** – X-rays from the X-ray tube or target strike the atom without promoting fluorescence. In this scenario, energy is lost in the collision process, and scatter appears as a source peak in the line spectrum, but slightly lower in energy than the Rayleigh scatter. Compton scatter is often referred to as 'inelastic' scatter.

Interferences

Interferences can be divided into three categories:

1. **Spectral interferences** – These are seen as peaks in the spectrum, from other sources, that overlap with the spectral peak of the element to be analysed. Examples include K and L line overlaps for sulphur and molybdenum, chlorine and rhodium, and arsenic and lead. In addition, adjacent element overlap can occur, examples being aluminium and silicon, sulphur and chlorine, and potassium and calcium. In these situations, it is the resolution of the detector that determines the significance of the overlap.
2. **Environmental interferences** – Lighter elements, such as those between sodium and chlorine in the Periodic Table, emit weak X-rays, whose signal can be reduced by air. The remedy is to either (a) urge the instrument with an inert gas such as helium (as helium is less dense than air, it results in less attenuation of the signal) or (b) vacuate air from the sample chamber via a vacuum pump. The removal of air from the sample chamber also has additional benefits, such as the elimination of spectral interferences resulting from argon, which is present in small quantities in air, has a spectral overlap with chlorine.
3. **Matrix interferences** – Two types of matrix interferences can result in absorption or enhancement effects. In absorption, any element can absorb or scatter the fluorescence of the element of interest; whereas in enhancement, characteristic X-rays of one element can excite another element in the same sample resulting in signal enhancement. These matrix interferences can be

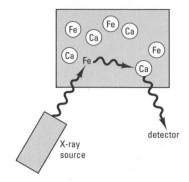

Fig. 18.7 Absorption-enhancement effects in XRF.

mathematically corrected by the use of influence coefficients, or alpha corrections. This is demonstrated in Fig. 18.7, where the incoming source X-ray causes iron in the sample to fluoresce. The resultant iron fluorescence is sufficient in energy to cause calcium to fluoresce. In this situation calcium is detected, but iron is not. The resultant signal responses are proportional to the concentrations of both calcium and iron.

Sample preparation

XRF is often regarded as requiring minimal or no sample preparation. However, for reproducible results consideration needs to be given to the type and form of sample to be analysed. Often the sample can be placed directly in a sample cup holder in the XRF instrument. A typical sample cup is normally 2–4 cm in diameter, and is no higher than it is wide. In addition, the sample cup holder can be obtained in a variety of configurations, including as a single open-ended cup (the obvious benefit being that it requires no cover on the cup) or a double open-ended cup (allows flexibility in terms of selecting the cover for the sample, e.g. Mylar™ film). You should always use covers for solution or powder samples, to prevent contamination and/or loss of material.

The most common window (i.e. sample support) film is Mylar. This has the combined benefits of low cost and high tensile strength, allowing it to be produced in a thin form (down to 1.5 mm), and thereby leading to highly reproducible results. However, Mylar has poor resistance to acids, preventing its use in many applications where acid may have been used in the preparation of the sample. Other materials used include polypropylene, polycarbonate, polyimide (Kapton™) and Teflon. It is also possible to use cups with solid beryllium windows for analysis of very light elements.

Sample preparation for liquid samples

Liquid samples can be analysed directly by three-quarters filling the sample cup and placing it in the EDXRF spectrometer. However, problems can arise due to the liquid sample evaporating, stratifying (forming layers) and/or precipitating (see Box 18.1). In addition, the liquid sample itself may react with the window cup film or be absorbed by it. In order to minimise these effects, it is appropriate to prepare all liquid samples immediately before analysis.

Alternative procedures for liquid samples include the addition of a solidifying agent to the liquid sample (e.g. cellulose, alumina or gelatin) to form a solid

---

Box 18.1 How to avoid problems with liquid samples in XRF

1. **Reduce evaporation of liquid samples by preparing and analysing samples immediately.** Evaporation can be reduced by placing a cover over the cup holder, though this can lead to bulging of the window film resulting in poor reproducibility of measurement. Some manufacturers produce baffled cups to help to reduce evaporation.

2. **Mixtures or immiscible liquids can give rise to stratification problems.** In order to assist in their analysis,

it may be necessary to separate the two liquids and analyse them separately. Alternatively, mix the solution rapidly to form an emulsion and then analyse immediately.

3. **If precipitation occurs, remove the liquid (supernatant) from the precipitate using a pipette.** This then allows analysis of both liquid and solid fractions. Alternatively, rapidly mix the liquid sample and the precipitate prior to analysis.

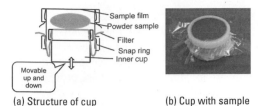

(a) Structure of cup   (b) Cup with sample

Fig. 18.8   Cup arrangement.

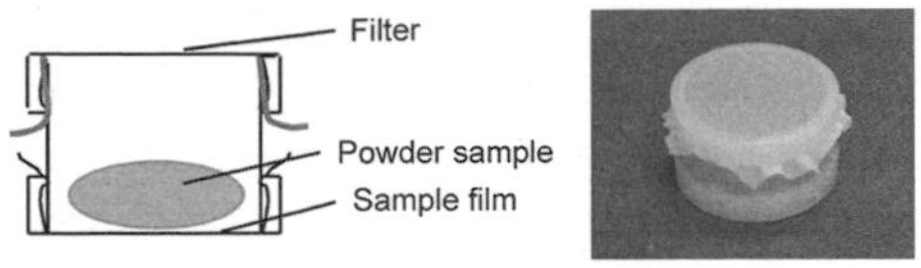

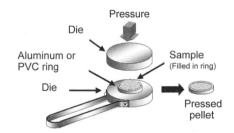

(a) Structure of cup   (b) Cup with sample

Fig. 18.9   Alternative cup arrangement.

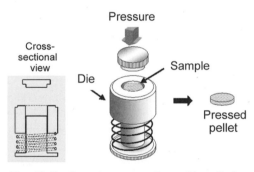

Fig. 18.10   Sample preparation with flat type dies.

Fig. 18.11   Sample preparation with cylinder type dies.

support. Alternatively, the sample can be presented as a thin film by applying the liquid sample to the surface of a support material (e.g. filter paper or the sample cup itself). The liquid sample can then be analysed directly, wet in the case of the filter paper, or dry by evaporating the sample directly in the cup. A variation on this approach is to use an ion-exchange resin to pre-concentrate the elements from the liquid sample, filter the resin (now containing the elements) and analyse this directly.

Sample preparation for solid samples

Solid objects can be placed directly into the sample chamber of the XRF spectrometer. However, several factors can influence the analysis of solid samples – surface roughness, particle shape and size, homogeneity, particle distribution and mineralisation.

Loose powders can be analysed by simply filling a sample cup to approximately three-quarters without any need for additional sample preparation. However, while this approach will give results, it has significant shortcomings due in part to the heterogeneity of most samples and to variation in particle size of most loose powders. Figure 18.8 shows a sample cup where the loose powder is supported between a sample film attached to the sample cup and a semi-permeable (microporous) filter. An alternative approach is shown in Fig. 18.9. In each case the sample cups are reusable when cleaned.

When pelletising samples, there is a possibility that contamination can occur due to previously pelletised sample remaining on the die surface. Therefore, it is recommended to clean the die surface every time before pel-letisation and to prepare samples starting with lower concentrations. Use of the film is effective not only to minimise contamination but also for samples such as iron or titanium oxides, which cannot be easily pelletised since a significant amount of powder can stick to the die surface. Sample films such as polypropylene or polyester can be used as a film for pelletisation. If a sample needs to be repelletised due to breakage, contamination due to ring or cup material can occur.

Pressed pellets can be prepared by pressing powders filled in a ring or a cup using a set of dies and a press machine. There are two types of dies – namely flat disc (Fig. 18.10) and cylinder types (Fig. 18.11). The type used depends on the characteristic of the powder sample. Ease of pelletisation depends on sample characteristics and grain size, and can be improved by sufficient pulverisation.

Box 18.2   How to prepare a loose powder sample for XRF analysis

1. **Dry and grind the loose powder sample** to a particle size corresponding to 300–400 mesh (15–35 μm) or better.

2. **Mix a portion of the dried powder with a binder** – for example, paraffin or cellulose (10:2 w/w). The binder helps to hold the finished pellet together.

3. **Clean the die** – this can be done by wiping with methanol or another solvent.

4. **Insert the backing (i.e. an aluminium cap) into the die and accurately weigh the sample added** – for

example, 4 g. It is important to keep the weight constant to allow consistent results.

5. **Place a polished pellet over the sample** – to produce a smooth finish.

6. **Insert the plunger and position the die in the press** – press the pellet at a pressure of 5–30 tonnes maintained for approximately 60 s.

7. **Remove the pellet from the die** – taking care not to crack it in the process. The pellet is then ready for analysis.

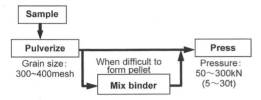

Fig. 18.12 Process for making a pressed pellet.

Forensic environmental application

A forensic environmental sample was subjected to EDXRF. The soil sample was prepared by air-drying it for 48 h prior to grinding and sieving. The sample was prepared as indicated in Box 18.2. The pelletised soil sample was then analysed. The results, shown in Fig. 18.15 as a plot of energy against signal, identify the range of elements present in the sample. By calibration of the EDXRF, the elements identified can be converted into quantitative data.

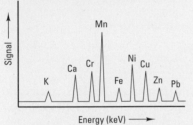

Fig. 18.15 Representative EDXRF trace of a forensic sample.

Mixing the powder sample with a forming agent ('binder') is another solution if pelletisation is difficult (Fig. 18.12). Without a binder, fine powder particles may fall off or scatter from the pellet surface and cause contamination of the spectrometer's sample chamber in vacuum mode. Powders in which particles are spherically shaped, such as SiO_2 or burned ash, are difficult to pelletise. Mixing ratio of sample to binder is typically 10 (sample):1(binder) or 10:2. It is also necessary to determine the purity of the binder as the binder choice should not include the elements to be analysed. Binders typically used are wax types – for example, SpectroBlend®, polystyrene-based powders, or boric acid and cellulose powders. Accurate weighing and complete mixing is essential to minimise analysis errors. An example of pressed pellets is shown in Fig. 18.13.

Manual press machines are available capable of delivering a 300 kN maximum load (Fig. 18.14). The press can be used for pelletisation with flat and cylinder type dies. The procedure for preparation of a pressed pellet is shown in Box 18.2.

Fig. 18.13 Pressed samples.

Fig. 18.14 A manual press.

Sources for further study

Jenkins, R. (1999) *X-ray Fluorescence Spectrometry,* 2nd edn. Wiley, Chichester.

Potts, P.J. and West, M. (eds) (2008) *Portable X-ray Fluorescence Spectrometry: Capabilities for in situ Analysis.* Royal Society of Chemistry, Cambridge.

Ritz, K, Dawson, L. and Miller, D. (eds) (2009) *Criminal an Environmental Soil Forensics.* Springer, Netherland

Vandecasteele, C. and Block, C.B. (1993) *Modern Methods for Trace Element Determination.* Wiley, Chichester.

Study exercises

18.1 Explain the principle of X-ray fluorescence spectroscopy – in a manner that would be understandable in court. Ask a colleague to listen to your explanation and provide feedback.

18.2 Test your knowledge. What are the main types of interferences associated with XRF and explain how they occur and how to avoid them.

18.3 Analysing a sample of soil by XRF. After reading this chapter, prepare a detailed stepwise protocol explaining how to prepare the soil sample and analysing it by XRF. Ask another student to evaluate your protocol and provide you with written feedback – either simply by reading through your protocol, or by trying it out as part of a class exercise (check with a member of staff before you attempt this in a laboratory).

Identifying compounds – the combination of techniques described in this and the following chapters can often provide sufficient information to identity a compound with a low probability of error.

Definitions

Spectrometry – any technique involving the measurement of a spectrum, e.g. of electromagnetic radiation, molecular masses.

Spectroscopy – any technique involving the production and subsequent recording of a spectrum of electromagnetic radiation, usually in terms of wavelength or energy.

Wavenumber – the reciprocal of the wavelength (expressed as cm^{-1}): a term used widely in IR spectroscopy, but rarely in other types of analysis.

Interpreting spectra – the spectrum produced in UV–vis, IR and NMR spectroscopy is a plot of wavelength or frequency or energy (x-axis) against absorption of energy (y-axis). Convention puts high frequency (high energy, short wavelength) at the left-hand side of the spectrum.

Understanding the origins of IR and Raman spectra – the IR spectrum is due to changes in charge displacement in bonds. The Raman spectrum is due to changes in polarisability in bonds.

In addition to ultraviolet–visible (UV–vis) spectroscopy (p. 154), there are three other essential techniques that you will encounter during your laboratory course. They are:

1. *Infrared (IR) and Raman spectroscopy* – this is concerned with the energy changes involved in the stretching and bending of covalent bonds in molecules.
2. *Nuclear magnetic resonance (NMR) spectroscopy* – this involves the absorption of energy by specific atomic nuclei in magnetic fields and is probably the most powerful tool available for the structural determination of molecules (Chapter 20).
3. *Mass spectrometry (MS)* – this is based on the fragmentation of compounds into smaller units. The resulting positive ions are then separated according to their mass-to-charge ratio (m/z) (Chapter 15).

As with UV–vis spectroscopy, IR and NMR spectroscopy are based on the interaction of electromagnetic radiation with molecules, whereas MS is different in that it relies on high-energy particles (electrons or ions) to break up the molecules. The relationship between the various types of spectroscopy and the electromagnetic spectrum is shown in Table 19.1.

Infrared and Raman spectroscopy

Both of these techniques involve the measurement of frequencies produced by the vibration of chemical bonds (bending and stretching). The IR/Raman region is generally considered to be from 800 to 2,500 nm (for near-IR) and up to 16,000 nm (for mid-IR). Near-IR spectroscopy involves recording the spectrum in that region in a manner analogous to UV/visible spectroscopy, and quantitative analysis is possible. However, the most widely used technique is mid-IR spectroscopy, which allows identification of groups or atoms in a sample compound, but is inappropriate for quantitative measurement. A peak at a particular frequency can be identified by reference to libraries or computer databases of IR spectra – e.g. a peak at a wavenumber of 1,730–1,750 cm^{-1} corresponds to a carbonyl group that is present in fatty acids and proteins. The 1,400–600 cm^{-1} region is known as the 'fingerprint' region (see p. 187) because no two compounds give identical spectra.

A covalent bond between two atoms can be crudely modelled as a spring connecting two masses and the frequency of vibration of the spring is defined by Hooke's law (eqn [19.1]), which relates the frequency of the vibration (v) to the strength of the spring, expressed as the force constant (k), and to the masses (m_1 and m_2) on the ends of the spring (defined as the reduced mass $\mu = (m_1 \times m_2) \div (m_1 + m_2)$).

$$v = \frac{1}{2\pi}\sqrt{\frac{k}{\mu}}$$ [19.1]

In simple terms, this means that:

● the stretching vibration of a bond between two atoms will increase in frequency (energy) on changing from a single bond to a double bond and then to a triple bond between the same two atoms (masses), i.e. the spring gets stronger. For example,

$$v \text{ for } C\equiv C > v \text{ for } C = C > v \text{ for } C - C$$

Table 19.1 The electromagnetic spectrum and types of spectroscopy

Type of radiation	Origin	Wavelength	Type of spectroscopy
γ-rays	Atomic nuclei	<0.1 nm	γ-ray spectroscopy
X-rays	Inner shell electrons	0.01–2.0 nm	X-ray fluorescence (XRF)
Ultraviolet (UV)	Ionisation	2.0–200 nm	Vacuum UV spectroscopy
UV/visible	Valency electrons	200–800 nm	UV/visible spectroscopy
Infrared	Molecular vibrations	0.8–300 mm	IR and Raman spectroscopy
Microwaves	Molecular rotations	1 mm to 30 cm	Microwave spectroscopy
	Electron spin		Electron spin resonance (ESR)
Radio waves	Nuclear spin	0.6–10 m	Nuclear magnetic resonance (NMR)

- as the masses of the atoms on a bond increases, the frequency of the vibration decreases, i.e. the effect of reducing the magnitude of μ. For example,

$$v \text{ for } C\text{—}H > v \text{ for } C\text{—}C > v \text{ for } C\text{—}H > v \text{ for } C\text{—}D;$$

$$v \text{ for } O\text{—}H > v \text{ for } S\text{—}H$$

Bonds can also bend, but this movement requires less energy than stretching and thus the bending frequency of a bond is always *lower* than the corresponding stretching frequency. When IR radiation of the same frequency as the bond interacts with the bond, it is absorbed and increases the amplitude of vibration of the bond. This absorption is detected by the IR spectrometer and results in a peak in the spectrum. For a vibration to be detected in the IR region, the bond must undergo a change in dipole moment when the vibration occurs. Bonds with the greatest change in dipole moment during vibration show the most intense absorption, for example $C\text{=}O$ and $C\text{—}O$.

Since bonds between specific atoms have particular frequencies of vibration, IR spectroscopy provides a means of identifying the type of bonds in a molecule – for example all alcohols will have an $O\text{—}H$ stretching frequency and all compounds containing a carbonyl group will have a $C\text{=}O$ stretching frequency. This property, which does not rely on chemical tests, is extremely useful in diagnosing the functional groups within a covalent molecule.

IR absorption bands – *since the frequency of vibration of a bond has a specific value, you would expect to see line spectra on the chart. However, each vibration is associated with several rotational motions and bands (peaks) are seen in the spectrum.*

IR spectra

A typical IR spectrum is shown in Fig. 19.1 and you should note the following points:

- **The *x*-axis, the wavelength of the radiation,** is given in wavenumbers ($\bar{v}$) and expressed in reciprocal centimetres (cm^{-1}). You may still see some spectra from old instruments using microns (m, equivalent to the SI unit 'micrometres', mm, at 1×10^{-6} m) for wavelength – the conversion is given by eqn [19.2]:

$$\text{wavenumber (cm}^{-1}\text{)} = \frac{1}{\text{wavelength (cm)}} = \frac{10{,}000}{\text{wavelength (}\mu\text{m)}} \quad [19.2]$$

- **The *y*-axis, expressing the amount of radiation absorbed by the molecule,** is usually shown as% transmittance (Fig. 19.1). When no radiation is absorbed (all is transmitted through the sample) we have 100% transmittance, and 0 % transmittance implies that all radiation is absorbed at a particular wavenumber. Since the *y*-axis scale goes from 0 to 100%

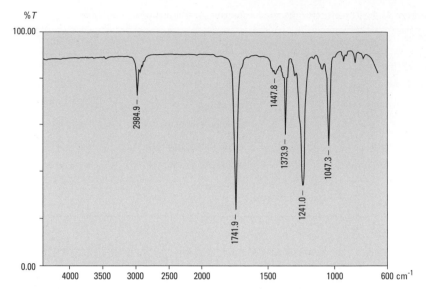

Fig. 19.1 IR spectrum of ethyl ethanoate $CH_3COOCH_2CH_3$ as a liquid film.

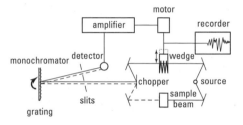

Fig. 19.2 Schematic diagram of a double-beam IR spectrometer.

> **The use of wavenumber** – this is a long-established convention, since high wavenumber = high frequency = high energy = short wavelength. Expression of the IR range, 4,000 cm^{-1} to 650 cm^{-1}, is in 'easy' numbers and the high energy is found on the left-hand side of the spectrum. Note that IR spectroscopists often refer to wavenumbers as 'frequencies', e.g. 'the peak of the $C = O$ stretching 'frequency' is at 1,720 cm^{-1}'.

> **Using double-beam instruments** – you can identify the sample beam by quickly placing your hand in the beam. If the pen records a peak, this is the sample beam, but if the pen moves up, then this is the reference beam.

> **Using the 100% control** – if you use this control to set the base line for the sample, you must turn down the 100% control when you remove the sample, otherwise the pen-drive mechanism may be damaged in trying to drive off the top of the chart.

transmittance, the absorption peaks are displayed *down* from the 100% line; this is *opposite* to most other common spectra.

- **The cells holding the sample** usually display imperfections and are not completely transparent to IR radiation, even when empty. Therefore, the base line of the spectrum is rarely set on 100% transmittance and quantitative applications of IR spectroscopy are more complex than for UV–vis (p. 154).

IR spectrometers

There are two general types:

1. **Double-beam or dispersive instruments** – in which the IR radiation from a single source is split into two identical beams. One beam passes through the sample, and the other is used as a reference and passes through air or the pure solvent used to dissolve the sample. The difference in intensity of the two beams is detected and recorded as a peak. The principal components of this type of instrument are shown in Fig. 19.2. The important controls on the spectrometer are:

   (a) **scan speed** – this is the rate at which the chart moves; slower for greater accuracy and sharp peaks;

   (b) **wavelength range** – the full spectrum or a part of the IR range may be selected;

   (c) **100% control** – this is used to set the pen at the 100% transmittance line when no sample is present (base line). It is usual practice to set the pen at 90% transmittance at 4,000 cm^{-1} when the sample is present, to give peaks of the maximum deflection.

   You should remember that this is an electromechanical instrument and you should always make sure that you align the chart against the calibration marks on the chart holder. In the more advanced instruments, an on-board computer stores a library of standard spectra, which can be compared with your experimental spectrum.

2. **Fourier transform infrared (FTIR) spectrometer** – the value of IR spectroscopy is greatly enhanced by Fourier transformation, named after the mathematician J.B. Fourier. The FT is a procedure for interconverting frequency functions and time or distance functions. In FTIR, information is

Box 19.1 How to run an infrared spectrum of a liquid or solid film, mull or KBr disk

A. Double-beam spectrometer

1. **Ensure that the instrument is switched on** and that it has had a few minutes to warm up.

2. **Make sure that the chart is aligned with the calibration marks on the chart bed or chart drum.** Most spectrometers scan from 4,000 cm^{-1} to 650 cm^{-1} and the pen should be at the 4,000 cm^{-1} mark.

3. **Adjust the 100% transmittance control to about 90%,** if necessary.

4. **Place the sample cell in the sample beam and adjust the 100% transmittance control to 90%,** or the highest value possible.

5. **Select the scan speed.** You must balance the definition required in the spectrum with the time available for the experiment. For most qualitative applications, the fastest setting is satisfactory.

6. **Press the 'scan' or 'start' button to run the spectrum.** The spectrum will be recorded and the spectrometer will automatically align itself at the end of the run. *Do not press* any other buttons while the spectrum is running or the instrument may not realign itself at the end of the run.

7. **Adjust the 100% transmittance control to about 50%,** remove the sample cell from the spectrometer and turn the 100% transmittance control to about 90%.

8. **Enter all of the following data on the spectrum –** name, date, compound and phase (liquid film, Nujol® mull, KBr disk, etc.).

B. FTIR spectrometer

1. **Make sure that the sample compartment is empty** and close the lid.

2. **Select the number of scans** – usually four is adequate for routine work.

3. **Select 'background' on the on-screen menu,** and scan the background. *Do not press* any other buttons or icons while the spectrum is running.

4. **Place the sample cell in the beam,** close the lid, select 'sample' and scan the sample. *Do not press* any other buttons or icons while the spectrum is running.

5. **Select 'customise',** or a similar function, and enter all the data – name, date, compound, phase (liquid film, Nujol mull, KBr disk, etc.) – on the spectrum.

6. **Select 'print'** to produce the spectrum from the printer.

Problems with IR spectra (and solutions)

These are usually caused by poor sample preparation and the more common faults are:

1. **The large peaks have tips below the bottom of the chart or the large peaks have 'squared tips' near the bottom of the chart** – the sample is too thick; remove some sample from the cell and rerun the spectrum.

2. **The spectrum is 'weak', i.e. few peaks** – the sample is too thin; add more sample or remake the KBr disk.

3. **The base line cannot be adjusted to 90% transmittance** – the NaCl plates or KBr disk are 'fogged', scratched or dirty; replace or remake the KBr disk.

4. **The pen tries to 'go off' the top of the spectrum** – obviously due to some absorption at 4,000 cm^{-1} when you were setting the base line. Repeat baseline set-up but at 80% transmittance; and bear in mind that dirty plates, above, can be the cause.

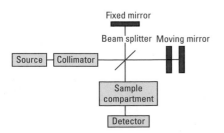

Fig. 19.3 Schematic diagram of an FT-IR spectrometer.

obtained from an interferometer, which splits the incident beam so that it passes through both the sample and a reference. When the beam is recombined, interference patterns arise because the two path lengths are different. The interference pattern has the same relationship to a normal spectrum as a hologram has to a picture, and integral computers use FT to convert the pattern into a spectrum in under a minute. A simple schematic diagram of an FT-IR spectrometer is shown in Fig. 19.3. The overall result is a greatly enhanced signal:noise ratio. The advantages of FTIR are:

(a) **rapid scanning speed** – typically four scans can be made per minute, allowing addition of the separate scans to enhance the signal:noise ratio and improve the resolution of the spectrum;

Infrared and Raman spectroscopy

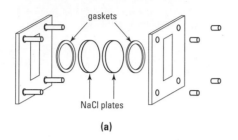

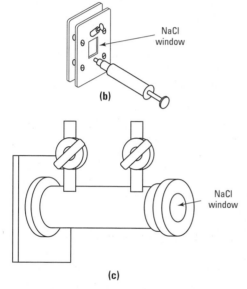

Fig. 19.4 Cells for IR spectroscopy: (a) demountable cell for liquid and solid films and mulls; (b) solution cell; (c) gas cell.

(b) **simplicity of operation** – the reference is scanned first, stored and then subtracted from the sample spectrum;

(c) **enhanced sensitivity** – the facility of spectrum addition from multiple scans permits detection of smaller quantities of chemicals;

(d) **the integral computer system** enables the use of libraries of spectra and simplifies spectrum manipulation – such as the subtraction of contaminant or solvent spectra.

The procedures for running IR spectra on double-beam and FT spectrometers are described in Box 19.1.

Sample handling

You can obtain IR spectra of solids, liquids and gases by use of the appropriate sample cell (sample holder). The sample holder must be completely transparent to IR radiation – consequently glass and plastic cells cannot be used. The most common sample cells you will encounter are made from sodium chloride or potassium bromide and you cannot use aqueous solutions or very wet samples, otherwise the sample cells will dissolve. A typical range of sample cells is shown in Fig. 19.4 and for routine qualitative work you will regularly use NaCl plates and KBr disks to obtain spectra of solids and liquids. Solution cells and gas cells are utilised in more specialised applications and require specific instructions and training.

Liquid samples

The most convenient way to obtain the IR spectrum of a pure, dry liquid is to make a thin liquid film between two NaCl disks (plates). Since the film thickness is unknown, this procedure is not applicable to quantitative work.

Solid samples

If you were to place a fine powder between two NaCl plates, a usable spectrum would not be obtained because the IR radiation would be scattered by diffraction at the edges of the particles and would not pass through to the detector. There are three solutions to this problem:

1. **Mulls** – in which the finely ground solid is mixed with a liquid, usually Nujol (liquid paraffin) or, less frequently, HCB (hexachloro-1,3-butadiene). This mulling liquid does not dissolve the chemical but fills the gaps round the edges of the crystals preventing diffraction and scattering of the IR radiation. Remember that these mulling liquids have their own IR spectrum, which is relatively simple, and can be subtracted either 'mentally' or by the computer. The choice of mulling liquid depends on the region of the IR spectrum of interest – Nujol is a simple hydrocarbon containing only $C=H$ and $C=O$ bonds, whereas HCB has no $C=H$ bonds, but has $C-Cl$, $C=C$ and $C-C$ bonds. Examination of the separate spectra of your unknown compound in each of these mulling agents enables the full spectrum to be analysed.

2. **KBr disks** – the finely ground solid compound is mixed with anhydrous KBr and squeezed under pressure. The KBr becomes fluid and forms a disk containing the solid compound dispersed evenly within it and suitable for obtaining a spectrum. The advantage of the KBr disk technique is the absence of the spectrum from the mulling liquid; the disadvantages are the equipment required (Fig. 19.5) and the practice required to obtain suitable transparent disks, which are very delicate and rapidly absorb atmospheric moisture.

3. **Thin solid films** – a dilute solution of the compound in a low-boiling-point solvent such as dichloromethane or ether is allowed to evaporate on a NaCl plate producing a thin transparent film. This method gives excellent results but is slightly limited by solubility factors.

When you are recording spectra of mulls, KBr disks and thin solid films, air is used as the reference and they are suitable for qualitative analysis only. The procedure for the preparation of liquid and solid films and mulls is described in Box 19.2 and that for KBr disks in Box 19.3.

Box 19.2 How to prepare liquid and solid films and mulls

A. Preparing a liquid film

1. **Select a pair of clean NaCl plates from a desiccator.** Clean them by wiping with a soft tissue soaked in dichloromethane and place them on the bench on a piece of filter paper or tissue paper to prevent scratching by the bench surface.

2. **Using a glass rod or boiling stick, place a small drop of liquid in the centre of one of the plates.** Do not use a Pasteur pipette, which may scratch the surface of the plate.

3. **Carefully, holding it by the edge, place the other plate on top and see if a thin film spreads between the plates, covering the centres.** Do not press to force the plates together. If there is not enough liquid, carefully separate the plates by lifting at the edge and add another drop of liquid. If there is too much liquid, separate the plates and wipe the liquid from one of them using a soft tissue.

B. Preparing a thin solid film

1. **Dissolve the sample (about 5 mg) in a suitable low-boiling-point solvent (about 0.25 mL),** such as DCM or ether.

2. **Place two drops of the solution on to the centre of an NaCl plate.** Allow the solvent to evaporate. Use a Pasteur pipette, but *do not* touch the surface of the plate.

3. **If the resulting thin film of solid does not cover the centre of the plate,** add a little more solution.

4. **Mount the *single* NaCl plate in the spectrometer and run the spectrum.** Note that the NaCl plate can rest on the V-shaped wedge on the sample holder in the spectrometer.

Preparing a mull

1. **Grind a small sample of your compound (about 5 mg) using a small agate mortar and pestle for at least 2 min.** The powder should be as fine as possible.

2. **Add one drop of mulling agent (Nujol or HCB) and continue grinding until a smooth paste is formed.** If the mull is too thick, add another drop of mulling agent; or if it is too thin, add a little more solid. Only experience will give you the correct consistency of mull – the key to a good spectrum is a mull of the correct fluidity.

3. **Transfer the mull to the centre or along the diameter of an NaCl plate** on a piece of filter paper or tissue paper to prevent scratching by the bench surface, using a small plastic spatula or a boiling stick.

4. **Carefully, holding it by the edge, place the other plate on top and very gently press to ensure that the mull spreads as a thin film between the plates.** If there is not enough liquid, carefully separate the plates by lifting at the edge and add another drop of mull. If there is too much liquid (poor spectrum), separate the plates and wipe the mull from one of them using a tissue.

C. Setting up the cell holder for liquid films and mulls

1. **Place the back-plate of the cell holder on the bench, position the rubber gasket, place the NaCl plates on the gasket and then put the second gasket on top of the plates.** These gaskets are essential to prevent fracture of the plates when you tighten the locking nuts.

2. **Carefully place the cell holder top-plate on the top gasket, drop the locking nuts into place and carefully tighten each in rotation.** These are safety nuts and if you overtighten them or if the back- and top-plates are not parallel, they will spring loose to prevent the NaCl plates being crushed.

3. **Transfer the cell holder assembly to the spectrometer and make sure it is securely mounted in the cell compartment.**

4. **Clean the plates in the fume cupboard by wiping them with a tissue soaked in DCM.** Stand them on filter paper or tissue paper to allow the solvent to evaporate and put them in the desiccator. Allow the DCM to evaporate from the tissue swab and dispose of it in the chemical waste.

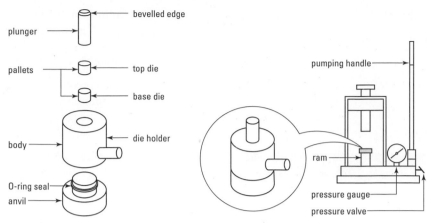

Fig. 19.5 Equipment for preparation of a KBr disk.

Box 19.3 How to prepare a KBr disk

1. **Take spectroscopic-grade KBr powder from the oven** and allow it to cool in a desiccator.

2. **Grind your compound (1–2 mg) in an agate mortar for 2 min, then add the KBr (0.2 g) and continue grinding to a fine powder.** Put the KBr powder back in the oven.

3. **Obtain a 'disk kit'** and make sure that:
   (a) it is complete – comprising a plunger, two dies (base and top), a die holder and an anvil, as shown in Fig. 19.5;
   (b) the components are for the same device – they are not interchangeable with other disk kits – and should be numbered.

4. **Press the die holder on to the anvil ensuring a proper fit.**

5. **Lower the base die, numbered-side down, into the die holder.** Make sure it slides in to a depth of about 50 mm.

6. **Pour some of the compound/KBr powder mixture, about one-third to one-half of the amount prepared, into the die holder.** Tap gently to produce an even layer on the base die.

7. **Lower the top die, numbered-side up, on top of the KBr mixture and make sure it slides down on to the powder.**

8. **Slide the plunger, with the bevelled edge at the top, into the die holder.** Ensure that it is touching the top die and press down gently so that the dies slide to the bottom, ensuring that you do not then push off the anvil.

9. **Place the assembled disk kit in the hydraulic press.** Tighten the top screw so that it touches the top of the plunger.

10. **Connect the anvil to a source of vacuum,** for example a rotary vacuum pump.

11. **Close the hydraulic release valve on the side of the press and gently pump the handle** until the pressure gauge reads between 8 and 10 tonnes and leave for 30 s.

12. **Open the hydraulic release valve gently.** When the pressure has fallen to zero, disconnect the vacuum from the anvil.

13. **Loosen the top screw.** Remove the disk kit from the press.

14. **Turn the disk kit upside down and carefully pull off the anvil.** Make sure that the plunger does not slide out by supporting it in the palm of your hand.

15. **Gently push the plunger and the base die will emerge from the die holder.** Take off the base die leaving the KBr disk exposed.

16. **Carefully slide the KBr disk into the special disk holder** using a microspatula.

17. **Run the IR spectrum immediately** because the disk will begin to cloud over as it absorbs atmospheric moisture.

18. **Clean the disk kit components with a tissue and check that all parts are present.**

19. **If the dies or the plunger stick in the die holder, tell your instructor.**

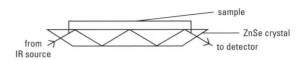

Fig. 19.6 Schematic of an ATR cell.

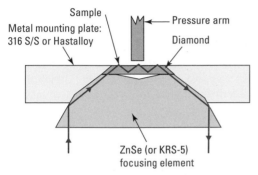

Fig. 19.7 Schematic diagram of an ATR 'diamond' anvil.

Attenuated total reflectance (ATR) sample holders

The principle of this technique depends on the fact that when light passes from a dense medium to a less dense medium, and the angle of the incident light is at a critical angle, then the light is reflected back into the dense medium, having penetrated a short distance into the less dense medium (see Fig. 19.6). In effect, the infrared spectrum of the less dense medium is recorded.

The ATR 'diamond anvil' cell comprises an infrared transparent zinc selenide (ZnSe) focusing element with a small circular diamond crystal (~1.5 mm diameter) on top, mounted in a stainless steel top plate (Fig. 19.7). In order to maintain good contact with the diamond, solids are pressed into contact using the pressure arm. In most cases sample handling is facilitated without recourse to Na Cl cells, mulls or solid films and only a small quantity of sample is required. As a result of the durability of diamond and stainless steel, clean-up of the 'diamond anvil' is an easy 'wipe clean' with no possibility of damaging the cell window. The major advantage of the 'diamond anvil' cell is that many samples can be analysed without the need for sample preparation and the only minor disadvantage is the slight reduction in intensity of the IR absorption peaks between 2,500 cm^{-1} and 1,650 cm^{-1} resulting from absorption of IR radiation by the diamond.

Applications of IR and Raman spectroscopy

Paper (with print), fabrics, polymer films, powders, gels and even aqueous solutions can produce high quality infrared spectra but the principal use of IR and Raman spectroscopy is in the identification of drugs (e.g. penicillin), small peptides, pollutants and food contaminants. When an IR spectrometer is coupled to a gas–liquid chromatograph, it can also be used for the analysis of drug metabolites. In forensic science, applications are varied and can include, for example:

- non-destructive detection of bloodstains (Doty *et al.*, 2016);
- trace evidence (e.g. paint, ink, plastic, fibres) (Zieba-Palus *et al.,* 2008);
- detection of drugs of abuse (Penido *et al.*, 2016).

Interpretation of IR spectra

To identify compounds from their IR spectrum you should know at which frequencies the stretching and bending vibrations occur. A detailed analysis can be achieved using the correlation tables found in specialist textbooks. For interpretation, the spectrum is divided into three regions:

Region 1   *(4000−2000 cm^{-1})* – this region contains the high frequency vibrations such as C—H, N—H and O—H stretching, together with C=C and C≡N stretching vibrations.

Region 2   *(2000−1500 cm^{-1})* – this is known as the 'functional group region' and includes the stretching frequencies for C=C, C=O, C=N, N=O and N—H bending vibrations.

Region 3 *(1500–650 cm⁻¹)* – this region contains stretching bands for C—O, C—N, C—Hal and the C—H bending vibrations. It is known as the 'fingerprint region' because it also contains complex low-energy vibrations resulting from the overall molecular structure and these are unique to each different molecule. Figure 19.8 shows the spectra of propan-1-ol and butan-1-ol, which show almost identical peaks for the O—H, C—H and C—O stretching frequencies and the C—H bending frequencies, but the spectra are different in the number and intensity of the peaks between 1,500 and 650 cm⁻¹, resulting from the presence of the additional CH_2 group in butan-1-ol. These highly specific bands in the 'fingerprint' region are useful for identification of molecules by comparison with authentic spectra via a database.

A simple correlation chart indicating the three regions of the spectrum and their associated bond vibrations is shown in Fig. 19.9. You can obtain most diagnostic information from spectral regions 1 and 2, since these are the simplest regions containing the peaks related to specific functional groups, while region 3 is normally used for confirmation of findings. Another important aspect of the IR spectrum is the relative intensities of the commonly found peaks and you should become familiar with peak sizes. A chart indicating the positions, general shapes and relative intensities of commonly found peaks is shown in Fig. 19.10. When you are attempting to interpret an IR spectrum you should use the approach described in Box 19.4.

If you are studying complexes formed from metals and organic ligands, the metal–ligand stretching vibration will occur below 600 cm⁻¹ and special IR spectrometers are used to observe this region. However, changes in the IR spectrum of the organic ligand on complexation can be detected in the normal 4,000–650 cm⁻¹ range.

Fourier transform infrared (FTIR) microscope – *The modification of a conventional infrared spectrometer by the addition of a microscope attachment offers considerable advantages in forensic science. The recovery of small samples from a crime scene can be examined using a FTIR microscope. Using FTIR-microscopy, small samples (down to 10 mm) can be viewed under the microscope and their composition determined by IR analysis.*

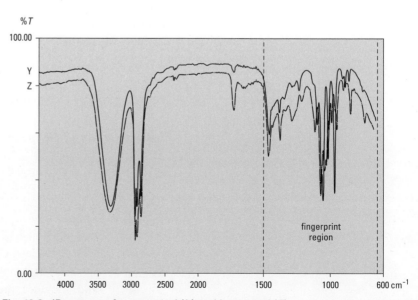

Fig. 19.8 IR spectra of propan-1-ol (*Y*) and butan-1-ol (*Z*).

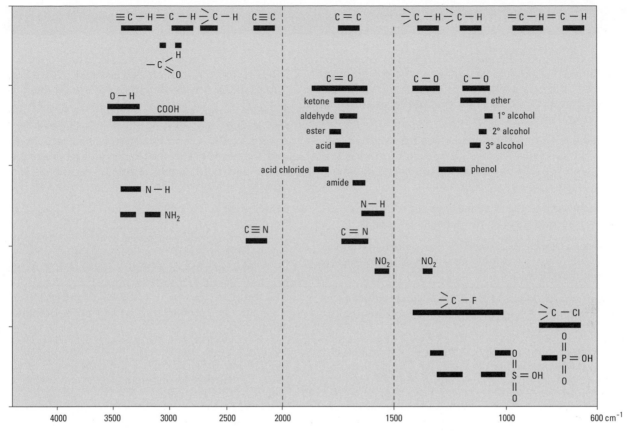

Fig. 19.9   Simplified correlation chart of functional group absorptions.

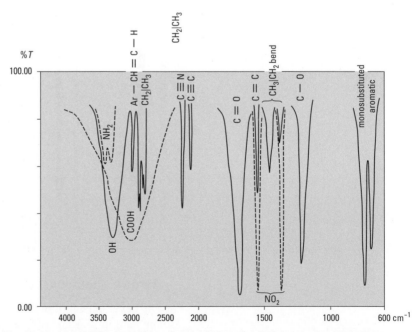

Fig. 19.10   Idealised intensities of some IR bands of common functional groups.

Box 19.4   How to interpret an IR spectrum

1. **Note the conditions under which the spectrum was obtained.** This should be written on the spectrum as 'phase'. If it was a solution or a mull, you will need to identify and 'subtract' the spectrum of the mulling agent or solvent.

2. **Consider carefully the reaction you have carried out.** You should know, from the correlation table, the functional groups and peaks in the starting materials and those expected in the product.

3. **Remember that the absence of peaks may be as useful in interpretation as the presence of peaks.**

4. *Do not attempt to identify all the peaks,* just those that are relevant to your interpretation. Go for the large peaks first.

5. **Many sharp peaks of medium to strong intensity** throughout the spectrum generally indicate an aromatic compound.

6. **Examine region 1 (4,000 – 2,000 cm^{-1}).** It is useful to draw a line on the chart at 3,000 cm^{-1}, just above the line (3,000–3,100 cm^{-1}) you will find the stretching frequencies for C_{sp}—H and C_{sp^2}—H indicating un-saturation, while just below (2,980–2,800 cm^{-1}) you

will find the C_{sp^3}—H stretching frequencies for CH_3, CH_2 and CH in saturated systems. Other bands for O—H, N—H, C≡C and C≡N are obvious.

7. **Examine region 2 (2,000–1,500 cm^{-1}).** Here you will find stretch, usually the most intense band in the spectrum; C=C and C=N stretches, less intense and sharper; N=O stretch (from NO_2) intense and sharp and with a twin band in region 3; N—H bending vibrations – do not confuse with C=O.

8. **Examine region 3 (1,500 – 650 cm^{-1}).** The large bands here are C—O, C—N, C—Cl, S=O, P=O, N=O (twin from region 2) stretches and C—H 'breathing' bands (900–700 cm^{-1}), which indicate the number and position of substituents on a benzene ring. Medium-intensity peaks of importance include the CH_3 and CH_2 bands at 1,460 cm^{-1} and 1,370 cm^{-1} from the carbon skeleton, which are also found in Nujol.

9. **Tabulate your results and make the appropriate deductions** after consulting the detailed correlation table. Remember to correlate the spectroscopic data with the chemical data.

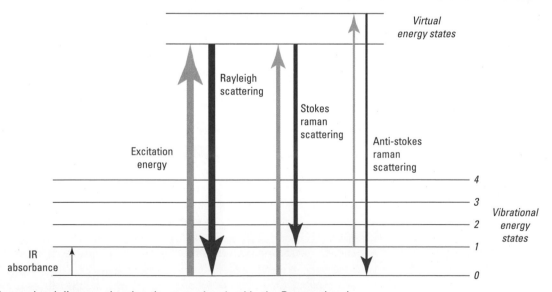

Fig. 19.11   Energy level diagram showing the states involved in the Raman signal.

Raman spectroscopy

The development of high-powered lasers has resulted in the development and application of Raman spectroscopy. Figure 19.11 shows the energy levels involved in the production of Raman spectra. The upper energy levels to which a molecule is excited by the incident light are referred to as the 'virtual levels'. The excitation in this case is not quantised; however, the method provides

Example – the symmetrical stretching mode of CO_2 involves a polarisability change in both $C = O$ bonds as they lengthen and contract (Fig. 19.13). This is therefore a Raman active vibration (at approximately $1,480$ cm^{-1}). In contrast in the asymmetrical stretching mode one $C = O$ bond lengthens as the other contracts; therefore, no change in polarisabilty takes place-so no Raman activity. In addition, in the bending mode the CO_2 molecule has no bond length changes – so it is also Raman inactive. For a simple linear centrosymmetrical molecule (e.g. CO_2), infrared active modes are Raman inactive (and vice versa).

information on the quantised vibrational levels of the molecule's ground state (as the molecule must return to one of those levels when the scattering event is complete). Most of the photons scattered by the Raman mechanism have a higher wavelength (i.e. lower energy) than the incident light – these are called the '**Stokes**' lines. In addition, it is also possible for Raman scattering to take place at shorter wavelengths (i.e. higher energy) – these are called the '**Anti-Stokes**' lines. Anti-Stokes lines are normally weaker in intensity and so are not usually used in analytical work.

Raman spectroscopy is essentially a scattering method. Most scattering takes places via the **_Rayleigh_** mechanism – this is where the photon-molecule collisions are **elastic** (i.e. do not involve any exchange of energy). As a result, the scattered photons have the same wavelength (and energy) as the incident photons (Fig. 19.11). Under normal conditions, however, a small proportion of photons are scattered **inelastically**; in this case, some energy is exchanged between a photon and the molecule it collides with. The quanta of energy involved corresponds to the vibrational energy levels of the molecules involved. Often the molecule will be in its ground vibrational state, so will accept energy from the photon (rather than vice versa). The Raman scattered light thus has a higher wavelength (i.e. lower energy) than the incident light; this principle is illustrated in Fig. 19.12 using the water molecule as an example.

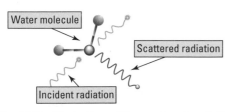

Fig. 19.12 Illustration of the scattered radiation from a water molecule.

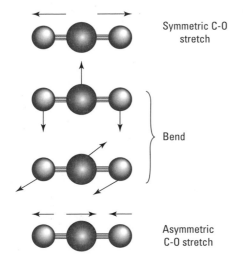

Fig. 19.13 The vibrational modes of carbon dioxide.

Principle of Raman spectroscopy

In infrared spectroscopy, absorption only occurs when a vibration causes a change in the diploe moment. In Raman spectroscopy, the principle is different even though it is the same bonds and vibrations that are involved. When the electric field associated with the incident radiation interacts with a bond it causes a momentary distortion in the associated electron cloud and a short lived induced dipole moment, which disappears when the radiation is re-emitted. The magnitude of this induced dipole moment is proportional to the polarisability of the bond (i.e. the extent to which the electron cloud is distorted by the electric field). As bonds lengthen they become more polarisable. Raman scattering only takes place when a molecular vibration is accompanied by a change in polarisability.

Resonance Raman spectroscopy

Normally, the Raman scattering effect is weak and hence the technique has had limited applicability. The development of **_Resonance Raman spectroscopy_** (RRS) has evolved due to the development of tunable lasers. In RRS it is possible to excite the sample at a wavelength at or near an electronic absorption maximum of the analyte (in aqueous solution), using a tunable laser, thereby increasing the sensitivity of the technique. A schematic diagram of a typical Raman spectrometer is shown in Fig. 19.14. A further development that has

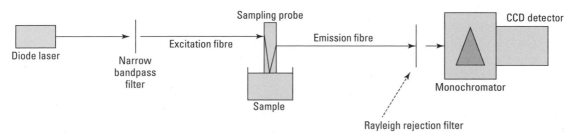

Fig. 19.14 Schematic diagram of a Raman spectrometer.

Example Raman spectroscopy has been used to identify cocaine and other illicit drugs in seized samples. For a review of the Raman spectroscopic techniques for identification of cocaine, see Penido et al. (2016).

enhanced Raman intensities is *surface-enhanced Raman spectroscopy* (SERS). In contrast to RRS, the sample is not investigated in an aqueous solution but is instead adsorbed onto a surface of a colloidal preparation of silver or gold. The combination of RRS and SERS has also led to the development of *surface-enhanced resonance Raman spectroscopy* (SERRS), which provides the enhanced sensitivity of both techniques.

The main advantages of Raman spectroscopy are as follows:

- non-destructive technique;
- no sample preparation;
- ability to collect information at low wavenumbers (i.e. 100 cm^{-1});
- fast collection of data;
- high spectral resolution is possible (typically 1 cm^{-1});
- high spatial information ($<1 \text{ } \mu\text{m}$);
- line width of spectral features generally sharp, offering good chemical distinguishing power;
- water is a weak Raman scatterer and does not mask the spectrum, enabling the analysis of aqueous solutions.

Text references

Doty, K.C., McLaughlin, G and Lednev, I.K. (2016) A Raman 'spectroscopic clock' for bloodstain age determination: The first week after deposition. *Analytical and Bioanalytical Chemistry* 408: 3993–4001.

Penido, C.A.F. de O., Pacheco, M.T.T., Lednev, I.K. and Jr. Silveira, L. (2016) Raman spectroscopy in forensic analysis: identification of cocaine and other illegal drugs of abuse. *Journal of Raman Spectroscopy* 4: 28–38.

Zieba-Palus, J., Borusiewicz, R. and Kunicki, M. (2008) PRAXIS – combined μ-Raman and μ-XRF spectrometers in the examination of forensic samples. *Forensic Science International* 175(1), 1–10.

Sources for further study

Chalman, J.M., Edwards, H.G.M. and Hargreaves, M.D. (2012) *Infra-red and Raman Spectroscopy in Forensic Science.* Wiley, Chichester.

Chapman, D. and Mantsch, H.H. (1995) *Infrared Spectroscopy of Biomolecules.* Wiley, New York.

Farquarson, S. (2010) *Applications of Surface Enhanced Raman Spectroscopy.* CRC Press, Boca Raton.

Smith, B.C. (2009) *Fundamentals of Fourier Transform Infrared Spectroscopy,* 2nd edn. CRC Press, Boca Raton.

Stuart, B. (1997) *Biological Applications of Infrared Spectroscopy.* Wiley, New York.

Virkler, K. and Lednev, I.K. (2008) Raman spectroscopy offers great potential for the nondestructive confirmatory identification of body fluids. *Forensic Science International* 181(1–3): e1–e5.

Study exercises

19.1 Interpret IR signals. The figure shows the IR spectra of acetic acid (ethanoic acid). Using the information provided below, identify the resonance corresponding to (a) the O—H and (b) C—O of the carboxylic acid group in the acetic acid spectrum.

Typical IR absorption ranges for different functional groups

Bond	Location	Wavenumber (cm⁻¹)
C—O	esters, alcohols	1,000–1,300
C—O	ketones, aldehydes, carboxylic acids, esters, amides	1,680–1,750
O—H	carboxylic acids (H-bonded)	2,500–3,300
O—H	alcohols (H-bonded)	3,230–3,350
O—H	free	3,580–3,670
N—H	amines	3,100–3,500

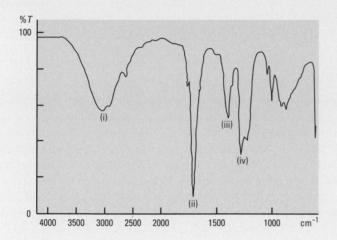

19.2 Forensic applications of FTIR. Read the case about the murder of Sarah Payne and discuss with colleagues how FTIR played a vital role in the examination of this case.

19.3 Future applications of IR and Raman spectroscopy. Using peer-reviewed journals, see if you can find some novel applications of this technology in forensic science. Devise a computer database for keeping details of your references. Keeping these records up to date will help you in your academic studies (see Chapter 48 for guidance).

Forensic applications – NMR can be used in conjunction with other analytical techniques such as GCMS (Chapter 15) for the characterisation of illicit drugs (Chapter 39). For example, 2 Chloro-4,5-methylenedioxymethylamphetamine was identified in an illicit drug seizure (Lewis et al., 2000).

Electromagnetic radiation (typically at radio frequencies of 60–600 MHz) is used to identify compounds in a process known as nuclear magnetic resonance (NMR) spectroscopy. This is possible because of differences in the magnetic states of atomic nuclei, involving very small transitions in energy levels. The atomic nuclei of the isotopes of many elements possess a magnetic moment. When these magnetic moments interact with a uniform external magnetic field, they behave like tiny compass needles and align themselves in a direction 'with' or 'against' the field. The two orientations, characteristic of nuclei with a nuclear spin quantum number $I = \frac{1}{2}$, have two different energies – the orientation aligned 'with' the field has a lower energy than that aligned 'against' the field (Fig. 20.1).

Basic principles

Typical magnetic nuclei of general use to chemists and biochemists are ^{1}H, ^{13}C, ^{19}F and ^{31}P, all of which have nuclear spin quantum numbers $I = \frac{1}{2}$. The energy difference between the two levels (ΔE) corresponds to a precise electromagnetic frequency (v), according to similar quantum principles for the excitation of electrons (p. 154). When a sample containing an isotope with a magnetic nucleus is placed in a magnetic field and exposed to an appropriate radio frequency, transitions between the energy levels of magnetic nuclei will occur when the energy gap and applied frequency are in *resonance* (i.e. when they are matched exactly in energy). Differences in energy levels, and hence resonance frequencies (v_0), depend on the magnitude of the applied magnetic field (B_0) and the magnetogyric ratio (γ), according to the equation:

$$v_0 = \frac{\gamma B_0}{2\pi}$$ [20.1]

For a given value of the applied field (B_0), nuclei of different elements have different values of the magnetogyric ratio (γ) and will give rise to resonance at various radio frequencies. The principal components of an NMR spectrometer are shown in Fig. 20.2.

For magnetic nuclei in a given molecule, an NMR spectrum is generated because, in the presence of the applied field, different nuclei of the same atoms experience small, different, local magnetic fields depending on the arrangement of electrons (i.e. in the chemical bonds) in their vicinity. The effective field at the nucleus can be expressed as:

$$B - B_0 (1 - \sigma)$$ [20.2]

where σ (the shielding constant) expresses the contribution of the small secondary field generated by the nearby electrons. The magnitude of σ depends on the

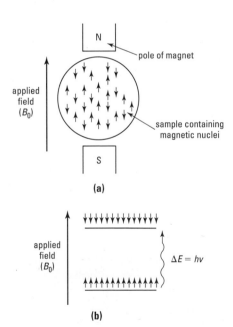

Fig. 20.1 Effect of an applied magnetic field, B_0, on magnetic nuclei: (a) nuclei in the magnetic field have one of two orientations – either with the field or against the field (in the absence of an applied field, the nuclei would have random orientation); (b) energy diagram for magnetic nuclei in an applied magnetic field.

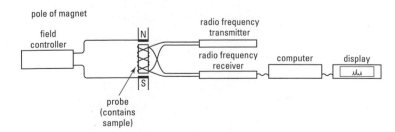

Fig. 20.2 Components of an NMR spectrometer.

electronic environment of a nucleus, so nuclei of the same isotope give rise to small different resonance frequencies according to the equation:

$$v_0 = \frac{\gamma B_0 (1 - \sigma)}{2\pi}$$

[20.3]

 KEY POINT *The variation of resonance frequencies with surrounding electron density is crucial to the usefulness of the NMR technique. If it did not occur, all nuclei of a single isotope would come into resonance at the same combination of magnetic field and radio frequency and only one peak would be observed in the spectrum.*

Chemical shift

The separation of resonance frequencies resulting from the different electronic environments of the nucleus of the isotope is called the *chemical shift*. It is expressed in dimensionless terms, as parts per million (ppm), against an internal standard, usually *tetra*methyl*s*ilane (TMS). By convention, the chemical shift is positive if the sample nucleus is less shielded (lower electron density in the surrounding bonds) than the nucleus in the reference, and negative if it is more shielded (greater electron density in the surrounding bonds). The chemical shift scale (δ) for a nucleus is defined as:

$$\delta = \frac{\left[(v_{\text{sample}} - v_{\text{reference}}) \times 10^6 \right]}{v_{\text{reference}}}$$

[20.4]

This means that the chemical shift of a specific nucleus in a molecule is at the same δ value, no matter what the operating frequency of the NMR spectrometer.

An NMR spectrum is a plot of chemical shift (δ) on the x-axis against absorption of energy (resonance) on the y-axis. On the right-hand side of the spectrum, at $\delta = 0$ ppm, there may be a small peak, which is due to the reference (TMS). A typical ^{1}H–NMR spectrum is shown in Fig. 20.3.

NMR spectrometers

These can operate at different radio frequencies and magnetic fields and are usually referred to in terms of radio frequency (e.g. 60 MHz, 270 MHz and 500 MHz spectrometers). Spectrometers operating above 100 MHz require expensive superconducting magnets to generate the strong magnetic fields. In

Nuclear spin quantum numbers and NMR *– other common nuclei with non-zero quantum numbers are 14N, 2D (I = 1) and ^{11}B and ^{35}Cl $\left(I = \frac{3}{2} \right)$. Their NMR spectra are not used on a routine basis.*

Example For an external magnetic field of 2.5T (tesla) , ΔE for ^{1}H is 6.6×10^{-26} J and since $\Delta E = hv$, the corresponding frequency (v) is 100 MHz; for ^{13}C in the same field, ΔE is 1.7×10^{-26} J, and v is 25 MHz.

Specificity of molecules *– every molecule that contains one or more magnetic nuclei has its own characteristic NMR fingerprint that may be used for identification and analysis.*

Measuring chemical shifts *– ppm is not a concentration term in NMR but is used to reflect the small frequency changes that occur relative to the reference standard, measured in proportional terms.*

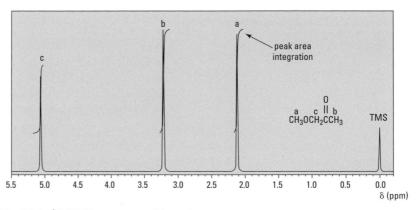

Fig. 20.3 ^{1}H–NMR spectrum of 1-methoxypropanone.

routine laboratory work 60 MHz and 90 MHz instruments are common, but 270 MHz machines are becoming more affordable. Increasing the operating frequency of the spectrometer effectively increases the resolution of the chemical shifts of the nuclei under examination. For example, the difference in frequency between 0 and 1δ is 60 Hz in a 60 MHz spectrometer but 270 Hz for a 270 MHz instrument.

Spectrometers can be divided into two types:

1. **Continuous-wave (CW) spectrometers** – which use a permanent magnet or an electromagnet, usually operating at 60 or 90 MHz. In practice, the radio frequency is held constant and small electromagnets on the faces of the main magnet (sweep coils) vary the magnetic field over the chemical shift range. The spectrometer sweeps through the spectroscopic region plotting resonances (absorption peaks) on a chart recorder (cf. dispersion IR spectrometers). CW spectrometers are usually dedicated to observation of a specific nucleus such as ^{1}H.

2. **Fourier transform (FT) spectrometers** – using superconducting magnets containing liquid nitrogen and liquid helium for cooling. Here the magnetic field is held constant and the sample is irradiated with a radio frequency pulse containing all the radio frequencies over the chemical shift region of the nucleus being examined (cf. FTIR p. 182). Computer control allows rapid repeat scans to accumulate spectra, presenting the data as a standard CW-type spectrum via FT processing. Simple variation of the radio frequencies permits observation of different nuclei (multinuclear NMR spectrometers). Thus an FT–NMR spectrometer can be used for obtaining ^{1}H, ^{13}C, ^{19}F, ^{15}N and ^{31}P NMR spectra.

Sample handling

The majority of NMR spectra are obtained from samples in solution and therefore the solvent should preferably not contain atoms of the nuclei being observed (except in the case of ^{13}C–NMR). The most common solvents are those in which the hydrogen atoms have been replaced by deuterium, which is not observed under the conditions under which the spectrum is obtained. $CDCl_3$ (deuteriochloroform, chloroform-d) is often the solvent of choice, but others such as dimethylsulphoxide-d^6 [$(CD_3)_2SO$], propanone-d^6 [$(CD_3)_2CO$], methanol-d^4 (CD_3OD) and deuterium oxide (D_2O) are in common use.

As it is unlikely that you will be allowed 'hands-on' use of an NMR spectrometer, the best approach you can take to obtain a good spectrum is to ensure good sample preparation. The quality of an NMR spectrum is degraded by:

- inappropriate solvent;
- inappropriate concentration of solute;
- inappropriate solvent volume;
- solid particles in the solution;
- water in the sample (inefficient drying);
- paramagnetic compounds.

Sample preparation for NMR spectroscopy is described in Box 20.1.

Interpreting NMR spectra

As a matter of routine in your laboratory work, you will be required to interpret ^{1}H–NMR spectra (also known as proton spectra). ^{13}C–NMR spectra are becoming more common, while ^{19}F and ^{31}P spectra may be obtained in specialised

Using deuterated solvents – these are expensive and should not be wasted. $CDCl_3$ is 100 times more expensive than spectroscopic-grade $CHCl_3$ and the others are at least 10–15 times more expensive than $CDCl_3$.

Using $CDCl_3$ – when using this solvent, additional peaks can appear in the spectrum. **^{1}H spectra** – a sharp single peak at $\delta_H = 7.26$ ppm due to the presence of $CHCl_3$ as an impurity. **^{13}C spectra** – a triplet at $\delta_C = 77.41$ ppm due to coupling between 13_C and D ($I = 1$)

Box 20.1 How to prepare a sample for NMR spectroscopy

1. **Make sure that your compound is free from water and solvent.**

2. **Test the solubility of your compound in cold CH_2Cl_2.** If it is soluble you can use $CDCl_3$ as the solvent for the NMR experiment. If it is insoluble, consult your instructor for the availability of other deuterated solvents.

3. **Dissolve your compound $CDCl_3$ (about 2 mL) in a clean, dry sample tube.** Use about 10mg of sample for CW–NMR or 5 mg of sample for FT–NMR. Check to see if the solvent contains TMS; if it does not, consult your instructor.

4. **Make a simple filter** in a new Pasteur pipette to remove insoluble material and water (Fig. 20.4). Check that your compound does not react with cotton wool and neutral alumina (alcohols and acids are strongly adsorbed on neutral alumina). If it does, replace the cotton wool with glasswool and do not use alumina. You *must* wear gloves when handling glasswool.

5. **Put the filter into a suitable clean, dry NMR tube** and, using a clean, dry Pasteur pipette, filter the solution into the NMR tube.

6. **Fill the NMR tube to the appropriate level** – between 30 and 50 mm in height is sufficient.

7. **Cap the NMR tube with the correct-size tube cap.** Make sure that it is correctly fitted to prevent oscillation when the tube is spinning in the spectrometer. Make sure that the cap is fitted correctly so that it will not fall off when the tube is in the spectrometer.

8. **Wipe the outside of the tube with a clean, dry tissue** to make sure that the spectrometer will not be contaminated. Cleaning the spectrometer probe is a very difficult task.

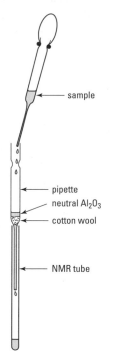

sample

pipette
neutral Al_2O_3
cotton wool

NMR tube

Fig. 20.4 Filtration of solutions for NMR.

^{1}H–NMR spectra – most of the spectra shown in this chapter do not extend over the normal spectral range $\delta = 0$–10 ppm. They are expanded to show the details of coupling patterns.

experiments. Therefore, you should concentrate on the interpretation of ^{1}H and ^{13}C spectra in the first instance.

^{1}H–NMR spectra

These normally cover the range between $\delta = 0$ and 10 ppm but the range is increased to $\delta = 15$ ppm when acidic protons are present in the molecule. The ^{1}H–NMR spectrum of a molecule gives three key pieces of information about the structure of a molecule:

1. **Chemical shift (δ)** – the peak positions indicate the chemical (magnetic) environment of the protons; i.e. different protons in the molecule have different chemical shifts.
2. **Integration** – the relative size of peak area indicates how many protons have the δ value shown.
3. **Coupling** – the fine structure on each peak (coupling) indicates the number of protons on adjacent atoms.

These three features make ^{1}H–NMR a powerful tool in structure determination and there are two extreme approaches to it:

1. **Prediction of the spectrum** of the expected compound from theoretical knowledge and then comparison with the spectrum obtained. You should recognise 'patterns' (e.g. triplet and quartet for an ethyl group; a singlet of peak area six for two identical methyl groups) that were present in the starting materials, but the δ_H values may have changed in the 'new' molecule. There are computer programs, such as g–NMR®, which will simulate the NMR spectrum from a structural formula.
2. **Interpretation of the spectrum** from correlation tables, but this is very difficult for the inexperienced.

In practice, a combination of the two approaches is used with cross-referencing and checking the proposed structure with tabulated d_H values and reference spectra until a satisfactory answer is found.

 KEY POINT *Always make sure that your predicted structure is consistent with the spectrum.*

Factors affecting chemical shift (δ_H)

The δ values of protons can be predicted to a general approximation from knowledge of the effects which produce variations in chemical shift.

1. **The hybridisation of the carbon atom** to which the hydrogen atom is attached:
   (a) sp^3 hybridised carbon – peaks occur between $\delta = 0.9$ and 1.5 ppm in simple hydrocarbon systems. The peaks move downfield with change of structure from CH_3 to CH_2 to CH.
   (b) sp hybridised carbon – peaks occur at about $\delta = 1.5$–3.5 ppm in alkynes.
   (c) sp^2 hybridised carbon – in alkenes the resonances occur around $\delta = 4$–8 ppm and the C—H peaks of aromatic rings are found between $\delta = 6$ and 9 ppm. The large downfield shifts of these C_{sp^2}—H nuclei result from deshielding of the protons by fields set up by circulation of the π electrons in the magnetic field. The proton of the aldehyde group (CHO) is particularly deshielded by this effect and is found at $\delta = 9$–10 ppm.

2. **Electron attraction or electron release** by substituent atoms attached to the carbon atom. Electron attracting atoms, such as N, O, Hal attached to the carbon, attract electron density from the C—H bonds and thus deshield the proton. This results in movement of the chemical shift to higher δ values (Table 20.1). Conversely, electron-releasing groups produce additional shielding of the C—H bonds resulting in upfield shifts of δ values.

3. **All the protons in benzene are identical** and occur at $\delta = 7.27$ ppm. In substituted aromatic compounds, the overall electron-attracting or releasing effect of the substituent(s) alters the δ values of the remaining ring protons making them non-equivalent. The *ortho* protons are affected most.

4. **For protons attached to atoms other than carbon,** the chemical shifts of protons attached to oxygen increase with increasing acidity of the O—H group; thus $\delta = 1$–6 ppm for alcohols, 4–12 ppm for phenols and 10–14 ppm for carboxylic acids. Hydrogens bound to nitrogen (1° and 2° amines) are found at $\delta = 3$–8 ppm. The approximate chemical shift regions are shown in Fig. 20.5.

Table 20.1 Chemical shifts of methyl protons

Compound	Chemical shift (ppm)
$(CH_3)_4Si$	0.00
CH_3R	0.90
CH_3I	2.16
CH_3Br	2.65
CH_3Cl	3.10
CH_3OR	3.30
CH_3F	4.26

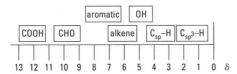

Fig. 20.5 Approximate chemical shift positions in the ^{1}H–NMR spectrum.

Proton chemical shifts – only hydrogen atoms bonded to carbon will be considered in this simplified treatment.

Interpreting NMR spectra: changes of δ – the terms used to indicate the movement of a particular peak with change in its chemical (magnetic) environment are: upfield – towards $\delta = 0$ ppm; downfield – towards $\delta = 10$ ppm; shielded – increased electron density near the proton; deshielded – decreased electron density near the proton.

Integration of peak areas

The area under each peak gives the relative number of protons and is produced directly on the spectrum (Fig. 20.6). On CW–NMR spectrometers, the height of the peak area integration line must be measured using a ruler, whereas on FT–NMR machines the area is calculated and displayed as a number. Points to remember are that:

- **The areas are *ratios*,** not absolute values, and you must find a peak attributable to a specific group to obtain a reference area – for example a single peak at $\delta = 1.0$ ppm is likely to be a CH_3 group and thus the area displayed or measured is equal to three protons.

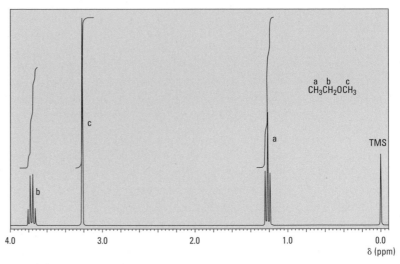

Fig. 20.6 ¹H–NMR spectrum of methoxyethane.

Integration of coupled peaks – the area under a singlet, doublet, triplet, quartet, etc., is still that of the type of hydrogen being considered. For example, if the peak for the three protons of a methyl group is split into a triplet by an adjacent methylene group, the area of the triplet is three.

- **You must ensure that you include integrations from all the fine-structure (coupling) peaks** in the peak area.
- **Do not expect the peak area integrations to be exact whole numbers** – for example, an area of 2.8 is probably three protons (CH_3), 5.1 is probably five protons (e.g. a C_6H_5 group), but 1.5 is probably a CH_3 and all the peak area integrations must be doubled.

Coupling (spin–spin splitting)

Many ¹H–NMR signals do not consist of a single line but are usually associated with several lines (splitting patterns). Protons giving multi-line signals are said to be *coupled*. This coupling arises from the magnetic influence of protons on one atom with those on an adjacent atom(s). Thus information about the nature of adjacent protons can be determined and fed into the structural elucidation problem. To a simple first approximation, the following three general points are useful in the interpretation of coupling patterns:

1. **Aliphatic systems** – if *adjacent* carbon atoms have *different types* of protons (a and b), then the protons will couple. If a proton is coupled to n ($n = 1, 2, 3, 4, 5$, etc.) other protons on an adjacent carbon atom, the number of lines observed is $n + 1$, as shown in the examples below.

$CH_3CH_2OCH_3$ Protons a are coupled to two protons b so $n = 2$;

a   b   c   therefore the peak for protons a is split into three lines (a triplet).

Protons b are coupled to three protons a so $n = 3$; therefore the peak for protons b is split into four lines (a quartet).

Protons c have no adjacent protons and therefore are not coupled and give a single line (singlet) (Fig. 20.6).

$CH_3CHBrCH_2Br$ Protons a are coupled to one proton b so $n = 1$;

a   b   c   therefore, the peak for protons a is split into two lines (doublet).

Protons b are coupled to three protons a and two protons c so $n = 5$; therefore the peak for protons b is split into six lines (sextet).

Protons c are coupled to one proton b so $n = 1$; therefore, the peak for protons c is split into two lines (doublet).

Protons a and protons c are not adjacent and do not couple (Fig. 20.7).

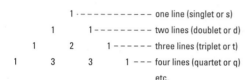

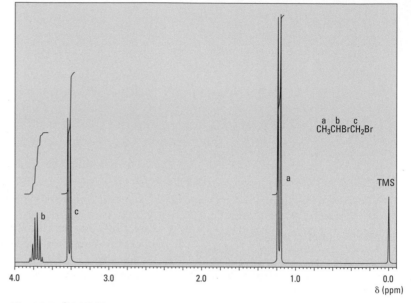

Fig. 20.7 ^{1}H–NMR spectrum of 1,2-dibromopropane.

Fig. 20.8 Intensities of coupled peaks from Pascal's triangle.

The intensity of each peak in the resulting singlet, doublet, triplet, quartet, etc. is calculated from Pascal's triangle (Fig. 20.8).

The separation between the coupled lines is called the coupling constant, J, and for aliphatic protons CH, CH_2 and CH_3 it is usually ~8 Hz.

KEY POINT *The (n + 1) rule applies only in systems where the coupling constant (J) between the protons is the same. Fortunately, this is common in aliphatic systems.*

2. **Alkene hydrogens** – hydrogen atoms on double bonds have different coupling constants depending on the stereochemistry of the alkene. Alkene hydrogens in the Z (*cis*) configuration have $J = 5–14$ Hz, whereas those in the E (*trans*) configuration have $J = 11–19$ Hz (Figs. 20.9(a) and (b)).

3. **Aromatic hydrogens** – coupling of hydrogens, which are non-adjacent, is readily observed in aromatic compounds. Different protons *ortho* to each other couple with $J = 7–10$ Hz, while those in a *meta* relationship have $J = 2–3$ Hz. *Para* coupling ($J = 0–1$ Hz) is not usually seen on the spectrum. The types of aromatic compound you are likely to meet most often are:

(a) Monosubstituted aromatic compounds – in which three basic patterns are found in the aromatic region of the spectrum. If the substituent exerts a weak electronic effect on the ring, the δ values of the ring protons are similar and the protons appear as a single peak of relative area five (Fig. 20.10(a)). If the group is strongly electron releasing (OH, NH_2, OCH_3, etc.), the

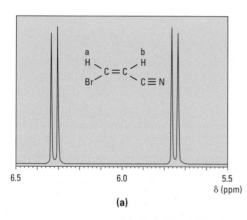

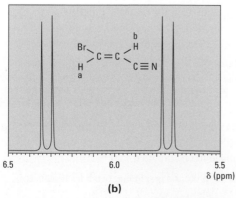

Fig. 20.9 ^{1}H–NMR spectra of: (a) (*Z*)-3-bromo-propenonitrile; (b) (*E*)-3-bromopropenonitrile.

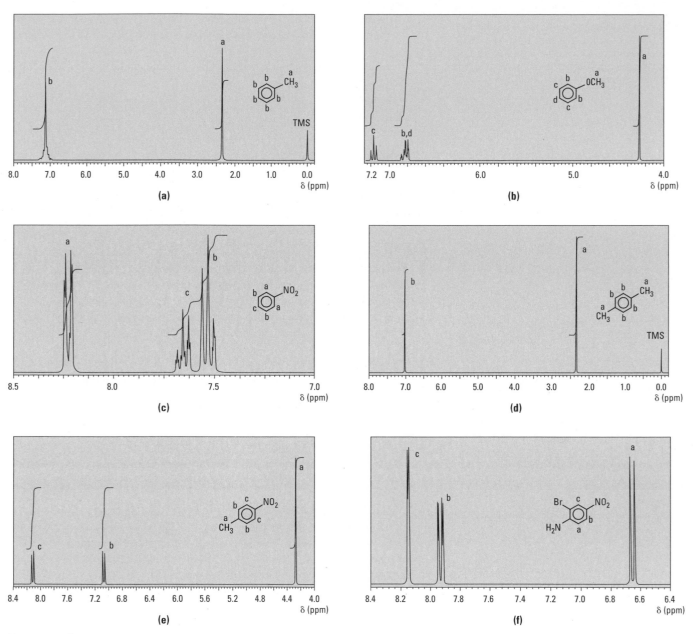

Fig. 20.10 ^{1}H–NMR spectra of: (a) methylbenzene; (b) methoxybenzene; (c) nitrobenzene; (d) 1,4-dimethylbenzene; (e) 4-methoxy nitrobenzene; (f) 4-amino-3-bromonitrobenzene (NH$_2$ protons not shown).

protons appear as complex multiplets (*ortho* and *meta* coupled) , below $\delta = 7.27$ ppm of relative areas two to three (Fig. 20.10(b)). If the group is electron attracting (e.g. NO$_2$, COOH, etc.), then the complex multiplets have $\delta = 7.27$ ppm (Fig. 20.10(c));

(b) *para*-disubstituted aromatic compounds – which are of two types. If the substituents are the same, then all the ring protons are identical and a singlet of relative area four is seen (Fig. 20.10(d)). If the substituents are different, then the pairs of hydrogens *ortho* to each substituent are different and *ortho*-couple to give what appears to be pair of doublets, each of relative area two (Fig. 20.10(e)).

Spin-lattice relaxation time – can affect signal intensities (peak sizes), and resonances may be split into several lines due to spin–spin coupling (interactions between neighbouring nuclei) (Gadian, 1996).

(c) Increasing numbers of substituents – which decrease the number of aromatic hydrogens and the spectrum becomes simpler. Thus the common 1,2,4-trisubstituted pattern (Fig. 20.10(f)) is recognised easily as an *ortho*-coupled doublet, a *meta*-coupled doublet and a doublet of doublets (coupled *ortho* and *meta*).

The chemical shifts of aromatic protons can be calculated from detailed correlation tables.

^{13}C–NMR spectra

The ^{13}C nucleus has $I = \frac{1}{2}$, like ^{1}H, and the ^{13}C–NMR spectrum of a compound can be observed using a different radio frequency range (in the same magnetic field) to that for ^{1}H. The ^{13}C spectrum will give peaks for each different type of carbon atom in a molecule, but the properties of the ^{13}C nucleus give some important and useful differences in the spectrum obtained:

- **The natural abundance of ^{13}C** is only 1.1% compared with 98.9% for ^{12}C – in any molecule no two adjacent atoms are likely to be ^{13}C and therefore coupling between ^{13}C nuclei will not be seen, giving a very simple spectrum.
- **In a sample of a compound, which contains many molecules,** the ^{13}C isotope is randomly distributed and all the different carbon atoms in a sample of a compound will be seen in the ^{13}C–NMR spectrum.
- **The sensitivity of the ^{13}C nucleus is low** and this, together with its low natural abundance, means that FT–NMR is the only practical system for producing a spectrum by accumulation of spectra by repetitions. Larger sample size in bigger NMR tubes also assist in solving the sensitivity/abundance problem.
- **The chemical shift range for ^{13}C** is greater ($\delta_C = 0$–250 ppm) than for ^{1}H ($\delta_H = 0$–15 ppm) giving greater spectral dispersion, i.e. the peaks for carbons with very slight differences in chemical shifts are separated and do not overlap.
- **^{13}C nuclei will couple with the ^{1}H nuclei** to which they are bonded directly – for example CH_3 will appear as a quartet, CH_2 as a triplet, CH as a doublet, but C with no hydrogen atoms attached will appear as a singlet. This introduction of complexity in the ^{13}C–NMR spectrum is removed by broadband decoupling (see below).
- **The peak areas of the different carbon atoms are *not* related** to the number of carbon atoms having the same chemical shift, as is the case for ^{1}H–NMR spectra.

Interpreting ^{13}C–NMR spectra

Normally you will be given two ^{13}C–NMR spectra (Fig. 20.11). The upper spectrum, which is more complex (more lines) is called the *off-resonance decoupled* spectrum and shows the ^{13}C –^{1}H coupling to enable you to determine which carbon signals are CH_3, CH_2, CH and C. Then overlapping of peaks may make the identification of different carbon atoms difficult. The lower spectrum is a *broadband decoupled* spectrum in which the molecule is irradiated with a second radio frequency range for the protons in the molecule and effectively removes all the ^{13}C–^{1}H couplings from the spectrum. The resulting simplicity of the spectrum makes identification of the different types of carbon in the molecule relatively easy.

Interpretation of ^{13}C–NMR spectra – the spectrum is that of all the carbon atoms in the molecule. It is easy to forget that the peaks for carbon atoms carrying no hydrogen atoms are present.

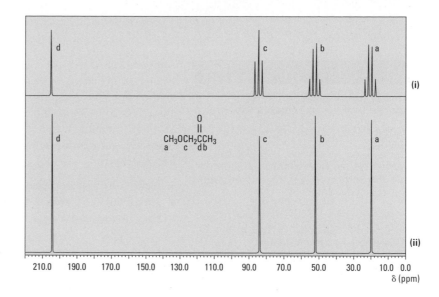

Fig. 20.11 ^{13}C–NMR spectra of 1-methoxypropa-none: (i) off-resonance decoupled; (ii) broadband decoupled.

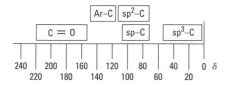

Fig. 20.12 Approximate chemical shift positions in ^{13}C–NMR.

The chemical shifts of ^{13}C atoms (δ_C) vary in the same manner as those of protons (Fig. 20.12):

1. **δ_C moves downfield** as the hybridisation of the carbon atom changes from sp^3 (0–50 ppm) to sp (75–105 ppm) to sp^2 (100–140 ppm).
2. **For sp^3 hybridised carbon,** δ_C moves further downfield with the change from CH_3 to CH_2 to CH to C.
3. **For sp^2 hybridised carbon,** aromatic carbons occur further downfield (δ_C = 115–145 ppm) than alkene carbon atoms (δ_C = 100–140 ppm).
4. **Bonding more electronegative atoms to carbon** deshields the carbon atom and moves the peaks downfield, e.g. CH_3—C (δ_C ~ 6 ppm) and CH_3—O (δ_C ~ 55 ppm), C=C (δ_C ~ 123 ppm) and C—O (δ_C ~ 205 ppm).

Text references

Gadian, D.G. (1996) *NMR and its Applications to Living Systems,* 2nd edn. Oxford University Press, Oxford.

Lewis, R.J., Reed, D., Service, A.G. and Langford, A.M. (2000) The identification of 2 Chloro-4,5-methylenedioxy-methyl amphetamine in an illicit drug seizure. *Journal of Forensic Sciences* **45**(5): 1119–1125.

Sources for further study

Callaghan, P.T. (1993) *Principles of Nuclear Magnetic Resonance Microscopy.* Oxford University Press, Oxford.

Gunther, H. (2013) *NMR Spectroscopy: Basic Principles, Concepts and Applications in Chemistry,* 2nd edn. Wiley & Sons, USA.

Levitt, M.H. (2008) *Spin Dynamics: Basics of Nuclear Magnetic Resonance,* 2nd edn. Wiley, Chichester.

Silverstein, R.M., Webster, F.X., Kiemle, D.J. and Bryce, D.L. (2015) *Spectroscopic Identification of Organic Chemicals,* 8th edn. Wiley, Chichester.

Study exercises

20.1 Investigate appropriate reference compounds for biological applications of NMR. Why are reference compounds important when measuring chemical shifts in NMR? Which compounds are suitable references for (a) ^1H and (b) ^{13}C?

20.2 Test your understanding of the NMR terminology. Distinguish between the term ppm as used in NMR and as a concentration term (p. 25).

Antibody (immunoglobulin) – a protein produced in response to an antigen.

Antigen – any antibody-generating molecule.

Epitope – a site on an antigen that determines its interaction with a particular antibody.

Hapten – a substance that contains at least one epitope, but is too small to induce antibody formation unless it is linked to a macromolecule.

Ligand – a molecule or chemical group that binds to a particular site on another molecule.

Monoclonal antibody – an antibody produced by a single clone of B lymphocytes. Monoclonal antibodies are highly specific for a particular antigen.

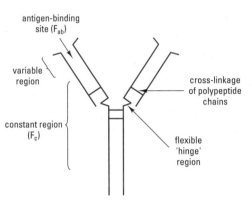

Fig. 21.1 Diagrammatic representation of IgG (antibody).

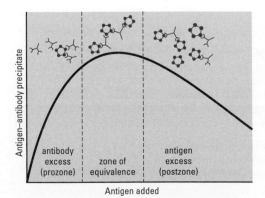

Fig. 21.2 Precipitation curve for an antigen titrated against a fixed amount of antibody.

Antibodies are important components of the immune system, protecting against a range of infectious diseases. They are protein molecules with two or more binding sites for a specific foreign substance (antigen). This specificity has allowed the development of a variety of immunoassays where the ability of an antibody to bind to an antigen, forming an antibody–antigen complex, can be measured. In forensic science, immunological assays use the specificity of this interaction for:

- identifying animal species, using the precipitin test;
- identifying the presence of a drug (or group of drugs) in blood or urine using enzyme immunoassays.

Antibody structure

An antibody is a complex globular protein, or immunoglobulin (Ig). While there are several types, IgG is the major soluble antibody in vertebrates and is used in most immunological assays. Its main features are:

- **Shape** – IgG is a Y-shaped molecule (Fig. 21.1), with two antigen-binding sites.
- **Specificity** – variation in amino acid composition at the antigen-binding sites explains the specificity of the antigen–antibody interaction.
- **Flexibility** – each IgG molecule can interact with epitopes which are different distances apart, including those on different antigen molecules.
- **Labelling** – regions other than the antigen-binding sites can be labelled, e.g. using a radioisotope or an enzyme with fluorogenic or chromogenic detection.

> **KEY POINT** *The ease of use and short analysis time involved in immunoassays mean that they can provide useful preliminary tests to indicate the presence of certain substances, where further investigation/quantification is required, using more sophisticated techniques described in Chapters 14–20, 22.*

The precipitin test

Immune complexes of antibodies and soluble antigens usually settle out of solution as a visible precipitate. In forensic science, this is usually termed a precipitin test (or precipitation test) and can be used to identify, for example, whether blood found at a scene is of human or other animal origin. The formation of visible immune complexes in agglutination and precipitation reactions only occurs if antibody and antigen are present in an optimal ratio (Fig. 21.2). It is important to appreciate the shape of this curve – cross-linkage is maximal in the zone of equivalence, decreasing if either component is present in excess. A single drop of the suspect blood is mixed with a drop of anti-human serum (produced by injecting a small amount of human blood into laboratory rabbits) and the mixture is placed on a card or slide and then rocked gently for a short time (up to 1 min). If the blood is of human origin, then visible precipitation (clumping) will occur, giving a positive reaction. If the anti-human serum gives a negative reaction, other antisera can be used to establish the type of animal, if necessary.

Radioimmunoassay (RIA)

This is based on competition between a radioactively labelled antigen (or hapten) and an unlabelled antigen for the binding sites on a limited amount of antibody. The quantity of antigen in a test solution can be determined using a known amount of radiolabelled antigen and a fixed amount of antibody. As with other immunoassay methods, it is important to perform appropriate controls to screen for potentially interfering compounds. With the increased use of enzyme immunoassay in forensic science, this technique is rarely used nowadays.

Enzyme immunoassays

These techniques are also known as enzyme-linked immunosorbent assays (ELISA). They combine the specificity of the antibody–antigen interaction with the sensitivity of enzyme assays using either an antibody or antigen conjugated (linked) to an enzyme at a site that does not affect the activity of either component. The enzyme is measured by adding an appropriate chromogenic substance, which yields a coloured product. Enzymes offer the following advantages over radioisotopic labels:

- **increased sensitivity** – a single enzyme molecule can produce many product molecules, amplifying the signal;
- **improved stability of reagents** – components are generally more stable than their radio labelled equivalents, giving them a longer shelf life;
- **automation is straightforward** – using disposable microtitre plates and an optical scanner;
- **no radiological hazard** – no requirement for specialised containment/disposal facilities.

ELISA can be used to provide a preliminary test for the presence of a specific drug or class of drugs in biological specimens including blood, *post-mortem* blood, urine, serum or plasma. The test is usually qualitative and any positive result would normally be confirmed and quantified by another analytical technique, such as HPLC, LC–MS or GC–MS (Chapter 14). The principal techniques are given below.

Double antibody sandwich ELISA

This is used to detect specific antigens, involving a three-component complex between a capture antibody linked to a solid support, the antigen and a second, enzyme-linked antibody (Fig. 21.3). This can be used to detect a particular antigen in a biological fluid or to quantify the amount of that antigen.

Indirect ELISA

This is used for antibody detection, with a specific antigen attached to a solid support. When the appropriate antibody is added, it binds to the antigen and will not be washed away during rinsing. Bound antibody is then detected using an enzyme-linked anti-immunoglobulin (Fig. 21.4), for example an anti-mouse antibody, raised by inoculating another animal (e.g. a rabbit) with mouse antibodies. One advantage of the indirect assay is that a single enzyme-linked anti-immunoglobulin can be used to detect several different antibodies, since the specificity is provided by the bound antigen.

ELISA testing in the forensic laboratory – substances commonly assayed by ELISA include amphetamine and related compounds, benzodiazepines, cannabinoids, cocaine, methadone, methylamphetamine and related compounds, morphine (specific) and opiates (general).

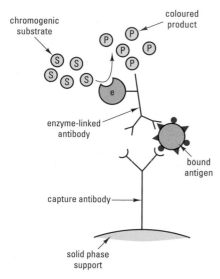

Fig. 21.3 Double antibody sandwich ELISA.

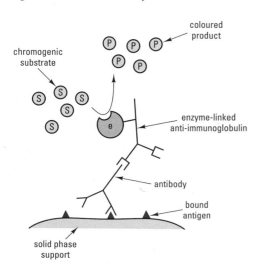

Fig. 21.4 Indirect ELISA.

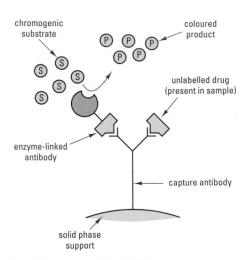

Fig. 21.5 Competitive ELISA.

(a) Positive result (indicated by the presence of one line)

(b) Negative result (indicated by the presence of two lines)

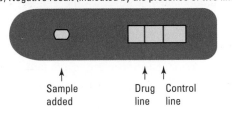

Sample added   Drug line   Control line

Fig. 21.6 Lateral Flow Immunoassay (LFIA): (a) positive result; (b) negative result.

Type approval – *any device must meet rigorous standards before being adopted for use. Only on successful completion of these standards a certificate can be granted (see also p. 358).*

Example – Legal limits (blood drug concentrations) for driving in the UK
  Cocaine *10* µg L^{-1}
  Benzoylecgonine *50* µg L^{-1}
  11 nor *δ9* tetrahydrocannabinol
  2 µg L^{-1}

Competitive ELISA

Commercially available kits are usually made up of a 96-well microplate (12 columns by 8 rows), coated with the relevant antibody for the class of drugs being investigated. A fixed volume, usually 10 or 25 µL of the case sample, calibrator or control is added to each well. A fixed volume, typically 100 µL, of enzyme-labelled drug is then added. Direct competition between this enzyme-labelled drug and the sample occurs for the binding sites of the antibody fixed to the wall of the microplate wells (Fig. 21.5). The wells are rinsed to remove excess enzyme and a chromogenic substrate is added and incubated for 30 min to visualise the enzyme as a coloured reaction. After the incubation period has elapsed, the reaction is stopped with dilute acid and the absorbance of each well is measured. Further details are given in Box 21.2. The absorbance produced at a particular wavelength is inversely proportional to the concentration of drug present in the case sample or calibrator/control.

Roadside testing for drugs of abuse

With an increasing incidence of drug driving (see Chapter 38), a number of roadside drug-testing devices have been developed to allow police officers to determine whether a suspect is under the influence of a substance other than alcohol. In the UK, legal limits for driving have been prescribed for 16 drugs including cocaine, morphine and diazepam under the Drug Driving (Specified Limits) (England and Wales) Regulations 2014. The Securetec Drugwipe™ S5 was granted type approval for roadside testing of cannabis and cocaine in 2015. These types of hand-held portable devices are based on lateral flow immunoassay techniques, a variant on the competitive immunoassay. On a nitrocellulose strip, an antibody to a drug and the drug itself are immobilised. Once the sample is added to the strip it moves by capillary action along this strip. If no drug is present, the antibody binds to immobilised drug and appears as a visible line. However, if a drug is present in the sample it binds to the antibody such that none is available to bind to the immobilised drug in the nitrocellulose strip. In this case no line appears and is indicative of a positive result (Fig. 21.6).

An alternative to this type of device is the biochip array technology, e.g. Randox Evidence Investigator™, based on chemiluminescent immunoassay where immobilised antibodies specific to different drugs are spotted at discrete test regions. The addition of the sample and an enzyme-labelled drug allows for competitive binding to these discrete sites. When viewed, if a drug is present it generates a light signal that can be read by the analyser. The advantage of this technology is that simultaneous classes of drugs can be determined in a single run.

Any roadside device (alcohol or otherwise) must be approved by the Secretary of State before 'evidence' obtained from them can then be used in court proceedings. Although type approval has been granted for the Securetec Drugwipe™ 3S, the device can only give an indication of whether cocaine or cannabis is present in the oral fluid. It remains the role of the forensic scientist to analyse a blood or urine sample that would be subsequently taken to determine whether a drug is present and whether, in their opinion, it could cause impairment.

Quality assurance and controls in enzyme immunoassays

You should always run samples in duplicate. You must be certain that the assay has performed satisfactorily, so you must include a series of controls.

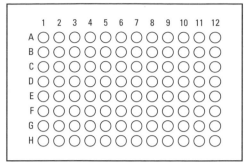

Add assay-specific enzyme conjugate to all wells

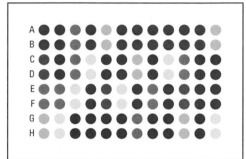

Add the chromogenic substrate to all wells

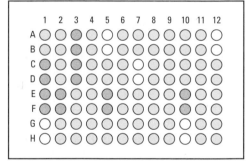

Stop the reaction

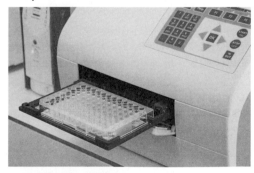

Read the plate at 450 mm using an ELISA plate reader

Fig. 21.7 Commercial ELISA 96-well kits

The first column of a commercially available ELISA kit (Fig. 21.7) is used to calibrate the plate, the results of which will be used to produce a calibration curve (see Fig. 21.8) from which all sample results will be read. The calibration is set up as follows:

- **Negative** – drug-free serum standard.
- **Negative control** – a serum standard spiked with a very low concentration of drug; this is below the cut-off concentration and therefore indicates a negative result.
- **Cutoff** – a serum standard spiked with a concentration of drug, which will be used to determine whether the result of the assay is positive or negative. This concentration is usually recommended by the manufacturers of the kits.
- **Positive control** – a serum standard spiked with a high concentration of drug; this is above the cutoff concentration and therefore indicates a positive result.

The second column typically contains matrix control samples, in duplicate, as follows:

- **Biological matrix** – the matrix that best represents the case samples, for example *post-mortem* blood, urine or serum, but you must be certain this is drug-free. You need to include these samples to be sure that the matrix does not interfere with the assay and gives a false positive result.
- **Diluent** – the case samples, calibrators and controls are diluted with either distilled water or a commercially available diluent from the ELISA kit. This diluent should also be included separately, to show that no interference has occurred.
- **Cutoff** – you should include the kit cutoff calibrator again as a check that the calibration is acceptable.
- **Known positive** – you should include a previous case sample in which the drug has already been confirmed as a 'true' positive.

Column three then contains your own spiked standards in the most appropriate biological matrix to the case samples. These should be spiked at the kit's cutoff concentration. Immunoassay is a sensitive technique to use for drug analysis in biological fluids operating effectively at concentration ranges from 5 ng mL^{-1} up to 1,000 ng mL^{-1}, hence the need to dilute the biological case samples. The same applies to the preparation of the spiked standards, an example of which is illustrated in Box 21.1.

Using the result of this sample, read from the curve, the remaining case samples can be determined to be either positive or negative – for example, if lower absorbance then the case is positive, if higher absorbance then the case is negative. A final spiked control should be at a high concentration and is used to confirm that the assay has worked successfully.

All of the other wells can be used for the case samples in duplicate, as described in Box 21.2.

Reporting the results

You should report the results as either positive or negative for the group of drugs assayed. Since the assays are usually non-specific, e.g. for benzodiazepines, a positive result does not identify a particular drug, such as diazepam, but indicates that one of the benzodiazepines is present. When presenting the results, you should include the case number, who carried out the analysis, which

Immunoassay

Definitions

Cutoff – the concentration that will indicate a positive result. Any case sample result greater than the cutoff can be reported as a positive result.

Spiking – the addition of a known concentration of drug to a drug-free matrix. This matrix should be similar to your case samples.

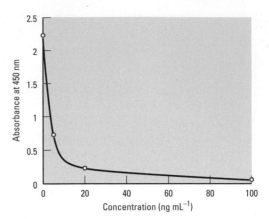

Fig. 21.8 A typical calibration curve for methadone.

Example – Common benzodiazepines that cross react with the benzodiazepine ELISA kit include:

   Chlordiazepoxide;
   Diazepam;
   Temazepam;
   Nitrazepam;
   Flunitrazepam.

assay was used and the sample(s) tested. The control values (spiked matrix cutoffs and positive) are entered on the report sheet, along with the expected concentration from your calculation, and the actual concentration calculated from the assay curve. These are recorded in full since they are the measure of how well the assay has performed and should be recorded in the case file. Since the assays are qualitative for forensic purposes, the results of the case samples are reported only as positive – in which case further screening and quantification of the drug will be requested – or negative – in which case no further analysis will be required. Finally, once the report sheet is completed it should be signed and dated.

Box 21.1   Calculating the drug concentration required for a 'spiked' standard

1. **Establish the cutoff concentration for the drug and test kit used** – for example, a manufacturer's stated cutoff concentration for a particular drug is stated to be 100 ng mL^{-1}.

2. **Establish the concentration of drug in your reference standard solution** – for example, a particular reference standard drug solution might have a concentration of 1 mg mL^{-1}.

3. **Calculate the dilution required for your standard solution to obtain the cutoff concentration required** – in this instance, the required final concentration is 100 ng mL^{-1} in your spiked standard.

Calculation (*Note:*   1 mg mL^{-1} ≅ 1,000 µg mL^{-1}; 1 µg mL^{-1} ≅ 1,000 ng mL^{-1}; and 1 mL ≅ 1,000 mL):

> ***Step 1 (initial dilution):*** 10 µL of the reference ≅ standard solution (1 mg mL^{-1}) in 1 mL methanol is a 1:100 dilution, giving a concentration of 0.01 mg mL^{-1} ≅ 10 µg mL^{-1}.

> ***Step 2 (final dilution in appropriate biological fluid):*** a further 1:100 dilution (10 mL of the diluted standard from step 1) into 1 mL blood, gives a final concentration of 0.1 µg mL^{-1} ≅ 100 ng mL^{-1}.

Box 21.2 How to perform an ELISA screen for drugs of abuse

1. **Prepare the apparatus** – switch on:
   (a) the microplate reader – the equipment that will measure the absorbance of the wells at a specific wavelength;
   (b) the microplate washer – each well is washed at various stages during the procedure. When using an automated washer, you should first check that the wash bottle has sufficient diluent and then use an 'old' microplate, to make sure that all wells are receiving the same volume of diluent to ensure that the wells are washed properly. Where necessary, use a wire needle cleaner to clean any blocked wash delivery tubes and repeat the process;
   (c) the computer – contains the software to label the wells, draw the calibration curve and calculate the results. Using the computer software, fill out the ELISA template with details of the test to be carried out.

2. **Prepare the solutions to be analysed** – these include:
   (a) samples – make sure that each sample tube is labelled with an identification number and create a key, so you know what each tube contains;
   (b) calibrators (negative, negative control, cutoff, positive control);
   (c) controls – calculate your control concentrations (Box 21.1). You should also include one 'drug-free' blank sample.
   In each instance each solution should normally be diluted, typically by adding 100 μL of solution to 400 μL of diluent, and then vortex mixed for at least 1 min so that the diluted solution is fully mixed.

3. **Add the individual solutions to the wells** – typically, 10 or 25 μL of the diluted calibrator/control/case sample solution is added to each designated well in the microplate.

4. **Add assay-specific enzyme conjugate to all wells** – typically 100 μL of horseradish peroxidase labelled drug is added to each well and the microplate is then placed in the dark at room temperature for 30 min to allow the competitive antibody – antigen interaction to take place (Fig. 21.5).

5. **Wash the wells** – transfer the microplate to the plate washer and wash the wells six times to remove excess enzyme conjugate. The final 'rinse' should be programmed to not fill the wells with diluent.

6. **Add the chromogenic substrate to all wells** – for example, 100 mL of a standard solution of 3,3′,5,5′-tetramethylbenzidine (TMB) is added to each well and re-incubated in the dark for 30 min, to allow colour development. The TMB substrate is oxidised in the presence of hydrogen peroxide to produce a blue colour. The colour is inversely proportional to the amount of drug that is present (competitive assay), so an intense blue indicates that no drug is present, for example in negative control wells (Fig. 21.7).

7. **Stop the reactions** – for example, by adding 100 mL of 1 mol L^{-1} HCl to denature the enzyme. The TMB colour will change from blue to yellow, due to the pH shift (p. 57). The human eye can distinguish shades of blue quite easily, but it is much more difficult to visually determine different shades of yellow once the reaction has been stopped.

8. **Measure the absorbance of each sample/calibrator/control well** – transfer the microplate to the plate reader and read at an appropriate wavelength. For TMB, use a wavelength of 450 nm. Check that the absorbance values in duplicate wells are in agreement with each other. If they are not, then the result cannot be accepted and the tests must be repeated – it may be that the plates were not washed adequately at each stage.

9. **Interpret the results** – for each case sample, you should check that the calibration curve (Fig. 21.8) is acceptable compared to the expected absorbance values supplied by the kit and record in your notes whether the measured concentration of your samples is greater or lower than the cutoff value. If it is greater, then it indicates a positive result. The case sample should then be analysed by another technique to determine which particular drug was initially detected using ELISA.

Sources for further study

Diamandis, E.P. and Christopoulos, T.K. (1997) *Immunoassay.* Academic Press, New York.

The Drug Driving (Specified Limits) (England and Wales) Regulations 2014. Available at: http://www.legislation.gov .uk/uksi/2014/2868/regulation/2/made. Last accessed: 17/08/2017.

Gee, S.J and Hammock, B.D. (2004) *A User's Guide to Environmental Immunochemical Analysis.* Available at: https://www.epa.gov/nscep. Last accessed: 17/08/2017.

Moffat, A.C., Osselton, M.D. and Widdup, B. (eds) (2004) *Clarke's Analysis of Drugs and Poisons,* 3rd edn. Pharmaceutical Press, London.

Study exercises

21.1 Roadside drug-testing devices. For a roadside drug-testing device to be accepted, what parameters do you think it should have? Discuss with colleagues and try to list at least five. Do you think that there will be a single device developed?

21.2 Test your knowledge of enzyme immunoassay. Without further reference to p. 205, what are the advantages of enzyme immunoassay over radioimmunoassay?

21.3 Explain your knowledge of enzyme immunoassay. Explain, in a manner understandable to a court, how ELISA works. Try your explanation with a colleague and get them to ask you questions about it.

22 Electrophoresis

Understanding electrophoresis – this is, in essence, an incomplete form of electrolysis, since the applied electrical field is switched off well before sample molecules reach the electrodes.

Table 22.1 pKa values of ionisable groups in selected amino acid residues of proteins

Group/residue	pK_a^1
Terminal carboxyl	3.1
Aspartic acid	4.4
Glutamic acid	4.4
Histidine	6.5
Terminal amino	8.0
Cysteine	8.5
Tyrosine	10.0
Lysine	10.0
Arginine	12.0

[1] Note that these are typical values – the pKa will change with temperature and ionic strength. Acidic residues will tend to be negatively charged at pH values above their pKa, whereas basic residues will tend to be positively charged below their pKa.

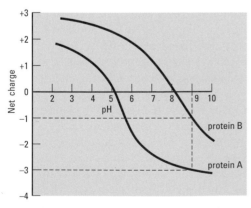

Fig. 22.1 Titration curves for two proteins, A and B, containing different proportions of acidic and basic amino acid residues.

KEY POINT *Electrophoresis is a separation technique based on the movement of charged molecules in an electric field. Dissimilar molecules move at different rates and the components of a mixture will be separated when an electric field is applied. It is a widely used technique, particularly for the analysis of complex mixtures such as DNA fragments or for the verification of purity (homogeneity) of isolated biomolecules.*

While electrophoresis is mostly used for the separation of charged macro molecules, techniques are available for high-resolution separations of small molecules such as nucleotides (e.g. by capillary electrophoresis, p. 220). Although this chapter deals mainly with the electrophoretic separation of proteins, the principles apply equally to other molecules, such as in the separation of nucleic acids, which is considered in more detail in Chapter 13).

The electrophoretic mobility of a charged molecule depends on:

- **Net charge** – negatively charged molecules (anions) migrate towards the anode ($+$), while positively charged molecules (cations) migrate towards the cathode ($-$); highly charged molecules move faster towards the electrode of opposite charge than those with lesser charge.
- **Size** – frictional resistance exerted on molecules moving in a solution means that smaller molecules migrate faster than large molecules.
- **Shape** – the effect of friction also means that the shape of the molecule will affect mobility – for example, globular proteins compared with fibrous proteins, linear DNA compared with circular DNA.
- **Electrical field strength** – mobility increases with increasing field strength (voltage), but there are practical limitations to using high voltages, especially due to heating effects.

The combined influence of net charge and size means that mobility (μ) is determined by the charge:density ratio or the charge:mass ratio, according to the formula:

$$\mu = \frac{qE}{r} \tag{22.1}$$

where q is the net charge on the molecule, r is the molecular radius and E is the field strength.

Electrophoresis and the separation of proteins

The net charge of a sample molecule determines its direction of movement and significantly affects its mobility. The net charge of a protein is pH dependent and is determined by the relative numbers of positively and negatively charged amino acid side chains at a given pH (Table 22.1). The degree of ionisation of each group is pH dependent, resulting in a variation of net charge on the molecule at different pH values (Fig. 22.1). Thus, electrophoresis is always carried out at *constant* pH and a suitable buffer must be present along with the sample in order to maintain that pH (Chapter 9). For example, if the proteins shown in Fig. 22.1 were subjected to electrophoresis at pH 9.0, and if the proteins were of similar size and shape, then the rate at which protein A (net charge, -3) migrates towards the anode would be faster than that for protein B (net charge, -1).

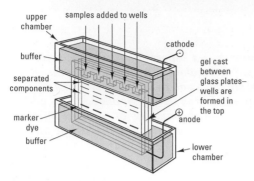

Fig. 22.2 Apparatus for vertical slab electrophoresis (components move downwards from wells, through the gel matrix).

Separation of proteins is usually carried out at alkaline pH, where most proteins carry a net negative charge.

Ionisable groups in nucleic acids include the phosphate of the phosphodiester bond and the purine and pyrimidine bases. Most nucleic acid electrophoresis is carried out at alkaline pH values at which the negatively charged phosphate group predominates. Each nucleotide moiety of nucleic acids contributes one negatively charged phosphate group, so the charge:mass ratio for molecules of different sizes will be constant. Nucleic fragments of different sizes will migrate toward the anode, but separation can only be achieved by running the sample in a gel that is able to act as a 'molecular sieve' (p. 108).

Basic apparatus

Most types of electrophoresis using a supporting medium (described below) are simple to carry out and the apparatus can be easily constructed, although inexpensive equipment is commercially available. High-resolution techniques such as 2D-electrophoresis and capillary electrophoresis require more sophisticated equipment, both for separation and analysis.

Simple electrophoretic separations can be performed either vertically (Fig. 22.2) or horizontally (Fig. 13.9, p. 109). The electrodes are normally made of platinum wire, each in its own buffer compartment. In vertical electrophoresis, the buffer solution forms the electrical contact between the electrodes and the supporting medium in which the sample separation takes place. In horizontal electrophoresis, electrical contact can be made by buffer-soaked paper 'wicks' dipping in the buffer reservoir and laid upon the supporting medium. The buffer reservoir normally contains a divider acting as a barrier to diffusion (but not to electrical current), so that localised pH changes that occur in the region of the electrodes (as a result of electrolysis) are not transmitted to the supporting medium or the sample. Individual samples are spotted on to a solid supporting medium containing buffer or are applied to 'wells' formed in the supporting medium. The power pack used for most types of electrophoresis should be capable of delivering ≈ 500 V and ≈ 100 mA.

Using a supporting medium

The effects of convection currents (resulting from the heating effect of the applied field) and the diffusion of molecules within the buffer solution can be minimised by carrying out the electrophoresis in a porous supporting medium. This contains buffer electrolytes and the sample is added in a discrete location or zone. When the electrical field is applied, individual sample molecules remain in sharp zones as they migrate at different rates. After separation, post-electrophoretic diffusion of selected biomolecules (e.g. proteins) can be avoided by 'fixing' them in position on the supporting medium, for example using trichloracetic acid (TCA).

The heat generated during electrophoresis is proportional to the square of the applied current and to the electrical resistance of the medium. Even when a supporting medium is used, heat production will lead to zone broadening by increasing the rate of diffusion of sample components and buffer ions. Heat denaturation of sample proteins may also occur, resulting in loss of biological activity, for example with enzymes. Another problem is that heat will reduce buffer viscosity, leading to a decrease in resistance. If the electrophoresis is run at constant voltage, Ohm's law dictates that as resistance falls, the current will increase, leading to further heat production. This can be avoided by using a

Minimising diffusion – *make the sample zone as narrow as possible, and fix and/or stain the bands as soon as possible after the run.*

Definition

Ohm's law $V = IR$, where V = voltage, I = current and R = resistance.

Optimising electrophoresis – attempting to minimise heat production using very low currents is not practical, since it leads to long separation times, and therefore to increased diffusion.

power pack that provides constant power. In practice, most electrophoresis equipment incorporates a cooling device – even so, distortions of an electrophoretic zone from the ideal 'sharp, linear band' can often be explained by inefficient heat dissipation.

Types of supporting medium

These can be subdivided into:

- **Inert media** – these provide physical support and minimise convection; separation is based on charge density only (e.g. cellulose acetate).
- **Porous media** – these introduce molecular sieving as an additional effect; their pore size is of the same order as the size of molecules being separated, restricting the movement of larger molecules relative to smaller ones. Thus, separation depends on both the charge density and the size of the molecule.

With some supporting media (e.g. cellulose acetate), a phenomenon called electro-endosmosis or electro-osmotic flow (EOF) occurs. This is due to the presence of negatively charged groups on the surface of the supporting medium, attracting cations in the electrophoresis buffer solution and creating an electrical double layer. The cations are hydrated (surrounded by water molecules) and when the electric field is applied, they are attracted towards the cathode, creating a flow of solvent that opposes the direction of migration of anionic biomolecules towards the anode. The EOF can be so great that weak anionic biomolecules (e.g. antibodies) may be carried towards the cathode.

Where necessary, EOF can be avoided by using supporting media such as agarose or polyacrylamide, but it is not always a hindrance to electrophoretic separation. Indeed, the phenomenon of EOF is used in the high-resolution technique of capillary electrophoresis (p. 220).

Cellulose acetate

Acetylation of the hydroxyl groups of cellulose produces a les hydrophilic structure than cellulose in the form of paper: as a result, it holds less water and diffusion is reduced, with a corresponding increase in resolution. Cullulose acetate is often used in the electrophoretic separation of plasma proteins in clinical diagnosis – it can be carried out quickly (~45 min) and its resolution is adequate to detect gross differences in various types of protein (e.g. paraproteins in myeloma). Cellulose acetate has a fairly uniform pore structure and the pores are large enough to allow unrestricted passage of all but the largest of molecules as they migrate through the medium.

Agarose

Agarose is the neutral, linear polysaccharide component of agar (from seaweed), consisting of repeating galactose and 3,6-anhydrogalactose subunits (Fig. 22.3). Powdered agarose is mixed with electrophoresis buffer at concentrations of 0.5–3.0%w/v, boiled until the mixture becomes clear, poured onto a glass plate, then allowed to cool until it forms a gel. Gelation is due to the formation of hydrogen bonds both between and within the agarose polymers, resulting in the formation of pores. The pore size depends on the agarose concentration. Low concentrations produce gels with large pores relative to the size of biological macromolecules, allowing them to migrate relatively unhindered through the gel, as determined by their individual charge densities. Low concentrations of agarose gel are suitable for techniques such as isoelectric

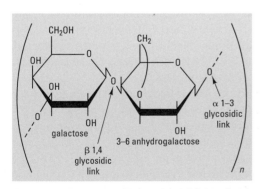

Fig. 22.3 Structure of agarose. Additional sulphate and pyruvyl groups are attached at selected hydroxyls in the polymer.

Box 22.1 How to carry out agarose gel electrophoresis of DNA

1. **Prepare the gel.** Typically, a small volume (10–20 mL) of buffer plus agarose is heated gently until the powder dissolves – take care not to overheat, or it will boil over. Nowadays, gels are often cast with a small amount of visualizing dye, such as SYBR®Safe (p. 109).

2. **Prepare the samples.** A small amount of sucrose or glycerol is usually added, to increase the density of the sample. A water-insoluble anionic 'tracking' dye (e.g. bromophenol blue or xylene cyanol) is also added to each sample, so that migration can be followed visually.

3. **Load the samples onto the gel.** Individual samples are added to the preformed wells using a pipettor (the sample should be retained within the well owing to its higher density, compared with the buffer solution). The volume of sample added to each well is small – typically less than 25 μL – so a very steady hand and careful dispensing are needed to pipette each sample accurately.

4. **Load the DNA markers onto the gel.** Typically, these standards of known size are added to the first and last wells of the gel; after electrophoresis, the relative positions of the bands of known size can be used to prepare a calibration curve (p. 477), usually by plotting $\log_{10}$ size (length) against distance travelled.

5. **Carry out ('run') the electrophoresis.** DNA separation is usually carried out at 100–150 V for 30–60 min (see manufacturer's instructions for specific details, according to which 'power pack' you are using); the gel should be run until the 'tracking' dye has migrated across 80% of the gel.

6. **Examine the result.** If you have used a visualising dye within the agarose, then you simply transfer the gel to a UV transilluminator and look for the 'bands' of fluorescence corresponding to each DNA fragment.

7. **Extract any DNA bands of interest.** If a particular band is required for further study, the piece of gel containing that band can be cut from the gel using either a clean scalpel or a specialised gel band cutter.

SAFETY NOTE – always wear suitable UV-filtering safety glasses when working with UV radiation to protect your eyes. Use a digital camera to photograph your gel. Alternatively, a dedicated image capture system can be used, e.g. GelDoc®.

Advantages of polyacrylamide gels – in addition to their versatility in terms of pore size, these gels are chemically inert, stable over a wide range of pH, ionic strength and temperature, and are transparent.

If polyacrylamide gels fail to set – polymerisation is inhibited by oxygen, so solutions should be degassed, and the surfaces of the polymerisation mixture exposed to air should be overlayed with water; if a gel still does not polymerise, the most common cause is the use of 'old' ammonium persulphate stock solution. If low pH buffers are used, polymerisation may be delayed because TEMED is required in the free base form.

focusing (p. 217), where charge is the main basis of separation. The smaller pores produced by higher concentrations of agarose may result in molecular sieving.

When agarose gels are used for the separation of DNA, the large fragment size means that molecular sieving is observed, even with low concentration gels. This is the basis of the electrophoretic separation of nucleic acids (Chapter 13). The process of DNA gel electrophoresis is shown in Box 22.1.

Polyacrylamide

Polyacrylamide gel electrophoresis (PAGE) has a major role in protein analysis and in separation of smaller DNA fragments (p. 108). The gel is formed by polymerising acrylamide monomer into long chains and cross-linking these chains using N,N'-methylene bisacrylamide (often abbreviated to 'bis'). The process is shown in Fig. 22.4. In most protocols, polymerisation is initiated by free radicals produced by ammonium persulphate in the presence of N,N,N',N'-tetramethylethylenediamine (TEMED). The photodecomposition of riboflavin can also be used as a source of free radicals.

The formation of polyacrylamide from its acrylamide monomers is extremely reproducible under standard conditions, and electrophoretic separations are correspondingly precise. The pore size, and hence the extent of molecular sieving, depends on the total concentration of monomer (%T), i.e. acrylamide plus bisacrylamide in a fixed ratio. This means that pores in the gel can be 'tailored' to suit the size of biomolecule to be separated – gels containing 3% acrylamide have large pores and are used in methods where molecular sieving should be avoided (e.g. in isoelectric focusing, p. 217), while higher concentrations of acrylamide (5–30%T) introduce molecular sieving to various degrees

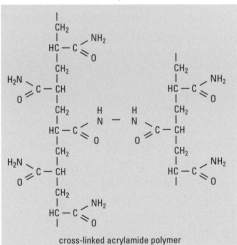

Fig. 22.4 Reactions involved in the formation of polyacrylamide gels.

depending on the size of the sample components (e.g. with 30% acrylamide gels, molecules as small as M_r 2,000 may be subject to molecular sieving). Gels of $<2.5\%$ are necessary for molecular sieving of molecules of $M_r > 10^6$, but such gels are almost fluid and require 0.5% agarose to make them solid. Note that a gel of 3% will separate DNA by molecular sieving owing to the large size of the nucleic acid molecules (p. 108).

SDS-polyacrylamide gel electrophoresis (SDS–PAGE)

The most widely used PAGE protein separation technique uses an ionic detergent, usually sodium dodecyl sulphate (SDS), which dissociates proteins into their individual polypeptide subunits and gives a uniform net charge along each denatured polypeptide. This technique, known as SDS–PAGE, requires only μg amounts of sample and is quick and easy to carry out. On the other hand, if it is necessary to preserve the native protein conformation and biological activity, non-dissociating conditions are used, i.e. no SDS is added. In SDS–PAGE the sample protein is normally heated to 100 °C for 2 min, in buffer containing 1% (w/v) SDS and 1% (w/v) 2-mercaptoethanol, the latter to cleave any disulphide bonds. The resultant polypeptides bind to SDS in a constant weight ratio, with 1.4 g of SDS per gram of protein. As a result, the intrinsic net charge of each polypeptide is 'swamped' by the negative charge imposed by SDS, and there is a uniform negative charge per unit length of polypeptide. Since the polypeptides now have identical charge densities, when they are subject to PAGE (with SDS present) using a gel of appropriate pore size, molecular sieving will occur and they will migrate strictly according to polypeptide size. Box 22.2 gives details on how to carry out SDS-PAGE for protein separation. This not only gives effective separation, but the molecular mass of a given polypeptide can be determined by comparing its mobility to polypeptide of known molecular mass run under the same conditions (Fig. 22.5). Several manufacturers (e.g. Amersham, Sigma) supply molecular mass standard kits, which may include polypeptides of M_r 11,700 to 212,000 (Table 22.2), together with details of their preparation and use. Where necessary, the treated sample can be concentrated by ultrafiltration and the buffer composition can be altered by diafiltration.

The principle of electrophoretic separation involving molecular sieving also applies to DNA fragment analysis using agarose (for larger fragments) or polyacrylamide gels (for smaller fragments).

Continuous and discontinuous PAGE systems

A continuous system is where the same buffer ions are present in the sample, gel and buffer reservoirs, all at the same pH. The sample is loaded directly on to a gel (the 'separating gel' or 'resolving gel') that has pores small enough to introduce molecular sieving. In contrast, discontinuous systems have different buffers in the gel compared to the reservoirs, both in terms of buffer ions and pH. The sample is loaded on to a large-pore 'stacking gel', previously polymerised on top of a small-pore separating gel (Fig. 22.6). The individual proteins in the sample concentrate into very narrow zones during their migration through the large-pore gel and stack up according to their charge densities, prior to separation in the small-pore gel, giving enhanced results compared with continuous systems.

Practical details of the preparation of PAGE and SDS–PAGE gels are given in Table 22.3 (see Westermeier (2004) or Gersten (1996) for further details).

Box 22.2 How to carry out SDS-PAGE for protein separation

1. **Prepare the gel.** Nowadays, many laboratories use pre-cast gels, bought from a manufacturer (e.g. BioRad®). If you are preparing your own gel, you will need to follow the protocol very carefully. Typically, the correct proportions of acrylamide, bisacrylamide and SDS are mixed together and degassed, under vacuum. Then ammonium persulfate and tetramethylenediamine (TEMED) are added to trigger the polymerisation. Once the latter two constituents are added, the gel should be poured immediately into the casting tray (including the well former 'comb').

2. **Prepare the samples.** The protein sample is mixed with a buffer solution containing SDS (to bind to the dissociated proteins), plus dithiothreitol (DTT) (to cleave disulfide bonds in the proteins) and a 'tracker' dye (e.g. bromophenol blue), then heated for 5 min at 95°C, to disrupt the tertiary structure and 'linearise' the polypeptide chains.

3. **Load the samples onto the gel.** Individual samples are added to the wells using a pipettor (p. 38). The volume of sample added to each well is typically less than 100 μL, so a very steady hand and careful dispensing are needed to pipette each sample accurately (steady the pipettor using both hands if this helps). To optimise the separation of proteins, the volume added should be kept as small as possible.

4. **Load the molecular mass standards.** Nowadays, many labs use 'rainbow' markers, with a wide range of proteins of known molecular mass, each of which is stained with a different colour, to enable estimation of the molecular masses of unknown proteins, by visual comparison.

5. **Run the electrophoresis.** The gel is positioned with the well/samples closest to the cathode (negative electrode), since they will move towards the anode during electrophoresis as a result of their negative charge. Protein separation is typically carried out at 80–100 V for 1–2 h (see manufacturer's instructions for specific details, according to which 'power pack' you are using); the gel should be run until the 'tracking' dye has migrated across 80% of the gel. Higher voltages give faster separation, but poorer separation of protein 'bands', and may cause denaturation of proteins due to heating.

6. **Fix and stain the gel.** One of the most widely used approaches uses Coomassie Brilliant Blue stain. Typically, this involves immersing the gel in 0.25% w/v Coomassie Brilliant Blue for 1 h then destaining overnight in a methanol/acetic acid solution (alternative staining/destaining procedures are given on pp. 218–219). A safer, water-based alternative can be bought from a manufacturer (e.g. Bio-Rad Bio-Safe Coomassie Stain), which allows the gel to be destained in water overnight. For higher resolution, a silver stain can be used instead of Coomassie Brilliant Blue.

7. **Examine the results.** After destaining, separated proteins are visible as blue bands against an unstained background (Fig. 22.5(a)). The position of these bands can be compared with the molecular mass standards to determine the size of each band in the test sample. For greater accuracy, the distance moved by the molecular mass standards can also be plotted against $\log_{10}$ relative molecular mass and the resulting relationship used to determine the size of unknown bands (Fig. 22.5(b)).

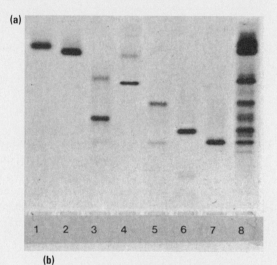

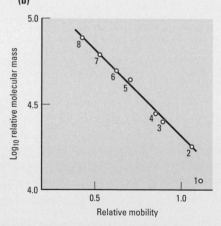

Fig. 22.5 Determination of relative molecular mass (M_r) of proteins by SDS–PAGE: (a) gel samples: 1,cytochrome c; 2,myoglobin; 3,γ-globulin; 4,carbonic anhydrase; 5,ovalbumin; 6,albumin; 7,transferrin; 8,mixture of samples 1–7 (photo courtesy of Pharmacia Biotech); (b) plot of log M_r against distance travelled through the gel.

Table 22.2 Molecular masses of standard proteins used in electrophoresis

Protein	M_r	$\log_{10}M_r$
Cytochrome c	11,700	4.068
Myoglobin	11,200	4.236
γ-globulin (light chain)	23,500	4.371
Carbonic anhydrase	29,000	4.462
Ovalbumin	43,000	4.634
γ-globulin (heavy chain)	50,000	4.699
Human albumin	68,000	4.832
Transferrin	77,000	4.886
Myosin (heavy chain)	212,000	5.326

Table 22.3 Preparation of gels for PAGE and SDS–PAGE. The gel solutions are made by mixing the components in the proportions and in the order shown. Figures are mL of each solution required to give the stated 90% gel strength

Solution (added in order shown)	PAGE		SDS–PAGE	
	3.5% gel (T = 3.6%)	7.5% gel (T = 7.7%)	5% gel (T = 5.1%)	10% gel (T = 10.2%)
1. Distilled water	19.3	7.5	14.9	—
2. Tris-glycine buffer, pH 8.9, 0.1 mol L^{-1}	33.0	33.0	—	—
3. Imidazole buffer, plus 0.2% w/v SDS	—	—	33.0	33.0
4. Acrylamide solution 22.2% w/v and 0.6% w/v bis	10.4	22.2	14.8	29.7
5. Ammonium persulphate solution, 0.15% w/v	3.2	3.2	3.2	3.2
6. TEMED	0.1	0.1	0.1	0.1
Final volume (ml)	66.0	66.0	66.0	66.0

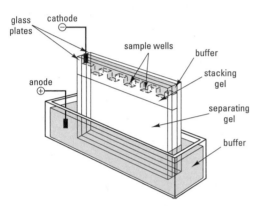

Fig. 22.6 Apparatus for discontinuous electrophoresis.

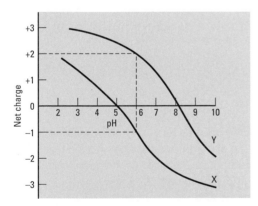

Fig. 22.7 Titration curves for two proteins, X and Y.

SAFETY NOTE *Preparing gels for PAGE* – *both acrylamide and bisacrylamide are extremely potent neurotoxins, so you must wear plastic gloves when handling solutions containing these reagents. Although the polymerised gel is non-toxic, it is still advisable to wear gloves when handling the gel, because some monomer may still be present.*

Isoelectric focusing (IEF)

In contrast to electrophoresis, which is carried out at constant pH, IEF is carried out using a pH gradient. The gradient is formed using small molecular mass ampholytes, which are analogues and homologues of polyamino-, polycarboxylic acids that collectively have a range of isoelectric points (pI values) between pH3 and 10. The mixture of ampholytes, either in a gel or in free solution, is placed between the anode in acid solution (e.g. H_3PO_4), and the cathode in alkaline solution (e.g. NaOH). When an electric field is applied, each ampholyte migrates to its own pI and forms a stable pH gradient which will persist for as long as the field is applied. When a protein sample is applied to this gradient, separation is achieved since individual proteins will migrate to their isoelectric points. The net charge on the protein when first applied will depend on the specific 'titration curve' for that protein (Fig. 22.7). As an example, consider two proteins, X and Y, having pI values of pH 5 and pH 8 respectively, which are placed together on the gradient at pH 6 (Fig. 22.8). At that pH, protein X will have a net negative charge and will migrate towards the anode, progressively losing charge until it reaches its pI (pH 5) and stops migrating. Protein Y will have a net positive charge at pH6 and so will migrate towards the cathode until it reaches its pI (pH 8).

Using a polyacrylamide gel as a supporting medium and a narrow pH gradient, proteins differing in pI by 0.01 units can be separated. Even greater resolution is possible in free solution (e.g. in capillary electrophoresis, p. 220). Such resolution is possible because protein molecules that diffuse away from the pI will acquire a net charge (negative at increased pH, positive at decreased pH) and immediately be focused back to their pI. This focusing effect will continue for as long as the electric field is applied.

In IEF, it is important that electro-osmotic flow (EOF) is avoided, as this would affect the ability of the proteins to remain stationary at their pIs. For gel IEF, polyacrylamide minimises EOF, while capillary IEF uses narrow bore tubing with an internal polymer coating.

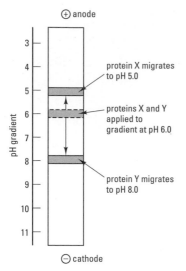

⊕ anode

protein X migrates
to pH 5.0

proteins X and Y
applied to
gradient at pH 6.0

protein Y migrates
to pH 8.0

⊖ cathode

Fig. 22.8 The migration of two proteins, X and Y, in response to a pH gradient.

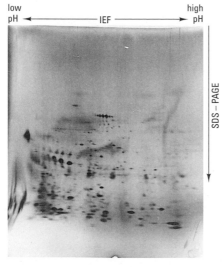

low
pH ◄──────── IEF ──────► high
pH

SDS – PAGE

Photo 22.1 Two-dimensional separation of proteins from 100 × concentrated urine (2.5μg total protein; silver stain. (Courtesy of T. Marshall and K.M. Williams.)

Preparing polyacrylamide gels – *most solutions used for gel preparation can be made in advance, but the ammonium persulphate solution must be prepared immediately before use.*

Following the progress of PAGE – *add bromophenol blue solution (0.002% w/v) to the sample in the ratio 1:25 (dye:sample). This highly ionic, small M_r dye migrates with the electrophoretic front.*

Two-dimensional electrophoresis

The most commonly used version of this high-resolution technique involves separating proteins by charge in one dimension using IEF in polyacrylamide gel, followed by separation by molecular mass in the second dimension using denaturing SDS-PAGE (p. 215). The technique allows up to 1,000 proteins to be separated from a single sample. Typically, the first dimension IEF run (pH 3–10) is carried out on gel strips of length 7–24 cm. Strips are run at a voltage of 500–3,500 V for 1.5 h, then at 3,500 V for a further 4 h. Gel strips can be used immediately, or frozen until required.

It is common for the second-dimension SDS-PAGE separation to be carried out on a discontinuous slab gel 0.5–1.5 mm thick, which includes a low percentage T stacking gel and a separating gel with an exponential gradient of 10–16% T. The separating gel can be prepared in advance, but the stacking gel must be formed shortly before addition of the rod gel from the 1D run.

After equilibration with the buffer used in SDS–PAGE, the 1D rod gel is loaded on to the 2D gel (still between the glass plates in which it was formed) and sealed in position using acrylamide or agarose. Before the sealing gel sets, a well should be formed in it at one end to allow addition of molecular mass markers. The second-dimension is run at 100–200 V until the dye front is ≈ 1 cm from the bottom edge of the slab. After running, the gel is processed for the detection of polypeptides, e.g. using Coomassie Brilliant Blue or silver stain. Analysis of the complex patterns that result from 2D electrophoresis requires computer-aided gel scanners to acquire, store and process data from a gel, such as that shown in Photo 22.1. These systems can compare, adjust and match up patterns from several gels, allowing both accurate identification of spots and quantification of individual proteins. Allowance is made for the slight variations in patterns found in different runs, using internal references ('landmarks'), which are either added standard proteins or particular spots known to be present in all samples.

Post-electrophoretic procedures – handling of the supporting medium, staining and analysis

For protein electrophoresis, the following stages are appropriate – details for nucleic acids are given on pp. 108–111.

Handling

All types of supporting medium should be handled carefully – wearing gloves is advisable, for safety and to avoid transfer of proteins from the skin. Agarose gels should be dried quickly before staining for proteins. Polyacrylamide gels in vertical slabs must be freed carefully from one of the glass plates in which they are formed, taking care to lever the glass at a point well away from the part of the gel containing the wells. Once free, the gels should be immediately transferred to fixing or staining solution.

Fixing, staining and destaining

To prevent the separated proteins from diffusing, they are usually fixed in position (Box 22.2). For most types of gel electrophoresis, 3%v/v TCA is often used. The most widely used stain for protein separations in gels is Coomassie Blue R-250 (where R = reddish hue): the detection limit is ≈ 0.2 μg and staining is quantitative up to 20 μg for some proteins. It is normal for background staining of the gel to occur, and removal of background colour ('destaining')

Use of isoelectric focusing – *it has been shown that IEF can be used for detection of transferrin phenotypes in serum samples and also to validate carbohydrate-deficient transferrin (CDT) assays for the identification of chronic alcohol abuse (see Chapter 38) (Arndt et al., 1998).*

Choosing a buffer system – *discontinuous systems are more time-consuming to prepare, but have the advantage over continuous systems in that relatively large volumes of dilute sample can be used and good resolution is still obtained.*

Choosing a pH for electrophoresis – *many proteins have isoelectric points in the range pH 4–7 and in response to electrophoresis with buffers in the region pH 8.0–9.5, most proteins will migrate towards the anode. With nucleic acid electrophoresis using agarose, tris acetate EDTA (TAE) buffer, pH 8.0, is routinely used to ensure that the DNA fragments are negatively charged.*

Avoiding streaking in 2D electrophoresis – *check carefully to ensure that the sample contains no particulate material (e.g. from protein aggregation); filter or centrifuge before use.*

Maximising resolution in 2D electrophoresis of proteins – *try to minimise nucleic acid contamination of your sample as they may interact with poly peptides/proteins, affecting their movement in the gel.*

Freezing gel strips – *be sure to mark the identity and orientation of each gel strip before freezing, e.g. by inserting a fine wire into one end of the strip. Note that, if urea is used in the gel strip, it will form crystals on freezing.*

Handling gels – *avoid touching gels with paper as it sticks readily and is difficult to remove without tearing.*

can be achieved either by diffusion or electrophoresis. To destain by diffusion, transfer the gel to isopropanol:acetic acid:water (12.5:10:77.5 v/v/v) and allow to stand for 48h, or change the solution several times to speed up the staining process. Electrophoretic destaining can remove Coomassie Blue, which is anionic – stained gels are placed between porous plastic sheets with electrodes on each side, and the tank is filled with 7% acetic acid. Passing a current of up to 1.0 A destains the gel in ≈ 30 min.

If you need greater sensitivity (e.g. for ng to fg amounts), or when using high-resolution techniques such as 2D-electrophoresis (p. 218), silver staining can be used. Depending on the protocol chosen and the proteins being stained, the silver technique can be 5- to 200-fold more sensitive than Coomassie Blue. The method involves a fixation step (e.g. with TCA), followed by exposure to silver nitrate solution and development of the stain. The silver ions are thought to react with basic and thiol groups in proteins, and subsequent reduction (e.g. by formaldehyde at alkaline pH, or by photodevelopment) leads to deposits of silver in the protein bands. Most proteins stain brown or black, but lipoproteins may stain blue, and some glycoproteins stain yellow or red. Some proteins lacking in amino acids with reducing groups (e.g. those lacking cysteine residues) may stain negatively, i.e. the bands are more transparent than the background staining of the gel. Although many protocols have been published, silver stain kits are commercially available (e.g. from Bio-Rad).

Although silver staining has clear advantages in terms of sensitivity, for routine work it is more laborious and expensive to carry out than the Coomassie Blue method. It also requires high-purity water, otherwise significant background staining occurs. Another feature is that the staining can be non-specific, since DNA and polysaccharides may stain on the same gel as proteins.

Blotting

The term 'blotting' refers to the transfer of separated proteins from the gel matrix to a thin sheet such as nitrocellulose membrane (commercially available from e.g. Millipore, Amersham). The proteins bind to this membrane and are immobilised. Blotting of proteins is usually achieved by electrophoretic transfer, and this process is normally referred to as Western blotting (see also Southern blotting and Northern blotting for DNA and RNA respectively, pp. 110–111). Its major advantage is that the immobilised proteins on the surface of the membrane are readily accessible to detection reagents, and staining and destaining can be achieved in less than 5 min. Use of labelled antibodies to detect specific proteins (immunoblotting) can take less than 6 h. In addition, it is easy to dry and store Western blots for long periods, for further analysis.

Recording and quantification of results

A number of expensive, dedicated instruments are available for the analysis of gels (e.g. laser densitometers). Alternatively, gel scanning attachments can be purchased for standard spectrophotometers, allowing measurement and recording of the absorbance of the Coomassie Blue stained bands at 560–575 nm. For instruments connected to a computer, quantification of individual components can be achieved by integrating the areas under the peaks.

You can photograph gels using a conventional camera (fine-grain film), digital camera or using a photocopier. Alternatively, a dedicated image capture and analysis system may be used (e.g. GelDoc®). The gel should be placed on a white glass transilluminator. A red filter will increase contrast with bands

Electrophoresis

Avoiding overloaded gels and band distortion – determine the protein concentration of the sample beforehand. Around 100 µg of a complex mixture, or 1–10 µg of an individual component, will be sufficient, but bear in mind that underloading may result in bands being too faint to be detected.

Optimising resolution – keep the sample volume as small as possible. For vertical slab gels and for rod gels, include 10% w/v sucrose or glycerol to increase density and allow buffer solution to be overlaid on the sample without dilution.

Origins of 'Western' blotting – following the description of 'Southern' blotting of DNA by Dr Ed Southern (p. 110), other points of the compass have been used to describe other forms of blotting, with 'Western' blotting for proteins.

Measuring peak areas – a valid 'low-tech' alternative to computer-based systems is to cut out and weigh peaks from a recorder chart.

Capillary electrophoresis is the method of choice for DNA.

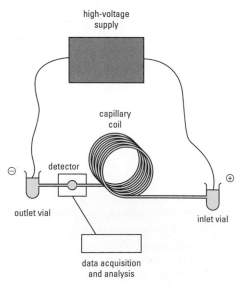

Fig. 22.9 Components of a capillary electrophoresis system.

stained with Coomassie Blue. If the gels themselves need to be retained, they can be preserved in 7% acetic acid. Alternatively, they can be dried using a commercially available gel dryer.

Capillary electrophoresis

The technique of capillary electrophoresis (CE) combines the high-resolving power of electrophoresis with the speed and versatility of HPLC (p. 131). The technique largely overcomes the major problem of carrying out electrophoresis without a supporting medium, i.e. poor resolution due to convection currents and diffusion. A capillary tube has a high surface area:volume ratio, and consequently the heat generated as a result of the applied electric current is rapidly dissipated. A further advantage is that very small samples (5–10 nL) can be analysed. The versatility of CE is demonstrated by its use in the separation of a range of biomolecules, for example amino acids, proteins, nucleic acids, drugs, vitamins, organic acids and inorganic ions. CE can even separate neutral species, for example steroids, aromatic hydrocarbons (see Weinberger, 2000). This versatility, coupled with its ability to analyse very small samples, makes CE a powerful technique for forensic analysis.

The components of a typical CE apparatus are shown in Fig. 22.9. The capillary is made of fused silica and externally coated with a polymer for mechanical strength. The internal diameter is usually 25–50 µm, a compromise between efficient heat dissipation and the need for a light path that is not too short for detection using UV/visible spectrophotometry. A gap in the polymer coating provides a window for detection purposes. Samples are injected into the capillary by a variety of means, for example electrophoretic loading or displacement. In the former, the inlet end of the capillary is immersed in the sample and a pulse of high voltage is applied. The displacement method involves forcing the sample into the capillary, either by applying pressure in the sample vial using an inert gas, or by introducing a vacuum at the outlet. The detectors used in CE are similar to those used in chromatography (p. 133), for example UV/visible spectrophotometric systems. Fluorescence detection is more sensitive, but this may require sample derivitisation.

Electro-osmotic flow (EOF), described on p. 213, is essential to the most commonly used types of CE. The existence of EOF in the capillary is the result of the net negative charge on the fused silica surface at pH values over 3.0. The resulting solvent flow towards the cathode is greater than the attraction of anions towards the anode, so they will flow towards the cathode (note that the detector is situated at the cathodic end of the capillary). The greater the net negative charge on an anion, the greater is its resistance to the EOF and the lower its mobility. Separated components migrate towards the cathode in the order: (1) cations, (2) neutral species, (3) anions.

Capillary zone electrophoresis (CZE)

This is the most widely used form of CE and is based on electrophoresis in free solution and EOF, as discussed above. Separations are due to the charge:mass ratio of the sample components, and the technique can be used for almost any type of charged molecule – it is especially useful for peptide separation and confirmation of purity.

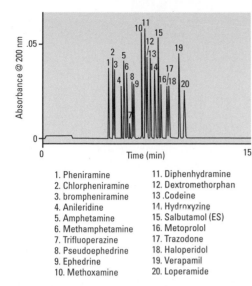

1. Pheniramine
2. Chlorpheniramine
3. brompheniramine
4. Anileridine
5. Amphetamine
6. Methamphetamine
7. Trifluoperazine
8. Pseudoephedrine
9. Ephedrine
10. Methoxamine
11. Diphenhydramine
12. Dextromethorphan
13. Codeine
14. Hydroxyzine
15. Salbutamol (ES)
16. Metoprolol
17. Trazodone
18. Haloperidol
19. Verapamil
20. Loperamide

Fig. 22.10 MEKC separation of a range of drugs.
Source: https://www.beckmancoulter.com/wsrportal/
bibliography?docname=br-9515a1.pdf, with permission
of Beckman Coulter, Inc.

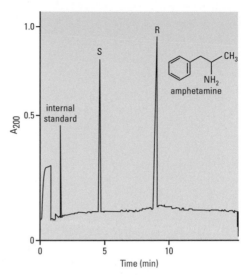

Fig. 22.11 CE separation of the R and S enantiomers of amphetamine using Beckman Coulter highly sulphated gamma cyclodextrin. Reprinted by permission of Beckman Coulter, Inc.

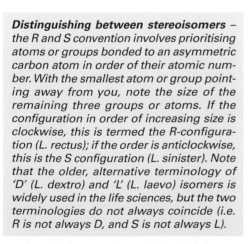

Distinguishing between stereoisomers – *the R and S convention involves prioritising atoms or groups bonded to an asymmetric carbon atom in order of their atomic number. With the smallest atom or group pointing away from you, note the size of the remaining three groups or atoms. If the configuration in order of increasing size is clockwise, this is termed the R-configuration (L. rectus); if the order is anticlockwise, this is the S configuration (L. sinister). Note that the older, alternative terminology of 'D' (L. dextro) and 'L' (L. laevo) isomers is widely used in the life sciences, but the two terminologies do not always coincide (i.e. R is not always D, and S is not always L).*

Micellar electrokinetic chromatography (MEKC)

This technique involves the principles of both electrophoresis and chromatography. Its main strength is that it can be used for the separation of neutral molecules as well as charged ones. This is achieved by including surfactants (e.g. SDS, Triton X-100) in the electrophoresis buffer at concentrations that promote the formation of spherical micelles, with a hydrophobic interior and a charged, hydrophilic surface. When an electric field is applied, these micelles will tend to migrate with or against the EOF depending on their surface charge. Anionic surfactants such as SDS are attracted by the anode, but if the pH of the buffer is high enough to ensure that the EOF is faster than the migration velocity of the micelles, the net migration is in the direction of the EOF, i.e. towards the cathode. During this migration, sample components partition between the buffer and the micelles (acting as a pseudo-stationary phase) – this may involve both hydrophobic and electrostatic interactions. For neutral species, it is only the partitioning effect that is involved in separation – the more hydrophobic a sample molecule, the more it will interact with the micelle, and the longer will be its migration time, since the micelle resists the EOF. The versatility of MEKC enables it to be used for separations of molecules as diverse as amino acids, polycyclic hydrocarbons and drugs of abuse. Figure 22.10 shows a MEKC separation of a range of drugs. MEKC is also known as micellar electrokinetic capillary chromatography (MECC).

Chiral capillary electrophoresis (CCE)

Resolution of a pair of chiral enantiomers (optical isomers) represents one of the biggest challenges for separation science, because each member of the pair will have identical physico-chemical properties. CE offers an effective method of separating enantiomers by inducing a 'chiral selector' in the electrophoresis medium. The most commonly used chiral selectors are cyclodextrins such as the highly sulphated cyclodextrins (HSCDs). As the enantiomers migrate along the capillary, one will tend to interact more strongly than the other and its mobility will be reduced relative to the other. Figure 22.11 shows separation of

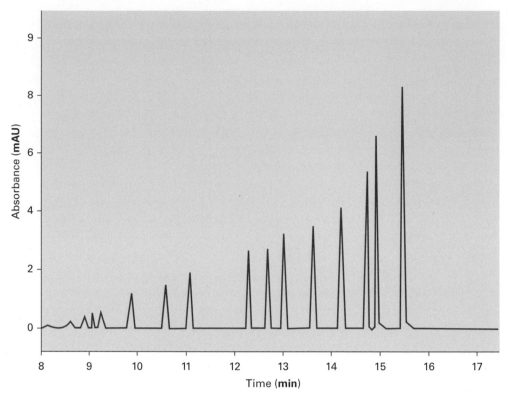

Fig. 22.12 CGE separation of a range of oligonucleotides.

the R and S forms of amphetamine using 5% HSCD in the electrophoresis buffer. The R-form has greater affinity for the HSCD used, so its retention time on the capillary is longer than that of the S-form. Note that HSDCs can also be used in HPLC, but CCE is more effective, with shorter development times and lower reagent costs.

Capillary gel electrophoresis (CGE)

The underlying principle of this technique is directly comparable with that of conventional PAGE – i.e. the capillary contains a polymer that acts as a molecular sieve. As charged sample molecules migrate through the polymer network, larger molecules are hindered to a greater extent than smaller ones and will tend to move more slowly. CGE differs from CZE and MEKC in that the inner surface of the capillary is polymer-coated in order to prevent EOF. This means that for most applications (e.g. polypeptide or oligonucleotide separations) sample components will migrate towards the anode at a rate determined by their size. The technique also differs from conventional PAGE in that a 'polymer network' is used rather than a gel – the polymer network may be polyacrylamide or agarose. A typical separation of oligonucleotide fragments by CGE is shown in Fig. 22.12.

CGE offers the following advantages over conventional electrophoresis:

- **efficient heat dissipation** means that a high electrical field can be applied, giving shorter separation times;
- **detection of the separated components** as they move towards the anodic end of the capillary (e.g. using a UV/visible detector) means that staining is unnecessary;
- **automation is feasible.**

Text references

Arndt, T., Hackler, R., Kleine, T.O. and Gressner, A.M. (1998) Validation by isoelectric focusing of the anion-exchange iso-transferrin fractionation step involved in determination of carbohydrate-deficient transferrin by the CDTect assay. *Clinical Chemistry* **44**(1): 27–34.

Gersten, D. (1996) *Gel Electrophoresis: Proteins* (Essential Techniques Series). Wiley, New York.

Weinberger, R. (2000) *Practical Capillary Electrophoresis.* Academic Press, New York.

Westermeier, R. (2004) *Electrophoresis in Practice: A Guide to Methods and Applications of DNA and Protein Separation,* 4th edn. VCH, Berlin.

Sources for further study

Anon. *British Society for Proteome Research Homepage.* Available at: http://www.bspr.org. Last accessed 17/08/2017.

Anon. *The Electrophoresis Society Homepage* (2009). Available: http://www.aesociety.org. Last accessed 17/08/2017.

Cunico, R.L., Gooding, K.M. and Wehr, T. (1998) *Basic HPLC and CE of Biomolecules.* Bay Bioanalytical, Hercules.

Guttman, A., Cohen, A.S., Heiger, D.N. and Karger, B.L. (1990) Analytical and micropreparative ultrahigh resolution of oligonucleotides by polyacrylamide gel high performance capillary electrophoresis. *Analytical Chemistry* **62**: 137–146.

Hames, B.D. and Rickwood, D. (1998) *Gel Electrophoresis of Proteins: A Practical Approach,* 3rd edn. Oxford University Press, Oxford.

Heiger, D.N., Cohen, A.S. and Karger, B.L. (1990) Separation of DNA restriction fragments by high performance capillary electrophoresis with low and zero crosslinked polyacrylamide using continuous and pulsed electric fields. *Journal of Chromatography* **516**: 33–48.

Khaledi, M.G. (1998) *High Performance Capillary Electrophoresis: Theory, Techniques and Applications.* Wiley, New York.

Link, A.J. (1998) *2-D Proteome Analysis Protocols.* Humana Press, Totowa.

Martin, R.M. (1996) *Gel Electrophoresis: Nucleic Acids* (Introduction to Biotechniques Series). Bios, Oxford.

Palfrey, S.M. (1999) *Clinical Applications of Capillary Electrophoresis.* Humana Press, New Jersey.

Strenge, M.A. and Lagu, A.L. (2004) *Capillary Electrophoresis of Proteins and Peptides.* Humana Press, New Jersey.

Tietz, D. (1998) *Nucleic Acid Electrophoresis.* Springer-Verlag, Berlin.

Weinberger, R. (2002) *Practical Capillary Electrophoresis,* 2nd edn. Academic Press, New York.

Study exercises

22.1 Find out why the net charge on a protein molecule varies with pH. Identify the amino acids primarily responsible for determining the net charge on a protein molecule and draw simple diagrams to represent the ionisation of their side chains, indicating how you would expect these side chains to be charged at acid, neutral and alkaline pH values.

22.2 Test your knowledge of 'blotting' terminology. What is Western blotting, and how does it differ from Northern and Southern blotting?

22.3 Consider the requirements for sample application in PAGE and IEF. Explain why in PAGE the sample is applied in a discrete narrow band, usually at the cathodic end of the gel, while in IEF the sample can be applied at any point along the length of the gel without concern about location or narrowness of the sample zone.

The investigative approach to crime scene investigation

The crime scene is probably the most important part of any criminal investigation. It is where forensic science starts. Locard's Principle states that every contact leaves a trace (Locard, 1928). This is the fundamental principle of scene investigation – you are looking for 'contact' evidence that will help solve the crime. This physical evidence must be protected against loss and contamination and be collected in an appropriate manner so that its evidential value is not lost during its collection, nor on transfer to the forensic laboratory and on to the courtroom. The crime scene is therefore initially cordoned off to restrict access to the evidence, thereby protecting it against contamination.

The first question you should ask at a crime scene is:

- What has happened?

At this stage, we don't know whether a crime has been committed. This is addressed later and is often informed by the 'evidence' at the scene and by law. Subsequent questions can then include:

- Has a crime been committed?
- How was it committed?
- When was it committed?
- Where was it committed?
- Who was involved?

Typical cases in forensic biology and chemistry – forensic biology crime scenes include murder, suicide, accidental death, road traffic (hit and run), assaults and serious sexual assaults. Forensic chemistry crime scenes include burglary, drug analysis, toxicology, road traffic (hit and run, driving under the influence), arson, fires and hydroponics (cultivation of narcotic plants).

 KEY POINT *The aims of a crime scene investigation are to determine what happened, to reconstruct the events leading up to the incident, to obtain as much information as possible and recover evidence that may help to determine who might (or might not) be involved. All evidence must be recovered and not compromised through contamination, cross-contamination or poor or inappropriate recovery methods.*

Crime scene personnel

Who attends a crime scene depends very much on the nature of that scene. For instance, in a frequently encountered volume crime such as burglary it would be very unusual to call out a senior ranking officer or forensic scientist, whereas in a case of murder, all members of crime scene personnel would be called out.

Members of the public

It is a common fact that most crime scenes are discovered by the public, as in the case of walking a dog and coming across a body in the bushes. The main problems with members of the public inadvertently finding a crime scene include:

- **the scene's unnecessary disturbance;**
- **their lack of awareness of forensic issues,** which could potentially destroy valuable evidence;
- **loss of time in reporting the incident.**

Police officer (first officer attending)

The role of this police officer is to secure and preserve the scene, but first and foremost he/she also has a duty to assist any complainer/victim present. He/she must also check the scene and surrounding area for potential evidence that will

Definitions

Contamination – when any crime scene has had something else added to it that is unrelated to the incident being investigated – e.g. ambulance personnel leaving a footwear impression (Chapter 27).

Cross-contamination – when trace evidence is transferred from one object or person to another via a third party – e.g. a police officer, present at a crime scene, coming into contact with the suspect could potentially allow the transfer of fibres inadvertently picked up from the scene to the suspect.

need protecting, as well as any possible assailant, but also make sure that nothing is touched or moved unless absolutely necessary. This officer also has the responsibility of taking detailed contemporaneous notes about the scene – such as whether the windows and doors were secure or whether there was evidence of forced entry, any unusual smells, lights on/off, heating, presence of weapons or drugs, etc., and positions of bodies. He/she will also need to note who was present (eyewitness, paramedics, etc., whose fingerprints and footprints will need to be taken for elimination purposes) and also minimise further disturbance of the scene. All the information that this officer has gained will be delivered to the senior investigating officer.

Senior investigating officer (SIO)/crime scene manager (CSM)

The senior investigating officer is responsible for making decisions on how to proceed with the investigation including:

- **police response** (uniformed and detective);
- **what is already known,** what it tells you and what else needs to be known;
- **how and where to find further information** to inform the investigation.

This process draws on information obtained from scientific support, intelligence, police search advisors (POLSA), the pathologist and forensic scientists.

The crime scene manager is responsible for making sure that the SIO forensic strategy is delivered during the investigation.

Scene of crime officer (SOCO)

The SOCO, also known as crime scene examiners (CSE) or crime scene investigators (CSI), can be either a police officer or civilian support staff. Their role in the investigation is to record the scene, and to search and recover evidence. The CSI is also responsible for the photography of the scene (p. 231), which orients the viewer to the evidence within the scene. He/she must also take meticulous notes during the examination, recover footwear impressions (Chapter 27) and fingerprints (Chapter 26), and correctly document the evidence recovered. There are two types of CSI – those who attend the more routine crime scenes, known as volume crime scenes (for example house break-ins) and the more experienced CSIs who attend the serious crime scenes such as murder scenes.

Forensic scientists

These are the independent forensic experts (not police) who will be called into the scene by the senior investigating officer to provide expert knowledge in either the interpretation of the scene or in the recovery of evidence. They are supplementary to the CSI, but will adhere to the same procedures as the CSI. They may also take photographs using an appropriate digital camera that is fully programmable. Digital images can complement the notes taken at the scene by the scientist to assist in the preparation of a scene statement (Chapter 60), although these images are not admissible as court exhibits (see p. 235). Scientific staff will be expert in their own discipline – a forensic chemist will be asked to attend a hydroponics scene (cannabis cultivation), whereas a forensic biologist will be asked to attend a murder scene (blood pattern interpretation, collection of trace evidence, hairs, fibres, blood, semen, etc.).

Other persons

Other people may also be asked to attend. For example, if an injured person is at the scene, paramedics will be asked to provide medical assistance, or if a person has been found dead then a forensic pathologist would be asked to

---

Taking photographs – *basic rules you should remember include:*

- *photograph everything;*
- *photograph the exhibit in situ before you do anything to it;*
- *photograph the exhibit after you have added a scale;*
- *photograph the same location after you have swabbed, added anything (e.g. arrows) and collected the evidence.*

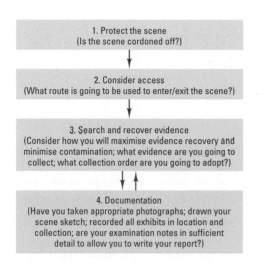

1. Protect the scene
(Is the scene cordoned off?)

2. Consider access
(What route is going to be used to enter/exit the scene?)

3. Search and recover evidence
(Consider how you will maximise evidence recovery and minimise contamination; what evidence are you going to collect; what collection order are you going to adopt?)

4. Documentation
(Have you taken appropriate photographs; drawn your scene sketch; recorded all exhibits in location and collection; are your examination notes in sufficient detail to allow you to write your report?)

Fig. 23.1 Flowchart to show the steps in crime scene examination, and associated questions.

Continuity of evidence – *the CSI or scientist who collects the evidence will record in his/her own scene log book exactly what has been collected and from where. The exhibit will be given a reference number (usually the person's initials followed by a number to indicate the order in which it was collected, i.e. 001 would have been collected before 002). This reference number identifies the exhibit and provides a written record to trace it back to its origin. This is known as continuity of evidence and all the exhibit details will appear in:*

- *the log book of the person who collected it;*
- *the label attached to the exhibit;*
- *the log book of the exhibits officer;*
- *documentation presented to the court.*

Health and Safety – *consideration must be given to the safety of the personnel as well as the protection of the scene. For example, any bodily fluid or presence of drug paraphernalia, e.g. used syringe, represents an unknown pathological risk.*

certify the death and interpret the scene, with a view to establishing the manner, mechanism and cause of death. Other experts may also be called depending on the nature of the scene – for example, if a gun is found then a firearms officer would be asked to attend to make the gun safe (Chapter 43) before anyone else can enter the scene, or if skeletal remains were found then a forensic anthropologist (Chapter 33) would be asked to attend. An exhibits officer would be present to log all evidence that is collected from the scene before transporting it to a secure storage facility. Journalists, or members of the public, may also try to attend the scene – however, they should be restricted to beyond an outer cordon (see below).

The crime scene

The purpose of the scene examination is to locate, identify, collect and preserve evidence. When working at the crime scene, you have to be aware of what evidence can be collected, how it should be collected to prevent contamination and what the evidential value is and what examinations can be performed on the evidence to further the case to its conclusion.

 KEY POINT *One of the most important aspects of scene examination is the recording/documenting of evidence before anything else takes place.*

Every scene will be different but there are some general rules (Fig. 23.1) which apply in all investigations, including:

1. **Protection of the scene** – initially the scene should be cordoned off using police tape. Two cordons should be established. The inner cordon should cover the area where you think you will find most of the evidence directly related to the incident. The outer cordon should cover an area where you think possible evidence could have been discarded, but it also allows you to maintain a distance between the evidence and the public. All personnel entering or leaving the scene can use the barrier between the inner and outer cordon to change into and out of their protective clothing. If the scene is outdoors, consideration must be given to the weather conditions. If a body has been found and it is raining, then a scene tent should be erected to preserve any trace evidence on the body. The appropriate personnel will be appointed and a log of who is present, whoever enters the scene and their purpose in entering the scene must be recorded.

2. **Access** – once the scene has been cordoned off, a decision has to be made as to the access route that will be used. Try to use points of access and egress that the suspect has not used – for example, come in through the back door of a house if the suspect has entered the property through a window and left through the front door. There will only be one entry/exit route used at the scene.

3. **Searching the scene and collecting evidence** – there is no definitive way of investigating a scene, since each is different and one method may apply to one set of circumstances but not to another. It may be that the scene is searched in parallel lines, appropriate for a large expanse of ground in an outside scene but not practical for the search of a three-storey town house. Division into grids may work, as would spiralling inwards from the edge of the cordon to the centre of the scene. The best method of searching a particular crime scene is up to the individual and the practice and advice of experienced practitioners.

4. **Documentation** – the scene has to be thoroughly documented throughout the examination. It must be recorded correctly otherwise all the subsequent examinations will be rendered meaningless. The following details should be included in standard examination forms, which should be written at the scene in sufficient detail for anyone reading them to understand and follow exactly what was done, when it was done and the order in which it was done:

(a) The initial stages of the examination should include location, date, time, who is present and any information already obtained from other persons attending the scene.

(b) The scene should be photographed (p. 239). Box 23.1 gives the guidelines for photographing a crime scene. The film will be given a unique identification number using the initials of the CSI who has taken the photographs followed by a number. The next item collected by the CSI will be given the next sequential number and so on for all other items collected.

(c) The scene should be sketched (p. 240) indicating the relative positions of the evidence. Your sketch does not have to be a work of art, but should include the dimensions of the scene and the type and exact location of the evidence.

Using photography and imaging for recording information

As a student, you may be able to request professional technical assistance for some of this type of work, but there is an important role for you in defining your requirements precisely. A basic understanding of the key factors that affect the final product will help you do this and this section aims to provide broad general guidance and advice.

Crime scene photography is usually carried out where many factors may be difficult to control. Photographs can be taken using two main systems – the digital camera and the film camera. Although the basic operation of both types is similar, they differ in their light-capturing and image-recording systems.

Film photography

Black-and-white or colour print photography involves capturing images on a film of plastic coated with light-sensitive silver halide salts. When exposed to light and subsequently chemically treated (developed), silver grains are produced to form a negative image, later converted to a positive image during printing. Transparency (slide or positive) films are based on colour dyes and are effectively grainless. The choice of film is a compromise between speed and resolution – use slower film for fine detail; faster film is more suitable for moving subjects or when light levels are low, but there is a loss of contrast and detail.

Digital photography and imaging

This is the production of an electronically stored image, produced using a digital camera (still or video/movie). The image is held as a series of discrete picture elements called pixels – the larger the number of pixels per unit surface area, the better the potential resolution of the image and the greater amount of detail captured.

Comparing digital and film systems

Despite advances in digital image technology and reductions in the price of digital cameras and associated memory systems, even the best digital images are of somewhat lower quality (resolution) than high-quality film images. However, digitised images have the advantages of speed and ease of production

Definition

Aperture – a hole through which the light travels to reach the film, set by the f-stop number seen on the lens ring (see Photo 23.1).

Depth of field – the amount of the image that is in focus from foreground to background.

Focal length – the length, in mm, of the lens.

Overexposure – excessive light is allowed to reach the film, resulting in an image that is overly bright. Any detail within this image will be lost.

Shutter speed – the time for which the shutter remains open allowing light to reach the film.

Underexposure – insufficient light is allowed to reach the film, resulting in a dark and blurry image.

Types of lenses – the most common lens is a 50 mm, which is equivalent to the same angle of view observed by the human eye:

- *wide angle – extends the angle of view to 84° but likely to get some minor distortion round the edges of the image;*
- *fish eye – extends to 180° with extensive distortion round the image;*
- *telephoto – increasing the focal length to 600 mm increases the magnification of the image;*
- *macro – a lens specifically designed for close-up imagery, less than 0.5 m distance from source.*

(since a developing stage is avoided) and are more readily manipulated. Because of the preview facility, they are also useful when it is important to confirm that a successful image has been taken, e.g. when an event is unrepeatable. On the other hand, images stored in magnetic form are not secure from computer failure, or damage from strong magnetic fields (see Box 46.1).

The role of photography in the recording of an incident

The purpose of recording an incident, whether it is still imagery or video recording, is to capture the scene as it was found. As a general rule, the scene is initially recorded by video to record the processing of the scene from start to finish. In conjunction with video footage, still imagery, traditionally through the use of conventional photography but more often nowadays through the use of digital imagery (see p. 235), is taken – the purpose of this is to record the scene *in situ* for presentation in court for illustrative purposes as well as for use during the investigative debrief. Interior images should be taken from each corner of the room, using a wide-angle lens, showing 'obvious' close-ups of evidence *in situ*, using a normal lens, as well as 360° views of rooms of significance during the investigation when 'evidence' is located.

Photography using a single lens reflex (SLR) camera

An SLR camera is composed of two parts (Photo 23.1):

- **the camera body**;
- **the lens** – normally detachable and interchangeable and essentially a series of prisms designed to focus light on to a single point, known as the focal point.

As light enters through the lens, it travels through to the focal point of the camera body, where a mirror angled at 45° is situated, just in front of where the film sits. The light is reflected vertically upwards to a pentaprism and projected through to the eyepiece that you are looking through. When the shutter is pressed to take a photo, this mirror flips up exposing the film for a controlled period of time determined by the shutter speed selected.

Photo 23.1 The single lens reflex (SLR) camera. (Image courtesy of Philip Gatward/ DK Images).

In order to take the perfect picture, there are a number of conditions that must be adopted:

- appropriate amount and angle of light;
- correct focus;
- appropriate aperture setting;
- appropriate shutter speed.

Focusing the camera

When looking through the eyepiece of the camera, depending on the model, you will see a circle in the centre of the lens. By turning the focusing ring (Photo 23.1) you can align the image such that both segments appear continuous and not disjointed (Photo 23.2). Alternatively, some models, for example Canon 5D, have a series of squares in the shape of a diamond that will flash red when the image is in focus.

Correct settings for taking the photograph

The first thing to choose is which lens to use. By reducing the focal length of the lens the image becomes smaller but the angle of view increases. Conversely, by increasing the focal length of the lens the size of the image increases but reduces the angle of view. Once selected and the image is in focus, ensure that the correct exposure settings are chosen.

 KEY POINT *The combination of the shutter speed and the aperture settings determines whether the photograph taken is correctly exposed.*

Example For a 50 mm lens do not use a shutter speed less than 1/60 unless on a tripod. The aperture is set by an f stop number, usually ranging from f22 to f1.7. Each stop reduces or enlarges the aperture in the lens by half. The f stop number represents the number in mm by which the focal length of the lens must be divided to yield the aperture diameter.

Example A 50 mm focal length lens set with an f stop of f22 has an aperture diameter of 50/22 = 2.27 mm. A 50 mm focal length lens set with an f stop of f1.7 has an aperture diameter of 50/1.7 = 29.41 mm.

Thus, where the image is in direct sunlight you would want to select a small aperture, thereby reducing the amount of light reaching the film. Conversely, in poorer light you would want to open up the aperture to allow more light to enter the camera.

The shutter speed can be set to open for 1/1,000th to 1 s. The length of the exposure time is proportional to the amount of light that exposes the film. If the subject you are taking is in broad daylight, then a fast shutter speed should be used (i.e. only opens the shutter for a very small period of time). Conversely, if the image is in poorer light, then you should open the shutter for longer to allow as much light as possible, without overexposing the image, to reach the film. If the subject is in darkness, then a flash-gun or artificial lighting should be used to illuminate the subject.

 KEY POINT *When the shutter is held open longer, the camera body must be held stationary or the image will appear blurry, known as 'camera shake'. As a general rule, the camera should always be*

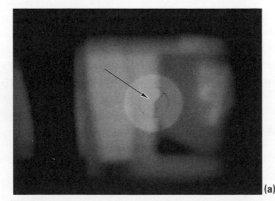

(a)   (b)

Photo 23.2 Illustration of an incorrectly focused image (a) and a correctly focused image (b). Note the disjointed image in the centre of the screen in (a), indicating that the image is not in focus (arrow).

placed on a tripod when the shutter speed 1/focal length is selected, to eliminate the risk of camera shake.

If both the subject in the foreground and the background are to be in focus, then an f11 or f16 aperture should ideally be used. If only the foreground is desired with the background blurry, an f2 aperture would suffice.

 KEY POINT *The aperture also controls the depth of field, therefore you should be careful when selecting the aperture setting.*

In combination, you have to decide whether there is sufficient light available to correctly expose the film, but you must have the correct aperture/shutter speed settings to take the image.

Types of photographic film

When using a traditional non-digital SLR camera, there are four important decisions to make when choosing a film:

1. what size of film you require in terms of both negative size and number of negatives on the film – this depends on the camera system used;
2. whether to use colour or black and white film;
3. whether to use transparency (slide or reversal) film or negative film;
4. what speed of film to use.

Film is classified by its sensitivity to light (its 'speed') and this is measured in either ISO (=ASA) or DIN units – do not confuse them. Black-and-white films and colour negative films use an emulsion that contains crystals and, therefore, has 'grain'. Table 23.1 summarises the relationship between speed, grain and definition for such films. Colour transparency films, although classified using the same speed criteria, are based on colour dyes and are effectively grainless. Slow film is used when fine detail and/or saturated colour is required, such as in microphotography, or when considerable enlargement may be required. Slow films have inherently more contrast than fast films. Use fast film when light levels are low, but remember that this results in reduction of contrast and detail. Films faster than 200 ISO (24 DIN) are only recommended for use in exceptional circumstances.

The choice of film is often a compromise between speed and detail, and a good general choice is film of about 100–160 ISO (21–23 DIN). There are many subtle differences between different makes of film, particularly with respect to colour balance, saturation and contrast, and choice is a matter of personal preference.

- **Black-and-white films** – all the usual types of modern film are panchromatic, i.e. sensitive to ultraviolet light and all the colours of the visible spectrum. Special films are available that respond only to selected wavelengths (such as infrared or X-ray) or are orthochromatic, responding only to blue, green and yellow but not to red light – such films are often used in copying and graphics work.

Table 23.1 The speed and grain relationship in film

Speed of film	ISO number	DIN number	Grain	Definition
Slow	25–64	15–19	Very fine	Very sharp
Medium	64–200	19–24	Fine	Sharp
Fast	200–400	24–27	Medium	Medium
Extra fast	400–1,600	27–32	Coarse	Poor to medium

Example In direct sunlight you could select a fast shutter speed with a wide aperture to achieve the correct exposure.

The camera has a built-in check for correct exposure. If the camera settings indicate a particular combination of shutter speed and aperture, then moving each control in opposite directions by the same increment will not affect the exposure.

Example 1/60 at f8 will be the same at 1/30 at f11, or 1/125 at f5.6

When looking through the eyepiece, you can press the shutter release button half-way down, and in your field of view the camera will indicate whether or not correct exposure has been set through the use of red − or + symbols. A green o indicates correct exposure.

Correct exposure – when a red '−' symbol appears, this tells you that the image is underexposed and you will need to increase the amount of light entering the camera – achieved through either widening the aperture or reducing the shutter speed. Likewise, a red '+' symbol indicates overexposure and you will need to reduce the amount of light entering the camera.

Definitions

Contrast – the degree of gradation between colours or the number of grey shades in black-and-white film; the higher the contrast, the sharper the gradation.

Saturation – the term used to describe the intensity of a colour; a saturated colour is an intense colour.

Storing colour film – colour film is highly sensitive to environmental factors such as heat and humidity, which cause changes in film speed and colour rendition. Make sure that your film has a sufficiently long expiry date. Store film for extended periods in a refrigerator or freezer; if stored in a freezer, allow a 24-h thawing period before use.

- **Colour films** – the main classification is into positive (reversal) film and negative film. The former is used to produce slides (transparencies) and the latter to produce colour prints. Prints can be produced from transparencies, and slides from negatives, but the former is the better process. Most negative films are colour masked giving them an overall orange tint when developed – this makes the colours purer when printed. Colour films must be balanced for the colour temperature of the light source used. Colour temperature is measured in kelvin (K; see Fig. 23.2). There are two main types of film: (a) daylight film is balanced for daylight conditions (5,400K) and for electronic flash; (b) artificial light types A (3,400K) and B (3,200K), designed for studio lighting conditions. Filters must be used if colour temperature corrections are necessary.

Types of lighting

The quantity and quality of the light is a critical factor in all photography except in electron microscopy. The quantity of light is measured by a photographic light meter, which may be external or built-in. The more light there is, the smaller the lens aperture you can use (larger 'f' number), and the greater will be the depth of field (= depth of focus). Therefore, the more light available, the better. By using the camera on a tripod, you can use slow shutter speeds and allow larger 'f' numbers to be used to maximise depth of focus. The use of an electronic flash system to provide some or all of the lighting makes this even easier, since the effective shutter speed with electronic flash is extremely short (1 ms). Modern electronic flash systems are computerised, making them easy to use.

The quality of light affects the colour balance of the film being used, even for black-and-white film. This is important under artificial light conditions when the spectrum can be different from that of sunlight. Always be sure to know the quality of light required for your film.

Remember that your choice of lighting arrangement will affect the quality of the picture – shadowless lighting is appropriate in some situations, but often shadows help to give three-dimensional form to the objects. In general, the use of more than one light source is advisable to prevent hard shadows.

 KEY POINT *For crime scene photography the position of the light is important. The purpose of the light in this case is to ensure the image is fully detailed with a minimum shadow.*

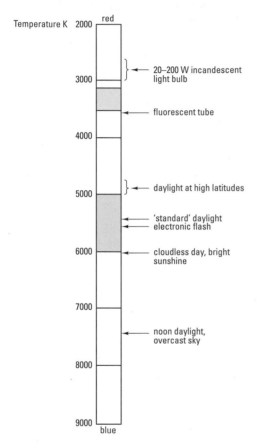

Fig. 23.2 Colour temperature and the kelvin scale in relation to sensitivity of film type.

Direction of the light

If the light is projected directly on to the surface, there is a possibility that the light will be projected directly back through the camera lens, resulting in overexposure of the film. When light is projected from behind the subject, then it is likely that the subject will appear as a silhouette. When projecting light from the side, this will emphasise shadows coming off the subject and its surroundings. Ideally, the lighting should be projected on to a white or neutral coloured surface that will reflect this light back on to the subject. This will ensure light reaches the subject to provide the detail of the image, but also reduces the potential for shadows (Photo 23.3).

 KEY POINT *To use a conventional camera properly, you need to understand the relationship between aperture (f-number), shutter speed and depth of field. For moving objects, give fast shutter speed priority by opening the lens aperture (small f-number). Where depth*

 (a)
 (b)

Photo 23.3 Illustration of the importance of the use of an external light source to visually enhance the image. Note the shadow and indistinct features when no flash is used (a) and note that the pattern and the staining on the sole of the shoe is apparent when flash is used (b).

of field is required, close the lens aperture (high f-number) – this will result in slower shutter speeds, so take care to avoid camera shake. Bracket your exposures (plus or minus 1 f-number at same shutter speed) to ensure good results.

Tips for better photography– use your camera on a tripod whenever possible, and use high shutter speed to minimise the effect of movements.

Use electronic flash wherever possible as it provides uniformity of colour balance. Unless you want shadowless lighting, do not place the flash on the camera (hot-shoe) connection.

Shadowless lighting of smaller objects is usefully obtained through a ring-flash system.

Film development (black and white)

Remember that the image quality is influenced not only by the conditions under which the film was exposed, but also by development conditions. The main factors include the type of developer used, the temperature and the duration of development. It is possible, therefore, to modify development when it is known that a film has been exposed under less than ideal light conditions and thus maximise the quality of the negative produced. If this is necessary, tell the photographer exactly what the conditions of exposure were so that adjustment of the development process can be considered. Do this only with the help of a professional photographer – it is just as easy to ruin a film as it is to improve it!

Digital imaging

An increasingly used alternative to photography is digital imaging – the production of an electronically stored image in digital format, for use by computer systems. These are usually produced using either a scanning device from a pre-existing image, or some form of digital camera (still or video). The image is held as a series of discrete units called pixels (Photo 23.4); the greater the number of pixels per unit surface area, the better the potential resolution of the image and the better the detail captured. The image may be in black/white, greyscale or colour. Image size and resolution are constrained by the amount of memory available for recording – file sizes can be very large. The quality will also depend on the printer available to you.

Digital photography for crime scene investigation

Many police forces have adopted digital photography as the norm following guidelines originally set out by the Association of Chief Police Officers (ACPO) in conjunction with Home Office Scientific Development Branch (HOSDB). These guidelines were originally produced in 2002 and were subsequently updated in 2007 and again in 2012 – they focus on image capture, retrieval, storage and use (Fig. 23.3). Evidentially, there is a need to be able to prove that the image originated from the camera in question and has remained unaltered

Photo 23.4 Pixel structure in a digital image.

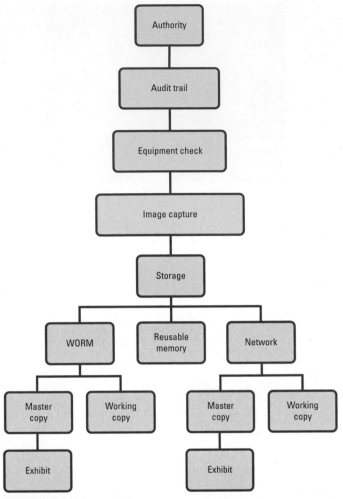

Fig. 23.3 The audit trail required to ensure that the image can be traced from its original capture to presentation in court. Adapted from Cohen and MacLennan-Brown (2007) p. 36

Digital cameras – either charged-couple devices (CCD) or complementary metal oxide semi-conductors (CMOS). Put simply, an array of light-sensitive cells absorbs light to different degrees, the energy of which is converted into a binary format, and thus a digital image.

Compression and admissibility – the issue of compression has been debated at length and it has now been agreed that provided the image illustrates the fact of the offence then evidentially it does not matter whether the image has been compressed or not.

Camera software – it is good practice to also copy the camera software on to the CD-R to allow the images to be read by any external media, i.e. in court.

Any copy of digital media is bit-for-bit identical to the original.

from its original state. An audit trail is put into place to ensure this continuity of digital evidence.

The audit trail begins with the person who is taking the image. They have to be authorised to be able to do so – for example, a crime scene photographer is authorised by virtue of their contract but a forensic scientist is not. The upshot of this is that any images taken by the scientist can be used for the investigation process, but not presented as evidence in court. The audit trail remains in place throughout the investigative process and continues until such time as disposal of the images is granted, which may be several years after the incident.

It is important to ensure that the camera has the correct time and date settings as this will be imprinted digitally on to the captured image. Any image will be stored temporarily on storage media appropriate to the camera used. This storage medium is not secure and as such is really only a transport medium until the images can be copied on to a secure medium such as CD-R or a secure network. The image should be captured in the highest definition available, usually a .RAW file, although the standard JPEG format can also be adopted and therefore it is essential that sufficient storage media are available for completion of the incident in question.

One of the advantages of the digital era is the speed with which image capture and subsequent use from a policing point of view take place. For example, Livescan is used routinely for the digital capture of palm and fingerprint taken from those arrested for any recordable offence. Immediate upload to IDENT1, the National Automated Fingerprint Identification System, has significantly increased the speed of fingerprint identification. Similarly, IRIS (integrated rapid imaging system) is currently being evaluated for the digital capture of fingerprints taken at an incident.

Optimising print quality – *remember that the quality of your negative is vital; you cannot get a good print from a poor-quality negative.*

The advantage of digital image capture is the immediacy of the image view. It is of utmost importance that no image, no matter how out of focus it appears, is deleted from the storage media and this is easily identifiable because the camera imprints a sequential number on to the image. It is also worth considering assigning a hash function to the image – assigned by a mathematical algorithm and imprinted on to the image. Any subsequent alteration of the image, even by 1 pixel, results in an alteration of the hash function (Fig. 23.4) Once the image capture is complete, the medium needs to be transported securely and the images copied on to a secure storage site. The most appropriate is CD-R (also known as Write Once, Read Many or WORM media). This initial copy is referred to as the master copy from which a working copy can be obtained simultaneously. The master copy, should be stored as any exhibit would be, and is the one that is of evidential value such that it is presented in court.

Type of print

The type of print used depends on its purpose. Glossy-finish prints generally appear sharper than matt or other finishes and are usually required for publication – the addition of lettering and scales is often only possible on the smooth surface of a glossy print. However, if preparing prints for display on a poster, the matt/velvet finishes are often preferable. The contrast of the image is determined by the choice of paper, which comes in a variety of grades of contrast. If your photo has too much contrast, reprint using a 'softer' grade of paper. You may be able to learn to develop and print your own black-and-white films, but colour printing is particularly difficult and best left to professionals.

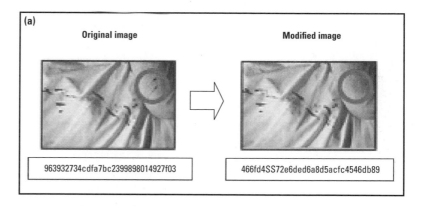

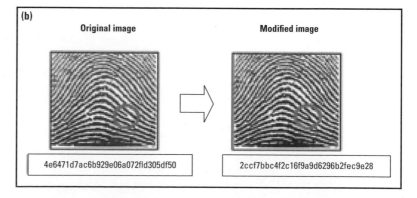

Fig. 23.4 Alteration of digital images alters the hash function, allowing the viewer to easily identify a manipulated image. In image (a) a bloodstain has been digitally removed (circled area) and in image (b) a ridge ending has been converted to a bifurcation (circled area). From Wen and Yang (2006).

Storing and mounting photographs

Both slides and negatives should be stored and maintained in good condition and be well organised. Avoid dampness, which is very destructive to all photographic materials – use silica gel desiccant in damp climates/environments. Record-keeping should be done carefully and include all relevant details, both of the subject and of the relevant processing procedures.

- **Transparencies** (slides) should be mounted in plastic mounts, but not between glass as this often causes more problems than it solves. Beware of cheap plastic filing materials as some contain residual chemicals that can damage transparencies over long time periods. Labelling of transparencies is best done on the mount using small, self-adhesive labels.
- **Negative strips** should be stored in transparent or translucent paper filing sheets. Obtain a set of contact prints for each film and store this with the negatives for easy reference.
- **Prints** should be stored flat in Boxes or in albums. When used for display, mount on stiff board either with modern photographic adhesives or dry-mounting tissue.

Drawing diagrams within a crime scene

Here, it is important to pay particular attention to the full and correct documentation of the scene. This is usually achieved by photographing the scene (Box 23.1), but your scene notes should also accurately record the scene and its components using one or more drawings. These are often referred to as 'scene sketches' and should be drawn in ink, to make a permanent record. The first sketch should show the entire scene (this is known as the scene overview) to give an indication of the overall plan, for example the position of a body in relation to items of furniture and other scene components, as shown in Fig. 23.5. Further ink sketches will also need to be drawn, to show the exact positions of the evidence within the scene – for example, location of a footwear impression on the floor, or a bloodstain on a wall. It is a good idea to indicate bloodstains on such scene sketches in red ink. The sketch should be signed and dated, as a permanent record of the scene.

If a CSI and a scientist have been asked to attend the scene, then each will produce a separate forensic statement (Chapter 60) for court purposes. A scene statement will be written by the scientist (Box 23.2), which details the scene in a descriptive format including such things as the point of entry, environmental conditions, date, time, location and position of bloodstains and any other observations. The CSI will produce a statement (Box 23.3) for court indicating what has been collected, along with the unique reference numbers and description of each type of evidence collected. A CSI, however, is not entitled to give his/her opinion in court, whereas a forensic scientist is (Chapter 60).

The types of case likely to be encountered fall loosely into the disciplines of biology (Chapters 30–36) and chemistry (Chapters 37–44). The types of evidence, also known as exhibits, that can be recovered from these cases are varied and depend on the nature of the crime scene and are discussed further in Chapter 24.

Crime scene photographs – are printed in chronological order and added to a photo album. This album is presented in court as a visual aid. Nowadays, it is becoming more common for digital multimedia presentations to be used in court.

Documenting the scene – this should include as a minimum:

- location of furniture;
- location of evidence;
- dimensions of the room and evidence as appropriate. When a scientist is requested to attend a scene, they can document the scene, but also offer an interpretation, for example, of the blood patterns observed.

Box 23.1 Guidelines for photographing a crime scene for court purposes

Photographs should be taken to document the evidence found *in situ*. As a general rule, photographs should be taken before the scene is disturbed, after the addition of a measurement scale and after the evidence has been collected.

Each room should be photographed from each corner to show the room from each angle, as well as photographing specific items following what is known as a 'three-shot rule' using a single lens reflex (SLR) camera (p. 231). In the UK, this rule has been adopted as best practice for forensic photography by the National Training Centre for crime scene investigators. Details such as date, time, film roll number, film speed, lighting conditions, distance, use of flash, exposure and aperture settings must be recorded in the scene log book, which will be used as a reference to produce the CSI statement (Chapter 60). Digital photography has now been adopted across the UK, but while the image capture and storage differs from conventional photography, the process ensuring the continuity and origination of the image does not (p. 229).

The three-shot rule includes:

1. **A long-range shot** – taken to enable the viewer to locate the area where the exhibit is in relation to the general surroundings (Photo 23.5(a)).

2. **A medium-range shot** – taken to clearly show the exhibit and anything immediately around it (Photo 23.5(b)).

3. **A close-up view or views** – taken to show the exhibit itself. The exhibit should fill most of the picture frame and should initially be taken exactly as the exhibit appears. Further photographs should be taken with a measurement scale included (Photo 23.5(c)).

4. **Additional photographs** should be taken if the exhibit has been made more visible by, for example, the removal of leaves, and also when the exhibit has been removed from its location to illustrate it in its entirety. A final photograph of the location where the exhibit was removed from should also be taken.

(a)

(b)

(c)

Photo 23.5 Photography of a crime scene: (a) long-range shot; (b) medium-range shot; (c) close-up view showing right-angled measurement scale.

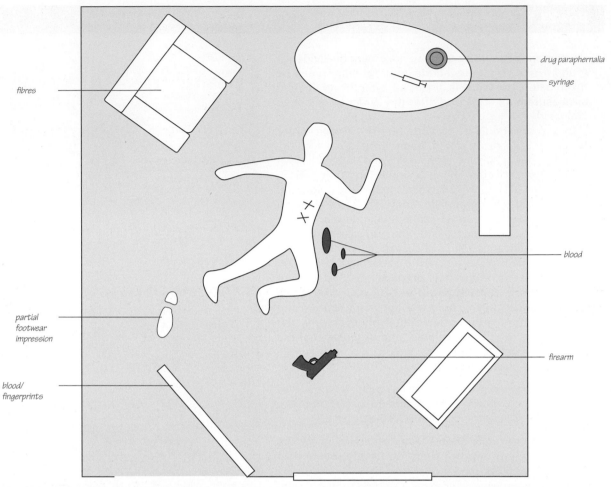

Fig. 23.5 A simple crime scene sketch. Note this has been oversimplified (see Chapter 24 for further details).

Box 23.2 Redacted example of a scene statement

64 Redrum Terrace

I, A. Boffin, hereby state that on the 1st June 2017, at the request of University Police, I attended 64 Redrum Terrace. Prior to my examination I was provided with the following information: the body of Mr D. Ceased was found on the morning of the 1st June 2017. He has been removed from the scene by the paramedics. He was last seen alive at 00:30 hours on the 1st June, when he was involved in an altercation with an as yet unidentified male.

Examination of 64 Redrum Terrace

The property was a ground-floor flat. The front door opened on to a hallway. Access to the living room was at the end of the hallway to the right of the front door. To the left of the front door was a bathroom. Adjacent to this bathroom was access to a double bedroom. Adjacent to the bedroom there was access to a dining room, with further access to a kitchen.

Front door

The front door to the property appeared unforced and undamaged. Heavy dripped blood was present on the external and internal handles of the front door. In my opinion these findings support the view that someone has entered the front door while dripping blood. Representative blood samples have been taken from the work surfaces and floor (AB0001; AB0002; AB0003).

Hallway

Heavy dripped blood was present on the hallway carpet leading from the front door to the living room. In my opinion these findings support the view that someone has moved around while dripping blood. In addition, a bloodstained footwear mark (AB0004) was present among the dripped blood on the floor suggesting that someone had walked across the floor while this blood was still wet. Representative blood samples have been

Box 23.2 (Continued)

taken from the work surfaces and floor (AB0005; AB0006; AB0007).

Living room

Heavy dripped blood was present on the carpet leading from the hallway to the settee.

Heavy bloodstaining was present to the settee, where Mr D. Ceased lay, and to the carpet below. In my opinion the nature and distribution of the blood to and around Mr D. Ceased is what I would expect if Mr D. Ceased had lain on the settee while bleeding heavily. Representative blood samples have been taken from the living room (AB0008; AB0009; AB0010).

Kitchen

There was nothing of apparent significance in this room.

Bathroom

There was nothing of apparent significance in this room.

Double bedroom

There was nothing of apparent significance in this room.

Signed : A. Boffin
Dated: 3rd October 2017

Box 23.3 Example of a CSI statement

UNIVERSITY POLICE WITNESS STATEMENT

Statement of: Jenny Brown
Age: Over 21

This statement (consisting of 1 page signed by me) is true to the best of my knowledge and belief and I make it knowing that, if it is tendered in evidence, I shall be liable to prosecution if I have wilfully stated in it anything which I know to be false or do not believe to be true.

Dated: 1st April 2017
Signature: J. Brown

I am a civilian Crime Scene Examiner employed by University Police. At 10:30 hours on 1st April 2017, I was on duty when I attended an incident at 64 Redrum Terrace, a two-storey semi-detached dwelling house.

On arrival at the scene I took a series of photographs of the outside of the property. This film roll number was L/454/04A, and I refer to this film as JB001. This film was further used to photograph the exhibits *in situ,* details of which are listed below and annotated in my scene log.

Under instruction from A. Boffin, I collected the following samples from the premises:
JB002 fibre lifts from seat of settee in livingroom of dwelling house 64 Redrum Terrace.
JB003 fibre lifts from back of settee in livingroom of dwelling house 64 Redrum Terrace.
JB004 fibre lifts from left arm of settee in livingroom of dwelling house 64 Redrum Terrace.
JB005 cellular material from floor in livingroom of dwelling house 64 Redrum Terrace.
JB006 blood lift from left arm of settee in livingroom of dwelling house 64 Redrum Terrace.
JB007 blood lift from sink in kitchen of dwelling house 64 Redrum Terrace.
JB008 blood lift from hot water tap in bathroom of dwelling house 64 Redrum Terrace.

JB009 New film roll number L/455/04A used to photograph the following exhibits:
JB010 cellular material (1) from floor in bedroom one of dwelling house 64 Redrum Terrace.
JB011 cellular material (2) from floor in bedroom one of dwelling house 64 Redrum Terrace.
JB012 cellular material (3) from floor in bedroom one of dwelling house 64 Redrum Terrace.
JB013 stained jeans from bed in bedroom one of dwelling house 64 Redrum Terrace.
JB014 stained shirt from bed in bedroom one of dwelling house 64 Redrum Terrace.
JB015 swab of blood fingerprint on lightswitch of bathroom of dwelling house 64 Redrum Terrace.
JB016 fingerprint lift bedroom one door of dwelling house 64 Redrum Terrace.

Box 23.3 (Continued)

JB017 fingerprint lift outside kitchen door of dwelling house 64 Redrum Terrace.
JB018 fingerprint lift inside front door of dwelling house 64 Redrum Terrace.

All exhibits were packaged, sealed and labelled by me at the time of collection. On completion of my examination, at 14:15 hours I handed all the exhibits to Ian Custodier for transport to the Forensic Science Laboratory.

Signed J. Brown
Dated 1st April 2017

Sources for further study

Cohen, N. and MacLennan-Brown, K. (2007) *Digital Imaging Procedure v2.1*. Available at: http://scienceandresearch.homeoffice.gov.uk/hosdb/publications/cctv-publications/DIP_2.1_16-Apr-08_v2.3_(Web).pdf?view=Binary). Last accessed 12/06/09.

Curtin, D.P. (2004) *The Textbook of Digital Photography*. Available at: http://www.photocourse.com/. Last accessed 17/08/2017.

Edwards, B. (2000) *The New Drawing on the Right Side of your Brain*. Souvenir Press, London.

Forensic Science Service (2004) *The Scenes of Crime Handbook*.

Gardner, R.M. (2004) *Practical Crime Scene Processing and Investigation*. CRC Press, Boca Raton.

Gookin, D. (2000) *Digital Scanning and Photography*. Microsoft Press International, Redmond, USA.

Lee, H.C. (2001) *Henry Lee's Crime Scene Handbook*. Academic Press, New York.

Locard, E. (1928) Dust and its Analysis. *Police Journal* **1**(2): 177–192.

McCartney, S. (2001) *Mastering the Basics of Photography*. Allworth Press, New York.

Nickell, J. and Fischer, J.F. (1999) *Crime Scene: Methods of Detection*. University Press of Kentucky, Lexington.

Pepper, I.K. (2005) *Crime Scene Investigation: Methods and Procedures*. Open University Press.

Redsicker, D.R. (2000) *The Practical Methodology of Forensic Photography*. CRC Press, Boca Raton.

Stelfox, P. (2009) *Criminal Investigation: An Introduction to Principles and Practice*. Willan Publishing, Devon.

Sutton, R. and Trueman, K. (ed.) (2009) *Crime Scene Management: Scene Specific Methods*. Wiley, Chichester.

Weiss, S.L. (2008) *Forensic Photography: Importance of Accuracy*. Prentice Hall, New York.

Wen, C. and Yang, K. (2006) Image authentication for digital image evidence. *Forensic Science Journal* **5**: 1–11.

White, P. (2004) *Crime Scene to Court: The Essentials of Forensic Science,* 2nd edn. Royal Society of Chemistry, London.

Zweifel, F.W. (1988) *A Handbook of Biological Illustration,* 2nd edn. University of Chicago Press, Chicago.

Study exercises

23.1 Draw a scene sketch. Draw a sketch of your living room annotating the diagram with key features and dimensions. Show your sketch to a colleague and ask them to indicate whether you have included all the appropriate details.

23.2 Take a correctly exposed photograph using an SLR camera. Practise taking photographs using an SLR camera for long-distance, medium and close-up images with and without a measurement scale, and with/without the use of external flash.

23.3 Take a correctly exposed photograph using a digital camera. Practise taking photographs using a digital camera for long-distance, medium and close-up images with and without a measurement scale, and with/without the use of external (forced) flash. Copy these images into a Word document.

Exhibit recovery with appropriate packaging (pp. 248–250), labelling (pp. 247–248) and storage is crucial to any investigation. The exhibit that has been identified at the scene and packaged is transported to the police station where it is retained in an exhibit store. Depending on the evidence, it will either remain in this store, or be sent internally to the scientific support unit or externally to a forensic science laboratory for subsequent examination. These exhibits will always be retained throughout the course of an investigation and may be produced during the court proceedings. It is of utmost importance that this 'journey' from crime scene to court can be accounted for with a solid audit trail throughout, a process known as continuity of evidence.

This section will briefly describe some of the common evidence types encountered, but more detail can be found in the following chapters.

Types of forensic evidence

Fingerprints

The most important points in relation to examining fingerprints at a scene (Chapter 26) are:

- the order of collection in terms of maximising recovery of evidence and minimising contamination (see Box 24.1);
- photographing the evidence *in situ*;
- appropriate recording of the positioning of the marks;
- the appropriate choice of visualisation techniques.

For example, if you discover a fingerprint in blood, there are a number of possible aspects you should consider. The pressure used to apply the print will have displaced the liquid blood to the edges of the bloodstain. As blood dries the surface hardens to form a raised crust around the edge of the stain. It may be possible to swab the raised upper surface of this crust without disturbing the print itself. If the ridge pattern (Chapter 26) is clearly defined, then the evidence should be collected as a whole for fingerprint examination at the laboratory. If the blood is smudged and the ridge details indiscernible, then there is no usable fingerprint evidence and the blood could be swabbed (Chapter 30).

> **Order and priority of examination** *is extremely important in the recovery of evidence – you have always to think of its evidential value.*

You also need to think about whether powder-dusting fingerprints will contaminate other valuable evidence (see Box 24.1). Every scene is different; therefore you should take a logical, systematic approach, at all times thinking about the evidential value of the exhibits. You will need to make the judgement as to whether or not you think one exhibit will yield more useful information.

 KEY POINT *It should be documented in the scene examination notes how the evidence is processed – e.g. fingerprint enhancement using aluminium powder, lifted by J-LAR® and secured onto acetate (Chapter 26).*

Footwear impressions

Footwear impressions should always be photographed (p. 231) and should include two measurement scales at right angles to each other around the impression (2D or 3D) to indicate the size before recovery is made. This should be undertaken at 90° to prevent any distortion in the image taken. A cast using, for

---

Box 24.1   How to consider the sequential nature of evidence collection

If a glass tumbler implicated in a murder scene is found to contain a small volume of liquid, then from an evidential point of view you would:

1. **Collect the remaining liquid contents** of the glass using a Pasteur pipette without touching the sides of the glass – this preserves the liquid evidence without contaminating the rim or fingerprint evidence.

2. **Swab the rim of the glass** for saliva to recover DNA evidence, first using a sterile cotton swab wetted

with sterile water and then using a second, dry, sterile cotton swab.

3. **Dust the glass for latent fingerprints** using aluminium powder (see p. 258).

Using this approach, you will have maximised recovery of three types of evidence – the liquid, DNA from saliva if the glass has been drunk from, and fingerprints of the person who handled the glass.

Packaging ESLA footwear lifts – these should be mounted into hard folders, secured in the base of a box. It is important that these are secured in place as any movement will disrupt the lifted print and make the evidence unusable.

Intelligence value of packaging – many illicit drugs are packaged in Beechams wraps (see Chapters 39 and 41). This packaging can be extremely useful in linking scene to scene and scene to individual.

Control sample – at least six glass samples should be collected from around the broken area, but not from the floor, to be a representative sample. You can mark which side is inside/outside using a black marker pen (FSS, 2004).

Clothing – never dry out clothing before packaging if an accelerant use has been implicated.

Definition

Control samples – reference samples to which all similar evidence will be compared.

example, dental stone can be used to recover 3D impressions, whereas an electrostatic lifting apparatus (ESLA) or gelatine lifter can be used for the recovery of 2D impressions (Chapter 27).

Drugs

Bulk drugs are relatively easy to identify. If drugs are found at a scene then a presumptive test, also known as a field test, can be performed to give an indication of the type of drug (for details see Chapter 39). The collection of bulk drugs is straightforward and, as a general rule, if different bulk drugs are found in the same location, for example under a bed, then they can be packaged together since there is no further risk of contamination other than that which has already occurred. The label description (p. 247), however, should include exactly what was found. If drugs are found in the same room, but in different locations within that room, then these should be packaged separately.

Paint and glass

Recovery of paint and glass fragments are very much case-dependent (Chapters 40–41). At a crime scene, control samples should be collected from as near to the damaged area as possible and clearly labelled as being a 'control' sample.

Fire debris

The most important point regarding fire scenes is whether the fire was started accidentally or deliberately and whether an accelerant such as petrol had been used.
    Types of evidence encountered include:

- liquid – accelerants;
- clothing;
- debris;
- control samples (air, unburned, debris).

It is crucial that a control air sample is collected in a nylon bag prior to entry into the fire scene (Chapter 44).

Hairs and fibres

Hair and fibre evidence (Chapters 32, 42) is the most likely trace evidence to be lost at a crime scene. Recovery of hairs and fibres using tape lifts (p. 410) would occur at the scene, but this evidence type can also be collected through

Box 24.2 How to recover blood from a scene

If the bloodstain is dry:

- moisten *a sterile cotton swab with sterile water* and touch the tip of the swab on to the bloodstain to concentrate the blood on the swab. Return the swab to its container. Label the swab and detail this in your scene notes, and package in a tamper-evident bag, and seal and label (p. 249). It should then be frozen at −20°C as soon as possible.

- If the area is large, using a sterile scalpel cut the stain away leaving 2–3 cm around. Recover a non-stained equivalent area as a control sample and package separately.

If the bloodstain is still wet:

- You could swab this wet stain or you could collect the liquid using a *sterile Pasteur pipette* to draw the liquid up and transfer it to a sterile container, which should then be securely packaged and labelled.

- If an item is wet with blood (e.g. clothing), allow it to dry naturally *in situ* as much as possible. If this is not practical/feasible then it should be packaged in a polythene bag and submitted to the laboratory as soon as possible. Here, the item of clothing will be placed to dry in a drying cabinet before being packaged securely for examination. If the item was left in the polythene bag, then it is likely that it would become contaminated from bacterial or fungal degradation.

the examination of exhibits within the laboratory, so providing that it is collected and securely packaged at the scene it should not be lost subsequently. In the case of large items that do not lend themselves to collection, such as settees, the item should be examined at the scene.

Biological fluids

There are many different types of biological fluids – such as blood, semen or saliva – that you will come across at a crime scene, or from the exhibits recovered from a crime scene (Chapter 30). When blood is found at a crime scene there are three things you will need to do:

1. **Identify that the stain is likely to be blood** – e.g. using presumptive tests (p. 294).
2. **Interpret any bloodstain patterns** – in order to reconstruct the events that led to their appearance.
3. **Recover representative bloodstains** for further analysis (see Box 24.2).

Evidential value of exhibits

When collecting evidence you must understand:

The evidential value – can vary depending on the circumstances and can change as the case is investigated.

The intelligence value – information that assists the investigation and crime reduction

- the potential evidential value;
- the purpose of recovering the evidence;
- how much you will need;
- what the evidence will be used for;
- the analysis to be performed.

The evidential value, in simple terms, is the likely importance of the evidence in relation to the investigation – remember the evidence may support *or* refute an individual's involvement. Some types of evidence have greater importance than others, in terms of what the analysis will tell you. This is also important when considering the order in which you intend to collect the evidence (Box 24.1).

Collecting evidence – basic principles

 KEY POINT *At any crime scene you must always maximise the recovery of evidence and minimise its contamination.*

Contamination – *this can occur at several points including:*

- *at the crime scene;*
- *during the collection of evidence;*
- *during transport of evidence;*
- *on submission of evidence;*
- *during analysis;*
- *on final storage of the exhibits.*

The risk of contamination – *depends to some extent on the number of personnel who have entered the scene. At a volume crime scene there may be only a few people involved (perhaps a police officer, the victim and a CSI) compared with a violent crime where police officers, members of the public, a pathologist, forensic scientist(s), CSI(s) and members of the emergency services may have been present.*

Avoiding contamination – *can be achieved by wearing full personal protective equipment (PPE)*

Collecting the evidence

The order of collection requires thought and planning. Non-fixed trace evidence (e.g. fibres caught on a broken window pane) should be identified first, to prevent loss. Thereafter, the sequence should be chosen to avoid contamination of other evidence. Generally the development of latent fingerprints will be performed last, unless the fingerprint evidence would be lost by the movement of other items or the collection of other exhibits.

Contamination and deterioration of evidence

This is one of the most important issues in forensic science and has the potential to occur throughout the investigation – unless you are aware of how contamination can occur, consider where it might occur and then take appropriate steps to prevent it from happening. The particular circumstances and nature of a crime scene under investigation must be taken into account, since if the evidence is contaminated then its evidential value will be lost.

Contamination of evidence can occur by events beyond your control, for example by weather conditions prior to the arrival of key personnel at the scene. The extent of contamination can be minimised by simple protective measures – for example, protecting latent fingerprints on glass shards from being lost by rain. Contamination can occur due to poor scene control, poor collection techniques – for example, dusting prior to collection of DNA evidence, or finding that wet exhibits have leaked through their packaging on to other exhibits.

It is easy to understand why the chance of contamination is higher in scenes involving a large number of personnel, but if the appropriate personal protective equipment is used (see Photo 24.1) before entering the inner cordon (p. 229), then this risk is minimised.

Appropriate personal protective equipment should include:

- **scene suit** – hood should be worn for serious offences;
- **mob cap** – to retain hair;
- **face masks** – avoid talking and manipulating the mask;
- **overshoes**;
- **powder-free gloves worn over the cuffs of the scene suit.** By double gloving, one pair of gloves can be removed after handling a particular exhibit without the potential of contamination from bare hands.

Contamination during the collection of evidence is rare if the appropriate procedures are used. However, there will be instances where you will have to choose between two types of evidence. In order for you to make a judgement regarding which one should you collect, you need to think about the evidential value of each type of evidence and choose the exhibit that you think will yield the most useful information when analysed.

Within the laboratory there is a potential for airborne contamination of the evidence. Therefore, appropriate measures should be in place to prevent this from occurring – for example, filters in air conditioning units. With respect to the final storage of the exhibits, they should be stored in the same condition as they were received in the laboratory and again this movement of the exhibit would be logged on the continuity part of the label (Fig. 24.1(b)). Biological fluids must

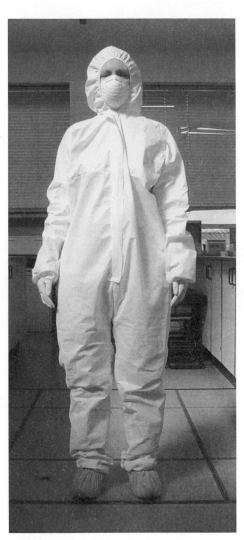

Photo 24.1 An example of personal protective clothing worn by a forensic scientist at a murder scene, including scene suit, mask, gloves and scene overshoes.

R. V. _____

Court use only
Court Exhibit No.
Court   Date

Police use only
Crime Ref. No: _____
Officer in case: _____
Force: _____
Description of item: _____
_____
_____
Where seized/produced: _____
_____
Time/date seized/produced:
_____
Seized/produced by: _____
Signed: _____
Exhibit Number: _____

Lab use only:

(a)

(Continuity)
Name/Rank/No. (Block Letters)
....
Signed...
Date...

(Continuity)
Name/Rank/No. (Block Letters)
....
Signed...
Date...

(Continuity)
Name/Rank/No. (Block Letters)
....
Signed...
Date...

(Continuity)
Name/Rank/No. (Block Letters)
....
Signed...
Date...

(b)

Fig. 24.1 (a) The CJA label is where you would record your full description of the item recovered. (b) The continuity of the CJA label is where you would record the signatures to account for the movement of the exhibit.

CJA label – provides an accurate record of the exhibit and includes what it is, where it was recovered from and the date and time it was recovered. A unique reference number will be allocated to the exhibit and will be recorded on this label, which ensures the continuity of evidence from when it was collected to its potential presentation in court.

be kept in a freezer to prevent microbial degradation. Storage is important should the need arise to re-analyse the exhibits, either as a consequence of a legal request or where a defence scientist has been instructed to do so.

Labelling the exhibit

Once the evidence is collected it must be properly documented with appropriate details recorded on the label. The exhibit is sealed in a secure package in order to avoid transfer of contamination – for example, from scene to suspect. It is also important that any person attending the scene does not subsequently come into contact with the suspect.

The exhibit label is known as a CJA label and derives its name from the Criminal Justice Act. It is this label that enables the continuity to be recorded, in that any movement of the packaged exhibit from one location to another will be signed for and recorded, i.e. from the exhibit store to the laboratory (Fig. 24.1(b)). The scientist performing the examination will also sign this part of the label once the item has been collected, as well as recording the full CJA label transcript (Fig. 24.1(a)) in their contemporaneous notes prior to any examination commencing.

The transcript on the label must match that which has been documented in the log book of whoever collected the evidence at the scene. Depending on the packaging, the label can either be pre-printed onto the bag or can be attached with Sellotape and initialled across the Sellotape onto the packaging. Label details should include:

- name(s) of suspect(s) (if known) plus each of their dates of birth;
- the exact identity of what the evidence is – for example, 103 white tablets or red woollen jumper;
- the exact location of where it was found;
- the date when it was collected – which may be only a date or inclusive of time and date depending on the nature of the evidence;
- the signature of the person who collected the evidence.

KEY POINT *When the exhibit is transferred from one person to the next it is the responsibility of whoever is taking charge of the exhibit to ensure that it is correctly labelled and documented, sealed and signed, until it reaches the laboratory. Thereafter anyone opening the bag for examination must reseal the bag when finished and sign the label to maintain continuity of evidence (p. 229).*

Equipment for collection of evidence

The equipment taken to the scene will depend on your role at the scene, whether you are the CSI or the investigating scientist. An important point is to ensure that the reagents that you will take with you for presumptive testing are effective, so these should be tested before leaving the laboratory. Box 24.3 gives details.

Packaging the evidence

Once the evidence has been collected it must be appropriately packaged to prevent loss or contamination, and to ensure the continuity of evidence. You must be able to identify the exhibit that was collected at the scene by its label details (Fig. 24.1(a)) and be able to account for its movement from the scene to the laboratory and finally to court (Fig. 24.1(b)). Every time the exhibit is

---

Box 24.3 Checklist of equipment required for examination of a crime scene

- **Protective clothing** – to include disposable gloves, disposable face mask, scene suit, disposable overshoes.

- **Recording equipment** – to include permanent fine tip pen, tape measure, paper, clipboard, coloured pens (e.g. red for noting presence of blood, purple for semen), marking arrows and numbers, labels, measuring scales, camera and film.

- **Evidence collection containers** – to include polythene bags, brown paper bags, boxes, selection of sizes of weapons tubes, biohazard containers, bubble wrap, Sellotape™, tamper-proof tape, brown parcel tape, biohazard tape.

- **Search equipment** – to include torch (preferably high-intensity, white-light), magnifying glass, stepping plates, measuring tapes.

- **Fingerprint and footwear impressions** – to include aluminium powder and brush, black powder and brush, gel lifters, casting powder, impression compound for small and large casts, water container, mixing spatula.

- **Presumptive test reagents** – to include Marquis (Chapter 39), Kastle Meyer (Chapter 30) – these should be tested before leaving the laboratory.

- **Miscellaneous items** – to include cleaning tissues, disposal equipment ('sharps' bin, yellow waste bags, etc.).

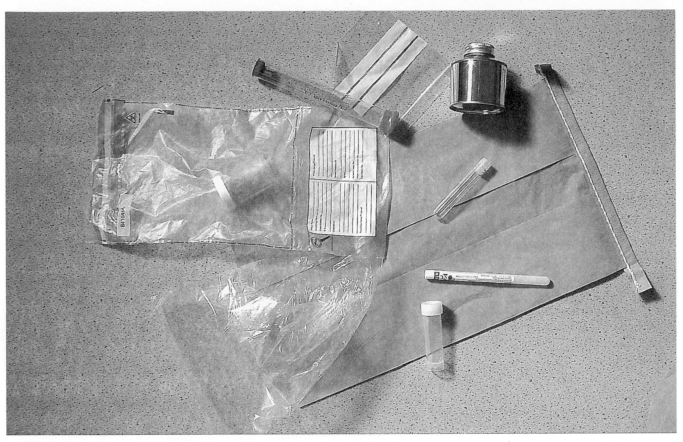

Photo 24.2 Examples of typical packaging/containers. Clockwise from top left – tamper-proof evidence bag, syringe biohazard container, polythene bag, metal flame tin, brown paper bag, 10mL sample tube, sterile medical swab, 25 mL sample tube and nylon bag.

moved, a log of its movement has to be recorded and whoever has transported it or examined it must sign the label attached to the exhibit to provide a written record of movement. In doing so, the continuity of the evidence can be accounted for.

You must have an awareness of the correct packaging to use for each type of evidence. Examples of appropriate packaging (see Photo 24.2) are:

- **Brown paper bags** – these should be used for all items of clothing/fabric, unless the exhibits are wet, in which case they should be dried as much as possible *in situ* or placed into a polythene bag and placed in a coolbox containing ice packs for immediate transportation to the laboratory for drying.
- **Tamper-proof evidence bags** – these polythene bags usually have the CJA label preprinted on them and have a self-adhesive tamper proof seal that can be applied when the plastic coating is removed
- **Polythene bags** – these can be sealed with a heat sealer or by tape with a signature across the seal and can be used for the majority of items unless there is a danger of the item penetrating/compromising the bag (for example, broken glass).
- **Weapons tubes** – these should be used for small weapons such as knives. An appropriate size should be chosen, taking care not to overtighten the tube. The tube should be sealed and placed into a polythene bag or tamper-evident bag.

Sealing a brown paper bag – the top of the bag should be folded over twice before tamper-evident tape is used to seal all the edges before signing (Photo 24.3).

- **Cardboard boxes** – these are useful for items that are fragile or may be broken (for example, footprint casts), or for items that could damage other packaging (for example, glass fragments).
- **Sterile medical swabs** – these are used for bloodstain evidence and for collection of 'intimate' samples from a victim.
- **Sterile biological fluid containers** – these are standard clinical/medical containers and are used for liquid blood or urine evidence. Label details should be added onto the container to identify what it is. The container should then be placed into a polythene bag or tamper-evident bag and sealed.
- **Nylon bags for fire debris** – these are used for the collection of volatile compounds (accelerants) that would diffuse through a polythene bag. The bag should be tied in a swan neck (p. 426) and secured with string (see Chapter 44). Brown tape should not be used to seal this packaging type.
- **Metal flame tins** – these are used for the collection of non-biological liquids that are liable to evaporate (e.g. petrol or alcohol). The tins have an inner push-top airtight seal and a secondary screw-top outer seal, to prevent any evaporation.
- **Anti-static bag/bubble wrap** – these are used for electronics (hardware/software) and should be placed in boxes and sealed. It is important to avoid any magnetic items and any material that may cause static for these exhibits.

For each form of packaging you should ensure that all sides are sealed and, where appropriate, that the edges are secured with tamper-proof tape over which you must mark your initials and usually the date (see Photo 24.3). This will ensure that the next time the package is seen it will be obvious if the packaging has been compromised. If this has occurred, then no examination should be carried out since you cannot guarantee what has happened to the evidence from its time of collection to its time of examination.

> **Hazard labels** – these should be added as appropriate e.g. blood = biohazard.

> **Additional fingerprint examination** – if an item is recovered and packaged but will also require fingerprint examination it is important to write on the label 'preserve for fingerprints' to notify the person conducting the examination to handle the item carefully.

Photo 24.3 Packaging of exhibits. Illustrated on the left is a correctly packaged exhibit showing the opening of the bag folded over and sealed with tamper-proof tape – including the fold, with a signature of the person who collected the exhibit and date it was collected across the seal. A label has been attached with tamper-proof tape, also signed and dated. On the right is an incorrectly packaged exhibit – the bag is folded, but not sealed. The fold is held in place with Sellotape and there are no details to indicate who has collected the exhibit.

Sources for further study

Gardner, R.M. (2004) *Practical Crime Scene Processing and Investigation.* CRC Press, Boca Raton.

Lee, H.C. (2001) *Henry Lee's Crime Scene Handbook.* Academic Press, New York.

Nickell, J. and Fischer, J.F. (1999) *Crime Scene: Methods of Detection.* University Press of Kentucky, Lexington.

Pepper, I.K. (2005) *Crime Scene Investigation: Methods and Procedures.* Open University Press.

Redsicker, D.R. (2000) *The Practical Methodology of Forensic Photography.* CRC Press, Boca Raton.

Stelfox, P. (2009) *Criminal Investigation: An Introduction to Principles and Practice.* Willan Publishing, Devon.

Sutton, R. and Trueman, K. (ed.) (2009) *Crime Scene Management: Scene Specific Methods.* Wiley, Chichester.

Weiss, S.L. (2008) *Forensic Photography: Importance of Accuracy.* Prentice Hall, New York.

White, P. (2004) *Crime Scene to Court: The Essentials of Forensic Science,* 2nd edn. Royal Society of Chemistry, London.

Study exercises

24.1 List the common types of evidence you would be likely to encounter at a volume crime scene. Consider where you are likely to find this evidence.

24.2 What would you consider the evidential value to be of the following evidence types?

(a) fingerprints;
(b) fibres;
(c) blood;
(d) glass.

24.3 Prepare a CJA label of one of the 'blood lifts' in the example given in Box 24.2.

Computer Misuse Act 1990 – legislates for offences including: unauthorised access to computer material; intent to commit further offences; intent to impair the operation of a computer; making supplying or obtaining articles for use in an offence (legislation. gov.uk, 2017).

Proportion of adults – in the UK who own/ use a smartphone is 74% in the last quarter of 2016. Eighty per cent of 16–34 year olds have used their smartphone for an online purchase compared to 40% of 35+ age category (Techtracker, 2017).

Definitions

Firewall – a network security system that controls incoming and outgoing network data traffic.

Malware – malicious software that prevents your device from working normally. This software often captures data from your device and includes viruses, worms, spyware.

Phishing – an attempt to obtain sensitive information (personal/security/ banking details) by electronic means (i.e. by email).

Smishing – an attempt to obtain sensitive information (personal/security/ banking details) by short message service (SMS) text messaging.

Spyware – malicious software that captures your browsing history.

Digital Forensics Specialist Group – this group has been established in England and Wales has been established to develop standards meeting ISO17025 (p. 475) for geolocation activities, network data analysis and social media analysis (Forensic Science Regulator, 2016).

The modern world has seen a proliferation of digital information being stored and used on a regular basis. As more digital technology enabled devices become available, so has an increase in new types of crime – collectively called cyber-crime, ranging from phishing emails, storage and dissemination of indecent images through to cyber attacks on homes and business enterprises.

Cyber attacks are becoming more frequently encountered with two predominant routes to gain unauthorised access or cause significant disruption to a network:

- **hacking** – where the unauthorised user gains access to personal or commercial data stored within the networked system through the use of specialist software;
- **denial of service (DOS)** – where the networked system links are overloaded by auto-generated messages resulting in the system crashing owing to the volume of traffic received.

Prevention of attacks such as these can be facilitated by installing commercial anti-virus, anti-spyware/malware software, using a firewall and not opening any attachments that may contain a virus in email messages from an unknown origin that have been sent to you.

 KEY POINT *There is a continually evolving cycle between new viruses emerging and new anti-virus software, so in order to keep your own electronic systems safe you must ensure that your anti-virus software is up-to-date.*

As technology evolves, so does the route by which digital information can be accessed. In 2016, 90% of UK adults accessed the Internet; however, smartphones have been estimated to be used by 74% of the UK population (Techtracker, 2017). This shift towards mobile technology use, as well as the speed by which the smartphone manufacturers update their devices, also has an impact on how a digital investigation will ensue. It would not be unusual to find several devices in a single location, with each offering different challenges for the investigator. The type of information that can be recovered is wide and varied depending on the case but can include email, texts, documents (including dates), photographs, video or global positioning system (GPS) data.

The work of the forensic document examiner (see Chapter 29) has in recent years been extended to include fraud using the Internet, desktop publishing, imaging programs, scanners and digital cameras, all of which have created new areas for investigation.

Nowadays, it is not uncommon to find that individuals no longer sign documents by hand in ink. The Internet has brought with it the digital signature which, in turn, has created new opportunities for fraud. For example, a document can now be scanned using optical character recognition (OCR) software, and then be modified, printed and redistributed. The addition of an electronic signature does not guarantee the authenticity of the document unless safeguards are employed for verification purposes. A document stored electronically can be modified by first printing it on an inkjet or laser printer. Then, a forged document can be produced by simply attaching a scanned signature using a printer similar to the original. The quality produced by modern colour printers is such that documents can be altered by simply cutting and pasting, and then reprinting with hardly any discernible trace of the changes made. However, these alterations may be detected by examining files on the computer used to modify the document (p. 458).

You should also be aware that other evidence may be present, e.g. finger-prints, but the use of powder enhancement (Chapter 27) is not appropriate as this can result in loss of the digital evidence. Alternatively, gel lifters (p. 259) can be used safely on the device.

Devices

Computer networks exist when two or more computers are connected together by cables (wired) or remotely by wireless connection (wireless), typically via a local area network (LAN). Data transmission will occur every time the computer is connected to a website and as such, a record of the Internet Protocol (IP) address is logged. Similarly, the operating system continually runs without you being aware and, as such, data transmission continually occurs in the background. Once a suspect device has been identified, time is therefore of utmost importance to prevent the loss of any digital data.

Locards principle (p. 227) remains the same, but this time you would be looking for a digital trace rather than a physical trace. As with all forensic evidence, key stages involved in the investigation of digital devices can be identified:

- **Identification of the devices** – simply where potential relevant sources are located, e.g. computer, smartphone, cloud storage, and which would be the most appropriate resource to examine.

- **Preservation of the data** – this is a key stage as this can have an impact on whether data can be recovered and used evidentially in court. Consideration must be given to isolating the device, for example, from a network without the loss of information as data can be remotely accessed and altered. If the suspect is still at a scene, they should be prevented from having any contact with the device.

If the computer is switched off, it should never be switched back on. The power cable should be removed from the device first and not from the wall socket. The computer, cables and ports should all be photographed and notes recorded of the connections during this process.

 KEY POINT **Make sure the computer is not in standby mode prior to removing the power cable as this may lose valuable data.**

If the computer is still switched on simply switching the device off is likely to lose valuable information. The screen should be photographed and recorded with details of all content and processes that are visible. If the screen is blank then a short movement of the mouse will restore the screen but this will also have an impact on the data stored in the volatile memory (p. 254). The screen should then be photographed as a permanent record of its display screen, and a note of the time and activity of the mouse use must be recorded. It is likely that the computer will be encrypted (password protected). The password may be obtained from the owner of the device or potentially from any notebooks in close proximity to the computer. If not available, it may be possible to recover it from the volatile memory, but this may have been overwritten depending on how many processes have been run since the last time the password was used. Software has also been developed–for example, Password Recovery Toolkit (PRTK) by AccessData®, to recover passwords and open encrypted files.

Digital information can be obtained from many sources including:

- ***storage media*** *– e.g. USB sticks, SD/xD cards, CD/DVD, external hard drives;*
- ***mobile technology*** *– e.g. mobile phone, smartphones, satellite navigation systems, digital cameras;*
- ***computers*** *– e.g. desktop, laptop, Apple Macintosh, websites, social media sites, remote cloud storage.*

Consider the location of the device *– a mobile phone found on a person is more likely to be relevant to an investigation than an 'old' phone found in a box in a cupboard. That is not to say that it should not be recovered, but there must be reasonable grounds for doing so.*

KEY POINT *Ideally the device would be in an unlocked state otherwise, if it has encryption or a password, access to the data may not be feasible. Specialist advice must be sought prior to any action that may result in the loss of digital evidence.*

Definition

Volatile memory – unlike hard disks, the volatile memory has no defined file structure system and is continually modified when a user performs any action on the device. It may be possible to retrieve passwords that have been stored in these locations temporarily until they are overwritten, but also locate data, which can give an indication of how an application or process was being used (including potential identification of malware).

Typical packaging – *anti-static bags should be used. Any device recovered should avoid any strong magnetic fields, excessive heat/cold/humidity and should also avoid Styrofoam as this can cause static to build up.*

Searching for deleted files on a computer – *in some cases, it may simply be a case of looking in the 'recycle bin' and using the command to Restore all files.*

Data storage – *typical computer hard drive storage 2 TB, smartphone storage up to 128 GB.*

- **Immediate extraction and identification from digital storage media** – software tools such as memdump or FATKit can be used to capture the information in the volatile memory of the computer, although it should be noted that using this software can also alter the contents of the memory and potentially overwrite data that could be used in an investigation. It is important, though, that this volatile memory is captured, as this represents active or very recent processes. The power cable should then be removed from the device first and not from the wall socket. The computer, cables and ports should all be photographed and appropriate detailed notes recorded during this process.

After photographic record, mobile phones, if switched off, should not be powered on. Typically, if they are switched on then power them down as in this mode they would not be able to receive any network signal that would enable a remote user to wipe the content, nor would they receive any messages or phone calls that would potentially overwrite existing data.

- **Physical recovery of the device**– the device should be packaged appropriately in anti-static evidence bags (see Chapter 24).

- **Examination and analysis** – all documents produced on a computer exist as electronic files. These files are divided up into many small segments (clusters) that are stored on the computer (e.g. on the hard drive), wherever there is space. Data will also be stored temporarily in the volatile memory. A duplicate copy of the contents of the volatile memory (or RAM) should be recovered first, followed by a duplicate copy of the data stored from this structured hard drive system. It is good practice to make two copies using appropriate software and to check that they have extracted the information needed e.g. hidden files. The location of these clusters is usually not contiguous, but via a file allocation table (FAT) links the clusters so that the entire file can be recovered in its entirety. By deleting a file, you might assume that all of the information is lost. However, this is not the case. Although the means of putting all the clusters together (the FAT) is deleted, not all of the clusters will be lost and these can be reassembled using appropriate software. Essential in this type of forensic work is speedy recovery of the computer. This is because each new file subsequently created on the computer overwrites existing clusters. Even if this approach proves fruitless, all is not lost. It may be possible to find other copies of the original document in other directories on the computer, for example in *.tmp files (temporary files), on the server or its back-up drives (for network-linked computers) or on removable media (USB, flashdrives or CDs). In these cases, all equipment should be seized at the earliest opportunity including USBs, external hard drives and CDs. The data storage capacity of the devices means that there is potentially a vast amount of data that would be available. The increased use of cloud storage represents a further challenge in this respect. A number of commercial tools are available for the examination to ensure as much information is recovered as possible – for example, Encase® Forensic, which can also recover digital evidence from mobile phones.

- **Interpretation** – once the information is recovered it has to be made sense of, which can then be reported in the form of a statement or in expert testimony in court (Chapter 60). It is not sufficient to merely find the digital evidence, but to show that the owner is aware of its existence or had intent to commit a criminal action. The likelihood of this knowledge can be ascertained by examining the recent file history (evidence of recently opened files, locations of files or folders), browsing history (recent search terms), file encryption (files with password protection) and so on, or even alteration of the suffix – for example, changing the name of the file from photograph.jpg to an .exe file. These actions may lend support to the owner being aware that the files exist on their device. Another consideration in the interpretation is determining how the files were obtained. In other words, whether it was accidental or a deliberate action, the latter strengthening the support that the user was aware of their actions. It is of course possible that the user's system has been 'hacked' and they were unaware of the data traffic occurring on their device.

Text references

Computer Misuse Act 1990 Available at http://www.legislation.gov.uk/ukpga/1990/18/contents.Lastaccessed01/08/2017.

Forensic Science Regulator (2016) Forensic science providers: codes of practice and conduct. Available at: https://www.gov.uk/government/collections/forensic-science-providers-codes-of-practice-and-conduct. Last accessed 14/08/2017.

Techtracker (2017) Available at https://www.ipsos-mori.com/researchpublications/publications/1901/80-of-1634-year-olds-use-a-smartphone-in-their-purchase-journey.aspx. Last accessed 01/08/2017.

Sources for further study

ACPO Good Practice Guide for Digital Evidence (2012) Available at: http://library.college.police.uk/docs/acpo/digital-evidence-2012.pdf. Last accessed 01/08/2017.

ACPO Good Practice Guide for Computer Based Electronic Evidence (2007). Available at: https://www.cps.gov.uk/legal/assets/uploads/files/ACPO_guidelines_computer_evidence[1].pdf. Last accessed 01/08/2017.

Casey, E. (2011) *Digital Evidence and Computer Crime Forensic Science, Computers, and the Internet,* 3rd edn. Elsevier, Burlington.

ENSFI (2015) *Best Practice Manual for the Forensic Examination of Digital Technology.* Available at: http://enfsi.eu/wp-content/uploads/2016/09/1._forensic_examination_of_digital_technology_0.pdf. Last accessed 01/08/2017.

National Institute of Justice (2009) *Electronic Crime Scene Investigation: An On-the-Scene Reference for First Responders.* Available at: https://www.ncjrs.gov/pdffiles1/nij/227050.pdf. Last accessed 01/08/2017.

History of fingerprinting – the concept of fingerprinting as a means of identification was introduced in the 1870s by Dr Henry Faulds, who recognised the importance of fingerprints as a means of identification. This was followed by a detailed study by Sir Francis Galton who, in 1892, published a book on 'fingerprints'. Included within this book was a classification for finger-printing, the essentials of which are still used today. This led in 1901 to its incorporation in criminal investigation by Sir Richard Edward Henry and its first use in court in England and Wales in 1902.

The uniqueness of fingerprints has made them an indispensable means of personal identification. Essentially, the patterns of ridges and troughs that are a vital component of any fingerprint provide a unique identifier. The pattern remains unchanged for life unless, damaged by burning or scarring.

Touching an object or surface with a hand leaves behind a characteristic mark retaining features of the ridges and troughs of a fingerprint. The skill of the crime scene investigator (CSI) is to recover the fingerprint from the object or surface even when it is virtually invisible (latent).

In the UK, fingerprints are not examined in a forensic science laboratory by a forensic scientist. Instead they are examined by a fingerprint examiner in the scientific support unit of the police force. The scientific support unit typically comprises teams of CSIs, photographers, chemical enhancement unit, finger-print examiners, footwear examiners and technical support staff. Some forces also have a specific digital evidence unit.

KEY POINT *Essentially, a fingerprint is a deposit of fatty residue left after sweat has evaporated. The pattern within the deposit provides a mirror image of the ridges and troughs of the finger or other part of the body that made it.*

The nature of fingerprints

Eccrine glands – are present over all the body and secrete sweat (predominantly water with a combination of inorganic and organic constituents)

Sebaceous glands – are present over all the body and secrete sebum, which mixes with the sweat to produce latent marks.

A layer of skin covers the entire body and approximately 95% is relatively smooth. However, in certain areas, for example fingers and palms of the hand, and toes and soles of the feet, friction ridges occur (Fig. 26.1). They are called friction ridges because they help us to grasp and hold on to objects. Within the friction ridges are pore openings, each of which is associated with a sweat gland. The outer layer of skin consists of stratified epithelium called the epidermis, with an underlying layer called the dermis. It is this latter layer, the dermis, that contains the sweat glands. Fingerprint deposits are produced from the eccrine and sebaceous glands. While the majority of sweat is moisture, typically 98.5% or more, it does contain trace amounts of other chemicals (Table 26.1). It is the deposition of these components that allow the characteristic pattern of the fingerprint to be left on a surface that has been touched. It should be noted that in the ridged epidermis, the eccrine ducts open out on the tip of the ridges. Therefore, the position of the secreted deposits mark the line of the ridges. On close examination, a print will have small voids in the ridge detail where the pores surface (Fig. 26.1).

The main problems in fingerprint recovery arise due to the following:

- the nature of the surface on which the mark is present;
- the method used to recover the mark;
- deposition conditions of the mark (humidity and light can alter the quality of the mark).

Where to look for fingerprints

This will depend on the circumstances of the crime. For example, in burglary investigations the point of entry is the obvious place to start the search. The

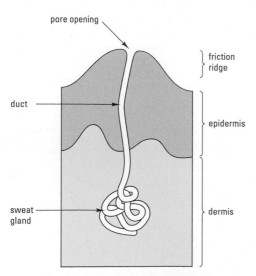

Fig. 26.1 Cross-section of skin through a friction ridge.

Labels: pore opening, duct, sweat gland, friction ridge, epidermis, dermis

Table 26.1 Typical chemical composition of the eccrine and sebaceous gland secretions

Eccrine gland

Water (98.5%+)

Amino acids (0.2-1μg)

(typically in order of abundance – lysine,ornithine, alanine, aspartic acid)

Urea

Lactic acid

Sugars

Creatinine

Choline

Uric acid

Chlorides (1–15 μg)

Metal ions

Ammonia

Sulphate

Phosphate

Sebaceous glands

Fatty acids – approximately 38% of which dodecanoic acid is predominant

Glycerides

Hydrocarbons – e.g. squalene – a 30 carbon hydrocarbon – approximately 15%

Cholesterol – approximately 4%

Alcohols

Modified from Cadd et al., 2015

Recording fingerprints – *always photograph a fingerprint prior to lifting, and also make sure you record appropriate identification details.*

Searching for fingerprints – *when searching the surface of an object for fingerprint deposits, ensure that it is well-illuminated.*

Types of brush – *fibreglass, animal hair, synthetic or natural fibre brushes are used to develop fingerprints. Care needs to be taken to ensure that the bristles of the brush do not make a significant contact with the surface being examined for fingerprints – valuable evidence may be destroyed.*

---

point of entry may have been a door, forced open or not (see Chapter 28) or via a window that has been broken. All of these sites are appropriate places to begin the search for fingerprints. Once this has been done it will be necessary to check for fingerprints in locations within the building that have been disturbed by the burglar. Another important area to check for fingerprints is on or near light switches, light bulbs, door handles, drawer openings and other places where hands may have made contact. However, fingerprints may not be left on some surfaces, for example carpet, or when the perpetrator has worn gloves, washed their hands or their hands were very cold.

How to recover a fingerprint

Various approaches are available for recovering fingerprints from a crime scene or objects recovered from a crime scene, victim or suspect.

Fingerprints are normally distinguishable in three forms:

1. those that are visible (or 'patent') prints;
2. those that are invisible to the naked eye ('latent' prints);
3. those that are formed in or on a substrate ('plastic' prints).

The recovery of visible fingerprints is more straightforward since they do not require any means of development or enhancement for their visualisation. For example, fingerprints may have been left on substances that melt easily or soften when held in the hand, such as chocolate, layers of dust, flour, soap, greasy surfaces, ink, etc. Another obvious approach is to look for fingerprints in blood present at a crime scene. A hand placed in spilled blood will leave fingerprints on everything that is subsequently touched until the blood dries. Once a fingerprint has been found it should be recorded using photography (p. 231).

The most common approaches for visualisation of latent fingerprints are powder dusting, chemical enhancement and illumination methods (Fig. 26.2) – their main features are described below.

Powder dusting

The simplest procedure for latent fingerprint recovery is powder dusting. The process relies on the mechanical adherence of powder particles to the sweat components of the skin ridge deposits. The application of the powder is carried out with a hand-held brush but it is important to choose the correct brush for the appropriate powder.

Similarly, it is important that the brushes are used in the appropriate manner – for example, swirling the brush in contact with the mark versus a brushing stroke. The most common types of powder that are recommended for crime scene use are aluminium powder and carbon black (Table 26.2). Details of the procedure for recovery of fingerprints using powder dusting are given in Box 26.1.

There are a variety of other powders that could potentially be used – for example, magnetic powders that contain fine ferromagnetic particles and are applied with a magnetic applicator, for example a Magna-Brush. The process of application is the same as that in Box 26.1. One benefit is that excess powder can be recovered with the magnetic applicator and reused. More recently, SupraNano™ fingerprint powders have been developed that could perhaps offer an alternative means of visualisation, although to be adopted for routine use, they would have to be validated to meet the accreditation standard ISO17025 that forces in England and Wales are currently undertaking as of 2017. The

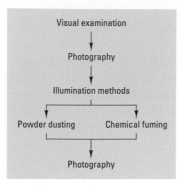

Fig. 26.2 Procedure for developing latent fingerprints.

Table 26.2 Some common dusting powders used for fingerprint recovery

Powder type	Application
Carbon black	Universal powder, ideal for smooth non-porous surfaces, e.g. table tops. Especially good for light-coloured surfaces.
Aluminium	Universal powder, especially good for dark-coloured surfaces, e.g. door frames.
Magnetic powder	Ideal method to minimise excess powder. Can be used only on non-magnetic surfaces, e.g. wood or plastic.

choice of which powder to use depends on the colour and surface type on which the mark has been deposited.

 KEY POINT *These fine powders can cause respiratory problems so it is always advisable to wear a mask when using powders.*

Based on trials (Bandey and Gibson, 2006) conducted by The UK Home Office Scientific Development Branch (HOSDB), the following uses are recommended:

- **flake powders,** e.g. aluminium powder; these can also be used for clean, dry, smooth and non-porous surfaces and would be applied using a Zephyr® brush in a light rotation motion;
- **granular powders,** e.g. black powder; these can be used for semi-rough, non-porous, textured or weathered surfaces and would be applied using a squirrel brush in a light brushing motion;

Box 26.1   How to locate, enhance and recover a latent fingerprint using dusting powder

1. **Locate the mark** – you need to sequentially examine an item making sure that you have covered all surfaces that could possibly have a latent mark on them. Visually examine the surface, making sure that you have looked for any marks at differing angles, followed by re-examination using a white light source, e.g. Maglite®. In the case of a window, examine the window ledge first, then sequentially the window glass.

2. **Assess which powder you should use** – decide which powder you should use (see p. 257). Remember to use the appropriate application brush, e.g. synthetic brush for flake powders, i.e. Zephyr®, Lightning Powder, USA; animal hair brush for granular powders, i.e. squirrel, Lightning Powder, USA; and a magnetic applicator (Lightning Powder, USA) for magnetic powders.

3. **Carefully apply the dusting powder** – apply a small amount of powder to the surface of the object using the appropriate brush by lightly dusting the latent print in the same direction as the ridge pattern (do not brush too hard or you will smear the print). Remove excess dusting powder carefully to allow the optimum fingerprint image to be observed. Take care not to overload the mark.

4. **Apply fingerprint-lifting tape to the print** – place the sticky side of a low-tack adhesive sheet over the dusted print and, taking care not to move it sideways, press gently and evenly over the print to transfer the image to the sheet, then remove carefully from the object.

5. **Place the recovered mark on a fingerprint card** – attach the adhesive sheet to the fingerprint card, taking care not to trap any air bubbles between the two. The card should be fully labelled with the crime reference number, details of who recovered the mark, the date on which it was recovered, the specific location where it was found, including directional markers (or gravity arrow) to indicate which side of the tape was at the top, and an exhibit number for continuity purposes.

Flake powders – *are more sensitive as the particle shape of the powder is such that more contact with the latent mark occurs.*

Directional arrows – *these are important to include on the recovery of the mark as they give context to the positioning of any marks that have been visualised.*

Recovery of latent marks – *this can be achieved by using optically clear, low-tack adhesive fingerprint lifting tape, or alternatively by using a gel lifter. These can be either white or black and the appropriate colour can be chosen to offer a contrast depending on the colour of the powder used.*

- **magnetic granular powders,** e.g. black magnetic powder; these can be used on unplasticised polyvinyl chloride (uPVC) windows and doorframes or rough-grained surfaces and would be applied using a magna brush®, but care must be taken not to touch the mark with the end of the wand. These may be convenient but are not as effective as the flake or granular powders.

Chemical enhancement

Chemical enhancement is a common method for visualising fingerprints from recovered objects.

 KEY POINT *Remember that where there may be a possibility that DNA can be obtained from the fingerprint, you should make sure that the chemical enhancement technique does not destroy any DNA evidence.*

Examples of the variety of visualisation techniques are given in Table 26.3.

This type of processing is normally performed at the chemical enhancement laboratory in the scientific support unit and includes techniques such as chemically treating the marks with dyes, fluorescent dyes or superglue® fuming, followed by dyes/fluorescent dyes. The technique used depends on the surface on which the fingerprint is found – e.g. latent mark on paper, in which case, the sequential processing using DFO, ninhydrin and photographic developer may be used for visualisation; or whether a patent fingerprint is found in, for example, blood in which case amido black (acid dyes) could be used for enhancement. These dyes target specific components in the fingerprint

Table 26.3 Selected techniques used to chemically enhance latent marks (recommended by Bowman (ed), *Fingerprint Development Handbook*) (2005)

Developer	Application
Wet white powder	Used to develop latent marks on the adhesive side of sticky tape.
Amido black (methanol base)	Used to enhance visible marks or to develop latent marks that have been deposited in blood.
Sudan black	Used to develop marks on non-porous surfaces, especially if contaminated with grease or oil. Can also be used to stain prints fumed with cyanoacrylate resin (Superglue)®.
Cyanoacrylate (Superglue®) fuming	Used to develop latent marks on non-porous objects.
Cyanoacrylate fluorescent dye	Used to dye cyanoacrylate (Superglue) developed latent marks. Marks can then be visualised by laser or UV light.
DFO (1,8-diazafluoren-9-one)	Used to develop latent marks on porous surfaces. DFO reacts with the amino acids from the eccrine secretions. When complete, the developed print will fluoresce under laser or UV light.
Ninhydrin (petroleum ether base)	Used to develop latent marks on porous surfaces. Ninhydrin reacts with amino acids present in eccrine secretions.
Photographic developer	Used to develop latent marks on porous surfaces. The photographic developer with surfactant reacts with the insoluble lipids in eccrine secretions resulting in silver nitrate being reduced to metallic silver.
Vacuum metal deposition	Used to develop latent marks on non-porous surfaces. The method involves coating or depositing a thin layer of metal on to a surface by vaporising metals under vacuum.

It is important to consult appropriate health and safety procedures in the laboratory before dealing with these chemicals.

composition – for example, ninhydrin reacts with the amino acids associated with eccrine secretions (see Table 26.1), whereas the acid dyes target the proteins associated with the blood rather than the constituents of the latent mark.

An alternative approach to the use of dyes is exposing the object to the fumes from Superglue® (methyl or ethyl cyanoacrylate). Care needs to be taken to ensure that the fingerprint examiners are not exposed to the fumes – the process should be carried out in a suitably vented container (e.g. MVC1000 cyanoacrylate fuming cabinet, Foster and Freeman UK, or the MVC® Lite portable system, Foster and Freeman UK), for cyanoacrylate fuming at a scene, with fixed humidity and temperature control. The humidity is important to be in excess of 75% in order for the chlorides in the latent mark to absorb water. This acts as the initiation step in the polymerisation of the cyanoacrylate monomer, resulting in white deposits appearing on the friction ridges. If cyanoacrylate fuming is to be carried out at the scene, it is recommended that non-porous surfaces are first examined by powder techniques (p. 257) (Bandey and Kent, 2003). In the case of Superglue®, any finger prints on the objects are exposed as white deposits. These can be further enhanced by exposure to a fluorescent dye, e.g. Basic Yellow 40 (BY40). This process has been applied to fingerprints on various materials, including plastics, metals and wood. The procedure is described in Box 26.2.

 KEY POINT *– it is important to recognise that some formulations will interfere with other evidence, e.g. DNA. In these instances, alternative formulations, e.g. water-based, may be more appropriate to use.*

Photography – after each stage you should photograph the fingerprint to record the enhancement.

There are many more dyes available – the choice is largely dependent on the substrate, but consideration also has to be given to the chemical composition (p. 257) of the latent mark itself. The composition, while similar among donors, is not identical between donors and this may give rise to differences

---

Box 26.2 How to develop a latent fingerprint with Superglue®

The following procedure can be used to recover a fingerprint using Superglue® in a temperature-controlled and humidity-controlled cabinet.

1. **Place the object(s) in a ventilated cabinet** before exposure to the fumes. Ideally they should be suspended from the top of the cabinet, to allow maximum exposure.

2. **Place 1-2 g of liquid Superglue® in a small dish** (aluminium or porcelain) and place this inside the cabinet on the hot plate and secure in place.

3. **Allow the cabinet to run through its automated cycle,** checking that the humidity has reached 80 °C to allow the polymerisation process to initiate.

4. **Allow the object(s) to be exposed to the fumes at the appropriate cycle time (typically 1 h)** until visible whitish-coloured fingerprint patterns appear.

5. **Allow the cabinet to run through its automated purge cycle** – the door will not release until the cabinet has purged all the cyanoacrylate vapour and is safe to open.

6. **Further enhance the Superglue-developed prints** by using a post-fuming fluorescent dye – typically BY40, although the choice will be substrate dependent.

7. **Observe any marks that have been visualised** – when using a fluorescent dye you should observe the marks at the optimised wavelength for excitation and emission of the light, e.g. BY40 can be excited at 430–470 nm and viewed with an emission filter of 495 nm.

8. **Photograph any observed marks** – specialised photography should be undertaken, taking into account the lighting used. Any image should be photographed with no distortion and on a 1:1 scale.

in how the donor mark will be enhanced – for example, with ninhydrin the reaction of ninhydrin with the amino acids results in the mark being visualised as purple (Ruhemanns purple) friction ridges. However, with some donors, only a slight reaction occurs, leading to a very faint orange/red colouration. The composition can change according to gender, ethnicity, psychological state and diet, as well as environmental conditions that occur following deposition (Cadd *et al.*, 2015). It is also known that some individuals are also known to be poor or good secretors and, in combination, these factors will play a part in the successful effective chemical enhancement of any mark. Consult the *Fingerprint Development Handbook* (2005) or the *Fingerprint Source Book* (2012) for further advice.

Illumination and enhancement methods

These are based on exposing the fingerprint to UV light or laser light. Certain substances present in perspiration (including body oils and/or foreign bodies contained in a latent fingerprint residue) fluoresce when exposed to laser or UV light. In this situation, no pre-treatment of the fingerprint is necessary. If fingerprints are not detected using UV or laser light, then enhancement can be performed. This is usually done after application of a dye – for example, BY40 post-Superglue® fuming. The dye will stain the polycyanolacrylate deposits, which can be photographed (p. 230).

As can be seen from the above, the choice of techniques for visualisation of latent fingerprints is varied. For this reason, a process has been developed to allow the fingerprint examiner to systematically apply the correct procedures with the minimum risk of destroying valuable information. The procedures are subdivided in to those that are applied to porous surfaces and those to non-porous surfaces (Table 26.4). It should be noted that the first procedures, irrespective of surface type, are both visual inspections with either the naked eye or different light sources. Only when this has been completed, and taking into consideration any other non-destructive techniques, should you apply powder dusting or chemical enhancement.

Examination of fingerprint characteristics

Comparison of a recovered mark with a reference fingerprint will need to be performed. To do this, the photograph of the mark is compared against a reference set of fingerprints taken from a suspect or for elimination purposes.

Table 26.4 Typical process to be considered in relation to marks on porous and non-porous surfaces Bowman (ed), (*Fingerprint Development Handbook, 2005*)

Porous surfaces	Non-porous surfaces
1. Visual examination	1. Visual examination
2. Inherent fluorescence by laser or UV light	2. Inherent fluorescence by laser or UV light
3. Other non-destructive considerations, e.g. ESDA (p. 282)	3. Cyanoacrylate fuming
4. DFO (1,8-diazofluoren-9-one) with visualisation at 473–548 nm; viewing goggles/filter 550 nm	4. Laser or UV light
5. Re-examine after 10 days	5. Fluorescent dye
6. Ninhydrin	6. Laser or UV light - with visualisation using for example BY40 at 400–469 nm; emission viewing goggles/filter at 495 nm
7. Re-examine after 10 days	
8. PD	

Note: Any marks that are observed will be photographed. Not all processes need to be performed; this is left to the discretion of the examiner.

arch

whorl

loop

Fig. 26.3 Some of the principal characteristic fingerprint patterns.

Pattern occurrence – *in the general population it is accepted that loops are most commonly encountered (approximately 70%), followed by whorls (25%) and arches (5%).*

 KEY POINT   Fingerprint comparisons are always performed from mark to reference print and never the other way round.

Reference fingerprints are obtained at a police station and serve a two-fold function – as a set of elimination fingerprints and also from the suspect arrested for the recordable offence. Ink is applied to a glass plate and firmly rolled out to form a thin film. Each of the fingers is then rolled on to this film, and then rolled on to a standard ten-print form in a designated box for each finger – this should capture the ridge pattern from nail bed to nail bed.

 KEY POINT   This rolling procedure must be performed in a single motion for each finger and not by forwards and backwards movements.

Likewise, in a single motion the inked fingers are also placed together on the bottom of the form and rolled forward to capture the ridge pattern to the tip of the finger. Palms can also be inked and their prints placed on to the reverse of the form, providing a full record of the ridge detail of the whole hand. If a person has been arrested for a recordable offence then this ten-print card, including palm print, is uploaded to IDENT1 – the UK's national fingerprint database.

Automated fingerprint identification systems

Automated fingerprint identification systems, or AFISs, are computer-based databases that allow rapid searching of archive fingerprint information against a fingerprint found at a crime scene.

The UK National Fingerprint database is known as IDENT1. Recent developments in fingerprint technology include the use of scanning devices at the police station, e.g. LiveScan, and mobile fingerprint devices that link directly to the IDENT1 database. This allows for rapid and effective screening for verification of the identity of an individual.

Fingerprint patterns can be divided into three main groups. The groups are arches, loops and whorls – the words accurately describe the shapes you would be looking at (Fig. 26.3).

There are also further subdivisions – for example, tented arches (where the ridge pattern extends to a point rather than a smooth curve), left or right loops (where the ridge pattern extends on a particular direction, also known as ulnar or radial loops), twinned loops (where two loop patterns converge at the core, with one overlapping the other – typically the ridge pattern here appears as an 'S' shape) and elongated whorls (where the characteristic whorl pattern has been elongated). These groups are easily identified and are designated as class characteristics.

In all patterns other than arches, there are areas close to the core known as 'deltas' (Fig. 26.3) where the ridges appear as a triangular feature. Loops have only one delta, with the exception of the twinned loop where you would find two deltas, the same as you would find for whorls, but you can still readily distinguish this pattern.

To be able to take a comparison further, a series of classifiable characteristic 'points' are required. These ridge characteristics are essentially the minutiae (the Galton characteristics) and are used to identify the individual and are designated as individual characteristics. There are seven basic ridge characteristics (ridge ending, bifurcation, lake, independent ridge, dot or island, spur and crossover) (Fig. 26.4). The comparison will start at the class characteristic

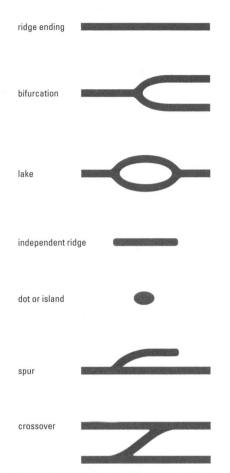

ridge ending

bifurcation

lake

independent ridge

dot or island

spur

crossover

Fig. 26.4 Characteristics of fingerprint ridges.

Accreditation – All police forces in the UK currently in 2017 are pursuing accreditation to ISO17025 see also (p. 475), a process that includes organisational and operational parameters such as method validation and competency testing of all fingerprint examiners.

(level 1) that identifies the overall ridge pattern. Level 2 records the individual minutae characteristics, with a further level 3 where the examiner may observe similarities in the distribution of the pores (although this latter is dependent on the quality of the enhanced mark). Examples of fingerprints are shown in Photo 26.1. Careful examination of Photo 26.1 will allow you to identify many of the basic ridge characteristics of fingerprints – a few are highlighted.

The ACE-V process

It is a combination of the class and individual characteristics that allow the fingerprint examiner to offer an opinion on whether or not a positive identification between the recovered fingerprint mark and the reference fingerprint card can be made.

In the UK, the process of comparison of a crime scene mark to a referent print is based on the examiner following the ACE-V process – **A**nalysis, **C**omparison, **E**valuation and **V**erification. In the analysis stage, the mark is assessed for quality and whether any ridge detail that can be observed is sufficient to proceed to comparison. If it is, then the mark will be compared to (i) a suspect or (ii) if unknown, then the mark can be searched against IDENT1 and any possible suspects can then be used for comparison. The comparison stage involves the examiner observing points of similarity (the minuate) on the mark and the corresponding points of similarity on the reference print. This process is now non-numerical and is based on the competence, experience, skill and opinion of the fingerprint examiner.

If sufficient points of similarity are found (the evaluation stage), then the examiner, in their opinion, may conclude that the mark can be identified to the person. Alternatively, in the absence of points of similarity, they may conclude that the mark cannot be identified to the person – i.e. exclusion. Two alternative evaluations may arise – insufficient, where there are simply not sufficient points of similarity to come to a conclusion, or inconclusive, where the quality of the mark is such that no conclusion can be attained.

The final stage in the process, and part of the accreditation process, is the verification stage, where the opinion has to be corroborated by one to two further fingerprint examiners. Ideally, this should be undertaken as a blind verification to ensure an independent conclusion is arrived at, rather than simply 'checking' someone else's work.

It is only at this stage, once the opinion is in agreement, that the results can be reported.

Sources for further study

Bowman, V. (ed.) (1998) *Manual of Fingerprint Development Techniques,* 2nd edn. Home Office Police Scientific Development Branch, Sandridge.

Pepper, I.K. (2005) *Crime Scene Investigation Methods and Procedures.* Open University Press.

Lee, H.C. and Gaensslen, R.E. (eds) (2001) *Advances in Fingerprint Technology,* 2nd edn. CRC Press, Boca Raton.

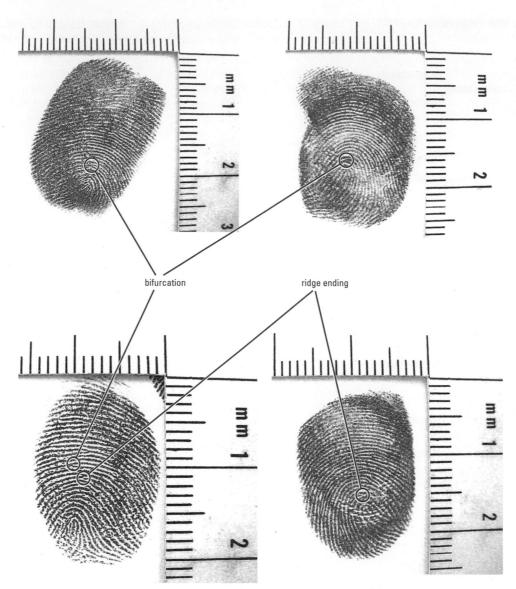

Photo 26.1 Examples of fingerprints taken from a suspect: note the use of a right-angled measurement scale.

Text references

Bandey, H. and Hardy, T. (2006) The powders process, study 3: Evaluation of fingerprint powders on textured surfaces and u-PVC. *Fingerprint and Forensic Science Newsletter,* 67/06. UK Home Office Scientific Development Branch, St Albans.

Bandey, H.L. and Gibson, A.P. (2006) The powders process, study 2: Evaluation of fingerprint powders on smooth surfaces. *Fingerprint and Forensic Science Newsletter,* 08/06. UK Home Office Scientific Development Branch, St Albans.

Bandey, H. and Kent, T. (2003) *Superglue Treatment of Crime Scenes: A Trial of the Effectiveness of the Mason Vactron,*

SUPERfume Publication 30/03. UK Home Office Police Scientific Development Branch, St Albans.

Bowman, V. (ed.) (2005) *Home Office Scientific Development Branch Fingerprint Development Handbook,* 2nd edn. UK Home Office Scientific Development Branch, St Albans

Cadd, S, Islam, M, Manson, P. and Bleay, S. (2015) Fingerprint composition and aging: A literature review. *Science and Justice* **55**(4): 219–318.

Fingerprint Source Book (2013) Available at: https://www.gov.uk/government/publications/fingerprint-source-book. Last accessed 07/09/2017/

Study exercises

26.1 Test your knowledge. What method of visualisation would you use to enhance a fingerprint on the following surfaces?

(a) Glass
(b) Blood
(c) Paper
(d) Black car door.

26.2 Practise recovering a fingerprint. Apply a fingerprint to a glass surface. Using Box 26.1 as a guide, practise the recovery of the fingerprint.

26.3 Practise a fingerprint examination. Using the same finger that you used for Study exercise 2, obtain a reference fingerprint of this finger on to plain paper, or on to a 10-print card if your university has access to them. Identify the class and 10 individual characteristics from your reference print. Compare the recovered print and the reference print and see if you find the same characteristics.

A footwear mark is made every time a person takes a step, irrespective of the surface. Someone walking across soft ground – for example, a freshly prepared flower-bed, will leave a visible indentation in the soil. However, not all impressions can be seen with the naked eye and they may require special lighting, powder dusting, chemical enhancement or an electrostatic charge to make them visible. All personnel involved at the crime scene, such as crime scene investigator (CSI), forensic scientist and police, will wear shoe covers and use stepping plates, where appropriate, at the crime scene. This ensures that no one investigating the crime ever stands on the floor of the crime scene, thereby preventing the risk of contamination. The practical skills required when investigating footwear marks include:

- finding the footwear mark;
- making an accurate representation of the mark;
- identifying any characteristic features of the footwear, including any patterns of wear or damage;
- comparing the mark with a suspect's shoe.

Footwear marks – can be 2D, e.g. on a hard surface, or 3D, e.g. on a soft surface.

Usually, the first two of these would be the responsibility of the CSI, whereas the last two can be the responsibility either of a footwear examiner within the scientific support unit of a police force or of an external forensic scientist. It is essential that all evidence is formally recorded at the crime scene for future use.

KEY POINT *Footwear marks are influenced by both the weight of the person and the surface over which the person has travelled. The mark can be made by either the undersole of the shoe worn by the suspect (footwear) or by the suspect's bare foot (footprint).*

Finding footwear marks at the scene of a crime

Specific areas to check for footwear impression evidence include the following:

- **The point of occurrence of the crime** – here, you might find marks because there may have been a struggle, or someone may have trodden in spilled blood, or items may have been walked over and a mark left – for example, on a carpet or documents lying on the ground; objects may have been moved, such as a dustbin placed under a window to aid climbing in through the window.
- **The point of entry to a building** – check for marks on, for example, broken glass or doors. Also, check the adjacent external surfaces, for example flower-bed, woodwork, etc.
- **The path through the crime scene** – search with an oblique light to find shallow impressions and surface prints on hard surfaces, where small particles of dust forming the impression will be picked up in the light beam (see Fig. 27.1).
- **The point of egress and other exterior areas** – these are important to check, though if this is the common exit route from the area then it may be difficult to establish which impressions belong to the suspect. As part of the investigation it is important to analyse, identify and eliminate every single footwear mark from a scene of crime.
- **Near other footwear marks** – find one and you may find another.

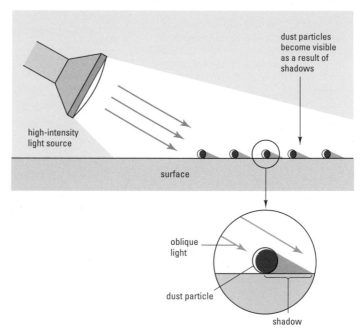

Fig. 27.1 Searching with an oblique light source.

Reconstruction of movement – of an individual can be made by examining the footwear marks left at a scene.

Checking the periphery of the crime scene for footwear marks – there is the possibility that footwear marks may have been left in locations that are not central to the scene. It is important to consider where you think the boundaries of the scene are (Chapter 23).

Protecting the crime scene – all personnel involved (crime scene examiners, police officers and forensic scientists) must wear shoe covers (scene overshoes Photo 24.1, p. 229) and use stepping plates where appropriate, to avoid damage to footwear marks.

Using gait analysis to identify individuals – while not directly based on footwear impressions, the analysis of walking patterns has the potential to be used to identify possible suspects with evidence from CCTV footage and crime scene information (for a case example, see Lynnerup and Vedel, 2005). The UK forensic science regulator in the 2015–16 annual report, has highlighted the need for further research in gait analysis as well as the impact of wear on marks (Tully, 2017).

 KEY POINT Consideration must be given to the outside environmental conditions and whether these would be likely to account for any immediate loss of evidence – for example, rainy conditions.

Footwear marks may provide information about the number of people involved, and their movements within the crime scene area – crime scene investigators should record and recover all impressions that could prove relevant to the case.

The investigator should be aware that:

- Footwear marks may have been intentionally destroyed by those involved in the crime.
- The weather may have degraded any marks left on open ground (e.g. during rainfall).
- Footwear marks may be destroyed when the crime scene is walked over by others. The area of the crime scene should be sealed off immediately upon arrival by the first officer attending (Chapter 23).
- Particular combinations of shoe and surface may not produce good marks.

Recording and recovering footwear marks at a crime scene

These may be either two-dimensional (2D) or three-dimensional (3D) in form, depending on whether the surface is hard or soft. In the case of 2D marks, these may be left on a flat surface, due to static electric charge on the undersole transferring particles on to the mark, or wet deposits on the undersole being left behind on a hard surface (positive marks), e.g. mud transferred from a shoe onto a windowsill, or in liquid present on the surface (negative marks), e.g. on a bloodstained laminate flooring. In contrast, a 3D impression may be left on a surface that was soft, where the undersole left an imprint as it was pressed on the surface, e.g. in a flowerbed.

Footwear marks are left ON a surface, whereas footwear impressions are left IN a surface. It is important to differentiate these because there are different techniques that can be used to recover each type of evidence.

The best lighting source is a high-intensity white light, for example Crimelite® or Maglite.

Example Typical hard surfaces for footwear marks include tiles, laminates, vinyl and wood.
Typical soft surfaces for footwear impressions include soil, snow and, occasionally, some deep-pile carpets (many other carpets are elastic and do not always retain a visible indentation).

When photographing the mark, make sure that the angle is 90° to prevent any distortion of the image.

Packaging of an ESLA lift *– the foil should be placed with the lifted mark uppermost into a box with the edges of the foil taped to the box to prevent any movement. The box should then be sealed and the CJA label completed appropriately (p. 247)*

 KEY POINT *Non-destructive visualisation and recording methods should always be used before more destructive chemical techniques.*

Locating marks and/or impressions

Many footwear marks are not readily visible with the naked eye (latent marks). Consequently, a search of the scene using a high-intensity light source, e.g. Maglite™, shone at an oblique angle (Fig. 27.1) is a useful starting point in a similar fashion to locating finger marks (Chapter 26). Examination with a UV lamp can also assist in circumstances where residues are fluorescent, e.g. biological fluids. Chemical enhancement and powder 'dusting' techniques (pp. 257–261) can also help visualise latent marks.

Direct photographic recording

This is the only approach when visible impressions have been left at the crime scene – for example, in spilled blood or on an oil-stained floor. In such circumstances, photographs will provide a permanent record (Box 23.1 gives further advice). Photographs should be taken at angles/distances that show the location of the impressions in relation to the crime scene, and directly from above at 90 °C using a right-angled measurement scale (Photo. 23.5, p. 239). An alternative approach is to physically remove the floor covering onto which the mark or impression has been left and after appropriate packaging (p. 248) and labelling (p. 247) can be transported either to scientific support if the police force internally employs a footwear examiner or externally to a forensic scientist for analysis.

Electrostatic lift (two-dimensional impressions)

Here, a mark is recovered directly from a crime scene, often in circumstances where a latent mark has been detected using an oblique light source to examine the area through a full 360° rotation. The electrostatic lift method works by capturing dust particles that have been temporarily subjected to electrostatic charge. Electrostatic lifts are not permanent records and must be photographed without delay. The method for preparing an electrostatic lift of a footwear mark is described in Box 27.1, and Photo 27.1 shows a footwear mark prior to and after an electrostatic lift.

Box 27.1 Preparation of an electrostatic lift of a footwear impression

To avoid fingerprints use suitable protective equipment throughout, such as latex gloves. Then employ an appropriate electrostatic lift kit – for example, the K9 Pathfinder® electrostatic dustprint system, as follows:

1. **Place the lifting material onto the mark.** Cut an appropriately sized piece of the lifting material. Typically, this is a foil with a black surface and a metallic surface. Place the black surface directly on top of the mark to be lifted.

2. **Place the electrostatic metal plate close to the covered impression.** Typically, the plate will need to be around 2 cm or so from the impression.

3. **Connect the electrostatic generator.** Making sure that it is turned off beforehand, this should be connected so that it makes contact both with the electrostatic metal plate and with the metallic upper surface of the lifting material.

4. **Operate the electrostatic generator.** Typical operating times are 10–30 s. If the lifting material forms ridges on the flat surface containing the mark, an insulated roller can be used to flatten the lifting material. Note that you must be very careful not to touch the electrostatically charged lifting material with any part of your body at this stage, to avoid the risk of electric shock. After switching off the generator, it should be removed from the lifting material.

5. **Carefully peel off the lifting material from the mark.** The underside (black surface) will now contain the lifted mark. Be careful not to touch the mark on this surface or you will destroy the detail present. Photograph the lifted mark at this stage, in case of subsequent damage. Package the electrostatic lift black side upwards in a box, until required.

6. **Record appropriate details.** Complete the full CJA label transcript. (see p. 247).

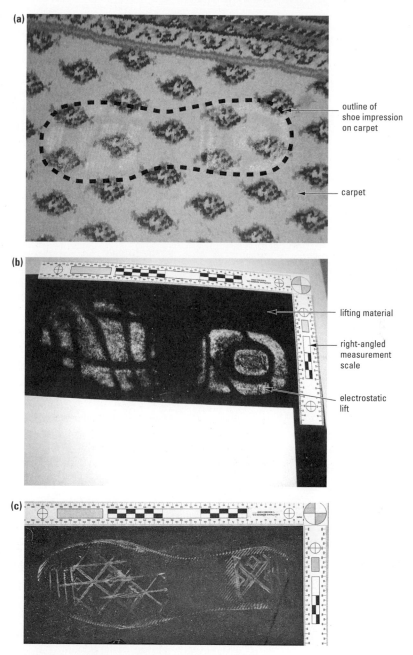

Photo 27.1 Footwear mark on carpet: (a) before; (b) after an electrostatic lift (but note the distortion as this image has been photographed at an oblique angle); and (c) a footwear mark recovered by electrostatic lift.

Gelatine lifting technique

Gel lifters are commonly used to recover latent and powdered footwear marks. Black gel lifts are commercially available, e.g. BVDA Gelatin lifter and Evident. They comprise three layers – an outer protective layer and a thick gelatine layer bonded on to a carrier plate. By placing the gelatine layer on the mark, it can be recovered without the gelatine layer adhering to the surrounding surface. Once a mark has been recovered, the gel lifter should be stored uncovered and secured in a box for photography at the earliest opportunity for subsequent examination, as it has been found that the image fades over time (Bandey, 2008).

Gel lifter or ESLA? – *The advantage of ESLA is that a speculative search can be undertaken, whereas for the gel you have to 'see' where the mark is. The gel can also lift surface texture, which may obscure some of the features of the mark lifted.*

Enhancement (two-dimensional marks)

A number of methods can be used to visualise faint marks – these are based on similar principles to those used for fingerprints (Chapter 26), within two broad groups:

1. **Chemical enhancement** – for example, by spraying with a chemiluminescent reagent, e.g. amido black, to visualise impressions in dried blood, or using a suitable dye for particular residues, e.g. ninhydrin (p. 259) or Sudan black for fats and oils. Superglue® fuming (p. 259) is another general approach that can then be dyed using an appropriate fluorescent dye. Luminol can be used if the impression is located in blood; however, although the subsequent fluorescence is intense and renders the impression clearly visible, it has to be performed in darkness, has a health and safety risk associated with the spraying of the chemicals and it is only a temporary fluorescence, meaning that immediate photography is required to capture the image.

2. **Powder-based techniques** – for wet marks that have dried out, most commonly in the form of powder dusting, e.g. using aluminium, titanium dioxide or carbon black (p. 258), although more recent research has demonstrated that powder suspensions can give good results for a range of residue types (Bandey, 2008). The newer Supranano® fluorescent suspension powders may prove effective for this purpose, but as with any new enhancement technique it will have to be fully validated prior to its incorporation into routine casework. Recovery of these visualised marks can be undertaken using gel lifters or low-tack adhesive tape in a similar manner to that associated with the recovery of finger marks.

Casting (three-dimensional impressions)

This is the usual approach when a visible indentation has been made, for example in soil. An ideal casting medium should have the following properties:

- **be readily obtainable at reasonable cost,** in consistent form and quality;
- **have a capacity to reproduce very fine detail;**
- **be easy to prepare and use,** under a range of environmental conditions, with no requirement for specialised equipment or complex procedures;
- **have the fluidity necessary to flow evenly into the impression,** but not to be absorbed or pass through it;
- **have a reasonable setting time,** creating a durable cast with dimensional stability;
- **have the capacity to be released from the material** in which the impression was made;
- **be readily cleaned,** without loss of detail;
- **have an extended shelf life.**

Historically, the choice of casting material was Plaster of Paris. However, casts prepared from this material are 'soft' and it is often difficult to remove attached material, for example soil, from the impression. As a result, Plaster of Paris has largely been replaced by dental impression materials, for example dental stone, which forms a hard cast and is easily cleaned with no loss of detail.

The procedure for the preparation of a dental stone cast at a crime scene is described in Box 27.2. This can be adapted for use in a laboratory class, for example using a mixing bowl or bucket, stirred by a gloved hand or stick. Photographs of footwear impressions in soft surfaces and their respective casts are shown in Photo 27.2.

Luminol spray – the spray is prepared using luminol powder, potassium hydroxide and hydrogen peroxide (3%). The associated COSHH and risk assessment MUST take place (Chapter 2) for its preparation and its subsequent use. Note the hazard phrases associated with this preparation include IRRITANT to eyes, skin and respiratory tract, harmful and corrosive.

Visible marks – should always be photographed prior to lifting.

Definition

Casting – filling a three-dimensional impression with a material that will acquire and retain the characteristics of the impression (the 'cast').

Casting on a slope – you can use casting frames to make sure that the casting material remains in place while it hardens.

Box 27.2　Preparation of a dental stone cast at a crime scene

The following procedure can be used to cast footwear impressions on reasonably flat surfaces. You should not remove anything that is part of the impression or that was there at the time the impression was made – any attempt to remove debris is likely to result in loss of detail in that part of the impression. Where the ground slopes, you may need to make a barrier (a 'bund') to retain the wet dental stone mixture when poured. Remember that a full-frame close-up photograph should be taken before you begin preparing the cast (p. 239 gives further details).

1. **Prepare a dental stone slurry.** To a 1 kg bag of dry dental stone in a zip-lock bag add approximately 0.5 litre of water using a graduated jug. Secure the bag and mix the contents by 'kneading' the contents of the bag, until it forms a slurry. Once prepared, this mixture has a working time of approximately 5 min, though this is affected by the water content of the slurry and the ambient temperature.

2. **Pour the dental stone slurry into the impression.** Sufficient material must be added to allow the slurry to flow into all parts of the impression, with sufficient overlap of adjacent areas. Tap the top of the slurry to remove any air bubbles that may be present during the pouring process.

3. **Allow the mixture to set fully.** This takes approximately 10–30 min, depending on the type used, the ambient conditions (e.g. the slurry will take longer to set in cold weather) and the water content of the slurry (wetter slurry will take longer to set). Check the material has set by gently placing a finger on top to identify whether the dental stone feels hard. Be careful, however, as it is the underside of the cast into which the impression has been made.

4. **Lift the cast.** Place your fingertips underneath the edges of the cast and lift gently. This should be done on the longer edges of the cast first and then the shorter edges. Do not rush this process, or you are likely to destroy valuable impression information by, for example, breaking the cast. After lifting, the underneath of the cast may be covered with debris from the surface on which it was formed, for example soil. Do not attempt to remove this material at this stage.

5. **Place the cast and any attached material in a clearly labelled container.** Wrap the cast with tissue and secure in a box. You will need to puncture the base of the box to allow the string to pass through and be tied. Remember to reseal these puncture holes using tape and sign across this new seal to maintain the integrity of this packaging.

6. **Complete the CJA label** - once packaged, transport to a secure location completing the continuity form as appropriate (p. 247).

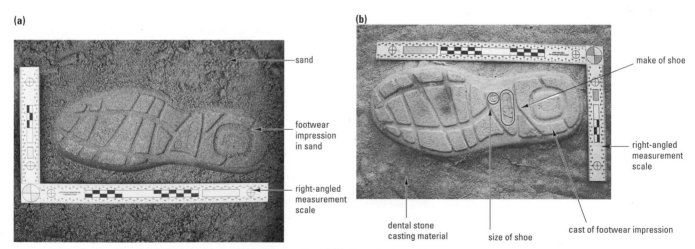

(a)　sand　footwear impression in sand　right-angled measurement scale

(b)　make of shoe　right-angled measurement scale　dental stone casting material　size of shoe　cast of footwear impression

Photo 27.2　Examples of (a) footwear impression in sand and (b) dental stone cast.

Casting in snow requires particular care since the impressions are delicate and heat-sensitive. A wax hardener, such as Snow Print Wax™, should be sprayed on to the impression to prevent the snow melting as a result of the heat generated by the hardening dental stone casting material. The dental stone slurry should be prepared with cold water and should be given time to fully set before its removal.

Box 27.3 Preparation of an inkless footwear impression

Inkless impressions are often most easily recorded by wearing a shoe, as follows.

1. **Place a new piece of pressure-sensitive paper on the chemically treated pad.** Make sure that the paper is placed directly over the waxed part of the pad.

2. **Create an impression of the shoe on the paper.** Walk over the paper in a normal movement. The natural 'rolling' action of the shoe will mean that the heel of the shoe touches the paper first and the toe last, transferring the weight of the person across the paper as the impression is made.

3. **Lift the paper from the pad and record appropriate details.** – for example, shoe size, make, suspect, etc. The paper record of the footwear impression can be retained for subsequent examination.

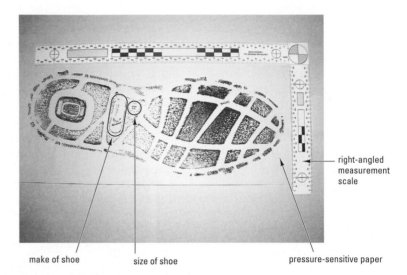

make of shoe   size of shoe   pressure-sensitive paper

right-angled measurement scale

Photo 27.3   An inkless footwear impression.

Preparing a two-dimensional mark of a suspect item of footwear

In contrast to the earlier examples, where the mark or impression was photographed, lifted or cast from the crime scene, here the footwear examiner will have access to the actual footwear and a 'positive' reference mark can be obtained simply by pressing the shoe onto a chemically treated pad, then onto pressure-sensitive paper (e.g. using the K9 Shoe Print Inkless Kit). It is, however, essential that the shoe is worn and that the inkless print is taken as if walking to produce a like-for-like print to compare. By recording multiple shoe marks, a database can be established (p. 274) and it is common that each force will have its own. Across forces it can be used as an intelligence tool and is continually updated to maintain its currency and effective use. The method for preparing an inkless shoe impression is described in Box 27.3 and an inkless shoe impression is shown in Photo 27.3.

Appreciating the diversity of sports footwear – visit your local sportswear shops, where you will find that most training shoes have complex undersole patterns, with each manufacturer creating unique and distinctive undersole styles.

Comparing crime scene evidence with suspect footwear

The information available from a footwear mark can be summarised in terms of: the pattern (or 'tread') on the undersole; the dimensions of the mark and the size of the shoe that formed it; the degree of wear present; the presence of any damage.

Table 27.1 Shoe conversion chart

Men's shoes						
British	6	7	8	9	10	11
USA	7	8	9	10	11	12
European	39.5	40.5	41.5	42.5	43.5	44.5
Women's shoes						
British	3	4	5	6	7	8
USA	4.5	5.5	6.5	7.5	8.5	9.5
European	35	36	37	38	39	40

Note: Use the above table as an approximate guide only as sizes are not exactly equivalent.

Pattern

It is important to see whether there is a sufficient similarity between the mark made at the crime scene and a suspect's footwear. There are many different undersole patterns present on footwear. While this may make it more difficult to find the exact match, it is also an advantage, since it provides the high level of diversity required in an effective matching process. A major aspect of the work of forensic footwear specialists is to keep up to date with the latest trends in footwear and, more importantly, to obtain impressions of the various undersoles available.

The two main questions to consider are:

1. **What make of shoe could have made the impression at the scene of a crime?** This question is most readily answered by comparing the impression with a database of undersole patterns.
2. **How common are these undersoles and how does the pattern vary between different pairs of the same shoe?** Some shoe undersoles are manufactured either by being cut out from a large piece of pre-moulded rubber, which can result in some individual features, especially around the edges of the undersole. Alternatively, for injection-moulded undersoles all shoes made from the same mould should have an identical undersole pattern. However, if the manufacturer uses several moulds to make the 'same' undersole, there may be differences between them. It is not uncommon for one shoe manufacturer to stop making a particular shoe design and the moulds be sold to a different manufacturer.

Size

Shoe size can sometimes be difficult to establish from the dimensions of an impression, since it is determined by the space in which the foot fits, rather than the size of the undersole. It is also more difficult if only a partial impression of the undersole is available. However, the overall length of the undersole is an important measurement.

Four common shoe size systems are used in different parts of the world. They are based on the overall length of the foot, as follows:

1. **The UK system** (sizes in increments of $\frac{1}{3}$ inch in length with half sizes $\frac{1}{6}$ of inch). The scale starts at child's size 0, which is 4 inches in length. After child size 13, which measures $8\frac{1}{3}$ inches, the sizing begins again at adult (male) size 1, increasing in $\frac{1}{3}$ inch increments.
2. **The USA system** (sizes in increments of $\frac{1}{3}$ inch in length with half sizes of $\frac{1}{6}$ inch). The scale begins at $3\frac{11}{12}$ inches, giving a quarter-size difference between the UK and US systems. After child's size 13, the sizing begins again with adult (male) size 1.

Interpreting footwear impressions – it should be noted that many shoes/trainers have the size descriptor imprinted in the sole (see, e.g., Photo 27.3). This information will also leave an impression in soft surfaces and hence will be visible in any cast produced. This type of information can assist the forensic scientist in either eliminating a suspect, or not.

Interconverting shoe sizes – while Table 27.1 provides a rough guide, a shoe will normally be designed and manufactured on one sizing system, with the closest equivalent sizes of the other systems sometimes being recorded on the label.

Using shoes to confuse – Theodor Kakzynski, the Unabomber, was known to wear specially adapted shoes with smaller soles attached to the base, to deliberately mislead investigators.

Individuality in footwear impressions – it is important to appreciate that features such as wear and damage provide characteristics that may enable a forensic scientist to demonstrate a potential match between an impression left at a crime scene and a particular shoe.

Case example Successful appeal of conviction, based on footwear impression evidence.

George McPhee was convicted in 1985 of the murder of Elizabeth MacKenzie of Culbokie, Scotland, based on testimony of police officers that linked him to footwear impressions at the crime scene. However, an appeal in 2005 concluded that a miscarriage of justice had occurred, since forensic evidence from the Grampian Police Laboratory – that the shoeprints were incomplete and could not be used to provide any reliable information as to size, etc. – had not been presented to the court (for further details, see https://www.scotcourts.gov.uk/search-judgments/judgment?id=2b7986a6-8980-69d2-b500-ff0000d74aa7).

SICAR6® – is a commercial database system that has images and characteristic details of shoe prints. These are coded using a shoe pattern coding technique and are also linked with the Solemate® footwear database. As of August 2016, this database contains 35,404 items of footwear.

3. **The European system,** also known as the Paris points system (sizes in increments of $\frac{2}{3}$ cm in length). The most common sizes are 38 $\left(25\frac{1}{3} \text{ cm}\right)$ to 48 (32 cm).
4. **The centimetre system** corresponds directly to foot length in centimetres.

It should also be remembered that, in addition to shoe size (and foot length), width is another important characteristic, especially for footprints/footwear of unusual width.

Degree of wear

As a shoe wears, the pattern on the undersole will change. Some features will be reduced in depth, or may disappear altogether. In addition, people walk in different ways, placing their weight on different parts of the undersole and creating unique patterns of wear – providing features by which the shoe can be recognised.

Factors influencing the wear of a shoe's undersole include:

- the wearer's weight, body type, occupation and habits;
- the shoe style and materials;
- the surfaces that the shoe passes over as it is worn.

Damage

Contact between a shoe and the ground causes the undersole to acquire cuts, scratches and other features of random damage. Over time, two shoes that started out with identical undersole patterns will acquire unique damage features and a measurable degree of individuality. Damage provides the greatest opportunity to identify a suspect from other individuals who may also be wearing the same make and type of footwear.

By careful examination of footwear for the above features, it can be matched to an impression at a crime scene. This information, along with other evidence from the crime scene, for example fingerprints (Chapter 26), can assist in the conviction or elimination of a suspect. It should also be noted that many of the same procedures of recovery and comparative analysis can be applied to tyre marks (p. 277) at a crime scene.

Database comparisons

Several databases exist for comparison of footwear impressions – for example, SICAR6® (Shoe Print Identification and Casework Management System; Foster and Freeman, 2017); these are used across Europe and the USA. In the UK, recent changes to legislation allow police officers to record the footwear impressions of suspects in cases of serious crimes, including burglary, violent crime and sexual offences, and to search these using the National Footwear Reference Collection (NFRC) and the National Footwear Database (Bluestar Software, 2017). Newer methodologies and algorithms are under development, e.g. by AlGarni and Hamiane (2008), which should lead to further refinements in database matching.

Text references

AlGarni, G. and Hamiane, M. (2008) A novel technique for automatic shoeprint image retrieval. *Forensic Science International* **181**: 10–14.

Bandey, H. (2008) Footwear mark recovery. *Fingerprint and Forensic Science Newsletter* 24/08, UK Home Office Scientific Development Branch, St Albans.

Bluestar Software (2017) The NFRC and NFD. Available at: https://www.scotcourts.gov.uk/search-judgments/judgment?id=2b7986a6-8980-69d2-b500-ff0000d74aa7. Last accessed 18/08/2017.

Foster and Freeman (2017) Shoe Print Identification and Casework Management System. Available at:

http://www.fosterfreeman.com/trace-evidence/356-sicar-6-solemate.html. Last accessed 18/08/2017.

Lynnerup, N. and Vedel, J. (2005) Person identification by gait analysis and photogrammetry. *Journal of Forensic Sciences* **50**: 112–18.

Sources for further study

Bodziak, W.J. (2016) *Forensic Footwear Evidence.* CRC Press, Boca Raton.

Buck, U., Albertini, N., Naether, S. and Thali, M.J. (2007) 3D documentation of footwear impressions and tyre tracks in snow with high resolution optical surface scanning. *Forensic Science International* **171**: 157–164.

Federal Bureau of Investigation (2008) *FBI Handbook of Crime Scene Forensics.* Skyhorse Publishing, New York.

Fisher, B.A.J. and Fisher D.R. (2012) *Techniques in Crime Scene Investigation,* 8th edn. CRC Press, Boca Raton.

Tully, G. (2017) Forensic Science Regulator Annual report 2015–2016. Available at: https://www.gov.uk/government/publications/forensic-science-regulator-annual-report-2016. Last accessed 18/08/2017.

Gardner, R.M. (2011) *Practical Crime Scene Processing and Investigation,* 2nd edn. CRC Press, Boca Raton.

Shor, Y., Chaikovsky, A. and Tsach, T. (2006) The evidential value of distorted and rectified digital images in footwear imprint examination. *Forensic Science International* **160**: 59–65.

Vernon, W. (2006) The development and practice of forensic podiatry. *Journal of Clinical Forensic Medicine* **13**: 284–287.

Study exercises

27.1 Specify details for labelling footwear impressions. What would you include on the labels for a shoe imprint or cast?

27.2 Select appropriate methods for use with different evidence types. Draw a simple flow diagram to show the main stages in the investigation of marks or impressions made in:

(a) soft soil;
(b) a blood-stained cement floor;
(c) a dusty warehouse, with wooden floorboards.

27.3 Investigate the chemical reaction responsible for the hardening of dental stone. Using the Internet and suitable search terms, research the underlying chemical reaction of this process.

Tool marks

Forced entry or physical violence using a tool can lead to surface indentations, for example in wood, plastic or skin. By its very nature, the tool is usually made of material harder than the surface it strikes. The work of the tool mark specialist involves initial examination of the surface in which the indentation has been made. It may, at a later stage in an investigation, involve a comparison of that surface (or its representation in the form of a mould or cast) with an object recovered from the crime scene or found as a result of police investigations.

 KEY POINT *When finding tool marks, you should adopt the same basic procedures as those for footwear impressions, described in Chapter 27.*

Recognising the tools used to commit crime

These can be divided into three main types:

1. **Those that cut** – for example, saws.
2. **Those that can be used as levers** – for example, jemmies and chisels.
3. **Those used as drilling/striking tools** – for example, hammers, drills and bats.

The marks made by each type are likely to be different. For example, saws tend to leave jagged edges, often with a linear repeating pattern because of the teeth; levers tend to leave angled depressions (fulcrum marks) as well as splinters where the surface has broken; striking tools tend to leave round, oval or square indentations. Tools cause marks on surfaces due either to compression (leaving a negative impression of the tool) or to scraping (scratching striations into the surface), or to a combination of both.

 KEY POINT *Remember to collect full thickness control paint samples from both damaged surfaces (Chapter 40).*

Recovering and recording tool mark impressions at a crime scene

A tool mark impression is typically three-dimensional in form. For example, forced entry into a house may have resulted from levering open a door made of wood or UPVC. This act will have caused both indentation into the wood or UPVC surface and a leverage/fulcrum mark (Fig. 28.1). In either case, it is then possible to, first, photograph the tool mark and, second, make a cast or mould of the impression.

Direct photographic recording

This is the only approach when visible tool marks have been left at the crime scene, for example on a window frame or on a victim's body. In such circumstances, a photograph will provide a permanent record (Box 24.1 gives further advice, including the use of UK National Training Centre guidelines). In the case of a door frame it may be possible to remove the affected area by carefully cutting it out to retain the evidence for further study, or to make a mould or cast of the impression *in situ* at the crime scene. If possible, the whole

---

Locating tool marks at a crime scene – typically, criminals will use tools to force entry, so doors, windows and their frames should be examined carefully.

Identifying tool marks at a crime scene – it is often possible to establish the general size and shape of a tool or weapon by impressions left at the scene. It should be noted that a tool mark can be recovered by a crime scene investigator, but it is only a forensic scientist who can offer an opinion on the instrument used based on that tool mark and other information given in the case.

Examining tool marks – remember that there are often two sides to the mark: (a) indentation and (b) leverage/fulcrum marks. Both are important.

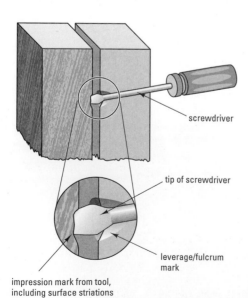

Fig. 28.1 Tool mark impressions in wood.

screwdriver

tip of screwdriver

leverage/fulcrum mark

impression mark from tool, including surface striations

of the item containing the mark should be submitted, e.g. a timber door frame. Alternatively, for example, if a victim has been assaulted with a weapon it will be necessary to photograph any injury as soon as possible. Visualisation of bruises may require alternative light sources, for example, polarised, UV or IR. However, changes that may develop as a result of bruising, which may only appear some time later, may also require photographing at a later stage – the bruising may reveal characteristics of the weapon used, e.g. parallel bruising implies a linear instrument. However, it should be noted that not all weapons used will leave a characteristic pattern.

Casting (three-dimensional impressions)

This is the usual approach when a visible indentation has been made, for example on a door frame (Fig. 28.2). The choice of casting material includes dental stone, casting putty (e.g. Mikrosil) (see Box 28.1), silicone rubber (e.g. Silmark™) and jewellery/modelling wax (Petraco *et al.*, 2009).

Note that tool mark examination sometimes provides only general class characteristics, such as the size and shape of the implement involved. However, it is the minor marks and striations (sometimes termed 'minutiae') that can point to the use of a particular tool (Nichols, 2007); such marks are the result of a combination of:

1. **manufacturing imperfections** – e.g. moulding 'flash' and machining marks;
2. **wear marks** – e.g. nicks and scratches in the working surface of the tool.

Comparing the negative impression marks from a crime scene with the positive imperfections present in a specific tool can enable the forensic investigator to link an individual implement to a particular crime. However, it is important *never* to try to fit a suspect tool directly into a tool mark from a crime scene, since this can cause cross-contamination and may also damage the surface of the mark. Instead, test marks/impressions and casts must be taken, to compare against marks from the crime scene (e.g. using a comparison microscope (p. 65). Chips of paint (Chapter 40) can provide further information that strengthens the evidential value of the material, as long as appropriate care has been taken to handle and package the items correctly (p. 395).

Tyre marks

The examination of motor vehicles is encountered in investigation of accidents or criminal investigations, for example hit-and-run, but also, fairly obviously, as a means of transportation. Tyre marks are commonly found at scenes and are typically categorised as visible (patent) surface marks, invisible (latent) surface marks or three-dimensional (plastic) impressions.

 KEY POINT *Tyre impressions are investigated using broadly similar techniques to those described for footwear impressions and fingerprints (Chapters 26 and 27).*

The procedure for examining tyre marks is initiated by full documentation and recording by photography (Box 23.1), using oblique, high-power lighting where necessary, followed by either:

- **removal of the item** containing the tyre mark (e.g. an item of clothing from a hit-and-run incident);

Mikrosil - *this silicone casting material is available in brown, black, white and grey colours. The brown Mikrosil is recommended to cast tool marks.*

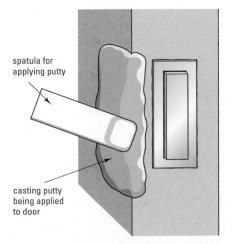

spatula for applying putty

casting putty being applied to door

Fig. 28.2 Applying casting putty to a tool mark indentation in a door.

Box 28.1 Casting a tool mark using Mikrosil

Mikrosil is an excellent casting material since it dries rapidly and is formulated to preserve the minute detail needed for this type of examination. It is available in three colours (white, brown and black) depending on the contrast colour that is required. As with all evidence, the process should be fully documented including photography prior to the recovery of the tool mark. The process is simple to use and is as follows:

1. **Preparation of Mikrosil** – depending on the size of the tool mark, squeeze 1–2 cm of Mikrosil and an equal length of hardener paste on to a piece of card. Mix the two parts together using a spatula for 30 s to 1 min.

2. **Apply the paste to the tool mark** – using the spatula apply the paste directly on to the tool mark, making sure that it is fully covered. You should try to carry out this stage within 1 min.

3. **Recover the tool mark** – the length of time required for the Mikrosil to harden depends on the ambient temperature. At 20 °C, you should leave it for 5–8 min to fully harden. At lower temperatures, you should leave it for longer (up to 15 min at −10 °C). The time is also determined by the amount of hardener paste that is mixed – by adding more, the time taken for hardening is reduced. Once the Mikrosil has set, it can simply be peeled from the surface, taking care not to damage any of the external edges of the cast as you do so.

4. **Examine the tool mark** – the cast should be securely stored and sent for examination. If a tool has been submitted that is suspected to have been used, a visual and low-power microscopy (Chapters 10 and 11) comparison can be performed to identify the class and individual characteristics of the tool and the recovered tool mark.

Case example Using surface scanning techniques with tyre tracks in snow – a young man was assaulted by three other men, who left tyre tracks in snow at the scene in Berne, Switzerland. Snow Print Wax failed to set, due to a low ambient temperature (−15 °C), so the investigators used surface scanning and 3D reconstruction to record the crime scene details. The tracks were subsequently matched to those of a suspect vehicle, confirming the value of this approach (see Buck *et al.*, 2007 for further details).

TreadMate is a reference collection over 8,500 tyres and can be used in conjunction with SICAR®6 evidence management system (Foster and Freeman, 2017)

- **'lifting' of a surface mark or impression** – using a suitable lifting method (pp. 268–269);
- **2D mark** – e.g. by recovering a full revolution of the tyre on to a suitable medium;
- **casting of an imprint** – e.g. using dental stone covering as much of the tread as possible (p. 270).

If the vehicle in question has been submitted, then the distances of the tyre marks should be noted including accurate measurements between the tyres (internal distance as well as outside to outside and internal to outside) as well as the tyre width.

Since tyre tread designs are almost as varied as those for footwear, they can be used to identify the manufacturer of the tyre and the make/model of vehicles on which such tyres were originally fitted, e.g. through a database such as TreadMate (Foster and Freeman, 2017). As with shoe prints, wear and damage can create a unique pattern in a tyre imprint, enabling individual matching by:

- comparison of 2D tyre mark and a suspect tyre (Screenshot 28.1);
- matching of test impressions (plastic prints) from a suspect tyre, made on a suitable surface, and casts of impressions from the crime scene.

As with tool marks, trace evidence (e.g., soil matching that of the crime scene found within the tyre tread) can provide corroborating information to incriminate a particular tyre.

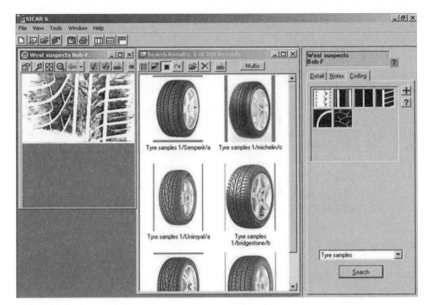

Screenshot 28.1   Tyre mark search result using SICAR® 6. Reproduced with permission from the Commercial Manager, Foster & Freeman.

Text references

Buck, U., Albertini, N., Naether, S. and Thali, M.J. (2007) 3D documentation of footwear impressions and tyre tracks in snow with high resolution optical surface scanning. *Forensic Science International* **171**: 157–164.

Foster and Freeman (2009) *TreadMate Tyre Pattern Database.* Available at: http://www.fosterfreeman.com/index.php/component/content/article/20-products/shoe-print-identification/119-treadmate. Last accessed 18/08/2017.

Foster and Freeman (2017) *SICAR®6 For the Management of Shoe Print and Tyre Mark Evidence Recovered from Scenes-of-Crime.* Available at: http://www.fosterfreeman.com/

trace-cvidence/356-sicar-6-solemate.html. Last accessed 18/08/2017.

Nichols, R.G. (2007) Defending the scientific foundations of the firearms and tool mark identification discipline: Responding to recent challenges. *Journal of Forensic Sciences* **52**: 586–594.

Petraco, N., Petraco, N.D.K., Faber, L. and Pizzola, P.A. (2009) Preparation of tool mark standards with jewelry modelling waxes. *Journal of Forensic Sciences* **54**: 353–358.

Sources for further study

Federal Bureau of Investigation (2008) *FBI Handbook of Crime Scene Forensics.* Skyhorse Publishing, New York.

Fisher, D.R. and Fisher, B.A.J. (2012) *Techniques of Crime Scene Investigation,* 8th edn. CRC Press, Boca Raton.

Gardner, R.M. (2004) *Practical Crime Scene Processing and Investigation.* CRC Press, Boca Raton.

Petraco, N. (2009) *Color Atlas of Forensic Tool Mark Identification.* CRC Press, Boca Raton.

White, P. (ed.) (2004) *Crime Scene to Court: The Essentials of Forensic Science,* 2nd edn. Royal Society of Chemistry, Cambridge.

Study exercises

28.1 Test your knowledge of tool mark procedures.
Place the following in logical sequence, in terms of their relative position within an investigation:

(a) Cast an impression of a crime scene mark using dental stone.

(b) Compare a crime scene impression against a test impression made using a suspect tool.

(c) Remove the cast containing a tool mark from a crime scene, taking care to package and label appropriately.

(d) Locate and recover any 'trace' evidence on/near to the tool mark at the scene.

(e) Photograph the tool mark incorporating a suitable right-angled measurement scale.

28.2 Fill in the blanks in the following paragraph.

_____ is the usual approach when a visible indentation has been made in a door frame. Choice of casting material includes _____ _____ and _____ _____. Likely marks in such circumstances include a leverage or _____ mark, as well as an impression from the _____ of the tool itself. Marks on the tool resulting from _____ or _____ can be used to provide _____ characteristics, enabling a specific implement to be linked to a particular crime scene. A _____ microscope can be used to compare the _____ from the scene with a _____ casting from the tool.

28.3 Research a specific case involving a motor vehicle.
Using the Internet and your library's databases, find out about the Stephen Barnes case (1989, Oneida County, USA) and the role that evidence from the motor vehicle played in the original conviction.

- *personal preference;*
- *teaching style;*
- *choice of writing instrument;*
- *writing surface and what lies beneath it;*
- *injury;*
- *illness;*
- *medication, drug or alcohol use;*
- *stress;*
- *attempted disguise.*

The examination of documents is one of the oldest forms of forensic investigation and is mainly associated with forgeries, i.e. the obtaining of goods or information by deception.

 KEY POINT *When a document is found it is imperative that fingerprints (Chapter 26) or any other impressions are not left on it prior to submission to the laboratory. Consideration must be given to how the document is handled, stored and packaged to prevent this.*

The work of the forensic scientist specialising in document analysis now covers a wide variety of topics, including:

- the identification of handwriting and signatures;
- material produced by computers;
- the analysis of inks, papers and writing media;
- distinguishing forged documents from genuine items;
- detecting additions and substitutions in a document;
- the restoration or deciphering of erased and obliterated writing, as well as being able to visualise/enhance any fingerprints (Chapter 26).

 KEY POINT *It is important that any document examination is performed prior to fingerprint examination.*

Examining handwriting and signatures

The majority of work undertaken by forensic document examiners is concerned with the identification of handwriting and signatures. Everyone is capable of recognising another person's handwriting – for example, a member of their close family – by simply gaining familiarity with characteristic elements of their style.

Characteristics of writing and signatures

Most people are taught from an early age the basic shapes and construction of letters that are used to produce words and sentences. Thus handwriting skills are acquired by a child via teachers and parents. However, as children progress to adolescence they are influenced by different styles. Modifications are then introduced over a period of time, such that from early adulthood the handwriting of an individual tends to remain consistent in style and presentation.

 KEY POINT *Characteristic handwriting is, in most cases, likely to remain with an individual throughout most of his/her adult life.*

Comparison of handwriting

The forensic document analysis expert is often asked to compare different forms of handwriting to find out whether they come from the same individual or not. This is not always easy, as the individual might be deliberately trying to disguise his/her handwriting, or can be under the influence of alcohol or drugs, resulting in a lack of hand control and hence pen movement. Deciding whether a signature is forged is a common example. The forensic document analysis expert is required to painstakingly examine the design, shape and structure of

(a)

note the spacing
between the 'f' and 'o'

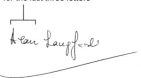

Alan Langford

'A' and 'l' are not joined, whereas 'a' and 'n' are

(b) alan Langford

Note the printing of all letters

(c) **Note the division of the
surname into two parts**

Alan Langford.

(d) alan Langford

Note the grouping of pairs of
letters. Also use of 'a' and not 'A'.

(e) Note the joined up writing
for the last three letters

Alan Langford

Fig. 29.1 Forged signatures – examples (a) to
(e) show different individual handwriting styles.

Principal features considered in handwriting analysis – *these are:*

- *letter formation;*
- *connecting strokes between letters;*
- *upstrokes;*
- *retraces;*
- *downstrokes;*
- *spacing;*
- *baseline;*
- *curves;*
- *size;*
- *distortion;*
- *hesitations.*

Only writing that is in the same case can be compared – *for example, BLOCK CAPITALS could not be compared with lower case writing in continuous prose.*

---

the handwriting to determine authorship. Look at the signatures of the first named author of this book in Fig. 29.1. You can clearly identify different styles and word construction.

The main signs of forged signatures are:

- blunt line endings and beginnings;
- retracing and 'patching';
- poor line quality with wavering and tremor of the line;
- stops in places where writing should be free-flowing.

While all of these signs would immediately alert the forensic document examiner to the potential that the signature has been forged, it is also worth considering the additional features of forged signatures:

- Any forged signature will, out of necessity, be similar to the genuine signature in terms of the main features of letter design.
- It is likely that some forgeries will resemble at least one genuine signature in almost every major detail.
- Genuine signatures, of any length, are never replicas of each other.

Signature identification normally requires a minimum of 15 to 20 genuine signatures for comparison with a signature that is unknown or disputed. When obtaining known comparison signatures, use the following approach (listed in order of importance):

1. Obtain genuine signatures written nearest the date of the questioned signature.
2. Obtain genuine signatures written on similar material (e.g. credit card receipts).
3. Obtain genuine signatures written under the same alleged or known circumstances.
4. Obtain genuine written material produced with a similar instrument (e.g. ball-point pen).

Where continuous prose is requested, it should be dictated to the writer and this should be repeated at least five times to ensure that a representative sample of writing is obtained.

Paper impressions

Examination of paper for indented writing is commonly requested. The pressure imposed on a pen when writing on a piece of paper within a writing pad not only leaves the ink impression on the top layer, but also makes indentations on paper layers below. These indentations are often not visible with the naked eye but can be detected using electrostatic detection apparatus (ESDA). This technique (Photo 29.1) was first used for case work in the UK in 1977 as an alternative to the use of an oblique light source (p. 267). The operation of ESDA is described in Box 29.1. ESDA enhances fingerprints that have been transferred on to a document; therefore to prevent any further impression or fingerprints from being introduced, cotton gloves should be worn when handling these documents.

 KEY POINT   All pages of the questioned document should be submitted in the same order as that in which they were found.

Box 29.1 How to use electrostatic detection apparatus (ESDA) to recover handwriting

This technique is used to recover indentations of handwriting from, for example, paper.

1. **Place the document to be examined in the ESDA[2] humidifier.**

2. **Place the document onto the platen (Photo 29.1) and switch on the vacuum.**

3. **Place an ultra-thin-sheet of plastic film over the document to be examined** – this allows the plastic film to be pulled down into the contours of the paper.

4. **Apply an electric charge to the plastic film and paper** – by passing a corona wire over the top. This allows a static charge to be imparted on to the plastic film and paper.

5. **Add powdered toner on top of the plastic sheet** – lift the platen so it is angled towards the toner tray and cascade the toner across the plastic sheet. The application of toner causes indentations in the document to become visible. This is achieved because the toner will be attracted to areas where impressions exist, thereby creating a contrasting image which exposes any impressions.

6. **Photograph the document** – to provide a permanent record and allow further examination.

7. **Plastic covering** – a low-tack, optically clear plastic covering can be applied to the plastic sheet, providing a protective covering to the impression evidence recovered.

8. **Switch off the vacuum** – the plastic sheet can now be removed from the original intact document for further examination.

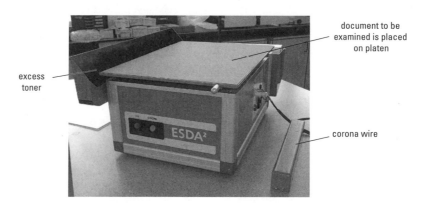

excess toner

document to be examined is placed on platen

corona wire

Photo 29.1 ESDA apparatus.

ESDA – is a non-destructive technique and should always be conducted prior to fingerprint examination using chemical enhancement techniques (p. 259)

When using ESDA, a 200 g commercial toner, also known as the cascade developer (so-called due to it being mixed with small diameter glass beads) can be distributed across the paper when the lid of the ESDA has been raised at an angle. The glass beads are collected in the excess toner tray (Photo 29.1). The cascade developer has been shown to be the most effective for at least 30 examinations of an A5-sized paper before the quality of the enhanced image is reduced. The glass beads can be recharged with toner after this time; however, it would also appear that the glass beads become smoother on continual use, and as such become less effective at delivering this toner to the impression (Daéid *et al.,* 2008).

An alternative additional approach for document examination, other than ESDA and oblique lighting, has been suggested by de Koeijer *et al.* (2006) who have shown the potential of a gelatine lifter (Chapter 27) for examination of

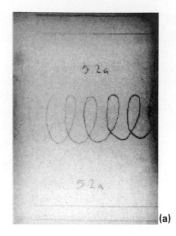

(a)

(b)

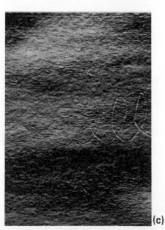

(c)

Photo 29.2 A comparison of the use of (a) gelatine lifter, (b) ESDA and (c) oblique lighting for the examination of a document. More definition was observed when the gelatine lifter was used in this instance. (Images from de Koeijer *et al.,* 2006.)

(a) Arial, 12 point

Forensic science is the application of science to questions which are of interest to the legal system.

Times New Roman, 12 point

Forensic science is the application of science to questions which are of interest to the legal system.

Courier New, 12 point

Forensic science is the application of science to questions which are of interest to the legal system.

Examples of the same text in different fonts printed from an inkjet printer.

(b) Forensic science is the application of science to questions which are of interest to the legal system.

Fig. 29.2 Examples of (a) ink-jet printer, (b) typescript.

documents in certain instances (Photo 29.2). It should be noted that subsequent ESDA examinations could not be performed, but the use of the gelatine lifter did not seem to have any impact on subsequent fingerprint enhancement providing the contact time was kept to a minimum. If this technique was to be considered, ESDA must be performed beforehand.

Examining typescript and printed text

Traditionally this aspect of document analysis focused on the use of typewriters. However, the rapid increase in the use of computer and information technology in recent years has widened this area of activity considerably. It is now possible to examine and identify printouts produced by different printing devices, for example computers using inkjet printers (Fig. 29.2(a)) and typewriters (Fig. 29.2(b)).

However, the three main questions asked of document examiners considering typescript and other printing devices are as follows:

1. Were the documents produced on the same printer (e.g. a typewriter or an inkjet printer)?
2. Is it possible to identify the make and model of the printer used?
3. Is it possible to put a timescale on when the document was produced?

The individual characteristics produced by printing devices are either inherent in the ink-depositing method or are arrived at through normal wear and tear of the device itself. It is the latter approach that offers the greatest advantage in detection, as it allows matching between the printed output and a particular printer. These defects on the printed page can occur as a result of misalignment within the printer, for example a slight offset in letter printing, or indentations introduced in the paper as a result of the paper passing through the printer.

Providing proof of identity – it is not uncommon to be asked for original documents to prove your identity. For example, when you enrolled on your degree programme you may have been asked to provide original documents showing your full name, examination grades and awarding body. By providing these at enrolment you have not only confirmed your eligibility for the programme but also allowed the university staff to examine the documents for any alterations.

Authenticating faxed documents – one reason faxed documents are not accepted as proof, in the case of legal documents, certificates, etc., is that they can be easily altered prior to sending. The often poor quality of the faxed document makes it difficult to detect such alterations.

Typewriters

Natural wear and tear of typewriters leads to variations in the printed word. Developments in typewriters from manual through to electric typewriters have made the work of the forensic document examiner more difficult. Distinguishing features to look for in typescript are:

- changes in horizontal or vertical alignment as a result of amendments made after reinserting the paper in a typewriter;
- changes in the type of ribbon used;
- corrections to the typed text.

Sometimes the forensic scientist is asked to investigate a document where the original typescript has been removed at some stage. Three common approaches are possible to erase typewritten text:

1. chemical solvents;
2. abrasives erasers;
3. lift-off tape/ribbon.

All of these methods of correction provide identifiable detection to the experienced document examiner. For example, the erasure of text using an eraser will create distortion in the paper fibres, which can be detected under a microscope. Removal of text by lift-off ribbon can be detected under an oblique light (p. 267), where indentations in the paper will be revealed. Chemical erasure can be detected under UV light, where disturbances to the surface of the paper will be exposed.

Photocopiers and laser printers

With a photocopier, an original document is placed on a glass platen and covered with a lid. Then the document is exposed to light that is reflected on to a drum coated in a photosensitive material. This creates an image of the document on the drum in the form of an invisible positive photoelectric charge. On application of negatively charged toner (black powder), the toner is attracted only to the sites where the image was created on the drum. The toner image is then transferred to paper, again by attraction (the paper has a positive charge), and the toner is then heat-sealed to the paper creating the final printed copy. The process is similar with a laser printer, but the image of the original document is held in the computer's memory and is written to the photosensitive drum using a laser.

In terms of document analysis, the use of photocopiers and laser printers will often leave identifying characteristics. The forensic document examiner may be able to identify a particular manufacturer and model of photocopier from a single reproduction from that machine.

 KEY POINT In order for this type of examination to occur, it is important that the photocopier is not cleaned. At least six copies should be obtained using clean paper that is of an equivalent size to the original questioned document.

Photocopying terminology – the black specks on a photocopy, often called 'trash marks', can be used for identification purposes.

This identification is achieved as a result of defects that are introduced into the paper as a result of the copying process. For example, the transport of the paper through the printer via belts, pinchers, rollers and gears can leave marks on the

Case example Charles A. Lindbergh Jr, the 20-month-old son of the famous aviator, was kidnapped on 1st March 1932. Extensive negotiations with several purported kidnappers resulted in a ransom of $50,000 being paid to a 'foreign-sounding stranger' by an intermediary. Seventy-three days after his abduction, the badly decomposed body of the child was discovered close to the family home. Extensive efforts by the FBI resulted in no new leads on the case until September 1935 when a gold certificate from the ransom money was found with a license plate number on it. The plate belonged to Bruno Hauptmann. So ended the hunt for the murderer of Charles A. Lindbergh Jr. Hauptmann was indicted on charges of extortion and murder and sent to trial. At the trial, forensic handwriting experts were able to link Hauptmann's writing with that found on the gold certificates. They concluded that the handwriting on the certificates had remarkable similarities in its personal characteristics to that of the suspect. Hauptmann was convicted of murder and sentenced to death. He was executed on 3rd April 1936.

paper. Marks on the glass platen that is used to create an image on the paper may contain defects (e.g. scratches), which become characteristic to the photocopier used and produce marks on the printed page. Also, dust and dirt particles can introduce defects into the photocopy. In some circumstances, these dark specks can also be used to 'date' the photocopy. This is because the defects are often temporary and, after periodic cleaning, disappear or change. If dated copies can be obtained, the shape and position of marks can be compared to arrive at a possible date. In addition, the toner itself can have unique chemical characteristics that can be identified by analytical techniques (see Chapters 17 and 18) and hence provide valuable information.

Preventing forgery of official documents

Some documents, such as the new biometric British passport or Bank of England banknotes, have a number of security features that are designed to prevent forgery. On banknotes, for example, these include raised print, metallic thread, watermarks, holograms, UV features detectable under 365 nm and microlettering. With the advent of the new polymer banknotes in circulation from 2016, this new design should help to prevent counterfeit production. For further information refer to the Bank of England website. The biometric passport now incorporates facial recognition (Chapter 33), as well as additional security features such as complex watermarks and a chip antenna that stores the photograph and personal data of the passport holder. This chip is secured by a digital certificate that can be readily identified as being altered (p. 237). For further information refer to the Home Office Identity and Passport Services website.

Text references

Bank of England (2017). Available at: http://www.bankofengland.co.uk/banknotes/pages/counterfeitadvice.aspx. Last accessed 18/08/2017.

Daéid, N.N., Hayes, K. and Allen, M. (2008). Investigations into factors affecting the cascade developer used in ESDA-A review. *Forensic Science International* **181**: 1–9.

de Koeijer, J.A., Berger, C.E.H., Glas, W. and Madhuizen, H.T. (2006) Gelatine lifting, a novel technique for the examination of indented writing. *Journal of Forensic Sciences* **51**(4): 908–914.

Home Office Identity and Passport Services (2009). Available at: http://www.ips.gov.uk/passport/about-biometric.asp. Last accessed 18/08/2017.

Sources for further study

Ellen, D.M., Foster, D.J. and Morantz, D.J. (1980) The use of electrostatic imaging in the detection of indented impressions. *Forensic Science International* **15**: 53–60.

Ellen, D. (2005) *The Scientific Examination of Documents: Methods and Techniques,* 3rd edn. Taylor and Francis, London.

Fisher, D.R. and Fisher, B.A.J. (2012) *Techniques in Crime Scene Investigation,* 8th edn. CRC Press, Boca Raton.

Foster, D.J. and Morantz, D.J. (1979) An electrostatic imaging technique for the detection of indented impressions in documents. *Forensic Science International* **13**, 51–54.

Koppenhaver, K. (2007) *Forensic Document Examination: Principles and Practice.* Humana Press, New York.

Study exercises

29.1 Compare your signature. On a piece of clean blank paper, sign your normal signature 15 times. Ask a colleague to do the same and identify the differences between your two signatures, as well as identifying any differences between your first and last signature.

29.2 Identify defects in a photocopier. Using your department's photocopier, obtain six copies using clean blank paper. Can you identify any defects on these sheets, and do these change between the first and last photocopy?

29.3 Impression evidence. On a pad of paper, write your signature using light, medium and hard pressure. On the underlying sheets, count the number of pages on which you can still see your signature (oblique lighting will help). If you have access to an ESDA, develop your sheets to confirm your observation.

Forensic biology

Biological fluids of relevance in forensic science include semen, blood, saliva, vomit, urine and faeces. It is the responsibility of the forensic biologist to examine these fluids, and stains arising from them, to determine, firstly, what they are and, secondly, to whom they belong. If a stain is found at a crime scene, it may or may not be of forensic importance. A simple presumptive test will indicate whether it is biological in origin (Boxes 30.1 and 30.3) and therefore of potential evidential value to the criminal investigation and worthy of further investigation. This may involve determining:

- **the type of fluid or stain** – this will indicate whether it is of biological origin;
- **the location of the fluid or stain** – this may corroborate one version of events said to have taken place;
- **the identity of the individual who left the fluid or stain** – this may link a suspect to a crime scene or eliminate him/her as the source.

KEY POINT **The examination of biological fluids can yield DNA evidence to provide information as to the identity of the individual who left them. However, it should be noted that DNA evidence does not prove identification. This forensic information is vital to the success of many prosecutions.**

Examination of biological fluids

Biological materials such as blood, semen, urine and faeces represent a potential microbiological hazard, for example hepatitis B, HIV+, throughout any forensic investigation from collection at a crime scene and analysis in a forensic laboratory, to possible presentation of the exhibit in court and the final storage location. At any crime scene, you should be aware of this potential risk and endeavour to protect yourself by wearing the appropriate personal protective equipment (p. 246). Any items collected from a crime scene that are contaminated with a biological material (e.g. bloodstained shirt) should be carefully packaged and labelled as a biohazard for submission to the forensic laboratory. If you are examining any such exhibit then you should be wearing gloves, laboratory coat and safety glasses. You should handle any 'wet' items, including liquids, in a bio-safety cabinet. Those items with dried biological stains can initially be examined on your prepared bench surface as long as you are fully protected. The risk, although still present, is not quite as great when the biological material is dry – for example, there is no risk of spillage when opening a vial containing blood.

Drawings of examined objects or exhibits

When an item such as a stained cushion, bedding or clothing has been submitted to the laboratory, any biological evidence must first be documented (p. 292 and 410–11) so you should include in your examination notes a written description of the exhibit. To complement this, you should also make sketches of the exhibit – for example, the location, size and description of bloodstains on an item of clothing or in the case of drug examination, the front, back and side profiles of a tablet (p. 384). Even though the stains may have been presumptively tested (p. 295) at the crime scene by the forensic scientist you should retest the samples to corroborate the positive result before proceeding with more detailed analysis. This should also include making an interpretation of the blood pattern observed. You should annotate your sketches to note whether you have carried out any analytical tests on any evidence (e.g. blood or semen) recovered from the exhibit, indicating the tests performed and their outcomes – for example, by drawing a purple stain on your drawing of an item of clothing to indicate a positive test for semen.

Examination of items should follow a set format and be documented on a standard examination form. Your notes should include the following sections:

- **description** – a full description of the item;
- **label** – full details of the label, if present, on the item;
- **damage** – noting the presence of any rips of tears in the documentation – the location is recorded as if you were wearing the item;
- **condition** – noting normal wear and tear of the item;
- **hair and fibres** – noting the presence of any trace evidence that does not naturally belong to the garment;
- **blood** – noting the location, size and type of bloodstaining present on the item.

Once the documentation of the item is complete, the examiner will sign and date the examination forms and the reporting scientist (Chapter 60) will check the findings, and in addition document any immediate interpretation on to the examination form. They will also sign and date the examination form. By following the same format every time an examination is conducted, you are less likely to miss crucial evidence.

Once you have tested the stain, you need to recover the stain from the item. This process of recovery varies according to the particular type of fluid in question. You should also remember that other trace evidence such as hairs (Box 32.1), fibres (Box 42.1) or glass debris (Box 41.1) may also be present and will require collection before analysis of the bloodstains.

Blood samples and stains

At the scene of a violent crime, blood may be present. One of the roles of the forensic biologist at this type of crime scene is to offer expertise in the reconstruction of events leading up to the formation of the bloodstains present. This is known as blood pattern analysis. The information that can be gained through the examination of bloodstains includes:

- direction of travel;
- angle of impact;
- nature of the force;
- relative positions of individuals at a scene;
- the sequence of events that may have occurred (Bevel and Gardner, 2008).

The size and appearance of a bloodstain depends on the volume of blood, the speed at which the blood was travelling and the surface on which it impacts. If a blood drop falls under gravity at 90° to the impact surface, the stain formed on impact will have a circular shape (Photo 30.1). As the height from which it falls increases, so does the diameter of the spot. If the height is greater than 30 cm, then 'spikes' may appear at the edges of the stain, which can be used to indicate the height. At heights greater than 2 m there will be no change in the diameter

Examination of an item for blood – this should follow the order:

- *presumptive testing;*
- *blood pattern interpretation;*
- *recovery of blood;*
- *DNA extraction.*

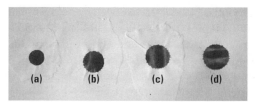

Photo 30.1 Typical bloodstain patterns observed from free-falling blood of the same volume on to a surface at 90° from a height of (a) 10 cm, (b) 50 cm, (c)1 m and (d) 2 m. Note that as height increases, the diameter of the bloodstain increases and the edges show the appearance of spikes or scalloped edges, but caution needs to be exerted as these can also form from impact on to non-smooth surfaces.

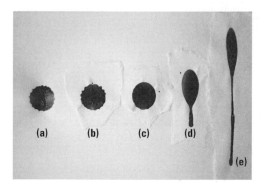

Photo 30.2 Typical bloodstain patterns observed from the same volume of blood at angles of impact of (a) 90°, (b) 70°, (c) 45°, (d) 25° and (e) 10°. Note that as the angle of impact becomes shallower, the shape of the bloodstain becomes more elliptical.

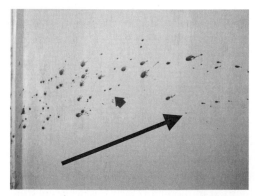

Photo 30.3 Photograph illustrating the direction of bloodstains. Note that the arrow indicates which bloodstain was sampled and not the direction.

of the spot, providing the volume remains unchanged, since the terminal velocity, or speed, of the blood drop will have been reached. The shape observed is largely dependent on the surface texture on which it impacts. If the surface is smooth, a circular shape is observed (providing it fell perpendicular to the surface), whereas if the surface is rough, the impact will result in an irregular shape.

By measuring the width and the length of the impacted blood, the angle of impact can be determined (Photo 30.2). This can be used to reconstruct the direction from which the blood originated, and hence, potentially, the relative position of an assailant or victim.

> 🔑 **KEY POINT** *When measuring the dimensions of the stain, the width should be measured at the widest point, and for the length you visually assign the start and end point by assuming a symmetrical shape of the stain and measure this distance.*

The direction of travel can be determined visually, by the appearance of the shape of the stain. The stain will appear elongated with a trailing edge in the direction that the stain was travelling (Photo 30.3). The direction can also be indicated by the linearity of a series of bloodstains. When blood impacts on a surface at an angle, the surface tension is broken such that some of the blood is broken from the original, and continues travelling forward leaving a thin line of blood. This phenomenon is known as wave cast-off.

Another type of cast-off is that associated with the use of a weapon. As the weapon impacts in wet blood, transfer of blood occurs. When the weapon is withdrawn, any motion will result in the blood transferring from the weapon on to another surface, e.g. wall or ceiling. This phenomenon is known as cast-off from a weapon and should not be confused with wave cast-off. The more times the weapon is used, the greater the transfer of blood, resulting in characteristic linear blood patterns being observed. The number of these linear patterns can give an indication of the number of blows that were struck, but it should be noted that the first impact does not generate any pattern, given that there is a short delay before the onset of bleeding. If several lines of blood can be identified, it is possible to determine whether each trail originated from a single point. This area is known as the point of convergence and represents a 2D view of the position of the person the blood originated from. For each trail that you have identified, you can place a length of string along the 'line of best fit' of the blood drops. By extrapolating the strings back towards the direction the blood drops came from, they will eventually overlap – the point of convergence. This point should never be forced and is usually an area rather than a fixed point. You can further determine the 3D position of this person, known as the point of origin. To do so you need to identify several large drops of blood on each trail.

Accurately measure the width and the length of each of these blood drops using Vernier calipers (p. 50). Using the following formula, you can determine the angle of impact:

$$\text{angle of impact} = \sin^1\left(\frac{\text{width}}{\text{length}}\right) \qquad [30.1]$$

Attach a length of string adjacent to each blood drop used to calculate the angle of impact. Extrapolate these strings back towards the direction the drops came from at the calculated angle until they overlap, and that is the point of origin.

Types of bloodstains observed in blood pattern analysis:

Low velocity – *these include dripping single drops or multiple, splashing including dripping into wet blood, cast-off from weapon.*

Medium velocity – *these include patterns associated with beating, stamping, expirational spatter.*

Arterial – *a category in its own right, typically characterised by an arcing pattern associated with the cardiac rhythm.*

High velocity – *a category associated with gunshot wounds.*

Transfer – *contact with wet blood either on a surface, or transfer of blood on to a surface; also includes smears and wipes.*

Example Two bloodstains were found at a crime scene. Stain (A) was measured as 3.3 mm wide, by 19 mm long; and stain (B) 17 mm wide by 19 mm long. Use eqn [30.1] to determine the angle of impact for each stain:

$$\text{stain (A)} = \sin^{1}\left(\frac{3.3}{19}\right) = 10°$$

$$\text{stain (B)} = \sin^{1}\left(\frac{17}{19}\right) = 63.5°$$

Case example Billie Jo Jenkins was unlawfully killed in 1997. Sion Jenkins was charged and subsequently acquitted in 2005. Central to the case was the fact that minute blood stains were found on his clothing. Two hypotheses were proposed – the pattern was consistent with that from a weapon, and the alternative explanation was that the blood was transferred on to the clothing from expirational blood.

The force used to injure an individual can be relatively easily determined from blood pattern analysis. For example, bloodstains produced where no force has been applied are typically classified as low velocity and are in the region of 4–8 mm in diameter, unless high volumes of free-flowing blood are involved. When greater force has been applied, for example using a baseball bat as a weapon, the blood droplets formed are broken up into smaller droplets, typically 1–4 mm in diameter, which radiate away from the point of impact. These types of stains are classified as medium velocity. Within this category there are occasions where expirational blood (coughing) occurs, which gives the characteristic pattern associated with this type of force. Stains from high-velocity impact are only associated with gunshot wounds, and are typically characterised by a solid mass of blood surrounded by a mist-like pattern of blood droplets of less than 1 mm diameter (Bevel and Gardner, 2008). Since their size is minimal, the distance travelled is typically less than 1m.

In cases where blood is found, it is likely to be transferred in a forward direction as well as backward. In other words, blood found at a scene will have impacted on a surface in the characteristic pattern associated with the force used, but will also appear on the individuals involved, for example on the hands and clothing. The location, size and patterns on the clothing are equally important in terms of blood pattern analysis and can be used to corroborate or refute a version of events, e.g. dripping blood versus medium velocity impact. Stained items of clothing can be submitted to the laboratory for examination and blood samples recovered from the clothing can then be recovered for DNA analysis (Box. 30.2) to assist in the identification of the individual it has originated from.

Bloodstains

The process of examination of an exhibit should follow a logical order (p. 292) to maximise the recovery of all potential evidence. This process should allow you to identify each potential bloodstain visually using, for example, light sources, i.e. Maglite and low-power microscopy. In your examination notes you should record the location and the sizes of the bloodstains using general descriptors including:

- minute – up to 1 mm;
- small – 1–2 mm;
- large – subjective size;
- spots of blood – deposition at 90°;
- splashes – deposition at any angle other than 90°;
- contact and smears – transfer stains from direct contact with wet blood.

Any stain believed to be blood should be indirectly tested with a presumptive test, such as the Kastle Meyer (KM) test (Box 30.1), at the crime scene prior to collection, or on any item submitted to the laboratory, e.g. a t-shirt from an alleged assault. This test should be corroborated in the laboratory using a different presumptive test (e.g. the leucomalachite green (LMG) test) to ensure that the sample has not given a false-positive result. The traditional tests are based on peroxidise activity of haemoglobin. However, there are newer commercially available tests, for example Hexagon OBTI (Johnston *et al.*, 2008) based on immunological techniques (Chapter 21). These tests are specific to anti-human haemoglobin antibodies and have the obvious

Box 30.1 How to carry out a presumptive test for blood

Kastle Meyer (KM) and leucomalachite green (LMG) tests detect the presence of peroxidase enzyme activity of the sample. When hydrogen peroxide is introduced, if peroxidase is present, hydrogen peroxide is reduced and oxygen is released, which catalyses the oxidation of the colourless dyes (phenophthalein or LMG) to their respective coloured forms.

1. **Prepare the reagents** – there are two main types of presumptive test used for blood. KM is used primarily at a crime scene since it is more stable than LMG. You can prepare both reagents as follows:
   (a) KM reagent – accurately weigh 12 g phenol phthalein, 120 g potassium hydroxide and 30 g zinc dust. Add to 600 mL distilled water and stir for 3 h on a hotplate.
   (b) LMG reagent – accurately weigh 2 g leucomalachite green and 5 g zinc dust. Add to 200 mL acetic acid and add a further 300 mL distilled water and mix thoroughly.
   (c) Hydrogen peroxide (3% v/v) – add 3 mL hydrogen peroxide to 100 mL distilled water and mix thoroughly.

   Before using these reagents on case samples, you should test them on a known blood sample (control) in order to make sure that your reagents are working properly. If a positive reaction occurs, then you can use them for your analysis. If no reaction occurs, you must prepare the reagents again.

2. **Identify each potential bloodstain at a crime scene** – you need to photograph the suspected bloodstain *in situ* (see Chapter 23). Add an arrow label (Photo 30.3) close to the stain to indicate which one you are going to examine. Re-photograph the stain with the arrow attached.

3. **Recover a small sample of the stain** – fold a circular filter paper in half, then half again to obtain a sharp point. Scrape the point of the filter paper over a small section of the stain. Open the filter paper and check that you can see the stain on the point (or centre) of the filter paper. If it cannot be seen, then refold the filter paper and scrape over the stain again. Re-photograph the stain.

4. **Test the stain** – pipette one drop of KM reagent on to the stain on the filter paper. The stain should not change colour. Pipette one drop of hydrogen peroxide on to the stain on the filter paper. You should observe and record in your notes whether there is a colour change. A positive reaction is characterised by a colour change to pink within 1–2 s.

5. **Collect the bloodstain from the crime scene.**

6. **Once you have tentatively identified the stain as blood** – you can recover it from the scene for further examination, as detailed in Box 24.2.

7. **Test each bloodstain you intend to analyse in the forensic laboratory** – bloodstain evidence, such as items of clothing or objects recovered from a crime scene or from a suspect or victim, will have been submitted to the laboratory for further examination. You should examine these items for trace evidence before any analysis of blood is carried out (see Chapters 32, 41 and 42) and then:

   (a) examine the exhibit and record in your notes the position of the suspected bloodstain – once tested positive, you should draw the exhibit indicating the position of the bloodstain in red ink. You should also indicate in your notes which stain you intend to analyse;
   (b) fold a circular filter paper in half, then half again – using the point of the filter paper, scrape over a small section of the stain;
   (c) open the filter paper and check that a stain can be seen on the point (or centre) of the filter paper – if it cannot be seen, then refold the filter paper and scrape over the stain again;
   (d) pipette one drop of LMG reagent to the stain on the filter paper – the stain should not change colour.
   (e) pipette one drop of hydrogen peroxide to the stain on the filter paper – observe and record whether there is a colour change and the time it took to produce the colour change. A positive reaction is characterised by a change to an intense blue-green colour within 1–2 s.

advantage that the incidence of false-positives should be reduced. It has been shown that Hexagon OBTI has an equal sensitivity to diluted blood as both KM and LMG (Johnston *et al.*, 2008), but only when the buffer volume has been optimised. Johnston *et al.* (2008) have also shown that Haemastix®, a peroxidise-based commercial test, had superior sensitivity, but only a partial DNA profile (p. 303) could be obtained from this 'superior' dilution of blood.

Any critical findings, e.g. KM positive result for blood, will need to be checked by the reporting officer on the examination notes as well as offering an opinion on the pattern observed. If no bloodstains are visible, a screening procedure should also be undertaken.

This process involves 'segmenting' the item into appropriate sizes, but this time rather than using the point of a filter paper to perform the presumptive test (Box 30.1), you firmly rub the side of the filter paper across the segment. By applying the presumptive test reagents to the filter paper, you can observe whether a positive or negative result occurs according to the colour change.

In very rare instances you can also do a direct test, although this is usually a last resort as it is a destructive test and is only performed by the scientist who will be the reporting officer. You can use this on dilute or very faint stains that have given a negative result by conventional methods, but have an appearance that suggests it could be blood. Taking great care, a single thread can be removed from the item and tested directly using the presumptive tests as before (Box 30.1).

There are other tests that can be employed, such as the Takayama test, where the presence of haemoglobin results in the formation of pink needle-like crystals that can be identified using low-power microscopy (Chapters 10 and 11).

It may be relevant in some cases to establish that a bloodstain is human in origin, rather than animal. In such instances, a simple immunological test known as the precipitin test can be employed (Chapter 21).

The stain, now identified as blood, can be extracted (see Box 30.2) and submitted for DNA analysis. Such analyses allow reliable identification of the person from whom the stain originated, so long as a reference sample exists or has been taken previously (see Chapter 23).

Semen

Detection of semen can be important to provide evidential support that sexual contact has occurred. This type of examination will usually be performed in the laboratory following submission of appropriate items, such as bedding, underclothes and oral or genital swabs taken during medical examination. Semen can usually be found in oral swabs for up to 12 h after an incident involving oral sex and in internal vaginal swabs for up to 72 h if ejaculation took place and a condom was not worn.

An item of clothing or bedding submitted to the laboratory should be thoroughly examined, including examination for other types of trace evidence, such as hairs (Chapter 32) or fibres (Chapter 42). If a stain has been located, a presumptive test, known as the acid phosphatase (AP) test (see Box 30.3) should be performed. It should be noted, though, that semen stains are not always evident, and therefore the AP presumptive screening test should be performed regardless of whether a visible stain has been identified. This test is based on the fact that acid phosphatase, an enzyme secreted by the prostate gland, is high in concentration in semen samples. The standard acid phosphatase test works by catalysing the conversion of a-sodium naphthylphosphate to free naphthyl, which in turn converts the dye from a colourless form to a purple stain.

Once the stain has been tentatively identified as semen, the presence of sperm heads should be confirmed. This process involves the extraction of the stain from the garment, or swab, to make the sample to be stained using

Validity of presumptive tests – these are not 100% accurate. They can give false-positives if the suspect stain contains, for example, chemical oxidants, which will react and produce a colour change. This can be distinguished from a true positive if the colour change is not immediate and remains faint.

Testing a sample for the presence of yeast – extract the semen sample and prepare a microscope slide (see Box 30.3). Add 0.025% w/v acridine orange, prepared in 2% v/v acetic acid. Gently rinse the slide with 2% v/v ethanol in saline and finally with saline. Using a fluorescence microscope equipped with a broad blue band filter, the sperm heads can be identified as those with a yellow/green colour, whereas yeast cells will appear red.

Box 30.2   Extraction of DNA from bloodstains

Once a bloodstain has been identified by a preliminary test, a sample of the stain must be extracted for DNA amplification (see Chapter 31) to produce a DNA profile. This process involves extracting the bloodstain from the material it has landed on, chemically digesting the blood cells and then analysing the DNA.

Extracting the bloodstain

1. **Locate the stain and remove a sample** – using a sterile scalpel, carefully cut a small amount of the stain, approximately 2–3 mm², into a sterile labelled microcentrifuge tube.

2. **Lyse the blood cells** – add 1 mL of sterile deionised water and vortex mix for 15 min; this should disrupt the cells, in particular the white blood cells which contain DNA. Collect the supernatant following centrifugation for 5 min at 10,000 × g – remove the supernatant to a second sterile, labelled microcentrifuge tube.

3. **Remove polyvalent metal ions** – add 100 mL of 5% Chelex 100® and incubate the tube at 56°C in a heating block for 30 min, with occasional vortex mixing of the sample. Chelex 100 is a chelating ion-exchange resin that removes cations that might interfere with subsequent DNA assay and is certified free of endonuclease and ligase activity (see Walsh *et al.*, 1991 for more details).

4. **Denature and remove proteinaceous material** – centrifuge the tube at 10,000*g* for 4 min, then return to a heating block at 100°C for 8 min.

5. **Harvest the soluble DNA extract** – vortex mix and re-centrifuge at 10,000 × *g* for 4 min. and then transfer the supernatant (containing extracted DNA) to a clean, sterile, labelled microcentrifuge tube. Discard the pellet.

6. **Store the DNA extract until required for analysis,** for example at −20°C (Chapter 31).

Note that other methods can be used, for example proteinase K/alcohol precipitation (see Box 31.1).

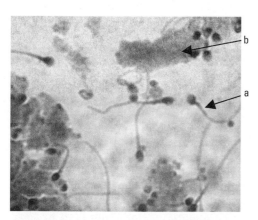

Photo 30.4 A sample of semen. Individual spermatozoa (arrow 'a') are characterised by a head and tail, and are approximately 7 μm × 4 μm (head), total length 55 μm. Partially broken cells where the nucleus is absent (arrow 'b') can also be seen.

haemotoxylin and eosin (H&E) for microscopic examination (see Box 30.4). This method has now been updated to include preferential lysis to separate DNA from sperm in mixed-fluid samples (e.g. semen and vaginal epithelial cells) using proteinase K and sodium dodecyl sulphate (SDS) (Chapter 31), but is still useful for cell harvesting (steps 1–5) and microscopic slide preparation for this sample type. There have also been several published improvements in the efficiency of sperm cell recovery including differential lysis with proteinase K, SDS and dithiotheritol (DTT) (Yoshida *et al.*, 1995) and more recently with the use of sodium lauroyl sarconsinate (sarkosyl) (Norris *et al.*, 2007). One of the main problems encountered in the examination of semen, from cases of alleged sexual assault, is that of fungal infection, particularly by yeast, but this is restricted to vaginal samples. When viewing a contaminated sample with low-power microscopy, any sperm cells will be masked by an abundance of dark purple-stained yeast cells. If the sample is contaminated, then the cell pellet should be digested by pipetting 20 μL proteinase K (10 mg mL⁻¹) and leaving the pellet to digest for 2 min. This will digest the yeast cells, but you should wash the pellet immediately after 2 min to prevent digestion of the sperm heads. Wash the cell pellet with 1 mL water, centrifuge at ~10,000*g* and discard the water. Repeat this process three times to ensure that all proteinase K has been removed. Prepare another slide and stain with haemotoxylin and eosin.

During microscopic examination of the slide, spermatozoa (Photo 30.4) and nucleated epithelial cells should be identified. The spermatozoa are scored according to the numbers present. The presence of tails is also noted, although a scoring system is not applied in this case. This is a critical

Box 30.3 Testing a stain for the presence of semen

Once the garment or other item has been fully described and any other trace evidence (e.g. hairs) has been recovered (Boxes 32.1, 41.1, 42.1), the suspect stain should be tested to determine whether or not the signs of semen are present. As with all biological fluids, you should take adequate precautions to ensure your safety and be wearing your personal protective equipment (p. 246). The procedure is as follows:

1. **Prepare the reagent** – the acid phosphatase reagent is made up in two steps. First, accurately weigh 1 g 1-naphthyl phosphate disodium salt, 2 g fast blue B salt, 6 g sodium acetate and 105 g sodium chloride and mix thoroughly. Then, accurately weigh 45.6 g of this mixture and add to 200 mL distilled water and 1mL glacial acetic acid. Transfer this solution into a bottle that has a fine spray. Fill a second bottle with a fine spray with sterile water. Store in the dark at 4°C, but bring to room temperature before use.

2. **Test the AP reagent** – collect a control sample of semen. In a bio-safety cabinet, carefully pipette one drop of this semen on to a circular filter paper and leave to dry, otherwise the intensity will not be comparable. Spray the filter paper with AP reagent. The stain should change from colourless to a purple colour. If it does not, you must make the reagent again.

3. **Prepare your work surface** – your bench surface should be prepared, ready for examination of the exhibit, as described in steps 1–7, Box 41.1. You also need to collect a sheet of plastic and, using scissors, cut a section of plastic to cover your bench surface. Tape this section on to your bench and place your exhibit on to this piece of plastic with the stain facing upwards. Cut two further sections of plastic slightly larger than the item you are examining.

4. **Recover the stain from the exhibit** – place one of the cut sections of plastic sheets between the layers of the item being examined. Spray the upper surface of the exhibit with water, making sure it is evenly wetted. Collect a piece of clean white blotting paper and place this on the wetted upper surface of the exhibit. Spray the paper with water, making sure it also is evenly wetted. Place the second section of plastic on top of the wet paper and apply even pressure on the exhibit so that the water from the item being examined is transferred to the paper.

5. **Test the stain** – remove the plastic sheet keeping the wet paper attached to it and place paper-side up on your bench. Gently trace the outline of the item on the paper using a black chinagraph pencil. Transfer the plastic and paper to a bio-safety cabinet and spray the paper with AP reagent.

6. **Record your results** – your notes should include a written description of the exhibit you have examined, complemented by a drawing. Observe and record in your notes any colour changes that occur after 2 min. If a colour change to purple is observed, you should annotate the picture in your notes, using a purple pencil, with the exact location where the stain is located. On the actual exhibit, you should mark the exact location using a chinagraph pencil that provides a contrasting colour to the exhibit – for example, if the exhibit was black, the stain should be marked using a yellow chinagraph pencil. This indicates the region of the stain for further analysis.

Definition

Buccal swab – a sterile medical swab scraped over the inside of the cheek to collect epithelial cells.

Reporting colour changes with the Phadebas amylase test tablets – *the colour change is a critical finding and should be witnessed and agreed by another scientist – i.e. the reporting officer. The colour changes are measured as a scale, ranging as shown here:*

weak   moderate   strong   very strong

Reporting colour changes with the Phadebas amylase test tablets.

finding and should be checked by a second scientist who will be the reporting officer of the case.

 KEY POINT *A minimum of 1 spermatozoon is required to allow you to report a positive result.*

Even if sperm heads have not been detected, a further test can be performed to corroborate a positive AP result, known as the choline test. Here a different microscope slide is prepared and placed in close contact with potassium iodide solution. The iodine will form crystals in the presence of seminal fluid, such that if a positive AP and choline test are found, the presence of seminal fluid can still be reported.

Once the microscopic examination is complete, if sufficient sperm heads (++ or more, see Table 30.1) have been identified then the cell pellet will be sent for DNA analysis (Box 30.4). It is important to remember, however, that internal and external vaginal swabs, even if they both have identified sperm heads, should not be sent for analysis together. This is to ensure that cross-contamination cannot occur, since the charges against the male will be different depending on whether or not penile penetration has occurred.

Box 30.4   How to extract sperm heads from a semen stain or swab

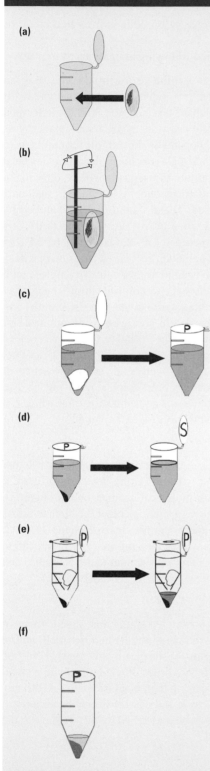

(a)

(b)

(c)

(d)

(e)

(f)

Fig. 30.1 Steps in semen testing. (Courtesy of L. Barnes.)

Unlike extraction of bloodstains, the purpose of this extraction is to recover whole cells. If the cells are undamaged they can be used for microscopic identification and then subsequent DNA examination. For this reason, there is no cell digestion stage in the procedure.

1. **Isolate the stain or swab** – for a swab, cut the end of the cotton swab off and transfer it to a 1.5 mL sterile microcentrifuge tube (Fig. 30.1(a)); for fabric, cut a piece of the fabric the stain is present on, approximately 2–3 mm², remembering that as semen dries the sperm heads may migrate to the edges of the stain.

2. **Cut the fabric into small pieces** – use a sterile scalpel and transfer the pieces into a sterile 1.5 mL microcentrifuge tube.

3. **Extract the semen** – pipette 0.5 mL sterile water (microbiological grade), which has been certified as DNA and RNA free, and vortex mix the microcentrifuge tube for 30 min. Agitate the cut fabric or cotton swab with a sterile disposable stirrer for 2 min (Fig. 30.1(b)).

4. **Recover the cellular material** – pipette the liquid to another sterile microcentrifuge tube labelled 'P' (pellet) and centrifuge at 10,000*g* for 4 min (Fig.30.1(c)). Place the microcentrifuge tube containing the cut pieces of fabric to one side.

5. **Pipette the supernatant (liquid) to a micro centrifuge tube** – labelled 'S' (supernatant) without disturbing the cell pellet (Fig. 30.1(d)).

6. **Prepare a 'spinaroo' to recover the remaining cellular material from the fabric** – a 'spinaroo' is produced when two microcentrifuge tubes are placed one on top of the other. The upper tube has a hole pierced in the base, which will allow any liquid in this tube to flow into the lower tube when spun in a centrifuge. Heat a mounted needle in a Bunsen flame until it glows, to sterilise the needle, and pierce a hole in the lid and base of the microcentrifuge tube containing the cut pieces of fabric, then place it into the tube labelled 'P' (Fig.30.1(e)). Centrifuge the 'spinaroo' at 8,000*g* for 4 min. The speed needs to be slightly lower than before, so that the tubes can be separated from each other after centrifugation.

7. **Remove the upper fabric tube and re-centrifuge the lower tube** – now containing the supernatant and cell pellet, at 10,000*g* for 4 min.

8. **Combine the supernatant** – pipette this supernatant to the microcentrifuge tube labelled 'S' without disturbing the cell pellet.

9. **Make a microscope preparation** – resuspend the pellet in 20 mL of supernatant (Fig.30.1(f)) and then add 1 mL of this to a microscope slide. Allow to thoroughly dry before staining. If contamination by yeast is suspected, then perform the acridine orange test. If not, then stain the slide with haematoxylin for 2 min and rinse the slide under very gently running water.

10. **Counter-stain the slide** – with eosin for 30 s and rinse the slide under very gently running water. Allow the slide to dry completely.

11. **View the slide under low-power magnification (p. 69)** – for example, 25× magnification (objective) for nucleated epithelial cells, and 40× magnification (objective) for sperm heads.

Table 30.1 Scoring system for sperm heads

0	No spermatozoa
Trace	Less than 10 spermatozoa overall
+	10–20 spermatozoa overall
++	20–30 spermatozoa overall
+++	>30, usually with 1–2 spermatozoa in each field of view
++++	Abundant number of spermatozoa

Preparation of p-dimethylaminocinnamaldehyde (DMAC) – *prepare a 0.1% w/v solution in absolute alcohol. For the working reagent, carefully pipette 1 mL of concentrated HCl to 9 mL 0.1% w/v DMAC.*

Saliva

In forensic science, saliva is a useful biological fluid for two main reasons:

- DNA can be extracted from the epithelial cells obtained from buccal swabs (see Box 30.4);
- the presence of semen can be identified following allegations of oral sex.

Occasionally a stain on clothing, or an exhibit at a crime scene (e.g. an envelope), may be found that is suspected to be saliva. To determine whether it is saliva, a simple test known as the Phadebas® test (see Box 30.5) is performed (Auvdel, 1986). Phadebas is commercially available as pre-treated paper or as Phadebas amylase test tablets and it will depend on the exhibit submitted as to whether the paper or tablets are used. When a glass or equivalent item has been submitted, Phadebas paper is not appropriate to use, as it will be difficult to apply the pressure required for the test to be successful. In this instance, Phadebas amylase test tablets can be used. These should only be handled by sterile forceps and never by hand, even when gloves are worn. Initially, any cellular material will have to be recovered by a standard cell harvesting technique (steps 1–5, Box 30.4). The supernatant recovered from this process is placed into an eppendorf tube and then used to test for salivary amylase with the addition of a Phadebas tablet. By reference to control samples (negative, i.e. sterile distilled water, and positive, i.e. sterile swab of your mouth) any colour changes can be observed and recorded in your examination notes. For further details on this technique you can refer to the Phadebas website referenced at the end of this chapter. This test indicates the presence of amylase activity. Phadebas is a starch polymer that has been dyed blue. In the presence of amylase, the water-insoluble starch polymer becomes soluble, releasing the dye. By measuring the absorbance of the solution, the concentration of amylase can be determined by reference to a calibration curve (see Chapter 51).

Urine

Occasionally, a light-coloured stain needs to be identified to determine whether or not it is urine. The most common test is based on the detection of urea. It should be remembered, though, that other biological samples contain urea. To determine whether the stain is urine, remove a small piece of the stained fabric from the garment and add one drop of p-dimethylaminocinnamaldehyde (DMAC) reagent. If a purple colour change occurs within 15 s, this is a strong indication of the presence of urine. If it takes up to 1 min for the colour to develop, the stain could be a dilute urine stain, or from another source (e.g. sweat).

Faeces

On rare occasions, you may be asked to examine stains that appear to be of faecal origin. These should initially be examined visually and by smell, noting the colour and odour. A small scraping of the surface of the stain should be removed using a scalpel and macerated in 2–3 drops of water. Transfer a small sample to a microscope slide and observe using high magnification ($\times 100$) any plant cells, undigested muscle fibres, bacteria and yeast that may be identified. Confirmation of the presence of faeces can be performed by testing the sample for urobilinogen.

Reporting results

The results of the analysis, for example whether a stain has been identified as blood or semen etc., should be stated. If samples have been removed for further testing, such as DNA analysis, then this should also be included

Box 30.5 Examination of a garment for saliva

Once the garment has been submitted for examination and has been fully described (p. 292) and any other trace evidence has been recovered (Box 32.1, 41.1, 42.1), an examination for the presence of saliva can be performed. As with all biological fluids, you should take adequate precautions to ensure your safety and wear your personal protective equipment (p. 247). The procedure is very similar to screening a garment for semen (Box 30.3), but this time uses paper that has been pre-treated with Phadebas granules.

1. **Examine the garment** – place the garment with the side you wish to examine directly facing you. Place a cut section of plastic sheet between the layers of the garment being examined. Dampen the upper surface of the exhibit with water, making sure it is evenly wetted.

2. **Prepare the garment** – cover the wetted area with Phadebas paper, but make sure that the reagent-treated side is in contact with the garment. Dampen the Phadebas paper with water, making sure it is evenly wetted. Gently trace the outline of the garment on to the Phadebas paper.

3. **Prepare a control sample** – using a sterile swab, swab the inside of your mouth, making sure the swab is moistened. Place this swab on to a corner of the Phadebas paper as far from the garment as possible. You must make sure that this corner does not come into contact with the garment at any time during the examination.

4. **Record your results** – place another plastic sheet on top of the paper and, using weights, make sure there is even contact across the exhibit. Start a timer and observe the paper every 10 min until a maximum of 40 min has elapsed. Record in your examination notes the location and time taken for any colour change to occur (a positive reaction is visualised by a diffuse blue colour on the paper) of both the garment itself and the control sample in the corner of the paper. Trace the outline of the positive reaction on to the garment using a chinagraph pencil and remove the Phadebas paper.

(see Chapter 31). An opinion can be offered for the interpretation of the distribution, location and significance of the biological fluid found in context with the information that has been received in the case.

Text references

Auvdel, M. (1986) Amylase levels in semen and saliva stains. *Journal of Forensic Science,* **2**: 426–431.

Bevel, T. and Gardner, R.M. (2008) *Bloodstain Pattern Analysis: With an Introduction to Crime Scene Reconstruction,* 3rd edn. CRC Press, Boca Raton.

Johnston, E., Ames, C.E., Dagnall, K.E., Foster, J. and Daniel, B.E. (2008) Comparison of presumptive blood test kits including Hexagon OBTI. *Journal of Forensic Sciences* **53**(3): 687–689.

Norris, J.V., Manning, K., Linke, S.J., Ferrance, J.P. and Landers, J.P. (2007) Expedited, chemically enhanced sperm cell recovery from cotton swabs for rape kit analysis. *Journal of Forensic Sciences* **52**(4): 800–805.

Phadebas webpage. Available at: http://www.phadebas.com/tibet/template/Index.vm?pageid=2680. Last accessed 18/08/2017.

Walsh, P.S., Metzger, D.A. and Higuchi, R. (1991) Chelex 100 as a medium for simple extraction of DNA for PCR-based typing from forensic material. *Biotechniques* **10**: 506–513.

Yoshida, K., Sekiguchi, K., Mizuno, N., Kasai, K., Sakai, I., Sato, H. and Seta, S. (1995) The modified method of two-step differential extraction of sperm and vaginal epithelial cell DNA from vaginal fluid mixed with semen. *Forensic Science International* **72**: 25–33.

Sources for further study

James, S.H., Eckert, F. and Eckert, W.G. (1998) *Interpretation of Bloodstain Evidence at Crimescenes.* CRC Press, Boca Raton.

James, S.H., Kish, P.E. and Sutton, T.P. (2005) *Principles of Blood Pattern Analysis – Theory and Practice.* CRC Press, Boca Raton.

James, S.H. and Nordby, J.J. (2002) *Forensic Science: An Introduction to Scientific and Investigative Techniques.* CRC Press, Boca Raton.

Myers, J.R. and Adkins, W.K. (2008) Comparison of modern techniques for saliva screening. *Journal of Forensic Sciences* **53**(4): 862–867.

Saferstein, R. (2000) *Criminalistics: An Introduction to Forensic Science.* Prentice Hall, Harlow.

Saferstein, R. (2002) *Forensic Science Handbook,* Vol. I, 2nd edn. Prentice Hall, Harlow.

Virkler, K. and Lednev, I.K. (2009) Analysis of body fluids for forensic purposes: From laboratory testing to non-destructive rapid confirmatory identification at a crime scene. *Forensic Science International* **188**: 1–17.

Wonder, A. (2007) *Bloodstain Pattern Evidence: Objective Approaches and Case Application.* Academic Press, New York.

Study exercises

30.1 Test your knowledge. What presumptive tests would you choose to perform for the following biological fluids:

(a) blood;
(b) semen;
(c) saliva;
(d) urine.

30.2 Consider the importance of the order of examination. Place the following in an appropriate sequence for the examination of a garment for blood: blood, glass, hair and fibre, critical finding agreement, initial examination, KM test – case, KM test – control.

30.3 Calculate the angles of impact for the following bloodstain measurements:

(a) width 16.6 mm, length 21.1 mm;
(b) width 4 mm, length 12.7 mm;
(c) width 7.6 mm, length 13.3 mm;
(d) width 18.3 mm, length 18.3 mm.

The DNA within the human genome contains several billion base pairs (p. 104), whose sequence is identical in every cell of a particular individual. Analysing this entire sequence would be impractical, and forensic scientists use a range of techniques to compare samples of DNA with respect to certain genetic sequences, or 'markers', as described below. Typical cases include:

- **violent crimes** – for example, where blood from the perpetrator is left at the scene, or where blood from the victim is found on a suspect's clothing, or on a weapon;
- **sexual assaults** – for example, where semen from the assailant can be recovered from the victim or from the victim's clothing;
- **burglary** – for example, where a perpetrator has left biological trace evidence (e.g. bodily fluids (p. 291)) at the scene.
- **crimes where there is no suspect** – in the UK, any DNA obtained from a crime scene can be compared with the UK National DNA database (NDNAD®). The NDNAD Strategy Board has representatives from a number of advisory groups including the Home Office, DNA Ethics Group, Forensic Science Regulator and Scottish Police Authority and is responsible for the policy on how DNA samples and profiles can be accessed and used.

Profiles in the DNA database include:

- **criminal justice samples** taken under the Police and Criminal Evidence (PACE) Act;
- **elimination samples**;
- **volunteer samples** (victims, third parties, intelligence screening);
- **police personnel samples.**

Current legislation in the UK allows for DNA samples to be obtained from those arrested for a recordable offence and then retained on the database. In 2001, there was an amendment to PACE such that there is now no requirement to remove or destroy DNA samples from those individuals found to be not guilty or from those where the charges against them were dropped, and a further amendment in 2003 allows samples to be obtained without consent from those arrested for a recordable offence. From 2005, reference samples from suspects who have not been charged with an offence can also be retained indefinitely. For further information, refer to the web pages referenced in the margin note above and at the end of this chapter. Similar databases are available in other countries – for example, the Combined DNA Index System (CODIS) in the USA.

 KEY POINT *DNA analysis is used in an increasing number of forensic science cases because it provides a powerful and effective means of comparing biological material from a crime scene with a particular suspect, together with a specific estimate of the probability of a false-positive match. When several DNA markers are used, the probability of a false-positive match is extremely low.*

DNA profiling

Provided that biological material left at a crime scene contains nucleated cells, the DNA in those cells can be analysed to obtain a genetic profile that is highly specific to the individual perpetrator.

NDNAD Strategy Board – *is responsible for overseeing the use of the NDNAD. For further details see https://www.gov.uk/government/groups/national-dna-database-strategy-board.*

NDNAD Ethics Group – *is responsible for providing advice on the ethical issues and operation use of the database. For further details see https://www.gov.uk/government/organisations/national-dna-database-ethics-group.*

Forensic Science Regulator – *is responsible for ensuring the quality of forensic science provision across the criminal justice sector. For further details see https://www.gov.uk/government/organisations/forensic-science-regulator.*

DNA profiles – *the majority of the profiles on the NDNAD are based on* SGM+ *profiles. From 2014, DNA$_{17}$ profiles were authorised for submission to the NDNAD.*

Sources of DNA – *all nucleated cells will contain the complete genome, so blood (e.g. from weapons and clothing), saliva (e.g. from cigarette ends, chewing gum, the rim of a glass) hair follicles (e.g. from the inside of hats, clothing), tissue (e.g. from nail scrapings), semen (e.g. from vaginal swabs, stains on underwear, clothing and bedding) and skin (e.g. from flakes of dandruff) can all be used as sources of DNA. Don't forget that there is also the possibility of a mixture of two bodily fluids, e.g. blood/saliva.*

The UK National DNA Database (NDNAD) – *launched in 1995, this contains several million DNA profiles and can be used to link people to a scene of crime, one crime scene to another, or people to people.*

DNA analysis – forensic applications

Case example In 1983 and 1986, two schoolgirls were murdered in Narborough, Leicestershire. Semen samples from both cases were found to belong to a person of type A blood group and an enzyme profile that matched 10% of the male population. A local youth confessed to the second murder, but not to the first. Police then contacted Professor Sir Alec Jeffreys, who analysed semen samples from both murders using his novel DNA profiling technique. The results showed conclusively that the semen samples from both cases came from the same man, but not from the youth, who became the first person in the world to be exonerated by DNA evidence. The police and FSS then undertook the first DNA screen of several thousand men with the same blood type as the killer in three local villages. The murderer, Colin Pitchfork, almost evaded detection by persuading a friend to give blood in his name, but that friend was overheard talking about the deception. As a result, Pitchfork was arrested and his DNA profile was found to match that of the semen samples from both murders. In 1988, he was sentenced to life imprisonment, the first person to be convicted of murder on the basis of DNA evidence.

Types of STR – simple STRs have the same repeat sequence throughout. Complex STRs have either incomplete versions of the core sequence in places or several variations of the core repeat sequence.

Genetic mapping and sequence studies have led to the discovery of several distinguishing features within the non-coding regions of DNA that can be used to differentiate between individuals. Non-coding DNA represents around 99% of the human genome and contains certain differences in DNA sequence (polymorphisms) that are inherited, but do not influence an individual's physical characteristics and therefore provide no information of genetic significance – for example, about an individual's predisposition to a particular medical condition. Such polymorphisms exist throughout the genome and the major types are outlined below.

Minisatellites or variable number tandem repeats (VNTRs)

Each minisatellite contains a defined sequence of nucleotides (about 9–50 bp long), repeated a number of times in a tandem fashion (Fig. 13.16(a)). The greater the number of repeats, the longer the minisatellite, which can vary from several hundred bp to over 20 kbp. The repeats of different lengths represent distinct alleles that are carried on chromosomes and are inherited in a Mendelian fashion (Chapter 13). The genetic differences that exist between individuals in terms of the number of tandem repeats can be recognised by treating DNA with restriction enzymes, each of which recognises and cleaves DNA at a particular sequence of bases (e.g. *Hae* III which cuts the base sequence at GGCC), and analysing the different-sized fragments produced, using electrophoresis (Fig. 13.16(b)). This is the basis of 'DNA fingerprinting', as first described in the 1980s by Sir Alec Jeffreys. Although still a very powerful analytical technique, VNTR analysis is limited by the quantity and quality of the DNA recovered, with about 50 ng of non-degraded DNA being required. It should be noted that individuals can share similar-sized VNTRs at a given repeat locus (location on a chromosome), so it is not possible to verify the source of the sample using only one locus. Several loci must be investigated. By using the known odds of someone other than the suspect producing an identical pattern for each locus and then multiplying the individual odds for each locus studied (p. 311), a profile with a very high degree of discrimination is obtained.

Amplified fragment length polymorphisms (AMPFLPs)

These have a core repeat of 10–20 bp; alleles are smaller than VNTRs and range in size from 100 to 1000 bp. Whereas most VNTR alleles are too long to be amplified by PCR (p. 114), the smaller size of AMPFLPs makes efficient amplification possible. When PCR is used to amplify AMPFLPs, the length of the fragment produced is defined by the primer sites (p. 115) rather than the restriction sites (p. 108) that are a feature of VNTR analysis. The stages in DNA profiling using PCR are summarised in Fig. 31.1. There are really three key stages in PCR (see pp. 114–117) broadly categorised into:

- **denaturing** – double-stranded DNA is denatured;
- **annealing** – primers bind to target sequences;
- **extending** – target sequences are extended/synthesised.

Microsatellites or short tandem repeats (STRs)

These 1–6 bp repeats are considerably shorter than VNTRs and AMPFLPs, and are constituents of alleles varying between 100 and 400 bp. A comparison of VNTR and STR sequences is shown in Fig. 31.2. STRs are highly suitable for amplification by PCR, and this allows ng or pg quantities of DNA, including degraded samples, to be analysed. Each cycle follows the stages described above. Ten cycles in PCR would generate 256 PCR products whereas 20 cycles

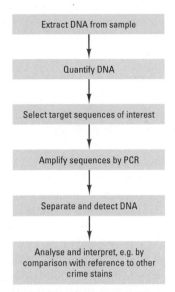

Fig. 31.1 The stages in DNA profiling.

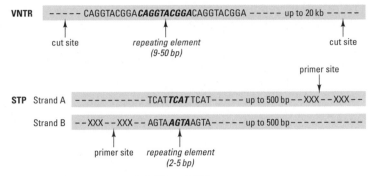

Fig. 31.2 Comparison of VNTR and STR sequences.

Requirements for successful PCR – during the annealing stage, primers are needed to attach to the ends of target sequences, as is magnesium chloride to stabilise the binding of these primers. Taq polymerase, e.g. AmpliTaqGold®, which has 5' exonuclease activity, is needed during the extending/synthesis stage.

Average quantity of DNA – in liquid blood ~ 20–40 ng mL^{-1}; in 1 cm^2 bloodstain ~ 0.5–2 ng mm^2.

generate 262,144. Second generation multiplex (SGM+) consists of 28 cycles and would generate 67,108,864 products with low copy number (LCN), now known as low template DNA (p. 311) consisting of 34 cycles and generating 4,294,967,296 PCR products. Tetranucleotide repeats (i.e. four bases, repeated in an array) are used most frequently in DNA testing, partly because they have a low mutation rate compared to dinucleotides or trinucleotides. With advancing technology, it is probable that complex STRs will have a role to play in future developments.

Compared to VNTRs, STRs show considerable variation in the length of the alleles within the 100–400 bp size range. This facilitates identification of amplified fragments (e.g. by PAGE, p. 214) and enables several STR loci to be amplified simultaneously (a 'multiplex' system), thus reducing the effort required in producing a DNA profile. The first-generation multiplex, introduced in the UK in 1994, amplified only four STRs. In the second-generation multiplex (SGM) system, six STR markers were used. The SGM Plus® system (Applied Biosystems) looks at 10 STRs, together with the sex chromosome marker, amelogenin. SGM Plus requires 1 ng DNA, or ~160 somatic cells, and will be run through 28 PCR cycles. The amelogenin gene codes for a protein involved in tooth enamel development and is located on both the X and Y chromosomes. Amplification of part of the amelogenin gene produces fragments of slightly different lengths from the X and Y chromosomes, allowing the sex of the DNA donor to be determined (Fig. 31.5, p. 310 gives an example of a profile for a male). Since there are two alleles for each STR (one from each parent) a genetic profile for the NDNAD contains 20 markers, plus the sex marker. Analysis of STRs has been enhanced by the introduction of dye-labelling of PCR products, allowing even fragments of similar size to be differentiated. Using SGM Plus it is recognised that the probability that someone other than the individual in question would share that same DNA profile is in the order of 1 in a billion.

KEY POINT *The probability is based on the profile, and not the probability that they were the offender.*

DNA$_{17}$

From July 2014, this new next-generation system for DNA profiling was introduced. It replaces the SGM Plus system and is now harmonised across Europe, allowing for cross-border exchange of information. The kits are available from commercial suppliers e.g. AmpFLSTR®NGM Select ™ from Thermo Fisher, and comprises the same amelogenin and ten regions of SGM Plus with an additional six regions (Fig. 31.7, p. 312). It is more sensitive than SGM Plus but caution will need to be exerted when interpreting low levels of DNA when

Home Office approved systems – to generate a profile that can be uploaded to the NDNAD the Home Office have approved the following PCR amplification kits: AmpFLSTR®NGM SElect byThermo Fisher; Powerplex® ESI 17 Pro and Fast by Promega and ESS Plex SEPlus by Qiagen.

Home Office, 2017

1000 Genomes Project – this is a useful resource for accessing genotypes, sequences and genome mapping, available at: www.1000genomes.org

considering source and activity. Even though the sensitivity is increased, the match probability (p. 305) remains the same as it currently is for an SGM Plus profile (1 in a billion).

Single nucleotide polymorphisms (SNPs)

These are the most common type and occur frequently throughout the genome (about every 300–500 bp), making them a potentially powerful tool for distinguishing between individuals. Well over a million SNPs have been characterised by the HapMap Project, however this was decommissioned in 2016. Fragments containing SNPs can be amplified readily by PCR. Products can be base-sequenced but more rapid analysis can be achieved using mass spectrometry (p. 144) or DNA microchips (p. 310). However, for the analyses to be statistically significant, many SNPs would need to be analysed. This is because at any SNP locus only two alleles would exist, differing by a single base (e.g. G or A, C or T, p. 104). For comparison, to obtain the same level of discrimination attained by a 13-locus multiplex STR analysis, up to 50 SNPs would need to be studied. The additional workload involved means that widespread routine use of SNPs in forensic science awaits further technical advances in automated analysis.

Mitochondrial DNA

Although most of the DNA in human cells is found in the chromosomes in the nucleus, mitochondria also contain DNA (mtDNA, Fig. 31.3). In contrast to chromosomal DNA, mtDNA is circular rather than linear and is considerably smaller (16,659bp). It contains 37 genes, coding for only 13 proteins and 24 types of RNA, and includes a non-coding region of 1.1kb (the D-loop).

There are several features of mtDNA that make it very useful in forensic analysis, including:

- **Maternal inheritance** – all members of a maternal lineage will share the same mtDNA sequence and standards for comparison can be collected from any maternal relative.
- **Lack of recombination** – unlike chromosomal DNA, it does not undergo recombination, although its rate of mutation is higher.
- **Presence in high copy number (100–1,000s) within a cell** – in cases where the amount of extracted DNA is small or degraded (e.g. from hair, bone, or teeth) there is a much better chance of obtaining successful typing results from mtDNA than from nuclear DNA. In the case of analysis of hair shafts, which contain minute amounts of DNA, use of mtDNA is usually the only viable option.

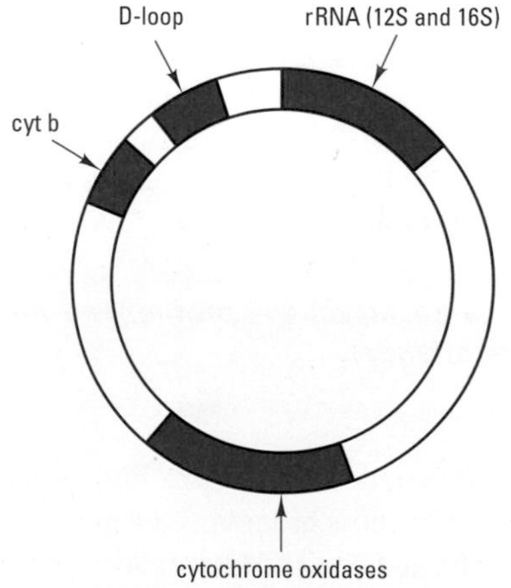

The mtDNA genome has been completely sequenced, and some regions of mtDNA are known to be highly polymorphic. These are located in the D-loop (Fig. 31.3) and are known as hypervariable regions (HVI, HVII and HVIII). Sequencing of PCR-amplified mtDNA in these regions allows samples to be compared in terms of their similarities and differences in base sequence. If the match between two samples is identical, the odds of such a match occurring by chance can be expressed in terms of relative frequency. The sequence of interest is compared to the Cambridge Reference Sequence for mtDNA (reported in 1981 by Anderson *et al.* and hence also known as the Anderson sequence). Using data provided by laboratories worldwide, a database exists of anonymous population profiles of mtDNA. All forensic profiles include, as a minimum, a

Fig. 31.3 Schematic diagram of mtDNA, to show major components, including the non-coding D-loop (containing hypervariable regions I–III).

Understanding the maternal inheritance of mtDNA – the ovum contains many mitochondria and the much smaller sperm relatively few. On fertilisation, the maternal mitochondria predominate, and there is some evidence that sperm mtDNA may be eliminated post-fertilisation. After conception, mitochondria replicate by binary fission (splitting in two) so mitochondria produced subsequently will contain only maternal mtDNA.

Case example In 1991 a group of skeletons discovered in a shallow grave in Yekaterinberg were tentatively identified as the remains of the Romanov family – the last Tsar, Tsarina and three of their children. The family had been executed by Bolshevik troops in 1918; their bodies had been buried, then sprayed with acid to make them unidentifiable. In 1992, the FSS was approached by the Russian authorities to authenticate the remains. Using samples from the surviving bones, DNA-based sex testing (amelogenin, p. 310) and STR analysis (p. 304) were carried out and the results confirmed that a family group was present in the grave. Further testing was carried out using mitochondrial DNA (mtDNA) from the bone samples. Such mtDNA is more likely to survive for longer than chromosomal DNA and, since it is maternally inherited, it is very useful for testing relatedness between generations. Samples of mtDNA from the adult female and the three children were matched with those from Prince Philip, Duke of Edinburgh, who is maternally related to Tsarina Alexandra. On the basis of the extensive DNA analysis, the FSS concluded that the Yekaterinberg bones were those of the last Tsar and his family (Gill *et al.*, 1994).

sequence region in hypervariable region I (HVI), defined by nucleotide positions 16,024–16,365, and a sequence region in hypervariable region II (HVII), defined by nucleotide positions 73–340. Data on the HVII region are accumulating and will provide powerful additional information in the future.

A systematic naming scheme exists for each mtDNA profile in the database. Each profile is indexed by the population group assigned by the contributor, as well as the continent, country or region of specimen origin. A standard 14-character nucleotide sequence identifier is assigned to each profile, using the structure XXX.YYY.ZZZZZZ. The first three characters (XXX) reflect the country of origin, using codes defined by the United Nations (1997). The second three characters (YYY) describe the group or ethnic affiliation to which a particular profile belongs. The final six characters (ZZZZZZ) are sequential acquisition numbers – e.g. for the 105th nucleotide sequence in each section of the database: JPN.ASN.000105 designates an individual of Asian origin from Japan; USA.ASN.000105 an Asian-American; and USA.008.000105 refers to an individual from the Apache tribe sampled in the USA.

An important potential complication in mtDNA analysis is the existence of heteroplasmy, i.e. more than one mitochondrial sequence in a single individual, particularly in hair samples. This is probably due to the rapid cell division associated with hair growth, and can result in the sequence found in one hair taken from an individual being different from his/her other hairs. Three types of heteroplasmy exist: site heteroplasmy, involving one base position; length heteroplasmy, where a section of mtDNA has an additional stretch of bases, usually cytosine; and deletion heteroplasmy.

DNA extraction and purification

 KEY POINT *It is really important that all appropriate anti-contamination procedures are adopted when analysing DNA.*

As the techniques for DNA extraction and analysis have improved, so has the need to ensure that the appropriate anti-contamination procedures are adopted to prevent extraneous DNA from being introduced either at the scene or in the laboratory. These procedures include:

- **Appropriate personal protective equipment** – to ensure that no extraneous DNA has been introduced at the scene, by the analyst, or even during the production of the consumables used in the laboratory. Disposable, certified DNA-free consumables should be used. Ideally, PPE should be colour coordinated to differentiate between LCN and standard DNA analysis.
- **Samples, collection, storage and examination** – samples taken from the victim and the suspect should never be stored together. You should ensure that there is no contact between the scene and the suspect. Different laboratories can be used during the examination process.
- **Negative controls** – these are really important in order to demonstrate that there has been no contamination during the analysis.
- **Quality control checks** – these should include consumables and reagents.
- **Cleaning and routine maintenance** – a rigorous cleaning regime must be adopted and include transportation vehicles as well as bench surfaces and instrumentation used.
- **Elimination databases** (see p. 303) – these also include laboratory-specific databases as well as staff databases for those involved in DNA consumable preparation.

Box 31.1 How to extract DNA from blood by the phenol–chloroform method

In the following procedure, a reagent blank and an extraction positive control must be included in every batch, and every transfer step should be witnessed and signed off. The various buffer solutions should be filter-sterilised (0.45 μm filter), or autoclaved.

1. **Collect the blood samples** – (e.g. in EDTA vacutainer tubes), remove aliquots and store at 4°C. If samples are not to be used within 5 days, freeze the blood in 700 μL aliquots at −80°C.

2. **Lyse the red cells** – by adding 800 μL of SCC buffer (containing NaCl at 175.3 g L^{-1}, sodium citrate dihydrate at 88.2 g L^{-1}, adjusted to pH7.0 with NaOH) to 700 μL of liquid (or thawed) blood; mix, and centrifuge for 1 min in a microfuge at maximum speed ($\approx$12,000$\times g$). Nucleated white cells are left intact at this stage.

3. **Repeat the red cell lysis stage** – remove 1.0 mL of supernatant and discard into a disinfectant solution (1% Vircon). Then, add 1.0 mL SCC buffer to the tube, mix thoroughly using a vortex mixer, and re-centrifuge for 1 min.

4. **Lyse the white cells** – remove as much of the supernatant as possible, taking care not to disturb the pellet (containing the white cells). To this pellet, add 375 μL of 0.2 mol L^{-1} sodium acetate (16.4 g L^{-1}), 25 μL of 10% w/v sodium dodecyl sulphate (SDS), and 5 μL of proteinase K solution (20 mg mL^{-1}) to digest proteinaceous material. Mix briefly and incubate at 56°C for 1 h. This releases DNA into solution.

5. **Remove proteinaceous material** – in a fume cupboard, add 120 μL of phenol/chloroform/isoamyl alcohol [25:24:1] (PCIA) to the tube and mix for 30 s to extract the DNA. Centrifuge for 2 min – protein collects at the interface between the aqueous and organic layers, and the upper aqueous layer contains the DNA.

6. **Harvest the soluble DNA fraction** – carefully remove the upper aqueous layer containing the DNA, being extremely careful not to disturb the denatured protein layer, and place in a microcentrifuge tube. Discard the original tube and the PCIA into a waste container in a fume cupboard.

7. **Precipitate the soluble DNA** – add 1.0 mL of cold, 100% ethanol to the aqueous layer, mix by inversion, and store the tube at −20°C for 15 min. Centrifuge, then decant and discard the supernatant; remove any remaining alcohol with a micropipette, taking care not to disturb the precipitate.

8. **Resolubilise the DNA** – add 180 μL of TE buffer (pH 7.4; containing 5 parts of 1 molL^{-1} tris-HCl to 1 part of 0.5 mol L^{-1} EDTA) to the pellet and vortex-mix briefly. Incubate at 56°C for 10min, then add 20 μL of 2.0 mol L^{-1} sodium acetate (164.0 g L^{-1}) and mix gently for 5 s.

9. **Reprecipitate the purified DNA** – add 500 μL of cold, 100% ethanol and gently mix until the solution is homogeneous. Centrifuge for 1 min, decant and discard the supernatant.

10. **Wash the DNA pellet** – at room temperature with 1 mL 70% v/v ethanol. Centrifuge for 1 min, decant and discard the supernatant; remove any visible alcohol with a micropipette, taking care not to disturb the precipitate. To remove residual ethanol, centrifuge the tube under vacuum for 10 min (e.g. using a Speed-Vac).

11. **Resolubilise the purified DNA** – resuspend the DNA in 200 μL of TE buffer; mix and incubate the contents at 56°C overnight. Finally, to prepare the DNA for quantification, vortex-mix the tubes for $\approx$30 s.

Qiagen® extraction – *Qiagen is a DEAE anion-exchange resin that interacts with the negatively charged phosphates of the DNA backbone. Qiagen-tips are small gravity-flow columns containing Qiagen resin to which DNA in the sample becomes tightly bound. Impurities such as RNA, protein, carbohydrates and small metabolites are washed from the column with medium ionic strength buffers (<1.0 mol L^{-1} NaCl). The DNA remains bound until eluted with a high-salt buffer (1.2–1.6 mol L^{-1} NaCl).*

Extraction is required for the maximal recovery of DNA from the matrix submitted and to remove any interference that would inhibit or affect PCR.

Several procedures exist for the extraction of DNA from human cells: for example, phenol–chloroform of DNA (Box 31.1); DNA from blood using a chelating resin such as Chelex 100 (Bio-Rad) (Box 30.2); and use of an anion exchange resin (Qiagen extraction), which is suitable for automation. Each laboratory will have a specific method that they will always follow for a specific bodily fluid.

Particular samples require specific protocols, including:

- **Liquid blood and bloodstains cut from clothing** – lyse the red cells and the extract and precipitate DNA from the nucleated white cells (Box 30.2 and Box 31.1).

Comparison of Chelex and Qiagen techniques for DNA extraction from blood

Chelex	Qiagen
Lysis using phosphate buffered saline and ProK	Lysis using SDS and ProK
Supernatant removed 5% Chelex and proK added, heated to 56° 1 h	Qiagen silica beads added and heated to 56°
Heated at 100°, 1 h	DNA binds to beads
Pellet centrifuged	Beads rinsed with sterile water and collected
DNA available in supernatent	DNA available in water

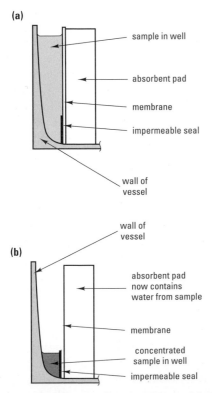

(a)

sample in well

absorbent pad

membrane

impermeable seal

wall of vessel

(b)

wall of vessel

absorbent pad now contains water from sample

membrane

concentrated sample in well

impermeable seal

Fig. 31.4 Minicon ultrafiltration system: (a) with sample added; (b) after ultrafiltration.

- **Vaginal swabs and stained clothing** – in rape cases these may contain DNA from both the male (e.g. nucleated sperm, Box 30.4) and the female (e.g. epithelial cells) involved. Differentiation between the two potential sources of DNA depends on the relative sensitivity of the cells to reducing agents. Sperm cell membrane contains thiol-rich proteins and are resistant to lysis unless a reducing agent such as dithiothreitol (DTT) is present in the medium. Initially, use a lysing solution containing no reducing agent to ensure epithelial cells from the female are lysed first. Then, centrifuge and remove the supernatant containing epithelial cell DNA. To the pellet, add a buffer containing a reducing agent to lyse any sperm cells.
- **Envelope flaps and non-self-adhesive stamps** – use steam and sterile forceps to prise open the flap or remove the stamp, and swab the gummed flap or stamp with a sterile swab or cotton bud soaked in sterile, deionised water; cut off the cotton from the stick and place in a microcentrifuge tube ready for DNA extraction and then dot blotting (p. 111). Alternatively, gum can be scraped off using a sterile scalpel and the DNA extracted using a suitable protocol. Note that self-adhesive stamps are unsuitable for DNA profiling, but a conventional fingerprint (p. 256) might be obtained from the surface.
- **Cigarette ends** – collect a portion of the filter that would have been in contact with the mouth, cut into small pieces and place in a sterile microcentrifuge tube for extraction.
- **Soft tissues** – store at $-20\,°C$ until they are processed.
- **Hair** (see also Chapter 32) – for nuclear DNA typing at least three individual whole hairs (including roots) of the same type are required; wash the hair in ethanol followed by deionised water, then place at least 1 cm of the hairs (root end) into a sterile microcentrifuge tube ready for DNA extraction. For mtDNA extraction, after treatment with ethanol and detergent the hair should be ground using a micro tissue grinder.
- **Bone** (see also Chapter 33) – remove traces of soft tissue and marrow and crush the bone into small fragments. Grind the fragments into a fine powder in the presence of liquid nitrogen and decalcify over several days using a buffer containing EDTA (a calcium-chelating agent). Once decalcified, DNA can be extracted from the remaining material.

Budowle *et al.* (2000) provide further details of DNA extraction methods for a range of samples. Note that protocols for preparation of DNA prior to analysis normally involve a final concentration step using commercially available concentrators such as the Minicon® (Fig. 31.4).

DNA fragment analysis

While Jeffreys' original DNA fingerprinting technique utilised Southern blotting (p. 110) for VNTR analysis, several methods of varying complexity are now available for PCR product analysis, including:

- **Allele-specific oligonucleotide assays** (ASOs – see pp. 110–112 for an explanation of probes, dot-blotting, and hybridisation). In the 'reverse dot-blot' technique, different ASO probes for multiple alleles at several loci are immobilised onto a nylon membrane strip. Corresponding regions of sample DNA are amplified by PCR, and added to the immobilised probes. Hybridisation will take place where complementarity exists, and this can be detected by the use of suitable labels (p. 112). A well-established locus suitable for dot-blot analysis is HLA-DQA1, which has eight common alleles, most of which have subtypes. A commercially available kit can be used for typing

Fig. 31.5 Scan of a polyacrylamide get of PCR products from amelogenin and three D loci. Of the two peaks at each position (Am, D8, D21 and D18), one is derived from the chromosome inherited by that individual from his father and one from his mother. The numbers below the scan indicate the specific alleles identified.

Example   Quantifying the results – the following information can be used as a guide to relate to the amount of DNA that is available:

Level of DNA	Amount of DNA (ng)
No DNA detected	Negative
Very low levels	0.01–0.02
Low levels	0.1–0.2
Reasonable levels	0.5

Example   Comparison of SGM +, Low Copy Number DNA and DNA$_{17}$

SGM +	Low copy number DNA	DNA$_{17}$
10 loci	10 loci	16 loci
PCR 28 cycles	PCR 34 cycles	PCR 29 cycles (optimum)
0.5–2 ng DNA	0.1–0.2 ng DNA	<0.1 ng DNA
Sample types include: bloodstains (1 mm+); semen; saliva; dandruff	Sample types include: touch DNA; historic samples; fingerprints	Sample types include: touch DNA; historic samples; fingerprints

the HLA-DQA1 locus (Amplitype® PM+DQA1 PCR Amplification and Typing Kit:PE Biosystems).

- **Polyacrylamide gel electrophoresis** (PAGE – pp. 214–217). This is utilised for the analysis of AMPFLPs and STRs; in the latter case, most separations are carried out using denaturing PAGE conditions so that amplified fragments are separated as single-stranded DNA. Multiplex analyses involve the labelling of PCR products from different loci. An example of a simplified multiplex analysis is shown in Fig. 31.5. This shows an electrophoresis scan of PCR products of amelogenin, and three of the D loci (D8, D21 and D18). The two amelogenin peaks are derived from the X and Y chromosomes and indicate that the DNA sample originated from a male (samples from females would produce a single peak corresponding to that represented by X). The genotypes assigned to the D8, D21, and D18 peaks are derived from tables that match the sizes of fragment peaks to individual alleles. This information, together with results from other D loci, constitutes the DNA profile of the individual.

- **Capillary gel electrophoresis** (p. 222). This is especially useful for separation of oligonucleotides (Fig. 22.12, p. 222) and is ideal for STR typing. It has advantages over conventional electrophoresis in terms of faster separation times, resolution and the potential for automation. A further important advantage is real-time detection, allowing direct input of results on a computer facilitating subsequent analysis.

- **Fluorescence spectroscopy** such as Fluoroscan® – this is a fluorometric technique that is used to quantify DNA by using appropriate dyes, e.g. for double-stranded DNA picogreen dye is used; for single stranded DNA oligreen dye is used.

- **Real-time PCR** – this technique allows the detection of PCR products as the amplification process progresses through the initial cycles, rather than waiting until all cycles have been completed. By coupling the Taq polymerase with fluorescence resonance energy transfer (FRET), data can be collected cycle by cycle in real time – e.g. StepOne™ Real time PCR system, Applied Biosystems.

- **DNA microchips/microarrays** – this is an area of rapid development. It involves fixing single-stranded probes for a wide range of informative nucleotide sequences onto specific sites on an electronic chip, and linking each probe site to a computer that can independently control the charge applied to each site. When amplified and labelled single-stranded sample DNA is added, it will hybridise to the probes. On computer-controlled reversal of polarity, only DNA with identical sequences to specific probes will remain bound; these can be detected by the presence of the attached label. Future development of microchip technology may lead to DNA profiles being generated at the crime scene.

Peak areas – *these are measured in relative fluorescence units (rfu).*

Interpretation of mixed profiles can be based on:

- **blind** – *based on the absence of any information;*
- **conditional** – *based on comparisons to reference samples.*

Low-template DNA analysis

Low-template DNA analysis was the general term that has been adopted for the analytical techniques that are currently used for samples containing 200 pg of DNA (Caddy *et al.*, 2008). Low copy number (LCN) is one such technique adopted by the FSS and is an extension of SGM Plus technology (p. 305), and is sensitive enough to analyse DNA from only a few cells (Gill, 2001). The lower limit of DNA required for multiplex systems is about 250pg, but they work most effectively when 1ng of DNA is analysed and no more than 28 PCR cycles are used. In low copy number DNA analysis, increased sensitivity can be achieved by increasing the number of PCR cycles to 34, but beyond that artefact production causes major difficulties. Even using 34 cycles, extremely rigorous practice is required to avoid contamination, both in the laboratory and at the crime scene, and special considerations are required to interpret results. Nevertheless, low-template DNA analytical techniques have been used successfully to provide evidence from tiny samples, such as a flake of dandruff, a few skin cells obtained from a fingerprint and archived microscope slides. The next-generation technique, DNA_{17}, is more sensitive than SGM Plus and will be seen to replace this system.

Interpreting and reporting DNA profiles

DNA profiling is a comparative approach, involving the analysis of two or more profiles under identical conditions to see whether the same fragment pattern is obtained. Typically, the samples compared are those from a crime scene and those from a particular suspect or suspects.

 KEY POINT *Reference samples are crucial to allow any interpretation to be made.*

Profiles can exist as individual or mixed, either as an equivalent 1:1 ratio or a major/minor component, or can be even more complex when there are more individuals involved. In order to determine whether there is more than one individual, you should identify on the electropherogram (Fig. 31.6) (EPG) whether:

- **the heights of the peaks are consistent** with that expected for either a hetero- or homozygote formation – with heterozygote pairs, the smaller peak should be at least 60% of its partner;

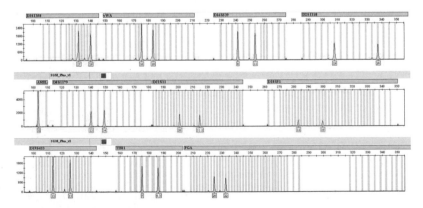

Fig. 31.6 SGM + electropherogram (EPG) illustrating the 10 loci and amelogenin. Permission from Dr E. Graham.

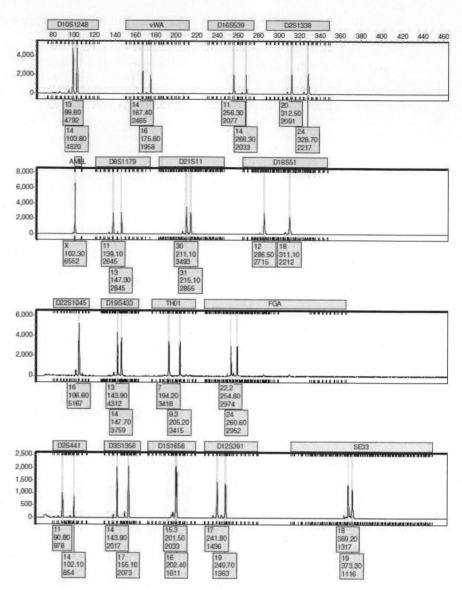

Fig. 31.7 SGM + electropherogram (EPG) illustrating the 10 loci and amelogenin. Permission from Dr E. Graham.

- **the heights of homozygote peaks are greater than 150 rfu;**
- **there are any additional peaks** and if any minor peaks could be accounted for by stutters – generally these can be identified by the number of base pairs apart (typically 4) and approximately 15% of the larger peak.

To be able to report DNA, all peaks observed on the EPG must have a peak height greater than 50 rfu. The interpretation must be corroborated and the examination notes signed by both scientists to confirm that there is agreement in the interpretation. With low-template DNA, the peak heights can fall below 150 rfu and in these cases there may only be a partial representation of the individual. With DNA_{17} the profile is also evaluated using an electropherogram, but this time each of the 10 loci and the amelogenin are represented (Fig. 31.7).

KEY POINT *In DNA profiling, it is essential that reference samples are taken from the suspect for comparison with the case samples. Suitable reference samples include buccal swabs (taken from the inside of the mouth, e.g. by a police officer, Box 31.2) or blood (taken by a medical examiner). These samples must be placed in tamper-proof bags and coded with details of the alleged crime, date of sampling, suspect's name and age, and the name, rank and number of the officer taking the sample. In the UK, samples taken for referencing are called criminal justice (CJ) samples.*

If any two compared profiles do not match then the interpretation is straightforward and conclusive – the DNA samples cannot be from the same person. In a criminal case, such a non-match can be used to *exclude* a particular person, as in the youth in the Colin Pitchfork case (p. 304). However, in those instances where there *is* a match between the two profiles, it is necessary to consider the likelihood that such a match was obtained by random chance (i.e. a false-positive match). In order to do this, it is necessary to know the relative occurrence of particular profiles (genotypes) in the population, based on Hardy–Weinberg principles (p. 101). Once such relative frequencies have been established, it is possible to calculate the odds that an unrelated person selected at random from the population would have the same profile, by multiplying together the relative frequencies of each locus. For example, if four VNTR (or STR) loci were used to produce a DNA profile, and the relative frequencies of occurrence of each pattern in the general population were 1:20 at locus 1, 1:30 at locus 2, 1:50 at locus 3, and 1:40 at locus 4, then the likelihood of finding an unrelated person with the same profile would be $1/20 \times 1/30 \times 1/50 \times 1/40 = 1/1,200,000$, or 1 in 1,200,000. Note that a probability-based approach can *never* prove absolute identity, since there is always a finite chance of a random false-positive match, especially where a large database is used. Your forensic statement (see Box 31.3 for an example) should conclude with a statement of the probability value of a false-positive match, so that a court can then decide on the likely significance of the result in the wider context of the case. Statistical comparison of a DNA profile is only performed when the scientist believes there to be a match and it is based on calculating probabilities for each of the loci identified using the Balding–Nichols product rule formula and by reference to population specific databases, assuming the Hardy–Weinberg principle (p. 101) holds true. It is important to recognise that the probability calculated and reported is related to the profile

Box 31.2 How to collect buccal swab samples for DNA analysis

1. **First, put on latex gloves** – to prevent transfer of your DNA to the swab samples.

2. **Take a first swab sample** – place a sterile swab in the individual's mouth. Move the swab firmly around the inside of the left cheek for around 10 s, using both sides during the swabbing – the swab may become moist but should not lose its overall shape. You must avoid touching the head of the swab at all times, or you may transfer your DNA to the sample.

3. **Take a second swab sample** – repeat the above on the inside of the right cheek, using a new sterile swab. When analysed, these two samples provide an internal quality control check, since the results should match.

4. **Prepare swabs for storage/transport** – usually, each swab is returned to its swab tube and then placed into a bag, sealed and labelled (p.249) with appropriate information.

Box 31.3 An example of a case statement involving DNA analysis

The following is an extract from a typical DNA statement for a physical assault case. Your report should include a background to DNA profiling, including relevant technical issues (e.g. what an SGM Plus profile is, p. 305), and an explanation of how the results have been interpreted (e.g. how the probability value was derived for the matched comparison, p. 311).

Summary of items received for DNA analysis

Reference samples
<u>Blood</u> labelled 'taken from Ann Offender on 1st April 2017'.
<u>Blood</u> labelled 'taken from Vic Tim on 1st April 2017'.

Case samples
<u>T-shirt</u> labelled 'taken from Ann Offender on 1st April 2017'.

Two stains labelled as 1A and 1B were extracted and submitted for DNA analysis.

Examination and results
DNA was extracted from the blood samples of Ann Offender and Vic Tim and full SGM Plus DNA profiles were obtained.

DNA was extracted and a full SGM Plus DNA profile was obtained from samples 1A and 1B. The DNA profiles obtained were the same as each other and matched the DNA profile of Vic Tim.

I have estimated a probability of 1 in a billion for obtaining this matching DNA profile, if the DNA from samples 1A and 1B originated from another male unrelated to Vic Tim.

and not to the guilt or innocence of an individual. Bayes theorem (Chapter 57) has also been adopted for use in explaining the strength of DNA matches to the court and jury by applying likelihood ratios for given circumstances based on the information that has been supplied in the case – for example, the likelihood ratio for findings in given circumstances, such as the probability of the profile originating from the suspect versus the probability of the profile originating from another unrelated person in the population.

Text references

Anderson, S., Bankier, A.T., Barrell, B.G., de Bruijn, M.H.L., Coulson, A.R., Drouin, J., Eperon, I.C., Nierlich, B., Roe, A., Sanger, F., Schrier, P.H., Smith, A.J.H., Staden, R. and Young, C. (1981) Sequence and organization of the human mitochondrial genome. *Nature* **290**: 457–465.

Budowle, B., Smith, J., Moretti, T. and DiZinno, J. (2000) *DNA Typing Protocols: Molecular Biology and Forensic Analysis.* Eaton Publishing, Natick.

Caddy, B., Taylor, G.R. and Linacre, A.M.T. (2008) A review of the science of low template DNA analysis. Available at: https://www.gov.uk/government/publications/review-of-the-science-of-low-template-dna-analysis. Last accessed 18/08/2017.

Gill, P. (2001) Application of low copy number DNA profiling. *Croatian Medical Journal* **42**: 229–232.

Gill, P., Ivanov, P.L., Kimpton, C., Piercy, R., Benson, N., Tully, G., Evett, I., Hagelberg, E. and Sullivan, K. (1994) Identification of the remains of the Romanov family by DNA analysis. *Nature Genetics* **6**: 130–135.

Jobling, M.A. and Gill, P. (2004) Encoded evidence: DNA in forensic analysis. *Nature Reviews Genetics* **5**: 739–751.

NDNAD Strategy Board (2017) Available at: https://www.gov.uk/government/groups/national-dna-database-strategy-board. Last accessed 19/08/2017.

NDNAD Ethics Group (2017) Available at: https://www.gov.uk/government/organisations/national-dna-database-ethics-group. Last accessed 19/08/2017.

Forensic Science Regulator (2017) Available at: https://www.gov.uk/government/organisations/forensic-science-regulator. Last accessed 19/08/2017.

Thermo Fisher Ltd (2017) AmpFlSTR®NGM SElect™ PCR Amplification Kit User Guide Available at: https://tools.thermofisher.com/content/sfs/manuals/cms_089008.pdf. Last accessed 19/08/2017.

Sources for further study

Balding, D.J. and Nichols, R.A. (1994) DNA profile match probability calculation: How to allow for population stratification, relatedness, database selection and single bands. *Forensic Science International* **64**(2–3): 125–140.

Balding, D.J. (2005) *Weight of Evidence for Forensic DNA Profiles.* Wiley, Chichester.

Butler, J.M. (2005) *Forensic DNA Typing: Biology, Technology and Genetics of STR Markers.* Elsevier Amsterdam.

Goodwin, W., Linacre, A. and Hadi, S. (2007) *An Introduction to Forensic Genetics.* Wiley, Chichester.

Graham, E.A.M. (2008) DNA reviews: Low level DNA profiling. *Forensic Science Medicine and Pathology* **4**(2): 129–131.

McClintock, J.T. (2008) *Forensic DNA Analysis; A Laboratory Manual.* CRC Press, Boca Raton.

National DNA Database Annual Report 2014–15. Available at: https://www.gov.uk/government/publications/ national-dna-database-annual-report-2014-to-2015. Last accessed 19/08/2017.

Promega (2017) PowerPlex® ESI 17 Fast System Technical Manual. Available at: https://www.promega.co.uk/-/media/ files/resources/protocols/technical-manuals/101/powerplex- esi-17-fast-system-protocol.pdf. Last accessed 19/08/2017.

Qiagen (2017) *Bench Guide: Protocols, Hints and Tips for Molecular Biology Laboratories.* Available at: http://www1 .qiagen.com/literature/BenchGuide/default.aspx. Last accessed 19/08/2017.

Rapley, R. and Whitehouse D. (ed.) (2007) *Molecular Forensics.* Wiley, Chichester.

Rudkin, N. and Inman, K. (2001) *An Introduction to Forensic DNA Analysis,* 2nd edn. CRC Press, Boca Raton.

Walsh, P.S., Metzgar, D.A. and Higuchi, R. (1991) Chelex 100 as a medium for the simple extraction of DNA for PCR based typing from forensic material. *Biotechniques* **1:** 91–98.

Study exercises

31.1 Find out more information about the NDNAD. Access the NDNAD pages using the Internet address above and find the latest NDNAD annual report. Using this report, try to find out:

(a) how many crime scene samples were loaded on to the NDNAD during the year;

(b) how many individuals are currently on the database;

(c) how many of the subject sample profiles relate to volunteer samples.

31.2 Test your knowledge. Without referring back to this chapter, write out as many ways you can think of to prevent contamination of DNA from occurring. Once you have finished your list, check it against the anti-contamination procedures listed in this chapter. Did you cover everything?

31.3 Test your knowledge. What are the key stages in DNA extraction?

Hair analysis as a multi-disciplinary activity – the forensic chemist will analyse hair for drugs and the forensic biologist will search and recover hair evidence from exhibits submitted into the laboratory and analyse them for DNA. However, they work as part of a team, along with police officers who will seize the clothing and interview the persons involved. Forensic scientists must be aware of contamination issues in order to ensure that the evidential value of the hair is not lost.

During the course of a forensic investigation, the main evidence that connects a suspect to a crime scene may be the transfer of hair from one person to another person, or object. In the absence of any other biological samples, hair can prove to be a vital link in the investigation. The examination of hair in such cases includes:

- establishing the identity of an individual – for example, linking a suspect to a crime scene by analysing the hair for DNA;
- suggesting a source – for example, identifying whether hair is human (head, pubic, body hair, racial origin) or animal;
- determining the mode of removal – for example, whether the hair was forcibly removed;
- providing long-term drug history of an individual – for example, the pattern of drug use, or abstinence, can be determined over a long period of time.

In a forensic investigation, for hair samples to be useful they should:

1. for DNA analysis, comprise at least three individual hairs of the same type; they must have the root sheath/cellular material present.
2. possess features that allow them to be identified, either to the suspect, the victim or to an animal species;
3. for drug analysis, comprise at least 30 individual hairs collected from the scalp of the person.

 KEY POINT *Hair analysis is a universal technique in forensic investigation and can give useful information on a number of different aspects, from the identity of an individual to whether a person has used drugs.*

General characteristics of hair

Hair is composed of three layers (see Fig. 32.1), which include:

- **the cuticle** – the outer protective layer consisting of overlapping scales;
- **the cortex** – cells containing keratin (protein), which contain melanin granules producing the colour and texture of the hair;
- **the medulla** – the inner layer, which essentially is an air-filled channel.

At the bottom of the hair shaft is the root, which is encased in a hair follicle, connecting the hair to a blood capillary (dermal papilla).

There are three distinct phases in the growth of a hair (Robertson, 1999), which are:

- **Anagen phase** – this is the main growth phase, typically lasting for between 3 and 5 years. The root/follicle cells are metabolically active and will produce hair upward from the dermal papilla at a growth rate of approximately 1 cm per month. Approximately 90% of all head hair is within this phase at any one time.
- **Catagen phase** – a transitional phase, usually lasting 1–2 weeks, between the growth phase and the final phase. During this transitional period, the follicle shrinks and breaks away from the blood supply.

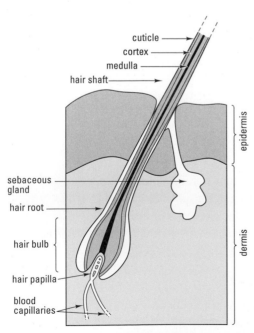

Fig. 32.1 The structure of hair.

- **Telogen phase** – the resting phase of hair growth, typically lasting 5–6 weeks, where the follicle is dormant with no hair growth. It is during this stage that hair is naturally shed.

Identification of the source of hair

The source of the hair is of paramount importance in a forensic investigation. The hair sample may have been shed naturally with the root still intact, may have been forcibly removed in which case the root will be damaged, or it may be surrounded by tissue fragments. Alternatively, the hair may have been cut, i.e. without the root, in which case the examination will focus only on the hair shaft. Sources of hair, for forensic investigation, include:

- recovery from a crime scene;
- reference samples obtained from a suspect, victim or deceased person;
- recovery from items of clothing worn by a suspect, victim or deceased person.

 KEY POINT *Reference samples of head hair must be obtained – typically at least 10 strands for DNA or 25 strands as a control for microscopic examination, should be plucked from the head of the suspect or victim, packaged, sealed and labelled in their presence and the label signed by the officer and the individual to identify the exhibit.*

Obtaining DNA from hair – *a hair shaft has no nuclei, therefore a full DNA profile (Chapter 31) can only be obtained if the root is still attached. It is possible, however, to extract mitochondrial DNA from the shaft (p. 306).*

Often these reference hair samples are secured in a paper package prior to sealing in a tamper-evident bag. All hair samples recovered from the scene or on clothing, etc. will be compared against this reference sample. In the case of a suspected sexual assault, hair combings of the pubic region should also be carried out by a police surgeon during the medical examination and the hair packaged as before. If other hair types are implicated, such as facial hair or body (arm/leg) hair, then a sample of these should be taken for examination.

Transfer and persistence

It is important to note that hair is not fixed in location on objects at a scene. It can move when transferred on to clothing and may be lost through people's natural movement after an incident.

In many cases, proof of association and/or guilt may rely on evidence of transfer from a source to another location. Transfer of trace evidence can occur in a number of ways, including:

Example Secondary transfer in practice. An assault has taken place and a transfer of hairs has occurred between the two persons involved. The victim sits down on a chair and transfers some of this evidence on to the chair. A third person comes along and sits down on the same chair. Transfer from the chair to this third person may occur but the act of transfer is completely unrelated to the initial assault.

- **one-way transfer** – where there is only one direction of transfer of evidence – for example, hair is transferred only on to the recipient;
- **two-way transfer** – where hair from one person is transferred on to another person and *vice versa;*
- **secondary transfer** – where the transfer occurs completely independently of the event under investigation (White, 2010).

This has implications regarding possible contamination of evidence (see Chapters 24 and 41). When investigating cases involving hair, it is crucial to exclude all other modes of transfer other than that which is suspected to have taken place during the event under investigation – for example, checking

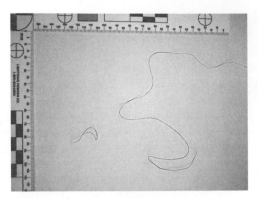

Photo 32.1 Typical hair samples submitted to the laboratory. The colour, length, straightness of the hair should be recorded in your examination notes.

the case details to confirm that the police officer attending an incident was not the same officer who arrested the suspect, or checking the custody record to confirm that the suspect and victim were not interviewed or examined in the same room. If there is a possibility that transfer may have occurred, then any hair evidence related to the case would be inadmissible in court.

The persistence of hairs depends very much on the physical nature of the object or material on to which it has been transferred. For example, if a hair sample comes into contact with skin with minimal contact, then it will not be fixed in location and will probably fall from the person immediately. However, if a struggle ensued, the contact time will have been greater and the hair may be more strongly fixed in location – for example under a fingernail, in which case it may remain until physically removed.

Dachs *et al.* (2003) investigated the phenomenon of persistence of hair on clothing and found that the type of fabric influenced the length of time the hair remained on the clothing. Hairs on woollen fabrics tended to be lost in a linear (constant) fashion over time, whereas the rate of loss of hairs on cotton, polyester and cotton/acrylic mixes followed an exponential curve.

The same logic applies to clothing – a fluffy woollen jumper is more likely to retain a hair sample than a smooth, cotton one. The persistence of hairs on clothing is also determined by the activity of the individual – for example,strenuous actions are more likely to dislodge the evidence than gentle movement.

Examination of hair samples

Once the hair sample (Photo 32.1) has been received in the laboratory, the forensic scientist will examine it within the polythene bag it is packaged in an attempt to identify its origin, unless it has been placed in a paper package inside a tamper-evident bag, in which case the bag will have to be opened. You should describe the visual characteristics, such as length, shape, size, colour, degree of stiffness or straightness. If an exhibit, such as an item of clothing, has been submitted for examination, then a process known as 'search and recover' is initiated (see Box 32.1).

To examine the recovered hair, the same protocol as for the reference hair sample (p. 317) is used, taking note of the visual characteristics of the strand while the hair is within the polythene bag. Once these have been described, the hair should be examined using a low-power microscope. Using this approach, it is possible to identify hair strands that will be used for comparison purposes (e.g. ones without the root attached) or those to be used for DNA analysis (e.g. ones with a root attached).

If the root is present, the hair can be removed from the bag using gloved hands and the root can be cut from the shaft of the hair using a clean sterile scalpel. This root can be examined for DNA profiling if required (see Chapter 31). It is still possible to recover DNA from mounted hair samples, but it is good practice to remove the root prior to mounting for microscopic analysis.

It is recognised that mitochondrial DNA (p. 306) can be obtained from the hair shaft, but this is not the case for nuclear DNA where little or no nuclear DNA will be detected (Andréasson *et al.*, 2006). It has also been shown that there is a wide variation in the DNA content between the root and shaft of plucked and naturally shed hairs (Andréasson *et al.*, 2006). Further studies have indicated the feasibility that nuclear DNA can potentially be obtained from the medulla in the hair shaft using a multiplex STR typing system (p. 309) in sufficient quantity to obtain a partial DNA profile (Barbaro *et al.*, 2008).

Photo 32.2 Comparison microscopy of a reference hair sample (picture on the right) and a hair sample (left) recovered from a crime scene. (Image courtesy of SPSA Forensic Services.)

Box 32.1 How to 'search and recover' hair evidence

There is a possibility that other trace evidence may also be present on an exhibit that you have been requested to examine. Before you begin any examination of an exhibit, you should ensure that you are wearing full personal protective equipment (p. 246), that your bench space is clean and that the integrity of the packaging of the exhibit is not compromised, as described in Box 41.1, p. 403.

1. **Consider the sequence in which evidence is to be collected** – remember that there may be more than one type of evidence on the exhibit, for example fibres, blood or glass debris. Therefore, the order of examination is very important to ensure the optimal recovery of all types of evidence. The simple rule is that the evidence that is most likely to be lost should be collected first, i.e. hairs and fibres, before glass debris and bloodstains.

2. **Make a thorough systematic examination of the item** – for example, a piece of clothing should be examined using oblique lighting and with the aid of a stereoscopic microscope (p. 73). It is best to adopt a systematic and consistent method of examination – for example, starting on the outside with the front of a jumper, examine the right-hand sleeve, the chest and then the left-hand sleeve, then repeat the process for the back of the jumper and again for the inside of the jumper.

3. **Locate and document hair evidence recovered** – for example, if a hair strand is found it should be picked up using gloved hands or forceps and transferred to a small polythene bag. The location of the hair should be documented in the examination notes, along with the number of hairs recovered. You should then tape the garment following the procedure adopted for fibre recovery (Box. 42.1).

(a)

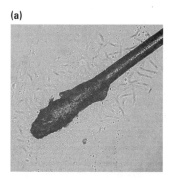

(b)

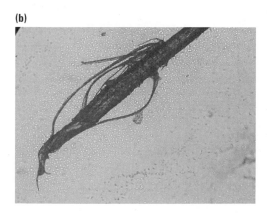

Photo 32.3 Human hair roots showing difference between naturally shed and forcefully plucked (×10 magnification): (a) root of a naturally shed hair showing an intact bulbous-shaped root at the end of the shaft; (b) root of a forcibly removed hair showing a distended root shape and remnants of the root sheath.

The mounted hair samples can then be examined in detail using a comparison microscope (p. 65). The reference hair sample should be examined (×10 magnification) on one side of the microscope and the physical appearance, hair length, hair shape, colour, cross-section, tip and root features recorded. Hair has recently been shown to exhibit marked intra-individual differences, even within a single hair that has not been subjected to any cosmetic treatment (Birngruber *et al.*, 2009). The recovered hair sample is then viewed at the same magnification and the same type of details are recorded. Both the images can be viewed together (Photo 32.2) when the microscope is connected to a video screen. By manipulating the positions of the hairs, the images can be aligned to determine whether or not they appear similar. Microscopic features should be recorded accurately and include, for example:

- **cuticle** – appearance of the cuticle structures such as coronal (crown like), spinous (petal), imbricate (flattened);
- **pigmentation** – distribution of the granular material throughout the hair;
- **medulla** – whether it is continuous or discontinuous;
- **cortical fusi** – presence of irregular-shaped air spaces;
- **ovoid bodies** – presence of small solid spherical structures.

Differences between human hair and that of other animal species can be determined when viewing the hair samples under high-power microscopy by comparison with reference hair samples. Differences such as the thickness of the cuticle and pigmentation patterns may be identified and should be recorded. The force with which the hair was removed can also be determined by examination of the root, but consideration must be given to the case circumstances and other evidence when offering such an opinion. If a hair is shed naturally, then the root will be intact and should have a bulbous appearance (see Photo 32.3 (a)). When the hair has been plucked, the root is often distended or damaged and will no longer have the typical bulbous shape. In addition, the epithelial sac and/or root sheath material surrounding the root may still be attached in these cases. (see Photo 32.3(b)) The racial origin can also be determined by observing the hair's surface morphology – such as whether the hair is fine, coarse, straight or curly with differing pigmentation patterns and diameter. For example, Caucasian hair is typically oval in shape when observing a cross-section, with an even distribution of pigmentation granules compared to Negroid hair, which is typically flattened in cross-section, with pigmentation densely distributed in clumps along the shaft of the hair, giving an opaque appearance (Robertson, 1999).

Analysis of hair for the presence of drugs

Drug content analysis of hair is becoming a routine procedure in the forensic laboratory. The advantages of hair as evidence in this context are that it is an unobtrusive sample, cannot be adulterated, does not require refrigeration and can, if the hair is long enough, provide information on the long-term drug use by an individual. This type of evidence should be regarded as a complementary test to blood drug analysis (Chapter 38) for establishing drug use, but cannot be used to determine the tolerance of an individual nor to determine the precise date on which a drug was taken.

A sample of hair collected for analysis of drugs should comprise approximately 30 hairs, taken from the back of the head. Once collected, the bundle should be tied with cotton thread, to keep the root ends together, and placed into a sterile, plastic, screw-top container, packaged in a polythene bag, sealed and labelled. Ideally the hair should be plucked, but it can be cut as close to the scalp as possible. In the case of drug-facilitated sexual assault (Chapter 38), a hair sample should be obtained during the initial medical examination and again one month later.

 KEY POINT *During the first month after an alleged incident the victim must not dye or cosmetically treat their hair.*

Cosmetic treatment of hair has been shown to reduce the potential to obtain drug evidence from this sample matrix; for example, Martins *et al.* (2008) have demonstrated a reduction in amphetamine and methamphetamine analogues in cases where hair has been cosmetically treated.

It is generally accepted that, for the average person, each hair grows approximately 1cm per month, although there are differences between racial groups. The basis of this method is that if an individual ingests a drug, then during its circulation in the bloodstream a proportion of the drug will enter the hair follicle, via the dermal papilla (see Fig. 32.1), and become incorporated into the growth of the hair shaft. Therefore, recent exposure to a drug will mean that the concentration of drug will be greater in the section of hair shaft closest to the scalp. After collecting hair samples, the root, or the end of the shaft closest to the scalp, i.e. the thicker end, needs to be identified. The hair sample should be measured and cut into segments every 2 cm from the root of the hair across the whole length of the hair sample. Each segment will be analysed separately for the presence of drugs (see Box 32.2). Combined with an estimate of the rate of growth of the hair, this allows the determination of a long-term drug use history for an individual, but such an opinion should only be offered if the hair sample analysed is greater than 6 cm (i.e. three segments) from scalp to hair tip. Any fewer than three segments will not provide a representative pattern of drug use.

It is important to consider which drug(s) might be relevant, as the most appropriate extraction method differs among drugs (see Box 32.2). For example, digesting the hair with an alkali will convert benzodiazepine drugs to benzophenones, and therefore the parent drug will not be detected on analysis.

Case example Detection of gamma-hydroxy butyrate (GHB) in hair following an alleged drug-facilitated sexual assault (DFSA) (Kintz *et al.*, 2003).

A 19-year-old female alleged that she had been sexually assaulted after drinking a spiked drink. A sample of head hair was taken during the initial examination and again one month later.

Each hair sample was cut into segments and the segments were analysed for the presence of GHB. It was shown that in the hair sample taken one month after the alleged assault, there was an increase in the GHB concentration of the hair, indicating that exposure to the drug had occurred. This evidence could be used to support the allegation of sexual assault in a criminal court.

Box 32.2 Stages in the analysis of a hair sample for the presence of drugs

To optimise the recovery of drug from a hair sample, there are four distinct steps that should always be followed:

1. **Sample preparation.** This should be performed on the open bench and not in a Class 1 bio-safety cabinet usually used for biological sample preparation. This is important, since the air flow within the cabinet would blow away the hair strands. The hair sample should be placed on to a clean sheet of white paper, and a stereoscopic microscope used to identify the roots, or the ends of the hair that are larger in diameter if the roots are absent. The strands should be combined and tied together with cotton thread. The bundle should be washed in a phosphate buffer (0.1 mol L^{-1}, pH 7.4) for 5 min to remove environmental contamination. It should then be washed with acetone, which will start to extract the fatty acids from the hair. Once dried, the hair sample is cut finely (< 1 mm) into a small glass phial.

2. **Sample digestion.** This is necessary to optimise the recovery of the drug, but you should remember that there may be more than one drug type in the hair sample. The choice of digestion method may destroy one or more of the drugs to be analysed so care

should be exercised, taking into account other information available about the case. There are several means of digestion, including:

- acid digestion (hydrochloric acid (1 mol L^{-1}) at 90 °C for 2 h – suitable for opiates and cocaine;
- alkali digestion (sodium hydroxide (1 mol L^{-1}) at 60 °C for 2 h – also suitable for opiates and cocaine, but also benzodiazepines, amphetamine, methadone, i.e. basic drugs (see Chapter 38);
- enzyme digestion (phosphate buffer, pH 7.4, containing 10,000 units b-glucuronidase at 37 °C for 12 h – suitable for cases where multiple drugs are to be investigated.

3. **Sample extraction.** This is performed using solid phase extraction (Chapter 12), for example with an anion exchange cartridge for cannabis, or a C18 cartridge for the basic drugs.

4. **Sample analysis.** This is performed using GC–MS or LC–MS, usually monitoring in the single ion mode (Chapter 14). Depending on the drug, the sample may need to be derivatised prior to analysis to improve the sensitivity of detection.

There are other complications regarding analysis of hair for drugs, including the effect of cosmetics – for example, when hair has been bleached, it can interfere with the drug's stability resulting in a negative test result. It has been argued by some defence counsels that environmental contamination, or passive exposure to drugs, such as being in a room where cannabis (see Chapter 38) is smoked, is the reason why their client tested positive. To avoid this possibility, the hair should be washed in buffer followed by acetone to ensure that the drug that is measured originates from the inner portion (cortex) of the hair and not from the protective outer layer (cuticle), where contamination may have occurred.

Reporting results of hair analysis

When reporting forensic biology cases involving the examination of hair, a list of all the reference samples examined should be included, along with a brief description of their visual appearance.

The statement (Box 32.3) should also contain a list of the hair samples that were recovered, including the location(s) from where they were recovered, a description of the number of hairs and their visual appearance. At this point it should be noted whether any of the hairs were suitable for DNA analysis and if so whether the root was removed for this purpose. The results of comparison microscopy should be included, stating whether a positive or negative match was found. It is recognised that in DNA analysis using SGM Plus®, or the newer multiplex DNA$_{17}$ kits (Chapter 31), the probability that someone other than the

Box 32.3 An example of a case statement involving analysis of hair

The following is an extract from a typical statement following the examination of an exhibit for hair.

Following an incident where Mr Hare is accused of assaulting Miss Curlee, the following samples were submitted for hair analysis.

Reference samples

Head hair labelled 'taken from accused Hare on the 1st April 2017'.
The hair was examined and found to have the appearance of human head hair. The hair is black in colour, straight with an average length of 3 cm. All roots were visible with sheath material.

Head hair labelled 'taken from complainant Curlee on 01/04/17'.
The hair was examined and found to have the appearance of human head hair. The hair is light brown in colour, curly with an average length of 12 cm. All roots were visible with sheath material.

Item from Mr Hare

Blue jumper labelled 'taken from accused Hare on the 1st April 2017'.
One light brown curly hair, with the appearance of human head hair, was recovered from the left sleeve of the jumper. This hair measured 12 cm in length. No root was visible. Both ends had the appearance of possibly being cut.

The recovered hair sample appears to be identical, in terms of shape and colour. However, in the absence of any root it is not possible to determine whether this hair originated from Miss Curlee. Therefore, this hair provides weak scientific evidence to support the view that the hair originated from Miss Curlee.

individual in question would share that same DNA profile is of the order 1 in a billion. There is no equivalent probability with hair analysis. Bayesian statistics (Chapter 57) can be adopted in these cases by applying likelihood ratios for given circumstances based on the information that has been supplied in the case. As a result, an opinion can be offered on the significance of the results of the case.

When reporting forensic chemistry cases, you should include the identity of the drug and the concentration in the hair sample, typically expressed in terms of mass concentration (e.g. as milligrams per gram). A summary of the effects of the drug may also be included (see Chapter 38). An opinion as to recent exposure to drugs may be offered, but you cannot specify how much or exactly when the drug was taken.

Text references

Andréasson, H., Nilson, M., Budowle, B., Lundberg, H. and Allen, M. (2006) Nuclear and mitochondrial DNA quantification of various forensic materials. *Forensic Science International* **164**: 56–64.

Barbaro, A., Cormaci, P., Binns, C. and Grant, P. (2008) Hair typing in a cold case. *Forensic Science International: Genetics Supplement Series* **1**: 396–7.

Birngruber, C., Ramsthaler, F. and Verhoff, M.A. (2009) The color(s) of human hair – forensic hair analysis with Spectracube®. *Forensic Science International* **185**: e19–e23.

Dachs, J., McNaught, I.J. and Robertson, J. (2003) The persistence of human scalp hair on clothing fabrics. *Forensic Science International* **138**: 27–36.

Kintz, P., Cirimele, V., Jamey, C. and Ludes, B. (2003) Testing for GHB in hair by GC/MS/MS after a single exposure: Application to document sexual assault. *Journal of Forensic Science* **48**: 1–6.

Martins, L.F., Yegles, M., Thieme, D. and Wennig, R. (2008) Influence of bleaching on the enantiomeric disposition of amphetamine type stimulants in hair. *Forensic Science International* **176**: 38–41.

Robertson, J. (ed.) (1999) *Forensic Examination of Hair.* Taylor & Francis, London.

White, P. (2010) *Crime Scene to Court: The Essentials of Forensic Science,* 3rd edn. Royal Society of Chemistry, London.

Sources for further study

Kintz, P. (2007) *Analytical and Practical Aspects of Drug Testing in Hair.* CRC Press, Boca Raton.

Ogle, R. and Fox, M. (1999) *Atlas of Human Hair Microscopic Characteristics.* CRC Press, Boca Raton.

Wheeler, B. and Wilson, L.J. (2008) *Practical Forensic Microscopy: A Laboratory Manual.* Wiley, New York.

Study exercises

32.1 Examination of hair. Brush your own hair and obtain a naturally shed sample. Pluck one of your own hairs out and identify the differences between the two hairs.

32.2 Document your results. Using both macroscopic and microscopic techniques, record the features you think are important.

32.3 Practice recovery of hair/fibres. Using the tape lifting technique (Chapter 42), tape lift an item of your clothing. How many hairs did you recover?

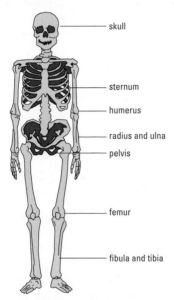

Fig. 33.1 Major bones of the human skeleton.

Forensic investigations may include the examination of skeletal remains. Examples include: cases where a body is found after a long period of time in a remote outside location; cases where the identity of a body is obscured, for example by fire; examination of the body of a murder victim buried in a shallow grave; identification of individuals from a plane crash; and investigations of war crimes from skeletal remains in mass graves. In such circumstances, skeletal remains may be useful because of the following features of human bones:

- **they survive for longer than the soft body parts** – they are the last part of the body to decompose;
- **they are physically strong** – they will not be distorted without breaking, unlike soft tissues;
- **they possess useful diagnostic traits** – for example, for determining age, racial origin and whether an injury occurred in life or *post mortem*;
- **they may show the presence of wounds** – for example, bullet holes or knife wounds.

The examination of skeletal remains is a specialist discipline and requires a detailed knowledge of the human skeletal structure (see Fig. 33.1) including the connective tissue, cartilage and bone types. Bone is rigid and has a supportive role in the body – it acts as protection for vital organs, provides the mechanical basis for movement and is the site of development of red blood cells (bone marrow). Cartilage and connective tissue are also an integral part of the skeleton, for example in the rib cage.

> **KEY POINT** *The examination of human skeletal remains can provide useful information, such as the identity of an individual and how he/she died, including cause, manner and approximate time since death. The discovery of human remains may also link one forensic case to another.*

Methods of analysis

If skeletal remains have been discovered in a shallow grave, the excavation must be handled with care. Once the grave has been found, the individual bones must be carefully removed and separately labelled. In the case of large numbers of skeletons, the difficulty of attributing loose bones to one individual arises. As with all forensic investigations it is of key importance to document, through photography and detailed notes, exactly what has been done and exactly what has been found. You are possibly dealing with a criminal investigation and the evidence you find is likely to be heard in court.

On investigating one or more bone samples, questions a forensic anthropologist should seek to answer include how long the bones have been present at the location where they were found and whether the skeletal remains can be attributed to a particular sex, age, height and racial origin to allow the identification of a person. Where many bones are found in a single location it is possible to determine whether they originated from one or more individuals – you can count the number of specific bones, for example the number of left femurs; since no one has two left legs, then you deduce the number from this.

Measuring the nitrogen content of a femur:

1. *Remove excess soil from the bone using a brush.*
2. *Cut a 2 cm section from the midshaft and leave to dry completely for 2 weeks at room temperature.*
3. *Remove 0.5–1 g of the cut piece of bone and measure the nitrogen content using the macro Kjeldahl method.*

If the nitrogen content is less than 3 g per 100 g bone mass then it indicates that the skeleton is likely to be greater than 300 years old (Jarvis, 1997).

Estimating the time since death

The time since death (*post-mortem* interval) may not be the same as the time since burial. If a body remains unburied then it is subject to the environmental conditions and associated insect colonisation (see Chapter 35). In contrast, a buried body will decompose at a different rate and will be colonised by different insects. The presence of clothing on the deceased also plays a significant part in the decomposition rate and colonisation – for example, a naked body is open to the elements and insects are not restricted in access to the body. On the other hand, for a body clothed in synthetic, tight-fitting garments, these would provide a barrier against the climate and insect access to the body.

A number of techniques are available to determine the length of time the bones have been present at a site. The process of skeletonisation is the last part of the process of decomposition and is very much dependent on the environmental conditions in which a body is kept. In the UK, skeletonisation will probably take about a year for a body left in the open and this will generally be more rapid in warmer countries. On examination, you may still find small remnants of soft tissue remaining on the bone, which can be useful for DNA evidence (Chapter 31) and also gives a tentative indication that the body has been there for some time, but probably less than 5 years. If the skeleton appears to disintegrate easily, i.e. crumbles readily, this tends to suggest that the age of the skeleton exceeds 100 years.

Estimating the age of the skeletal remains

Testing the age of bones, in the forensic laboratory, can be done relatively easily – you can examine the bones for the presence of blood (see Chapter 30). A positive reaction indicates that the skeleton is likely to be less than 10 years old. Alternatively, if the bones appear to be old, the nitrogen content of the bones can be analysed. This can give an indication of the age of the bones in terms of how many centuries have passed. The nitrogen content of fresh bones is approximately 4 g per 100 g bone mass, which will gradually be lost over a period of years (Jarvis, 1997). A further test to distinguish recent or ancient bones uses ultraviolet light – for example, using the hand-held Crime-lite® torch, set between 425 and 500 nm in a darkroom in the forensic laboratory, fluorescence of the bones can be detected. If the bones do not fluoresce, it indicates that they are likely to be greater than 100 years old.

There has been a further development in these techniques to include the use of luminol-chemiluminescence. Ramsthaler *et al.* (2009) have shown that bone samples taken from femoral shafts from known burial periods (ranging from 1st century to 2003) gave a positive reaction with luminol with an 88.75% correct burial period classification. In order to have confidence in the age of the skeletal remains it is advisable that you should adopt a combination of the methods rather than rely on a single method.

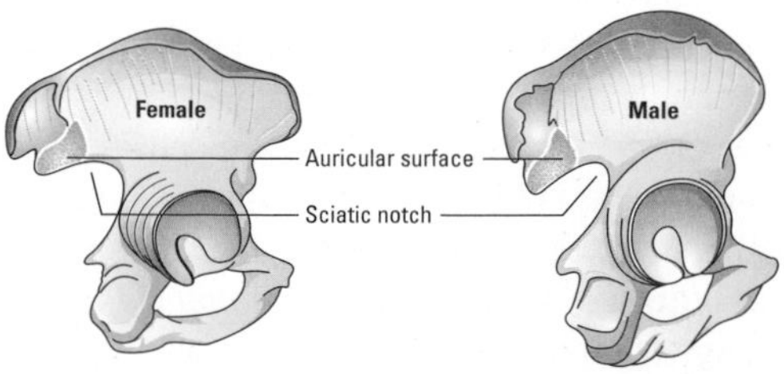

Fig. 33.2 The pelvis of female and male skeletons showing the narrower angle of the sciatic notch in the male (arrowed). (Adapted from Burns, 1999.)

Determining the sex of a skeleton

While there are some basic differences between the skeletons of the two sexes, in some cases it can be extremely difficult to interpret whether the skeleton is male or female. Within the population there are females who express male characteristics and vice versa, and the same applies for their skeletal structures. In general, though, there are four main areas to focus on:

1. **Pelvis** – the length of the pubic bone is longer in females than in males. During puberty in females, the hips move outwards and in the process the sciatic notch (Fig. 33.2) becomes considerably wider than seen in the male pelvis. The subpubic angle is also wider in females than in males and is

equivalent to the angle formed by stretching your thumb and forefinger apart. The subpubic angle in a male pelvis is the equivalent angle of stretching the forefinger and middle finger apart. In females, the measurement of the pubic symphysis (where the pubic bones meet together) is longer and the angle of the iliac crest (known as flaring) is more pronounced.

2. **Skull** – the ridges around the eye socket are prominent in males but absent in females and the bony lump behind the earhole, commonly referred to as the mastoid process, is larger in males than in females. The lower jaw, or mandible, is usually wider and more sharply angled with a more square-shaped chin in males than in females.

3. **Sternum** – the sternum is the bone to which the ribs attach and consists of three regions: the sternum, the manubrium joined at the top and the xiphoid process at the bottom. If the whole sternum is greater than twice the length of the manubrium then this usually indicates that the skeleton is male.

4. **Long bones** – if the pelvis is not available for examination then the femur head diameter can be measured. In males, the diameter is greater than in females. If greater than 47.5 mm the bone is likely to be of male origin, if less than 42.5 mm, it is likely to be female (Stewart, 1979).

Estimating the age of an individual from skeletal remains

Age can be estimated from the developmental stage of the skeleton looking specifically at:

- **the length of the femur** – this increases until adulthood (and at different rates between the two sexes);
- **the proportion of bone to cartilage** – this changes with age, with more cartilage being present in younger skeletons;
- **the pubic bones** – these can show signs of nodules forming as age increases;
- **the rib ends** – these will change from having a sharp, scalloped appearance in early teens to elongated, ragged with a central core appearing in late fifties;
- **the presence of degenerative changes** – these can indicate advancement of years;
- **the stage of dentition** (see Chapter 34);
- **the organic and inorganic contents of the bone** – these tend to decrease reducing the bone elasticity and quantity with an increased likelihood of fractures in the elderly (osteoporosis).

Estimating the height of an individual from skeletal remains

In order to be able to do this, the sex and racial origin of the skeleton need to be determined. Once this has been done, the height can be estimated by accurately measuring the length of the long bones of the arms and legs. A mathematical relationship can be used to relate such lengths to the height of an individual, which differs between the sexes and people of different racial origins. The femur is the ideal bone to use for this type of calculation, but to be more confident in your estimate the other long bones (e.g. tibia, fibia, humerus, ulna and radius) can also be accurately measured using Vernier calipers (p. 50). By reference to commercial databases, such as the Forensic Anthropology Databank Fordisc 2.0 (Jantz and Ousley, 2005), the height of the individual from a particular sex and race can be estimated using an appropriate mathematical formula. Similarly, population studies, for example in Portuguese adults (de Mendonca, 2000), published in peer-reviewed journals can also be consulted to help you to estimate the height of an individual belonging to a specific population.

Sex determination techniques – for a review of techniques see Krishan et al. (2016). The authors discuss the reliability of existing and new emerging techniques.

Case example   Identifying a murder case from analysis of skeletal remains
Human skeletal remains were discovered in a forest in Denmark in 1994. Examination of the bones indicated that it was likely to be a male, aged early 20s with a height of approximately 170 cm. Numerous cut marks were noted on the ribs, vertebrae and the tibia.

During the police investigation, an Iranian refugee had been reported missing. The dentition of the skeleton was examined and the identity of the person was confirmed. Subsequently, a suspect was arrested who confessed to stabbing the refugee to death 18 months earlier (Vesterby and Poulsen, 1997).

Predicting the height of an individual person from skeletal remains – this can be performed by accurately measuring one of the long bones and then using a mathematical formula to estimate the height.

For example, for a skeleton identified as a European male, with a left femur accurately measured at 49.6 cm, using the formula (2.32 × femur length) + 65.53 ± 3.94 cm (Burns, 1999), the height can be determined to be 180.4 cm ± 3.94 cm.

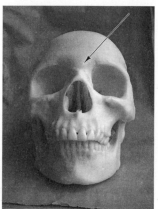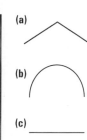

Photo 33.1 A typical skull showing the location of the quonset hut (arrowed) and its appearance in (a) European, (b) Asian and (c) African people.

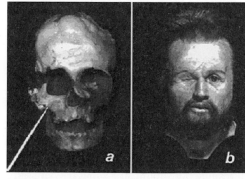

Photo 33.2 Facial reconstruction from a skull depicting (a) a wound to the orbit of the eye and (b) a possible facial reconstruction of the skull. (From Wilkinson and Neave, 2003 Copyright © 2003, with permission from Elsevier.)

Determining the racial origin of a skeleton

There are a number of traits, particularly in the skull, that can be related to the ethnicity of an individual. You should observe the skull with the face towards you, and also from a side profile. The slope of the skull is more pronounced in people of African origin when compared to European or Asian. Looking at the nasal bones you can observe the appearance of the 'quonset hut' (Photo 33.1). In people of European origin, this line appears as an inverted 'V', compared to an arch in Asian and horizontal in African people. The dentition can also be used (Chapter 34), in particular the location of Carabelli's cusp – an extra raised area found on the surface of the molars. If this cusp appears on the lingual, or tongue, side of the molar then it indicates European origin. If it is on the buccal, or cheek, side then it indicates Asian origin.

Differences between **ante-mortem** *and* **post-mortem** *injuries*

If any injury is noted on the bones, e.g. a fracture or a hole in skull, you can determine whether it was as a result of an injury during life (the *ante-mortem* period), whether it might have been the cause of death or whether it has happened after the person died.

If an injury occurs in life, a physiological process of healing will begin. In the case of fractures, a callus will form where the fracture occurred. This callus formation will remain on the bone and is a clear indicator that the injury occurred during the *ante-mortem* period.

If the injury was the result of the death, then no such healing will have occurred. In this instance you would look for signs of weathering of the bone – does the colour of the bone appear different to the bones immediately adjacent? If it appears to be the same colour (outer and inner surfaces) as the remainder of the skeleton, then it would be likely that the weathering of the surfaces has occurred at the same rate, suggesting that the injury was present prior to skeletonisation.

Equally, when the individual is living, the bones will break in a different manner to those broken in the *post-mortem* period. In the latter case, the bones will be brittle and will tend to splinter rather than form the characteristic greenstick or transverse fracture associated with an *ante-mortem* injury.

Facial reconstruction

The aim of facial reconstruction is to reproduce the face of an individual from a skull's characteristics (see Photo 33.2). The technique uses the skull morphology as a starting point and layers of modelling clay are placed over the skull, their thickness being defined by average values for the thickness of flesh in the relevant area. The limiting factor in this procedure is that many soft tissue features (such as the eyes, nose, lips and ears) are not related to skeletal features and hence are subject to speculation as to what they actually looked like. There have been studies carried out looking at features, such as nose projection and the pronasale position – the most forward point of the tip of the nose. It was found that in a study of 29 adult males, the average nose projection measured 30.9 ± 4.7 mm, with an average pronasale height of 44.3 ± 3.5 mm. In a comparison of 30 adult females, the average nose projection measured 28.1 ± 4.1 mm, with an average pronasale height of 43.0 ± 3.5 mm (Stephan *et al.*, 2003). These types of studies can be very useful to help you to reconstruct the soft tissue, but data are limited and therefore any facial reconstruction can only be an approximation of how the person may have looked in life.

Disaster Victim Identification (DVI) – mass disasters usually result in a large number of fatalities and involve a multi-agency approach in the investigation. General examples include: natural – e.g. floods, cyclone, earthquake; manmade – e.g. terrorism, war; historical – e.g. mass war graves.

Mass grave sites – these can be located and evaluated using aerial photography, ground penetrating radar (GPR), Geographic Information System (GIS) or even volatile organic compound (VOC) analysis associated with decomposition.

DVI – the simplified steps in a DVI investigation

Locate the scene – locate, identify and preserve the scene.

Process the scene – identification of remains and personal artefacts.

Post mortem examination – can be either in a temporary mortuary or transferred to a permanent facility. The examination also includes photography, fingerprint, radiology, odontology, DNA sampling in addition to the routine pathological examination.

Comparison with ante-mortem data (biometric, physical and circumstantial) – assessment will also include family and friend interviews, reference against missing person database.

Identification Board – the board is presided by a Coroner or equivalent, whereupon a death certificate can be granted and the body/remains can be released.

Reconciliation – if the ante- and post mortem data result in a positive identification, the body/remains can be recommended for repatriation with the family.

Determining the identity of an individual

Whenever a mass disaster (e.g. plane crash, Asian tsunami in 2004, act of terrorism resulting in multiple fatalities such as the World Trade Centre in 2001, or if the site of a mass burial, e.g. Crni Vrh, Bosnia and Herzegovina, has been located), there is a need for the identity of the individuals to be established. The process of the investigation of these sites should follow the same procedure as that for crime scene investigation (Chapter 23).

A mass grave site can be identified by disturbance of the top soil, which may have an obvious mound, perhaps accompanied by a lack of vegetation growth (see Chapter 36), especially when the grave is only a few months old. A double cordon should be erected and the site should be searched and fully documented. Care has to be taken during the process of excavation of the site and exhumation of the remains – the bodies are likely to be commingled and will require careful separation for re-assembly or re-association at the mortuary (usually established as a temporary mortuary on site). This can give an indication of the number of individuals found. As with all crime scenes, the full chain of custody and documentation processes should be in place. A *post-mortem* examination will be performed on the remains, inclusive of a full description of the clothing and personal effects, external and, where appropriate, internal examination, teeth examination (Chapter 34) and facial reconstruction.

Comparisons can then be made from *ante-mortem* data such as clothing, personal effects, dental records and, in combination with the criteria described earlier in this chapter (sex, age, stature), an attempt made to identify the individual. This process was successfully applied for the identification of bodies recovered from two mass graves in Bajajnica, Serbia (Djuric *et al.,* 2007). Recommendations for best practice have been proposed (Baraybar, 2008) and include:

- *ante-mortem* **data** – usually obtained by interview but should follow guidelines so that it can be presented in court at a later stage;
- **age** – reference has to be made to population specific standards;
- **dental records** – useful but only when the *ante-mortem* records are current and available;
- **DNA** – useful for corroboration in combination with other information obtained from the examination.

DNA (Chapters 13 and 31) has been shown to be successfully obtained from the femur, ribs and tooth samples (Westen *et al.,* 2008), but it has to be recognised that in a temporary mortuary the potential for contamination is increased. This can be minimised by adopting a standard operating procedure in these types of investigation.

Reporting forensic anthropology cases

These types of case form a useful part of the forensic investigation. Examination of skeletal remains can provide vital information about an individual, which may assist in identification in combination with further studies. Examination of the bones may also indicate whether the person has died in suspicious circumstances, which may then require further forensic investigations. The report should include the analytical results, but should stress that they are only estimates and not exact figures.

In other words, while the examination of the skeleton *in situ* and in the laboratory follows the stringent controls that would be expected in a forensic investigation, the report of the analytical findings is most useful for internal forensic science purposes – i.e. informing other specialist disciplines of the preliminary results from which they can direct further analytical tests in order that their results can help in the investigation of a crime.

Text references

Baraybar, J.P. (2008) When DNA is not available, can we still identify people? Recommendations for best practice. *Journal of Forensic Sciences* **53**(3): 533–540.

Burns, K. (1999) *Forensic Anthropology Training Manual.* Prentice Hall, New Jersey.

de Mendonca, M.C. (2000) Estimation of height from the length of long bones in a Portuguese adult population. *American Journal of Physical Anthropology* **112**: 39–45.

Djuric, M., Dunjic, D., Djonic, D. and Skinner, M. (2007) Identification of victims from two mass-graves in Serbia: A critical evaluation of classical markers of identity. *Forensic Science International* **172**: 125–129.

Jantz, R.L. and Ousley, S.D. (2005) *FORDISC 3.1. Personal Computer Forensic Discriminant Functions.* Available at: https://fac.utk.edu/fordisc-3-1-personal-computer-forensic-discriminant-functions/. Last accessed 20/08/2017.

Jarvis, D.R. (1997) Nitrogen levels in long bones from coffin burials interred for periods of 26–90 years. *Forensic Science International* **85**: 199–208.

Krishan, K. Chatterjee, P.M., Kanchan, T, Kaur, S, Baryah, N. and Singh, R.K. (2016) A review of sex estimation techniques during examination of skeletal remains in forensic anthropology casework. *Forensic Science International* **261**: 165e1–e8.

Ramsthaler, F., Kreutz, K., Zipp, K. and Verhoff, M.A. (2009) Dating skeletal remains with luminol-chemilumiscence. Validity, intra- and inter-observer error. *Forensic Science International* **187**: 47–50.

Stephan, C.N., Henneberg, M. and Sampson, W. (2003) Predicting nose projection and pronasale position in facial approximation: A test of published methods and proposal of new guidelines. *American Journal of Physical Anthropology* **122**: 240–250.

Stewart, T.D. (1979) *Essentials of Forensic Anthropology, Especially as Developed in the United States.* Charles C. Thomas, Springfield.

Vesterby, A. and Poulsen, L.W. (1997) The diagnosis of a murder from skeletal remains: A case report. *International Journal of Legal Medicine* **110**: 91–100.

Westen, A.A., Gerretson, R.R.R. and Maat, G.J.R. (2008) Femur, rib, and tooth sample collection for DNA analysis in disaster victim identification (DVI): A method to minimise contamination risk. *Forensic Science Medicine and Pathology* **4**: 15–21.

Wilkinson, C. and Neave, I. (2003) The reconstruction of a face showing a healed wound. *Journal of Archeological Science* **30**: 1343–1348.

Sources for further study

Adams, B.J. and Byrd, J.E. (eds) (2008) *Recovery, Analysis, and Identification of Commingled Human Remains.* Humana Press, New Jersey.

Black, S. and Ferguson, E. (2011) *Forensic Anthropology 2000–2010.* CRC Press, Boca Raton.

British Association for Human Identification. Available at: http://www.bahid.org/. Last accessed 20/08/2017.

Disaster Victim Identification (2017) Available at: https://www.interpol.int/INTERPOL-expertise/Forensics/DVI. Last accessed 20/08/2017.

Nafte, M. (2008) *Flesh and Bone: An Introduction to Forensic Anthropology,* 2nd edn. Carolina Academic Press, Durham.

Skinner, M., Alempijevic, D. and Djuric-Srejic, M. (2003) Guidelines for international forensic bio-archaelogy monitors of mass grave exhumations. *Forensic Science International* **134**: 81–92.

Study exercises

33.1 Test your knowledge. List eight methods that could be used to help establish the identity of an individual from skeletal remains.

33.2 Find out more information. Facial reconstruction techniques are developing rapidly. Using reference to online journals, try to find a current technique and discuss with your colleagues the key issues associated.

33.3 Test your knowledge. How would you determine the sex of an individual from their skeletal remains?

Bitemark – a mark left in an object that resembles the dental structure.

Canines – teeth for holding and ripping.

Deciduous dentition – teeth found from the age of 6 months to 2 years.

Eruption – the process of the tooth emerging from the gum.

Incisors – teeth for biting.

Molars – teeth for chewing/grinding.

Odontogram – dental record chart.

Odontology – the study of teeth, including development and degeneration.

Permanent dentition – teeth found from the age of 6 years, which last the duration of life.

Positive identification – no difference between the dentition in the human remains and *ante-mortem* dental records can be found.

Presumptive identification – this is a circumstantial identification based on, for example, a driver's licence.

Forensic odontology is a scientific discipline applying dental expertise in any legal investigation of an accident or crime. The forensic odontologist is a qualified dental surgeon, who has taken further training in forensic odontology. These specialists are most often asked to assist the forensic investigation in cases where a body is severely decomposed, when there is a case of multiple fatalities, such as a mass disaster (e.g. a plane crash), or in cases where a victim has been bitten. There are two distinct areas of expertise:

1. **positive identification of unknown human remains** – for example, comparing the dentition of the deceased with *ante-mortem* records to determine identity;
2. **bitemark analysis** – for example, identifying an individual from an impression left on a person or object.

 KEY POINT *Human teeth are resistant to degradation and the dentition is often the last structure in the body to decompose. Teeth can provide useful information about the deceased, including age, sex and possible identity.*

Human dentition and its development

Teeth develop following a regular developmental pattern. It is thus possible to estimate the age of a person from the stage of development of the dentition. From the age of 6 months, the deciduous dentition appears and is usually complete by 2 years, with a complement of 20 teeth. During the age of 6 to 14 years, the permanent teeth appear, with the exception of the third molars (wisdom teeth). During this time, there is a mixture of deciduous and permanent dentition, hence this transition period is known as mixed dentition. The appearance of the wisdom teeth is variable and may occur between 18 and 25 years, although they may not erupt at all. The adult human dentition consists of 32 teeth arranged in arches, one in the upper jaw and the second in the lower jaw (Fig. 34.1). Each tooth is given a number starting from the upper right third molar (number 1) to upper left third molar (number 16). The lower jaw begins from the lower left third molar (number 17) and finishes with the lower right third molar (number 32).

Examining human remains

Even though a body may not be identified visually, there is often a presumptive identification available from, for example, personal effects found on or close by the deceased. In cases where there is no presumptive identification, there are several techniques that can be used to aid the police in the investigation, which rely on the expertise of the forensic anthropologist (see Chapter 33), as well as the forensic odontologist.

Estimating the age of an individual

The method most commonly used when human remains cannot be identified visually is known as Gustafson's method (Box 34.1) and is based on the histology of the lower central incisor. It is important to know the structure of a tooth (see Fig. 34.2) in order to be able to use this method.

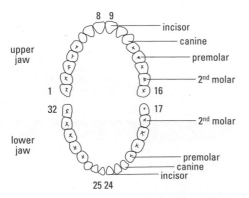

Fig. 34.1 Human adult dentition, indicating position of the types of teeth and the universal numbering system.

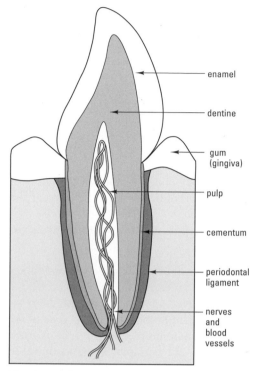

Fig. 34.2 Structure and major components of a tooth.

The tooth is primarily composed of three distinct regions:

- **enamel** – an outer, dense, hard, mineralised layer known as the crown;
- **dentine** – an inner layer of dense, tubular mass of collagen and elastin, containing inorganic compounds, such as calcium, fluoride, magnesium salts and hydroxyapatite;
- **pulp** – soft connective tissue in the central region of the tooth connected to nerves and blood supply.

The tooth remains in place in the socket (alveolus) in the jaw-bone by means of a layer of cementum (a porous layer of calcified tissue) and the periodontal ligament (a soft connective tissue that anchors the cementum, and so the tooth, to the jaw).

An alternative to the microscopic examination of the age changes in teeth is to analyse the amino acid content of the enamel and dentine (Mörnstad *et al.*, 1994). By using HPLC (Chapter 14), the D and L configuration of aspartic acid can be determined. Aspartic acid is usually found in the L configuration in biological materials, but as age increases it is converted into the D configuration by natural isomerisation. Therefore, a ratio between the D and L configuration, known as the racemisation ratio, changes as age increases. This technique can estimate the age to ± 12 years.

Determining the sex of an individual

The sex of human remains can be determined by examination of key skeletal structures (Chapter 33). If the sex of the human remains cannot be determined from the skeleton, for example because of *post-mortem* damage to the pelvis and skull, then the teeth can be examined. Although there are no sex differences in the surface morphology of teeth, it may be possible to extract the pulp of the teeth, which can then be used for DNA analysis (Chapter 31).

Box 34.1 How to estimate the age of an individual from teeth using Gustafson's method

1. **Remove the lower central incisor** (see Fig. 34.1) – this tooth is used primarily because it is least affected by dental decay and is the one that is usually retained for the longest period of time in the adult dentition.

2. **Cut the tooth** – the tooth should be cut vertically in half using a low-speed diamond saw, such as a Buehler Isomet™ precision saw.

3. **Prepare sections of the tooth** – the tooth should then be sliced into sections, using the precision saw, approximately 100 μm in diameter to allow the section to be viewed under a microscope.

4. **Mount the sections on to a microscope slide** – observe the microscopic features at ×100 total magnification with a low-power microscope (see Chapter 10).

5. **Record your observations** – details of the microscopic features should be recorded in your examination notes and should include:

- the extent of the wear of the surface of the tooth, also known as attrition, on a scale of 0–3 (see Fig. 34.3);
- the extent of deposition of minerals into the pulp, known as secondary dentine, resulting from attrition;
- whether the periodontal ligament has detached from the root;
- the thickness of the layer of cementum – as age increases, more cementum is produced;
- whether the root is transparent – a root becomes more transparent as age increases;
- the shape of the root – as age increases, the root becomes more flattened.

6. **Calculate the age of the tooth** – using regression formulae from published tables (Vystrcilova and Novotny, 2000) the age of the tooth can be estimated. This form of age estimation is not exact, but age can usually be determined to ± 6 years.

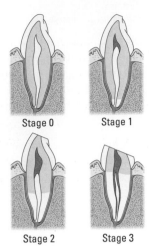

Fig. 34.3 The three stages of wear in teeth according to Gustafson. (From Burns, 1999, Copyright © 1999, by permission of Pearson Education, Inc. Upper Saddle River, NJ.)

Stage 0   Stage 1
Stage 2   Stage 3

Definitions

Chromatin – the stainable substance of a cell that contains DNA and RNA.

Racemisation – the process by which an amino acid is converted from an L isomeric configuration to its mirror image, a D isomeric configuration.

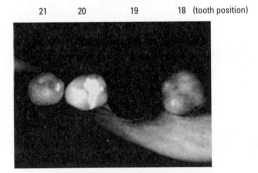

Photo 34.1 Mandible illuminated at 380 nm showing restorations in teeth (left-hand side positions 21 and 20). (Image from Bush *et al.*, 2008.)

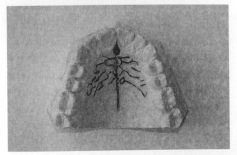

Photo 34.2 Dental cast illustrating the ridge pattern of palatal rugae (note that the rugae have been coloured for illustration purposes only).

Post-mortem comparisons

The most reliable way to determine identity is to compare the dentition of the deceased to *ante-mortem* dental records of the person you believe the individual to be. Typically, a *post-mortem* dental chart, or odontogram, is produced detailing the examination of each tooth and the surrounding structures (Pretty and Sweet, 2001). The examination should be thorough and should include details such as:

- **teeth** – stage of development, crown, root and pulp morphology, if all teeth are present (erupted or unerupted), if any teeth are missing and the presence of any restoration work, such as crowns and fillings;
- **periodontal region** – general morphology and pathology of the gums (if available), general morphology and disease of the periodontal ligament and the alveolus;
- **general anatomical features of the jaw** – presence of any disease and signs of trauma.

By checking a list of missing persons, it is possible to narrow down possibilities of who the person was. *Ante-mortem* dental records can be obtained from a dental surgeon where the person was registered and compared with the *post-mortem* odontogram to see if there are any similarities in the positions of the teeth or any dental treatment. One of the main problems with *ante-mortem* dental records is when you change dentist – for example, when you move to another city, your dental records are not transferred, unlike your medical records. Therefore, there is a possibility that the dental records obtained for comparison may not be the most up-to-date records. It is recognised that there are difficulties with *ante-* and *post-mortem* comparisons including angulation (the angles at which both records were taken may differ slightly), distances of images, positioning of images, coupled with changes associated with *rigor mortis* (Mincer *et al.,* 2008). An alternative to radiography is the use of ultraviolet illumination (Bush *et al.,* 2008). Restorative composite resins are now more commonly used rather than amalgams and these have been shown to have different fluorescent properties. Although dentition and enamel do fluoresce, the extent of the fluorescence is increased when observing resins at 380 nm (Bush *et al.,* 2008, Photo 34.1). If there are no *ante-mortem* records against which to compare the deceased's dentition, DNA analysis (see Chapter 31) can be used. Both genomic and mitochondrial DNA can be extracted from the roots of the teeth, which can be used to determine the sex of the individual as well as providing a DNA profile from which a possible identification can be made.

A proposed alternative to identification by dentition is the use of the palatoscopy (the examination of the palatal rugae). The palatal rugae appear in the upper surface of the mouth and are characterised by assymetrical ridges (Photo 34.2). Just as fingerprints are unique, so it is believed that this ridge pattern is as well. There are a number of recognised techniques adopted to classify the ridge patterns, but these appear to be subjective between users. As with *ante-* and *post-mortem* comparisons with dental records, the same could be applied to palatal rugae patterns, the primary advantage being that the ridge pattern is persistent and does not alter during life. Ohtani *et al.* (2008) have demonstrated a similar success rate between dental record identification and identification by the palatal rugae. Obviously the disadvantage at the moment is a lack of *ante-mortem* data from which the comparison can be made. For further information about the different classification types, see Caldas *et al.* (2007) referenced at the end of this chapter.

Case example In 1989, a skeletonised body was found under a tree. A rope was found loosely attached to a branch of the tree above where the remains lay, supporting the proposition of suicide. A forensic anthropologist examined the human remains and determined that they belonged to a middle-aged man. A forensic odontologist performed a *post-mortem* dental examination and found a distinctive gold-plated tooth at position 19. A subsequent search of missing persons revealed two possibilities. The *ante-mortem* dental records were obtained for each and one was immediately discounted. The other matched all but one tooth (position 30), which in the skeletonised body contained an occlusal filling, whereas in the *ante-mortem* records the tooth was intact. This discrepancy was accounted for by dental treatment carried out by a different dentist and therefore not included on the *ante-mortem* record that had been obtained. The body was thereby identified (Kullman *et al.*, 1993).

Ageing bruises by their colour – the appearance of a bruise is variable, but in general will follow this pattern:

Initial	purple red/blue;
1–3 days	brown, due to the breakdown of haemoglobin;
4–5 days	greenish brown, greenish yellow;
7–10 days	yellowish brown, tan and yellow;
over 14–15 days	normal skin colour returns.

Bitemark analysis

A bitemark is, in simple terms, a bruise characterised by opposing arches matching the natural shape of a perpetrator's dentition. A bruise is a common injury, but is not permanent, lasting only for a few days. Specific teeth in the dentition produce different types of bruising – for example, canines tend to produce triangular bruising, whereas the incisors produce rectangular bruising. Thus both class and individual characteristics can be determined. There are key stages in the examination of bitemark evidence and these, according to Bernitz *et al.* (2008), should include:

- **Identification of a mark** – if a mark is visually identified you must consider whether or not it is of human origin. A bitemark is characterised by bruising associated with opposing arches, but these will differ among species, e.g. dog versus human. It is also important to differentiate patterns associated with inanimate objects that could mislead the interpretation.

- **Direct comparison** – once a bitemark is identified, a 2D representation can be obtained (Box 34.2) and compared with a 3D reference dental cast (Photo 34.2). An alternative technique for performing this comparison is using 'invisible ink' to mark the key edges of the dentition. By observing this at 395 nm, the ink fluoresces and the image can be digitally captured and used to compare against the actual bitemark (Metcalf, 2008).

- **Metric analysis** – this is fundamental in providing an opinion as to the likelihood of a match. Measurements should be taken from canine → canine, as well as the effects that rotation has on this measurement. Other measurements include left and right canine → central incisor and the calculation of the angle of torsion between these (De Angelis *et al.*, (2007).

- **Comparison with a population database** – this allows common data to be identified within a particular ethnic population.

 KEY POINT *The most important aspect of bitemark analysis is photographing the evidence as soon as is practically possible, to provide a permanent record of the bitemark.*

Box 34.2 How to examine bitemark evidence

1. **Prepare initial documentation** – you should include the case number, name, age and sex of the victim, the place, date and time of the examination.

2. **Observe the bitemark** – you should record the anatomical position of the mark, the coloration of the mark, shape, size (diameter and length) and whether the skin has been broken.

3. **Photograph the bitemark** – using both black-and-white and colour film (Chapter 23), initially without a measurement scale. The photographs should illustrate the bitemark in location to a recognisable anatomical site, and close-up photographs should show the detail of the bruising pattern. The close-up photographs should also include a scale from which the dimensions of the mark can be later examined. If it is possible, the victim should be asked to return in a few days and the bitemarks photographed again to record any changes over time. When you are photographing the bitemark, you should vary the lighting (e.g. flash fill and angles). Of all the photographs that you take, the one that is most important is that which is taken vertically over the bitemark – this is the photograph that shows minimal distortion and that will be used in any subsequent superimposition.

4. **Swab the skin surface** – use a sterile medical swab, moistened with sterile deionised water, to wipe over the entire area of the bitemark. Return the swab to its tube, package it and seal with a tamper-proof tape in a

Box 34.2   (continued)

polythene bag. A second swab should be taken in the same way of an unmarked site, which should be recorded in your examination notes. This sample should be packaged in the same way as the bitemark swab, but should be clearly labelled as a control reference sample.

5. **Analyse the bitemark from the photographs** – you should be able to determine the upper and lower arches of the teeth (see Fig. 34.1) by examining the pattern of bruising and measuring the diameter between the marks. The canines and first premolars are likely to have caused the greatest degree of bruising – therefore between these points you can identify the position of the central incisors. In so doing, the direction of the bite can be determined. You should count the number of tooth marks and the number of gaps, taking note of any faint bruising in a gap that may represent a tooth lower in height than the others.

6. **Compare the bitemark to the dentition of a suspect** – a dental impression should be made of a suspect's dentition in the presence of a qualified dentist and police officer. This dental impression should be cast in dental stone providing a permanent record. This cast should be packaged securely to prevent damage and sent to the laboratory for comparison with the bitemark photographs. The diameter of the arches can be measured and any specific characteristic features of the dentition noted. A vertical photograph can be taken of the upper and lower arches of the cast, using exactly the same parameters that have been recorded in the examination notes for the photograph of the bitemark. Using a computer, directly superimpose one image on top of the other and compare the arches and prominent bruising to see if the bitemark impression matches the teeth of the cast.

Case example   The first bitemark case to be heard in court related to the conviction of Theodore Bundy, who stood accused of the rape and murder of at least 23 women during 1974–78. Along with other trace evidence, a bitemark was found on the buttock of one of the victims. This bitemark proved to be a positive match to Bundy, who had unusually distorted dentition, which was crucial in securing his conviction.

Bitemark evidence – In 2016, bitemark evidence was reviewed in a landmark case (case against Chaney, TSFS case No. 1109.15.07) in the United States of America. Following the review, the Texas Forensic Science Commission has, at the moment, recommended that bitemark evidence should not be admissible in courts of law in Texas. The review highlighted the necessity for proficiency testing and to establish robust 'criteria for identifying when a patterned injury constitutes a human bitemark. These criteria should be expressed clearly and accompanied by empirical testing to demonstrate sufficient inter and intra-examiner reliability and validity when the criteria are applied.' TSFS (2017). The American Board of Forensic Odontologists (ABFO) are currently undertaking further research to address such issues to prevent any miscarriages of justice from occurring. For more information see the TSFS website available at: http:// www.fsc.texas.gov/cases?field_complaint_ number_value=1109.15.07&field_complainant_value=&field_laboratory_value=&field_ forensic_discipline_value=&field_status_ value=&items_per_page=10 and the ABFO website available at: http://abfo.org/

A bitemark (Box 34.2) inflicted on a victim can be identified to a particular individual because of differences in:

- the natural shape, size and abnormalities of the teeth and jaws;
- the stage of development of the dentition;
- changes associated with ageing;
- pathology of the teeth and periodontal regions;
- restoration by a dentist.

Since the process of biting is likely to involve the transfer of saliva on to the skin, the bitemark can be swabbed and analysed for the presence of DNA (see Chapter 31), thus providing a further possible means of identification.

Significance of bitemark evidence

When pressure is exerted on skin, it can be pulled or stretched due to its elasticity, leaving an indentation that differs from individual to individual. Bush *et al.* (2009) have illustrated that distortion is most pronounced when there is movement in the biting action, and least pronounced when the bite occurs along natural tension lines within the body. The degree of severity of a bitemark has been proposed by Pretty (2007) to encompass a range from 1–6, from mild bruising to full avulsion of tissue. The two extremes of this range offer little evidential value, whereas those towards the middle of the scale illustrate class and individual characteristics associated with this type of injury and can thus be utilised for comparisons with reference material.

Text references

American Board of Forensic Odontologists website (2017) Available at: http://abfo.org/ Last accessed 20/08/2017.

Bernitz, H., Owen, J.H., van Heerden, W.F.P. and Solheim, T. (2008) An integrated technique for the analysis of skin bite marks. *Journal of Forensic Sciences* **53**(1): 194–198.

Burns, K. (1999) *Forensic Anthropology Training Manual.* Prentice Hall, New Jersey.

Bush, M.A., Hermanson, A.S., Miller, R.G. and Bush, P.J. (2008) Ultraviolet illumination as an adjunctive aid in dental inspection. *Journal of Forensic Sciences* **53**(2): 408–411.

Bush, M.A., Miller, R.G., Bush, P.J. and Dorion, R.B.J. (2009) Biochemical factors in human dermal bitemarks in a cadaver model. *Journal of Forensic Sciences* **54**(1): 167–176.

Caldas, I.M., Magalhaes, T. and Alfonso, A. (2007) Establishing identity using cheiloscopy and palatoscopy. *Forensic Science International* **165**: 1–9.

De Angelis, D., Cattaneo, C. and Grandi, M. (2007) Dental superimposition: a pilot study for standardising the method. *International Journal of Legal Medicine* **121**: 501–506.

Kullman, L., Solheim, T., Grundin, R. and Teivins, A. (1993) Computer registration of missing persons: A case of Scandinavian co-operation in identification of an unknown male skeleton. *Forensic Science International* **60**: 15–22.

Metcalf, R.D. (2008) Yet another method for marking incisal edges of teeth for bitemark analysis. *Journal of Forensic Sciences* **53**(2): 426–429.

Mincer, H.H., Chaudrey, J., Blankenship, J.A. and Turner, E.W. (2008) Postmortem dental radiography. *Journal of Forensic Sciences* **53**(2): 405–407.

Mörnstad, H., Pfeiffer. H. and Teivens, A. (1994) Estimation of dental age using HPLC-technique to determine the degree of aspartic acid racemization. *Journal of Forensic Sciences* **39**: 1425–1431.

Ohtani, M., Nishida, N., Chiba, T., Fukuda, M., Miyamoto, Y. and Yoshioka, N. (2008) Indication and limitations of using palatal rugae for personal identification in edentulous cases. *Forensic Science International* **176**: 178–182.

Pretty, I.A. (2007) Development and validation of a human bitemark severity and significance scale. *Journal of Forensic Sciences* **52**(3): 687–691.

Pretty, I.A. and Sweet, D. (2001) A look at forensic dentistry Part1: The role of teeth in determination of human identity. *British Dental Journal* **190**: 359–366.

Texas Forensic Science Commission website (2017) Available at http://www.fsc.texas.gov/sites/default/files/Final%20Bite%20Mark%20Report%20no%20exhibits.pdf. Last accessed 01/10/17

Vystrcilova, M. and Novotny, V. (2000) Estimation of age at death using teeth. *Variability and Evolution* **8**: 39–49.

Sources for further study

Adams, C., Carabott, R. and Evans, S. (eds) (2014) *Forensic Odontology: An Essential Guide.* Wiley-Blackwell.

Bowers, C.M. (2011) *Forensic Dental Evidence: An Investigators Handbook.* Elsevier, Amsterdam.

British Association of Forensic Odontology Website (2009). Available at: http://www.bafo.org.uk/. Last accessed 12/06/09.

Dorion, R.B.J. (2011) *Bitemark Evidence: A Color Atlas and Text,* 2nd edn. CRC Press, Boca Raton.

Forensic Dentistry On-line (2009). Available at: http://www.forensicdentistryonline.org/. Last accessed 12/06/09.

Pretty, I.A. and Sweet, D.J. (2007) *Color Atlas of Forensic Dentistry.* Springer-Verlag, New York.

Stimson, P.G. and Mertz, C.A. (1997) *Forensic Dentistry.* CRC Press, Boca Raton.

Study exercises

34.1 Test your knowledge of the structure of teeth. Cover up the legend on the right-hand side of Fig. 34.2 with a piece of paper or card. Now identify the key components of the tooth. Check your answers from the legend.

34.2 Test your knowledge of the arrangement of teeth. Name the types and position of teeth found in the normal human adult dentition.

34.3 Test your knowledge of the steps involved in bitemark analysis. Name the key stages involved in the examination of a bitemark.

Forensic entomology involves the study of insects, and other arthropods, to support legal investigations and includes:

- **Medico-legal investigations** – usually related to criminal aspects of the legal system and dealing with the necrophagous (carrion-feeding) insects that infest human remains.
- **Urban investigations** – dealing with insects that affect humans (living or dead) and their immediate environment; this may include both civil and criminal components.
- **Studies of stored product insects** – commonly found in foodstuffs (civil and criminal components).

This chapter deals primarily with the use of insects in medico-legal investigations related to the investigation of human remains, but the same principles apply to the other areas.

The forensic use of insects is founded on two important features of their biology:

1. insects are important carrion feeders in all terrestrial environments;
2. they have rigid and repeatable life cycles that provide a capacity for retrospective interpretation in forensic investigations.

KEY POINT *Forensic entomology requires a proper understanding of a number of insect features: a knowledge of their biology and ecology; the identification of the organisms; an understanding of their life cycles; and an appreciation of the factors that influence the timing of the life cycle components.*

Basic principles of insect biology

You will need to understand the key features of insect anatomy in order to identify specimens, both adult and larval. The basic adult form has three clearly identifiable functional regions (Fig. 35.1) – the head, the thorax and the abdomen – each of which may have been modified during evolution and often provides diagnostic features for the particular insect family/species.

The insect body wall is termed an exoskeleton and is characterised by the durable cuticle that allows the bodies/fragments of insects to remain in the environment for extended periods of time – allowing forensic use long after the organism is dead. Some components are sclerotised (e.g. the jaws) and remain usable in identification for extended periods.

The head of most adult insects is a hardened capsule bearing eyes, antennae and mouthparts that are important diagnostic characteristics for identification. The majority of necrophagous insects have a sponging mouth type allowing the non-invasive sucking of liquids.

Directly behind the head is the thorax (Fig. 35.1), a region composed of three fused body segments that bear the six legs (one pair per segment) characteristic of insects and the wings, one pair in the flies or, in the other taxonomic groups, two pairs borne on the posterior thoracic segments. Each leg usually has five major parts and terminates in a region called the tarsus, itself made up of up to five segments and often ending in a tarsal claw.

Making the most of forensic entomology – appropriate and detailed sampling is the key to success.

Fig. 35.1 Insect body structure (common house fly, Musca domestica).

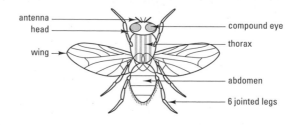

antenna — head
wing
compound eye
thorax
abdomen
6 jointed legs

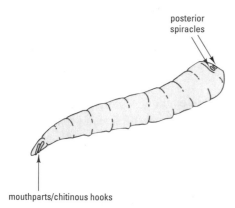

posterior spiracles

mouthparts/chitinous hooks

Fig. 35.2 Maggot – key features.

The third and final region is the abdomen (Fig. 35.1), which is typically composed of 11 segments, although it may be reduced in some groups. There are paired, feeler-like structures at the posterior end of the abdomen (cerci) whose presence or structure can be useful in identification. Female insects also bear an ovipositor at the tip of the abdomen; this is used when laying eggs. Each abdominal segment bears a pair of spiracles, visible as small oval spots – these are openings to the respiratory system.

The structure of maggots and larval stages (instars) is generally very different from adults, usually comprising a form with much-reduced complexity in which identification features may be very limited (Fig. 35.2). Larval stages such as maggots have a thoracic spiracle on each side of the body, as well as a pair of posterior spiracles at the tip of the abdomen, and the shape and coloration of these structures is valuable for identification.

Insect development and life cycle

Insects pass through a number of stages when developing from egg to adult. The process is termed metamorphosis and is associated with shedding of the exoskeleton (ecdysis) at various points as they grow – the shed skin is persistent and called an exuvium. The appearance and duration of the life stages is species-specific and influenced by environmental conditions – this is why appropriate temperature data in the form of isomegalens (growth curves) are essential for forensic analysis (Fig. 35.3). The time spent in any particular life stage is called a stadium. Each growth stage within a particular life stage is called an instar.

Life cycles may be of three main types:

1. **Ametabolous** – in which the young hatch from the egg as small adult forms with no intermediate larval/pupal stages.
2. **Hemimetabolous** (gradual metamorphosis) – where eggs hatch out into nymphs, small adult-like forms lacking only the wings typical of the adult form. With each ecdysis, they become more like the final adult form.
3. **Holometabolous** (complete metamorphosis) – with both larval (feeding stage) and pupal (resting and metamorphosis stage) components.

The morphology and ecology of these forms can be very important in forensic analysis. In particular, the holometabolous fly (Diptera) egg that is laid directly on to potential food sources such as human bodies in early stages of decomposition – typically in a natural opening, e.g. nose, ears, mouth, site of wound – develops into a larval stage called a maggot. This passes through three instars before migrating away from the food source and pupating, usually taking place in the soil, but this can be up to several metres from the food source, e.g. *Calliphora vicina*. Some species of fly then molt to form an exarate pupa but they do it inside the old skin of the final larval stage, which then shrinks and hardens forming a puparium. This puparium darkens with time to brown, reddish-brown or black depending on the species.

> **Using terminology correctly** – note that the second larval instar has moulted once since hatching from the egg.

> **Effect of temperature** – as temperature decreases, the amount of time required for development increases.

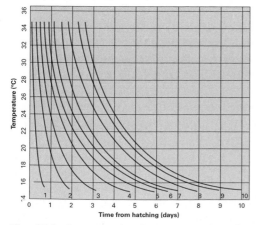

Temperature (°C)
Time from hatching (days)

Fig. 35.3 An example of an isomegalen diagram. The time since hatching (x axis) is plotted against temperature (y axis). For further details and species specific isomegalen diagrams refer to entomology scientific publications, for example, Grassberger and Reiter, 2001.

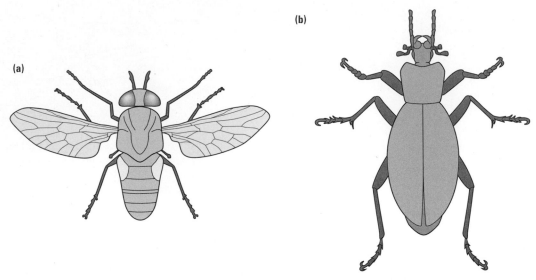

Fig. 35.4 Insects: (a) a Dipteran fly; (b) a cole opteran beetle.

Morphological characteristics of the larvae are retained in the outer layer of the puparium and are often sufficient to allow species identification.

Identification

This is a crucial component of forensic entomology. Taxonomic identification of insects found on corpses is essential to the reconstruction of events. It allows the appropriate developmental data and distribution ranges to be applied to an investigation, and any error in identification will invalidate any estimates of *post-mortem* intervals.

There are two main orders of insects that are of importance in forensic analysis, namely the Diptera (flies) and the Coleoptera (beetles) (Fig. 35.4). Identification of a specimen to species level will require access to specialist texts. Although some species of insects can be identified from photographs, this is rarely sufficient and wet mount microscopic examination is frequently required.

 KEY POINT *As the insect exoskeleton is hard, it can be softened by clearing the specimen in methyl benzoate or Hoyer's medium before examination (Table 35.1) – this will also aid mounting and examination of specimens.*

A useful review of the principal insect groups of forensic importance is provided by Byrd and Castner (2009). The main taxonomic groups are summarised in Table 35.2.

Table 35.1 Composition of Hoyer's medium

Distilled water	50 mL
Arabic gum (acacia)	30 g
Choral hydrate	200 g
Glycerin	16 mL

Preparation: dissolve Arabic gum *completely* in the distilled water. Then, and only then, completely dissolve in choral hydrate, then add glycerin and mix well. Before using Hoyer's medium, let it stand undisturbed for several days in order to clarify. Store the mixture at 4°C. The medium may be diluted when needed with small amounts of distilled water.

SAFETY NOTE *Choral hydrate is used as a hypnotic and a sedative. Abuse may lead to habituation or addiction. Some individuals are extremely sensitive to the vapours of Hoyer's medium and develop headaches, etc.*

Further advice on taxonomic terminology – for terminology and phylogeny of insects and other arthropods, see Chapter 38 of Jones et al. (2003).

Equipment needed for the collection of entomological evidence *(adapted from Amendt et al., 2007)*

Documentation and recording includes:

- *Notes – a protocol should be followed to document where the body was found (inside/outside), state of dress (clothing/ partial undress/unclothed), description of the body, state of decomposition, temperature (ambient, ground and body) and where the entomological evidence was found.*
- *Other useful items include pencil, labels, camera, thermometer – for the measurement of temperature (ambient, ground and body) or a temperature data logger that can be left to monitor temperature fluctuations over a period of days.*

Collection of entomological evidence includes:

- **Forceps** – *these are required for collection of the adult species. Care must be taken so as not to damage the immature insects when these are collected.*
- **Spoons** – *useful for the collection of larvae.*
- **Paintbrush** – *useful for the collection of eggs.*
- **Trowel** – *useful for the collection of soil.*
- **Insect net** – *useful for the collection of adult airborne insects.*
- **Ethanol** – *80% v/v for the preservation of the insect.*
- **Thermos flask** – *filled with hot water, above 80 °C for killing the insect.*

Storage of entomological evidence includes:

- **Vials** – *these containers should allow entry of air into the vessel, but not allow release of the specimens. It is also useful to have a layer of sawdust or tissue paper in these vials to absorb any fluids expelled from the larvae.*
- **Coolbag** – *required for the transport of live specimens and should ideally be kept at a temperature of 2–6 °C.*

Table 35.2 The main taxonomic groups of insects of forensic importance

Order Diptera	Family Calliphoridae (blow flies)
	Family Sarcophagidae (flesh flies)
	Family Muscidae (muscid flies)
	Family Piophilidae (skipper flies)
	Family Scathophagidae (dung flies)
	Family Sepsidae (black scavenger flies)
	Family Sphaeroceridae (small dung flies, minute scavenger flies)
	Family Stratiomyidae (soldier flies)
	Family Phoridae (humpbacked flies or scuttle flies)
	Family Psychodidae (moth flies, sand flies, and owl midge)
Order Coleoptera	Family Silphidae (carrion beetles)
	Family Dermestidae (skin beetles, leather beetles, hide beetles, carpet beetles and larder beetles)
	Family Saphylinidae (rove beetles)
	Family Histeridae (clown beetles)
	Family Cleridae (checkered beetles)
	Family Trogidae (hide beetles)
	Family Scarabaeidae (scarab beetles)
	Family Nitidulidae (sap beetles)

Sampling

Forensic entomologists must use precise methods to collect and present the evidence correctly, as this is a vital requirement for accurate interpretation (Haskell *et al.*, 2001). Central to this process is the proper collection, preservation, transportation and recognition of the entomological material. It is highly recommended that information, whether derived from field or laboratory work, is recorded on pre-printed data collection forms such as those given in Haskell *et al.* (2001).

 KEY POINT *All samples must be very carefully labelled and must contain at least information on the date and time of collection, case number, location and sample number. Such labels should be duplicated – one, printed in indelible ink or pencil on heavy bond paper should be placed inside the specimen container, while the other should be printed on adhesive paper and be fixed to the outside of the sample container.*

The use of forensic entomology is increasing in criminal investigations and recently a protocol of best practice has been proposed (Amendt *et al.*, 2007) for the collection of entomological evidence. This includes appropriate methods of collecting specimens, documentation and methods for the estimation of the *post-mortem* interval.

Investigation at the field site can be divided into several major stages:

1. Assessment, measurement and recording of general scene characteristics.
2. Observation and recording of insect infestations at the site.
3. Collection and recording of climatological (especially temperature and humidity) data at the site.
4. Collection and appropriate preservation of adult flies and beetles.
5. Collection and appropriate treatment of eggs, larvae and puparia.
6. Collection of insect specimens from the surrounding area (up to 6 m from the body). Remember that post-feeding larvae will migrate for pupation.
7. Collection of insect specimens from directly beneath, and in close proximity to (1 m or less), the remains after the body has been removed.

8. Documentation of recent historical climatic data, especially temperature.
9. Assessment of the ecological characteristics of the site – soil, water, plants, etc.

A detailed exposition of the methods appropriate for these tasks is provided by Haskell *et al.* (2001).

When investigating human remains, you should collect samples from a variety of body regions including orifices, wounds, corpse (surface and underneath) and clothing, especially in folds, carefully recording the environmental parameters that might affect insect development rates. The largest, and thus oldest, maggots are the most important and must be collected, together with representatives of the complete developmental range of maggots present. Record accurate information on where they were found on the body, times of collection and ambient temperatures, both of the body and the surrounding environment. It is also advisable to collect soil samples (Chapter 36) from up to 2 m from the corpse as well as leaf litter detritus (Amendt *et al.*, 2007).

Preservation of samples

All specimens must be preserved immediately unless it is intended to rear some to adult stage, to assist with *post-mortem* interval (PMI) determinations. The most widely used method used to kill non-adult specimens (eggs, larvae or pupae) is by plunging them into water just below boiling point for 10–15 s. They should then be transferred rapidly to a solution of 80% ethanol in carefully labelled containers – this prevents the discoloration and shrinkage that would occur if they were just plunged into common preservative solutions such as ethanol and formaldehyde while still alive.

 KEY POINT *This treatment is important, as shrinkage would make the maggots appear younger than they really and since size is an important indicator of age.*

Killing specimens – *the purpose of killing the larvae collected is so that larval length can be measured and compared with reference data to identify the age and estimate the time since death.*

Adult specimens (aerial or crawling insects primarily) should be killed in a freezer set at $-20\,°C$ for 1 h. These can then be transferred to 80% ethanol for storage.

 KEY POINT *Do not place living specimens directly into ethanol as this will cause shrinkage as well as alteration of colour.*

The insects may then be preserved in liquid as described above or may be pinned for identification.

Providing information on the possible cause of death

Venomous insects might occasionally be the cause of death themselves but they can also assist in the identification of chemicals, e.g. cocaine or heroin, normally determined from blood, urine or stomach contents after these sources have become difficult to use due to decomposition. It is, however, impossible to determine a cause of death of an individual from toxicological data obtained from entomological specimens alone.

The sites of blowfly infestation may also be important – heavy infestation of particular locations might indicate that these were the original sites of trauma. The usual sites of oviposition on dead human remains are the natural openings, although even here there are preferences – blowflies favour the facial region and concentrations in other regions may indicate specific types of attack. The position of clothing may also influence oviposition.

> **KEY POINT** *Insects can be useful in assisting a pathologist to assign a cause of death – sampling maggots, empty puparia or larval cast skins for a specific chemical compound (including poisons) can provide a 'body burden' for that compound.*

Estimating the time of death using forensic entomology

Under normal conditions, insects arrive at the body very soon after death, and determination of the age of the insect populations can provide an estimate of the *post-mortem* interval (PMI) that may not be obtainable by other methods. After death, it is the flies (order Diptera) that arrive first, particularly the blowflies (Calliphoridae) and the flesh flies (Sarcophagidae) and, after the eggs have been laid, the insects go through their life stages in a sequence that is generally predictable and, consequently, the age of the population (and thus the PMI of the corpse) may be estimated.

However, the success of this procedure requires that:

- the insects are correctly and precisely identified, since different species differ in their rates of development;
- information on the development times of life stages of the particular species found is available or can be determined;
- the environmental factors that may influence the development times can be determined – these are primarily temperature and humidity but can also include chemicals within the decomposing body.

It is also possible to rear captured life stages of uncertain age to support stage estimations and times, but this requires considerable care and an appropriate setup. This approach is mainly used as a research tool or is a method required for poorly known species where appropriate life stage development information does not already exist (see Byrd and Castner, 2009).

Figure 35.5 illustrates the life cycle of a blowfly. Typically, the egg stage lasts for a day or so, and the larval stage (maggot) has three instars (reaching a length of 5 mm by 1.8 days; 10 mm after 2.5 days; 17 mm after 4–5 days). Identification of a blowfly instar is easy, being based on size, size of mouth parts and the morphology of the posterior spiracles. Note that the duration of each stage is dependent on both temperature and humidity, and size alone may not be sufficient. For example, *Calliphora vicina* appears to be cold adapted and has a complete and normal pupariation at temperatures below 16 °C, but the growth rate is slowed significantly at low temperatures, e.g. 4 °C, and high temperatures, e.g. 35 °C, appear to be fatal for this species (Donovan *et al.*, 2006). The prepupa is about 12mm long and is seen 8–12 days after oviposition. The prepupa gradually becomes a pupa, which darkens with age, known as tanning. Pupae (9 mm long) are seen 18–24 days after oviposition. (Empty puparia indicate that the remains must be > 20 days old.)

Using this knowledge, the instar stage (1st, 2nd and 3rd) can be identified. The size of the instar is also a function of age up until post-feeding but is dependent on the food source and whether or not it is drug laden. Temperature, both environmental and maggot mass, is another factor that can influence the growth rates of the insects. It is therefore crucial that a detailed knowledge of the

Establishing body burdens of chemical compounds – where these are to be determined, specimens should be frozen without chemical fixation unless the chemical procedure to be used requires other treatments.

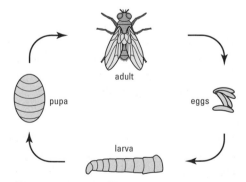

Fig. 35.5 Blowfly life cycle.

species is known before any interpretation can be made for the estimation of the *post-mortem* interval.

 KEY POINT *It is really important to record the temperature (ambient, ground, soil and body) accurately at the time of discovery. You will also need to obtain weather data from the closest meteorological station over the past few days/months as appropriate to the case.*

There are many factors other than temperature that influence development and these should be considered when estimating the time of death. These include:

- **Larval crowding** – also known as maggot mass. Large numbers competitively feeding in the same place can form a large mass and generate heat. Given that temperature is known to influence the rate of development, it follows that the development rate of these maggots would be artificially altered, leading to a misinterpretation of the development age and size. Ireland and Turner (2006) have shown an increased development rate of *Calliphora vomitoria* with larval crowding and have also illustrated a variation in rate according to location of feeding (liver, brain and muscle).
- **Limited/delayed access to food source** – if a human body is found within a house or car there will be an inherent delay in the insect succession. Voss *et al.* (2008) have shown that the rate of decomposition, using a pig carcass as a model, was faster within an enclosed vehicle and that there was a delay of 16–18 h for the appearance of the first insects and a delay of 24–48 h before oviposition.
- **Presence of drugs** – in cases of drug-related deaths (Chapter 38) a drug-laden body can influence the rate of growth, leading to either an over- or underestimation of the *post-mortem* interval. For example, *Lucilia sericata* feeding on liver spiked with codeine showed significantly faster development (Kharbouche *et al.*, 2008), *Chrysoma putoria* and *Chrysoma albiceps* (Calliphoridae) feeding on liver spiked with diazepam also developed faster (Carvalho, 2001) and even liver spiked with paracetamol slightly accelerates the growth of *Calliphora vicina* (O'Brien and Turner, 2004).
- **Different food sources** – growth rates have been shown to vary considerably depending on the tissues that the larvae are feeding on. For example, *Lucilia sericata* larval length varies according to whether the larvae are feeding on lung, heart or liver, although similar lengths of larvae were noted irrespective of the species on which the larvae were feeding (Clark *et al.*, 2006). This phenomenon does appear to differ between species of insect, therefore it is crucial that as much information about the species is known before any conclusions can be drawn in relation to the *post-mortem* interval.

Another approach to estimating the PMI is to use the fact that a cadaver is subjected to a fairly predictable succession of organisms that thrive on different parts of the body, although the details of this succession are dependent on the geographical area, the season and the details of the location. This will be true also for the soil fauna beneath the body, if present. However, organisms that may visit and leave a corpse several times (e.g. ants and adult flies) are considered relatively poor indicators of time since death. Succession data can be recorded and used to estimate PMI – by identifying the appropriate species present in the insect community, the stage in the development of the succession can be identified and the time taken for the development of this stage can be estimated. However, this approach is very dependent on a detailed knowledge of the probable succession existing within a particular location.

An alternative approach to estimation of time of death – Tarone et al. (2007) have shown that mRNA of the following three genes of Lucilia sericata were profiled:

- *bicoid* – responsible for early egg development;
- *slalom* – responsible for the dorsal pattern;
- *chitin synthase* – responsible for the larval cuticle.

It was found that there was a predictable change in gene expression during development, accurate to within 24 h of time age.

Methods for the calculation of *post-mortem* interval

Where there are known fluctuations of temperature, it is more accurate to use accumulated degree hours (ADH) or accumulated degree days (ADD) for the estimation of the *post-mortem* interval, rather than relying on the isomegalen diagrams (Fig. 35.3). This calculation is based on a linear relationship with temperature, providing it is above the base temperature for development and below that which is known to cause development to stop. Simply, it is based on adding together the minimum times required for each stage development identified to reach the 3rd instar, e.g. cumulative minimum time (hours) taken for egg stage + 1st instar + 2nd instar. This is multiplied by the measured ambient temperature to give the accumulated degree hours. To obtain the accumulated degree days, this figure is divided by 24. There are several more complex models to determine the ADD, each having been shown to be successful in the determination of the *post-mortem* interval (VanLaerhoven, 2008). You can then estimate how many days have elapsed, but this still needs caution as the calculation assumes a constant ambient temperature and does not take into account the temperature fluctuations that may have occurred during this time period.

Calculating the ADH – if under controlled conditions, the development rate at 23 °C is:

egg stage – 13.3 h

1st instar – 10.3 h

2nd instar – 24.6 h

Then the ADH can be calculated as $(13.3 + 10.3 + 24.6) \times 23 = 1,108.6$ h

Post-mortem submersion interval

There are data available for the estimation of the *post-mortem* interval from corpses found on land, but there are limited data available for the estimation of the *post-mortem* submersion interval. It is possible to use invertebrate succession in these cases as well as algal and diatom (Chapter 36) analysis (Zimmerman and Wallace, 2008). Wallace *et al.* (2008) have shown that the Order: Trichoptera, which includes the caddisflies (specifically the limnephilid family, where the life cycles are known), can be used successfully to estimate the *post-mortem* submersion interval.

Midge larvae (Diptera: Chironomidae) appeared to be the dominant species found on a pig carcass submerged in water. Keiper *et al.* (1997) noted that differences were observed, however, in the rate of colonisation between free flowing (13 days post submersion) and pooled water (20 days post submersion).

Definition

Post-mortem submersion interval – the time taken from when the body enters the water until the time of discovery.

Example Following the death of a female by drowning, a PMSI of 16–17 days was estimated by using the development rates of the aquatic midge (Medina et al., 2015).

Text references

Amendt, J., Campobasso, C.P., Gaudry, E., Reiter, C., LeBlanc, H.N. and Hall, M.J.R. (2007) Best practice in forensic entomology – standards and guidelines. *International Journal of Legal Medicine* **121**: 90–104.

Byrd, J.H. and Castner, J.L. (eds) (2009) *Forensic Entomology: The Utility of Arthropods in Legal Investigations,* 2nd edn. CRC Press, Boca Raton.

Carvalho, L. (2001) Determination of drug levels and the effect of diazepam on the growth of necrophagous flies of forensic importance in southeastern Brazil. *Forensic Science International* **120**(1): 140–144.

Clark, K., Evans, L. and Wall, R. (2006) Growth rates of the blowfly, *Lucilia sericata,* on different body tissues. *Forensic Science International* **156**: 145–149.

Donovan, S.E., Hall, M.J.R., Turner, B.D. and Moncrieff, C.B. (2006) Larval growth rates of the blowfly, *Calliphora vicina,* over a range of temperatures. *Medicine and Veterinary Entomology* **20**: 106–114.

Grassberger, M. and Reiter, C. (2001) Effect of temperature on Lucilia sericata (Diptera: Calliphoridae) development with special reference to the isomegalen and isomorphen diagram. *Forensic Science International* **120**: 32–36.

Haskell, N.H., Lord, W.D. and Byrd, J.H. (2001) Collection of Entomological Evidence during Death Investigations, Chapter 3 in *Forensic Entomology,* Byrd, J.H. and Castner, J.L. (eds), pp. 81–120. CRC Press, Boca Raton.

Ireland, S. and Turner, B. (2006) The effects of larval crowding and food type on the size and development of the blowfly, *Calliphora vomitoria. Forensic Science International* **159**: 175–181.

Jones, A.M., Reed, R.H. and Weyers, J.D.B. (2003) *Practical Skills in Biology,* 3rd edn. Pearson Education, Harlow.

Keiper, J.B., Chapman, E.G. and Foote, B.A. (1997) Midge larvae (*Diptera: Chironomidae*) as indicators of postmortem submersion interval of carcasses in a woodland stream: A preliminary report. *Journal of Forensic Sciences* **42**(6): 1074–1079.

Kharbouche, H., Augsburger, M., Cherix, D., Sporkert, F., Giroud, C., Wyss, C., Champod, C. and Mangin, P. (2008) Codeine accumulation and elimination in larvae, pupae, and imago of the blowfly Lucilia sericata and effects on its development. *International Journal of Legal Medicine* **122**(3): 205–211.

Medina, A.G., Hernando, O.S. and Rios, J.G. (2015) The Use of the developmental rate of the aquatic midge *Chironomus riparius* (Diptera, Chironomidae) in the Assessment of the Postsubmersion Interval. *Journal of Forensic Sciences* **60**(3): 822–826.

O'Brien, C. and Turner, B. (2004) Impact of paracetamol on Calliphora vicina larval development. *International Journal of Legal Medicine* **118**(4): 188–189.

Tarone, A.M., Jennings, K.C. and Foran, D.R. (2007) Aging blow fly eggs using gene expression: A feasibility study. *Journal of Forensic Sciences* **52**(6): 1350–1354.

VanLaerhoven, S.L. (2008) Blind validation of post-mortem interval estimates using developmental rates of blow flies. *Forensic Science International* **180**: 76–80.

Voss, S.C., Forbes, S.L. and Dadour, I.R. (2008) Decomposition and insect succession on cadavers inside a vehicle environment. *Forensic Science Medicine and Pathology* **4**: 22–32.

Wallace, J.R., Merritt, R.W., Kimbirauskas, R., Benbow, E. and McIntosh, M. (2008) Caddisflies assist with homicide case: Determining a post-mortem submersion interval using aquatic insects. *Journal of Forensic Sciences* **53**(1): 219–221.

Zimmerman and Wallace (2008) The potential to determine a post-mortem submersion interval based on an algal/diatom diversity on decomposing mammalian carcasses in brackish ponds in Delaware. *Journal of Forensic Sciences* **53**(4): 935–941.

Sources for further study

European Association of Forensic Entomology Available at: http://www.eafe.org/. Last accessed 21/08/2017.

Gennard, D.L. (2012) *Forensic Entomology: An Introduction,* 2nd ed. Wiley, Chichester.

Grassberger, M. and Reiter, C. (2002) Effect of temperature on development of the forensically important holarctic blow fly *Protophormia terranovae* (Robinson-Desvoidy)(Diptera: Calliphoridae). *Forensic Science International* **128**: 177–182.

Kulshrestha, P. and Satpathy, D.K. (2001) Use of beetles in forensic entomology. *Forensic Science International* **120**: 15–17.

Unwin, D.M. (1981) A key to the families of British Diptera. *Field Studies* **5**: 5135–5153.

Study exercises

35.1 Test your knowledge of the life cycle of *Calliphora vicina* . What are the stages and minimum development times for this species of insect?

35.2 Apply your knowledge. What methods can be used to estimate the *post-mortem* interval?

35.3 Perform a calculation of the *post-mortem* interval. Using the following information, calculate the ADH and ADD for a blow fly species to reach the 3rd instar:

Rearing temperature 21 °C
Minimum development egg stage = 15 h, 1st instar = 12.4 h, 2nd instar = 24.1 h, 3rd instar = 35.4 h.

36 Forensic botany

The forensic botanist as one of a team – *in practice, a plant scientist working in forensic science is usually part of a multidisciplinary approach to a problem. For example, a plant ecologist searching for a hidden grave might work in a team that could include experts using ground-penetrating radar together with search dogs and their handlers. The team might also rely on aerial photography and ultimately on molecular (e.g. DNA) or dental evidence to confirm identity.*

Forensic botany is an emerging specialism that involves the application of plant science to resolve legal questions. As such, it calls upon an extremely wide range of skills and techniques – from traditional, key-based plant identification to contemporary molecular biology. Valuable applications of forensic botany include:

- **suggesting a point of origin of a specimen** – for example, when linking an object or person to a scene of a crime, or supporting an alibi;
- **dating a specimen or estimating a time of death** – for example, in determining how long a body could have been buried;
- **providing evidence as to the nature and/or location of death** – for example, to demonstrate that a person is likely to have died by drowning.

To be useful in forensic science, a plant specimen should:

1. possess features that allow it to be identified to species level or below;
2. be specific to certain locations and/or times of year, either in isolation or in combination with other specimens;
3. persist well through time, being resistant to decomposition by natural and/or organic processes.

Microscopic samples, such as pollen, have the additional advantage that suspects cannot easily detect them or remove them from clothing and other sources of evidence.

 KEY POINT *Botanical evidence may be combined with information from forensic zoology and other sources to provide a more complete reconstruction of past events.*

Identification of plant specimens

Alternative expressions – *some authorities use the term 'systematics' to cover methods of biological identification within forensic science. This term refers to the study of classification and nomenclature, while the word 'taxonomy' usually refers to the system of classification. It is worth noting that classification systems can differ according to botanical authority.*

The correct identification of plant specimens is crucial to some forensic investigations. The specimens themselves can vary in scale from whole plants (either alive or dead and possibly dehydrated) through leaves, flowers, roots and stems, down to single cells such as fruit stone cells or fibres and including single-celled organisms (microalgae, diatoms) and even gametes (pollen) and subcellular parts (cell walls, starch grains). In the case of cannabis cultivation, the number of plants found can range from a few (amateur production) to hundreds grown under optimum conditions (professional production) to ensure a harvest throughout the year. When submitted to the laboratory, the plants should be intact and sampled such that they are representative of each stage of development found. At the molecular level, detection of toxins and drugs of botanical origin (Chapters 38 and 39) and DNA 'signatures' may also be important (see below).

Case example   Importance of correct botanical identification in narcotics investigations
This can be essential when investigating controlled substances obtained from plants, for example heroin (derived from *Papaver somniferum*, the opium poppy) and marijuana (derived from *Cannabis sativa*, hemp). In some states in the USA, possession of only certain species of *Cannabis* is illegal, so a conviction may depend on the exact identification of specimens (see Lane *et al.*, 1990 for further information).

Whatever the nature of the plant material, identification is often carried out with the aid of a key. This will contain a set of branching statements, often in a dichotomous series that asks you to choose at successive stages between two possibilities, each of which sets up yet more paired possibilities until you arrive at a tentative identification (see Box 36.1). Ideally, you should then compare your specimen with a detailed description based on a 'type' herbarium specimen. It is only if your specimen and the description match closely that you can be certain of your identification.

Box 36.1 An example of a botanical key and description

This is part of a key to a British species of the genus *Draba,* taken, with permission, from Stace (1997). The first section takes the form of an indented key where same-numbered choices are compared before either making a tentative identification or moving to another pair of choices within the key. Having made a tentative identification, the specimen is compared with the detailed description for the species – that for *D. aizoides* is given in the second section below. Clearly, use of this key requires a fair amount of terminology (available from a glossary) and in the flora a series of line diagrams is provided to illustrate the fruit, which is an important diagnostic feature in this instance.

```
21. DRABA L. - Whitlowgrasses
Annuals to perennials; hairs unbranched or branched, often stellate; leaves simple; pet-
als white or yellow; fruit a latiseptate silicula or sometimes short siliqua, ± not
inflated; seeds in 2 rows under each valve.

1   Petals yellow; style >1 mm in fruit; hairs all unbranched      1. D. aizoides

1   Petals white; style <1 mm in fruit; at least some hairs
    branched and stellate                                          2

    2 Annual; stem-leaves < 2x as long as wide, cordate and-       4. D. muralis
      clasping stem at base

    2 Perennial; at least some stem-leaves > 2x as long as wide
      or stem-leaves 0, tapered to rounded at base at & not
      clasping stem                                                3

3   Stems with 0-2(3) leaves, <8 cm; fruit 3-8 mm, not twisted     2. D. norvegica

3   Stems normally with >3 leaves, normally >10 cm; fruit 7-12 mm
    usually twisted

                                                                   3. D. incana
```

1. D. aizoides L. - <u>Yellow Whitlowgrass.</u> Tufted perennial with all leaves in basal rosettes; leaves linear, entire; stems to 15 cm, erect, few-flowered; petals yellow; fruit 5-10 mm, with style 1.2-3 mm. Probably native; limestone rocks and walls near sea; Gower peninsula, Glam (known since 1795); European mountains.

Table 36.1 The hierarchy of taxa as applied to botany, and specifically the English oak tree. Below the species level there are further sub divisions – subspecies, cultivars and forms which, if distinguishable, may add power to forensic investigations. The word taxon (plural taxa) describes a taxonomic assemblage of organisms sharing basic features

Taxon	Name
Kingdom	Plantae
Division	Anthophyta
Class	Dicotyledonae
Order	Fagales
Family	Fagaceae
Genus	*Quercus*
Species	*Q. robur*

The process of identification does not always require knowledge of the taxonomy of the group in question – although this often helps – but keys do generally assume quite a detailed knowledge of relevant anatomical and morphological terms. Fortunately, they usually contain helpful glossaries and the most user-friendly also include illustrations that help the diagnostic process. An experienced worker may be able to skip straight to the stage of comparison with a description if he/she recognises the main diagnostic features of the specimen. CD-ROM and Web-based keys have been developed and these can speed up the process of plant identification by proposing candidate species on the basis of surprisingly little information.

The norm in many botanical investigations is to identify the level of species (see Table 36.1). This usually requires detection of key diagnostic features at macroscopic level. If the specimen includes flowers, this is especially valuable – floral characteristics are important because they are usually conserved regardless of the environment in which a plant grows, whereas vegetative characteristics (e.g. leaf shape) can be more variable and therefore less reliable for diagnosis.

The chief molecular techniques used to identify plant specimens are the randomly amplified polymorphic DNA (RAPD) and the amplified fragment length

Case example   DNA typing in botanical identification

A murder suspect denied having been near to the site where the victim's body was found. Seed pods identified as those of the tree *Parkinsonia microphylla* (palo verde) were found in the back of the suspect's truck – these trees grew close to the site of the murder, but also in many other places in the neighbourhood. DNA typing through RAPD analysis revealed high genetic variability among various trees sampled from a range of locations. It could be stated from the genetic 'fingerprints' obtained that there was a very high probability that the seeds in the truck were from the trees at the murder site. This indicated that the suspect's truck had been at the site, linking him to the murder. See Yoon (2013) for further details.

polymorphism (AFLP) methods. Both techniques are based on the polymerase chain reaction (PCR, p. 114) – however, in RAPD numerous short (10 base pairs) primers are used to amplify the genome in various random locations to produce a unique 'genetic fingerprint' of the sample. AFLP is more sensitive and more reproducible than RAPD.

Analysis of pollen and aquatic microorganisms

Palynology

Pollen analysis, or palynology, is well established in plant ecology as a means of tracking temporal changes in plant composition and climate through tens or thousands of years. Applied to forensic science, it is especially useful for providing evidence of location or of linkage between locations – each site possesses a characteristic pollen 'signature' based on the local flora, their pollen-releasing activity and the characteristics of the various pollen types. There are many potential sources of pollen evidence. Typical items or places where useful samples could be obtained include dirt, mud or dust; hair or fur; fabric; packing materials; the nasal cavity or stomach of human remains; air filters; and bank notes.

Microscopic pollen grains are produced by male flowers of 'higher' plants (gymnosperms and angiosperms) and carry the male gamete to the female parts, where fertilisation may take place after growth of a pollen tube to an ovule. Transfer of pollen between male and female parts is brought about by several mechanisms – for example wind, animal, e.g. bees, butterflies, rodents or self-pollination (not many pollen grains are produced due to the short distances that they have to travel, but finding them can indicate that the parent plant is in close proximity). The size and characteristics of the grains of each species are determined by both the physics and physiology of the mechanism, as well as the taxonomy of the species (for examples, see Fig. 36.1).

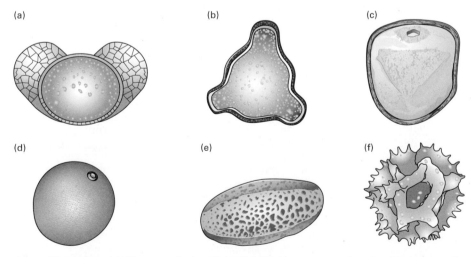

Fig. 36.1   Representative pollen grains: (a) *Pinus,* a wind-pollinated gymnosperm tree showing air sacs to allow transportation over large distances; (b) *Epilobium,* an insect-pollinated angiosperm herb; (c) *Carex,* a wind-pollinated sedge; (d) *Bromus,* a self-pollinated angiosperm grass; (e) *Salix,* a wind-pollinated angiosperm tree; and (f) *Taraxacum,* a self-cloning (apomictic) angiosperm herb, probably insect-pollinated in the past. (Diagram after Scagel *et al.* (1984). Parts (b)–(f) Copyright © 1984. Reprinted with permission of Brooks/Cole, a division of Thomson Learning: www.thomson rights.com. Fax 800 730-2215. Part (a) Copyright © Schweizerbart-Publishers. www.schweizerbart.de.) Note that the grains are not drawn to the same scale, but range between 25 and 125 μm in diameter.

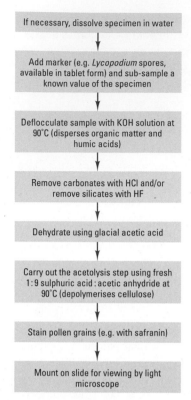

Fig. 36.2 Flowchart for preparation of a pollen sample. Washing, filtering and centrifugation steps are frequent, but are not included here. Due to safety considerations, it is unlikely that undergraduates would be allowed to prepare specimens, so this may be done for you.

Example descriptions of common pollen types (see Fig. 36.1):
Pine – Pinus sylvestris, 75 μm, two sacs with no apertures.
Willow – Salix caprea, 22 μm, oval with long colpi, reticulate sculpture.
Dandelion – Taraxacum vulgare, 35 μm, round, echinate edges.

The value of pollen in forensic science is due to its extremely resilient coat, which is made from a substance known as sporopollenin. This outer coat (exine) is resistant to mechanical, biological and chemical degradation. This cannot be broken down by microbes and, indeed, is resistant to attack by the strongest of acids. This last fact allows pollen samples to be separated from other specimens by digesting all other organic materials present (Fig. 36.2).

> **KEY POINT** *The acids used in producing a pollen sample are extremely dangerous and appropriate safety procedures must be used.*

Surface features (sculpturing) of the pollen coat can be used diagnostically, as can number, shape, size and possession of apertures (pores can be single or multiple), furrows (colpi), pores and bladders or whether the grains are single or attached together (e.g. in 'tetrads' of four grains). The shape can be spherical, triangular or multi-type, with different sculpturing patterns on the surface including:

- **reticulate** – characterised by spots on the surface;
- **scabrate** – characterised by elongated dots on the surface;
- **rugliate** – characterised by the appearance of wavy lines on the surface;
- **psilate** – characterised by a smooth surface;
- **echinate** – characterised by spikes on the surface.

The wall thickness can also be determined when viewed under low-power microscopy (p. 65) or scanning electron microscopy (p. 66). Wind-pollinated forms tend to be typically 20–60 μm, although variation is known to occur across the range 7–200 μm. Typically they will disperse up to 100 m from their origin; however, if the wind conditions are favourable they can be dispersed to distances up to 2 km.

These differences allow a trained palynologist to identify the species involved using a key, ideally photographic rather than an illustration. For more information on pollen identification, refer to Institute of Botany, University of Vienna palynology database, available at: http:www.paldat.org/. If reasonable numbers of the different types of pollen present in a sample are counted, then inferences can be made about the geographical and ecological origin of the specimen. However, when arriving at conclusions, several factors must be taken into account:

- Some species, especially those that are wind pollinated, produce vastly more pollen than others.
- Depending on the mass, size and shape of the grains, pollen may travel different distances from its point of origin.
- Different types of pollen may decompose at different rates.

Due to the resilient coat, pollen persists for many years after dispersal; therefore when it is collected there is the possibility that it originated from the current season or from previous years. There is also the possibility that it will have been transferred from subject to soil and *vice versa*.

Sample collection
As with all types of evidence, a reference control sample should be obtained as early as possible to prevent transfer of further evidential, or erroneous, material. Small 'pinch' samples should be taken of the surface soil and stored in clean, sterile airtight containers. Where vegetation is sampled, this should be dried as soon as possible.

Studies of plankton

Similar principles to those discussed for pollen also apply to evidence from phytoplankton and microalgae, which may be characteristic of a type of body of water or a specific aquatic location, and which, even when dead, leave cell walls with characteristic shapes and patterned silica deposits (for examples, see Fig. 36.3).

An important forensic use of plankton samples is in the diagnosis of death by drowning, which can otherwise be especially difficult for decomposed human remains where other physiological indicators of drowning may be absent. The method relies on the fact that when water is taken into the lungs, the planktonic diatoms are also taken in. There is a suggestion that diatoms can enter the systemic circulation via the lung, but also by other means of transportation throughout the body, especially from foodstuffs, e.g. prawns, where it has been estimated that over 8,000 diatoms (centric, oval pennate, pennate and naviculoid types) per 50 g has been found (Yen and Jayaprakash, 2007). This should therefore be taken into consideration when considering whether death

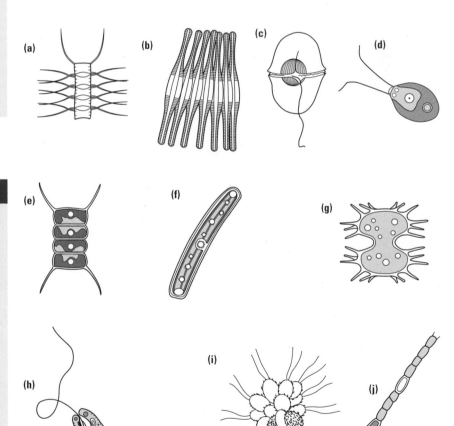

Fig. 36.3 Representative diatom and phytoplankton types (a) *Chaetoceros* and (b) *Fragilaria* (Bacillariophyta); (c) *Gymnodinium* (Pyrrophycophyta); (d) *Chlamydo monas*; (e) *Scenedesmus*; (f) *Roya* and (g) *Xanthidium* (Chlorophyta); (h) *Euglena* (Euglenophycota); (i) *Hymenomonas* (Chrysophyta); and (j) *Anabena* (Cyanophyta). (Diagram after Boney, 1989). Note that the organisms are not drawn to the same scale, but range between 25 and 250 μm in diameter/length.

Case example   Use of evidence from pollen analysis

After a plane crash in New Mexico, a lawsuit was brought against the plane's manufacturers, claiming that an in-flight blockage in the fuel line might have caused engine power loss and loss of control by the pilot. The wreckage was stored in an open-air yard, pending an investigation into the incident. On detailed examination of the plane's components, a mass of organic material was found to be blocking a part of the fuel line. Forensic examination revealed (a) that the mass consisted of pollen and plant material; (b) that grains present came from insect-pollinated plant species growing near to the storage yard; and (c) that the pollen was still viable. Since the pollen could not have survived the fire that followed the accident, and because of the species make-up of the pollen mass and associated debris, it was concluded that the blockage had been created after the accident and could not have been its cause. See Yoon (2013) for further details.

Definition

Plankton – tiny plants, animals or bacteria that live in open water. Plankton have limited or no motility and are generally transported through the water by currents and tides. There are three major plankton groups: **phytoplankton** – microscopic plants and bacteria; **zooplankton** – microscopic animals; and **macro-zooplankton** – larger fish eggs or larvae and invertebrates. Among the phytoplankton are included:

- diatoms (phylum Bacillariophyta);
- golden-brown algae (Chrysophyta);
- green algae (Chlorophyta);
- blue-green algae (Cyanophyta, or Cyanobactena);
- dinoflagellates (Pyrrophycophyta);
- cryptomonads (Cryptophyta);
- microflagellates (Prasinophyta, Euglenophycota, Protozoa).

was due to drowning. Later, they may become associated with other bodily organs as decay occurs. For example, one criterion for a diagnosis of drowning is 20 diatoms per 100 μL of pellet taken from a 10 g lung sample – or five diatoms from other organs (Ludes *et al.*, 1996), e.g. bone marrow. By standardising a microalgae test (to include diatoms as well as other microalgae, e.g. dinoflagellates and chlorophytes), it has been suggested that it can be used as an adjunct to other biochemical tests, e.g. strontium, for the diagnosis of drowning (Díaz-Palma *et al.*, 2009). Extraction methods include acid digestion (which may destroy other useful organisms such as zooplankton) and, more recently, ultrasonic digestion and specialised techniques normally used for DNA extraction. A digestion technique is needed to remove the organic matter to allow the diatoms to be visualised and identified. An effective digestion method appears to be enzyme digestion, using proteinase K (Ming *et al.*, 2007), but it has also been shown that proteinase K in combination with chemical digestion (trishydrochloric acid with sodium dodecyl sulphate) improves the efficiency of digestion, allowing a more effective identification of diatom and microalgae species (Díaz-Palma *et al.*, 2009).

Plankton sampling can also help to identify the site of drowning, if the relative abundance and species diversity of the lung or other sample matches the flora found at a suspected aquatic location. In some cases, the relative abundance of species present can even help to specify a date in the year when the drowning occurred, owing to the sequential nature of blooms of algae and other species through the seasons.

> **Case example   Exploiting characteristic plankton samples**
> The phytoplankton and larger algae present in flowing rivers are different from those found near static bodies of water such as lakes. Identification of characteristic species in mud recovered from footwear has been used to link victims and suspects to a common crime scene. See Yoon (2013) for further details.

Bryophytes

Bryophytes (Plantae; bryophytae) are ground-growing mosses typically 1–10 cm tall. Virtanen *et al.* (2007) have shown that bryophyte fragments transfer to footwear when walked across and appear to persist on the footwear for an extended period of time (in excess of 24 h). DNA can also be extracted successfully from the plant material, making this species a potentially useful botanical marker.

> **Common bryophyte species found in the UK include:**
>
> | Species | Common name | Height | Characteristic | Location |
> |---|---|---|---|---|
> | Brachythecium albicans | Whitish feather moss | 2–5 cm | Long slender branches | Sandy soil/sand dunes |
> | Bryum rubens | Crimson tuber thread moss | 1 cm | Leaves tinged red | Bare soil including gardens/roadside |

Algal colonisation

Another method of estimating the *post-mortem* submersion interval (see also p. 343), applicable to cases where a body has lain under water, is to study colonisation of the remains by micro- and macroalgae. The diversity of species found in such situations increases through time and after several weeks might approach some 50 different types. Some species are known to be 'late colonisers' and can support the evidence from studies of diversity. Such studies would be likely to be allied to examination of insect larvae, as covered in Chapter 35. Algae will need to be kept wet and not allowed to dry out. It can be packaged in a polythene bag but should not be stored for longer than 24 h in this condition.

Techniques for dating specimens using plant material

Several methods of dating events rely on the recovery and analysis of organic plant material. Carbon dating involves determining the ratio of carbon isotopes (^{14}C to ^{12}C) in an organic specimen but will not be discussed in detail here because the timescales it applies to (hundreds or thousands of years) are generally longer than those involved in crime investigations.

> **Identifying the source of wood samples –** *to a trained eye, the nature of the cells and tissues present in woody specimens can be used to identify the source species. Particularly important features are the size and shape of xylem and fibres cells in transverse section; the presence or absence of differences in the diameters of the cells; and the nature of 'rays' arising from cells aligned radially from the centre to the outside of the stem, branch or trunk.*

Box 36.2 Principles of dendrochronology

The following are the key assumptions made when dating specimens through analysis of tree-ring width:

- **Tree-ring growth can be described by a mathematical model** that represents relative growth as an aggregate of five factors: (i) the trend in growth due to tree age; (ii) the weather during the year in question; (iii) disturbance factors internal to the forest stand (e.g. fall of a neighbouring tree due to wind); (iv) disturbance factors external to the forest stand (e.g. infestation by an insect pest); and (v) random error. This assumption allows different samples to be compared on the same 'scale'.

- **The physical and biological processes affecting relative tree-ring width** today also operated in the past. This assumption means that no unexpected causes of variation are expected to interfere with the conclusions.

- **Cross-dating of relative tree-ring width series** from different samples is valid for exact year dating. This assumption allows a sample to be dated against a reference sample or database.

- **The greater the number of subsamples and replicates that are available,** the less the interference from statistical 'noise'. This assumption indicates that there will be greater confidence in a conclusion when replicate specimens are available.

Note that the amplitude of differences in tree growth rates can vary among specimens and is generally higher under growth-limiting conditions or at the extremes of a species' natural ecological range.

Dendrochronology

A more frequently used technique for dating is that of dendrochronology, or the study of tree 'rings' – the cylinders of secondary growth that occur on an annual basis in long-lived perennial plants as their stems thicken, and which appear as concentric rings in transverse section (Fig. 36.4). The ring patterning is due to differences in the wood produced early and late in the season – the former appears light in colour as it has larger cells with relatively thin cell walls, while the latter is darker due to the predominance of smaller cells with thicker walls (see inset in Fig. 36.4). The result is a distinct banding effect that allows each year's growth to be measured. Dendrochronology relies on the fact that the extent of growth, and hence ring width, can be related to weather conditions in different years (see Box 36.2).

It is possible to match the 'standardised' width of tree rings or sequences of relative widths to those from other samples (known as cross-dating). An unknown sample can be dated by reference to this standard, according to the sequence of relatively strong and weak growth years that it exhibits. This often requires computer-based statistical and database analysis.

The simple counting of numbers of annual rings can also be useful in dating, especially when 'year zero' can be identified. An example might be where the root of a perennial species has grown within a buried body. So long as it can be established that penetrative growth has occurred since burial, then the highest number of annual rings found on specimens sets an upper limit on the date of burial. It is also possible to make inferences from the recovery growth made by roots damaged by spades, etc., during burial.

Applications of plant ecology

Plant ecology is a broad subject that encompasses a wide range of methods. A tentative description of a source ecosystem can be derived from various botanical sources (e.g. pieces of plants or plant propagules found on clothing) and linked to a likely or known habitat within a search area. If several species can

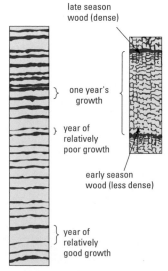

late season
wood (dense)

} one year's growth

} year of relatively poor growth

early season
wood (less dense)

} year of relatively good growth

Fig. 36.4 Transverse section through a wood sample, showing various features of tree rings.

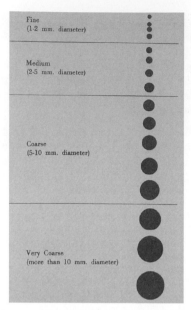

Photo 36.1 Munsells soil colour chart illustrating the varying particle sizes of soil. (Image courtesy of X-rite.)

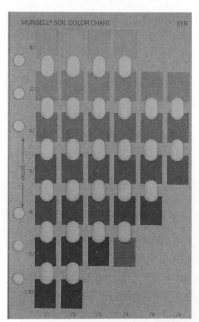

Photo 36.2 Munsells soil colour chart illustrating the various hues of soil. (Image courtesy of X-rite.)

be obtained, their known or likely habitat preferences might indicate, for example, that the sample came from a site at the margin of a lake. Plant samples might also indicate a time of year through the flowering or seeding time of specimens obtained. The plant identification techniques and skills noted above (pp. 345–347) are likely to be required when reconstructing a habitat, and evidence may be extremely limited or have come from several sources, such as fragments of plants combined with samples of pollen.

A specific area where plant ecology has been demonstrated to be important is in the identification of hidden graves. Where disturbance of the ground has taken place, a succession of plant species will then colonise any bare soil. The early colonisers are likely to be annual species, especially those with airborne seeds and fruits, while longer-lived perennials and plants reproducing vegetatively will take longer to establish. The pattern of succession is predictable, depending on geographical location, and a trained ecologist can recognise such areas against a background of mature ecosystem, even after 20 years have elapsed, and thereby identify potential sites for further investigation.

Typically, soil consists of a mineral content (sand, silt, clay) and an organic content (vegetation/animal in various states of decomposition – humus and microorganisms). While an exact area cannot be pinpointed, examination of soil can give an indication of the similarities of two samples in respect of the elemental, mineralogical, vegetative (e.g. pollen) composition. Soil appears in a layered format, which can be used to identify soil movement in, for example, a burial site. These layers consist of:

Depth Layer of soil

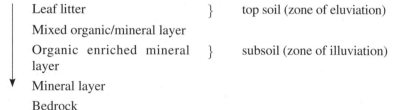

When examining soil there are a number of parameters that can be used for identification purposes. These include:

- **Particle size** – measured on a scale from fine to very coarse (Photo 36.1).
- **Texture** – whether the texture is clay based, loam or sand. The surface texture can be examined by the use of a scanning electron microscope (p. 66).
- **Colour** – a visual comparison with reference to Munsells® colour charts (Photo 36.2). These colour charts are based on three colour parameters:
  - hue – the dominant colour, e.g. red, yellow, green, blue or purple, and abbreviated to the first letter, so for yellow red colour the designation would be YR;
  - value – the lightness of the colour measured on a scale of 0 (black) to 10 (white);
  - chroma – the intensity or strength of the colour, measured on a scale of 0 (neutral) to 20 (intense colouration).
- **Determination of the inorganic composition** – by, for example, XRF (p. 174) or ICP–MS (p. 168), but this is likely to vary significantly with particle size (Pye *et al.*, 2007).

- **Determination of the organic content** – for example by pyrolysis GC–MS (Chapter 14) or for the detection and identification of pollen (p. 347).

The process of soil examination for the organic and inorganic content will often involve soil digestion. For example, Brown (2006) used the following techniques for the removal of:

- carbonates – digestion in weak hydrochloric acid;
- silicates – digestion by hydrofluoric acid;
- organic content – an acetylating mixture of sulphuric acid and acetic anhydride.

By using these techniques Brown (2006) was able to show similarities between primary and secondary burial sites in Bosnia.

Examination of the soil for volatile organic compounds (VOCs) can also assist in the location of clandestine burial sites, as these compounds are released into the soil from decomposing bodies. Hoffman *et al.* (2009) have characterised the VOCs and found that there is a similar profile across different tissues that could be used to aid in the detection of a burial site. The effects on the biochemistry of the soil have also been studied using an animal model and it has been shown that pH increases at the burial site, along with prolonged elevation of nitrogen and phosphorus levels (Benninger *et al.*, 2008).

Example   Dendrochronology in action
A dispute about the provenance of two antique violins was solved by analysis of the tree rings in their wooden sounding boards. These were non-destructively examined using X-rays and the relative ring widths compared with standards for the region in which Stradivari, the purported maker, had lived. It was concluded from this dendrochronological analysis that the parts could not have been made before 1910. Since Stradivari died in 1737, it was concluded that the instruments were fakes. See Yoon (2013) for further details.

Recent developments – it has been proposed that the use of microbial ecogenomics can assist in the investigation of clandestine graves (Ralebitso-Senior et al., 2016).

Text references

Benninger, L.A., Carter, D.O. and Forbes, S.L. (2008) The biochemical alteration of soil beneath a decomposing carcass. *Forensic Science International* **180**: 70–75.

Boney, D.A. (1989) *Phytoplankton,* 2nd edn. Cambridge University Press, Cambridge.

Brown, A.G. (2006) The use of forensic botany and geology in war crimes investigations in NE Bosnia. *Forensic Science International* **163**: 204–210.

Díaz-Palma, P.A., Alucema, A., Hayashida, G. and Maidana, N.I. (2009) Development and standardization of a microalgae test for determining deaths by drowning. *Forensic Science International* **184**: 37–41.

Hoffman, E.M., Curran, A.M., Dulgerian, N., Stockham, R.A. and Eckenrode, B.A. (2009) Characterization of the volatile organic compounds present in the headspace of decomposing human remains. *Forensic Science International* **186**: 6–13.

Lane, M.A., Anderson, L.C., Barkley, T.M., Bock, J.H., Gifford, E.M., Hall, D.W., Norris, D.O., Rost, T.L. and Stern, W.L. (1990) Forensic botany: Plants, perpetrators, pests, poisons and pot. *Bioscience* **40**: 34–39.

Ludes, B., Coste, M., Tracqui, A. and Mangin, P. (1996) Continuous river monitoring of the diatoms in the diagnosis of drowning. *Journal of Forensic Sciences* **41**: 425–428.

Ming, M., Meng, X. and Wang, E. (2007) Evaluation of four digestive methods for extracting diatoms. *Forensic Science International* **170**: 29–34.

Munsells Soil Colour Charts (2000). Gretag Macbeth, New York.

Palynological database Available at: http:www.paldat.org/. Last accessed 22/08/2017.

Pye, K., Blott, S.J., Croft, D.J. and Witton, S.J. (2007) Discrimination between sediment and soil samples for forensic purposes using elemental data: An investigation of particle size effects. *Forensic Science International* **167**: 30–42.

Ralebitso-Senior, T.K., Thompson, T.J.U. and Carney, H.E. (2016) Microbial ecogenomics and forensic archaeology: New methods for investigating clandestine graves. *Human Remains and Violence* **2** (1): 41–57.

Scagel, R.F., Bandoni, R.J., Maze, J.R., Rouse, G.E., Schofield, W.B. and Stein, J.R. (1984) *Plants: An Evolutionary Survey.* Wadsworth, Inc., Belmont.

Stace, C.A. (1997) *New Flora of the British Isles,* 2nd edn. Cambridge University Press, Cambridge.

Virtanen, V., Korpelainen, H. and Kostamo, K. (2007) Forensic botany: Usability of bryophyte material in forensic studies. *Forensic Science International* **172**: 161–163.

Yen, L.Y. and Jayaprakash, P.T. (2007) Prevalence of diatom frustules in non-vegetarian foodstuffs and its implications in interpreting identification of diatom frustules in drowning cases. *Forensic Science International* **170**: 1–7.

Yoon CK (1993) Forensic Science: Botanical witness for the prosecution. *Science* **260**(5110): 894–895.

Sources for further study

Bock, J.H. and Norris, D.O. (1997) Forensic botany: An under-utilized resource. *Journal of Forensic Science* **42**: 364–367.

Bock, J.H. and Norris, D. (2016) *Forensic Plant Science.* Academic Press, Elsevier, London.

British Bryological Society Available at: http:www.britishbryo-logicalsociety.org.uk/. Last accessed 22/08/2017.

Coyle, H.M. (2004) *Forensic Botany: Principles and Applications to Criminal Casework.* CRC Press, Boca Raton.

Faegri, K., Kaland, P.E. and Krzywinski, K. (eds) (1992) *Textbook of Pollen Analysis.* Wiley, New York.

Grissino-Mayer, H.D. *Ultimate Tree-Ring Web Pages.* Available at: http:web.utk.edu/ăgrissino/. Last accessed 22/08/2017.

Study exercises

36.1 Test your knowledge. What are the principles of dendrochronology?

36.2 Test your knowledge of soil examination. If a sample of soil was submitted for examination, what tests could you perform in the laboratory?

36.3 Find more information. Using appropriate sources, find a different example from that given in this chapter of the following species of plant, and list the key characteristics of each that could be used to identify the plant:

(a) bryophyte;
(b) diatom;
(c) pollen.

Forensic chemistry

Examples   Typical alcohol content in beverages
Beer 3–5% v/v
Wine 10–13% v/v
Spirits 35–45% v/v

Volume to volume (v/v) is the term used to indicate the alcohol content expressed as a percentage. For example, to prepare 1000 mL of a 40% v/v solution of ethanol, pipette 40 mL of ethanol into a 1000 mL volumetric flask (p. 37) and dilute to the mark with water.

Example   Spirits formed from distillation of natural fermentation products

Spirit	Fermentation source
Brandy	Grape
Gin	Maize/rye
Whisky	Malted barley
Vodka	Grain

Prosecution in the UK – this is controlled by Sections 12–16 of the **Criminal Justice and Police Act 2001**, which prohibits the drinking of alcohol in public places. Any person suspected of drinking alcohol would have their drink seized and sent to the forensic laboratory for examination. If the alcohol content is greater than 0.5% v/v, then it is classed as alcoholic liquor and the person would be prosecuted.

Driving under the influence (UK legislation) – drivers believed to be under the influence of alcohol will be charged under terms of Section5 of the **Road Traffic Offenders Act 1988**. The analysis of the sample submitted to the forensic laboratory is restricted to alcohol only. If no alcohol is found then no further analysis, e.g. for drugs, can legally be performed. If drugs were suspected to have caused impairment, then the person would be charged under Section 4 of the **Road Traffic Offenders Act 1988**. In this instance alcohol analysis would still be performed and if the person was found to be over the legal limit for driving then no further analysis would be carried out irrespective of whether drugs were also involved. If no alcohol was found, then a drug screen (Chapter 38) would be performed.

Alcohol (ethanol, ethyl alcohol) is a social drug in beverages such as beer, wine and spirits and is one of the most common drugs encountered in forensic science. The forensic scientist is often required to measure alcohol concentrations, whether in an alcoholic drink (e.g. where its alcohol content needs to be quantified) or in a biological fluid (e.g. in blood from a person charged with being under the influence of alcohol). It is also sometimes necessary to estimate a person's blood alcohol concentration at a certain point in time, based on such values.

 KEY POINT   In court, questions often asked of the forensic scientist are whether an individual was under the influence of alcohol at the time of an incident, and whether such a concentration might explain the behaviour of that person.

Alcoholic beverages are produced in a fermentation process, the specifics of which determine the type of alcoholic drink produced. For example, the fermentation of malted barley, water and hops results in the production of beer, whereas the fermentation of apple juice results in cider, and the fermentation of the sugars in grapes results in wine. Spirits, on the other hand, are distilled products from the natural fermentation process and as such have a higher alcohol content, usually in the region of 35–45%. The illicit production of spirits is often observed and, unlike the commercial products that are governed by the Food and Drugs Act 1955, the alcohol content is highly variable. Likewise, the alcohol present can be a mixture of both ethyl alcohol and methyl alcohol (methanol), the latter causing serious toxicity when ingested.

Types of forensic case involving alcohol

Liquor licensing

All commercial sources of alcohol (off-licence shops, pubs, hotels, etc.) by law are required to inform the customer of the amount of alcohol in the liquor. This is specified in notices and on the labels of bottles and canned drinks. The forensic scientist may be asked to determine whether a liquid contains alcohol or whether the percentage of alcohol matches that claimed.

Drinking in public areas

An analyst might be asked to examine seized bottles, cans, etc. to analyse their contents for alcohol. This is also the case where underage drinking is suspected, with a view to prosecuting the supplier of the alcohol. Any drink suspected of containing alcohol would be seized, collected in a flame tin and submitted to the laboratory for examination.

Being under the influence of alcohol (driving and behavioural changes)

This is one of the most important analyses that the forensic scientist is asked to perform, to determine whether someone was under the influence of alcohol at the time he/she was stopped from driving or at the time of an incident or accident. The legal limit for driving has been set according to the known effects of alcohol at a given concentration, but differs between countries – values for the UK (note the differences) are given in Table. 37.1.

Alcohol analysis

Table 37.1 Legal limits for alcohol for driving in the UK

Sample	Legal limit (England, Wales and Northern Ireland)	Legal limit (Scotland as of 2014)
Breath	35 µg per 100 mL	22 µg per 100 mL
Blood	80 mg per 100 mL	50 mg per 100 mL
Urine	107 mg per 100 mL	67 mg per 100 mL

Alcohol is always reported as 'not less than xx mg per 100 mL' in the UK and unless otherwise specified refers to ethanol.

Impairment tests – these are (1) pupil examination; (2) a walk and turn test; (3) one-leg stand; (4) 30-s (modified Romberg) test; (5) finger-to-nose test. The overall impression/demeanour of the driver will be documented.

Biological samples – blood, urine and vitreous humour should be collected and preserved in a sample tube containing sodium oxalate and potassium fluoride.

Two samples should be obtained; one for analysis in the forensic laboratory, the other for defence analysis should it be required by the defendant.

Roadside breath tests for alcohol – these used to be carried out using an instrument such as the Lion Alcolmeter®. There were three possible readings from such a test:

1. *Green light indicates no alcohol present.*
2. *Orange light indicates alcohol. The person would be conveyed to a police station to either provide a further breath test using, for example, Lion Intoximeter®, or a blood/urine sample for alcohol analysis in the laboratory.*
3. *Red light indicates alcohol present that exceeds the legal limit. The person would be charged with drink driving.*

These hand-held devices have been replaced by digital devices such as the Drager 6510 that have received type approval where the result is displaced in mg 100 mL^{-1} rather than the 'traffic light' system of its predecessors. The accuracy of these devices is recorded as +−0.008 mg L^{-1}.

The typical steps in the process of a Section 5 offence include:

- **Erratic driving** – recognition of poor driving ability, e.g. swerving on road, driving extremely slowly, mounting pavement, etc.
- **Police stop vehicle** – the police have the power to stop a vehicle where there is a suspicion of the driver driving under the influence (DUI).
- **Recognition of impairment** – only a police officer who has been approved to carry out impairment tests under Section 6B (6) Road Traffic Act 1988 can administer impairment tests. Currently there are five impairment tests (pupil examination and four psychomotor tests) that can be used to indicate whether a person is impaired.
- **Roadside breath test** – a roadside breath test can be carried out (see p. 359).
- **Arrest and transfer to police station** – if a positive result is obtained from the breath test the person is arrested and conveyed to the police station.
- **Evidential breath test** – a commercial breath-alcohol measurement system is used (see p. 359) to record an accurate breath-alcohol concentration.
- **Blood or urine sample obtained** – if the evidential breath test fails (see p. 359) or falls between 35 and 45 µg alcohol per 100 mL then a forensic medical examiner is called and a blood sample obtained for alcohol analysis in the laboratory. The blood sample is divided into two parts – one is sent to the forensic laboratory and the other is given to the defendant as a 'defence' sample should they wish to have it tested independently.
- **Prosecution** – if the results are above the legal limit for drink driving then the individual is prosecuted.

Note that for a Section 4 offence a similar process is adopted but alcohol and/or drugs are examined for in the blood or urine sample (see Chapter 38).

Samples and sampling

Four main types of biological sample are presented for alcohol analysis depending on the case:

1. **Breath** – for example, taken in relation to driving under the influence of alcohol.
2. **Blood** – for example, taken in relation to driving under the influence of alcohol, or *post mortem* to determine whether the death was alcohol related, such as acute alcohol poisoning or the pathological changes associated with chronic alcohol abuse. A clinical blood sample may also be taken to determine whether the amount of alcohol present could account for someone's behaviour, or whether that person would be fully aware of his/her actions.
3. **Urine** – for example, taken in relation to driving under the influence of alcohol where a blood sample is refused, or taken *post mortem*.
4. **Vitreous humour** – the fluid from the eyeball is only taken *post mortem* and is most useful when *post-mortem* blood is either not available or is unsuitable for analysis.

Alcohol is both a volatile and an oxidisable compound and correct storage conditions are required to minimise the loss of alcohol and the preservation of the evidence. Any biological material should be stored at 4 °C prior to analysis and thereafter stored at −20 °C. This is necessary in case the sample needs to be re-examined at a later date and thus ensures minimum loss of the volatile component.

The process for Type Approval involves the devices being tested by two or more police forces, allocated by ACPO Road Policing on behalf of the Public Order Unit. The device is also tested by an accredited laboratory and further

Type Approval – any device that is used at the roadside in the UK has to have type approval authorisation granted by the Secretary of State. Guidance on the procedure and technical specifications for type approval was published in 2013. (Home Office, 2014.)

tested by a Home Office accredited (UKAS) (p. 474) facility. On successful completion of these tests a type approval certificate is granted.

Any suspect liquid would be collected in a flame tin, essentially a metal tin sealed with two caps, an inner airtight seal and an outer screw-top cap. These seals prevent any evaporation of the volatile components, including alcohol. The tin is placed into a polythene bag and sealed with tamper-proof tape, and a label detailing what the sample is and where it was taken from (see p. 247), is attached to the tin for submission to the forensic laboratory.

Methods of analysis

There are several ways to analyse alcohol. However, the following three are common in forensic analysis:

1. **Roadside breath test** – a hand-held breathalyser used as soon as a person has been stopped by a police officer. A recent study assessing the accuracy and reliability of these hand-held alcohol detectors has determined that they are accurate when compared with the confirmatory test (Zuba, 2008) and as such are of an appropriate standard to be presented evidentially.
2. **Calibrated breathalyser** – a commercial instrument such as the Lion Intoxilyser (Photo 37.1). The instrument is calibrated to 35 µg alcohol per 100 mL with certified reference material and the subject is required to blow into the instrument. The alcohol concentration in the breath is calculated and, in the UK, if it is more than 45 µg alcohol per 100 mL the person is automatically prosecuted. Between 35 and 45 µg alcohol per 100 mL, a blood or urine sample is normally required to confirm the alcohol concentration.
3. **Gas chromatography** – headspace analysis (p. 80, Chapter 14) in which a blood or urine sample is taken from a person by a police surgeon, more commonly known as a forensic medical examiner, and submitted to the laboratory for alcohol analysis.

To convert the breath alcohol concentration to blood alcohol concentration a ratio of 1:2,300 can be applied for conversions in the UK or 1:2,100 in the USA and many European countries, according to differences in their legal limits for driving (Jones and Andersson, 1996).

Alcohol analysis for all other samples can be analysed using headspace gas chromatography (GC) with a flame ionisation detector (see Chapter 14). This allows detection of ethanol, as well as other similar volatile compounds, such

Photo 37.1 A typical commercial breath alcohol measurement system. The model illustrated is a Lion Intoxilyzer model 6000. Image from Lion-Breath.

Definition

Henry's Law – the concentration of a volatile substance in solution is directly proportional to its concentration in the atmosphere above the solution when in a sealed system at a given temperature.

Fig. 37.1 A typical time course profile in blood following ingestion of alcohol. Note the linear elimination rate which for the average individual is assumed to be 18 mg per 100 mL per hr^{-1}. Further information on how this can be used to estimate the blood alcohol at a given point in time is given in Box 37.2, p. 361.

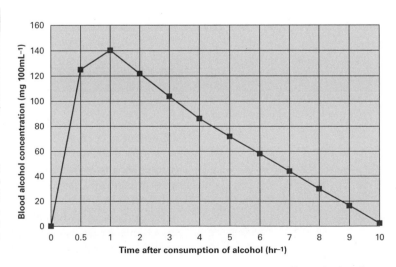

Alcohol analysis

as methanol (often found in illicitly produced liquor) and acetone (often found when investigating deaths associated with chronic alcoholism).

The principle of headspace sampling is based on Henry's Law. When a liquid sample is placed into a sealed headspace vial and heated, the alcohol within the liquid is distributed equally between the liquid and the atmosphere above it. The injector takes a sample of this atmosphere (the headspace) and injects this into the gas chromatograph. This method is used for:

- **the analysis of blood or urine samples** submitted from subjects suspected of drinking and driving;
- **biological samples** (blood, plasma, serum, vitreous humour) in both criminal and *post-mortem* cases;
- **samples of alcoholic beverages.**

Two independent megabore columns, e.g. RTX-1 BAC1 and BAC2, are used in the GC system, so for a single injection the sample is split between the two columns which, on detection by the FID, give two sets of results. These results should be in agreement with each other – if they are not the analysis must be repeated. All samples are also analysed in duplicate. As with all forensic toxicology analyses, the purpose of the examination is to accurately determine the concentration of a drug, especially for:

- **drink driving cases** – whether an individual was over the legal limit for drink driving;
- **criminal cases** – whether the suspect or victim was under the influence of alcohol;
- ***post-mortem* material** – whether the concentration of alcohol could account for the cause of death or be contributory to the cause of death.

You should create a calibration curve (see Chapter 51) consisting of a minimum of five standards to cover the range 20–300 mg per 100 mL. Certified reference standards (p. 474) can be purchased directly from a commercial supplier or can be prepared in-house. The analysis will also require an internal standard, such as *tert*-butyl alcohol. Once the calibration curve has been produced, the curve should be checked against a certified 80 mg per 100 mL ethanol standard from a different commercial supplier (see Chapter 50). The concentration calculated from the curve should fall within $\pm$ 1.5% of the actual certified concentration to be accepted (p. 376). If this is so then you can proceed with your case samples. You should, however, run a quality control sample, 80 mg per 100mL, at the beginning and end of your test samples to ensure that the system has continued to operate at the level of precision and accuracy required (p. 473).

Normally the samples you would analyse would be contained in 5 mL sealed glass vials containing a preservative (sodium fluoride). To maintain the continuity of evidence (p. 247), road traffic samples should arrive in a glass vial sealed within a small container that is labelled with appropriate details of the accused, the time that the sample was taken and by whom. This information has to be corroborated by checking against the paperwork submitted for the case *before* the sample is opened. In the laboratory, the vials containing the sample would be placed in an automated system which would remove, via a syringe, 100 µL of specimen to a sealed headspace vial, mixed with a known volume of the internal standard (200 µL). At no point should you have to open the sample vial or the sealed headspace vial. If the sample has to be manually diluted, then you should pipette the volumes accurately using a positive displacement pipette (p. 38) into the headspace vial.

The identification of ethanol is achieved by the comparison of the retention times of any compounds with that of the certified ethanol standard, and quantified by measuring the ratio of the peak area of ethanol to the peak area of the internal standard. The concentration can then be calculated from the calibration curve (Chapter 51). After the concentration has been calculated from the mean of the duplicate samples, each of which has been through the two GC columns (total of four results), a further 6% of this mean value is subtracted, representing the possible margin of error based on a typical normal distribution of results. This subtraction of 6% is only performed for road traffic cases and back-calculations. For all other cases, there is no need to take this margin of error into account as they are not being prosecuted for being over the legal limit for driving. This result would then be reported as being 'not less than x milligrams of alcohol per 100 millilitre'.

 KEY POINT *Alcohol results are only ever reported as a whole number.*

Alcohol back-calculations

When a sample of blood has been taken several hours after an incident, the forensic scientist may be asked to estimate the alcohol concentration at the time the incident took place. This is known as a back-calculation. While there are too many variables involved to give an exact concentration, these calculations have a place in the legal system providing that the full restrictions and limitations of the calculations are made clear in the courtroom. In order to perform the calculation, it is assumed that the individual is fit and healthy, has no pre-existing medical condition and that alcohol absorption is complete.

Elimination rates – a recent study has shown that women tend to eliminate alcohol at a faster rate than men and this difference appears to be related to progesterone levels (Dettling et al., 2008).

Circumstances where no post-incident drinking is involved

The simplest calculation to perform is that when there has been no post-incident drinking (see Box 37.1). With this type of calculation, the minimum information you require is the date, time and result for the sample taken from the individual, and the date and time the incident took place. The calculation has to compensate for the amount of alcohol that would have been eliminated from the time the incident took place up to the time the sample was taken. For

---

Box 37.1   How to back-calculate a blood alcohol concentration when no alcohol has been consumed post-incident

After leaving a public house in a small village in England, Ada Little was seen driving erratically by an eye witness, who contacted the police.

The police managed to apprehend Ms Little. She failed the roadside breath test and so she was arrested and transported to a police station. A police surgeon was called who obtained a blood sample from Ms Little at the police station, two hours after she had been seen driving erratically. Ms Little made a written statement indicating that she had consumed no alcohol since leaving the pub.

1. Measured blood alcohol concentration of Ms Little's sample = 64 mg per 100 mL

2. Time elapsed from incident to sample being taken = 2 h.

3. Alcohol eliminated within this time period = 2 h × 18 mg per 100 mL = 36 mg per 100 mL (range 2 × 10 = 20 to 2 × 25 = 50).

4. Concentration at the time of the incident = 64 + 36 = 100 mg per 100 mL (range 84–114 mg per 100 mL).

5. As the legal limit in England and Wales is 80 mg per 100 mL, Ms Little would be prosecuted.

example, an average individual is generally assumed to eliminate alcohol at a rate of 18 mg per 100 mL of blood per h (Fig. 37.1) with a range from 10 to 25 mg per 100 mL per h. This range is assumed to cover approximately 80% of the population. If calculating using breath alcohol values rather than blood concentrations, an elimination rate of 7.8 μg per 100 mL per h is generally assumed (range 4–12 μg per 100 mL per h). The results obtained can then be compared with legal limits for breath samples (Table. 37.1).

If the back-calculated concentration is above the legal limit for driving (Table. 37.1) then the individual would be prosecuted in a court of law and the forensic scientist may be asked to give expert witness testimony to explain the calculation and how the result was obtained.

KEY POINT *You cannot perform any calculation on an alcohol concentration that has been measured as zero. If no alcohol is present, it is not possible to estimate an alcohol concentration at any time prior to the sample being taken, since you do not know the exact time at which all alcohol was eliminated.*

Circumstances where alcohol has been consumed post-incident

For situations where post-incident drinking is involved, the calculation becomes more complex, taking into account the body mass index (mass and height), mass of fat and total body water to give a dimensionless corrective factor (*r*) known as the Widmark factor (Barbour, 2001; see Box 37.2).

There are other correction factors that have been proposed including:

- **Watson** – this method takes into account total body water according to sex, age, weight and height.
- **Seidl** – this method takes into account total body water according to weight, height and blood water.

The adoption of a specific method for the calculation can result in differences in the final calculation (see Box 37.3) and thus the interpretation.

In order to perform this calculation, you need to know the sex, height and mass of the individual, the date and time the incident took place, the time the blood or breath sample was taken, what alcohol was consumed and how much. Details of how to calculate the concentration of alcohol at a given time following post-incident drinking are given in Box 37.3. Note that if the mass

---

Box 37.2   How to calculate a Widmark factor (*r*) according to Forrest (1986)

Before calculating a Widmark factor you will first need to obtain the following information:

1. Body mass index (BMI) = $\dfrac{\text{mass (weight), in kg}}{\text{square of height, in m}}$

[37.1]

2. Fat as percentage of body weight:

(a) men = (1.34 × BMI) − 12.469
(b) women = (1.371 × BMI) − 3.467   [37.2]

3. mass of body fat = $\dfrac{\% \text{ fat} \times \text{body mass (kg)}}{100}$ [37.3]

4. Total body water
= 0.724 × (body mass−mass of body fat)   [37.4]

The Widmark factor is then calculated from the following relationship:

Widmark factor = $\dfrac{\text{total body water}}{\text{body mass} \times 0.8}$ [37.5]

Most values of Widmark factor lie between 0.66 and 0.84 for men, and 0.57 and 0.75 for women.

The type of alcohol consumed – beer, wine and spirits each have different concentrations (v/v) of alcohol.

(weight) and height are given in imperial measurements then these will have to be converted into their metric equivalents using the following formula:

for mass (weight):   1 stone = 6.3503 kg; 1 pound = 0.4536 kg

for height: 1 foot = 30.48 cm; 1 inch = 2.54 cm

Interpretation of results

Effects of alcohol

The effects of alcohol are enhanced as more is consumed. At low doses there is little change to the individual, but as the concentration increases, loss of inhibitions can give the person a feeling of euphoria. As the concentration increases further, a sedative effect begins to come into play, with slurring of speech, disturbance of balance, impaired co-ordination, reduction in visual, audio and spatial awareness, and diminished reaction times. These adverse effects are further enhanced as more alcohol is consumed, until vomiting or unconsciousness is reached. Impairment of respiration and circulation can be obtained if sufficient alcohol is consumed in a short period of time, which is potentially life-threatening.

Factors influencing an individual's reactions to alcohol

There are many factors that will affect how a person will react to a given amount of alcohol, including:

- **The speed at which the individual drinks** – rapid consumption of alcohol results in a high peak blood concentration.
- **The type and amount of food in the stomach** – the presence of partially digested food in the stomach can delay the rate of absorption of alcohol.
- **The body mass of the individual** – the effects of alcohol on an individual are partly a function of the blood volume of the individual. A larger individual has a larger volume of blood, therefore the alcohol entering the bloodstream is diluted to a greater extent, i.e. he/she would have a lower blood alcohol concentration for a given amount of alcohol consumed.
- **Previous drinking history** – if an individual is used to drinking alcoholic beverages on a regular basis he/she will become psychologically and physically dependent on alcohol (this is known as tolerance). More alcohol is then required to produce the physical and behavioural changes associated with a small amount of alcohol in a non-tolerant person. Tolerant individuals will also express higher levels of the enzymes associated with alcohol metabolism.
- **The social environment** – the effects of alcohol can partly be attributed to where the individual is drinking (e.g. at home, in a pub, etc.).
- **Health** – if the individual is tired, recovering from an illness or under stress then the effects of alcohol may be more pronounced.
- **Other drugs** – these can interact with alcohol and may enhance its effects. As a result, many prescription medications come with a warning label.
- **The individual's expectation** – if someone thinks he/she is going to get drunk then he/she may feel intoxicated on a relatively small amount of alcohol.

Metabolism of alcohol

Alcohol has a low volume of distribution ($0.43–0.59$ L kg^{-1}), indicating it is not lipophilic and will distribute evenly throughout the body. The distribution within an individual depends to a large extent on the fat content of the individual, which must be taken into account when performing back-calculations (see p. 362).

Definition

Volume of distribution *(V_d)* is the theoretical volume of blood, per kg of body weight, that would be required if the drug were distributed in equilibrium throughout the body. This value represents the partitioning of a drug between the blood and tissues.

Metabolism – the process by which a drug is converted to a more polar form to facilitate excretion.

Box 37.3   How to calculate a blood alcohol concentration when alcohol has been consumed post-incident – a worked example

A blue car was involved in an accident at 1800 hours on 24/3/17. The driver failed to stop at the scene, but his number was taken and reported to the police.

The police traced the owner, Ben Drinking, and questioned him regarding the offence. At this time, he smelled of alcohol, which he claimed was due to him panicking when the accident occurred and subsequently having a drink to calm his nerves. The police arrested him and conveyed him to the police station for a breath examination. At 1927 hours on the 24/3/17 a breath test was carried out, but the breathalyser failed to calibrate.

A blood sample was obtained at 2134 hours on 24/3/17. Mr Drinking's mass (weight) is 10st 4lb and his height is 5ft 9in. The blood alcohol concentration was measured and found to be not less than 183 mg per 100 mL. Mr Drinking claims he drank four normal measure vodkas and three pints of beer (5% v/v) between the time of the accident and the police arriving at his home.

You have been asked to perform a back-calculation to determine whether he was over the legal limit for driving at the time of the incident.

1. **Convert the weight (p) and height of the individual to metric units**
   Weight (p) = 10 st 4 lb = $(10 \times 6.3503) + (4 \times 0.4536)$
   = 65.3 kg
   Height 5 ft 9 in = $(5 \times 30.48) + (9 \times 2.54)$ = 1.75 m

2. **Calculate the Widmark factor (r) for the individual**
   Body mass index = 21.3 kgm^{-2} (see eqn [37.1])
   Percentage of fat = 16.1 (see eqn [37.2])
   Mass of body fat = 10.5 kg (see eqn [37.3])
   Total body water = 39.7 kg (see eqn [37.4])
   Widmark factor (r) = 0.76 (see eqn [37.5])

3. **Record the date and time the incident took place**
   1800 hours on 24/3/17

4. **Record the date and time the blood/breath sample was taken**
   2134 hours on 24/3/17

5. **Record the measured blood (GC–FID) or breath (intoxilyser) result as C_b.**
   183 mg per 100 mL

6. **Calculate compensation for elapsed time**
   Time of incident (T1) = 1800 hours on 24/3/17

Time blood sample was taken (T2) = 2134 hours on 24/3/17
Elapsed time = 3h 34 min = 3.56 h (always **round down**)
   Amount of alcohol that would have been eliminated during this time, assuming an average elimination rate of 18 mg per 100 mL (range 10–25 mg per 100 mL) = 3.56 × 18 = 64 mg per 100 mL, range 35–89 mg per 100mL.

7. **Calculate the volume of alcohol consumed**
   Alcohol consumed was three pints of beer (5% v/v) = 3 × 568 m L = 1,704 mL; and 4 measures of vodka (unknown v/v) = 4 × 25 mL = 100 mL. A measure is assumed to be 25 mL unless otherwise specified.

8. **Convert total volume of alcohol consumed to mass of alcohol consumed (A)**
   Use the formula:

$$g \text{ of alcohol } (A) = \frac{\text{volume} \times \% \text{ alcohol v/v} \times 0.789}{100}$$

[37.6]

where 0.789 = density of ethanol. Ideally the alcohol concentration (% v/v) should be supplied as well, but if it is unknown then it should be assumed to be 3.345% v/v for beer, 12% v/v for wine, and 40% v/v for spirits.
   3 pints = 1704 mL of beer (5% v/v) = 68 g (always **round up**)
   4 measures of vodka = 100 mL vodka (assumed to be 40% v/v) = 32 g (always **round up**).

9. **Calculate the alcohol concentration in blood $Co(A)$**

Use the formula

$$Co(A) \text{ mg per 100 mL} = 100 \times \frac{A}{p \times r}$$

= 202 mg per 100 mL (always **round up**)   [37.7]

10. **Calculate blood alcohol concentration at the time of the incident (C_a)**

C_a = measured alcohol result (C_b) − Co(A)
     + compensation for elapsed time
   = (183 − 202) + 64 = 45 mg per 100 mL,
   range 16 − 70 mg per 100 mL.

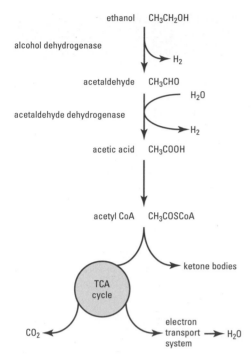

Fig. 37.2 Pathway for the metabolism of alcohol.

The absorption of alcohol from the stomach begins immediately after ingestion and is assumed to give a peak blood alcohol concentration 1 h after complete ingestion. Once absorbed, it is transported in the bloodstream through the liver to the heart and thereafter distributed around the body. As the alcohol passes through the liver it begins to be metabolised (so called 'first pass metabolism') initially to acetaldehyde (Fig. 37.2). This reaction is catalysed by the enzyme alcohol dehydrogenase. This enzyme is also found in the intestines and as the alcohol passes around the body it is continually metabolised. Acetaldehyde is further metabolised to acetic acid by the enzyme acetaldehyde dehydrogenase and then finally oxidised to water and carbon dioxide for elimination, primarily in the urine.

Further metabolism can occur via minor routes of metabolism such as the phase II conjugation mechanisms, including:

- sulphotransferase activity to ethyl sulphate;
- glucuronosyl transferase activity to ethyl glucuronide.

Ethyl glucuronide usually constitutes 0.02% of an ethanol dose excreted in the urine (Dahl *et al.,* 2002) but has been shown to increase when alcohol has been consumed recently (within 3–5 hours) (Høiseth *et al.,* 2007) and as such could offer supplementary evidence of recent alcohol consumption. It has also been used as a marker for chronic alcohol consumption in segmented hair samples (see p. 372) where ethyl glucuronide levels have been reported in the $pgymg^{-1}$ to $ng\ mg^{-1}$ range (Jurado *et al.,* 2004).

Other markers of chronic alcoholism include:

- **Acetone** – this ketone, formed as a result of ketoacidosis (Fig. 37.2), is a good indicator of sustained alcohol misuse when the concentration exceeds 7 mg alcohol per 100 mL.
- **γ-glutamyl transferase (GGT)** – the normal clinical range for GGT is reported to be $5–42\ U/L^{-1}$ with an elevated GGT level believed to be indicative of alcohol-induced liver damage as shown by Sadler *et al.* (1996) where GGT levels in chronic alcoholics were found to be $27–2840\ U/L^{-1}$.
- **Carbohydrate deficient transferrin (CDT)** – CDT is the name given to the different types of human transferrin including the isoforms asialo-, monosialo- and disialo-transferrin. CDT was examined by capillary electrophoresis (Chapter 22) in a study of individuals driving under the influence of alcohol and was found to be elevated in a high proportion of cases (Bortolotti, 2007). CDT/transferrin ratios (CDT in % of total serum transferrin) greater than 20% appear often in cases of chronic alcohol abuse (Arndt, 2008).

Frequently, in the case of chronic alcoholism, there is no, or little, alcohol found in the blood at autopsy. In these cases, you can look at the associated changes to the liver – for example, cirrhosis or fatty liver.

Problems with interpretation – post-mortem production of alcohol

There are some instances where alcohol can be produced during the *post-mortem* period. If an individual died in a temperate climate and was not found for a period of time, the body will begin to decompose. During the decomposition period, bacteria from the gut can contaminate the blood vessels. During the *post-mortem* period, if the blood sample has been contaminated with such bacteria, then it is possible that alcohol production can be caused by the anaerobic fermentation of glucose, lactic acid and/or fatty acids. This can, in severe cases, reach alcohol levels of 40 mg per 100 mL. This possibility must be taken into account before the results are interpreted.

Reporting results

Once you have measured or calculated an alcohol concentration, you must be able to convey to the court what this number actually means. The forensic scientist cannot say that an individual was drunk – it is for the court to make that judgement. You must, therefore, convey to the court what the concentration means in context, for example in terms of the legal limits for driving. You can add to this by explaining what the known effects of this concentration are for the average individual, stressing that this is only the average and not necessarily for this person, since you do not know exactly how they react to alcohol.

Text references

Arndt, T., Guessregen, B., Hallermann, D., Nauck, M., Terjung, D. and Weckesser, H. (2008) Forensic analysis of carbohydrate-deficient transferrin (CDT) by HPLC – Statistics and extreme CDT values. *Forensic Science International* **175**(1): 27–30.

Barbour, A.D. (2001) Simplified estimation of Widmark 'r' values by the method of Forrest. *Science and Justice* **41**(1): 53–54.

Bortolotti, F., Trettene, M., Gottardo, R., Bernini, M., Ricossa, M.C. and Tagliaro, F. (2007) Carbohydrate-deficient transferrin (CDT): A reliable indicator of the risk of driving under the influence of alcohol when determined by capillary electrophoresis. *Forensic Science International* **170**(2)–(3): 175–178.

Criminal Justice and Police Act 2001, ss.12–16, Pt 1. Available at: http://www.legislation.gov.uk/ukpga/2001/16/pdfs/ukpga_20010016_en.pdf. Last accessed 22/08/2017.

Dahl H., Stephanson N., Beck O. and Helander A. (2002) Comparison of urinary excretion characteristics of ethanol and ethyl glucuronide. *Journal of Analytical Toxicology* **26**(4): 201–204.

Dettling, A., Skopp, G., Graw, M. and Haffner, H.-Th. (2008) The influence of sex hormones on the elimination kinetics of ethanol. *Forensic Science International* **177**(2)–(3): 85–89.

Forrest, A.R.W. (1986) The estimation of Widmark's factor. *Journal of Forensic Science Society* 26: 249–252.

Høiseth, G., Bernard, J.P., Karinen, R., Johnsen, L., Helander, A., Christophersen, A.S. and Mørland, J. (2007) A pharmacokinetic study of ethyl glucuronide in blood and urine: Applications to forensic toxicology. *Forensic Science International* **172**(2)–(3): 119–124.

Home Office (2014) *Evidential Breath Alcohol Analysis Instruments A Guide to Type Approval Procedures for Evidential Breath Alcohol Analysis Instruments used for Law Enforcement in Great Britain.* Available at: https://www.gov.uk/government/uploads/system/uploads/attachment_data/file/362271/MEBTIguideV2.pdf. Last accessed 22/08/2017.

Jones, A.W. and Andersson, L. (1996) Variability of the blood/breath alcohol ratio in drinking drivers. *Journal of Forensic Sciences* 41: 916–921.

Jurado, C., Soiano, M., Giménez, P. and Menéndez, M. (2004) Diagnosis of chronic alcohol consumption: Hair analysis for ethyl-glucuronide. *Forensic Science International* **145**(2)–(3): 161–166.

Posey, D. and Mozayami, A. (2007) The estimation of blood alcohol concentration: Widmark revisited. *Forensic Science, Medicine, and Pathology* **3**(1): 33–40.

Road Traffic Offenders Act 1988, ss. 4–5, Pt 1. Available at: http://www.legislation.gov.uk/ukpga/1988/53/pdfs/ukpga_19880053_en.pdf. Last accessed 22/08/2017.

Sadler, D.W., Girela, E. and Pounder, D.J. (1996) Post mortem markers of chronic alcoholism. *Forensic Science International* **82**(2): 153–163.

Zuba, D. (2008) Accuracy and reliability of breath alcohol testing by handheld electrochemical analysers. *Forensic Science International* **178**(2)–(3:, e29–e33.

Sources for further study

Denney, R.C. (1997) *None for the Road: Understanding Drink Driving.* Shaw & Sons, Crayford.

Karch, S. (2007) *Forensic Issues in Alcohol Testing.* CRC Press, Boca Raton.

Ley, N. (1997) *Drink Driving Law and Practice.* Sweet & Maxwell, London.

Study exercises

37.1 Perform a simple back-calculation. Use the following information to determine the amount of alcohol at the time of the incident:

Time of incident:	15:45; 01/01/17
Time blood sample was obtained:	18:32; 01/01/17
Measured blood alcohol concentration:	67 mg alcohol per 100 mL

37.2 Calculate the Widmark factor. Use the following information to calculate the Widmark factor for both individuals (see p. 362):

(a) female, weight 9 stone 3 pounds, height 5 feet 2 inches

(b) male, weight 11 stone 7 pounds, height 6 feet 3 inches

37.3 Test your knowledge of the effects of alcohol. What are the effects of alcohol at the following concentrations?

(a) 40 mg alcohol per 100 mL;

(b) 80 mg alcohol per 100 mL;

(c) 150 mg alcohol per 100 mL;

(d) 250 mg alcohol per 100 mL;

(e) 350 mg alcohol per 100 mL.

***Toxicology is not a recent discipline** – Paracelsus (1492–1541) is recognised as the forefather of toxicology, and Orfila was the first to use toxicology for court purposes in a case of arsenic poisoning in 1813.*

Sub-disciplines of toxicology:

***Clinical toxicology** – the clinical toxicologist assists in the diagnosis of drug-related illness. If an individual presents at hospital with symptoms of drug overdose, the clinical toxicologist must analyse the sample in as short a time as possible to allow a medical practitioner to administer the correct antidote. The clinical toxicologist is also responsible for monitoring drug concentrations in selected patients (therapeutic drug testing), to ensure that the correct dose is administered to give the desired response.*

***Eco-toxicology** – the eco-toxicologist monitors pollutant levels in, for example, air, water, soil, crops to ensure that industry is complying with government limits.*

***Sport toxicology** – the toxicologist analyses biological fluids for the presence of performance-enhancing drugs, such as anabolic steroids, that may have been used by athletes, as well as those being administered to animals (e.g. horses). The role of this toxicologist is to identify whether or not a performance-enhancing drug has been administered and to report to the appropriate sports body.*

***Employment drug testing** – in this role, the toxicologist examines samples from a company's employees to determine whether they have been taking drugs. This is more common in the USA. However, some employers in the UK and Europe demand participation in a drug-testing programme.*

***Sudden deaths** – any unexplained death in the UK will be investigated under instruction by a procurator fiscal in Scotland, or a coroner in England, Wales and Northern Ireland.*

Toxicology is the scientific study of drugs and poisons. The role of the forensic toxicologist is to identify, quantify and confirm the presence of any drug or poison in a biological sample or paraphernalia associated with a drug-related incident, for example the contents of a syringe. Once the concentration of the drug is known, the toxicologist can then form an opinion as to whether the concentration found could have caused the death of the individual or could account for the behaviour of that individual.

 KEY POINT *It is not so much the substance that is poisonous but the dose at which it is applied. The forensic toxicologist must identify and quantify any drug in relevant case materials. He or she is also responsible for the interpretation of these drug levels and presenting an opinion in court.*

The types of case that are likely to be encountered by the forensic toxicologist fall into two categories – where the drug may have caused death or may have contributed to the death; and where the behaviour of an individual may be explained by the drugs found in his/her body. The analysis could be used to assist in court proceedings of a criminal case, but also in routine death investigation. In all cases it is crucial that detailed notes are taken at the time of any analysis and the results of the analysis recorded. There may be more than one drug in question, and the toxicologist will need to give an opinion on what the results mean as opposed to merely confirming the drugs' presence. The time constraints on the analysis are different to those of other sub-disciplines. For example, a clinical toxicologist is usually required simply to identify the drug as rapidly as possible, whereas a forensic toxicologist is required to identify and *quantify* any drug that may have caused a death, or contributed to the behaviour of an individual. In the latter case, the analysis is limited only by the time constraints set by the court.

Non-criminal cases of sudden death

This type of case is probably the most common and falls into two categories:

1. **Deliberate** – in this type of sudden death, an excessive amount of a drug is taken with the intention of causing harm or to commit suicide.
2. **Accidental** – drug overdoses can occur among people who inadvertently exceed the stated dose of a drug that has been prescribed for them by their doctor – for example, in the belief that by increasing the amount of drug taken they will obtain more immediate action, by miscalculating the amount or by forgetting that the dose had already been taken.

For officers attending a crime scene, it is important to record and preserve all medication containers found there, noting the identity of the drug and its purpose, the instructions for use, when the medication was prescribed and the number of pills remaining. This can give an immediate indication of the drug(s) that are potentially responsible for the death, but these would have to be confirmed by the toxicologist as having been ingested.

Criminal cases

Criminal cases are varied. If the person is living, then the analysis is often to determine whether the victim or accused were under the influence of alcohol (Chapter 37) or drugs (Chapter 39) at the time an incident took place

Drug-facilitated sexual assault (DFSA) – defined by the Advisory Council on the Misuse of Drugs (ACMD) (2007), as 'all forms of non-consensual penetrative sexual activity whether it involves the forcible or covert administration of an incapacitating or stupefying substance by an assailant for the purposes of serious sexual assault'. The definition also includes 'sexual activity by an assailant with a victim who is profoundly intoxicated by his or her own actions to the point of near or actual unconsciousness'.

Questions to be asked in DFSA cases – *to help the forensic scientist, the answers to the following questions should be supplied:*

- *What symptoms did the victim describe?*
- *How long was the victim unconscious?*
- *What specimens were collected?*
- *How much time passed between the alleged drugging and the collection of specimens?*
- *How much alcohol did the victim consume?*
- *Did the victim take any drugs (recreational or prescription)?*
- *Did the victim urinate prior to the collection of a urine sample? If so, how many times?*
- *What drugs does the suspect have access to?*

Driving under the influence – *in the UK it is an offence to drive, attempt to drive or be in charge of a motor vehicle on a road or other public place when under the influence of alcohol. If a person is suspected of driving when under the influence of alcohol, he or she will be charged under Section 5 of the* Road Traffic Offenders Act 1988 (Chapter 37).

It is an offence to drive, attempt to drive or be in charge of a motor vehicle on a road or other public place when under the influence of drink or drugs. If a person is suspected of driving when under the influence of drugs, he or she will be charged under Section 4 of the Road Traffic Offenders Act 1988.

(e.g. assault, road traffic cases). If a person died from a drug overdose, then the person who supplied the drug could be prosecuted for supplying that drug.

Criminal cases of sudden death

In cases where large quantities of drug (typically 1 kg) are transported in the body following ingestion (body-packing), there are occasions when one of the small packets, usually condoms containing 1–3 g of the drug, ruptures resulting in an 'accidental' overdose.

Drug-facilitated sexual assault (DFSA)

These cases are different from the normal cases encountered, in that the analysis is focused on screening the biological samples for evidence of administration of a single acute dose of a drug, which could render the victim unconscious or unable to prevent a sexual assault occurring. The Sexual Offences Act (2003) was amended and came into force in 2004 and now states that it is an offence to administer a stupefying substance with the intent of overpowering the victim to engage him or her in sexual activity, either with the offender or with another person. It may be that the time between the assault taking place and the blood or urine sample being collected is several hours or even several days after the event, in which case the original drug is unlikely to be found and the evidence may be in the form of a metabolite.

As soon as an allegation of rape or sexual assault has been made, a urine sample must be obtained from the victim. Time is critical if the forensic toxicologist is to have a chance of being able to identify any drug present that could corroborate the victim's recollection of events. The drugs involved in these cases may render the victim unconscious for several hours and, coupled with the time delay in reporting the case to the authorities, this may result in the drug being eliminated from the body.

The urine sample, although intimate, should be taken in the presence of a police officer to ensure the provenance of the sample, but with due consideration for the feelings of the victim. Ideally it should be the first void after the incident as this will yield the most evidential value. If it is not, the number of voids should be recorded. A blood sample, on the other hand, must be obtained by a forensic medical examiner.

DFSA cases are particularly difficult for the forensic toxicologist since the time from the assault to the sample being taken is usually long enough for the drug to have been metabolised by the body. Therefore, analysis of drugs in hair can be a useful tool in corroborating that the assault has taken place (Chapter 32). Hair should be collected during the medical examination, cut from the scalp. The victim is requested to return after one month to give a further hair sample. This period of time should be sufficient to allow any drug that had been administered to be incorporated into shafts of the hair. Analysis of the hair could corroborate the victim's statement. However, the exact time, date and dose of any drug found cannot be determined other than to say it had occurred within that month. Hair is also useful to give an indication of the longer-term drug history of that individual (p. 320). Vomit is also useful in these cases since an unabsorbed drug could be detected in it, though only qualitatively.

If glassware has been seized in connection with the case, then any liquid residues remaining in a glass or bottle can be analysed for the presence of any drug.

Road traffic offences

Within this category, the forensic toxicologist would analyse blood or urine in cases submitted to the laboratory from persons believed to have been driving under the influence of alcohol (Chapter 37) or other drugs/controlled substances (Chapter 39).

Impairment by drugs is initially determined by the police officer at the roadside, after first ruling out impairment by alcohol using a roadside breath-screening device (see Chapter 37). In the UK, in 2015 type approval (p. 206) was granted for two preliminary roadside drug-testing devices – the Securetec Drugwipe 3S by Securetec Detection Systems Ag (granted on 22/2/15) and the Drager Drug Test 5000 by Drager Safety Ltd (granted on 13/3/15). Both devices, however, are based on immunoassay techniques (p. 206) and are limited to the detection of cocaine and cannabis, and unlike the evidential roadside alcohol devices, the presence of the drugs still needs to be confirmed by the toxicologist. If deemed to be, or suspected to be, impaired, the suspect would be arrested and conveyed to the police station, and a police surgeon, also known as a forensic medical examiner, would be called. If the police surgeon considers the driver to be impaired, then a specimen of blood or urine would be obtained for analysis.

Fatal accident inquiries

In the case of a death in custody, or an accident at work resulting in the death of an employee, there will be an investigation known as a fatal accident inquiry. In terms of the toxicological analysis, the question that must be addressed is whether the person was under the influence of drugs at the time of accident/death.

Defence analysis

Defence solicitors may also instruct the forensic toxicologist to examine a sample to confirm the identity and quantity of a drug or alcohol, or to give his/her opinion of an analysis based on the final statement written for the court and the notes/results that are in the case file (p. 554).

Samples submitted for analysis

All biological samples should be obtained by a qualified medical practitioner. In the case of a sudden death, the samples should be obtained by a forensic pathologist during the *post mortem*. If a person has been admitted to hospital, then a blood sample is likely to have been obtained by a doctor as soon as possible for analysis by a clinical toxicologist. For a clinical sample (serum, plasma, whole blood) then you should be aware:

- **that it does not contain any preservative** – this may have an impact on the detection of specific drugs, e.g. alcohol;
- **that the storage conditions were not in your control** – degradation of a drug can occur if the sample has not been refrigerated;
- **of the provenance of the sample** – the sample has been obtained in the absence of a police officer, therefore you cannot account for what has happened to the sample from the time it was taken to the time it was seized, although there is a barcoded audit trail within the hospital service.

This sample can then be seized by the police and submitted to a forensic laboratory for further analysis. Other non-biological samples may also be submitted for analysis, such as tablets, powders, liquids, solvent containers and syringes that have been recovered from a house or a person.

In cases of sudden death, the purpose is to determine as accurately as possible the concentration(s) of the drug(s) that existed in the blood at the time of death and to give an opinion as to whether the death can be explained by the drug concentration(s) found.

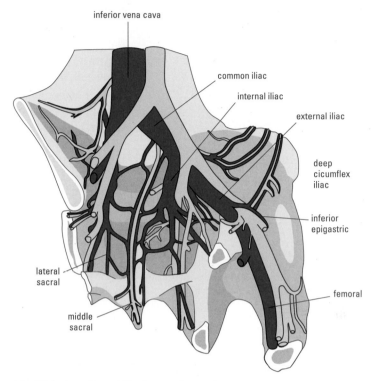

inferior vena cava

common iliac

internal iliac

external iliac

deep cicumflex iliac

inferior epigastric

lateral sacral

middle sacral

femoral

Fig. 38.1 Location of the femoral vessels.

Typical examples include:

- **Blood** – *post-mortem* blood can either be fluid, clotted or a mixture of both. Blood is the only sample in which a drug can be quantified and a meaningful interpretation in respect of intoxication be made. It is therefore the most important matrix for analysis. If a drug is found in the blood it is usually indicative of recent use (within hours) of that drug.

  When investigating a death, a blood sample must be obtained from a peripheral site, such as the femoral vessels (Fig. 38.1), and not from any central blood vessel, such as the cardiac vessels or inferior vena cava. The inferior vena cava, the major vein of the human body, splits into the left and right iliac vein at the lower part of the abdomen, which become the left and right femoral veins at the top of each leg. Blood sampled from these veins is more likely to be fluid, but also minimises the risk of contamination from *post-mortem* drug redistribution (p. 378). In life, drugs are actively transported around the body, either in solution in plasma, by partitioning in the red blood cells, or bound to plasma proteins. Analysis of a blood clot rich in red blood cells may give an artificially elevated result. In cases of an orally administered overdose (usually by ingestion of a large quantity of drug) the drugs essentially exist as a reservoir in the stomach. After death, although the drug will not be actively absorbed and distributed around the body, it continues to be distributed by simple diffusion into the vessels and organs close by. This diffusion can be extensive as autolysis proceeds and will affect the great blood vessels in the central region of the torso (i.e. aorta, vena cava) as well as diffusion into the liver (the left and caudate lobes that lie adjacent to the stomach). If a blood sample is taken from a peripheral source, such as the femoral vessels, this *post-mortem* artefact is minimised and any drug concentration found in the blood will be most representative of that at the time of death.

If the sample is to be analysed for alcohol or other volatile compounds, then it should have potassium oxalate added as an anti-coagulant and sodium fluoride as a preservative (see Chapter 37). If a person has received a blood transfusion during medical treatment, then any drug analysis should be performed on the pre-transfusion blood sample.

- **Urine** – if a drug is found in urine it indicates use of that drug at some time prior to the collection of the specimen, but does not give an indication of the time or the dose. Usually, it reflects use within the last few days, depending on the drug. However, with the exception of alcohol, the influence of a drug on behaviour cannot be assessed by the finding of a drug in a urine sample.
- **Hair** – this is a useful medium when the long-term drug history of the individual needs to be known (Chapter 32). Since hair grows on average 1 cm per month (Wennig, 2000), segmental sections along the length of hair, when analysed for drug content, give a history of drug use. These samples cannot be used to give a precise time, date or dose of the drugs identified, but can give the pattern of usage, for example periods of abstinence, continual use and increased use. They cannot be used as in indicator of tolerance of the individual (see p. 380).

Approximate detection times for some commonly encountered drugs in blood and urine

	Blood (h^{-1})	*Urine* (h^{-1})
MDMA	*24*	*48*
Cocaine	*12*	*-*
Benzoylecgonine (BZE)	*48*	*48–72*
11-nor-Δ9-Tetrahydrocannabinol (THC)	*5*	*-*
11-nor-Δ9-Tetrahydrocannibinol-9-carboxylic acid	*36*	*34–87*

Modified from Verstraete A.G. (2004)

Blood, urine and hair can be obtained from living persons as well as deceased. The following samples may also be submitted to the laboratory but can only be obtained at a *post mortem*:

- **Vitreous humour** – this is the clear colourless liquid within the eyeball and is an ideal sample for toxicological analysis, since it is the one sample that is likely to be free from contamination and *post-mortem* artefact. It is obtained at the *post-mortem* using a needle and syringe and serves as a useful sample for corroborating a blood alcohol concentration in the absence of a urine sample, but has limited value in drug analysis, primarily due to the volume that can be recovered.
- **Liver** – this is the largest organ in the body and is largely responsible for the metabolism of many drugs. The right lobe of the liver is larger than the left lobe, but is also furthest away from the stomach and diaphragm. Therefore when sampling this organ, a small section from deep within this lobe (Fig. 38.2) should be taken to minimise any *post-mortem* redistribution artefact. Liver can be used for qualitative analysis in cases when extensive

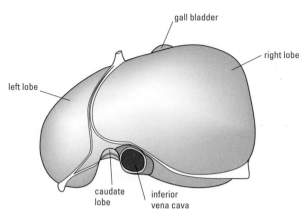

Fig. 38.2 Lobes of the liver.

decomposition has occurred, or when the person has survived for several days following the ingestion of a drug.

- **Lungs** – these are the organs that control respiration. At the *post mortem,* the whole left or right lung should be collected and placed into a nylon bag and sealed with a swan neck (see p. 426). These organs are primarily used where gases or volatile compounds (butane lighter fuel, etc.) are implicated. The lungs are analysed as this will be where the greatest concentration of the toxic substance will be found, simply because in the process of respiration this is the first organ that the drug will enter.
- **Gastric contents** – the gastric (stomach) contents can be obtained from a sample of vomit or by collection of the contents at the *post mortem.* The sample may contain large quantities of the original drug/poison, allowing immediate identification. The analysis usefully complements the results obtained from blood or urine, especially in cases where absorption is incomplete, such as in the ingestion of a large quantity of tablets.
- **Oral fluid** – this non-invasive sample can be used on site (e.g. at the roadside) and is collected by the use of a swab or oral fluid collection device.
- **Sweat** – the composition of sweat is similar to that of plasma but contains no protein. Water-soluble drugs can be excreted via this route, believed to occur due to passive diffusion. The samples can be obtained by the use of sweat patches.

Oral fluid – *can be collected by expectorant or stimulation methods. Commercial oral fluid collection tubes are available – for example, Quantisal™ Oral Fluid Collection Device by Alere or OralEze™ Collection Device by Thermo Fisher Ltd.*

Toxicological analysis

No single analytical test is capable of detecting all drugs. Therefore, any drug in the sample must first be identified by a screening process before it can be quantified. However, not all drugs that have been identified in the screening process need to be quantified. For example, Lansoprazole is a drug that is prescribed to protect the stomach when other tablets are taken. It has low toxicity and no deleterious effects, so therefore it is not likely to be contributory to the cause of death or influence the behaviour of an individual.

A basic strategy should be employed for toxicological analysis, including:

1. analysis of blood, urine and/or vitreous humour for alcohol (Chapter 37);
2. examination of blood for the presence of carbon monoxide, if appropriate, using a CO oximeter;
3. preliminary screen of blood/urine for drugs of abuse using immunoassay (Chapter 21);

4. preliminary screen of blood/urine or other samples for prescription drugs and drugs of abuse using chromatographic techniques (Chapter 14);
5. quantification of any drugs in blood provisionally identified in earlier screens (Chapter 51).

Alcohol analysis

Blood, urine and vitreous humour submitted to the laboratory should be analysed for alcohol, providing that an appropriate sample type and volume have been supplied (see Chapter 37 for further details).

Carbon monoxide

This toxic gas is produced by incomplete combustion of carbon compounds. It is clear, colourless, tasteless and non-irritating, making its detection by the individual impossible unless CO monitors have been installed. An analysis of samples for carbon monoxide is a common request for forensic analysis when there is a fatality in a house fire, a sudden death (e.g. suspected faulty gas heater), an accident at work (where oxygen is limited, e.g. grain storage) or a motor vehicle accident.

A carbon monoxide oximeter is typically used to measure the haemoglobin content of the blood sample. Haemoglobin is present in the blood as oxygenated haemoglobin (oxyHb), deoxygenated haemoglobin (HHb), met-haemoglobin and sulph-haemoglobin. The CO-oximeter measures each of these, as well as the percentage of oxygen saturation. These instruments are designed for *ante-mortem* samples rather than *post-mortem* samples and as such you often get an error message associated with a high met-haemaglobin concentration, but this has been demonstrated to have no effect on the measurement of carboxyhaemoglobin (COHb) – the important analyte when exposed to carbon monoxide (Lee *et al.*, 2003). The instrument is calibrated using three certified reference serum samples, each containing different concentrations of carboxyhaemoglobin. The case blood sample is directly aspirated into the oximeter and the carboxyhaemoglobin concentration is calculated by reference to the calibration standards. This value is expressed as a percentage of haemoglobin saturation and gives an indication as to whether the individual was breathing in, for example, a fire, or, if sufficiently high, can indicate the cause of death.

Typical COHb concentrations in carbon monoxide poisonings are in the region of 59–88%, compared with 5–6% in smokers and 10% in city dwellers. The effects of COHb concentrations include:

- at 10–20% – headaches, weakness and nausea;
- at 30–40% – severe headaches, dizziness, likelihood of collapse;
- at 40–50% – blurred vision, difficulty in breathing, loss of consciousness;
- at 50% and over – likelihood of respiratory failure and death.

Drugs of abuse (preliminary screen)

Preliminary immunoassay screens (Chapter 21), each of which cover a specific drug or drugs of a single class, are used to detect drugs of abuse. Standard screens should include tests for cannabis, amphetamines and related compounds, cocaine, methadone, opiates and benzodiazepines. It is important to remember that the immunoassay only gives a preliminary result. It does not conclusively identify the drug and cannot be used for quantification. Any positive result obtained by this technique must be confirmed and quantified using an appropriate technique such as GC–MS or LC–MS (Chapters 39).

Other drugs (general screen)

The purpose here is to identify prescription drugs, for example antidepressants, analgesics, anticonvulsants, etc. (see Table. 38.1). These fall into the category of acidic, basic or neutral drugs according to their chemical composition and are extracted from samples either by liquid–liquid extraction or solid phase extraction (see Chapter 12) before analysis by gas chromatography–mass spectrometry (GC–MS) (see Chapters 14–15). There are many thousands of drugs that could potentially be looked for and it is beyond the scope of this chapter to discuss these in detail. The toxicologist is directed to a large extent by the case history, or the circumstances of the case. An example of how to extract drugs from a blood sample for a general screen using liquid–liquid extraction is given in Box 38.1.

Quantifying drugs and assessing toxicity

Once the case sample has been screened for the presence of any drugs, the forensic toxicologist must decide which, if any, of the drugs should be quantified. By reference to relevant monographs and other texts (e.g. Baselt (2002), Moffat *et al.* (2011)), the toxicity of each drug can be evaluated. If the drug is indicated in the literature as potentially harmful, or known to impair behaviour/brain function, then it should be quantified. The forensic toxicologist should be aware of potential interactions between drugs that may have been administered (see p. 380). This may mean that more than one drug needs to be quantified, when taking into account drug interactions.

To quantify a drug, you should prepare a calibration curve (Chapter 51), covering a range of concentrations from therapeutic to fatal levels in the same matrix as the sample being quantified (e.g. in blood). A quality control sample (Chapter 50) should also be spiked (see p. 473) with a drug concentration, which falls on the midpoint of the calibration curve. Case blood samples should be extracted, at least in duplicate, at the same time as the spiked blood standards for the calibration curve and quality control. The extracted samples can be analysed by liquid chromatography or gas chromatography (Chapter 14), depending on the drug being quantified. For the calibration curve to be accepted, the correlation coefficient of the curve should be r>0.99 and the quality control sample should fall within $\pm$ 20% of its actual value when calculated from the curve (SOFT, 2006). For road traffic offences involving alcohol, the quality

Internal standard – should be used where appropriate. The best internal standard to use for analysis of drugs using MS technology (see Chapter 15) is the deuterated form of the drug. e.g. d^5 diazepam.

Validation – any protocol involving quantitative analysis should have been validated prior to its use (see Chapter 51).

Table 38.1 Common drugs tested for in forensic toxicology

Antidepressants	For the treatment of depression e.g. amitriptyline
Anticonvulsants	Combat seizures, such as in epilepsy e.g. carbamazepine
Narcotic analgesics	Alleviate severe pain e.g. methadone, morphine
Analgesics	Alleviate mild to moderate pain e.g. paracetamol, dextropropoxyphene
Anxiolytics	For the treatment of anxiety e.g. diazepam
Benzodiazepines	Sedatives, and for anxiety e.g. diazepam, temazepam
Drugs of abuse	Including amphetamines and related compounds, methadone, opiates and opioids, benzodiazepines, cannabinoids, cocaine

Box 38.1 Extraction of blood for a general drugs screen

The purpose of a general drug screen is to identify whether or not any drugs, or drug metabolites, are present. If a drug is identified that is of toxicological importance, then it would be quantified. A screen is usually performed using GC–MS (Chapters 14–15) since the majority of drugs can be identified in a single run.

1. **Prepare the samples for analysis** – for example, collect blood samples from the refrigerator and record the label and sample details in your examination notes. Accurately pipette 1 mL of each sample into a test tube labelled with the case details in a biosafety cabinet.

2. **Add internal standards** – for example, a fixed amount of a basic internal standard such as Proadifen, and a fixed amount of an acidic internal standard, such as Brallobarbitone, using an appropriate positive displacement pipette (p. 38).

3. **Extract neutral compounds** – accurately pipette 5 mL of ether (solvent) into each blood sample. Seal the top of the test tube and rotate the tube for 15 min on a rotator mixer. Neutral compounds will be extracted from the aqueous blood sample into the solvent layer.

4. **Extract acidic compounds** – accurately pipette 1 mL of 0.025 mol L^{-1} hydrochloric acid into the test tube, seal the top of the test tube and rotate the tube for 15 min on a rotator mixer. Any acidic compounds will be extracted from the blood sample into the solvent layer.

5. **Separate the solvent from the sample** – first centrifuge the test tube at low speed, approx. $800 \times g$, for 5 min, then carefully aspirate (remove) the solvent (upper) layer to a clean test tube using a Pasteur pipette and label this as the acidic/neutral fraction, along with the case details.

6. **Extract basic compounds** – to the acidified blood, accurately pipette 1 mL of 3% (w/v) sodium hydroxide and 5 mL of ether solvent. Seal the top of the test tube and rotate the tube for 15 min on a rotator mixer. This will extract any basic compounds from the blood sample to the solvent layer.

7. **Separate the solvent from the sample** – again, centrifuge the test tube at approx. $800 \times g$ for 5 min, then carefully aspirate the solvent (upper) layer to a clean test tube and label this as the basic fraction, along with case details.

8. **Redissolve the fractions in methanol** – first, transfer the two test tubes to a heating block set at $60\,°C$ and dry under a stream of nitrogen, to remove the ether. Then, re-suspend the basic fraction solvent residue in methanol (50 μL) and the acidic/neutral fraction solvent residue in methanol (100 μL).

9. **Analyse by GC–MS** – inject 1 μL of the extract into a GC-MS (Chapters 14–15), programmed to start at a low temperature, such as $100\,°C$, increasing in temperature to $300\,°C$ by the end of the programme, to ensure that all components in the extract have been eluted from the column.

10. **Interpret the results** – examine the chromatogram produced and identify, by retention time and mass spectrum, any drugs present. The internal standards should be identified. If they cannot be identified, then the sample should be injected again, and if they are still not detected then either the appropriate parts of the GC–MS may need to be cleaned or the sample will have to be re-extracted and re-analysed. Any positive result found should then be quantified where appropriate – however, if the screen was negative for drugs it could mean that the person has not taken the drug, has not taken a large enough dose of the drug to be detected, or the biological sample was taken too long after the drug was ingested.

control should fall within $\pm$ 1.5% of its actual value. If it does not fall within this percentage error, then the calibration curve will have to be repeated. The concentration of the drug in the case samples can be calculated directly by reference to the calibration curve using the equation of the straight line (p. 503) and should be reported as the average of the duplicate samples. If the case samples are not in agreement, then the case sample should be re-extracted. If there is insufficient case sample left for further extraction, then the case may be reported as, for example, 'examination of the blood indicated the presence of paracetamol, but there was insufficient sample to quantify this drug' or 'paracetamol was found at approximately 120 mg L^{-1}'.

Definitions

Pharmacodynamics – *the study of the dose versus pharmacological response.*

Pharmacokinetics – *the study of the ADME processes over a period of time.*

Example Routes of administration to facilitate absorption

Route	Location	Example
Parental (intravenous, intra muscular, subcutaneous)	Vein, muscle, under skin	heroin
Enteral (or oral)	Gastrointestinal tract	MDMA
Buccal/ sublingual	Mouth	LSD
Rectal	Rectum	diazepam
Inhalation	Lungs	cannabis
Topical	Skin/eye	hydrocortisone

Definition

Volume of distribution (V_d) – the theoretical volume of body fluid that would be necessary if the total amount of drug in the body were distributed at the same concentration as in plasma. It can be calculated, providing distribution equilibrium is attained, using the following formula:

$$V_d = \frac{A_p}{C_p}$$

where A_p = amount of drug in the body, and C_p = plasma concentration.

Pharmacokinetics

In order to be able to interpret a drug concentration at a given time point, it is first import and to understand the concept of pharmacokinetics. When a drug is ingested it undergoes a series of processes, commonly referred to as the ADME processes:

- **A**bsorption;
- **D**istribution;
- **M**etabolism;
- **E**xcretion.

While these processes can be monitored during life to obtain therapeutic blood drug concentrations and half-life data, it poses a more difficult issue for the interpretation of blood drug concentrations in *post-mortem* toxicology. During life, drugs are actively transported to their sites of action, whereas after death you can still have drug movement, a phenomenon known as *post-mortem* drug redistribution, that can significantly affect the concentration found in the blood and/or organ sample.

Absorption

The route of administration controls the transfer of drug into the systemic circulation and the time taken, or rate, for the process.

Distribution

Once the drug is absorbed into the systemic circulation it is transported around the body to its site of action. The extent of distribution can be indicated by the volume of distribution (V_d) of the drug and is affected by, for example, blood flow, the ability to pass through biological membranes (partition coefficient), lipophilicity of the drug, size, ionisation and degree of plasma protein binding. Drugs that are lipohilic (sequester easily into fatty tissue) in nature tend to have a high V_d value, for example the tricyclic antidepressant amitriptyline, and as such are more likely to redistribute after death (see p. 378). Once the drug reaches the site of action it mediates a response. It is presumed that the response of an individual follows a normal population distribution (see Fig. 38.3); however, in reality there is likely to be considerable intra-variation in terms of therapeutic and fatal blood drug concentrations observed (Fig. 38.4).

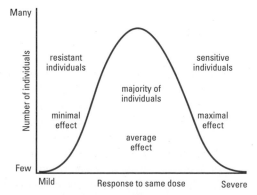

Fig. 38.3 An individual response to a drug is predicted to follow a normal distribution profile.

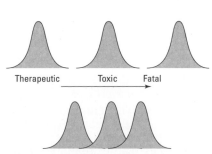

Fig. 38.4 A more realistic illustration of the response to a drug on an individual.

Example   Examples of metabolic routes
Phase I includes:

oxidation – wide variety of substrates;

reduction – compounds with reducible groups, i.e. aldehyde, ketones;

hydrolysis – compounds with ester or amide groups.

Phase II includes:

glucuronidation – carboxylic acids, phenols, alcohols;

sulphation – alcohols, phenols, primary aromatic amines;

acetylation – aromatic amines, phenols;

methylation – phenols, amines, alcohols.

Probably the most important phase I metabolic route is that associated with the cytochrome P450 family accounting for approximately 70–80% of activity. These are subdivided into subfamilies (CYP1, CYP2 and CYP3), and within these there are a wide number of isoforms that are associated with drug metabolism, collectively known as mixed function oxidases. Of note is the CYP2 sub family which, although is not the most prevalent, is the one with the greatest drug activity – for example, CYP2A6 metabolises nicotine, CYP2D6 methadone. The CYP2 subfamily is also known to show genetic polymorphisms, which may play a part in the death of an individual at low concentration if they have a genetic mutation of one of the CYP2 isoforms.

KEY POINT   *The effect of a drug after administration is controlled by the rate of absorption, distribution, concentration and sensitivity of the individual to the drug.*

Metabolism

This is the process by which the drug is transformed into either an inactive form (more polar metabolite) to facilitate excretion or bioactivated to a pharmacologically active form. Metabolic routes within the body fall under two categories – phase I (modification of the chemical structure) and phase II (conjugation reaction), with most drugs undergoing a combination of the two phases.

When a drug is ingested it immediately undergoes the process of metabolism, such that the parent drug (i.e. the one originally taken) concentration is reduced and the metabolite concentration is increased. If the drug is taken repeatedly, this process continues until steady state (therapeutic) levels are achieved. The ratio between the parent drug and metabolite can be calculated and gives an indication as to whether the concentration is due to acute or chronic exposure, which may influence your interpretation.

It is also worth pointing out that some metabolites are also pharmacologically active, e.g. diazepam and its metabolites – temazepam and oxazepam. As such, any pharmacological effect will be a result of the combination of the parent drug and metabolite as opposed to any one single drug. Metabolites also have their use in determining what parent drug has been taken – for example, the presence of 6-monoacetylmorphine is indicative of heroin use.

Excretion

As drugs become metabolised to their more polar, water-soluble forms they can then be more easily excreted from the body, with the major route being in the urine, but other smaller excretory routes such as sweat and breath (for the more volatile compounds) also exist.

Post-mortem *drug redistribution*

The phenomenon of the movement of drugs in the body is known to occur following death. Drugs can diffuse from tissues of high concentration, e.g. stomach contents, into the surrounding tissues and blood vessels. As a consequence, drug concentration may be subject to elevated levels that do not necessarily reflect the concentration at the time of death. In general terms you can predict whether or not a drug is likely to redistribute in this manner by the volume of distribution (V_d). As there can be substantial differences in concentration of drug found in different blood vessels (see Table. 38.2), it is crucial that the blood sample obtained at autopsy is that from a ligated peripheral blood vessel (femoral vein) to minimise the extent of this redistribution artefact. Similarly, the distribution of drug in the liver or lung is not homogeneous (Pounder *et al.*, 1996), nor is the distribution homogeneous in muscle when proposed as an alternative to blood (Langford *et al.*, 1998). The extent of redistribution remains unknown for all drugs and is clearly a confounding factor in the interpretation of *post-mortem* toxicological results.

There are currently no accepted biochemical markers that indicate whether or not this artefact has taken place, although there does appear to be some correlation with the parallel redistribution of the amino acids leucine, methionine and serine when compared with the movement of amitriptyline (Langford and Pounder, 1997).

Table 38.2 The distribution of the tricyclic antidepressant amitriptyline in blood and tissues and its potential for redistribution (data courtesy of Langford and Pounder, 1997)

Sample	Amitriptyline (mg L^{-1})
Femoral vein	1.8
Left and right iliac veins	2.6
Lower inferior vena cava	3.5
Inferior vena cava	2.4
Superior vena cava	2.8
Right heart	2.7
Pulmonary artery	3.4
Left pulmonary vein	18.8
Right pulmonary vein	20.2
Aorta	11.7
Vitreous humour	0.8
Bile	42.1
Urine	13.6

Interpretation

Once the drug concentration has been determined it has to be interpreted, taking into account all the available information regarding the case. This interpretation should be based partly on reference to published tables of drug data (Table. 38.3), which categorise the drug concentrations in therapeutic, toxic and fatal ranges (Uges, 1996; Druid and Holmgren, 1997), but also taking into account other factors such as age, body mass, presence of natural disease, dose, drug interactions and tolerance of the individual.

A novel alternative approach has been proposed where a Bayesian network (Chapter 57) was demonstrated to be successful in corroborating previously reported cases where drugs had been ingested by taking into account both pathological and toxicological findings (Langford *et al.*, 2015).

The dose is of significant importance. Drug concentrations found in the body depend on the dose given and how frequently that dose is taken. A higher dose, in general, produces higher drug concentration in plasma and urine.

 KEY POINT The exact dose cannot be predicted from the drug concentration found in these fluids.

When a drug is taken over a period of time, the accumulation in the blood of the drug or its metabolite(s) may occur if elimination of the drug or its metabolites is not complete in the interval between doses. By looking at the ratios of the parent drug to its metabolite(s) you may be able to determine the frequency of use and whether this is an acute or chronic dose. For example, smoking a single cannabis reefer may result in a positive blood or urine test for cannabinoids for up to 1 or 2 days. Continued use of cannabis on a daily basis, however, may result in a positive blood or urine test for 3 or more weeks after drug use has stopped. This is explained by the fact that cannabis is highly lipophilic, with a high affinity for adipose tissues/fat stores. These tissues, in effect, act as a drug reservoir from which the drug is slowly released.

Drugs with a high V_d are more likely to undergo substantial redistribution following death.

Example Interpreting a case involving more than one drug A drug dealer was suspected of supplying heroin to a regular drug user, who subsequently died. The drug dealer was charged with manslaughter on the basis that he supplied the drug user with the heroin.

A blood sample was obtained from the drug user at the *post mortem* and examined for the presence of drugs. The toxicological analysis of the blood indicated the presence of: alcohol (at 140 mg per 100 mL); morphine (at 0.04 mg L^{-1}); diazepam (at 0.7 mg L^{-1}); desmethydiazepam, a metabolite of diazepam (at 0.6 mg L^{-1}).

In this case, there are three drugs present that can cause central nervous system depression. By reference to drug tables (e.g. Uges, 1996), individually the estimated concentrations of these drugs would be unlikely to be fatal. However, in combination, since each has a depressant activity, the likelihood of fatality is greatly increased (Stockley, 1999) and the death in this case could be attributed to the combination of drugs, rather than specifically to the heroin especially given that no 6 monoacetyl morphiine was found.

Table 38.3 Reference table for therapeutic, toxic and fatal drug concentrations in blood-plasma

Drug	Therapeutic range	Toxic range	Fatal dose
Amitriptyline	0.05–0.3	0.5-0.6	1.5–2
Nortriptyline®	0.02–0.2	0.3	1–3
Cocaine	0.05–0.3	0.25–1	0.9–2.1
Diazepam	0.1–2	3–5	–
Paracetamol	10–25	100–150	200–300

Extracted from Schulz *et al.* (2012): all results expressed as mg L^{-1}.

Drug interactions

Drugs will produce either an antagonistic or synergistic effect in the body. This is of particular importance when interpreting those drugs affecting the central nervous system, i.e. antidepressants in combination with narcotic analgesics. The combination of the drugs may prove fatal even if the individual drug concentrations are not in the fatal category.

Post-mortem production of alcohol

It is known that in a decomposing body, microbiological degradation of the tissues around the gastro-intestinal region can result in the production of significant amounts of alcohol (de Lima and Midio, 1999). Therefore, interpretation of alcohol concentrations in a decomposed body should be treated with caution (Chapter 37).

Tolerance

The more frequently a drug is used, then the more likely a person is to build up tolerance to the drug, i.e. more of the drug is needed to produce the same physiological effects. Data regarding how long tolerance takes to build up are limited, but it is believed that tolerance for most drugs will be established in 7–10 days of repeated use. If the drug is no longer taken, then this acquired tolerance will be lost in approximately 3–4 days. This phenomenon is particularly important in interpreting cases where death may be due to abuse of drugs. In the case of a naïve user, the death may be explained relatively easily in terms of an overdose. If a regular user abstains from taking the drug, for example during a prison term, then death may be explained due to a breakdown in tolerance. The one type of death that may be difficult to explain is that of a regular tolerant drug user who dies suddenly. At the *post mortem* there may be no pathological cause (usually only circumstantial evidence) or toxicological cause (usually only low levels of drug), other than long-term drug misuse, which doesn't explain why the person died on this occasion.

Understanding heroin addiction – the route of administration is usually by intravenous injection, but it can also be smoked. Acute intoxication with the drug gives a rush of euphoria, but also decreases the heart and breathing rate, with potentially fatal consequences. Chronic effects are characterised by physical and psychological dependence and tolerance to the drug.

Reporting toxicology cases

When producing a toxicological statement (Chapter 60) you should include the analytical findings, a brief summary of each of the drugs that have been found and your interpretation of the drug concentration found, including the effects of multiple drugs in combination.

 KEY POINT *As a toxicologist you must be careful not to say in your statement that a death was caused by a drug. It is only the forensic pathologist who can assign a cause of death.*

In a case involving a drug overdose, it is possible to report your result using a form of words that implies that the person would have died from the drug concentration found – for example, 'the concentration of paracetamol lies in the range associated with fatality reported in the scientific literature'. When reporting cases where there is an allegation of regular illicit drug use, you do not know the tolerance of the individual and therefore you can make no such comment on the likelihood of fatality, as illustrated in Box 38.2.

Box 38.2 An example of a statement for a case involving heroin

The following is an extract from a typical toxicology statement.

Blood for alcohol labelled 'taken at autopsy from Ann Addict on 1st April 2017'.

The blood was examined for alcohol with a negative result.

Femoral blood sample labelled 'taken at autopsy from Ann Addict on 1st April 2017'.

Morphine was found in the blood (0.27 mg per L).

6-monoacetyl morphine (a metabolite of diamorphine) was found in the blood (14 mg per L)

The blood was further examined for other drugs, with negative results.

Diamorphine (heroin) *per se* only lasts for a few minutes in the body before being converted to an intermediate, 6-monoacetyl morphine, and then more slowly to morphine. The conversion to 6-monoacetyl morphine is completed within 30 min and the complete conversion to morphine within a few hours.

The range of blood morphine concentrations that produce toxicity vary considerably depending on the tolerance of the individual. Blood morphine concentrations observed in individuals using diamorphine or morphine on a regular basis may be sufficient to cause serious (if not fatal) effects in non-tolerant individuals. The concentration of morphine detected in the blood of Miss Ann Addict may be sufficiently high to cause toxic symptoms in the absence of tolerance.

A similar approach should be adopted for reporting each drug found. You should refer to the scientific literature (see Chapters 45 and 47) to research the most up-to-date information regarding the drug, which may help in the interpretation of the specific case you are dealing with, but make sure you use appropriate peer-reviewed sources.

Text references

Advisory Council for the Misuse of Drugs (ACMD) (2007) Drug Facilitated Sexual Assault. Available at: https://www.gov.uk/government/publications/acmd-drug-facilitated-sexual-assault-dfsa-2007. Last accessed 22/08/2017.

Baselt, R.C. (2002) *Disposition of Toxic Drugs and Chemicals in Man,* 6th edn. Biomedical Publications, Foster City.

de Lima, I.V. and Midio, A.F. (1999) Origin of ethanol in decomposed bodies. *Forensic Science International* 106: 157–162.

Department of Transport, Road Safety Drug Driving collection. Available at: https://www.gov.uk/government/collections/drug-driving\#table-of-drugs-and-limits. Last accessed 22/08/2017.

Druid, H. and Holmgren, P. (1997) A compilation of fatal and control concentrations of drugs in postmortem femoral blood. *Journal of Forensic Sciences* **41**(1): 79–87.

Langford, A.M. and Pounder, D.J. (1997) Possible markers for postmortem drug redistribution. *Journal of Forensic Sciences* **42**(1): 88–92.

Langford, A.M., Taylor, K.K. and Pounder, D.J. (1998) Drug concentration in selected skeletal muscles. *Journal of Forensic Sciences* **43**(1): 22–27.

Langford, A.M., Bolton, J.R., Carlin, M.G. and Palmer, R. (2015) Post mortem toxicology: A pilot study to evaluate the use of a Bayesian Network to assess the likelihood of fatality. *Journal of Forensic and Legal Medicine* 33: 82–90.

Lee, C., Tam, J.C.N, Kung, L. and Yim, L. (2003) Validity of CO-oximetric determination of carboxyhaemoglobin in putrefying blood and body cavity fluid. *Forensic Science International* **132**(2): 153–156.

Moffat, A.C., Osselton, D., Widdop, B., Watts, J. (eds) (2011) *Clarke's Analysis of Drugs and Poisons,* 4th edn. Pharmaceutical Press, London.

Pounder, D.J., Adams, E., Fuke, C. and Langford, A.M. (1996) Site to site variability of postmortem drug concentrations in liver and lung. *Journal of Forensic Sciences* **41**(6): 927–932.

Schulz, M., Iwersen-Bergmann, S., Andresen, H and Schmoldt, A. (2012) Therapeutic and toxic blood concentrations of nearly 1000 drugs and other xenobiotics. *Critical Care* **16**(4):R136

Sexual Offences Act 2003. Available at: http://www.legislation.gov.uk/ukpga/2003/42/contents. Last accessed 22/08/2017.

SOFT (2006) *Forensic Toxicology Laboratory Guidelines.* Society of Forensic Toxicologists (SOFT). Available at: http://www.soft-tox.org/files/Guidelines_2006_Final.pdf. Last accessed 22/08/2017.

Stockley, I.H. (1999) *Drug Interactions.* Pharmaceutical Press, London.

Uges, D. (1996) Therapeutic and toxic drug concentrations. *TIAFT Bulletin* **26**(1): 1–34.

Verstraete, A.G. (2004) Detection times of drugs of abuse in blood, urine and oral fluid. *Therapeutic Drug Monitoring* 26: 200–205.

Wennig, R. (2000) Potential problems with the interpretation of hair analysis results. *Forensic Science International* 107: 5–12.

Sources for further study

Flanagan, R.J., Taylor, A., Watson, I.D. and Whelpton, R. (2007) *Fundamentals of Analytical Toxicology.* Wiley, Chichester.

Gray, H. (1918) *Anatomy of the Human Body.* Philadelphia. Available at: http://www.bartleby.com/. Last accessed 22/08/2017.

Jickells, S. and Negrusz, A. (eds) (2008) *Clarke's Analytical Forensic Toxicology.* Pharmaceutical Press, London and Chicago.

Karch, S.B. (2015) *Karch's Pathology of Drug Abuse,* 5th edn. CRC Press, Boca Raton.

LeBeau, M.A. and Mozayani, A. (eds) (2001) *Drug-Facilitated Sexual Assault.* Academic Press, New York.

Liska, K. (2007) *Drugs and the Human Body with Implications for Society,* 8th edn. Prentice Hall, Harlow.

Uges, D. (2004) The International Association of Forensic Toxicologists (TIAFT). Available at: http://www.tiaft.org (members only website). Last accessed 22/08/2017.

Wills, S. (2005) *Drugs of Abuse,* 2nd edn. Pharmaceutical Press, London and Chicago.

Study exercises

38.1 Test your understanding of the interpretation of *post-mortem* blood drug concentrations. How would you interpret a methadone blood drug concentration of 0.6 mg L^{-1} in (a) a naïve user and (b) a known chronic drug user regularly attending a methadone maintenance clinic?

38.2 Write a protocol for a general drug screen. After reading this chapter, prepare a detailed stepwise protocol, including instrumental parameters, explaining how you would perform a general drug screen on a *post-mortem* blood sample. Ask another student or a tutor to evaluate your protocol and provide you with feedback. You may wish to read peer-reviewed journals to help with your protocol. Discuss how the methods differ from your protocol.

38.3 Recognition of *post-mortem* redistribution. Discuss this issue with a colleague or in a group and list key points that could affect your interpretation of *post-mortem* blood concentrations. Consider how these issues could be resolved.

Drug legislation in the UK – drugs are controlled under the Misuse of Drugs Act 1971. The details of control are legislated through the Misuse of Drugs Regulations 2001.

Example Drug seizures in England and Wales 2016–2017

Class A – 29,807 (of which 8092 were heroin (equating to 783 kg), 14,892 were cocaine (equating to 5,516 kg), 3,174 were ecstasy (equivalent to 498,331 tablets)

Class B – 104,236, the majority of which (99,779) related to cannabis (resin 5,838 kg), herbal (11,861 kg) and a total of 318,988 plants seized

Class C – 5,016 seizures, including 1,945 benzodiazepines equating to 567,438 doses

Total seizures 138,955

Figures courtesy of Home Office Statistical Bulletin (2017)

A forensic chemist may be asked to examine illicit drugs that have been found or seized from a person, e.g. cannabis resin or heroin. The purpose of the examination may be:

- **to identify the type of drug(s)** – including illicit drugs and proprietary preparations;
- **to determine the amount of drug(s) submitted for examination** – for example, to indicate whether the person was intending to supply the drug, rather than for personal use;
- **to determine the purity of the drug(s)**;
- **to determine the impurity profile of the drug(s)** – for example, to indicate whether the drug has been manufactured by a particular clandestine laboratory.

Production, possession and supply of all drugs are governed by law, including national and international legislation as well as the United Nations treaties, the Single Convention on Narcotic Drugs, the Convention on Psychotropic Substances and the Convention Against Illicit Traffic in Narcotic Drugs and Psychotropic Substances (King, 2003).

 KEY POINT *A forensic chemist analyses samples submitted to the laboratory for controlled drugs, the results of which may determine whether a person will face a charge in the criminal justice system (e.g. of possession, supply or production). Any drug seizures are monitored and information is shared with Customs & Excise to track illicit drug movement, and for public safety when, for example, a new source of pure heroin appears in a city.*

Stages in bulk drug analysis

There are four stages in the examination of drugs that have been submitted to the forensic laboratory:

1. **Initial examination** – at this stage you should examine the integrity of the packaging, check that the contents of the bag match the label details and the submission paperwork, and record your observations in your examination notes.
2. **Presumptive tests** – through experience of analysing illicit drugs you may be able to form a visual impression of the identity of a drug. However, a chemical test is still required to support your initial impression prior to further analysis. For example, a fake ecstasy tablet may not contain 3,4-methylenedioxymethylamphetamine (MDMA). Using a simple presumptive test such as the Marquis test (see Box 39.1), the presumptive identity of MDMA can be determined by a colour change to blue/black, whereas it would remain colourless if no MDMA were present.
3. **Quantification and confirmation** – by using a technique such as high-performance liquid chromatography or gas chromatography (Chapter 14) the identity of the drug can be confirmed and the purity of the drug can be calculated.
4. **Reporting the results** – once you are confident that the drug has been identified conclusively, then a report can be written.

Bulk drug analysis

Initial examination

You should always record a detailed description of the bag and its contents in your examination notes, including:

- **The exact transcript of the label details (inclusive of spelling mistakes)** – this is important in terms of the continuity of evidence (Chapter 23).
- **The type of bag the drugs have been supplied in** – some police forces use bags specifically designed for drug seizures that come with a pre-printed unique reference number. Other bags that can be used are standard polythene evidence bags. You should check the integrity of the seal, record the drug bag number and the type of bag.
- **The number of tablets of each type** – there may be tablets of different colours or embossed with different logos, which should be treated as different populations.
- **The colour and appearance of the drug** – e.g. white/cream, flecked/mottled, flat/concave, the presence of brand marks on either side, any other distinguishable features.
- **Accurate dimensions** of the diameter and height of the tablets/compressed drug block measured using Vernier calipers (p. 50).
- **A drawing of the front, side and reverse profiles.**
- **Mass of the drugs** – bulk powder, powders obtained from individual wraps, cannabis (herbal and resin) must be weighed. It is not usually necessary to weigh tablets, unless the seizure is large. In these situations, you can count 100 manually or by using a drugs counter (p. 20) and accurately weigh them. Weigh the total to provide an estimate of the total number of tablets. However, if the seizure contains different tablets, then this process cannot be done and the populations must be separated and weighed individually.

In cases involving the submission of, for example, cannabis resin, tablets or powder wraps, you must decide the appropriate size of sample to ensure that the analysis is representative of the whole seizure. According to the United Nations Drug Control Programme, if the total number is between 1 and 10, then all 10 should be examined, between 1 and 100, then 10 should be examined and for more than 100, the square root of the total number should be examined (Cole, 2003). In practice, this would prove costly and time consuming. Therefore, in the UK a process known as random sampling is adopted based on each tablet in the population having an equal chance of being sampled (see Table 39.1). If different populations of tablets occur within the same seizure, then the same sampling procedure is also applied to them.

Presumptive tests

The purpose of these tests, also known as spot tests, is to provide a rapid presumptive identification of drugs or their precursors. There are many different reagents that can be used for this purpose, including Ehrlich's reagent for hallucinogens, cobalt thiocyanate for cocaine or the Duquenois test for cannabis. However, one test commonly used in forensic chemistry involves using Marquis reagent (see Box 39.1), which reacts with a variety of drugs including ecstasy, opiates, cocaine and amphetamine. With heroin, Marquis reagent produces a purple coloration due to the formation of an oxonium-carbenium salt, whereas with amphetamine the orange colour is produced due to the formation of a carbenium ion.

Thin-layer chromatography (TLC)

This analytical method (Chapter 14) should be performed after the spot test. It separates out the individual components of the tablet, powder or resin using a

Reference standard mixes for TLC – these standards should include the components that are likely to be found in the unknown drug sample, for example:

Drug	Standard mix
Amphetamine	methanol; amphetamine; caffeine
Benzodiazepine	methanol; diazepam; temazepam
Cannabis	methanol; known cannabis resin standard
Cocaine	methanol; cocaine
Diamorphine	methanol; diamorphine; noscapine; monoacetylmorphine
Ecstasy	methanol; N-hydroxy methylene dioxyamphetamine (MDA); 3,4-methylenedioxy methylamphetamine (MDMA); 3,4-methylenedioxy ethylamphetamine (MDEA), N-methyl-1-(1,3-benzodioxol-5-5-yl)-2-butanamine (MBDB)
LSD	methanol; lysergide (LSD); ergotamine; methylsergide; ergometrine

Box 39.1 How to perform a presumptive Marquis test on an unknown powder or tablet

1. **Prepare the Marquis reagent** – measure 10 mL formaldehyde into a beaker and add 100 mL of concentrated sulphuric acid slowly, continually stirring the mixture.

2. **Prepare the bench top** – clean the bench top using methanol and then wipe down with a clean tissue. Discard the tissue into a bin designated for bulk drug waste. Collect a large sheet of brown paper and place on the clean bench surface.

3. **Prepare the drug** – clean a scalpel blade and spatula with methanol. If the drug seized is a tablet, then record all appropriate details (see p. 384) in your examination notes. Using the scalpel, carefully scrape the surface of the tablet on to the brown paper. Collect this sample into a small glass screw-top vial. If a powder has been submitted, then accurately weigh the powder and, using a small spatula, transfer a small sample into a small glass screw-top vial.

4. **Perform the test** – pipette 3–4 drops of Marquis reagent into a spotting well (a ceramic tile with indentations). The reagent should always be added to the well first as a check, to see if the well is contaminated (the reagent should remain colourless). If a colour reaction does occur, the well is contaminated and should not be used. Add a small amount (1 mg) of the drug to the reagent using a small spatula. Record any colour change that occurs during the first five seconds of the test.

5. **Interpret the colour changes** – the colour change should be noted in your examination notes and can give an indication of the type of drug present. Examples of colours produced include:
   - diamorphine (heroin) – purple;
   - ecstasy – blue/black;
   - amphetamine – orange;
   - methylamphetamine – orange/brown;
   - cocaine – no colour change, but will effervesce.

Table 39.1 Random sampling of tablets – one approach for deciding on the number of tablets you need to examine increases with the number in the population is as follows:

Population size	Number of tablets
1	1
2–4	2
5–20	3
21+	4

Thus, even if the seizure contains 1,000 tablets, only four randomly sampled tablets need to be examined. (see p. 384 for more information). Alternative approaches to random sampling include the square root of n, by management discretion or by the judicial requirement.

silica-coated TLC plate (see Box 39.2). Although it can be used tentatively to identify a drug based on the R_f values of the drug compared to known reference standards (Chapter 14), it cannot be used without further testing to report a drugs case. The exception to this is cannabis, since a visual and microscopic comparison should have already been performed (p. 391).

Confirmation of the identity of the drug

Presumptive tests only give an indication of the group a drug belongs to, therefore the identity of a drug needs to be confirmed by another technique, usually HPLC or GC–MS (Chapters 14–15). These techniques will provide you with a definitive identification of the drug. When you confirm the presence of any bulk drug it is important to recognise that contamination between injections can occur in HPLC or GC–MS. It is important to place blank, drug-free samples between case samples, to ensure that the appearance of 'ghost' peaks from the previous injection are not confused with the actual case sample. Using these techniques, the identity of the drug can be determined using retention time, UV absorbance or mass spectrum data when compared to reference standards.

Box 39.2 How to analyse bulk drugs using thin-layer chromatography

It is important to have some indication of the type of drugs that might be present in a sample before using TLC (see Chapter 14), since the type of drug will influence which solvent system will be used. Although a general TLC solvent system can be prepared for the separation of most drugs encountered in the forensic laboratory, there are drugs, such as cannabis and lysergic acid (LSD), that require a different system (see below).

1. **Prepare an appropriate solvent system** – example solvent systems include:

   - a general solvent system – measure 750 mL cyclohexanone, 150 mL toluene and 10 mL diethylamine into a 1 L flask and mix well;

   - for LSD, measure 900 mL chloroform and 100 mL methanol into a 1 L flask and mix well;

   - for cannabis, measure 950 mL toluene and 50 mL diethylamine into a 1 L flask and mix well.

   There are other solvent systems that can be used, such as those described in Moffat et al. (2004). Pour the solvent into a TLC reservoir to a depth of 0.5 cm and cover the tank with a lid.

2. **Prepare the visualisation reagent** – once the separation of the drugs has occurred, you need to be able to observe how far the components in the drug have moved along the TLC plate. The reagents used to visualise the spots can differ according to the drug being analysed. As with the solvent systems, different reagents can be used, including:

   - A general visualisation reagent, such as acidified iodoplatinate – accurately weigh 0.25 g platinic chloride and 5 g potassium iodide. Add to 100 mL water, mix thoroughly and add 5 mL concentrated hydrochloric acid. Transfer to a bottle that has a fine spray.

   - for the visualisation of cannabis, measure 50 mL water and add to 50 mL methanol. Add 50 mg fast blue BB dye and mix thoroughly. Transfer to a bottle that has a fine spray.

3. **Prepare the TLC plates** – pipette 1 mL methanol to the sample of drug you collected for the presumptive test (see Box 39.1) and vortex mix. Allow the insoluble material to settle to the bottom of the vial. Collect a silica gel TLC plate and, using a pencil, lightly draw a line 1 cm from the bottom edge of the plate. Mark on this line at 1-cm spaces a series of crosses, and under each cross write a reference number to indicate whether the sample to be loaded at that position is a reference standard or a case sample.

4. **Load ('spot') the samples on to the plate** – place a capillary tube into the drug solution prepared in step 3. 'Steady' your hand with your other hand and gently touch the end of the capillary tube on to the TLC plate ('spotting') at the appropriately labelled position on the baseline. You should repeat this process for all case samples, appropriate reference standards and a sample of methanol. The reference standards should be a mix of known pure drugs that will elute across the length of the plate as an indicator that the plate is functioning, but also to serve as a reference to possibly identify a drug in the unknown sample (p. 385). The major problem with TLC when used for bulk drug analysis is that the concentration of the drug is unknown. If the drug has been diluted, or cut, several times, then it may be too weak to be detected using TLC. By checking the spots on the baseline under a UV light source, you can determine whether you have spotted enough drug on the plate – if you cannot see a spot then you need to add more sample. Care has to be taken though not to overload the plate, as this will give a long, elongated spot that will be difficult to identify when compared to a reference standard.

5. **Develop the plate** – place the TLC plate into the TLC reservoir and allow the solvent to rise up the plate until it reaches 1 cm from the top. Remove the plate and score the solvent front (see Chapter 14) with a pencil.

6. **Visualise the 'spots'** – once the plate is dry, spray the plate with the appropriate visualisation reagent. Using acidified iodoplatinate the spots will develop as a darker area, from which the R_f (p. 129) can then be calculated and a tentative identification of the drug made. For cannabis, spraying the plate with fast blue BB identifies the many individual components of cannabis. The bands you specifically need to identify are cannabinol (purple), cannabidiol (yellow) and tetrahydrocannabinol (red) to provide a positive identification (see p. 392).

For some drugs, for example amphetamine and ecstasy, derivatisation of the drug is required prior to analysis by GC–MS. This increases the polarity of the drug, increases the sensitivity of detection and produces a more characteristic fragmentation pattern. Amphetamine should be derivatised with carbon disulphide (CS_2) and ecstasy heptafluorobutyric anhydride (HFBA), both of which attach to the amine group of the drugs (p. 389).

These techniques are also the method of choice for analysis of trace drug evidence, such as drug paraphernalia (e.g. scales or exhibits collected from a clandestine laboratory) or a drug deal (e.g. a large seizure of money, small scales, knives, pipes or even burnt foil in cases of drug use). It is important to recognise the potential for contamination of such trace evidence in a bulk drug laboratory. In these cases, trace drug analysis cannot be performed in the same laboratory as bulk drug analyses. For similar reasons, if a person enters the bulk drug laboratory, then he/she should not enter the trace laboratory during the same working day.

Purity

HPLC and GC–MS can also provide information on the purity and impurity profile of the drug. The purpose of calculating the purity of the drug is to determine the percentage of the controlled drug that is present in the sample (see Box 39.3). It is possible that a powder may have a high percentage of drug from which it can be diluted with other compounds, known as cutting agents. This can be a significant finding in terms of the amount of drug that would be potentially available for supply, which can influence the charge levied against a person and ultimately the term of imprisonment.

Profiling

The purpose of profiling a drug is to determine whether two independently seized drugs have originated from the same source. This can be carried out either by (i) chemical profiling (e.g. for synthetic drugs), or by (ii) DNA profiling for naturally occurring drugs, such as cannabis (Linacre and Thorpe, 1998, see also Chapter 31), morphine or cocaine. It may be possible that markers produced during the manufacturing process are unique to a particular plant species. The intelligence value of such markers means that if identified in, for example, illicit heroin seizures, then it has to have originated from this source.

Using GC–MS, the chemical profile of the drug can be established. The relative amounts of the drug (active ingredient) and the impurities that are present in the sample can be determined, as well as the cutting agents that may have been used. You can also determine chemical impurities that have become incorporated into the drug during its manufacture. These impurities can be used to

---

Determination of drug purity in the UK – this will only be carried out if sufficient quantity of the drug is submitted for analysis, for example:

Amphetamine – if the quantity is greater than 10 g;

Diamorphine – if the quantity is greater than 1 g.

Example Calculating the free base mass for cocaine.HCl

In order to calculate the free base mass, you need to know the relative molecular mass (M_r) of the drug and the drug in the salt.

cocaine.HCl (salt) $\quad M_r = 339.8$

cocaine $\quad M_r = 303.4$

Proportion of free base $= \dfrac{303.4}{339.8} = 0.893$

If 10 mg cocaine.HCl had been weighed, then the actual mass of cocaine as a free base is $0.893 \times 10 = 8.93$ mg. If this was added to 10 mL methanol, then the concentration of your stock solution would be 0.893 mg mL^{-1}.

Box 39.3   Calculating the purity of a drug

1. **Prepare a reference drug standard** – accurately weigh approximately 10 mg of the relevant pure drug standard and take note of the exact weight. Pipette 1 mL of methanol into a vial and add the drug. The actual concentration of the drug is based on its free base form and not as a salt. Therefore, to calculate the concentration you need to know the mass of the drug and the salt.

2. **Create a calibration curve** – using the stock solution of the drug standard, create a calibration curve (Chapter 51) and run the samples through an HPLC.

3. **Prepare the unknown sample** – accurately weigh 50 mg of the case sample and dilute in 50 mL methanol. This sample will be the equivalent of 1 mgmL^{-1} (w/v). A small amount of this solution can then be injected into the HPLC.

4. **Calculate the concentration of the drug** – calculate the concentration from the calibration curve (Chapter 51).

5. **Calculate the percent purity of the drug** using the formula:

$$\% \text{ purity} = \frac{\text{calculated concentration of drug (from step 4)(mg mL}^{-1})}{\text{weighed concentration of drug (from step 3)(mg mL}^{-1})} \times 100 \qquad [39.1]$$

Bulk drug analysis

Definitions

Opiate – natural (morphine, codeine) or semi-synthetic (diamorphine, dihydro-codeine) drugs derived from the poppy, *Papaver somniferum*.

Opioid – synthetic drugs similar in nature to the opiates (methadone, fentanyl, buprenorphine).

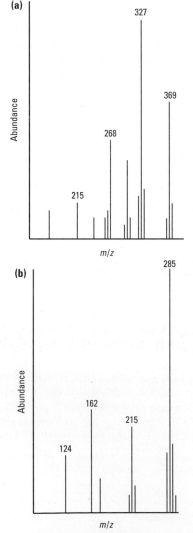

Fig. 39.1 GC–MS chromatograms for (a) diamorphine and (b) morphine.

determine whether one batch of drugs can be linked to another and may also indicate the country of origin.

Bulk drugs are broadly categorised as:

- natural products, e.g. cannabis, cocaine;
- semi-synthetic, e.g. heroin;
- synthetic, e.g. methadone, synthetic cannabinoids, substituted cathinones.

Semi-synthetic drugs typically include a natural product that has undergone a chemical process to derive the 'active' drug. For example, heroin is derived from the plant *Papaver somniferum*. The isoquinoline alkaloids (morphine, thebaine, codeine) and the phenanthrene alkaloids (noscapine, papaverine) can be found in the latex in the flowering head of the plant. These are extracted and purified, from which diamorphine can be synthesised. The synthesis reaction processes and the natural variation of the plant result in a mixture of diamorphine and these alkaloids. It is this mixture that can be used for chemical profiling for intelligence purposes.

Examples of bulk drug analysis

Semi-synthetic drugs – diamorphine (heroin)

Diamorphine can be submitted to the laboratory either as a bulk drug or individual wraps, or as paraphernalia such as burnt foil, spoons or even syringes, following abuse of the drug. Once the exhibit has been fully described in your examination notes, the drug type should be determined. Use Marquis reagent (see Box 39.1) to initially identify the generic group of the drug.

If a positive result is obtained, you need to then identify the individual components in the sample. Prepare a TLC plate (see Box 39.2) and 'spotdrug and reference standard. After running the plate, visualise the spots with acidified iodoplatinate and determine the R_f values of the individual components.

The identity of these components can be confirmed using GC–MS. The GC should be programmed to operate from a low temperature (90 °C) to a high temperature (300 °C) in order to elute all potential components (Chapter 14). A small sample (10–50 mg) can be dissolved directly in methanol for injection into the GC (the greater the concentration, the stronger the response on the GC; however, care should be taken not to overload the instrument). The advantage of using this technique is that the impurities, or cutting agents, commonly caffeine or paracetamol, can also be determined at the same time as the main drug. Typically, you would find diamorphine along with papaverine, noscapine and thebaine as impurities formed during the manufacturing process. It may also indicate the presence of other drugs, or components, that the two presumptive tests have not identified. Diamorphine can be identified by monitoring ions at *m/z* values 327, 369 and 268 and morphine at 285, 162 and 124 (see Fig. 39.1).

If the weight of diamorphine is greater than 1 g, then the purity of the drug should be determined. If the sample is not homogeneous you should grind the powder in a pestle and mortar. Accurately weigh 10 mg and dissolve in 100 mL methanol. Prepare a free base diamorphine standard (see Box 39.3) and create a calibration curve. Prepare a mobile phase by diluting (a) 18 mL concentrated ammonia into 675 mL water and (b) dissolving 24 g ammonium nitrate in 500 mL water. Mix 500 mL of reagent (a) with 250 mL of reagent (b). Inject all samples into an HPLC using, for example, a Spherisorb™ column connected to a UV detector set at 280 nm (Chapter 14), making sure a methanol blank is tested in-between the calibration curve and each case drug sample. From the calibration curve, you can calculate the purity of the drug.

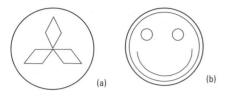

Fig. 39.2 Representative logos seen on ecstasy tablets.

Synthetic drugs – ecstasy

Ecstasy is the common name for 3,4-methylenedioxymethylamphetamine (MDMA). However, there are several other drugs that come under this general heading, including methylenedioxyamphetamine (MDA) and 3,4-methylenedi oxyethylamphetamine (MDEA).

These drugs primarily come in tablet form in a variety of colours, shapes and sizes. The tablets can appear to be professionally made, inclusive of a logo (see Fig. 39.2) that can be used to identify a particular source or dealer. Common logos include the Mitsubishi, Superman and Ferrari symbols, but the logo can be anything – for example when the Teletubbies programme was first broadcast, a Teletubby logo was launched. Recognition of the logo can give an indication that the tablet is a designer drug such as ecstasy, but this cannot be used as a parameter for positive identification. A typical tablet will contain approximately 100 mg of the drug.

When tablets are submitted to the laboratory, the packaging and contents should be examined as detailed on p. 384. A Marquis test should be performed, noting that a positive result is indicated by a colour change to blue/black. This test can be confirmed by TLC and the presence of the particular components can be confirmed using GC–MS following derivatisation with, for example, heptafluorobutyric anhydride (HFBA) (see Box 39.4).

As with other drugs, chemical profiling can also be performed for the ecstasy-related drugs. In ecstasy seizures, it has been reported that the precursor 3,4-methylenedioxyphenyl-2-propanone is found, along with palmitic and stearic acid (Waddell-Smith, 2007). The chemical profile of the drug can be determined by:

- profiling the organic impurities – e.g. by GCMS (see Chapters 14–15);
- profiling the composition of the drug – e.g. by Raman or near IR spectroscopy (see Chapter 19);
- profiling the trace metals within the drug – e.g. by ICP-MS (see Chapter 17). (Waddell-Smith, 2007)

Other adulterants can also be found – for example, ketamine or caffeine, incorporated into the tablet to enhance the stimulant effect.

Novel psychoactive substances (NPS)

Prior to 2016 these types of compounds were termed 'legal highs'. As of 2016, the Psychoactive Substances Act has come into force in the UK and this now

---

Box 39.4 Derivatisation of ecstasy tablets using HFBA

1. **Prepare the reagents** – (i) Tris buffer – weigh 121 g tris (hydroxymethyl) methylamine and add to 1 L water, (ii) 10% sodium bicarbonate solution – weigh 10 g sodium bicarbonate and add to 100 mL water.

2. **Extract the drug from the tablet** – prepare a scraping of the tablet (see part 3 of Box 39.1), weigh approximately 10 mg of the powder and add to a glass vial. Pipette 250 μL tris buffer and 500 μL toluene to the vial and vortex mix the sample. Pipette 50 μL of this toluene into a clean glass vial and add a further 450 μL of toluene.

3. **Derivatise the sample** – pipette 10 μL of HFBA into the glass vial and add 500 μL of 10% sodium bicarbonate solution. Vortex mix the sample. Transfer the toluene to a GC–MS autosampler vial ready for injection. Using a temperature program from 100 °C to 300 °C the derivatised ecstasy type drugs can be identified, for example:

MDA – ions monitored at m/z 240, 135, 162, 375;
MDMA – ions monitored at m/z 254, 135, 162, 389;
MDEA – ions monitored at m/z 268, 135, 162, 240, 403.

restricts the supply, synthesis of any substance that can produce a psychoactive effect. These compounds, typically in powder form, represent a continual evolvement of chemical structure hence the legal status was continually catching up with new compounds until this new act was passed. The chemical composition of the marketed powder, albeit declared as not for human consumption, would for the user be unknown. This also poses an analytical problem for the scientist, especially in respect of reference standards (p. 474) to confirm the identity.

Of note in this category of synthetic drugs are the synthetic cannabinoids, piperazines and cathinones and their derivatives. The synthetic cannabinoids are further subdivided into three types:

- classical, e.g. HU210 that has been suggested to have 100 times the potency of tetrahydrocannabinol;
- non-classical, e.g. cyclohexylphenols; aminoalkylindoles, e.g. JWH-01;8
- endocannabinoids.

These usually are fine crystalline powders that can be solvent extracted (Chapter 12) and analysed using TLC (Chapter 14) and GCMS (Chapters 14–15). Regioisomers can be determined using NMR (Chapter 20). There is currently limited data relating to the toxicological effects of these drugs, however it is noted that they have been linked to fatality.

Cathinone itself is a natural product obtained from the plant Catha edulis, but what has appeared are the synthetic cathinones, so called 'bath salts', which are chemically similar to the phenethylamines but not as potent. As with the synthetic cannabinoids, there are limited data on the toxicological effects, and with the chemical composition the chemical structures are continually modified leading to a wide variance in composition.

Natural drugs – cocaine

When a suspected cocaine sample is submitted to the laboratory, not only will you need to identify it as cocaine, but you will also need to identify whether it is a salt or a free base (see Box 39.5). Record the packaging and description details of the exhibit in your examination notes. Test the drug sample with Marquis reagent and note whether the reagent effervesces. Prepare a TLC plate and spot the case drug sample, methanol and reference standard (cocaine, lignocaine and procaine). Visualise the plate using acidified iodoplatinate and record your results.

Box 39.5 How to determine whether cocaine is present in a sample as a free base or salt

This method is based on the fact that cocaine as a free base is soluble in hexane, but not in water; and vice versa for cocaine hydrochloride (salt) (Logan *et al.*, 1989):

1. **Dissolve a small amount of the case drug sample in a suitable solvent** – for example, 5–10 mg into 1 mL hexane, and vortex mix.

2. **Centrifuge, to remove any insoluble tablet debris** – for example, $800–1,000 \times g$ for 5 min.

3. **Test for free base cocaine** – pipette some of the supernatant layer into a clean test tube – for example, 300 μL of the supernatant, and add 200 μL of cobalt

thiocyanate solution. If a blue precipitate is formed, then cocaine is present as a free base.

4. **If no precipitate is formed, extract in water** – for example, add 1 mL of distilled water to the supernatant and vortex mix.

5. **Partition into chloroform** – pipette 500 μL of chloroform into a clean test tube and add 300 μL of the aqueous (lower) layer obtained from step 4.

6. **Test for cocaine present as a salt** – add 200 μL of cobalt thiocyanate solution. If a blue precipitate is formed in the chloroform (lower) layer, then cocaine is present as a salt.

The presence of cocaine can be confirmed using GC–MS, monitoring ions at m/z 82, 182, 105 (Moffat *et al.*, 2004). With cocaine, a simple extraction should be carried out prior to injection. Weigh approximately 50 mg of the case drug into a microcentrifuge tube, add 200 μL of 20% ammonia and 1 mL ethyl acetate. Vortex mix and add 100 mg of sodium sulphate to remove any moisture in the liquid. Transfer the liquid layer into a GC–MS autosampler vial ready for injection.

If the drug has been identified as cocaine and the weight is greater than 1 g then a purity analysis should be performed as described on page 387. The HPLC detector should be set at a wavelength of 233 nm, using a column such as Inertsil ODS2™ and a mobile phase consisting of 850 mL water and 150 mL acetonitrile, acidified with 1mL 2.5 mol L^{-1} sulphuric acid.

Natural drugs – cannabis

Analysis of cannabis is slightly different from other drugs in that a positive result can be reported following a positive TLC result and visual identification using microscopy (see Chapter 10). With all bulk drug analyses, you are trying to identify a drug that would normally require some form of analytical chemistry to extract the drug (e.g. from a powder or tablet). With cannabis, visual identification serves the same purpose – i.e. it provides a feature that, in combination with a positive TLC result, is sufficient for you to be confident to confirm to a court that the sample you examined was cannabis.

Cannabis can be submitted in the form of a plant (see Photo 39.1), herbal material (dried plant material, including leaves and stalks) or resin. In each case you should record in your examination notes the following:

- **Visual identification** – you should include a description of the sample, including the characteristic smell, number of pieces of resin, brand marks, shape and appearance of the leaves, whether the plant is flowering and weight of the plant or herbal material.
- **Microscopic analysis** – the leaves of cannabis plants should be examined for the presence of glands and bracts (see Fig. 39.3). Using a scalpel, you can dissect these and transfer them to a microscope slide. Alternatively, a scraping of cannabis resin can be obtained using a scalpel, and transferred into a vial containing methanol. Pipette a drop of the methanolic extract on to a microscope slide. Using a low-power microscope ($\times$40 total magnification), identify the hairs (cystolithic, glandular and unicellular-trichomes) and at higher magnification ($\times$100 total magnification) identify the glands and stalks protruding from the edge.
- **Chemical analysis** – the methanolic extract containing cannabis should be spotted on to a TLC plate (see Box 39.1) and visualised using fast blue BB dye. There are many different individual components in cannabis, but the ones you need to identify are cannabidiol (yellow spot), tetrahydrocannabinol (red spot) and cannabinol (purple spot) (see Photo 39.2).

Reporting results

These types of cases should include the specific exhibit examined and the results of the analysis. A brief statement of the classification of the drug and relevant law(s) should also be included. The following examples are extracts from typical bulk drug reports. For complete details of how to write your report see p. 555.

A case involving diamorphine

Bag containing brown powder labelled 'found in possession of Dee Lar on 25/12/17'.

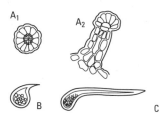

Photo 39.1 The head of a cannabis plant. (Image courtesy of SPSA Forensic Services)

Fig. 39.3 Features of cannabis that can be used to identify the plant. Shown are specific features from a bract – a leaf-like structure associated with the flowering part of the plant: A_1, view of the upper surface (head) of a glandular hair; A_2, stalked glandular hair – these are usually found on the bract and on the lower surface of the leaves to facilitate the secretion of cannabis resin; B, cystolithic hair – so called because of the presence of calcium carbonate in the body of the hair; C, unicellular hair – an abundant hair type covering most of the plant.

Photo 39.2 Separation of individual components of cannabis using TLC. The spots within the lines correspond to the elution order of cannabidiol, cannabinol and 11nor δ9 tetrahydrocannabinol respectively. (Image courtesy of SPSA Forensic Services)

The above item was examined and found to consist of a clear polythene bag containing a small plastic coin bag and a quantity of brown powder. The brown powder (9.32 g) was analysed and found to contain diamorphine (approximately 61% pure, calculated as base).

Diamorphine (ClassA) is a controlled drug within the meaning of Section 2 of the Misuse of Drugs Act 1971.

A case involving cocaine

Wrap containing white rocks labelled 'found in possession of A. Dict on 01/04/17'.

The above item was examined and found to consist of a polythene wrap containing a quantity of lumpy, off-white powder. The powder (625 mg), now in a separate container, was analysed and found to contain cocaine (approximately 82% pure, calculated as base).

Cocaine (ClassA) is a controlled drug within the meaning of Section 2 of the Misuse of Drugs Act 1971, subject to Schedule 5 of the Misuse of Drugs Regulations 2001.

A case involving ecstasy tablets

Bag containing 15 tablets labelled 'found in possession of Sue Spect on 24/06/17'.

The above item was examined and found to consist of a polythene bag containing 15 complete tablets. The complete tablets were examined and found to be similar in terms of appearance. Three of the tablets, selected at random and now in separate containers, were analysed and each found to be an illicit preparation containing 3,4-methylenedioxymethylamphetamine (MDMA).

3,4-methylenedioxymethylamphetamine (ClassA), a compound structurally derived from an N-alkyl-α-methylphenethylamine by substitution in the ring with an alkylene-dioxy substituent, is a controlled drug within the meaning of Section 2 of the Misuse of Drugs Act 1971.

Text references

Araujo, A.M., Valente, M.J., Carvalho, M. (2015) Raising awareness of NPS chemical analysis and in vitro toxicity screening of legal high packages containing synthetic cathinones. *Archives of Toxicology* **89**(5): 757–771.

Cole, M.D. (2003) *The Analysis of Controlled Substances.* Wiley, Chichester.

Home Office Statistical Bulletin (2017) Available at: https://www.gov.uk/government/uploads/system/uploads/attachment_data/file/657872/seizures-drugs-mar2017-hosb2217.pdf Last accessed 12/12/2017.

King, L. (2003) *The Misuse of Drugs Act: A Guide for Forensic Scientists.* Royal Society of Chemistry, Cambridge.

Linacre, A. and Thorpe, J. (1998) Detection and identification of cannabis by DNA. *Forensic Science International* 91: 71–76.

Logan, B.K., Nichols, H.S. and Stafford, D.T. (1989) A simple laboratory test for the determination of the chemical form of cocaine. *Journal of Forensic Sciences* 34: 678–681.

The Misuse of Drugs Regulations 2001, Schedules 1–7. Available at: http://www.opsi.gov.uk/si/si2001/20013998.htm. Last accessed 12/06/09.

Moffat, A.C., Osselton, M.D. and Widdup, B. (eds) (2004) *Clarke's Analysis of Drugs and Poisons,* 3rd edn. Pharmaceutical Press, London.

Scientific Working Group for Analysis of Seized Drugs (2016) Recommendations Edition 7.1 Available at: http://swgdrug.org/. Last accessed 23/08/2017.

Waddell-Smith, R.J.H. (2007) A review of recent advances in impurity profiling of illicit MDMA Samples. *Journal of Forensic Sciences* **52**(6): 1237–1497.

Sources of further study

Drugwise (2016) Promoting evidence based information on drugs, alcohol, tobacco. Available at: www.drugwise.org.uk. Last accessed 23/08/2017.

Psychoactive Substances Act (2016) Available at: www.legislation.gov.uk/ukpga/2016/2/pdfs/ukpga_20160002_en.pdf. Last accessed 23/08/2017.

Smith, F.P. (ed.) (2005) *Handbook of Forensic Drug Analysis.* Academic Press, New York.

Study exercises

39.1 Test your knowledge of presumptive tests. For the following drugs, what colour change is likely to be observed when using Marquis reagent?

(a) amphetamine;
(b) methylamphetamine;
(c) cocaine;
(d) diamorphine;
(e) ecstasy.

39.2 Write a protocol for determining the purity of a sample of cocaine. After reading this chapter, prepare a detailed stepwise protocol, including instrumental parameters, explaining how to determine the purity of the sample. Ask another student or a tutor to evaluate your protocol and provide you with feedback.

39.3 Test your knowledge of the Misuse of Drugs Act. If you do not have a copy of the current Misuse of Drugs Act, you can access the document on the UK Government website (http://www.legislation.gov.uk/ukpga/1971/38/contents). Read this document and have a look in other appropriate sources so that you can list five drugs in each of the five schedules of the Misuse of Drugs Act.

Binder (or film former) – provides the solid matrix that binds the pigment particles together.

Dyes – soluble colour material.

Extenders – compounds used to increase the bulk of the paint and to determine the type of finish, e.g. sheen, matt.

Paint – a decorative liquid polymer preparation containing binder, pigments, extenders and solvent. As the paint dries, the solvent evaporates leaving a hard surface.

Pigments – insoluble colour materials.

Primers – provide strong adhesion between the surface and paint layer.

Paint is a mixture of dyes or pigments, extenders and other chemicals suspended in an organic liquid medium. When applied to a surface, this medium will dry out, either by the evaporation of solvent or by a chemical reaction with air. Once the paint has dried, if the painted surface is damaged then there is a possibility of transfer of paint fragments on to the object causing the damage – for example, a tool used to open a window. It is these paint fragments or 'flakes' that, when compared to control reference samples obtained from a crime scene, can potentially link a suspect to a particular crime.

Forensic examination of paint fragments includes:

- **microscopy** – the surface and cross-section (layers) of the suspect paint flake can be compared using light and comparison microscopy (p. 65) with a control paint fragment;
- **spectroscopy** – most synthetic paints can be analysed using Fourier transform infrared (FTIR) spectroscopy (p. 182);
- **chromatography** – a chemical profile of the polymers in the paint can be determined using pyrolysis gas chromatography–mass spectrometry (p. 398).

 KEY POINT   Paint flakes must be properly recovered and collected from a crime scene. These flakes should, wherever possible, be of full paint thickness, e.g. covering all the layers of paint from under-coat to topcoat.

Types of cases

The most commonly encountered forensic cases involving paint include:

- **Breaking and entering** – for example, where a tool has been used to prise open a window, fragments of wood and small flakes of paint may be transferred on to the perpetrator and remain on the tool. Subsequent examination of both may link the perpetrator to the scene.
- **Road traffic accidents** – any force on impact will damage the paintwork of a vehicle. The paint may be transferred to another vehicle, or even to an individual in a hit-and-run case.
- **Vandalism (e.g. graffiti)** – for example, paint from an aerosol may persist on clothes or the hands/face. Since this type of paint is usually present as a single surface layer, the chemical composition will need to be examined to determine whether the paint seized from an individual can be linked to a particular act of vandalism.
- **Authentication of paintings** – for example, this may involve the analysis of oil paints and their corresponding pigments to determine whether an oil painting is original or is of a certain age.

Paint samples – the majority of paint samples submitted to the forensic laboratory for examination are multi-layered household or motor vehicle samples.

Major types of paints encountered in forensic science:

Water-based acrylic emulsions – e.g. undercoat paint for woodwork;

Solvent-based acrylic emulsions – e.g. touch-up paints for motor vehicles;

Paints containing nitrocellulose – e.g. touch-up paints for motor vehicles;

Oil-based paints containing epoxy resins – e.g. for motor vehicles.

Collection of paint samples

As with any trace evidence, care is required in the collection of paint samples at a crime scene (see Box 40.1). If possible, a control paint sample should be collected, which will be used as a reference against which all other paint flakes, recovered from a suspect, will be compared. If a suspect has been arrested, then his/her clothing should be seized by a police officer once they have been

Box 40.1 How to collect paint fragments from a crime scene

In a case of breaking and entering, you should:

1. **Locate the point of entry** – examine the scene (Chapter 23) and locate where the perpetrator has gained access into the property. This is usually through a window, so you should take note that there may be other types of evidence at this location, such as fingerprints (Chapter 26), footwear impressions (Chapter 27) or tool marks (Chapter 28).

2. **Recover control paint samples** – examine the point of entry for signs of damage to the woodwork, which may be indicative of a tool that has been used. Make sure this damaged area has been photographed (Chapter 23) and a cast of the tool mark has been made. Use a scalpel to cut a small paint sample, approximately 1 cm^2, from the woodwork as near to the damaged paint area as possible. This sample should traverse the full thickness of the paint layers and extend into the wood. This process should be repeated from different areas to obtain a representative sample of the paint.

3. **Package the control paint samples** – place the individual paint fragments into separate polythene bags, seal with tamper-proof tape and attach labels detailing the position the samples were taken from, making sure they are clearly marked as controls.

In a case of an accident involving a vehicle, you should:

1. **Recover all associated debris at the scene** – examine the scene and systematically collect all debris: for example, glass fragments, broken plastic moulding, bumpers.

2. **Recover control paint samples from the vehicle(s) involved** – locate the point(s) of impact and, using a scalpel, cut through the paint layer to the metal underneath. Ideally the paint sample recovered should be 1 cm^2; however, in practice it is often quite difficult to obtain this size, so a representative sample should be obtained. A similar paint sample should be obtained from an undamaged area. If there is transfer of paint on to, for example, the bumper of the motor vehicle, this should be recovered in the same way, obtaining a full thickness sample.

3. **Package the control paint samples** – place the individual paint fragments into a glass screw-top vial and package in a polythene bag, seal with tamper-proof tape and attach labels detailing the position the samples were taken from – make sure they are clearly marked as controls.

Examination protocol – includes visual examination, microscopy, chemical testing, chemical composition (FTIR, pyrolysis GC) and elemental composition (SEM/EDX,XRF).

conveyed to the police station. The removal of clothing should be supervised while the suspect is standing on a sheet of brown paper. The clothing, as well as any surface debris that falls off the clothing, should be packaged by the officer, sealed, labelled and signed in the presence of the suspect and submitted to the laboratory. The clothing and debris may be examined for all types of trace evidence including blood (Chapter 30), hairs (Chapter 32), glass (Chapter 41) and fibres (Chapter 42) as well as paint, depending on the circumstances of the case.

Analysis of paint samples

There are a number of ways that paint can be analysed. These draw on the various properties and features of paint samples, including surface characteristics, organic or inorganic composition and number of layers (Caddy, 2001).

Paint samples are typically multi-layered, therefore a cross-section of the paint sample needs to be prepared prior to analysis. There are several techniques that can be used to prepare a cross-section, such as:

- **Embedding the paint sample in a transparent polymer resin** – once the resin has cured, the surface can be ground down using a rotating grinder to expose the cross-section of the sample for microscopic examination.
- **Sections of the embedded paint sample can be cut at predetermined thicknesses** (typically in the μm range) using a microtome, e.g. Leica

---

Box 40.2 How to prepare a paint sample for cross-sectional examination by embedding in plastic

1. **Prepare your bench surface** – clean the bench thoroughly before you start any examination.

2. **Examine the packaging** – make sure that the contents of the packaging match the CJA label details, that the bag and seals are intact. Record initial details in your examination notes.

3. **Examine the paint sample** – visually examine the fragment and document the colour, shape, size, thickness, visible layers, general condition (i.e. weathering) in your examination notes.

4. **Prepare the plastic bag** – cut a clear plastic bag to give you a double-layered section that is slightly larger than the paint sample and place towards the end of a glass microscope slide. On the other end of the microscope slide, label with the details of the sample.

5. **Embed your paint sample** – place the paint sample between the two plastic layers, making sure that it is not close to any of the edges of the plastic. Place another microscope slide on top. Place the microscope slide (paint-sample side) 'sandwich' on to a hotplate that has been set to a low heat. The heat should be sufficient only to melt the plastic bag slowly (within 1–2 min) so as not to damage the paint sample itself. The plastic should melt evenly and form a seal around the paint sample.

6. **Prepare the cross-section** – remove the microscope slide from the hotplate and allow it to cool. Using a scalpel, carefully prise one of the microscope slides away from the melted plastic without damaging the plastic layer. Place the remaining slide containing the embedded paint sample on to a stereo microscope (p. 73) stage. Look through the eyepiece and focus the image. Using a scalpel, very carefully trim excess plastic from the one edge of the embedded paint sample. Using a Teflon-coated blade, cut a very thin section along the length of the paint sample and repeat this process until you have obtained at least three full-thickness sections. Using the scalpel, you can gently prise the remaining plastic away from the cross-section.

7. **Examine the cross-section** – by using low-power microscopy you can determine the number, sequence, thickness and colours of the paint sample.

RM2165, for further examination by FTIR (Flynn *et al.*, 2005) (see Chapter 19).

- **Embedding the paint sample in a plastic coating** (see Box 40.2) – once the paint sample has been embedded it is possible to cut a thin section by hand using a Teflon-coated razor blade, e.g. GEM® stainless-steel coated, single-edge industrial blades. The limitation of this method is that the thickness of the section is greater than that produced by a microtome, but with practice you can improve your technique to ensure a reproducible uniform cut, time after time.

 KEY POINT It is important that the cuts made with the Teflon blade are perpendicular to the paint sample. Any distortion will lead to a misinterpretation of the thickness (relative to each other) of individual layers.

Microscopy

- **Light microscopy** – the morphology of the paint surface can be examined initially at low magnification ($\times 100$ total magnification). You should record:

  1. the colour, shapes and any differences in size across the whole sample;
  2. what the outer surface looks like;
  3. whether the fragments have uniform surface characteristics (homogeneous).

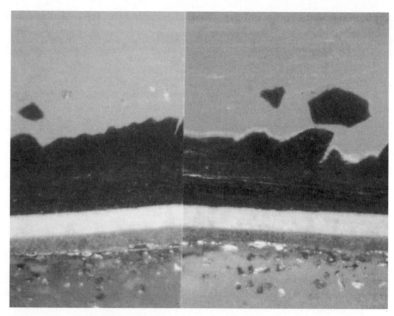

Photo.40.1 A suspect paint sample (right) compared with the crime scene control paint sample (left) using a comparison microscope. (Image courtesy of SPSA Forensic Services)

Repeat this process under $\times$ 400 total magnification, but this time also rotate the slide and record any changes in colour of the sample.

- **Comparison microscopy** (p. 65) – paint is seldom a single layer, and therefore the cross-section (e.g. the diameter of each of the paint layers in a control sample and a test sample), can be examined by direct visual comparison (Photo 40.1).
- **Polarising microscopy** – the pigments in the paint sample can be differentiated by the way they absorb light and the degree by which they refract light (p. 65). The paint sample is mounted on to a microscope slide (Box 40.3) using a reference mounting material such as Meltmount™. This reference material has a known refractive index (R_f = 1.66), which is used for comparison against paint samples. This is known as the Becke test. Some paint samples will only have a single refractive index, but others may have two, the difference of which is known as birefringence.
- **Scanning electron microscopy** – this technique can also be used when a high degree of magnification (see p. 66) is required to identify minute surface features of the paint samples.

Spectroscopy

The chemical composition of organic paint samples can be determined using spectroscopic techniques such as Fourier transform infrared (FTIR) spectroscopy (Fig. 40.1). The combined technique of microscopy and FTIR, e.g. Bruker FTIR Hyperion, proves to be an invaluable tool in the analysis of individual layers from cross-sectional paint samples. If the pigment is inorganic in origin, then the elemental composition can be determined using X-ray fluorescence (XRF) spectroscopy or scanning electron microscopy with energy dispersive X-ray (SEM/EDX) analysis (Chapter 18). The advantage of using SEM/EDX is that an elemental profile of the individual layers of the paint can be determined. This is particularly useful when a paint fragment, recovered from a

Box 40.3 How to prepare paint samples using Meltmount® for analysis of pigments using a polarising microscope

1. **Prepare the Meltmount** – place the bottle containing Meltmount on a hotplate until it appears thin and watery. Place a small empty glass bottle on the hotplate containing a glass eyedropper and allow the barrel of the eyedropper to warm up – this will prevent the Meltmount from hardening in the eyedropper.

2. **Prepare the paint sample** – recover a small paint sample and place on a microscope slide. Cover with a coverslip and place on the hotplate. Slightly raise the coverslip and, using the warm eyedropper, apply one drop of the Meltmount on to the slide. Lower the coverslip down on to the sample and press firmly to distribute the mounting medium evenly. Remove the slide from the hotplate and allow to cool – the Meltmount will harden.

3. **Set up the microscope** – turn on the transmitted light source on the polarising microscope. Using the Bertrand lens – a refractive lens located between the objective and eyepiece – fully open the iris under the mounting stage of the microscope and adjust until the circle of light is reduced to half of its original size. This will allow the sample on the microscope stage to be illuminated in polarised light. Remove the Bertrand lens before examining your sample.

4. **Examine the sample** – you can determine whether Meltmount or the case paint sample has the higher refractive index. Place the microscope slide on the stage and view under high magnification (×400 total magnification). A band of light, known as the Becke line, appears at the edge of the fragment. Adjust the focus and observe what happens to the Becke line. If it moves in towards the fragment, then the R_f of the fragment is higher than that of the Meltmount. If the line moves away from the fragment, then the R_f of the fragment is lower than that of the Meltmount. This is a simple test that can easily discriminate between pigments in a paint sample and a control paint sample if the R_f values of the two are different.

Fig. 40.1 A typical infrared spectrum of an acrylic emulsion (undercoat paint layer). Identifying features include:

peaks at 2900: stretching;
peaks at 1732: strong carbonyl band;
peaks at 1233: ester;
peaks at 1433 and 1371: CH_2 and CH_3 bands.

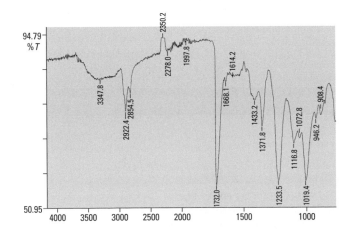

FTIR – *can be used to obtain information on the binder, pigments and additives used across each layer.*

Common paint types – *these include PVA emulsion (polyvinyl acetate, pigments and water), acrylic emulsion (poly-n-butyl-methylacrylate and NC paints (nitrocellulose oil paints).*

suspect, is not full thickness. The profile of the layers of paint that are present in the sample can be compared and possibly matched to the layers of the reference paint sample, i.e. a physical match can be determined by finding exactly the same elemental profile in sequential layers.

Chromatography

If the pigment used to dye the paint sample is organic in origin (e.g. Hansa Yellows), then the paint fragment can be examined using thin-layer chromatography or high-performance liquid chromatography (Chapter 14) to separate individual colours. Alternatively, pyrolysis gas chromatography–mass spectrometry (Chapter 14) may be used. Here, paint fragments are heated in the absence of air (McMinn *et al.*, 1985). This causes the paint polymers to break down to their constituent monomers. These can then be separated by GC and identified by their mass spectral data, (Chapter 14) which can be used to discriminate between one paint sample and another.

Interpretation and reporting paint cases

The purpose of the analysis of paint fragments from a suspect is to determine whether or not they match those from a crime scene. Therefore, your statement (Chapter 60) should include your opinion as to whether or not the results of your analysis support or refute the proposition that the suspect was present at the crime scene, as illustrated in the example shown in Box 40.4.

When making your interpretation you should consider:

- **the number and type of fragments** – how common the paint is, e.g. blue motor-vehicle paint;
- **nature of contact** – whether the fragment has been crushed, for example, by the pressure applied by a tool (see Chapter 28) or smeared by contact with wet or dry paint;
- **whether the paint samples are full-thickness/multi-layered** – if only one layer is found, then the strength of the evidence is limited when compared with evidence of bi-layer or multi-layer samples;
- **how the paint was transferred** – if a tool was used, it is likely that primary transfer will have occurred from the paint on to the tool. If this tool is subsequently used in another location, then further primary transfer can occur, but, equally, secondary transfer can occur from the tool to the surface. This phenomenon of two-way transfer has been demonstrated in simulated burglary cases (Buzzini *et al.*, 2005);
- **likelihood of transfer and persistence.**

The Bayesian approach (Chapter 57) can also be adopted to assess the significance of the paint evidence in a similar fashion to other trace evidence.

Box 40.4 An example of a case statement involving the analysis of paint

Circumstances of the case

A Ford Escort car was involved in an accident resulting in damage to a fence. The driver failed to stop at the scene of the accident. However, a car matching the description was traced by the police and a sample of paint was recovered from the bumper of the vehicle.

The following is an extract from a typical statement:

Summary of examination

I have examined a paint sample taken from a Ford Escort motor vehicle Reg. No. PA 1NT and compared it to a sample of paint removed from the fence opposite 39 Dented Row.

Results

Paint sample (1) labelled 'found nearside front bumper of PA 1NT on 01/04/17'.

The above item contained several fragments of black paint, with the following layer sequence:
Black; black; dark grey; yellow; black; light grey; orange.

Paint sample (2) labelled 'found on fence opposite 39 Dented Row on 01/04/17'.

The above item consisted of several fragments of black paint with the following layer sequence:
Black; black; dark grey; yellow; black; light grey; orange.

Conclusion

Paint sample (1) was found to be indistinguishable in terms of colour, appearance and layer sequence from paint sample (2).

It is my opinion that there is strong evidence to support the proposition that paint recovered from the Ford Escort Reg. No. PA 1NT originated from the fence opposite 39 Dented Row.

Text references

Buzzini, P., Massonnet, G., Birrer, S., Egli, N.M., Mazzella, W. and Fortini, A. (2005) Survey of crowbar and household paints in burglary cases – population studies, transfer and interpretation. *Forensic Science International* 152: 221–234.

Caddy, B. (2001) *Forensic Examination of Glass and Paint: Analysis and Interpretation.* Taylor and Francis, London.

Flynn, K., O'Leary, R., Lennard, C., Roux, C. and Reedy, B.J. (2005) Forensic applications of infrared chemical imaging:

Multi-layered paint chips. *Journal of Forensic Sciences* **50**(4): 832–841.

McMinn, D.G., Carlson, T.L. and Munson, T.O. (1985) Pyrolysis capillary gas chromatography/mass spectrometry for the analysis of automotive paints. *Journal of Forensic Sciences* 30: 1064–1073.

Sources for further study

Forensic paint analysis and comparison guidelines (2000). *Forensic Science Communications,* 1 Available at: https://archives.fbi.gov/archives/about-us/lab/forensic-science-communications/fsc/july1999/painta.htm. Last accessed 23/08/2017.

Lucy, D. (2005) *An Introduction to Statistics for Forensic Scientists.* Wiley, Chichester.

Study exercises

40.1 Observation of paint transfer. In a vice, tighten together two blocks of painted wood. Using a screwdriver, or equivalent, lever in between the painted surfaces. Observe and record the appearance of the wood as well as any transfer of paint material on to the tool. You could also consider making a cast of the tool mark (Chapter 27).

40.2 Examination of paint samples. Examine different common multi-layered paint samples using low-power and polarising microscopy and record the differences observed in each case.

40.3 Test your knowledge. List the common techniques available to examine paint samples.

Glass is a hard, amorphous, brittle substance, usually transparent, made by the fusing together of one or more oxides of silicon, boron or phosphorus with certain other basic oxides (e.g. sodium, magnesium, calcium, potassium). This process is performed at high temperature and the product is cooled rapidly to prevent crystallisation. Therefore, glass is essentially a supercooled liquid.

Glass provides useful evidence in many forensic investigations for a number of reasons, including:

- **Physical composition** – the various methods used to manufacture glass create features that can be used to physically match glass fragments recovered from an individual or object with those from a specific location.
- **Robustness** – glass is resistant to environmental conditions; therefore, freshly broken glass can be readily identified at a crime scene. Weathering of glass can occur, but only over a long period of time.
- **Fingerprints** – if a broken window is the point of entry to a house, then it is possible that latent fingerprints (Chapter 26) may have been left on the inner and/or outer surface of the glass.
- **Sharp edges** – when glass is freshly broken, the edges may cause a tear to clothing, yielding fibre evidence (see Chapter 42) or may cut the person trying to gain access through the window, leaving blood evidence (Chapter 30).
- **Fragments** – microscopic fragments can be transferred to clothing and to hair. A suspect may not be able to remove all traces of these fragments.

 KEY POINT The properties of glass can be used to give an indication of whether a person can be linked to a scene by the analysis of the physical, chemical and optical properties of glass fragments recovered from the person, or his/her property.

Types of forensic cases involving glass

Forensic cases involving glass are varied and can involve any type of manufactured glass, such as window panes, car headlights, drinking glasses, etc. The most commonly encountered cases are:

- **Breaking and entering** – for example, a broken pane of glass may have allowed entry into a property. Glass evidence from the window will be found at the scene and may be matched to fragments found on the suspect.
- **Vandalism** – if a window has been deliberately broken, glass fragments may have been transferred on to the suspect.
- **Assaults** – for example, if a person has been assaulted using a broken bottle there may be blood left on the glass (Chapter 30) or glass fragments may be left embedded in the skin.
- **Road-traffic accidents** – for example, in the case of a hit-and-run incident a forensic scientist would examine the car headlight or windscreen glass fragments from the vehicle and compare these to fragments found on the victim.

Understanding the different types of glass – the glass manufacturing process involves various stages, including:

- *fusing the glass components together under high temperature;*
- *shaping the glass into its desired form;*
- *cooling the glass under controlled conditions (annealing).*

This process produces glass of many types, such as:

- *float* – *most modern glass is made using this process, where molten glass is fed through rollers on to a bed of molten tin;*
- *patterned sheet* – *fed through rollers, one of which is engraved with a pattern;*
- *toughened sheet* – *using a process of rapid cooling, the normal stresses in the glass are removed; this type of glass is commonly found in car windscreens and on breaking will form cubes rather than the typical glass shards;*
- *laminated* – *layers of glass are interspersed with a sheet of plastic flexible film; this type of glass, common in shop windows, does not shatter as the film holds the shards in place;*
- *non-sheet* – *glass that has been formed by being pressed in moulds, e.g. bottles.*

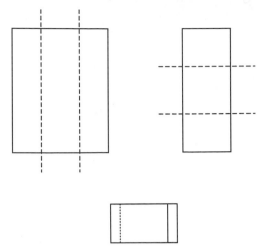

Fig. 41.1 Preparation of a Beecham's wrap.

 KEY POINT *You should be aware that there may be other evidence types on the glass (e.g. fingerprints, fibres, blood) and so you should adopt appropriate precautions to maximise the recovery of all evidence.*

Collection of glass evidence

Obtaining a control glass sample

At a crime scene, it is important to be aware of contamination issues (see p. 316) when collecting samples. Any fragments recovered from a scene should be kept separate from evidence collected from the suspect at all times. Methods of recovery depend on the nature of the crime scene. For example, if at a volume crime (see p. 227), such as house break-in, then a glass fragment must be lifted from the window frame of the pane of glass that was broken and not from the floor or the window sill. This fragment is known as a control glass sample and is the one to which all other fragments will be compared. If any of the glass fragments found on the ground show signs of other types of evidence, then these can also be collected – for example, fingerprints (Chapter 26), footwear marks (Chapter 27) or blood (Chapter 30). On the other hand, in the case of a road-traffic incident all glass fragments and associated debris should be collected, including those found on the ground. Control glass samples, however, should be collected only from the actual vehicle windscreen, window or headlight.

To be useful in forensic science, a control glass sample must:

- **be collected only from the glass that remains in the frame** and not from the ground. Use a permanent marker to indicate which side of the glass was inside/outside;
- **have a number of 'full thickness' pieces** – i.e. not those showing fracture lines;
- **be collected from each individual window pane that has been broken** – glass from different window panes will need to be packaged separately;
- **include all types of glass that has been broken**;
- **be packaged in a secure manner**, remembering that glass is sharp. Caution needs to be exercised, not just for health and safety reasons, but also in context of keeping the integrity of the packaging when in storage, i.e. a polythene bag may be penetrated by the sharp edge of the glass and would thus render the evidence unusable. A more suitable packaging would be a cardboard box, with the sample secured to the inside using Sellotape®.

In all cases, full details should be recorded in your examination notes, including the extent of glass damage, the position and height relative to the ground, the amount of glass missing and the exact location from which the control samples were taken.

Glass evidence – *Typical fragment sizes are 0.1–1 mm.*

Consider the order of collection and other evidence – *hairs (Chapter 32) should be collected during visual examination; fibres (Chapter 42) should be collected before shaking any garment.*

Collection of glass fragments from clothing

Once a suspect has been identified, his/her clothing can be seized for examination. The forensic scientist will examine the item of clothing and collect any glass fragments found for further analysis – a process known as search and recover (see Box 41.1).

Since glass is trace evidence, the clothing should be collected and packaged at the earliest opportunity (see p. 248). Important points to note are:

- the clothing must not be taken by officers who have attended the scene;
- if there is more than one suspect then different officers must attend each suspect;
- not only should the clothing be seized, but hair combings must also be taken prior to the removal of the clothing (see p. 317).

Box 41.1 How to, search and recover, trace evidence

This describes how to examine a sample of clothing for fragments of glass. However, the methods described also apply to other searches (e.g. fibres). In some cases, several types of evidence may appear during the examination.

1. **Wearing full personal protective equipment, clean the examination table with disinfectant prior to any examination.** A clean sheet of Benchkote® should be taped to the bench surface on to which the bag containing the exhibit will be examined.

2. **Examine the bag before opening it** – noting the integrity of the seals (tamper-proof seal and the normal bag seal) (see p. 250).

3. **Brush the outside of the bag and note if any debris is recovered** – if there is, then there is the possibility that the integrity of the bag has been compromised. If the debris has come from the bag, there is the possibility that it has contaminated other evidence. If it has come from another source then there is a possibility that the evidence you are examining has been contaminated. The brushing process should be repeated and any further debris noted – if there is no debris then the packaging is intact and the debris found has not contaminated the inside of the bag. If, however, on the third time of brushing debris is still found, then the packaging is compromised and no further examination can be carried out.

4. **Locate where you are going to cut open the bag** – the packaging should be opened as far from the tamper-proof seal as possible. It should not be immediately adjacent to the original bag seal either, nor should it be along any of the seams or by undoing the flap of an envelope. It is important to keep all the seals intact, as it may be required to illustrate this on the exhibit in court. Once any examination is complete, the bag should be re-sealed immediately. If a second examination is required then a further opening can be made, this time protecting the opening that has already been made as well as the original seals. This provides a record of how many times the bag has been opened.

5. **Cut open the bag using scissors** – making sure the cut is made on one side of the bag, with care not to damage the contents of the bag. The bag must be opened on the table to prevent any contamination of the contents, and also to protect you from the contents that may, on occasion, include lice or fleas but also may present a microbiological hazard if stained with body fluids.

6. **Match the contents of the bag to the label details and associated paperwork before commencement of the examination** – the packaging and label details should be recorded in your examination notes.

7. **Lay the item out flat on the Benchcote and visually examine the surface for trace evidence** – including hairs and fibres, glass and biological stains. For example, an item of clothing should be drawn in your examination notes and the position of any evidence found recorded on the drawing. If obvious hairs or fibres are noted these can be removed with tweezers into a polythene bag for analysis later. Use a stereoscopic microscope (Chapter 11) to locate any glass fragments; if they are 'visible' then they can be easily recovered using tweezers. Remember to recover fibres prior to shaking (step 8).

8. **With one hand, hold the item of clothing over the Benchcote and with your other hand gently tug at the garment so that any debris caught in the clothing surface is shaken off the surface** – repeat this process in different directions across the whole of the garment. Don't forget that if the garment contains pockets then these should also be examined by turning them inside out. If trousers have been submitted, then turn-ups should also be examined. These should be separately recovered into Beecham's wraps (p. 402) and fully documented in your examination notes (pp. 410–411).

9. **Shake the contents of the bag on to the Benchcote and record if any debris falls out of the bag** – this debris should be collected into a Beecham's wrap (see Fig. 41.1). See Chapter 24, p. 250 for further details of tamper-evident packaging types.

10. **Make a full record in your examination notes** – to include the following:

    - number of glass fragments that have been recovered, and from where;
    - colour – the colour of any glass fragments, which can give an indication if more than one type of glass is present;
    - size – typically the fragment size will be 0.1 to 1 mm, although larger fragments may be recovered and examined when the need arises;
    - thickness – whether the fragment is full thickness or not;
    - appearance – whether the fragments appear flat, patterned, toughened, etc.;
    - retention properties – if on clothing, the type of clothing and its composition;
    - other types of debris found, if present.

Analytical techniques

Once the glass has been recovered from the clothing, it will be examined and compared with the reference control sample that was obtained from the scene. Several methods are available for the analysis of glass fragments.

Surface examination

This can give useful information, but is dependent on the size of the fragment. Microscopy (Chapters 10–11) can identify scratches on the surface of the glass, can identify whether the glass is freshly broken, and is especially useful in determining whether the fragment is curved or patterned.

Whether the original glass was flat can be determined from the larger fragment sizes, i.e. those greater than 0.5 mm, since these are likely to be representative of the original item.

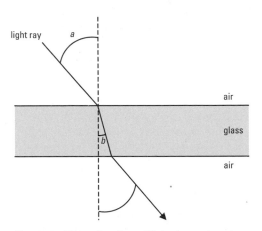

Fig. 41.2 The refraction of light through a sheet of glass: *a* is the angle of incidence; *b* is the angle of refraction.

Refractive index measurement

This is the main discriminatory technique and is based on the principle that light passing through glass is refracted, or bent (Locke and Underhill, 1985), as shown in Fig. 41.2. The refractive index is measured using glass refractive index measurement (GRIM), which comprises a microscope, equipped with a monochromatic light source usually set at 589 nm, a microscope stage that can be heated, a video display and a computer. The system is calibrated using three silicone oils covering a refractive index range of 1.45 to 1.53. Certified glass reference samples are supplied with known refractive indices for each of these three oils (Caddy, 2001). The glass sample is immersed in a silicone oil and placed on the microscope hot stage, which is coupled to the video display. The stage is subsequently heated and cooled. Initially, the glass is visible, but as the temperature of the hot stage is increased, the oil reaches a point where it matches the refractive index of the glass. At this point the glass becomes invisible and the temperature change of the oil, monitored by the computer, is converted into the refractive index of the glass sample. The largest change in refractive index is noted in toughened glass.

Table. 41.1 Typical elements found in glass

Element	Elemental composition (%)			
	Float	Boro-silicate	Lead crystal	Green bottle
SiO_2	72.8	80.2	54.9	72.0
Al_2O_3	1.4	2.6	0.1	1.1
Fe_2O_3	0.1	0.07	0.02	0.96
CaO	8.2	0.1		8.4
MgO	3.8			2.1
Na_2O	12.8	4.5	0.2	15.1
K_2O	0.8	0.3	12.3	
Cr_2O_3				0.19
PbO			31.9	
B_2O_3		12.3	0.5	
As_2O_5			0.5	

Modified from Caddy (2001)

Elemental composition

An alternative to refractive index measurement is to establish the elemental composition of the glass (Table. 41.1). Glass is primarily silica with different metal oxides, depending on the manufacturing process. The elemental composition is particularly useful for determining the type of glass – for example, during the manufacture of float glass, molten tin is incorporated into the surface of the glass, while in the production of crystal, lead is incorporated into the glass.

Glass composition can be examined using scanning electron microscopy (Chapter 10) coupled with energy dispersive X-ray detectors (SEM/EDX) or X-ray methods (XRF) (Chapter 18) and, more recently, using ICP–MS (see Chapter 17). These techniques will give a profile of all the elements that are found in the glass fragment, which can then be compared with the reference control sample.

Box 41.2 An example of a case statement involving the analysis of glass

The following is an extract from a typical statement.

PURPOSE

I have been asked to examine the items detailed in this report and to give an opinion as to whether, or not, the accused, Wendy Brekker (01/01/1966), was in close proximity to the breaking window at 16 Glasshouse Road on the 12th February 2004.

SUMMARY OF EXAMINATION

Particulate debris from the surface of the items of clothing was collected and examined for the presence of glass fragments with a freshly broken appearance. Recovered glass fragments were compared with the control glass sample taken from the locus.

RESULTS

Control glass sample

Glass samples labelled 'taken from left window pane, living room of 16 Glasshouse Road on the 12th February 2004'.
The above item consisted of four large fragments of glass approximately 3.94 mm thick, and a number of smaller fragments. A representative sample was taken for analysis using glass refractive index measurement (GRIM).

Items Attributed to Wendy Brekker

Sweatshirt labelled 'taken from Wendy Brekker on 3/2/17'.
The above item, a dark green sweatshirt, was examined and eight fragments of glass with a freshly broken appearance were recovered from the surface debris.

All of the glass fragments were further examined, and found to be indistinguishable in terms of refractive index from the control glass sample.

Jeans labelled 'taken from Wendy Brekker on 3/2/17'.
The above item, a pair of light-blue denim jeans, was examined and seven fragments of glass with a freshly broken appearance were recovered from the surface debris. These fragments were further examined, and six were found to be indistinguishable in terms of refractive index from the control glass sample.

Ten fragments of glass with a freshly broken appearance were recovered from the pockets of the garment and were further examined, and nine were found to be indistinguishable in terms of refractive index to the control glass sample.

Left shoe labelled 'taken from Wendy Brekker on 3/2/17'.
The above item, a left adidas™ trainer, was examined and four fragments of glass with a freshly broken appearance were recovered from the upper of the shoe and seven fragments of glass with a freshly broken appearance from the sole.

Four glass fragments from the upper and three glass fragments from the sole were examined and found to be indistinguishable in terms of refractive index from the control glass sample.

INTERPRETATION

The finding of glass fragments with a freshly broken appearance on the surface of an item of clothing is significant as I would not expect such findings on a person chosen at random from the population and is indicative of recent contact with breaking or broken glass.

CONCLUSION

It is my opinion that there is strong evidence to support the proposition that the accused, Wendy Brekker, was within 3 metres of the window being broken at 16 Glasshouse Road on the 12th February 2017.

Hicks *et al.* (2003) have demonstrated that, where refractive index measurements have not been able to discriminate between glass fragments, the use of non-destructive energy dispersive X-ray fluorescence has been successful when the fragment size > 0.3 mm. Time-of-flight mass spectrometry (p. 150) has the potential to be used in forensic applications for the determination of the elemental composition of glass. Coumbaros *et al.* (2008) have investigated the elemental distribution in clear float and non-float surface regions of glass using traditional methods (refractive index, p. 404) in comparison with time-of-flight mass spectrometry. It was concluded that, although the refractive indices were notably different between float and non-float surfaces, there was no significant variation in the elemental distribution across the bulk pane, but care must be taken to ensure the correct identification and examination of float glass, rather than the examination of the more variable non-float surface regions that did show variations in Si, Ca, Mg and Na levels.

Transfer and persistence

When a window is broken by force, if the individual is in close proximity (less than 3 metres) to the window, then transfer of glass fragments will often occur. Large fragments of glass (bigger than 0.5 mm) are mostly lost from clothing within 30 min of the glass being broken, although smaller fragments (up to 0.5 mm) can still be recovered 8 h after the event (Caddy, 2001). Persistence also very much depends on the 'knit' of the clothing – for example, a smooth, tightly woven garment is less likely to retain glass fragments than a loosely knitted fabric.

The evidential value of this type of trace evidence is greatest when glass fragments are found in hair combings of the suspect, or where the fragments are embedded in the uppers of the suspect's shoes. There is less value when it is found in surface debris, i.e. from trousers, jacket, etc., although this does depend on the number of fragments recovered, and of even less value when found in pockets or trouser turn-ups – the fragments may have been there for a long time, and natural wear will change their appearance over a period of time. There is little evidential value (p. 245) when the only glass fragments recovered are found embedded in the sole of a suspect's shoes.

Interpreting and reporting glass evidence

Once the analysis is complete and the fragments have been identified, you need to make an interpretation as to the significance of your findings. In order to make this interpretation you need to consider the following questions:

- What types of fragments are present? Do they appear to be from the same source and do they match the 'control' glass sample?
- How many fragments were found on the clothing and where on the clothing were the fragments found?
- What are the retentive properties of the suspect's clothes – i.e. how likely is the clothing to retain the fragments over a period of time?
- How was the glass broken? What distance was the individual from the breakage?

Your interpretation should adopt a Bayesian statistical approach (Chapter 57) and address the likelihood of the following hypotheses, based on proposition arguments:

1. the probability that the glass fragments found on the individual's clothing:

   a. originated from the window that was broken (null hypothesis is true);
   b. originated from a different source (null hypothesis is not true);

2. the probability that the glass fragments found on the individual's clothing:

   a. originated by a particular activity – e.g. breaking the window using a hammer (null hypothesis is true);
   b. originated by the same activity but by another individual other than the suspect (null hypothesis is not true).

For further information on the use of Bayesian analysis in this context, refer to Curran *et al.* (1999) and Zadora (2009).

Your statement should specify the appearance of the glass, especially in relation to whether or not it has a freshly broken appearance. The size and number of fragments recovered also needs to be specified, as do the results of the analytical technique used to examine the glass fragments.

 KEY POINT *If the glass fragments recovered from the suspect's clothing match the control glass sample, then these can be expressed as 'indistinguishable from the control sample'. This phrase does not specify that the glass fragments originate from the source, merely that they match the glass found at the scene.*

An interpretation should be included that states whether or not your results support or refute the person being present when the glass was broken, taking into account all your analytical findings (see Box 41.2)

Text references

Caddy, B. (2001) *Forensic Examination of Glass and Paint: Analysis and Interpretation.* Taylor and Francis, London.

Coumbaros, J., Denman, J., Kirkbride, K.P., Walker, G.S. and Skinner, W. (2008) An investigation into the spatial elemental distribution within a pane of glass by time of flight secondary ion mass spectrometry. *Journal of Forensic Sciences* **53**(2): 312–320.

Curran, J.M., Buckleton, J. and Triggs, C.M. (1999) The robustness of a continuous likelihood approach to Bayesian analysis of forensic glass evidence. *Forensic Science International* **104**: 91–103.

Hicks, T., Sermier, F., Goldmann, T., Brunelle, A., Champod, C. and Margot, P. (2003) The classification and discrimination of glass fragments using non-destructive energy dispersive X-ray fluorescence. *Forensic Science International* **137**: 107–118.

Locke, J. and Underhill, M. (1985) Automated refractive index measurement of glass particles. *Forensic Science International* **27**: 247–260.

Zadora, G. (2009) Classification of glass fragments based on elemental composition and refractive index. *Journal of Forensic Sciences* **54**(1): 49–59.

Sources for further study

Aitken, C.G.G. and Taroni, F. (2004) *Statistics and the Evaluation of Evidence for Forensic Scientists,* 2nd edn. Wiley, Chichester.

Allen, T.J. and Scranage, J.K. (1998) The transfer of glass 1. Transfer of glass to individuals at different distances. *Forensic Science International* 93: 167–174.

Curran, J.M., Hicks, T.N. and Buckleton, J.S. (2000) *Forensic Interpretation of Glass Evidence.* CRC Press, Boca Raton.

Lucy, D. (2005) *An Introduction to Statistics for Forensic Scientists.* Wiley, Chichester.

Newton, A.W.N., Curran, J.M., Triggs, C.M. and Buckleton, J.S. (2004) The consequences of potentially differing distributions of the refractive indices of glass fragments from control and recovered sources. *Forensic Science International* 140: 185–193.

Analysis of glass

Study exercises

41.1 Preparation of Beecham's wraps. Using Fig. 41.1 as a guide, practice the preparation of a Beecham's wrap for the storage of trace evidence – note that the dotted lines represent folds in the paper.

41.2 Practice recovery of trace evidence. Using any item of clothing, practice the process of 'search and recovery' for trace evidence. Document the process as if you were in a forensic science laboratory. You will find that Boxes 41.1 and 32.1 will assist you.

41.3 Interpretation of scientific findings. From your library obtain the following reference: Allen, T.J. and Scranage, J.K. (1998) The transfer of glass – part 1. Transfer of glass to individuals at different distances. *Forensic Science International* 93: 167–174. Read the paper and discuss with your peers the key points that the experiments have shown.

Natural fibres – these include those of animal origin, such as wool or silk, of vegetable origin, such as cotton or hemp, and of mineral origin, such as asbestos.

Synthetic fibres – these are man-made polymer-based fibres, such as polyester, but can also be fibres synthesised from natural polymers, such as viscose.

The discovery of fibres at a crime scene may eventually provide the link between a suspect and a particular event. Fibres can be unknowingly transferred from a perpetrator's clothes to the crime scene, or on to another person, if in close contact. In the context of forensic science, fibres are regarded as distinct from hairs (Chapter 32), although there are similarities in how they are transferred and how they can be recovered. The examination of fibre evidence by the forensic scientist includes:

- **microscopic analysis** – to determine the surface morphology, cross-section, colour and type of the fibre;
- **spectroscopic analysis** – to determine the chemical composition and dye colour of the fibre;
- **numerical/statistical analysis** – to determine the most likely mode of transfer between the source of the fibre and the recipient.

Types of fibre and their relevance

In the context of forensic science, the term 'fibre' refers to those individual components of textiles that make up, for example, garments or upholstery. These fibres fall into two categories, natural and synthetic. These differ in properties, from their surface morphology to their features at the molecular level (see Fig. 42.1). These differences allow the forensic scientist to arrive at an opinion as to the significance of the analytical findings. In order for fibres to have a strong evidential value, they should be:

- readily distinguishable from other fibres present at the scene;
- ideally from a source that does not shed fibres easily;
- linked to an item of clothing belonging to a suspect;
- shown to have been transferred only during the event under investigation and not by another means;
- examined in separate laboratories if the items, suspected of being linked by transfer, are collected from the scene and the suspect, or clothing from the suspect.

 KEY POINT *Fibres can be transferred from one person to another, or from one object to another, if they have been in close contact. Since these transferred fibres are usually loosely attached to a person, or object, they are always the first evidence type collected from a crime scene and the first recovered from an exhibit submitted to a forensic laboratory.*

Factors affecting transfer between garments include:

- pressure of contact;
- length of contact;
- texture of both the donor and recipient garments.

Determination of fibre type

The first stage in any examination is to start documenting the process using standard examination notes (Box 42.1). These should follow the same format every time you examine an item – in so doing this ensures that you don't miss

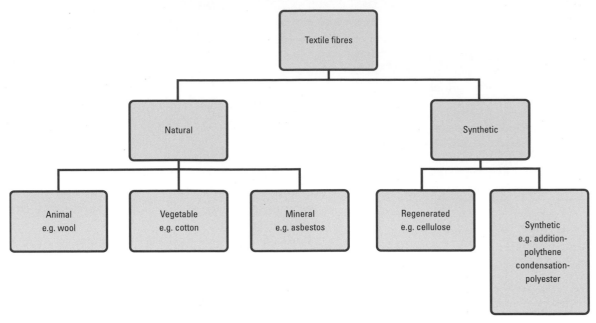

Fig. 42.1 Fibre types.

Box 42.1 How to 'search and recover' fibre evidence from exhibits recovered from a crime scene and from a victim's or a suspect's clothing

Fibre evidence is collected from exhibits in a slightly different way to that of hair evidence (Box 32.1), although the initial preparation of the exhibit remains the same as for all trace evidence (Box 41.1, p. 403).

1. **Perform an initial examination** – carefully unfold and visually inspect the item, making written descriptive examination notes. If any obvious fibres are easily identified under the naked eye, lift these off the item using forceps and place into a Beecham's wrap (see p. 402).

2. **Recover the fibres** – use J-LAR tape, which is similar to Sellotape, to sequentially lift the fibres from the item. It is good practice to adopt a particular sequence of sampling and to use this approach throughout, to ensure a thorough examination of the item. For the examination of a jumper, or similar item, you should apply the sticky surface of the tape to the garment, ensuring good contact, and then lift

the tape. You should repeat this process at least eight times across the most appropriate sections of the garment – i.e. across the back of the left sleeve, the chest and the right sleeve. Each section should be lifted with a different piece of tape. If appropriate, you can repeat the process for the front of the garment, and for the inner surfaces (e.g. in cases of sexual assault). With trousers, a minimum of four tape lifts should be performed on each leg, front and back.

3. **Secure the tape lift** – each time a tape lift is completed, you should transfer the tape, sticky-side down, on to a sheet of acetate. You should then label the acetate sheet using a permanent marker pen with the case number, a brief description of the item, a description of the location of the tape lift and a sequential number indicating the order of all the tape lifts.

any valuable evidence in your examination protocol. Your notes should include, in the following order:

- **Description** – a written description of the item you are examining.
- **Label** – any label details on the item and its location.

- **Condition** – your judgement on the wear condition of the item, i.e. new or old.
- **Damage** – visual and low-power microscopy for examination and judgement of damage features, i.e. buttons missing, pulled threads attached, tearing of garment, and a judgement on whether the item could still be worn. Any damage features should be measured, as well as assessing underlying damage to other clothing types.
- **Hairs and fibres** – details should be recorded of tape lifts taken, including the number taken and location (outside/inside).
- **Blood** – location of any bloodstaining on the item (Chapter 30), as well as any presumptive screening tests performed.

 KEY POINT *The edges of the tape may have fibres attached to them, so you should seal them using Sellotape to prevent any risk of contamination.*

Your examination notes should also be accompanied by drawings of the item indicating the position of any evidence, directionality of bloodstaining and your opinion based on the evidence in each section.

Once the initial documentation is noted, you can then recover any fibres from items submitted to the forensic laboratory (see Box 42.1). The case details should be assessed to determine the most appropriate part of the item to examine – for example, if a suspect was sitting in a car, then the most likely area for transfer is from the back of the shirt or trousers to and from the seat, but don't forget to tape lift the seatbelts as well as the headrest. Once the fibres have been recovered and secured on to acetate sheets, they can then be further examined to compare with reference fibres taken from the suspect and victim. The control samples should be obtained from items that are considered to be from where the fibres originated. Ideally, the control sample would be submitted in its entirety, but where this is not possible representative tape lifts (approximately 10 cm in length) should be obtained covering all the fibre types from the source. The fibres observed will either belong to the exhibit (normal population) or have been transferred on to the exhibit (extraneous fibres). It is the fibres that don't naturally belong to the exhibit that should be examined further.

The forensic scientist must also determine how easily the item will lose fibres (see Box 42.2), since this will have a significant impact on the strength of the evidence once the examination is complete. In terms of the strength of evidential value, the ideal is to find a large number of fibres from a garment of clothing that does not shed fibres readily. The evidential value would be further strengthened if these fibres were identified and found to be an uncommon fibre, rather than, for example, white cotton. Since sources of white cotton are varied and the different sources cannot be distinguished either by microscopy or spectroscopy, they have little evidential value in supporting or refuting a suspect's involvement.

Case example Fibre evidence in practice
On 1st July 2000, Sarah Payne disappeared in Sussex, UK. On 17th July a decomposed body was found. A muscle was examined for DNA and a profile obtained (see Chapter 31), identifying the body as the missing child. At the scene, fibres were found that were collected and submitted to the forensic laboratory. Roy Whiting was arrested and his van was seized. The van was examined, tape lifted and the contents submitted to the forensic laboratory, including a clown-pattern curtain, a red sweatshirt and a pair of socks.

Fibres were examined using microscopy, Fourier transform infrared (FTIR) spectroscopy, microspectro-photometry (MSP) (see Chapter 19) and thin-layer chromatography (TLC) (see Chapter 14). A comparison of the fibres recovered at the scene and those recovered from the van revealed that the fibres from the scene were consistent with the red sweatshirt and the socks recovered from the van. A further single fibre matched the material from the van seat.

On the basis of this evidence Roy Whiting was convicted of murder.

Box 42.2 Performing a 'shed test' on a garment

The purpose of a shed test is to determine how many fibres would be lost under normal wear conditions.

1. **'Tape lift' the garment** (see Box 42.1) – to ensure it is free from any extraneous fibres.

2. **Repeat the tape lift** – but this time apply the tape only once to the area in question.

3. **Count the number of fibres recovered** – if a large number of fibres are recovered then the garment can be said to shed fibres easily, whereas if only a few fibres are recovered then the item does not shed fibres easily.

Also important is the retention of the fibres on the person or object, known as transfer and persistence (p. 317). As with hair, the retention of fibres depends on the physical nature of the object or material it has been transferred on to, as well as the duration and type of physical contact and the physical activity after contact (see Chapter 32). However, fibres can be surprisingly persistent – it has been demonstrated that, even after washing, clothes may retain fibres accumulated after contact with another garment (Palmer, 1998). Therefore, although fibre collection is one of the more time-consuming and laborious tasks a forensic scientist carries out, it is worthwhile, especially when there is an absence of other evidence types.

Analytical techniques

The fibres collected on the acetate sheet should first be examined directly with a stereomicroscope (p. 73). Any fibres that appear to be different from those of the source garment should be carefully removed from the acetate sheet, by cutting a flap around the fibre in the lifting tape using a scalpel, taking care not to cut through the acetate sheet. This flap can be lifted and the fibre removed using forceps, placed on to a microscope slide and secured with a coverslip. It should now be examined using high-power, comparison (using white, blue, fluorescence and ultraviolet light) and polarising microscopy (see Chapter 10) and spectroscopic techniques (see Chapter 19) to determine its identity. Microscopic identification features can include:

- presence of delustrant particles or the presence of other pigments;
- scales;
- cross markings;
- striations – whether they are present and the length of the striations;
- cross-sectional shape.

Once the microscopic examination is complete, further techniques using spectroscopy can be applied to identify the composition of the fibres.

Since most synthetic fibres are carbon-based polymers, Fourier transform infrared (FTIR) spectroscopy is a particularly useful tool for discriminating among fibre types. Fibre colour under visible, ultraviolet and infrared spectra gives further discrimination. Raman spectroscopy (Chapter 19) may prove useful in some cases, but it is important to remember that the cellulose backing of the tape used for lifting the fibres can interfere with the Raman analysis.

Once the microscopy and spectroscopy examination is complete, and if the fibre sample is large enough, further examination can be carried out to determine the dyes present in the fibre. This is a destructive technique and should only be considered when all other tests have been completed. The dyes can easily be extracted into solvent, for example pyridine:water, in a 4:3 ratio (Robertson and Grieve, 1999), and individually separated using thin-layer chromatography (Chapter 14) or high-performance liquid chromatography (Chapter 14), or even LC–MS (Chapter 15). Petrick *et al.* (2006) used this technique successfully to differentiate dyes in polyester and acrylic fibres. The dyes extracted from fibres recovered from the crime scene can then be compared with control samples.

An additional technique that could potentially be employed is the use of DNA extracted from natural fibres. Dunbar and Murphy (2009) have shown that it is possible to obtain DNA from the parenchymal cells that have been incorporated into, for example, ropes and hemp and further identified to a specific species of plant. Caution should still be exerted, though, when considering the use of this technique, especially where contamination, for example from grass staining, has occurred.

Typical order of examination

Comparison Microscopy
→ MSP → FTIR → TLC

Microspectrophotometry (MSP) – *measures absorption of electromagnetic radiation in the short UV or Vis spectral region. This technique can be used for comparison purposes rather than identification.*

Thin-layer chromatography (TLC) – *this can be used to analyse the dye of the fibre. The dye can be extracted by heat, solvent or glacial acetic acid or oxalic acid; the choice is dependent on which dye has been used.*

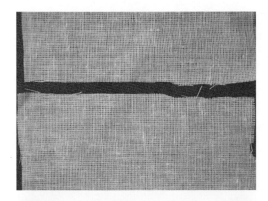

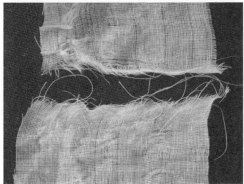

Photo 42.1 Characteristics of cut and torn fabrics.

Cut fabric – usually shows little distortion of the fibres, the ends appear sharp and can easily be matched together (physical fit).

Torn fabric – usually distorted, with the edges of the fabric frayed and of different lengths. The direction of the tear can usually be determined by the bunching of the individual fibres.

Textile damage

Fibre analysis extends beyond the examination and identification of individual fibres. Fibres can be examined as part of an investigation to determine the nature of damage to clothing, which can be used to corroborate, or refute, a particular version of events. The forensic scientist can normally distinguish between a fabric sample that has been forcibly torn and one that has been cut. A combination of visual inspection and low-power microscopy can be used to distinguish between the two types (Photo 42.1). This is important in terms of the nature of the allegation – for example, in determining whether force has been used or whether the damage is consistent with a penetrating weapon having been used, in which case the position of the wound should be matched up to the position of the damage in the clothing, before the item of clothing has been submitted to the laboratory. Being able to recognise the differences between the two types of damage is equally important for allegations of violent attack, where the alleged victim may be suspected of damaging clothing, for example using scissors, after the event.

Your examination should offer an opinion to differentiate between cut fabric (e.g. by scissors), tears (e.g. pulled threads), rips (e.g. along a seam) and normal wear and tear (e.g. tears at a cuff), as well as assessing whether the garment could still be worn, the direction of the tears and the sequence in which the damage was produced. If a garment is damaged, a duplicate garment should be obtained where possible, so that the damage features observed in the submitted item can be recreated on this duplicate. This process allows the scientist to offer an opinion on the force used, how easy the garment was to damage, the strength of the garment and whether the damage feature produced is consistent with that observed on the original.

It is important, therefore, to form an opinion as to the likelihood of a particular weapon being used. Daéid *et al.* (2008) have attempted to correlate damage on clothing (natural and synthetic fabrics) from different knives, and length of wounds observed from a stabbing action. Significant differences were observed in the fabric and the underlying wound when tight-fitting clothing was worn, and indeed differences were also observed between natural and synthetic fabrics.

Interpretation and reporting fibre cases

What you need to know for interpretation is the length of time for which contact occurred, along with how the transfer might have occurred, the type and number of fibres that have been identified and how long the fibres are likely to persist on the recipient item. Persistence depends very much on the fibre in question, the nature of the recipient and the force of contact, as well as the number of times contact has actually occurred. Generally speaking, if fewer than three fibres are recovered, this is not considered significant, unless the fibres are not commonly encountered, in which case the evidential value is significantly improved.

 KEY POINT *Your interpretation should be made based on the findings from the examination in the context of the circumstances of the case. Care needs to be exerted when interpreting damage, especially in the context of normal wear-and-tear features.*

Box 42.3 Examples of case statements involving the analysis of fibres

The following two examples illustrate extracts from typical statements involving fibres.

Case 1 – involving cut fabric

Circumstances

I understand that, following a domestic dispute, Mr Cotton was stabbed with a kitchen knife. This knife was cleaned but later recovered during the scene investigation. Mr Cotton was given medical assistance by the paramedics who attended the scene. During the medical examination, they cut his T-shirt to examine the wound.

Items submitted for analysis

Knife labelled 'found in wheelie bin, 11 Laundry Road on 01/04/17'.
The knife was examined and found to be a kitchen knife measuring 140 mm long and 25 mm maximum width. No blood was found on the knife.

T-shirt labelled 'taken from Mr Cotton on 1/04/17'.
The T-shirt was examined and large bloodstains found on the lower right front. The T-shirt was cut from the bottom middle to the neckline and parallel across the chest in a T shape, consistent with being cut during medical intervention. There was a further cut in the lower right front, 18 mm long. This cut was consistent with a stab-type cut and the knife found.

Case 2 – involving an allegation of rape

Circumstances

An allegation of rape has been made by Miss Ny Lon. She claims that she was tied with a blue dressing gown belt belonging to the suspect, Mr Wooler.

Items received for examination

Blue dressing gown labelled 'taken from Mr Wooler on 2nd July 2017'.
The dressing gown was examined and found to be a blue cotton towelling robe. Attached to the gown is a belt of the same material. The colour and microscopic appearance of its constituent fibres were noted for comparison purposes. The belt was found to shed fibres very readily.

Blouse labelled 'found in possession of Miss Lon on the 2nd July 2017'.
The blouse was examined and the surface debris removed. No fibres similar to those of the dressing gown belt were found. The blouse shed fibres very poorly and was therefore unsuitable as a source of shed fibres. It would also retain fibres very poorly.

Opinion

In my opinion, based on the information available to me at present, these findings provide no scientific evidence to support or refute the assertion that the blouse and the belt had been in contact with each other.

Consideration must be given to other factors, such as washing the garment, the activity levels from the time of the incident to the time of collection and the textures of the donor and recipient garments.

The interpretation is based either on statistical probability, the odds of recovering the number of fibres found, or Bayesian statistics (Chapter 57), expressing the likelihood that the number of fibres found were due to the suspect being involved (see Chapter 55).

Text references

Daéid, N.N., Cassidy, M. and McHugh, S. (2008) An investigation into the correlation of knife damage in clothing and the length of skin wounds. *Forensic Science International* **179**: 107–110.

Dunbar, M. and Murphy, T.M. (2009) DNA analysis of natural fiber rope. *Journal of Forensic Sciences* **54**(1): 108–113.

Palmer, R. (1998) The retention and recovery of transferred fibres following the washing of recipient clothing. *Journal of Forensic Sciences* **43**: 502–504.

Petrick, L.M., Wilson, T.A. and Fawcett, R. (2006) High performance liquid chromatography-ultraviolet spectroscopy-electrospray ionization mass spectrometry method for acrylic and polyester forensic fiber dye analysis. *Journal of Forensic Sciences* **51**(4): 771–779.

Robertson, J. and Grieve, M. (1999) *Forensic Examination of Fibres,* 2nd edn. Taylor and Francis, London.

Sources for further study

Aitken, C.G.G. and Taroni, F. (2004) *Statistics and the Evaluation of Evidence for Forensic Scientists,* 2nd edn. Wiley, Chichester.

Grieve, M.C. (1994) Fibres and forensic science: New ideas, developments and techniques. *Forensic Science Review* **6**: 60–80.

Lucy, D. (2005) *Introduction to Statistics for Forensic Scientists.* Wiley, Chichester.

Robertson, J.R. Roux, C. and Wiggins, K. (2017) *Forensic Examination of Fibres,* 3rd edn. CRC Press, Boca Raton

Sawbridge, M. and Ford, J.E. (1987) *Textile Fibres under the Microscope*, Shirley Institute, Manchester.

Taupin, J.M. and Cwiklik, C. (2009) *Scientific Protocols for Forensic Examination of Clothing.* CRC Press, Boca Raton.

Study exercises

42.1 Document your examination. Using the information given in Box 42.1 and pp. 410–411, fully examine and document an item of your clothing.

42.2 Practise recovery of hair/fibres. Using the tape lifting technique (Box 42.1), tape lift the item of clothing used in study exercise 42.1. Observe the tape lift using macroscopic and microscopic techniques, documenting what you think is important.

42.3 Test your knowledge. What other tests could you do to identify the fibres?

Ammunition – comprises the cartridge case, primer, propellant and bullet in its entirety.

Bullet – the part of the ammunition that is projected from the firearm.

Ballistics – the scientific study of projectiles in flight.

Cartridge – metal casing, or plastic wadding, that contains the primer and propellant and forms a gas-tight seal with the bullet.

Firearm – in the UK, a lethal, barrelled weapon of any description from which any shot, bullet or other missile can be discharged (Section 57 Firearms Act 1968).

Gunshot residue – trace residue of the metals from the ammunition released when the weapon is fired.

Primer – a mixture of compounds that explode when compressed, igniting the propellant.

Propellant – a compound, such as nitrocellulose, that will burn explosively to produce a large volume of gas within the cartridge.

NABIS – there are four NABIS hubs in the UK – Birmingham, London, Manchester and Strathclyde.

Types of firearm – include:

- *Air-gun* – a hand-fired weapon that does not contain any explosive. As the trigger is pulled, the pellet is expelled by release of compressed gas. Suitable for short-distance shooting.
- *Handgun* – a hand-fired weapon, including pistols and revolvers. Suitable for short-distance shooting.
- *Machine-gun* – automatically loading weapon, capable of rapidly firing multiple rounds.
- *Rifle* – a weapon fired from the shoulder, with a rifled bore (p. 417). Suitable for long-distance shooting.
- *Shotgun* – smooth-bored barrel; ammunition is small spherical pellets in a plastic cartridge. Suitable for short-distance shooting.

Firearm analysis is a specialist discipline involving the application of a wide range of forensic techniques. It includes recovery of evidence at the crime scene, search and recovery of trace evidence from clothing, hands, wounds, etc., and the study of ballistics, i.e. what happens to a projectile, such as a bullet, in flight.

Potential applications of forensic science include:

- **Identifying who fired a weapon** – for example, determining whether a particular individual was responsible for causing an injury to another party.
- **Matching weapons and comparing used bullets** – for example, when linking a weapon to a particular crime scene.
- **Providing evidence in the reconstruction of events** – for example, establishing the likely distance from which a weapon was fired, to corroborate the version of events of a suspect or witness.

A forensic scientist will focus his/her analysis on particular aspects including:

1. **Ballistics** – examining what happens to the bullet inside the barrel of a firearm, during flight and when it reaches its target.
2. **Analysis of gunshot residue**, also known as firearm discharge residue (FDR) – examining hands or clothing for primer residue from a person who has fired a weapon.
3. **Physical fits and microscopic comparisons** – examining any marks that may have been transferred to a bullet as it is fired from the weapon.
4. **Determination of the serial number of the firearm** – examining an obliterated serial number using chemical treatment.

The National Ballistics Intelligence Services (NABIS) was developed via a jointly funded programme by the Home Office and Association of Chief Police Officers (ACPO). NABIS delivers a national database that contains confidential information on all the firearms that have been recovered by the UK police forces and associated ballistic information including, for example, bullet and cartridge casings. Further to this it also serves as a fast and very effective intelligence tool by providing potential links to suspects, incidents, locations and weapons.

 KEY POINT *Apart from the highly visible effects of bullets, evidence obtained from firearms will often remain unnoticed by the casual observer; however, microscopic trace evidence may link an individual to a particular crime.*

Ballistics

There are many different types of firearms available, each of which will have projectiles with distinctive forensic characteristics. For example, a rifle and a shotgun have dissimilar mechanisms of discharge, which will result in characteristic features imprinted on the bullet casing or bullet itself, as well as different patterns of damage on impact.

As a general rule, ammunition (Fig. 43.1) is composed of:

- **a cartridge case or jacket,** typically of brass (70% copper, 30% zinc), but can also include nickel, or plastic in the case of a shotgun;

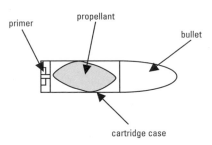

Fig. 43.1 A typical example of ammunition showing the location of the four main components.

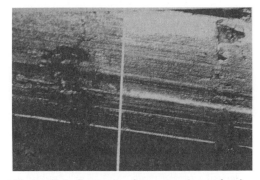

Photo 43.1 Example of a comparison of striation marks on a bullet, illustrating the associated characteristic longitudinal pattern using comparison microscopy (Chapter 10). (Image from Heard, 2008.)

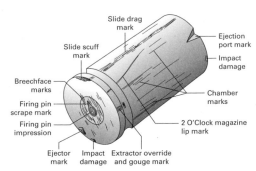

Fig. 43.2 Illustration of marks that could be transferred on to a cartridge case:
(a) Chamber marks – occur as a result of the cartridge being loaded into the firearm, characterised by scuff marks on the sides of the cartridge case as they are located/moved in the magazine.
(b) Firing marks – occur as a result of the firing pin making contact with the primer – in the illustration is an example where the primer is retained in a primer cap in the centre of the cartridge base (known as centre fire). If the primer was retained in the rim, the cartridge is known as rim fire.
(c) Ejection marks – occur as a result of the cartridge being ejected after discharge.
(d) Impact marks – occur when the ejected cartridge impacts on to a hard surface.
(From Haag and Haag, 2011)

- **a primer,** consisting of barium nitrate, as an oxidiser, lead styphnate, tetracene and antimony trisulphide;
- **a propellant,** such as nitrocellulose or nitroglycerin;
- **a bullet,** usually lead-based, with various combinations of steel, tin, antimony or copper jackets (Warlow, 2011).

A plastic cartridge of a shotgun does not contain a solid bullet mass, but rather a selected weight of small, round pellets. The close-range destructive force is enhanced with this type of ammunition, but for distances in excess of 40 m, bullets are more effective.

All commercially available ammunition (civilian or military) is stamped with a mark, known as a cartridge headstamp, that can be found on the base of the cartridge and can be used to identify, for example, the manufacturer, calibre and date of production.

Internal ballistics

As soon as the trigger of a firearm is fired, the primer explodes igniting the propellant, which results in a controlled expansion of gas. This creates an increased pressure within the barrel and the force produced propels the bullet forward, as well as the expulsion of the gaseous gunshot residue. The degree of acceleration to some extent depends on the length of the barrel, since this determines the length of time the force is applied. During the manufacture of any firearm the inside of the barrel is initially smoothed so the bullet does not deviate from its intended path. Typically, the barrel will then be further modified to contain a series of grooves, known as rifling, either in a right- or left-hand spiral. These grooves are normally less than 0.1 mm thick, with the upper ridges known as lands. As the bullet travels along the barrel, the pattern of the grooves marks the surface of the bullet, appearing as a series of fine lines or striations (see Photo 43.1).

As with other forensic evidence types such as fingerprints (Chapter 26) and footwear impressions (Chapter 27), the marks associated with internal ballistics are also categorised into class and individual characteristics. As indicated above, class characteristics include the direction of the rifling, along with the number and width of lands and grooves. Individual characteristics, on the other hand, are introduced predominantly by manufacturing imperfections and are observed as small imperfections within the rifling.

 KEY POINT *The striations on a bullet are unique to a particular gun, and therefore become a distinctive characteristic for forensic investigation.*

It is not only the bullet that will pick up impression characteristics when the weapon is chambered, fired or ejected. Marks can be transferred to the cartridge case from the primer, as well as from the bullet chamber, from the magazine movement and during ejection from the weapon. On firing the weapon, the base of the cartridge will receive an impression mark from the firing pin (see Fig. 43.2). If the cartridge cases are recovered from a crime scene, then these can be examined in the same way as the bullets.

The evidence associated with internal ballistics falls into three broad categories:

1. **Microscopic examination of the recovered bullet** – this should be performed using a comparison microscope (see Chapter 10). If a weapon has been recovered, it should be test fired and the bullet compared with that recovered from the scene. The bullets should be examined under low

Identifying striation marks – *matching striation marks will identify a bullet with a specific gun. No two guns, even if sequentially manufactured, have exactly the same internal marks or defects, which are transferred to the bullet or its soft metal casing as it passes along the barrel.*

Examination of exhibits for lead residue – *prepare sodium rhodizonate solution by adding 0.2 g of this salt to 100 mL distilled water. Swab the exhibit with water and using a Pasteur pipette add, dropwise, the sodium rhodizonate solution. In the presence of lead, the solution will change from orange to red-brown in colour (Walker and Rodacy, 2002).*

Swabbing a hand for gunshot residue – *the area from the trigger finger to the thumb should be swabbed with isopropanol and water using a medical swab (Photo 43.2). Substances present can then be extracted by solid phase extraction (see Chapter 12) using, for example, Chromosorb 104 and the extract analysed using SEM–EDX.*

A recent development *in characterising FDR from swabs has been demonstrated using MSI-TOF-SIMS, with the advantage of this technique showing organic, inorganic and morphological data with no/little damage to the sample (Castellanos et al., 2016).*

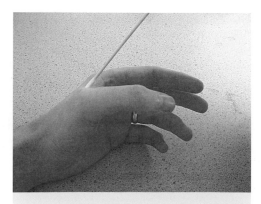

Photo 43.2 Swabbing a hand for gunshot residue. The main areas to focus on are the thumb and forefinger as these are the ones in closest proximity to the residue when the weapon is fired.

magnification ($\times$10) to maintain an appropriate field of view and depth of focus, and then at 40$\times$ magnification using a comparison microscope (Chapter 10) so that the bullet can be rotated and the striation marks compared between both bullets (Warlow, 2011) (Photo 43.1).

2. **Determination of the composition of the bullet** – this can be performed using simple chemical tests – for example, addition of sodium rhodizonate to identify lead residue or dithiooxamide (DTO) for the presence of copper residues (from the jacket) on exhibits through which the bullet has passed.

 KEY POINT *If you need to test for both copper and lead, you must perform the dithiooxamide test prior to the sodium rhodizinate test. Lead will not transfer into the alkaline solution used in the dithiooxamide test.*

In the case of cartridges, it is equally important to determine whether a latent fingerprint is present (see Chapter 26).

3. **Gunshot residue analysis, also known as firearm discharge residue (FDR)** – this can be carried out using scanning electron microscopy, coupled with an energy-dispersive X-ray detector (SEM–EDX) (Romolo and Margot, 2001), as described in Chapter 18. It is extremely important to minimise contamination for FDR analysis. Any person who has had contact with a firearm should not be the person who collects the FDR exhibits. It is also important to collect a control sample from the examiner who is conducting the examination for comparison purposes. Residue can be deposited on the person who fired the weapon, on the intended victim and also on any other object or person in close proximity, so interpretation of a positive test for gunshot residues should be treated with caution. The primer mainly consists of a unique combination of lead, barium and antinomy. Other elements are present including aluminium, sulphur, tin and calcium but these are not specific for gunshot residue. The persistence of residue on the hands is limited, typically lasting only 2–4 h. However, it may be trapped in clothing and hair, which can be detected for several days after firing the weapon (Warlow, 2011). An alternative to SEM–EDX for identifying whether an individual has recently held a weapon is spraying the hand with pyridyldiphenyl triazine (PDT). This compound reacts in the presence of any ferrous metal, so therefore is non-specific, and initiates a colour change from colourless to magenta, indicating a positive result (Leifer *et al.*, 2001).

An alternative approach to the collection of firearm discharge residue is the use of specifically designed pre-carbon-coated adhesive disks for SEM-EDX analysis. These disks, known as SEM stubs, can be applied to the surface in question and can then be directly transferred into the SEM chamber for analysis.

External ballistics

In terms of forensic importance, external ballistics usually involves reconstructing the point of origin, i.e. where the bullet was fired from, as well as giving an indication of the type of weapon used and the distance from which it was fired, most notably when a person has been shot. The angle of impact can be determined by placing thin probes, such as dowelling rods, into the bullet holes and photographing these *in situ*. By extrapolating a line from the terminal position of the bullet, for example embedded in a wall, along the dowelling rod, the direction of the bullet can be determined.

Bullets do not follow a straight line to the target. They obey the physical laws that apply to any projectile, such as kinetic energy of the bullet as it leaves the muzzle of the firearm, drag, air resistance and gravity. Furthermore, the presence of grooves within the barrel of the firearm cause the bullet to spin on its axis during flight, in a manner similar to the throwing of a rugby ball. The speed of the bullet is dependent on the initial force applied to it, but as it travels through the air, the forces of air resistance and drag reduce its energy. Hence, handguns cannot be used over distances greater than 50 m, whereas high-velocity rifles are specifically designed to maintain the energy of the bullet for distances up to several hundred metres.

Terminal ballistics

What happens when bullets hit the intended target depends on the energy of the bullet that remains on impact and also on the target itself. If the target is a dense material (e.g. brick) then the kinetic energy of the bullet will be dissipated quickly and the depth of penetration will be minimal. Damage will usually be caused by penetration and crushing forces in low-velocity weapons, i.e. less than 300 ms^{-1}, whereas with high-velocity weapons, i.e. greater than 500 ms^{-1}, penetration of the target is immediately followed by the production of a cavity, as a result of oscillating shock waves after the bullet has passed through.

When a gunshot injury has been inflicted on an individual, the resultant blood pattern (p. 294) will appear as a mist-like dispersion of blood, confluent in the main stain but with droplet sizes usually less than 0.1 mm in the surrounding area. There are also some key features of the wounds, which can help in determining the distance from which they were shot (Mason and Purdue, 2000). These include:

- **Contact wounds** – associated with contact of the barrel of the gun with the skin of the person. These wounds can be found on any part of the body, but if they occur over bony prominences, they give the appearance of a ragged stellate wound, formed by the explosive force of the bullet being forced from the barrel and splitting or tearing the skin. The burning mixture of primer and propellant gases is forced from the barrel and sears the edges of the contact wound. If the weapon was fired through clothing then the searing appears on the edges of the damage to the clothing and not on the skin. Any unburned powder may be forced into the track of the wound, which can later be examined for its composition by SEM–EDX. In some cases, the impression of the muzzle can be seen imprinted on to the skin, which can be matched to the actual weapon used.
- **Wounds at distances up to 1 m** – characterised by a stippling of the skin around a circular entrance wound, caused by the burning primer and propellant residues impacting and sticking to the skin. This pattern of stippling is termed 'powder tattooing'. If it is concentric around the wound then the weapon was fired at approximately 90°. If the bullet was fired at an angle then the powder tattooing will appear elliptical, with the area of least stippling indicating the direction from which the bullet was fired. A more reliable technique for the determination of distance (up to 1 m) has been reported to be the analysis of lead patterns using atomic absorption spectroscopy (see Chapter 17) surrounding the wound (Gagliano-Candela *et al.*, 2008), where a linear relationship has been found between the firing distance and the lead concentration in defined areas of the target.
- **Wounds arising from a weapon from a distance greater than 1 m** – these are much more difficult to characterise. Although there will be no powder tattooing or other indications of a close-range shot, the primer residue can

Examining a weapon at a crime scene – the safety of everyone in attendance at the scene is paramount. In cases where a firearm is found, the weapon must first be made safe by an appropriately trained person before any further examination can be performed.

1. First engage the safety catch and then remove the magazine.
2. Next, open the breech and take a photograph to indicate where bullets are located.
3. Swab any spent cartridges with isopropanol and water for analysis of gunshot residue.
4. Record details of the make, model and serial number along with the barrel length, diameter and weight of the weapon.
5. Package the weapon in a cardboard box and add an evidence label (see Chapter 24).

Contamination – remember that the firearm could be a source of FDR contamination and should be stored separately from other exhibits.

Preparation of Fry's reagent – add 80 mL concentrated hydrochloric acid to 60 mL of water containing 12.9 g copper(II) chloride and 50 mL of ethanol.

Comparison of bullets – if a bullet fired from a suspect weapon is compared with a bullet collected from a crime scene and found to be a physical match, it should appear in the report using the words 'is consistent with'.

adhere to the fired bullet and may be detected in the track of a wound. Bullets fired at long distances, typically from high-velocity weapons, have a significant amount of energy to propel them. The bullet, on impact, is much more destructive as a result, and therefore the internal injuries that are observed are usually more severe.

Examining crime scenes where firearms have been used

A thorough examination of the scene should be carried out (see Chapter 23). If a weapon has been found at a scene of crime the first thing that must be done is to make sure it is safe for any examination to proceed to ensure the safety of anyone attending the scene. During the process, you should consider where potential evidence might be located, for example fingerprints that might be contaminated or smudged by the process of making the weapon safe, or saliva (Chapter 30) if the weapon was placed in the mouth. You need to make sure that any reagents/powders used do not enter the barrel of the firearm.

Discharged casings and live ammunition should be photographed *in situ* and recorded in detail in your scene examination notes, (p. 230) – for example, the number of shots that were fired, which you can determine by counting the number of cartridge cases found at the scene, and the make and the calibre of the bullet, which can be obtained from the cartridge cases. You can reconstruct the events by examining the number of bullet holes and the direction of bullets, as well as examining the blood patterns found (p. 294). If the person firing the weapon was in close proximity, there may well be back-spatter from the wound on to that person and on to the weapon; therefore, if the weapon was found it should also be examined for the presence of blood (see Chapter 30), as well as determining the serial number.

The serial number is imprinted into the metal of the firearm at a certain depth. When the serial number is scratched, it is usually only the surface that is obliterated and not the indentation underneath. You can attempt to identify the number by microscopy (Chapter 10), or under oblique lighting. If you cannot determine the serial number by these techniques then you can use chemical visualisation. When an acid is added to the obliterated section, the scratched or etched surface is dissolved at a faster rate than the underlying metal, which results in the reappearance of the serial mark. A typical process for weapons made of iron is the use of Fry's reagent, as follows:

1. Apply the reagent to the obliterated serial mark using a cotton swab and leave for approximately 1 min.
2. Apply 15% v/v nitric acid to the obliterated serial mark with a cotton swab and leave for approximately 1 min.

Repeat this process several times and the obliterated serial numbers should appear.

Reporting firearms cases

When spent bullets have been recovered from a scene, and subsequently a firearm is recovered during the investigation, then the firearm will be test fired and the bullets compared with each other. In this instance, the report will simply state whether or not the striation marks are consistent with having been fired from the same weapon.

When gunshot residue collected from a suspect has been examined, it will have been compared with residue collected from a particular weapon, or if no weapon has been recovered, compared with an exhibit found at a crime scene. However, it is not possible to determine with certainty who fired the weapon, since residue will be readily transferred on to any person, or object, that was in close proximity to the weapon.

Text references

Castellanos, A., Bell, S. and Fernandez-Lima, F. (2016) Characterisation of FDR recovered from skin swabs using sub micrometric spectrometry imaging. *Analytical Methods* **8**(21): 4300–4305.

Gagliano-Candela, R., Colucci, A.P. and Napoli, S. (2008) Determination of firing distance. lead analysis on the target by atomic absorption spectroscopy (AAS). *Journal of Forensic Sciences* **53**(2): 321–324.

Haag, M. and Haag, L. (2011) *Shooting Incident Reconstruction*, 2nd edn. Academic Press, London.

Heard, B. (2008) *Handbook of Firearms and Ballistics: Examining and Interpreting Forensic Evidence*, 2nd edn. Chancery Wiley Law Publications, New York.

Leifer, A., Avissar, Y., Berger, S., Wax, H., Donchin, Y. and Almog, J. (2001) Detection of firearm imprints on the hands of suspects: Effectiveness of PDT reaction. *Journal of Forensic Sciences* **46**(6): 1442–1446.

Mason, J.K. and Purdue, B.N. (2000) *The Pathology of Trauma*, 3rd edn. Arnold, London.

Romolo, F. and Margot, P. (2001) Identification of gunshot residue: A critical review. *Forensic Science International* **119**: 195–211.

Walker, P. and Rodacy, P. (2002) *Field Test Kit for Gunshot Residue Detection*. Available at: http://prod.sandia.gov/techlib/access-control.cgi/2001/013942.pdf. Last accessed 24/08/2017.

Warlow, T.A. (2011) *Firearms, the Law and Forensic Ballistics*, 3rd edn. Taylor and Francis, London.

Sources for further study

Association of Firearm and Toolmark Examiners Website. Available at: https://afte.org/

Dimaio, V. (1999) *Gunshot Wounds: Practical Aspects of Firearms, Ballistics, and Forensic Techniques* (Practical Aspects of Criminal & Forensic Investigation). Interpharm/CRC, Boca Raton.

National Ballistic Intelligence Service website. Available at: http://nabis.police.uk/

Nichols, R. (2003) Firearm and toolmark identification criteria: A review of the literature, Part II. *Journal of Forensic Sciences* **48**(2): 1–10.

Sinha, J.K. (2014) *Forensic Investigation of Unusual Firearms.* CRC Press, Boca Raton

Wallace, S.J. (2008) *Chemical Analysis of Firearms, Ammunition and Gunshot Residue.* CRC Press, Boca Raton.

Study exercises

43.1 Test your knowledge of firearm terminology. Define the following terms and give examples of each:

  (a) bullet;
  (b) cartridge;
  (c) primer;
  (d) propellant;
  (e) ammunition.

43.2 Test your knowledge of FDR analysis. List five elements that would be found in FDR analysis.

43.3 Discuss the interpretation of FDR. Using the Jill Dando case as an example, discuss in a group why Barry George was convicted in 2001 and subsequently acquitted in 2008. Consider the importance of the FDR in this case.

Definitions

The following terms have specific meanings in relation to fire investigation:

Accelerant – a flammable liquid fuel used to accelerate and direct the spread of a fire, typically containing aromatic compounds and/or long hydrocarbon chains.

Arson – wilful fire-raising.

Exothermic – a reaction that produces heat.

Flame – a hot glowing mass of burning vapour.

Fuel – any combustible material that will be burned for the duration of the fire.

Means of ignition – any means of raising the temperature above a critical value to allow an item to combust.

Pyrolysis – burning.

Pyrolysis products – gases, soot, etc. produced from burning fuel.

Seat of fire – the starting point of the fire.

The underlying process leading to a fire is an uncontrolled exothermic oxidation reaction. In other words, heat (fire) is produced when a combustible material interacts with oxygen in the air and the chemical reaction that occurs releases a significant amount of energy. There are really two types of fire – those that burn with flames (the most common and destructive type) and those that burn without flames.

For a fire to occur, there must be:

- **a combustible material present**;
- **an adequate oxygen supply** to maintain the burning process;
- **a means of ignition**, such as heat, electrical or accelerant (DeHaan, 2007).

Oxygen in air exists at a concentration of 21%. If this content drops below 15% then most flames can no longer be supported and the flame will go out (e.g. a fire in a sealed room). If, however, air is allowed in through a door or a window, then there may be sufficient oxygen to re-ignite the fire on entry into that room, which may have an implication in determining the development of the fire.

The most common request of forensic scientists is to determine the means of ignition of a fire, as this may result in an individual being prosecuted – for example, for willful fire-raising or arson.

 KEY POINT *The purpose of fire investigation is generally to establish the seat (origin) of the fire, to determine whether there is evidence that the fire was started deliberately and to collect and analyse fire debris.*

Common causes of fires

All fires require an input of energy (heat) to start. Establishing the means of ignition is the most difficult part of investigating a fire, simply because the starting point of the fire is likely to have been destroyed during the burning process. Common means of ignition include:

- **Arson** (intentional fire) – this is the main type of fire investigation that the forensic scientist will be asked to attend. The fire scene may be located outdoors, in a disused building, a road vehicle or house. In these cases, determining the seat of the fire is of great importance. For instance, if the seat of the fire was determined to be behind the front door, then the implication is that the means of ignition may have been directed through the letterbox. This may have been as a result of lighting papers or by the use of an accelerant such as petrol, diesel, turpentine or lighter fuel. It is not uncommon for an accelerant to be used in close proximity to an electrical appliance, which is then subsequently suggested as a cause for the start of the fire.
- **Hot objects** or surfaces overheating – for example, ceramic hobs of cookers or irons that come into close contact with a combustible material may be sufficient to ignite a fire, which can then spread to other combustible materials (Table 44.1). The same applies to someone sitting in close proximity to a heater (e.g. gas heater, electric bar heater or open fire), which may transfer sufficient heat to ignite clothing.
- **Electrical sources** – with the advent of modern electrical wiring, circuit breakers and fuses, electrical ignition is not as common as it used to be. Proving this

Table 44.1 Incidence of fires reported in England and Wales in 2014–15

Cause	Occurrence (no. of cases)
Cooking	16,549
Heating appliance	1,968
Electrical	9,561
Arson	3,012
Candles	1,025
Cigarette-related	2,974
Children playing with matches	388

Adapted from www.gov.uk/government/collections/fire-statistics (2016)

Understanding arson – *arson is governed by the Criminal Damage Act 1971. In 2016 the Home Office counting rules for recording offences changed to distinguish between arson endangering life and arson not endangering life.*

Case example An elderly gentleman, with a travel rug wrapped around his knees, has fallen asleep while sitting close to an electric bar heater. The ends of the rug reach ignition point and start to burn, but the fire does not extend beyond the chair. This scene is typical of a fatal fire investigation and on entry into the room, the temperature of the room, condition of the heater (and the fact it is turned on), the proximity of the chair to the fire and the localised area of burning, including the charring on the ceiling should be recorded. In this instance, the cause of death would be likely to be recorded as accidental.

Understanding fires – *the intensity (heat) of the fire can be approximated as follows:*

Flame colour	Temperature
faint red	500–550 °C
orange	650–750 °C
yellow	850–1,000 °C
white	1,200 °C

Consider CCTV – *check CCTV footage of the area to see whether the building/scene has been recorded prior to the onset of the fire.*

to be the case is difficult, as the cabling surrounding the wires is likely to have melted due to the heat. In the case of a suspect portable electrical appliance, this could be submitted for further analysis along with the damaged wiring. If the insulation of two wires becomes damaged and the two wires come into close proximity to each other, then arcing can occur between the two, which may produce a significantly higher temperature than for most fires. In this case, the copper in the wires will melt at a localised point forming a bead at the point of arcing, and if this can be traced then an electrical fault can be confirmed.

- **Cigarette smoking** – there are three sources of ignition in these cases: as a result of primary ignition – for example, by a match used for lighting the cigarette (a basic flame that can reach temperatures of up to 1,200 °C); from the cigarette itself (a glowing, smouldering source); and from lighter fuel (accelerant).
- **Chip-pan fires** – a common cause of fire where the fat or oil overheats. These types of fires are commonly localised to the cooker and the ceiling immediately above. However, they are often accelerated into a more serious and intense fire when water is added. Here the water immediately turns into steam, which results in an explosive mixture with the hot oil.
- **Other causes** – for example, children playing with matches, the use of candles, especially tea-lights which may ignite the surface that the candle is placed on, and, occasionally, lightning.

Fire scene examination

These types of scene are unlike others in that you, as a forensic scientist, are not in control of the scene. The fire service will be in attendance and will be in the process of putting the fire out, or will have put the fire out, by the time you arrive. Your safety and the safety of others is paramount and you should ensure that you have spoken to the fire officer in charge and the police to make sure it is safe to enter the premises. On arrival at the scene it is also important to find out and record a number of facts before proceeding with the scene examination (see Box 44.1), including:

- The date and time of the initial call to you and the time of your arrival at the scene.
- The weather conditions.
- Who is present at the scene, and whether anyone is acting unusually. It is often the case in arson that the perpetrator will remain and observe the actions of the fire brigade.
- External damage to the property, if any.
- The action of the fire brigade – in particular how they gained access to the property (e.g. forced doors, broken windows).
- The degree/intensity of the fire when you arrive, which can be determined by observing the flame intensity if the fire is still burning, or discussing with the fire officers. You should also document the colour of the smoke, which may give an indication of the type of combustible material that has burned.
- The state and extent of the fire in its initial stages, where the fire was intense (which could be in more than one location) and furnishing and contents of the building.

 KEY POINT It is of great importance to identify yourself and work in conjunction with the fire service in the investigation of fire scenes.

Box 44.1 Main stages in a fire scene examination

1. **Locate the seat (origin) of the fire** – observe the pattern of burning to try to determine the order and direction in which burning occurred. Heat rises, as well as flames and the gases produced from the fire, therefore more damage will be observed in an upward direction from this point. Look for the areas with the most severe damage as these are most likely to be those closest to the seat of the fire. If there is insufficient fuel for the fire to continue to burn it will be localised and there will be evidence of the soot and other pyrolysis products on the surfaces above this localised area. The same principle can be applied on a larger scale to identify the room where the fire started.

2. **Study the development of the fire** – the position of the seat of the fire will determine the direction the fire will take; fire needs material to burn as well as oxygen to support combustion. Fires tend to burn in a predictable manner, although the time-scales involved in the sequence may differ according to the fuel, ventilation and source of ignition. The fire starts at the ignition stage, which will always be with a small flame. Oxygen will have been plentiful and the temperature will not have risen significantly within the room. Soot and gases (carbon monoxide and carbon dioxide) will have been produced that may have resulted in the death of a person in a fatal fire. Observe the ceiling of the rooms, which may have become charred. These may also become fuel for the fire, allowing its spread. The floor of the room where the fire started will have remained fairly cool compared with the ceiling. However, as the heat intensity in the room increases, this is usually sufficient to cause ignition of other materials, even at floor level. Each item that ignites will add to the heat intensity and aid the fire's growth. Observe the extent of the damage in each room, which can indicate the intensity of heat and duration of the exposure, taking into account that once the flames have subsided (fuel has been nearly exhausted) then fire enters the post-flame stage and becomes smouldering. Smouldering fires can maintain a high temperature though, and will continue to burn solid fuels for as long as some oxygen is available. Fresh entry of oxygen into the room may cause re-ignition to the flaming stage. Look for barriers (i.e. flame-resistant materials) that may have altered the course of the fire.

3. **Take into account the weather conditions** – the environmental temperature should be noted. A fire is more likely to occur in dry, hot conditions where the air is likely to contain less moisture (humidity). The condition of the combustible fuel should also be noted – obviously if it is wet it is less likely to burn, unless an accelerant has been used. The wind conditions should also be recorded because an adequate supply of air (oxygen) is required. The wind can also influence the direction and spread of the fire.

Investigating fatal fires

When a body is found in a fire it should be treated as a potential crime scene. As with all crime scenes, the appropriate personnel are employed to offer their expertise and to attempt to reconstruct events (see Chapter 23). As with all deaths, the cause and manner of death has to be established by the forensic pathologist. At autopsy, samples of blood can be obtained that will be sent to the forensic laboratory to determine whether or not the person died from inhaling carbon monoxide, one of the gaseous products produced from a fire. By measuring carboxyhaemoglobin levels in the blood (Chapter 38) it can be determined whether the person was breathing at the onset of the fire, as can the presence of soot in the trachea extending deep into the lung. The body must be identified, but given that it may have been engulfed by the fire this may prove visually difficult depending on the duration and intensity of the fire. With a severely burned body, the most useful means of identification is usually the teeth (Chapter 34), provided an up-to-date record of dental treatment is available.

Fires can be deliberately started to conceal a murder, in which case the absence of carboxyhaemoglobin (see p. 374) or lack of soot in the airways will indicate that the individual was not breathing at the onset of the fire. A careful examination of the body must be carried out by the forensic pathologist to

The extent of burning of a body – *this depends on the intensity of the heat, duration of exposure and the position of the body, i.e. whether parts of the body are exposed to the fire. For example, in a fire burning at 680 °C, the extent of burning likely to be seen in general terms is:*

up to 15 min – *the face, arms and legs will become charred;*

by 20 min – *the arm bones, ribs and skull will be clearly visible;*

by 25 min – *the shin bones will be clearly visible;*

by 35 min – *all leg bones will be clearly visible.*

Using a nylon bag – *it is important to collect all fire debris samples, including control reference samples, in nylon bags and not polythene bags. Nylon bags are impermeable to accelerants; therefore, if an accelerant has been used to start a fire, this trace evidence will not be lost between the time of collection and the time of analysis.*

Unburned items – *these are more likely to retain an accelerant; search the debris thoroughly for any unburned material and recover into a nylon bag (see p. 426).*

establish whether or not any injuries are present that would be consistent with the person being murdered.

Sample collection

Appropriate selection and storage of containers is really important because you do not want to lose any of the accelerant by evaporation. Williams and Sigman (2007) have demonstrated that some storage containers leak when stored over a period of time at 66 °C. Glass mason jars leaked most and to a lesser extent metal flame tins. Debrispak® polymer (nylon) bags exhibited the slowest leak rate. It should be noted, however, that it is highly unlikely that exhibits would be stored at this temperature.

 KEY POINT *The most important practical step of any fire investigation is to collect a reference sample of air (control sample) prior to entry into the building, especially when accelerants are suspected. You need to do this to show that there is no accelerant in the air prior to you entering the building. When you collect fire debris you will compare it with the control air bag. If an accelerant is found in the debris but not in the control air bag then you can say that an accelerant may have been used. If, however, a control air bag is not collected you cannot state whether any accelerant found is due to residual levels in the atmosphere or specifically from the fire debris.*

Collecting the control air sample is easily done by simply opening a fresh nylon bag and collecting an air sample, at least 10 m from the building. To tie the bag a swan neck procedure is used (see Photo 44.1). It is important that this sample is clearly labelled as 'Control' with the location, time and date it was collected. This procedure should be repeated twice to give two control air samples.

 KEY POINT *Never store control bags in close proximity to any other samples suspected of containing an accelerant.*

Once you have entered the building and have established the possible seat of the fire (see Box 44.1) you should collect debris samples into nylon bags. These debris samples should include two samples of debris collected remotely from the seat of the fire, for example from another room, or, if the fire was contained within a single room, then the furthest point away from the seat of the fire. A further two debris samples should be collected from the actual seat of the fire.

Appropriate rules for collection of evidence from fires for debris are:

- always prepare a control bag prior to entering the scene;
- always use a fresh nylon bag;
- use an appropriately sized bag for the sample – only fill the bags half full and never overfill them;
- tie the bag with the 'swan-neck' procedure (Photo 44.1);
- attach a label, with the sample details, using string around the tied neck.

If a liquid or spillage is observed at the scene, which you suspect may be an accelerant, then:

- take a swab of an area that does not appear to have any spillage present – this will be used as a control reference swab;
- take a control sample of any carpet, or other fabrics that have not been contaminated, either by the fire or by the liquid;

Suspect's clothing – remember to search clothing prior to submission, for any other items of evidential value.

Photo 44.1 How to tie a nylon bag by the swan-neck procedure.

- if possible, transfer a sample of the liquid to a metal tin (see Chapter 24);
- if the volume of liquid is insufficient, swab the sample and place the swab into a nylon bag;
- if a container suspected of being the one used to transport the accelerant is found at the scene, then submit the entire sample to allow the volume of liquid to be measured;
- take a swab of any spillage;
- package red metal tins and swabs in nylon bags.

If a suspect has been identified and arrested, then his/her clothing can be seized by the police.

 KEY POINT   Never dry any clothing or items suspected to contain an accelerant prior to packaging in a nylon bag for submission to the laboratory.

In this instance, the clothing should be placed inside a nylon bag and sealed using the swan-neck procedure, and appropriate label details should be attached to the bag. The clothing will be submitted to the laboratory for analysis for the presence of accelerants, but kept isolated from other items, and should be treated in the same way as a fire debris sample.

You have to consider alternative hypotheses to explain an accelerant on a suspect's clothing. One such hypothesis is the claim that the presence of petrol was from legitimate contact, for example filling a car up with petrol at a petrol station. Coulson *et al.* (2008) examined shoes and items of clothing from 29 individuals who had recently filled their cars with petrol. No petrol residues were detected on any of the items examined, suggesting that theoretically the transfer of petrol could occur, but in practice it does not. Consideration should be given to the experimental design (see Chapter 5) and the population size of this study before robust conclusions can be drawn.

Analysis of fire debris

Each debris sample must be examined and the label details and description of the sample recorded in your examination notes. This description should include an accurate weight of the sample. The process of debris analysis is similar to that for alcohol analysis (Chapter 37) in that the sample, in its sealed nylon bag, is heated at 100 °C for a given time. This pre-heating time is sufficient to allow equilibration of volatile compounds between the sample and the air (headspace) above it. The time taken for equilibration depends on the mass of the sample, which is why it is important to record the weight of the debris.

Once the sample bags, including the control reference bag, have been pre-heated, the smell of the vapour should be assessed and recorded as they are removed from the oven. Each bag is cut open in turn and a maximum volume of 200 mL should be sampled, by withdrawing the air (headspace) using a graduated syringe.

These headspace samples are then adsorbed on to a cartridge, such as Tenax TA (Jackowski, 1997) (see Chapter 12), by passing the contents of the syringe through the cartridge. The volatile compounds (accelerants) will adsorb on to the cartridge.

Time required for pre-heating debris samples – as the mass of the debris increases so will the time required for pre-heating the sample. The ASTM have published guidelines for the standard practice for the analysis of fire debris samples. For more information see ASTM E1388-17 available at HYPERLINK "http://www.astm.org" www.astm.org (Last accessed 19/02/18).

It has been noted that when using Tenax TA the cartridge has to be optimised to 60 °C to ensure the maximal adsorption of polar and non-polar components (Borusiewicz and Zie$_{t}$ba-Palus, 2007). An alternative to Tenax TA is the use of solid phase micro extraction (SPME) (see Chapter 12), e.g. 100 µm polydimethylsiloxane (PDMS) with direct contact of the fibre and the fire debris. Yoshida *et al.* (2008) demonstrated the effectiveness of this technique for the extraction of petrol, paraffin and diesel and found that there was an increased recovery of low-volatile components from diesel in fire debris samples.

These compounds can be eluted from the cartridge directly into a gas chromatograph (Chapter 14) with FID or MS detection. This process is known as thermal desorption and occurs by rapidly heating the cartridge to 300 °C. Most accelerants are long-chain hydrocarbons, typically between 8 and 22 hydrocarbon units (e.g. diesel). These hydrocarbons will be detected as a series of equally spaced peaks by the gas chromatograph (Fig. 44.1(a) – (d)), the number of which can give an indication as to which accelerant may have been used. In a fire, the lower boiling point chemicals in an accelerant will partially evaporate (Fig. 44.1(c) and (d)), altering the typical reference profile. By comparison to known reference samples the identification of an accelerant may be confirmed. If petrol vapour were subsequently found on the clothing of an individual, a gas chromatography (GC) profile could be produced on analysis and compared with that found at the scene.

Reporting fire cases

When reporting the results of fire cases, it is almost always in relation to whether or not an accelerant has been used to deliberately start a fire and whether or not an accelerant has been found on an individual. The results can report that an accelerant, such as petrol, was present or was not present (Box 44.2).

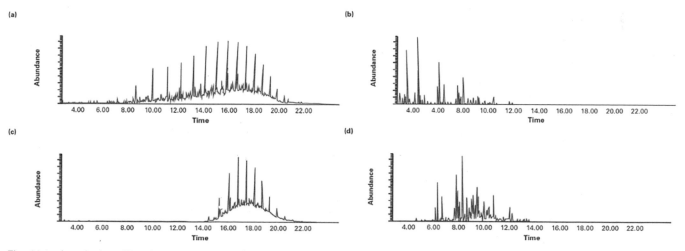

Fig. 44.1 A typical profile of petrol and diesel (unevaporated and evaporated).

Box 44.2 An example of a statement for a case involving arson

The following is an extract from a typical fire report. For details of how to write your report see Chapter 60.

Purpose

I have been asked to analyse the items detailed in this report for the presence of common fire accelerants (e.g. petrol, paraffin, diesel, white spirit).

Results

Petrol vapour was detected with the following two items:

Sample of debris (1) labelled 'found seat of fire within Flue Manor on 23rd February 2017'.

Sample of debris (2) labelled 'found seat of fire within Flue Manor on 23rd February 2017'.

No common fire accelerant was detected with the following item:

Control bag labelled 'prepared at Flue Manor on 23/02/17'.

***Forensic evidence from deliberate explosions** – this might include:*

- *the power supply, usually in the form of batteries of any size;*
- *the presence of any circuit boards;*
- *timers, for a delayed detonation;*
- *detonator and associated wiring;*
- *residues of the actual explosive itself, for instance that found on any wrappers;*
- *evidence of the container the explosive was housed in.*

***Bombing and explosions** – accounted for 16,747 of 31,646 worldwide incidents in 2014/15. In the UK, this type of case was attributed to 108 of 218 incidents. (Data derived from Global Terrorism Database.)*

***Chemical profile** – you should examine the item for the explosive but you should also consider the chemicals that were used to construct the device, e.g. fertiliser, solvents, weedkiller, etc.*

Explosions

Essentially, an explosion can be characterised as a near-instantaneous release of energy from a chemical reaction. This results in shock waves and, depending on the container used, projectiles that are capable of causing severe damage remote to the explosion site. Explosions can occur either deliberately (e.g. explosive devices, such as home-made pipe bombs) or accidentally (e.g. gas leaks).

Many different types of explosive are available commercially, including dynamite or nitroglycerin, and military explosives, including the more recently developed plastic explosives (e.g. Semtex, C4).

When an explosive device detonates, the surrounding area is subjected to a high degree of force causing severe damage, often structural, so care must be taken regarding safe working at the scene. Just as with all other forensic investigations, the scene should be cordoned off, documented and searched systematically for evidence (Chapter 23) that could explain the cause of the explosion.

 KEY POINT *The purpose of the investigation of explosions is to determine whether the event was accidental or deliberate, what materials were used to make the explosive device, where the device was made and how the device was made.*

At the scene, there is likely to be a significant amount of debris, with dispersal over a widespread area. The scene search can therefore be laborious and will typically involve systematically sifting through the debris in a structured manner until the seat of explosive is reached. The explosive device itself may not be totally destroyed and parts of it should be searched for.

Examination of samples in the laboratory requires various techniques, according to the type of explosive and the nature of the evidence that is submitted. For example, explosive vapours on clothing can be examined by desorption on to Tenax TA cartridges, as described for fire debris (p. 426). For the explosive materials themselves, the tentative identity of the material can be determined by thin-layer chromatography (TLC: Chapter 14), as shown in Box 44.3.

Box 44.3   How to identify an explosive by TLC

Explosives can be tentatively identified using TLC (see also Chapter 14). If this test gives a positive result, a confirmatory test should be performed before the results are reported.

1. **Prepare the solvent system** – measure 900 mL toluene and 100 mL ethyl acetate into a 1 L flask and mix well. This solvent system can separate the majority of organic explosives. Pour the solvent into a TLC reservoir to a depth of 0.5 cm and cover the tank with a lid.

2. **Prepare the visualisation reagent** – once the separation of the explosive has occurred, you need to be able to observe how far the components in the drug have moved along the TLC plate. The reagent used to visualise the spots is known as Griess reagent:
   (i)   reagent A – accurately weigh 0.5 g α – naphthol. Add to 165 mL 30% v/v acetic acid/water;
   (ii) reagent B – accurately weigh 1 g sulphanilic acid. Add to 100 mL 30% v/v acetic acid/water;
   (iii) measure 50 mL reagent A into a 250 mL beaker. Add to 50 mL reagent B and mix thoroughly. Transfer to a bottle that has a fine spray;
   (iv) prepare a 1 mol L^{-1} sodium hydroxide solution and transfer to a bottle that has a fine spray.

3. **Prepare the TLC plates** – pipette 1 mL acetone to the sample of explosive and vortex mix. Collect a normal phase silica gel TLC plate and, using a pencil, lightly draw a line 1 cm from the bottom edge of the plate. Mark on this line at 1 cm spaces a series of crosses; under each cross write a reference number to indicate whether the sample to be loaded at that position is a reference standard or a case sample.

4. **Load ('spot') the samples on to the plate** – as described in step 4, Box 39.2, 'spot' acetone, a standard mix containing common explosives such as nitrocellulose, nitrogylcerin, trinitrotoluene (TNT), tetryl (2,4,6-trinitrophenylmethylnitramine) and pentaerythritol tetranitrate (PETN) and the test sample on to the TLC plate. Place the plate into the reservoir chamber and cover with a lid.

5. **Develop the plate** – allow the solvent to rise up the plate until it reaches 1 cm from the top. Remove the plate and score the solvent front (see Chapter 14) with a pencil.

6. **Visualise the TLC plates** – once the plate is dry, spray it with 1 mol L^{-1} sodium hydroxide. Transfer the TLC plate into an oven set at 100 °C for 10 min. This will convert any nitrate esters and nitramines into nitrites. Remove the TLC plate from the oven and spray the plate with Griess reagent. The spots will develop as an orange colour, from which the R_f (p. 129) can then be calculated and a tentative identification of the explosive made.

(Adapted from Beveridge, 1998.)

Microscopy (see Chapter 10) can also be used to identify the colour, consistency and physical appearance of the explosive. Commercial explosives contain a substance, known as a tag, which is added during the manufacturing process, for example Microtaggant, a multi-layered melamine resin (Yinon, 1999). This tag is not destroyed when the explosive detonates and can be retrieved from the debris and examined under the microscope (340 to 3,100 overall magnification).

Confirmation of explosive chemicals or products of explosions can be carried out using chromatography (Chapter 14) or spectroscopy (Chapter 17). With HPLC, a reversed phase (p. 131) C18 column can be employed with UV detection at 215 nm, for example in the detection of nitroglycerin. A normal phase CN column (p. 131) can also be used, coupled with a thermal energy analyser (TEA) for the detection of nitrate or nitrose compounds. For this type of analysis an aqueous free mobile phase, such as isooctane:methylene chloride:2-propanol (90:9:1, v/v/v) is appropriate (Beveridge, 1998).

GC can also be used when coupled with a variety of detectors ranging from TEA, FID, ECD (Chapter 14) and MS (Chapter 15). GC–FID is more suitable for those explosive devices containing hydro carbons, as well as oils or plasticisers associated with plastic explosives.

Photo 44.2 Microtaggant identification particles used for tracing the origin of an explosive post-detonation. (*Source:* microtracesolutions.com)

Thermal energy analyser (TEA) – this detector operates at a temperature of 550 °C. Any compound passing through the detector is pyrolysed, releasing nitrogen dioxide, which reacts with ozone to produce 'excited' nitrogen dioxide. As this returns to its non-excited state it emits light that is proportional to the amount of compound that is present.

Ion chromatography can also be employed, i.e. Dionex® (Chapter 14). If an oxidiser has been used in the manufacture of the explosive device, such as sodium nitrate or potassium nitrate, the inorganic anion or cation that remains after detonation can be detected and a profile produced.

Infrared spectroscopy (Chapter 19) can be used to identify the functional groups of the explosive material. The advantage of this technique is that a profile of the explosive as a whole can be determined. For example, explosives with a nitro group (NO_2) will show strong absorption bands (e.g. bands at wavelengths of 1,534 and 1,354 in the case of TNT).

Text references

ASTM (2018) American Society for Testing and Materials, ASTM E 1388-17 Standard practice for static headspace sampling of vapors from fire debris samples.available at www.astm.org/Standards/E1388.htm last accessed 19/02/18

Beveridge, A. (1998) *Forensic Investigation of Explosions.* Taylor and Francis, London.

Borusiewicz, R. and Zie̦ba-Palus, J. (2007) Comparison of the effectiveness of Tenax TA® and Carbotrap 300® in concentration of flammable liquids compounds. *Journal of Forensic Sciences* **52** (1): 70–74.

Coulson, S., Morgan-Smith, R., Mitchell, S. and McBriar, T. (2008) An investigation into the presence of petrol on the clothing and shoes of members of the public. *Forensic Science International* **175** (1): 44–54.

Criminal Damage Act 1971 Available at: http://www.legislation. gov.uk/ukpga/1971/48/contents. Last accessed 24/08/2017.

DeHaan, J. (2007) *Kirk's Fire Investigation.* Brady Fire Series. Prentice-Hall, Harlow.

Fire Statistics. Available at: www.gov.uk/government/ collections/fire-statistics. Last accessed 24/08/2017.

Global Terrorism Database. Available at: https://www.start. umd.edu/gtd/. Last accessed 24/08/2017.

Jackowski, J.P. (1997) The incidence of ignitable liquid residues in fire debris as determined by a sensitive and comprehensive analytical scheme. *Journal of Forensic Sciences* 42: 828–832.

Microtrace Solutions Website. Available at: http://www. microtracesolutions.com/. Last accessed 12/06/09.

Newman, R., Gilbert, M. and Lothridge, K. (1998) GCMS Guide to Ignitable Liquids CRC Press, Boca Raton.

Williams, M. and Sigman, M. (2007) Performance testing of commercial containers for collection and storage of fire debris evidence. *Journal of Forensic Sciences* **52** (3): 579–585.

Yinon, J. (1999) *Forensic and Environmental Detection of Explosives.* Wiley, Chichester.

Yoshida, H., Kaneko, T. and Shinichi, S. (2008) A solid-phase microextraction method for the detection of ignitable liquids in fire debris. *Journal of Forensic Sciences* **53** (3): 668–769).

Sources for further study

Almirall, J.R. and Furton, K.G. (2004) *Analysis and Interpretation of Fire Scene Evidence.* CRC Press, Boca Raton.

Daéid, N. (2002) *Using Analytical Techniques to Combat Arson.* Presented at The Royal Society of Chemistry meeting 2002.

Daéid, N. (2004) *Fire Investigation.* CRC Press, Boca Raton.

Redsicker, D. and O'Connor, J. (1997) *Practical Fire and Arson Investigation,* 2nd edn. CRC Press, Boca Raton.

Study exercises

44.1 Write a protocol for the examination of a fire scene. After reading this chapter, prepare a detailed stepwise protocol explaining how you would proceed with the investigation of a fire scene. Ask another student or a tutor to evaluate your protocol and provide you with feedback.

44.2 Practise tying a nylon bag. Using the instructions on how to tie a nylon bag on p. 426, practise your tying technique.

44.3 Test your knowledge of analytical techniques. Discuss in a group what techniques are available for the determination of the following compounds:

(a) nitroglycerin;
(b) nitrates;
(c) hydrocarbons;
(d) potassium nitrate.

Information technology
and library resources

The ability to find scientific information is a skill required for many exercises in your degree programme. You will need to research facts and published findings as part of writing essays, literature reviews and project introductions, and when amplifying your lecture notes and revising for exams. You must also learn how to follow scientific convention in citing source material as the authority for the statements you have made.

Sources of information

For essays and revision

You are likely to use primary scientific papers as well as secondary literature (p. 453). If a lecturer or tutor specifies a particular book, then it should not be difficult to find out where it is shelved in your library, using the computerised index system. Library staff will generally be happy to assist with any queries. If you want to find out which books your library holds on a specified topic, use the system's subject index. You will also be able to search by author or by key words.

There are two main systems used by libraries to classify books – the Dewey Decimal system and the Library of Congress system. Libraries differ in the way they employ these systems, especially by adding further numbers and letters after the standard classification marks to signify shelving position or edition number, for example. Enquire at your library for a full explanation of local usage.

The Internet is an expanding resource for gathering both general and specific information (see Chapter 46). Sites fall into analogous categories to those in the printed literature – there are sites with original information, sites that review information and bibliographic sites. One considerable problem is that websites may be frequently updated, so information present when you first look may be altered or even absent when the site is next consulted. Further, very little of the information on the Internet has been monitored or refereed. Another disadvantage is that the site information may not state the origin of the material – who wrote it or when it was written.

For literature surveys and project work

For these you will probably need to consult the primary literature. If you are starting a new research project or writing a report from scratch, you can build up a core of relevant papers by using the following methods:

- **Asking around** – supervisors or their postgraduate students will almost certainly be able to supply you with a reference or two that will start you off.
- **Searching a computer database** – these cover very wide areas and are a convenient way to start a reference collection, although a charge is often made for access and sending out a listing of the papers selected (your library may or may not pass this on to you).
- **Consulting the bibliography of other papers in your collection** – an important way of finding the key papers in your field. In effect, you are taking advantage of the fact that another researcher has already done all the hard work!
- **Referring to 'current awareness' journals or computer databases** – these are useful for keeping you up to date with current research; they usually provide a monthly listing of article details (title, authors, source, author

---

Browsing in a library – this may turn up interesting material, but remember the books on the shelves are those not currently out on loan. Almost by definition, the latter may be more up-to-date and useful. To find out a library's full holding of books in any subject area, you need to search its catalogue (normally available as a computerised database). An online search will also bring up electronic versions of textbooks (ebooks).

Example The book *Handbook of Forensic Pathology*, 2nd edn by DiMaio and Dana (2007, CRC Taylor and Francis) is likely to be classified as follows:

Dewey Decimal system: 614.4

where	614	refers to public health, incidence of disease, forensic medicine
	614.1	refers to forensic medicine

Library of Congress system: RB57

where	R	refers to medicine
	RB	refers to pathology
	RB57	*refers to post-mortem examinations, autopsies*

Internet resources – your university library will provide you with access to a range of web-based databases and information systems. The library web pages will list these and provide links, which may be worth bookmarking on your web browser. Resources especially useful to scientists include:

- *Web of Science (including the citation index);*
- *Ingenta Connect (including Ingenta Medline);*
- *PubMed;*
- *ScienceDirect;*
- *Scopus;*
- *Zetoc.*

Most of these electronic resources operate on a subscription basis and may require an 'Athens' username and password – for details of how to obtain these, consult library staff or your library's website.

Researching a new topic – reading reviews (secondary sources) can provide you with a useful overview at the start of a new project.

Finding and citing published information

Computer databases – several databases are now produced on CD-ROM for open use in libraries (e.g. Applied Science and Technology Index). Some databases can be accessed via the Internet, such as Science Direct®, a service providing access to information from over 7,000 periodicals (username and password required via your library). Each of these databases usually has its own easy-to-follow menu instructions. It is worthwhile to consider key words for your search beforehand, to focus your search and save time.

Definitions

Abstracts – shortened versions of papers, often those read at scientific meetings. These may later appear as full papers.

Bibliography – a summary of the published work in a defined subject area.

ebook – a book published online in downloadable form.

ebrary – a commercial service offering ebooks and other online resources.

ejournal – a journal published online, consisting of articles structured in the same way as a paper-based journal. A valid username and password may be required for access.

Journal/periodical/serial – any publication issued at regular intervals. In biosciences, usually containing papers describing original research findings and reviews of literature.

Monograph – a specialised book covering a single topic.

Proceedings – volume compiling written versions of papers read at a scientific meeting on a specific topic.

Review – an article in which recent advances in a specific area are outlined and discussed.

The primary literature – comprises original research papers, published in specialist scientific periodicals.

address) arranged by subject and cross-referenced by subject and author. Current-awareness journals cover a wider range of primary journals than could ever be available in any one library. Examples include:

(a) *Current Contents* – published by the Institute of Scientific Information, Philadelphia, USA, which reproduces the contents pages of journals of a particular subject area and presents an analysis by author and subject.

(b) *Current Advances* – published by Pergamon Press, Oxford, UK, which subdivides papers by subject within research areas and cross-references by subject and author.

(c) *Biological Abstracts* – in which each paper's abstract is also reproduced. Papers may be cross-referenced according to various taxa, which is useful in allowing you to find out what work has been done on a particular organism.

- **Using the *Science Citation Index* (SCI)** – this is a very valuable source of new references, because it lets you see who has cited a given paper; in effect, SCI allows you to move forward through the literature from an existing reference. The index is also available online *via* ISI® Web of Science. Some libraries have copies on CD-ROM, which allows rapid access and output of selected information.

For specialised information

You may need to consult reference works, such as encyclopaedias, pharmacopeias, maps and books providing specialised information. Much of this is now available on CD-ROM or online (consult your library's information service or Internet pages). Three books worth noting are:

- The *Handbook of Chemistry and Physics* (Haynes, 2014) – the Chemical Rubber Company's publication (affectionately known as the 'Rubber Bible'), giving all manner of physical constants, radioisotope half-lives, etc.
- The *Merck Index* (O'Neil *et al.*, 2013) – which gives useful information about organic chemicals (e.g. solubility, whether poisonous), now available online from the Royal Society of Chemistry.
- The *Geigy Scientific Tables* (8th edn) – a series of six volumes (Lentner, 1981; 1984; 1986; 1990; 1992; Lentner *et al.*, 1982), provides a wide range of information centred on biochemistry, e.g. buffer formulae, properties of constituents of living matter.
- The *British Pharmacopeia* – provides detailed reference information on pharmaceutical and medicinal compounds for research and development, manufacture, analysis and quality-control measures.

Obtaining and organising research papers

Obtaining a copy

It is usually convenient to have personal copies of key research articles in print or electronic format for direct consultation when working in a laboratory or writing. The simplest way of obtaining these is to photocopy the originals or to download and/or print off copies online (e.g. as '.pdf' files). For academic purposes, this is normally acceptable within copyright law. If your library does not take the journal, it may be possible for them to borrow

Storing printed research papers – these can easily be kept in alphabetical order within filing boxes or drawers, but if your collection is likely to grow large, it will need to be refiled as it outgrows the storage space. An alternative is to keep an alphabetical card index system (useful when typing out lists of references) and file the papers by 'accession number' as they accumulate. New filing space is only required at one 'end' and you can use the accession numbers to form the basis of a simple cross-referencing system.

Using commercial bibliographic database software to organise your references – for those with large numbers of references in their collection, and who may wish to produce lists of selected references in a particular format – e.g. for inclusion in a project report or journal paper – systems such as EndNote, Reference Manager or ProCite can reward the investment of time and money required to create a personal reference catalogue. Appropriate bibliographic data must first be entered into fields within a database (some versions assist you to search online databases and upload data from these). The database can then be searched and used to create customised lists of selected references in appropriate citation styles.

it from a nearby institute or obtain a copy via a national borrowing centre (an 'inter-library loan'). If the latter, you will have to fill in a form giving full bibliographic details of the paper and where it was cited, as well as signing a copyright clearance statement concerning your use of the copy.

Your department or school might be able to supply 'reprint request' postcards to be sent to the designated author of a paper. This is an unreliable method of obtaining a copy because it may take some time (allow at least 1–3 months!) and some requests will not receive a reply. Taking into account the waste involved in postage and printing, it is probably best simply to photocopy or send for a copy via inter-library loan.

Organising papers

Although the number of papers you accumulate may be small to start with, it is worth putting some thought into their storage in electronic and/or printed format and indexing before your collection becomes disorganised and unmanageable. Few things are more frustrating than not being able to lay your hands on a vital piece of information, and this can seriously disrupt your flow when writing or revising.

Indexing your references

Whether you have obtained a printed copy, have stored downloaded files electronically or have simply noted the bibliographic details of a reference, you will need to index each resource. This is valuable for the following reasons:

- You will probably need the bibliographic information for creating a reference list for an assignment or report.
- If the index also has database features, this can be useful, allowing you to search for key words or authors.
- If you include an 'accession number' and if you then file printed material sequentially according to this number, this will help you to find the hard copy.
- Depending on the indexing system used, you can add comments about the reference that may be useful at a later time, e.g. when writing an introduction or conclusion.

The simplest way to create an index system is to put the details on reference cards, but database software e.e. Endnote X7 can be more convenient and faster to sort, once the bibliographic information has been entered. If you do not feel that commercial software is appropriate for your needs, consider using a word processor or spreadsheet; their rudimentary database sorting functions (see Chapters 48 and 49) may be all that you require. If you are likely to store lots of references and other electronic resources digitally, then you should consider carefully how this information is kept – for example, by choosing file names that indicate what the file contains, and that will facilitate sorting.

Making citations in text

It is particularly important to cite all sources of information used in your work. This will demonstrate to assessors that you have used appropriate source material and it will also avoid any possibility of plagiarism (using another person's work without acknowledgement, p. 451).

There are two main ways of citing articles and creating a bibliography (also referred to as 'references' or 'literature cited').

The parenthetical system (e.g. Harvard, author date)

For each citation, the author name(s) and the date of publication are given at the relevant point in the text. The bibliography is organised alphabetically and by date of publication for papers with the same authors. Formats normally adopted are, for example, 'Smith and Jones (1983) stated that. . . ' or 'it has been shown that. . . (Smith and Jones, 1983)'. Lists of references within parentheses are separated by semi-colons (e.g. '(Smith and Jones, 1983; Jones and Smith, 1985)', normally in order of date of publication. To avoid repetition within the same paragraph, an approach such as 'the investigations of Smith and Jones indicated that' could be used, following an initial citation of the paper. Where there are more than two authors it is usual to write 'et al.' (or *et al.* if an italic font is available); this stands for the Latin *et alia* meaning 'and others'. If citing more than one paper with the same authors, put, for example, 'Smith and Jones (1987; 1990)' and if papers by a given set of authors appeared in the same year, letter them (e.g. Smith and Jones, 1989a; 1989b).

The numerical system (e.g. Vancouver)

Papers are cited via a superscript or bracketed reference number inserted at the appropriate point. Normal format would be, for example: 'DNA sequences[4,5] have shown that . . . ' or 'Jones [55,82] has claimed that. . . ' Repeated citations use the number from the first citation. In the true numerical method (e.g. as in *Nature*), numbers are allocated by order of citation in the text, but in the alpha-numerical method (e.g. the *Annual Review* series), the references are first ordered alphabetically in the bibliography, then numbered, and it is this number that is used in the text. Note that with this latter method, adding or removing references is tedious, so the numbering should be done only when the text has been finalised.

 KEY POINT   *The main advantages of the Harvard system are that the reader might recognise the paper being referred to and that it is easily expanded if extra references are added. The main advantages of the Vancouver system are that it aids text flow and reduces length.*

How to list your citations in a bibliography reference list

Whichever citation method is used in the text, comprehensive details are required for the bibliography so that the reader has enough information to find the reference easily. Citations should be listed in alphabetical order with the following priority: first author, subsequent author(s), date. Unfortunately, in terms of punctuation and layout, there are almost as many ways of citing papers as there are journals! Your department or school may specify an exact format for project work; if not, decide on a style and be consistent – if you do not pay attention to the details of citation you may lose marks. Take special care with the following aspects:

- **Authors and editors** – give details of *all* authors and editors in your bibliography, even if given as *et al.* in the text.
- **Abbreviations for journals** – while there are standard abbreviations for the titles of journals (consult library staff), it is a good idea to give the whole title, if possible.
- **Books** – the edition should always be specified as contents may change between editions. Add, for example, '(5th edition)' after the title of the book.

You may be asked to give the International Standard Book Number (ISBN), a unique reference number for each book published.

- **Unsigned articles** – e.g. unattributed newspaper articles and instruction manuals – refer to the author(s) in text and bibliography as 'Anon'.
- **Unread articles** – you may be forced to refer to a paper *via* another without having seen it. It is best to refer to another authority who has cited the paper, e.g. '. . . Jones (1980), cited in Smith (1990), claimed that. . . ' Alternatively, you could denote such references in the bibliography by an asterisk and add a short note to explain at the start of the reference list.
- **Websites** – there is no widely accepted format at present. You should follow departmental guidelines if these are provided, but if these are not available we suggest providing author name(s) and date in the text when using the Harvard system (e.g. Hacker, 2009), while in the bibliography giving the URL details in the following format: Hacker, A. (2009) University of Anytown Homepage on Aardvarks. Available at: http://www.myserver.ac.uk/homepage. Last accessed 23/02/09. In this example, the Web page was constructed in 2009, but accessed in February 2009. If no author is identifiable, cite the sponsoring body, e.g. University of Anytown, 2009, and, if there is no author or sponsoring body, write 'Anon.' for 'anonymous', e.g. Anon. (2009), and use Anon. as the 'author' in the bibliography. If the Web pages are undated, either use the 'Last accessed' date for citation and put no date after the author name(s) in the reference list, or cite as 'no date' (e.g. Hacker, no date) and leave out a date after the author name(s) in the reference list – you should be consistent whichever option you choose.
- **Personal communications** – information received in a letter, seminar or conversation can be referred to in the text as, for example, '. . . (Smith, pers. comm.)'. These citations are not generally listed in the bibliography of papers, though in a thesis you could give a list of personal communicants and their addresses.
- **Online material** – some papers and articles are published solely online and others are available online ahead of publication in printed form. The item may be given a digital object identifier (DOI), allowing it to be cited and potentially tracked before and after it is allocated to a printed issue (see http://www.doi.org/). DOIs also allow for Web page redirection by a central agency, and CrossRef (http://www.crossref.org/) is the official DOI registration organisation for scholarly and professional publications. DOIs can be used as 'live' hyperlinks in online articles, or cited in place of the volume and page numbers for the article, with the remainder of the details cited in the usual fashion, e.g. 'Smith. A. and Jones B. (2009). Our latest important research in the form of a Web-published article. Online Forensic Sciences 8/2009 (p. 781). Published online: 26 March 2009. DOI: 0.1083/ mabi.200980019.'

Text references

Fruchtenicht, T.L., Herzig, W.P. and Blackledge, R.D. (2002) The discrimination of two dimensional military boot impressions based on wear patterns. Science and Justice **42**(2): 97-104

Haynes, W.M. (ed.) (2014) *CRC Handbook of Chemistry and Physics,* 95th edn. CRC Press, Boca Raton, Florida.

Lentner, C. (ed.) (1981) *Geigy Scientific Tables, Vol. 1: Units of Measurement, Body Fluids, Composition of the Body, Nutrition,* 8th edn. Ciba-Geigy, Basel.

Lentner. C. (ed.) (1984) *Geigy Scientific Tables, Vol. 3: Physical Chemistry, Composition of Blood, Hematology, Somatometric Data,* 8th edn. Ciba-Geigy, Basel.

Lentner, C. (ed.) (1986) *Geigy Scientific Tables, Vol. 4: Biochemistry, Metabolism of Xenobiotics, Inborn Errors of Metabolism, Pharmacogenetics, Ecogenetics,* 8th edn. Ciba-Geigy, Basel.

Lentner, C. (ed.) (1990) *Geigy Scientific Tables, Vol. 5: Heart and Circulation*, 8th edn. Ciba-Geigy, Basel.

Lentner, C. (ed.) (1992) *Geigy Scientific Tables, Vol. 6: Bacteria, Fungi, Protozoa, Helminths*, 8th edn. Ciba-Geigy, Basel.

Lentner, C., Diem, K. and Seldrup, J. (eds) (1982) *Geigy Scientific Tables, Vol. 2: Introduction to Statistics, Statistical Tables, Mathematical Formulae*, 8th edn. Ciba-Geigy, Basel.

McMillan, K.M. and Weyers, J.D.B. (2013) *Smarter Student: Skills and Strategies for Success at University*. Pearson Education, Harlow.

O'Neil, M.J., Heckelman, P.E., Koch, C.B. and Roman, K.J. (2013) *The Merck Index: An Encyclopedia of Chemicals, Drugs and Biologicals*, 15th edn. Merck & Co., Inc., Rahway, New Jersey.

Pears, R. and Shields, G. (2005) *Cite them Right: The Essential Guide to Referencing and Plagiarism*. Pear Tree Books, Newcastle upon Tyne.

Spence, L. and Asmussen, G. (2003) Spectral enhancement of leucocrystal violet treated footwear impression evidence in blood. Forensic Science International **132**(2): 117-124.

Sources for further study

BIDS UK: The BIDS 'for users' page (2017). Available at: http://www.bids.ac.uk/info/fs_forusers.htm Last accessed 24/08/2017.

ISI Web of Science (2017). Available at: http://wok.mimas.ac.uk. Last accessed 24/08/2017.

Scopus (2017) Available at: https://www.scopus.com/home.uri. Last accessed 24/08/2017.

Zetoc (2017) Available at: http://zetoc.jisc.ac.uk/. Last accessed 24/08/2017.

Study exercises

45.1 Test your library skills. This exercise relies on the fact that most university-level libraries serving forensic science departments will take the scientific journal, *Journal of Forensic Sciences*. To help you answer these questions, it may be beneficial to attend a library induction session, if you haven't already. Alternatively, the library's help or enquiry desks may be able to assist you if you are having problems.

(a) First, find out and provide the name of the classification system that your university uses for cataloguing its books and periodicals.

(b) Using your library's cataloguing system (online, preferably), find out the appropriate local classification number for the *Journal of Forensic Sciences*.

(c) Where is *Journal of Forensic Sciences* shelved in your library? (Your answer need refer only to most recent issues if some have been archived.)

(d) What is the exact title of the landmark papers in the following two volumes? (i) *Journal of Forensic Sciences* **53**(2): 325–30 (2008); (ii) *Journal of Forensic Sciences* **52**(1): 16–20 (2007).

45.2 Explore different methods of citing references. Go to your library and seek out the journal area for biology, chemistry or forensic science. Choose three different journals in your subject area and from a recent edition write down how they would print a typical citation for a multi-author journal paper in the 'references' or 'literature cited' section. Where used, indicate italicised text with normal underline and bold text with wavy underline. Pay attention to punctuation. Compare these methods with each other, with the methods recommended on pp. 437–8 of this book and with the recommendations your department or your course handbook makes. Are they all the same?

45.3 Make website citations. Use a search engine (p. 445) to find an informative website that covers each of the following:

(a) the use of SI units;

(b) information about the cases published by the Forensic Science Service;

(c) Code C of the Police and Criminal Evidence Act.

Indicate how you would cite each website at the end of an essay (follow your department's guidelines or use those in this chapter).

45.4. Compare the Harvard and Vancouver methods of citation. Pair up with a partner in your class. Each person should then pick one of the two main methods of citation and consider its pros and cons independently. Meet together and compare your lists. Given the choice, which method would you choose for (a) a handwritten essay, (b) a word-processed review, (c) an article in an academic journal, and why?

Information and communication technology (ICT) is vital in the modern academic world and 'IT literacy' is a core skill for all scientists. This involves a wide range of subsidiary computer-based skills, including:

- **accessing Web pages** using a Web browser such as Internet Explorer, Firefox, Safari or Chrome;
- **searching the Web** for useful information and resources using a search engine such as Google, or a meta-search engine such as Dogpile;
- **finding what you need** within online databases, such as library catalogues, or complex websites, such as your university's;
- **downloading, storing and manipulating files;**
- **communicating** via the Internet;
- **using e-learning** facilities effectively;
- **working with 'Office'-type programs and other software** (dealt with in detail in Chapters 48 and 49).

You will probably receive an introduction to your university's networked IT systems and will be required to follow rules and regulations that are important for the operation of these systems. Whatever your level of experience with PCs and the Internet, you should also follow the basic guidelines shown in Box 46.1. Reminding yourself of these from time to time will reduce your chances of losing data.

The Internet as a global resource

The Internet is a complex network of computer networks; it is loosely organised and no one group organises it or owns it. Instead, many private organisations, universities and government organisations fund and operate discrete parts of it. The Web is the most popular application of the Internet. It allows easy links to information and files that may be located on networked computers across the world. The Web enables you to access millions of 'home pages' or 'websites' – the initial point of reference with many individuals, institutions and companies. Besides text and images, these sites may contain 'hypertext links', highlighted words or phrases that take you to another Internet location via a single mouse click. You can gain access to the Internet either through a network at your university, at most public libraries, at a commercial 'Internet café' or from home via a modem connected to a broadband or dial-up Internet service provider (e.g. Virgin Media, BT or Sky).

 KEY POINT *Most material on the Internet has not been subject to peer review or vetting. Information obtained from the Web or posted on newsgroups may be inaccurate, biased or spoof; do not assume that everything you read is true or even legal.*

Online communication

You will be allocated an e-mail account by your university and should use this routinely for communicating with staff and fellow students, rather than using a personal account. You may be asked to use e-mail to submit work as an attachment, or you may be asked to use a 'digital drop-Box' within the university's e-learning system (Box 46.2). When using e-mail at university, follow conventions, including etiquette, carefully:

Academic use of ICT resources – a range of inappropriate activities will be identified in your university's rules for use of ICT systems. They may include: hacking, spamming, using another person's account, and copyright infringement, as well as broader aspects of behaviour covered by a code of conduct or student charter.

Understanding the technology – you do not need to understand the workings of the Internet to use it; most of it is invisible to the user. To ensure you obtain the right facilities you may need to know some jargon, such as terms for speed of data transfer (megabits) and the nature of Internet addresses. Setting up a modem and/or local wireless network can be complex, but instructions are usually provided with the hardware. White and Downs (2014) and Gralla (2006) are useful texts if you wish to learn more about computing and the Internet.

Box 46.1 Important guidelines for using PCs and networks

Hardware

- Don't drink or smoke around the computer.
- Try not to turn the computer off more than is necessary.
- Never turn off the electricity supply to the machine while in use.
- Switch off the computer and monitor when not in use (saves energy and avoids dangers of 'hijacking').
- Rest your eyes at frequent intervals if working for extended periods at a computer monitor.
- Never try to reformat the hard disk without the help of an expert.

CDs and USB drives

- Protect CDs when not in use by keeping them in holders or Boxes.
- Label USB (Universal Serial Bus) drives with your name and return details, and consider adding these to a file stored on the drive.
- Try not to touch the surface of CDs, and if they need cleaning, do so carefully with a clean cloth avoiding scratching. If floppy disks are used, keep these away from sources of magnetism (e.g. speakers).
- Keep disks away from moisture, excess heat or cold.
- Keep disks and USB drives well away from magnets; remember these are present in loudspeakers, TVs, etc.
- Don't use disks from others, unless you first check them for viruses.
- Don't insert or remove a disk or USB drive when it is operating (drive light on). Close all files before removing a USB drive and use the Safely Remove Hardware feature.
- Try not to leave a disk in the drive when you switch the computer off.

File management

- Organise your files in an appropriate set of folders.

- Always use virus-checking programs on copied or imported files before running them.
- Make back-ups of all important files at frequent intervals (say, every ten minutes or half-hour), e.g. when using a word processor or spreadsheet.
- Periodically clear out redundant files.

Network rules

- Never attempt to 'hack' into other people's files.
- Do not give out any of your passwords to others. Change your password regularly. Make sure it is not a common word, is longer than eight characters, and includes numerical characters and punctuation symbols, as well as upper- and lower-case letters.
- Never use network computers to access or provide financial or other personal information – spyware and Trojan programs may intercept your information.
- Never open e-mail attachments without knowing where they came from – always virus-check attachments before opening.
- Remember to log out of the network when finished – others can access your files if you forget to log out.
- Be polite when sending e-mail messages.
- Periodically reorganise your e-mail folder(s). These rapidly become filled with acknowledgements and redundant messages that reduce server efficiency and take up your allocated filespace.
- Do not play games without approval – they can affect the operation of the system.
- If you are setting up your own network, say in your flat, always install up-to-date firewall software, anti-spyware and anti-virus programs.

The Golden Rule – always make back-up copies of important files and store them well away from your working copies. Ensure that the same accident cannot happen to both copies.

Spam, junk mail and phishing – these should be relatively easy to identify, and should never be responded to or forwarded. Some may look 'official' and request personal or financial details (for example, they may pretend to come from your bank, and ask for account details). Never send these details by e-mail or your identity may be used illegally.

- **Check your e-mail account regularly (daily).** Your tutors may wish to send urgent messages to you in this way.
- **Respond promptly to e-mails.** Even if you are just acknowledging receipt, it is polite to indicate that you have received and understood a message.
- **Be polite.** E-mail messages can seem to be abrupt and impersonal.
- **Take care to read your messages through before sending** and, if you are at all in doubt, do not send your message right away: re-read at a later time and consider how others might view what you say.

Box 46.2　Getting to grips with e-learning

Some key aspects of tackling e-learning are outlined below.

1. **Develop your basic IT skills, if required.** e-learning requires only basic IT skills, such as: use of keyboard and mouse; word processing; file management; browsing and searching. If you feel weak on any of these, seek out additional courses offered by the IT administration or your department.

2. **Visit your e-learning modules regularly.** You should try to get into a routine of doing this on a daily basis at a time that suits you. Staff will present up-to-date information (e.g. lecture room changes) via the 'announcements' section, may post information about assessments or links to the assessments themselves, and you may wish to provide feedback or look at discussion threads.

3. **Participate.** e-learning requires an active approach:

   - At the start of each new course, spend some time getting to know what has been provided online to support your learning. As well as valuable resources, this may include crucial information such as learning objectives (p. 601), dates of submission for coursework and weighting of marks for different elements of the course.

   - If you are allowed to download lecture notes (e.g. in the form of PowerPoint presentations), do not think that simply reading through these will be an adequate substitute for attending lectures and making further notes (see p. 594).

   - Do not be tempted to 'lurk' on discussion boards – take part. Ask questions; start new threads; answer points raised by others if you can.

   - Try to gain as much as you can from formative online assessments (p. 601). If these include feedback on your answers, make sure you learn from this, and if you do not understand it consult your tutors.

   - Learn from the critical descriptions that your lecturers provide of linked websites. These pointers may help you to evaluate such resources for yourself in future (p. 448).

   - Don't think that you will automatically assimilate information and concepts, just because you are viewing them online. The same principles apply as with printed media – you must apply active learning methods (p. 603).

   - Help your lecturers by providing constructive feedback when they ask for it. You may find this easier to do online than hurriedly filling out a feedback sheet at the end of a session.

4. **Organise files and Web links.** Take the time to create a system of folders and files for downloaded material in tandem with your own coursework files, and set up folders on your browser for bookmarked websites ('Favourites' in Internet Explorer).

5. **Take care when submitting coursework.** Make sure you keep a back-up of any file you e-mail or submit online and check the version you are sending carefully. Follow instructions carefully, for example regarding file type, or how to use your system's 'digital drop-Box'.

Examples　Common domains and sub-domains include:

.ac	academic
.com	commercial (USA mainly)
.co	commercial (UK)
.edu	education (USA mainly)
.gov	government (USA and UK)
.mil	military (USA only)
.net	Internet-based companies
.org	organisation
.uk	United Kingdom

- **Consider content carefully.** A useful approach is only to send what you would be happy to hear being read out loud to classmates or family.
- **When communicating with tutors,** take care with language and names. Slang phrases and text message shorthand are unlikely to be understood. Be friendly without being overfamiliar.
- **Use e-mail for academic purposes** – this includes discussing coursework with classmates, but not forwarding questionable jokes, potentially offensive images, links to inappropriate websites, etc. In fact, doing so may break regulations and result in disciplinary action.
- Beware of spam, junk and 'phishing' via e-mail.

Similar rules apply to discussion boards and the learning management system. The Usenet Newsgroup service is an electronic discussion facility, and there are thousands of newsgroups representing different interests and topics. Any user can contribute to the discussion within a topic by posting their own message – it is like e-mail, but without privacy, since your message becomes

Definition

Bookmark – a feature of browsers that allows you to save details of websites you have visited. This is termed 'add to favourites' in Internet Explorer. Bookmarks save you the trouble of remembering complex URL names and typing them into the browser's address window.

Examples
Useful Web portals
Anil Aggrawal's Internet Journal of Forensic Medicine and Toxicology at: http://anilaggrawal.com/ij/indexpapers.html
   Zeno's Forensic Science Site at: http://forensic.to/forensic.html
   Organic Chemistry portal at http://organic-chemistry.org
   PLOS – open-access publisher for science and medicine at http://plos.org/which-journal-is-right-for-me

Locating information on the Internet – useful searching systems are located at the following URLs (some may be directly accessible from your browser):

http://www.altavista.com/sites/search/webadv/ (advanced search page)

http://www.google.com/advanced_search (advanced search page)

http://www.scirus.com/ (subject-specific searching in Science/Engineering)

http://uk.searchengine.com/ (UK-restricted search engine)

Google® Scholar can be used to search for peer-reviewed articles, for example, scientific papers: http://scholar.google.com/ © 2015 Google Inc. All rights reserved. Google and the Google Logo are registered trademarks of Google Inc. (Locating information on the Web)

available to all other subscribers. To access a newsgroup, your system must be running, or have access to, a newsgroup server that has subscribed to the newsgroup of interest.

Your university may also make use of social media, including Facebook and Twitter. Often these systems will be explained during the initial orientation period, including how to 'follow' the university so that you can keep up to date through news feeds.

Internet tools

The specific programs you will use for accessing the Internet will depend on what has been installed locally, on the network you are using and on your Internet service provider. The best way to learn the features of the programs is to try them out, making full use of whatever Help services are available.

e-learning systems
Most university departments present their courses through a mixture of face-to-face sessions (e.g. lectures, tutorials, practicals) and online resources (e.g. lecture notes, websites, discussion boards, computerised tests and assessments). This constitutes 'blended learning' on your part, with the online component also being known as e-learning. The e-learning element is usually delivered through an online module within a virtual learning environment (e.g. Blackboard, Moodle). It is important not to neglect the e-learning aspects of your course just because it may not be as rigidly timetabled as your face-to face sessions. This flexibility is to your advantage as you can work when it suits you, but it requires discipline on your part. Box 46.2 provides tips for making the most of the e-learning components of your courses.

Internet browsers
These are software programs that interact with remote server computers around the world to carry out the tasks of requesting, retrieving and displaying the information you require. Many different browsers exist, but the most popular are Internet Explorer, Firefox and Google Chrome. These browsers dominate the current market and have plug-ins and add-on programs available that allow, for example, video sequences to be seen online. The standard functions of browsers include:

- accessing Web documents;
- following links to other documents;
- printing the current document;
- maintaining a history of visited URLs (including 'bookmarks' for key sites);
- searching for a term in a document;
- viewing images and image maps.

Browsers provide access to millions of websites. Certain sites specialise in providing catalogued links to other sites – these are known as portals and can be of enormous help when searching within a particular area of interest. Your university's library website will almost certainly provide a useful portal to catalogues and search services, often arranged by subject area, and this is often the first port of call for electronic resources; get to know your way around this part of the website as early as possible during your course.

When using a Web browser program to get to a particular page of information on the Web, all you require is the location of that page, i.e. the URL (Uniform Resource Locator). The URL normally uses a standard format, generally beginning with https:// (secure) and followed by the various terms that direct the system to the appropriate site. If you don't have a specific URL in mind but wish to explore appropriate sites, you will need to use a search tool with the browser.

Search tools

With the proliferation of information on the Web, one of the main problems is finding the exact information you require. There are a variety of information services that you can use to filter the material on the network. These include:

- search engines (Boxes 46.3 and 46.4);
- meta-search engines;
- subject directories;
- subject gateways (portals).

Search engines such as Google (http://www.google.com/), Bing (http://bing.com/) and DuckDuckGo (http://www.duckduckgo.com/) are tools designed to search, gather, index and classify Web-based information. Searching is usually by key word(s), although specific phrases can be defined. Many search engines offer advanced searching tools, such as the use of Boolean operators to specify combinations of key words to more precisely filter the sites. Box 46.3 provides tips for refining key word searches, while Box 46.4 provides tips for enhanced searching with Google.

It is important to realise that each search engine will cover at most about 40% of the available sites, and if you want to carry out an exhaustive search it is necessary to use several to cover as much of the Web as possible. Meta-search engines make this easier. These operate by combining collections of search engines. Examples include Dogpile (http://www.dogpile.com/index.gsp/) and Mamma (http://www.mamma.com/).

Some useful approaches to searching include the following:

- **For a comprehensive search,** use a variety of tools including search engines, meta-search engines and portals or directories.
- **For a complex, finely specified search,** employ Boolean operators and other tools to refine your key words as fully as possible (Box 46.3). Some search engines allow you to include and exclude terms or restrict by date.
- **Use 'cascading' searching when available** – this is searching within the results of a previous search.
- **Use advanced search facilities to limit your search,** where possible, to the type of medium you are looking for (e.g. graphics, video), language, sites in a specific country (e.g. UK) or to a subject area (e.g. news only).

However well-defined your search is, you will still need to evaluate the information obtained. Chapter 47 covers general aspects of this topic while Box 46.5 provides specific advice on assessing the quality of information provided on websites.

Directories

A directory is a list of Web resources organised by subject. It can usually be browsed and may or may not have a search facility. Directories often contain better-quality information than the lists produced by search engines because they have been evaluated, often by subject specialists or librarians. Check your library's subject resources for relevant directories.

'Dissecting' a Web address – *if a URL is specified, you can often find out more about a site by progressively deleting sections of the address from the right-hand side. This will often take you to 'higher levels' of the site, or to the home page of the organisation or company involved.*

Definition

Search engine – a software system that returns hyperlinks to websites ('hits') based on keywords specified by the user.

Examples

Some useful Web portals and databases
Drugwise
http://drugwise.org.uk
European Pollen Database
http://www.europeanpollendatabase.net
Molecular Biology gateway (molecular biology;microbiology;PCR;virology)
http://highveld.com
NIST Chemistry WebBook
http://webbook.nist.gov/chemistry/
NIST Forensic Science Reference Data
http://www.nist.gov/topics/forensic-science/reference-materials-standards-and-guidelines/reference-data
Reddy's Forensic Page – Forensic Databases
http://www.forensicpage.com/
Short Tandem Repeat DNA Internet Database
http://www.cstl.nist.gov/strbase/
United States National Library of Medicine: Medline
http://www.nlm.nih.gov/bsd/pmresources.html

Box 46.3 Useful tips for using search engines

- **Key words should be chosen with care.** Try to make them as specific as possible, e.g. search for 'blow-flies', rather than 'flies' or 'insects'.

- **Most search engines are case-insensitive.** Thus 'Nobel Prize' will return the same number of hits as 'nobel prize'. If in doubt, use lower case throughout.

- **Putting key word phrases in double quotes (e.g. "blood pattern analysis") will result in a search for sites with the phrase as a whole** rather than sites with both (all) parts of the phrase as separate words (i.e. 'blood' and 'pattern' and 'analysis' at different places within a site). This feature allows you to include common words normally excluded in the search, such as 'the'.

- **Use multiple words/phrases plus similar words to improve your search,** for example 'insects "common bluebottle fly" United Kingdom'. If you use scientific terms, you are likely to find more relevant sites – for example, search for the name of a particular species such as '*Calliphora vicina*'.

- **Adding words preceded by + or − will add or exclude sites with that word present** (e.g. 'blood diseases – leukaemia' will search for all blood diseases excluding leukaemia). This feature can also be used to include common words normally excluded by the search engine.

- **Check that your search terms have the correct spelling,** otherwise you may only find sites with the same misspelled word. In some cases, the search engine may prompt you with an alternative (correct) spelling. If a word has an alternative US spelling (e.g. color, hemoglobin), then a search may only find hits from sites that use the spelling you specify.

- **Boolean operators (AND, OR, NOT) can be used to specify combinations of key words** to more precisely filter the sites identified (e.g. 'plant NOT engineering' will avoid sites about engineering plants and focus on botanical topics).

- **Some search engines allow 'wildcards' to be introduced with the symbol** *. For example, this will allow you to specify the root of a word and include all possible endings, as with anthropomorph*, which would find anthropomorphic, anthropomorphism, etc. If the search engine does not allow wildcards, then you will need to be especially careful with the key words used, including all possible words of relevance.

- **Numbers can be surprisingly useful in search engines.** For example, typing in EC 1.1.1.1 will find sites concerned with alcohol dehydrogenase as this is its code number. If you know the phone number for a person, institute or company or the ISBN of the book, this can often help you find relevant pages quickly.

- **If you arrive at a large site and cannot find the point at which your searched word or phrase appears, press Control and F together** and a local search window will appear, allowing you to find the point(s) where it is mentioned.

Downloading files from the Internet and e-mails – read-only files are often available as 'pdf' files that can be viewed by Adobe Acrobat reader software (available free from http://www.adobe.com), while other files may be presented as attachments to e-mails or as links from Web pages that can be opened by suitable software (e.g. Microsoft Word or 'paint' programs such as Paint Shop Pro. Take great care in the latter cases as the transfer of files can result in the transfer of associated viruses. Always check new files for viruses (especially .exe files) before running them, and make sure your virus-detecting software is kept up to date.

FTP (File Transfer Protocol) and file transmission

FTP is a method of transferring files across the Internet. In many cases the files are made available for 'anonymous' FTP access, i.e. you do not need a previously arranged password. Log in as 'anonymous' and give your e-mail address as the password. Use your Web browser to locate the file you want and then use its FTP software to transfer it to your computer.

 KEY POINT *The transfer of files can result in the transfer of associated viruses. Always check new files for viruses before running them. Make frequent updates to your virus-checking software.*

Using the Internet as a resource

A common way of finding information on the Web is by browsing or 'surfing'. However, this can be time-consuming. Try to restrict yourself to sites known

Box 46.4   Getting the most from Google searches

Google (http://www.google.com) has become the search engine of choice for millions of people, due to its simplicity and effectiveness. However, you may be able to improve your searches by understanding its default settings and how they can be changed.

- **Download the Google toolbar to your browser.** This is available from the Google homepage and will give you quick access to the Google search facility.

- **Understand how standard operators are used.** For combinations of key words Google uses the 'minus' operator '−' instead of NOT (exclude) and '+' instead of AND (include). Since Google usually ignores small words ('stop words' such as 'in' or 'the'), use '+' to include them in a search. Where no operator is specified, Google assumes that you are looking for both terms (i.e. '+' is default). If you want to search for alternative words, you can use 'OR' (e.g. *sulphur* OR *sulfur*). Google does not allow brackets and also ignores most punctuation marks.

- **While wildcard truncation of words using '*' is not allowed, you can use '*' to replace a whole word (or number).** For example, if you type the phrase *'a hair shaft is approximately* * nanometres'* your results will give you results for Web pages where the wildcard is replaced by a number.

- **Search for exact wording.** By placing text in inverted commas, you can ensure that only websites with this exact phrasing will appear at the head of your search results.

- **Search within your results to improve the outcome.** If your first search has produced a large number of results, use the Search within results option near the bottom of each page to type in a further word or phrase.

- **Search for words within the title of a Web page.** Use the command 'intitle:' to find a Web page, for example intitle: "*blood pattern*" returns Web pages with this phrase in the title (note that phrases must always be in double speech marks, not single quotes).

- **Search within a website.** Use the 'site:' command to locate words/phrases on a specific website, for example 'site:gov.uk forensic science regulator newsletter' returns only those results for newsletters on the Forensic Science Regulators website (https://www.gov.uk/government/organisations/forensic-science-regulator). Pressing Control + F when visiting a Web page will give you a pop-up search window.

- **Locate definitions, synonyms and spellings.** The operator 'define:' enables you to find the meaning of a word. If you are unsure as to the spelling of a word, try each possibility – Google will usually return more results for the correct spelling and will often also prompt you with the correct spelling (Did you mean . .).

- **Find similar Web pages.** Simply click the Similar pages option at the end of a Google search result to list other sites (note that these sites will not necessarily include the term(s) searched for).

- **If a Web link is unavailable, try the cached (stored) page.** Clicking on Cached at the end of a particular result should take you to the stored page, with the additional useful feature that the search term(s) will be highlighted.

- **Using the calculator functions.** Simply enter a calculation and press Enter to display the result, for example $10 + (2 \times 4)$ returns 18. The calculator function can also carry out simple interconversion of units, e.g. '2 feet 6 inches in metres' returns 0.762 (see Box 4.1 for interconversion factors between SI and non-SI units).

- **Try out the advanced search features.** In addition to the standard operators, these include the ability to specify the number of results per page (e.g. 50, to reduce the need for the next button), language (e.g. English), file format (e.g. for PDF files), recently updated Web pages (e.g. past 3 months), usage (e.g. free to use/share).

- **Find non-text material.** These include images, video and maps – always check that any material you use is not subject to copyright limitations (p. 452). Use Google alerts to keep up to date. This function (http://www.google.co.uk/alerts) enables you to receive regular updated searches by e-mail.

- **Use Google Scholar™ to find articles and papers.** Go to http://scholar.google.co.uk/ and type in either the general topic or specific details for a particular article, e.g. author names or words from the title. Results show titles/authors of articles, with links to either the full article, abstract or citation. A useful feature is the Cited by . . . link, taking you to those papers that have cited the article in their bibliography and enabling you to carry out forward citation searching to locate more recent papers. Also try out the advanced scholar search features to limit your search to a particular author, journal, date or subject area. However, you should note that Google Scholar™ provides only a basic search facility to easily accessible articles and

Using online resources

Box 46.4 (Continued)

should not be viewed as a replacement for your library's electronic journal holdings and searching software. For example, if you find the title of a paper via Google Scholar™ you may be able to locate the electronic version through your own library's databases, or request it via inter-library loan (p. 437). Another significant limitation is that older (more cited) sources are typically listed first. Use Advanced Search to find sources between years X and Y.

- **Use Google Earth to explore locations.** This allows you to zoom in on satellite images to find locations.

Box 46.5 How to evaluate information on the Internet

It is often said that 'you can find anything on the Internet'. The two main disadvantages of this are, first, that you may need to sift through many sources before you find what you are looking for and, second, that the sources you find will vary in their quality and validity. *It is important to realise that evaluating sources is a key aspect of using the Internet for academic purposes, and one that you will need to develop during the course of your studies.* The ease with which you can 'point and click' to reach various sources should not make you complacent about evaluating their information content. The following questions can help you to assess the quality of a website – the more times you can answer 'yes', the more credible the source is likely to be, and vice versa:

Authority

- Is the author identified?
- Are the author's qualifications or credentials given?
- Is the owner, publisher or sponsoring organisation identified?
- Is an address given (postal and/or e-mail)?

It is sometimes possible to get information on authority from the site's metadata (try the 'View' 'Source' option in Internet Explorer, or look at the URL to see if it gives any clues as to the organisation, e.g. does the domain name end in .ac, .edu, .gov or .org, rather than .co or .com).

Content

- Is there any evidence that the information has been peer-reviewed (p. 453), edited or otherwise validated, or is it based on such sources?
- Is the information factual rather than based on personal opinions?
- Is the factual data original (primary) rather than derived from other sources (secondary)?

- Are the sources of specific factual information detailed in full (p. 438)?
- Is there any indication that the information is up to date, or that the site has been recently updated?
- Is the purpose of the site clear and is the target audience identified?
- Is the content relevant to the question you are trying to answer?
- Is there any evidence of a potential conflict of interest, or bias? (Is the information comprehensive and balanced, or narrowly focused?)
- Did you find the information via a subject-specific website (e.g. a bioinformatics resources portal such as ExPASy), or through a more general source, such as a search engine (e.g. Google)?

The above questions are similar to those that you would use in assessing the value of a printed resource (pp. 451–455), and similar criteria should be applied to Web-based information. You should be especially wary of sites containing unattributed factual information or data whose primary source is not given.

Presentation

- Do you have a positive overall impression of how the site has been put together?
- Are there many grammatical or spelling mistakes?
- Are there links to other websites, to support statements and factual information?

The care with which a site has been constructed can give you an indication of the credibility of the author/organisation. However, while a poorly presented site may cause you to question the credibility of the information, the reverse is not always necessarily true. Don't be taken in by a slick, well-presented website – authority and content are *always* more important than presentation.

Using traditional sources – remember that using the Internet to find information is not a substitute for visiting your university library. Internet resources complement rather than replace CD-ROM and more traditional printed sources.

Remembering useful websites – create a 'bookmark' ('add a 'favourite') for the ones you find of value, to make revisiting easy. This can be done from the menu of your browser program. Make a copy of your bookmark file occasionally, to avoid loss of this information.

Examples   Selected websites of forensic science interest:
American Academy of Forensic Sciences
http://www.aafs.org/
American Board of Forensic Document Examiners
http://www.abfde.org/
American Board of Forensic Odontology
http://www.abfo.org/
American Board of Forensic Toxicology
http://www.abft.org/
American Society of Questioned Document Examiners
http://www.asqde.org/
British Academy of Forensic Sciences
http://www.bafs.org.uk/
British Association for Human Identification
http://www.bahid.org/
European Network of Forensic Science Institutes
http://www.enfsi.org/cms.php
Forensic Science Society.
http://www.csofs.org/
Forensic Science Regulator
https://www.gov.uk/government/organisations/forensic-science-regulator
National Crime Agency
http://www.nationalcrimeagency.gov.uk/
National Police Chiefs Council
http://www.npcc.police.uk/
Skills for Justice
http://www.sfjuk.com/

Note that URLs may change – make a key word search using a search engine to find a particular site if the URL information you have does not lead you to an active page.

to be relevant to the topic of interest. Some of the most useful sites are those that provide hypertext links to other locations. Some other resources you can use on the Internet are:

- **Libraries, publishers and commercial organisations.** Your university library is likely to subscribe to one or more databases providing access to scientific articles; these include Web of Science (http://wok.mimas.ac.uk/), and Science Direct (http://www.sciencedirect.com/). A password is usually required, especially for off-campus use – consult your library staff for further details. Some scientific database sites give free access, without subscription or password. These include PubMed/Medline (http://www.ncbi.nlm.nih.gov/) and the Highwire Library of Sciences and Medicine (http://www.jlr.org/site/misc/HWPortal.xhtml). Others allow free searching but require payment for certain articles. Publishers such as Pearson Education and booksellers such as Amazon® provide online catalogues and e-commerce sites that can be useful sources of information (see http://www.pearsoneduc.com/ and http://www.amazon.co.uk/).

- **Online journals and e-books.** A number of traditional journals have websites. You can keep up to date by visiting the websites of *Nature* (http://www.nature.com/), *New Scientist* (http://www.newscientist.com/) and *Scientific American* (http://www.sciam.com/). Some scientific societies make their journals and other publications available via their websites, e.g. the Royal Society of Chemistry at http://www.rsc.org. Journals solely published in electronic format are also available but some require a subscription password for access – check whether your institute is a subscriber. An example of an e-book is *Misleading DNA Evidence: Reasons for Miscarriages of Justice* (2014) at (https://www.elsevier.com/books/misleading-dna-evidence/gill/978-0-12-417214-2?start_rank=1&producttype=books&sortby=sortByDateDesc&author=peter%20gill&q=peter%20gill)

- **Data and images.** Archives of text material, video clips and photographs can be accessed, and much of the material is readily available. The Biological Image Gallery (http://www.academicinfo.net/bioimage.html/) is a good example and Internet Pathology Lab for Medical Education includes forensic pathology images (http://library.med.utah.edu/WebPath/FORHTML/FORIDX.html). When downloading such material, you should (a) check that you are not breaching copyright and (b) avoid potential plagiarism by giving a full citation of the source if you use such images in an assignment (see p. 452).

- **Databases.** In addition to those covering the scientific literature, others focus on specific topics (e.g. academic employment, http://www.jobs.ac.uk/).

Using online resources

Text references

Gralla, P. (2006) *How the Internet Works,* 8th edn. Pearson, Harlow.

White, R. and Downs, T. (2014) *How Computers Work,* 10th edn. Pearson, Harlow.

Sources for further study

Hewson, C., Vogel, C. and Laurent, D. (2016) *Internet Research Methods,* 2nd edn. Sage Publishing, Thousand Oaks, CA.

Hock, R. (2013) *The Extreme Searchers' Internet Handbook: A Guide for the Serious Searcher* 4th edn. Cyber Age Books, New Jersey.

Isaacs, T. and Isaacs, M. (2000) *Internet Users' Guide to Network Resource Tools,* 2000 edn. Addison-Wesley, Harlow.

Winship, I. and McNab, A. (2000) *Students' Guide to the Internet 2000–2001.* Library Association, London.

Study exercises

46.1 Explore the resources of the Internet using a search engine. Using a search engine, find the answers to the following questions:

    (a) Who is Graham Young, and what is he famous for?

    (b) What is the common name for *Erythroxylum coca?*

    (c) What is the postal address of the Chartered Society of Forensic Sciences?

46.2 Compare results from a variety of search engines. First, think of an appropriate biological or chemical key word or phrase (e.g. a drug name) and enter this into several search engines. Make sure that you include meta-search engines such as Mamma. Compare the outcomes to reveal the strengths and weaknesses of the individual search engines. Work with a colleague to compare different searches on a quantitative (i.e. number of hits) and qualitative (quality of hits) basis.

46.3 Organise your bookmarks. Enter the 'Organise favourites' menu for your preferred browser and create folders with appropriate headings. Move existing bookmarks to these folders and save any new ones appropriately. Doing this will help you find bookmarks more easily, rather than searching through long lists.

Example An internet search for the letters 'NPCC' (e.g. using Google®) will reveal that this acronym appears in over 1 million websites. Not all of these deal with The National Police Chiefs Council – a UK website to help transform policing strategies. The other listed websites include: *Northeast Power Coordinating Council; National Projects Construction Corporation Limited; Novogradac Property Compliance Certification; National Power Construction Corporation,* which obviously are easy to identify as irrelevant to policing, reform and transformation. When assessing the usefulness of any websites, you should consider the questions set out in Box 47.1.

Plagiarism – the unacknowledged use of another's work as if it were one's own. In this definition, the concept of 'work' includes ideas, writing, data or inventions and not simply words; and the notion of 'use' does not only mean copy 'word-for-word', but also 'in substance' (i.e. a copy of the ideas involved). Use of another's work is acceptable, if you acknowledge the source. Therefore, to avoid unintentional plagiarism (Box 47.1), if you think a particular author has said something particularly well, then quote him or her directly (using inverted commas) and provide a reference to the relevant article or book beside the quote. For example:

'Plagiarize? \'pla-je-,riz also j--\ vb-rized; -riz?ing vt [plagiary]:to steal and pass off (the ideas or words of another) as one's own: use (a created production) without crediting the source vi: to commit literary theft: present as new and original an idea or product derived from an existing source – **pla.gia.riz.er** *n*'

From: *Webster's New Collegiate Dictionary,* 9th edn (Springfield: Merriam, 1981, p. 870).

Note that this is not plagiarism because the source has been cited and the material is shown within quotation marks.

Checking the reliability of information, assessing the relative value of different ideas and thinking critically are skills essential to the scientific approach. You will need to develop your abilities to evaluate information in this way because:

- **You will be faced with many sources of information,** from which you will need to select the most appropriate material.
- **You may come across two conflicting sources of evidence** and may have to decide which is the more reliable.
- **The accuracy and validity of a specific fact** may be vital to your work.
- **You may doubt the quality of the information** from a particular source.
- **You may wish to check the original source** because you are not sure whether someone else is quoting it correctly.

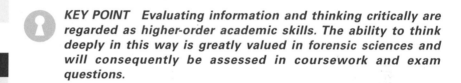 **KEY POINT** *Evaluating information and thinking critically are regarded as higher-order academic skills. The ability to think deeply in this way is greatly valued in forensic sciences and will consequently be assessed in coursework and exam questions.*

The process of evaluating and using information can be broken down into four stages:

1. **Selecting and obtaining material.** Library books and journals remain a prime source of information (Chapter 45). This can lead to difficulties because not every source is instantly available, and you may have to wait for weeks for an inter-library loan or photocopy to arrive. Nowadays, the Internet is increasingly a first port of call if you want to find something out. This has the advantage of being faster, but the authenticity of information on the Internet can be more difficult to establish than for a conventional printed source (see Box 46.3).
2. **Assessing the content.** You will need to understand fully what has been written, including any technical terms and jargon used. Establish the relevance of the information to your needs and assure yourself that the data or conclusions have been presented in an unbiased way.
3. **Modifying the information.** In order to use the information, you may need to alter it to suit your needs. This may require you to make comparisons, interpret or summarise. Some sources may require translation. Some data may require mathematical transformation before they are useful. There is a chance of error in any of these processes, and also a risk of plagiarism.
4. **Analysis.** This may be your own interpretation of the information presented, or an examination of the way the original author has used the information.

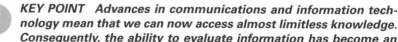 **KEY POINT** *Advances in communications and information technology mean that we can now access almost limitless knowledge. Consequently, the ability to evaluate information has become an extremely important skill.*

Box 47.1 How to avoid plagiarism and copyright infringement

Plagiarism is defined on p. 451. Examples of plagiarism include:

- **copying the work of a fellow student** (past or present) and passing it off as your ow;

- **using 'essay-writing services',** such as those on offer on certain websites;

- **copying text or images from a source** (book, journal article or website, for instance) and using this within your own work without acknowledgement;

- **quoting others' words** without indicating who wrote or said them;

- **copying ideas and concepts** from a source without acknowledgement, even if you paraphrase them.

Most students would accept that some of the above can only be described as cheating. However, many students, especially at the start of their studies, are unaware of the academic rule that they must always acknowledge the originators of information, ideas and concepts, and that not doing so is regarded as a form of academic dishonesty. If you adopt the appropriate conventions that avoid such accusations, you will achieve higher marks for your work as it will fulfil the markers' expectations for academic writing. Universities have a range of mechanisms for identifying plagiarism, from employing experienced and vigilant coursework markers and external examiners to analysing students' work using sophisticated software programs. Plagiarism is always punished severely when detected. Penalties may include awarding a mark of zero to all involved – both the copier(s) and the person whose work has been copied (who is regarded as complicit in the crime). Further disciplinary measures may be taken in some instances. In severe cases, such as copying substantive parts of another's work within a thesis, a student may be dismissed from the university. If you wish to avoid being accused of plagiarism, the remedies are relatively simple:

1. **Make sure the work you present is always your own.** If you have been studying alongside a colleague, or have been discussing how to tackle a particular problem with your peers, make sure you write on your own when working on your assignments.

2. **Never be tempted to 'cut and paste'** from websites or online sources such as word-processed handouts.

Instead, read these carefully, decide what the important points are, express these in your own words and provide literature citations to the original sources (see Chapter 45). In some cases, further investigations may be required to find out details of the original sources. The lecturer's reading list or a book's references may help you here.

3. **Take care when note-taking.** If you decide to quote word-for-word, make sure you show this clearly in your notes with quotation marks. If you decide to make your own notes based on a source, make sure these are original and do not use phrases from the original. In both cases, write down full details of the source at the appropriate point in your notes.

4. **Place appropriate citations throughout your text where required.** If you are unsure about when to do this, study reviews and articles in your subject area to get the picture (see Chapter 45).

5. **Show clearly where you are quoting directly from a source.** For short quotes, this may involve using quotation marks and identifying the source afterwards, as in the example . . . as Samuel Butler (1877) wrote: 'a hen is only an egg's way of making another egg'. For longer quotes (say 40 words or more), you should create a separate paragraph of quoted text, usually identified by inverted commas, indentation, italicisation or a combination of these. A citation must always be included, normally at the end. Your course handbook may specify a layout. Try not to rely too much on quotes in your work. If a large proportion of your work is made up from quotes, this will almost certainly be regarded as lacking in originality. Copyright issues are often associated with plagiarism, and refer to the right to publish (and hence copy) original material, such as text, images and music. Copyright material is indicated by a symbol © and a date (see, for example, p. iv of this book). Literary copyright is the aspect most relevant to students in their academic studies. UK Copyright Law protects authors' rights for life and gives their estates rights for a further 70 years. Publishers have 'typographical copyright' that lasts for 25 years. This means that it is illegal to photocopy, scan or print out copyright material unless you have permission, or unless your copying is limited to an extent that could be considered 'fair dealing'. For educational purposes – private study or research – in a scientific context, this generally means:

- no more than 5% in total of a work;

- one chapter of a book;

- one article per volume of an academic journal;

- 20% of a short book;

- one separate illustration or map.

You may take only one copy within the above limits, may not copy for others and may not exceed these amounts, even if you own a copy of the original. These rules also apply to Web-based materials, but sometimes you will find sites where the copyright is waived. Some copying may be licensed; you should consult with your library's website or helpdesk to see whether it has access to licensed material.

Distinguishing between primary and secondary sources – try the 'IMRaD test'. Many primary sources contain information in the following order: Introduction, Materials and Methods, Results and Discussion. If you see this format, and particularly if data from an experiment, study or observation are presented, then you are probably reading a primary source.

Example If a journalist wrote an article about a new technique for DNA analysis for the *New York Times* that was based on an article in *Forensic Science International*, the *New York Times* article would be the secondary source, while the *Forensic Science International* article would be the primary source.

Taking account of the changing nature of websites and wikis – by their very nature, these sources may change. This means it is important to quote accurately from them and to give a 'Last accessed' date when citing (see p. 439).

Finding out about authors and provenance – these pieces of information are easy to find in most printed sources and may even be presented just below the title, for convenience. In the case of the Internet, it may not be so easy to find what you want. Relevant clues can be obtained from 'home page' links and the header, body and footer information. For example, the domain (p. 443) may be useful, while the use of the tilde symbol (~) in a URL usually indicates a personal, rather than an institutional, website.

Evaluating sources of information

One way of assessing the reliability of a piece of scientific information is to think about how it was obtained in the first place. Essentially, 'facts' originate from someone's research or scholarship, whether they are numerical data, descriptions, concepts or interpretations. Sources are divided into two main types:

1. **Primary sources** – those in which ideas and data are first communicated. The primary literature is generally published in the form of 'papers' (articles) in journals. These are usually refereed by experts in the academic peer group of the author, and they will check the accuracy and originality of the work and report their opinions back to the editors. This peer-review system helps to maintain reliability, but it is not perfect. Books and, more rarely, articles in magazines and newspapers, can also be primary sources but this depends on the nature of the information published rather than the medium. These sources are not formally refereed, although they may be read by editors and lawyers to check for errors and unsubstantiated or libellous allegations.

2. **Secondary sources** – those that quote, adapt, interpret, translate, develop or otherwise use information drawn from primary sources. It is the act of quoting or paraphrasing that makes the source secondary, rather than the medium. Reviews are examples of secondary scientific sources, and books and magazine articles are often of this type.

When information is modified for use in a secondary source, alterations are likely to occur, whether intentional or unintentional. Most authors do not deliberately set out to change the meaning of the primary source, but they may unwittingly do so, for example by changing text to avoid plagiarism or by oversimplification. Others may consciously or unconsciously exert bias in their reporting, for example by quoting evidence that supports only one side of a debate. Therefore, the closer you can get to the primary source, the more reliable the information is likely to be. On the other hand, modification while creating a secondary source could involve correcting errors, or synthesising ideas and content from multiple sources.

Authorship and provenance

Clearly, much depends on who is writing the source and on what basis (e.g. who paid them?). Consequently, an important way of assessing sources is to investigate the ownership and provenance of the work (who and where it originated from, and why).

Can you identify who wrote the information? If it is signed or there is a 'by-line' showing who wrote it, you might be able to make a judgement on the quality of what you are reading. This may be a simple decision, if you know or can assume that the writer is an authority in the area; otherwise a little research might help (e.g. by putting the name into a search engine). Of course, just because Professor X thinks something does not make it true. However, if you know that this opinion is backed up by years of research and experience, then you might take it a little more seriously than the thoughts of a junior-school pupil. If an author is not cited, effectively nobody is taking responsibility for the content. Could there be a reason for this?

Is the author's place of work cited? This might tell you whether the facts or opinions given are based on an academic study. Is there a company with a vested interest behind the content? If the author works for a public body, there may be publication rules to follow, and they may even have to submit their work to a publications committee before it is disseminated. They are certainly more likely to get into trouble if they include controversial material.

Evaluating facts and ideas

However reliable the source of a piece of information seems to be, it is probably a good idea to retain a slight degree of scepticism about the facts or ideas involved. Even information from impeccable primary sources may not be perfect – different approaches can give different outcomes, and interpretations can change with time and with further advances in knowledge.

Critically examining facts and ideas is a complex task depending on the particular issues involved, and a number of different general approaches can be applied. You will need to decide which of the following general tips are useful in your specific case:

- **Make cross-referencing checks triangulation** – look at more than one source and compare what is said in each. The cross-referenced sources should be as independent as possible (e.g. do not compare a primary source together with a secondary review based on it). If you find that all the sources give a similar picture, then you can be more confident about the reliability of the information.

- **Look at the extent and quality of citations** – if references are quoted, these indicate that a certain amount of research has been carried out beforehand, and that the ideas or results are based on genuine scholarship. If you are doubtful about the quality of the work, these references might be worth looking at. How up-to-date are they? Do they cite independent work, or is the author exclusively quoting their own work, or solely the work of one person?

- **Consider the age of the source** – the fact that a source is old is not necessarily a barrier to truth, but ideas and facts may have altered since the date of publication, and methods may have improved. Can you trace changes through time in the sources available to you? What key events or publications have forced any changes in the conclusions?

- **Try to distinguish fact from opinion** – to what extent has the author supported a given viewpoint? Have relevant facts been quoted, *via* literature citations or the author's own researches? Are numerical data used to substantiate the points used? Are these reliable and can you verify the information, for example by looking at the sources cited? Might the author have a reason for putting forward biased evidence to support a personal opinion?

- **Analyse the language used** – words and their use can be very revealing. Subjective wording might indicate a personal opinion rather than an objective conclusion. Propaganda and personal bias might be indicated by absolute terms, such as 'everyone knows . . . ', 'It can be guaranteed that . . . ', or a seemingly one-sided consideration of the evidence. How carefully has the author considered the topic? A less studious approach might be indicated by exaggeration, ambiguity or the use of 'journalese' and slang. Always remember, however, that content should be judged above presentation.

- **Look closely at any numbers** – if the information you are looking at is numerical in form, have statistical errors been taken into consideration and, where appropriate, quantified? If so, does this help you arrive at a conclusion about how genuine the differences are between important values?

- **Think carefully about any hypothesis-testing statistics used** – are the methods appropriate? Are the underlying hypotheses the right ones? Have the results of any tests been interpreted correctly in arriving at the conclusion? To deal with these matters, you will need at least a basic understanding of the statistical approach to data analysis and of commonly used techniques (see Chapters 55 and 56).

Table 47.1 Checklist for assessing information in science. How reliable is the information you have been reading? The more 'yes' answers you can give below, the more trustworthy you can assume it to be

Assessing sources

❑ Can you identify the author's name?
❑ Can you determine what relevant qualifications he/she holds?
❑ Can you say who employs the author?
❑ Do you know who paid for the work to be done?
❑ Is this a primary rather than secondary source?
❑ Is the content original or derived from another source?

Evaluation information

❑ Have you checked a range of sources?
❑ Is the information supported by relevant literature citation?
❑ Is the age of the source likely to be important regarding the accuracy of the information?
❑ Have you focused on the substance of the information presented rather than its packaging?
❑ Is the information fact or opinion?
❑ Have you checked for any logical fallacies in the arguments?
❑ Does the language used indicate anything about the status of the information?
❑ Have the errors associated with any numbers been taken into account?
❑ Have the data been analysed using appropriate statistics?
❑ Are any graphs constructed fairly?

Learning from examples – *as your lecturers introduce you to case studies, you will see how forensic scientists have applied critical thinking to understand the nature of a particular case. Some of your laboratory sessions may mimic the processes involved. These skills and approaches can be applied in your course, e.g. when writing about a forensic science issue or carrying out a research project.*

Table 47.1 provides a checklist to use when evaluating sources.

Critical thinking

Critical thinking involves the application of logic to a problem or case study or issue. It requires a wide range of skills. Key processes involved include acquiring and processing information, creating appropriate hypotheses and formulating conclusions and acting on the conclusions towards a specific objective.

 KEY POINT *Critical thinking needs reliable knowledge, but it requires you to use this appropriately to analyse a problem. It can be contrasted with rote learning – where you might memorise facts without an explicit purpose other than building your knowledge base.*

Critical thinking is particularly important in science because the subject deals with complex and dynamic systems. These can be difficult to understand for several reasons:

- **they are often multi-faceted, involving many interactions**;
- **it can be difficult to alter one variable in an experiment without producing confounding variables** (see p. 31);
- **many variables may be unmeasured or unmeasurable**;
- **heterogeneity (variability) is encountered at all scales** (not one case in forensic science is identical to another);
- **perturbation of systems can lead to unexpected ('counter-intuitive') results.**

As a result, conclusions in scientific research are seldom clear-cut. Critical thinking allows you to arrive at the most probable conclusion from the results at hand; however, it also involves acknowledging that other conclusions might be possible. It allows you to weigh up these possibilities and find a working hypothesis or explanation, but also to understand that your conclusions are essentially dynamic and might alter when new facts are known. This is an important aspect of forensic science. Hypothesis-testing with statistics (Chapter 55) is an important adjunct to critical thinking because it demands the formulation of simple hypotheses and provides rational reasons for making conclusions.

Recognising fallacies in arguments is an important aspect of critical thinking, especially when considering the interpretation of a DNA profile (Chapter 31). Philosophers and logicians recognise different forms of argument and many different fallacies in each form. Damer (2013) provides a broad overview of this wide-ranging and complex topic.

Interpreting data

Numerical data

Information presented in public, whether as a written publication or spoken presentation, is rarely in the same form as it was when first obtained. Chapters 3 and 54 deal with processes in which data are recorded, manipulated and transformed, while Chapter 55 describes the standard descriptive statistics used to 'encapsulate' large data sets. Chapter 56 covers some relevant mathematical techniques. Sampling (essentially, obtaining representative measurements) is at the heart of many observational and experimental approaches in forensic

'*You can prove anything with statistics*' – leaving aside the issue that statistical methods deal with probability, not certainty (Chapter 55), it is possible to analyse and present data in such a way that they support one chosen argument or hypothesis rather than another. Detecting a bias of this kind can be difficult, but the critical thinking skills involved are essential for all scientists (see p. 455).

science (see Chapters 37–39), and analysis of samples is a key component of hypothesis-testing statistics (Chapter 56). Understanding these topics and carrying out the associated study exercises will help you improve your ability to interpret numerical data.

Graphs

Frequently, understanding and analysis in science depends on your ability to interpret data presented in graphical form. The process of analysing a graph can be split into five phases:

1. Consider the context and aims.
2. Recognise the graph form and examine the axes.
3. Look closely at the scale of each axis.
4. Examine the symbols and curves.
5. Evaluate errors and statistics.

These processes are covered in more detail in Chapter 52.

Sometimes, graphs may mislead. This may be unwitting, as in an unconscious effort to favour a 'pet' hypothesis of the author. Graphs may be used to 'sell' a product, for example in advertising, or to favour a viewpoint as, perhaps, in politics. Experience in drawing and interpreting graphs will help you spot these flawed presentations, and understanding how graphs can be erroneously presented (Box 52.3) will help you avoid the same pitfalls.

Tables

Tables, especially large ones, can appear as a mass of numbers and thus be more daunting at first sight than graphs. In essence, however, most tables are simpler than most graphs. The process of analysing a table is similar to that of analysing graphs:

1. Consider the context and aims.
2. Examine what information is contained in the rows and columns.
3. Consider the units used and check any footnotes.
4. Compare the data values across rows and/or down columns. Look for patterns, trends, unusual values, etc.
5. Take into account any statistics that are presented.

The construction of tables is dealt with in Chapter 53.

Explaining your thoughts

The context for your evaluation of the literature and the associated critical thinking will normally be an essay, report, expert witness statement (p. 555) or similar piece of academic writing (Chapters 61–62). The skills involved in marshalling and explaining your thoughts are regarded as highly important in employment and research.

You may have a very specific remit, as defined in the instruction for the assignment (Chapter 60), or the topic may be open. In either case, your reading around the topic should result in an overarching position or argument you wish to put forward – this is sometimes termed the 'thesis' for your writing. You may be explaining an established viewpoint or creating an original perspective on a topic. For both situations, the same principles apply when setting out your thoughts. You should:

- **make a clear statement of the issue being considered,** if necessary defining terms and boundaries;

Good writing requires good logic – understanding the logic behind what you want to write is a prerequisite for creating high-quality text. Creating a plan for your writing (Chapter 62) will help you to both recognise and organise what you want to say.

- **consider the issue from different perspectives,** providing evidence for or against different propositions;
- **ensure your viewpoint is logical and internally consistent;**
- **structure your writing appropriately** – for example, by first considering evidence for a particular view and then evidence against it, or by considering the development of evidence through time;
- **use an academic style of writing,** avoiding personal statements (p. 540)
- **arrive at a conclusion,** even if this is that the evidence is not sufficient to allow firm statements to be made.

In the sciences, the norm is to use inductive reasoning – that is, to state observed facts and assumptions at the outset, then draw a logical conclusion based on these. The alternative, deductive reasoning, starts from a general statement, premise or law that is held to be true and then reaches a conclusion by considering facts logically. You should look for these types of arguments in texts and papers, and also think about possible flaws in such arguments.

Text reference

Damer, T.E. (2013) *Attacking Faulty Reasoning: A Practical Guide to Fallacy-Free Arguments,* 7th edn. Wadsworth, Belmont, CA.

Sources for further study

Barnard, C.J., Gilbert, F.S. and MacGregor, P.K. (2007) *Asking Questions in Biology: Key Skills for Practical Assessments and Project Work,* 3rd edn. Prentice Hall, Harlow.

Currano, J. and Roth, D. (2013) *Chemical Information for Chemists.* Royal Society of Chemistry, Cambridge

Shenton, A.K. and Pickard, A.J. (2014) *Evaluating Online Information and Sources.* UKLA.

Taylor, D., Abamo, D., Hicks, T and Champod, C. (2016) Evaluating forensic biology results given source level propositions. *Forensic Science International: Genetics* 21: 54–67.

Van Gelder, T. *Critical Thinking on the Web.* Available at: http://www.austhink.org/critical/. Last accessed 25/08/2017.

Study exercises

47.1 Distinguish between primary and secondary literature. Based on their titles and any research you can do in your library, determine whether the following journals are primary or secondary sources:

(a) *Scientific American;*
(b) *Journal of Forensic Sciences;*
(c) *Forensic Science International;*
(d) *The New Scientist;*
(e) *Journal of Clinical Forensic Medicine;*
(f) *The Lancet;*
(g) *Forensic Science Communications;*
(h) *Science and Justice.*

47.2 Consider a controversial issue from both sides. Select a current ethical topic being discussed in the newspapers or other media, e.g. the National DNA database. Next, write out a statement that you might use for a motion in a debate, such as 'Should everybody have their DNA uploaded on to the NDNAD?'. Then write at least five points in support of both sides of the argument, which you should organise in tabular form. If you can find more than five points, add these to your table, but for each point that you add to one side you should add one to the other side.

47.3 Analyse graphic presentations in the media. Many newspapers provide graphic presentations related to current issues, and graphs are frequently used in television news reports. Practise critical thinking skills by determining whether the graphs presented are a fair representation of the facts.

You will probably be familiar with a range of computer programs used for academic work, and may own a laptop or PC with this software installed. To support your studies, you will also have access to networked PCs and associated programs licensed for your use. However, the specific software and versions may vary between these systems, involving different menu protocols and commands for the same or similar functions. In addition, the specific demands of academic work may involve the use of sophisticated features or even new types of program. This chapter considers some common software applications in relation to relevant tasks. Spreadsheets and presentation software are considered in detail in Chapters 49 and 59.

Reassess your IT skills and knowledge in relation to your course – although you may be familiar with the 'office-style' software (e.g. Microsoft Office, Apple Mac® Pages), you may be required to use features in new or different ways. For example:

- *You may be asked to present documents and their components in very specific formats (such as defining fonts, line spacing, paragraph layout, margins, layout of tables and figures).*
- *You may benefit from using certain editing features to refine your writing (such as word counts, thesaurus, spelling and grammar checker).*
- *You may need to adapt your methods to longer writing exercises (such as creating an outline structure, writing parts out of sequence, creating a bibliography at the outset and contributing to it as you write).*

 KEY POINT *Even when you are familiar with the basics of a software program, it may be valuable to learn more about advanced features, to ensure that you are working efficiently and effectively.*

Word processors

The word processor has improved the process of writing because of the ease of revising text. Word processing is a transferable skill, valuable beyond the immediate requirements of your degree course. Using a word processor should improve your writing skills and speed because you can create, check and change your text on the screen before printing it as 'hard copy' on paper. Once entered and saved, multiple uses can be made of a piece of text with little effort.

When using a word processor you can:

- refine material many times before submission;
- insert material easily, allowing writing to take place in any sequence;
- use a spell-checker to check your text;
- use a thesaurus when composing your text;
- produce high-quality final copies;
- reuse part or all of the text in other documents.

Although use of computers to compose text is now almost universal, it is worth remembering certain disadvantages of this approach, including:

- the need to learn the operational details of the program;
- the temptation to make 'trivial' revisions, hence 'overworking' your text;
- the risk of losing files or forgetting to save work appropriately.

 KEY POINT *It is vital to save your work frequently to a memory stick, hard drive or network drive. This should be done every 10 min or so. If you do not save regularly, you may lose hours of work. Most programs can be set to 'autosave' every few mins – make sure you switch this feature on.*

Word processors come as 'packages' comprising the program and a manual, often with a tutorial program. Examples are Microsoft Word and WordPerfect®. Most word processors have similar general features but differ in operational detail – it is best to pick one and stick to it as far as possible so that you become familiar with it. Learning to use the package is like learning to drive a car – you need only to know how to drive the computer and its program, not to understand how the engine (program) and transmission (data transfer) work, although a

The computerised office – *many word processors are sold as part of an integrated suite, e.g. Microsoft® Office, with the advantage that they share a common interface in the different components (word processor, spreadsheet, database, etc.) and allow ready exchange of information (e.g. text, graphics) between component programs.*

Using textbooks, manuals and tutorials – *the manuals that come with some programs may not be very user-friendly and it is often worth investing in one of the textbooks that are available for most word-processing programs. Alternatively, use an online Help tutorial.*

Using a word processor – *take full advantage of the differences between word processing and 'normal' writing (which necessarily follows a linear sequence and requires more planning):*

- *Simply jot down your initial ideas for a plan, preferably at paragraph-topic level. The order can be altered easily, and if a paragraph grows too much it can easily be split.*
- *Start writing wherever you wish and fill in the rest later.*
- *Just put down your ideas as you think, confident in the knowledge that it is the concepts that are important to note – their order and the way you express them can be adjusted later.*
- *Don't worry initially about spelling and use of synonyms – these can (and should) be checked during a separate revision scan of your text, using the spell-checker first (beware of its shortcomings and make sure you select the correct version of English) to correct obvious mistakes, then the thesaurus to change words for style or to find the mot juste.*
- *Use a draft printout to check (a) for pace and spacing (difficult to correct on-screen) and (b) to ensure that words checked for spelling fit the required sense.*

Deleting and restoring text – *because deletion can sometimes be made in error, there is usually an 'undelete' or 'restore' feature that allows the last deletion to be recovered, usually available through the program's Edit menu or, in the case of Microsoft Word 2016, through the use of the Undo button on the top line menu (see Screenshot 48.1) or by pressing Control and Z.*

little background knowledge is often helpful and will allow you to get the most from the program.

In most word processors, the appearance of the screen realistically represents what the printout on paper will look like. Word-processing files actually contain large amounts of code relating to text format, etc., but these clutter the screen if visible. Some word processors are menu-driven, others require keyboard entry of codes – menus are easier to start with and the more sophisticated programs allow you to choose between these options.

Because of variation in operational details, only general and strategic information is provided in this chapter – you must learn the details of your word processor through use of the appropriate manual and Help facilities.

Before starting you will need:

- **the program** (usually installed on a hard disk or available via a network);
- **appropriate media** for storage, retrieval and back-up of your own files when created;
- **the appropriate manual** or textbook giving operational details;
- **a draft page layout design** – in particular you should have decided on page size, page margins, typeface (font) and size, type of text justification and format of page numbering;
- **an outline of the text content**;
- **access to a suitable printer** – this need not be attached to the computer you are using since your file can be taken to an office where a printer is available, providing that it has the same word processing program.

Laying out (formatting) your document

Although you can format your text at any time, it is good practice to enter the basic commands at the start of your document – entering them later can lead to considerable problems due to reorganisation of the text layout. If you use a particular set of layout criteria regularly, e.g. an A4 page with space for a letterhead, make a template containing the appropriate codes that can be called up whenever you start a new document. Note that various printers may respond differently to particular codes, resulting in a different spacing and layout.

Typing the text

Think of the screen as a piece of typing paper. The cursor marks the position where your text/data will be entered and can be moved around the screen by use of the cursor-control keys. When you type, don't worry about running out of space on the line because the text will wrap around to the next line automatically. Do not use a carriage return (usually the Enter key) unless you wish to force a new line, for example when a new paragraph is wanted. If you make a mistake when typing, correction is easy. You can usually delete characters or words or lines and the space is closed automatically. You can also insert new text in the middle of a line or word. You can insert special codes to carry out a variety of tasks, including changing text appearance such as underlining, **emboldening** and *italics*. Paragraph indentations can be automated using the Tab key, as on a typewriter, but you can also indent or bullet whole blocks of text using special menu options. The function keys are usually pre-programmed to assist in many of these operations.

Editing features

Word processors usually have an array of features designed to make editing documents easy. In addition to the simple editing procedures described above, the program usually offers facilities to allow blocks of text to be moved ('cut and paste'), copied or deleted.

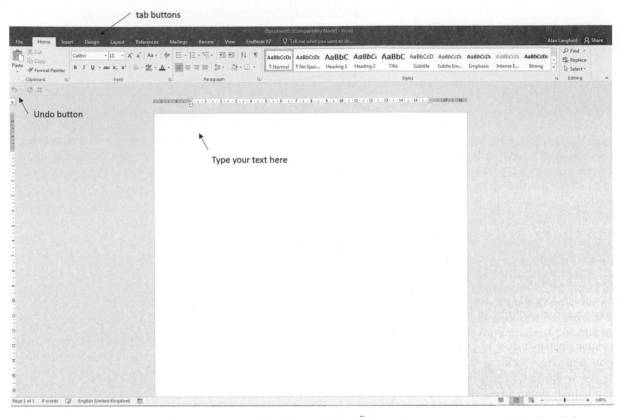

Screenshot 48.1 Example of screen display options within Microsoft Word®. The submenus are accessed via the tab buttons on the top line and allow you to insert graphics, adjust the margins, insert headers/footers, e-mail the document and review changes made to the document.

An extremely valuable editing facility is the Find or Search procedure – this can rapidly scan through a document looking for a specified word, phrase or punctuation. This is particularly valuable when combined with a Replace facility so that, for example, you could replace the word 'test' with 'trial' throughout your document simply and rapidly.

Most word processors have a command that reveals the normally hidden codes controlling the layout and appearance of the printed text. When editing, this can be a very important feature since some changes to your text will cause difficulties if these hidden codes are not taken into account – in particular, make sure that the cursor is at the correct point before making changes to text containing hidden code, otherwise your text will sometimes change in apparently mystifying ways.

Fonts and line spacing

Most word processors offer a variety of fonts depending on the printer being used. Fonts come in a wide variety of types and sizes, but they are defined in particular ways as follows:

● **Typeface** – the term for a family of characters of a particular design, each of which is given a particular name. The most commonly used for normal text is Times Roman (as used here for the main text) but many others are widely available, particularly for the better-quality printers. They fall into three broad groups: serif fonts with curves and flourishes at the ends of the characters (e.g. Times Roman); sans serif fonts without such flourishes, providing a clean, modern appearance (e.g. Helvetica, also known as Swiss); and decorative fonts used for special purposes only, such as the production of newsletters and notices.

> **Language setting** – remember to set up your document language before you start compiling text; this will ensure that the spell check and thesaurus provide the correct spellings by default within your document.

- **Size** – measured in points. A point is the smallest typographical unit of measurement, there being 72 points to the inch (about 28 points per cm). The standard sizes for text are 10, 11 and 12 point, but typefaces are often available up to 72 point or more.
- **Appearance** – many typefaces are available in a variety of styles and weights. Many of these are not designed for use in scientific literature but for desktop publishing.
- **Spacing** – can be either fixed, where every character is the same width, or proportional, where the width of every character, including spaces, is varied. Typewriter fonts such as Elite and Prestige use fixed spacing and are useful for filling in forms or tables, but proportional fonts make the overall appearance of text more pleasing and readable.
- **Pitch** – specifies the number of characters per horizontal inch of text. Typewriter fonts are usually 10 or 12 pitch, but proportional fonts are never given a pitch value since it is inherently variable.
- **Justification** – the term describing the way in which text is aligned vertically. Left justification is normal, but for formal documents both left and right justification may be used (as here).

You should also consider the vertical spacing of lines in your document. Drafts and manuscripts are frequently double-spaced. If your document has unusual font sizes, this may well affect line spacing, although most word processors will cope with this automatically.

Table construction

Tables can be produced by a variety of methods:

- **Using the Tab key as on a typewriter** – this moves the cursor to pre-determined positions on the page, equivalent to the start of each tabular column. You can define the positions of these tabs as required at the start of each table.
- **Using the inbuilt word processor table-constructing procedures.** Here the table construction is largely done for you and it is much easier than using tabs, providing you enter the correct information when you set up the table.
- **Using a spreadsheet to construct the table** and then copying it to the word processor. This procedure requires considerably more manipulation than using the word processor directly and is best reserved for special circumstances, such as the presentation of a very large or complex table of data, especially if the data are already stored as a spreadsheet.

Graphics and special characters

Many word processors can incorporate graphics from other programs into the text of a document. Files must be compatible (see your manual) but if this is so, it is a relatively straightforward procedure. For professional documents, this is a valuable facility, but for most undergraduate work it is probably better to produce and use graphics as a separate operation, for example using a spreadsheet.

You can draw lines and other graphical features directly within most word processors, and special characters (e.g. Greek characters) may be available depending on your printer's capabilities.

Tools

Many word processors also offer you special tools, the most important of which are:

- **Macros** – special sets of files you can create when you have a frequently repeated set of keystrokes to make. You can record these keystrokes as a 'macro' so that it can provide a shortcut for repeated operations.

Quick commands for commonly used functions – most word processors provide several routes to achieve the same end result. These include standard menus and commands; customisable toolbar commands and key combinations. Some useful examples include CTRL+C for copy; CTRL+F for find; CTRL+P for print; CTRL+V for 'paste'; CTRL+X for 'cut'.

Presenting your documents – it is good practice not to mix typefaces too much in a formal document; also the font size should not differ greatly for different headings, subheadings and the text.

Preparing draft documents – use double spacing to allow room for your editing comments on the printed page.

- **Thesaurus** – used to look up alternative words of similar or opposite meaning while composing text at the keyboard.
- **Spell-check** – a very useful facility that will check your spellings against a dictionary provided by the program. This dictionary is often expandable to include specialist words that you use in your work. The danger lies in becoming too dependent on this facility, as they all have limitations. In particular, they will not pick up incorrect words that happen to be correct in a different context (i.e. 'was' typed as 'saw' or 'see' rather than 'sea'). Be aware of American spellings in programs from the USA, e.g. 'color' instead of 'colour'. The rule, therefore, is to use the spell-check first and then carefully read the text for errors that have slipped through.
- **Word count** – useful when you are writing to a prescribed limit.

Printing from your program

Word processors require you to specify precisely the type of printer and/or other style details you wish to use. Most printers also offer choices as to text and graphics quality, so choose draft (low) quality for all but your final copy since this will save both time and materials.

Use a Print preview option to show the page layout, if it is available. Assuming that you have entered appropriate layout and font commands, printing is a straightforward operation carried out by the word processor at your command. Problems usually arise because of some incompatibility between the criteria you have entered and the printer's own capabilities. Make sure that you know what your printer offers before starting to type – although settings are modifiable at any time, changing the page size, margin size, font size, etc. all cause your text to be rearranged, and this can be frustrating if you have spent hours carefully laying out the pages!

Databases

A database is an electronic filing system whose structure is similar to a manual record-card collection. Its collection of records is called a file. The individual items of information on each record are called fields. Once the database is constructed, search criteria can be used to view files through various filters according to your requirements. The computerised catalogues in your library are just such a system – you enter the filter requirements in the form of author or subject key words.

You can use a database to catalogue, search, sort and relate collections of information. The benefits of a computerised database over a manual card-file system are:

- **The information content is easily amended/updated.**
- **Printouts of relevant items can be obtained.**
- **It is quick and easy to organise through sorting and searching/selection criteria,** to produce subgroups of relevant records.
- **Record displays can easily be redesigned,** allowing flexible methods of presenting records according to interest.
- **Relational databases can be combined,** giving the whole system immense flexibility. The older 'flat-file' databases store information in files that can be searched and sorted, but cannot be linked to other databases.

Relatively simple database files can be constructed within spreadsheets using the columns and rows as fields and records respectively. These are capable of reasonably advanced sorting and searching operations and are probably sufficient for the types of databases you are likely to require as an undergraduate. You may also make use of a bibliographic database specially constructed for that purpose, e.g. EndNote™ (see Chapter 45).

Preparing final documents – for most work, use a 12-point proportional serif typeface with spacing dependent on the specifications for the work.

Creating a table in Microsoft Word® 2016 – use the Insert tab (see Screenshot 48.1) and click on Table. Select the number of rows and columns by dragging the mouse over the template and the table will automatically appear in the document. By clicking the left-hand mouse button, the table is inserted into the document.

Inserting special characters – a wide range of symbols including Greek letters and characters from other languages is available within most word processor programs.

Using a spell-check facility – do not rely on this to spot all errors. Remember that spell-check programs do not correct grammatical errors.

Using the print preview mode – this can reveal errors of several kinds, e.g. spacing between pages, and prevent your wasting paper and printer ink unnecessarily.

Relational database – effectively a set of structured tables of data where information is formally related to others. This database can be used to construct new data sets without the need to adjust the original tables.

Choosing between a database and a spreadsheet – use a database only after careful consideration. Can the task be done better within a spreadsheet? A database program can be complex to set up and usually needs to be updated regularly.

Using spreadsheet statistics functions – before using a specific statistics package, check whether your spreadsheet is capable of carrying out the form of analysis you require as this can often be the simpler option.

Presentation using computer packages – while many computer programs enhance presentational aspects of your work, there are occasions when they can make your presentation worse. Take care to avoid the following common pitfalls:

- *Default or 'chart wizard' settings for graphs may result in output that is non-standard for the sciences (e.g. shaded background, gridlines, coloured symbols) or is missing key elements. Use the same criteria for producing graphs by computer as you would for hand-drawn ones (see Chapter 52).*
- *Selecting the wrong chart type can result in non-linear axes, or evenly spaced data on the x-axis, when they are not evenly spaced numerically.*
- *Fonts in labels and legends may not be consistent with other parts of your presentation.*
- *Some programs cannot produce Greek symbols (e.g. μ) – do not use 'u' as a substitute. The same applies to scientific notation and superscripts – do not use e.g. 1.4E + 09 for 1.4×10^9 or 14C for ^{14}C. It is better to draw the proper symbol or superscript by hand.*
- *Do not rely on spell-checkers. You should always proofread your work carefully in draft form.*
- *Do not rely on grammar-checkers. These often operate by making 'suggestions' for changes. This does not mean they are correct.*

Statistical analysis packages

Statistical packages vary from small programs designed to carry out very specific statistical tasks to large sophisticated packages (Statgraphics®, Minitab®, etc.) intended to provide statistical assistance, from experimental design to the analysis of results. Consider the following features when selecting a package:

- **The data entry and editing section should be user-friendly,** with options for transforming data.
- **Data exploration options** – these should include descriptive statistics and exploratory data analysis techniques.
- **Hypothesis-testing techniques** – these should include ANOVA, regression analysis, multivariate techniques and parametric and non-parametric statistics.
- **Support with research methods** – the program should provide assistance with experimental design and sampling methods.
- **Output facilities** – these should be suitable for graphical and tabular formats.

Some programs have very complex data entry systems, limiting the ease of using data in different tests. The data entry and storage system should be based on a spreadsheet system, so that subsequent editing and transformation operations are straightforward.

 KEY POINT *Make sure that you understand the statistical basis for your test and the computational techniques involved before using a particular program.*

Graphics/presentation packages

Many of these packages are specifically designed for business graphics rather than science. They do, however, have considerable value in the preparation of materials for posters and talks where visual quality is an important factor. There are many packages available such as Freelance Graphics®, Harvard Graphics®, Microsoft PowerPoint® and Sigmaplot®, which provide numerous templates for the preparation of overhead transparencies, slide transparencies and paper copy, both black and white and in colour. They usually incorporate a 'freehand' drawing option, allowing you to make your own designs.

Although the facilities offered are often attractive, the learning time required for some of the more complex operations is considerable and they should be considered only for specific purposes – routine graphical presentation of data sets is best done from within a spreadsheet or statistical package. There may be a service provided by your institution for the preparation of such material and this should be considered seriously before trying to learn to use these programs.

The most important points regarding the use of graphics packages are:

- **Graphics quality** – the built-in graphics are sometimes of only moderate quality. Use of annotation facilities can improve graphics considerably. Do not use inappropriate graphics for scientific presentation.
- **Producing colour graphics** – this requires a good-quality colour printer/plotter.
- **Importing graphics files** – graphs produced by spreadsheets or other statistical programs can usually be imported into graphics programs, and this is useful for adding legends, annotations, etc. when the facilities offered by the original programs are inadequate. Check that the format of files produced by your statistics/spreadsheet program can be recognised by your graphics program. The different types of file are distinguished by the three-character filename extension – e.g. .jpg and .bmp refer to specific image-file formats.

Word processors, databases and other packages

 KEY POINT *Computer graphics are not always satisfactory for scientific presentation. While they may be useful for exploratory procedures, they may need to be redrawn by hand for your final report. It may be helpful to use a computer-generated graph as a template for the final version.*

For more advanced tasks, additional software may be available on your network; for example, Sigma Plot can produce graphs with floating axes; Adobe Illustrator is useful for designing complex graphics; Adobe Dreamweaver® enables you to produce high-quality Web pages or Mind Genius® can be used to produce Mind Maps (Chapter 67).

Image storage and manipulation

With the widespread use of digital images (p. 237), programs that facilitate the storage and manipulation of electronic image files have become increasingly important. These programs create a library of your stored images and provide a variety of methods for organising and selecting images. Adobe Photoshop® and PaintShop Pro® are two of many programs for image manipulation. Many are highly sophisticated programs intended for graphic artists. However, for most scientific purposes relatively limited functions are required, such as image cropping and resizing.

Take care when copying images – *you may be at risk of committing plagiarism and copyright infringement (Chapter 47).*

Sources for further study

Alexander, M., Kusleika, R. (2015) *Access 2016 Bible.* Wiley, Chichester.

Lambert, J. and Frye, C. (2015) *Microsoft Office 2016 Step by Step.* Microsoft Press, Washington.

Wempen, F. (2015) *Word 2016 In Depth.* Pearson Que®. (And similar texts for other packages and release versions.)

Study exercises

48.1 Investigate intermediate/advanced Word features. The tasks in the following list are likely to be useful in preparing assignments and report writing within the sciences. Can you carry out all of the tasks? If not, use either a manual or the online Help feature to find out how to accomplish them. Tips are given in the answers section.

(a) Sort information in a list into alphabetical order.
(b) Replace a text string word or phrase with a new text string throughout your document.
(c) Replace a text string in normal font with the same text string in italics throughout your document.
(d) Add a 'header' and 'footer' to your document, the former showing the document's title and the latter containing page numbers in the bottom centre of the page.
(e) Adjust the margins of the page to give a 5 cm margin on the left and a 2 cm margin on the right.
(f) Change the type of bullets used in a list from standard form to a number form.

(g) Use the Thesaurus option to find a different or more suitable word to express your meaning. Try, for example, to find alternatives to the word 'alternative'.
(h) Carry out a spell-check on your document.
(i) Carry out a word count on your document and on a selected part of it.
(j) Open two documents and switch between them.

48.2 Make precise copies of tables. Copy the following table using a word processor such as Microsoft Word.

	Number of flies recorded		
Common fly type	**August**	**September**	**October**
Calliphora vicina			
Calliphora vomitoria			
Musca domestica			

48.3 Investigate what programs and packages are available to you as a student. Test each program with appropriate data, images, etc.

Definitions

Macro – a sequence of user-defined instructions, attached to a template or run independently, allowing complex repeated tasks to be 'automated'.

Office suite – a package of complementary and integrated programs such as a word processor, a spreadsheet and a database.

Spreadsheet – a display of a grid of cells into which numbers, text or formulae can be typed to form a worksheet. Each cell is uniquely identifiable by its column and row number combination (i.e. its 2D co-ordinates) and can contain a formula that makes it possible for an entry in one cell to alter the contents of one or more other cells.

Template – here, a pre-designed spreadsheet without data but including all formulae necessary for (repeated) data analysis.

Example (spreadsheets)

- Microsoft Excel®
- Apple Numbers®

Note: This chapter uses Microsoft Excel for illustrative purposes.

The spreadsheet is one of the most powerful and flexible microcomputer applications. It can be described as the electronic equivalent of a paper-based longhand calculation, where the sums are carried out automatically. Spreadsheets provide a dynamic method of storing, manipulating and analysing data sets. Advantages of spreadsheets include:

- **ease and convenience** – especially when complex calculations are repeated on different sets of data;
- **accuracy** – providing that the entry data and cell formulae are correct, the result will be free of calculation errors;
- **improved presentation** – data can be produced in graphical or tabular form to a very high quality;
- **integration with other programs** – graphs and tables can be exported to other compatible programs, such as a word processor in the same office suite;
- **useful tools** – advanced features include hypothesis-testing statistics, database features and macros.

Spreadsheets can be used to:

- **store and manipulate raw data** by removing the drudgery of repeated calculations, allowing easy transformation of data and calculation of statistics;
- **display your data as a graph or chart, for evaluation and/or presentation** – printouts can be used in practical and project reports;
- **carry out statistical analysis** by using built-in procedures or by allowing construction of formulae for specific tasks;
- **model 'what if' situations,** where the consequences of changes in data can be seen and evaluated.

The spreadsheet (Screenshot 49.1) is divided into rows (identified by numbers) and columns (identified by alphabetic characters). Each individual combination of column and row forms a cell that can contain either a data item, a formula or a piece of text called a label. Formulae can include scientific and/or statistical functions and/or a reference to other cells or groups of cells (often called a range). Complex systems of data input and analysis can be constructed (models). The analysis, in part or complete, can be printed out. New data can be added at any time and the sheet recalculated. You can construct templates, pre-designed spreadsheets containing the formulae required for repeated data analyses, adding the data when they become available.

The power a spreadsheet offers is directly related to your ability to create models that are accurate and templates that are easy to use. The sequence of operations required is:

1. **Determine what information/statistics you want to produce.**
2. **Identify the variables you will need to use,** both for original data that will be entered and for any intermediate calculations that might be required.
3. **Set up areas of the spreadsheet for data entry,** calculation of intermediate values (statistical values such as sums of squares, etc.), calculation of final parameters/statistics and, if necessary, a summary area.
4. **Establish the format of the numeric data** if this is different from the default values. This can be done globally (affecting the entire spreadsheet) or locally (affecting only a specified part of the spreadsheet).

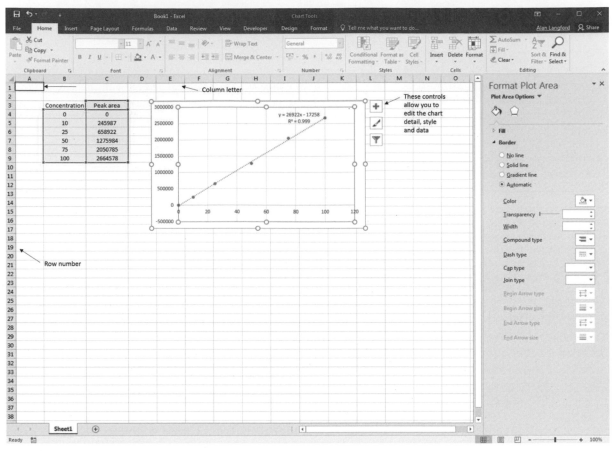

Screenshot 49.1   The appearance of a typical spreadsheet showing cells, rows and columns, toolbars, etc.

Templates – *these should contain:*

- *a data input section;*
- *data transformation and/or calculation sections;*
- *a results section, which can include graphics;*
- *text in the form of headings and annotations;*
- *a summary section.*

Constructing a spreadsheet – *start with a simple model and extend it gradually, checking for correct operation as you go.*

Using hidden (or zero-width) columns – *these are useful for storing intermediate calculations that you do not wish to be displayed on the screen or printout.*

5. **Establish the column widths required** for the various activities.
6. **Enter labels** – use extensively for annotation.
7. **Enter a test set of values to use during formula entry** – use a fully worked example to check that formulae are working correctly.
8. **Enter the formulae required to make all the calculations,** both intermediate and final. Check that results are correct using the test data.

The spreadsheet is then ready for use. Delete all the test data values and you have created your template. Save the template and it is then available for repeated operations.

Data entry

Spreadsheets have built-in commands that allow you to control the layout of data in the cells (see Screenshot 49.2). These include number format, the number of decimal places to be shown (the spreadsheet always calculates using eight or more places), the cell width and the alignment of the entry within the cell (left, right or centre). An auto-entry facility assists greatly in entering large amounts of data by moving the entry cursor either vertically or horizontally as data are entered. Recalculation default is usually automatic so that when a new data value is entered the entire sheet is recalculated immediately.

Screenshot 49.2 Example of cell formatting options within the Microsoft Excel® Spreadsheet. These menus are accessed via the Format > Cell option and would apply to all of a range of selected cells: (a) Use of the number formatting option to specify that data will be presented to three decimal places (the underlying data will be held to greater accuracy); (b) Use of the date formatting option to specify that dates will be presented in day/month/year format (spreadsheet dates are stored numerically and converted to appropriate formats). This allows a period between two dates to be calculated more easily.

(a)

(b)

Data output from analytical instruments – *many devices provide output in spreadsheet-compatible form (e.g. a 'comma delimited' file). Once you have uploaded the information into a spreadsheet, you can manipulate, analyse and present it according to your needs. Consult instrument manuals and the spreadsheet Help function for details.*

Operators and brackets in spreadsheets – *the standard mathematical operators ÷ and × are usually replaced by / and * respectively, while ^ signifies 'to the power'. In complex formulae, brackets should be used to separate the elements, otherwise the results may not be what you expect, e.g. Excel will calculate = A1 * B1/C1 − D1 differently from (A1 * B1)/(C1 − D1).*

Definition

Function – a pre-programmed code for the transformation of values (mathematical or statistical functions) or selection of text characters (string functions).

The parts of a spreadsheet

Labels

These identify the contents of rows and columns. They are text characters, and cannot be used in calculations. Separate them from the data cells by drawing lines, if this feature is available. Programs make assumptions about the nature of the entry being made – most assume that if the first character is a number, then the entry is a number or formula. If it is a letter, then it will be a label. If you want to start a label with a number, you must override this assumption by typing a designated character before the number to tell the program that this is a label – check your program manual for details (e.g. in Excel it is a single quote mark preceding the number).

Numbers

You can also enter numbers (values) in cells for use in calculations. Many programs let you enter numbers in more than one way and you must decide which method you prefer. The way you enter a number does not affect the way it is displayed on the screen as this is controlled by the cell format at the point of entry. There are usually special ways to enter data for percentages and currency, and scientific notation for very large and small numbers.

Formulae

These are the 'power tools' of the spreadsheet because they do the calculations. A cell can be referred to by its alphanumeric code – for example, A5 (column A, row 5) – and the value contained in that cell manipulated within a formula – for example = (A5 + 10) or = (A5 + B22) – in another cell. Formulae can include pre-programmed functions that can refer to a cell, so that if the value of that cell is changed, so is the result of the formula calculation. They may also include limited branching options through the use of logical operators (e.g. IF, TRUE, FALSE, OR, etc.).

Functions

Various functions may be offered, but only mathematical and statistical functions will be considered here.

Mathematical functions

Spreadsheets have program-specific sets of predetermined functions but they almost all include trigonometrical functions, angle functions, logarithms and random number functions. Functions are invaluable for transforming sets of

Using spreadsheets

Example = sin(A5) is an example of a function in Excel. If you write this in a cell, the spreadsheet will calculate the sine of the number in cell A5 (assuming it to be an angle in radians) and write it in the cell. Different programs may use a slightly different syntax.

data rapidly and can be used in formulae required for more complex analyses. Spreadsheets work with an order of preference of the operators in much the same way as a standard calculator and this must always be taken into account when operators are used in formulae. They also require a very precise syntax – the program should warn you if you break this!

Statistical functions

Modern spreadsheets incorporate many sophisticated statistical functions and, if these are not appropriate, the spreadsheet can be used to facilitate the calculations required for most of the statistical tests found in textbooks. The descriptive statistics normally available include:

- **the sum of all data** present in a column, row or block;
- **the minimum and maximum** of a defined range of cells;
- **counts of cells** – a useful operation if you have an unknown or variable number of data values;
- **averages** and other statistics describing location;
- **standard deviations** and other statistics describing dispersion;
- **frequency** – a useful function, where you have large sets of data, that allows you to create frequency distributions using pre-defined class intervals.

The hypothesis-testing statistical functions are usually reasonably powerful (e.g. t-test, ANOVA, regressions) and they often return the *probability* (P) of obtaining the test statistic (where $0 < P < 1$), so there may be no need to refer to statistical tables. Again, check on the effects of including empty cells within the statistical calculation.

Database functions

Many spreadsheets can be used as simple databases and offer a range of functions to support this, including filtering and sorting options. The rows and columns of the spreadsheet are used as the fields and records of the database (see Chapter 48). For many biological purposes, this form of database is perfectly adequate and should be considered seriously before using a full-feature database product.

(a)

	Cell	Formula	
Original → cell	A1	=B1+C1	← Original formula
Copied cells	A2	=B2+C2	Copied formulae (relative)
	A3	=B3+C3	
↓	A4	=B4+C4	

(b)

	Cell	Formula	
Original → cell	A1	=B1/$C$1	← Original formula
Copied cells	A2	=B2/$C$1	Copied formulae (mixed relative and absolute)
	A3	=B3/$C$1	
↓	A4	=B4/$C$1	

Fig. 49.1 Illustration of relative (a) and absolute (b) copying. In Excel, the $ sign before and after the column letter makes the cell reference absolute, as shown in (b).

Empty cells – note that these may be given the value 0 by the spreadsheet for certain functions. This may cause errors, e.g. by rendering a minimum value inappropriate. Also, an error return may result for certain functions if the cell content is zero.

Statistical calculations – make sure you understand whether any functions you employ are for populations or samples (see p. 517).

Copying

All programs provide a means of copying (replicating) formulae or cell contents when required and this is a very useful feature. When copying, references to cells may be either relative, changing with the row/column as they are copied, or absolute, remaining a fixed cell reference and not changing as the formulae are copied (Fig. 49.1).

KEY POINT *The distinction between relative and absolute cell references is very important and must be understood; it provides one of the most common forms of error when copying formulae.*

As an example, in Excel, copying is normally *relative* and if you wish a cell reference to be *absolute* when copied, this is done by putting a dollar ($) sign before the column reference letter and before the new reference number, e.g. $C$56.

Naming blocks

When a group of cells (a block) is carrying out a particular function, it is often easier to give the block a name that can then be used in all formulae referring to that block. This powerful feature also allows the spreadsheet to be more readable.

Graphics display

Most spreadsheets now offer a wide range of graph and chart options (Screenshot 49.1), which are easy to use, and this represents a way to examine your data sets rapidly and comprehensively. The quality of the final graphics output (to a printer) may be variable but is usually sufficient for data exploration and analysis. Many of the default options are business graphic styles but there are usually histogram, column and pie charts, X–Y plotting, line and area graphics options available. Note that some spreadsheet graphics may not come up to the standards expected for the formal presentation of scientific data, unless you manipulate the option settings appropriately.

Printing spreadsheets

This is usually a straightforward menu-controlled procedure, made difficult only by the fact that your spreadsheet may be too big to fit on one piece of paper. Try to develop an area of the sheet that contains only the data that you need to print, e.g. perhaps a summary area. Remember that columns and/or rows can usually be hidden for printing purposes and that you can control whether the printout is in portrait or landscape mode, and for page size and format. Use a screen preview option, if available, to check your layout before printing. A 'print to fit' option is also available in some programs, making the output fit the page dimensions.

Using a spreadsheet as a database

Many spreadsheets can be used as databases, using rows and columns to represent the fields and records (see Chapter 48). For many purposes, this form of database is perfectly adequate and should be considered seriously before using a full-feature database program.

Using text functions – these allow you to manipulate text within your spreadsheet and include functions such as 'find and replace' and alphabetical or numerical 'sort'.

Using string functions – these allow you to manipulate text within your spreadsheet and include functions such as 'search and replace' and alphabetical or numerical 'sort'.

Sources for further study

Hart-Davies, G. (2010) *Beginning Microsoft Office 2010.* Academic Press, New York.

(And similar texts for other release versions.)

Lambert J. and Frye, C. (2015) *Microsoft Office 2016 Step by Step.* Microsoft Press, Washington.

Using spreadsheets

Study exercises

The instructions and tips for these problems assume that you have Excel® (2016) available. If not, they should be readily modified for most advanced spreadsheet programs. If you have problems with any of the tasks, try using the program's Help facility.

49.1 Create a spreadsheet and graph (introductory).

(a) Copy the information in the table below into a spreadsheet. Name and save the spreadsheet file appropriately.

(b) From the copied information, create a pie chart using the *Insert* function on the top line menu.

(c) Adjust the colours selected so the chart will print out in black and white. Save the final version of your spreadsheet. Print the chart out directly from Excel.

Fingerprint classification	% of population
Whorl	33
Arch	6
Tented Arch	8
Right Loop	36
Left Loop	17

49.2 Create a spreadsheet and graph (advanced).

(a) Copy the data in the table below into a spreadsheet. Name and save the file appropriately.

(b) Use the spreadsheet and chart-making facilities to create a scatter plot and label appropriately.

(c) Add a linear trend-line and display the equation and R-squared value on the chart.

(d) Copy the graph to a file in Word and print out.

Concentration of phenobarbital (mg/L)	Peak area
0	0
10	101233
25	249324
50	506556
100	1005468
150	1542156

49.3 Use a spreadsheet as a simple database. Copy the data in the table below into cells within a spreadsheet. Modify the column widths so you can see all of the text on a single screen. Now sort the data in the following ways:

(a) by subject, in alphabetical order;
(b) by date and then by time of day;
(c) by topic, in reverse alphabetical order.

My Exam Timetable

Subject	Date	Time	Paper	Location	Question style
Chemistry	3 Jun	Morning	1	Great Hall	Multiple-choice
Chemistry	17 Jun	Morning	2	Exam Hall 5	Essay paper
Chemistry	2 Jun	Afternoon	3	Main Laboratory	Information processing
Genetics	3 Jun	Afternoon	A	Small Hall	Short-answer questions
Genetics	14 Jun	Afternoon	B	Exam Hall 5	Essay paper
Forensic Botany A	4 Jun	Morning	1	Small Hall	Short-answer questions
Forensic Botany B	1 Jul	Afternoon	1	Exam Hall 3	Short-answer questions
Chromatography A	13 Jun	Afternoon	2	Exam Hall 5	Essay paper
Chromatography B	2 Jun	Morning	2	Main Laboratory	Practical exam

Analysis and presentation of data

Definitions

Accuracy – the closeness of an individual measurement, or a mean value based on a number of measurements, to the true value.

Concentration range – the range of values from the detection limit to the upper concentration at which the technique becomes inaccurate or imprecise.

Detection limit – the minimum concentration of an analyte that can be detected at a particular confidence level.

Drift – 'baseline' movement in a particular direction. Drift can be a problem during analysis (e.g. when separating biomolecules by chromatography).

Noise – random fluctuations in a continuously monitored signal.

Precision – the extent of mutual agreement between replicate data values for an individual sample.

Quality control – measures in place to ensure that the result meets your laboratory's standard.

Quality assurance – measures in place to monitor and document the performance of a test procedure, e.g. proficiency testing schemes.

Replicate – repeat measurement.

Selectivity – the extent to which a method is free from interference due to other substances in the sample.

Sensitivity – the ability to discriminate between small differences in analyte concentration.

Validation – the process whereby the accuracy and precision of a particular analytical method are checked in relation to specific standards, using an appropriate reference material containing a known amount of analyte.

Useful websites
UKIAFT *http://www.ukiaft.co.uk/*

UNODC *https://www.unodc.org/*

Most analytical methods rely on one or more chemical or physical properties of the test substance (the analyte) for detection and/or measurement. There are two principal approaches:

1. **Qualitative analysis** – where a sample is assayed to determine whether a biomolecule is present or absent. For example, a blood sample might be analysed for a particular drug (see Chapter 38).
2. **Quantitative analysis** – where the quantity of a particular biomolecule in a sample is determined in terms of its concentration (e.g. as mgL^{-1}). For example, a blood sample might be analysed to determine its alcohol concentration in mg $100 \ mL^{-1}$ (see Chapter 37).

Cole (1995) and Moffat *et al.* (2004) give details of the chief methods used to analyse drugs and poisons. Your choice of approach will be determined by the purpose of the investigation and by the level of accuracy and precision required. Many of the basic quantitative methods rely on chemical reactions of the analyte, and involve assumptions about the nature of the test substance and the lack of interfering compounds in the sample – such assumptions are unlikely to be wholly valid at all times. If you need to make more exacting measurements of a particular analyte, it may be necessary to separate it from the other components in the sample – e.g. extraction of the analyte using solid phase extraction to remove interferences (Chapter 12), using chromatography (Chapter 14) or electrophoresis (Chapter 22), and then identify the separated components, e.g. using spectroscopic methods (see, for example, Chapter 19).

 KEY POINT *In general, you should aim to use the simplest procedure that satisfies the purpose of your investigation – there is little value in using a complex, time-consuming or costly analytical procedure to answer a simple problem when a high degree of accuracy is not required. In forensic science, these analytical procedures must be shown, with documented evidence, to be appropriate and to be working to an agreed laboratory standard.*

Most of the routine methods based on chemical analysis are destructive since the analyte usually has to be extracted from the matrix in which it is held – for example, extracting drugs from blood or urine (Chapter 38) or extracting a semen stain from clothing (Chapter 30). However, many analytical methods that are based on physical properties are non-destructive, for example fibre analysis using Fourier transform infrared (FTIR) spectroscopy (Chapter 42). Non-destructive methods are often preferred, as they allow further characterisation of a particular sample.

Validity and quantitative analysis

The United Kingdom and Ireland Association of Forensic Toxicologists (UKIAFT) has published guidelines for forensic toxicology. These include personnel, Standard Operating Procedures (SOPs), samples, chain of custody, analytical procedures, quality assurance and control, review of data, reporting results and interpretation. For more details, see Cooper *et al.,* 2010. The United Nations Office on Drugs and Crime (UNODC) has also published recommended methods for identification and analysis of (specific) drugs, for example synthetic cathinones (Chapter 39).

UKAS – *The United Kingdom Accreditation Service is the only national accreditation body appointed by the Accreditation Regulations, 2009 (SI No 3155/2009) to assess internationally agreed standards.*

ISO – *International Organisation for Standardisation.*

IEC – *International Electrotechnical Commission.*

For further information see UKAS https:// www.ukas.com/ and specifically for forensic science https://www.ukas.com/sectors/ forensic-science/.

Selected suppliers of forensic reference standards –
UK: LGC – *Laboratory of the Government Chemist is a UKAS accredited certified reference material supplier within the requirements of ISO Guide 34.*

USA: NIST – *National Institute of Science and Technology, Washington DC.*

For further information, see https://www .ukas.com/services/accreditation-services/ reference-material-producer-accreditation/. Last accessed 25/08/2017.

Before any analytical procedure can commence, a method has to be developed and validated. Validation parameters include accuracy, precision, linearity, specificity, range, limit of detection, limit of quantitation and robustness. In the UK, UKAS can provide accreditation, a means of assessing the competence of the laboratory to meet established criteria designated in ISO/IEC17025. This standard assesses the general requirements in order for a laboratory to conduct sampling, tests and calibration. In forensic science, this includes forensic analysis, examination and testing, continuity, case management, storage, staff competence, validity and suitability of methods, facilities and equipment used and quality assurance and quality control.

Before using a particular procedure, you should consider its possible limitations in terms of:

- **measurement errors, and their likely magnitude** – these might include processing errors (e.g. in preparing solutions and making dilutions), instrumental errors (e.g. a gas chromatography instrument that has not been set up correctly), calibration errors (e.g. converting a digital readout to an analyte concentration) and errors due to the presence of interfering substances (e.g. fatty acids in blood samples);
- **sampling errors** – these may occur if the material used for analysis is not representative, e.g. *post-mortem* blood may be either completely fluid, partially clotted or completely clotted, which may interfere with extraction of a drug.

The reliability of a particular method can be assessed by measuring 'standards' (sometimes termed 'controls'). These are often prepared in the laboratory by adding a known amount of analyte, or reference material, to a sample matrix similar to the forensic case sample. For example, when analysing a blood sample, controls should be prepared using real blood, such as horse blood or human transfusion blood (this is often termed 'spiking' a sample, see p. 208). The reference material used for spiking must be pure and supplied from a recognised source. These are available from commercial suppliers who will also provide a certificate of analysis indicating the exact concentration and purity of the compound. In most instances, several standards (including a 'blank' or zero) are assayed to construct a calibration curve (see Chapter 51), which is then used to convert sample measurements to amounts of analyte. The use of certified reference standards is particularly important when analysing blood or urine samples for alcohol in cases supplied to the laboratory where the person has been charged with driving under the influence of alcohol (Chapter 37). In this case, certified reference standards should be obtained from a commercial supplier and will be used to prepare a calibration curve (Chapter 51). A second set of certified reference standards should be obtained from a different supplier, which will be used to check the calibration of the analytical method, a process known as quality control – a mean value, based on repeated measurements of an individual 'standard', can be compared with the certified value.

Validation of a particular method is important in a forensic science laboratory, where the results of the analysis have important implications. Such laboratories operate strict validation procedures, which include:

- adherence to standard operating procedures (SOPs);
- calibration of assays using certified reference materials containing known amounts of analyte and traceable to a national reference laboratory;

- effective quality assurance and quality control systems;
- detailed record-keeping, covering all aspects of the analysis and recording of results.

Such rigour is required for all cases likely to be heard in court, but not, for example, in routine sudden cases (see Chapter 38), although the general principles of standardisation, calibration, assessment of performance and record-keeping are equally valid.

Accreditation – in the UK, forensic science laboratories should be accredited by UKAS (United Kingdom Accreditation Services) to ensure that all analytical procedures are performed to an internationally recognised standard (ISO/IEC 17025). Other international accreditation bodies include ASCLD/LAB (American Society of Crime Laboratory Directors/Laboratory Accreditation Board) (US) and NATA (National Association of Testing Authorities) (Australia).

Proficiency testing schemes

These are used by laboratories carrying out analytical measurements and will give a snapshot of a laboratory's performance and quality systems at any one point in time. By reviewing the performance over a period of time, the analytical quality of the laboratory can be determined. For example, the QUARTZ Proficiency Testing scheme for *post-mortem* blood toxicology is managed by the LGC as an independent means to assess the quality of the analytical and reporting of test results in accordance with ISO/IEC 17025. For further details, see https://www.lgcstandards.com/BF/en/proficiency-testing/forensics/forensic-blood-toxicology-proficiency-testing. Last accessed 25/08/2017.

Reporting analytical results

Biochemical analysis in forensic science demands both accuracy and precision (p. 15). In order to report the presence of, for example, a drug in a blood sample, you have to be certain that the drug is present. In order to be so, a combination of analytical procedures should be used. Presumptive tests, such as ELISA (Chapter 21) may give an indication of the presence of a particular type of drug. To ensure that the ELISA is performing satisfactorily, spiked standards are included in the assay at a known concentration (p. 208). GC–MS (Chapters 14-15) used for screening the blood sample may identify the specific drug using a combination of the retention time and the mass spectrum of the drug. Using this procedure, an internal standard (p. 376) is added to the blood sample prior to extraction. This ensures that the extraction process is working satisfactorily and that the instrument is operating correctly. If a drug has been identified using this process, a reference standard is analysed that should elute at the same retention time (2%, SOFT (2006)) of the drug in the case sample. Occasionally, after the extraction process, the extract will have to be derivatised prior to analysis by GC–MS, for example morphine is usually derivatised using N-methyl-N-trimethylsilyltrifluoroacetamide (MSTFA). If a drug has been derivatised, it can still be identified by the combination of retention time and mass spectrum in comparison to a derivatised reference standard. Once the drug has been identified, the presence of the drug can either be confirmed or quantified, usually by a technique based on a different chemical principle to that used for screening, such as HPLC or LC–MS (Chapters 14–15). It is only after the process of identification, quantification (if appropriate) and confirmation that the drug can be reported.

Criteria for the selection of a particular analytical method:

- the required level of accuracy and precision;
- the number of samples to be analysed;
- the amount of each sample available for analysis;
- the physical form of the samples;
- the expected concentration range of the analyte in the samples;
- the sensitivity and detection limit of the technique;
- the likelihood of interfering substances;
- the speed of the analysis;
- the ease and convenience of the procedure;
- the skill required by the operator;
- the cost and availability of the equipment.

Text references

Cole, M.D. (1995) *The Analysis of Drugs of Abuse: An Instruction Manual.* Ellis Horwood, Hemel Hempstead.

Cooper, G.A.A., Paterson, S. and Osselton, D. (2010) The UKIAFT forensic toxicology laboratory guidelines (2010). *Science and Justice* **50**: 166–176.

Forensic Toxicology Laboratory Guidelines (2006) Society of Forensic Toxicologists, SOFT. Available at: http://www .soft-tox.org/files/Guidelines_2006_Final.pdf. Last accessed 25/08/2017.

Moffat, A.C., Osselton, M.D. and Widdup, B. (eds) (2004) *Clarke's Analysis of Drugs and Poisons,* 3rd edn. Pharmaceutical Press, London.

Sources for further study

Baynes, S. and Carlin, M.G. (2010) *Forensic Applications of High-Performance Liquid Chromatography.* CRC Press, Boca Raton.

Guidance on Analytical Methods Validation (2015) Available at: http://www.fda.gov/downloads/drugs/guidancecomplian-ceregulatoryinformation/guidances/ucm386366.pdf Last accessed 13/08/2017

Jickells,S. and Negrusz, A., (2008) (eds) *Clarke's Analytical Forensic Toxicology.* Pharmaceutical Press, London and Chicago.

Prichard E. and Barwick, V. (2007) *Quality Assurance in Analytical Chemistry.* Wiley, Chichester.

Swartz, M.E. and Krull, I.S. (2012) *Handbook of Analytical Validation.* CRC Press, Boca Raton.

Study exercises

50.1 Test your knowledge of quality in analytical measurements. Explain the meaning of the following terms and why they are important in quantitative chemical analysis:

(a) accuracy;
(b) precision;
(c) quality control;
(d) quality assurance;
(e) accreditation;
(f) validation.

50.2 Offer your opinion. Discuss with your colleagues whether or not all forensic laboratories should be accredited to UKAS standards. Consider whether or not the results of the performance of the laboratory should be disclosed in court.

There are many instances where it is necessary to measure the quantity of a test substance using a calibrated procedure. You are most likely to encounter this approach in one or more of the following practical exercises:

- quantitative chromatographic analysis (e.g. GC or HPLC, Chapter 14);
- quantitative spectrophotometric assay (Chapter 16);
- atomic absorption spectroscopic analysis of metal ions in biological solutions (Chapter 17);
- quantitative element analysis of glass using XRF (Chapter 18);
- using a bioassay system to quantify a test substance – examples include immunoassay (Chapter 21).

> **Understanding quantitative measurement** – Chapter 50 contains details of the basic principles of valid measurement, while Chapters 14–22 deal with some of the specific analytical techniques used in forensic science. The use of internal standards is covered on p. 376.

 KEY POINT *In most instances, calibration involves the establishment of a relationship between the measured response (the 'signal') and one or more 'standards' containing a known amount of substance.*

In some instances, you can measure a signal due to an inherent property of the substance (e.g. the absorption of UV light p. 154), whereas in other cases you will need to react it with another substance to see the result (e.g. molecular weight measurements of DNA fragments after electrophoresis, visualised using SYBR® Safe, p. 109), or to produce a measurable response (e.g. the reaction of cupric ions and peptide bonds in the Biuret assay for proteins).

> **Calibrating laboratory apparatus** – this is important in relation to validation of equipment; e.g. when determining the accuracy and precision of a pipettor by the weighing method, see p. 39.

The different types of calibration curve

By preparing a set of solutions (termed 'standards'), each containing either (i) a known *amount* or (ii) a specific *concentration* of the substance, and then measuring the response of each standard solution, the underlying relationship can be established in graphical form as a 'calibration curve', or 'standard curve'. This can then be used to determine either (i) the amount or (ii) the concentration of the substance in one or more test samples. Alternatively, the response can be expressed solely in mathematical terms. An example of this approach is the determination of chlorophyll pigments in plant extracts by measuring absorption at particular wavelengths, and then applying a formula based on previous (published) measurements for purified pigments.

There are various types of standard curve. In the simplest cases, the relationship between signal and substance will be linear, or nearly so, and the calibration will be represented best by a straight-line graph (see Box 51.1). In some instances (Fig. 51.1(a)), you will need to transform either the *x* values or *y* values, in order to produce a linear graph. In other instances, the straight-line relationship may hold only up to a certain value (the 'linear dynamic range') and beyond this point the graph may curve (e.g. in quantitative spectrophotometry the Beer–Lambert relationship often becomes invalid at high absorbance, giving a curve, Fig. 51.1(b)). Some calibration curves are sigmoid (Fig. 51.1(c)). Finally, the signal may *decrease* in response to an increase in the substance (Fig. 51.1(d), e.g. radioimmunoassay), where an inverse sigmoid calibration curve is obtained. In some practical classes, you may be told that the relationship is expected to be linear, curvilinear or whatever, while in others you may be expected to decide the form of the standard curve as part of the exercise.

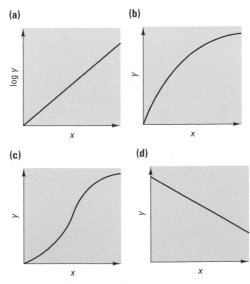

Fig. 51.1 Types of calibration curve.

Box 51.1 The stages involved in preparing and using a calibration curve

1. **Decide on an appropriate test method** – for example, in a project you may need to research the best approach to the analysis of a particular metabolite in your biological material.

2. **Select either (a) amount or (b) concentration, and an appropriate range and number of standards** – in practical classes, this may be given in your schedule, along with detailed instructions on how to make up the standard solutions. In other cases, you may be expected to work this out from first principles (Chapters 7, 14 and 17) give worked examples – aim to have evenly spaced values along the x-axis.

3. **Prepare your standards very carefully** – due attention to detail is required. For example, you should ensure that you check the calibration of pipettors beforehand, using the weighing method (p. 39). Don't forget the 'zero standard' plus any other controls required, for example to test for interference due to other chemical substances. Your standards should cover the range of values expected in your test samples.

4. **Assay the standards and the unknown (test) samples** – preferably all at the same time, to avoid introducing error due to changes in the sensitivity or drift in the zero setting of the instrument with time. It is a good idea to measure all of your standard solutions at the outset, and then measure your test solutions, checking that the 'zero standard' and 'top standard' give the same values after, say, every six test measurements. If the remeasured standards do not fall within a reasonable margin of the previous value, then you will have to go back and recalibrate the instrument, and repeat the last six test measurements. If your test samples lie outside the range of your standards, you may need to repeat the assay using diluted test samples (extrapolation of your curve may not be valid, see p. 488).

5. **Draw the standard curve, or determine the underlying relationship** – Figure 51.2 gives an example of a typical linear calibration curve, where the spectrophotometric absorbance of a series of standard solutions is related to the amount of substance. When using Excel or graphics packages, it is often appropriate to use type linear regression (p. 525) to produce a linear trend line (also termed the 'line of best fit') and you can then quote the value of r^2, which is a measure of the 'fit' of the measurements to the line (see p. 525). In forensic analysis the value of r^2 should normally be as close to 1.00 as possible. However, you should take care not to use a linear plot when the underlying relationship is clearly non-linear (Fig. 52.10) and you must consider whether the assumptions of the regression analysis are valid (e.g. for transformed data).

6. **Determine the amount or concentration in each unknown sample** – either by reading the appropriate value from the calibration curve, or by using the underlying mathematical relationship, i.e. $y = mx + c$ (p. 503). Make sure you draw any horizontal and vertical construction lines very carefully – many students lose marks unnecessarily by submitting poorly drawn construction lines in practical reports.

7. **Correct for dilution or concentration, where appropriate** – for example, if you diluted each test sample ten-fold, then you would need to multiply by 10 to determine the value for the undiluted test sample. As another example, if you assayed 0.2 mL of test sample, you would need to multiply the value obtained from the calibration curve by 5, to give the value per mL.

8. **Quote your test results to an appropriate number of significant figures** – this should reflect the accuracy of the method used (see p. 501), not the size of your calculator's display.

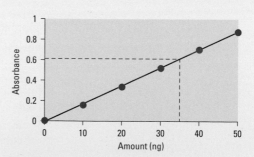

Fig. 51.2 Typical calibration curve for spectrophotometric analysis.

 KEY POINT *You should always aim for a linear regression value (r^2) > 0.99 in your calibration curve when you have a linear relationship between signal and substance.*

Practical considerations

Amount or concentration?

This first step is often the most confusing for new students. It is vital that you understand the difference between *amount* of substance (e.g. mg, ng, etc.), and *concentration* (the amount of substance per unit volume, e.g. mmol mmol L^{-1}, mol m^{-3}, % w/v, etc.) before you begin your practical work.

 KEY POINT *Essentially, you have to choose whether to work in terms of (i) the total amount of substance in your assay vessel (e.g. test tube or cuvette) or (ii) the final concentration of the substance in your assay vessel, which is independent of the volume used.*

Your pipetting skills are really important. Chapter 6 gives more details on the correct use of pipettors. It is also worth checking that the pipettors are correctly calibrated prior to their use.

Choice of standards

In your early practical classes, you may be provided with a stock solution (p. 46), from which you then have to prepare a specified number of standard solutions. In such cases, you will need to understand how to use dilutions to achieve the required amounts or concentrations (p. 47). In later work and projects, you may need to prepare your standards from chemical reagents in solid form, where the important considerations are purity and solubility (p. 45). For professional analysis in forensic science, it is often important to be able to trace the original standard or stock solution back to national or international standards (p. 473).

How many standards are required?

This may be given in your practical schedule, or you may have to decide what is appropriate (e.g. in project work and research). If the form and working range of the standard curve is known in advance, this may influence your choice – for example, linear calibration curves can be established with fewer standards than curvilinear relationships. In some instances, analytical instruments can be calibrated using a single standard solution, often termed a 'calibrator'. Replication of each standard solution is a good idea, since it will give you some information on the variability involved in preparing and assaying the standards. Consider whether it is best to plot mean values on your standard curve, or whether you should plot the individual values (if one value appears to be well off the line, you have made an error, and you may need to check and repeat).

Preparing your standards

Dealing with interfering substances – one approach is to use the method of 'standard additions', where the standards all contain a fixed additional amount of the sample (for more details of this approach see Dean, 1997). Internal standards can also be used to detect such problems.

It is extremely important to take the greatest care to measure out all chemicals and liquids very accurately to achieve the best possible standard curve. The grade of volumetric flask used and temperature of the solution also affect accuracy (grade A apparatus is best). You may also consider what other additives might be required in your standard solutions. For example, do your test samples have high levels of potentially interfering substances, and should these also be added to your standards? Also consider what controls and blank solutions to prepare.

 KEY POINT *The validity of your standard curve depends on careful preparation of standards, especially in relation to accurate dispensing of the volumes of any stock solution and diluting liquid (diluent) – the results for your test samples can only be as good as your standard curve!*

Preparing the calibration curve and determining the amount of the unknown (test) sample(s)

This is described in stepwise fashion within Box 51.1. Check you understand the requirements of graph drawing, especially in relation to plotted curves (p. 484) and the mathematics of straight-line graphs (p. 503). Spreadsheet programs such as Microsoft Excel® can be used to produce a regression line for a straight-line calibration plot (p. 465). Examples of how to do this are provided in Box 51.2.

Box 51.2 How to use a spreadsheet (Microsoft Excel® 2016) to produce a linear regression plot

In the example shown below, the following simple data set has been used:

Concentration (μg/mL^{-1})	Peak area
0	0
10	1002
20	2054
30	3089
40	4100
50	5007

Using the Trendline feature – this quick method provides a line of best fit on an Excel chart and can also provide a set of equation values for predictive purposes.

1. **Create a graph (chart) of your data.** Enter the data in two columns in your spreadsheet, select the data array (highlight using left mouse button) and then, using the Insert tab, select the Insert Scatter (X,Y) or Bubble Chart icon from the Charts subsection and then choose the Scatter icon.

2. **Add a trend line.** Click on the $\boxed{+}$ symbol (Chart Elements) to the right of the graph, and on the Trendline box, click on the right arrow button. Choose More Options and then select: (i) Display equation on chart and (ii) Display R-squared value on chart. Now click OK. Make sure the Trendline Options selection is set to Linear. The equation (shown in the form $y = mx + c$) gives the slope and intercept of the line of best fit, while the

R-squared value (coefficient of determination, p. 525) gives the proportional fit to the line (the closer this value is to 1, the better the fit of the data to the trend line).

3. **Modify the graph to improve its effectiveness.** For a graph that is to be used elsewhere (e.g. in a lab write-up or project report), adjust the display to remove the default background and gridlines and change the symbol shape. With the Format Trendline menu open, you can alter the Fill and Line options and the Effects options. Using the Fill and line options, the width and colour of the line can be adjusted to make it thinner or thicker. Drag and move the equation panel if you would like to alter its location on the chart.

4. **Add a title and axes labels.** Click on the $\boxed{+}$ symbol (Chart Elements) to the right of the graph and on the Axis Titles box, click on the right arrow button then select Primary Horizontal and Primary vertical boxes. These will automatically appear on your chart. Select the text on the chart and compose the axis and chart titles as appropriate. Figure 51.3 shows a calibration curve produced in this way for the data presented above.

5. **Use the regression equation to estimate unknown (test) samples.** By rearranging the equation for a straight line and substituting a particular y-value, you can predict the amount/concentration of substance (x-value) in a test sample. This is more precise than simply reading the values from the graph using construction lines. If you are carrying out multiple calculations, the appropriate equation, $x = (y - c)/m$, can be entered into a spreadsheet, for convenience.

Box 51.2   (Continued)

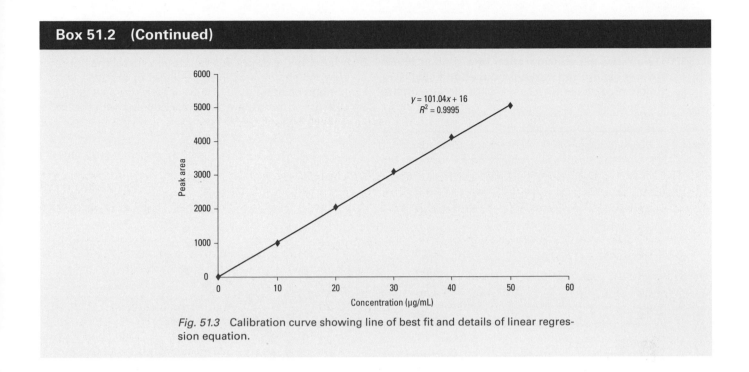

Fig. 51.3 Calibration curve showing line of best fit and details of linear regression equation.

Text reference

Dean, J.D. (1997) *Atomic Absorption and Plasma Spectroscopy,* 2nd edn. Wiley, Chichester. [Chapter1 deals with calibration, and covers the principle of standard additions.]

Sources for further study

Harris, D.C. (2010) *Quantitative Chemical Analysis,* 8th edn. Freeman, New York.

Miller, J.N. and Miller, J.C. (2010) *Statistics and Chemometrics for Analytical Chemistry,* 6th edn. Prentice Hall, Harlow.

Calibration and quantitative analysis

Study exercises

51.1 Determine the concentration of a drug in blood from a calibration curve produced in Excel. The following data are for a set of calibration standards for methadone.

Concentration mg/L^{-1}	Peak area
0	0
0.1	11412
0.2	21568
0.4	40235
0.6	61426
0.8	80002
1.0	104201
2.0	210546

Using PC-based software (e.g. Excel), fit a trend line (linear regression) and determine the methadone content of the following extracted blood samples with the following peak areas:

(a) 22,654; (b) 65,245; (c) 154,256.

51.2 Identify the errors in a calibration curve. The figure below shows a calibration curve of the type that might be submitted in a practical write-up. List the errors and compare your observations with the list given on p. 486.

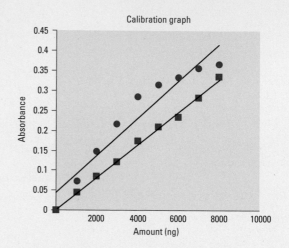

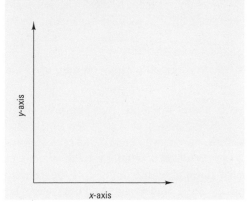

Graphs can be used to show detailed results in an abbreviated form, displaying the maximum amount of information in the minimum space. Graphs and tables present findings in different ways. A graph (figure) gives a visual impression of the content and meaning of your results, while a table provides an accurate numerical record of data values. You must decide whether a graph should be used–for example, to illustrate a pronounced trend or relationship, or whether a table (Chapter 53) is more appropriate.

A well-constructed graph will combine simplicity, accuracy and clarity. Planning of graphs is needed at the earliest stage in any write-up as your accompanying text will need to be structured so that each graph delivers the appropriate message. Therefore, it is best to decide on the final form for each of your graphs before you write your text. The text, diagrams, graphs and tables in a laboratory write-up or project report should be complementary, each contributing to the overall message. In a formal scientific communication, it is rarely necessary to repeat the same data in more than one place (e.g. as a table and as a graph). However, graphical representation of data collected earlier in tabular format may be applicable in laboratory practical reports.

Practical aspects of graph drawing

The following comments apply to graphs drawn for laboratory reports. Figures for publication or similar formal presentation are usually prepared according to specific guidelines, provided by the publisher/organiser.

> **KEY POINT** Graphs should be self-contained – they should include all material necessary to convey the appropriate message without reference to the text. Every graph must have a concise explanatory title to establish the content. If several graphs are used, they should be numbered, so they can be quoted in the text.

- **Consider the layout and scale of the axes carefully.** Most graphs are used to illustrate the relationship between two variables (x and y) and have two axes at right angles (e.g. Fig. 52.1). The horizontal axis is known as the abscissa (x-axis) and the vertical axis as the ordinate (y-axis).
- **The axis assigned to each variable must be chosen carefully.** Usually the x-axis is used for the independent variable (e.g. treatment), while the dependent variable (e.g. response) is plotted on the y-axis. When neither variable is determined by the other, or where the variables are interdependent, the axes may be plotted either way round.

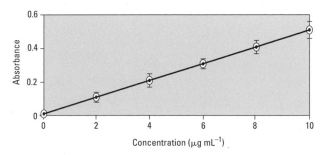

Fig. 52.1 Calibration curve for the determination of lead in soil using flame atomic absorption spectroscopy. Vertical bars show standard errors ($n=3$).

Using graphs

Choosing between a histogram and a bar chart – use a histogram for continuous quantitative variables and a bar chart for discrete variables (see Chapter 3 for details of these types of measurement scale).

- **Each axis must have a descriptive label showing what is represented,** together with the appropriate units of measurement, separated from the descriptive label by a solidus or 'slash' (/) or by *brackets,* as in Fig. 52.1.
- **Each axis must have a scale with reference marks** ('tics') on the axis to show clearly the location of all numbers used.
- **A figure legend should be used** to provide explanatory detail, including a key to the symbols used for each data set.

Handling very large and very small numbers

To simplify presentation when your experimental data consist of either very large or very small numbers, the plotted values may be the measured numbers multiplied by a power of 10; this multiplying power should be written immediately before the descriptive label on the appropriate axis. However, it is often better to modify the primary unit with an appropriate prefix (p. 24) to avoid any confusion regarding negative powers of 10.

Size

Remember that the purpose of your graph is to communicate information. It must not be too small, so use at least half an A4 page and design your axes and labels to fill the available space without overcrowding any adjacent text. If using graph paper, remember that the white space around the grid is usually too small for effective labelling. The shape of a graph is determined by your choice of scale for the x and y axes which, in turn, is governed by your experimental data. It may be inappropriate to start the axes at zero (e.g. Fig. 52.1). In such instances, it is particularly important to show the scale clearly, with scale breaks where necessary, so the graph does not mislead. For example, Fig. 56.5 is drawn with 'floating axes' (i.e. the x and y axes do not meet in the lower left-hand corner), while Fig. 51.2 does not need scale breaks on either the x or y axes.

Graph paper

In addition to conventional linear (squared) graph paper, you may need the following:

- **Probability graph paper** – this is useful when one axis is a probability scale.
- **Log–linear graph paper** – this is appropriate when one of the scales shows a logarithmic progression, for example the exponential growth of cells in liquid culture. Log–linear paper is defined by the number of logarithmic divisions covered (usually termed 'cycles'), so make sure you use paper with the appropriate number of cycles for your data. An alternative approach is to plot the log-transformed values on 'normal' graph paper.
- **Log–log graph paper** – this is appropriate when both scales show a logarithmic progression.

Types of graph

Different graphical forms may be used for different purposes, including:

- **Plotted curves** – used for data where the relationship between two variables can be represented as a continuum (e.g. Fig. 52.1).
- **Scatter diagrams** – used to visualise the relationship between individual data values for two interdependent variables (e.g. Fig. 52.2), often as a preliminary part of a correlation analysis (p. 525).

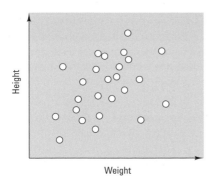

Fig. 52.2 Scatter diagram: height and weight of individual humans in a group.

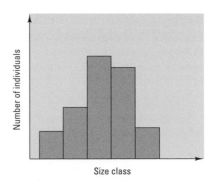

Fig. 52.3 Histogram: the number of plants within different size classes.

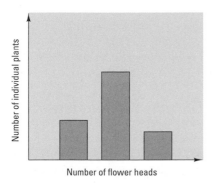

Fig. 52.4 Bar chart: number of flowering heads of a cannabis plant.

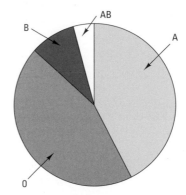

Fig. 52.5 Pie chart: relative abundance of blood groups in man.

- **Three-dimensional graphs** – show the interrelationships of three variables, often one dependent and two independent. A contour diagram is an alternative method of representing such data.
- **Histograms** – represent frequency distributions of continuous variables (e.g. Fig. 52.3). An alternative is a tally chart.
- **Frequency polygons** – emphasise the form of a frequency distribution by joining the co-ordinates with straight lines, in contrast to a histogram. This is particularly useful when plotting two or more frequency distributions on the same graph.
- **Bar charts** – represent frequency distributions of a discrete qualitative or quantitative variable (e.g. Fig. 52.4). An alternative representation is the line chart.
- **Pie charts** – illustrate portions of a whole (e.g. Fig. 52.5).
- **Pictographs** – give a pictorial representation of data.

Choosing graphical symbols – *plotted curves are usually drawn using a standard set of symbols:* ●, ○, ■, □, ▲, △, ◆, ◇. *By convention, paired symbols ('closed' and 'open') are often used to represent 'plus' (treatment) and 'minus' (control) treatments.*

The plotted curve

This is the commonest form of graphical representation used in forensic science. The key features are outlined below and given in checklist form in Box 52.1, while Box 52.2 advises on how to use Microsoft Excel 2016 – see also Box 51.2.

Using graphs

The following sequence can be used whenever you need to construct a plotted curve – it will need to be modified for other types of graph.

1. **Collect all of the data values and statistical values** – in tabular form, where appropriate.

2. **Decide on the most suitable form of presentation** – this may include transformation to convert data to linear form.

3. **Choose a concise descriptive title** – together with a reference (figure) number and date, where necessary.

4. **Determine which variable is to be plotted on the *x*-axis and which on the *y*-axis.**

5. **Select appropriate scales for both axes** – make sure that the numbers and their location (scale marks) are clearly shown, together with any scale breaks.

6. **Decide on appropriate descriptive labels for both axes** – with SI units of measurement, where appropriate.

7. **Choose the symbols for each set of data points** – decide on the best means of representation for statistical values.

8. **Plot the points** – to show the co-ordinates of each value with appropriate symbols.

9. **Draw a trend line for each set of points** – use a see-through ruler, so you can draw the line to have an equal number of points on either side of it.

10. **Write a figure legend** – to include a key that identifies all symbols and statistical values and any descriptive footnotes.

Box 52.2   How to create and amend graphs within a spreadsheet (Microsoft Excel 2016) for use in coursework reports and dissertations

Excel can be used to create plotted curves, bar charts and histograms of reasonable quality, but only if you know how to amend the default settings to improve the overall effect, so that they meet the standard required for practical and project reports. As with a hand-drawn graph, the basic stages in graph drawing (Box 52.1) still apply.

Producing a plotted curve or bar chart

1. **Create the appropriate type of graph (chart) for your data.** Enter your data into the spreadsheet (e.g. in two columns), select the data array (highlight the appropriate cells by clicking and holding down the left-hand mouse button and dragging), then use the 'Insert' tab to open the chart subsection and select a particular Chart type from the choice of icons. Clicking on the appropriate icon opens a drop-down sub-menu to choose a specific chart type. You have a choice of chart types including column, line, pie, bar, area, scatter; or you can choose to select the 'Other' option to select a different chart type.

    For a plotted curve, use the 'Insert Scatter (X,Y) or bubble chart' option with 'Scatter' as the Chart sub-type – the line will be added at a later stage. (Note: never use the line plot because this will create a graph with evenly spaced *x*-axis entries, regardless of their actual values – see Box 51.2).

2. **Change the default settings to improve the overall appearance.** For a graph that is to be used elsewhere (e.g. in a coursework report or a dissertation), adjust the display using the chart styles option that appears on the right of the graph to alter the style and colour and the $\boxed{+}$ option to add legends, error bars and gridlines.

    Consider each element of the image in turn, including the overall size, height and width of your graph (click on the chart using the left-hand mouse button to show the 'sizing handles' and drag these to resize). Other settings can be altered, typically by moving the cursor over the feature and clicking the right-hand mouse button to reveal an additional menu of editing/formatting options, or by clicking the icons that appear to the right of the graph. The examples given below are for illustrative purposes only, and should not necessarily be regarded as a prescriptive list. With Excel 2016, these examples apply to all chart types.

Examples

- **The colour of the markers** can be altered by clicking on the images in the colour section of the Chart style menu.

- **Horizontal gridlines** can be removed by clicking the left-hand mouse button on a gridline and pressing

Box 52.2 (Continued)

delete or by changing the line colour to match the background, i.e. no colour, by clicking the right-hand button and choosing the appropriate outline colour. Alternatively, you can select the Chart Elements option $+$ and, clicking on the right arrow of the gridlines box, deselect the Primary horizontal gridlines. Similarly, by choosing major and minor gridlines in both horizontal and vertical gridlines, you can make them more like those of conventional graph paper.

- **Axes** can be reformatted using the Chart Elements option $+$ and clicking on the right arrow of the Axes option. Choose more options and you open up the default settings, or can change to your desired option (e.g. thousands, millions, billions, log scales).

- **Axis label** changes can be achieved using the Chart Elements option $+$ and clicking on the right arrow of each of the elements you want to introduce. You can change the text by highlighting the text boxes and inserting your legends. You will need to click on the Home tab to alter font size, colour, superscript and subscript text.

- **Add a border to your chart** by clicking on the Format tab > Shape styles. Choose an appropriate style from the options available. You can also change the colour by clicking on the Shape outline icon.

- **Add a trendline**. Click on the $+$ symbol (Chart Elements) to the right of the graph, and on the Trendline box, click on the right arrow button. Choose More Options and then select: (i) Display equation on chart and (ii) Display R-squared value on chart. Now click OK. Make sure the Trendline Options selection is set to Linear. The equation (shown in the form $y = mx + c$) gives the slope and intercept of the line

of best fit, while the R-squared value (coefficient of determination, p. 525) gives the proportional fit to the line (the closer this value is to 1, the better the fit of the data to the trend line). Alternatively, you can right click on any of the data points, and select Add Trendline from the menu.

- **Add error bars** by clicking on the Chart Elements option $+$ and, clicking on the right arrow of Error bars option, you can choose between standard error, percentage or standard deviation. You can also choose more error bar options to change the style of the error bar. This will introduce error bars in both horizontal and vertical planes. Select the plane you don't require by simply clicking on the appropriate error bar to highlight it and press delete.

- **Using templates.** By clicking on the Design tab, there is a section called Chart styles. This section contains pre-loaded templates that you could use to improve your chart. Try clicking on these icons to see the different templates available. You can still alter the chart afterwards using the methods above.

Note that it is probably better not to use the default Chart Title option within Excel, which places the title at the top of the chart, but to cut-and-paste your untitled graph into a word processor such as Microsoft Word and then type a formal figure legend below the graph itself. However, once your graph is embedded into Word it is generally best not to make further amendments – go back to the original Excel file, make the required change(s) and re-insert the graph into Word.

Note: instructions illustrated here may vary among the different versions of Microsoft Office programs.

Data points

Each data point must be shown accurately, so that any reader can determine the exact values of x and y. In addition, the results of each treatment must be readily identifiable. A useful technique is to use a dot for each data point, surrounded by a hollow symbol for each treatment (see Fig. 52.1). An alternative is to use symbols only (Fig. 52.10), though the co-ordinates of each point are defined less accurately. Use the same symbol for the same entity if it occurs in several graphs and provide a key to all symbols.

Statistical measures

If you are plotting average values for several replicates and if you have the necessary statistical knowledge, you can calculate the standard error (p. 512), or the 95% confidence limits (p. 524) for each mean value and show these on your graph as a series of vertical bars (see Fig. 52.1). Make it clear in the legend whether the bars refer to standard errors or 95% confidence limits and quote the value of n (the number of replicates per data point). Another approach is to add a least-significant difference bar to the graph.

Interpolation

Once you have plotted each point, you must decide whether to link them by straight lines or a smoothed curve. Each of these techniques conveys a different message to your reader. Joining the points by straight lines may seem the simplest option, but may give the impression that errors are very low or non-existent and that the relationship between the variables is complex. Joining points by straight lines is appropriate in certain graphs involving time sequences (e.g. the number of animals at a particular site each year), or for repeat measurements where measurement error can be assumed to be minimal (e.g. recording a patient's temperature in a hospital, to emphasise any variation from one time point to the next). However, in most plotted curves, the best straight line or curved line should be drawn (according to appropriate mathematical or statistical models, or by eye) to highlight the relationship between the variables – after all, your choice of a plotted curve implies that such a relationship exists. Don't worry if some of your points do not lie on the line – this is caused by errors of measurement and by biological variation. Most curves drawn by eye should have an equal number of points lying on either side of the line. You may be guided by 95% confidence limits, in which case your curve should pass within these limits wherever possible.

Curved lines can be drawn using a flexible curve, a set of French curves or freehand. In the latter case, turn your paper so that you can draw the curve in a single, sweeping stroke by a pivoting movement at the elbow (for larger curves) or wrist (for smaller ones). Do not try to force your hand to make complex, unnatural movements, as the resulting line will not be smooth.

Extrapolation

Be wary of extrapolation beyond the upper or lower limit of your measured values. This is rarely justifiable and may lead to serious errors. Whenever extrapolation is used, a dotted line ensures that the reader will be aware of the uncertainty involved. Any assumptions behind an extrapolated curve should also be stated clearly in your text.

The histogram

While a plotted curve assumes a continuous relationship between the variables by interpolating between individual data points, a histogram involves no such assumptions and is the most appropriate representation if the number of data points is too few to allow a trend line to be drawn. Histograms are also used to represent frequency distributions (p. 485), where the y-axis shows the number of times a particular value of x was obtained (e.g. Fig. 52.3). As in a plotted curve, the x-axis represents a continuous variable which can take any value within a given range (e.g. plant height), so the scale must be broken down into discrete classes and the scale marks on the x-axis should show either the mid-points (mid-values) of each class, or the boundaries between the classes.

The columns are adjacent to each other in a histogram, in contrast to a bar chart, where the columns are separate because the x-axis of a bar chart represents discrete values.

Joining the points – Any graph should only ever have one line showing the relationship between the points. Never use a point-to-point style for a calibration curve; it should always be a line of best fit.

Conveying the correct message – the golden rule is 'always draw the simplest line that fits the data reasonably well and is scientifically reasonable'.

Extrapolating plotted curves – try to avoid the need to extrapolate by better experimental design.

Drawing a histogram – each datum is represented by a column with an area proportional to the magnitude of y: in most cases, you should use columns of equal width, so that the height of each column is then directly proportional to y. Shading or stippling can be used to identify individual columns, according to your needs.

Interpreting graphs

The process of analysing a graph can be split into five phases:

1. **Consider the context** – look at the graph in relation to the aims of the study in which it was reported. Why were the observations made? What hypothesis was the experiment set up to test? This information can usually be found in the Introduction or Results section of a report. Also relevant are the general methods used to obtain the results. This might be obvious from the figure title and legend, or from the Materials and Methods section.

2. **Recognise the graph form and examine the axes** – first, what kind of graph is presented (e.g. histogram, plotted curve)? You should be able to recognise the main types summarised on pp. 484–485 and their uses. Next, what do the axes measure? You should check what quantity has been measured in each case and what units are used.

3. **Look closely at the scale of each axis** – what is the starting point and what is the highest value measured? For the x-axis, this will let you know the scope of the treatments or observations (e.g. whether they lasted for 5 min or 20 years; whether a concentration span was two-fold or fifty-fold). For each axis, it is especially important to note whether the values start at zero; if not, then the differences between any treatments shown may be magnified by the scale chosen (see Box 52.3).

4. **Examine the symbols and curves** – information will be provided in the key or legend to allow you to determine what these refer to. If you have made your own photocopy of the figure, it may be appropriate to note this directly on it. You can now assess what appears to have happened. If, say, two conditions have been observed while a variable is altered, when exactly do they differ from each other, by how much and for how long?

5. **Evaluate errors and statistics** – it is important to take account of variability in the data. For example, if mean values are presented, the underlying errors may be large, meaning that any difference between two treatments or observations at a given x value could simply have arisen by chance. Thinking about the descriptive statistics used (Chapter 55) will allow you to determine whether apparent differences could be significant in both statistical and scientific senses.

Sometimes graphs are used to mislead. This may be unwitting, as in a subconscious favouring of a 'pet' hypothesis of the author. Graphs may be used to 'sell' a product in the field of advertising or to favour a viewpoint as, perhaps, in politics. Experience in drawing and interpreting graphs will help you spot these flawed presentations, and understanding how graphs can be erroneously presented (Box 52.3) will help you avoid the same pitfalls.

Using computers to produce graphs – never allow a computer program to dictate size, shape and other aspects of a graph. Find out how to alter scales, labels, axes, etc., and make appropriate selections. Draw curves freehand if the program only has the capacity to join the individual points by straight lines.

Examining graphs – don't be tempted to look at the data displayed in a graph before you have considered its context, read the legend and the scale of each axis.

Understanding graphs in scientific papers – the legend should be a succinct summary of the key information required to interpret the figure without further reference to the main text. This is a useful approach when 'skimming' a paper for relevant information (p. 596).

Box 52.3 How graphs can misrepresent and mislead

1. **The 'volume' or 'area' deception** – this is mainly found in histogram or bar chart presentations where the size of a symbol is used to represent the measured variable. For example, the amount of hazardous waste produced in different years might be represented on a chart by different sizes of a chemical drum, with the *y*-axis (height of drum) representing the amount of waste. However, if the symbol retains its *shape* for all heights, as in Fig. 52.6(a), its *volume* will increase as a cubic function of the height, rather than in direct proportion. To the casual observer, a two-fold increase may look like an eight-fold one, and so on. Strictly, the *height* of the symbol should be the measure used to represent the variable, with no change in symbol width, as in Fig. 52.6(b).

2. **Effects of a non-zero axis** – a non-zero axis acts to emphasise the differences between measures by reducing the range of values covered by the axis. For example, in Fig. 52.7(a) it looks as if there are large differences in mass between males and females; however, if the scale is adjusted to run from zero, then it can be seen that the differences are not large as a proportion of the overall mass. Always scrutinise the scale values carefully when interpreting any graph.

3. **Use of a relative rather than an absolute scale** – this is similar to the above, in that data compared using relative scales (e.g. percentage or ratio) can give the wrong impression if the denominator is not the same in all cases. In Fig. 52.8(a), two treatments are shown as equal in *relative* effect, both resulting in 50% relative response compared (say) to the respective controls. However, if treatment A is 50% of a control value of 200 and treatment B is 50% of a control value of 500, then the actual difference in *absolute* response would have been masked, as shown by Fig. 52.8(b).

4. **Effects of a non-linear scale** – when interpreting graphs with non-linear (e.g. logarithmic) scales, you may interpret any changes on an imagined linear scale. For example, the pH scale is logarithmic, and linear changes on this scale mean less in terms of absolute H^1 concentration at

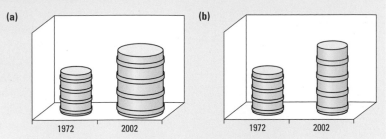

Fig. 52.6 Increase in pesticide use over a 30-year period.

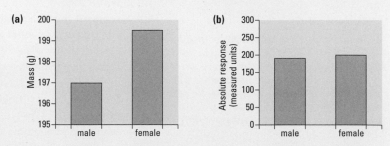

Fig. 52.7 Average mass of males and females in test group.

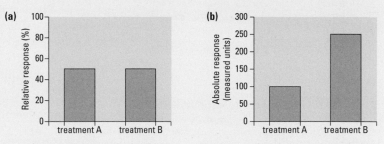

Fig. 52.8 Responses to treatments A and B.

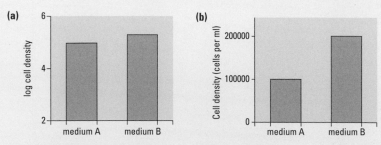

Fig. 52.9 Effect of different media on cell density.

Box 52.3   (Continued)

high (alkaline) pH than they do at low (acidic) pH. In Fig. 52.9(a), the cell density in two media is compared on a logarithmic scale, while in Fig. 52.9(b), the same data are graphed on a linear scale. Note, also, that the log y-axis scale in Fig. 52.9(a) cannot be shown to zero, because there is no logarithm for 0.

5. **Unwarranted extrapolation** – a graph may be extrapolated to indicate what would happen if a trend continued, as in Fig. 52.10(a). However, this can only be done under certain assumptions (e.g. that certain factors will remain constant or that relationships will hold under new conditions). There may be no guarantee that this will actually be the case. Figure 52.10(b) illustrates other possible outcomes if the experiment were to be repeated with higher values for the x-axis.

6. **Failure to account for data point error** – this misrepresentation involves curves that are overly complex in relation to the scatter in the underlying data. When interpreting graphs with complex curves, consider the errors involved in the data values. It is probably unlikely that the curve would pass through all the data points unless the errors were very small. Figure 52.11(a) illustrates a curve that appears to assume zero error and is thus overly complex, while Fig. 52.11(b) shows a curve that takes possible errors of the points into account.

7. **Failure to reject outlying points** – this is a special case of the previous example. There may be many reasons for outlying data, from genuine mistakes to statistical 'freaks'. If a curve is drawn through such points on a graph, it indicates that the point carries equal weight with the other points, when in fact, it should probably be ignored. To assess this, consider the accuracy of the measurement, the number and position of adjacent points, and any special factors that might be involved on a one-off basis. Figure 52.12(a) shows a curve where an outlier has perhaps been given undue weight when showing the presumed relationship. If there is good reason to think that the point should be ignored, then the curve shown in Fig. 52.12(b) would probably be more valid.

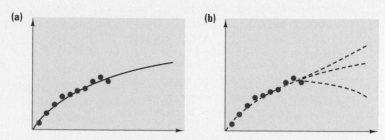

Fig. 52.10   Extrapolation of data under different assumptions.

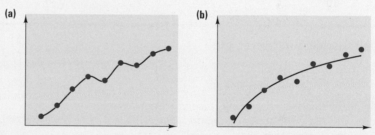

Fig. 52.11   Fitted curves under different assumptions of data error.

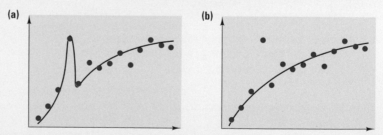

Fig. 52.12   Curves with and without outlier taken into account.

Box 52.3   (Continued)

8. **Inappropriate fitted line** – here, the mathematical function chosen to represent a trend in the data might be inappropriate. A straight line might be fitted to the data, when a curve would be more correct, or *vice versa*. These cases can be difficult to assess. You need to consider the theoretical validity of the model used to generate the curve (this is not always stated clearly). For example, if a straight line is fitted to the points, the implicit underlying model states that one factor varies in direct relation to another, when the true situation may be more complex. In Fig. 52.13(a), the relationship has been shown as a linear relationship, whereas an exponential relationship, as shown in Fig. 52.13(b), could be more correct.

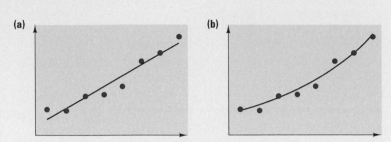

Fig. 52.13   Different mathematical model used to represent trends in data.

Sources for further study

Billo, E.J. (2011) *Excel for Chemists: A Comprehensive Guide*, 3rd edn. Wiley, Chichester.

Briscoe, M.H. (1996) *Preparing Scientific Illustrations: A Guide to Better Posters, Presentations and Publications.* Springer-Verlag, New York.

Currell, G. and Dowman, T. (2009) *Essential Mathematics and Statistics for Science*, 2nd edn. Wiley, Chichester.

De Levie, R. (2001) *How to use Excel in Analytical Chemistry and in General Scientific Data Analysis.* Cambridge University Press, Cambridge.

Miller, J.N. and Miller, J.C. (2010) *Statistics and Chemometrics for Analytical Chemistry*, 6th edn. Prentice Hall, Harlow.

More Charts, Graphs and Tables (2000). Open University, Milton Keynes.

Study exercises

52.1 Select appropriate graphical presentations (see also study exercise 51.2, p. 482). Choose an appropriate graphical form for each of the following examples:

(a) Correlation between drug concentration and peak area.
(b) Proportion of different fingerprint class characteristics in a survey of undergraduates attending your university.

(c) Relationship between growth rate and drugs in maggots.
(d) Number of sperm heads per field of view for several different evidential samples.

52.2 Find examples of misleading graphs. Create a portfolio of examples of misleading graphs taken from newspapers. For each graph, state what aspect is misleading (see Box 52.3) and, where possible, attempt to show the data correctly in a new graph.

A table is often the most appropriate way to present numerical data in a concise, accurate and structured form. Assignments and project reports should contain tables that have been designed to condense and display results in a meaningful way and to aid numerical comparison. The preparation of tables for recording primary data is discussed on p. 456.

Decide whether you need a table or a graph. Histograms and plotted curves can be used to give a visual impression of the relationships within your data (pp. 484–485). On the other hand, a table gives you the opportunity to make detailed numerical comparisons.

 Always remember that the primary purpose of your table is to communicate information and allow appropriate comparison, not simply to put down the results on paper.

Preparation of tables

Title

Every table must have a brief descriptive title. If several tables are used, number them consecutively so they can be quoted in your text. The titles within a report should be compared with one another, making sure they are logical and consistent and that they describe accurately the numerical data contained within them.

Structure

Display the components of each table in a way that will help the reader understand your data and grasp the significance of your results. Organise the columns so that each category of like numbers or attributes is listed vertically, while each horizontal row shows a different experimental treatment, class of drug, recovery, etc. (as in Table 53.1). Where appropriate, put control values near the beginning of the table. Columns that need to be compared should be set out alongside each other. Use rulings to subdivide your table appropriately, but avoid cluttering it up with too many lines.

Alternatives to tables for presenting numerical data – *if you have only a few numbers, consider simply presenting these within the text. An alternative approach is to show the data values on a graph.*

Constructing titles – *it is a common mistake in student practical reports to present tables without titles, or to misconstruct the title. Take care.*

Saving space in tables – *you may be able to omit a column of control data if your results can be expressed as percentages of the corresponding control values.*

Table 53.1 Analytical results for drugs in blood plasma

Class of drug	Name of drug	% recoveries	
		SPE–HPLC–UV	LLE–HPLC–APCI–MS
Benzodiazepines	Diazepam	92.4	89.2
	Temazepam	90.2	83.1
	Oxazepam	92.3	86.5
Opiates	Morphine	83.4	78.2
	Codeine	87.6	74.2
	Acetylcodeine	88.4	79.8

SPE–HPLC–UV: solid phase extraction followed by high-performance liquid chromatography separation with ultraviolet detection.
LLE–HPLC–APCI–MS: Liquid–liquid extraction followed by high-performance liquid chromatography separation with atmospheric pressure chemical ionisation mass spectrometry detection.

Examples If you measured the width of a fibre to the nearest one-tenth of a micrometre, quote the value in the form '52.6 μm'.

Quote the width of a fibre as 52.6 μm, rather than 0.0000526 m or 52.6 × 10^{-6}m.

Saving further space in tables – in some instances a footnote can be used to replace a whole column of repetitive data.

Using computers and word processing packages – these can be used to prepare high-quality versions of tables for project work (p. 463). (See also Box 53.2.)

Headings and subheadings

These should identify each set of data and show the units of measurement, where necessary. Make sure that each column is wide enough for the headings and for the longest data value.

Numerical data

Within the table, do not quote values to more significant figures than necessary, as this will imply spurious accuracy (p. 15). By careful choice of appropriate units for each column, you should aim to present numerical data within the range 0 to 1,000. As with graphs, it is less ambiguous to use derived SI units with the appropriate prefixes, in the headings of columns and rows, rather than quoting multiplying factors as powers of 10. Alternatively, include exponents in the main body of the table (see Table 9.1), to avoid any possible confusion regarding the use of negative powers of 10.

Other notations

Avoid using dashes in numerical tables, as their meaning is unclear – enter a zero reading as '0' and use 'NT' not tested or 'ND' if no data value was obtained, with a footnote to explain each abbreviation. Other footnotes, identified by asterisks, superscripts or other symbols in the table, may be used to provide relevant experimental detail (if not given in the text) and an explanation of column headings and individual results, where appropriate. Footnotes should be as condensed as possible. Table 53.1 provides examples.

Statistics

In tables where the dispersion of each data set is shown by an appropriate statistical parameter, you must state whether this is the (sample) standard deviation, the standard error (of the mean) or the 95% confidence limits, and you must give the value of n (the number of replicates). Other descriptive statistics should be quoted with similar detail, and hypothesis-testing statistics should be quoted along with the value of P (the probability). Details of any test used should be given in the legend, or in a footnote.

Text

Sometimes a table can be a useful way of presenting textual information in a condensed form (see examples on pp. 58 and 87).

When you have finished compiling your tabulated data, carefully double-check each numerical entry against the original information, to ensure that the final version of your table is free from transcription errors. Box 53.1 gives a checklist for the major elements of constructing a table.

Box 53.1 Checklist for preparing a table

Every table should have the following components:

- **a title,** plus a reference number and date where necessary;
- **headings for each column and row,** with appropriate units of measurement;
- **data values,** quoted to the nearest significant figure and with statistical parameters, according to your requirements;
- **footnotes** to explain abbreviations, modifications and individual details;
- **rulings to emphasise groupings** and distinguish items from each other.

Box 53.2 How to use a word processor (Microsoft Word 2016) or a spreadsheet (Microsoft Excel 2016) to create a table

Creating tables with Microsoft Word – word-processed tables are suitable for text-intensive or number-intensive tables, although in the second case entering data can be laborious. When working in this way, the natural way to proceed is to create the 'shell' of the table, add the data, and then carry out final formatting on the table.

1. **Move the cursor to the desired position in your document** – this is where you expect the top left corner of your table to appear. Click the Insert icon, then choose Table.

2. **Select the appropriate number of columns and rows** – don't forget to add rows and columns for headings. As default, a full-width table will appear, with single rulings for all cell boundaries, with all columns of equal width and all rows of equal height.

   Example of a 4 × 3 table:

3. **Customise the columns** – by placing the cursor over the vertical rulings then 'dragging', you can adjust their width to suit your heading text entries, which should now be added.

Heading 1	Heading 2	Heading 3	Heading 4

4. **Work through the table adding the data** – entries can be numbers or text.

Heading 1	Heading 2	Heading 3	Heading 4
xx	xx	xx	xx
xx	xx	xx	

5. **Make further adjustments to column and row widths to suit** – for example, if text fills several rows within a cell, consider increasing the column width, and if a column contains only single or double-digit numbers, consider shrinking its width. To combine cells, first highlight them, then right-click the mouse button and click on Merge cells. You may wish to reposition text within a cell by right-clicking the mouse button and choosing an appropriate position in the cell alignment menu.

Heading 1	Heading 2	Heading 3	Heading 4
xx	xx	xx	xx
	xx	xx	

6. **Finally, remove selected borders to cells** – one way is to highlight the table, then click on the Design icon and choose an appropriate style from the template options. If you don't want any shading, click on Design > Shading and choose No colour. Another way is to highlight the cells in the table, then right-click the mouse button and choose Borders and shading. You can choose the style you wish from this submenu so that your table looks like the examples shown in this chapter.

7. **Add a table title** – this should be positioned above the table (cf. a figure title and legend, p. 493), legend and footnotes.

Final version of the table:

Table xx. A table of some data

Heading 1	Heading 2	Heading 3	Heading 4
xx	xx	xx	xx
	xx	xx	

[a]An example of a footnote.

Box 53.2 (continued)

Creating tables with Microsoft Excel – tables derived from spreadsheets are effective when you have lots of numerical data, especially when these are stored or created using the spreadsheet itself. When working in this way, you can design the table as part of an output or summary section of the spreadsheet, add explanatory headings, format, then possibly export to a word processor when complete.

1. **Design the output or summary section** – plan this as if it were a table, including adding text headings within cells.

17				
18	Heading 1	Heading 2	Heading 3	Heading 4
19				
20				
21				
22				

2. **Insert appropriate formulae within cells to produce data** – if necessary, formulae should draw on the other parts of the spreadsheet.

17				
18	Heading 1	Heading 2	Heading 3	Heading 4
19	Aaa	=A1	=C3*5	=SDEV(A1:A12)
20	Bbb	=A2	=F45/G12	=SDEV(B1:B12)
21				
22				

3. **Format the cells** – this is important to control the number of decimal places presented. Use Format cells > Number.

4. **Adjust column width to suit** – you can do this via the column headings, by placing the cursor over the rulings between columns then 'dragging'.

17				
18	Heading 1	Heading 2	Heading 3	Heading 4
19	Aaa	=A1	=C3*5	=SDEV(A1:A12)
20	Bbb	=A2	=F45/G12	=SDEV(B1:B12)
21				
22				

5. **Add rulings as appropriate** – click Home and then choose an appropriate template in the Format as table menu in the Styles subsection, or use the Borders menu on the toolbar (Home > Font), as described above.

17				
18	Heading 1	Heading 2	Heading 3	Heading 4
19	Aaa	=A1	=C3*5	=SDEV(A1:A12)
20	Bbb	=A2	=F45/G12	=SDEV(B1:B12)
21				

The table can now be copied and pasted to a Word document.

Sources for further study

Evergreen, S.D.H. (2014) *Presenting Data Effectively: Communicating Your Findings for Maximum Impact.* SAGE Publishing, California.

Kirkup, L. (1995) *Experimental Methods: An Introduction to the Analysis and Presentation of Data.* Wiley, New York.

Lambert, J. (2015) *Microsoft Office 2016 Step by Step.* Microsoft Press, Washington.

MacFarland, T.W. (2014) *Introduction to Data Analysis and Graphical Presentation in Biostatistics with R: Statistics in the Large.* Springer International Publishing, Cham.

Walkenbach, J. (2015) *Excel 2016 Bible.* Wiley, Chichester.

Study exercises

53.1 Redesign a table of data. Using the following example, redraft the table to improve layout and correct inconsistencies.

Concentrations of drug and metabolites found in a blood sample

Diazepam	0.2	$\mu g\ L^{-1}$
Desmethyl diazepam	0.075	$\mu g\ ml^{-1}$
Temazepam	0.1	$mg\ L^{-1}$
Methadone	0.23	$\mu g\ ml^{-1}$
Alcohol	86	$mg\ 100\ mL^{-1}$
Caffeine	–	–
Nicotine	–	–

* Nicotine and caffeine were not quantified.

53.2 Devise a text-based table. After reading through this chapter, and working from memory, draw up a table listing the principal components of a typical table in the first column, and brief comments on the major features of each component in the second column.

Science often requires a numerical or statistical approach. Not only is mathematical modelling an important aid to understanding, but computations are often needed to turn raw data into meaningful information or to compare them with other data sets. Moreover, calculations are part of laboratory routine, perhaps required for making up solutions of known concentration (see p. 47 and below), or for the calibration of a microscope (see p. 74). In research studies and project work, 'trial' calculations can reveal what input data are required and where errors in their measurement might be amplified in the final result (see p. 164).

 KEY POINT *If you find numerical work difficult, practising problem-solving is especially important.*

Practising at problem-solving:

- **demystifies the procedures involved,** which are normally just the elementary mathematical operations of addition, subtraction, multiplication and division (Table 54.1);
- **allows you to gain confidence** so that you don't become confused when confronted with an unfamiliar or apparently complex form of problem;
- **helps you recognise** the various forms a problem can take , such as crossing experiments in classical genetics.

Table 54.1 Sets of numbers and operations

Sets of numbers	
Whole numbers:	0, 1, 2, 3, ...
Natural numbers:	1, 2, 3, ...
Integers:	... −3, −2, −1, 0, 1, 2, 3, ...
Real numbers:	integers and anything between (e.g. −5, 4.376, 3/16, π, $\sqrt{5}$)
Prime numbers:	subset of natural numbers divisible by 1 and themselves only (i.e. 2, 3, 5, 7, 11, 13, ...)
Rational numbers:	p/q where p (integer) and q (natural) have no common factor (e.g. 3/4)
Fractions:	p/q where p is an integer and q is natural (e.g. −6/8)
Irrational numbers:	real numbers with no exact value (e.g. π)
Infinity:	(symbol ∞) is larger than any number (technically not a number as it does not obey the laws of algebra)
Operations and symbols	
Basic operators:	$+, -, \times$ and $\div$ will not need explanation; however, / may substitute for $\div$ and * may substitute for $\times$ or this operator may be omitted
Powers:	a^n, i.e. 'a to the power n', means a multiplied by itself n times (e.g. $a^2 = a \times a =$ 'a squared', $a^3 = a \times a \times a =$ 'a cubed'). n is said to be the index or exponent. Note $a^0 = 1$ and $a^1 = a$
Logarithms:	the common logarithm (log) of any number x is the power to which 10 would have to be raised to give x (i.e. the log of 100 is 2; $10^2 = 100$); the antilog of x is 10^x. Note that there is no log for 0, so take this into account when drawing log axes by breaking the axis. Natural or Napierian logarithms (ln) use the base e (= 2.71828...) instead of 10
Reciprocals:	the reciprocal of a real number a is $1/a$ $(a \neq 0)$
Relational operators:	$a > b$ means 'a is greater (more positive) than b', $<$ means less than, $\leq$ means less-than-or-equal-to and $\geq$ means greater-than-or-equal-to
Proportionality:	$a \propto b$ means 'a is proportional to b' (i.e. $a = kb$, where k is a constant). If $\propto 1/b$, a is inversely proportional to b $(a = k/b)$
Sums:	$\sum_{x_i}$ is shorthand for the sum of all x values from $i = 0$ to $i = n$ (more correctly the range of the sum is specified under the symbol)
Moduli:	$\|x\|$ signifies modulus of x, i.e. its absolute value (e.g. $\|4\| = \|-4\| = 4$)
Factorials:	$x!$ signifies factorial x, the product of all integers from 1 to x (e.g. 3! = 6). Note 0! = 1! = 1

Table 54.2 Simple algebra – rules for manipulating

If $a = b + c$, then $b = a - c$ and $c = a - b$

If $a = b \times c$, then $b = a \div c$ and $c = a \div b$

If $a = b^c$, then $b = a^{1/c}$ and $c = \log a \div \log b$

$a^{1/n} = \sqrt[n]{a}$

$a^{-n} = 1 \div a^n$

$a^b \times a^c = a^{(b+c)}$ and $a^b \div a^c = a^{(b-c)}$

$(a^b)c = a^{(b \times c)}$

$a \times b = \text{antilog} (\log a + \log b)$

Steps in tackling a numerical problem

The step-by-step approach outlined below may not be the fastest method of arriving at an answer, but most mistakes occur when steps are missing, combined or not made obvious – so a logical approach is often better. Error tracing is distinctly easier when all the stages in a calculation are laid out.

Have the right tools ready

Scientific calculators greatly simplify the numerical part of problem-solving. However, the seeming infallibility of the calculator may lead you to accept an absurd result that could have arisen because of faulty key-pressing or faulty logic. Make sure you know how to use all the features on your calculator, especially how the memory works, how to introduce a constant multiplier or divider and how to obtain an exponent (note that the 'exp' button on most calculators gives you 10^x, not 1^x or y^x; so 1×10^6 would be entered as $\boxed{1}\ \boxed{\text{exp}}\ \boxed{6}$, *not* $\boxed{10}\ \boxed{\text{exp}}\ \boxed{6}$).

Approach the problem thoughtfully

If the individual steps have been laid out on a worksheet, the 'tactics' will already have been decided. It is more difficult when you have to adopt a strategy on your own, especially if the problem is presented as a story and it isn't obvious which equations or rules need to be applied.

- **Read the problem carefully** as the text may give clues as to how it should be tackled. Be certain of what is required as an answer before starting.
- **Analyse what kind of problem it is,** which effectively means deciding which equation(s) or approach will be applicable. If this is not obvious, consider the dimensions/units of the information available and think how they could be fitted to a relevant formula. In examinations, a favourite ploy of examiners is to present a problem such that the familiar form of an equation must be rearranged (see Table 54.2 and Box 54.1). If you are unsure whether a recalled formula is correct, a dimensional analysis can help – write in all the units for the variables and make sure that they cancel out to give the expected answer.
- **Check that you have, or can derive, all of the information required** to use your chosen equation(s). It is unusual but not unknown for examiners to supply redundant information. So, if you decide not to use some of the information given, be sure why you do not require it.
- **Decide in what format and units the answer should be presented.** This is sometimes suggested to you. If the problem requires many changes in the prefixes to units, it is a good idea to convert all data to base SI units (multiplied by a power of 10) at the outset.
- **If a problem appears complex,** break it down into component parts.

Present your answer clearly

The way you present your answer obviously needs to fit the individual problem. Multiple examples are shown throughout this book that illustrate several important points. Guidelines for presenting an answer include:

1. **Make your assumptions explicit.** Most mathematical models of biological phenomena require that certain criteria are met before they can be legitimately applied (e.g. 'assuming the tissue is homogeneous. . . '), while some approaches involve approximations that should be clearly stated (e.g. 'to estimate the mouse's skin area, its body was approximated to a cylinder with radius x and height y . . . ').

Hints for solving numerical problems

Box 54.1 Example of using the rules of Table 54.2

Problem: if $a = (b - c) \div (d + e^n)$, **find** e

1. Multiply both sides by $(d + e^n)$; formula becomes: $a(d + e^n) = (b - c)$

2. Divide both sides by a; formula becomes: $d + e^n = \dfrac{b - c}{a}$

3. Subtract d from both sides; formula becomes: $e^n = \dfrac{b - c}{a} - d$

4. Raise each side to the power $1/n$; formula becomes: $e = \dfrac{b - c}{a} - d^{1/n}$

Units – *never write any answer without its unit(s) unless it is truly dimensionless.*

Rounding off – *do not round off numbers until you arrive at the final answer.*

2. **Explain your strategy for answering,** perhaps giving the applicable formula or definitions that suit the approach to be taken. Give details of what the symbols mean (and their units) at this point.
3. **Rearrange the formula to the required form** with the desired unknown on the left-hand side (see Table 54.2).
4. **Substitute the relevant values into the right-hand side of the formula,** using the units and prefixes as given (it may be convenient to convert values to SI beforehand). Convert prefixes to appropriate powers of 10 as soon as possible.
5. **Convert to the desired units step-by-step,** i.e. taking each variable in turn.
6. **When you have the answer in the desired units,** rewrite the left-hand side and underline the answer. Make sure that the result is presented with an appropriate number of significant figures (see below).

Check your answer

Having written out your answer, you should check it methodically, answering the following questions:

- **Is the answer of a realistic magnitude**? You should be alerted to an error if an answer is absurdly large or small. In repeated calculations, a result standing out from others in the same series should be double-checked.
- **Do the units make sense and match up with the answer required**? Don't, for example, present a volume in units of m^2.
- **Do you get the same answer if you recalculate in a different way**? If you have time, recalculate the answer using a different 'route', entering the numbers into your calculator in a different form and/or carrying out the operations in a different order.

Rounding: decimal places and significant figures

In many instances, the answer you produce as a result of a calculation will include more figures than is justified by the accuracy and precision (p. 15) of the original data. Sometimes you will be asked to produce an answer to a specified number of decimal places or significant figures, and other times you will be expected to decide for yourself what would be appropriate.

Examples

The number 4.123 correct to two decimal places is 4.12
The number 4.126 correct to two decimal places is 4.13
The number 4.1251 correct to two decimal places is 4.13
The number 4.1250 correct to two decimal places is 4.12
The number 4.1350 correct to two decimal places is 4.14
The number 99.99 correct to one decimal place is 100.0

Examples

The number of significant figures in 194 is three.
The number of significant figures in 2,305 is four.
The number of significant figures in 0.003482 is four.
The number of significant figures in 210×10^8 is three (21×10^9 would be two).

Examples

The number of significant figures in 3,051.93 is six.
To five significant figures, this number is 3,051.9
To four significant figures, this number is 3,052
To three significant figures, this number is 3,050
To two significant figures, this number is 3,100
To one significant figure, this number is 3,000
3,051.93 to the nearest 10 is 3,050
3,051.93 to the nearest 100 is 3,100

Note that in this last case you must include the zeros before the decimal point to indicate the scale of the number (even if the decimal point is not shown). For a number less than 1, the same would apply to the zeros before the decimal point. For example, 0.00305193 to three significant figures is 0.00305. Alternatively, use scientific notation (in this case, 3.05×10^{-3}).

 KEY POINT *Do not simply accept the numerical answer from a calculator or spreadsheet, without considering whether you need to modify this to give an appropriate number of significant figures or decimal places.*

Rounding to n decimal places

This is relatively easy to do.

1. **Look at the number to the right of the *n*th decimal place.**
2. **If this is less than five,** simply 'cut off' all numbers to the right of the *n*th decimal place to produce the answer (i.e. round down).
3. **If the number is greater than five,** 'cut off' all numbers to the right of the *n*th decimal place and add one to the *n*th decimal place to produce the answer (i.e. round up).
4. **If the number is 5,** then look at further numbers to the right to determine whether to round up or not.
5. **If the number is *exactly* 5** (i.e. there are no further numbers to the right), then round to the nearest *even* *n*th decimal number (round to the nearest even number). *Note:* When considering a large number of calculations, this procedure will not affect the overall mean value. Some rounding systems do the opposite to this (i.e. round to the nearest odd number), while others always round up where the number is exactly 5 (which *will* affect the mean). Take advice from your tutor and stick to one system throughout a series of calculations.

Whenever you see any numbers quoted, you should assume that the last digit has been rounded. For example, in the number 22.4, the '.4' is assumed to be rounded and the calculated value may have been between 22.35 and 22.45.

Quoting to n significant figures

The number of significant figures indicates the degree of approximation in the number. For most cases, it is given by counting all the figures except zeros that occur at the beginning or end of the number. Zeros *within* the number are always counted as significant. The number of significant figures in a number like 200 is ambiguous and could be one, two or three; if you wish to specify clearly, then quote as e.g. 2×10^2 (one significant figure), 2.0×10^2 (two significant figures), etc. When quoting a number to a specified number of significant figures, use the same rules as for rounding to a specified number of decimal places, but do not forget to keep zeros before or after the decimal point. The same principle is used if you are asked to quote a number to the 'nearest 10', 'nearest 100', etc.

When deciding for yourself how many significant figures to use, adopt the following rules of thumb:

- **Always round *after* you have done a calculation.** Use all significant figures available in the measured data during a calculation.
- **If adding or subtracting with measured data,** then quote the answer to the number of decimal places in the data value with the least number of decimal places (e.g. $32.1 - 45.67 + 35.6201 = 22.1$, because 32.1 has one decimal place).
- **If multiplying or dividing with measured data,** keep as many significant figures as are in the number with the least number of significant places (e.g. $34,901 \div 3,445 \times 1.3410344 = 13.59$, because 3,445 has four significant figures).

Examples
1/8 as a percentage is
$1 \div 8 \times 100 = 100 \div 8 = 12.5\%$
0.602 as a percentage is
$0.602 \times 100 = 60.2\%$

Examples
190% as a decimal fraction is
$190 \div 100 = 1.9$
5/2 as a percentage is $5 \div 2 \times 100 = 250\%$

Example A population falls from 4 million to 3.85 million. What is the percentage change? The decrease in numbers is $4 - 3.85 = -0.15$ million. The fractional decrease is $-0.15 \div 4 = -0.0375$ and we multiply by 100 to get the percentage change = minus 3.75%.

Take care with percentages – *for example, if a number was increased by 50% and then decreased by 50%, it would not return to the original value (e.g.* $200 + 100 (50\%) = 300 - 150 (50\%) = 150$).

Example $2^3 = 2 \times 2 \times 2 = 8$

Example Avogadro's number,
$\approx 602,352,000,000,000,000,000,000$,
is more conveniently expressed as
6.02352×10^{23}

- **For the purposes of significant figures,** assume 'constants' have an infinite number of significant figures.

Some reminders of basic mathematics

Errors in calculations sometimes appear because of faults in mathematics rather than computational errors. For reference purposes, Tables 54.1 and 54.2 give some basic mathematical principles that may be useful. Eason *et al.* (1992) should be consulted for more advanced needs.

Percentages and proportions

A percentage is just a fraction expressed in terms of hundredths, indicated by putting the percentage sign (%) after the number of hundredths. So, 35% simply means 35 hundredths. To convert a fraction to a percentage, just multiply the fraction by 100. When the fraction is in decimal form, multiplying by 100 to obtain a percentage is easily achieved just by moving the decimal point two places to the right.

To convert a percentage to a fraction, just remember that, since a percentage is a fraction multiplied by 100, the fraction is the percentage divided by 100. For example, $42\% = 42/100 = 0.42$. In this example, since we are dealing with a decimal fraction, the division by 100 is just a matter of moving the decimal point two places to the left (42% could be written as 42.0%). Percentages greater than 100% represent fractions greater than 1. Percentages less than 1 may cause confusion. For example, 0.5% means half of 1% (0.005) and must not be confused with 50% (which is the decimal fraction 0.5).

To find a percentage of a given number, just express the percentage as a decimal fraction and multiply the given number. For example, 35% of 500 is given by $0.35 \times 500 = 175$. To find the percentage change in a quantity, work out the difference (= value 'after' −value 'before'), and divide this difference by the original value to give the fractional change, then multiply by 100.

Exponents

Exponential notation is an alternative way of expressing numbers in the form a^n ('a to the power n'), where a is multiplied by itself n times. The number a is called the base and the number n the exponent (or power or index). The exponent need not be a whole number, and it can be negative if the number being expressed is less than 1. See Table 54.2 for other mathematical relationships involving exponents.

Scientific notation

In scientific notation, also known as 'standard form', the base is 10 and the exponent a whole number. To express numbers that are not whole powers of 10, the form $c \times 10^n$ is used, where the coefficient c is normally between 1 and 10. Scientific notation is valuable when you are using very large numbers and wish to avoid suggesting spurious accuracy. Thus if you write 123,000 this may suggest that you know the number to ± 0.5, whereas 1.23×10^5 might give a truer indication of measurement accuracy (i.e. implied to be ± 500 in this case). Engineering notation is similar, but treats numbers as powers of ten in groups of 3, i.e. $c \times 10^0, 10^3, 10^6, 10^9$, etc. This corresponds to the SI system of prefixes (p. 24).

A useful property of powers when expressed to the same base is that when multiplying two numbers together you simply add the powers, while if dividing

Example (Use to check the correct use of your own calculator)
102,963 as a log $= 5.012681$ *(to six decimal places)*
$10^{5.012681} = 102,962.96$
(Note loss of accuracy due to loss of decimal places.)

you subtract the powers. Thus, suppose you counted eight bacteria in a 10^{-7} dilution (see p. 47), there would be 8×10^7 in the same volume of undiluted solution; if you now dilute this 500-fold (5×10^2), then the number present in the same volume would be $8/5 \times 10^{(7-2)} = 1.6 \times 10^5 = 160,000$.

Logarithms

When a number is expressed as a logarithm, this refers to the power n that the base number a must be raised to give that number, e.g. $\log_{10}(1,000) = 3$, since $10^3 = 1,000$. Any base could be used, but the two most common are 10, when the power is referred to as $\log_{10}$ or simply log, and the constant e (2.718 282), used for mathematical convenience in certain situations, when the power is referred to as $\log_e$ or ln. Note that logs need not be whole numbers; there is no log value for the number zero; and that $\log_{10} = 0$ for the number 1.

To obtain logs, you will need to use the log key on your calculator, or special log tables (now largely redundant). To convert back ('antilog'), use:

- the $\boxed{10^x}$ key, with $x = $ log value;
- the $\boxed{\text{inverse}}$ then the $\boxed{\text{log}}$ key; or
- the $\boxed{y^x}$ key, with $y = 10$ and $x = $ log value.

If you used log tables, you will find complementary antilogarithm tables to do this.

There are many uses of logarithms in biology, including pH ($= -\log[H^+]$), where $[H^+]$ is expressed in mol L^{-1} (see p. 57) and the exponential (logarithmic) growth of microorganisms.

Linear functions and straight lines

One of the most straightforward and widely used relationships between two variables x and y is that represented by a straight-line graph, where the corresponding mathematical function is known as the equation of a straight line, where:

$$y = a + bx \qquad [54.1]$$

In this relationship, a represents the intercept of the line on the y (vertical) axis, i.e. where $x = 0$, and therefore $bx = 0$, while b is equivalent to the slope (gradient) of the line, i.e. the change in y for a change in x of 1. The constants a and b are sometimes given alternative symbols, but the mathematics remains unchanged, e.g. in the equivalent expression for the slope of a straight line, $y = mx + c$. Figure 54.1 shows what happens when these two constants are changed, in terms of the resultant straight lines.

The two main applications of the straight-line relationship are:

1. **Function fitting** – here, you determine the mathematical form of the function, i.e. you estimate the constants a and b from a data set for x and y, either by drawing a straight line by eye and then working out the slope and y intercept, or by using linear regression (p. 525) to obtain the most probable values for both constants. When putting a straight line of best fit by eye on a hand-drawn graph, note the following:
   - **Always use a transparent ruler,** so you can see data points on either side of the line.
   - **For a data series where the points do not fit a perfect straight line,** try to have an equal number of points on either side of the line, as in Fig. 54.2(a), and try to minimise the average distance of these points from the line.

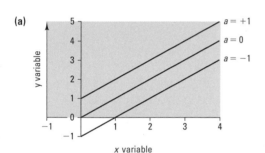

(a)

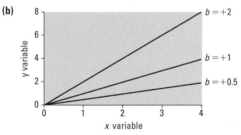

(b)

Fig. 54.1 Straight-line relationships ($y = a + bx$), showing the effects of (a) changing the intercept at constant slope, and (b) changing the slope at constant intercept.

Hints for solving numerical problems

(a)

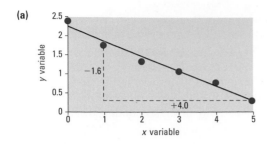

(b)

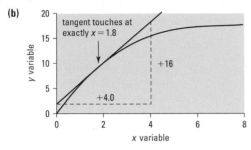

Fig. 54.2 Drawing straight lines: (a) simple linear relationship, giving a straight line with an intersect of 2.3 and a slope of $-1.6 \div 4.0 = 0.4$; (b) tangent drawn to a curve at $x = 1.8$, giving a slope of $16 \div 4 = 4$.

Examples

Using eqn [54.1], the predicted value for y for a linear function where $a = 2$ and $b = 0.5$, where $x = 8$ is:
$y = 2 + (0.5 \times 8) = 6$.
Using eqn [54.2], the predicted value for x for a linear function where $a = 1.5$ and $b = 2.5$, where $y = -8.5$ is:
$x = (-8.5 - 1.5) \div 2.5 = -4$.
Using eqn [54.2] the predicted x intercept for a linear function where $a = 0.8$ and $b = 3.2$ is: $x = (0 - 0.8) \div 3.2 = -0.25$.

Example (unitary method) A lab schedule states that 5 g of a compound with a relative molecular mass of 220 are dissolved in 400 mL of solvent. For writing up your Materials and Methods, you wish to express this as mol L^{-1}.

1. If there are 5 g in 400 mL, then there are $5 \div 400$ g in 1 mL.
2. Hence, 1,000 mL will contain
   $5 \div 400 \times 1,000$ g $= 12.5$ g.
3. 12.5 g $= 12.5 \div 220$ mol $= 0.0568$ mol, so [solution]
   $= 56.8$ mmol L^{-1} ($= 56.8$ mol m^{-3}).

- **Once you have drawn the line of best fit, use this line,** rather than your data values, in all subsequent procedures (e.g. in a calibration curve, Chapter 51).
- **Tangents drawn to a curve give the slope (gradient) at a particular point,** e.g. in an enzyme reaction progress curve. These are best drawn by bringing your ruler up to the curve at the exact point where you wish to estimate the slope and then trying to make the two angles immediately on either side of this point approximately the same, by eye (Fig. 54.2(b)).
- **Once you have drawn the straight line,** or tangent, choose two points reasonably far apart at either end of your line and then draw construction lines to represent the change in y and the change in x between these two points – make sure that your construction lines are perpendicular to each other. Determine the slope as the change in y divided by the change in x (Fig. 54.2).

2. **Prediction** – where a and b are known, or have been estimated, you can use eqn [54.1] to predict any value of y for a specified value of x, for example during exponential growth of a cell culture, where $\log_{10}$ cell number (y) increases as a linear function of time (x) – note that in this example the dependent variable has been transformed to give a linear relationship. You will need to rearrange eqn [54.1] in cases where a prediction of x is required for a particular value of y (e.g. in calibration curves, Chapter 51, or bioassays), as follows:

$$x = (y - a) \div b \qquad [54.2]$$

This equation can also be used to determine the intercept on the x (horizontal) axis, i.e. where $y = 0$.

Hints for some typical problems

Calculations involving proportions or ratios

The 'unitary method' is a useful way of approaching calculations involving proportions or ratios, such as those required when making up solutions from stocks (see also Chapter 6) or as a subsidiary part of longer calculations.

1. **If given a value for a multiple,** work out the corresponding value for a single item or unit.
2. **Use this 'unitary value'** to calculate the required new value.

Calculations involving series

Series (such as those used in dilutions, see also p. 47) can be of three main forms:

1. **arithmetic** – where the *difference* between two successive numbers in the series is a constant (e.g. 2, 4, 6, 8, 10, . . .);
2. **geometric** – where the *ratio* between two successive numbers in the series is a constant (e.g. 1, 10, 100, 1,000, 10,000, . . .);
3. **harmonic** – where the values are reciprocals of successive whole numbers (e.g. 1, $\frac{1}{2}$, $\frac{1}{3}$, $\frac{1}{4}$, . . .).

Note that the logs of the numbers in a geometric series will form an arithmetic series (e.g. 0, 1, 2, 3, 4, . . . in the above case). Thus, if a quantity y varies with a quantity x such that the rate of change in y is proportional to the value of y (i.e. it varies in an exponential manner), a semi-log plot of such data will form a straight line. This form of relationship is relevant for exponentially growing cell cultures and radioactive decay.

Statistical calculations

The need for long, complex calculations in statistics has largely been removed because of the widespread use of spreadsheets with statistical functions (Chapter 49) and specialised programs such as Minitab® (p. 463). It is, however, important to understand the principles behind what you are trying to do (see Chapters 51 and 55) and interpret the program's output correctly, either using the 'help' function or a reference manual.

Problems in Mendelian genetics

These cause difficulties for many students. The key is to recognise the different types of problem and to practise so you are familiar with the techniques for solving them (see Chapter 13).

Text reference

Eason, G., Coles, C.W. and Gettinby, G. (1992) *Mathematics and Statistics for the Bio-Sciences*. Ellis Horwood, Chichester.

Sources for further study

Adam, C. (2010) *Essential Mathematics and Statistics for Forensic Science*. Wiley, Chichester.

Harris, D.C. (2016) *Qualitative Chemical Analysis*, 9th edn. W.H Freeman & Company, New York.

Lucy, D. (2006) *Introduction to Statistics for Forensic Scientists*. Wiley, Chichester.

Miller, J.N. and Miller, J.C. (2010) *Statistics and Chemometrics for Analytical Chemistry*, 6th edn. Prentice Hall, Harlow.

Monk, P. and Munro, L.J. (2010) *Maths for Chemists: A Chemists' Toolkit of Calculations*. Oxford University Press, Oxford.

Study exercises

54.1 Rearrange a simple formula. The Beer–Lambert relationship, eqn [16.3] (p. 154), is written in the form $A = \varepsilon l\,[C]$. Rearrange, in the form:

(a) $[C] =$;   (b) $\varepsilon =$

54.2 Rearrange the following formulae:

(a) If $y = ax + b$, find b;
(b) If $y = ax + b$, find x.

54.3 Work with decimal places or significant figures. Give the following numbers to the accuracy indicated:

(a) 214.51 to three significant figures;
(b) 107,029 to three significant figures;
(c) 0.0450 to one significant figure;
(d) 99.817 to two decimal places;
(e) 99.897 to two decimal places;
(f) 99.997 to two decimal places;
(g) 6,255 to the nearest 10;
(h) 134,903 to the nearest ten thousand.

State the following:

(i) the number of significant figures in 3,400;
(j) the number of significant figures in 3,400.3;
(k) the number of significant figures in 0.001 67;
(l) the number of significant figures in 1.001 67;
(m) the number of decimal places in 34.46;
(n) the number of decimal places in 0.001 67.

54.4 Practise working with linear functions (note also that Chapter 51 includes study exercises based on linear functions and plotting straight lines). Assuming a linear relationship between x and y, calculate the following (giving your answers to three significant figures):

(a) x, where $y = 7.0$, $a = 4.5$ and $b = 0.02$;
(b) x, where $y = 15.2$, $a = -2.6$ and $b = -4.46$;
(c) y, where $x = 10.5$, $a = 0.2$ and $b = -0.63$;
(d) y, where $x = 4.5$, $a = -1.8$ and $b = 4.1$.

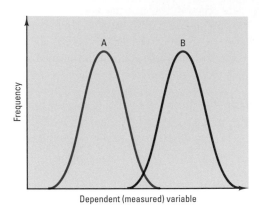

Fig. 55.1 Two distributions with different locations but the same dispersion. The data set labelled B could have been obtained by adding a constant to each datum in the data set labelled A.

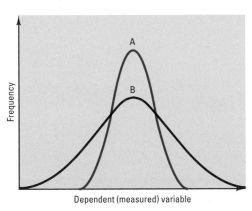

Fig. 55.2 Two distributions with different dispersions but the same location. The data set labelled A covers a relatively narrow range of values of the dependent (measured) variable, while that labelled B covers a wider range.

Example Box 55.1 shows a set of data and the calculated values of the measures of location, dispersion and shape for which methods of calculation are outlined here. Check your understanding by calculating the statistics yourself and confirming that you arrive at the same answers.

Whether obtained from observation or experimentation, most scientific data exhibit variability. This can be displayed as a frequency distribution. Descriptive (or summary) statistics are useful because they enable you to quantify aspects of the frequency distribution of a sample. You can use them to:

- **condense a large data set for presentation in figures or tables** – for example, in a practical write-up or project report;
- **provide estimates of parameters of the frequency distribution** of the population being sampled (p. 513).

KEY POINT The appropriate descriptive statistics to choose depend on both the type of data, i.e. quantitative, ranked or qualitative (p. 13), and the nature of the underlying population frequency distribution.

If you have no clear theoretical grounds for assuming what the underlying frequency distribution is like, then graph one or more sample frequency distributions, ideally with a sample size >100.

The methods used to calculate descriptive statistics depend on whether data have been grouped into classes. You should use the original data set if it is still available, because grouping into classes loses information and accuracy. However, large data sets may make calculations unwieldy, and are best handled by computer programs.

Three important features of a frequency distribution that can be summarised by descriptive statistics are:

- **the sample's location** – i.e. its position along a given dimension representing the dependent (measured) variable (Fig. 55.1);
- **the dispersion of the data** – i.e. how spread out the values are (Fig. 55.2);
- **the shape of the distribution** – i.e. whether symmetrical, skewed, U-shaped, etc. (Fig. 55.3).

Measuring location

Here, the objective is to pinpoint the 'centre' of the frequency distribution, i.e. the value about which most of the data are grouped. The chief measures of

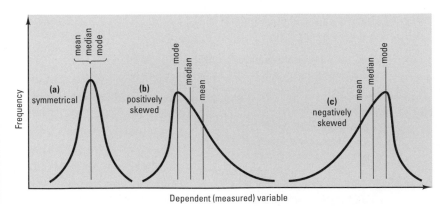

Fig. 55.3 Symmetrical and skewed frequency distributions, showing relative positions of mean, median and mode.

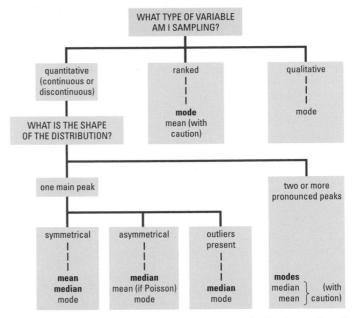

Fig. 55.4 Choosing a statistic for characterising a distribution's location. Statistics written in bold are the preferred option(s).

location are the mean, median and mode. Figure 55.4 shows how to choose among these for a given data set.

Mean

The mean (denoted $(\overline{Y})$ and also referred to as the arithmetic mean) is the average value of the data. It is obtained from the sum of all the data values divided by the number of observations (in symbolic terms, $\sum Y/n$). The mean is a good measure of the centre of symmetrical frequency distributions. It uses all of the numerical values of the sample and therefore incorporates all of the information content of the data. However, the value of a mean is greatly affected by the presence of outliers (extreme values). The arithmetic mean is a widely used statistic in science, but there are situations when you should be careful about using it (see Box 55.2 for examples).

Median

The median is the mid-point of the observations when ranked in increasing order. For odd-sized samples, the median is the middle observation; for even-sized samples it is the mean of the middle pair of observations. Where data are grouped into classes, the median can only be estimated. This is most simply done from a graph of the cumulative frequency distribution, but can also be worked out by assuming the data to be evenly spread within the class. The median may represent the location of the main body of data better than the mean when the distribution is asymmetric, or when there are outliers in the sample.

Mode

The mode is the most common value in the sample. The mode is easily found from a tabulated frequency distribution as the most frequent value. If data have been grouped into classes then the term modal class is used for the class containing most values. The mode provides a rapidly and easily found estimate of sample location and is unaffected by outliers. However, the mode is affected by chance variation in the shape of a sample's distribution and it may lie distant

---

Use of symbols – *Y is used in Chapters 55 and 56 to signify the dependent variable in statistical calculations (following the example of Sokal and Rohlf, 2011, Heath, 1995 and Wardlaw, 2000). Note, however, that some authors use X or x in analogous formulae and many calculators refer to $\overline{x}$, $\sum x^2$, etc. for their statistical functions.*

Definition

An outlier – any datum that has a value much smaller or bigger than most of the data.

Definition

Rank – the position of a data value when all the data are placed in order of ascending magnitude. If ties occur, an average rank of the tied variates is used. Thus, the rank of the datum 6 in the sequence 1, 3, 5, 6, 8, 8, 10 is 4; the rank of each datum with value 8 is 5.5.

Box 55.1 Descriptive statistics for a sample of data

Value (Y)	Frequency (f)	Cumulative frequency	fY	fY^2
1	0	0	0	0
2	1	1	2	4
3	2	3	6	18
4	3	6	12	48
5	8	14	40	200
6	5	19	30	180
7	2	21	10	98
8	0	21	0	0
Totals	$21 = \Sigma f(=n)$		$104 = \Sigma fY$	$548 = \Sigma fY^2$

In this example, for simplicity and ease of calculation, integer values of Y are used. In many practical exercises, where continuous variables are measured to several significant figures and where the number of data values is small, giving frequencies of 1 for most of the values of Y, it may be simpler to omit the column dealing with frequency and list all the individual values of Y and Y^2 in the appropriate columns. To gauge the underlying frequency distribution of such data sets, you would need to group individual data into broader classes (e.g. all values between 1.0 and 1.9, all values between 2.0 and 2.9, etc.) and then draw a histogram. Calculation of certain statistics for data sets that have been grouped in this way (e.g. median, quartiles, extremes) can be tricky and a statistical text should be consulted.

Statistic	Value*	How calculated
Mean	4.95	$\Sigma fY/n$, i.e. 104/21
Mode	5	The most common value (Y value with highest frequency)
Median	5	Value of the $(n + 1)/2$ variate, i.e. the value ranked $(21 + 1)/2 = 11$th (obtained from the cumulative frequency column)
Upper quartile	6	The upper quartile is between the 16th and 17th values, i.e. the value exceeded by 25% of the data values
Lower quartile	4	The lower quartile is between the 5th and 6th values, i.e. the value exceeded by 75% of the data values
Semi-interquartile range	1.0	Half the difference between the upper and lower quartiles, i.e. (6−4)/2
Upper extreme	7	Highest Y value in data set
Lower extreme	2	Lowest Y value in data set
Range	5	Difference between upper and lower extremes
Variance (s^2)	1.65	$s^2 = \dfrac{\Sigma fY^2 - (\Sigma fY)^2/n}{n - 1}$ $= \dfrac{548 - (104)^2/21}{20}$
Standard deviation (s)	1.28	$\sqrt{s^2}$.
Standard error (SE)	0.280	$s/\sqrt{n}$.
95% confidence limits	4.36−5.54	$\overline{Y} \pm t_{0.05}[20] \times$ SE (where $t_{0.05}[20] = 2.09$, Table 56.2)
Coefficient of variation (CoV)	25.9%	$100\, s/\overline{Y}$

* Rounded to three significant figures, except when it is an exact number.

Box 55.2 Three examples where simple arithmetic means are inappropriate

Mean	n
6	4
7	7
8	1

pH	$[H^+](mol\ L^{-1})$
6	1×10^{-6}
7	1×10^{-7}
8	1×10^{-8}
mean	3.7×10^{-7}
$-\log_{10}$ mean	6.43

1. **If means of samples are themselves meaned, an error can arise if the samples are of different size.** For example, the arithmetic mean of the means in the table shown left is 7, but this does not take account of the different 'reliabilities' of each mean due to their sample sizes. The correct weighted mean is obtained by multiplying each mean by its sample size (n) (a 'weight') and dividing the sum of these values by the total number of observations, i.e. in the case shown, $(24 + 49 + 8)/12 = 6.75$.

2. **When making a mean of ratios (e.g. percentages) for several groups of different sizes,** the ratio for the combined total of all the groups is not the mean of the proportions for the individual groups. For example, if 20 rats from a batch of 50 are male, this implies 40% are male. If 60 rats from a batch of 120 are male, this implies 50% are male. The mean percentage of males $(50 + 40)/2 = 45\%$ is *not* the percentage of males in the two groups combined, because there are $20 + 60 = 80$ males in a total of 170 rats $= 47.1\%$ approx.

3. **If the measurement scale is not linear, arithmetic means may give a false value.** For example, if three media had pH values 6, 7 and 8, the appropriate mean pH is not 7 because the pH scale is logarithmic. The definition of pH is $-\log_{10}[H+]$, where $[H+]$ is expressed in mol L^{-1} ('molar'); therefore, to obtain the true mean, convert data into $[H+]$ values (i.e. put them on a linear scale) by calculating $10^{(-pH\ value)}$ as shown. Now calculate the mean of these values and convert the answer back into pH units. Thus, the appropriate answer is pH 6.43 rather than 7. Note that a similar procedure is necessary when calculating statistics of dispersion in such cases, so you will find these almost certainly asymmetric about the mean.

Mean values of log-transformed data are often termed geometric means – they are sometimes used in microbiology and in cell culture studies, where log-transformed values for cell density counts are averaged and plotted, rather than using the raw data values. The use of geometric means in such circumstances serves to reduce the effects of outliers on the mean.

from the obvious centre of the distribution. Note that the mode is the only statistic to make sense of qualitative data – for example 'the modal (most frequent) eye colour was blue'.

The mean, median and mode have the same units as the variable under discussion. However, whether these statistics of location have the same or similar values for a given frequency distribution depends on the symmetry and shape of the distribution. If it is near-symmetrical with a single peak, all three will be very similar; if it is skewed or has more than one peak, their values will differ to a greater degree (see Fig. 55.3).

Describing the location of qualitative data – the mode is the only statistic that is suitable for this task. For example, the modal (most frequent) fingerprint pattern was a loop.

Measuring dispersion

Here, the objective is to quantify the spread of the data about the centre of the distribution. Figure 55.5 indicates how to decide which measure of dispersion to use.

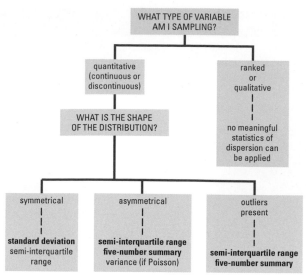

Fig. 55.5 Choosing a statistic for characterising a distribution's dispersion. Statistics written in bold are the preferred option(s). Note that you should match statistics describing dispersion with those you have used to describe location, i.e. standard deviation with mean, semi-interquartile range with median.

Example In a sample of data with values 3, 7, 15, 2, 5, 10 and 4, the range is 12 (i.e. the difference between the highest value, 15, and the lowest value, 3).

Range

The range is the difference between the largest and smallest data values in the sample (the extremes) and has the same units as the measured variable. The range is easy to determine, but is greatly affected by outliers. Its value may also depend on sample size – in general, the larger this is, the greater will be the range. These features make the range a poor measure of dispersion for many practical purposes.

Semi-interquartile range

The semi-interquartile range is an appropriate measure of dispersion when a median is the appropriate statistic to describe location. For this, you need to determine the first and third quartiles, i.e. the medians for those data values ranked below and above the median of the whole data set (see Fig. 55.6). To calculate a semi-interquartile range for a data set:

1. **Rank the observations** in ascending order.
2. **Find the values** of the first and third quartiles.
3. **Subtract the value** of the first quartile from the value of the third.
4. **Halve this number.**

For data grouped in classes, the semi-interquartile range can only be estimated. Another disadvantage is that it takes no account of the shape of the distribution at its edges. This objection can be countered by using the so-called 'five-number summary' of a data set, which consists of the three quartiles and the two extreme values – this can be presented on graphs as a box and whisker plot (see Fig. 55.7), and is particularly useful for summarising skewed frequency distributions. The corresponding 'six-number summary' includes the sample's size.

Variance and standard deviation

For symmetrical frequency distributions, an ideal measure of dispersion would take into account each value's deviation from the mean and provide a measure of the average deviation from the mean. Two such statistics are the sample variance, which is the sum of squares ($\sum(Y - \overline{Y})^2$) divided by $n - 1$ (where n is the sample size), and the sample standard deviation, which is the positive square root of the sample variance.

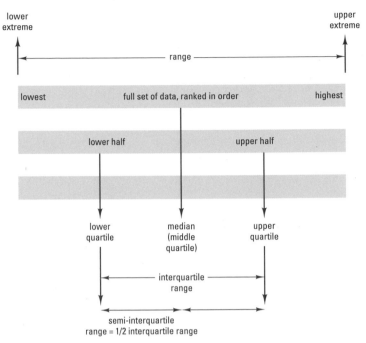

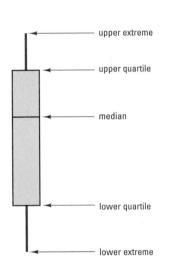

Fig. 55.7 A box and whisker plot, showing the 'five-number summary' of a sample as it might be used on a graph.

Fig. 55.6 Illustration of median, quartiles, range and semi-interquartile range.

The variance (s^2) has units that are the square of the original units, while the standard deviation (s, or SD) is expressed in the original units – one reason s is often preferred as a measure of dispersion. Calculating s or s^2 longhand is a tedious job and is best done with the help of a calculator or computer. If you don't have a calculator that calculates s for you, an alternative formula that simplifies calculations is:

$$s = \sqrt{\frac{\sum Y^2 - (\sum Y)^2/n}{n - 1}}$$ [55.1]

To calculate s using a calculator:

1. Obtain $\sum Y$, square it, divide by n and store in memory.
2. Square Y values, obtain $\sum Y^2$, subtract memory value from this.
3. Divide this answer by $n - 1$.
4. Take the positive square root of this value.

Take care to retain significant figures, or errors in the final value of s will result. If continuous data have been grouped into classes, the class mid-values or their squares must be multiplied by the appropriate frequencies before summation (see example in Box 55.1). When data values are large, longhand calculations can be simplified by coding the data – for example, by subtracting a constant from each datum, and decoding when the simplified calculations are complete (see Sokal and Rohlf, 2011).

Coefficient of variation

The coefficient of variation (CoV) is a dimensionless measure of variability relative to location, which expresses the sample standard deviation, usually as a percentage of the sample mean:

$$\text{CoV} = \frac{100s}{\bar{Y}(\%)}$$ [55.2]

Using a calculator for statistics – make sure you understand how to enter individual data values and which keys will give the sample mean (usually shown as $\bar{X}$ – or $\bar{x}$) and sample standard deviation (often shown as σ_{n-1}). In general, you should not use the population standard deviation (usually shown as σ_n).

Example Consider two methods of bioassay for a toxin in freshwater.

For a given standard, Method A gives a mean result of = 50 'response units' with s = 8, while Method B gives a mean result of = 160 'response units' with s = 18. Which bioassay gives the more reproducible results? The answer can be found by calculating the CoV values, which are 16% and 11.25% respectively. Hence, Method B is the more precise (= reproducible), even though the absolute value of s is larger.

This statistic is useful when comparing the relative dispersion of data sets with widely differing means or where different units have been used for the same or similar quantities.

A useful application of the CoV is to compare different analytical methods or procedures, so that you can decide which involves the least proportional error – create a standard stock solution, then base your comparison on the results from several subsamples analysed by each method. You may find it useful to use the CoV to compare the precision of your own results with those of a manufacturer (e.g. for an autopipettor, p. 38). The smaller the CoV, the more precise (repeatable) is the apparatus or technique (note: this does not mean that it is necessarily more *accurate*, see p. 15).

Measuring the precision of the sample mean as an estimate of the true value using the standard error

Most practical exercises are based on a limited number of individual data values (a sample), which are used to make inferences about the population from which they were drawn. For example, the haemoglobin content might be measured in blood samples from 100 adult human females and used as an estimate of the adult human female haemoglobin content, with the sample mean ($\overline{Y}$) and sample standard deviation (s) providing estimates of the true values of the underlying population mean (μ) and the population standard deviation (σ). The reliability of the sample mean as an estimate of the true (population) mean can be assessed by calculating a statistic termed the standard error of the sample mean (often abbreviated to standard error or SE), from:

$$\mathrm{SE} = \frac{s}{\sqrt{n}}$$ [55.3]

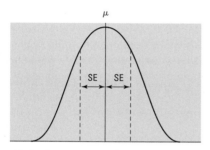

Fig. 55.8 Frequency distribution of sample means around the population mean (μ) Note that SE is equivalent to the standard deviation of the sample means, for sample size = n.

Strictly, the standard error is an estimate of the dispersion of repeated sample means around the true (population) value – if several samples were taken, each with the same number of data values (n), then their means would cluster around the population mean (μ) with a standard deviation equal to SE, as shown in Fig. 55.8. Therefore, the *smaller* the SE, the more reliable the sample mean is likely to be as an estimate of the true value, since the underlying frequency distribution would be more tightly clustered around μ. At a practical level, eqn [55.3] shows that SE is directly affected by the dispersion of individual data values within the sample, as represented by the sample standard deviation (s). Perhaps more importantly, SE is inversely related to the *square root* of the number of data values (n). Therefore, if you wanted to increase the precision of a sample mean by a factor of 2 (i.e. to reduce SE by half), you would have to increase n by a factor of 2^2 (i.e. four-fold).

Summary descriptive statistics for the sample mean are often quoted as $\overline{Y} \pm \mathrm{SE}(n)$, with the SE being given to one significant figure more than the mean. For example, summary statistics for the sample mean and standard error for the data shown in Box 53.1 would be quoted as 4.95 $\pm$ 0.280 ($n = 21$). You can use such information to carry out a t-test between two sample means (Box 56.1); the SE is also useful because it allows calculation of confidence limits for the sample mean (p. 524).

Calculating the extent of skew and kurtosis of a data set – use the SKEW and KURT functions in Microsoft Excel.

Fig. 55.9 Frequency distributions with different numbers of peaks. A unimodal distribution (a) may be symmetrical or asymmetrical. The dotted lines in (b) indicate how a bimodal distribution could arise from a combination of two underlying unimodal distributions. Note here how the term 'bimodal' is applied to any distribution with two major peaks – their frequencies do not have to be exactly the same.

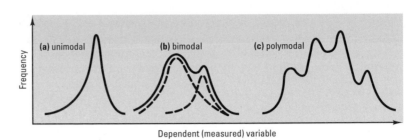

Describing the 'shape' of frequency distributions

Frequency distributions may differ in the following characteristics:

- **number of peaks;**
- **skewness or asymmetry;**
- **kurtosis or pointedness.**

The shape of a frequency distribution of a small sample is affected by chance variation and may not be a fair reflection of the underlying population frequency distribution – check this by comparing repeated samples from the same population or by increasing the sample size. If the original shape were due to random events, it should not appear consistently in repeated samples and should become less obvious as sample size increases.

Genuinely bimodal or polymodal distributions may result from the combination of two or more unimodal distributions, indicating that more than one underlying population is being sampled (Fig. 55.9). An example of a bimodal distribution is the height of adult humans (females and males combined).

A distribution is skewed if it is not symmetrical, a symptom being that the mean, median and mode are not equal (Fig. 55.3). Positive skewness is where the longer 'tail' of the distribution occurs for higher values of the measured variable; negative skewness where the longer tail occurs for lower values. Some biological examples of characteristics distributed in a skewed fashion are volumes of plant protoplasts, insulin levels in human plasma and bacterial colony counts.

Kurtosis is the name given to the 'pointedness' of a frequency distribution. A platykurtic frequency distribution is one with a flattened peak, while a leptokurtic frequency distribution is one with a pointed peak (Fig. 55.10). While descriptive terms can be used, based on visual observation of the shape and direction of skew, the degree of skewness and kurtosis can be quantified and statistical tests exist to test the 'significance' of observed values (Sokal and Rohlf, 2011), but the calculations required are complex and best done with the aid of a computer.

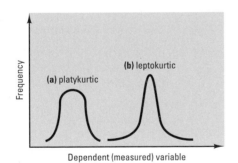

Fig. 55.10 Examples of the two types of kurtosis.

Using computers to calculate descriptive statistics

There are many specialist statistical packages (e.g. SPSS) that can be used to simplify the process of calculation of statistics. Note that correct interpretation of the output requires an understanding of the terminology used and the underlying process of calculation, and this may be best obtained by working through one or more examples by hand before using these tools. Spreadsheets offer increasingly sophisticated statistical analysis functions, some examples of which, for Microsoft Excel, are provided in Box 55.3.

Box 55.3 How to use a spreadsheet (Microsoft Excel) to calculate descriptive statistics

Method 1: Using spreadsheet functions to generate the required statistics. Suppose you had obtained the following set of data, stored within an array (block of columns and rows) of cells (A2:L6) within a spreadsheet. The following functions could be used to extract descriptive statistics from this data set:

	A	B	C	D	E	F	G	H	I	J	K	L
1	My data set											
2	4	4	3	3	5	4	3	7	7	3	5	3
3	6	2	9	7	3	4	5	6	6	9	4	8
4	5	3	2	5	4	5	7	2	8	3	6	3
5	11	3	5	2	4	3	7	8	4	4	4	3
6	3	6	8	5	6	4	3	4	3	6	10	5

Descriptive statistic	Example of use of function[a,b]	Result for the above data set
Sample size n	= COUNT((A2:L6)	60
Mean	= AVERAGE(A2:L6)[c]	4.9
Median	= MEDIAN(A2:L6)	4.0
Mode	= MODE(A2:L6)	3
Upper quartile	= QUARTILE(A2:L6,3)[d]	6.0
Lower quartile	= QUARTILE(A2:L6,1)	3.0
Semi-interquartile range	= QUARTILE(A2:L6,3)-QUARTILE(A2:L6,1)	3.0
Upper extreme	= QUARTILE(A2:L6,4) *or* = MAX(A2:L6)	11
Lower extreme	= QUARTILE(A2:L6,0) *or* = MIN(A2:L6)	2
Range	= MAX(A2:L6) − MIN(A2:L6)[e]	9.0
Variance	= VAR(A2:L6)	4.464
Standard deviation	= STDEV(A2:L6)	2.113
Standard error	= STDEV(A2:L6)/(SQRT(COUNT(A2:L6)))[f]	0.273
Coefficient of variation	= 100*STDEV(A2:L6)/AVERAGE(A2:L6)	43.12%

Notes:

[a] Typically, in an appropriate cell, you would click Insert . Function . COUNT, then select the input range and press return.

[b] Other descriptive statistics can be calculated – these mirror those shown in Box 66.1, but for this specific data set.

[c] There is no 'MEAN' function in Microsoft Excel.

[d] The first argument within the brackets relates to the array of data, the second relates to the quartile required (consult Help feature for further information).

[e] There is no direct 'RANGE' function in Microsoft Excel.

[f] There is no direct 'STANDARD ERROR' function in Microsoft Excel. The SQRT function returns a square root and the COUNT function determines the number of filled data cells in the array.

Method 2: Using the Tools > Data Analysis option. This can automatically generate a table of descriptive statistics for the data array selected, although the data must be presented as a single row or column. This option might need to be installed for your network or personal computer before it is available to you (in the latter case use the Add Ins > Analysis ToolPak option from the File Options menu – consult the Help feature for details). Having entered or rearranged your data into a row or column, the steps involved are as follows:

1. Select Data > Data Analysis.

2. From the Data Analysis box, select Descriptive Statistics.

3. Input your data location into the Input Range (left click and hold down to highlight the column of data).

Box 55.3 (Continued)

4. From the menu options, select Summary Statistics and Confidence Level for Mean: 95%.

5. When you click *OK,* you should get a new worksheet, with descriptive statistics and confidence limits shown. Alternatively, at step 3, you can select an area of your current worksheet as a data output range (select an area away from any existing content as these cells would otherwise be over-written by the descriptive statistics output table).

6. Change the format of the cells to show each number to an appropriate number of decimal places. You may also wish to make the columns wider so you can read their content.

7. For the data set shown above, the final output table should look as shown alongside:

Descriptive statistics for a data set

Column 1[a,b]

Mean	4.9
Standard error	0.27
Median	4.0
Mode	3
Standard deviation	2.113
Sample variance	4.464
Kurtosis	0.22
Skewness	0.86
Range	9.00
Minimum	2.0
Maximum	11.0
Sum	294
Count	60
Confidence level (95.0%)	0.55

Notes:

[a] These descriptive statistics are specified (and are automatically presented in this order) – any others required can be generated using Method 1.

[b] A more descriptive heading can be added if desired – this is the default.

Text references

Heath, D. (1995) *An Introduction to Experimental Design and Statistics for Biology.* UCL Press Ltd, London.

Sokal, R.R. and Rohlf, F.J. (2011) *Biometry,* 4th edn. W.H. Freeman and Co., San Francisco.

Wardlaw, A.C. (2000) *Practical Statistics for Experimental Biologists,* 2nd edn. Wiley, New York.

Sources for further study

Adam, C. (2010) *Essential Mathematics and Statistics for Forensic Scientists.* Wiley, Chichester.

Aitken, C. and Taroni, F. (2004) *Statistics and the Evaluation of Evidence for Forensic Scientists,* 2nd edn. Wiley, Chichester.

Lucy, D. (2005) *An Introduction to Statistics for Forensic Scientists.* Wiley, Chichester.

MacFarland, T.W. (2014) *Introduction to Data Analysis and Graphical Presentation in Biostatistics with R.* Springer, New York.

Walkenbach, T. (2015) *Excel 2016 Bible.* Wiley, Chichester.

Descriptive statistics

55.1 Practise calculating descriptive statistics. Using the data set given in the table in Box 55.3, calculate the following statistics:

(a) range;
(b) variance;
(c) standard deviation;
(d) coefficient of variation;
(e) standard error.

Answers (b) to (e) should be given to four significant figures.

55.2 Calculate and interpret standard errors. Two samples, A and B, gave the following descriptive statistics (measured in the same units): Sample A, mean = 16.2, standard deviation = 12.7, number of data values = 12; Sample B, mean = 13.2, standard deviation = 14.4, number of data values = 20. Which has the lower standard error in absolute terms and in proportion to the sample mean? (Express your answers to three significant figures.)

55.3 Compute a mean value correctly. A researcher finds that the mean size of larvae in three replicate samples designated A, B and C is 3.0, 2.5 and 2.0 mm respectively. He computes the mean larval size as 2.5 mm, but forgets that the sample sizes were 24, 37 and 6 respectively. What is the true mean size of the larvae? (Answer to three significant figures.)

Using Bayesian statistics – *in forensic science one of the approaches is to use Bayesian statistics that estimate the probability of guilt based on the evidence found. It is calculated using a likelihood ratio and the hypotheses that have been presented to court by prosecution (suspect linked to crime) and defence (suspect not linked to crime). For further details, see Robertson and Vignaux (1995), Taroni et al. (2010).*

This chapter outlines the philosophy of hypothesis-testing statistics, indicates the steps to be taken when choosing a test and discusses features and assumptions of some important tests. This approach may be useful in your final-year project (Chapter 61). For details of the mechanics of tests, consult appropriate texts (e.g. Heath, 1995; Wardlaw, 2000; Sokal and Rohlf, 2012). Most tests are now available in statistical packages for computers (see p. 463) and many in spreadsheets (Chapter 49).

To carry out a statistical test:

1. Decide what it is you wish to test – create a null hypothesis and its alternative.
2. Determine whether your data fit a standard distribution pattern.
3. Select a test and apply it to your data.

Setting up a null hypothesis

Hypothesis-testing statistics are used to compare the properties of samples either with other samples or with some theory about them. For instance, you may be interested in whether two samples can be regarded as having different means, whether the counts of the insect *Calliphora vicina* in different locations can be regarded as randomly distributed, or whether property A of an illicit drug is related to property B.

> **KEY POINT** *You can't use statistics to prove any hypothesis, but they can be used to assess how likely it is to be wrong.*

Statistical testing operates in what at first seems a rather perverse manner. Suppose you think a treatment has an effect. The theory you actually test is that it has no effect – the test tells you how improbable your data would be if this theory were true. This 'no effect' theory is the null hypothesis (NH). If your data are very improbable under the NH, then you may suppose it to be wrong, and this would support your original idea (the 'alternative hypothesis'). The concept can be illustrated by an example. Suppose two groups of subjects were treated in different ways, and you observed a difference in the mean value of the measured variable for the two groups. Can this be regarded as a 'true' difference? As Fig. 56.1 shows, it could have arisen in two ways:

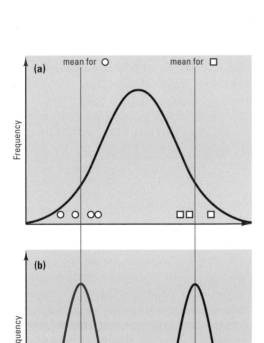

- because of the way the subjects were allocated to treatments – i.e. all the subjects liable to have high values might, by chance, have been assigned to one group and those with low values to the other (Fig. 56.1(a));
- because of a genuine effect of the treatments – i.e. each group came from a distinct frequency distribution (Fig. 56.1(b)).

A statistical test will indicate the probabilities of these options. The NH states that the two groups come from the same population (i.e. the treatment effects are negligible in the context of random variation). To test this, you calculate a test statistic from the data, and compare it with tabulated critical values giving the probability of obtaining the observed or a more extreme result by chance (see Boxes 56.1 and 56.2). This probability is sometimes called the *significance* of the test.

Fig. 56.1 Two explanations for the difference between two means. In case (a) the two samples happen by chance to have come from opposite ends of the same frequency distribution, i.e. there is no true difference between the samples. In case (b) the two samples come from different frequency distributions, i.e. there is a true difference between the samples. In both cases, the means of the two samples are the same.

Understanding 'degrees of freedom' – this depends on the number of values in the data set analysed, and the method of calculation depends on the statistical test being used. It relates to the number of observations that are free to vary before the remaining quantities for a data set can be determined.

Definition

Modulus – the absolute value of a number, e.g. modulus $-3.385 = 3.385$.

Quoting significance – the convention for quoting significance levels in text, tables and figures is as follows:

$P > 0.05 = $ *'not significant' (or NS)*
$P = 0.05 = $ *'significant' (or *)*
$P = 0.01 = $ *'highly significant' (or **)*
$P = 0.001 = $ *'very highly significant' (or ***)*

Thus, you might refer to a difference between means as being 'highly significant (P > 0.01)'. For this reason, the word 'significant' in its everyday meaning of 'important' or 'notable' should be used with care in scientific writing. The asterisk coding shown above is most often used as a shorthand in tables and should be explained in the table legend, or in a footnote

Choosing between parametric and non-parametric tests – always plot your data graphically when determining whether they are suitable for parametric tests, as this may save a lot of unnecessary effort later.

Note that you must take into account the degrees of freedom (d.f.) when looking up critical values of most test statistics. The d.f. is related to the size(s) of the samples studied – formulae for calculating it depend on the test being used. Scientists normally use two-tailed tests – i.e. we have no expectation beforehand that the treatment will have a positive or negative effect compared to the control (in a one-tailed test we expect one particular treatment to be bigger than the other). Be sure to use critical values for the correct type of test.

By convention, the critical probability for rejecting the NH is 5% (i.e. $P = 0.05$). This means we reject the NH if the observed result would have come up less than one time in twenty by chance. If the modulus of the test statistic is less than the tabulated critical value for $P = 0.05$, then we accept the NH and the result is said to be 'not significant' (NS for short). If the modulus of the test statistic is greater than the tabulated value for $P = 0.05$, then we reject the NH in favour of the alternative hypothesis that the treatments had different effects and the result is 'statistically significant'.

Two types of error are possible when making a conclusion on the basis of a statistical test. The first occurs if you reject the NH when it is true, and the second if you accept the NH when it is false. To limit the chance of the first type of error, choose a lower probability (e.g. $P = 0.01$), but note that the critical value of the test statistic increases when you do this and results in the probability of the second type of error increasing. The conventional significance levels given in statistical tables (usually 0.05, 0.01, 0.001) are arbitrary. Increasing use of statistical computer programs now allows the exact probability of obtaining the calculated value of the test statistic to be quoted (e.g. $P = 0.037$).

Note that if the NH is rejected, this does not tell you why many alternative explanations may be possible. Also, it is important to distinguish between statistical significance and scientific relevance, which must be considered separately.

Comparing data with parametric distributions

The distribution pattern of a set of data values may be biologically relevant, but it is also of practical importance because it defines the type of statistical tests that can be used. A parametric test is one that makes particular assumptions about the mathematical nature of the population distribution from which the samples were taken. If these assumptions are not true, then the test is obviously invalid, even though it might give the answer we expect. A non-parametric test does not assume that the data fit a particular pattern, but it may assume characteristics of the distributions. Used in appropriate circumstances, parametric tests are better able to distinguish between true but marginal differences between samples than their non-parametric equivalents (i.e. they have greater 'power').

The properties of the main distribution types found in biology are given below, with both rules-of-thumb and more rigorous tests for deciding whether data fit these distributions.

Binomial distributions

These apply to samples of any size from populations when data values occur independently in only two mutually exclusive classes (e.g. type A or type B). They describe the probability of finding the different possible combinations of the attribute for a specified sample size k (e.g. out of 10 specimens, what is the chance of 8 being type A). If p is the probability of the attribute being of type A and q the probability of it being type B, then the expected mean sample number of type A is kp and the standard deviation is $\sqrt{kpq}$. Expected

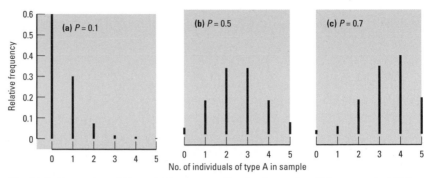

Fig. 56.2 Examples of binomial frequency distributions with different probabilities. The distributions show the expected frequency of obtaining *n* individuals of type A in a sample of 5. Here *P* is the probability of an individual being type A rather than type B.

frequencies can be calculated using mathematical expressions (see Sokal and Rohlf, 2012). Examples of the shapes of some binomial distributions are shown in Fig. 56.2. Note that they are symmetrical in shape for the special case $p = q = 0.5$ and the greater the disparity between p and q, the more skewed the distribution.

Some examples of data likely to be distributed in binomial fashion are possession of two alleles for seed coat morphology (e.g. smooth and wrinkly) and whether an animal is male or female. Binomial distributions are particularly useful for predicting gene segregation in Mendelian genetics (p. 99) and can be used for testing whether combinations of events have occurred more frequently than predicted (e.g. more siblings being of the same sex than expected). To establish whether a set of data is distributed in binomial fashion we calculate expected frequencies from probability values obtained from theory or observation, then test against observed frequencies using a χ^2-test (p. 103) or a *G*-test (see Wardlaw, 2000).

Quantifying skew – the Microsoft Excel SKEW function can be used to assess the extent of skewness in a data set.

Poisson distributions

These apply to discrete characteristics that can assume low whole-number values, such as counts of events occurring in area, volume or time. The events should be 'rare' in that the mean number observed should be a small proportion of the total that could possibly be found. Also, finding one count should not influence the probability of finding another. The shape of Poisson distributions is described by only one parameter, the mean number of events observed, and has the special characteristic that the variance is equal to the mean. The shape has a pronounced positive skewness at low mean counts, but becomes more and more symmetrical as the mean number of counts increases (Fig. 56.3).

Some examples of characteristics distributed in a Poisson fashion are the number of microbes per unit volume of medium and the number of radioactive disintegrations per unit time. One of the main uses for the Poisson distribution is to quantify errors in count data, such as estimates of a radioactive isotope in a sample. To decide whether data are Poisson distributed:

Tendency towards the normal distribution – under certain conditions, binomial and Poisson distributions can be treated as normally distributed:

- where samples from a binomial distribution are large (i.e. >15) and p and q are close to 0.5;
- for Poisson distributions, if the number of counts recorded in each outcome is greater than about 15.

- use the rule-of-thumb that if the coefficient of dispersion ≈ 1, the distribution is likely to be Poisson;
- calculate 'expected' frequencies from the equation for the Poisson distribution and compare with actual values using a χ^2-test (p. 103) or a *G*-test.

Definition

Coefficient of dispersion $= S^2/\overline{Y}$. This is an alternative measure of dispersion to the coefficient of variation (p. 511).

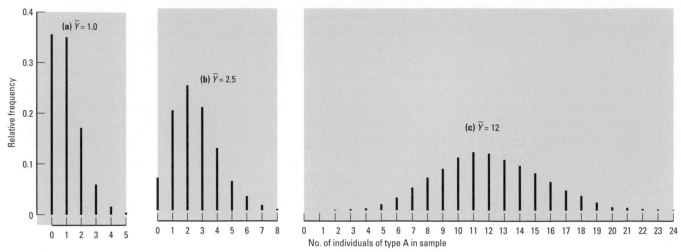

Fig. 56.3 Examples of Poisson frequency distributions differing in mean. The distributions are shown as line charts because the independent variable (events per sample) is discrete.

Normal distributions (Gaussian distributions)

These occur when random events act to produce variability in a continuous characteristic (quantitative variable). This situation occurs frequently in various types of scientific data, so normal distributions are very useful and much used. The bell-like shape of normal distributions is specified by the population mean and standard deviation (Fig. 56.4) – it is symmetrical and configured such that 68.27% of the data will lie within ± 1 standard deviation from the mean, 95.45% within ± 2 standard deviations from the mean, and 99.73% within ± 3 standard deviations from the mean.

Some examples of data likely to be distributed in a normal fashion are the dimensions of cells and the height of either adult female or male humans. To check whether data come from a normal distribution, you can:

- **use the rule-of-thumb that the distribution should be symmetrical** and that nearly all the data should fall within $\pm 3s$ of the mean and about two-thirds within $\pm 1s$ of the mean;
- **plot the distribution on normal probability graph paper** – if the distribution is normal, the data will tend to follow a straight line (see Fig. 56.5);

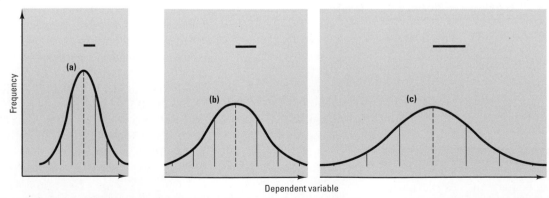

Fig. 56.4 Examples of normal frequency distributions differing in mean and standard deviation. The horizontal bars represent population standard deviations for the curves, increasing from (a) to (c). Vertical dashed lines are population means, while vertical solid lines show positions of values ±1, 2 and 3 standard deviations from the means.

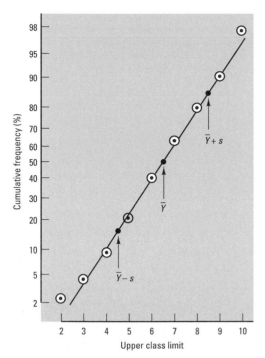

Fig. 56.5 Example of a normal probability plot. The plotted points are from a small data set where the mean $\bar{y} = 6.93$ and the standard deviation $s = 1.895$. Note that values corresponding to 0% and 100% cumulative frequency cannot be used. The straight line is that predicted for a normal distribution with $\bar{y} = 6.93$ and $s = 1.895$. This is plotted by calculating the expected positions of points for $Y \pm s$. Since 68.3% of the distribution falls within these bounds, the relevant points on the cumulative frequency scale are 50;34.15%; thus this line was drawn using the points (4.495, 15.85) and (8.285, 84.15) as indicated on the plot.

Definition

Homogeneous variance – uniform (but not necessarily identical) variance of the dependent variable across the range of the independent variable. The term homoscedastic is also used in this sense. The opposite of homogeneous is heterogeneous (= heteroscedastic).

Table 56.1 Suggested transformations altering different types of frequency distribution to the normal type. To use, modify data by the formula shown and then examine effects with the tests described on pp. 521–526.

Type of data; distribution suspected	Suggested transformation(s)
Proportions (including percentages); binomial	arcsin $\sqrt{X}$ (also called the angular transformation)
Scores; Poisson	$\sqrt{X}$ or $\sqrt{x + 1/2}$ (if zero values are present)
Measurements; negatively skewed	x^2, x^3, x^4, etc. (in order of increasing strength)
Measurements; positively skewed	$1/\sqrt{X}$, $\sqrt{X}$, ln x, $1/x$ (in order of increasing strength)

Deviations from linearity reveal skewness and/or kurtosis (see p. 513), the significance of which can be tested statistically (see Sokal and Rohlf, 2012);

- **use a suitable statistical computer program to generate predicted normal curves** from the $\bar{Y}$ and s values of your sample(s) – these can be compared visually with the actual distribution of data and can be used to give 'expected' values for a χ^2-test (p. 103) or a G-test.

The wide availability of tests based on the normal distribution and their relative simplicity means you may wish to transform your data to make them more like a normal distribution. Table 56.1 provides transformations that might be applied. The transformed data should be tested for normality as described above before proceeding – don't forget that you may need to check that transformed variances are homogeneous for certain tests (see definition below).

A very important theorem in statistics, the central limit theorem, states that as sample size increases, the distribution of a series of means from any frequency distribution will become normally distributed. This fact can be used to devise an experimental or sampling strategy that ensures that data are normally distributed, i.e. using means of samples as if they were primary data.

Choosing a suitable statistical test

Comparing location (e.g. means)

If you can assume that your data are normally distributed, the main test for comparing two means from independent samples is Student's t-test (see Boxes 56.1 and 56.2, and Table 56.2). This assumes that the variances of the data sets are homogeneous. Tests based on the t-distribution are also available for comparing means of paired data or for comparing a sample mean with a chosen value. When comparing means of two or more samples, analysis of variance (ANOVA) is a very useful technique. This method also assumes that data are normally distributed and that the variances of the samples are homogeneous. The samples must also be independent (e.g. not subsamples). The nested types of ANOVA are useful for letting you know the relative importance of different sources of variability in your data. Two-way and multiway ANOVAs are useful for studying interactions between treatments.

For data satisfying the ANOVA requirements, the least significant difference (LSD) is useful for making planned comparisons among several means (Sokal and Rohlf, 2012). Any two means that differ by more than the LSD will be significantly different.

Table 56.2 Critical values of Student's *t*-statistic (for two-tailed tests). Reject the null hypothesis at probability *P* if your calculated *t* value exceeds the value shown for the appropriate degrees of freedom $= (n_1 - 1) + (n_2 - 1)$

Degrees of freedom	Critical values for $P = 0.05$	Critical values for $P = 0.01$	Critical values for $P = 0.001$
1	12.71	63.66	636.62
2	4.30	9.92	31.60
3	3.18	5.84	12.94
4	2.78	4.60	8.61
5	2.57	4.03	6.86
6	2.45	3.71	5.96
7	2.36	3.50	5.40
8	2.31	3.36	5.04
9	2.26	3.25	4.78
10	2.23	3.17	4.59
12	2.18	3.06	4.32
14	2.14	2.98	4.14
16	2.12	2.92	4.02
20	2.09	2.85	3.85
25	2.06	2.79	3.72
30	2.04	2.75	3.65
40	2.02	2.70	3.55
60	2.00	2.66	3.46
120	1.98	2.62	3.37
∞	1.96	2.58	3.29

Checking the assumptions of a test – *always acquaint yourself with the assumptions of a test. If necessary, test them before using the test.*

The chief non-parametric tests for comparing the locations of two samples are the Mann–Whitney *U*-test and the Kolmogorov–Smirnov test. The former assumes that the frequency distributions of the samples are similar, whereas the latter makes no such assumption. In both cases the sample's size must be ≥4 and for the Kolmogorov–Smirnov test the samples must have equal sizes. In the Kolmogorov–Smirnov test, significant differences found with the test could be due to differences in location or shape of the distribution, or both.

Suitable non-parametric comparisons of location for paired data (sample size ≥6) include Wilcoxon's signed rank test, which is used for quantitative data and assumes that the distributions have similar shape. Dixon and Mood's sign test can be used for paired data scores where one variable is recorded as 'greater than' or 'better than' the other.

Non-parametric comparisons of location for three or more samples include the Kruskal–Wallis *H*-test. Here, the number of samples is without limit and they can be unequal in size, but again the underlying distributions are assumed to be similar. The Friedman *S*-test operates with a maximum of five samples and data must conform to a randomised block design. The underlying distributions of the samples are assumed to be similar.

Comparing dispersions (e.g. variances)

If you wish to compare the variances of two sets of data that are normally distributed, use the *F*-test. For comparing more than two samples, it may be sufficient to use the F_{max}-test, on the highest and lowest variances. The Scheffé–Box

Box 56.1 How to carry out a *t*-test

The *t*-test was devised by a statistician who used the pen-name 'Student', so you may see it referred to as Student's *t*-test. It is used when you want to decide whether two samples come from the same population or from different ones (Fig. 56.1). The samples might have been obtained by observation or by applying two different treatments to an originally homogeneous population.

The null hypothesis (NH) is that the two groups can be represented as samples from the same overlying population (Fig. 56.1(a)). If, as a result of the test, you accept this hypothesis, you can say that there is no significant difference between the group means.

The alternative hypothesis is that the two groups come from different populations (Fig. 56.1(b)). By rejecting the NH as a result of the test, you can accept the alternative hypothesis and say that there is a significant difference between the sample means, or, if an experiment were carried out, that the two treatments affected the samples differently.

How can you decide between these two hypotheses? On the basis of certain assumptions (see below), and some relatively simple calculations, you can work out the probability that the samples came from the same population. If this probability is very low, then you can reasonably reject the NH in favour of the alternative hypothesis, and if it is high, you will accept the NH.

To find out the probability that the observed difference between sample means arose by chance, you must first calculate a '*t*-value' for the two samples in question. Some computer programs (e.g. Excel and Minitab) provide this probability as part of the output, otherwise you can look up statistical tables (e.g. Table 56.2). These tables show 'critical values' – the borders between probability levels. If your value of *t* exceeds the critical value for probability *P*, you can reject the NH at this probability ('level of significance').

Note that:

- for a given difference in the means of the two samples, the value of *t* will get larger the smaller the scatter within each data set;
- for a given scatter of the data, the value of *t* will get larger the greater the difference between the means.

So, at what probability should you reject the NH? Normally, the threshold is arbitrarily set at 5% – you quite often see descriptions like 'the sample means were significantly different ($P < 0.05$)'. At this 'significance level' there is still up to a 5% chance of the *t*-value arising by chance, so about 1 in 20 times on average, the conclusion will be wrong. If *P* turns out to be lower, then this kind of error is much less likely.

Tabulated probability levels are generally given for 5%, 1% and 0.1% significance levels (see Table 56.2). Note that this table is designed for 'two-tailed' tests, i.e. where the treatment or sampling strategy could have resulted in either an increase or a decrease in the measured values. These are the most likely situations you will deal with in, for example, biology.

Examine Table 56.2 and note the following:

- The larger the size of the samples (i.e. the greater the 'degrees of freedom'), the smaller *t* needs to be to exceed the critical value at a given significance level.
- The lower the probability, the greater *t* needs to be to exceed the critical value.

The mechanics of the test

A calculator that can work out means and standard deviations is helpful.

1. **Work out the sample means $\overline{Y}_1$ and $\overline{Y}_2$ and calculate the difference between them.**

2. **Work out the sample standard deviations s_1 and s_2.** (NB if your calculator offers a choice, choose the '$n - 1$' option for calculating s – see p. 511).

3. **Work out the sample standard errors $SE_1 = s_1/\sqrt{n_2}$ and $SE_2 = s_2/\sqrt{n_2}$; now square each, add the squares together, then take the positive square root of this** – n_1 and n_2 are the respective sample sizes, which may, or may not, be equal.

4. **Calculate *t*:**

$$t = \frac{\overline{Y}_1 - \overline{Y}_2}{\sqrt{(SE_1)^2 + (SE_2)^2}} \qquad [56.1]$$

The value of *t* can be negative or positive, depending on the values of the means. This does not matter, and you should compare the modulus (absolute value) of *t* with the values in tables.

5. **Work out the degrees of freedom** $= (n_1 - 1) + (n_2 - 1)$.

6. **Compare the *t*-value with the appropriate critical value (see Table 56.2).**

Box 56.2 provides a worked example – use this to check that you understand the above procedures.

Assumptions that must be met before using the test

The most important assumptions are:

- The two samples are independent and randomly drawn (or, if not, are drawn in a way that does not create bias). The test assumes that the samples are quite large.
- The underlying distribution of each sample is normal. This can be tested with a special statistical test, but a rule-of-thumb is that a frequency distribution of the data should be (a) symmetrical about the mean and (b) nearly all of the data should be within three standard deviations of the mean and about two-thirds within one standard deviation of the mean (see p. 520).
- The two samples should have uniform variances. This again can be tested (by an F-test), but may be obvious from inspection of the two standard deviations.

Box 56.2 Worked example of a *t*-test

Suppose the following data were obtained in an experiment (the units are not relevant):

Control: 6.6, 5.5, 6.8, 5.8, 6.1, 5.9
Treatment: 6.3, 7.2, 6.5, 7.1, 7.5, 7.3

Using the steps outlined in Box 56.1, the following values are obtained (denoting control with subscript 1, treatment with subscript 2):

1. $\overline{Y}_1 = 6.1167$; $\overline{Y}_2 = 6.9833$: difference between means $= \overline{Y}_1 - \overline{Y}_2 = 0.8666$

2. $s_1 = 0.49565$; $s_2 = 0.47504$

3. $SE_1 = 0.49565/2.44949 = 0.202348$

   $SE_2 = 0.47504/2.44949 = 0.193934$

4. $t = \dfrac{-0.8666}{\sqrt{(0.202348^2 + 0.193934^2)}} = \dfrac{-0.8666}{0.2802777} = -3.09$

5. d.f. $= (5 + 5) = 10$

6. Looking at Table 56.2, we see that the modulus of this *t*-value exceeds the tabulated value for $P = 0.05$ at 10 degrees of freedom ($= 2.23$). We therefore reject the NH, and conclude that the means are different at the 5% level of significance. If the modulus of *t* had been <2.23, we would have accepted the NH. If modulus of *t* had been >3.17, we could have concluded that the means are different at the 1% level of significance.

(log-anova) test is recommended for testing the significance of differences between several variances. Non-parametric tests exist but are not widely available – you may need to transform the data and use a test based on the normal distribution.

Confidence limits for statistics other than the mean – consult an advanced statistical text (e.g. Sokal and Rohlf, 2012) if you wish to indicate the reliability of estimates of, for example, population variances.

Determining whether frequency observations fit theoretical expectation

The χ^2-test (p. 103) is useful for tests of 'goodness of fit' – for example, comparing expected and observed progeny frequencies in genetical experiments or comparing observed frequency distributions with some theoretical function. One limitation is that simple formulae for calculating χ^2 assume that no expected number is less than 5. The *G*-test (2*I* test) is used in similar circumstances.

Comparing proportion data

When comparing proportions between two small groups (e.g. whether 3/10 is significantly different from 5/10), you can use probability tables such as those of Finney *et al.* (1963), or calculate probabilities from formulae – however, this can be tedious for large sample sizes. Certain proportions can be transformed so that their distribution becomes normal.

Placing confidence limits on an estimate of a population parameter

On many occasions, a sample statistic is used to provide an estimate of a population parameter, and it is often useful to indicate the reliability of such an estimate. This can be done by putting confidence limits on the sample statistic, i.e. by specifying an interval around the statistic within which you are confident that the true value (the population parameter) is likely to fall, at a specified level of probability. The most common application is to place confidence limits on the mean of a sample taken from a population of normally distributed data values. In practice, you determine a confidence factor for a particular level of probability, which is added to and subtracted from the

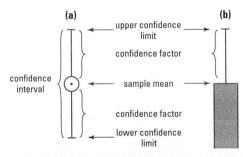

Fig. 56.6 Graphical representation of confidence limits as 'error bars' for: (a) a sample mean in a plotted curve, where both upper and lower limits are shown; and (b) a sample mean in a histogram, where, by convention, only the upper value is shown. For data that are assumed to be symmetrically distributed, such representations are often used in preference to the 'box and whisker' plot shown on p. 510. Note that SE is an alternative way of representing sample imprecision/error (e.g. Fig. 52.1).

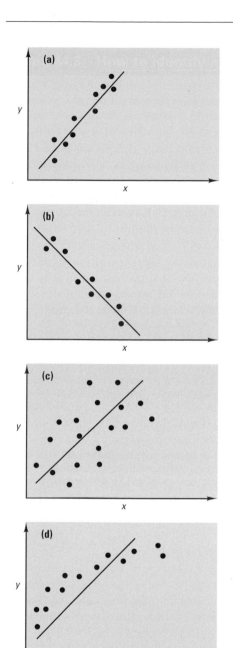

Fig. 56.7 Examples of correlation. The linear regression line is shown. In (a) and (b), the correlation between x and y is good: for (a) there is a positive correlation and the correlation coefficient, r, would be close to −1; for (b) there is a negative correlation and the correlation coefficient would be close to 1. In (c) there is a weak positive correlation and r would be close to 0. In (d) the correlation coefficient may be quite large, but the choice of linear regression is clearly inappropriate.

sample mean ($\overline{Y}$) to give the upper confidence limit and lower confidence limit respectively. These are calculated as:

$$\overline{Y} + (t_{P[n+1]} \times \text{SE}) \text{ for the upper limit}$$

$$\overline{Y} - (t_{P[n-1]} \times \text{SE}) \text{ for the lower limit} \qquad [56.2]$$

where $t_{P[n-1]}$ is the tabulated critical value of Student's t-statistic for a two-tailed test with $n - 1$ degrees of freedom at a specified probability level (P) and SE is the standard error of the sample mean (p. 512). The 95% confidence limits (i.e. $P = 0.05$) tells you that, on average, 95 times out of 100 the interval between the upper and lower limits will contain the true (population) value. Confidence limits are often shown as 'error bars' for individual sample means plotted in graphical form. Figure 56.6 illustrates how this is applied to plotted curves and histograms (note that this can be carried out for data series within a Microsoft Excel graph (chart – see Box 52.2, pp. 486–487).

Correlation and regression

These methods are used when testing the relationship between data values for two variables. Correlation is used to measure the extent to which changes in the two sets of data values occur together in a linear manner. If one variable can be assumed to be dependent on the other (i.e. a change in X causes a particular change in Y), then regression techniques can be used to provide a mathematical description of the underlying relationship between the variables – for example, to find a line of best fit for a data series. If there is no *a priori* reason to assume dependency, then correlation methods alone are appropriate.

A correlation coefficient measures the strength of the linear relationship between two variables, but does not describe the relationship. The coefficient is expressed as a number between −1 and +1; a positive coefficient indicates a direct relationship, where the two variables change in the same direction, while a negative coefficient indicates an inverse relationship, where one variable decreases as the other increases (Fig. 56.7). The nearer the coefficient is to −1 or +1, the stronger the linear relationship between the variables, i.e. the less 'scatter' there would be about a straight line of best fit (note that this does *not* imply that one variable is dependent on the other). A coefficient of 0 implies that the two variables show no linear association and therefore the closer the correlation coefficient is to zero, the weaker the linear relationship. The importance of graphing data is shown by the case illustrated in Fig. 56.7(d).

Pearson's product moment correlation coefficient (r) is the most commonly used statistic for testing correlations. The test is valid only if both variables are normally distributed. Statistical tests can be used to decide whether the correlation is significant – e.g. using a one-sample t-test to see whether r is significantly different from zero, based on the equation $t = r \div \sqrt{[(1 - r^2) \div (n - 2)]}$ at $n - 2$ degrees of freedom. If one or both variables are not normally distributed, then you should calculate an alternative non-parametric coefficient, for example Spearman's coefficient of rank correlation (r_S) or Kendall's coefficient of rank correlation (τ). These require the two sets of data to be ranked separately, and the calculation can be complex if there are tied (equal) ranks. Spearman's coefficient is said to be better if there is any uncertainty about the reliability of closely ranked data values.

If underlying theory or empirical graphical analysis indicates a linear relationship between a dependent and an independent variable, then linear regression can be used to estimate the mathematical equation that links the two

Using more advanced types of regression *– these include:*

- *Model II linear regression, which applies to situations where a dependent variable Y varies with an independent variable X, and where both variables may have error terms associated with them.*
- *Multiple regression, which applies when there is a relationship between a dependent variable and two or more independent variables.*
- *Non-linear regression, which extends the principles of linear regression to a wide range of functions. Technically, this method is more appropriate than transforming data to allow linear regression.*

Advanced statistics books should be consulted for details of these methods, which may be offered by some statistical computer programs.

Example If a regression analysis gives a value for r^2 of 0.75 (i.e. $r = 0.84$), then 75% of the variance in Y can be explained by the trend line, with $1 - r^2 = 0.25$ (25%) remaining as unexplained (residual) variation.

variables. Model I linear regression is the standard approach, and is available within general-purpose software programs such as Excel, and on some scientific calculators. It is suitable for experiments where a dependent variable Y varies with an *error-free* independent variable X in accordance with the relationship $Y = a + bX + e_Y$, where e_Y represents the residual (error) variability in the Y variable. For example, this relationship might apply in a laboratory procedure where you have carefully controlled the independent variable and the X values can be assumed to have zero error (e.g. in a calibration curve, see Chapter 51, or in a time-course experiment where measurements are made at exact time points). The regression analysis gives estimates for a and b (equivalent to the slope and intercept of the line of best fit, p. 478). Computer-based programs usually provide additional features – for example, residual values for (e_Y), estimated errors for a and b, predicted values of Y along with graphical plots of the line of best fit (the trend line) and the residual values. In order for the model to be valid, the residual (error) values should be normally distributed around the trend line and their variance should be uniform (homogenous) – i.e. there should be a similar scatter of data points around the trend line along the x-axis (independent variable).

If the relationship is not linear, try a transformation. For example, this is often done in analysis of enzyme kinetics. However, you should be aware that the transformation of data to give a straight line can lead to errors when carrying out linear regression analysis – take care to ensure that the assumptions listed in the previous paragraph are valid for the transformed data set and that the data points are evenly distributed throughout the range of the independent variable. If these criteria cannot be met, non-linear regression may be a better approach, but for this you will require a suitable computer program (e.g. GraphPad Prism®).

The strength of the relationship between Y and X in model I linear regression is best estimated by the coefficient of determination (r^2 or R^2), which is equivalent to the square of the Pearson correlation coefficient. The coefficient of determination varies between 0 and $+1$ and provides a measure of the goodness of fit of the Y data to the regression line – the closer the value is to 1, the better the fit. In effect, r^2 represents the fraction of the variance in Y that can be accounted for by the regression equation. Conversely, if you subtract this value from 1, you will obtain the residual (error) component, i.e. the fraction of the variance in Y that cannot be explained by the line of best fit. Multiplying the values by 100 allows you to express these fractions in percentage terms.

Using computers to calculate hypothesis-testing statistics

As with the calculation of descriptive statistics (p. 506), specialist statistical packages such as SPSS and Minitab can be used to simplify the calculation of hypothesis-testing statistics. The correct use of the software and interpretation of the output require an understanding of relevant terminology and of the fundamental principles governing the test, which is probably best obtained by working through one or more examples by hand before using these tools (e.g. Box 13.2; Box 56.2). Spreadsheets offer increasingly sophisticated statistical analysis functions.

Text references

Heath, D. (1995) *An Introduction to Experimental Design and Statistics for Biology.* UCL Press Ltd, London.

Robertson, B. and Vignaux, G.A. (1995) *Interpreting Evidence: Evaluating Forensic Science in the Courtroom.* Wiley, London.

[Explains the Bayesian approach with minimal mathematics.]

Schmuller, J. (2005) *Statistical Analysis with Excel for Dummies.* Wiley, Hoboken.

Sokal, R.R. and Rohlf, F.J. (2012) *Biometry,* 4th edn. W.H. Freeman and Co., San Francisco.

Taroni, F., Bozza, S., Biedermann, A, Garbolino, P. and Aitken, C. (2010) *Data Analysis in Forensic Science – A Bayesian Perspective.* Wiley, Chichester.

Wardlaw, A.C. (2000) *Practical Statistics for Experimental Biologists,* 2nd edn. Wiley, New York.

Sources for further study

Aitken, C.G.G. and Taroni, F. (2004) *Statistics and the Evaluation of Evidence for Forensic Scientists,* 2nd edn. Wiley, Chichester.

Balding, D.J. (2005) *Weight of Evidence for Forensic DNA Profiles.* Wiley, Chichester.

Dytham, C. (2003) *Choosing and Using Statistics: A Biologists' Guide,* 2nd edn. Blackwell, Oxford.

Finney, D.J., Latscha, R., Bennett, B.M. and Hsu, P. (1963) *Tables for Testing Significance in a 2 × 2 Table.* Cambridge University Press, Cambridge.

Lee, P.M. (2004) *Bayesian Statistics: An Introduction,* 3rd edn. Arnold, London.

Lucy, D. (2005) *An Introduction to Statistics for Forensic Scientists.* Wiley, Chichester.

Taroni, F., Aitken, C., Garbolini, P. and Biedermann, A. (2006) *Bayesian Networks and Probabilistic Inference in Forensic Science.* Wiley, Chichester.

Study exercises

56.1 Calculate 95% confidence limits. What are the 95% confidence limits of a sample with a mean = 24.7, standard deviation = 6.8 and number of data values = 16? (Express your answer to three significant figures.)

56.2 Practise using a *t*-test. A forensic science student examined the effect of adding cocaine to foodstuff that maggots were feeding on. She dosed the foodstuff with an appropriate amount of cocaine in methanol: water (1:100) and allowed the maggots to feed for 7 days. With the controls, she applied the same amount of methanol: water without the cocaine. After a further 7 days, she measured the length of the maggots and obtained the results shown below. Carry out a *t*-test on the data and draw appropriate conclusions.

Maggot length in mm

Control	7.5	8.1	7.6	6.2	7.5	7.8	8.9
Cocaine	5.6	7.5	8.2	6.7	3.5	6.5	5.9

Chemometrics has been defined as the chemical discipline that uses mathematical and statistical methods to design or select optimal measurement procedures and experiments and to provide maximum chemical information by analysing chemical data (Kowalski, 1978). It can assist with (i) the planning of experiments, and (ii) the manipulation and interpretation of large data sets. Some aspects of chemometrics can be done using an appropriate spreadsheet but the majority of applications require the use of dedicated software. The fundamental principles of most of the processes involved in chemometrics are those of statistics. You are therefore advised to become familiar with the material in Chapters 55 and 56 before proceeding.

When carrying out any experimental work, e.g. an undergraduate practical, you should always read the entire practical script before starting the experimentation. This is important as it allows you to plan each step of the process and to organise space and time to perform the experiment. This initial planning is further complicated in project work and research projects when, often, there is no laboratory script to follow. In these situations, you finally come down to planning the initial experiments after background research (e.g. reading the appropriate scientific literature on the subject area to be investigated), purchasing/obtaining the appropriate chemicals/reagents, etc. It is at this stage that chemometrics can be of some assistance. Assuming that you are able to identify the dependent variables in the experiment, then you can apply 'experimental design', which allows you to gain the maximum amount of knowledge about the system you are investigating from a limited number of experiments.

Once the experimental work has been completed you then need to consider how to interpret the results, i.e. how to maximise the chemical information inherent in the data. Initial attempts are often centred around plotting the data, to visualise trends and to allow conclusions to be drawn. The simplest form of data visualisation is simply to tabulate the results (Chapter 53). As an example, if a drug has been determined in bodily fluids and tissues, it is a relatively simple matter to tabulate the data (see Table 38.2). One possibility for the data is then to calculate the mean and standard deviation, although in this case this would not be appropriate to do so as each sampling site is variable. Another approach would be to plot the data as a histogram, as in Figure 52.3, so we are then able to make a visual interpretation of the quality of these data.

However, what if we had more than one variable to consider? In other words, we have multivariate data. For example, what if we want to identify trends in fingerprint composition? The variables we might want to consider could be: gender, ethnicity, body mass, age and diet. We can, of course, tabulate the data, as before, but this does not allow us to consider any trends in the data. To do this we need to be able to plot the data. However, once we exceed three variables (which we need to be able to plot in three dimensions) it becomes impossible to produce a straightforward plot. It is in this context that chemometrics offers a solution, reducing the dimensionality to a smaller number of dimensions and hence the ability to display multivariate data. The most important technique in this context is called principal component analysis (PCA).

The following discussion highlights only the basic principles. For more detailed information you are advised to consult the literature and dedicated chemometric software packages. It should always be borne in mind, however, that the choice of which variables to optimise should be selected (i) by someone with prior knowledge of the system under investigation, or (ii) after performing preliminary experiments to determine which are the most important variables.

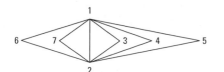

Fig. 57.1 Step-size simplex.

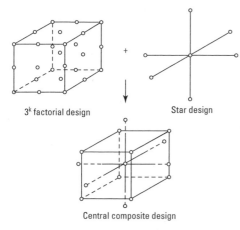

3^k factorial design

Star design

Central composite design

Fig. 57.2 Central composite design.

Experimental design

There are two main multivariate optimisation strategies: those based on sequential designs and those based on simultaneous designs.

Sequential design

Sequential optimisation is based on the one-at-a-time approach. The major limitation of this approach is that it assumes that no interaction effects occur between the variables. Unfortunately this is not always the case. A sequential design strategy involves carrying out a few experiments at a time and using the results of those experiments to determine the next experiment to be done. The best known of the sequential design approaches is called the simplex method. A simplex is essentially a geometric figure having a number of vertices equal to one more than the number of variables. For example, if we have two variables, the simplex is a triangle, three variables a tetrahedron, and so on.

Let us consider the case of two variables, x_1 and x_2. An algorithm describes the initial simplex to be performed (Fig. 57.1). By performing experiments 1–3, described by the initial simplex, and recording their responses, the next set of experiments can be described. If we obtain the lowest response for experiment 2, it can therefore be assumed that a higher response would be obtained in the opposite direction. By reflecting point 2, we can obtain point 4. By performing the experiment described by point 4 we obtain its response, thereby perpetuating the simplex.

Four rules can be described for a simplex design:

1. **A new simplex is formed** by rejecting the point with the lowest response and replacing it with its mirror image across the line defined by the two remaining points.
2. **If the new point in the simplex** has the lowest response, return to the preceding simplex and create the new simplex by using instead the point with the second-lowest response.
3. **If a point is retained in three consecutive simplexes,** then it can be assumed that an optimum has been reached. (Note: it may be that this optimum is not the true optimum, but that the simplex has been trapped at a false optimum. In this situation, it is necessary to start the simplex again, or use a modified simplex in which the step size is not fixed but variable, see Fig. 57.2.)
4. **If a point is suggested by the simplex** algorithm that is beyond the limit of the variables, i.e. it is beyond the safe working limits of an instrument, then the point is rejected and an artificially low response is assigned to it, and the simplex is continued with rules 1–3.

Simultaneous design

In a simultaneous approach, the relationship between variables and results is studied as follows: carry out an appropriate design, apply a mathematical model to the design and then apply a response surface method to the data. Appropriate designs might be based on factorial designs (full or fractional) or a central composite design. Response surface methods frequently rely on visualisation of the data for interpretation.

Factorial design

In general terms, consider the case of two variables at two levels, e.g. a high value and a low value. This is termed a two-level design or a (full) 2^k factorial design, where k is the number of variables. Therefore we have $2^2 = 4$ experiments to be done. Often the values of the variables are coded; this is done for

Box 57.1 Example of a two-level factorial design

The recovery of methadone by liquid–liquid extraction, from 1 litre of river water, and subsequent analysis by high-performance liquid chromatography is to be optimised. It has been determined that the following are critical to achieving an optimum extraction: the volume of extraction solvent, the mass of salt added and the pH of the water sample. Therefore, a 2^3 design is required. The experimental levels are: volume of extraction solvent (5 and 50 mL); mass of salt added (0.0 and 1.0 g); and pH (4 and 7). The coded values for the experiment are shown in Table 57.1. The +1 values represent the higher value, e.g. pH 7, while −1 represents the lower value, e.g. pH 4. The number of experiments can be reduced if a fractional factorial design is used. For example, in this situation the fractional factorial design would become $2^{3-1} = 4$ experiments. In this situation, the experiments labelled with an asterisk in Table 57.1 would be done.

Table 57.1 Two-level factorial design

Experiment	Volume of solvent	salt	pH	Result
1	−1	−1	−1	Y_1
2*	+1	−1	−1	Y_2
3	+1	+1	−1	Y_3
4*	−1	+1	−1	Y_4
5*	−1	−1	+1	Y_5
6	+1	−1	+1	Y_6
7	+1	+1	+1	Y_7
8*	−1	+1	+1	Y_8

convenience purposes only. In this example, high and low values will be coded as (+) and (−). Alternatively, it might be the case that the number of variables is three. In this situation, we would have a 2^3 factorial design, requiring eight experiments. An example of a two-level factorial design is shown in Box 57.1.

The limitation of the two-level factorial design approach is that no estimation of curvature can be determined. In order to take this into account, the use of designs with at least three levels is required. Three-level designs are therefore often known as response surface designs. Probably the most important design in this context is the central composite design (CCD). Central composite designs consist of a full (or fractional) factorial design onto which is superimposed a star design. The number of experiments to be done (R) can be worked out as follows:

$$R = 2^k + 2k + n_0 \qquad [57.1]$$

Response surface methodology allows the relationship between the responses and variables to be quantified, using a mathematical model, and to be visualised. Thus the equation for a straight-line graph can be written as:

$$y = mx + c \qquad [57.2]$$

where m is a constant and c is the intercept. This describes the relationship between a single variable (x) and its response (y). Using the previous example, with three variables (x_1, x_2 and x_3) it is possible to extend this mathematical model.

Table 57.2 Central composite design for three variables

Experiment	Variable 1	Variable 2	Variable 3	Result
Factorial design, 2^3				
1	−1	−1	−1	Y_1
2	+1	−1	−1	Y_2
3	+1	+1	−1	Y_3
4	−1	+1	−1	Y_4
5	−1	−1	+1	Y_5
6	+1	−1	+1	Y_6
7	+1	+1	+1	Y_7
8	−1	+1	+1	Y_8
Star design, 2 k				
9	−α	0	0	Y_9
10	+α	0	0	Y_{10}
11	0	−α	0	Y_{11}
12	0	+α	0	Y_{12}
13	0	0	−α	Y_{13}
14	0	0	+α	Y_{14}
Centre points				
15	0	0	0	Y_{15}
16	0	0	0	Y_{16}

First of all, we can consider how each of the variables influences the response (y) in a linear manner. However, the relationship between y and x_1, x_2 and x_3. may not be linear, so it is necessary to consider the possibility of curvature. This is done in terms of a quadratic variable, i.e. a squared dependence (x_1^2, x_2^2 and x_3^2). Finally, it is also important to consider the effects of possible interactions between the variables, $x_1 \rightarrow x_2 \rightarrow x_3$, i.e. x_1x_2, x_1x_3 and x_2x_3. The overall general equation can therefore be written as:

$$Y = b_0+b_1x_1+b_2x_2+b_3x_3+b_4x_2+b_5x_2+b_6x_2+b_7x_1x_2+b_8x_1x_3+b_9x_2x_3 \quad [57.3]$$

where b_0 is the intercept parameter and $b_1 - b_9$ are the regression coefficients for linear, quadratic and interaction effects.

This equation can be analysed using multiple linear regression and tested for statistical significance at, for example, the 95% confidence interval (see p. 524). In addition, the response can be explored by plotting a three-dimensional graph. Unfortunately, in the above example, three variables are present. This immediately constrains what it is possible to plot on the graph (one of the axes must be the response). One way to select the two variables to plot is by considering their statistical significance and then selecting two variables that are significant at the 95% confidence interval. An alternative approach might be simply to plot the two variables you might wish to discuss in your experimental report. A typical response surface is shown in Fig. 57.3. It can be seen that the 'time' variable has a maximum at 8–12 min, while the 'temperature' variable has a maximum at 160–180 °C. Further experiments might be carried out at these two

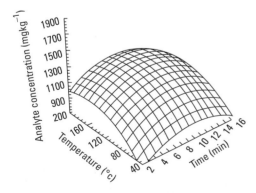

Fig. 57.3 Example of a response surface.

Table 57.3 A typical randomised CCD

Original experiment (from Table 57.2)	(New) experiment run order	Variable 1	Variable 2	Variable 3	Result
8	1	−1	+1	+1	Y_1
3	2	+1	+1	−1	Y_2
14	3	0	0	+α	Y_3
6	4	+1	−1	+1	Y_4
12	5	0	+α	0	Y_5
13	6	0	0	−α	Y_6
4	7	−1	+1	−1	Y_7
1	8	−1	−1	−1	Y_8
7	9	1	1	1	Y_9
15	10	0	0	0	Y_{10}
10	11	+α	0	0	Y_{11}
16	12	0	0	0	Y_{12}
9	13	−α	0	0	Y_{13}
2	14	+1	−1	−1	Y_{14}
5	15	−1	−1	+1	Y_{15}
11	16	0	−α	0	Y_{16}

maxima to determine the repeatability of the approach. However, it is necessary to plot all variables consecutively to identify all maxima.

In general, it is important to consider the following issues when carrying out an experimental design:

- **Carry out repeat measurements** for a particular combination of variables, to determine the repeatability of the approach.
- **To remove systematic error (bias),** you should randomise the order in which experiments are done (p. 31).
- **It is important to eliminate intervariable effects (confounding),** i.e. the situation where one variable is interrelated to another.
- **Often, the large number of experiments to be carried out makes it impossible to run all of them on the same day.** If this happens run your experiments in discrete groups or 'blocks'.

Principal component analysis

The use of modern automated instrumentation allows the acquisition of large amounts of chemical data. As well as simply tabulating the data, other forms of 'analysis' are required to interrogate the chemical information contained within the data. One such approach, enabling the simplification of large data sets by reducing the number of independent variables, is principal component analysis (PCA). The basis of this approach is:

- **to reduce the number of original independent variables** into new axes, so-called 'principal components' (PCs), each of which can be estimated unambiguously – the data contained in these new PCs, and which are expressed as 'scores', are uncorrelated with each other;

- **to express, in a few PCs,** the amount of variation in the data;
- **to have each new PC** express a decreasing amount of variation.

An example of the application of PCA is shown in Box 57.2.

Box 57.2 Example of principal component analysis

Consider a chemical reaction where reactants, X and Y, produce product Z. The yield of Z is dependent upon the temperature of the reaction and its pH. And suppose that the reaction has been carried out by a class of students, providing a large amount of data. By plotting temperature against pH (Fig. 57.4), we can identify a single new variable, PC_1, which obviously contains aspects of pH and temperature, i.e.

$$PC_1 = a(temperature) = b(pH) \qquad [57.4]$$

PC_1 can then be used to replace the original two variables. In addition, the direction of PC_1 indicates where the greatest variation in the data lies. The other information that can be obtained is the scatter of the data on either side of the regression line. This is due to random variation rather than a trend. In this example, therefore, it is not possible to extract any further PCs.

In eqn [57.4], the coefficients a and b indicate the relative importance of the two variables to PC_1, and are called factor loadings. In general, therefore, the plotting of factor loadings between any two PCs can provide useful information as to the relationship of variables to the PCs. Figure 57.5 shows such a plot. It is seen that variables 1–3 contribute strongly (positively) and variable 5 negatively to PC_1. Variable 6 contributes strongly to PC_2, whereas variable 4 contributes significantly to both PCs.

Bayesian statistics

To evaluate evidence you need to consider how the material has been transferred from object A to object B, how far it has travelled from, how long it remains on the object and whether this transfer can occur by an unrelated mechanism to that proposed. When a case is presented to court, it is essentially done so using a prosecution hypothesis, H(p) the suspect is linked to the crime versus a defence hypothesis, H(d) the suspect is not linked to the crime, to enable the jury to assess the relationship between two individuals - the defendant and victim. Holistically the outcome of the case is based on the strength or evidential weighting of each of the evidence types presented in the context of the circumstances of the case.

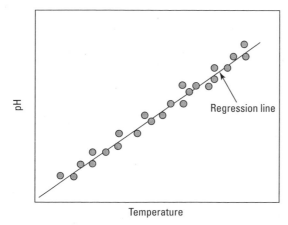

Fig. 57.4 Determination of principal component 1.

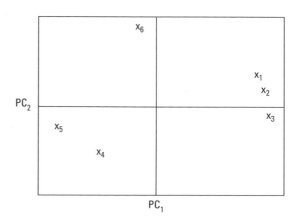

Fig. 57.5 Principal component analysis.

When two competing hypotheses or propositions are presented, a Bayesian approach to probability can be applied to the interpretation and evaluation of forensic evidence types that takes into account this context sensitivity. The basic concept in Bayesian statistics is therefore that of conditional probability – i.e. it takes into account a belief regarding an event based on a number of factors that may condition its significance. This can be translated to the following statement of probability.

Given the event B, the probability of the event A is x, and is represented as:

$$P(A|B) = x \tag{57.5}$$

This equation of the statement of probability (P) of an event A, is given under the condition of other known factors – hence a conditional rather than frequentist probability approach. It is important to recognise, though, that $P(A|B)$ is not the same as $P(B|A)$. This is known as transposing the conditional, or prosecutor's fallacy – for example, if $P(A|B) = 95\%$ probability that the offender has blue eyes, it does not mean that there is a 95% probability that any blue-eyed person is the offender.

Bayes theorem can therefore be defined as:

$$P(A|B) = \frac{P(B|A)P(A)}{P(B)} \tag{57.6}$$

This defines the relationship between the probabilities of A and B and the conditional probabilities of A given B and B given A, where: $P(A)$ and $P(B)$ are the prior probabilities and $P(A|B)$ is the posterior probability.

Applied to a forensic context where two competing propositions (p) are considered (p(Hp) and p(Hd)), the equation needs to take into account the evidence (E) and contextual information (I).

Simplified, this relates to:

$$\text{Posterior odds} = \text{likelihood ratio} \times \text{prior odds} \tag{57.7}$$

where the likelihood ratio is a measure of the belief of a hypothesis based on the evidence presented, commonly expressed as a verbal scale in case reporting (Table 57.1) and the prior odds (the contextual information) is based on the initial belief given the information you already have.

This translates to:

$$\frac{p(Hp|I,E)}{p(Hd|I,E)} = \frac{p(E|Hp,I)}{p(E|Hd,I)} \times \frac{p(Hp,I)}{p(Hd,I)} \tag{57.8}$$

Bayesian networks

A Bayesian network can be used for complex probabilistic cases to calculate the likelihood ratio when there are a number of interdependent factors that condition the probability. Commercially available software, e.g. Hugin Researcher can be used to construct a network for application to a number of evidence types. Each piece of evidence or event/proposition is commonly termed a node, and these are linked together using arrows. This graphical structure allows for the description and modelling of these interdependent relationships that are connected together. It is within these connections that the uncertainty is modelled, using conditional probabilities to form the basis of the

Table 57.4 The likelihood ratio expressed as a verbal scale of strength of evidence. From AFSP, 2009

Verbal scale	LR value in support of Hp	LR value in support of Hd
Weak support	1–10	1–0.1
Moderate support	10–100	0.1–0.01
Moderately strong support	100–1000	0.01–0.001
Strong support	1,000–10,000	0.001–0.0001
Very strong support	10,000–1,000,000	0.0001–0.00001
Extremely strong support	1,000,000+	<0.000001

relationship interactions between the various components of the problem under investigation. The underlying Bayesian algorithms use these conditional probabilities to calculate the probability of different hypotheses given a series of specific observations. This approach has been recently successful in assigning a likelihood of fatality based on toxicological and pathological findings (Langford *et al.*, 2015) as well as having being developed for DNA modelling (Cereda *et al.*, 2014) and individualisation (Biedermann *et al.*, 2013).

The Bayesian statistical approach can provide a logical coherent evaluation of the strength of the evidence. However, one of the criticisms of this approach is that the use of likelihood ratios is subjective. Caution needs to be exerted when using such an approach in the court to make sure that the jurors understand the significance of the evidence being presented in such a manner and that the Bayesian approach is not misunderstood. For further information and a more in-depth explanation of the use of Bayesian forensic data analysis, see Taroni *et al.*, 2010.

Text references

Association of Forensic Science Providers (2009) Standards for the formulation of evaluative forensic science expert opinion. *Science and Justice* **49**: 161–164.

Biedermann, A., Garbolini, P. and Taroni, F. (2013) The subjectivist interpretation of probability and the problem of individualisation in forensic science. *Science and Justice* 53: 192–200.

Cereda, G., Biedermann, A., Hall, D and Taroni, F. (2014) Object-orientated Bayesian networks for evaluating DIP-STR profiling results from unbalanced DNA mixtures. *Forensic Science International – Genetics* **8**: 159–168.

Kowalski, B.R. (1978) *Chemometrics.* Taylor and Francis, Abingdon, Oxford.

Langford, A.M., Bolton, J.R, Carlin, M.G. and Palmer, R. (2015) Post-mortem toxicology: A pilot study to evaluate the use of a Bayesian Network to assess the likelihood of fatality. *Journal of Forensic and Legal Medicine* **33**: 82–90.

Taroni, F., Bozza, S., Biedermann, A., Garbolino, P. and Aitken, C. (2010) *Data Analysis in Forensic Science: A Bayesian Decision Perspective.* Wiley, Chichester.

Sources for further study

Beebe, K.R., Pell, R.J. and Seasholz, M.B. (1998) *Chemometrics: A Practical Guide.* Wiley, Chichester.

Brereton, R.G. (2003) *Chemometrics: Data Analysis for the Laboratory and Chemical Plant.* Wiley, Chichester.

Brereton, R.G. (2007) *Applied Chemometrics for Scientists.* Wiley, Chichester.

Brereton, R.G. (2009) *Chemometrics for Pattern Recognition.* Wiley, Chichester.

Jensen, F and Nielsen, T. (2007) *Bayesian Networks and Decision Graphs.* Springer, New York.

Miller, J.N. and Miller, J.C. (2005) *Statistics and Chemometrics for Analytical Chemistry,* 5th edn. Prentice Hall, Harlow. [Gives detailed coverage of calibration methods and the validity of analytical measurements.]

Otto, M. (2007) *Chemometrics: Statistics and Computer Application in Analytical Chemistry,* 2nd edn. Wiley, Chichester.

Steiner, E. (2008) *The Chemistry Maths Book,* 2nd edn. Oxford University Press, Oxford.

Taroni, F. Aitken, C.G.G., Garbolino, P and Biedermann, A. (2006) *Bayesian Networks and Probabilistic Inference in Forensic Science.* Wiley, Chichester.

Varmuza, K. and Filzmoser, P. (2009) *Introduction to Multivariate Statistical Analysis in Chemometrics.* CRC Press, Boca Raton.

Study exercises

57.1 Search the scientific literature and find a journal article in which a factorial design or central composite design has been used to optimise a set of variables. Consider how they selected the boundaries of their chosen variables.

57.2 Search the scientific literature and find a journal article in which a principal component analysis has been used to interrogate data and identify patterns within the data. Consider how the visualisation of data using PCA may be beneficial.

57.3 Consider how you might use either optimisation or pattern recognition techniques in your work, such as a research project.

57.4 Conduct a literature search on the current use of Bayesian networks in forensic science and evaluate how effective this approach could be.

Communicating information

Written communication is an essential component of all sciences. Most courses include writing exercises in which you will learn to describe ideas and results accurately, succinctly and in an appropriate style and format. The following are features common to all forms of scientific writing.

Organising time

Making a timetable at the outset helps ensure that you give each stage adequate attention and complete the work on time (e.g. Fig. 58.1). To create and use a timetable:

1. Break down the task into stages.
2. Decide on the proportion of the total time each stage should take.
3. Set realistic deadlines for completing each stage, allowing some time for slippage.
4. Refer to your timetable frequently as you work – if you fail to meet one of your deadlines, make a serious effort to catch up as soon as possible.

 KEY POINT *The appropriate allocation of your time to reading, planning, writing and revising will differ according to the task in hand (see Chapters 60–62).*

Organising your information and ideas

Before you write, you need to gather and/or think about relevant material (Chapters 45–47). You must then decide:

- what needs to be included and what doesn't;
- in what order it should appear.

Start by jotting down headings for everything of potential relevance to the topic (this is sometimes called 'brainstorming'). A spider diagram (Fig. 58.2) or a mind map (Fig. 67.2) will help you organise these ideas. The next stage is to create an outline of your text (Fig. 58.3). Outlines are valuable because they:

- force you to think about and plan the structure;
- provide a checklist so nothing is missed out;
- ensure the material is balanced in content and length;
- help you organise figures and tables by showing where they will be used.

In an essay or review, the structure of your writing should help the reader to assimilate and understand your main points.

 KEY POINT *A suitable structure is essential to the narrative of your writing, and should be carefully considered at the outset.*

Subdivisions of the topic could simply be related to the nature of the subject matter (e.g. estimating the *post mortem* interval (PMI)) and should proceed logically (e.g. time discovered to *post-mortem* findings).

A chronological approach is good for evaluation of past work (e.g. the development of fingerprint analysis), whereas a step-by-step comparison might be best for certain exam questions (e.g. 'Discuss methods of analysis for drugs of abuse'). There is little choice about the structure of most practical and project reports (see p. 560).

Time management – practical advice is given in Chapter 65, pp. 585–588.

Creating an outline – an informal outline can be made simply by indicating the order of sections on a spider diagram (as in Fig. 58.2).

Monday:	morning	Lectures (University)
	afternoon	Practical (University)
	evening	Initial analysis and brainstorming (Home)
Tuesday:	morning	Lectures (University)
	afternoon	Locate sources (Library)
	evening	Background reading (Library)
Wednesday:	morning	Background reading (Library)
	afternoon	Squash (Sports hall)
	evening	Planning (Home)
Thursday:	morning	Lectures (University)
	afternoon	Additional reading (Library)
	evening	Prepare outline (Library)
Friday:	morning	Lab class (University)
	afternoon	Write first draft (Home)
	evening	Write first draft (Home)
Saturday:	morning	Shopping (Town)
	afternoon	Review first draft (Home)
	evening	Revise first draft (Home)
Sunday:		Free
	morning	Produce final copy (Home)
	afternoon	Proofread and print
	evening	essay (Home)
Monday:	morning	Final read-through and check Submit essay (deadline midday)

Fig. 58.1 **Timetable for writing a short essay.**

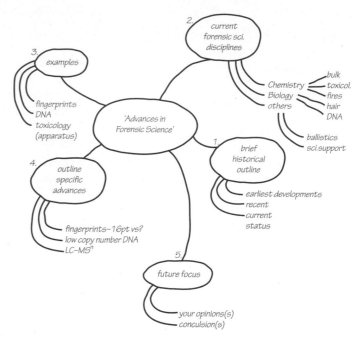

Fig. 58.2 Spider diagram showing how you might 'brainstorm' an essay with the title 'Advances in Forensic Science'. Write out the essay title in full to form the spider's body, and as you think of possible content, place headings around this to form its legs. Decide which headings are relevant and which are not, and use arrows to note connections between subjects. This may influence your choice of order and may help to make your writing flow because the links between paragraphs will be natural. You can make an informal outline directly on a spider diagram by adding numbers indicating a sequence of paragraphs (as shown). This method is very effective when you must work quickly, as with an essay written under exam conditions.

Writing

Adopting a scientific style

Your main aim in developing a scientific style should be to get your message across directly and unambiguously. While you can try to achieve this through a set of 'rules' (see Box 58.1), you may find other requirements driving your writing in a contradictory direction. For instance, the need to be accurate and complete may result in text littered with technical terms, and the flow may be

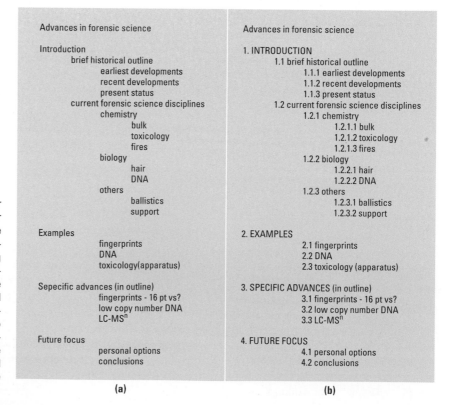

Fig. 58.3 Formal outlines. These are useful for a long piece of work where you or the reader might otherwise lose track of the structure. The headings for sections and paragraphs are simply written in sequence with the type of lettering and level of indentation indicating their hierarchy. Two different forms of formal outline are shown – a minimal form (a) and a numbered form (b). Note that the headings used in an outline are often repeated within the essay to emphasise its structure. The content of an outline will depend on the time you have available and the nature of the work, but the most detailed hierarchy you should reasonably include is the subject of each paragraph.

Box 58.1　How to achieve a clear, readable style

Words and phrases

- Choose short, clear words and phrases rather than long ones – e.g. use 'build' rather than 'fabricate'; 'now' rather than 'at the present time'. At certain times, technical terms must be used for precision, but don't use jargon if you don't have to.
- Don't worry too much about repeating words – especially when to introduce an alternative might subtly alter your meaning.
- Where appropriate, use the first person to describe your actions ('We decided to'; 'I conclude that'), but not if this is specifically discouraged by your supervisor.
- Favour active forms of writing ('the observer completed the survey in ten minutes') rather than a passive style ('the survey was completed by the observer in ten minutes').
- Use tenses consistently – past tense is always used for Materials and Methods ('samples were taken from. . . ') and for reviewing past work ('Smith (1990) concluded that. . . '). The present tense is used when describing data ('Fig. 1 shows. . . '), for generalisations ('Most authorities agree that. . . ') and conclusions ('I conclude that. . . ').
- Use statements in parentheses sparingly – they disrupt the reader's attention to your central theme.
- Avoid clichés and colloquialisms – they are usually inappropriate in a scientific context.

Punctuation

- Try to use a variety of types of punctuation – to make the text more interesting to read.
- Decide whether you wish to use 'closed' punctuation (frequent commas at the end of clauses) or 'open' punctuation (less frequent punctuation) and be consistent.
- Don't link two sentences with a comma – use a full stop, this is an example of what *not* to do.
- Pay special attention to apostrophes, using the following rules:
  - To indicate possession, use an apostrophe before an 's' for a singular word (e.g. the rat's temperature was. . . ') and after the 's' for a plural word ending in 's' (e.g. the rats' temperatures were = 'the temperatures of the rats were'). If the word has a special plural (e.g. woman → women) then use the apostrophe before the s ('the women's temperatures were. . . ').
  - When contracting words, use an apostrophe (e.g. do not = don't; it's = it is), but remember that contractions are generally *not* used in formal scientific writing. Note that we have used 'don't' and some other contractions in this textbook to avoid a dry, formal writing style, aiming for a user-friendly and accessible approach.
  - Do *not* use an apostrophe for 'its' as the possessive form of 'it' (e.g. 'the university and its surroundings'). Note that 'it's' is reserved for 'it is'. This is a very common mistake.
  - Never use an apostrophe to indicate plurals. Even for abbreviations, the accepted style is now to omit the apostrophe for the plural (e.g. 'the ELISAs were').

Sentences

- Don't make them overlong or complicated.
- Introduce variety in structure and length.
- If unhappy with the structure of a sentence, try chopping it into a series of shorter sentences.

Paragraphs

- Get the paragraph length right – five sentences or so. Do *not* submit an essay that consists of a single paragraph, nor one of single-sentence paragraphs.
- Make sure each paragraph is logical, dealing with a single topic or theme.
- Take care with the first sentence in a paragraph (the 'topic' sentence) – this introduces the theme of the paragraph. Further sentences should then develop this theme (e.g. by providing supporting information, examples or contrasting cases).
- Use 'linking' words or phrases to maintain the flow of the text within a paragraph: 'for example'; 'in contrast'; 'however'; 'on the other hand'.
- Make your text more readable by adopting modern layout style – the first paragraph in any section of text is usually *not* indented, but following paragraphs are (by the equivalent of three character spaces). In addition, the space between paragraphs should be slightly larger than the space between lines. Follow departmental guidelines if these specify a format.
- Group paragraphs in sections under appropriate headings and subheadings to reinforce the structure underlying your writing.
- Think carefully about the first and last paragraphs in any piece of writing – these are often the most important as they respectively set the aims and report the conclusions.

Note: If you're not sure what is meant by any of the terms used here, consult a guide on writing (see the sources for further study section at the end of the chapter).

continually interrupted by references to the literature. The need to be succinct also affects style and readability through the use of, for example, stacked noun-adjectives (e.g. 'single nucleotide polymorphism) and acronyms (e.g. 'SNP'). Finally, style is very much a matter of taste and each tutor, examiner, supervisor or editor will have pet loves and hates, which you may have to accommodate. Different assignments will need different styles – Box 58.2 gives further details.

Developing technique

Writing is a skill that can be improved, but not instantly. You should analyse your deficiencies with the help of feedback from your tutors, be prepared to change work habits (e.g. start planning your work more carefully) and be willing to learn from some of the excellent texts that are available on scientific writing (p. 544).

Getting started

A common problem is 'writer's block' – inactivity or stalling brought on by a variety of causes. If blocked, ask yourself these questions:

- Are you comfortable with your surroundings? Make sure you are seated comfortably at a reasonably clear desk and have minimised the possibility of interruptions and distractions.
- Are you trying to write too soon? Have you clarified your thoughts on the subject? Have you done enough preliminary reading?
- Are you happy with the underlying structure of your work? If you haven't made an outline, try this. If you are unhappy because you can't think of a particular detail at the planning stage, just start writing – it is more likely to come to you while you are thinking of something else.
- Are you trying to be too clever? Your first sentence doesn't have to be earth-shattering in content or particularly smart in style. A short statement of fact or a definition is fine. If there will be time for revision, get your ideas down on paper and revise grammar, content and order later.
- Do you really need to start writing at the beginning? Try writing the opening remarks after a more straightforward part. With reports of experimental work, the Materials and Methods section may be the easiest to start at.
- Are you too tired to work? Don't try to 'sweat it out' by writing for long periods at a stretch – stop frequently for a rest.

Revising your text

Wholesale revision of your first draft is strongly advised for all writing, apart from in exams. If a word processor is available, this can be a simple process. Where possible, schedule your writing so you can leave the first draft to 'settle' for at least a couple of days. When you return to it fresh, you will see more easily where improvements can be made. Try the following structured revision process, each stage being covered in a separate scan of your text:

1. **Examine content** – have you included everything you need to? Is all the material relevant?
2. **Check the grammar and spelling** – can you spot any 'howlers'?
3. **Focus on clarity** – is the text clear and unambiguous? Does each sentence really say what you want it to say?
4. **Be succinct** – what could be missed out without spoiling the essence of your work? It might help to imagine an editor has set you the target of reducing the text by 15%.
5. **Improve your style** – could the text read better? Consider the sentence and paragraph structure and the way your text develops to its conclusion.

*Improving your writing skills – you need to take a long-term view if you wish to improve your writing skills. An essential preliminary is to invest in and **make full use of** a personal reference library (see Box 58.3).*

Writing with a word processor – use the dynamic/interactive features of the word processor (Chapter 48) to help you get started: first make notes on structure and content, then expand these to form a first draft and finally revise/improve the text.

Benefits of talking about your work – discussing your topic with a friend or colleague might bring out ideas or reveal deficiencies in your knowledge.

Revising your text – to improve clarity and shorten your text, 'distil' each sentence by taking away unnecessary words, and 'condense' words or phrases by choosing a shorter alternative.

Box 58.2 Using appropriate writing styles for different purposes (with examples)

Note that courses tend to move from assignments that are predominantly descriptive in the early years to a more analytical approach towards the final year (see Chapter 68). Also, different styles may be required in different sections of a write-up – for example, descriptive for introductory historical aspects and becoming more analytical in later sections.

Descriptive writing

This is the most straightforward style, providing factual information on a particular subject. This approach is most appropriate:

- in essays where you are asked to 'describe' or 'explain' (p. 569);
- when describing the results of a practical exercise, such as, 'The experiment shown in Figure 1 confirmed that alcohol stability was strongly influenced by temperature, as the rate observed at 20°C was more than double that seen at 4°C.'

However, in literature reviews and essays where you are asked to 'discuss' (p. 569) a particular topic, the descriptive approach is mostly inappropriate – as in the following example where a large amount of specific information from a single scientific paper has been used without any attempt to highlight the most important points:

'In a study carried out between July and October 2006, a total of 350 blood samples were screened for alcohol. Alcohol was detected in 74% of these cases. Blood alcohol concentrations greater than 200 mg per 100 mL were found in 34% of these cases, with 18% of the samples also positive for acetone (Grey and Gray, 2006).'

In the most extreme examples, whole paragraphs or pages of essays may be based on descriptive factual detail from a single source, often with a single citation at the end of the material. Such essays often score low marks in project work where a more analytical approach is required (such as using spreadsheets, Chapter 62).

Comparative writing

This technique is an important component of academic writing, and it will be necessary to develop your comparative writing skills as you progress through your course. Its applications include:

- answering essay questions and assignments of the 'compare and contrast' type (p. 569);
- comparing your results with previously published work in the Discussion section of a practical report.

To use this style, first decide on those aspects you wish to compare and then consider the material (e.g. different literature sources) from these aspects – in what ways do they agree or disagree with each other? One approach is to compare/contrast a different aspect in each paragraph. At a practical level, you can use 'linking' words and phrases to help orientate your reader, as you move between aspects where there is agreement and disagreement. These include, for agreement: 'in both cases'; 'in agreement with'; 'is also shown by the study of'; 'similarly'; 'in the same way'. And, for disagreement: 'however'; 'although'; 'in contrast to'; 'on the other hand'; 'which differs from'. The comparative style is fairly straightforward, once you have decided on the aspects to be compared. The following brief example compares two different studies using this style:

'While Grey and Gray (2006) reported that acetone and alcohol was present in 46 cases out of 350 blood samples, Black and White (2007) showed that 132 cases from 1432 cases were positive for acetone.'

Comparative text typically makes use of two or more references per paragraph.

Analytical writing

Typically, this is the most appropriate form of writing for:

- a review of scientific literature on a particular topic;
- an essay where you are asked to 'discuss' (p. 568) different aspects of a particular topic;
- evaluating a number of different published sources within the Discussion section of a final-year project dissertation.

By considering the significance of the information provided in the various sources you have read, you will be able to take a more critical approach. Your writing should evaluate the importance of the material in the context of your topic (see also Chapter 47). In analytical writing, you need to demonstrate critical thinking (p. 455) and personal input about the topic in a well-structured text that provides clear messages, presented in a logical order and demonstrating synthesis from a number of sources by appropriate use of citations (p. 437). Detailed information and relevant examples are used only to explain or develop a particular aspect, and not simply as 'padding' to bulk up the essay. The following example shows how detail can be used for explanation:

'acetone can be found in conjunction with alcohol (ethanol) in blood samples. A short-term study with a relatively small number of cases (350 samples) indicated that acetone was found in a relatively small number of cases (Grey and Gray, 2006). This observation was confirmed by a larger study where 132 cases from 1432 cases were positive for acetone (Black and White, 2007).'

Analytical writing is based on a broad range of sources, typically with several citations per paragraph.

Box 58.3 Improving your writing ability by consulting a personal reference library

Using dictionaries

We all know that a dictionary helps with spelling and definitions, but how many of us use one effectively? You should:

- Keep a dictionary beside you when writing and always use it if in any doubt about spelling or definitions.
- Use it to prepare a list of words that you have difficulty in spelling – apart from speeding up the checking process, the act of writing out the words helps commit them to memory.
- Use it to write out a personal glossary of terms – this can help you memorise definitions. From time to time, test yourself.

Not all dictionaries are the same! Ask your tutor or supervisor whether he/she has a preference and why. Try out the *Oxford Advanced Learner's Dictionary*, which is particularly useful because it gives examples of use of all words and helps with grammar – for example, by indicating which prepositions to use with verbs. Dictionaries on forensic science tend to be limited in scope. However, *Forensic Science: An Illustrated Dictionary* by J.C. Brenner (CRC Press) covers a wide range of areas and topics, including commonly used forensic terms.

Using a thesaurus

A thesaurus contains lists of words of similar meaning grouped thematically; words of opposite meaning always appear nearby.

- Use a thesaurus to find a more precise and appropriate word to fit your meaning, but check definitions of unfamiliar words with a dictionary.
- Use it to find a word or phrase 'on the tip of your tongue' by looking up a word of similar meaning.
- Use it to increase your vocabulary.

Roget's Thesaurus is the standard. Several publishers produce a combined dictionary and thesaurus.

Using guides for written English

These provide help with the use of words.

- Use guides to solve grammatical problems such as when to use 'shall' or 'will', 'which' or 'that', 'effect' or 'affect', etc.
- Use them for help with the paragraph concept and the correct use of punctuation.
- Use them to learn how to structure writing for different tasks.

Common errors

These include (with examples):

- **Problems over singular and plural words** – 'the results shows'.
- **Verbose text** – 'One definition that can be employed in this situation is given in the following sentence.'
- **Misconstructed sentences** – 'Health and safety regulations should be made aware of . . .'
- **Misuse of punctuation, especially commas and apostrophes** – for examples, see Box 58.1.
- **Poorly constructed paragraphs** – for advice/examples, see Box 58.1.

Sources for further study

Beyer, R.E. (2014) *A Scientific Approach to Writing for Engineers and Scientists.* Wiley, Chichester.

Butterfield, J. (ed.) (2015) *Fowler's Dictionary of Modern English Usage,* revised 4th edn. Oxford University Press, New York.

Clark, R. *The English Style Book: A Guide to the Writing of Scholarly English.* Available at: http://www.litencyc.com/stylebook/stylebook.php. Last accessed 29/08/2017.

Kane, T.S. (2000) *The Oxford Essential Guide to Writing.* Oxford University Press, New York.

Lindsay, D. (2011) *Scientific Writing = Thinking in Words.* CSIRO, Collingwood.

McMillan, K.M. and Weyers, J.D.B. (2008) *The Smarter Study Skills Companion.* Pearson, Harlow.

Partridge, E. (1990) *You Have a Point There.* Routledge and Kegan Paul, London.

Study exercises

58.1 'Brainstorm' an essay title. Pair up with a partner in your class. Together, pick a suitable essay title from a past exam paper. Using the spider diagram or another technique, individually 'brainstorm' the title. Meet afterwards, compare your ideas and discuss their relative merits and disadvantages.

58.2 Improve your writing technique. From the following checklist, identify the three weakest aspects of your writing, either in your own opinion or from essay/assignment feedback:

- grammar;
- paragraph organisation;
- presentation of work;
- punctuation;
- scientific style;
- sentence structure/variety;
- spelling;
- structure and flow;
- vocabulary.

Now either borrow a book from a library or buy a book that deals with your weakest aspects of writing. Read the relevant chapters or sections and for each aspect write down some tips that should help you in future.

58.3 Improve your spelling and vocabulary with two lists. Create a pair of lists and pin these up beside your desk. One should be entitled 'Spelling Mistakes' and the other 'New Words'. Now, whenever you make a mistake in spelling or have to look up how to spell a word in a dictionary, add the problem word to your spelling list, showing where you made the mistake. Also, whenever you come across a word whose meaning is unclear to you, look it up in a dictionary and write the word and its meaning in the 'new words' vocabulary list.

Most students feel very nervous about speaking in public. This is natural, since very few people are sufficiently confident and outgoing that they look forward to such events. Additionally, the technical nature of the subject matter may give you cause for concern, especially if you feel that some members of the audience have a greater knowledge than you have. However, this is a fundamental method of scientific communication and it therefore forms an important component of many forensic science courses.

The comments in this chapter apply equally to informal talks, for example those based on assignments and project work, to more formal conference presentations and to (mock) court appearances (expert testimony). It is hoped that the advice and guidance given below will encourage you to make the most of your opportunities for public speaking, but there is no substitute for practice. Do not expect to find all of the answers from this, or any other, book. Rehearse, and learn from your own experience.

 KEY POINT *The 'three Rs' of successful public speaking are: reflect – give sufficient thought to all aspects of your presentation, particularly at the planning stage; rehearse – to improve your delivery; rewrite – modify the content and style of your material in response to your own ideas and to the comments of others.*

Whatever discipline in forensic science you choose to follow in your career, from crime scene investigation through laboratory analysis to defence consultancy, at some point you are likely to be required to give expert witness oral testimony in a court of law. Giving evidence in court has many similarities to the general principles of public speaking described in this chapter, but there are key differences and responsibilities, detailed on pp. 556–559. Your course is likely to include role-play sessions where you will gain practical experience in expert witness testimony under mock trial conditions.

Preparing for a spoken presentation

Preliminary information

Begin by marshalling the details needed to plan your presentation, including:

- the duration of the talk (if defined);
- whether time for questions is included;
- the size and location of the room;
- the projection/lighting facilities provided, and whether pointers or similar aids are available.

It is especially important to find out whether the room has the necessary equipment for digital or slide projection (projector and screen, black-out curtains or blinds, appropriate lighting) or overhead projection before you prepare your audio-visual aids. If you concentrate only on the spoken part of your presentation at this stage, you are inviting trouble later on. Have a look around the room and try out the equipment at the earliest opportunity, so that you are able to use the lights, projector, etc. with confidence. For digital projection systems, check that you can load/present your material.

Opportunities for practising speaking skills include:

- *answering lecturers' questions;*
- *contributing in tutorials;*
- *talking to informal groups;*
- *stating your views at formal (committee) meetings;*
- *demonstrating or explaining to other students, e.g. during a practical;*
- *asking questions at seminars;*
- *answering an examiner's questions in an oral exam;*
- *taking part in role-play, e.g. courtroom testimony.*

Learning from experience – *use your own experience of good and bad lecturers to shape your performance. Some of the more common errors include:*

- *speaking too quickly;*
- *reading from notes and ignoring the audience;*
- *unexpressive, impersonal or indistinct speech;*
- *distracting mannerisms;*
- *poorly structured material with little emphasis on key information;*
- *factual information too complex and detailed;*
- *too few or too many visual aids.*

Using slides – check that the lecture the-atre has a lectern light, otherwise you may have problems reading your notes when the lights are dimmed.

Prezi – is an alternative online electronic presentation software that allows users to zoom in and out of their presentation content.

Pitching your talk at the right level – the general rule should be 'do not overesti-mate the background knowledge of your audience'. This sometimes happens in stu-dent presentations, where fears about the presence of 'experts' can encourage the speaker to include too much detail, over-loading the audience with facts.

Managing your time when speaking – avoid looking at your watch as it gives a negative signal to the audience. Use a wall clock, if one is provided, or take off your watch and put it beside your notes, so you can glance at it without distracting your audience.

Audio-visual aids

Find out whether your department has facilities for preparing overhead trans-parencies or slides, whether these facilities are available for your use and the cost of materials. Adopt the following guidelines:

- **Keep text to a minimum** – present only the key points, with up to 20 words per slide/transparency.
- **Make sure the text is readable** – try out your material beforehand.
- **Use several simpler figures** rather than a single complex graph.
- **Avoid too much colour on overhead transparencies** – blue and black are easier to read than red or green.
- **Use electronic presentation software (e.g. PowerPoint)** as long as the necessary facilities are available for your talk (see Box 59.1).

Audience

You should consider your audience at the earliest stage, since they will deter-mine the appropriate level for your presentation. If you are talking to fellow students you may be able to assume a common level of background knowledge. In contrast, a research lecture given to your department, or a paper at a meeting of a scientific society will be presented to an audience from a broader range of backgrounds. An oral presentation is not the place for a complex discussion of specialised information – build up your talk from a low level. The speed at which this can be done will vary according to your audience. As long as you are not boring or patronising, you can cover basic information without losing the attention of the more knowledgeable members in your audience.

Box 59.1 How to use PowerPoint to deliver a talk

When creating a PowerPoint talk, you should bear the following points in mind:

- **Background** – choose whether you wish to present your talk as a light font on a dark background (more restful) or a dark font on a light background (more lively). Avoid flat and dull backgrounds as these will seem uninteresting, and brightly coloured ones as these will distract. A number of pre-set backgrounds are available (PowerPoint 2016, use the Design tab), but bear in mind that your audience may have seen these before.

- **Layout** – as you create each new slide, you can choose different layouts for the material (PowerPoint 2016, use the Home tab and choose Layout). Areas designated for text or images can easily be modified later.

- **Font** – the default fonts for headings and bullet points are large (intentionally so, for clarity). Do not be tempted to reduce them to less than 18–20 points to cram more words into the slide. If you have too much material, create a new slide and divide your information. Aim for no more than 40 words per slide, preferably fewer. Try to use more

than one font colour, perhaps to fit with levels of hierarchy in the material. Ensure that the colours are complementary with each other and with the background.

- **Images** – slides simply made up of text alone can be very uninteresting. Adding images or diagrams can brighten up your talk considerably (use the Insert menu, Picture option). Images can be taken with a digital camera, scanned or copied from the Web, but you must take care not to break copyright regula-tions. Clipart is copyright free, but use it sparingly as most people will have seen the images before, and they are rarely wholly relevant. Diagrams can be made from components created using the Shapes menu.

- **Animation** – avoid excessive use of animation fea-tures such as movement of text on to the slide and sound effects, as these will distract both you and your listeners.

When delivering your talk, don't forget to engage the audience. Don't let the computer gadgetry or presenta-tion 'gimmicks' distract you from the essential rules of good speaking (Box 59.2).

Using PowerPoint

The PowerPoint presentation program can be used to produce high-quality aids for a spoken presentation (Box 59.1), assuming a computer and digital projector are available where you intend to speak. PowerPoint can also be used to create high-quality overheads and handouts, and for poster production (Chapter 63). The program is relatively easy to use if you are familiar with others in the Microsoft Office suite. Your presentation is produced as a series of slides with a choice of backgrounds on to which you can insert headings, bullet points, digital images (e.g. in 'jpg' format), clipart and diagrams, in a similar way to that discussed in Chapter 63 (see also Box 63.1). An 'animation' (or 'build') feature allows you to reveal parts of each slide in sequence and this will help you pace your talk.

Content

While the specific details in your talk will be for you to decide, most spoken presentations share some common features of structure, as described below.

Introductory remarks

It is vital to capture the interest of your audience at the outset. Consequently, you must make sure your opening comments are strong, otherwise your audience will lose interest before you reach the main message. Remember that it takes a sentence or two for an audience to establish a relationship with a new speaker. Your opening sentence should be some form of preamble and should not contain any key information. For a formal lecture, you might begin with 'Thank you for that introduction. My talk today is about . . .' then restate the title and acknowledge other contributors, etc. You might show a slide or transparency with the title printed on it, or an introductory photograph if appropriate. This should provide the necessary settling-in period.

After these preliminaries, you should introduce your topic. Begin your story on a strong note – avoid timid or apologetic phrases.

Opening remarks are unlikely to occupy more than 10% of the talk. However, because of their significance, you might reasonably spend up to 25% of your preparation time on them (Box 59.2).

 KEY POINT Make sure you have practised your opening remarks, so that you can deliver the material in a flowing style, with less chance of mistakes.

The main message

This section should include the bulk of your experimental results or literature findings, depending on the type of presentation. Keep technical details of methods to the minimum needed to explain your data. This is *not* the place for a detailed description of equipment and experimental protocol (unless it is a talk about methodology). Results should be presented in an easily digested format.

 KEY POINT Do not expect your audience to cope with large amounts of data – use a maximum of six numbers per slide. Remember that graphs and diagrams are usually better than tables of raw data, since the audience will be able to see the trends and relationships in your data (p. 483).

Box 59.2   Hints on presenting your talk

Notes (see p. 547 for further advice)

Many accomplished speakers use abbreviated notes for guidance, rather than reading from a prepared script. In planning the writing and delivery of your talk:

- Prepare a first draft as a full script – write in spoken English, keeping the text simple and avoiding an impersonal style. Aim to *talk* to your audience, not read to them.

- Use note cards with key phrases and words – it is best to avoid using a full script at the final presentation. As you rehearse and your confidence improves, a set of cards may be a more appropriate format for your notes.

- Consider the structure of your talk – keep it as simple as possible and announce each subdivision, so your audience is aware of the structure.

- Mark the position of slides/key points, etc. – each note card should contain details of structure, as well as content.

- Memorise your introductory/closing remarks – you may prefer to rely on a full written version for these sections in case your memory fails.

- Write on only one side of the card/paper, in handwriting large enough to be read easily during the presentation. Each card or sheet must be clearly numbered, so that you do not lose your place.

- Rehearse your presentation – ask a friend to listen and to comment constructively on parts that were difficult to follow.

- Use 'split times' to pace yourself – following rehearsal, note the time at which you should arrive at key points of your talk. These timing marks will help you keep to time during the 'real thing'.

Consider your image

Make sure that the image you project during your talk is appropriate for the occasion:

- Consider what to wear – aim to be respectable without 'dressing up', otherwise your message may be diminished.

- Develop a good posture – it will help your voice projection if you stand upright, rather than slouching or leaning over the lectern.

- Project your voice – speak towards the back of the room.

- Make eye contact – look at members of the audience in all parts of the room. Avoid talking to your notes, to the screen or to only one section of the audience.

- Deliver your talk with expression – arm movements and (subdued) body language will help maintain the interest of your audience. However, you should avoid extreme gestures (it may work for some TV personalities, but it isn't recommended for the beginner!). Expressive gestures should be particularly avoided in expert witness testimony (Box 59.1).

- Try to identify and control any distracting repetitive mannerisms (e.g. repeated empty phrases, fidgeting with pens, keys, etc.) as this will distract your audience. Practising in front of a mirror may help.

- Practise your delivery – use the comments of your friends to improve your performance.

Allowing time for slides – as a rough guide you should allow at least two minutes per illustration, although some diagrams may need longer, depending on content.

Show the final results of any analyses in terms of the statistics calculated, and their significance (p. 507), rather than dwelling on details of the procedures used. However, figures should not be crowded with unnecessary detail. Every diagram should have a concise title and the symbols and trend lines should be clearly labelled, with an explanatory key where necessary. When presenting graphical data, always 'introduce' each graph by stating the units for each axis and describing the relationship for each trend line or data set.

 KEY POINT   Use summary slides at regular intervals, to maintain the flow of the presentation and to emphasise the main points.

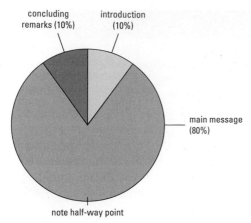

Fig. 59.1 Pie chart showing time allocation for a typical presentation.

Final remarks – *make sure you give the audience sufficient time to assimilate your final slide; some of them may wish to write down the key points. Alternatively, you might provide a handout with a brief outline of the aims of your study and the major conclusions.*

Take the audience through your story step-by-step at a reasonable pace. Try not to rush the delivery of your main message due to nervousness. Avoid complex, convoluted storylines – one of the most distracting things you can do is to fumble back and forth through slides or overhead transparencies. If you need to use the same diagram or graph more than once then you should make two (or more) copies. In a presentation of experimental results, you should discuss each point as it is raised, in contrast to written text where the results and discussion may be in separate sections. The main message typically occupies approximately 80% of the time allocated to an oral presentation (Fig. 59.1).

Concluding remarks

Having captured the interest of your audience in the introduction and given them the details of your story in the middle section, you must now bring your talk to a conclusion. At all costs do not end weakly, for example by running out of steam on the last slide. Provide your audience with a clear 'take-home message' by returning to the key points in your presentation. It is often appropriate to prepare a slide or overhead transparency listing your main conclusions as a numbered series.

Signal the end of your talk by saying 'finally . . .', 'in conclusion . . .' or a similar comment and then finish speaking after that sentence. Your audience will lose interest if you extend your closing remarks beyond this point. You may add a simple end phrase (e.g. 'thank you') as you put your notes into your folder, but do not say 'that's all folks!' or make any similar offhand remark. Finish as strongly and as clearly as you started.

Think about questions

Many speakers are worried by the prospect of questions after their oral presentation. Once again, the best approach is to prepare beforehand:

- Consider what questions you may be asked – prepare brief answers.
- Do not be afraid to say 'I don't know' – your audience will appreciate honesty, rather than vacillation, if you don't have an answer for a particular question.
- Avoid arguing with a questioner – suggest a discussion afterwards rather than becoming involved in a debate about specific details.
- If no questions are forthcoming you may pose a question yourself, and then ask for opinions from the audience – if you use this approach you should be prepared to comment briefly if your audience has no suggestions. This will prevent the presentation from ending in an embarrassing silence.

 KEY POINT *Never get angry, defensive or argumentative if giving evidence in court. Your testimony thereafter will not be as good and your credibility may be put into question.*

Sources for further study

Alley, M. (2007) *The Craft of Scientific Presentations: Critical Steps to Succeed and Critical Errors to Avoid,* 5th edn. Springer-Verlag, New York.

Capp, C.C. and Capp, G.R. (1989) *Basic Oral Communication,* 5th edn. Prentice Hall, Harlow.

Kranz, W.B. (2016) *Oral Communication Strategies for Scientific Presentations.* Academic Press, New York.

Radel, J. (2004) *Oral Presentations.* Available at: http://people. eku.edu/ritchisong/oralpres.html. Last accessed 29/08/2017.

Zandes, E. and Macleod, L. (2010) *Presentation Skills for Scientists – A Practical Guide.* Cambridge University Press, New York.

Study exercises

59.1 Prepare a checklist for assessing the quality of an oral presentation. After reading through this chapter, prepare a 10-point checklist of assessment criteria under the heading 'What makes a good oral presentation?'. Compare your list with the one that we have provided – do you agree with our criteria, or do you prefer your checklist (and can you justify your preferences)?

59.2 Evaluate the presentation styles of other speakers. There are many opportunities to assess the strengths and weaknesses of academic 'public speakers', including your lecturers, seminar speakers, presenters of TV documentaries, etc. Decide in advance how you are going to tackle the evaluation (e.g. with a quantitative marking scheme, or a less formal procedure).

59.3 Prepare a testimony for court explaining how a complex scientific instrument works, e.g. GC–MS. Identify questions that are likely to be asked and rehearse appropriate answers. Practise these question-and-answer sessions with one or more partners within your year group. You may wish also to refer to Chapters 14–15.

The end point of any forensic investigation of a crime is usually the presentation of evidence in court, in written or oral form. Written evidence comes in the form of a forensic statement and you are likely to be given opportunities to practise writing such statements during your degree course. You may also be required to attend court to give evidence. This court appearance allows the lawyers, both for the prosecution and defence, to query the results and opinion offered in your statement. Oral presentations in general are covered in Chapter 59.

While the various types of case encountered by a forensic scientist have similarities, each one is unique. Apart from the basic requirements, there is no common approach to what is included in a forensic statement. There are also differences between statements prepared in different countries. Individual forensic science laboratories will have their own set of guidelines.

As part of your training, you will need to develop your skills in judging what to include in your statement, the appropriate level of detail and how to organise it so that it is understandable to a court of law.

 KEY POINT *The purpose of a forensic statement is to summarise and explain, in layman's terms, what you have done and what you have found – you must always keep this in mind when writing.*

It is important to make sure that your forensic statements are precise in terms of content, grammar, spelling and wording. The statement must be clear and concise and be readily understandable by the lawyers for both prosecution and defence. For example, if several spelling errors were included then a defence lawyer could use this against you in an attempt to discredit your evidence in court, by implying that you are not careful in your work. The only evidence for how careful you are is the final statement, so the impression the jury has of you as the expert witness is exactly as the lawyer has suggested.

Similarly, you should always think about what questions a lawyer is likely to ask. If you have adequately answered all potential questions in your statement then you are less likely to be called to court to give oral testimony, and your evidence, as put forward in your statement, will be agreed between prosecution and defence. You have to make sure, though, that what you have written is factually correct.

Types of forensic statement and their authors

Different statements may be made available to the court and their content will depend on the context of the case. For example, during a murder trial written statements presented in court might include information from the following people:

- **The first police officer on the scene** – this is the only time where an officer can refer to his/her notes written at the time of the incident.
- **The scene of crime officer (SOCO)** – more commonly referred to as crime scene examiner (CSE) or crime scene investigator (CSI) – attending the scene. The statement might include details of the location and what was collected, together with unique reference numbers for each item.
- **The identification bureau staff** – the statement may provide details of the analysis of fingerprints and footwear marks found.
- **The investigating police officers** – information might include items seized from the accused.
- **The forensic medical examiner** – who may provide details of the medical examination of the accused and any biological samples obtained.

Different procedures exist across the UK – this reflects the differences in the legal systems. For example, Scotland is governed under Scottish Law, whereas the rest of the UK (England, Wales and Northern Ireland) is governed under English Law. Many forensic statements in Scotland require a corroboratory signature, while elsewhere this is not necessary.

The Criminal Procedure Rules (2015) provide guidance for the duty of the expert witness to the court and the content of expert witness reports in England and Wales.

Types of forensic statement – apart from the forensic pathologist's statement, the other examples given here are typical of the types of statement you might prepare during your degree course. You may also take part in role-play exercises, where your statement has to be presented in a mock trial.

Differences in the statements – a CSI statement is a statement of fact (i.e. what was observed, collected, documented), whereas a forensic scientist statement is one that includes an expert opinion based on the information received regarding the case and an appropriate interpretation of results from the analytical findings.

An interim statement may be produced during the investigation, which will be amended as the results of the investigation/analyses are completed.

The following statements are classed as coming from an 'expert witness'. The expert witness is the only person qualified to offer an opinion in court. For example, in a murder case these might include:

- **forensic pathologist's statement** – providing details of the location where the body was found, identification of the body, external and internal examination, cause of death;
- **forensic toxicologist's statement** – giving details of examination, analysis and interpretation of any biological samples obtained (Chapters 37–38);
- **forensic biologist's statement** – this may include details of examination of weapons, hairs/fibres from clothing, evidence of sexual activity (Chapters 30, 32, 42);
- **forensic DNA scientist's statement** – detailing the results of DNA profiles from samples (Chapter 31);
- **defence scientist's statement** – this may agree or disagree with the statements from any of the prosecution forensic scientists.

The structure of each of the main types of statement, and examples of content and phrasing, are given below.

Forensic pathologist's statement

While you are unlikely to be asked to write this type of statement during your course, you may be given a *post-mortem* statement in order to assist with your interpretation of other analytical findings. It is included here for reference and to illustrate what may be covered. In England and Wales only one doctor is required to perform the autopsy and sign the statement, whereas in Scotland two doctors are required (known as a double-doctor *post-mortem*) and both need to sign the statement.

1. **Title page** – showing date and location of autopsy, name and other information on the deceased, place, time and cause of death, examining doctors and authorising coroner.
2. **Declaration** – a statement from the doctor(s) carrying out the autopsy, giving their names and the qualifications that entitle them to make the statement.
3. **Identification of the deceased** – details of those persons who made the formal identification.
4. **Clothing** – a description of whether the body was fully clothed, partially clothed or stripped prior to autopsy.
5. **External examination** – including descriptions of medical condition, race, height, weight, hair colour, eye colour, presence of significant natural disease, piercings, tattoos, teeth, circumcision, scars.
6. *Post-mortem* **changes** – such as the presence of rigor mortis, hypostasis.
7. **Recent injuries** – bruising, needle marks, etc., as well as old and healing injuries (e.g. obvious signs of chronic intravenous drug abuse).
8. **Marks of medical intervention** – all signs of medical intervention should be recorded, including the positioning of catheters, endotracheal tubes, vascular infusion, etc.
9. **Internal examination** – this will include details of the cardiovascular, respiratory, digestive, genitourinary, lymphatic, endocrine, cranial, nervous and musculoskeletal systems, noting any gross pathologies or whether the organs are 'unremarkable'.
10. **Samples taken** – for the purposes of continuity of evidence (Chapter 24) this should include full details of which samples were retained for histology and toxicology, including those seized from admission to hospital, if relevant.
11. **Opinion as to cause of death** – this is based on the information available to the medical practitioners at the time the *post-mortem* was carried out. The cause

---

Defence statement – produced by a second scientist working for the defence lawyers. It may be that the scientist is only asked to produce a statement stating whether they agree with the opinion of the prosecution scientist, or it may be that they repeat the analysis performed by the prosecution scientist to see if they obtain the same results, from which they will produce their own statement.

Example (declaration in Scotland)
We, Dr W. Burke and Dr W. Hare, registered medical practitioners, hereby certify on Soul and Conscience as follows: On the instructions of the Procurator Fiscal at Edinburgh we performed a *post-mortem* examination and dissection on the body of Mr D. Ceased at the Mortuary, Edinburgh Royal Infirmary, on 1st April 2017 commencing at 9.00am.

Definitions

Hypostasis – the accumulation of blood in an organ under the influence of gravity.

Rigor mortis – temporary muscle rigidity and stiffening of joints occurring after death.

of death may be obvious or may require further laboratory analysis, and supplementary statements, before an opinion can be provided. In any forensic investigation, the forensic pathologist is the only person who can assign cause of death.

12. **Commentary** – this should include comments on, for example, drug use, injuries and their likelihood of fatality, etc.
13. **Signatures** – by the doctor(s) who performed the *post-mortem*.

Supplementary statements may also be required, to include post-autopsy analyses – for example, toxicological investigation of the samples taken (Chapter 38) or histological examination of internal organs, for example brain, lung, thymus, before an opinion can be offered as to the cause of death. As with the main statement, any supplementary statements will also have the same reference number, name of deceased and address, and will be signed by the doctor(s).

Forensic scientist's statement

This is the type of statement that you are most likely to come across during your studies, either by writing an expert witness statement or in giving evidence based on a statement supplied to you. The content of the statement is broadly similar to that written when reporting any practical or project work (p. 561). The main features of a typical statement are given in Box 60.1 and an example is given in Figure 60.1.

As with all statements, it is essential that a declaration be written that indicates that the person has the authority to write the statement. In England and Wales, the words of the declaration are defined by Section 9 of the Criminal Justice Act (see margin).

 KEY POINT *For any forensic statement, all exhibits that have been examined must be included, irrespective of whether the results are positive or negative, or whether they support or refute the involvement of a particular person. In no circumstances should any exhibit be omitted from the statement, as there is a legal requirement to disclose information on all items examined.*

Scene of crime officer (SOCO) statement

This type of statement is also known as a CSI statement. It is essentially a list of each exhibit seized from the locus and should be recorded with the officer's initials and unique reference number (see pp. 241–242 for an example of a statement). This reference number should appear throughout the history of the exhibit and must be consistent across all statements, indicating continuity of evidence.

Scene statements

When a forensic scientist is called to a scene to offer his or her professional expertise, a scene statement is written detailing the address, officers in attendance, descriptions of the overview of the scene and each of the rooms examined (see pp. 240–241 for an example of this type of statement). In each case, the forensic scientist can instruct the officers to seize certain items for laboratory examination, which will be appropriately packaged (Chapter 24).

Defence statement

These follow the same protocol as for all other expert witness statements. If you are asked to prepare a defence statement, the main difference is that you will also have a prosecution statement to review and you will be able to make comments or express opinions on what has already been analysed. There may also be a need for you to re-analyse exhibits and compare results. Remember that you must be *impartial* – you are not writing a statement to assert someone's guilt or innocence, but presenting the facts to the court and offering your opinion on them. If you do not agree with the prosecution statement, then you must provide evidence to support your arguments – for example, citation of studies in peer-reviewed journals or other appropriate reference materials.

Working with autopsy samples – typical samples that might be sent for forensic analysis include blood from a ligated femoral vein, urine, vitreous humour (fluid from the eye), plus a small sample of liver (from deep within the right lobe), bile, stomach contents and head hair.

Declaration – 'This statement, consisting of X pages signed by me, is true to the best of my knowledge and belief and I make it knowing that, if it is tendered in evidence, I shall be liable to prosecution if I have wilfully stated in it anything which I know to be false or do not believe to be true.' Criminal Proc. Rules r27.2; Criminal Justice Act 1957, s9, Magistrates Court Act 1980, s.53.

There are many different types of statements that can be produced, including abbreviated statements, in response to the procurement process, but the scientist can only give evidence on a full statement.

Your statement – this should always be:

- written in third party;
- with correct grammar and free from typographical errors;
- written in a language that is easily understood;
- factually correct;
- signed on every page.

Box 60.1 The structure of a typical forensic scientist's statement

Most forensic science statements cover the following main aspects, though you may be given more detailed guidelines to follow – for example, in the form of a typical laboratory standard operating procedure (SOP).

Section	Contents/purpose	Checklist for reviewing content
Authorisation statement or declaration	A declaration is provided according to Section 9 of the Criminal Justice Act (see p. 534).	Have you included your declaration or authorisation statement? Have you signed and dated it?
Laboratory address	Descries where the statement and results originated from.	Are the details correct?
Qualifications and experience	Informs the court of your suitability to be an expert witness.	Have you listed all your relevant qualifications, your job title and specialism, your length of service?
Case against	The full name(s) and date(s) of birth of the defendant(s).	Do you have the correct defendant? Is the date of birth correct?
Laboratory reference number	A unique identifying mark for the case.	Is it present and correct?
Circumstances	A brief description of what you understand to have happened. This is the background information that a scientist would use to base their interpretation on, so if it changes, or new information comes to light, then the scientist can re-evaluate their findings.	Does this explain succinctly what the case is about?
Receipt of exhibits	A list of all the exhibits that were received *and* examined including which police force submitted them, on what date, exhibit numbers and description of the exhibits, and who/where they relate to/from. Given that over a hundred exhibits may have been presented for laboratory examination, it is sufficient to include at the end of the statement that *n* exhibits were received but not examined.	Have you identified all the exhibits received? Do the total numbers match? Do the label details correspond to the exhibits?
Request/purpose	A statement of what you have been asked to do. This can be brief and generic. Remember that it is your decision, as the impartial analyst, what to examine. This section should state the question(s) that you are addressing/the points to prove.	Does this explain what you have been asked to do and what you intend to do?
Technical issues	A basic background to the instrumentation, examination and interpretation of the evidence on cases such as blood pattern analysis or DNA.	Do you understand what you have written? Would a layperson understand what you have written?
Results of examination of exhibits	A section including the *exact transcript* of the label details of each exhibit, inclusive of any spelling mistakes. The exhibit, if presented in court, can then be linked directly to the statement, for continuity of evidence. This transcript should then be followed by what the exhibit was examined for. You should include all the final results of the examination, whether they are positive or negative findings. Standard scientific nomenclature, including appropriate units (Chapter 4), should be followed and should be consistent throughout the statement. It may be appropriate to include details of the instrumentation used and the SOP that was followed. In cases of visual examination, a description of the exhibit is included and if trace evidence is recovered it is referred to by the analyst's reference number.	Have you copied the label details *exactly?* Have you included what the exhibit was analysed for? Have SI units been used properly throughout? Have you included appropriate statistical analysis? Have you statemented to appropriate significant figures?

Box 60.1 (Continued)

Section	Contents/purpose	Checklist for reviewing content
Interpretation and conclusions	A section where you include background information on the examination results. For example, if it is a drug, then you should include reference to a monograph for that drug – for bulk drug analysis in the UK, include the class of drug under the Misuse of Drugs Act 1971. For toxicology, the result you found should be related to that recorded in the scientific literature (i.e. 'therapeutic, toxic or fatal'). It is within this section that your opinion is offered, while remaining within your area of expertise – for example, 'it is my opinion that the liquid is non-flammable and so could not be used to accelerate a fire'. If appropriate to the evidence type, you should consider a Bayesian approach to your interpretation (Chapter 57). You should also include a caveat that you have the right to reconsider your findings/conclusions if any further information is forthcoming.	Is the information provided appropriate? Does it address what you have been asked to do? Have you compared your data with other published work? Have you included your opinion and conclusion?
Use of additional staff	Assistants are often used to perform the analysis and they should be mentioned here – it is often the case that the statementing officer is not the one who carried out all the analysis.	Have you acknowledged that additional staff have been involved in the analysis?
Signatures	You are the author and ultimately responsible for the statement, therefore you must sign the statement on every page. The statement cannot go to court without a signature.	Have you signed the statement? Are your qualifications correct?
Date of statement	The date on which you sign the statement.	Have you dated the statement?

Speaking in court – remember this is the first time that the jury will see you and first impressions are important, so make sure you are dressed appropriately and are well-practised at stating the preliminary material, including the oath or affirmation, and your personal and professional details.

Swearing an oath or making an affirmation – the oath is a promise on the Bible to tell the truth, and in the UK, the oath is: 'I swear by Almighty God that the evidence I shall give shall be the truth, the whole truth and nothing but the truth'.

Where a witness follows another faith, an appropriate form of oath can be taken, for example the Muslim faith can be sworn on the Koran, with the form of words 'I swear by Allah. . . . '

The affirmation is a promise to tell the truth and is: 'I do solemnly, sincerely and truly declare, and affirm, that the evidence I shall give shall be the truth, the whole truth and nothing but the truth.' Both the oath and the affirmation carry equal weight in court.

In England and Wales, you would be asked by the usher whether you wish to swear or affirm prior to entering the courtroom, whereas in Scotland the judge will assume that you wish to swear in unless you inform them otherwise.

Your defence statement should include:

1. The name of the defendant.
2. A s.9 declaration or authorisation statement.
3. Your qualifications – a list of qualifications, membership of learned societies, areas of expertise and any previous experience of giving evidence in court.
4. Purpose – a comment that you have been instructed by solicitors that their client is accused of a particular crime and that you have been asked to provide a statement addressing whether you agree with the prosecution statements or addressing specific questions that may not be elucidated from the case for the prosecution.
5. Background and circumstances – list all statements and all information supplied to you in order for you to prepare your statement.
6. Analysis of statements/commentary – normally, you would include brief background information of, for example, an outline of the techniques used in DNA profiling (Chapter 31), followed by your opinion as to whether the analytical results support the prosecution's case. Scientific literature to support the commentary should also be included, appropriately referenced (Chapter 45).
7. Conclusion – here you should draw attention to points in the prosecution statement that you feel may be inappropriate, or which you think can be interpreted differently. Equally, it may be that you agree entirely with the case for the prosecution, in which case you must state this.
8. Signature – your statement must be signed and dated.

Giving evidence in court

Any witness giving evidence in court is not there to 'win' the case. They are there to inform the court of what was seen, heard or, in the case of the expert witness, give their interpretation and opinion based on experimental findings.

Forensic Science Agency
23 Examiner Road
Kingstown

Case Against **Ian E. Briate (13041972)**

Ref No FSA 001
Statement of A. Boffin BSc(Hons), PhD, MRSC, CChem
Age of Witness   over 21
Occupation   Forensic Scientist

This statement, consisting of 1 page signed by me, is true to the best of my knowledge and belief and I make it knowing that, if itis tendered in evidence, I shall be liable to prosecution if I have wilfully stated in it anything which I know to be false or do notbelieve to be true.

Dated the 1st day of April 2017.
Signature A Boffin

Qualifications and experience
I am a Bachelor of Science (BSc), having obtained an Honours degree in Biological sciences and a PhD in Toxicology. I have been employed by the Forensic Science Agency since 1987, as a forensic scientist, specialising in the analysis of body fluids and other materials for the presence of alcohol, drugs and poisons.

Receipt of exhibits
On the 18th March 2017 the following item was received for examination:
Blood for drugs labelled 'taken from Ian E. Briate on 17th March 2017'.

Circumstances
I understand that Mr Briate was arrested on suspicion of driving whilst under the influence of alcohol or drugs following an incident at 1800 hours on the 17th March 2017.

Request
I have been asked to analyse the above blood sample for the presence of any drugs that might have impaired Mr Briate's ability to drive.

Technical details
The blood sample was further analysed for the presence of a wide range of drugs which could have an adverse effect on the ability to drive safely, including alcohol, using GC-headspace analysis, common drugs of abuse (opiates and opioids, cocaine, amphetamine and related compounds, cannabinoids and benzodiazepines) using ELISA and common over-the-counter medications using GC-mass spectrometry. Methadone quantification was performed using HPLC.

Results
Methadone was found in the blood (0.27 milligram per litre).
The blood was further examined for alcohol and other drugs with a negative result.

Comment
The presence of methadone in the blood sample is consistent with Mr Briate having consumed methadone at *some time* prior to the provision of the sample. Methadone is prescribed to treat dependence on opioid drugs such as heroin. Methadone is widely abused.

The concentration of methadone found in the blood lies in the range of values found following the normal medical use, and illicit abuse, of this drug.

Reported side effects of methadone include nausea, vomiting, drowsiness and confusion, which can adversely affect the performance of skilled tasks such as driving.

Conclusions
The presence of methadone was detected in the blood sample from Mr Ian E. Briate.
Methadone can give rise to effects that can impair the ability to drive safely.

Signature A Boffin   Date 1st April 2017

Fig. 60.1 Example of a typical forensic scientist's statement.

The role of a forensic scientist in court is to state the facts, justified by scientific reasoning, and to offer an opinion as an expert witness (note that non-expert witnesses cannot offer such opinions). If you were giving expert witness testimony in court you would have specialist expertise in one or more forensic science disciplines – for example, toxicology, pathology, DNA analysis. The British judicial system is adversarial – the role of the expert witness is to explain the scientific evidence to the jury. Your opinion as a prosecution expert witness is based on the original information provided to you, alongside this scientific evidence. Similarly, a defence expert witness will also offer their opinion, but this may differ if the original information supplied to them is different, therefore leading to an alternative interpretation. As a result, your opinions would be subject to question and challenge in order to progress either side of the case. Advice is given in Box 60.2 on oral examinations that is pertinent to preparation for expert witness testimony.

> **KEY POINT** *When giving evidence as an expert witness you should restrict your comments to your areas of expertise and you should not answer questions on other specialist disciplines in which you have not been trained. Remember, you are the expert and you know your discipline. The judge and the barristers do not have this expert knowledge, therefore your role is to explain complex science in a way that is understandable to the court.*

The first stage in the process of any testimony in court is the oath or affirmation, depending on your religious conviction. You are then required to state your full name and professional address, followed by your qualifications and experience, to provide the court with the information that justifies your ability to give expert testimony.

Following these preliminaries, the sequence of questioning is as follows:

1. **Examination in chief** – whoever called you as a witness, either the prosecution or the defence, will question you about the statement you have written for the court's benefit. In essence, they will lead you carefully through the statement, asking you appropriate questions about your results, emphasising key aspects and presenting you as a credible expert to enhance their case.

2. **Cross-examination** – the opposing barrister will then ask questions, often in order to give the jury a reason to doubt the validity your findings or opinions, and thereby to support the opinions of their expert witness. You must be fully prepared for any questions that could raise doubt in the jury's mind about your expertise or your statement. You need to think very carefully about each question before answering, and if it requires more than a yes or no answer, then you should ask the judge to allow you to explain in more detail if you feel that you have not been able to adequately explain or clarify your answer. Although it may seem that the barrister asking the questions is attacking you personally, this is not the case. Remember they are trying to win the case for their client and will do so by any means possible, whether it is by questioning your credibility as an expert or any weaknesses in your experimental findings.

3. **Re-examination** – it may be necessary for the first lawyer to ask additional questions, in order to clarify certain points raised during the cross-examination.

Box 60.2 gives practical advice on expert witness testimony and these are also useful hints for any mock courtroom presentations at university.

What to expect during cross-examination – lawyers may use tactics intended to disconcert you, including:

- shuffling their papers;
- interrupting your replies;
- insisting on 'yes' or 'no' answers;
- making asides to their colleagues;
- repeating questions.

Addressing the judge – in the UK, you should use 'sir' or 'madam' in a Magistrates' Court or Sheriff's Court, 'your Honour' in a Crown Court and either 'your Lordship/my Lord' or 'your Ladyship/my Lady' at the Old Bailey Crown Court.

Box 60.2   Some hints on giving evidence in court

Consider your appearance – you should aim to look smart and professional. Formal clothes will give the best impression (e.g. for a man, a suit and tie; for a woman, a trouser-suit or formal blouse, skirt and jacket).

Be prepared – anticipate the questions you are likely to be asked, prepare written answers for them and rehearse the delivery of your answers. Know your statement in detail and identify its strengths and weaknesses. Under cross-examination, questions will be asked to expose these weaknesses. Be up to date in your knowledge of the relevant scientific literature.

Box 60.2 (Continued)

Use your voice effectively – how you project your voice is important (p. 546). You should try to avoid speaking in a monotone, and you should also be careful not to be overdemonstrative or theatrical in your 'performance', as this will undermine your credibility. Presentation of expert testimony is a more formal occasion than a general talk (p. 546), and you should avoid overexpressive body language.

Pause before you answer – give yourself enough time to think about the question, even if it seems straightforward.

Always tell the truth – you will swear to tell the truth in court. Perjury is a criminal act and could result in you being prosecuted.

Be impartial – this is the keystone of all forensic science testimony. It is not up to you to decide guilt or innocence; that is the responsibility of the judge and jury.

Be clear and concise – make sure you answer the questions asked, and do not stray into other areas. If the lawyers require more information, they will ask you further questions.

Do not give too much technical detail – provide your answers in layman's terms. Remember that the members of the jury are not likely to have a scientific background and so are unlikely to understand complex scientific explanations. Avoid jargon.

Know your limitations – make sure you understand in advance what you can and cannot say within your area of expertise. Be prepared to say 'I do not know', or 'this is outside my area of expertise' where this is appropriate.

Who to speak to – always face the judge (and jury). In the witness stand, position yourself so that your feet point towards them. Turn on your hips to receive questions from the barristers and then relax your body. Your natural posture returns you to face the judge so you can direct your answer to him/her.

Text references and sources for further study

Babitsky, S. and Mangraviti, J.J. (2002) *Writing and Defending Your Expert Statement: The Step by Step Guide with Models.* SEAK Inc., Falmouth, MA.

Bond, C., Solon, M., Harper, P. and Davies, G. (2007) *The Expert Witness in Court: A Practical Guide,* 3rd edn. Shaw & Sons, London.

Criminal Procdures Rules (2015) http://www.legislation.gov.uk/uksi/2015/1490/contents/made. Last accessed 29/08/2017.

Expert Evidence Available at: http://www.cps.gov.uk/legal/assets/uploads/files/expert_evidence_first_edition_2014.pdf. Last accessed 29/08/2017.

Expert Witness Institute Available at: http://www.ewi.org.uk. Last accessed 29/08/2017.

Guidance booklet for expert witnesses: Role of the expert witness and disclosure. Available at: http://www.copfs.gov.uk/images/Documents/Prosecution_Policy_Guidance/Guidelines_and_Policy/Guidance%20booklet%20for%20expert%20witnesses%20%20June%2015.pdf. Last accessed 29/08/2017.

Hadley, K. and Fereday, M.J. (2007) *Ensuring Competent Performance in Forensic Practice -Recovery, Analysis, Interpretation and Reporting.* CRC Press, Boca Raton.

Hall, J.G. and Smith, G.D. (2001) *The Expert Witness,* 3rd edn. Barry Rose Law, Chichester.

Hannibal, M. and Mountford, L. (2002) *The Law of Criminal and Civil Evidence: Principles and Practice.* Longman, Harlow.

Robertson, B. and Vignaux, G. (1995) *Interpreting Evidence: Evaluating Forensic Science in the Courtroom.* Wiley, New York.

Wall, W. (2009) *Forensic Science in Court: The Role of the Expert Witness.* Wiley, Chichester.

Study exercises

60.1 Prepare a written explanation to explain how a presumptive test works, e.g. Kastle Meyer. Identify questions that are likely to be asked and rehearse appropriate answers. Ask a colleague or tutor to comment on what you have written.

60.2 Summarise the main differences between an expert witness statement and a CSI statement. From the information in this chapter and other sources of information, write down the ways in which these two types of statements differ.

60.3 Prepare an expert witness statement. Use the results you have obtained from one of your practical classes to prepare a statement for court giving details of your experimental findings and interpretation.

Typical structure of scientific reports – this usually follows the 'IMRAD' acronym: Introduction, Materials and Methods, Results and Discussion; or the 'IERAD' acronym: Introduction, Experimental, Results and Discussion.

Practical reports, project reports, theses and scientific papers differ greatly in depth, scope and size, but they all have the same basic structure. Some variation is permitted however (see Box 61.1), and you should always follow the advice or rules provided by your department or school.

Additional parts may be specified – for theses, a title page is often required and a List of Figures and Tables as part of the Contents section. When work is submitted for certain degrees, you may need to include certain declarations and statements made by the student and supervisor. In scientific papers, a list of Key Words is often added following the Abstract – this information may be combined with words in the title for computer cross-referencing systems.

KEY POINT *University regulations may specify a precise format for producing your report or thesis. Obtain a copy of these rules at an early stage and follow them closely to avoid losing marks.*

Steps in the production of practical reports

These are exercises designed to make you think more deeply about your experiments and to practise and test the skills necessary for writing up research work. You can see the standard format to use in Box 61.1. Special features are:

- **Introductory material** is generally short and, unless otherwise specified, should outline the aims of the experiment(s) with a minimum of background material.
- **Materials and methods/experimental** may be provided by your supervisor for practical reports. If you make changes to this, you should state clearly what you did. With extended projects, your lab notebook (see p. 17) should provide the basis for writing this section.
- **Great attention in assessment** will be paid to presentation and analysis of data. Take special care over graphs (see p. 483). Make sure your conclusions are justified by the evidence you present.

Choosing between graphs and tables – graphs are generally easier for the reader to assimilate, while tables can be used to condense a lot of data into a small space.

Repeating your experiments – remember, if you do an experiment twice, you have repeated it only once!

Options for discussing data – the main optional variants of the general structure include combining Results and Discussion into a single section and adding a separate Conclusions *section.*

- *The main advantage of a joint Results and Discussion section is that you can link together different experiments, perhaps explaining why a particular result led to a new hypothesis and the next experiment. However, a combined* Results and Discussion *section may contravene your department's regulations, so you should check before using this approach.*
- *The main advantage of having a separate* Conclusions *section is to draw together and emphasise the chief points arising from your work, when these may have been 'buried' in an extensive* Discussion *section.*

Choose the experiments you wish to describe and decide how best to present them

Try to start this process before your lab work ends, because at the stage of reviewing your experiments a gap may become apparent (e.g. a missing control) and you might still have time to rectify the deficiency. Irrelevant material should be ruthlessly eliminated, at the same time bearing in mind that negative results can be extremely important. Use as many different forms of data presentation as are appropriate, but avoid presenting the same data in more than one form. Graphs are generally easier for the reader to assimilate, while tables can be used to condense a lot of data into a small space. Relegate large tables of data to an appendix and summarise the important points within the main text, with a cross-reference to the appendix. Make sure that the experiments you describe are representative – always state the number of times they were repeated and how consistent your findings were.

Make up plans or outlines for the component parts

The overall plan is well defined (see Box 61.1), but individual parts will need to be well organised, as with any other form of writing (see Chapter 58).

Box 61.1   The structure of reports of experimental work

Undergraduate practical and project reports are generally modelled using the IMRAD structure (p. 560), or a close variant of it, because this is the structure used for nearly all research papers and theses. The more common variations include Results and Discussion combined into a single section, and Conclusions appearing separately as a series of points arising from the work. In scientific papers, a list of Key Words (for computer cross-referencing systems) may be included following the Abstract. Acknowledgements may appear after the Contents section, rather than near the end. Department or school regulations for producing theses and reports may specify a precise format – they often require a title page to be inserted at the start and a List of Figures and Tables as part of the Contents section, and may specify declarations and statements to be made by the student and supervisor.

Part (in order)	Contents/purpose	Checklist for reviewing content
Title	Explains what the project was about	Does it explain what the text is about succinctly?
Authors plus their institutions	Explains who did the work and where; also where they can be contacted now	Are all the details correct?
Abstract/Summary	Synopsis of methods, results and conclusion of work described. Allows the reader to grasp quickly the essence of the work	Does it explain why the work was done? Does it outline the whole of your work and your findings?
List of Contents	Shows the organisation of the text (not required for short papers)	Are all the sections covered? Are the page numbers correct?
Abbreviations	Lists all the abbreviations used (but not those of SI, chemical elements, or standard biochemical terms)	Have they all been explained? Are they all in the accepted form? Are they in alphabetical order?
Introduction	Orientates the reader – explains why the work has been done and its context in the literature, why the methods used were chosen, why the experimental organisms were chosen. Indicates the central hypothesis behind the experiments	Does it provide enough background information and cite all the relevant references? Is it of the correct depth for the readership? Have all the technical terms been defined? Have you explained why you investigated the problem? Have you outlined your aims and objectives? Have you explained your methodological approach? Have you stated your hypothesis?
Materials and Methods/Experimental	Explains how the work was done. Should contain sufficient detail to allow another competent worker to repeat the work	Is each experiment covered and have you avoided unnecessary duplication? Is there sufficient detail to allow repetition of the work? Are proper scientific names and authorities given for all organisms? Have you explained where you got them from? Are the correct names, sources and grades given for all chemicals?
Results	Displays and describes the data obtained. Should be presented in a form that is easily assimilated (graphs rather than tables, small tables rather than large ones)	Is the sequence of experiments logical? Are the parts adequately linked? Are the data presented in the clearest possible way? Have SI units been used properly throughout? Has adequate statistical analysis been carried out? Is all the material relevant? Are the figures and tables all numbered in the order of their appearance? Are their titles appropriate? Do the figure and table legends provide all the information necessary to interpret the data without reference to the text? Have you presented the same data more than once?

Box 61.1 (Continued)

Part (in order)	Contents/purpose	Checklist for reviewing content
Discussion/ Conclusion	Discusses the results – their meaning, their importance; compares the results with those of others; suggests what to do next	Have you explained the significance of the results? Have you compared your data with other published work? Are your conclusions justified by the data presented?
Acknowledgements	Gives credit to those who helped carry out the work	Have you listed everyone who helped, including any grant-awarding bodies?
Literature Cited (Bibliography)	Lists all references cited in appropriate format – provides enough information to allow the reader to find the reference in a library	Do all the references in the text appear on the list? Do all the listed references appear in the text? Do the years of publications and authors match? Are the journal details complete and in the correct format? Is the list in alphabetical order, or correct numerical order?

Presenting your results – remember that the order of results presented in a report need not correspond with the order in which you carried out the experiments – you are expected to rearrange them to provide a logical sequence of findings.

Using the correct tense – always use the past tense to describe the methodology used in your work, since it is now complete. Use the present tense only for generalisations and conclusions (p. 541).

Save your documents – at regular intervals and don't restrict to one copy.

Write!

The Materials and Methods/Experimental section is often the easiest to write once you have decided what to report. Remember to use the past tense and do not allow results or discussion to creep in. The Results section is the next easiest as it should only involve description. At this stage, you may benefit from jotting down ideas for the Discussion – this may be the hardest part to compose as you need an overview both of your own work and of the relevant literature. It is also liable to become wordy, so try hard to make it succinct. The Introduction shouldn't be too difficult if you have fully understood the aims of the experiments. Write the Abstract and complete the List of References at the end. To assist with the latter, it is a good idea as you write to use an appropriate electronic management system for your references, e.g. Endnote™ (Chapters 45–47).

Revise the text

Once your first draft is complete, try to answer all the questions listed in Box 61.1. Show your work to your supervisors and learn from their comments. Let a friend or colleague who is unfamiliar with your subject read your text; they may be able to pinpoint obscure wording and show where information or explanation is missing. If writing a thesis, double-check that you are adhering to your institution's thesis regulations.

Prepare the final version

Markers appreciate neatly produced work but a well-presented document will not disguise poor science. If using a word processor, print the final version with the best printer available. Make sure figures are clear and in the correct size and format.

Submit your work

Your department or school will specify when to submit a thesis or project report, so plan your work carefully to meet this deadline or you may lose marks. Tell your supervisor early of any circumstances that may cause delay and check to see whether any forms are required for late submissions, or evidence of extenuating circumstances.

Project work

Deciding on a topic to study

Assuming you have a choice, this important decision should be researched carefully. Make appointments to visit possible supervisors and ask them for advice on topics that you find interesting. Use library texts and research papers to obtain further background information. Perhaps the most important criterion is whether the topic will sustain your interest over the whole period of the project. Other things to look for include:

- **Opportunities to learn new skills** – ideally, you should attempt to gain experience and skills that you might be able to 'sell' to a potential employer.
- **Ease of obtaining valid results** – an ideal project provides a means to obtain 'guaranteed' data for your report, but also the chance to extend knowledge by doing genuinely novel research.
- **Assistance** – what help will be available to you during the project? A busy lab with many research students might provide a supportive environment should your potential supervisor be too busy to meet you often. On the other hand, a smaller lab may provide the opportunity for more personal interaction with your supervisor.
- **Impact** – it is not outside the bounds of possibility for undergraduate work to contribute to research papers. Your prospective supervisor can alert you to such opportunities.

The Internet as an information source – since many university departments or schools have home pages on the Internet, searches using relevant key words may indicate where research in your area is currently being carried out. Academics usually respond positively to being e-mailed.

Asking around – one of the best sources of information about supervisors, laboratories and projects is past students. Some of the postgraduates in your department or school may be products of your own system and they could provide an alternative source of advice.

Liaising with your supervisor(s) – this is essential if your work is to proceed efficiently. Specific meetings may be timetabled, e.g. to discuss a term's progress, review your work plan or consider a draft introduction. Most supervisors also have an 'open-door' policy, allowing you to air current problems or discuss your results. Prepare well for all meetings – have a list of questions ready before the meeting; provide results in an easily digestible form (but take your lab notebook along); be clear about your future plans for work.

Planning your work

As with any lengthy exercise, planning is required to make the best use of the time allocated (p. 585). This is true on a daily basis, as well as over the entire period of the project. It is especially important not to underestimate the time it will take to write and produce your thesis. If you wish to benefit from feedback given by your supervisor, you should aim to have drafts in his/her hands in good time. Since a large proportion of marks will be allocated to the report, you should not rush its production.

If your department requires you to write an interim report, look on this as a good opportunity to clarify your thoughts and get some of the time-consuming preparative work out of the way. If not, you should set your own deadlines for producing drafts of the Introduction and Materials and Methods/Experimental sections.

 KEY POINT *Project work can be very time-consuming. Try not to neglect other aspects of your course – make sure your lecture notes are up to date and collect relevant supporting information as you go along.*

Getting started

Figure 61.1 is a flowchart illustrating how a project might proceed. At the start, don't spend too long reading the literature and working out a lengthy programme of research – get stuck in and do an experiment. There is no substitute for 'getting your hands dirty' to stimulate new ideas:

- even a 'failed' experiment will provide some useful information that may allow you to create a new or modified hypothesis;
- pilot experiments may point out deficiencies in experimental technique that will need to be rectified;
- the experience will help you create a realistic plan of work.

Choosing a project subject area – a good place to start is reviewing current research published in the latest issues of journals, e.g. Forensic Science International, Science and Justice or research databases, e.g. Innovate UK forensic science research.

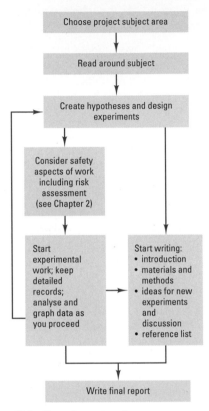

Fig. 61.1 Flowchart showing a recommended sequence of events in carrying out an undergraduate research project.

Sources of further information for project work – experimental design checklist (Box 5.1); advice on recording results (Chapter 20); describing and analysing numerical data (Chapter 3).

Brushing up on IT skills – word processors and spreadsheets are extremely useful when producing a thesis. Chapters 48 and 49 detail key features of these programs. You might benefit from attending courses on the relevant programs or studying manuals or texts so that you can use them more efficiently.

Designing experiments or sampling procedures

Design of experiments and sampling procedure is discussed in Chapter 5. Avoid being too ambitious at the start of your work. It is generally best to work with a simple hypothesis and design your experiments or sampling around this. A small pilot experiment or test sample will highlight potential stumbling blocks including resource limitations, whether in materials or time, or both.

Working in a laboratory environment

During your time as a project student, you are effectively a guest in your supervisor's laboratory.

- **Be considerate** – keep your 'area' tidy and offer to do your share of lab duties such as calibrating the pH meter, replenishing stock solutions, distilled water, etc.
- **Use instruments carefully** – they could be worth more than you would think. Careless use may invalidate calibration settings and ruin other people's work as well as your own.
- **Do your homework on techniques you intend to use** – there is less chance of making costly mistakes if you have a good background understanding of the methods you will be using.
- **Always seek advice** if you are unsure of what you are doing.

 KEY POINT *It is essential that you follow all the safety rules applying to the laboratory or crime scene investigation. Make sure you know all relevant procedures – normally there will be prominent warnings about these. If in doubt, ask.*

Keeping notes and analysing your results

Tidy record-keeping is often associated with good research, and you should follow the advice and hints given in Chapter 3. Try to keep copies of all files relating to your project. As you obtain results, you should always calculate, analyse and graph data as soon as you can (p. 483). This can reveal aspects that may not be obvious in numerical or readout form. Don't be worried by negative results – these can sometimes be as useful as positive results if they allow you to eliminate hypotheses – and don't be too dispirited if things do not work first time. Thomas Edison's maxim 'Genius is one per cent inspiration and ninety-nine per cent perspiration' certainly applies to research work.

Writing your project report

The general structure of scientific reports is dealt with in Box 61.1. For advice on how to write up your research project and methods of accumulating relevant information, see Box 61.2.

Box 61.2 How to write up your research project (dissertation) or thesis

1. **Getting started.** Writing a research project or thesis will probably constitute the biggest writing task that you will have undertaken to date. It will be the result of you undertaking a major research project in forensic science. While the layout of the research project or thesis can vary depending on your university, department or supervisor, they generally follow a certain pattern (or style) – the IMRAD/IERAD style. In addition to these, additional information is also required, specifically an Abstract (one page), Acknowledgements, Bibliography (References) and Appendices (contains details not included in the Results and Discussion section).

2. **Effective writing.** You will be aware already because of your past academic career that your concentration to work effectively is time limited. In this context you need to maximise your creative writing time, i.e. writing the research project or thesis, alongside activities that can support this writing. Such 'support activities' might include the preparation of figures, tables and schemes.

3. **Where to start.** It is important to identify a style that you propose to follow to write up your research project or thesis prior to starting. This can be achieved by looking at research projects or theses from previous students, ideally in your specific research area. Before commencement of the writing, it is a good idea to arrange a meeting with your research supervisor to discuss the content of your research project or thesis. Following this meeting, map out an outline table of contents, including major chapter headings, then subheadings per chapter and any other detail you can add. Practically, a good place to start is the Experimental and Results and Discussion sections, although the order in which you start is up to you.

4. **Introduction.** This section can be very time-consuming. Therefore, the more work you can do on it early on, the better. You should allocate some time at the start for library work (without neglecting field or bench work), so that you can build up a database of references (Chapter 45). While photocopying can be expensive, you will find it valuable to have copies of key reviews and references handy when writing away from the library. Discuss proposals for content and structure with your supervisor to make sure your effort is relevant. Leave space at the end for a section on aims and objectives. This is important to orientate readers (including assessors), but you may prefer to finalise the content after the results have been analysed.

5. **Materials and methods.** You should note as many details as possible in your laboratory notebook *when doing the experiment or making observations.* Don't rely on your memory or hope that the information will still be available when you come to write it up. Even if it is, chasing these details can waste valuable time.

6. **Results.** Show your supervisor graphed and tabulated versions of your data promptly. These can easily be produced using a spreadsheet (p. 465), but you should seek your supervisor's advice on whether the design and print quality is appropriate for inclusion in your report. You may wish to access a specialist graphics program to produce publishable-quality graphs and charts – allow some time for learning its idiosyncrasies. If you are producing a poster for assessment (Chapter 63), be sure to mock up the design well in advance. Similarly, think ahead about your needs for any seminar you will present.

7. **Discussion.** Because this comes at the end of your report, and some parts can only be written after you have all the results in place, the temptation is to leave the discussion to last. This means that it might be rushed – this is not a good idea because of the weight attached by assessors to your analysis of data and thoughts about future experiments. It will help greatly if you keep notes of aims, conclusions and ideas for future work as you go along (Fig. 61.1). Another useful tip is to make notes of comparable data and conclusions from the literature as you read papers and reviews.

8. **Acknowledgements.** Make a special place in your notebook for noting all those who have helped you carry out the work, for use when writing this section of the report.

9. **References.** Because of the complex formats involved (p. 437), these can be tricky to type. To save time, process them in batches as you go along using a bibliographic software, e.g. Endnote, that can help in the organisation of your references (Chapter 45).

10. **The final draft.** It is highly probable that you will produce multiple drafts of your research project or thesis until you get to the point where it is done. Deciding it is done and complete can be a significant and difficult decision to make. While a deadline is critical, it is also important that you time manage (Chapter 65) your writing to optimise the final research project or thesis. Having a final proofread is crucial prior to submission. Be aware of inconsistencies in text, figures and tables. Finally, after making any last modifications, you will be ready to submit your work.

Using drawings and photographs – these can provide valuable records of sampling sites or experimental set-ups and could be useful in your report. Plan ahead and do the relevant work at the time of carrying out your research rather than afterwards. Refer to Chapter 3 for tips on technique.

Oral assessments – there may be an oral exam (viva voce) *associated with the submission of a thesis or dissertation. The primary aim of the examiners will be to ensure that you understand what you did and why you did it.*

Definition

Peer review – the process of evaluation and review of a colleague's work. In scientific communication, a paper is reviewed by two or more expert reviewers for comments on quality and significance.

 KEY POINT *Make sure you are absolutely certain about the deadline for submitting your report and try to submit a few days before it. If you leave things until the last moment, you may find that access to printers, photocopiers and binding machines is difficult.*

Producing a scientific paper

Scientific papers are the means by which research findings are communicated to others. Peer-reviewed papers are published in journals – each journal covers a well-defined subject area and publishes details of the format they expect.

 KEY POINT *Peer review is an important component of the process of scientific publication – only those papers whose worth is confirmed by the peer-review process will be published.*

It would be very unusual for an undergraduate to submit a paper on his or her own – this would normally be done in collaboration with your project supervisor, and only then if your research has satisfied appropriate criteria. However, it is important to understand the process by which a paper comes into being (Box 61.3), as this can help you understand and interpret the primary literature.

Box 61.3   Steps in producing a scientific paper

Scientific papers are the lifeblood of any science and it is a major landmark in your scientific career to publish your first paper. The main steps in doing this should include the following:

Assessing potential content

The work must be of an appropriate standard to be published and should be 'new, true and meaningful'. Therefore, before starting, the authors need to review their work critically under these headings. The material included in a scientific paper will generally be a subset of the total work done during a project, so it must be carefully selected for relevance to a clear central hypothesis – if the authors won't prune, the referees and editors of the journal certainly will!

Choosing a journal

There are thousands of journals covering science and each covers a specific area (which may change through time). The main factors in deciding on an appropriate journal are the range of subjects it covers, the quality of its content and the number and geographical distribution of its readers. The choice of journal always dictates the format of a paper since authors must follow to the letter the journal's 'Instructions to Authors'.

Deciding on authorship

In multi-author papers, a contentious issue is often who should appear as an author and in what order they should be cited. Where authors make an equal contribution, an alphabetical order of names may be used. Otherwise, each author should have made a substantial contribution to the paper and should be prepared to defend it in public. Ideally, the order of appearance will reflect the amount of work done rather than seniority. This may not happen in practice!

Writing

The paper's format will be similar to that shown in Box 61.1 and the process of writing will include outlining, reviewing, etc. as discussed elsewhere in this chapter. Figures must be finished to an appropriate standard and this may involve preparing photographs or digital images of them.

Submitting

When completed, copies of the paper are submitted to the editor of the chosen journal with a simple covering letter. A delay of one to two months usually follows while the manuscript is sent to one or more

---

Box 61.3 (Continued)

anonymous referees, who will be asked by the editor to check that the paper is novel and scientifically correct, and that its length is fully justified. It is becoming increasingly common to submit papers electronically (e-submission). An electronic copy of the paper may also be made available online (e.g. in a pdf file format).

Responding to referees' comments

The editor will send on the referees' comments to the authors, who will then have a chance to respond. The editor will decide, on the basis of the comments and replies to them, whether the paper should be published.

Sometimes quite heated correspondence can result if the authors and referees disagree!

Checking proofs and waiting for publication

If a paper is accepted, it will be sent to the typesetters or, increasingly, transformed into an electronic format (pdf file). The next the authors see of it is the proofs (first printed version in style of journal), which have to be corrected carefully for errors and returned. Eventually, the paper will appear in print, but a delay of six months following acceptance is not unusual. Most journals offer the authors reprints, which can be sent to other researchers in the field or to those who send in reprint request cards.

Sources for further study

Berry, R. (2004) *The Research Project: How to Write it,* 5th edn. Routledge, London.

Davis, M. and Davis, K.J. (2012) *Scientific Papers and Presentations: Navigating Scientific Communication in Today's World,* 3rd edn. Academic Press, London.

Day, R.A. and Gastel, B. (2012) *How to Write and Publish a Scientific Paper,* 7th edn. Cambridge University Press, Cambridge.

Hofmann, A.H. (2014) *Scientific Writing and Communication: Papers, Proposals and Presentations,* 2nd edn. Oxford University Press, Oxford.

Lobban, C.S. and Schefter, M. (1992) *Successful Lab Reports: A Manual for Science Students.* Cambridge University Press, Cambridge.

Luey, B. (2002) *Handbook for Academic Authors,* 4th edn. Cambridge University Press, Cambridge.

McMillan, K.M. and Weyers, J.D.B. (2014) *How to Complete a Successful Research Project.* Pearson Education, London.

Matthews, J.R., Bowen, J.M. and Matthews, R. (2007) *Successful Science Writing: A Step-by-Step Guide for the Biological and Medical Sciences,* 3rd edn. Cambridge University Press, Cambridge.

Valiela, I. (2009) *Doing Science: Design, Analysis and Communication of Scientific Research,* 2nd edn. Oxford University Press, Oxford.

Study exercises

61.1 Write a formal Materials and Methods section. Adopting the style of a research paper (e.g. past tense, all relevant detail reported such that a competent colleague could repeat your work), write out the Materials and Methods for a practical you have recently carried out. Ask a colleague or tutor to comment on what you have written.

61.2 Describe a set of results in words. Again, adopting the style of a research paper, write a paragraph describing the results contained in a particular table or graph. Ask a colleague or tutor to comment on your description to identify what is missing or unclear.

61.3 Write an Abstract for a paper. Pair up with a colleague. Each of you should independently choose a different research paper in a current journal. Copy the paper, but mask over the Abstract section, having first counted the words used. Swap papers. Now, working to the same amount of words as in the original, read the paper and provide an Abstract of its contents. Then, compare this with the real Abstract and with each others'.

The function of an essay is to show how much you understand about a topic and how well you can organise and express your knowledge. A literature survey or review is a specialised form of essay that summarises and reviews the evidence and concepts concerning a particular area of research.

Writing essays

Organising your time for writing essays

The way you should divide your time when producing an essay depends on whether you are writing it for in-course assessment or under exam conditions (Fig. 62.1). Essays written over a long period with access to books and other resources will probably involve a research element, not only before the planning phase but also when writing (Fig. 62.1(a)). For exams, it is assumed that you have revised appropriately (Chapter 68) and essentially have all the information at your fingertips. To keep things uncomplicated, the time allocated for each essay should be divided into three components – planning, writing and reviewing (Fig. 62.1(b)), and you should adopt time-saving techniques whenever possible (Box 65.1).

Making a plan for your essay
Dissect the meaning of the essay question or title
Read the title very carefully and think about the topic before starting to write. Consider the definitions of each of the important nouns (this can help in approaching the introductory section). Also think about the meaning of the verb(s) used and try to follow each instruction precisely (see Table 62.1). Don't get side-tracked because you know something about one word or phrase in the title – consider the whole title and all its ramifications. If there are two or more parts to the question, make sure you give adequate attention to each part.

Consider possible content and examples
Research content using the methods described in Chapters 45 and 46. If you have time to read several sources, consider their content in relation to the essay title. Can you spot different approaches to the same subject? Which do you prefer as a means of treating the topic in relation to your title? Which examples are most relevant to your case, and why?

Construct an outline
Every essay should have a structure related to its title.

> **KEY POINT** *Most lost marks for essays are because the written material is badly organised or is irrelevant. An essay plan, by definition, creates order and, if thought about carefully, should ensure relevance.*

Your plan should be written down (but crossed out later if written in an exam book). Think about an essay's content in three parts:

1. **The introductory section**, in which you should include definitions and some background information and the context for the topic being considered. You should also tell your reader how you plan to approach the subject.

> **Essay content** – *it is rarely enough simply to lay down facts for the reader – you must analyse them and comment on their significance.*

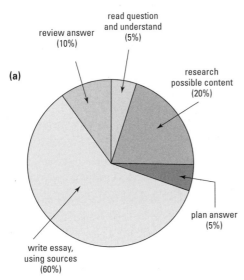

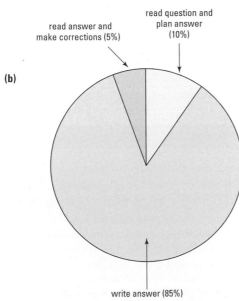

Fig. 62.1 Typical division of time for an essay written as part of in-course assessment (a) or under exam conditions (b).

Ten Golden Rules for essay writing – these are framed for in-course assessments (p. 606), though many are also relevant for exams (see also Box 69.2).

1. Read the question carefully, and decide exactly what the assessor wants you to achieve in your answer.
2. Make sure you understand the question by considering all aspects – discuss your approach with colleagues or a tutor.
3. Carry out the necessary research (using books, journals, Internet), taking appropriate notes. Gain an overview of the topic before getting involved with the details.
4. Plan your work in outline before you start writing. Check that your plan covers the main points and that it flows logically.
5. Introduce your essay by showing that you understand the topic and stating how you intend to approach it.
6. As you write the main content, ensure it is relevant by frequently looking back at the question.
7. Use headings and subheadings to organise and structure your essay.
8. Support your statements with relevant examples, diagrams and references where appropriate.
9. Conclude by summarising the key points of the topic, indicating the present state of knowledge, what we still need to find out and how this might be achieved.
10. Always re-read the essay before submitting it. Check grammar and spelling and confirm that you have answered all aspects of the question.

Using diagrams – give a title and legend to each diagram so that it makes sense in isolation and point out in the text when the reader should consult it (e.g. 'as shown in Fig. 1. . .' or 'as can be seen in the accompanying diagram, . . .').

Table 62.1 Instructions often used in essay questions and their meanings. When more than one instruction is given (e.g. compare and contrast; describe and explain), make sure you carry out *both* or you may lose a large proportion of the available marks

Account for:	give the reasons for
Analyse:	examine in depth and describe the main characteristics of
Assess:	weigh up the elements of and arrive at a conclusion about
Comment:	give an opinion on and provide evidence for your views
Compare:	bring out the similarities between
Contrast:	bring out dissimilarities between
Criticise:	judge the worth of (give both positive and negative aspects)
Define:	explain the exact meaning of
Describe:	use words and diagrams to illustrate
Discuss:	provide evidence or opinions about, arriving at a balanced conclusion
Enumerate:	list in outline form
Evaluate:	weigh up or appraise; find a numerical value for
Explain:	make the meaning of something clear
Illustrate:	use diagrams or examples to make clear
Interpret:	express in simple terms, providing a judgement
Justify:	show that an idea or statement is correct
List:	provide an itemised series of statements about
Outline:	describe the essential parts only, stressing the classification
Prove:	establish the truth of
Relate:	show the connection between
Review:	examine critically, perhaps concentrating on the stages in the development of an idea or method
State:	express clearly
Summarise:	without illustrations, provide a brief account of
Trace:	describe a sequence of events from a defined point of origin

2. **The middle of the essay**, where you develop your answer and provide relevant examples. Decide whether a broad analytical approach is appropriate or whether the essay should contain more factual detail.
3. **The conclusion**, which you can make quite short. You should use this part to summarise and draw together the components of the essay, without merely repeating previous phrases. You might mention such things as the broader significance of the topic; its future; its relevance to other important areas of forensic science. Always try to mention both sides of any debate you have touched on, but beware of 'sitting on the fence'.

 KEY POINT *Use paragraphs to make the essay's structure obvious. Emphasise them with headings and subheadings unless the material beneath the headings would be too short or trivial.*

Start writing

- **Never lose track of the importance of content and its relevance**. Repeatedly ask yourself: 'Am I really answering this question?' Never waffle just to increase the length of an essay. Quality is important rather than quantity.
- **Illustrate your answer appropriately**. Use examples to make your points clear, but remember that too many similar examples can stifle the flow of an essay. Use diagrams where a written description would be difficult or take too long. Use tables to condense information.
- **Take care with your handwriting**. You can't get marks if your writing is illegible! Try to cultivate an open form of handwriting, making the individual letters large and distinct. If there is time, make out a rough draft from which a tidy version can be copied.

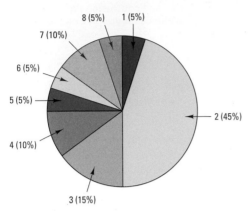

Fig. 62.2 Pie chart showing how you might allocate time for a literature survey:

1. select a topic;
2. scan the literature;
3. plan the review;
4. write first draft;
5. leave to settle;
6. prepare a structured review of text;
7. write final draft;
8. produce top copy.

Reviewing your answer

Don't stop yet!

- **Re-read the question** to check that you have answered all points.
- **Re-read your essay** to check for errors in punctuation, spelling and content. Make any corrections obvious. Don't panic if you suddenly realise you've missed a large chunk out, because the reader can be redirected to a supplementary paragraph if necessary.

Writing literature surveys and reviews

The literature survey or review is a specialised form of essay that summarises and reviews the evidence and concepts concerning a particular area of research.

> **KEY POINT** *A literature review should not be a simple recitation of facts. The best reviews are those that analyse information rather than simply describe it.*

Organising your time

Figure 62.2 illustrates how you might divide up your time for writing a literature survey. There are many subdivisions in this chart because of the size of the task – in general, for lengthy tasks, it is best to divide up the work into manageable chunks. Note also that proportionately less time is allocated to writing itself than with an essay. In a literature survey, make sure that you spend adequate time on research and revision.

Selecting a topic to review

You may have no choice in the topic to be covered, but if you do, carry out your selection as a three-stage process:

1. **Identify a broad subject area** that interests you.
2. **Find and read relevant literature in that area**. Try to gain a broad impression of the field from books and general review articles. Discuss your ideas with your supervisor.
3. **Select a relevant and concise title**. The wording should be considered very carefully as it will define the content expected by the reader. A narrow subject area will cut down on the amount of literature you will be expected to review, but will also restrict the scope of the conclusions you can make (and vice versa for a wide subject area).

Scanning the literature and organising your references

You will need to carry out a thorough investigation of the literature before you start to write. The key issues are as follows:

- **Make a start with relevant literature** – seek help from your supervisor, who may be willing to supply a few key papers to get you started. Hints on expanding your collection of references are given on p. 436.
- **Assessing the relevance and value of each article** – this is the essence of writing a review, but it is difficult unless you already have a good understanding of the field (Catch 22!). Try reading earlier reviews in your area.
- **Clarifying your thoughts** – you may find subdividing the main topic and assigning your references to these smaller subject areas can help you gain a better overview of the literature.

Deciding on structure and content

The general structure and content of a literature survey is described below.

Introduction

The introduction should give the general background to the research area, concentrating on its development and importance. You should also make a statement about the scope of your survey – as well as defining the subject matter to be discussed, you may wish to restrict the period being considered.

Main body of text

The review itself should discuss the published work in the selected field and may be subdivided into appropriate sections. Within each portion of a review, the approach is usually chronological, with appropriate linking phrases (e.g. 'Following on from this, . . .'; 'Meanwhile, Bloggs (2016) tackled the problem from a different angle. . .'). However, a good review is much more than a chronological list of work done. It should:

- **allow the reader** to obtain an overall view of the current state of the research area, identifying the key areas where knowledge is advancing;
- **show how techniques** are developing and discuss the benefits and disadvantages of using particular organisms or experimental systems;
- **assess the relative worth** of different types of evidence – this is the most important aspect (see Chapter 47). Do not be intimidated from taking a critical approach as the conclusions you may read in the primary literature aren't always correct;
- **indicate where there is conflict** in findings or theories, suggesting if possible which side has the stronger case;
- **indicate gaps** in current knowledge.

You do not need to wait until you have read all the sources available to you before starting to write the main body. Word processors allow you to modify and move pieces of text at any point and it will be useful to write paragraphs about key sources or groups of related papers as you read them. Try to create a general plan for your review as soon as possible. Place your draft sections of text under an appropriate set of subheadings that reflects your plan, but be prepared to rearrange these and re-title or re-order sections as you proceed. Not only will working in this way help to clarify your thoughts, but it may help you avoid a last-minute rush of writing near to the submission date.

Conclusions

The conclusions should draw together the threads of the preceding parts and point the way forward, perhaps listing areas of ignorance or where the application of new techniques may lead to advances.

References, etc.

The References or Literature Cited section should provide full details of all papers referred to in the text (see p. 437). It is a good idea to use bibliographic software, e.g. Endnote™, to assist you (Chapters 45–47). The regulations for your department may also specify a format and position for the Title page, Contents, Acknowledgements, etc.

Defining terms – *the Introduction is a good place to explain the meaning of the key terms used in your survey or review.*

Balancing opposing views – *even if you favour one side of a disagreement in the literature, your review should provide a balanced and fair description of all the published views of the topic. Having done this, if you do wish to state a preference, give reasons for your opinion.*

Making citations – *a review of literature poses stylistic problems because of the need to cite large numbers of papers; in the Annual Review series this is overcome by using numbered references (see p. 438).*

Style of literature surveys and reviews – *The Annual Review series (available in most university libraries) provides good examples of the style expected in scientific reviews.*

Sources for further study

Good, S. and Jensen, B. (1995) *The Student's Only Survival Guide to Essay Writing.* Orca Book Publishers, Victoria, USA.

McMillan, K.M. and Weyers, J.D.B. (2011) *How to Write Essays and Assignments,* 2nd edn. Pearson Education, London.

McMillan, K.M. and Weyers, J.D.B. (2012) *The Study Skills Book.* Pearson Education, London.

Shields, M. (2010) *Essay Writing: A Students Guide.* Sage Publishing, London.

Study exercises

62.1 Practise dissecting essay titles. Use past exam papers, or make up questions based on learning objectives for your course and your lecture notes. Take each essay title and carefully 'dissect' the wording, working out exactly what you think the assessor expects you to do (see Table 62.1).

62.2 Write essay plans under self-imposed time limits. Continuing from 62.1, outline plans for essays from a past exam paper. Allow yourself a maximum of 5 minutes per outline. Within this time your main goal is to create an essay plan. To do this, you may need to 'brainstorm' the topic.

Alternatively, if you allocate 10 minutes per essay, you may be able to provide more details, e.g. list the examples you could describe.

62.3 Summarise the main differences between a review and a scientific paper. From the many subject areas in the *Annual Review* series (find via your library's periodical indexing system), pick one that matches your subject interests, and within this find a review that seems relevant or interesting. Read the review and write down five ways in which the writing style and content differ from those seen in primary scientific papers.

Learning from others – look at the various types of posters around your university and elsewhere. The best examples will be visual, not textual – with a clear structure that helps get the key messages across.

A scientific poster is a visual display of the results of an investigation, usually mounted on a rectangular board. Posters are used at scientific meetings to communicate research findings, and in undergraduate courses to display assignment work or project results.

In a written report you can include a reasonable amount of specific detail and the reader can go back and re-read difficult passages. However, if a poster is long-winded or contains too much detail, your reader is likely to lose interest, so you should aim to be focused and succinct.

 KEY POINT *A poster session is like a competition – you are competing for the attention of people in a room. Because you need to attract and hold the attention of your audience, make your poster as interesting as possible. Think of it as an advertisement for your work and you will not go far wrong.*

Preliminaries

Before considering the content of your poster, you should find out:

- **the linear dimensions of your poster area,** typically up to 1.5 m wide by 1.0 m high;
- **the composition of the poster board** and the method of attachment, whether drawing pins, Velcro® tape or some other form of adhesive; and whether these will be provided – in any case, it's safer to bring your own;
- **the time(s)** when the poster should be set up and when to attend;
- **the room** where the poster session will be held.

Design

Plan your poster with your audience in mind, as this will dictate the appropriate level for your presentation. Aim to make your poster as accessible as possible to a broad audience. Since a poster is a *visual* display, you must pay particular attention to the presentation of information – work that may have taken hours to prepare can be ruined in a few minutes by the ill-considered arrangement of items (Fig. 63.1). Begin by making a draft sketch of the major elements of your poster.

It is worth discussing your intended design with someone else, as constructive advice at the draft stage will save a lot of time and effort when you prepare the final version. Alternatively, consult Simmonds and Reynolds (1994) or the other sources for further study at the end of this chapter.

Layout

Usually the best approach is to divide the poster into several smaller areas, and prepare each as a separate item on a piece of card. Some people prefer to produce a single poster on one sheet of paper or card and store it inside a protective cardboard tube. However, a single large poster will bend and crease, making it difficult to flatten out. In addition, photographs and text attached to the backing sheet often work loose. A more common and preferred approach is to use software such as PowerPoint (Box 63.1 on p. 575) or Publisher.

If you are not using PowerPoint, then subdividing your poster means that each smaller area can be prepared on a separate piece of paper or card, of A4 size or slightly larger, making transport and storage easier. It also breaks the

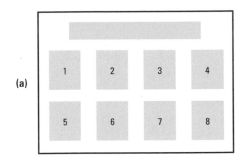

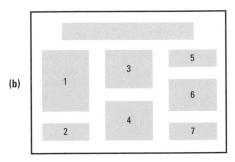

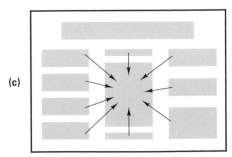

(a)

(b)

(c)

Fig. 63.1 Poster design: (a) an uninspiring design – sub-units of equal area, reading left to right, are not recommended; (b) this design is more interesting and the text will be easier to read (column format); (c) an alternative approach, with a central focus and arrows/tapes to guide the reader.

reading matter up into smaller pieces, looking less formidable to a potential reader. By using pieces of card of different colours you can provide emphasis for key aspects, or link text with figures or photographs.

You will need to guide your reader through the poster. It is often appropriate to use either a numbering system, with large, clear numbers at the top of each piece of card, or a system of arrows (or thin tapes) to show the relationship of sections within the poster (see Fig. 63.1(c)). Make sure that the relationship is clear and that the arrows or tapes do not cross.

Title

Your chosen title should be concise (ideally no more than eight words), specific and interesting, to encourage people to read the poster. Make the title large and bold – it should run across the top of your poster in letters at least 4 cm high, so that it can be read from the other side of the room. Details of authors, together with their addresses (if appropriate), should be given, usually in the top right-hand corner in somewhat smaller lettering than the title.

Text

Write in short sentences and avoid verbosity. Keep your poster as visual as possible and make effective use of the spaces between the blocks of text. Your final text should be double-spaced and should have a minimum capital letter height of 8 mm (minimum font size 24 point or less if more text is required in your assignment – you will be advised on this in your assignment brief), preferably greater, so that the poster can be read at a distance of 1m. One method of obtaining text of the required size is to photo-enlarge standard typescript (using a good-quality photocopier), or use a high-quality (laser) printer. It is best to avoid continuous use of text in capitals, since it slows reading and makes the text less interesting to the reader. Also avoid italic, 'balloon' or decorative styles of lettering.

 KEY POINT *Keep text to a minimum – aim to have a maximum of 500 words in your poster, or as specified in your assessment instructions.*

Subtitles and headings

These should have a capital letter height of 12–20 mm, and should be restricted to two or three words. They can be produced by photo-enlargement, by stencilling, Letraset® or by hand, using pencilled guidelines (but make sure that no pencil marks are visible on your finished poster).

Colour

Consider the overall visual effect of your chosen display, including the relationship between text, diagrams and the backing board. Colour can be used to highlight key aspects of your poster. However, it is very easy to ruin a poster by the inappropriate choice and application of colour. Careful use of two, or at most three, complementary colours will be easier on the eye and may aid comprehension. Colour can be used to link the text with the visual images (e.g. by picking out a colour in a photograph and using the same colour on the mounting board for the accompanying text). For PowerPoint posters, careful choice of colours for the various elements will enhance the final product (Box 63.1). Use coloured inks or water-based paints to provide colour in diagrams and figures, as felt pens rarely give satisfactory results.

PowerPoint *– when using PowerPoint 2016 set the poster orientation and size by Design>Slide size>Custom slide size.*

Presenting a poster at a formal conference *– it can be useful to include a photograph of the contributor for identification purposes.*

Making up your poster *– text and graphics printed on good-quality paper can be glued directly on to a contrasting mounting card – use photographic spray mountant or Pritt® rather than liquid glue. Trim carefully using a guillotine to give equal margins, parallel with the paper. Photographs should be placed in a window mount to avoid the tendency for their corners to curl. Another approach is to trim pages or photographs to their correct size, then encapsulate in plastic film – this gives a highly professional finish and is less weighty to transport.*

Producing composite material for posters *– PowerPoint is generally more useful than Word when you wish to include text, graphics and/or images on the same page. It is possible to use PowerPoint to produce a complete poster, although it can be expensive to have this printed out commercially to A1 or A0 size.*

Box 63.1 How to create a poster using Office PowerPoint 2016

Software such as PowerPoint can be used to produce a high-quality poster, providing you have access to a good colour printer. However, you should avoid the standard templates available on the Internet as they encourage unnecessary uniformity and stifle creativity, leading to a less satisfying end-result. The following steps give practical advice on creating a poster as a single PowerPoint slide:

1. **Sketch out your plans.** Decide on the main poster elements (images, graphs, tables and text sections) and their relationship with each other and draw out a one-page 'storyboard' (see Fig. 63.1). Think about colours for background, text and graphics (use two or three complementary colours) – dark text on a light background is clearer (high contrast), and uses less ink when printing. Also, consider how you will link the elements in sequence, to guide readers through your 'story'.

2. **Get your material ready.** Collect together individual files for pictures, figures and tables. Make any required adjustments to images, graphs or tables before you import them into your poster.

3. **Create a new/blank slide.** Open PowerPoint and click on the Blank presentation icon. Then use the Design tab > Slide size > Custom slide size menu to select either Landscape or Portrait orientation and to set the correct page size (use Width and Height commands, or select a standard size like A4, A3, A2 etc.). Right-click on the slide and select Ruler and Grid and Guides (to help position elements within the slide – the horizontal and vertical guidelines can be dragged to different positions at later stages, as required). Use the templates on the top line menu to select an appropriate Background style and colour. In general, avoid setting a picture as your background as these tend to detract from the content of the poster. Before going further, save your work. Repeat this frequently and in more than one location (e.g. hard drive and USB memory stick).

4. **Add graphics.** For images, use the Insert tab, select Pictures and browse to Insert the correct file. The Insert, Chart command performs a similar function for Excel charts (graphs). Alternatively, use the copy-and-paste functions of complementary software. Once inserted, resize using the sizing handles in one of the corners (for photographs, take care not to alter one dimension relative to the other, or the image will be distorted). To re-position, put the mouse pointer over the image, left-click and hold, then drag to new location. While the Insert tab offers standard shapes and other useful features, you should avoid clipart (jaded and overused) and poor-quality images from the Internet (always use the highest resolution possible) – if you do not have your final images, use blank text boxes to show their position within the poster.

5. **Add text.** Use the Insert tab to select a Text box and place this on your slide, then either type in your text (use the Enter key to provide line spacing within the box) or copy-and-paste text from a word-processed file. You will need to consider the font size for the printed poster (e.g. for an A0 poster (size 1189 × 841 mm), a printed font size of 24 point is appropriate for the main text, with larger fonts for headings and titles. If you find things difficult to read on-screen, use the Zoom function (either select a larger percentage in the Zoom box on the bottom right toolbar, or hold down the Control key and use the mouse wheel to scroll up (magnify) or down (reduce). Use a separate text box for each element of your poster and don't be tempted to type too much text into each box – write in phrases, using bullet points and numbered lists to keep text concise (aim for approximately 50 words per text box, or as appropriate for your poster). Select appropriate font styles and colours using the Home > Drawing Shape Fill, Outline and Effects options (line thickness and colour can then be altered). Present supplementary text elements in a smaller font – for example, details of methodology, references cited.

6. **Add boxes, lines and/or arrows** to link elements of the poster and guide the reader (e.g. Fig. 63.1). These features are available from the Insert tab Shapes drop-down menu in the Illustrations sub section. Note that new inserts are overlaid on older inserts – if this proves to be a problem, select the relevant item and use the Arrange > Order functions to change its relative position.

7. **Review your poster.** Get feedback from another student or tutor, e.g. on a small printed version, or use a projector to view your poster without printing (adjust the distance between projector and screen to give the correct size).

8. **Revise and edit your poster.** Revisit your work and remove as much text as possible. Delete any component that is not essential to the message of the poster. Keep graphs simple and clear (p. 483 gives further advice). White space is important in providing structure.

9. **Print the final version.** Use a high-resolution colour printer (this may be costly, so you should wait until you are sure that no further changes are needed).

Content

The typical format is that of a scientific report (see Box 61.1), i.e. with the same headings, but with a considerably reduced content. Keep references within the text to a minimum – interested parties can always ask you for further information or it may be prudent to use the Vancouver system (or equivalent) (see Chapter 45), given the space constraints, unless a specific referencing style is requested. Also note that most posters have a Summary/Conclusions section, rather than an Abstract.

Introduction

This should give the reader background information on the broad field of study and the aims of your own work. It is vital that this section is as interesting as possible, to capture the interest of your audience. It is often worth listing your objectives as a series of numbered points.

Materials and Methods/Experimental

Keep this short, and describe only the principal techniques used. You might mention any special techniques, or problems of general interest.

Results

Don't present raw data: use data reduction wherever possible, i.e. figures and simple statistical comparisons. Graphs, diagrams, histograms and pie charts (Chapter 52) give clear visual images of trends and relationships and should be used in place of tabulated data. Final copies of all figures should be produced so that the numbers can be read from a distance of 1m. Each should have a concise title and legend, so that it is self-contained: if appropriate, a series of numbered points can be used to link a diagram with the accompanying text. Where symbols are used, provide a key on each graph (symbol size should be at least 5 mm). Avoid using graphs straight from a written version, for example a project report, textbook, or a paper, without considering whether they need modification to meet your requirements.

Conclusions

This is where many readers will begin, and they may go no further unless you make this section sufficiently interesting. This part needs to be the strongest part of your poster, summarising the main points. Refer to your figures here to draw the reader into the main part of your poster. A slightly larger or bolder typeface may add emphasis, though too many different typefaces can look messy. For the reference list, a smaller font can be used.

The poster session

If you stand at the side of your poster throughout the session, you are likely to discourage some readers, who may not wish to become involved in a detailed conversation about the poster. Stand nearby. Find something to do – talk to someone else or browse among the other posters, but remain aware of people reading your poster and be ready to answer any queries that may raise. Do not be too discouraged if you aren't asked lots of questions – remember, the poster is meant to be a self-contained, visual story without need for further explanation.

A poster display will never feel like an oral presentation, where the nervousness beforehand is replaced by a combination of satisfaction and relief as you unwind after the event. However, it can be a very satisfying means of communication, particularly if you follow these guidelines.

Text reference

Simmonds, D. and Reynolds, L. (1994) *Data Presentation and Visual Literacy in Medicine and Science.* Butterworth-Heinemann, London.

Sources for further study

Alley, M. (2007) *The Craft of Scientific Presentations: Critical Steps to Succeed and Critical Errors to Avoid,* 5th edn. Springer-Verlag, New York.

Briscoe, M.H. (2000*) Preparing Scientific Illustrations: A Guide to Better Posters, Presentations and Publications,* 2nd edn. Springer-Verlag, New York.

Davis, M.F. (2012) *Scientific Papers and Presentations,* 2nd edn. Academic Press, New York.

Gosling, P.J. (1999) *Scientist's Guide to Poster Presentations.* Kluwer, New York.

Hess, G. and Liegel, L. *Creating Effective Poster Presentations.* Available at: http://www.ncsu.edu/project/posters Last accessed 30/08/2017.

Study exercises

63.1 Design a poster. Working with one or more partners from your year group, decide on a suitable poster topic (perhaps something linked to your current teaching programme). Working individually, make an outline plan of the major elements of the poster, with appropriate subheadings and a brief indication of the content and relative size of each element (including figures, diagrams and images). Exchange draft plans with your partners and arrange a session where you can discuss their merits and disadvantages.

63.2 Prepare a checklist for assessing the quality of a poster presentation. After reading through this chapter, prepare a 10-point checklist of assessment criteria under the heading 'What makes a good poster presentation?' Compare your list with the one that we have provided – do you agree with our criteria, or do you prefer your own list (and can you justify your preferences)?

63.3 Evaluate the posters in your university. Most universities have a wide range of academic posters on display. Some may cover general topics (e.g. course structures), while others may deal with specific research topics (e.g. poster presentations from past conferences). Consider their good and bad features (if you wish to make this a group exercise, you might compare your evaluation with that of other students, in a group discussion session).

Study and examination skills

This chapter outlines the range of transferable skills and their significance to students of forensic science. It also indicates where practical skills fit into this scheme. Having a good understanding of this topic will help you place your studies at university in a wider context. Awareness of these matters will help when carrying out personal development planning (PDP) (see p. 583). You will also gain an insight into the qualities that employers expect you to have developed by the time you graduate.

The range of transferable skills

Table 64.1 provides a comprehensive listing of university-level transferable skills under six skill categories. There are many possible classifications – and a different one may be used in your institution or field of study. Note particularly that 'study skills', while important, and rightly emphasised at the start of many courses and programmes, constitute only one area of skills acquired by most university students.

The phrase '*Practical Skills*' in the title of this book indicates that there is a special subset of transferable skills related to practical work. However, although this text deals primarily with the skills and techniques required for laboratory practicals, crime scene and associated studies at university, a broader range of material is included. This is because the skills concerned are important, not only in forensic science but also in the wider world. Examples include time management, evaluating information and communicating effectively.

 KEY POINT *Forensic science is essentially a practical subject, and therefore involves highly developed laboratory and crime scene skills. The importance that your lecturers place on practical skills will probably be evident from the large proportion of curriculum time you will spend on practical work in your course or programme.*

The word 'skill' implies much more than the robotic learning of, for example, a laboratory routine. Of course, some of the tasks you will be asked to carry out in practical classes *will* be repetitive. Certain techniques require manual dexterity and attention to detail if accuracy and precision are to be attained, and the necessary competence often requires practice to make perfect. However, a deeper understanding of the context of a technique is important if the skill is to be appreciated fully and then transferred to a new situation. That is why this text is not simply a 'recipe book' of methods and why it includes background information, tips and worked examples, as well as study exercises to test your understanding.

Transferability of skills

Transferable skills are those that allow someone with knowledge, understanding or ability gained in one situation to adapt or extend this for application in a different context. In some cases, the transfer of a skill is immediately obvious. Take, for example, the ability to use a spreadsheet to summarise biological and

---

Skills terminology – different phrases may be used to describe transferable skills, depending on place or context. These include: 'personal transferable skills' (PTS), 'key skills', 'core skills' and 'competences'.

Using course materials – study your course handbook and the schedules for each practical session to find out what skills you are expected to develop at each point in the curriculum. Usually the learning outcomes/objectives will outline the skills involved.

Example The skills involved in teamwork cannot be fully developed without a deeper understanding of the interrelationships involved in successful groups. The context will be different for every group and a flexible approach will always be required, according to the individuals involved and the nature of the task.

The importance of transferable skills

Table 64.1 Transferable skills identified as important in forensic science. The list has been compiled from several sources, including the UK Quality Assurance Agency for Higher Education subject benchmark statement for forensic science (QAAHE, 2012)

Skill category	Examples of skills and competences
Generic skills for forensic scientists	Having an appreciation of the complexity and diversity of crime scene investigation, forensic chemistry and forensic biology
	Reading and evaluating scientific literature with a full and critical understanding Ability to communicate a clear and accurate account of a forensic science topic, both verbally and in writing Applying critical and analytical skills to evaluate evidence regarding theories and hypotheses in forensic science Using a variety of methods for studying forensic science Having the ability to think independently, set personal tasks and solve problems
Intellectual skills	Recognising and applying forensic scientific theories, concepts and principles Analysing, synthesising and summarising information critically Obtaining evidence to formulate and test hypotheses; applying knowledge to address familiar and unfamiliar problems
Experimental and observational skills	Carrying out basic laboratory and crime scene techniques and understanding the principles that underlie them Working in a lab or crime scene safely, responsibly and legally, with due attention to ethical aspects Designing, planning, conducting and reporting on forensic investigations and data arising from them Obtaining, recording, collating and analysing data at the crime scene and in the laboratory
Numeracy, communication and IT skills	Understanding and using data in several forms (e.g. numerical, textual, verbal and graphical) Communicating in written, verbal, graphical and visual forms Citing and referencing the work of others in an appropriate manner Obtaining data, including the concepts behind sampling and sampling errors, calibration and types of error Processing, interpreting and presenting data, and applying appropriate statistical methods for summarising and analysing data Solving problems with calculators and computers, including the use of tools such as spreadsheets Using computer technology to communicate and as a source of information in forensic science
Interpersonal and teamwork skills	Working individually or in teams as appropriate; identifying individual and group goals and acting responsibly and appropriately to achieve them Recognising and respecting the views and opinions of others Evaluating your own performance and that of others Appreciating the interdisciplinary nature of forensic science
Self-management and professional development skills	Working independently, managing time and organising activities Identifying and working towards targets for personal, academic and career development Developing an adaptable and effective approach to study and work

chemical data and create a graph to illustrate results. Once the key concepts and commands are learned (Chapter 49), they can be applied to many instances outside a forensic science degree course where this type of output is used. This is not only true for similar data sets, but also in unrelated situations, such as making up a financial balance sheet and creating a pie chart to show sources of expenditure. Similarly, knowing the requirements for good graph drawing and tabulation (Chapters 52 and 53), perhaps practised by hand in earlier work, might help you use spreadsheet commands to make the output suit your needs.

The science-related cognitive abilities, practical and professional skills

Other cases may be less clear but equally valid. For example, towards the end of your undergraduate studies you may be involved in designing experiments as part of your project work. This task will draw on several skills gained at earlier stages in your course, such as preparing solutions (Chapters 6–9), deciding about numbers of replicates and experimental layout (Chapter 5) and perhaps carrying out work as part of crime scene investigation (Chapters 23–28), analytical techniques (Chapters 14–22), forensic chemistry (Chapters 37–44), or forensic biology (Chapters 30–36). How and when might you transfer this complex set of skills? In the workplace, it is unlikely that you would be asked to repeat the same process, but in critically evaluating a problem or in planning a complex project for a new employer, you will need to use many of the time-management, organisational and analytical skills developed when designing and carrying out experiments. The same applies to information retrieval and evaluation and writing essays and dissertations, when transferred to the task of analysing or writing a business report.

Personal development planning

Many universities have schemes for personal development planning (PDP), which may go under slightly different names such as progress file or professional development plan. You will usually be expected to create a portfolio of evidence on your progress, then reflect on this, and subsequently set yourself plans for the future, including targets and action points. Analysis of your transferable skills profile will probably form part of your PDP. Other aspects commonly included are:

- your aspirations, goals, interests and motivations;
- your learning style or preference (see p. 598);
- your assessment transcript or academic profile information (e.g. record of grades in your modules);
- your developing CV (see p. 614).

Taking part in PDP can help focus your thoughts about your university studies and future career. This is important, as many science degrees do not lead to a single, specific occupation. The PDP process will introduce you to some new terms and will help you to describe your personality and abilities. This is important when constructing your CV and when applying for jobs.

What your future employer will be looking for

At the end of your course or programme, which may seem some time away, you will aim to get a job and start on your chosen career path. You will need to sell yourself to your future employer, first in your application form and curriculum vitae (Chapter 70), and perhaps later at interview. Many forensic science students seek employment across a broad range of occupations on completion of their degree programmes, and companies rarely employ graduates simply because they know how to carry out a particular lab routine or because they can remember specific facts about their chosen degree subject. Instead, employers tend to look for a range of qualities and transferable skills that together define an attribute known as 'graduateness'. This encompasses, for example, the ability to work in a team, to speak effectively and write clearly about your work,

Opportunities to develop and practise skills in your private or social life – you could, for example, practise spreadsheet skills by organising personal or club finances using Microsoft® Excel® or teamwork skills within any university clubs or societies you may join (see Chapter 66).

Types of PDP portfolio and their benefits – some PDP schemes are centred on academic and learning skills, while others are more focused on career planning. Some are carried out independently and others in tandem with a personal tutor or advisory system. Some PDP schemes involve creating an online portfolio, while others are primarily paper-based. Each method has specific goals and advantages, but whichever way your scheme operates maximum benefit will be gained from being fully involved with the process.

Your transferable skills audit:

- Create a list of appropriate skills.
- Rate your skills using a scale 1–10.
- Think about ways to improve your scores – is there a training workshop? Could you speak to a skills advisor?
- Add comments as you progress to give a sense of achievement/self-awareness.

Definition

Employability – the combination of in-depth subject knowledge, work awareness, subject-specific, generic and career management skills, and personal attributes and attitudes that enable a student to secure suitable employment and perform excellently throughout a career spanning a range of employers and occupations.

to understand complex data and to manage a project to completion. All of these skills can be developed at different stages during your university studies.

 KEY POINT *Factual knowledge can be important in degrees with a strong vocational element and this will be important to students who become forensic science practitioners. However, for others, understanding how to find and evaluate information is usually rated more highly by employers than the narrow ability to memorise facts.*

Most likely, your future employer(s) will seek someone with an organised yet flexible mind, capable of demonstrating a logical approach to problems – someone who has a range of skills and who can transfer these skills to new situations. Many competing applicants will probably have similar qualifications. If you want the job, you will have to show that your additional skills and personal attributes place you above the other candidates.

Text reference

QAAHE (2012) *Subject Benchmark Statement for Forensic Science.* Quality Assurance Agency for Higher Education, Gloucester.

Sources for further study

Drew, S. and Bingham, R. (2010) *The Guide to Learning and Study Skills.* Gower Publishing Ltd, Aldershot.

McMillan, K. and Weyers, J.D.B. (2012) *The Study Skills Book,* 3rd edn. Pearson Education, Harlow.

Race, P. (2007) *How to get a Good Degree: Making the Most of Your Time at University,* 3rd edn. Open University Press, Buckingham.

Study exercises

64.1 Evaluate your skills. Examine the list of skill topics shown in Table 64.1. Now create a new table with two columns. The first half of this table should indicate five skills you feel confident about and show where you demonstrated this skill (for example, 'working in a team' and 'in a first-year group project in fingerprint examination'). The second half of the table should show five skills you do not feel confident about, or you recognise need development (e.g. 'communicating in verbal form'). List these and then list ways in which you think the course material for your current modules will provide opportunities to develop these skills, or what activities you might take to improve them (e.g. 'forming a study group with colleagues').

64.2 Find skills resources. For at least one of the skills in the second half of Table 64.1, check your university's library database to see if there are any texts on that subject. Alternatively, carry out a search for relevant websites (there are many); decide which are useful and 'bookmark' them for future use (Chapter 46).

64.3 Analyse your goals and aspirations. Spend a little time thinking about what you hope to gain from university. See if your friends have the same aspirations. Think about and/or discuss how these goals can be achieved, while keeping the necessary balance between university work, paid employment and your social life.

65 Managing your time

Definition

Time management – a system for controlling and using time as efficiently and as effectively as possible.

Advantages of a good time management system:

- *a much greater feeling of control over your activities;*
- *avoidance of stress.*
- *improved productivity – achieve more in a shorter period;*
- *improved performance levels – work to higher standards because you are in charge;*
- *an increase in time available for non-work matters – work hard, but play hard too.*

Example   The objective to spend an extra hour each week on directed study on toxicology principles fulfils the SMART criteria, in contrast to a general intention to study more.

One of the most important activities that you can do is to organise your personal and working time effectively. There is a lot to do at university and a common complaint is that there just isn't enough time to accomplish everything. In fact, research shows that most people use up a lot of their time, without realising it, through ineffective study or activities such as extended coffee breaks. Developing your time management skills will help you achieve more in work, rest and play, but it is important to remember that putting time management techniques into practice is an individual matter, requiring a level of self-discipline not unlike that required for dieting or for sporting success. A new system won't always work perfectly straightaway, but through time you can evolve a system that is effective for you.

An inability to organise your time effectively results in feelings of failure, frustration, guilt and being out of control in your life.

Setting your goals

The first step is to identify clearly what you want to achieve, both in work and in your personal life. We all have a general idea of what we are aiming for, but, to be effective, your goals must be clearly identified and priorities allocated. Clear, concise objectives can provide you with a framework in which to make these choices. Try using the 'SMART' approach, in which objectives should be:

- **S**pecific – clear and unambiguous, including what, when, where, how and why.
- **M**easurable – having quantified targets and benefits to provide an understanding of progress.
- **A**chievable – being attainable within your resources.
- **R**ealistic – being within your abilities and expectations.
- **T**imed – stating the time period for completion.

Having identified your goals, you can now move on to answer four very important questions:

1. Where does your time go?
2. Where should your time go?
3. What are your time-wasting activities?
4. What strategies can help you?

Analysing your current activities

The key to successful development of time management is a realistic knowledge of how you currently spend your time. Start by keeping a detailed time log for a typical week (Fig. 65.1), but you will need to be truthful in this process. Once you have completed the log, consider the following questions:

- How many hours do I work in total and how many hours do I use for 'relaxation'?
- What range of activities do I do?
- How long do I spend on each activity?
- What do I spend most of my time doing?
- What do I spend the least amount of my time doing?

Time slots	Activity									Notes
7.00–7.15										
7.15–7.30										
7.30–7.45										
7.45–8.00										
8.00–8.15										
8.15–8.30										
8.30–8.45										
8.45–9.00										
9.00–9.15										

Fig. 65.1 Example of how to lay out a time log. Write activities along the top of the page, and divide the day into 15-minute segments as shown. Think beforehand how you will categorise the different things you do, from the mundane (laundry, having a shower, drinking coffee, etc.) to the well-timetabled (tutorial meeting, sports club meeting) and add supplementary notes if required. At the end of each day, place a dot in the relevant column for each activity and sum the dots to give a total at the bottom of the page. You will need to keep a diary like this for at least a week before you see patterns emerging.

- Are my allocations of time in proportion to the importance of my activities?
- How much of my time is ineffectively used, e.g. for uncontrolled socialising or interruptions?

Managing your time

If you wish, you could use a spreadsheet (Chapter 49) to produce graphical summaries of time allocations in different categories as an aid to analysis and management. Divide your time into:

- **committed time** – timetabled activities involving your main objectives/goals;
- **maintenance time** – spent supporting your general life activities (shopping, cleaning, laundry, etc.);
- **discretionary time** – for you to use as you wish, e.g. recreation, sport, hobbies, socialising.

Avoiding time-wasting activities

Look carefully at those tasks that could be identified as time-wasting activities. They include gossiping, overlong breaks, uninvited interruptions and even ineffective study periods. Try to reduce these to a minimum, but do not count on eliminating them entirely. Remember also that some relaxation *should* be programmed into your daily schedule.

Organising your tasks

Having analysed your time usage, you can now use this information, together with your objectives and prioritised goals, to organise your activities, both on a short-term and a long-term basis. Consider using a diary-based system (such as those produced by Filofax®, TMI® and Day-timer®) that will help you plan ahead and analyse your progress.

Divide your tasks into several categories, such as:

- **urgent** – must be done as a top priority and at short notice (e.g. doctor's appointment);

Quality in time management – avoid spending a lot of time doing unproductive studying, e.g. reading a textbook without specific objectives for that reading. Make sure you test your recall of the material, if you are working towards an examination.

Being assertive – if friends and colleagues continually interrupt you, find a way of controlling them before they control you. Indicate clearly on your door that you do not wish to be disturbed and explain why. Otherwise, try to work away from disturbances.

Matching your work to your body's rhythm – everyone has times of day when they feel more alert and able to work. Decide when these times are for you and programme your work accordingly. Plan relaxation events for periods when you tend to be less alert.

Use checklists as often as possible – post your lists in places where they are easily and frequently visible, such as in front of your desk. Ticking things off as they are completed gives you a feeling of accomplishment and progress, increasing motivation.

- **routine** – predictable and regular, and therefore easily scheduled (e.g. preparation, lectures or playing sport);
- **one-off activities** – usually with rather shorter deadlines and which may be of high priority (e.g. a tutorial assignment or seeking advice);
- **long-term tasks** – sometimes referred to as 'elephant tasks', which are too large to 'eat' in one go (e.g. learning a language). These are best managed by scheduling frequent small 'bites' to achieve the task over a longer timescale.

You should make a weekly plan (Fig. 65.2) for the routine activities, with gaps for less predictable tasks. This should be supplemented by individual daily checklists, preferably written at the end of the previous working day. Such plans and checklists should be flexible, forming the basis for most of your activities except when exceptional circumstances intervene. The planning must be kept brief, however, and should be scheduled into your activities. Box 65.1 provides tips for effective time management during your studies.

 KEY POINT *Review each day's plan at the end of the previous day, making such modifications as are required by circumstances - for example, adding an uncompleted task from that day or a new and urgent task.*

WEEKLY DIARY   Week beginning:

	Sunday	Monday	Tuesday	Wednesday	Thursday	Friday	Saturday
DATE							

	Sunday	Monday	Tuesday	Wednesday	Thursday	Friday	Saturday
7–8 am		Breakfast	Breakfast	Breakfast	Breakfast	Breakfast	
8–9		Preparation	Preparation	Preparation	Preparation	Preparation	Breakfast
9–10	Breakfast	PE112(L)	PE112(L)	PE112(L)	PE112(L)	BIOL(P)	Travel
10–11	FREE	CHEM(L)	FOR SCI(L)	FOR SCI(L)	CHEM(L)	BIOL(P)	WORK
11–12	STUDY	STUDY	STUDY	STUDY	STUDY	BIOL(P)	WORK
12–1 pm	STUDY	BIOL(L)	BIOL(L)	BIOL(L)	BIOL(L)	TUTORIAL	WORK
1–2	Lunch	Lunch	Lunch	Lunch	Lunch	Lunch	Lunch
2–3	(VOLLEY-	CHEM(P)	STUDY	SPORT	FOR SCI(P)	STUDY	WORK
3–4	BALL	CHEM(P)	STUDY	(VOLLEY	FOR SCI(P)	STUDY	WORK
4–5	MATCH)	CHEM(P)	STUDY	BALL	FOR SCI(P)	SHOPPING	WORK
5–6	FREE	STUDY	STUDY	CLUB)	STUDY	TEA ROTA	WORK
6–7	Tea	Tea	Tea	Tea	Tea	Tea	Tea
7–8	FREE	STUDY	STUDY	FREE	STUDY	FREE	FREE
8–9	FREE	STUDY	STUDY	FREE	STUDY	FREE	FREE
9–10	FREE	FREE	STUDY	FREE	STUDY	FREE	FREE

	Sunday	Monday	Tuesday	Wednesday	Thursday	Friday	Saturday
Study (h)	2	10	11	4	11	6	0
Other (h)	13	5	4	11	4	9	15

Total study time = 44 h

Fig. 65.2 A weekly diary, with examples of entries for a first-year science student with a Saturday job and active membership of a volleyball club. Note that 'free time' changes to 'study time', e.g. for periods when assessed work is to be produced or during revision for exams. Study time (including attendance at lectures, practicals and tutorials) thus represents between 42% and 50% of the total time.

Box 65.1 Tips for effective planning and working

- Set guidelines and review expectations regularly.

- Don't procrastinate – don't keep putting off doing things you know are important; they will not go away, but they will increase to crisis point.

- Don't be a perfectionist – perfection is paralysing.

- Learn from past experience – review your management system regularly.

- Don't set yourself unrealistic goals and objectives – this will lead to procrastination and feelings of failure.

- Avoid recurring crises – they are telling you that something is not working properly and needs to be changed.

- Learn to concentrate effectively and don't let yourself be distracted by casual interruptions.

- Learn to say 'no' firmly but graciously when appropriate.

- Know your own body rhythms – e.g. are you a morning person or an evening person?

- Learn to recognise the benefits of rest and relaxation at appropriate times.

- Take short but complete breaks from your tasks – come back feeling refreshed in mind and body.

- Work in suitable study areas and keep your own workspace organised.

- Avoid clutter – physical and mental.

- Learn to access and use information effectively (Chapters 45–47).

- Learn to read and write accurately and quickly (Chapters 61, 62 and 67).

Sources for further study

Anon (2016) Study Guides and Strategies: Time Management. Available at: http://www.studygs.net/timman.htm. Last accessed 30/08/2017.

Bird, P. (2011) *Effective Time Management.* Hodder Ed, London.

Drew, S. and Bingham, R. (2010) *The Guide to Learning and Study Skills.* Gower Publishing Ltd, Aldershot.

McMillan, K. and Weyers, J.D.B. (2012) *The Study Skills Book,* 3rd edn. Pearson Education, Harlow.

Study exercises

65.1 Evaluate your time usage. Compile a spreadsheet to keep a record of your daily activities in 15-minute segments for a week. Analyse this graphically and identify areas for improvement.

65.2 List your short-, medium- and long-term tasks and allocate priorities. Produce several lists, one for each of the three timescales, and prioritise each item. Use this list to plan your time management, by scheduling high-priority tasks and leaving low-priority activities to 'fill in' the spare time that you may identify. This task should be done on a regular (monthly) basis to allow for changing situations.

65.3 Plan an 'elephant' task. Spend some time planning how to carry out a large or difficult task (such as learning a language or learning to use a complex computer program) by breaking it down into achievable segments ('bites').

Team – a team is not simply a group of people with job titles, but a collaborative group of individuals, each of whom has a role in a shared task that is understood by other members. Members of a team may seek out certain roles and they may perform most effectively in the ones that are most natural to them.

Team role – a tendency to behave, contribute and interrelate with others in a particular way (Belbin, 2010).

Peer assessment – this term applies to marking schemes in which all or a proportion of the marks for a teamwork exercise are allocated by the team members themselves. Read the instructions carefully before embarking on the exercise, so you know which aspects of your work your fellow team members will be assessing. When deciding what marks to allocate yourself, try to be as fair as possible with your marking.

Gaining confidence through experience – the more you take part in teamwork, the more you know how teams operate and how to make teamwork effective for you.

It is highly likely that you will be expected to work with fellow students during practicals and in mock-ups of crime scene work. This might take the form of sharing tasks, or casual collaboration through discussion, or formally directed teamwork such as problem-based learning (Box 69.1) or preparing a poster (Chapter 63). Interacting with others in this way can be rewarding and realistically represents the professional world, where teamworking is common. The advantages of such collaborative work include:

- **synergistic interactions/teamwork** – it often results in better ideas, produced by the interchange of views;
- **support can be provided** to individuals by other members of the team;
- **enhanced levels** of personal commitment;
- **eharing of responsibilities** for complex or difficult tasks.

However, some people approach teamwork with negative feelings. Reasons for this include:

- **initial reservations about working with strangers** – not knowing whether you will be able to form a friendly and productive relationship;
- **lack of personal commitment to the specified task** – perhaps due to unfamiliarity or perceived dislike concerning the topic;
- **fear of being held back by others** – especially for those who have been successful in individual work already;
- **lack of previous experience** – worries about the kinds of personal interactions likely to occur and the team role likely to suit you best;
- **concerns about the outcomes of peer assessment** – and in particular whether others will give you a fair mark for your efforts.

In most cases, these feelings can be transformed through positive participation and a common desire to do well, so that the team as a whole achieves its target.

Teamwork skills

Some of the key skills you will need to develop to maximise the success of your teamworking activities include:

- **interpersonal skills** – these include the way in which you react to new people, how you listen to and communicate with others and how you deal with conflict and disagreemen.
- **e**ffort and responsibility, are willing to trust your fellow team members and have mechanisms to deal with unexpected outcomes or even failure to contribute.
- **Effective listening** – this involves giving others the opportunity and time to express their views and to take these seriously, however expressed.
- **Speaking clearly and concisely** – effective communication is a vital part of teamwork, not only between team members, but also when presenting team outcomes to others (Chapter 59).
- **Providing constructive criticism** – it is all too easy to be negative, but only constructive criticism will have a positive effect on interactions with others.

Collaboration for learning

Much collaboration is informal and consists of pairs or groups of individuals getting together to exchange materials and ideas while studying. It may consist of a 'brainstorming' session for a topic or piece of work, or sharing efforts to research a topic. This has much to commend it and is generally encouraged. However, it is vital that this collaborative learning is distinguished from the collaborative writing of assessed documents: the latter is not usually acceptable and, in its most extreme form, is plagiarism, usually with a heavy punishment in university assessment systems. Make sure you know what plagiarism is, what unacceptable collaboration is, and how they are treated within your institution (see p. 451).

KEY POINT *Collaboration is inappropriate during the final phase of an assessed piece of work unless you have been directed to produce a group report. Collaboration is encouraged during research and learning activities, but the final write-up must normally be your own work. The extreme of producing copycat write-ups is regarded as plagiarism (p. 451) and will be punished accordingly.*

The dynamics of teamworking

It is important that team activities are properly structured so that each member knows what is expected of them. Allocation of responsibilities usually requires the clear identification of a leader. Several studies of groups have identified different team roles that derive from differences in personality. You should be aware of such categorisations, both in terms of your own predispositions and those of your fellow team members, as it will help the group to interact more productively. Belbin (2010) identified eight such roles, recently extended to nine, as shown in Table 66.1. Several of the categories shown in this table are suitable for a leader, including a co-ordinator and shaper.

In formal team situations, your course organiser should deal with these issues; even if they do not, it is important that you are aware of these roles and their potential impact on the success or failure of teamwork. You should try to identify your own 'natural' role: if asked to form a team, bear the different roles in mind during your selection of colleagues and your interactions with them. The ideal team should contain members capable of adopting most of these roles. However, you should also note the following points:

- **People will probably fit one of these roles naturally** as a function of their personality and skills.
- **Group members** may be suited to more than one of these roles.
- **In some circumstances**, team members may be required to adapt and take a different role from the one that they feel best suits them.
- **No one role is 'better' than any other**. For good teamwork, the group should have a balance of personality types present.
- **People may have to adopt multiple roles**, especially if the team size is small.

KEY POINT *In formal teamwork situations, be clear as to how individual contributions are to be identified and recognised. This might require discussion with the course organiser. Make sure that recognition, including assessment marks, is truly reflective of effort. Failure to ensure that this is the case can lead to disputes and feelings of unfairness.*

Studying with others – teaming up with someone else on your course for revision (a 'study buddy') is a potentially valuable activity and may especially suit some types of learners (p. 591). It can help keep your morale high when things get tough. You might consider:

- *sharing notes, textbooks and other information;*
- *going through past papers together;*
- *dissecting the questions and planning answers;*
- *talking to each other about a topic (good for aural learners, p. 591);*
- *giving tutorials to each other about parts of the course that have not been fully grasped.*

Avoiding plagiarism – make sure you understand the assessment requirements of any team task, so that you avoid any possible charge of plagiarism when you submit your work for assessment. Universities often have formal mechanisms for dealing with such academic misconduct, and the best way to avoid such procedures is to be aware of the assessment criteria.

Recording group discussions – make sure you structure meetings (including writing agendas) and note their outcomes (taking minutes and noting action points).

Table 66.1 A summary of the team roles described by Belbin (2012). No one role should be considered 'better' than any other, and a good team requires members who are able to undertake appropriate roles at different times. Each role provides important strengths to a team, and its compensatory weaknesses should be accepted within the group framework

Team Role Summary Descriptions

Team Role	Contribution	Allowable Weaknesses
Plant	Creative, imaginative, free-thinking. Generates ideas and solves difficult problems.	Ignores incidentals. Too preoccupied to communicate effectively.
Resource Investigator	Outgoing, enthusiastic, communicative. Explores opportunities and develops contacts.	Over-optimistic. Loses interest once initial enthusiasm has passed.
Co-ordinator	Mature, confident, identifies talent. Clarifies goals. Delegates effectively.	Can be seen as manipulative. Offloads own share of the work.
Shaper	Challenging, dynamic, thrives on pressure. Has the drive and courage to overcome obstacles.	Prone to provocation. Offends people's feelings.
Monitor Evaluator	Sober, strategic and discerning. Sees all options and judges accurately.	Lacks drive and ability to inspire others. Can be overly critical.
Teamworker	Co-operative, perceptive and diplomatic. Listens and averts friction.	Indecisive in crunch situations. Avoids confrontation.
Implementer	Practical, reliable, efficient. Turns ideas into actions and organises work that needs to be done.	Somewhat inflexible. Slow to respond to new possibilities.
Completer Finisher	Painstaking, conscientious, anxious. Searches out errors. Polishes and perfects.	Inclined to worry unduly. Reluctant to delegate.
Specialist	Single-minded, self-starting, dedicated. Provides knowledge and skills in rare supply.	Contributes only on a narrow front. Dwells on technicalities.

Your lab partner(s)

Many laboratory sessions in the sciences (chemistry and biology) involve working in pairs or small groups. In some cases, you may work with the same partner(s) for a series of practicals or for a complete module. The relationship you develop as a team is important to your progress, and can enhance your understanding of the material and the grades you obtain. Tips for building a constructive partnership include:

- Introduce yourselves at the first session and take a continuing interest in each other's interests and progress at university.
- At appropriate points, discuss the practical (both theory and tasks) and your understanding of what is expected of you.
- Work jointly to complete practical work effectively, avoiding the situation where either partner dominates the activities and gains most from the practical experience.

Making the most of lab partnerships – make sure that you share the different practical tasks across all members of your lab group, otherwise some will miss one of the opportunities afforded by practical classes. This is particularly important in subjects involving a practical exam at the end of term.

Make sure that when you acquire shared data – you write your practical report (Chapter 61) individually, otherwise you could face a penalty associated with academic misconduct (Box 47.1 or p. 452).

- Share tasks according to your strengths, but do this in such a way that one partner can learn new skills and knowledge from the other.
- Make sure you ask questions of each other and communicate any doubts about what you have to do.
- Discuss other aspects of your course – e.g. by comparing notes from lectures or ideas about in-course assessments.
- Consider meeting up outside the practical sessions to study, revise and discuss exams.

Tutorial groups

Making the most of tutorials – *most tutorials require preparation in advance of each session; this can include pre-tutorial reading(s), literature-based research and/ or the completion of specific tutorial questions.*

Tutorials are a group learning environment. Discussions in tutorials can help you to develop your ideas by observing others' approaches, views and ideas and assimilating the facts and concepts that they introduce (see p. 590). This depends on all present participating fully and enthusiastically, while at the same time respecting the rights of others to make a contribution and express their opinions.

Text reference

Belbin, R.M. (2010) *Team Roles at Work,* 2nd edn. Butterworth Heinemann, Oxford.

Source for further study

Belbin, R.M. The Belbin® Team Roles. Available at: http://www.belbin.com. Last accessed 30/08/2017.

Study exercises

66.1 Evaluate your 'natural' team role(s). Using Table 66.1 as a source, decide which team role best fits your personality.

66.2 Keep a journal during a group activity. Record your feelings and observations about experiences of working with other students. After the event, review the journal and then draw up a strategy for developing aspects where you feel you might have done better.

66.3 Reflect upon your teamwork abilities. Draw up a list of your reactions to previous efforts at collaboration or teamwork and analyse your strengths and weaknesses. How could these interactions have been improved or supported more effectively?

Note-taking is an essential skill that you will require in many different situations, such as:

- listening to staff in lectures, seminars and practical classes;
- attending meetings and tutorials;
- reading texts and research papers;
- finding information on the Internet.

 KEY POINT *Good performance in assessments and exams is built on effective learning and revision (Chapters 68 and 69). However, both ultimately depend on the quality of your notes.*

Taking notes from lectures

Taking legible and meaningful lecture notes is essential if you are to make sense of them later, but many students find it difficult when starting their university studies. Begin by noting the date, course, topic and lecturer on the first page of each day's notes. Number every page in case they get mixed up later. The most popular way of taking notes is to write in a linear sequence down the page, emphasising the underlying structure via headings, as in Figure 58.3. However, the 'pattern' and 'Mind Map' methods (Figs. 67.1 and 67.2) have their advocates: experiment, to see which method you prefer.

Whatever technique you use, don't try to take down all the lecturer's words, except when an important definition or example is being given, or when the lecturer has made it clear that he/she is dictating. Listen first, then write. Your goal should be to take down the structure and reasoning behind the lecturer's approach in as few words and phrases as possible. At this stage, follow the lecturer's sequence of delivery. Use headings and leave plenty of space, but don't worry too much about being tidy – it is more important that you get down the appropriate information in a readable form. Use abbreviations to save time. Recognise that you may need to alter your note-taking technique to suit different lecturers' styles.

Make sure you note down references to texts and take special care to ensure the accuracy of definitions and numerical examples. If the lecturer repeats or otherwise emphasises a point, highlight (e.g. by underlining) or make a margin note of this – it could come in useful when revising. If there is something you

---

Choose note-taking methods appropriately – the method you choose to take notes might depend on the subject, the lecturer and their style of delivery, or your own preference.

Compare lecture notes with a colleague – looking at your notes for the same lecture may reveal interesting differences in approach, depth and detail.

Adjusting to the styles of your lecturers – different approaches to lecture delivery demand different approaches to note-taking. For example, if a lecturer seems to tell lots of anecdotes or spend much of the time on examples during a lecture, do not switch off – you still need to be listening carefully to recognise the key take-home messages. Similarly, if a lecture includes a section consisting mainly of images, you should still try to take notes – e.g. fingerprint identification, key features, even quick sketches of the class and individual characteristics. These will help prompt your memory when revising. Do not be deterred by lecturers' idiosyncrasies; in every case you still need to focus and take useful notes.

Rather than printing the presentation – you may find it easier to add notes to your lecture using your laptop. If you open the presentation using PowerPoint, you can add directly to the notes section of the slides.

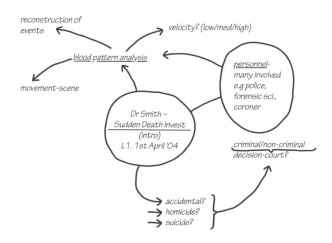

Fig. 67.1 An example of 'pattern' notes, an alternative to the more commonly used 'linear' format. Note the similarity to the 'spider diagram' method of brainstorming ideas (Fig. 58.2).

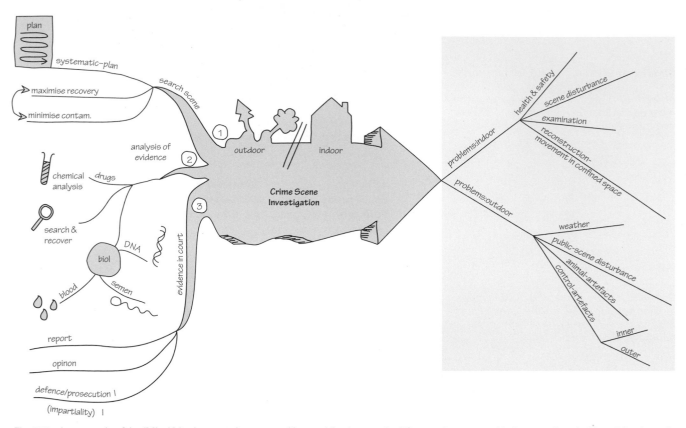

Fig. 67.2 An example of the 'Mind Map' approach to note-taking and 'brainstorming'. Start at the centre with the overall topic title, adding branches and sub-branches for themes and subsidiary topics. 'Basic' maps consist of a branched hierarchy overwritten with key words (e.g. shaded portion above). Connections should be indicated with arrows; numbering and abbreviations are encouraged. To aid recall and creativity, Buzan and Buzan (2009) recommends use of colour, different fonts, three-dimensional doodles and other forms of emphasis (e.g. non-shaded portion above).

Example Commonly used abbreviations include:

$\exists$	there are, there exist(s)
$\therefore$	therefore
$\because$	because
$\propto$	is proportional to
Σ	leads to, into
d	comes from, from
SS	involves several processes in a sequence
$1°, 2°$	primary, secondary (etc.)
$\approx, \cong$	approximately, roughly equal to
$=, \neq$	equals, not equal to
K, [	equivalent, not equivalent to
$<, >$	smaller than, bigger than
W	much bigger than
[X]	concentration of X
Σ	sum
Δ	change
f	function
#	number
q	infinity, infinite

You should also make up your own abbreviations relevant to the context, e.g. if a lecturer is talking about blood pattern analysis, you could write 'BPA' instead.

do not understand, ask at the end of the lecture, and make an appointment to discuss the matter if there is no time to deal with it then. Tutorials may provide an additional forum for discussing course topics.

Lectures delivered by PowerPoint® or similar presentation programs

Some students make the mistake of thinking that lectures delivered as computer-based presentations with an accompanying handout or Web-resource require little or no effort by way of note-taking. While it is true that you may be freed from the need to copy out large diagrams and the basic text may provide structure, you will still need to adapt and add to the lecturer's points. Much of the important detail and crucial emphasis will still be delivered verbally. Furthermore, if you simply listen passively to the lecture, or worse, try to work from the handout alone, it will be far more difficult to understand and remember the content.

If you are not supplied with handouts, you may be able to print out the presentation beforehand, perhaps in the 'three slides per page' format that allows space for notes alongside each slide (Fig. 67.3). Scan through this before the lecture if you can; then, during the presentation, focus on listening to what the lecturer has to say. Note down any extra details, points of emphasis and examples. After lectures, you could also add notes from supplementary reading. The text in

What form is cannabis seen in the Forensic Laboratory?

- Plant (male vs female)
- Herbal
- Resin
- Reefers
- Hashish oil
- Paraphernalia
- 'Blood/urine' - toxicology

Detection–Plant characteristics

- Leaves (appearance, hairs)
- Microscopy (glands, bracts)
- Characteristics smell
- Resin (colour, texture, brand marks/patterns)

A_1 A_2

B C

Detection–TLC

- Silica gel, 0.25 mm UV$_{254}$
- Toluene/diethylamine (95:5 v:v)
- Develop with fast blue BB

Fig. 67.3 An example of a printout from PowerPoint in 'Handouts (3 slides per page)' format. (Images courtesy of SPSA Forensic Services)

Printing PowerPoint slides – *use the 'Black and White' option on the Print menu to avoid wasting ink on printing of coloured backgrounds. If you wish to use colour, remember that slides can be difficult to read if printed in small format. Always print a sample page before printing the whole lecture.*

Sources of abbreviations for note taking – *general abbreviations can be found at http://public.oed.com/how-to-use-the-oed/abbreviations/*

presentations can be converted to word processor format if you have access to the electronic file. In PowerPoint®, this can be achieved from the Outline View option on the View menu. You can copy and paste text between programs in the normal fashion, then modify font size and colour as appropriate.

'Making up' your notes

As soon as possible after each lecture, work through your notes, tidying them up and adding detail where necessary. Add emphasis to any headings you have made, so that the structure is clearer. If you feel it would be more logical for your purposes, change the order. Compare your notes with material in a textbook and correct any inconsistencies. Make notes from, or photocopy, any useful material you see in textbooks, ready for revision.

Taking notes from books and journal papers

Scanning

Good reading skills are vital when taking notes from written sources. When consulting a new source for specific information, the first thing you need to do is to orientate yourself by understanding the text's scope and structure. This is often called 'scanning'.

- For books, this might involve a quick inspection of the contents section, a check on how each chapter is constructed and noting, for example, whether the book has a glossary that might be useful. Once you are familiar with the structure and layout, then you might either go to the appropriate chapter or section, or consult the index.
- For research publications, the best idea is to read the abstract before consulting specific text, figures or tables, as this should detail the essential methods and findings. The paper's layout thereafter will probably involve the same component sections (IMRAD, p. 560), but occasionally in a journal-specific order. Referencing systems may also differ (p. 438) and you may wish to note this.

Depending on your goal, there may be a specific key word or phrase for which you are searching, or you may wish to read paragraphs on a specific topic. As well as an index, most textbooks use systems of headings and subheadings that facilitate such searches. With digital or online resources you can press the ctrl and F keys together to access a 'find' dialog box that will speed up this process – however, take care to enter correctly spelled and relevant words, using alternatives if an initial search draws a blank.

KEY POINT *When taking notes, it is vital that you distinguish between your own paraphrasing or summarising of the text and situations where your notes are direct quotes, or you may be guilty of plagiarism (p. 451). If transcribing text word for word, always use quotation marks and always note the full citation details of the source at the same time.*

Skimming

This is a valuable way to gain the maximum amount of information in the minimum amount of time, by reading as much of a text as required. Essentially, the technique (also termed 'surveying') requires you to look at the organisation of the text, rather than the detail. In a sense, you are trying to see the writer's original plan and the purpose behind each part of the text. Look through the whole of the piece first, to gain an overview of its scope and structure. Headings provide an obvious clue to structure, if present. Next, look for the 'topic sentence' in each paragraph, which is often the first. You might then decide that the paragraph contains a definition that is important to note, or it may contain examples and so may not be worth reading for your purpose.

When you have found relevant material, note-taking fulfils the vital purpose of helping you understand and remember the information. If you simply read it, either directly or from a photocopy, you are at risk of accomplishing neither. The act of paraphrasing (using different words to give the same meaning) makes you think about the meaning and express this for yourself. It is an important active-learning technique. A popular method of describing skimming and note-taking is called the SQ3R technique (Box 67.1).

Scanning effectively – *you need to stay focused on your key words, otherwise you may be distracted by apparently interesting but irrelevant material. Working out how a piece of writing is structured will help you scan quickly for relevance, digest the content faster and find material of interest as soon as possible.*

Spotting sequences – *writers often number their points (firstly, secondly, thirdly, etc.), and looking for these words in the text can help you skim it quickly.*

Making sure you have all the details – *when taking notes from a text or journal paper, (a) always take full details of the source see (Chapter 45) and, if copying word-for-word, make sure you indicate this using quotation marks and take special care to ensure you do not alter the original.*

Box 67.1   The SQ3R technique for skimming texts

Survey   Gain a quick overview of the contents of the book or chapter, perhaps by rapidly reading the contents page or headings.

Question   Ask yourself what the material covers and how precisely it relates to your study objectives.

Read   Now read the text, paying attention to the ways it addresses your key questions.

Recall   Recite to yourself what has been stated every few paragraphs. Write notes of this if appropriate, paraphrasing the text rather than copying it.

Review   Think about what you have read and/or review your notes as a whole. Consider where it all fits in.

 KEY POINT   Obtaining information and then understanding it are distinct, sequential parts of the process of learning. You must be able to do more than recall facts to succeed.

Methods for finding and evaluating texts and articles are discussed further in Chapters 45–47.

Text reference

Buzan, T. and Buzan, B. (2009) *The Mind Map Book: Unlock Your Creativity, Boost Your Memory.* Pearson, Harlow.

Sources for further study

Lebauer, R.S. (2000) *Learn to Listen, Listen to Learn: Academic Listening and Notetaking.* WhitePlains, New York.

Morris, S. and Smith, J. (1998) *Understanding Mind Maps . . . in a Week.* [Foreword by Buzan, A.] Hodder and Stoughton, London.

Study exercises

67.1   Experiment with a new note-taking technique. If you haven't tried the pattern or mind-mapping methods (Figs. 67.1 and 67.2), carry out a trial to see how they work for you. Research the methods first by consulting appropriate books or websites.

67.2   Carry out a 'spring clean' of your desk area and notes. Make a concerted effort to organise your notes and handouts, investing if necessary in files and folders. This will be especially valuable at the start of a revision period.

67.3   Try out the SQ3R technique. The next time you need to obtain information from a text, compare this method (Box 67.1) with others you may have adopted in the past. Is it faster, and does it aid your ability to recall the information?

Be adaptable – *you should be prepared to adjust your study methods according to the topic, the learning environment and the approach of your lecturers, as well as your learning preferences.*

Aligning your learning with a specific approach – *it is important not to read too much into any formal 'diagnosis' of your preferred method of learning. You need to take a flexible approach, as no matter how you prefer to learn, many of the outputs assessed at university (for example, exam answers, essays and reports) are in a formal written format and you will need to apply what you have learned to these formats. Also, different aspects of your study will require different approaches, irrespective of personal preferences. For example, practical skills are best learned by 'hand-on' activities – learning by doing.*

Understanding your learning preferences – *in practice it can be helpful to reflect on your personal preferences and how you can make the most of these to enhance your learning.*

There are many different ways of learning, and at university you have the freedom to choose which approach to study suits you best. You should tackle this responsibility with an open mind, and be prepared to consider new options. Understanding how you learn best and how you are expected to think about your discipline will help you to improve your approach to study and to understand the principles of forensic science at a deeper level.

 KEY POINT *At university, you are expected to set your own agenda for learning. There will be timetabled activities, assessments and exam deadlines, but it is your responsibility to decide how you will study and learn, how you will manage your time and, ultimately, what you will gain from the experience. You should be willing to challenge yourself academically to discover your full potential.*

Thinking about thinking

The thinking processes that students are expected to carry out can be presented in a sequence, starting with less complex thought processes and ending with more complex processes, each of which builds on the previous level (see Table 68.1). The first two categories in this ladder apply to gaining basic knowledge and understanding–important when you first encounter a topic. Processes three to six are those carried out additionally by high-performing university students, with the latter two being especially relevant to final-year students, researchers and professionals. Naturally, the tutors assessing you will want to reward the deepest thinking appropriate for your level of study. This is often signified by the words used in assessment tasks and marking criteria (column three, Table 68.1) and while this is not an exact relationship, being more aware of this agenda can help you gain more from your studies and appreciate what is being demanded of you.

Identifying your personal learning preference

We do not all learn in the same way. Your preferred approach to learning is simply the one that suits you best for receiving, communicating and understanding information. It therefore involves selections that will help you learn and perform most effectively. There are many different ways of describing such learning strategies–for example, VARK and ASSIST, and you may be introduced to these specific schemes during your studies. Although methods and terminology may differ among these approaches, it is important to realise that it is the process of analysing your learning style that is critical, together with the way you use the information to modify your approach to studying, rather than the specific type of learner that you may identify yourself to be.

 KEY POINT *Having a particular learning preference or style does not mean that you are automatically skilled in using methods generally suited to that type of learner. You must work at developing your ability to take in information, study and cope with assessment.*

Table 68.1 A 'ladder of thinking' process, moving from 'shallower' thought processes (top of table) to 'deeper' levels of thinking (bottom of table). This table is derived from research by Benjamin Bloom. When considering the cue words in typical question instructions, bear in mind that the precise meaning will always depend on the context. For example, while 'describe' is often associated with relatively simple processes of recall, an instruction such as 'describe how GCMS works' demands that you exhibit higher-level understanding. Note also that while a 'cue word' is often at the start of a question/instruction, this is not universally so

Thinking processes and description (in approximate order of increasing 'depth')	Example of typical question structure with one word highlighted	Other cue words used in question construction
1. **Remembering (knowing facts)** – if you know information, you can recall or recognise it. this does not always mean you understand it at a higher level.	**Describe** the main components of a GCMS.	❏ Define ❏ List ❏ State ❏ Identify
2. **Understanding** – if you comprehend a fact, you understand what it means.	**Explain** how a fingerprint is deposited onto a surface.	❏ Distinguish ❏ Interpret ❏ Outline ❏ Illustrate
3. **Applying** – to apply a fact means that you can put it to use in a particular context.	Using the Forrest calculation, **calculate** the concentration of alcohol at the time of the incident.	❏ Demonstrate ❏ Illustrate ❏ Solve ❏ Show
4. **Analysing** – to analyse information means that you are able to break it down into parts and show how these components fit together.	Drawing on your understanding of blood pattern analysis, **defend** why the pattern observed is associated with blunt force trauma.	❏ Compare ❏ Explain ❏ Consider ❏ Discuss
5. **Evaluating** – if you evaluate information, you arrive at a judgement based on its importance relative to the topic being addressed.	**Evaluate** whether iris-recognition software can be used for biometric identification.	❏ Review ❏ Assess ❏ Consider ❏ Justify
6. **To create or synthesise** – you need to be able to extract relevant facts from a body of knowledge and use these to address an issue in a novel way or create something new.	**Devise** an experimental strategy to determine whether drugs were involved in the fatality of the now deceased.	❏ Design ❏ Integrate ❏ Test ❏ Create

Learning effectively in different settings

The approaches you use must suit the different modes of teaching you encounter.

Lectures

These are designed to impart knowledge and understanding efficiently on the part of the staff, who can teach large classes using this method. However, in some instances they can simply be note-taking exercises for you as a student. This may tempt you to approach such teaching in a 'passive' frame of mind, but this is almost certainly not the best way to learn. To get the most from lectures, you need to:

Be active in your learning – a common theme in all recommended approaches to effective learning is activity on the learner's part. Thus, note taking during lectures requires a greater level of engagement with the material than the passive action of simply listening; discussing concepts with others involves a deeper degree of thinking than solo thought processes when reading text.

- **Prepare beforehand** by finding out what the topic will be, what the learning outcomes are, and by doing some preliminary reading.
- **Arrive in good time,** sitting where you can see and hear the lecturer, with the right materials for taking notes.
- **Listen attentively,** particularly when the lecturer is stating key facts or definitions.
- **Make useful notes** – these will not be a transcript of the lecturer's words, but a personal digest of the key points that have been made (see Chapter 67).

- **Ask questions if you do not understand something.** This might not be at the point of delivery, because things may become clearer when you go over your notes, read a textbook or talk about the subject with a fellow student.
- **Above all, do attend lectures** even if they are recorded for playback during a revision period.

Practicals (lab classes)

In forensic science, practical work is essential so that your understanding is grounded in real examples of biological and chemical material, processes and equipment in both laboratory and (mock) crime scene facilities. Many practicals follow the 'scientific method' (Chapter 5) and illustrate how to design and carry out observations and experiments. They may help you to develop manipulative skills, as well as those associated with data recording, analysis and reporting. To maximise learning from practicals, you should:

- **Prepare as well as you can** by reading through the schedule in advance.
- **Make sure that you have all the equipment and PPE needed**.
- **Arrive at the lab in good time**.
- **Understand and observe safe practice** (Chapters 1–2).
- **Follow the advised procedures**.
- **Ask questions when you do not understand**.
- **Manage your time during practicals**.
- **Take relevant contemporaneous notes**.
- **Complete your write up/report** as soon as possible after the session.

e-learning (using technology to enhance your student experience)

These modes of learning allow easy access to learning material at a time of your choosing, but they also assume a personal discipline in your approach to study. Effective learning in this context requires the following:

- **making regular and frequent visits** to online modules and portals;
- **allocating time to study**;
- **paying special attention** to announcements, message pages or e-mail systems – note some platforms do not necessarily send notifications of updated content;
- **participating in online discussions**;
- **organising materials** provided in digital form;
- **reading the advised materials and more** – you may get access via a digital reading list to online texts;
- **making notes as appropriate**;
- **observing staff-set milestones** in study, assessment and submission of work – note where and how to submit your work electronically;
- **creating personal milestones** in study, self-assessment and preparation of work.

The only person who can judge the effectiveness of your learning at university is you: only you will know how much effort you put into your studies and what you are expecting, in terms of a mark or grade; only you will know how comfortable you feel with a particular approach; and only you can respond to the feedback you have been given, in terms of how you will learn for future assessments. Be prepared to change your learning methods if you find that they are unsuccessful or difficult to apply in particular circumstances.

The role of assessment and feedback in your learning

Your starting point for assessment should be the learning outcomes or objectives for each module, topic or learning activity. You will usually find them in your module handbook. They state in clear terms what your tutors expect you to be able to accomplish after participating in each part and reading around the topic. Also of value will be marking/assessment criteria or grade descriptors, which state in general terms what level of attainment is required for your work to reach specific grades. These are more likely to be defined at faculty/college/school/department level and consequently published in appropriate handbooks and websites. Reading learning outcomes and grade descriptors will give you a good idea of what to expect and the level of performance required to reach your personal goals. Relate them to both the material covered (e.g. in lectures and practicals, or online) and past exam papers. Doing this as you study and revise will indicate whether further reading and independent studying is required, and of what type. You will also have a much clearer picture of how you are likely to be assessed.

Learning objectives/outcomes – statements of the knowledge, understanding or skills that a learner will be able to demonstrate on successful completion of a module, topic or learning activity.

Preparing for revision and examinations

Before you start revising, find out as much as you can about each exam, including:

- its format and duration;
- the date and location;
- the types of questions;
- whether any questions/sections are compulsory;
- whether the questions are internally or externally set or assessed;
- whether the exam is 'open book' and, if so, which texts or notes are allowed.

Your course tutor is likely to give you details of exam structure and timing well beforehand, so that you can plan your revision; the course handbook and past papers (if available) can provide further useful details. Always check that the nature of the exam has not changed before you consult past papers.

 KEY POINT Use the learning objectives for your course (normally published in the handbook) as a fundamental part of your revision planning. These indicate what you will be expected to be able to do after taking part in the course, so exam questions are often based on them. Check this by referencing past papers.

There are essentially two types of assessment – formative and summative, although the distinction may not always be clear-cut (see p. 602). The first way you can learn from formative assessment is to consider the grade you obtained in relation to the work you put in. If this is a disappointment to you, then there must be a mismatch between your understanding of the topic and the marking scheme of the marker, or a problem in the writing or presentation of your assignment. If you do not understand the reason for your grade then contact your tutor.

The second way to learn from formative assessment is through the written feedback and notes on your work. These comments may be cryptic, or scribbled hastily, so if you don't understand or cannot read them, ask the tutor who marked the work. Most tutors will be pleased to explain how you could have improved your mark. If you find that the same comments appear frequently, it may be a good idea to seek help from your university's academic support unit. Take along examples of your work and feedback comments so they can give

Formative assessments – these may be mid-term or mid-semester tests and are often in the same format as later exams. They are intended to give you feedback on your performance. You should use the results to measure your performance against the work you put in, and to find out, either from grades or tutor's comments, how you could do better in future. If you don't understand the reason for your grade, talk to your tutor.

Summative assessments – these include end-of-year or end-of-module exams. They inform others about the standard of your work. In continuous or 'in-course' assessment, the summative elements are spread out over the course. Sometimes these assessments may involve a formative aspect, if feedback is given.

Using feedback from tutors – it is always worth reading any comments on your work as soon as it is returned. If you do not understand the comments, or are unsure about why you might have lost marks in an assignment, ask for an explanation while the topic is still fresh in your mind.

Filing lecture notes – make sure your notes are kept neatly and in sequence by using a ring binder system. File the notes in lecture or practical sequence, adding any supplementary notes or photocopies alongside, or in an appropriately organised electronic format.

Time management when revising – this is vital to success and is best achieved by creating a revision timetable (Box 68.1).

Recognise when your concentration powers are dwindling – take a short break when this happens and return to work refreshed and ready to learn. Remember that 20 minutes is often quoted as a typical limit to full concentration effort.

Aiding recall through effective note-taking – the Mind® Map technique (p. 594), when used to organise ideas, is claimed to enhance recall by connecting the material to visual images or linking it to the physical senses.

you the best possible advice. Another suggestion is to ask to see the work of another student who obtained a good mark, and compare it with your own. This will help you judge the standard you should be aiming for.

Organising and using lecture notes, assignments and practical reports

Given their importance as a source of material for revision, you should have sorted out any deficiencies or omissions in your lecture notes and practical reports at an early stage. For example, you may have missed a lecture or practical due to illness, etc., but the exam is likely to assume attendance throughout the year. Make sure you attend classes and keep your notes up to date. Ask fellow students for copies of any notes for any sessions missed. Your practical reports and any assignment work will contain specific comments from the teaching staff, indicating where marks were lost, corrections, mistakes, inadequacies, etc. It is always worth reading these comments as soon as your work is returned, to improve the standard of your subsequent reports. If you are unsure about why you lost marks in an assignment, or about some particular aspects of a topic, ask the appropriate member of staff for further explanation. Most lecturers are quite happy to discuss such details with students on a one-to-one basis and this information may provide you with 'clues' to the expectations of individual lecturers that may be useful in exams set by the same members of staff. However, you should never 'fish' for specific information on possible exam questions, as this will not be well received.

Preparing for revision

Begin early, to avoid last-minute panic. Start in earnest several weeks beforehand, and plan your work carefully:

- **Prepare a revision timetable** – an 'action plan' that gives details of specific topics to be covered (Box 68.1). Find out at an early stage when (and where) your examinations are to be held, and plan your revision around this. Try to keep to your timetable. Time management during this period is as important as keeping to time during the exam itself.
- **Study the learning objectives/outcomes for each topic** (usually published in the course handbook) to get an idea of what lecturers expect from you.
- **Use past papers as a guide to the form of exam** and the type of question likely to be asked (Box 68.2).
- **Remember to have several short (five-minute) breaks** during each hour of revision and a longer break every few hours. In any day, try to work for a maximum of three-quarters of the time.
- **Include recreation within your schedule** – there is little point in tiring yourself with too much revision, as this is unlikely to be profitable.
- **Make your revision as active and interesting as possible** (see below) – the least productive approach is simply to read and re-read your notes.
- **Ease back on the revision near the exam** – plan your revision to avoid last-minute cramming and overload fatigue.

Active revision

The following techniques may prove useful in devising an active revision strategy:

- **'Distil' your lecture notes** to show the main headings and examples. Prepare revision sheets with details for a particular topic on a single sheet of paper, arranged as a numbered checklist. Wall posters are another useful revision aid.
- **Confirm that you know about the material by testing yourself** – take a blank sheet of paper and write down all you know. Check your full notes to see if you missed anything out. If you did, go back immediately to a fresh blank sheet and redo the example. Repeat, as required.
- **Memorise definitions and key phrases**–definitions can be a useful starting point for many exam answers. Make up lists of relevant facts or definitions associated with particular topics. Test yourself repeatedly on these, or get a friend to do this. Try to remember *how many* facts or definitions you need to know in each case – this will help you recall them all during the exam.
- **Use mnemonics and acronyms** to commit specific factual information to memory. Sometimes, the dafter they are, the better they seem to work.
- **Use pattern diagrams or mind maps** as a means of testing your powers of recall on a particular topic (pp. 593–594).
- **Draw diagrams from memory**: make sure you can label them fully.
- **Try recitation as an alternative to written recall** –talk about your topic to another person, preferably someone in your class. Talk to yourself if necessary. Explaining something out loud is an excellent test of your understanding.
- **Associate facts with images or journeys** if you find this method works.
- **Use a wide variety of approaches** to avoid boredom during revision (e.g. record information on audio tape, use cartoons, or any other method as long as it is not just reading).
- **Form a revision group** to share ideas and discuss topics.
- **Prepare answers to past papers** – e.g. write essays or, if time is limited, write essay plans (see Box 68.2).
- **If your subject involves numerical calculations,** work through representative problems.
- **Make up your own questions** – the act of putting yourself in the examiner's mind-set by inventing questions can aid revision. However, you should not rely on 'question spotting': this is a risky practice!

Revision checks – *it is important to test yourself frequently during revision, to ensure that you have retained the information you are revising.*

Question spotting – *avoid this risky strategy. Lecturers are aware that this approach may be taken and try to ask questions in an unpredictable manner. You may find that you are unable to answer on unexpected topics that you failed to revise. Moreover, if you have a preconceived idea about what will be asked, you may also fail to grasp the nuances of the exact question set, and thereby fail to provide a focused answer.*

Final preparations – *try to get a good night's sleep before an exam. Last-minute cramming will be counter-productive if you are too tired during the exam.*

Box 68.1 How to prepare and use a revision timetable

1. **Make up a grid showing the number of days until your exams are finished.** Divide each day into several sections. If you like revising in large blocks of time, use am, pm and evening slots, but if you prefer shorter periods, divide each of these in two, or use hourly divisions (see also Fig. 65.2).

2. **Write in your non-revision commitments,** including any time off you plan to allocate and physical activity at frequent intervals. Try to have about one-third or a quarter of the time off in any one day. Plan this in relation to your best times for useful work – for example, some people work best in the mornings, while others prefer evenings. If you wish, use a system where your relaxation time is a bonus to be worked for – this may help you motivate yourself.

3. **Decide on how you wish to subdivide your subjects** for revision purposes. This might be among subjects, according to difficulty (with the hardest getting the most time), or within subjects, according to

Box 68.1 (Continued)

topics. Make sure there is an adequate balance of time among topics, and especially that you do not avoid working on the subject(s) you find least interesting or most difficult.

4. **Allocate the work to the different slots available on your timetable.** You should work backwards from the exams, making sure that you cover every exam topic adequately in the period just before

each exam. You may wish to colour-code the subjects.

5. **As you revise, mark off the slots completed** – this has a positive psychological effect and will boost your self-confidence.

6. **After the exams, revisit your timetable** and decide whether you would do anything differently next time.

Box 68.2 How to use past exam papers

Past exam papers are a valuable resource for targeting your revision.

1. **Find out where the past exam papers are kept.** Copies may be lodged in your department or the library; or they may be accessible online.

2. **Locate and copy relevant papers for your module(s).** Check with your tutor or course handbook that the style of paper will not change for the next set of examinations.

3. **Analyse the design of the exam paper.** Taking into account the length in weeks of your module, and the different lecturers and/or topics for those weeks, note any patterns that emerge. For example, can you translate weeks of lectures/practicals into numbers of questions or sections of the paper? Consider how this might affect your revision plans and exam tactics, taking into account (a) any choices or restrictions offered in the paper, and (b) the different types of question asked (i.e. multiple-choice, short-answer or essay).

4. **Examine carefully the style of questions.** Can you identify the expectations of your lecturers? Can you relate the questions to the learning objectives? How much extra reading do they seem to expect? Are the questions fact-based? Do they require a synthesis

based on other knowledge? Can you identify different styles for different lecturers? Consider how the answers to these questions might affect your revision effort and exam strategy.

5. **Practise answering questions.** Perhaps with friends, set up your own mock exam when you have done a fair amount of revision, but not too close to the exams. Use a relevant past exam paper; don't study it beforehand! You need not attempt all of the paper at one sitting. You'll need a quiet room in a place where you will not be interrupted (e.g. a library). Keep close track of time during the mock exam and try to do each question in the length of time you would normally assign to it (see p. 607) – this gives you a feel for the speed of thought and writing required and the scope of answer possible. Mark each other's papers and discuss how each of you interpreted the questions and laid out your answers, and your individual marking schemes.

6. **Practise writing answer plans and starting answers.** This can save time compared with the 'mock exam' approach. Practice in starting answers can help you get over stalling at the start and wasting valuable time. Writing answer plans gets you used to organising your thoughts quickly and putting your thoughts into a logical sequence.

 KEY POINT *When considering assessment questions, look carefully at words used in the instructions. These cues can help you identify what depth is expected in your answer (see Table 68.1). Take special care in multi-part questions, because the first part may require low-level thinking, while in later parts marks may be awarded for evidence of deeper thinking.*

The evening before your exam should be spent consolidating your material, and checking through summary lists and plans. Avoid introducing new material at this late stage – your aim should be to boost your confidence, putting yourself in the right frame of mind for the exam itself.

Sources for further study

Anderson, L.W., Krathwohl, D.R. and Bloom, B.S. (2001) *A Taxonomy for Learning, Teaching and Assessing: A Revision of Bloom's Taxonomy of Education Objectives.* Allyn and Bacon, London.

Burns, R. (1997) *The Student's Guide to Passing Exams.* Kogan Page, London.

Hamilton, D. (2003) *Passing Exams: A Guide for Maximum Success and Minimum Stress.* Cengage Learning, Boston.

McMillan, K. and Weyers, J.D.B. (2012) *The Study Skills Book,* 3rd edn. Pearson Education, Harlow.

O'Brien, D. (2007) *How to Pass Exams: Accelerate Your Learning – Memorise Key Facts – Revise Effectively,* 2nd edn. Baird, Winchester.

Many universities host study skills websites – these can be found using 'study skills', 'revision' or 'exams' as key words in a search engine.

Study exercises

68.1 Draw up a revision timetable. Use the techniques discussed in Box 68.1 to create a revision timetable for your forthcoming exams.

68.2 Make use of past exam papers. Use the techniques discussed in Box 68.2 to improve your revision strategy: assess their effectiveness in a particular exam, or series of exams.

68.3 Try out new active-revision techniques. Try any or all of the methods mentioned on pp. 603–604 when revising. Compare notes with a colleague – which seems to be the most successful technique for you and for the topic you are revising?

68.4 Review your note-taking methods. How well suited are they to your needs? How well suited are they to the lecture styles of the academic staff? Have you captured the important points, or are you merely transcribing exactly what the lecturer says? Where lecturers use PowerPoint slides, are you listening for, and capturing in note form, the additional spoken points and examples that the lecturer is adding during the live presentation?

Aiming high – *your goal should be to perform at your highest possible level and not simply to fulfil the minimum criteria for progression. This will lay sound foundations for your later studies. Remember, too, that a future employer might ask to see your academic transcript, which will detail all your module grades including any fails/resits, and will not just state your final degree classification.*

Definition

Transcript – this is your record of achievement at university. Normally it will consist of details of each module or course you have taken, and an indication of the grade or mark achieved. In the UK, your transcript will also show your final (honours) classification – that is, first class, upper second class (2.1), lower second class (2.2), third class or unclassified. (Note: some UK universities do not differentiate second class degrees.)

You are unlikely to have reached this stage in your education without being exposed to the examination process. You may not enjoy being assessed, but you probably want to do well in your course. It is therefore important to understand why and how you are being tested. Identifying and improving on the skills required for exam success will allow you to perform to the best of your ability.

Assessed coursework

There is a component of assessed coursework in most modules. This often tests specific skills, and may require you to demonstrate thinking at deeper levels. The common types of coursework assessment likely to be encountered in forensic science are covered at various points in this book:

- practical exercises (throughout);
- essays (Chapters 58 and 62);
- numerical problems (Chapter 54);
- data analysis (Chapters 50–57);
- poster and spoken presentations (Chapters 59 and 63);
- crime scene investigation (Chapters 23–29);
- literature surveys and reviews (Chapter 62);
- project work (Chapter 61);
- problem-based learning (Box 69.1).

At the start of each year or module, read the course handbook or module guide carefully to find out when any assessed work needs to be submitted. Note relevant dates in your diary, and use this information to plan your work. Take special note if deadlines for different modules clash, or if they coincide with social or sporting commitments.

 KEY POINT *If, for some valid reason (e.g. illness), you will be late with an assessment, speak to your tutors as soon as possible. They may be able to take extenuating circumstances into account by not applying a marking penalty. They will let you know what paperwork you may have to submit to support your claim.*

Summative exams – general points

Summative exams (p. 602) normally involve you answering questions without being able to consult other students or your notes. Invigilators are present to ensure appropriate conduct, but departmental or school representatives may be present for some of the exam. Their role is to sort out any subject-related problems, so if you think something is wrong, ask at the earliest opportunity. It is not unknown for parts of questions to be omitted in error, or for double meanings to arise, for example.

Planning

When preparing for an exam, make a checklist of the items you will need (e.g. pens, pencils, sharpener and eraser, calculator, paper tissues, watch, ID card or enrolment number). On the day of the exam, give yourself sufficient time to arrive at the correct room, without the risk of being late. Double-check

Box 69.1 Problem-based learning (PBL)

In this teaching method, you are presented with a 'real-world' problem or issue, often working within a team. As you tackle the problem, you are expected to gain factual knowledge, develop skills and exercise critical thinking (Chapter 47). Because there is a direct and relevant context for your work, and because you have to employ active-learning techniques, the knowledge and skills you gain are likely to be more readily assimilated and remembered. This approach also more closely mimics workplace practices. PBL usually proceeds as follows:

1. **You are presented with a problem** (e.g. a case study, a hypothetical crime scene, a topical issue).

2. **You consider what issues and topics you need to research,** by discussion with others if necessary. You may need to identify where relevant resources can be found (Chapters 45–47).

3. **You then need to rank the issues and topics in order of importance,** allocating tasks to group members, if appropriate.

4. **Having carried out the necessary research, you should review the information that has been obtained.** As a result, new issues may need to be explored and, where appropriate, allocated to group members.

5. **You will be asked to produce an outcome, such as a report, diagnosis, seminar presentation or poster.** An outline structure will be required and, for groups, further allocation of tasks to accomplish this outcome.

If asked to carry out PBL as part of your course, it is important to get off to a good start. At first, the problem may seem unfamiliar. However, once you become involved in the work, you will quickly gain confidence. If working as part of a group, make sure that your group meets as early as possible, that you attend all the sessions and that you do the necessary background reading. When working in a team, a degree of self-awareness is necessary regarding your 'natural' role in group situations (Table 66.1). Various methods are used for assessing PBL, and the assessment may involve peer marking.

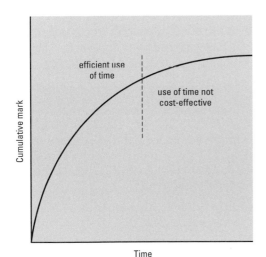

Fig. 69.1 Exam marks as a function of time. The marks awarded in a single answer will follow the law of diminishing returns – it will be far more difficult to achieve the final 25% of the available marks than the initial 25%. Do not spend too long on any one question.

Using the question paper – unless this is specifically forbidden, you should write on the question paper to plan your strategy, keep to time and organise your answers.

the times and places of your exams, both well before the exam and also on arrival. If you arrive at the exam venue early, you can always rectify a mistake if you find you have gone to the wrong place.

Tackling the paper

Begin by reading the instructions at the top of the exam paper carefully, so that you do not make any errors based on lack of understanding of the exam structure. Make sure that you confirm:

- how many questions are set;
- how many must be answered;
- whether the paper is divided into sections;
- whether any parts are compulsory;
- what each question/section is worth, as a proportion of the total mark;
- whether different questions should be answered in different books.

Do not be tempted to spend too long on any one question or section (see Box 69.2 for advice) – the return in terms of marks will not justify the loss of time from other questions (see Fig. 69.1). Take the first few minutes or so to read the paper and plan your strategy, before you begin writing. Do not be put off by those who begin immediately – it is almost certain they are producing unplanned work of a poor standard.

Underline the key phrases in the instructions, to reinforce their message. Next, read through the set of questions. If there is a choice, decide on those questions to be answered and the order in which you will tackle them. Quickly prepare a timetable that takes into account the amount of time required to complete each section and that reflects the allocation of marks – there is little point in spending one-quarter of the exam period on a question worth only 5% of the total marks. Use the exam paper to mark the sequence in which the questions will be answered and write the finishing times alongside; refer to this timetable during the exam to keep yourself on course.

Checking exam answers – look for:

- errors of fact;
- missing information;
- grammatical and spelling errors;
- errors of scale and units;
- errors in calculations.

Reviewing your answers

At the end of the exam, you should allow some time to check through your script. Make sure your name and/or ID number is on each exam book as required and on all other sheets of paper, including graph paper, even if securely attached to your script, as it is in your interest to ensure that your work does not go astray.

 KEY POINT *Never leave any exam early. Most exams assess work carried out over several months in a time period of 2–3 hours and there is always something constructive you can do with the remaining time to improve your script.*

Special considerations for different types of exam question

Essay questions

Essay questions let examiners test the depth of your comprehension and understanding as well as your recall of facts. Essay questions give you plenty of scope to show what you know. They suit those with a good grasp of principles, but who perhaps have less ability to recall details.

Before you tackle a particular question, you must be sure of what is required in your answer. Ask yourself 'What is the examiner looking for in this particular question?' and then set about providing a *relevant* answer. Consider each individual word in the question and highlight, underline or circle the key words. Make sure you know the meaning of the terms given in Table 62.1 (p. 569) so that you can provide the appropriate information, where necessary. Spend some time developing a structure for your writing (see Chapter 58). Refer back to the question frequently as you write, to confirm that you are keeping to the subject matter. Box 69.2 gives advice on writing essays under exam conditions.

Adopting different tactics according to the exam – you should adjust your exam strategy (and revision methods) to allow for the differences in question types used in each exam paper.

Box 69.2 Writing under exam conditions

Always go into an exam with a strategy for managing the available time.

- **Allocate some time (say 5% of the total) to consider which questions to answer and in which order.**

- **Share the rest of the time among the questions, according to the marks available.** Aim to optimise the marks obtained. A potentially good answer should be allocated slightly more time than one you don't feel so happy about. However, don't just concentrate on any one answer (see Fig. 69.1).

- **For each question, divide the time into planning, writing and revision phases** (see p. 606).

Employ time-saving techniques as much as possible.

- **Use spider diagrams** (Fig. 58.2) **or mind maps** (Fig. 67.2) to organise and plan your answers.

- **Use diagrams and tables** to save time in making difficult and lengthy explanations, but make sure you refer to each one in the text.

- **Use standard abbreviations** to save time repeating text, but always explain them at the first point of use, e.g. polymerisation chain reaction (PCR), high-performance liquid chromatography (HPLC).

- **Consider speed of writing and neatness,** especially when selecting the type of pen to use – ballpoint pens are fastest, but they tend to smudge. You can only gain marks if the examiner can read your script.

- **Keep your answer simple and to the point,** with clear explanations of your reasoning.

Make sure your answers are relevant.

- **Don't include irrelevant facts** just because you memorised them during revision, as this may do you more harm than good. You must answer the specific question that has been set.

- **Remember that time taken to write irrelevant material is time lost from another question.**

Penalties for guessing – if there is a penalty for incorrect answers in a multiple-choice test, the best strategy is *not to* answer questions when you know your answer is a complete guess. Depending on the penalty, it may be beneficial to guess if you can narrow the choice down to two options (but beware of false or irrelevant alternatives). However, if there are no such penalties, then you should *provide an answer to all questions.*

It is usually a good idea to begin with the question that you are most confident about. This will reassure you before tackling more difficult parts of the paper. If you run out of time, write in note form. Examiners are usually understanding, as long as the main components of the question have been addressed and the intended structure of the answer is clear. Common reasons for poor exam answers in essay-style questions are listed in Box 69.3. Try to avoid making these mistakes.

Multiple-choice and short-answer questions

Multiple-choice questions (MCQs) and short-answer questions (SAQs) are generally used to test the breadth and detail of your knowledge. The various styles that can be encompassed within the SAQ format allow for more demanding questions than MCQs, which may emphasise specific factual knowledge.

A good approach for MCQ papers if the exam is paper based is as follows:

1. **First trawl** –read through of all of the questions fairly rapidly, noting the 'correct' answer in those you can attempt immediately, perhaps in pencil.
2. **Second trawl** – go through the paper again, checking your original answers and this time answering any other straightforward questions.

Box 69.3   Reasons for poor exam answers to essay-style questions

The following are reasons that lecturers cite when they give low marks for essay answers:

- **Not answering the exact question set.** Either failing to recognise the specialist terms used in the question, or failing to demonstrate an understanding of the terms by not providing definitions, or failing to carry out the precise instruction in a question, or failing to address all aspects of the question.

- **Running out of time.** Failing to match the time allocated to the extent of the answer. Frequently, this results in spending too long on one question and not enough on the others, or even failing to complete the paper.

- **Failing to answer all parts** of a multiple-part question, or to recognise that one part (perhaps involving more complex ideas) may carry more marks than another.

- **Failing to provide evidence** to support an answer. Forgetting to state the 'obvious' – either basic facts or definitions.

- **Failing to illustrate an answer appropriately.** Either by not including a relevant diagram, or by providing a diagram that does not aid communication, or by not including examples.

- **Incomplete answer(s).** Failing to answer appropriately due to lack of knowledge.

- **Providing irrelevant evidence** to support an answer. 'Waffling' to fill space.

- **Illegible handwriting.**

- **Poor English,** such that facts and ideas are not expressed clearly.

- **Lack of logic** or structure to the answer.

- **Factual errors.** Indicating poor note taking, or poor revision, or poor recall.

- **Failing to correct obvious mistakes** by re-reading an answer before submitting the script.

At higher levels, the following aspects are especially important:

- **Not providing enough in-depth information.**

- **Providing a descriptive rather than an evaluative answer.** Focusing on facts, rather than deeper aspects of a topic (see Table 68.1).

- **Not setting a problem in context,** or not demonstrating a wider understanding of the topic. (However, make sure you don't overdo this, or you may risk not answering the question set.)

- **Not giving enough evidence of reading around the subject.** This can be demonstrated, for example, by quoting relevant papers and reviews and by giving author names and dates of publication.

- **Not considering both sides of a topic/debate, or not arriving at a conclusion if you have done so.**

Online MCQ exam – *the approach here is likely to be different as you are will have to submit your answer before moving on to the next question. In this instance, you should take your time in answering the questions but keeping a close eye on your overall time. The online exam may have been set up to allow backtracking, to allow you to change an answer to a question that has already been submitted – in which case you will be able to review all of your answers before finishing the exam.*

Answer the question as requested – *this is true for all questions, but especially important for SAQs. If the question asks for a diagram, make sure you provide one; if it asks for n aspects of a topic, try to list this number of points; if there are two or more parts, provide appropriate answers to all aspects. This may seem obvious, but many marks are lost for not following instructions.*

Applying your knowledge/skills to a practical exam in forensic science:

- **Read through the case assessment/ information supplied to you;**
- **Determine an examination strategy** – *what are you trying to ascertain? How can you do this? What do you need to examine?*
- **Undertake your examination/processing** – *consider continuity; contamination issues; order and priority of examination as well as health and safety and risk assessments;*
- **Interpretation of your results** – *what do your experimental results mean in relation to the information you have been given?*
- **Scientific conclusion** – *concluding remarks that are robust and unbiased.*

3. **Third trawl** – now tackle the difficult questions and those that require longer to answer (e.g. those based on numerical problems).
4. **Final review** – look again at all of your answers and check for obvious mistakes.

One reason for adopting this four-phase approach is that you may be prompted to recall facts relevant to questions looked at earlier. You can also spend more time per question on the difficult ones.

When unsure of an answer, the first stage is to rule out options that are clearly absurd or have obviously been placed there to distract you. Next, looking at the remaining options – can you judge between contrasting pairs with alternative answers? Logically, both cannot be correct, so you should see if you can rule one of the pair out. Watch out, however, in case *both* are irrelevant to the answer. If the question involves a calculation, try to work this out independently from the answers, so you are not influenced by them.

In SAQ papers, there may be a choice of questions. Choose your options carefully – it may be better to gain half marks for a correct answer to half a question, than to provide a largely irrelevant answer that apparently covers the whole question but lacks the necessary detail. For this form of question few, if any, marks are given for writing style. Think in 'bullet point' mode and list the crucial points only. The time for answering SAQ questions may be tight, so get down to work fast, starting with answers that demand remembered facts. Stick to your timetable by moving on to the next question as soon as possible. Strategically, it is probably better to get part-marks for the full number of questions than good marks for only a few.

Practical and information-processing exams

The prospect of a practical or information-processing exam in forensic science may cause you more concern than a theory exam. This may be due to a limited experience of practical examinations, or to the fact that practical and observational skills are tested, as well as recall, description and analysis of factual information. Your first thoughts may be that it is not possible to prepare for such exams but, in fact, you can improve your performance by mastering the various practical techniques described in this book.

You may be allowed to take your laboratory reports and other texts into the practical exam. Don't assume that this is a soft option, or that revision is unnecessary – you will not have time to read large sections of your reports or to familiarise yourself with basic principles, etc. The main advantage of 'open book' exams is that you can check specific details of methodology, reducing your reliance on memory, provided you know your way around your practical manual. In all other respects, your revision and preparation for such exams should be similar to theory exams. Make sure you are familiar with all of the practical exercises, including any work carried out in class by your partner (since exams are assessed on individual performance). If necessary, check with the teaching staff to see whether you can be given access to the laboratory to complete any exercises that you have missed.

At the outset of the practical exam, determine or decide on the order in which you will tackle the questions. A question in the latter half of the paper may need to be started early on in the exam period (e.g. an ELISA assay requiring 2-h processing time in a 3-h exam). Such questions are included to test your forward-planning and time-management skills. You may need to make additional decisions on the allocation of material – for example, if you are given 30 sterile test tubes, there is little value in designing an experiment that uses 25 of these to answer question 1, only to find that you need at least 15 tubes for subsequent questions.

Make sure you explain your choice of apparatus and experimental design. Calculations should be set out in a stepwise manner, so that credit can be given even if the final answer is incorrect. If there are any questions that rely on recall of factual information and you are unable to remember specific details (for example you cannot identify a particular specimen or slide), make sure that you describe the item fully, so that you gain credit for observational skills. Alternatively, leave a gap and return to the question at a later stage.

Oral exams and interviews

It is likely in your forensic science degree that you will face the challenge of expert witness testimony in a court environment (Chapter 60). The advice given below is applicable to this specific form of assessment. An oral interview is sometimes a part of final degree exams, representing a chance for the external examiner(s) to get to know the students personally and to test their abilities directly and interactively. In some departments, orals are used to validate the exam standard, or to test students on the borderline between exam grades. Sometimes an interview may form part of an assessment, as with project work or posters. This type of exam is often intimidating – many students say they don't know how to revise for an oral – and many candidates worry that they will be so nervous they won't be able to do themselves justice.

Preparation is just as important for orals as it is for written exams:

- **Think about your earlier performances** – if the oral follows written papers, it may be that you will be asked about questions you did not do so well on. These topics should be revised thoroughly. Be prepared to say how you would approach the questions if given a second chance.
- **Read up a little about the examiner** – he or she may focus their questions on their area of expertise.
- **Get used to giving spoken answers** – it is often difficult to transfer between written and spoken modes. Write down a few questions and get a friend to ask you them, possibly with unscripted follow-up queries.
- **Research and think about topical issues in your subject area** – some examiners will feel this reflects how interested you are in your subject.

Your conduct during the oral exam is important, too:

- **Arrive promptly and wear reasonably smart clothing** – not to do either might be considered disrespectful by the examiner.
- **Take your time before answering questions.** Even if you think you know the answer immediately, take a while to check mentally whether you have considered all angles. A considered, logical approach will be more impressive than a quick, but ill-considered, response.
- **Start answers with the basics, then develop into deeper aspects** – there may be both surface and deeper aspects to a topic and more credit will be given to students who put the latter into context.
- **When your answer is finished, stop speaking** – a short, crisp answer is better than a rambling one.
- **If you don't know the answer, say so** – to waffle and talk about irrelevant material is more damaging than admitting that you don't know.
- **Make sure your answer is balanced** – talk about the evidence and opinions on both sides of a contentious issue.
- **Don't disagree strongly with the examiner** – politely put your point of view, detailing the evidence behind it. Examiners will be impressed by

---

Examples These are principal types of question you are likely to encounter in a practical or information-processing exam:

Manipulative exercises Often based on work carried out during your practical course. Tests dexterity, specific techniques (e.g. dissection, sterile technique).

'Spot' tests Short questions requiring an identification, or brief descriptive notes on a specific item (e.g. a prepared slide). Tests the knowledge of seen material or the ability to transfer this to a new example.

Calculations May include the preparation of aqueous solutions at particular concentrations (Chapter 12) and statistical exercises (Chapters 55–57). Tests numeracy.

Data analyses May include the preparation and interpretation of graphs (Chapter 52) and numerical information, from data either obtained during the exam or provided by the examiner. Tests problem-solving skills.

Drawing observations Accurate representation and labelling will be important. Tests drawing and interpretation abilities (Chapter 3).

Preparing specimens for examination with a microscope Tests staining technique and light microscopy technique (Chapters 10–11).

Interpreting images Sometimes used when it is not possible to provide living specimens, e.g. in relation to crime scenes, or work microscopy. Can test a variety of skills.

Allow yourself to relax in oral exams – external examiners are experienced at putting students at ease. They will start by asking 'simple-to-answer' questions, such as what modules you did, how your project research went, and what your career aspirations are. Imagine the examiner is a friend rather than a foe.

Terminology – the oral exams are sometimes known simply as 'orals' or, borrowing Latin, as 'viva voce' (by or with the living voice) exams or 'vivas'.

students who know their own mind and subject area. However, they will expect you to support a position at odds with the conventional viewpoint.

- **Finally, be positive and enthusiastic about your topic.**

Counteracting anxiety before and during exams

Adverse effects of anxiety need to be overcome by anticipation and preparation well in advance (Box 69.4). Exams, with their tight time limits, are especially stressful for perfectionists. To counteract this tendency, focus on the fvollowing points during the exam:

- **Don't expect to produce a perfect essay** – this won't be possible in the time available.
- **Don't spend too long planning your answer** – once you have an outline plan, get started.
- **Don't spend too much time on the initial parts of an answer,** at the expense of the main message.
- **Concentrate on getting all of the basic points across** – markers are looking for the main points first, before awarding extra marks for the detail.
- **Don't be obsessed with neatness,** either in handwriting or in the diagrams you draw, but make sure your answers are legible.
- **Don't worry if you forget something.** You can't be expected to know everything. Most marking schemes give a first-class grade to work that misses out on up to 30% of the marks available.

 KEY POINT *Everyone worries about exams. Anxiety is a perfectly natural feeling. It works to your advantage, as it helps provide motivation and the adrenaline that can help you 'raise your game' on the day.*

Lack of preparation – the remedy, of course, is to adopt an effective approach to your revision (Chapter 68).

After the exam – try to avoid becoming involved in prolonged analyses with other students over the 'ideal' answers to the questions; after all, it is too late to change anything at this stage. Go for a walk, watch TV for a while, or do something else that helps you relax, so that you are ready to face the next exam with confidence.

Box 69.4 Strategies for combatting the symptoms of exam anxiety

Sleeplessness. This is commonplace and does little harm in the short term. Get up, have a snack, do some light reading or other work, then return to bed. Avoid caffeine (e.g. tea, coffee and cola) for several hours before going to bed.

Lack of appetite. Again commonplace. Eat what you can, but take sugary sweets into the exam to keep energy levels up in case you become tired.

Fear of the unknown. It might be a good idea to visit the exam room, so you can become familiar with the location. Confirm dates and times of exams. Go through your pre-exam checklist (p. 606). Check any paperwork you have been given regarding the format and timing of the exam. Take a mascot or lucky charm with you if this helps.

Worries about timekeeping. Get a reliable alarm clock, or a new battery for an old one. Arrange for an alarm phone call. Ask a friend or relative to make sure you are awake on time. Make reliable travel arrangements to arrive on time. If your exam is early in the morning, it

may be a good idea to get up early for a few days beforehand.

Blind panic during an exam. Explain how you feel to an invigilator. Ask to go for a supervised walk outside. Do some relaxation exercises (see below), then return to your work. If you are having problems with a specific question, it may be appropriate to speak to the departmental or school representative at the exam.

Feeling tense. Shut your eyes, take several deep breaths, do some stretching and relaxing muscle movements. During exams, it may be a good idea to do this between questions, and possibly to have a complete rest for a minute or so. Prior to exams, try some exercise activity or escape temporarily from your worries by watching TV or a movie.

Running out of time. Don't panic when the invigilator says 'five minutes left'. It is amazing how much you can write in this time. Write note-style answers or state the areas you would have covered; you may get some credit.

There is a lot to be said for treating exams as a game. After all, they are artificial situations contrived to ensure that large numbers of candidates can be assessed together, with little risk of cheating. They have conventions and rules, just like games. If you understand the rationale behind them and follow the rules, this will aid your performance.

Sources for further study

Acres, D. (1998) *Passing Exams Without Anxiety: How to Get Organised, Be Prepared and Feel Confident of Success.* How To Books, London.

McMillan, K.M. and Weyers, J.D.B. (2011) *How to Succeed in Exams and Assessments,* 2nd edn. Prentice Hall, London.

O'Brien, D. (2007) *How to Pass Exams: Accelerate Your Learning – Memorise Key Facts – Revise Effectively,* 2nd edn. Baird, Winchester.

Many universities host study skills websites that cover exam techniques; these can be found using 'study skills', 'revision' or 'exams' as key words in a search engine.

Study exercises

69.1 Analyse your past performances. Think back to past exams and any feedback you received from them. How might you improve your performance? Consider ways in which you might approach the forthcoming exam differently. If you have kept past papers and answers to continuous assessment exercises, look at any specific comments your lecturers may have made.

69.2 Share revision notes with other students. Make a revision plan (see Chapter 68) and then allocate some time to discussing your revision notes with a colleague. Try to learn from his or her approach. Discuss any issues you do not agree upon.

69.3 Plan your exam tactics. Find out from your module handbook or past papers what the format of each paper will be. Confirm this if necessary with staff. Decide how you will tackle each paper, allocating time to each section and to each question within the sections (see p. 607). Write a personal checklist of requirements for the exam (see p. 606).

<table>
<tr><td>

Definition

</td></tr>
</table>

Curriculum vitae (or CV for short) – a Latin phrase that means 'the course your life has taken'.

Personal development planning (PDP) and your CV – many PDP schemes (p. 583) also include an element of career planning that may involve creating a draft or generic CV. The PDP process can help you improve the structure and content of your CV, and the language you use within it.

Understanding skills and qualities – it may be helpful to think about how the skills and qualities in Tables 64.1 and 70.1 apply to particular activities during your studies, since this will give them a greater relevance.

Focusing on evidence – it is important to be able to provide concrete information that will back up the claims you make under the 'skills and personal qualities' and other sections of your CV. A potential employer will be interested in your level of competence (what can you actually do?) and in situations where you have used a skill or demonstrated a particular quality. These aspects can also be mentioned in your covering letter or at interview.

Many students only think about their curriculum vitae (CV) immediately before applying for a job. However, this should not be the case. Thinking about and drafting your CV at an early stage of your degree course is important. You can always add more (and revise it) as your degree progresses. There are four main reasons why this can be valuable:

1. Considering your CV and how it will look to a future employer will help you think more deeply about the direction and value of your academic studies.
2. Creating a draft CV will prompt you to assess your skills and personal qualities and how these fit into your career aspirations.
3. Your CV can be used as a record of all the relevant things you have done at university and then, later, will help you communicate these to a potential employer.
4. Your developing CV can be used when you apply for vacation or part-time employment.

 KEY POINT *Developing your skills and qualities needs to be treated as a long-term project. It makes sense to think early about your career aspirations so that you can make the most of opportunities to build up relevant experience. A good focus for such thoughts is your developing curriculum vitae, so it is useful to work on this from a very early stage.*

Skills and personal qualities

Skills (sometimes called competences) are generally what you have learned to do and have improved with practice. Table 64.1 summarises some important skills for forensic science students. This list might seem quite daunting, but your tutors will have designed your courses to give you plenty of opportunities for developing your expertise. Personal qualities, on the other hand, are predominantly innate. Examples include honesty, determination and thoroughness (Table 70.1). These qualities need not remain static, however, and can be developed or changed according to your experiences. By consciously deciding to take on new challenges and responsibilities, not only can you develop your personal qualities, but you can also provide supporting evidence for your CV.

Personal qualities and skills are interrelated because your personal qualities can influence the skills you gain. For example, you may become highly proficient at a skill requiring manual dexterity if you are particularly adept with your hands. Being able to transfer your skills is highly important (Chapter 64) – many employers take a long-term view and look for evidence of the adaptability that will allow you to be a flexible employee and one who will continue to develop skills.

Developing your curriculum vitae

The initial stage involves making an audit of the skills and qualities you already have, and thinking about those you might need to develop. Tables 70.1 and 64.1 could form a basis of this self-appraisal. Assessing your skills may be easier than critically analysing your personal characteristics. In judging

Table 70.1 Some positive personal qualities

- Adaptability
- Conscientiousness
- Curiosity
- Determination
- Drive
- Energy
- Enthusiasm
- Fitness and health
- Flexible approach
- Honesty
- Innovation
- Integrity
- Leadership
- Logical approach
- Motivation
- Patience
- Performance under stress
- Perseverance
- Prudence
- Quickness of thought
- Seeing other's viewpoints
- Self-confidence
- Self-discipline
- Sense of purpose
- Shrewd judgement
- Social skills (sociability)
- Taking initiative
- Tenacity
- Tidiness
- Thoroughness
- Tolerance
- Unemotional approach
- Willingness to take on challenges

Seeing yourself as others see you – *you may not recognise all of your personal qualities and you may need someone else to give you a frank appraisal. This could be anyone whose opinion you value – a friend, a member of your family, a tutor or a careers adviser.*

Setting your own agenda – *you have the capability to widen your experience and to demonstrate relevant personal qualities through both curricular and extracurricular activities.*

Paying attention to the quality of your CV – *your potential employer will regard your CV as an example of your very best work and will not be impressed if it is full of mistakes or badly presented, especially if you claim 'good written communication' as a skill!*

your qualities, try to take a positive view and avoid being overly modest. It is important to consider personal qualities in a specific context – for example. 'I have shown that I am trustworthy by acting as treasurer for the University Forensic Society', as this evidence will form a vital part of your CV and job applications.

If you can identify gaps in your skills, or qualities that you would like to develop, especially in relation to the needs of your intended career, the next step is to think about ways of improving them. This will be reasonably easy in some cases, but may require some creative thinking in others. A relatively simple example would be if you decided to learn a new language or maintain one you learned at school. There are likely to be many local college and university courses dealing with foreign languages at many different levels, so it would be a straightforward matter to join one of these. A rather more difficult case might be if you wished to demonstrate 'responsibility', because there are no courses available on this. One route to demonstrate this quality might be to put yourself up for election as an officer in a student society or club; another could be to take a leading role in a relevant activity within your community (e.g. voluntary work such as hospital radio). If you already take part in activities like these, your CV should relate them to this context.

Basic CV structures and their presentation

Box 70.1 illustrates the typical parts of a CV and explains the purpose of each part. Employers are more likely to take notice of a well-organised and presented CV, in contrast to one that is difficult to read and assimilate. They will expect yours to be concise, complete and accurate. There are many ways of presenting information in a CV, and you will be assessed partly on your choices.

- **Order.** There is some flexibility as to the order in which you can present the different parts (see Box 70.1). A chronological approach within sections helps employers gain a picture of your experience.
- **Personality and 'colour'.** Make your CV different by avoiding standard or dull phrasing. Try not to focus solely on academic aspects – you will probably have to work in a team and the social aspects of teamwork will be enhanced by your outside interests. However, make sure that the reader does not get the impression that these interests dominate your life.
- **Style.** Your CV should reflect *your* personality, but not in such a way that it indicates too idiosyncratic an approach. It is probably better to be formal in both language and presentation, because flippant or chatty expressions will not be well received.
- **Neatness.** Producing a well-presented, word-processed CV is very important. Use a laser-quality printer and good-quality paper; avoid poor-quality photocopying at all costs.
- **Layout.** Use headings for different aspects, such as personal details, education, etc. Emphasise words (e.g. with capitals, bold, italics or underlining) sparingly and with the primary aim of making the structure clearer. Remember that careful use of white space is important in design.
- **Grammar and proofreading.** Look at your CV carefully before you submit it, as sloppy errors give a very poor impression. Even if you use a spell-checker, some errors may creep in. Ask someone who you regard as a reliable proofreader to comment on it (many tutors will do this, if asked in advance).

Box 70.1 The structure and components of a typical CV and covering letter

There is no right or wrong way to write a CV, and no single format applies. It is probably best to avoid software templates and CV 'wizards' as they can create a bland, standardised result, rather than something that demonstrates your individuality. It is important to focus on the relevant information tailored to the position applied for, keeping your writing concise, well structured and well presented.

You should include the following components, with appropriate subheadings, generally in the order given below:

1. **Personal details.** This section *must* include your full name and date of birth, your address (both home and term-time, with dates, if appropriate) and a contact telephone number at each address. If you have an e-mail account, you should also include this but make sure that it is a sensible e-mail address, e.g. yourname@university.ac.uk. You need only mention gender if your name could be either male or female.

2. **Education.** Choose either chronological order or reverse chronological order, and make sure you take the same approach in all other sections. Give educational institutions and dates (month, year) and provide more detail for your degree course than for your previous education. Remember to mention any prizes, scholarships or other academic achievements. Include your overall mark for the most recent year of your course, if it seems appropriate. Make sure you explain any gap years.

3. **Work experience.** Include all temporary, part-time, full-time and voluntary jobs. Details include dates, employer, job title and major duties involved.

4. **Skills and personal qualities.** Tables 64.1 and 70.1 give examples of the aspects you might include under this heading. Emphasise your strengths, and tailor this section to the specific requirements of the post (the 'job description'). For example, you might emphasise the practical skills you have gained during your degree studies if the post is directly relevant to forensic science, but concentrate on generic transferable skills and personal qualities for other jobs. Provide supporting evidence for your statements in all cases.

5. **Interests and activities.** This is an opportunity to bring out the positive aspects of your personality, and explain their relevance to the post you are applying for. Aim to keep this section short, or it may seem that your social life is more important than your education and work experience. Include up to four separate items, and provide sufficient detail to highlight the *positive* aspects of your interests (e.g. positions of responsibility, working with others, communication, etc.). Use sections 4 and 5 to demonstrate that you have the necessary attributes to fulfil the major requirements of the post.

6. **Referees.** Include the names (and titles), job descriptions, full postal addresses, contact telephone numbers and e-mail addresses of two referees (rarely, some employers may ask for three). It is usual to include your personal tutor or course leader at university (who among other things will verify your marks) plus another person – perhaps a current or former employer, or someone who runs a club or society and who knows your personal interests and activities. Unless you have kept in touch with a particular teacher since starting university, it is probably best to choose current contacts, rather than those from your previous education.

Some other points to consider:

- Try to avoid jargon and overcomplicated phrases in your CV: aim for direct, active words and phrases (see Box 58.1, p. 539).

- Most employers will expect your CV to be word-processed (and spell-checked). Errors in style, grammar and presentation will count against you, so be sure to check through your final version (and ask a reliable person to second-check it for you).

- Aim for a *maximum* length of two pages, printed single-sided on A4 paper, using a 'formal' font (e.g. Times Roman or Arial) of no less than 12 point for the main text. Always print on to good-quality white paper. Avoid fussy use of colour, borders, fonts or icons.

- Don't try to cram in too much detail. Use a clear and succinct approach with short sentences and lists to improve 'readability' and create structure. Remember that your aim is to catch the eye of your potential employer, who may have many applications to work through.

- It is polite to check that people are willing to act as a referee for you and to provide them with an up-to-date copy of your CV.

Your covering letter should have four major components:

1. **Letterhead.** Include your contact details, the recipient's name and title (if known) and address, plus any job reference number.

2. **Introductory paragraph.** Explain who you are and state the post you are applying for.

3. **Main message.** This is your opportunity to sell yourself to a potential employer, highlighting particular attributes and experience. Keep it to three or four sentences at the most, and relate it to the particular skills and qualities demanded in the job or person specification.

4. **Concluding paragraph.** A brief statement that you look forward to hearing the outcome of your application is sufficient.

Finally, add either 'Yours sincerely' (where the recipient's name is known) or 'Yours faithfully' (in a letter beginning 'Dear Sir or Madam') and then end with your signature.

- **Relevance.** If you can, slant your CV towards the job description and the qualifications required (see below). Make sure you provide evidence to back-up your assertions about skills, qualities and experience.
- **Accuracy and completeness.** Check that all your dates tally – otherwise, you will seem careless. It is better to be honest about your grades and, for example, a period of unemployment, than to cover this up or omit details that an employer will want to know. They may be suspicious if you leave things out.

Adjusting your CV

Creating a generic CV – as you may apply for several jobs, it is useful to construct a CV in electronic format (e.g. as a Word® file), which includes all information of potential relevance. This can then be modified to fit each post. Having a prepared CV on file will reduce the work each time you apply, while modifying this will help you focus on relevant skills and attributes for the particular job.

You should fine-tune your CV for each post. Employers frequently use a 'person specification' to define the skills and qualities demanded in a job, often under headings such as 'essential' and 'desirable'. This will help you to decide whether to apply for a position and it assists the selection panel in filtering the applicants. Highlight relevant qualifications as early in your CV as possible. Be selective – don't include every detail about yourself. Emphasise relevant parts and leave out irrelevant details, according to the job. Similarly, your letter of application is not merely a formal document but is also an opportunity for persuasion (Box 70.1). You can use it to state your ambitions and highlight particular qualifications and experience. However, don't go over the top – always keep the letter to a single page.

 KEY POINT *A well-constructed and relevant CV won't necessarily guarantee you a job, but it may well get you on to the short list for interview. A poor-quality CV is a sure route to failure.*

Sources for further study

Anon (2000) *How to Write a Curriculum Vitae,* 4th edn. University of London, Careers Service, London.

Corfield, R. (2009) *Preparing the Perfect Job Application: Application Forms and Letters Made Easy,* 5th edn. Kogan Page, London.

Graduate Prospects website. Available at: http://www .prospects.ac.uk/ Last accessed: 31/08/2017.

Study exercises

70.1 Evaluate your personal attributes. Using Table 70.1, list five qualities that you would use to best describe yourself, and cite the evidence you might give to a potential employer to convince them that this was the case. List five attributes you could develop, then indicate how you might do this.

70.2 Create a generic CV. Drawing on your school record of achievement, or any CV already prepared (e.g. for a part-time job), create a word-processed generic CV. Save the file in an appropriate (computer) folder and make a back-up copy. Print out a copy for filing. Periodically update the word-processed version. If appropriate, save different versions to be used in different contexts (e.g. when applying for a vacation job).

70.3 Think about your future career and ask for advice. Make an appointment with one of the advisors in your university's careers service. Ask about career options for graduates with your intended degree, or determine what qualifications or module options might be appropriate for occupations that interest you.

Answers to study exercises

We have attempted to provide an 'answer' to all of the study exercises. Where the question is open-ended and no 'correct' answer can be given, we have provided tips, which should help with your general approach, indicate which resources are worth consulting or provide a pointer to relevant material within the book. Where a non-numerical question has a 'correct' answer, we have provided a model text-based answer. If a calculation is involved, we have shown the steps involved and have indicated the correct answer.

1 Essentials of practical work

1.1. Possible reasons why practical work might be of value in a university course include:

- practicals reinforce lecture material, in agreement with the adage: 'I hear and I forget, I see and I remember, I do and I understand';
- practical procedures provide students with an opportunity to develop their manual skills and laboratory competences;
- investigative procedures and problem-solving practical exercises enable students to improve their skills in experimental design and the application of the scientific method;
- practicals enable students to develop their abilities to observe and measure biological systems, and to record the outcome;
- students are able to analyse and interpret the data from practical exercises and to consider the validity of their results, including sources of error, etc.;
- the results of practical procedures give students an opportunity to develop skills in reporting and presenting 'experiments' in written format.

1.2. *Tip:* Possible items for a bulk drug examination: scalpel; brown paper; methanol; ammonia; ethyl acetate; sample tubes, vortex mixer; examination notes; paper tissues; water; Pasteur pipette; first-aid kit nearby – in case of accident.

1.3.
(a) 40
(b) 44.266 66, expressed to four significant figures = 44.27
(c) 0.019 531 25, expressed to three significant figures = 0.0195
(d) 1.6×10^5
(e) 0.0313, expressed to three decimal places = 0.031

2 Health and safety

2.1.
(a) See pp. 6–11.
(b) Fig. 2.1 (p. 7).
(c) Fig. 2.2 (p. 8).
(d)

International symbol for a biohazard. Usually red on a yellow background, or black on a red background.

2.2. *Tip:* The locations of each item will vary, according to the layout of your chosen laboratory. You should ask someone in charge (e.g. demonstrator, lecturer, technician or laboratory manager) if you are unable to find any of the items listed.

2.3.
(a) *Tip:* The answer will vary, according to your university.
(b) In the UK, water-filled fire extinguishers are red – use for wood, paper and textiles; CO_2 extinguishers are black, or have a black panel – use for flammable liquids and electrical fires; dry-powder extinguishers are blue, or have a blue panel – use for all types of fires (wood, paper, textiles, gaseous fires, flammable liquids and electrical fires); foam extinguishers are beige, or have a beige panel – use for flammable liquids (note that other colour conventions may apply outside the UK).
(c) *Tip:* This will vary, depending on your department's procedure. However, it is likely to include a specific written record book for accidents.
(d) *Tip:* There will often be separate codes of practice for work involving non-pathogenic microbes (e.g. general microbiology classes) and pathogenic microbes. The latter requires a higher level of safe working practice, and may include the use of disposable aprons, etc.

2.4. *Tip:* Use either your department's chemical hazard information system or an Internet database (e.g. the National Institute for Occupational Safety & Health Databases at: https://www.cdc.gov/niosh/data/; or the Agency for Toxic Substances and Disease Registry ToxFAQs database at: http://www.atsdr.cdc.gov/toxfaq.html.) Alternatively, you could use a 'portal' site such as Biochem Links at: http://biochemlinks.com/; or the material safety data sheet (MSDS) site at http://www.ilpi.com/msds/index.html).
(a) Cocaine is a narcotic and toxic – protective gloves and eye/face protection should be used during preparation of stock solutions. Cocaine can also cause allergic skin reactions in sensitive individuals and breathing the powder form should be avoided.
(b) Phenolphthalein is an irritant and potentially carcinogenic. Avoid contact with strong oxidising agents. It should be used in a well-ventilated room. Disposable gloves can be used to prevent skin contact.
(c) Sulphuric acid is highly corrosive and an irritant. Protective gloves and safety glasses should be worn when preparing stock solutions.

3 Making measurements and observations

3.1.
(a) Quantitative, discontinuous, ratio
(b) Quantitative, continuous, ratio
(c) Qualitative, discontinuous, nominal
(d) Quantitative, discontinuous, ratio
(e) Qualitative, discontinuous, nominal

3.2. The results indicate that balance A has a bias of $+0.05$ g across the weighing range, while balance B has a consistent bias of about $+0.04\%$. Both balances are precise, but not accurate.

3.3. *Tip:* Use a spreadsheet to lay out the table once you have decided what it needs to contain and what statistics you might wish to calculate. You can use spreadsheet functions to help you calculate some of the statistics.

4 SI units and their use
4.1. (a) 191 cm
(b) 568 mL
(c) 310 K
(d) 72.6 kg
4.2. (a) 10 m
(b) 15 mL
(c) 5 g J
(d) 65 km s^{-1}
(e) 100 pg
4.3. (a) 2.05 g L^{-1}
(b) 0.022 moles
(c) 26.5 mg 100 mL^{-1}

5 Scientific method and design of experiments
5.1. *Tip:* For Microsoft Excel, try the formula = INT(5*(RAND())+1)
5.2. *Tip:* Consider what the purpose of the practical is. You are the one who is carrying out the examination so make sure you understand why you are undertaking the work. If you were to repeat the work would you get the same result? Are you confident in your practical skills? Do you know if there is any instrumental error?
5.3. *Tip:* Consider what the purpose of the experiment is. Use the following questions to help you design your experiment: What are you trying to achieve? Are there any similar studies published? What is the 'normal' rate of growth? What variables can you control? What statistics could you apply to determine whether your results are significant? Are there any ethical considerations to your study?

6 Working with liquids
6.1. (a) Use measuring cylinders – e.g. measure out 700 mL of ethanol using a 1000 mL measuring cylinder, and measure out 300 mL of water using a 500 mL measuring cylinder; mix together in a large conical flask (e.g. 1000 mL capacity) or beaker.
(b) Use a pipettor (e.g. P200 Gilson Pipetman) set to deliver 200 μL and clean disposable tips.
(c) Weigh out 10.0 mg (0.0100 g) of methadone standard using a four-place balance, add this to a 10 mL volumetric flask and make up to 10 mL with methanol. Use a pipettor (e.g. P200 Gilson Pipetman) set to deliver 200mL and clean disposable tips and add this to a 10 mL volumetric flask and make up to 10 mL with methanol.
6.2. *Tip:* Box 6.1 (p. 39) gives stepwise details of how to use a pipettor.
6.3. *Tip:* You may find this type of calculation easier using a spreadsheet, rather than a calculator (Chapter 49 gives further details). The model A pipettor gave a mean delivery of 0.9795 mL, with a standard deviation of 0.010 40 mL (to five decimal places). The model B pipettor delivered, on average, 1.0107 mL, with a standard deviation of 0.001 25 mL. The model C pipettor gave an average delivery of 1.0009 mL, with

a standard deviation of 0.058 82 mL. Therefore, model C was the most accurate pipettor (with a mean value closest to the true value of 1.0000 mL) and model B was most precise (giving the most reproducible results, as shown by the lowest standard deviation). The model A pipettor was the least accurate (mean value furthest from the true value), while model C was the least precise (having the highest standard deviation).

7 Basic laboratory procedures
7.1. *Tip:* All of these can be calculated using the relationship $[C_1]V_1 = [C_2]V_2$ (eqn [7.2]). Do not forget to include the volumes of both solutions when calculating the final volume – e.g. in example (a) below, the final volume is 10 mL (1 + 9) and not 9 mL.
(a) $1 \times 0.4 = [C_2] \times 10$, therefore $[C_2] = (1 \times 0.4) \div 10 = 0.04$ mol L^{-1} and therefore $0.04 \times 1000 = 40.0$ mmol L^{-1}.
(b) $10 \times 25 = [C_2] \times 500$, therefore $[C_2] = (10 \diamond 25) \div 500 = 0.5$ μg mL and therefore $0.5 \times 1000 = 500$ ng mL^{-1}.
(c) $10 \times 10 = [C_2] \diamond 250$, therefore $[C_2] = (10 \times 10) \div 250 = 0.4$ mg L
(d) $200 \times [V_1] = 0.2 \diamond 10$, therefore $[V_1] = (0.2 \times 10) \div 200 = 0.01$ mL $= 10$ μL

9 pH and buffer solutions
9.1. *Tip:* Use eqn [9.5] to interconvert between pH and [H$^+$].
(a) $7.4 = -\log_{10}[H^+]$, therefore $[H^+] = 3.98 \times 10^{-8}$ mol L^{-1}.
(b) $4.1 = -\log_{10}[H^+]$, therefore $[H^+] = 7.94 \times 10^{-5}$ mol L^{-1} and therefore 7.94×10^{-8} mol m^{-3}.
(c) $pH = -\log_{10}[2 \times 10^{-5}]$, therefore $pH = 4.70$.
(d) $pH = -\log_{10}[10^{-12.5}]$, therefore $pH = 12.5$.

10 Introduction to microscopy
10.1. (a) T
(b) F
(c) F
(d) T
(e) T
(f) T
(g) T
(h) F
(i) F
(j) T
10.2. Missing words are: diffracted; near-transparent; resolution; interference; contrast; 3D; focus; optical sectioning; polarised; laser.

11 Setting up and using microscopes
11.1. *Tip:* To memorise the parts, it may help to imagine yourself setting up a microscope.
11.2. (a) Provides optimal resolution by ensuring that the light source is focused on the slide.
(b) Provides a magnified image to the eyepiece lenses.
(c) Enhances image contrast by cutting down on stray light reaching the objective lens.
(d) Sets up the microscope for the distance between your pupils, so you can use both eyepieces.
(e) Allows you to return to same place on a slide.
11.3. Answer (c) is correct (see pp. 69–71).

12 Sample preparation

12.1. (a) To extract the cannabinoids from a blood sample, either solid phase extraction or solvent (liquid–liquid) extraction would be suitable, but consideration has to be given to the extraction conditions, e.g. solvents used, pH.

(b) To extract pesticides from soil, Soxhlet extraction could be used.

(c) To extract accelerants from fire debris, thermal desorption should be used, e.g. Tenax.

(d) To extract heroin from bulk drug powder, solvent extraction should be used.

12.2. (a) Column preparation – you need to activate the adsorption sites on the SPE cartridge.

(b) Sample loading – you need to allow sufficient time for the analyte to adsorb on to the active sites, while the matrix passes through the cartridge to waste.

(c) Interference removal – any interfering compounds that remain in the cartridge need to be removed before analyte elution to ensure a clean extract before being presented to any instrumentation.

(d) Analyte elution – you need to choose the correct elution conditions to ensure you remove all the analyte from the cartridge.

12.3. *Tip:* When you are writing your protocol, consider whether someone else could pick it up and follow your instructions to achieve the same result. Remember you need to include sample preparation, extraction conditions and detection parameters.

13 DNA analysis – fundamental principles

13.1. The expected values are 137 : 274 : 137, based on a 1 : 2 : 1 ratio. The χ^2 value is 1.05 + 3.07 + 2.11 = 6.23 (see Box 13.2 for method of working). Since this value is greater than the critical value for χ^2 for two degrees of freedom ($n - 1$ categories = 3 − 1) at $P = 0.05$ (which is 5.99, Table 13.1), the geneticist should reject the null hypothesis of a 1 : 2 : 1 outcome.

13.2. (a) In aqueous solution, individual ethidium bromide molecules have a low fluorescence, due to the stacking of the planar molecules. When ethidium bromide intercalates between two strands of DNA, this leads to a substantial enhancement in fluorescence – intercalation prevents the molecular collisions that would otherwise decrease fluorescence.

(b) Ethidium bromide can also intercalate within double-stranded regions of RNA, e.g. hairpin loops.

13.3. *Tip:* Table 13.4 gives advice for standard polyacrylamide and agarose gels, while pulsed field gel electrophoresis is covered on the following page.

(a) Use an agarose gel, e.g. at a concentration of 0.3% w/v.

(b) Use a polyacrylamide gel, e.g. at a concentration of 5% w/v.

(c) Use PACE, which is a variant of pulsed field gel electrophoresis that is able to fractionate DNA molecules of widely different sizes.

13.4. Insufficient Mg^{2+} can impair the polymerisation reaction, since it is an essential co-factor for thermostable DNA polymerases. Excess Mg^{2+} stabilises double stranded DNA and may prevent complete denaturation of the PCR product after each cycle, thereby reducing yield. Excess Mg^{2+} can also promote spurious annealing of primers, and this can lead to production of non-specific products (for more details, see: https://www.promega.co.uk/resources/product-guides-and-selectors/protocols-and-applications-guide/pcr-amplification/).

14 Chromatography

14.1. *Tip:* Use eqn [14.4] to determine R_f, based on the measured distances travelled by each component, relative to the solvent front.

(a) The corresponding R_f values are:
pigment A = 63 ÷ 114 = 0.553;
pigment B = 76 ÷ 114 = 0.667;
pigment C = 86 ÷ 114 = 0.754.

14.2. (a) Flame Ionisation Detector.

(b) Thermal Conductivity Detector.

(c) Electron Capture Detector.

(d) Diode Array Detector.

14.3. Electrochemical detectors, then fluorescence detectors, then UV/visible detectors. Many biomolecules, either intrinsically or after reaction with a colour reagent, can be detected by UV/visible spectroscopy. However, fewer biomolecules show native fluorescence or the electrical properties necessary for electrochemical detection, making UV/visible detection the most versatile approach.

14.4. (a) *Tip:* Calculate the selectivity from eqn [14.2] using the elution time for the compound excluded from the stationary phase as the column dead time (t_0), with all times converted to seconds. Thus $\alpha = (372 - 95) \div (270 - 95) = 1.582\,857\,1 = 1.58$.

(b) *Tip:* Calculate the resolution using eqn [39.7]. Thus $R - (372 - 270) \div 0.5\,(40 + 44) = 2.428\,571\,4 = 2.43$. This is a good level of resolution for quantitative work, giving clear separation of the two peaks.

14.5. (a) A measure of retention time.

(b) Identifies when the peaks elute relative to each other.

(c) Measures the narrowness of a peak.

(d) A measure of peak shape.

15 Mass spectrometry

15.1. C_2H_3Cl, 62 a.m.u. m/z 27 = maximum 2 × C m/z 62:64 suggests Cl isotope 62 − 35 = 27; therefore 62 amu for ^{35}Cl & 64 amu for ^{37}Cl.

15.2. (a) EI^+ refers to electron impact ionisation (see p. 149).

(b) Cl^- refers to negative chemical ionisation (see p. 149).

(c) APCI refers to atmospheric pressure chemical ionisation (see p. 149).

(d) ESI refers to electrospray ionisation (see p. 149).

15.3.

Commonly find m/z 58, 135, 162 when MDMA is not derivatised.

16 Basic spectroscopy

16.1. *Tip:* Box 16.1 gives stepwise instructions for using a spectrophotometer – check that you have covered all of the major points. However, the exact details will vary from instrument to instrument.

16.2. *Tip:* Substitute values into eqn [16.3] and solve for [*C*] (margin examples are given on p. 154).

(a) Note that you must convert the path length from mm to cm beforehand: $0.57 = 20 \times 0.5 \times [C] = 0.057$ g L^{-1} = 57.0 µg mL^{-1}.

(b) First calculate the concentration, using eqn [16.3]: $0.31 = 20 \times 1 \times [C] = 0.0155$ g L^{-1}. Next, express the concentration in the required units: 0.0155×10^9 (convert to ng) $\div 10^6$ (convert to µL) = 15.5 ng mL^{-1}. Then, calculate the amount in 50 µL: $15.5 \times 50 = 775$ ng.

16.3. First determine the concentration of *p*-nitrophenol, in mol L^{-1}. Thus 8.8 µg mL^{-1} $\div 10^6$ (convert to g mL^{-1}) $\times 10^3$ (convert to g L^{-1}) $\div 291.27$ (convert to mol L^{-1}) = 0.000 030 212 5 mol L^{-1}. Next, substitute values into eqn [16.3] and solve for ε: $0.535 = e \times 1 \times 0.000\,030\,212\,5$, so $\varepsilon = 17\,707.902\,36 = 17\,700$ L mol^{-1} cm^{-1}. Note that you should use the full numerical value until the final stage, to avoid introducing 'rounding' errors.

17 Atomic spectroscopy

17.1. The calibration graph is shown below. The test solution has a K$^+$ concentration of 0.32 mmol L^{-1}. This is equivalent to $0.32 \div 1000 \times 25 = 0.008$ mmol in 25 mL (the test sample volume). Next, divide by the weight of tissue used in grams: $0.008 \div 0.482 = 0.016\,598$ mmol (g tissue)$^{-1}$ = 16.6 µmol (g tissue)$^{-1}$.

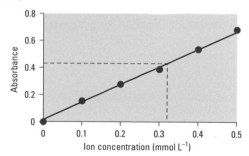

Calibration curve for a series of standards, assayed for K$^+$ and based on the data in the table in study exercise 17.1.

17.2. See the graph below – note that this calibration line is approximately linear up to ~4.0 µg mL^{-1} but it becomes increasingly curved above this point. Water sample (a) contains Zn at 1.70 µg mL^{-1}; water sample (b) contains Zn at $3.5 \times 20 = 70.0$ µg mL^{-1}; water sample (c) contains Zn at $8.3 \times 5 = 41.5$ µg mL^{-1} (note that the graph curves at higher concentrations, making the estimate for water sample (c) less reliable than the other two – a better approach might have been to dilute this sample further and reassay).

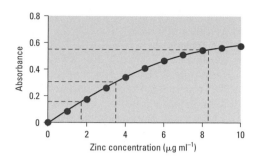

18 X-ray fluorescence spectroscopy

18.1. *Tip:* Write down the key points on how XRF works; consider whether a jury would understand the science of your explanation; prepare, practise and rehearse answers with your colleagues.

18.2. Interferences include:

(a) Spectral – occur from sources other than the analyte you wish to measure.

(b) Environmental – occur from lighter elements and can be avoided by purging the instrument with an inert gas or creating a vacuum by the removal of air.

(c) Matrix – any element can absorb or scatter the fluorescence of the element, but can be corrected mathematically by alpha corrections.

18.3. *Tip:* When you are writing your protocol, consider whether someone else could pick it up and follow your instructions to achieve the same result. Use Box 18.2 as a guide but you will have to consider how you could 'dry' the soil sample first.

19 Infrared and Raman spectroscopy

19.1. (a) Peak (i).

(b) Peak (ii).

19.2. *Tip:* Find an appropriate source to familiarise yourself with the case, as well as making reference to peer-reviewed journals or textbooks. Use this information to explain and understand why FTIR was used, how it was used and how it helped in this case.

19.3. *Tip:* Your database for references could simply be recorded in a spreadsheet or you could use Microsoft Access®. It is important that you keep up to date with the technology and associated applications, and consider their potential use in a forensic investigation (even if they haven't been previously adopted for this purpose). It is also important to consider whether or not the examination (preparation or detection) would be destructive to the evidence type.

20 Nuclear magnetic resonance spectroscopy

20.1. *Tip:* The term 'chemical shift' refers to the position in a spectrum of a signal from an absorbing magnetic nucleus relative to the signal from a reference compound. Ideally, the reference compound will give a single, unambiguous, sharp resonance at a frequency relatively far from the resonances of the compounds under analysis.

    (a) Tetramethylsilane (TMS) $[(CH_3)_4Si]$ is a suitable reference for ^1H as it contains 12 protons in identical environments, giving a single peak well separated from those of the protons of most other molecules.

    (b) TMS is also suitable as a reference compound for ^{13}C NMR in most biological applications.

20.2. In both instances, ppm is an abbreviation for 'parts per million', and the units must be established from the context in which the expression is used. In NMR, ppm refers to the small frequency changes that occur relative to the reference standard, expressed in proportional terms. Thus 1 ppm in NMR means a frequency difference of 1 Hz per MHz, e.g. 270 Hz in a 270 mHz spectrum. When used as a concentration term, ppm is equivalent to the expression of a concentration in parts per million, e.g. as $\mu g\ mL^{-1}$ ($10^{-6}\ g\ mL^{-1}$) in w/v terms, or $\mu g\ g^{-1}$ ($10^{-6}\ g\ g^{-1}$) in w/w terms.

21 Immunoassay

21.1. *Tip:* You need to consider the application of the device at the roadside. Use the following questions as a guide: Would the device be able to detect all drugs? What cut-off limits would it have? What sample would be required? Would the result be evidential in a court? Would the device be able to prove impairment? How could you prevent false positives or false negatives?

21.2. *Tip:* Try to remember the key functions of each as bullet points.

21.3. *Tip:* Write down the key points on how ELISA works; consider whether a jury would understand the science of your explanation; prepare, practise and rehearse answers with your colleagues.

22 Electrophoresis

22.1. *Tip:* The dissociation of two important amino acids is shown below:

Glutamate: $R\text{-}COOH \rightleftharpoons R\text{-}COO^- + H^+$

           low pH   neutral/high pH

Lysine: $R\text{-}NG_3^+ \rightleftharpoons R-NH_2 + H^+$

low/neutral pH   high pH

Note that the charge on a given amino acid side chain at a given pH will depend on the dissociation constant or pKa, (see p. 211) of the ionisable group.

22.2. *Tip:* The different forms of blotting are listed on p. 219. Transfer of proteins on to gels is termed Western blotting, while DNA transfer is known as Southern blotting and RNA transfer as Northern blotting (p. 219 explains the origins of the terms).

22.3. In PAGE any diffusion of sample proteins that occurs reduces resolution, so it is best to start with as narrow a sample zone as possible. For most protein separations, the buffer pH is chosen so that the proteins are negatively charged and will migrate from the cathodic end to the anodic end of the gel. In IEF, the separation is carried out on a pH gradient – because proteins will all migrate to their pI values irrespective of the starting point, the position of sample application is not important. The only exception would be if any of the proteins to be separated were unstable at extreme pH values, in which case it would be best to avoid application at either end of the pH gradient (e.g. pH 3.0 and pH 10.0). Once a given protein has reached the position corresponding to its pI, it will remain in a narrow band because any diffusion away from the pI will result in the protein acquiring a net charge and being focused back to its pI.

23 Personnel and recording the scene

23.1. *Tip:* When drawing your sketch, consider what is important. For example, dimensions of the room, location of doors, windows, state of the room, location of furniture, location of 'evidence'. Consider the use of 3D sketches for clarity.

22.2. *Tip:* Using an SLR camera, practise obtaining correct exposure. Adjust in turn the aperture or the shutter speeds until the correct exposure is obtained. Turn the focusing ring to ensure the correct focus is obtained. Practise setting the camera so that the image being photographed is exactly 90° to the camera.

22.3. *Tip:* Using a digital camera, practise obtaining image capture with/without the zoom function. Practise setting the camera so that the image being photographed is exactly 90° to the camera. Save the images to a media card (xD, SD or equivalent) and insert these images into a Word document using the Insert menu, Picture option. Browse the media card and insert the image.

24 Collecting evidence – basic principles

24.1. For example – fingerprints, footwear marks, tool marks, glass, paint, blood, hairs and fibres.

24.2. (a) High evidential value – can be used for identification.

    (b) Depends on rarity of fibre, how easily shed, number of fibres, and persistence.

    (c) High evidential value – can be used to obtain a DNA profile to potentially link scene to suspect or refute involvement.

    (d) Depends on location found, number of fragments, type of glass.

24.3. Your answer should have included a detailed description of the item, where it was found and the date it was found, an exhibit reference number that matches your contemporaneous notes. It should be signed and dated.

26 Investigating fingerprints

26.1. (a) Flake powders, e.g. aluminium

    (b) Amido black

    (c) Ninhydrin

    (d) Flake powders, e.g. aluminium; cyanoacrylate fuming

26.2. Refer to Box 26.1 to guide you through this process.

26.3. You should be able to identify your class characteristics (whorl, arch, loop). For the individual characteristics, you may find that a stereomicroscope, or if you have access to a comparison microscope, would help.

27 Footwear marks and impressions

27.1. Refer back to Chapter 24, p. 243.

27.2. (a) Photograph > cast.

    (b) Photograph (you could use amido black, if required, for visualisation) > blood sampling (Chapter 30).

    (c) Photograph, if possible with high-intensity oblique light source > electrostatic lift (negative impression).

27.3. Calcium sulphate hemihydrate reacts with water to form gypsum (calcium sulphate dehydrate), as follows:
$(CaSO_4)_2.H_2O + 3H_2O > 2CaSO_4.2H_2O$ (exothermic)

28 Investigating other marks

28.1. $e \rightarrow d \rightarrow a \rightarrow c \rightarrow b$

28.2. Missing words are: 'casting'; 'dental stone'; either 'casting putty' or 'silicone rubber'; 'fulcrum'; 'tip'; 'manufacture'; 'wear'; 'individual'; 'comparison'; either 'impression' or 'cast'; 'test'.

28.3. (i) Matching of soil in tyre tread on Barnes' truck with that from the crime scene, plus (ii) matching of fabric impressions on a panel of the truck with that of the jeans of the victim. Conviction overturned in 2008, on the basis of new DNA evidence and weakness of soil and fabric pattern evidence. See: https://www.innocenceproject.org/cases/steven-barnes/

29 Document analysis

29.1. When you write your signature, try to start at the centre of a blank piece of paper – this way the 'natural' slant of writing will become apparent. Your signature there will show slight differences from the first to last.

29.2. The defects will appear as small black marks, or they may even appear as smears. These will be different on different photocopiers.

29.3. Pressure is subjective, but use the format of light pressure just touching the paper, medium as you would write normally and hard by pressing firmly down on the paper. You will find that as pressure increases so does the impression that can be observed, but this will also depend on the type and thickness of the paper used.

30 Analysis of biological fluids

30.1. (a) Kastle Meyer or leucomalachite green are traditionally used.
(b) Acid phosphatase
(c) Phadebas
(d) *p*-dimethylaminocinnamaldehyde (DMAC)

30.2. Initial examination > hair and fibre > glass > blood > reagent testing > testing garment > agreement of critical findings.

30.3. (a) 51.88°
(b) 18.35°
(c) 34.85°
(d) 90°

31 DNA analysis – forensic applications

31.1. You should be able to find the answers in the annual report 2014–15 available https://www.gov.uk/government/publications/national-dna-database-annual-report-2014-to-2015 but you should always refer to the most current data reports.

31.2. Refer to p. 307 for a full list of anti-contamination procedures.

31.3. Cell lysis > denature proteins > annealing > synthesis.

32 Analysis of hair

32.1. This is a practical exercise, but you should find that naturally shed hair does not have a distended root.

32.2. You should be able to document exactly what you see visually and underneath the microscope. Do not forget to include all the features of the hair and not just the detail of the root appearance.

32.3. This is a practical exercise. Use Boxes 32.1 and 42.1 to help you in this process. You may wish to refer to Chapters 10 and 11 for assistance with setting up the microscope. Any hairs recovered are likely to be naturally shed and may be of animal origin if you have a pet.

33 Analysis of skeletal remains

33.1. You can estimate the **sex** of the remains by examining the pelvis, skull, sternum and/or long bones; **age** by the length of long bones, proportion of bone:cartilage, presence of degenerative diseases, stage of dentition; **height** can be used but there is a degree of variation, needs to be compared against population specific databases; **racial origin** can be determined predominantly by features on the skull; **facial reconstruction** techniques; **dental records** (see also Chapter 34); **comparison** with *ante-mortem* data can be used to assist identification by comparison with clothing, personal effects; **DNA** can also be used to corroborate findings.

33.2. There are many different techniques used for facial reconstruction, from 2D overlays to 3D computer-aided design software packages. Try searching in *Forensic Science International* or *Journal of Forensic Sciences* to find your information.

33.3. The sex can be determined by examining the **pelvis** – in females the iliac crest is more angled, pubic symphysis is longer, sub pubic angle is wider, sciatic notch is wider; **skull** – in males, the orbital ridges are more pronounced, mastoid process is larger, lower mandible is 'square' shaped; **sternum** – if the sternum length is 2 × or more than the length of the manubrium, the skeleton is more likely to be male; **femur head** – diameter > 47.5 mm more likely to be male, <42.5 mm more likely to be female.

34 Forensic odontology

34.1. Refer to Fig. 34.2 on p. 331, and check your answers.

34.2. Refer to Fig. 34.1 on p. 330. Each tooth is designated a number from upper right 3rd molar (number 1) to upper left 3rd molar (number 16) and the same for the lower jaw. Refer to Photo 34.1 and you will see that the teeth represented in the image are located on the lower left jaw.

34.3. Initial documentation > observation and identification of a mark (judgement for whether it is of human origin) > photographic capture of the mark > swab skin > analyse the photograph (measurements, assessment of key features, distortion artefacts) > compare with cast from suspect > comparison with population database (to assess whether there any common features within the specific population that the suspect belongs to).

35 Forensic entomology

35.1. Egg stage (1 day) > larval > 1st instar (1.8 days) > 2nd instar (2.5 days) > 3rd instar (4–5 days) > prepupae (8–12 days) > pupae (18–24 days) > adult, but you should remember that the stages of development are determined by temperature. You could try to source the isomegalen diagram for this species from peer-reviewed journals.

35.2. PMI can be determined, for example, by **insect succession,** which appears to follow a predictable pattern in a particular climate; **stages of development** – with knowledge of the minimum development times; the presence of different stages of development can give an indication of time; **ADH and ADD** – mathematical calculation of the time for development but this assumes a constant and unfluctuating temperature.

35.3. The ADH can be calculated as $(15 + 12.4 + 24.1) \times 21 = 1081.5$ hours

ADD $= 1081.5 \div 24 =$ approximately 45 days

36   Forensic botany

36.1. Dendrochronology is the examination of tree rings and represents seasonal difference in growth, allowing the age of the tree to be determined. There are a number of factors that affect the ring formation and these are described in Box 36.2 and p. 351.

36.2. If an item of clothing, e.g. shoes, was submitted then, after the full documentation of the exhibit, soil can be recovered by using a small toothbrush and collected for examination. There are a number of techniques that can be used and these are detailed on p. 352. Some techniques are non-destructive, whereas others, e.g. soil digestion for examining the soil for exchangeable bases (i.e. potassium, sodium), require a digestion with 0.05 mol L^{-1} EDTA, or for silicates digestion with hydrofluoric acid. Since it is a destructive technique you must make sure that all other non-destructive analyses are performed prior to this.

36.3. The following Web pages will be helpful: http://www.british-bryologicalsociety.org.uk/ – British Bryological Society http://rbg-web2.rbge.org.uk/ADIAC/pubdat/pubdat.html – Automatic Diatom Identification and Classification (ADIAC) database (a collaborative project between Royal Botanical Gardens, Edinburgh, and University of Newcastle-upon-Tyne). Within the Web pages is an introduction to diatom identification. http://www.botany.unibe.ch/paleo/pollen_e/ – Introduction to pollen analysis

37   Alcohol analysis

37.1. Not less than 117 mg alcohol per 100 mL (range 94–136 mg alcohol per 100 mL)

37.2. (a) $r = 0.644$

(b) $r = 0.774$

37.3. (a) Relaxation, but a possibility of delayed reaction times.

(b) This is the current drink drive limit in the UK and as such impairment of complex tasks will be noted as well as slurred speech, errors of judgement, some loss of co-ordination.

(c) Speech is slurred, co-ordination is significantly impaired.

(d) Effects become more pronounced, possibility of unconsciousness, memory loss.

(e) Coma is likely, death is possible due to depression of the central nervous system, or by inhalation of vomit.

38   Forensic toxicology

38.1. (a) Concentration lies in the range associated with fatal poisoning.

(b) Concentration lies in the range that is commonly associated with a tolerant drug user. While this concentration is known to cause death in a naive user, it may not have a fatal effect in this case.

38.2. You will need to include how you would prepare a blood sample, and the instrumental conditions for GC–MS (injection port, column, temperature programme and MS detection parameters). You should also include what you should do to make sure that the instrument is working effectively. i.e. tuning, quality control.

38.3. You should consider what *post-mortem* redistribution is, what drugs are likely to be affected, how the phenomenon occurs, what samples are most likely to be affected, whether there is a marker to indicate that the redistribution has occurred.

39   Bulk drug analysis

39.1. (a) Orange

(b) Orange/brown

(c) Remains colourless, but will effervesce

(d) Purple

(e) Black

39.2. You will need to include details for the preparation of a reference standard – refer to p. 44 if necessary to remind you how to prepare a standard from a stock solution. Construct a calibration curve, accurately weigh your cocaine sample and run these through an HPLC – you should also include the parameters used to set up the instrument from injection conditions, column used, mobile phase. You will then need to calculate the purity – you may wish to refer to Box 39.3.

39.3. Look up each of the schedules in the Misuse of Drugs Act, available at http://www.legislation.gov.uk/ukpga/1971/38/contents and list your five drugs from the documentation.

40   Analysis of paint

40.1. This is a practical exercise that will differ according to the different instruments used, different paint samples/layers and different types of wood. Assess for yourself the scientific evidence you can obtain.

40.2. This is a practical exercise that will differ according to the different paint samples obtained. Try to identify the different layers – you may wish to refer to Chapters 10 and 11 to help with the microscopy.

40.3. Low-power microscopy, polarising microscopy, scanning electron microscopy, FTIR, XRF, py GC–MS.

41   Analysis of glass

41.1. Divide a piece of clean paper into three. Open the paper out and repeat the process perpendicular to the previous folds. Turn the paper over and, using the existing fold lines as a guide, fold over one edge of the paper. Tuck the remaining 'leaf' into this fold.

41.2. Refer to Box 41.1 and 32.1 and the text in Chapter 32 to help make sure that you have fully documented the process.

41.3. This is a key paper to explain glass transfer and has formed the basis of subsequent interpretation. You may wish to look for more recent journal articles to see how interpretation has progressed since 1998.

42 Analysis of fibres

42.1. Remember that your notes should fully document the item you have examined in an appropriate order as follows: description > label > condition > damage > hairs and fibres > blood.

42.2. This is a practical exercise. Use Boxes 32.1 and 42.1 to help you in this process. You may wish to refer to Chapters 10 and 11 for assistance with setting up the microscope. The fibres recovered will belong predominantly to the item you have tape-lifted. You should try to identify whether there are any fibres that have been transferred on to the item.

42.3. Low-power microscopy, FTIR, microspectrophotometry, Raman, TLC, HPLC, LC–MS.

43 Firearms and ballistic evidence

43.1. (a) The part of the ammunition that is projected from the firearm.

(b) Metal casing, or plastic wadding, that contains the primer and propellant.

(c) A mixture of compounds that explode when compressed.

(d) A compound that burns explosively producing a large volume of gas.

(e) Comprises the case, primer, propellant and bullet.

43.2. Includes specifically lead, barium, antinomy, but also aluminium, sulphur, tin and calcium.

43.3. You may wish to search online to find out more about this case. Focus on why Barry George was originally convicted and the issues surrounding the FDR evidence in the subsequent appeal.

44 Analysis of fires and explosions

44.1. You should include in your answer who would be present at the scene, how to take control reference samples, how to locate the seat of the fire, how to take debris samples, unburned samples and control debris samples.

44.2. This is a practical-based exercise – refer to Box 44.1 to help you.

44.3. (a) HPLC, UV detection

(b) HPLC, normal phase, thermal energy analyser

(c) GC–FID

(d) Dionex, ion chromatography

45 Finding and citing published information

45.1. (a) The Dewey Decimal Classification system, the US Library of Congress system or other, as appropriate.

(b) *Journal of Forensic Science:* Dewey: 363.25; Library of Congress: Q1.N3; (or other, as appropriate). Note: the 'Per' or 'per' that may precede these numbers refers to the fact that this is a periodical, rather than a book.

(c) *Tip:* Answer as appropriate – this will depend on the layout of your particular library.

(d) (i) 'Repeatability and Reproducibility of Earprint Acquisition'

(ii) 'Frozen Human Bone: A Microscopic Investigation'.

45.2. *Tip:* The main point here is that methods of writing down references are diverse. You should also find that the details recorded are the same, although they may be in a different order or font style. You must pay attention to the precise instructions given for your course, to ensure that you get this right when writing up a project report or dissertation.

45.3. *Tip:* Two possible sites are:

(a) SI units: http://physics.nist.gov/cuu/Units/index.html (last accessed 31/08/2017)

(b) https://www.gov.uk/guidance/police-and-criminal-evidence-act-1984-pace-codes-of-practice (last accessed 31/08/2017)

45.4. *Tip:* When writing a handwritten essay, the variant of the Vancouver method, in which references are listed in the order cited, might be the most convenient to use, because you could write down all the references cited on a separate sheet as you wrote out the essay. However, if you felt that it was important for the reader to see the author(s) and publication dates of the papers, then the Harvard method might be more appropriate – however, you would need to wait until the essay was fully written before organising the literature-cited section in author and date order. In a word-processed review, you might prefer the Vancouver method as this might allow the text to flow more smoothly without being interrupted by lists of author names and dates. On the other hand, the Harvard system is easier to use as you write with a word processor because you can simply 'slot' each new reference into the correct place in the list. In an academic journal, it might be assumed that the readership would want to know the authors and dates of the references cited, so the Harvard system would probably be the most appropriate.

46 Using online resources

46.1. (a) Graham Young is famous for committing murder by the use of thallium.

(b) *Erythoxylum coca* is the name given to the species of plant from which cocaine is derived: See, for example, http://www.erowid.org/chemicals/cocaine/cocaine.shtml

(c) The postal address of the Chartered Society of Forensic Sciences is Copthall Bridge House, Station Bridge, Harrogate, North Yorkshire, HG1 1SP, United Kingdom.

46.2. *Tip:* Note the number of hits found for each search engine. Make a note or printout of the top 10 sites located by each search engine. Compare these site listings to reveal the quality of data obtained. Repeat this exercise for meta-search engines. Make lists of the component search engines used by the main meta-search engines to help you devise a strategy for the best coverage of the Internet.

46.3. *Tip:* Using the bookmark editor for your browser, create folders for each of your study courses and then create subfolders for each module that you are doing. Now use some searches to put relevant bookmarks in each folder. Don't forget to include a folder for transferable skills sites – there are lots of supportive sites available that are worth visiting.

47 Evaluating information

47.1. (a) P;

(b) P;

(c) P;

(d) P;

(e) P;

(f) P;

(g) P;

(h) P;

(i) P Where journals contain both original papers and reviews, we have classed them as primary.

47.2. Some potential debating points on whether 'everybody should have their DNA uploaded on to the NDNAD'

For	Against
Crime detection rates increased	Infringement of human rights
Intelligence value – linked cases	Issues related to informed consent
Non-coding information uploaded	Potential for misuse?
Cold case successes	Does it fairly represent the UK population?
Miscarriages of justice corrected	Ethical considerations of familial searching?

47.3. *Tip:* Use Box 52.3 as a source to indicate ways in which graphs may be used to misrepresent information. You may find this exercise easier to do with printed graphs. Those on television may not be shown for long enough to allow you to carry out a detailed analysis. Nevertheless, they represent a rich source of material to criticise!

48 Word processors, databases and other packages

48.1. *Tip:*

(a) Ensure that the list components are in separate paragraphs; highlight the list; from the Table menu select AZ↓ Sort function; ensure options are set to paragraphs, text, ascending.

(b) From the Home menu, select the Replace option, then fill in the relevant boxes.

(c) From the Home menu, select the Replace option, then fill in the relevant boxes; select More ≫ then Format, Font, Italic.

(d) From the Insert menu, select Header and Footer and use the small on-screen menu to add text and numbering as desired. Formatting commands (e.g. centre) will work in the header and footer boxes. As an alternative for adding page numbers, this can be done from the Insert menu, Page numbers . . . option.

(e) Margins can be adjusted from Page Layout menu, Margins.

(f) Select the list text, then use the Home menu, Bullets and Numbering option, using the 'Define new' option if the style you desire is not displayed in the panel.

(g) Type 'alternative' in a Word page. Ensure that the cursor is within the word (or highlight the word); from Review menu, select Thesaurus options. Perhaps 'option' might be a useful synonym?

(h) From the Review menu, select Spelling and Grammar to start a spell-check. Take care that the checker queries UK spellings (it may be set to accept US spellings). Note: this is not a substitute for reading your document – the spell-checker will miss typing errors like 'form' instead of 'from'.

(i) For a whole document, triple click in left margin to Select all, then use Review menu, ABC123 option. For selected text, highlight (select) the part you wish to count, then carry out same instructions.

(j) While in the first document, use the Office button, Open option to open another. You can switch between them using the Window menu, where you will see all open documents listed. Note: remember to save changes to all documents when closing down your editing session.

48.2. *Tip:* Although there are several ways to modify tables, you may find it useful to try the following commands (think carefully about their order).

- Table, Insert Table
- Table, Merge Cells
- Table, Distribute Columns Evenly
- Tables and borders, Modify borders commands (various)

Use the Help feature if you run into problems.

48.3. *Tip:* You might start your search on the networked 'desktop' and icons visible to you when you log on. Use 'Help' menus and 'Wizards' to investigate how to use the programs, or consult any manuals available in the computer suite.

49 Using spreadsheets

49.1. See the pie chart below. *Tip:* Depending on the precise method you use, you may need to provide the Name, Values and Category Labels for the Chart Wizard or adjust those assumed. When creating the graph, select the 'As new sheet' option when prompted for a Chart Location. For printing in black and white, select black and white hatching/shading options after click-selecting chart segments. Ensure the segments of the chart are labelled (i.e. not the default legend option) using the Chart/Chart Options menu.

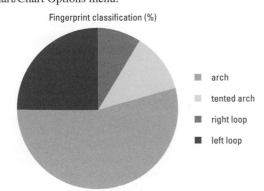

Fingerprint classification (%)

- arch
- tented arch
- right loop
- left loop

49.2. See the graph below. *Tip:* When setting up the spreadsheet, create appropriate formulae in new columns for the transformed data; graph using the 'XY (Scatter)' option in the Microsoft Excel Chart Wizard to make sure the data are correctly spaced on the *x*-axis. Plot the concentration on the *x*-axis and the peak area data on the *y*-axis. Using the right-hand button on the mouse, click any of the plotted data points and select 'Add trendline'. Make sure that the trendline option is set to linear and select the options 'Display equation on chart' and 'Display *R*-squared value on chart' and then click on the 'Close' option.

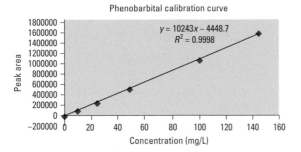

Phenobarbital calibration curve

$y = 10243x - 4448.7$
$R^2 = 0.9998$

49.3. *Tip:* Take care when entering the date data in the spreadsheet. You may need to specify the format of the cells for the date column (Format menu, Cells option). Highlight all parts of the spreadsheet table including column headers, and then use the Data menu, AZ↓ Sort option to rearrange data. You do not need to fill in all the response boxes and can select 'None' if a box contains criteria from a previous sort.

50 Fundamental principles of quantitative chemical analysis

50.1. (a) Accuracy – closeness to the 'true' value.
(b) Precision – measurement of the variability of data.
(c) Quality control – process of inspection, analysis and action required to ensure the quality of a process or product.
(d) Accreditation – competency to carry out specific assessment tasks assessed by an external body.
(e) Validation – a process to ensure that the analytical method is robust and reliable for the purpose for which it was designed (e.g. should define the selectivity, specificity, limit of detection and quantification, linear working range, accuracy and precision).

50.2. *Tip:* Consider what accreditation is and what its purpose is. You may wish to check out the UKAS website at https://www.ukas.com/

51 Calibration and quantitative analysis
51.1.

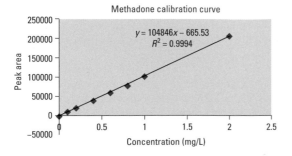

Methadone calibration curve

$y = 104846x - 665.53$
$R^2 = 0.9994$

(a) 0.222 mg L^{-1}
(b) 0.628 mg L^{-1}
(c) 1.47 mg L^{-1}

51.2. *Tip:* Check that you understand the general requirements for good graph drawing, detailed in Chapter 52.

(a) The title of the figure ('calibration graph') does not give sufficient information to enable the reader to understand the content.
(b) No details are given as to the nature of each set of data values – are these curves for two separate substances?
(c) The *x*-axis has a poor choice of units – it would be better to use mg, then all of the values would be 1000 times smaller.
(d) The *x*-axis runs beyond the highest value (8 mg), wasting around 20% of the horizontal space.
(e) The scale marks (tic marks) on the *x*-axis are missing.
(f) The *x*-axis has no zero shown.
(g) The *y*-axis has too many numbers, and too many minor scale marks – it is probably better to have a tic mark every 0.1 absorbance units. (Note that absorbance (*A*) is a dimensionless term, so no units are required – this is not an error.)
(h) The data values represented by the square symbols show a reasonable fit to the lower linear trend line, but the data values represented by the round symbols do not – the latter set of data shows a clear curvilinear relationship and therefore a linear trend line is not appropriate.
(i) Lines should not run through the symbols, as is the case for several of the square symbols.

52 Using graphs
52.1. (a) Plotted curve
(b) Pie chart
(c) Scatter diagram, possibly with a trend line
(d) Bar chart

52.2. *Tip:* The Sunday newspaper supplements often analyse news stories with the aid of graphs and might be a good source for material because their articles are often slanted towards a particular viewpoint, and you may find that the graphical presentation has been chosen to support this.

53 Presenting data in tables
53.1. Concentrations of drug and metabolites found in a blood sample (mg L^{-1}); alcohol expressed in mg per 100 mL^{-1}

Methadone	0.23
Diazepam	0.2
Desmethyl diazepam	0.075
Temazepam	0.1
Nicotine	NQ
Caffeine	NQ
Alcohol	86

NQ = positive result, but not quantified.

Answers to study exercises

53.2. *Tip:* Box 53.1 gives the key aspects. The following table gives one possible layout.

Component	Comment
Title	Concise, self-contained description of table contents, with numbering where appropriate
Column/row headings	Identifies the content of each column and row, showing units of measurement, where appropriate
Data values	Quoted to an appropriate number of significant figures/decimal places
Footnotes	All abbreviations and other individual details must be explained
Rulings	Used to emphasise any groupings within the table, and to separate individual items

54 Hints for solving numerical problems

54.1. (a) $[C] = A/\varepsilon l$
(b) $\varepsilon = A/[C]l$

54.2. (a) Subtract ax from both sides and then swap sides, so: $b = y - ax$
(b) 1. Subtract b from both sides and then swap sides, so: $ax = y - b$
2. Divide both sides by a, so: $x = (y - b)/a$

54.3. (a) 215
(b) 107 000
(c) 0.04
(d) 99.82
(e) 99.90
(f) 100.00
(g) 6,260
(h) 130 000
(i) 2
(j) 5
(k) 3
(l) 6
(m) 2
(n) 5

54.4. *Tip:* To calculate x, substitute values into eqn [54.4].
(a) $x = (7.0 - 4.5) \div 0.02 = 125$;
(b) $x = (15.2 + 2.6) \div -4.46 = -3.99\,103\,139 = -3.99$.
Tip: to calculate y, substitute values into eqn [54.3].
(a) $y = 0.2 + (-0.63 \times 10.5) = -6.415 = -6.42$;
(b) $y = -1.8 + (4.1 \times 4.5) = 16.65 = 16.6$.

55 Descriptive statistics

55.1. (a) Range $= 8$
(b) Variance $= 4.464$
(c) Standard deviation $= 2.113$
(d) Coefficient of variation $= 43.12\%$
(CoV $= 100 \Diamond 2.113/4.9$)
(e) Standard error $= 0.2728$

55.2. *Tip:* Substitute values into eqn [55.3] to calculate the SE of each sample.

For sample A: $12.7 \div 3.464\,101\,615 = 3.666\,174\,209 = 3.67$.
For sample B: $14.4 \div 4.472\,135\,955 = 3.219\,937\,888 = 3.22$.
Thus, in absolute terms, sample B has the lower standard error (note that the higher standard deviation of sample B is more than offset by the increased number of data values). To calculate the proportional standard error, divide the SE by the mean, as follows:
For sample A: $3.666\,174\,209 \div 16.2 = 0.226\,307\,05 = 0.226$.
For sample B: $3.219\,937\,888 \div 13.2 = 0.243\,934\,688 = 0.244$.
Thus, in proportion to the mean, sample A has the lower standard error.

55.3. Larval size data (recalculated)

Replicate sample	Mean sample larval size (mm)	Sample number	Mean size × sample size
A	3.0	24	72.0
B	2.5	37	92.5
C	2.0	6	12.0
Total		67	176.5

True mean $= 176.5/67 = 2.63$ mm

56 Choosing and using statistical tests

56.1. *Tip:* First calculate the standard error using eqn [55.3], as $6.8 \div 4 = 1.7$. Then, substitute values into eqn [56.2] to calculate the 95% confidence limits (note that you also need the value for $t_{0.05/15} = 2.131$). The upper limit is calculated as: $24.7 + (2.131 \times 1.7) = 28.3227 = 28.3$. The lower limit is calculated as $24.7 - (2.131 \times 1.7) = 21.0773 = 21.1$.

56.2. *Tip:* The calculated $t = 2.136$ with 12 degrees of freedom; the critical value at $P = 5\%$ is 2.18 (Table 56.2); hence you would accept the null hypothesis that the samples came from the same population, and thus conclude that the cocaine had no significant effect.

57 Chemometrics and advanced statistics

57.1. *Tip:* Use the information provided in Chapter 45 to identify a scientific paper that has used either a factorial or central composite design. The boundaries of their chosen variables may have been determined by some preliminary experiments or because of practical limitations, e.g. it was not possible to operate under the conditions.

57.2. *Tip:* Use the information provided in Chapter 45 to identify a scientific paper that has used a principal component analysis (PCA). The visualisation of large data sets to identify trends can be effectively done using PCA.

57.3. *Tip:* Discuss with other students or your project supervisor how you might use optimisation approaches to assist with identifying best operating conditions, e.g. designing a new organic synthesis and wanting to determine the optimum conditions for yield or to maximise the signal output from an instrumental analytical technique. Also how might you use PCA to visualise a large data set.

57.4. Search using Web of Science (or similar) for a most recent article, or use the references in the chapter as a starting point. Consider how effective this approach could be and whether it offers any further insight into data analysis for your chosen topic for review.

58 General aspects of scientific writing

58.1. *Tip:* When brainstorming, think of all aspects of the topic that could be relevant (even if you could not give precise details at this stage). When you meet together, discuss which of your combined ideas would be most important in crafting an answer and what order you might place them in.

58.2. *Tip:* Try to apply what you have learned in the next assignment you write – ask a tutor for specific feedback if you are unsure about whether your technique has improved.

58.3. *Tip:* Use the spelling list to help you when writing and make a conscious effort to memorise the spelling each time you use it. The act of writing the vocabulary list will assist you to memorise new words and their meanings. If you have trouble learning definitions – e.g. terms in molecular biology – you could extend these ideas to create a personal glossary of terms and acronyms.

59 Giving a spoken presentation

59.1. Ten-point checklist – what makes a good spoken presentation?

- Introduction – does the speaker explain the structure and rationale of the topic at the outset?
- Audience – is the material presented at an appropriate level?
- Content – does the presentation cover the topic effectively?
- Speed and structure – are the main elements of the presentation presented clearly, and at an appropriate pace?
- Voice – is the presentation delivered in an engaging, active vocal style?
- Audio-visual aids – does the speaker make good use of visual images (e.g. graphs, photographs, etc.)?
- Image – does the presenter make good use of body language?
- Notes – does the speaker use notes to structure the talk, rather than reading from a written text?
- Conclusion – is a clear 'take-home message' delivered in the final stages of the presentation?
- Questions – does the presenter deal with questions effectively?

59.2. *Tip:* You could try marking speakers out of 10 for each of the points listed in exercise 59.1 (either using the checklist provided above or your own version), or you could simply prepare a list of the good and bad points of the presentations you have evaluated.

59.3. *Tip:* Write down the key points on how the instrument works; consider whether a jury would understand the science of your explanation; prepare, practise and rehearse answers with your colleagues.

60 Writing a forensic statement and presenting evidence in court

60.1. *Tip:* Write down the key points on how the presumptive test works. Consider whether a jury would understand the science of your explanation; prepare, practise and rehearse answers with your colleagues.

60.2. The main difference is that the expert witness statement is one in which the author can express an interpretation and opinion of data/results. A CSI statement is a description of a scene examination and the evidence that was recovered from the scene.

60.3. *Tip:* Using the results you have obtained from a practical laboratory, write the statement. Use Box 60.1 and Fig. 60.1 as a reference and decide the format of the statement. Consider what you think is important that the Court needs to know. As a general rule, references would not be included in the statement – by the token that it is an expert witness statement, it is assumed that your information would be obtained from appropriate peer-reviewed sources. Don't forget to perform a spelling and grammar check (see Chapter 48).

61 Reporting practical and project work

61.1. *Tip:* To assimilate the required style for Materials and Methods, you may find it appropriate to read some research papers from the journal section of your library. Note particularly that the Materials and Methods section is a description of 'what was done', not a set of instructions.

60.2. *Tip:* Again, you may find it appropriate to read some research papers from the journal section of your library to assimilate the normal style for describing research results.

61.3. *Tip:* Abstracts are difficult to write. Try to include a synopsis of all the main sections of the paper, including its aims, methods, key results and conclusions. Ignore the word-length restriction until you have noted the main points, then try to reduce (or, less likely, expand) your effort to match the requirement.

62 Writing essays, literature surveys and reviews

62.1. *Tip:* Can you determine what lies behind each question? Some question titles are quite direct, but others ask for information in a more subtle way. Use your imagination to think beyond the immediate question, linking to learning objectives or to other relevant material covered in lectures.

62.2. *Tip:* Compare your ideas with those of a partner, or ask tutors or lecturers what they think of your efforts. A useful adjunct to this exercise is to write the first sentence of your answer to avoid writer's block.

62.3. Five differences between reviews and papers are:
1. Reviews deal with material in general terms, taking an overview, whereas papers tend to look at a focused, single aspect of a topic.
2. The subdivisions are generally not the same – papers usually follow the IMRAD format (p. 560), while reviews are structured according to the major components of the topic.
3. There is little or no reference to original data in reviews.
4. There is little detail of methods in reviews.

5. They tend to use different reference citation systems, with Harvard (p. 438) most commonly used in papers and Vancouver (p. 438) used in reviews.

63 Organising a poster display

63.1. *Tip:* Use Fig. 63.1 and the subheadings of Chapter 63 as a starting point for assessing the pros and cons of your designs.

63.2. Ten-point checklist – what makes a good poster presentation?
- Title – is it concise, specific and interesting?
- Author(s) – does the poster show details of the names and addresses of all the contributors?
- Structure – is the overall structure clear to the observer, with good use of subheadings?
- Flow – is the layout of the poster clear, in terms of how the audience is expected to 'read' each section?
- Content – does the presentation have a clear introduction, main message and conclusion?
- Text – does the poster contain an appropriate amount of written material in a readable font?
- Graphics – does the poster make good use of diagrams, figures and images?
- Size and scale – does the poster make effective use of the space available?
- Colour – does the presentation use colour effectively?
- Conclusion – is the 'take-home message' clear to the observer?

63.3. *Tip:* You might use the 10-point checklist given above, or your own version from exercise 63.2 to assess selected posters by giving a mark out of 10 for each item in the list. In a group exercise, you can see how your 'scores' compare with those of other students, and discuss items where scores are different.

64 The importance of transferable skills

64.1. *Tip:* Where you feel confident about skills you have learned at school, take care to consider whether they might need to be upgraded for university/college use. When thinking about opportunities for developing skills, remember that these may occur outside university, perhaps in work or social contexts.

64.2. *Tip:* Possible key words/phrases for an Internet search include: biology or chemistry skills, C&IT skills, numeracy skills, study skills, time management.

64.3. *Tip:* You could create a grid to record your thoughts, with column headings 'University' 'Work' and 'Social', and rows for 'Short term' 'Medium term' and 'Long term'. Short term and medium term could refer to your time at university, while long term could refer to after graduation.

65 Managing your time

65.1. *Tip:* Model your spreadsheet on Fig. 65.1. It isn't too difficult to fill in details at the end of each day, either directly into the spreadsheet or on a printed version. You will need to collect information for at least a week and possibly longer before you see patterns emerging.

65.2. *Tip:* It is important to include both social and study-related activities on your lists. Short-term lists deal with issues of the day or week, medium-term for the term or semester and longer term for one year onwards. Relate each of these lists to appropriate goals you may have over these time-scales.

65.3. *Tip:* This task could be related to (a) your self-analysis of transferable skills (Chapter 64), or (b) some large task such as carrying out a final-year project. In the latter case, for example, there are small jobs that can be done as you proceed with the larger task, such as writing parts of the Introduction or compiling a list of references, and these will reduce time pressure towards the end of the task.

66 Working with others

66.1. *Tip:* Think about your contributions to past group activities while doing this exercise and, if necessary, get feedback from friends and colleagues. You may feel that you fit into more than one 'natural' role – this is quite often the case.

66.2. *Tip:* This exercise might best be associated with a specific teamwork activity, but this need not be restricted to study – group contributions with clubs, societies or in employment are equally valid. Strategies for improvement will depend on your identified weaknesses. For example, if you felt too shy to contribute effectively, you might want to practise public speaking (see Chapter 59) or attend an assertiveness workshop.

66.3. *Tip:* Columns 4 and 5 of Table 66.1 are relevant, particularly if you are able to identify a 'natural' role or roles for yourself in group situations (as in exercise 66.1). Can you relate your strengths and weaknesses to specific events that have occurred during teamwork, and might you handle the situation differently in future?

67 Taking notes from lectures and texts

67.1. *Tip:* If you are used to using a particular note-taking method that seems to work well, you may feel reluctant to experiment. Try out the new method by taking notes at a seminar, tutorial or meeting where it will not matter so much if the technique does not work well at the first attempt.

67.2. *Tip:* Make a list of any missing notes or handouts and ask a colleague if you can work from their notes to fill in these gaps.

67.3. *Tip:* To compare methods, test your recall some time afterwards. Take a blank sheet of paper and see what you can write about each topic.

68 Learning and revising effectively

68.1. *Tip:* When constructing your revision timetable, remember the following important points:
- Break large topics into 'bite-sized' units.
- Mix up hard or less interesting topics with those you enjoy revising – don't ignore them.
- Keep an appropriate balance between work and relaxation.
- Offer yourself rewards if work targets are completed.

68.2. *Tip:* You may wish to keep one of the past papers (preferably a recent one) to use in a mock exam. Remember that learning objectives can be just as important as exam papers in helping you to revise.

68.3. *Tip:* Read through the list of active revision tips on p. 603 and decide which might work best for you. Carry out a trial of the method with one of your topics where the material has seemed difficult to learn. Experiment until you arrive at a solution that works, remembering (a) that different techniques might work best in different subjects and (b) a little variety might make the revision process more interesting.

68.4. *Tip*: Read through your notes and assess whether they still make sense after the lecture. How do you record your information. Could you change your style of note taking to improve?

69   Assessments and exams

69.1. *Tip:* Some questions to ask yourself about past exam performances . . . Did you prepare well enough? Did you run out of time during the exam? Did you spend too long on a particular question or section, and have to rush another? Were your answers direct and at the appropriate depth? Did you misinterpret any questions, or miss out part of any answers? Were your writing skills, including planning, up to the standard required?

69.2. *Tip:* When revising, try to find a topic you find hard to understand and see whether your colleague has approached it in the same way as you. If not, you may be able to learn from this.

69.3. *Tip:* Discuss your tactics with a colleague sitting the same exam. What topics do you agree are likely to come up?

70   Preparing your curriculum vitae

70.1. *Tip:* This exercise might be attempted with a friend you can trust to give you a frank opinion. Remember that your personal qualities can be developed in both curricular and extra-curricular activities.

70.2. *Tip:* Working with a friend or group from your class, compare notes on how you have organised your CVs and then modify your own CV, taking on board good ideas from your peers. Create a physical file for your revised CV and add handwritten notes, updating it as and when required.

70.3. *Tip:* Use the 'Prospects' website noted in the sources for further study to gain ideas before your appointment with the careers service. The library or careers resource centre may have useful information, often accessible via the Internet.

Index

Index

Index

Index

hypotheses 29–30, 533–4, 535, 564
   null hypothesis 407, 517–18, 522, 523
hypothesis-testing statistics 454, 455, 463, 468, 494, 517–26

ICP–AES (inductively coupled plasma–atomic emission spectroscopy) 167–8
ICP–MS (inductively coupled plasma mass spectrometry) 168–70, 404
ICT guidelines 442
ICT skills 441, 443, 458, 564, 582
ideal solutes 53
IDENT1 (National Automated Fingerprint Identification System) 262, 263
identification of individuals 328, 330, 332, 333, 334, 424, 553
IEC (ion-exchange chromatography) 124, 131, 141
IEF (isoelectric focusing) 217, 218, 219
image, personal 549, 556, 558, 611
images
   digital 230–1, 236, 237, 464, 547
   interpreting 19, 20, 73–5
immunoassay 204–10, 374
immunoblotting 219
immunoglobulin G (IgG) 204
impairment tests 358, 370
impartiality 554, 559
impurities, in drugs 383, 387–8
independent variables 13, 16, 31, 483, 525, 532–3
inductively coupled plasma–atomic emission spectroscopy (ICP–AES) 167–8
inductively coupled plasma–mass spectrometry 168–70
inductively coupled plasma–mass spectrometry (ICP–MS) 168–70, 404
information
   evaluating 443, 448, 451–7, 571
   finding and citing 435–9, 444–9, 451
   recording see drawing; photography
infrared spectroscopy see IR spectroscopy
injuries 277, 327, 419–20, 553
   see also wounds
insects 336–43
   colonisation of bodies 325, 340
   life cycles 337–8, 341–2, 343
instars (larval stages) 337, 340, 341, 343
instruments 15, 59–60
integration (NMR) 197, 198–9
intelligence value 245
interaction
   of drugs 375, 379, 380
   of treatments 33
   of variables 531–2
interdependent variables 13, 483, 484
interferences 165–6, 168, 170, 176–7
interfering substances 473, 474, 479

internal standards 142, 360, 361, 375, 376, 475
Internet 435, 436, 441–9, 451, 563
interpolation 488
interval scales 14
interviews 611–12
intimate samples 66, 250, 369
ion-exchange chromatography see IEC
ion-exchange sorbents 91–2
ionisation sources 148–9, 149–50, 168
IR (infrared) spectra 181–2, 183, 187–90
IR (infrared) spectrometers 182–4
IR (infrared) spectroscopy 180–90, 430
isoelectric focusing (IEF) 217, 218, 219
IT guidelines 442
IT skills 441, 443, 458, 564, 582

Jeffreys, Professor Sir Alec 304
Jenkins, Billie Jo 294
Jenkins, Sion 294
journals 435–7, 438, 449, 452, 453, 566–7, 596–7
Kakzynski, Theodor (Unabomber) 274
Kastle Meyer (KM) test 295
KBr disks 184–5, 186
ketamine 388, 389
key words 560, 561, 563, 596
keys, botanical 345–6
KM (Kastle Meyer) test 295
knives 249, 413
Kolmogorov–Smirnov test 522
Kruskal–Wallis H-test 522
kurtosis 512, 513, 521

lab books 3, 16–17, 560, 565
lab partners 591–2
labelling
   chemicals 40, 48
   exhibits 229, 247–8, 250, 291, 317, 555
   in laboratories 4, 89
   samples 317, 339, 359, 425, 426
laboratories, national reference 474
laboratory work 3–5, 10, 43–52, 483, 564, 581, 582, 591–2, 600
larval stages (instars) 337, 340, 341, 343
laser printers 285–6
latent fingerprints 244, 246, 257–61, 401, 418
lateral flow immunoassay (LFIA) 206
laws, scientific 29
LC–MS (liquid chromatography–mass spectrometry) 149–50, 321
lead residue from gunshots 418, 419
learning objectives/outcomes 601, 602
learning styles 598
least significant difference (LSD) 488, 521
lectures, taking notes 443, 593–7, 599–600, 602
'legal highs' see NPS (novel psychoactive substances)

legal issues, laboratory work 3–4
length, measuring 49–50, 74
lenses
   cameras 231, 232
   microscopes 64, 69, 70, 71, 73, 398
leucomalachite green (LMG) 295
LFIA (lateral flow immunoassay) 206
libraries 435–7, 445, 449
light
   absorption 154–5
   oblique 266, 267, 268, 284, 285, 319
   for photography 232, 234–5, 333
   units 27
light microscopy 64–6, 69–73, 396–7
light-sensitive chemicals 40
likelihood of harm, in risk assessment 7
likelihood ratio 534, 535
Lindbergh, Charles A. Jr. 286
line charts 485, 520
line of best fit 293, 478, 480, 481, 488, 503–4, 525
linear functions 503–4
liquid chromatography 128–30, 140, 141–2
liquid chromatography–mass spectrometry see LC–MS
liquid films 184, 185
liquid–liquid extraction 87–9, 376
liquids
   collecting as evidence 244, 245, 357, 359, 425–6
   holding and storing 40–2, 425
   measuring and dispensing 37–40
   sample preparation and handling 82–6, 177–8, 184
literature reviews 435–6, 453, 543, 570–1
liver 342, 365, 371, 372–3, 378
LMG (leucomalachite green) test 295
Locard's Principle 227, 253
location (frequency distributions) 485, 488, 506–9, 513
location (place), evidence of 345, 347, 348, 350
logarithms 484, 490–1, 503, 509
long-term drug history 320–1, 369, 372, 379
low copy number DNA 311
low template DNA analysis 311, 312
LSD (least significant difference) 488, 521
LSD (lysergic acid) 385, 386
luminescence 159
luminol 270, 325
lungs 342, 349, 373, 378, 424
lysergic acid (LSD) 385, 386

MacKenzie, Elizabeth 274
McPhee, George 274
MAE (microwave-assisted extraction) 79, 80

Index

Index